Wiliam Wood

American Druggist

Wiliam Wood

American Druggist

ISBN/EAN: 9783743316980

Manufactured in Europe, USA, Canada, Australia, Japa

Cover: Foto ©ninafisch / pixelio.de

Manufactured and distributed by brebook publishing software (www.brebook.com)

Wiliam Wood

American Druggist

The
American Druggist

AN

ILLUSTRATED MONTHLY JOURNAL

OF

Pharmacy, Chemistry and Materia Medica

FRED'K A. CASTLE, M.D.,
LATE PHYSICIAN TO THE PRESBYTERIAN HOSPITAL AND
LECTURER ON PHARMACOLOGY, BELLEVUE HOSPITAL
MEDICAL COLLEGE; MEMBER OF THE COMMITTEE ON
REVISION AND PUBLICATION OF THE PHARMA-
COPŒIA OF THE U. S. OF AMERICA.
EDITOR

CHARLES RICE, PH.D.,
CHEMIST OF THE DEPARTMENT OF PUBLIC CHARITIES AND
CORRECTION; CHAIRMAN OF THE COMMITTEE OF
REVISION AND PUBLICATION OF THE PHARMA-
COPŒIA OF THE U. S. OF AMERICA.
ASSOCIATE EDITOR

VOL. XVII.

WILLIAM WOOD & COMPANY
PUBLISHERS
56 & 58 LAFAYETTE PLACE, NEW YORK
1888

American Druggist

Vol. XVII. No. 1.   NEW YORK, JANUARY, 1888.   Whole No. 163.

GLEDITSCHIA TRIACANTHOS.

BY ABRAHAM L. METZ, PH.G.

Instructor in Practical Pharmacy, Tulane University,
New Orleans, La.

Through the kindness of Dr. J. F. Joor, Prof. of Botany of Tulane University, I was placed in possession of a letter from Dr. Claiborne, which gives the exact locality where Mr. Goodman claims to have first obtained the leaves from which he extracted the so-called alkaloid "*stenocarpine*;" and also a description of certain letters alleged to have been cut in the limb of the tree. As everything surrounding the supposed discovery of so valuable a medicament was clothed in mystery, I thought that, by making a personal inspection of the locality, I could possibly discover the marked tree, and clear up the mystery. I have made several further preliminary experiments in obtaining an alkaloidal or other proximate principle from *Gleditschia triacanthos*, the results of which will be seen further on; but, having failed to obtain the supposed anæsthetic, I set out on what proved to be a "wild-goose chase." The information given to Dr. Claiborne by Messrs. Goodman and Seward was to the effect, "that the tree from which they obtained the leaves is on the banks of the Mississippi River, between Donaldsonville and Placquemine, five or six miles from the former place. There are cuts in one limb of the tree the letters 'N. P.;' on another, just opposite, 'A. C.'" With this valuable information, I set out for Donaldsonville, on November 22d, for the purpose of obtaining any information on the subject, and at the same time make an inspection of the locality.

About three miles and a half above Donaldsonville, I met the first clump of trees on the banks. There are several trees, all along the bank, but these are Pecan trees (*Carya oliræformis* Nutt.). The before mentioned clump of trees consisted of willow trees (*Salix nigra* L.), cottonwood (*Populus angulata* Ait.), and a few trees of *Gleditschia triacantha* L. These failed to show the described letters.

About five miles above Donaldsonville, there is another clump of trees on the bank. This clump consisted of a few trees of *Gleditschia monosperma* Walt., *Gleditschia triacanthos* L., and such as were described above, and also a few scattered trees of *Catalpa bignonioides* Walt. These also failed to present the described letters, yet every tree was inspected and with special pains in regard to the letters said to have been cut in the trees.

About one mile above this clump, there are a few scattered trees of *Gleditschia triacanthos*; on one of these trees, there was a peculiar mark in the form of T, and another mark which appeared to have been obliterated with an axe. There are many scattered trees of *Gleditschia triacanthos* all along the bank, which I inspected for the described letters, but without success.

I still kept on my journey until I was about ten and a half miles above Donaldsonville. There are here quite a number of *Gleditschia triacanthos* trees, every one of which was inspected. On one tree the following marks were cut:

A N
T Vi
V

This was upon one of the *Gleditschia triacanthos* trees, and being informed that there were no more trees within five miles, I abandoned my journey with the conviction that it proved, as suspected, a "wild goose chase." I then set up an inquiry, and not even the plantation hands could give me any information regarding the gathering of leaves from any tree, or regarding the manufacture of anything along the banks of the Mississippi in that locality by any strange men, or by any one else.

One can rest assured that any unusual manipulations would soon have spread from one to another, had any one seen or heard of the gathering of leaves from any tree.

What the negro plantation hands do not see or hear occurring in their neighborhood is not worth while seeing or hearing. However, I learned from an old negro, to use his own words, that "a big, stout man, who said he was a horse-doctor, was in this neighborhood last May." He did not know his name, nor could I obtain further information from any one else in the vicinity. Why the originators of "stenocarpine" first spread the report that they obtained the leaves in West Feliciana Parish, when this parish is quite distant from Ascension Parish (in which lies Donaldsonville and the surrounding country I traversed in my search), is something I cannot understand; on the whole, everything connected with the alleged discovery does not hold together, and has, so far, proved a hoax.

The limited amount of time I have had at my disposal since September 12th was given to the above subject with the results presently to be given. All these experiments, however, are merely of a preliminary character, and on attempt was made to determine the nature of the crystallizable matters found, partly for want of time, as stated before, and partly through deficiency of sufficiently fresh material.

The late Prof. Gustav Robert Kirchhoff.
(See page 2.)

The first trial was upon 180 grammes of leaves, which were not quite dry. They were contused in an iron mortar, macerated for 48 hours, and percolated with a 2% solution of sulphuric acid until perfectly exhausted. The percolate was evaporated to a small bulk upon a water bath, and sodium carbonate added to saturation; quite a bulky precipitate was thrown down, which I extracted with benzene. This benzene solution was washed with acidulated water to obtain any alkaloid present in the acidulated solution. The latter was again super-saturated with sodium carbonate, the solution or mixture shaken with ether, and the latter evaporated spontaneously. As a result, I obtained a varnish-like film with *two small acicular crystals* of a brownish color, the solution of which, after acidulating, gave quite a reaction with Nessler's reagent. The varnish-like film felt resinous to the touch, the taste was slightly bitter, but did *not* possess any anæsthetic properties.

The second trial was made upon 250 grammes of leaves. These were dried in the sun, reduced to a No. 20 powder, macerated for 24 hours, and percolated with acidulated alcohol to exhaustion. I then distilled off most of the alcohol and evaporated the rest spontaneously until the odor of alcohol was no longer perceptible. The residuary liquid was then super-saturated with sodium carbonate and the liquid extracted with ether. The latter was evaporated spontaneously, and again the result was a varnish-like film, which appeared to have a crystalline structure. The alcoholic solution deposited a large amount of extractive matter, which was filtered off before saturating with sodium carbonate.

The third trial was upon 1,250 grammes of leaves, which were partly dried, contused in an iron mortar, macerated for 48 hours, and percolated with a 2% solution of hydrochloric acid to exhaustion. The percolate was evaporated on a water bath to the consistence of an extract, and an excess of lime added. The mass was thoroughly dried at 140° F., exhausted with a mixture of alcohol and ether, and this solution exposed in a wide porcelain dish to allow it to evaporate spontaneously. As a result I obtained a small quantity of a semi-liquid mass, having a distinctly crystalline structure, but resinous to the touch, and which, when dried in vacuo over sulphuric acid, yielded a yellow powder, which acquired a resinous and adhesive character when exposed to the atmosphere. This yellow powder was examined under the microscope by Dr. J. B. Elliott, Professor of the Theory and Practice of Medicine, Tulane University, when it was found to deliquesce on the slide, showing acicular crystals of a yellowish color.

Thinking that perhaps the product was contaminated with calcium chloride, I dissolved the product in alcohol and added a small quantity of dilute sulphuric acid. This produced a precipitate which I filtered off. I then evaporated the alcohol spontaneously, and my result was, as before, a resinous mass with a crystalline structure which, when examined by Prof. Elliott, exhibited the same peculiar phenomena under the microscope.

Assuming for the present that these results point to the presence of a peculiar proximate principle, it seemed to be of interest to ascertain whether a modification of the treatment would make it probable that there were more than one present.

I accordingly prepared a fresh solution, which was made strongly alkaline with ammonia water, and extracted with chloroform. The latter was then evaporated spontaneously, yielding, as a result, a resinous, varnish-like film, with the same peculiar crystalline formation as before described. The liquid residue was exposed to the atmosphere and, after the odor of chloroform was no longer perceptible, the alkaline solution was extracted with ether, and, upon evaporation of the latter, there was obtained a black amorphous residue insoluble in water and chloroform, which appears to belong to the class of resins, but was not further examined.

In another experiment, I used 2 kilos of leaves, dried them, reduced them to a No. 40 powder, using as a menstrum a 2% solution sulphuric acid. I employed the process of repercolation (to avoid the use of heat). The percolate was saturated with gaseous ammonia, which gave a very bulky precipitate; the percolate and precipitate were then extracted with chloroform and the latter evaporated spontaneously. As a result I obtained a semi-liquid mass of a brownish color, showing traces of crystalline structure.

On repeating this process, using only water as a menstrum, the same results were obtained. In every instance, the crystalline matter was observed to be in the form of acicular crystals arranged around a common centre, having a sort of stellate appearance.

The products of all the above processes had a slightly bitter taste, but not the remotest property of an anæsthetic, as I applied portions of each product to the tip of my tongue. A peculiar odor was manifested throughout the different processes of manipulation.

These results may possibly guide those making experiments.

THE LATE PROF. KIRCHHOFF.

Prof. Gustav Robert Kirchhoff, of the university of Berlin, died on October 17th at Berlin. His name will always rank among the pioneers of scientific research. In 1859 he announced the important discovery that the Fraunhofer lines in the solar spectrum were due to the existence of elementary bodies in a state of vapor; and that the spectrum differed, not only according to the presence or absence of any of the elements, but also according as the luminous vapor of the element itself was examined, or a ray of white light transmitted through the vapor. In the former case, the spectrum is dark, but traversed by certain colored bands in definite positions. In the latter case, the spectrum is luminous and colored, while the positions of the bands are occupied by exactly coinciding dark lines. This discovery not only opened an entirely new field in chemical analysis, enabling the most minute quantities of elementary bodies to be recognized, but it also led to the discovery of a number of new elements, and revealed much of the nature and composition of the stellar world. In the practical application of his discovery to chemical analysis, he had (while Professor at Heidelberg) the help and assistance of his colleague Prof. Robert W. Bunsen, and, in fact, the perfection of the method, for practical purposes, must be ascribed to these two scientists conjointly. Prof. Kirchhoff distinguished himself also in many other directions upon the field of natural philosophy.

Purification of Syrups by Dialysis.

What is called a "battery of dialyzers" has lately been introduced for the above purpose in Germany; it consists of a series of tall cylinders of fine wire-gauze, open at the top end, but not at the bottom, which is rounded. This gauze is coated on both sides with layers of paper pulp, and the cylinders, arranged in regular series depending from a frame-work above, are plunged into the molasses, juices, or syrups to be purified, and are filled almost to the top with clear water, and allowed to "dialyze" for twelve hours or more. The water (into with a large proportion of the salts contained in the syrups, etc., together with traces only of the saccharine matter, has permeated by "osmosis") is then pumped away through pipes reaching to the bottom of each cylinder, and fresh water pumped in to supply its place. After a further interval this is changed in the same manner, the operation being repeated until the syrup, or whatever fluid preparation is being treated, is considered to be sufficiently purified. This method is, after the first cost of the apparatus, a very simple and inexpensive one, and can be employed either upon a large or a small scale for extracting the salts and other crystalline matters from various chemical and pharmaceutical preparations.

THE UNITED STATES GALLON.

BY PROF. W. P. MASON.

"The gallon is a vessel containing 58,372.2 grains (8.3389 pounds avoirdupois) of the standard pound of distilled water, at the temperature of maximum density of water, the vessel being weighed in air in which the barometer is 30 inches, at 62° F." (See report on "Weights and Measures" by Secretary of the Treasury, Senate doc. 1857.)

This definition being somewhat obscure, occasion was taken to write to the Treasury Department, from which letter the following is quoted: "Does this wording mean that the 'gallon' is a *volume* equal to that occupied by the above quantity of water under the conditions named; or does it intend a 'gallon' to be understood as meaning the quantity of liquid capable of being held by such standard *vessel* as above referred to, even after such vessel has been expanded by elevation of temperature? I take it that the latter view, although certainly stated, can hardly be intended."

The reply to this came from the office of the "Coast Survey," and read as follows:

"The standard gallon is a measure of capacity or volume. Its capacity was derived from standard weights; and in verifying and standardizing capacity measures, it is the practice to determine the volumes by weighings. It is, therefore, to be understood that the capacity of a gallon is measured by the *weight* of a volume of distilled water at maximum density, whose weight in air, at 62° F.—bar. 30 inches—equals 58,372.2 grains.

"It follows, therefore, that a gallon is the measure of a *constant volume*, and that due allowance must be made for changes of temperature of a vessel used as a gallon measure."

A letter recently coming from the Treasury Department reads:

"The value adopted by this office for the weight of 231 cubic inches of distilled water, at its maximum density, is 8.3389 lbs.; or 8.3310 lbs. at 15° C. This reduced to 60° F. gives a value of 8.3312 lbs."

Desiring to obtain a value in pounds for a U. S. gallon of distilled water at 60° F.—said value to be carried beyond four decimal places—a very surprising degree of confusion was discovered among the authorities.

For instance:

		Grains		lbs.
U. S. Pharmacopœia 1870	58329.8862	grains or	8.333698	lbs.
" " 1880	58329.6	"	8.3376	"
Miller's Chemistry	58317.2	"	8.3310	"
Am. Chemist, vol. i., p. 318	58316.8	"	8.3314	"
U. S. Treasury Dept.	—	"	8.3312	"
U. S. Dispensatory (last edition)	58329.886	"	8.333698	"
Oldberg's "Weights and Measures," page 167	59,333.218	"	8.333609571	"

From Barnard's "Metric System" we have:
One cubic inch of pure water at 62° F., and under a pressure of 30 inches of mercury, weighs

in vacuo .... 252.75965 grains.

Using Kopp's tables (Watt's Dict., vol. iii., p. 58, and interpolating by formula number one), we have:
One cubic inch of water at 32° F. becomes

at 60° F. .... 1.000769074789 cu. in.
at 62° F. .... 1.000942763386 "

Hence:
One cubic inch at 62° F. becomes

at 60° F. .... 0.999826349101 cu. in.

Hence:
One cubic inch of water at 60° F. weighs

in vacuo .... 252.8085026 grains.

And one gallon (231 cubic inches) weighs

in vacuo .... 58397.8091006 grains, or 8.3425153858 lbs.

Referring again to Barnard's "Metric System" we find:

	Grains
1 cu. in. water at 62° F., in air at 62° F., weighs	252.49645
1 " dry air " 62° "	0.30909098
1 " " " 60° " "	0.31028673

Hence:

	Grains
1 cu. in. water at 62° F. in air at 60° F. weighs	252.49734343

Now:
One cubic inch of water at 62° F. becomes, as we have seen, 0.999826349101 cubic inch at 60° F., and the weight of this volume of water at 60° F. is equal to that of the entire cubic inch at 62° F., plus the weight of a volume of air at 60° F., equal to the difference between unity and said volume of water.

Hence:
0.999826349101 cubic inch of water at 60° F., and in air at 60° F., weighs 252.46729724 grains.

Hence:

One cubic inch of water at 60° F., weighed in air at 60° F., and under a pressure of 30 inches of mercury, weighs 252.33110257 grains.

From these results we obtain for the weight of one U. S. gallon (231 cubic inches) of pure water at 60° F., and weighed in dry air at 60° F. under a pressure of 30 inches of mercury:

58334.68469367 grains, or 8.33332638481 lbs.

RENSSELAER POLYTECHNIC INSTITUTE.
TROY, N. Y., Dec. 9th, 1887.

Note by Ed. Amer. Drugg.—This paper is an outcome of an inquiry set on foot by Prof. W. P. Mason, to ascertain in the first place upon what authority the U. S. Pharmacopœia had based the value in grains there given as being equivalent to a U. S. gallon. This inquiry was addressed to the Chairman of the Committee of Revision, who replied that so far as he was aware there was in reality no *legally* defined standard of measure or relation between weight and measure in existence in this country. A wine-gallon is reckoned as equivalent to 231 cubic inches, and this value had been taken over from the English system, though never expressly defined. The value required to connect weights and measures is the weight of a cubic inch of pure water of a known temperature, at a known temperature and pressure of the air. On looking up all the available authorities, and recalculating the value of a wine gallon, this was found to be

58335.21790875 grains, or 8.33360257 pounds.

In calculating these figures, use was made of the tables in Prof. Oldberg's "Weights and Measures," second edition, (chiefly the table on page 165). The result being communicated to Prof. Mason, the latter followed the authorities further, and in a paper recently read before the American Chemical Society, he reported having calculated and found the value of 1 U. S. Gallon (231 cub. inch.) of distilled water at 60° F. and 30 inches pressure to be

in vacuo....58397.6091006 grains, or 8.3425155658 lbs.
in air at 60° F, 58334.94840743 " " 8.3335637249 "

This last value, as will be seen, is very close to the one given by by Professor Oldberg, and that obtained by the writer of this note, and given above. Since the reading of this paper, Prof. Mason has given further attention to the subject, and as a result thereof, he finds it necessary to slightly alter the figures previously obtained by him. The new figures differ, for a value of a gallon of water in grains, only by a little over 0.26 of one grain, affecting only the fifth decimal of a fraction expressing the value in pounds.

Until further information is supplied, the value reported by Prof. Mason deserves preference before all others. It seems, however, highly desirable that this whole question of standards and relation of weight to measure, be finally settled by law, and preliminary to this, by a new scientific investigation which might be most suitably conducted under the auspices of the National Academy of Sciences or some other representative scientific body.

AIR-TIGHT TAPS.

MR ARNOLD EILOART draws attention to the air-tight tap which he devised some years ago, but the best form of which appears to have been overlooked, while others of his invention are quite commonly in use.

The plug of this tap has two grooves, G G, running around it, and is used with an ordinary socket, S. These grooves, filled with liquid, check any transfer of gas between the exterior and interior of the tap, and, if through bad grinding, such transfer takes place, it is at once detected by bubbles in the liquid. They may be supplemented by vertical grooves joining them in opposite quadrants of the plug-circumference, to stop the passage of gas around the plug, when the tap is turned off.

These taps were originally devised for apparatus used in the analysis of gases, but they will be found useful for various other purposes where an absolutely air-tight stopcock is required. Another form of air-tight stop-cock, not as serviceable for gas analysis as that just described, but nevertheless useful otherwise, is shown in Fig. II. Here there is a cup-shaped vessel around the neck of the stop cock, which is to be filled by a suitable liquid ('paraffin oil, etc., etc.]. It will be seen that this form of tap can only be used in an upright position, to prevent the liquid contents of the well from running out. The tap first described, however (Fig. I.), may be used in any position, as the liquid is contained in the grooves.—After *Chem. News*.

Creolin, an antiseptic, oily substance lately introduced, is separated from the tar oil of anthracite coal by treating it with a strong alkali, disengaging the creolin with acid, and distilling it with steam. It forms a milk-white emulsion with water, and in this form may be used as a disinfectant.

IMPROVED SPECIFIC GRAVITY BOTTLE.

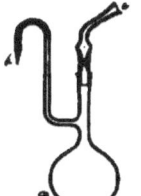

IN the course of a paper on the Analysis of Iron Ore, in the *Chem. News* (Nov. 18th), by A. A. Blair, the author describes his method of taking the specific gravity of the powdered ore, and in connection therewith recommends an improved form of specific gravity bottle. The latter was made with the view of overcoming two difficulties which occur when using the common flask, viz., the expansion and overflow consequent on transferring the flask at 60° F. to the higher temperature of the balance case, and the necessity for waiting until the finely powdered mineral—which was the special object of the author's investigations—had settled before the stopper could be inserted without loss of material. These ends were successfully met by melting on a capillary tubulus to the lower part of the neck, and grinding in a stopper having a small bulb above the capillary, to allow for expansion.

As the author's object was to take the specific gravity of a mineral powder, he had, of course, to insure the complete expulsion of air from between the solid particles. For this purpose he heated the contents of the flasks, after having introduced a weighed quantity of ore and enough water to cover it, almost to boiling by means of a water-bath. Next, the flask was placed under a bell-glass connected with the aspirator, and allowed to boil a few minutes at a reduced pressure. It was then filled with water almost to the tubulus, cooled, the stopper was inserted, and by suction it was then filled slightly above the

FIG. 1.

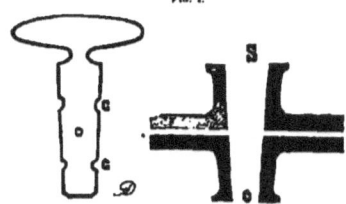

FIG. 2.

Eiloart's air-tight faucet.

mark on the capillary part of the stopper. [Suction is applied at *a*, while the tube *b* dips into water.]

The same manipulation is, of course, required when using the apparatus for any other specific gravity determinations.

When it has been filled to the point described by the author, so that it actually holds more liquid than is required at 60° F., the apparatus is put in a place where it will acquire the temperature just mentioned. The level of liquid in the capillary tube is then adjusted exactly to the mark either by touching the orifice of *b* with blotting paper to withdraw any excess, or by presenting to it a drop or two of the liquid to imbibe it.

The flask is then dried, transferred to the balance case, and when it has acquired the temperature of the room, weighed.

Antifebrin.

SINCE the first experiments with this valuable remedy performed by Drs. Cahn and Hepp, in Strasburg, antifebrin has been carefully studied by others, and with the same satisfactory results. It possesses the advantage of being low in price, and, moreover, the dose is small, two to ten grs. once, twice, or at most three times a day sufficing to produce a considerable reduction of temperature in cases of typhoid fever, pneumonia, also in erysipelas and acute rheumatic gout. It is given in powders as well as in solution; for the latter mode of administration, it will be found most advisable to dissolve it in brandy, subsequently adding a little water and syrup, as follows: Antifebrin, 1 drachm; brandy, 4½ ounces. Dissolve and add distilled water, 6 drachms; syrup, 6 drachms. One tablespoonful a dose. The remedy is thus rendered very pleasant to take.

A good preparation should be of pure white color, and form moderately large crystals, which are but very sparingly soluble in cold water, rather more readily in hot, and easily in alcohol. Antifebrin melts at 233.6°, and boils at 563°.—*Monthly Mag.*

Table Showing the Yield of Essential Oil as Obtained from Various Plants and Parts of Plants.

Messrs. Schimmel & Co., of Leipzig, have appended to their fall report on Essential Oils* a very valuable table, showing the average yield of essential oil, as obtained, on a manufacturing scale, from a large number of natural products. The original table contains the German name of the crude substance (plant or part of plant), the botanical name and the average yield from 100 kilos. We have omitted the column containing the botanical names, and have re-arranged the table so as to correspond to the English alphabet, but we have appended the botanical source of those substances which are not officinal or less well-known, reference being made to the running numbers of the table. In doing so we have sometimes deviated from the original by giving another botanical name, when this appeared to be more generally recognized by authorities.

As the table comprises only those essential oils which are actually distilled in the works of Messrs. Schimmel & Co., many will be found wanting. Regarding these, statistics must be obtained elsewhere. It may be added that the figures representing the average yield obtained by Schimmel & Co., on a manufacturing scale, are generally larger (in some cases very much larger) than those previously reported by other authorities who work only on a small or experimental scale.

Natural product.	Average yield, per cent.
1 Ajowan Seed	3.000
2 Almond, bitter	0.4–0.7
3 Angelica Root—	
Thuringia	0.750
Saxony	1.000
4 Angelica Seed	1.150
5 Anise Seed—	
Chili	2.400
Levant	1.800
Moravia	2.800
Russia	3.200
Spain	2.100
Thuringia	2.400
6 Arnica Flowers	0.040
7 Arnica Root	1.100
8 Asafœtida	3.250
9 Avens Root	0.040
10 Balsam Copaiba—	
Para	45.000
11 Balsam Gurjun	65.000
12 Balsam Peru	0.400
13 Basil, sweet (herb)	0.060
14 Bay Leaves	2.5–3.5
15 Buchu Leaves	2.600
16 Butter Bur Root	0.055
17 Calamus Root	2.300
18 Canella Bark	1.000
19 Caraway Seed, cult.—	
Germany	4.000
Holland	5.500
Moravia	5.000
East Prussia	5.000
20 Caraway Seed, wild—	
Germany	6.0–7.0
Norway	6.0–6.5
Russia	5.000
21 Cardamom Seed—	
Ceylon	4.0–6.0
Madras	5.000
Malabar	4.250
Siam	4.300
22 Carrot Seed	1.650
23 Cascarilla Bark	1.750
24 Cassia Buds	1.350
25 Cedar Wood	2.500

Natural product.	Average yield, per cent.
26 Celery Herb	0.200
27 Celery Seed	2.000
28 Chamomile, German	0.285
29 Chamomile, Roman	0.7–1.0
30 Chekan Leaves	1.000
31 Cinnamon, Ceylon	1.500
32 Cinnamon, Ceylon	0.9–1.25
33 Cloves—	
Amboina	19.000
Bourbon	18.000
Zanzibar	17.000
34 Clove Stems	6.000
35 Coriander—	
East Indies	0.150
Holland	0.600
Italy	0.700
Mogadore	0.600
Russia	0.900
Thuringia	0.800
36 Crisp Mint	1.000
37 Cubebs	12.0–16.0
38 Cullilaban Bark	3.400
39 Cumin Seed—	
East Indies	2.250
Malta	2.900
Mogadore	3.000
Syria	4.200
40 Dill Seed—	
Germany	3.500
Russia	4.000
41 Dill Seed, East Ind.	3.000
42 Elder Flowers	0.025
43 Elecampane Root	0.900
44 Elemi Resin	17.000
45 Eucalyptus Leaves	3.000
46 Fennel Seed—	
Galicia	6.000
Saxony	5.0–5.5
47 Fennel Seed, East Ind.	3.200
48 Galbanum	6.500
49 Galangal	0.750
50 Ginger Root—	
Africa	2.500
Bengal	2.000
Cochinchina	1.900

Natural product.	Average yield, per cent.
Japan	1.800
51 Heracleum Seed	1.000
52 Hops	0.700
53 Hyssop	0.400
54 Iva Herb	0.400
55 Juniper Berries—	
Germany	0.5–0.7
Hungary	1.0–1.1
Italy	1.1–1.2
56 Laurel Berries	1.000
57 Laurel Leaves	2.400
58 Laurel, California	7.500
59 Lavender Flowers—	
Germany	2.900
60 Linaloa Wood	5.000
61 Lovage Root	0.600
62 Lupulin	3.250
63 Mace	11.0–16.0
64 Marjoram—	
Fresh	0.250
Dry	0.900
65 Massoy Bark	
66 Masterwort	0.800
67 Matico Leaves	2.400
68 Melissa Herb	0.100
69 Michelia Bark	0.300
70 Milfoil	0.080
71 Mugwort Herb	0.045
72 Mugwort Root	0.100
73 Musk Seeds	0.280
74 Mustard—	
East Indies	0.590
Germany	0.750
Holland	0.850
Italy (Puglia)	0.750
75 Mustard, Russian	0.900
76 Myrrh	3.5–6.5
77 Nigella Seed	0.300
78 Nutmeg	8.0–10.0
79 Nard, Celtic, Root	1.000
80 Olibanum	6.300
81 Opoponax	6.500
82 Origanum (Creta)	3.500
83 Orris Root	0.200
84 Parsley Herb	0.300

Natural product.	Average yield, per cent.
85 Parsley Seed	3.000
86 Parsnip Seed	2.400
87 Patchouli Herb	1.5–4.0
88 Peach Kernels	0.8–1.0
89 Pepper, Black	2.200
90 Peppermint—	
Fresh	0.300
Dry	1.0–1.25
91 Pimenta	3.500
92 Pimpinella Root	0.025
93 Poplar Buds	0.500
94 Pyrethrum Herb	0.030
95 Rose, fresh	0.050
96 Rosemary, wild	0.350
97 Rosewood	6.040
98 Sage—	
Germany	1.400
Italy	1.700
99 Sandal—	
East Indies	4.500
Macassar	2.500
100 Sandal, West Indies	2.700
101 Sassafras	2.600
102 Savin	3.750
103 Snake Root, Canada	2.0–2.5
104 Snake Root, Virginia	2.000
105 Staranise, China	5.000
106 Staranise, Japan	1.000
107 Storax	1.000
108 Sumbul Root	0.300
109 Tansy	0.150
110 Thyme, wild	0.300
111 Turmeric Root	5.200
112 Uva Ursi Leaves	0.010
113 Valerian—	
German	0.950
Holland	1.000
114 Valerian, Japan	
115 Vetiver Root	0.2–0.35
116 Water Drop Wort	1.300
117 Wormseed, Levant	3.000
118 Wormwood Herb	0.3–0.4
119 Zedoary Root	1.300

*Bericht von Schimmel & Co. (Inhaber Gebr. Fritzsche), in Leipzig. Fabrik ätherischer Oele, Essenzen und chemischer Präparate. October, 1887. Leipzig.

Notes. 1.—From *Carum Ajowan* Benth. et Hook. (*Ammi copticum* L.—*Ptychotis coptica* et *Pt. Ajowan* DC.)—9. From *Geum urbanum* L.—11. From *Dipterocarpus turbinatus*, Gaert. fil., and other species of *Dipt.*—13. From *Ocimum Basilicum* L.—16. *Tussilago Petasites* L.—24. From the unripe fruits of the Chinese Cinnamon tree.—25. *Juniperus Virginiana* L.—26, 27. *Apium graveolens* L.—28. *Matricaria Chamomilla* L.—29. *Anthemis nobilis* L.—36. *Mentha crispa* L.—38. *Laurus Culilaban* L.—39. *Cuminum Cyminum* L.—40. *Anethum graveolens* L.—41. *Anethum Sowa* Roxb.; but this is identical with the preceding.—42. *Sambucus nigra* L.—44. *Icica Abilo* Blanco (doubtful).—45. *Eucalyptus globulus* Labill.—46. *Fœniculum Panmorium* DC., merely a variety of *F. vulgare* Gaert.—49. From *Alpinia Galanga* Willd. This is the so-called Greater Galangal (Radix Galangæ majoris) obtained from Java. It must not be confounded with the "Lesser Galangal," the root of *Alpinia officinarum* Hance, which comes from China. This contains, according to the Pharmacographia, 0.7 per cent of essential oil.—51. *Heracleum Sphondylium* L., cow parsley.—54. The herb formerly called *Herba Ivæ* or *Herba Genippi veri*, and usually referred to *Iva moschata* Schreb., now better referred to several species of *Ajuga*, chiefly *A. Iva*; also *A. Chamæpitys* Schreb., ground pine, or yellow bugle.—56, 57. *Laurus nobilis* L.—58. *Oreo-*

daphne Californica Nutt., bay-laurel or spice tree.—60. *Elaphrium graveolens* Kunth? It is now generally, and more correctly referred to species of *Burnera*.—61. *Ligusticum Levisticum* L.—64. *Origanum Majorana* L.—65. Referred to "Massoia aromatica" by Schimmel & Co. The precise source is undetermined. Some species of *Cinnamomum* have been regarded as the mother plant.—66. *Imperatoria Ostruthium* L.—69. *Michelia nilagirica*, according to Schimmel & Co. Probably *Michelia Champaca* L.—71, 72. *Artemisia Abrotanum* L.—73. *Abelmoschus moschatus* Moench. (*Hibiscus Abelmoschus* L.)—75. *Sinapis* (*Brassica*) *juncea* L.—77. *Nigella sativa* L.—79. *Valeriana celtica* L.—80. Various species of *Boswellia*.—81. The source is unknown. Has been referred to *Opoponax Chironium* Koch. (See special note at end of this article.)—82. *Origanum criticum* L.—83. The "oil of orris" is understood to be chiefly myristic acid containing a very small quantity of the essential oil. It is impracticable to separate the latter from the former.—86. *Pastinaca sativa* L.—87. *Pogostemon Patchouli* Pell.—92. *Pimpinella Saxifraga* L., common burnet saxifrage.—93. *Populus nigra* L.—93. In Schimmel & Co.'s list quoted as "Matricaria-Kraut" from *Matricaria Parthenium*. Now generally referred to *Pyrethrum Parthenium* Smith.—95. *Rosa centifolia* L.—96. *Ledum palustre* L.—97. *Convolvulus Scoparius* L., also called "rhodium wood" (see this JOURNAL, 1887, p. 35). The oil of rosewood mentioned in the table, of course, means the true essential oil distilled from this wood, and does not mean the so-called oil of rhodium, which is generally an artificial mixture of several oils.—100. Source unknown. The plant, however, has been ascertained to belong to the family Rutaceæ.—103. *Asarum Canadense* L.—106. *Illicium religiosum* L. Baillon and others now regard this identical with the common star-anise.—110. *Thymus Serpyllum* L.—111. *Curcuma longa* L.—114. *Patrinia scabiosæfolia* Link.—115. *Andropogon muricatus* Retz.—116. *Phellandrium aquaticum* L.—*Œnanthe Phellandrium* Lamb.—119. *Curcuma Zedoaria* Rosc.

Note on Opoponax. (By Ed. Am. Droin.)

Dr. Joh. L. Schlimmer, in his valuable work entitled "*Terminologie médico-pharmaceutique et anthropologique française-persane,*" (fol., Teheran, 1874 (lithographed), page 410, has the following note on opoponax:

Opoponax; angl. opoponax; allem. panax gummi; pers. djaw-chive. (After giving the statement of Persian authorities as to its medicinal properties, he continues as follows. We translate into English:)

"Dr. Polak (that is, Dr. I. E. Polak, of Vienna, professor at the Persian College) states (II. c. I., 119, and II., 209) that opoponax is the product of *Diplolænia cachrydifolia*, which occurs in the high mountains extending northwards of Teheran, particularly near Azadhar. The plants, when in buds, or the young shoots, are used by the Persian, as a culinary vegetable, both fresh and pickled in vinegar. I have not yet been able to ascertain whether the

Opoponax persicum, Boiss., which Mr. Kotchy ('Abhand. der Geogr. Gesellschaft') has found near Ostonbagh and Dermeri, in the same mountains, which furnishes opoponax ... is identical with the *Diplotænia* mentioned by Dr. Polak."

Note on Mitcham Oils of Peppermint and Lavender.*

The stem and leaves, or the leaves alone, of the lavender are placed in a huge iron container or still, and covered with water. A fire is then lighted under the container, and when the water in the latter commences to boil, the steam is forced through the only exit, viz., a worm-shaped pipe, which has been fixed to the still before the heat is applied. This pipe runs into a cooling-vat, where it is surrounded by cold water, and then the vapor passing from the still, which carries the essential oil with it, is condensed, the oil at the same time being liquefied. Oil and water together are then drawn from the worm by a tap and left to separate, the oil being subsequently drawn off. The steamed-out part of the plants is put aside, dried in the air, and burnt; but, especially just after the distillery season, the accumulation of this waste product causes much in convenience. The peppermint oil is usually sold as it comes from the still, this being the cheapest variety; but, in another part of the works, there is a rectifying apparatus in which the more expensive grades of oils are treated, in order to remove the resinous matter and improve the color. The oil which first runs out of this apparatus is placed aside and sold as "triple rectified;" the bulk following forms the second quality, and the remainder is simply "rectified" oil. After each distillation, or if a different material has to be distilled, the container is cleaned, and the odor which still adheres to it is destroyed by boiling water containing alkali in solution. A large proportion of the mint is raised on land belonging to the works, but part of the material is bought from farmers in the neighborhood, and it is said that the acreage devoted to the crop by growers in Mitcham and the surrounding villages is increasing every year. This year nearly 3,000 lbs. essential oil of peppermint were distilled at the Mitcham works, about 360 lbs. being obtained from the white mint—the most prized variety, which, of course, is always distilled separately. This oil of white mint sells at 45s. to 50s. per lb., but the cultivation of the white mint is not likely to extend in the same proportion as that of the black, the former only containing about one-half of the percentage of essential oil of the latter. Besides, white peppermint is a crop which is particularly sensitive to climatic influences, and suffers more severely from drought or frost than does the black mint. Of course, the quantity of 3,000 lbs., large as it is, only represents a fraction of the whole of the oil actually distilled at Mitcham. There are several works in that district, and many farmers are in the habit of getting their crops distilled at some of these, paying a royalty for the use of the stills. Lavender is also an important crop in Mitcham. At the distillery which we have described, only the leaves of the plant are placed in the still, the stems being thrown away, as they are thought to render less fragrant the aroma of the oil of the leaf. The lavender crop this season has been about the best for ten years, and nearly 500 lbs. of oil were obtained at the distillery. The proprietors are endeavoring to extend the growing of this crop, and to induce farmers to try the cultivation of new products. Chamomiles were a total failure this year, and only 30 or 40 lbs. of oil were obtained from Mitcham flowers. This had all been sold as soon as it was distilled. We were shown a fine sample of beautiful deep-green color and penetrating odor. Their oil averages from 30s. to 40s. per lb. in price; but this year the firm were able to make 80s. per lb. for the small quantity which they distilled.

Methylal.

Methylal is a soporific of very recent date. It is administered in doses of 20 to 25 grains in water, with a little syrup, thus: Methylal, 1 drachm; syr. orange flower, 4 ounces; water, 1 ounce. One tablespoonful for a dose. It has also been applied externally as a local anæsthetic dissolved in oil, or as an ointment with lard as a base. Both forms are made to contain 15 per cent of methylal. It is a colorless ethereal fluid, which smells like a mixture of chloroform and acetic ether, and tastes pungent and aromatic; it is readily soluble in water as well as in alcohol. The sp. gr. at 30° F. is 0.855; it boils at 107.6°.—*Monthly Mag.*

Hypnon.

By means of 3 to 8 grain doses of this very powerful soporific, a profounder sleep is produced than that caused by chloral hydrate. It possesses an agreeable(?) aroma, somewhat resembling a mixture of oil of bitter almonds and neroli, but its action on the mucous membrane of the mouth is almost caustic. It is dispensed, therefore, in capsules of gelatin, each of which contains 1 grain of the remedy, combined with 10 of almond oil, to prevent any risk of unpleasant effects. It is a colorless fluid, sparingly soluble in water, more readily so in alcohol, of the sp. gr. 1.032 at 59° F., the boiling point being 410° F.—*Monthly Mag.*

DRYING-FRAME FOR FUNNELS.

An easily adjustable frame for drying filters contained in funnels is shown in the accompanying cut. It is described by Victor Meurer in the *Zeitschr. f. Anal. Chemie* (1887, 514). It consists of two glass rods bent in the shape of a triangle, and two glass rods bent at each end under an angle of 90 degrees, which ends are slipped over the upward-pointing ends of the triangle. A small glass rod, with in-turned ends, serves to prevent the parallel tubes from spreading. The funnels are simply placed in the rack, and the whole arrangement made of such a size that it will go over a sand-bath.

Meurers' drying frame for funnels.

IMPROVED BUNSEN BURNER.

Mr. E. P. Venable has constructed a modified Bunsen burner, (see figure), in which the exit of the coal-gas, at the place where it mingles with the air, may be regulated by means of a screw at the bottom of the burner. The gas occupies the space surrounding the inner cone, which is adjustable by the screw. If the volume of gas were regulated by a stop-cock somewhere in the inlet-tube *a*, the pressure between the stop-cock and the exit of the gas would constantly vary according as the stop-cock is turned on full or in part. With the above-described new construction, the pressure of gas remains constantly uniform up to the point of exit.

The same construction may be applied in burners intended for gasolin.—*Journ. Anal. Chem.*

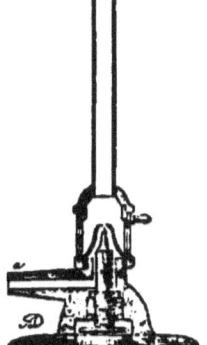

AN IMPROVED APPARATUS FOR ESTIMATING CARBONIC ACID.

Robert Muencke has made some improvements in the usual forms of Geissler's apparatus for estimating carbonic acid.

A is the receptacle for the carbonate. The acid is poured into the cup-shaped neck *B*, and by suitably turning the stopper—which bears the wash-apparatus and delivery, acid is admitted into *A*, through the interior tube *d*. The developed carbonic acid gas passes out in the direction of the arrows, being compelled to pass through the liquid surrounding the inner tube *c*, for the purpose of being washed. When the reaction is completed, air is aspirated through *e*, the stopper in the lower receptacle being removed.—*Chem. Zeit.* and *Chem. Centralbl.*

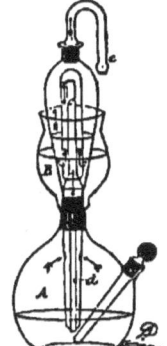

Saccharin when fused with sodium hydrate is decomposed, and salicylate of soda is contained in the mass formed. This on neutralization with hydrochloric acid yields with ferric salts the intense violet coloration which is so characteristic of salicylic acid. From this it is obvious how saccharin may be detected.

Detection of Vegetable Oils in Cod-Liver Oil.

PROF. E. SALKOWSKI has published a lengthy paper on methods of testing cod-liver oil and vegetable oils in the *Zeitsch. f. Anal. Chem.* (1887, 557-582), from which we take the more important portions.

The author paid special attention to methods by which the presence of *vegetable oils* could be detected. Probably, the conditions of the cod-liver oil trade in some sections of Europe are entirely different from what they are near the sea-coast, or in this country, for it is pretty well known that vegetable oils are of little use for adulterating cod-liver oil, as long as cheap fish-oils, such as dorsch oil, menhaden oil, etc., can be obtained in large quantities, of fair quality, and at low prices. However this may be, Prof. Salkowski's investigations have led to some very interesting results.

Instead of detailing at length the experiments regarding the melting and freezing point of the oil, or the quantity of volatile acid which may be distilled off from the fatty acids of a given quantity of the oil, we will at once state that no useful or practical test could be based on these data.

The author, thereupon, turned his attention to the well-known reaction, which has long been in use as a test of identity for cod-liver oil, namely that produced by mixing the oil with sulphuric acid. This test is best performed in two ways, namely, first, by allowing sulphuric acid to flow into cod-liver oil contained in a watch-glass, and second, by dissolving a few drops of cod-liver oil in chloroform, then adding the sulphuric acid and shaking.* The Pharm. Germ. II. directs a solution of the oil in disulphide of carbon; but Salkowski agrees with Hager, that a chloroform solution is much preferable, as the tints are more persistent. The mixture of sulphuric acid and chloroform solution of cod-liver oil, when shaken, assumes successively the following colors:

1. Violet-blue.   3. Brownish-red.
2. Purple.   4. Deep brown.

This remarkable and well-known reaction, which occurs also when the oil contains considerable proportions of foreign oils, is referred by all authorities to the presence of *biliary* constituents, without the latter having as yet been determined by any one. But the assumption of the presence of these biliary matters in cod-liver oil is altogether unsupported. Buchheim has proven that the oil contains no *biliary acids;* and the above test does not serve for the detection of *bile pigments.* On the other hand, the test has a remote resemblance to that for cholesterin, if the latter is dissolved in chloroform, as Salkowski advises. But it will not be proper to call cholesterin a constituent of the bile (though it occurs therein in small quantities), because it is so widely distributed through nature, and particularly the animal kingdom.

In order to determine which constituents of cod-liver oil produce this reaction, a number of samples (50 Gm. each) of cod-liver oil of different origin were saponified with alcoholic solution of potassa, the alcohol nearly all evaporated, the resulting soap solution dissolved in much water (2 liters), and the strongly alkaline solution shaken with ether. The separation of the ethereal layer requires a long time and can often be completed only by the addition of a little alcohol.

On distillation, the ethereal solution yielded a yellowish residue, which at once congealed to a solid mass, and consisted mainly of *cholesterin.*

By *recrystallization from hot alcohol,* and spreading the crystalline magma upon porous tiles, it was obtained as a brilliant white mass melting at 146° C. Microscopical appearance and reactions proved it conclusively to be pure cholesterin. Its chloroformic solution was perfectly colorless, and gave the typical reaction with sulphuric acid, *without showing the blue tint* which at first appears in cod-liver oil.

The amount of cholesterin in cod-liver oil is rather considerable, certainly much larger than in other animal oils. On an average, it amounted to 0.3 per cent. Regarding the reaction of sulphuric acid with the chloroform solution of cholesterin, the following new observations are given by Salkowski. If the purplish-violet chloroform solution which floats on top of the sulphuric acid is diluted by the further addition of chloroform, it is rendered almost colorless, or intensely blue; but on shaking it with the acid, it returns to its former tint. This is no doubt caused by a trace of water in the chloroform. For, if the purplish chloroform solution is poured into an absolutely dry test-tube, it retains its color; further addition of chloroform renders it light blue, and addition of sulphuric acid and shaking again turns it purplish-violet. If chloroform, which had previously been shaken with sulphuric acid, is used for dilution, no change of color occurs.

We now come back again to the residue obtained after distilling off the ether. If this is *not* recrystallized from alcohol, but at once treated with chloroform, it dissolves to a limpid *golden-yellow* liquid. This liquid assumes a magnificent *blue* color with sulphuric acid, but the blue tint soon disappears and makes room for the other normal cholesterin tints. Since *pure* cholesterin does not yield this blue reaction, but only when it contains the yellow coloring matter, the blue tint must be caused by the action of sulphuric acid upon the *latter*. Now this yellow coloring matter is *not* a bile pigment, because when its chloroformic solution is shaken with solution of carbonate of sodium, it is not taken up by the latter. It belongs to the series of bodies known as *lipochroms* ("fat-coloring matters"), studied by W. Kühne.

The fatty acids of cod-liver oil themselves, are, however, likewise involved in the color reaction with sulphuric acid, as is pointed out by the author.

Hence, the color reaction between sulphuric acid and cod-liver oil is attributable to three causes, viz., *cholesterin, lipochrom,* and *the fatty acids.*

The question now arose, how vegetable oils would behave under the same method of treatment. The author found that a coloring matter, yielding a *blue* tint in chloroformic solution with sulphuric acid, exists *only* in *palm oil,* and here in considerable quantity. Traces are also found in cotton-seed oil, but none whatever in all other oils that were examined.

Cholesterin, on the other hand, was met with in all examined oils, except *palm* oil. This oil is obtained from the *flesh of the fruit.* It may therefore be properly inferred that *cholesterin* is a constituent of all *seed oils.*

The fatty acids obtained from vegetable oils were found not to respond to the reaction with sulphuric acid. A trace of such reaction only occurred with linseed and palm oil.

Now it appeared at first quite doubtful whether the discovery of the true cause of the color reaction could be put to practical use for testing the identity or purity of an oil. On further examination, however, the prospect of utilizing it became much more favorable.

The presence of cholesterin in *vegetable oils* had been known for some time. In 1878, Hesse discovered, in Calabar beans, a substance much resembling cholesterin, and gave it the name *phytosterin.* Concerning this body, other authorities have varied considerably in their views. While Maly did not regard its existence as sufficiently proven, Beilstein (*Handbuch de Org. Chem.* 1st ed., p. 1,377) refers *all* statements of the occurrence of cholesterin in the vegetable kingdom to *phytosterin,* an assumption which Salkowski declares to be exceedingly probable. Maly had pointed out that Hesse's phytosterin may possibly be identical with the iso-cholesterin of wool-fat, and regretted that Hesse had not examined the behavior of the former with sulphuric acid, so as to ascertain whether it gave the same color reactions as cholesterin, or no color at all, like iso-cholesterin. Subsequently, however, Hesse supplied this information, stating that it *did* give the same color reaction as cholesterin.

Since there is no longer any reason to doubt the existence of phytosterin, it occurred to Salkowski that the "*cholesterin*" *of vegetable oils is identical with this phytosterin.* And this turned out to be so in reality.

The two substances, cholesterin and phytosterin (the latter including now the so-called "cholesterin" of vegetable oils) may be sharply distinguished by the following criteria. In the case of

Cholesterin		Phytosterin
a magma of lamellæ.	The hot saturated or nearly saturated alcoholic solution congeals, on cooling, to crystalline	bunches or groups of solid, and sometimes rather broad needles.
extremely thin, rhombic plates, frequently with an inturned angle.	Under the lens, the crystals appear as	long, rather solid needles arranged in form of stars or bunches.
(never like in phytosterin)	When slowly crystallized the crystals appear	as handsomely developed, rather elongated, six-sided plates.
(never like in phytosterin)	When rapidly crystallized	most of the needles show a characteristic double-pointed free end.
146° C.	Melting point	132°-134° C. (according to Hesse, 132°-133° C.).

In order to test the practical applicability of the different behavior of these two substances, the author prepared three mixtures of pure cod-liver oil with 20 per cent of rape oil, linseed oil, and cotton-seed oil, respectively, and tested them in the following manner:

10 Gm. of cod-liver oil were introduced into a flask, next 10 Gm. of potassa, dissolved in 10 Gm. of water, were added, and lastly 10 C.c. of alcohol. On shaking and gently heating, the mixture becomes quite hot, and the saponification is completed in a few minutes. The solution is then

---
*The U. S. Ph. (1880) gives this test in the following language: "On the addition of sulphuric acid, the Oil acquires a violet color, soon changing to brownish red, and if 1 drop of the oil be dissolved in 20 drops of disulphide of carbon, and the solution shaken with 1 drop of sulphuric acid, it will acquire a violet blue tint, rapidly changing to rose-red and brownish-yellow."

diluted with water to 600-700 C.c., and this thoroughly shaken (in a large separator) with about 500 C.c. of ether. After the ether has separated—which requires several hours, but which may be somewhat hastened by the addition of a small quantity of alcohol—the ethereal solution is removed, filtered through paper, if necessary, and the ether nearly all distilled off. Since the residue always contains a trifle of unsaponified fat it should be warmed once more with alcoholic solution of potassa. The resulting turbid solution is then again shaken with a little ether, the ethereal solution removed and washed several times with water in order to remove any traces of soap that might have been taken up by it. It is then evaporated in a deep glass capsule, the residue dissolved (in the same capsule) in hot alcohol, and this solution then evaporated to 1 or 2 C.c., the capsule being covered with a large watchglass. The soft crystalline magma which separates on cooling and standing is spread upon a porous tile, and after it has been dried, its melting point determined. In pure cod-liver oil this was found to be 145° C., while in the three samples purposely adulterated it was regularly between 139° and 140° C. These differences are not large, but, nevertheless, are large enough to form a definite decision.

The author also examined cod-liver oil with reference to the amount of *free fatty acids* it contains. The leading authorities in therapeutics maintain that the presence of free fatty acids in cod-liver oil is one of the most valuable features, inasmuch as these acids, after having passed the stomach, form soaps with the alkali of the bile and the pancreatic juice, and in this form (as soap emulsion) are most readily assimilated. Salkowski has, however, found that all *light-colored cod-liver oil* contains only minute quantities of free fatty acids (0.34 to 0.69 per cent calculated as oleic acid), consequently the above-mentioned theory is not applicable to these oils. Darker colored oils, however, do contain a notable quantity of free fatty acids; one sample examined by the author containing 6.5 per cent. This being the case, it would seem as if the dark cod-liver oils deserved the preference medicinally. On the other hand, their advantages might be neutralized by their bad odor and taste.

[It will be of interest to study the properties of the cholesterin obtained from other fish-oils, not derived from livers, for these are perhaps more commonly used as adulterants of cod-liver oil than any other.]

A FILLING FLASK FOR BURETTES.

Arthur Stein recommends a flask with two tubes for filling volumetric solutions into burettes. If small funnels are used, the liquid is sometimes apt to lose somewhat in strength, particularly if it contains volatile chemicals, such as ammonia or hydrochloric acid. Besides, the new device renders the use of a funnel altogether unnecessary. The arrangement and use of the apparatus are easily intelligible from the cut. The tubes *a c* and *d* have a calibre of 5 millimeters ; *c* is about ½ inch shorter than the other tube. Hence, when the flask is inclined so as to discharge liquid, the latter will cease to flow as soon as the orifice of the shorter tube is below the surface of the liquid.—*Chem. Zeit.* and *Chem. Centralbl.*

APPARATUS FOR SHAKING AND SEPARATING LIQUIDS.

A very handy apparatus, serving as a double separatory funnel, when immiscible liquids have to be first shaken with each other and afterwards separated, has been devised by Robert Schütze. It consists of two glass globes *A* and *B* connected together by a two-way cock. The latter, when in the position shown in the cut, establishes communication between the globe *A* and the exterior, so that a liquid may be drawn off into a suitable receptacle. In the same manner, the globe *B* may be connected with the exterior. If the stop-cock is turned through an angle of 90°, it establishes communication between the globes and shuts off that with the exterior. At *a* and *b* are two tubulures, for charging the globes with liquid.—*Chem. Zeit.*

[There is one point connected with this apparatus which seems to bear improvement. That is, the handles of the stop-cock and of the two glass stoppers should all be on one side, so that when the apparatus is held so that the central stop-cock is to discharge any of the within contained liquid, the stoppers may not be liable to fall out,

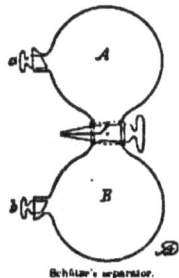

Schütze's separator.

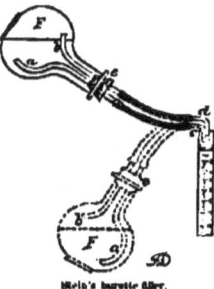

Stein's burette filler.

as would seem to be the case with the apparatus shown in the cut.

For support, two common straw-rings will answer.—Ed. Amer. Drug.]

The Manufacture of Cocaine.

H. T. Pfeiffer gives the following account of his process of manufacturing crude cocaine in Peru and Bolivia.

The disintegrated coca leaves are digested at 70° C. in closed vessels for two hours, with a very weak solution of sodium hydrate and petroleum (boiling between 200° and 250° C.). The mass is filtered, pressed while still tepid, and the filtrate allowed to stand until the oil has completely separated from the aqueous solution. The oil is drawn off and carefully neutralized with very weak hydrochloric acid. A white, bulky precipitate of cocaine hydrochloride is obtained, together with an aqueous solution of the same compound, while the petroleum is free from the alkaloid and may be used for the extraction of a fresh batch of leaves. The precipitate is dried, and by concentrating the aqueous solution a further quantity of the hydrochloride is obtained. Both can be shipped without risk of decomposition. The product is not quite pure, but contains some hygrine, traces of gum, and other matters. Its percentage of alkaloid is 75 per cent, while chemically pure cocaine hydrochloride ($C_{17}H_{21}NO_4.2N.Cl$) contains 80.6 per cent of the alkaloid. The sodium hydrate solution cannot be replaced by milk of lime, nor can any other acid be used for neutralization. Alcohol or ether are not suitable for extraction. A repetition of the process with once extracted coca leaves gave no further quantity of cocaine, proving that all the cocaine goes into solution by one treatment. The same process serves on the small scale for the valuation of coca leaves. 100 Gm. of coca leaves are digested in a flask with 400 C.c. of water and 250 C.c. of petroleum ; the flask is loosely covered and warmed on the water-bath, shaking it from time to time. The mass is then filtered, the residue pressed, and the filtrate allowed to separate in two layers. The oil layer is run into a bottle and titrated back with $\frac{1}{10}$ HCl (1 Gm. of HCl in 100 C.c.), until exactly neutral. The number of C.c. of hydrochloric acid required for titrating back, multiplied by 0.42, gives the percentage of cocaine in the samples. The following are some of the results with different samples of coca leaves of various age:

			Per cent of cocaine.	
Coca leaves from	Mapiri,	1 month old,	0.5%	
"	"	" Yungas	" 0.5%	
"	"	" Mapiri and Yungas,		
		6 months old,	0.4%	of the weight of the dry leaves.
"	"	" Cuzco (Peru), 8 months old,	0.3%	
"	"	" Mapiri and Yungas, 1 year old,	0.2%	
"	"	" Cuzco,	0.2%	
"	"	" Mapiri and Yungas, 2 years old,	0.15%	

Coca leaves from Yungas and Cuzco, 3 years old, contained no trace of the alkaloid, whereas fresh green leaves from Yungas contained 0.7 per cent of the weight of the dry leaves. The same process is also applicable for the manufacture of quinine from poor quinine bark, with the single alteration that weak sulphuric acid must be used for the neutralization of the alkaloid petroleum extract.—*Chem. Zeit.*

Cellulose for Finings.

Cellulose, in the form of paper and wood pulp, is now being extensively employed on the continent for the clarifying or "fining" of beer, wines, syrups, and pharmaceutical extracts; a little salicylic acid added to the pulp enables it to be kept in the flocculent or damp state without fear of decomposition. This salicylic cellulose seems to answer very well, and its popularity, accordingly, is rapidly increasing on either side of the Rhine.

Synthesis of a Sugar.—Prof. Fischer and Mr. Tafel, of Würzburg, announce that they have succeeded in producing artificially a substance possessing the properties and the composition of a true sugar, differing, so far as at present known, from glucose only by the fact that it is optically inactive.

[ORIGINAL TRANSLATION AND ABSTRACT.]

The Testing of Commercial Sulphate of Quinine.*

Drs. G. Kerner and A. Weller, the well-known authorities on the field of quinine manufacture, have for some time past been engaged in special studies of the recently proposed methods of testing commercial sulphate of quinine, with a view to ascertain whether Kerner's test could not be so modified as to be applicable to the conditions at present prevailing in the quinine market, or whether some other test should be substituted for it. The first portion of their paper was published in the beginning of this year, and in this part it was demonstrated by the authors that the optical method was inapplicable for an *official* test of sulphate of quinine. In the continuation of the paper, which has just reached us, the authors devote their attention chiefly to the ammonia test and its eventual improvement.

When Dr. Kerner first proposed his test—in 1863—the condition of the quinine market was materially different from what it is at present. At that time, manufacturers of quinine worked up, almost exclusively, only South American barks, which contained, besides quinine, chiefly cinchonine and quinidine, while *cinchonidine* was either entirely absent or played only a very inferior rôle. The cuprea barks which flooded the market some time about and after the year 1870, did not contain this alkaloid either. Consequently, the latter occurred but rarely in commercial sulphate of quinine as a natural constituent. Now, the ammonia test was originally designed for detecting the presence of cinchona alkaloids, other than quinine, when *mechanically mixed* with the latter for the purposes of fraud. And, indeed, it never failed to detect this, and it is even to-day capable of showing even the smallest quantities of other cinchona alkaloids when mechanically mixed with quinine.

For a number of years past, however, the cultivated East Indian barks have more and more been drawn upon by manufacturers, and in some of these, cinchonidine exists in very large proportion, often exceeding that of quinine itself. When the latter alkaloid is isolated and crystallized (as sulphate), it is exceedingly difficult to separate the cinchonidine completely from it. The reason is that during the crystallization a double salt of quinine and cinchonidine is formed, which has the property of being either not at all or but slightly split up by cold water. On testing such a sulphate of quinine with the ammonia test (Kerner's test), it had long been known that different results were obtained according as *cold* or *hot* water was used in treating the salt. With *cold* water, nearly every German quinine stood the test perfectly. But when hot water was employed, even the best German quinines required almost always more than 7 cubic centimeters of water of ammonia of spec. grav. 0.960.

[Since reference will be subsequently made to the wording of Kerner's test as given in the U. S. Pharm., we print it here. It will be noticed that the sample to be tested is first deprived of water, in order to ascertain the amount of the latter present. And to avoid waste of quinine by taking a separate sample for Kerner's test, it is directed that the dry residue be taken for this purpose. The passage in the U. S. Ph. reads as follows:

"If 1 Gm. of the salt be placed in a porcelain capsule, and dried at a temperature of 100° C. (212° F.) for three hours, or until a constant weight is attained, the remainder, cooled in a desiccator, should weigh not less than 0.838 Gm. (absence of more than 8 molecules, or 16.18 per cent of water). If the residue thus dried at 100° C. (212° F.) be agitated with 10 C.c. of distilled water, the mixture macerated at 15° C. (59° F.) for half an hour, then filtered through a small filter, 5 C.c. of the filtrate taken in a test-tube, and 7 C.c. of water of ammonia (spec. grav. 0.960) then added—on closing the tube with the finger and gently turning it until the ammonia is fully intermixed, a clear liquid should be produced. If the temperature of maceration has been 16° C. (60.8° F.), 7.5 C.c. of the water of ammonia may be added; if 17° C. (62.6° F.), 8 C.c. may be added. In each instance, a clear liquid indicates the absence of more than about 1 per cent of cinchonidine or quinidine, and of more than traces of cinchonine."]

Since the detection of cinchonidine by means of the officinal test depends upon the greater solubility of its sulphate compared with quinine sulphate, it follows that in a case where the two alkaloids have been crystallized together, and where *cold* water is used for preparing the test-liquid, the sample may be found apparently free from cinchonidine, while if *hot* water had been used, the latter alkaloid might have been easily detected.

The authors quote a series of parallel experiments, made with cold water and with water at 60° C. upon the same samples of commercial sulphate of quinine, which show conclusively that the use of *cold* water for preparing the test-liquid fails to reveal a large proportion of the cinchonidine. The following table shows the results:

Number of Sample.	Ammonia Required.	
	Test with cold water.	Test with water at 60° C.
1	5.45 C.c.	10.00 C.c.
2	5.50 "	10.00 "
3	7.55 "	10.75 "
4	6.20 "	9.50 "
5	5.80 "	8.40 "
6	6.45 "	8.35 "
7	6.40 "	11.75 "
8	6.65 "	12.70 "
9	6.85 "	10.80 "
10	6.30 "	11.50 "
11	7.00 "	15.00 "
12	7.05 "	13.50 "
13	5.85 "	10.25 "
14	6.80 "	13.00 "
15	6.90 "	11.20 "

It will be seen from this that, of all the samples which appeared to stand the test when *cold* water was used, only a single one stood it with *hot* water. The fact that the two series of figures are not proportionate to each other is simply due to the varying amount of splitting up of the double salt of the alkaloids, which does not always take place uniformly. The authors, therefore, declare that the test is unsuited for a quantitative determination of "latent" cinchonidine, though it may serve as such for the alkaloid when mechanically mixed with the quinine salt.

The occurrence and influence of "latent" cinchonidine may be shown still more prominently by a synthetic method—namely, by applying the test *first* to mechanical mixtures of the two sulphates, and afterwards to another portion of the same mixture, previously raised to boiling and again cooled.

	Requires ammonia.
1. Normal Quinine Sulph.	3.50 C.c.
2. do., mixed with 5% Cinchonidine Sulph.	18.00 "
3. do., do., and boiled	6.15 "
4. do., mixed with 10% Cinchonidine Sulph.	lim'd.*
5. do., do., and boiled	12.70 "

Under favorable circumstances, even larger percentages of cinchonidine may become latent and escape the test.

In order to make the ammonia test applicable to the kind of quinine at present available in the market, in the first place necessary to direct the sample to be treated with water at such a temperature as will be certain to split up any double salt of quinine and cinchonidine that may be present. Besides, the quantity of ammonia may be regulated according to the degree of purity which the officinal salt is required to have. It has been demonstrated that, when perfectly pure sulphate of quinine is extracted with cold water, as directed by the test, it does *not* require 7 C.c. of ammonia to dissolve it. In fact, the authors have found, from a large number of careful experiments, that an absolutely chemically pure sulphate of quinine, treated with water at 15° C., furnishes a solution, 5 C.c. of which require *only* 3.4 to 3.5 C.c. of water of ammonia of spec. grav. 0.960 for precipitating and redissolving the quinine. If, therefore, the market could be supplied with chemically pure sulphate of quinine, the preceding figures would represent the proportions to be used in the test.

The authors point out that sulphate of quinine may be regarded as absolutely chemically pure if, when treated with *any* proportion of cold water (insufficient for its complete solution), it always yields solutions requiring exactly identical amounts of ammonia for the end-reaction, and if these results remain unaffected even by repeated recrystallization of the salt and applying the test to the several mother-liquors.

The proposition had already been made by other experimenters, to modify the test by using hot or boiling water. But the authors, aware that too high a temperature would be liable to introduce other drawbacks, made a series of careful experiments to determine the most suitable temperature. In the course of these experiments it was found that the *size* of the crystals in which the salt exists exerts a considerable influence upon the amount of cinchonidine entering into solution.

This error may be avoided either by reducing the sample to powder, previous to macerating it in water, or to drive out the water of crystallization by exposure to a gentle heat (40–50° C.). The latter temperature is preferred by the authors to one at 100° C. (212° F.), because in the former case there is obtained a stable salt containing 2 molecules of water. On drying at 100° C., this is dissipated, but is again gradually reabsorbed by exposure to damp air.

The objection has been raised that if a temperature higher than 15° C. is used for maceration, the resulting solution is liable to be supersaturated. Although it is not likely that this can occur while a notable quantity of undissolved crystals are still present in the liquid, yet it has been found that there is some change produced in the salts, so far as to render them *basic*. That is, even a

---

* Abstract of a paper by Dr. G. Kerner and Dr. A. Weller, entitled "Prüfung des käuflichen schwefelsauren Chinins," in the Archiv der Pharmacie, 1887, pp. 711–733. Received as pamphlet from the authors.

* Even a very large excess of ammonia was unable to produce a clear solution.

short heating appears to separate a small proportion of the alkaloids in a *free* state. This may be shown by treating a sample of sulphate of quinine with ether, which will take up only faint traces of the salt, while the same agent will extract a notable quantity of free alkaloid, after it has been heated with water. However, the authors do not regard this as a valid objection, but state that any error resulting from this cause is avoided by allowing the mixture of water and sulphate of quinine to cool during a sufficiently long time.

In order to study the effect of time in cooling, normal or chemically pure sulphate of quinine was used—the same which required 3.4 to 3.5 C.c. of ammonia. One part of this was dissolved as far as possible in 30 parts of boiling water, then cooled, and portions of it tested with ammonia at stated intervals. One series of experiments was made so that the solution was allowed to cool in the air, and the respective sample was placed in a water-bath at 15° C. only half an hour before being tested. In the other series, the hot solution was at once transferred to the water-bath at 15° C., and left there until a sample was tested. The samples of the first series are quoted under the letter *a*, those of the second series under *b*. The figures indicate the amount of ammonia required:

Duration of Cooling.	Cooled in Air and Water. *a*	Cooled in Water. *b*
½ hour	—	5.35 C.c.
1 "	5.20 C.c.	4.85 "
2 "	5.00 "	4.30 "
3½ "	—	3.95 "
4 "	4.90 "	—
4½ "	—	3.85 "
5½ "	—	3.70 "
6 "	4.60 "	—
7 "	4.30 "	—

It will be seen that a perfect return to the constant titer possessed by the original sample requires a considerable time; but nevertheless it takes place much more quickly if the hot solution is at once cooled by being placed in cold water, 5½ hours being required to reach the original titer pretty closely, while in the other case 7 hours were insufficient to approach it even as far as the other.

The return to the original titer, however, is reached still more quickly by taking *less water*, and using a lower temperature for maceration. The following table gives the results of experiments made with 2 Gm. of partly dried sulphate of quinine (with 2 mol. of water) and 20 Gm. of water, four different sets of experiments being made at different temperatures, the time of heating being half an hour. In the sets quoted under *a* and *b*, the temperature was 100° C., in *c* it was 60° C., in *d* heat was not used at all, the salt being only macerated (and occasionally stirred up) with water at 18° C. during 5 hours. The samples were cooled as follows: *a* first in the air, and the portion to be tested cooled in a water-bath at 15° C. during half an hour preceding the test; *b*, *c*, and *d* were cooled by being at once placed into water at 15° C. The figures again denote the quantity of ammonia required:

Duration of Cooling.	*a* Digested at 100° C.	*b* Digested at 100° C.	*c* Digested at 60° C.	*d* Macerated cold.
½ hour	—	6.50	5.40	—
1 "	5.80	—	4.40	3.50
1½ hours	—	—	3.90	3.55
2 "	—	5.20	3.40	—
3 "	—	4.40	3.45	—
3½ "	—	—	3.55	3.50
4 "	—	—	3.50	—
6½ "	5.00	—	3.55	—
7½ "	4.30	—	—	—
18 "	3.45	3.50	—	3.50

From this it appears that a temperature of 60° C., and a cooling in water at 15° C. during two hours, is perfectly sufficient to obtain the correct titer, while, if boiling water is used, a constant titer is reached only after the lapse of a long time.

Upon the basis of the several experiments here outlined, the authors give the following modification of the test:

Modified Kerner's Test.

Allow the sample of sulphate of quinine to effloresce completely by exposure to a heat of 40–50° C. (104–122° F.); then put 2 Gm. of it together with 20 Gm. of distilled water into a test-tube, place this in a water-bath at a temperature of 60–65° C. (140–149° F.), and allow it to remain therein for half an hour, repeatedly shaking up the contents. Then transfer the test-tube to a water-bath at 15° C. (59° F.), and leave it in this for two hours, agitating the contents frequently and strongly. Care is to be taken that, before withdrawing the tube for the purpose of filtration, the temperature of the water-bath shall have been as near as possible to 15° C. (59° F.). [Then quickly filter through pure paper-filters of 7 centimeters diameter.] Transfer 5 C.c. of the filtrate to a test-tube, and add just enough water of ammonia of spec. grav. 0.960 to cause the resolution of the separated quinine. The quantity of ammonia required should not exceed ... cubic centimeters."

The authors temporarily left the amount of ammonia blank, as they were not fully prepared to make a definite proposition. While they themselves advocate a certain degree of purity in the commercial sulphate quinine, and while they feel that neither they nor other honest manufacturers need be suspected of seeking a justification for a low grade of quinine, by arguments against too high a degree of purity, they decidedly differ in opinion from those who want to reject quinine containing more than 1 per cent of cinchonidine, because they believe this to be against the interests of the consumers themselves. The removal of the last percentages of cinchonidine is a very expensive process. And the consumer alone has to pay for this without having the least benefit therefrom, or even without positively improving the medicinal power of the product. A quinine of such a degree of purity would cost about 15 per cent more than the commercial kind. The authors state that the best brands of quinine, for some time past, contain between 2 and 6 per cent of "latent" cinchonidine, which is not a worthless diluent, but is therapeutically nearly identical with the quinine itself. Regarding the ammonia titer, the authors state that, while chemically pure sulphate of quinine requires only 3.4 to 3.5 C.c. of water of ammonia, a mixture of 97 parts of sulph. of quinine and 3 parts of sulph. of cinchonidine requires 4 C.c., and a mixture containing 7 per cent, 6 C.c. of ammonia. Yet these figures are valid only for mixtures of the chemically pure salts. The commercial salt contains sometimes other substances, such as hydroquinine, which have a modifying effect upon the quantity of ammonia.

[We do not agree with our friends Drs. Kerner and Weller in their argument against strict purity of the commercial sulphate of quinine. While we are fully aware of the difficulties in the way, and without being puritanical theorists, we yet believe that sulphate of quinine should be put on the market in as pure a condition as it can be prepared. What if the price should be 15, or even 25 per cent higher? Quinine is so low now that few would feel this advance. We have paid this additional 25 per cent for the impure commercial quinine not a very long while ago. Why should he be unwilling to pay the same price now for a pure article? We believe the time will come when the pure quinine will be in chief demand. One of the principal objections to it has been the supposition that it could not be prepared in the light feathery condition in which the ordinary public has been accustomed to see and purchase it. As prepared from the bisulphate, it is indeed usually obtained in heavy, hard crystals. Yet a method of preparing it in a light condition has been found and announced not long ago. Hence this objection is no longer valid.—Ed. Am. Dr.]

The execution of the test as described above is very simple. The sample of quinine may be allowed to effloresce by exposure in a warm place, or this may be accomplished by means of a water-bath at 60–65° C. While the sample is in the cold-water bath, it is not necessary to keep this constantly and exactly at 15° C.; it is only desirable that it shall be as close to this temperature as convenient, and it is even preferable that the temperature shall be rather a little over 15° C. than below this. But special care must be taken that during the 15 or 30 minutes preceding the removal of the sample for filtration, the temperature shall be exactly 15° C. A difference of temperature of only 1° or 2° C. may raise the ammonia titer by ½ to ¼ cubic centimeter. After the mixture has stood the proper time at the required temperature, a portion of the liquid is passed through a small dry filter—7 centimeters in diameter—the filtrate usually amounting to more than 10 C.c., so that there is enough for two titrations. If desired, the filtration may be performed by means of a small aspirator. If sulphate of quinine is digested with water at 100° C., the mixture forms after cooling such a thick magma that it is difficult, even with an aspirator, to obtain 5 C.c. of filtrate. This is an additional reason why the authors prefer a temperature of 60–65° C. For the same reason it is necessary to employ 2 Gm. of the salt and 20 Gm. of water, since if only 1 Gm. of salt and 10 Gm. of water are taken, it is often difficult to obtain 5 C.c. of filtrate.

The water of ammonia must be exactly of the specific gravity 0.960 at 15° C. The titration is best performed in this way, that the *whole allowable quantity of ammonia is added at once*, in order to ascertain whether the sample will come up to the accepted standard, which is really the practical question to be decided. If it is then desired to find the limit up to which ammonia can or must be added so as to still produce a clear liquid, this may be done with another portion of 5 C.c., to which the ammonia may be added in small portions. The end reaction is easily recognised by the fact that, upon being *once* gently turned over, the liquid shows only a faint opalescence, which disappears either at once or within one or two seconds on turning the test-tube over once more. The *disappearance of the opalescence* is the important criterion, and no attention need be paid to any small, solitary specks floating about in the liquid. These specks consist of hydrate of quinine, and are formed now and then in minute quantity, particularly if the ammonia was added too slowly or in too long intervals. They may form in solutions of pure or impure quinine, but are always present in too small a quantity to have any influence upon the end-reaction. [The appearance of these specks may, however, be entirely prevented if, instead of the weaker ammonia (spec. grav. 0.960), the stronger (spec. grav. 0.920) is used. One of the authors had always advocated the use of the latter, but it appears that there are good reasons why the weaker ought to be preferred.] If the preceding details are observed, it is easy to obtain concordant results, though, of course, there will be cases where differences of 0.1 to 0.15 (and even 0.2) C.c. will be observed. In the case of normal or pure sulphate of quinine, or such as had the sulphate of one of the other alkaloids mechanically mixed with it, the end-reaction is much more sharply recognized. Finally, the authors point out that the duration of heating the sample (one-half hour) is to be observed as nearly as possible; while the cooling may be protracted for any desired period, as long as it exceeds two hours.

The authors append a number of analytical figures to show how the amount of ammonia required varies with samples of varying composition. It being impossible to prepare mixtures with pre-determined amount of latent cinchonidine—for, even if exactly known quantities of the two alkaloids are crystallized together, they will not each time form the same quantity of double-salt—the only way by which the authors could exactly determine the relative true proportions of the two alkaloids was by means of the optical method, based upon that of Oudemans.

For this purpose the efflorescent salt was used in each case, the quantity employed corresponding as nearly as possible to 0.745 Gm. (or $\frac{1}{1000}$ molecule) of the anhydrous sulphate. This quantity was dissolved in 6 C.c. of normal hydrochloric acid, diluted to 20 C.c. at 17° C., and the polarising angle determined in a 200 millimeter tube in Laurent's polarimeter. According to the formula $[\alpha] = \frac{a \cdot 20}{2 \cdot p}$, in which p represents the weight of anhydrous sulphate of quinine used, the following values were found as the means of a long series of determinations:
1, for chemically pure sulphate of quinine $[\alpha] = -237.71$
2, for chem. pure sulph. of cinchonidine $[\alpha] = -149.37$

By means of these constants the relation of the two salts in various artificially prepared mixtures was determined as follows:

Number of Mixture	Polarising Angle (α)	Per cent of Cinchonidine in the anhydrous salt	Per cent of Cinchonidine in the hydrous salt	Amount of Cinchonidine originally added
1	−235.8	3.2%	3.1%	2%
2	−233.3	2.8%	2.6%	4%
3	−234.7	8%	3.2%	6%
4	−231.8	7.0%	8.9%	10%
5	−231.1	7.7%	7.27%	10%
6	−229.1	9.7%	9.1%	20%

From the figures in the last columns it appears that with increased admixture of cinchonidine increased amounts of the latter become latent, though the proportions are not always the same.

The six samples, thus exactly determined, were now titrated with ammonia in the manner above described, and the following results obtained:

No. Containing sulphate cinchonidine	Tests made with hot water			With cold water
	I.	II.	III.	IV.
1.	3.1%	3.90−3.95	3.75−3.75	3.75−3.75	3.60−3.55
2.	1.6%	3.90−3.85	3.80−3.80	3.90−3.90	3.75−3.80
3.	3.2%	4.80−4.80	4.90−4.80	4.80−4.85	3.95−4.00
4.	5.9%	5.45−5.45	5.50−5.55	5.40−5.40	4.30−4.50
5.	7.2%	6.85−6.85	6.20−6.25	6.20−6.25	5.10−5.10
6.	9.1%	10.70−10.60	10.55−10.70	10.60−10.60	8.80−8.85

The titrations agree well among themselves. The quantity of ammonia in general increases with the percentage of cinchonidine, but in a more rapid proportion than the latter. Differences of one-half per cent of cinchonidine can be detected by this method only with difficulty, but differences of one per cent with certainty. If less than 1.5 or 2 per cent of cinchonidine is present in a latent condition, its detection becomes doubtful or impossible. But this limit of sensitiveness is perfectly sufficient for an official test. The figures in column IV. were obtained when the samples were macerated in cold water, and are appended only to again show the insufficiency of this solvent.

[If sulphate of cinchonidine were the only impurity occurring in sulphate of quinine, it would follow from the preceding figures that the test of the U. S. Pharm., if modified so as to use hot water for maceration, would permit the presence of about 7.5 per cent of sulphate of cinchonidine, and not one per cent. But, as cold water is directed by the U. S. Ph., the test really permits the presence of a still larger quantity. In reality, however, cinchonidine is not the only contamination.—ED. AM. DR.]

The authors, among other interesting facts (which we are compelled to omit) mention the proposition of Schaefer, to dry sulphate of quinine at 100° C., as this is able to break up the double salt, so that the latent cinchonidine becomes recognizable, whereby the ammonia titer is raised. They acknowledge that the latter is to some extent the case, but they also point out that Schaefer's proposition had long been anticipated by the U. S. Ph., where the salt is directed to be dried at 100° C.

It is now pretty well established that there is probably no commercial sulphate of quinine which does not contain some proportion of *hydroquinine* and probably also *hydrocinchonidine*, as sulphates. Hesse has found that 5 C.c. of a solution of sulphate of hydroquinine saturated at 15° C. require not less than 25 C.c. of ammonia of spec. gr. 0.960. In this respect, therefore, it shows a considerable similarity to cinchonidine. But the sulphate of hydroquinine resembles the latter still more in this respect, that it may form a double salt with sulphate of quinine, in which it is no longer detected by the officinal test (with cold water as macerating liquid), or which influences the ammonia titer but very slightly.

1. Normal sulph. quinine required ammonia 8.5 C.c
2. do with 5% sulph. of hy-
    droquinine, mixed " 11.4 C c.
3. do with 5% " boiled " 4.0 C c.
4. do with 10% " boiled " 6.5 C.c.

Hence, mechanically—added hydroquinine is easily demonstrated, but that which has been crystallized with the quinine is present in a latent form.

The modified ammonia test, however, is fully capable of revealing its presence, as the hot solvent helps to split up the double salt. The influence of the hydroquinine upon the ammonia is about of the same extent as that of cinchonidine.

Since commercial sulphate of quinine often contains a considerable proportion of sulphate of homoquinine—the authors have frequently found 4 to 7 per cent, and even in so-called Chininum sulfuricum *purissimum* they have sometimes found 2, 3 and 4 per cent—it will, of course, exert its influence upon the test. A portion of the titer of commercial sulphate of quinine, which even in the best brands is usually higher than 7 C.c., is, therefore, to be placed to the account of homoquinine. But as this latter alkaloid should not be regarded as a contamination of quinine (it certainly deserves this name much less than cinchonidine), it is but fair to make a corresponding deduction from the titer. The authors think that no great error will be committed if 1½ to 2 C.c. of the ammonia are credited to homoquinine, and simply deducted from the titer.

If it is, however, desired to detect, and approximately determine, the homoquinine, this may be done by means of permanganate of potassium in the following manner: Dissolve five grammes of sulphate of quinine with the aid of a little sulphuric acid in one-half liter of cold water, and add cautiously a dilute solution of permanganate, until a drop placed on a white surface, and touched with a drop of permanganate, does no longer discolor the latter at once, but allows it to retain its color for a short time. Then filter, wash the manganese oxide remaining on the filter with some water, and shake the united filtrates with ether and ammonia. On evaporating the separated ethereal layer (previously washed), the hydroquinine will remain, and if it is pure, may be recognized from its resistance to the action of permanganate. Should it be affected by the latter, this would show that it is still accompanied by undecomposed quinine. In this case the process would have to be repeated.

The Preparation of Infusion of Digitalis.

M. BROEKER, army pharmacist at Utrecht, has recently published a paper on the infusion of digitalis in the *Nieuw Tijdschrift voor d. Pharmacie in Nederland.* He shows that the preparation of this infusion presents certain difficulties which it is well to be aware of, and it becomes nowadays a very important matter to know exactly how much active principle is contained in the different preparations daily met with.

The author recommends pharmacists only to use the parenchyma of the leaf in making infusion of digitalis. This parenchyma contains, he says, about 1 per cent of *digitaline*, whilst the stalks and nerves of the leaves only contain about 0.02 per cent of the same active principle. These, the writer says, should be discarded. Moreover, his experience teaches him that, by leaving the stalks and leaf-nerves, the infusion becomes gelatinous.

With regard to the temperature of the water, and the time it should be allowed to remain in contact with the leaves, M. Broeker finds that a maceration of two hours' duration with water at a temperature of 20° C. gives the best result. The infusion may also be made at a temperature of 70° C., but the result is less satisfactory. [We do not approve the recommendations of the author, because they will necessitate an entire change of adjustment of the dosage of this much-employed preparation.—ED. AM. DR.]

The author says that the same remarks apply perfectly well to making infusion of senna; the best therapeutic preparation is that in which the infusion is obtained by macerating the leaves for two hours with water at a temperature of 15° to 20° C.—*Monthly Mag.*

---

* Namely, to the sulphate of quinine before dissolving and crystallizing the mixture.

Quinine Mixtures.

As regards the solution of quinine in acids, the fact that the mineral acids, strong or dilute, make presentable pill masses indicates that they should not be poured upon the quinine, but that the latter should be well diffused in water before acids are added. Very often, however, no acid is ordered in the prescription. In such a case it is extremely unwise to depart from the letter of the physician's order. The only admissible manner of compounding is to reduce the quinine to fine powder, and diffuse it in the liquids. In some cases, as when spirit of ether is an ingredient, the quinine in this form will tend to adhere to the bottle; but this may be avoided by the addition of a little mucilage of acacia to the mixture. Some dispensers advocate that the quinine should be dissolved in such circumstances, and the view is one for which there is much to be said; but in all cases quinine in solution is much more bitter than when in suspension, and this fact throws the balance of opinion in favor of the suspension method. The greater number of difficulties with quinine mixtures occur through the precipitation of the quinine after it has been brought into solution. The simplest of these, apart from those due to the action of ordinary alkaloidal precipitants, are caused by the formation of less soluble salts owing to double decomposition. For example, ammonium acetate may induce a precipitate. Apparently, nothing is to be dreaded by the mixture of a solution of quinine with spirit of mindererus; but it so happens that acetate of quinine is one of its least soluble salts, although it dissolves readily on heating, and in certain proportions it is possible to get a mixture of an alkaline acetate and quinine sulphate perfectly solid owing to the formation of quinine acetate. Salicylates also form sparingly soluble compounds with soluble quinine salts. The most intractable results are those caused by alkaloidal precipitants. The more common of these which are found associated with quinine in prescriptions are the alkaline carbonates and hydrates, iodides and (from them) iodine, perchloride of mercury and infusions or tinctures containing tannin. In all circumstances these substances precipitate the quinine as insoluble compounds, which in most cases are adhesive. The alkaline hydrates and carbonates precipitate quinine as hydrate, and there is no means of avoiding the precipitation. English prescribers appear to be fonder of ordering the alkalies—generally in the form of aromatic spirit of ammonia—with citrate of iron and quinine than with the plain salts of quinine, probably under the impression that the spirit does not affect the stability of the double citrate. Under the same impression, probably, ammoniated tincture of quinine is sometimes directed to be diluted with water. In this tincture, quinine exists as hydrate dissolved in alcohol, and when the alcohol is reduced to a certain point the quinine falls out of solution. The only way to make presentable mixtures in such cases is to dilute the alkaline solution well, and in the case of other compounds of quinine than the ammoniated tincture, the alkaloidal solution also, adding to the latter mucilage of acacia in the proportion of half a drachm to each ounce of the finished mixture; then mix the two solutions. In this way the quinine is deposited in a fine state of division, and, although it subsides, the precipitate is readily diffusible on shaking, which is not the case if the mucilage is not added, so that it may be considered an admissible alteration of the pharmacy of the prescription, and should therefore be noted thereon for the benefit of the next dispenser. Iodide of potassium forms variable compounds with solutions of quinine salts. Neutral solutions of quinine and iodide of potassium do not react chemically, but the presence of free acid invariably induces a chemical change, and this is increased if there is any substance in the mixture—such as nitric acid or spirits of nitre—which liberates iodine. It is seldom that herapathite is formed—a brown compound of quinine iodide, and free iodine being generally the product. If possible, the dispenser should communicate with the prescriber in such cases, so as to suggest the exclusion of the oxidizing body; failing that, the reaction between the iodide and oxidizing body should be carried out with as small a quantity of iodide as possible, and in a perfectly full phial. The rest of the iodide should be mixed with the quinine and mucilage mixture before the iodine solution is added to it. Bromides present no difficulty with quinine solutions, and it is seldom, fortunately, that perchloride of mercury is prescribed with quinine. The precipitate which it causes is a heavy one, and without something to suspend it, it is possible that the patient might get an excessive quantity of the quinine mercurate in the last dose. Some vegetable infusions containing tannin, particularly the acid infusion of roses, form abhorrent-looking mixtures with quinine, owing to the precipitation of quinine tannate. In these cases, it is best to use pure quinine in proper proportion rather than the sulphate, so that chemical reaction may be reduced to a minimum. Apart from the examples which are given, other kinds of difficulties occasionally occur. In all cases, however, the dispenser has only to adhere to the principles that (1) chemical reaction should be effected in the most dilute solutions, and (2) a means for the proper apportioning of the dose should be adopted; for the latter mucilage of acacia is not only generally suitable, but it has also been shown to retard or modify chemical reaction. Hence the necessity for adding it to the quinine solution before the reacting element.—*Chem. and Druggist.*

Note on Emulsions.*

Notwithstanding that the balance of opinion is greatly in favor of acacia for emulsions, there are still those who hold to tragacanth and continue to recommend it. This is matter for surprise, for the more fully we know the perfect character of acacia emulsions the more completely do those of tragacanth pass into the shade. Tragacanth gives magmas rather than emulsions; you can easily incorporate oils with it, but examine the product and you will see the oil globules are of a coarse character, visible to the unaided eyes. The difference obtainable by the two gums may reasonably be attributed to their difference of constitution. In a tragacanth emulsion, the swollen colloid bassorin appears to have the power of preventing the globules of oil coalescing, not by virtue of viscosity, but rather by providing an obstacle to the movement of the oil. On the other hand, a perfect acacia emulsion has each particle of oil surrounded by an envelope of soluble gum, both together forming a cell, having enough resistance to prevent coalescence with contiguous cells. At this point I am constrained to make a few remarks on the cod-liver oil emulsion of the "Unofficial Formulary," made as you know with tragacanth. Like Conroy, my attempt to make a good emulsion of it was a failure. The oil is well suspended, but badly divided. It would have been better, as Conroy suggests, to have made it with gum acacia.

Tinctures of senega and quillaia have remarkable properties as emulsifying agents, because of their power, in very small quantity, of dividing and pulverizing substances where gums fail. If you place in a bottle 1 oz. of chloroform, 20 minims of tincture of senega, and a few drachms of water, shake well, and make up to 5 oz. with water, you get a product in which the chloroform is divided into an immense number of globules; these globules readily subside, but will rest for hours without breaking down. Mercury, ether, or any essential oil can be divided in the same manner. Mr. H. Collier ("Yearbook of Pharmacy," 1879) gives some formulæ for senega-made emulsions; they are useful for hospital work, where time allowed for work done is much too brief. In private dispensing, senega will never be regarded with favor, as its emulsions are too temporary in character.

The flavoring and preservation of emulsions ought not to be overlooked. Although an emulsion may be therapeutically and mechanically perfect, it is often nauseating to the taste and offensive in odor. Flavoring, though only an adjunct, still does contribute elements of value to a medicine. The common favorites among flavors are those used in cookery, such as the volatile oils of almond, cinnamon, cassia, cloves, lemon, the essence of vanilla, and orange-flower water. My opinion of these as regards permanency, palatability, and power to disguise is in favor of almonds. An elegant cod-liver oil emulsion is made as follows: (The weights and measures are British.)

Cod-liver oil..................................4 oz.
Powdered gum acacia........................1 oz.
Oil of cassia..................................4 minims.
Oil of almonds (volatile)....................4 minims.
Saccharin.....................................2 grains.
Water to make................................8 oz.

Mix the oils with the gum and saccharin in a dry mortar, add 2 oz. of water, stir till the emulsion is formed; finally, add sufficient water to make 8 oz., then mix well. Castor-oil is well disguised in the following formula:

Castor oil....................................1 oz.
Powdered gum acacia........................3 drachms.
Oil of almonds (volatile)....................2 minims.
Oil of cloves (volatile).......................1 minim.
Saccharin.....................................1 grain.
Water to make................................

Mix the oils with the gum and saccharin in a dry mortar, add 4 drachms of water at once, stirring till the emulsion is formed, dilute to 4 oz. with water.

Having saccharin at our disposal provides us with a useful substitute for sugar in emulsions. Its advantages are that it adds nothing to the thickness of the product, and cannot give rise to fermentation. The method found most convenient for using saccharin is a 10-per-cent solution made by adding bicarbonate of sodium till effervescence ceases; 20 grains of saccharin take 8 grains of the soda salt.

To keep emulsions for long periods is not desirable; they are best freshly made. Should it be desired to preserve them, recourse must be had to such antiseptics as boric or salicylic acid, or, better perhaps, a simple tincture of benzoin, or even pure chloroform. The latter is a most powerful antiseptic, imparting an agreeable sweetness; 1 minim may be added to each ounce of emulsion.

---

* From a paper by Mr. A. W. Gerrard, F.C.S., teacher of Pharmacy to University College, London, in the *Chemist and Druggist.*

Improved Preparation of Oxyiodide of Bismuth.

VARIOUS methods have so far been proposed to prepare this compound, but there appears to be a disadvantage in the character of the solvent, viz., nitric acid, which is generally used to bring the bismuth into solution. Mr. O. Kaspar proposed to neutralize the injurious effects of the solvent by using very dilute solutions, which introduced another drawback, namely, that in the preparation of larger quantities of the salt, very large volumes of liquid were required to be handled. Mr. Bernhard Fischer has lately proposed to replace nitric by acetic acid. His process is the following:

25.4 parts of crystallized nitrate of bismuth are dissolved with the aid of a gentle heat, in 120-150 C.c. of glacial acetic acid (96% acid), and this solution is poured, under stirring, into a solution of 33.2 parts of iodide of potassium and 54.4 parts of crystallized acetate of sodium in 2 to 3 liters of water. Each portion of the bismuth solution, poured in, causes a greenish-brown precipitate, which, during the first stage of the operation, assumes, on being first formed, a lemon-yellow color, which, on further addition of bismuth passes more and more into brick-red.

The precipitate is washed first by decantation, then on the filter, and dried at 100° C. The oxyiodide of bismuth thus prepared is in form of a bright brick-red powder, containing on an average 67.21% of Bi_2O_3. Mr. O. Kaspar reviews this process, on the basis of new experiments, and says that there is some loss of iodine involved, as the liquid poured off from the precipitate contains this body in a free state. He also points out that the product becomes paler and more yellowish on exposure to light. Hence it ought to be kept in the dark.

Aplantesis.

THIS is a new term proposed by Prof. J. W. Mallet for a peculiar separation of a solvent from the dissolved substance upon an increase of temperature.

Prof. Mallet had made the observation that in an alcohol thermometer, the liquid contents of which were colored with cochineal, the upper part of the liquid column appeared *colorless* when the temperature increased, while at no other portion of the colored liquid column could there be seen any separation of coloring matter. It therefore appeared as if the alcohol had separated from the dissolved substance by mere expansion.

The author next examined aqueous and alcoholic solutions of various colloidal substances, such as starch, tannin, caramel, albumen, and gelatin. The experiments were conducted in flasks holding about ½ liter, and closed with corks through which passed a glass tube of 4 millimeters bore, and 15-20 Cm. long, provided in the middle with a glass stop-cock. Each flask was filled with the respective liquid until the latter stood in the glass tube a few centimeters below the stop-cock. The solutions had been carefully filtered through several layers of paper, so that they were absolutely free from any suspended matter. The flasks were then cooled for some time with ice, and next placed in a moderately warm room, until the liquid had risen, in consequence of its expansion, a few centimeters above the glass stop-cock. The latter was then carefully closed, the liquid above the stop-cock taken out by means of a capillary pipette, and examined for the quantity of dissolved substance contained therein. A portion of the liquid remaining in the flasks was also examined for the purpose of comparison. In all cases it was found that the portion removed by the pipette contained a more or less diminished quantity, and in some cases even none at all, of the originally dissolved substance.

The only explanation which the author can suggest for this phenomenon—which he proposes to call *aplantesis*—is this, that the solvent passes through between the molecules of the substance and thus becomes separated from it. A similar separation of colloids from their solvents, though in an opposite sense, takes place when the former gelatinize on cooling.—*After Chem. News.*

[Note by Ed. Am. Drugg.—The explanation given by the author amounts to this, that a certain number of molecules of the solvent—which are originally homogeneously distributed throughout the liquid, and uniformly mixed with the molecules of the substance dissolved—at an increase of temperature become detached from their place of lodgment and pass upwards between the superincumbent molecules of the solid and the solvent. To how great a depth this process can extend is not shown, but it would seem that, at least in narrow tubes, it may extend to a depth of one or even more centimeters. According to the author's theory, this separation is purely mechanical, and the separated molecules may be assumed *to remain at rest when they have arrived in the uppermost layer*, where they will be soon joined by others similarly disembarrassed of their former solid companion-molecules. But the question may be asked, Have such phenomena ever been observed in solutions prepared with *non-volatile* or *very difficultly volatile* liquids? If it shall be found that the phenomenon takes place only when the solvent is readily or moderately *volatile*, then an explanation may be found in the fact that the solvent, even at low temperatures, is slowly vaporised, and if inclosed in tubes such as described by the author, probably recondensed, falling back again and gradually collecting as a pure layer on the surface. It need not be assumed that the same molecules of liquid which are already thus collected as a layer, are the only ones which continue to be vaporised and recondensed, but it may readily be imagined and conceded that the loosening or starting action of an increase of temperature upon the molecules of the solvent may extend some distance downward from the surface. Beyond a certain depth, of course, the weight of the superincumbent column will counteract the tendency of the molecules to float upward. Consequently, it may be assumed, that fresh molecules from below the pure layer already collected, will constantly be thrown upwards with the others, whereby the layer of pure column will gradually increase up to a certain point. Then it might be asked, will not the superincumbent pure layer gradually diffuse itself again with the remainder of the liquid, thus reproducing the original uniform and homogeneous solution? The answer to this would be, that if the apparatus remains as it was, the action would probably go on continuously. The lower portion of the "pure" layer would gradually and constantly diffuse with the main body of the solution, while new layers of still purer liquid will collect on top, the purest of all being that which just reaches the surface, freshly condensed.]

Strophanthus.

THE British Consul at Zomba (East Central Africa) gives the following notes which he has obtained from Mr. Buchanan, in reference to this plant:

"Strophanthus is considered the most powerful poison the natives possess. It is found at a low level, and, as far as I can gather from personal observation and native sources, is not to be had on the high land. The supplies hitherto obtained have been drawn from the right bank of the River Shiré, below the Murchison Rapids. There is, apparently, more than one species, or, at least, variety; the distinguishing feature being a much smaller pod and fewer seeds. At present, information relative to these other varieties is scant. The Strophanthus is a strong climbing plant, and is always found in the vicinity of high trees, on which it supports itself. The stem varies in diameter, but has an average of a few inches. It lies on the ground in folds, the branches supporting themselves on the nearest trees. The young branches have a rod-like habit, and are in appearance not unlike elder; the fruit grows in pairs, and has a peculiar appearance, very like a pair of immense horns hanging on a slender twig. The fruit begins to ripen in July, and lasts till the end of September. Judging from the few plants I have reared here, it would appear to be a strong growing plant. The natives are quite ignorant of its age, or how old a plant may be before it bears fruit. The native method of preparing the poison is very simple. They first clean the seeds of their hairy appendages, and then pound them in a mortar until they have reduced them to a pulp. A little water is then added. To the pulp is then added the bark of a tree containing a gummy substance which helps to keep the poison on the arrow, in event of its striking against a stone. The poison thus prepared is spread upon the arrow and allowed to dry; game wounded by arrows poisoned with strophanthus die quickly. The flesh is eaten without evil effect. The only precaution taken is to squeeze the baobab bark on the wound made by the arrow, and this counteracts the evil effect of the poison. Buffalo and all smaller game are killed by this poison.—*Times.*

Opium and Ether—After-Effects Avoided.

IT frequently happens—more often, indeed, than not—that the administration of opium is attended with so many symptoms of the undesirable kind, such, for instance, as sickness, nausea, headache, and general interference with the digestive functions, that its use is necessarily abandoned or restricted on this account. Dr. A. G. Auld, of Wick, N. B., has lately discovered a plan whereby the valuable action of opium may be obtained without incurring any of the ill effects before alluded to. The method is a simple one, consisting merely in giving along with the tincture of opium (supposing this to be the preparation of the drug prescribed) an equal, or even a rather larger, proportion of spirit of ether. The latter stimulates the action of the alimentary canal, and the secretive organs generally, and thus neutralizes the effect produced upon those by the opium alone, while not interfering with its powers in any other respect. We trust that other practitioners will repeat Dr. Auld's practice with this valuable, yet much abused narcotic, as this method of getting all the good effects thereof, without any of its evils, cannot be too widely known or too greatly imitated.—*Monthly Mag.*

Prof. Bloxam, of London, well known as the author of a much-used and practical treatise on general chemistry, and several works on analytical chemistry, died on November 29th, 1887.

Insect Remedies.

THE report on entomology made by W. B. Alwood to the Columbus Horticultural Society, last winter, states that many remedies were employed on the two described cabbage worms, consisting of alum water of different degrees of strength, tansy water, tomato water, benzine, coal-oil emulsions of different strengths, Hammond's slug-shot, Cayenne pepper, half a dozen remedies from England, several preparations of tobacco and pyrethrum. None proved of any value, except the tobacco soaps and pyrethrum. The tobacco soaps, prepared with potash, were quite efficient, the value of which was ascribed to the potash. Pyrethrum is recommended as the best remedy, being perfectly safe, easy of application, and more deadly on the worms than any remedy used. Powder of good quality, mixed with three times its bulk of flour, was found perfectly effective, applied with a dusting-bellows. One pound, costing 50 cents, was enough to cover an acre, if properly handled.

Chinese Trade Guilds.

THOSE who think that the "cutter" is something new under the sun will be interested in the following account of how this evil is taken care of by the Druggists' Guild of Wênchow:

"From days of yore to the present, all occupations have commenced their organizations by establishing regulations, to be subject to modifications by time and circumstances. Accordingly, we of the drug trade, in the reign of Hsien Fêng (having previously been divided into two guilds), united and formed a compact body, without reconciling old and new rules, and, therefore, for the past ten years irregularities have occurred necessitating their codification. Consequently we assembled and agreed on the new rules hereto subjoined. Henceforth they are to be conformed to in their entirety; their violation, when discovered, will entail the penalty of two plays and liquor and viands for over twenty persons. This notice is given to caution against infringement of the following laws:

"It is agreed that all accounts shall be settled at each of the three terms of the year.

"It is agreed that deductions of 5 per cent be allowed for cash payments, but not on credit transactions.

"It is agreed that when a member is in debt to another, and transfers his dealing to a third party, the Guild shall bring the three members together, and that he shall not be allowed to trade with the latter until he liquidates his debt to the former.

"It is agreed that a member who allows a customer a higher rate for dollars than their market value for the day shall be mulcted.

"It is agreed that a druggist newly commencing business shall pay an initiation fee to the treasurer of the God of Medicine Temple; if failing to pay up the due amount in full, the member who transacts trade with him shall be fined to the full extent of the deficiency."—From a report by United States Minister to China, DENBY, to the Department of State on "Chinese Guilds."

Sandal-Wood.

FROM an article by David Hooper, in the *Chem. and Drugg.* (Nov. 26th), we take the following note on sandal-wood:

The chief article of commerce in Mysore, and the most important item in the forest revenue, is the sandal-wood. The *Santalum album* is from thirty to sixty feet high, with not a very robust habit; the color of the stem is darker than that of the figs and cassias in its vicinity; the flowers are small and red, but neither the bark, sap-wood, leaves, nor flowers have that fragrance which is found in the duramen or heart-wood. The sandal is propagated by seeds; and, as both the wood and the tree are a government monopoly, the fruits are carefully collected by servants, whether from forests or from the compounds of private houses. Natural-grown sandal is being attended to by having a system of special men, called "sandal-monegars," to look after their cultivation, as there is a doubt if the artificially-grown trees will have the same amount and quality of fragrance as the self-sown. The wood is sold by auction once a year, the larger portion being purchased by merchants of Bombay. Until the sales, it is stored in depots called "Kotes," situated in several towns in the province. Mysore sandal is appreciated above all other kinds, especially in the China market, and it has a steady net price of 45 l. per ton at the place of production, showing it to be the most valuable wood in the world. During the year 1886-1887, a better sale of the wood realized about 46,000 l.—a substantial increase to the Mysore forest revenue of 1 lakh of rupees, or 10,000 l., over the sales of the previous year.

Dispensing under Difficulties.

Pharmacist Aidmajor Lahache, a graduate of the Paris College of Pharmacy, writing from Biskra, the southernmost point of civilised Algeria, relates some of the difficulties encountered by the pharmacist who tries to follow the French Cordex near the Sahara desert. "After May," he says, "it is hardly possible to dispense an ointment or a salve in Biskra, both lard and vaseline remaining always constantly liquid; mercurial ointment separates into two layers, one quite fluid and transparent, and the other semi-liquid, but holding still the metal in suspension. Cocoa butter is useless, so are suppositories; the temperature of the human body being during the day inferior to that of the atmosphere, any composition that would be solid before introduction would not melt in the cavities for which such medicaments are intended, a state of things contrary to all pharmaceutical ethics. Woe to the pharmacist who would leave unstoppered any bottle of ammonia, collodion, or tincture! Crystallized sulphate of soda begins to liquefy in June, to become solid again only in September. The same is the case with carbolic acid. Adhesive, gold-beater's skin, and court plasters cannot be used. Infusions, decoctions, and emulsions spoil in a few hours. Licorice-root has to be rejected and replaced by glycyrrhizin. All india-rubber instruments must be abandoned. Some pill-masses cannot be made at all; for the others the excipients are to be altered, and what is worse, the familiar pill-machine, owing to the dilatation of the brass plates, either have their grooved portion bulging out of shape if the wooden frame is strong enough, or the wood cracked when the metal is stronger. The only drop of comfort is that ready-made solutions can be kept in stock at a degree of concentration impracticable in our climates. Such are boric acid, sodium borate, salicylic acid, and hypodermic solutions in general." As to the feelings of the pharmacists under such conditions, they may readily be imagined; no doubt he wished he had never left the green banks of the Seine.—*Chem. and Drugg.*

French Toilet Preparations.

In a report submitted to the Hygienic Council of Paris by Drs. Dubrisay and Chafin, the authors state that the perfumery and toilet products now sold contain so many noxious substances that it is desirable the factories should be placed under special surveillance. They give a number of instances in support of their statement. The so-called "harmless and purely vegetable" hair dyes, they say, are all poisonous. "Progressive dyes" are ammoniacal solutions of nitrate of silver. The "instantaneous dyes" are a solution of litharge in lime water. "Eau des Fées" is a solution of sulphate of lead in hyposulphite of soda. "Eau Figaro" consists of three solutions (1) of nitrate of silver and sulphide of copper; (2) sulphide of sodium; (3) cyanide of potassium (to remove the silver stains). "Eau des Fleurs" is composed of rose water, 93.5; flowers of sulphur, 2.7; acetate of lead, 2.8. Passing to cosmetics, they say "Lait antipelique" is composed of corrosive sublimate, 1.7; oxide of lead, 4.22; sulphuric acid and camphor. "Lait de Manille" is a mixture of borax, copper, tincture of benzoin, and essence of bitter almonds; "Lait de Ninon," of bismuth and zinc; "Eau Magique," oxide of lead and hyposulphite of zinc; "Eau de fleur de lys," protochloride of mercury; "Eau royal de Windsor," glycerin and oxide of lead; "Eau de Castille" hyposulphite of soda and acetate of lead. The "Poudre Pilivore de Laforet" contains mercury (!),50 grs.; sulphide of arsenic, 30 grs.; litharge, 30 grs. and starch, 30 grs. "Epiteine" is simply sulphite of calcium, and "Antiboldos" hypophosphite of soda. Pomades against baldness all contain cantharides and croton oil.

Some Phases of the Trade in Eau de Cologne.

IT is doubtful whether any article of commerce of the same proportion has given rise to so many lawsuits as the eau de Cologne industry generally, and more especially the respective degree of "genuineness" of the countless "Farinas" who are engaged in the manufacture of the perfume. In the early years of the present century, Cologne numbered sixty makers of the perfume, most of whom carried on business under the style of "Farina," having secured a bogus partner of that name in Italy, where in some provinces the patronymic is almost as common as are Brown, Jones, or Robinson in this country. A poet of the period went so far as to assert that—

... Chaque jour le Rhin vers Cologne charrie
De nombreux Farinas, tous " seuls," tous " Jean Marie; "

a verse which might be rendered in doggerel English as follows:

The Rhine towards Cologne does every day carry a
Number of Farinas, each " genuine John Maria."

The export trade in eau de Cologne is said to date from 1760, when, during the Seven Years' War, the French temporarily occupied Cologne. They carried away samples of the perfume to their own country, where it became very popular. At present Great Britain and the United States are the best foreign customers for the article.—*Chem. and Drugg.*

The new German Spirit Tax which went into effect on October 1st had induced foreign dealers to lay in as large stocks as possible previous to its introduction, so much so that the price advanced considerably from this excessive demand alone. Of course, since the tax has gone into effect, the price of the commodity has proportionally advanced, but is not quite settled yet.

Camphor Ice.—Spermaceti, 3 ounces; white wax, 4 ounces; oil almonds, exp., 8 ounces; camphor, 4 ounces; oil cajuput, 40 drops; oil lemon, 2 drachms.

Philicome Pomade.—Wax, 10 ounces; rose oil, 1 pound; sweet almond oil, 1 pound; cassia, jasmine, and tuberose oil, of each half a pound; oil of orange, essential, 1 drachm. Dissolve the wax in the rose and almond oil, and add the other oils as it cools, stirring all the time. ["Oil of Jasmine" is an alcoholic tincture made from the "pomade."]

Fluid Philicome.—White wax, 1 ounce; rose oil, 1 pound; oils of cloves, ½ drachm; bergamot, 1 ounce; lemon, ½ ounce; lavender (English), 2 drachms. Dissolve and mix.

Royal Windsor Pomade.—Lard, 2 pounds; spermaceti, 2 ounces; wax, 1 ounce; cassia pomade, 4 ounces; olive oil, 1 pound. jasmine oil (French), 3 ounces. Heat up well. Perfume: Oil of bergamot ½ ounce, oil of cloves, 1 drachm; oil of cinnamon (Ceylon), ½ ounce.

Oleine for Darkening the Hair.—Tannic acid, ½ drachm; glycerin, 2 drachms; oil of sweet almonds, 6 drachms; oil of neroli, 2 drops; oil of orange peel, 20 drops. Mix.

Castor-Oil Pomade.—Yellow wax, 3 ounces; castor oil and olive oil, of each, 16 ounces. Perfume, 1 ounce.

Convenient Glue.—Gelatin is dissolved in the water-bath in its own weight of strong vinegar, a quarter part of alcohol and a very little alum is then added. This glue, it is said, will remain liquid, and is much used for cementing mother-of-pearl, horn, etc., upon wood or metal.

Still Another suggestion for an adhesive gum for labels. It is a modification of the tragacanth paste which is so useful for mounting botanical specimens. Soak 30 Gm. of tragacanth in a little water until it is fully swelled, beat it up to the consistence of a thick homogeneous mucilage, and mix this with a mucilage made from 120 grammes of acacia, and pass the whole through a piece of "tammy." Add to this 120 C.c. of glycerin, in which 2.5 grammes of powdered thymol has previously been shaken up, and lastly make the whole up to 1 liter by measure.

To Remove Dandruff and Promote the Growth of Hair.—No. 1. The following is found to be very efficacious:—Acet. canthar., 2 drachms; aromatic vinegar, 2 drachms; spirit of rosemary, 2 drachms; elder-flower water, ad 4 ounces. Well sponge the roots of the hair every morning, and brush with a moderately hard brush. Or No. 2.—Ether, 1 ounce; tinct. of cantharid., 1 ounce; alcohol, 1 pint; rose oil, q. s. Well shake, and apply with a moderately hard brush at bedtime.

Bronchitis Cure (Dr. Dobell).—Carbonate of ammonium, 35 grains; wine of ipecac, 2 drachms; spirit of chloroform, 1 drachm (1 to 7); paregoric, 2 drachms; water, ad 8 ounces. Mix. One tablespoonful three times a day, or oftener if the cough is troublesome.

Neuralgia Powders.—Take of quinine, 16 grs.; carbonate of iron, 1 ounce; Dover's powder, 40 grs.; jalap, 40 grs.; essence of peppermint, 15 drops. Mix, and divide into eight powders, one to be taken twice a day.

Toothache Remedy.—E. S. Kirk finds that the ordinary paste used for filling hollow teeth, for the purpose of "deadening" the nerve, does not fulfil its purpose fully. He, therefore, recommends (in the *Dental Cosmos*) the following, which is said to be satisfactory in every respect:

Arsenious Acid	2 parts.
Hydrochlorate of Cocaine	2 "
Menthol	½ part.
Glycerin	enough to make a paste.

We give the above with the reservation that we deem it a *dangerous* compound for indiscriminate use. The application of arsenious acid or of compounds containing this to any portion of the fauces or interior of the mouth has more than once led to very serious results, even under professional supervision.

Elixir of Terpin.—Vigier recommends the following mixture for the administration of terpin or terpin hydrate:

	Gm.	One dose.
Terpin (hydrate)	0.500	gr. 8
Glycerin	7.000	fl. ʒ 1¾
Alcohol	7.000	fl. ʒ 2¼
Syrup of Honey	7.000	fl. ʒ 1¾
Vanillin	0.002	gr. 1/30

—*L'Union Pharm.*

Note.—Syrup of honey (*Codex*) is prepared by mixing 4 parts of honey with 1 part of distilled water, heating to a boil, clarifying, and straining.

Syrup of Saccharin.—The *Rundschau* gives the following proportions: Dissolve 10 parts of saccharin with 11 parts of carbonate (or 12 parts of bicarbonate) of sodium in 1,000 parts of distilled water at a temperature of 104° F.

Corn-Salve.—Black oxide of copper, 15 grains; lard, ½ oz. Mix well with aid of heat. After paring the corn as closely as possible, apply the ointment once daily.

Castor-Oil Mixture.—Guerman, a Roumanian apothecary, recommends the following combination which he improperly calls an emulsion. The taste of the oil is well disguised in it. It contains about 30 per cent of alcohol, which may make it unsuitable for administration in certain cases.

	Gm.	
Castor Oil	30	1 fl. oz.
Alcohol	15	5 fl. dr.
Syrup of Rhubarb	20	½ fl. oz.
Oil of Peppermint, drops	2	2 drops.

Mix and shake thoroughly.

A Natural Wine Containing Iron.—The wine grown at La Seyne, Department Var, France, is probably the only one so far known which contains more than traces of iron naturally. This is, no doubt, due to the peculiar condition of the iron in the soil. On analysis, the wine was found to contain in 1 liter:

Alcohol	67.54 Gm.
Extractive	20.50 "
Acid (calculated as sulphuric)	5.20 "
Ash	2.60 "

Among the latter 0.11 Gm. of ferric oxide. The usual quantity of iron found in wine varies from 0.01 to 0.02 Gm. per liter.—*Journ. Pharm. et Chim.*

Standardizing Volumetric Solution of Permanganate.—In place of oxalic acid, which is usually employed, the tetroxalate of potassium has recently been recommended by R. Ulbricht, because its solution may be kept a long time without deterioration. Fresenius, who quotes Ulbricht in the *Zeitsch. f. Anal. Chem.*, 1887, 629, points out that this salt has been recommended already in 1856 by K. Kraut, and that the latter has used it ever since with the greatest satisfaction.

Benzol in Whooping Cough.—Dr. J. Lowe highly recommends benzol as a remedy for whooping cough. To deprive the benzol somewhat of its hot, burning taste, and to prevent it from causing nausea, he advises it to be administered in a viscid mixture, and in small doses, usually in quantity of three or four minims. Yet even smaller doses are effective, and for a child of 4 or 5 years of age two minims every two hours will be sufficient. The following mixture is recommended by him:

℞ Benzol. puriss.	♏ 32
Glycerini	fl. ℥ 1½
Ol. Menthæ pip.	♏ 10
Syr. Mori	fl. ℥ ½

M. A teaspoonful every two hours.

[In place of syrup of mulberries, some other pleasant syrupy vehicle, such as syrup of raspberries, may be used.]—*Brit. Med. Journ.*

Oleate of Atropine in Suppositories is recommended by J. F. Brown, of Dover, England, as a substitute for extract of belladonna. Ten grains of atropine dissolved in a half-ounce of oleic acid and diluted with oil to a fluid-ounce and twenty minims, will form a solution of which each minim will represent one grain of the extract.—*Pharm. Journal.*

Test-Paper for Oxygen.—According to Wuerster (*Ber. Deutsch. Chem. Ges.*), a most delicate reagent for active oxygen, even when the latter is present only in traces, may be prepared by saturating paper with a solution of tetramethyl-paraphenylen-diamide. This substance is rendered of an intense violet color when coming in contact with oxidizing substances. Hence it will indicate active oxygen, either in a free state or in combination. It has been found perfectly indifferent towards other substances, and will, therefore, be preferable to other reagents for active oxygen.

Antipyrin may fairly be considered the most popular of modern antipyretics. The dose varies from 15 to 30 grains, twice, three, or more times a day. For children 3 to 12 grains will be found to be sufficient. It is of great value in all febrile diseases, reducing temperature very promptly. Of late it has been applied in subcutaneous injections as a local anæsthetic. In some cases a bright pink rash, like nettle rash, will suddenly appear during treatment; this is considered to be of no importance, as it causes no inconvenience, and soon disappears.

Antipyrin is readily soluble in water and alcohol; it possesses but little flavor, and that not unpleasant, and is, therefore, adapted for administration in solution. It thus possesses great advantages over quinine, especially in treating children, who take it very readily if mixed with a little syrup, thus: Antipyrin, 80 grains; simple syrup, 1 ounce; water, add to 4 ounces. Two teaspoonfuls for a dose.

It crystallizes in colorless laminæ, which melt at a temperature between 230° and 235.4° F.—*Monthly Mag.*

THE
American Druggist

AN ILLUSTRATED MONTHLY JOURNAL

OF

Pharmacy, Chemistry, and Materia Medica.

Vol. XVII., No. 1. Whole No. 163.

FREDERICK A. CASTLE, M.D. .... Editor.
CHARLES RICE, Ph.D. .... Associate Editor.

PUBLISHED BY

WM. WOOD & CO., 56 & 58 Lafayette Place, N. Y.

SUBSCRIPTION PRICE per year, ... $1.50
SINGLE COPIES, ...15

Address all communications relating to the business of the AMERICAN DRUGGIST, such as subscriptions, advertisements, change of Post-Office address, etc., to WILLIAM WOOD & CO., 56 and 58 Lafayette Place, New York City, to whose order all postal money orders and checks should be made payable. Communications intended for the Editor should be addressed in care of the Publishers.

The AMERICAN DRUGGIST is issued in the latter part of each month, dated for the month ahead. Changes of advertisements should reach us before the 18th. New advertisements can occasionally be inserted after the 18th. Regular Advertisements according to size, location, and time. Special rates on application.

ITEMS.

The **National Pure Food Convention** will hold its second session in Washington, D. C., in Willard's Hall, beginning Thursday, January 19th, 1888, at 12 o'clock.

All national, State, commercial, mercantile, agricultural, health, and other organizations favoring the enactment of a judicious national anti-adulteration act, which will supplement those of various States and municipalities by reaching imported commodities, interstate transactions, and territory exclusively under the jurisdiction of the United States authorities, are invited to send one or more delegates, not exceeding three in number, to this convention. Editors of trade and other journals favoring this object are also invited to attend as delegates.
Headquarters of the committee will be at Willard's Hotel. Organizations electing delegates will please communicate names of same to Elisha Winter, Secretary, 213 East 23d Street, New York, and any suggestions as to the welfare and conduct of the convention to Newton Dexter, Chairman Committee of Arrangements, Albany, N. Y.

Cincinnati College of Pharmacy.—The number of those who have already signified their intention of attending the spring session of the Cincinnati College of Pharmacy (which will be inaugurated in March next), and the letters of inquiry received, indicate that there will be a very full attendance.

Georgia.—The Governor has appointed the following-named gentlemen to serve as a Pharmaceutical Examining Board for the State, for the term of three years: J. W. Goodwin, of Macon; Theodore Schumann, of Atlanta; Osceola Butler, of Savannah; O. C. Durham, of Augusta; and H. R. Slack, Jr., of La Grange.

California.—The seventeenth annual meeting of the California Pharmaceutical Society was held in San Francisco on November 10th. Twelve new members were elected. In the address of the President, Mr. John Dawson, it was mentioned that 50 students had matriculated in the senior and 27 in the junior class, 34 junior students had been examined for the higher grade, and 14 out of 15 seniors had passed the examination for the degree of Ph.G. During the preceding year, the membership had been reduced to 135, and the receipts from dues amounted to $842.00. The following-named officers were elected: President, Fred. C. Heil; Vice-Presidents, Dr. R. H. Behr, Prof. William T. Wenzell; Treasurer, Henry Michaels; Secretary, Chas. M. Troppmann; Librarian, Miss Josephine Barbat; Editor, William T. Wenzell; Trustees, John Calvert, William M. Searby, Emil Huppersberger, J. Argenti, D. M. Fletcher, Charles Tropp-

mann, Henry Barbat. It was voted to reduce the dues of country members from $6.00 to $3.00, and of resident members from $8.00 to $4.00, and to request the Board of Trustees to arrange for a meeting in some interior town about the month of May next. A committee, consisting of Messrs. John Dawson, E. W. Runyon, and J. Calvert was appointed to solicit members for the American Pharmaceutical Association, and Prof. A. L. Longfeld and J. Dawson were appointed to prepare a list of queries.

Kansas.—Dr. Robert S. Drake, of Beloit, the President of the State Pharmaceutical Association, writes us the following encouraging account of pharmaceutical matters in that State:
"It is my pleasure to report that we are making rapid advances, in the State of Kansas, in the profession of pharmacy; at our last annual meeting we gained 50 new members, and the attendance was about 300. Our recent pharmacy law is giving entire satisfaction to the legitimate pharmacists of the State. We are enforcing the law. Our board prosecuted twelve violations of the law this month and were successful in every case.
"The next meeting of the board will be held in Altona.
"It is our intention to raise the standard each meeting. At our last examination twenty-three (23) passed, out of sixty candidates. The stigma of 'saloonist' is being removed. We are beginning to receive the recognition that we have a right to demand.
"I have only been in the State three years, and am surprised to see how fast the public is being educated to the fact of the necessity of competent pharmacists. In procuring the passage of our amended bill through the Legislature, last winter, I was gratified and encouraged at the support and help the public gave our Committee on Legislation. When we made our arguments to the different members of the legislature, in support of the various sections of the law, we were agreeably surprised at the prompt support they gave us.
"So far, we have not failed in any prosecution that the board has attempted. The most of the complaints of violations of the law come from the public, and *not* from the competing pharmacists. Very few of the pharmacists make complaints of their competitors; we are gratified to know that it is *not* jealousy, revenge, or competition that prompts the complaints. It is that the public are demanding that it should be served by competent pharmacists. This is as it should be. As long as this state of affairs exists, the profession of pharmacy will advance. It is an old law that supplies will be furnished as they are demanded. The rising generation of pharmacy sees the actual necessity of educated pharmacists, it is now the ambition of almost every drug clerk to take a course at some college of pharmacy; they realize that they cannot compete with their neighbor if they do not educate themselves. The next five years will work a great revolution in the drug trade in this State. The graduates of pharmacy will then be the *rule* and *not* the exception, *as it is now*. When this comes to pass, life will not tremble in the balance or be sacrificed on the altar of ignorance or carelessness."

Jobst-Zimmer.—The well-known manufacturing firms of Friedrich Jobst, of Feuerbach-Stuttgart, and C. Zimmer, Frankfurt on the Main, have been consolidated into one corporation. The several factories, consisting of the Wholesale Depot for Drugs and Chemicals in Stuttgart, the Quinine and Chemical Works in Feuerbach, near Stuttgart, and the Branch Depot at Milan, are thus united under the new name: "Vereinigte Fabriken chemisch-pharmaceutischer Produkte, Feuerbach-Stuttgart, und Frankfurt a. M., Zimmer & Co." It seems to us, a briefer title would have been more advantageous.

Menthol and Aconitine.—A combination of menthol with aconitine, for external application, in form of cones, is reported to have met with much success in England. The proportions used are:

Aconitine .... 1 part.
Menthol .... 500 parts.

The aconitine is dissolved in alcohol, and the solution added to the melted menthol. The mass is then made into cones of about 2 oz. each.—Schimmel & Co., Report on Oils.
Note by Ed. Am. Dr.—If commercial aconitine, without further designation, is used in this combination, it is possible that a rather weak alkaloid may happen to be chosen, or else, a very powerful variety may be pitched upon. We consider it improper and dangerous to countenance the use of such a compound without the advice and control of a physician, who will designate the kind of aconitine to be used, and will be able to watch and control its effects.

Saccharin has been introduced into pill-coating by an English drug firm.

The Toronto College of Pharmacy has 57 students, one of which is a woman.

QUERIES & ANSWERS.

Queries for which answers are desired, must be received by the 5th of the month, and must in every case be accompanied by the name and address of the writer, for the information of the editor, but not for publication.

No. 2,065.—Extraction of Essential Oil (Dr. B. M. C. V., Caracas, South America).

"What would be the most practical and economical method for extracting an essential oil contained in a tree in small quantity, being soluble in water, ether, and alcohol; if possible, mechanical? I have treated the green plant, reduced to pulp, with ether, and after evaporation I have distilled it with salt water, giving me the essential oil, but this method would be to me very expensive."

Based upon the information furnished, we think that a still such as was described in our last volume as being in use in the Southern States (page 204) would answer the purpose very well. The material to be treated should be cut as fine as possible, for which purpose such a machine as is used by farmers in this country for cutting straw might be employed in the case of small twigs or juicy plants.

No. 2,066.—Local Anæsthetic (Dr. J. M. S.).

One of the most efficient local anæsthetics, to be employed in form of spray, is the lightest boiling portion of petroleum which is known in the market as rhigolene. This boils at 1° C. (33.8° F.), and is a liquid which must be handled with great care, as it emits an inflammable vapor even at low temperatures. That portion of petroleum which boils below 50° C. (122° F.) is usually collected by itself, and as such is known as naphtha or gasolene. A certain fraction of this, having a boiling point of about 68° C. (152° F.), is known as Canadol. This has also been recommended for the same purpose. But it is not as efficient as the other. Chloride of methyl is probably the most efficient of all these volatile agents; but, as this is not readily obtainable—having to be sent out in strong cylinders, in which the gaseous chloride of methyl is compressed into a liquid—we advise the employment of rhigolene.

No. 2,067.—Armenian Pills (M.).

These pills contain copaiba and cubebs, and have received their euphemistic title from the fact that they also contain Armenian bole. According to Schacht, they are prepared thus:

Copaiba	14	parts.
Magnesia	2	"
Cubebs, powdered	7	"
Armenian Bole, powdered	7	"

Heat the Copaiba on a steam bath until it acquires the consistence of a plaster (that is until most of the volatile oil has been dissipated); then mix it with the magnesia and set it aside (that the mass may set). Next add the powdered Cubebs and Armenian Bole and mix intimately. Make the mass into pills of 0.5 Gm. (8 grains) each, and roll them in Armenian bole.

No. 2,068.—Penawar-Jambi (O. R.).

This substance, which is often spelled Pengwar-(or Pengwar) Jambi, is derived from several species of *Cibotium*, chiefly *Cibotium Baromez* Kg., and *C. glaucescens* Kg., and *C. glaucum* Hook. Cibotium is a tree-fern, the dense, frog hairs of which are found often as a thick covering upon contiguously growing trees. These hairs are light, soft, silky, and have almost a metallic lustre of a golden-yellow or bronze color. Each hair consists of a series of thin-walled cells, placed one over the other, and separated by horizontal, corrugated cell-walls. The cells are flat, and do not appear to have the power of taking up liquids by capillary attraction. Their hæmostatic properties are ascribed to the fact that the blood with which they are brought in contact softens the cell-wall, and dissolves the contents of the cell, which at the same time swell up. At least this is the explanation given by Vogl.

The Penawar-Jambi most generally met with in commerce is that which is derived from *Cibotium glaucum* Hook., native of the Sandwich Islands. This is also known by the special name *pulu*. This substance is exported largely as a stuffing material for mattresses, etc. Another kind, known as *pakoe-kidang* is derived from species of Alsophila and allied plants growing upon Java. This may be readily recognized by the fact that the hairs are twisted in an angle of 90 degrees at the point of juncture of the cells. This gives an extra lustre to this variety; besides, the hairs of the last-named are much longer and stronger.

As there are so many other, and more easily accessible hæmostatics, it is not likely that the demand for the above-described foreign articles, as surgical dressings, will ever again amount to much.

No. 2,069.—Sulphate of Zinc Caustic (M.).

Several prominent surgeons are in the habit of using a particular kind of caustic as an application to cancerous or other sores, when it is desired, not only to exert a powerfully escharotic action, but also to confine the action to a sharply circumscribed spot.

This caustic is prepared by mixing anhydrous sulphate of zinc with concentrated sulphuric acid to a paste.

Sulphate of zinc is exposed to the air in a warm room, until it has effloresced as far as possible (corresponding to a loss of 5 molecules of water). It is then dried at a temperature of 212° F. and afterwards at 230° F., until it is anhydrous. To make sure that all the water has passed off, the dry residue may be cautiously ignited, at a low red heat. A small loss of sulphuric acid will not interfere with its subsequent use. The residue is passed, while still warm, through a fine sieve, transferred to a glass-stoppered wide-mouthed bottle, and mixed with enough concentrated sulphuric acid, by means of a glass rod, to produce a paste of the consistence of honey. The bottle is then carefully stoppered, and the contents are ready for use. By keeping, the paste will become hard and dry.

No. 2,070.—Liquor Magnesii Bromidi (Oil City).

A solution of bromide of magnesium, containing 8 grains of the dry salt in a tablespoonful or ½ fluidounce, has been in use for some time, first in the Philadelphia Hospital, and lately also in other hospitals as well as in private practice. It may be prepared by the following process:

Diluted Hydrobromic Acid (U. S.)	3	fl. oz.
Carbonate of Magnesium	q.	s.
Water, enough to make	7	fl. oz.

Diluted hydrobromic acid contains 10 per cent, by weight, of the absolute acid. One fluidounce weighs about 491 grains; hence, this contains about 49 grains of HBr, and the 2 fl. oz. contain about 98 grains of HBr; and this is equivalent to about 97 grains of bromine. But 97 grains of bromine, when combined in molecular proportions with magnesium (forming $MgBr_2$, 24 + 160 = 184) produce, in round number, 112 grains of bromide of magnesium. If the solution is then made to measure 7 fluidounces, the product will be of the strength above indicated.

The formula suggested by our correspondent is not correct.

No. 2,071. Saccharin and its Solubility ("D.").

The rate of solubility of saccharin which we gave in our last volume (p. 202) correct, and has been confirmed by others, though of course the figures there given were not determined with scientific accuracy. Our attention has, meanwhile, been directed to the fact that the manufacturers of saccharin advise it to be always combined with an alkali (sodium carbonate or bicarbonate). This is, of course, an important point which ought to be communicated to every purchaser or user of the substance. Saccharin is chemically regarded an acid. As has been stated by us, it requires about 80 parts of diluted alcohol for solution. When it is, however, neutralized with soda, the resulting salt is very much more soluble, 1 part requiring only about 9 parts of diluted alcohol (mixture of equal volumes of 94% alcohol and water) for solution. This concentrated solution may be diluted with water to any extent, without precipitating. Saccharin is one of those substances which are very apt to form a supersaturated solution. For instance, after we had succeeded in dissolving 7 Gm. of the soda salt of saccharin in 80 C.c. of the above-mentioned diluted alcohol, to an apparently stable and perfectly transparent solution, we set it aside for about half an hour, when we found that a portion of the salt had separated as a soft, bulky, crystalline lump. It required only a small quantity of the solvent to bring this back into solution. One of our wholesale friends some time ago brought us several vials, containing solutions of saccharin itself (not neutralized with soda). One of them contained a clear solution of 1 in 30 parts of the same diluted alcohol, of which we had found 80 parts requisite.

We told him that we suspected his sample to be supersaturated, and indeed next morning, all the excess had crystallized out.

Regarding the sweetening power of saccharin, we may add that the soda salt leaves a much more decided impression of sweetness upon the tongue and palate than the saccharin itself. We have submitted a number of samples of mixtures sweetened with saccharin or its sodium salt on the one hand, and with sugar on the other hand, to unprejudiced persons, and find that individual judgments vary considerably as to the *degree* of sweetness—that is, as to what might be regarded an exact equivalent in sweetness to a given quantity of sugar. In making such experiments, it is necessary to equalize the conditions as much as possible. A good plan is to prepare jellies with sugar and with saccharin respectively, so that each preparation may have about the same *body*.

No. 2,072.—Tincture of Litmus ("Senior.")

A very delicate tincture of litmus may be prepared by following Kretschmar's directions.

Macerate commercial, whole litmus in water for several

days, draw off the solution, and repeat the extraction with water, until the latter takes up but little more of the coloring matter. Then add to the united liquids enough hydrochloric acid to render the solution permanently red, evaporate it to a small bulk, mix it with clean sand, and then evaporate to dryness. Reduce the mass to a granular powder, and wash it, first with boiling, and afterwards with cold water. The grains of sand then retain only the pure coloring matter (Kane's azolitmin) which is almost insoluble in water free from alkalies. On treating the colored sand with hot water, containing a little ammonia, the coloring matter is dissolved. Its tint should be adjusted so, between alkali and acid, that a small sample of the solution, when diluted with much water, produces a violet-colored liquid.

The solution may be used without the addition of alcohol. In this case it is well to saturate it with chloroform, using a sufficient quantity of it to have some of it remain undissolved at the bottom. The bottle, which should only be closed with a pellet of cotton (as complete exclusion of air soon renders the liquid colorless), may be shaken up occasionally to saturate the liquid again with chloroform.

Or the liquid may be mixed with about 20 per cent of alcohol.

One pound of litmus will furnish about 6 pints of solution, or tincture, of proper depth of color.

No. 2,073.—**Red Fire** (A Subscriber, Albany, N. Y.)
"Will you kindly give me a receipt for making red fire of the best kind: 1, for such as is ordinarily used on the street and 2, for such as is used in theatres ?"

Dr. Ure's dictionary gives the following formula in the article on Pyrotechny in general: 40 parts of nitrate of strontia, 13 of flowers of sulphur, 5 of chlorate of potash, and 4 of sulphuret of antimony.

Sergius Kern gives fifteen formulas for red fire on p. 715 of the supplement to Ure's dictionary, by which the time occupied in the burning can be regulated as desired, No. 1 being a quick burning compound and No. 15 the slowest.

On p. 215 of the AMERICAN DRUGGIST for 1885 you will find a variety of the latest formulas for Bengal lights, together with important information relating to them.

W. Canning says that mixtures of chlorate of potash, sulphur, and nitrate of strontium, in quantities larger than about an ounce, will frequently take fire within a few hours after they are made. When nitrate of baryta is substituted for strontia, the liability is nearly as great. When sulphuret of antimony or charcoal is added, the liability is greatly lessened, but probably not entirely done away with.

Erdman's formula for red fire for theatrical purposes or use in-doors consists of sulphur, 20 parts; saltpeter, 32 parts; chlorate of potash, 27 parts; chalk, 20 parts; charcoal, 1 part. This gives a rose-red light and is said to be perfectly harmless when used in a room.

The *Scientific American* some time since reported the death of a young lady in Bristol, New Hampshire, from inhaling the fumes of a red fire composed of nitrate of strontia, black sulphide of antimony, sulphur, and chlorate of potash.

In any case, the ingredients must be powdered separately and mixed without shock or friction—the best method being to use a bone paper-knife and a sheet of paper. It is also best to mix them only a short time before use.

No. 2,074.—**Agaricin** (St. Louis).
This acid principle derived from white agaric (*Polyporus officinalis* Fries), which is used with great success as a remedy for excessive or abnormal perspiration, is prepared in the following manner:

Powdered white agaric is exhausted with alcohol. The alcoholic solution, which contains four different resins, designated by Schmieder respectively as alpha-, beta-, gamma-, and delta-resin, is concentrated to a small bulk. This causes the separation of *white* resins containing the agaricin, while *red* resins remain in solution. The *white* resins are treated with alcohol with the addition of potassa. This causes the potassium salt of the alpha resin to go into solution, while the corresponding salt of the beta resin remains undissolved. The mixture is filtered, and the residue treated with water, which dissolves the potassium salt of the beta resin, while the gamma resin, which does not combine with potassa, remains undissolved. The aqueous solution of the *potassium salt of the beta resin* is now treated with solution of chloride of barium, causing the precipitation of agaricate of barium. This is dissolved in boiling 30-per-cent alcohol, and the solution decomposed by sulphuric acid. From the filtrate the agaricin gradually separates, and may be recrystallized from 30-per cent alcohol.

Agaricin is described by the Pharmacopœia Committee of the Germ. Pharm. Assoc., as a white, amorphous, or white silky crystalline powder of a faint odor and taste, appearing under the microscope to consist of four-sided lamellæ, little soluble in cold water; soluble in hot water to a turbid strongly-foaming liquid, which reddens litmus. It is soluble in about 130 parts of cold and 10 parts of hot alcohol, still more easily in hot acetic acid, only slightly in ether, and scarcely at all in chloroform. Caustic alkalies dissolve it to a liquid which foams strongly when shaken. At 80° C., or when kept over sulphuric acid, it loses 1 molecule of water of crystallization.

The chemical formula of agaricin is $C_{16}H_{30}O_5 \cdot H_2O$ (mol. w. 320).

No. 2,075.—**Insecticide for Bedbugs**, etc. (M. O. A.).
This correspondent states that he has used the best insect powder for some time past without any success. He asks us to suggest something better.

We would recommend that our correspondent try either of the following:

1. Prepare an alcoholic tincture of the best Dalmatian insect powder, in the proportion of 2 troy oz. to the pint. In this dissolve 1 tr. oz. of shellac, 2 tr. oz. of naphthalin, and ½ tr. oz. of picric acid. With this solution paint the fissures, cracks, recesses, etc., of the bedstead and mattress frame, wherever the obnoxious insects are wont to congregate or hide.

2. Paint the places with a solution of 1 tr. oz. of corrosive sublimate in 2 fl. oz. of glycerin, and tinted with a little fuchsine. Only a thin coat is required, and this may be dusted over with insect powder, so that it will not be sticky to the bed-clothing that may come in contact with it.

3. Mix 3 av. oz. of borax, 8½ oz. of salicylic acid, and 1½ oz. of bicarbonate of sodium with 15 fl. oz. of alcohol and 10 fl. oz. of water, in a capacious capsule, and stir until no more gas is given off. Then evaporate the mixture, on a water-bath, to a syrupy consistence, and add to it 1 oz. of sulphate of zinc, 1 oz. of tartar emetic, 1 oz. of inspissated ox-gall, 30 grains of strychnine sulphate, and enough aniline violet to color. Place the capsule on a water-bath, and heat the contents, under constant stirring, until they become stiff and doughy. Remove the mass, while still hot and pliable, and form it into a roll, which may be wrapped in tin-foil or paraffin paper. When wanted for use, a small portion of the hardened mass is broken off and dissolved in about 10 parts of water. A little mucilage may then be added to it. This liquid is painted or brushed on precisely like either of the preceding ones.

The peculiar aniline-color tints of both of the last-named preparations are a sufficient caution to prevent either of them from being accidentally mistaken for harmless substances. Of course, both being poisonous, they should be kept in a secure place.

No. 2,076.—**To Render Tincture of Iron "Tasteless"** (J. A.).

Our correspondent, as he himself states, is aware how the so-called tasteless tincture of iron is prepared, and it is *not* his object to have his query understood as referring to this. He desires to learn of some way by which tincture of iron, at the time of administration, can be rendered tasteless, or at least less unpleasant to the taste.

Any process or method by which the characteristic astringent and ferruginous taste of ferric chloride or of tincture of chloride of iron is modified or neutralized involves certain molecular changes or a decomposition, resulting in the production of a new compound. For example, the "tasteless tincture of iron" which our correspondent alludes to, owes its tastelessness to the fact that the iron no longer exists as a chloride, but most probably as a citrate. And so it is with any other process that accomplishes the same purpose. In many cases, it may be entirely immaterial whether the iron introduced into the system is offered to it in the form of tincture of chloride of iron or in any other form (reduced iron, saccharated carbonate, citrate, phosphate, sulphate, etc., etc.). And in these cases the physician will probably have no objection whatever, if his patient seeks to render the administration of the remedy as pleasant to his taste as possible. There are, however, some cases in which the astringent character of the tincture is desired to produce a certain impression, that is, where the ferric chloride, in its alcoholic solution, is intended, *as such*, to reach the place where it is to produce the special impression, or where it is to be absorbed. In such cases, it would be improper to counteract the physician's plan by causing a chemical change in the compound before it has reached the intended place.

Having premised these remarks we will append two methods which, in our experience, are very effective in accomplishing the result desired.

1. Pour the measured quantity of tincture of iron, immediately before administering or taking it, into a sufficient quantity of *milk*, about a wineglassful for every 10 drops of tincture. This method was first recommended by Hager. The iron probably changes to phosphate in this case.

2. Pour the tincture into a sufficient quantity of *Vichy water*—about 1 fl. oz. for every 10 minims of tincture. This method is often practised in the public hospitals of this city. Our attention was first drawn to it by Dr. A. B. Pope. In this case, of course, the iron changes to carbonate, the carbonic acid being speedily disengaged, and ferrous hydrate being deposited on standing. In this form it has been found to be quite easily taken, and, so far as known, with best results.

No. 2,077.—**Bland's Pills** (V.).
We have heretofore given several formulas for preparing Bland's Pills, but most of them contained acacia

as an ingredient. This is also the case with the formula of the French Pharmacopœia, in which the pills are contained under the title "Pilules Ferrugineux de Blaud," with the Latin (?) synonym "Pilulæ D. Blaud." It has, however, recently been pointed out that acacia is an undesirable constituent, as it is apt to react with the iron, and produce an insoluble compound in the course of time.

In order to enable our correspondent to examine the merits of formulæ omitting the acacia, we place here two from among those last published.

1. *Dieterich.*

	Gm.	Grains.
Sulphate of Iron, cryst.	100.	1540
Carbonate of Potassium	50.	775
Magnesia	5.	77
Sugar, in fine powder	100.	1540
Althæa, in fine powder	50.	775
Glycerin	q. s.	q. s.

Triturate the Sulphate of Iron to as fine a powder as possible, mix it with the Carbonate of Potassium and Magnesia, and then add the Sugar and Althæa. Finally mix it with enough Glycerin to form a pill mass.

If this mass is divided into 640 pills, each pill will contain about 1 grain of ferrous carbonate.

The mass should have and retain a handsome green color. This is best attained by using only so much carbonate of potassium as is necessary to decompose the iron salt.

The sugar and althæa may be omitted. But the mass will then gradually become hard and indigestible.

2. *British Formulary* ("B. P. C." Unofficial Formulary).

Sulphate of Iron	60 grains
Carbonate of Potassium	36 "
Sugar, in powder	12 "
Tragacanth, in powder	4 "
Glycerin,	
Distilled Water	āā 2½ min.

Reduce the Sulphate of Iron to a fine powder, add the Sugar and Tragacanth, and mix intimately. Finely powder the Carbonate of Potassium in another mortar, and thoroughly incorporate with it the Glycerin and Water. Transfer this to the mortar containing the Sulphate of Iron, beat thoroughly until the mass becomes green and assumes a soft, pillular consistence and divide into 24 pills.

Each pill contains about 1 grain of ferrous carbonate.

The theoretical quantity of ferrous carbonate obtainable from crystallised sulphate of iron is at once seen by inspecting the molecular weights:

$FeSO_4.7H_2O$	$FeCO_3$
ferrous sulphate	ferrous carbonate
278	116

or, in percentage, 100 parts, by weight, of ferrous sulphate yield 41.7 per cent of ferrous carbonate.

No. 2,078.—**Albuminate of Iron (Iowa).**

We have previously published several formulas for preparing this compound, but we have no means of ascertaining at the present time how the several products, as prepared by the given formulæ, compared with each other, or what keeping qualities they showed. From reports now and then published in the pharmaceutical press, however, it would appear that all known processes suffer from some defect or other. Recognizing this fact, W. Gruening has recently (*Pharm. Zeitsch. f. Russl.*, 1887, Nos. 34–36,) studied the features of these processes, and partly on the experience thus gained, but chiefly on the results of an analysis of a proprietary preparation made by Drees, he elaborated a new process, which is said to give an unexceptionable product. We have not tried it, as we had no demand for the preparation. But we understand that many physicians would be glad to employ this compound, even if only in an experimental way, as it is considered, theoretically, to contain iron in a most suitable condition for absorption. Gruening's process is as follows:

45 Gm. of dry egg-albumen are mixed with 270 Gm. of distilled water. When it is completely dissolved, 49 Gm. of liquor ferri acetatis (Russian Pharm.), of spec. grav. 1.134-1.138 [or the corresponding preparation of the U. S. P. diluted to the same density] are added, the mixture several times shaken, and, if necessary, passed through a small linen strainer. If any residue remains, this may be washed with 40–50 Gm. of water. The liquid is now transferred to a parchment-paper dialyzer, and dialyzed with fresh supplies of water until the contents form a jelly. This is now mixed with 10 Gm. of hydrochloric acid and dissolved by gentle agitation, and the resulting liquid dialyzed again, until the liquid has only a very faint acid reaction with litmus. When a small sample, poured into a flat capsule, and with a few drops of ammonia, and covered with a piece of paper saturated with sulphuric acid, remains liquid after the lapse of a few hours, the dialysis may be considered as completed. The liquid, which has now again assumed the consistence of a thin jelly, is removed from the dialyzer, and gradually mixed with dilute soda solution, until the precipitate first formed is again dissolved, but so that an excess of soda is carefully avoided, as this would produce a jelly of albuminate of sodium. For this reason it is advisable to add, at first, only enough soda to just start the solution of the jelly. The mixture is set aside for 12 hours, then strained, and if a residue has remained, this is cautiously dissolved by a few drops of soda solution. To the liquid are now added 75 Gm. of cinnamon water (spirituous; containing about 20% of alcohol), and enough water to make the liquid weigh 750 Gm. And, finally, 250 Gm. of alcohol of 90% are added, under brisk agitation.

The resulting product contains about 0.5% of ferric oxide and 3.04% of albumen, and about 29% of alcohol.

No. 2,079.—**Prescription Difficulty (E. A.).**

This correspondent sends us the following communication:

"In a recent issue of the *Pharmaceutical Journal*, a case of fatal poisoning is reported to have occurred in Australia (on the authority of the *Australian Journal of Pharmacy*) from the administration of the following mixture:

R) Potassii Chloratis	gr. 40
Syr. Ferri Iodidi	fl. ʒ 4
Syrupi	fl. ʒ 4
Spir. Chloroformi	♏ 20
Aquæ	q. s. ad fl. ʒ 3

"As reported there, 'the mixture, when dispensed, was of a light-brown color, which gradually darkened, and in a few hours iodine was deposited in abundance. In this condition, the mixture was administered to a child, eventually causing death. The prescriber condemned the dispensing of the mixture, which he said should have been almost colorless, and he held the dispenser to be liable for the consequences. But an expert to whom the subject was referred failed, after various trials, to prepare a presentable mixture.'"

We are asked to explain the cause of the decomposition, if possible.

On consulting the September number of the *Australian Journ. Pharm.*, we find the original report of Mr. J. M. Higgins, the expert who examined the prescription. He enumerates the several trials he made to prepare it as follows:

1. Mixed the syrup of iodide of iron and simple syrup together; then added the spirit of chloroform, and lastly the chlorate dissolved in cold water. The result was a yellowish-green mixture, which in a short time turned red, and in a few hours flocks of iodine appeared.

2. Mixed the solution of the salt with the simple syrup and spirit, and gradually added the syrup of iodide of iron. Same result as in No. 1.

3. Warm water employed to dissolve the salt. Decomposition took place immediately.

4. A drop or two of liquor potassæ added to the solution of the chlorate arrested the chemical action for a short time only.

Only pure substances were used.

On repeating the above-detailed experiments, we find that, when all the ingredients except the chlorate are mixed, the solution remains unaffected by starch, showing that no iodine is set free. On adding the chlorate, however, decomposition very soon begins, and if gelatinized starch had previously been added, a violet to blue tint is soon produced. Now this liberation of iodine can only be accounted for by the presence of some agent which will decompose the chlorate, so that chlorine is set free, the chlorine then liberating an equivalent amount of iodine. The only agents likely to be present which will accomplish this, are free acids. On examining any commercial sample of iodide of iron, it will be found that they all have an acid reaction, due to the presence of small quantities of hydriodic acid. If hydriodic acid is capable of eliminating chlorine from chlorate of potassium, a simple experiment will decide this. This is, in fact, the case, but only when the acid is moderately concentrated. The chlorine, however, at the moment of being liberated, in its turn liberates iodine, and this is revealed by its reaction with starch. Yet the whole reaction, even with a moderately strong hydriodic acid, is not very energetic, the amount of iodine altogether liberated and recognizable by starch being comparatively small. (If hydrochloric acid is substituted for hydriodic, a very small quantity is capable of causing the slow elimination of chlorine.) Another portion of chlorine probably combines with iodine and escapes the test. This reaction, thus observed to take place with a rather concentrated acid, does not, however, of itself account for the action of the exceedingly small quantity of hydriodic acid which is present in a well-made and fresh syrup of iodide of iron. It suggests itself here to make an attempt to remove all traces of free acid from the syrup of iodide of iron. We have endeavored to accomplish this by means of carbonate of calcium. On shaking equal volumes of the syrup and of water with an excess of carbonate of calcium and filtering, the excess of acid is, indeed, removed, and when such a syrup (which is only half strength, on account of the water present) is used in equivalent proportion for the preparation of the above-mentioned mixture, the result is a greenish-yellow liquid which does *not* give a reaction with starch at first. On standing, however, a slight reaction will be produced after some time, and this gradually becomes intensified on further standing. Now it is well known that, under the influence of light and air, and in the presence of water, ferric iodide constantly eliminates traces of hydriodic acid, which will, under certain conditions, decompose so that the iodine is set free, giving the solution a dark color. In the presence of sugar or certain other substances (such as hypophosphorous acid), however, the free iodine is again taken up and reconverted into hydriodic acid. As the process of eliminating hydriodic acid seems to go on continually, it appears to us that this body exerts its decomposing action on the chlorate while in a *nascent state*. But the eliminated chlorine immediately again decomposes the trace of iodide formed. We can account for the reaction in no other way, but would suggest that this subject be taken up by some one who has the necessary time to devote to its study. Incidentally we would remark that the presence of peroxide of hydrogen in the atmosphere, or the addition of peroxide of hydrogen to hydriodic acid or to iodides causes an abundant liberation of iodine. It is not impossible that the presence of this body may have something to do with the reaction.

No. 2,080.—Cod-Liver Oil Emulsion (Subscriber).
The use of lime-water for the purpose of preparing an "emulsion" of cod-liver oil is not at all uncommon, but does not deserve indorsement, unless it be the express desire of the prescriber to present the oil to the intestinal canal of his patient in form of a lime soap. Of course, a mixture of lime-water and cod-liver oil (or any other fixed oil) is no emulsion, in the true sense of the word, but produces a lime soap, which is but little soluble in water. Yet it is known that this compound is by no means rejected by the digestive organs, being sometimes (according to some authorities) even more easily taken up than the unchanged oil itself.

The question has been repeatedly put to us, and also by "Subscriber," whether it is not possible to replace gum arabic—which has become very expensive and almost a luxury—by some cheaper and equally efficient substitute. There are, indeed, various methods of preparing emulsions, besides that which requires the use of acacia, such as those made with Irish Moss, Glyconin, Tragacanth, Quillaja, etc., but each of these has slight drawbacks, either requiring some time and trouble to prepare, or being but little less expensive than the acacia emulsion. One of us has had this problem presented to him during the last year in a very prominent manner. The supply of cod-liver oil emulsions, prepared in considerable quantity by means of acacia, for the use in public dispensaries, is apt to become an expensive item, and induces a careful search after something equally serviceable and cheaper. Such a substitute has been found in *Dextrin*, and by means of this, an excellent emulsion may be prepared without the least trouble.

The market offers various qualities of dextrin. In tint it varies from yellowish or yellowish-gray to pure white. Some is prepared by more heat and subsequent washing. Another kind is prepared by means of acids (oxalic, etc.), and washing. It makes no difference by which of these processes it is prepared, so long as it is neutral to testpaper, of a white or whitish color, having not more than a slight yellowish tint, and, when dissolved in water, free from disagreeable odor and taste. Every kind of commercial dextrin, especially when mixed or dissolved in water, has more or less of an odor, but in the better grades this is so slight, and so easily overcome by suitable flavoring, that it may be disregarded. Pure dextrin is soluble to a clear, limpid liquid in less than its own weight of water. But commercial dextrin usually contains more or less unaltered starch. *For the purpose of making emulsions, the presence of a moderate proportion of starch in dextrin is an advantage.*

Having procured a dextrin corresponding to the description here given, the first step is to prepare a *mucilage of dextrin*. And it may be presumed that those who want to employ this method of making emulsions desire to keep the mucilage in stock, so as to enable them to prepare the emulsion quickly when wanted, we shall give the necessary direction for this purpose.

1. MUCILAGE OF DEXTRIN.
(*For Emulsions.*)

Dextrin .... 1 part
Water, enough to make .... 3 parts

Mix them in a tared vessel, and heat the mixture, under constant stirring, to near boiling, until it is limpid. Then restore any water lost by evaporation, strain the liquid through muslin, and transfer it, while hot, to bottles, which should be filled to the neck. Pour a sufficient quantity of bent olive oil on the surface, to form a protecting layer and set the bottles aside in a cool place, so that the contents may congeal to a jelly. Then cork them securely and keep them in a cool place, in an upright position.

Note.—When this mucilage is to be used for preparing emulsion of cod-liver oil, or for other mixtures, the protecting layer of oil on the surface is first poured off and the remainder removed by a pellet of absorbent cotton. The bottle is then gently warmed until the contents are melted, and allowed to cool again short of causing the mucilage to again solidify, when it may be mixed with the cod-liver oil or other ingredients.

2. DEXTRIN EMULSION OF COD-LIVER OIL.

Cod-liver oil .... 8 fluidounces
Mucilage of dextrin .... 5 "   "
Water .... 3 "   "
Syrup .... 1 fluidounce
Flavoring .... q. s.

To the mucilage of dextrin, contained in a capacious bottle, gradually add the cod-liver oil, first in small portions, and agitate thoroughly after each addition, until the oil is emulsified. Finally add the syrup, the water, and the flavoring, and mix the whole thoroughly together.

As in the case of other emulsions, when larger quantities are to be prepared, it is best to use some mechanical contrivance for incorporating the ingredients. Of all mixing appliances known to us, the Keystone Beater (to be obtained at 28 Vesey street, New York) seems to us the most simple and best.

If salts, such as hypophosphites, etc., are to be combined with the emulsion, they may be dissolved in a portion or the whole of the water directed to complete the 16 fluid ounces of emulsion.

If well made, a dextrin emulsion of cod-liver oil is *at least* as stable as one made with acacia. And even if it should be partially separate at first, it is so easily and quickly restored that any tendency to separation, due to hasty preparation, is no practical drawback. In fact, should it have separated, it will be found that the tendency to do so will disappear entirely after it has been kept a few days, and has meanwhile been occasionally reshaken. The quantity of mucilage of dextrin here given will make a rather dense emulsion. One of the consistence of thin cream may be made by reducing the mucilage to 4 fl. oz. Even if this should separate during the first few days, it will soon acquire stability.

No. 2,081.—Bleaching of Feathers and Hair (Boston).
The art of bleaching feathers or hair is one that requires considerable practice and experience. We can give here only an outline and must refer you for fuller information to special works on the subject.

Feathers as well as hair, in their crude condition (such, for instance, as are sold in quantities in the market) are usually covered with more or less fatty matter and dirt or dust. This must be carefully removed. For this purpose, the feathers are laid in a 10 per cent solution of carbonate of sodium (sal soda), and the latter then gradually heated to about 180° F. If the feathers, etc., are valuable, they must be fastened singly and in rows to sticks, and suspended in the liquid so that they do not touch each other.

When they have been in the liquid for about an hour, they are transferred to clean water and carefully washed. And until they are further manipulated, they are left in the water to prevent new dust, etc., from settling upon them.

The bleaching is done, either by hanging the wet feathers, etc., in a room, in which sulphur is afterwards burnt, or better, by macerating them in a solution of peroxide of hydrogen. For this purpose, the commercial 10 volume solution is sufficiently pure. It is best to use three baths (agate-ware, oblong pans are very useful). The feathers, etc., are first placed into No. 1 and covered with the solution. To economize the latter, some pieces of glass rod or plate may be laid upon them to keep them down. After 24 hours they are taken out, transferred to No. 2 and covered with a fresh quantity of solution, while a new supply of washed feathers is put into No. 1. After the next 24 hours, the contents of No. 2 are put in No. 3 and again treated with fresh solution, while the contents of No. 1 are put in No. 2, and No. 1 supplied with fresh feathers. Finally, after 24 hours more, the feathers, etc., in No. 3 have been acted upon by the bleaching liquid as far as possible. The process is kept up continuously, so that each lot of feathers, etc., is kept in bleaching liquid during 72 hours. When No. 1 becomes exhausted, the liquid is thrown away, fresh liquid put in, and the pan becomes then No. 3, the previous No. 2 and 3 becoming, respectively, No. 1 and 2.

Of course, dark colored feathers cannot be bleached completely white. If perfectly white feathers are wanted, the original feathers must have been at least whitish or grayish-white. In many cases, even the longest contact with bleaching material will not render the feather absolutely white. The manufacturer overcome this by the same trick which is used by the laundress in making up white goods (addition of bluing to the starch), namely by placing the feathers in an extremely dilute solution of an aniline violet having a bluish tint.

No. 2,082.—Solubility of Terpin ("Baltimore," and E. O.).
In answering a query as to a suitable solvent for terpin hydrate, in our December number (Query 2,062), we referred to page 140 of our last year's volume. The solvent there mentioned is the Acidum Nitricum Alcoholisatum of the French Pharm. As it is, however, doubtful whether this solvent will answer in all cases, we would, under ordinary circumstances, rather prefer alcohol as a solvent.

1 part of terpin hydrate requires about 7 parts (by weight) of 85% alcohol for solution, according to Deville. According to our own experience, 1 part is soluble in about 9 parts of officinal (94%) alcohol, which corresponds to a proportion of 1 troy ounce of terpin hydrate to about 11½ fluid-ounces of the alcohol.

Terpin hydrate is soluble also in 200 parts of cold, and in 27 parts of boiling water.

No. 2,083.—**Pharmaceutical Apparatus** (S.).
The address of Messrs. Canning and Patch is 109 Green str., Boston, Mass.

We shall be glad to give you the other desired information, if you will inform us what special kind of pharmaceutical apparatus you are in search of.

No. 2,084.—**Glycerite of Subacetate of Lead** (S.).
We are asked to state what the standard strength of this preparation is, that is, what percentage of subacetate—$Pb(C_2H_3O_2)_2 . PbO = 548$—the product should contain. The preparation is officinal in the British Pharm., and directed to be made by mixing together

Acetate of Lead	5 oz.
Oxide of Lead	3½ oz.
Glycerin	1 pint
Water	12 oz.

boiling for a quarter of an hour, then filtering, and evaporating until the water is dissipated.

Assuming that the whole of the acetate of lead taken is converted into the theoretically possible amount of subacetate, also assuming that all the water is dissipated, without loss of glycerin, the product would contain

Subacetate of Lead	3,166 grains.
Glycerin (1 pint, imper. meas., sp. gr. 1.250)	11,036 "
	14,202 grains.

This would be equivalent to about 22.3 per cent of subacetate.

No. 2,085.—**Spence Metal** (B.).
Our correspondent asks us several questions about the casting of Spence's Metal of which we have given a full account in NEW REMEDIES, 1880, page 137.

We regret to say that we have no practical experience with the metal, and would refer our querist to Messrs. Spence & Co., 31 Lombard street, London, E. C. We know of no depot in this city.

No. 2,086.—**"Churchill's Iodine"** (T.).
There are two iodine preparations known by Churchill's name, viz.:

1. *Churchill's Tincture of Iodine:*

Iodine	9½ tr. oz.
Iodide of Potassium	½ tr. oz.
Alcohol	15 fl. oz.
Water	8 fl. oz.

2. *Churchill's Iodine Caustic:*

Iodine	1 tr. oz.
Iodide of Potassium	2 tr. oz.
Water	4 fl. oz.

No. 2,087.—**Recognition of Graduates of Pharmacy by Boards of Pharmacy** (K.).
The Boards of Pharmacy of the State of New York are not all on the same basis, so far as the recognition of Graduates of Pharmacy is concerned. The State Board, having jurisdiction in all counties but New York, Kings, and Erie, is not required to accept diplomas as evidence. Hence even Graduates have to undergo an examination. In the three counties mentioned, which have, each, a separate pharmacy law, the act provides for the recognition of graduates.

The law makes no difference between Graduates of Colleges within or without the State. A graduate of the Chicago College of Pharmacy would, therefore, have as good a chance, in the three counties named, as a Graduate from New York. But if he wants to be registered by the State Board, he will have to stand an examination.

No. 2,088.—**Blue Prints** (J. D. C.).
A very full explanation of the details of the process of making blue prints has been given by us on page 117 of our last volume (under Query No. 1,956).

No. 2,089.—**Syrup of Lactophosphate of Calcium** (or Lime) (E. A. S.).
The so-called soluble lactophosphate of lime is not a true chemical compound, though it is believed to be pretty uniform, as found in the market. The above-named preparation may be made either by dissolving phosphate of calcium in lactic acid and syrup, or by dissolving lactate of calcium in phosphoric acid and syrup, or by dissolving the commercial "lactophosphate of calcium (lime)" in syrup.

The United States Pharm. gives a formula for the syrup, which starts from phosphate of calcium. This furnishes a satisfactory product. But in order to show how the several processes may be applied, upon quantities of 1 pint of product, each, we shall give formulas for all three methods, the products being practically identical, though there is always a factor of doubt in the case of the commercial lactophosphate.

It so happens that the molecular weights of calcium phosphate and calcium lactate are so nearly alike that equal quantities of the two salts may be regarded, practically, as containing equal quantities of calcium [*Calcium lactate:* $Ca(C_3H_5O_3)_2$—mol. w. 308. Calcium phosphate: $Ca_3(PO_4)_2$—mol. w. 310].

1, *U. S. Ph. process*, calculated for 1 pint of product, and modified so as to simplify the process.

Triturate 220 grains of Precipitated Phosphate of Calcium with 330 grains of Lactic Acid, 1½ fluidounces of Orange Flower Water, and 6 fluid ounces of Water gradually added, until the calcium salt is dissolved. Then add 13 troy ounces of sugar, and enough water to make 1 pint. Dissolve by agitation and strain if necessary.

2. *With Lactate of Calcium.*—Dissolve 220 grains of Lactate of Calcium with 220 minims of Phosphoric Acid (50%), 1½ fl. oz. of Orange Flower Water, and 6 fluidounces of Water, and proceed further as under No. 1.

3. *With Lactophosphate.*—Dissolve 330 grains of so-called soluble Lactophosphate of Calcium in 1½ fl. oz. of Orange Flower Water and 6 fl. oz. of Water, and continue as under No. 1.

No. 2,090.—**Cornutin** (H. W. I.).
Prof. Kobert's cornutin, a peculiar principle extracted from ergot, which is said to be the most prominent representative of the oxytocic properties of ergot, is manufactured by Gehe & Co., of Dresden. You may order it through any importing house. It is very expensive, and is likely to cost, delivered here, not much less than one dollar a grain.

No. 2,091.—**National Formulary** (H. and several other inquirers).
In reply to a number of inquiries received, it is here stated that the printing of the text of the National Formulary is progressing as rapidly as is consistent with careful editing. It is expected that the work will be out during the latter part of March, 1888.

No. 2,092.—**Bismuth Free from Arsenic** (J. A. H.).
There are several ways by which bismuth may be freed from arsenic. The U. S. Pharmacopœia of 1870 had a process for preparing bismuth salts in which provision is made for the removal of the arsenic in shape of arseniate of bismuth. But it is believed that it usually failed to remove the whole of it.

A very good process to accomplish the desired object is the following, originally devised by Biltz, and adopted in the last German Pharmacopœia.

Heat 8 parts of commercial bismuth with 1 part of nitrate of sodium, in an iron capsule or crucible, to a faint red heat. As soon as the mass begins to swell, stir it with an iron spatula continuously (for about one hour) until the metal is so finely distributed that it is scarcely possible to recognize it as such any longer. Then remove the vessel from the fire, allow the mass to cool somewhat, then add 5 parts of water and 3 parts of solution of soda, of spec. gr. 1.160. Boil the whole during a few minutes, constantly stirring, transfer it upon a filter, wash the mass until it is perfectly free from alkali, and dry. The residue consists of finely divided metallic bismuth and a little oxide of bismuth, which are both dissolved when nitric acid is made to act upon them. The original impurities, viz., arsenic, sulphur, and selenium, pass into solution in the alkaline liquid. According to Hirsch, however, a trace of arsenic may still be present in the residual mass, as basic arseniate of bismuth.

No. 2,093.—**Prescription Query** (B. J. K.).
This correspondent writes:
"I have a prescription for:
B Cinchonid. Sulph. Fort. Will you please state what the prescriber meant. I am told that physicians write the above for *Quinine*, when they do not want their patient to know that they are taking quinine."

The information given to our correspondent appears to be correct. In prescriptions coming under our experience, the above synonym for quinine has not yet been met with, and after consulting some of our friends, we believe that the above term is confined to the practice of a few physicians. It is not a practice to be recommended or approved, as it establishes a false position between physician, patient, and pharmacist; and besides, it is a weak concession to the unjust prejudice engendered in the minds of many gullible persons, by the venders of certain nostrums, who frighten them with the assertion that "quinine poisons the system, settles in the bones, etc., etc."

Information wanted.

1. What is Tomatin? Stated to be coloring matter used for coloring tomato catsup a dark "brick dust" color.
2. What is the composition of Dr. Wilhoft's Antiperiodic?
3. What is the composition of Kennedy's Medical Discovery?

American Druggist

Vol. XVII. No. 2.   NEW YORK, FEBRUARY, 1888.   Whole No. 164.

Emulsions.

BY A. W. GERRARD, F.C.S.

Twenty-five years ago, in the early days of my pupilage, I can well remember the rough and ready rule of thumb methods that often prevailed when an emulsion had to be made, also the thick gruel-like magmas or thin greasy stuff produced. Happily there has been a change for the better, and pharmacists now recognize that to make satisfactory emulsions certain rules must be observed as to quantities and careful attention given to the process.

The most generally useful and important emulsifying agents at our disposal are the gums of acacia and tragacanth, used either as a powder or mucilage, preferably I think, as powder; of less value, but still having some special qualities to recommend them, should be mentioned yolk of egg and the tinctures of quillaia and senega. Milk is an emulsion formed by nature, and closely allied to milk in character is the emulsion made by rubbing almonds with water; both of these, though providing the highest types of what emulsions should be, are certainly not good emulsifying agents, for they possess no more power to emulsify than does a well-made diluted emulsion of any fixed oil. It is the habit of some dispensers to speak of the solutions of potash, soda, and ammonia as emulsifying agents. The cases are very few indeed where they really act as such; for when we combine alkalies with an oil or resin, they form soaps or semisoaps, so that their action is chemical, whereas a true emulsion owes its condition to physical influences. These alkalies have, however, some small power to emulsify, for I have often noticed that when they are shaken with chloroform or ether in the presence of vegetable extractive an emulsion has formed; its character, however, is weak, as separation usually takes place in twenty-four hours.

There are a few remarkable examples of emulsification happening daily in pharmaceutical practice, to which hitherto little or no attention has been paid, although it seems almost impossible they can have been overlooked. Most dispensers, when making an ointment with vaseline, must have observed the change of color the vaseline undergoes, and how opaque it becomes on stirring; the explanation of this is, that an emulsion of air has been formed. The peculiar viscosity of the vaseline and the motion of the spatula causes imprisonment of air, which soon becomes distributed in an extremely fine state of division. The statement here made is easy to prove, and can be demonstrated by the following experiment: Dilute some spirit of wine with water until a piece of vaseline just sinks in the liquid, now take a fresh portion of vaseline, then stir it well to get the air taken up, place it also in the liquid, it will be seen to float. The difference in the behavior of the two portions is caused by their different gravities, one portion holding air in suspension. Under similar treatment it will be found that most unctuous bodies emulsify air. What influence emulsified air has upon the keeping properties of fats and ointments would form an interesting subject for research. It is worthy of remark that two at least of the official ointments cannot be properly made without containing emulsified air; these are the ointments of red oxide of mercury and of boric acid. Unless they are continuously stirred while cooling they set to hard masses; stirring causes them to take up air, the air by its presence giving the ointments a finely granular soft and smooth consistence.

Emulsification of water is a common operation of pharmacy, cold cream manufacture provides an example; it is well known that the white, soft, creamy unctuousness of that article depends almost entirely on the water it holds in suspension. Butter is sometimes adulterated by being made to contain emulsified water. If we desire to incorporate an aqueous extract with a fat, it is usual to thin the extract with water, then emulsionize with the fat. The value of lanolin as an ointment base largely depends upon its containing emulsified water; the water has a softening influence on the lanolin, rendering it pliant and easy to mix; without water its consistence would be much too stiff for a good ointment base.

Emulsions prepared from the same kind of ingredients are frequently seen to differ in appearance and stability. The product of one operator is pure white, of another whitish-brown; its consistency is thick or thin; it may either separate in a few hours, or remain permanent for weeks. Differences of this kind can be accounted for by two causes, one natural, depending upon variations in drugs, due to soil, climate, period of collection, or change effected by age; the other mechanical, in which the operator is usually at fault; for instance, the order of mixing may be varied, stirring in one case having been more vigorous or prolonged than in another, or dilution may have been effected with varying rapidity. Of the causes of variation alluded to, those which are natural are mainly outside the pharmist's control; the best and most he can do is to select good fresh drugs, taking care they are well preserved from atmospheric and other influences. Differences due to the mechanical steps of a process we may regard as entirely under control; they are faults either of judgment or of bad manipulation. Measuring oil in a watery measure should be avoided; likewise the use of a damp or warm mortar. It is a bad practice to leave off stirring whilst an emulsion is forming; when formed a little extra stirring is often advantageous. Never starve an emulsion by trying to be economical with the gum; the result is invariably a weak product, soon breaking down, or may be an utter failure, and however much you may try to coax it into form with more gum the result is commonly unsatisfactory. Overdoses of gum are almost as bad as deficiencies; you risk getting a thick magma flowing with difficulty, whereas good emulsions flow quite easily. For the patient, it is certainly far more pleasant to get a dose that flows easily down the throat, rather than one which hangs about the fauces and nauseates quite as much as the raw oil would.

A phenomenon commonly observed during the progress of making a gum emulsion, is a cracking noise, like the breaking of a small stick; this is due to the tearing action of the pestle, causing a series of fractures in the product. It has been asserted by many authorities that this click or cracking is positive evidence that the emulsion is a success. In my experience the sign is not infallible, for on numerous occasions students have shown me their products, with plenty of crack on stirring, but in such a spoilt condition that there was not the remotest hope of turning them into emulsions.

During the past fifteen years several contributions on emulsions have appeared in the *Pharmaceutical Journal*, and in the "Year Book of Pharmacy," chiefly the contributions of American pharmacists, to whom we are indebted for many useful hints and formulæ on emulsions. Having repeated some of the experiments of the authors, it was thought the results obtained might be a useful addition to these notes. R. Rother, *Pharm. Journ.*, May 11th, 1872, in a thoughtful paper says, "A perfect artificial emulsion is physically identical with the natural, that is as far as the extinction of the oil is concerned, and this peculiarity is the distinctive feature of an emulsion." There is one statement in the paper open to criticism, where the author says: "A concentrated perfect emulsion is in itself the most rapid and efficient emulsifier, possessing the property of emulsifying oil to an almost unlimited extent." The fault to be found with this statement is, that it creates an impression that a perfect emulsion can be utilized for the preparation of other emulsions, thus placing at our disposal an easy means of emulsification, besides economizing gum; such, however, is not the case, as the following experiment is intended to show: Eighty grains of powdered gum, half an ounce of castor oil, and three drachms of water were converted into a perfect emulsion. A further quantity of oil was added, and found, as stated by Rother, to be easily emulsified, or it would be more correct to say combined. Further it was found that dilution of the product with oil could be carried to an apparently unlimited extent. Though this experiment is interesting, its practical value is small, for as one would theoretically expect, it is found the excess of oil quite changes the character of the product; it no longer admits of dilution with water like an ordinary emulsion, but is changed to a magma, floating in and repulsing water, as if it were oil only. This change of character is due to the fact of the product being no longer, as Rother implies, an emulsion of oil, but an emulsion of mucilage; the oil being in excess constitutes the menstruum in which particles of mucilage are evenly distributed. The conditions of the case in analogous to those where ether dissolves water, and water dissolves ether. The knowledge to be gathered from the experiment is that, under certain conditions, mucilage will emulsify oil; on the other hand, oil being in excess, it emulsifies the mucilage, one product admitting of dilution with water, the other dilution with oil.

Another communication to which I would draw attention is by E. Gregory, "Year-Book of Pharmacy," 1887. The author discusses the question whether mucilage or powder of acacia gives the best emulsions; the conclusion being that the use of mucilage should be abandoned in favor of powdered gum. Gregory states that three drachms of powdered gum will emulsify one ounce of any of the volatile oils, but rather less (about 2 drachms) will answer for the fixed oils and balsams. The author's method of procedure is to mix the gum first with the oil, and, if the above quantities be used, neither more nor less than four and a half drachms of water all added at once. The method was tested upon one ounce each of the following fixed and volatile oils: castor, cod-liver, olive, almond, turpentine, eucalyptus, peppermint, and sandal wood. The result in each case was as follows: The fixed oils all gave exceptionally good emulsions, white and as perfect as could be desired. Cod-liver oil during the process became very pasty, but that condition did not in any way interfere with dilution or final completeness. Oil of turpentine was a failure, but on slowly adding two drachms more water than Gregory indicates, it gave a creamy emulsion. Oil of eucalyptus failed, and like turpentine took two drachms more water to recover it; the product was then imperfect. Oil of peppermint turned out fairly well, but a little more water improved it. Sandal wood oil gave a beautifully white and perfect emulsion, which I attribute to its having more body or viscosity than other volatile oils. Gregory's process was further applied to creasote, carbolic acid, copaiba, balsam of Peru, and extract of male fern. All of these gave excellent emulsions, those of creasote, carbolic acid, and copaiba, after resting a month, appearing as perfect as on the day they were made; the male fern and Peru formed creamy layers, which a gentle shake easily distributed. Taken as a whole, Gregory's process is as good as any examined; the only improvement I can suggest is that, when dealing with volatile oils, each ounce requires 5 drachms of powdered gum and at least 6 drachms of water.

P. H. Dilg (*Amer. Journ. Pharm.*, 1878) approves of powdered gum for emulsions, 4 drachms of which should be added to 8 drachms of oil, then 6 drachms of water in one volume. The rule the author attempts to establish is, that 2 parts of oil need 1 part each of gum and water. A trial of the formula, whilst giving good emulsions, turned them out much too thick; the gum is really in excess of what is needed, a 33-per-cent castor oil emulsion flowing with difficulty. On economical grounds Gregory's formula is preferable, giving better emulsions with one-third less gum.

Notwithstanding that the balance of opinion is greatly in favor of acacia over tragacanth for the production of emulsions, yet there are still those who hold to tragacanth and continue to recommend it; this is matter for surprise, for the more fully we know the perfect character of acacia emulsions, the more completely do those made with tragacanth pass into the shade. Tragacanth gives magmas rather than emulsions; you can easily enough combine and suspend oils with it, but examine the product, and you will plainly see that the oil globules are generally of a coarse character, distinctly visible to the unaided eye. Further, tragacanth emulsions lack that milk-like fluidity, pure whiteness, and capacity for easy dilution, so characteristic of acacia emulsions. The difference obtainable by the two gums may reasonably be attributed to their difference of constitution. In a tragacanth emulsion the swollen colloid bassorin appears to have the power of keeping the globules of oil from coalescing, not by virtue of its viscosity, but rather by providing an obstacle to the movement of the oil. On the other hand, in a perfect acacia emulsion each particle of oil is no doubt surrounded by an envelope of perfectly soluble gum, both together forming a cell, having enough resistance to prevent coalescence with contiguous cells. At this point I am constrained to make a few remarks on the cod-liver emulsion of the Unofficial Formulary made, as you know, with tragacanth. Like Conroy, my attempt to make a good emulsion of it was a failure. The oil is well incorporated and suspended, but badly divided; however well it may be shaken it shows, on inversion, oil globules flowing down the bottle side in a state of division that certainly would not satisfy a fair critic. It would have been better, as Conroy suggests, to have made it with gum acacia.

Tinctures of senega and quillaia possess remarkable properties as temporary emulsifying agents, remarkable because of their power, in very small quantity, to divide and pulverize substances when gums fail. If you place in a bottle 1 ounce of chloroform, 20 minims of tincture of senega, and a few drachms of water, then shake them well, and make up to 5 ounces with water, you get a product in which the chloroform is seen to be divided into an immense number of globules; these globules do not remain long suspended; they readily subside, but will rest together for hours without coalescence. After a day or two a portion of chloroform is found broken down. Mercury, ether, or essential oils can be divided in the same manner; a singular feature about the mercury is that it succeeds best when gently shaken, violent agitation restores it to its original form. Mr. H. Collier, of Guy's Hospital, "Year Book of Pharmacy," 1879, gives some formulæ for senega-made emulsions. These I find are very useful for hospital work, where, as a rule, the time allowed for the work done is much too brief; but in private dispensing, senega will never be regarded with much favor, on account of the temporary character of its products.

The flavoring and preservation of emulsion is a branch of the subject which certainly ought not to be overlooked. Although an emulsion may be therapeutically and mechanically perfect, it often is nauseating to the taste and offensive in odor. Flavoring, though only an adjunct, therefore of minor importance, still does contribute elements of value to a medicine. The pharmacist has a great variety of flavors at his command; his chief difficulty perhaps is to select the one which would give most general satisfaction. The common favorites among flavors are those used in cookery, such as the volatile oils of almond, cinnamon, cassia, cloves, lemon, the essence of vanilla, and orange-flower water. My own opinion of these, as regards permanency, palatability, and power to disguise, is in favor of essential oil of almonds, used in the proportion of 1 minim to each ounce of oil emulsified. An elegant cod-liver oil emulsion, in which taste and odor are well masked, is made as follows:

Take of:

Cod-liver Oil	4 ounces.
Powdered Gum Acacia	1 ounce.
Oil of Cassia	4 minims.
Oil of Almonds	4 minims.
Saccharin	2 grains.
Water to make	8 ounces.

Mix the oils with the gum and saccharin in a dry mortar, add 2 ounces of water in one volume, stirring till the emulsion is formed; finally, add sufficient water to make 8 ounces.

Castor oil is very well disguised in the following formula:

Take of:

Castor Oil	1 ounce.
Powdered Gum Acacia	3 drachms.
Essential Oil of Almonds	2 minims.
Oil of Cloves	1 minim.
Saccharin	1 grain.
Water to make	4 ounces.

Mix the oils with the gum and saccharin in a dry mortar; add 4 drachms of water at once, stirring till the emulsion is formed; dilute to 4 ounces with water.

My experience with yolk of egg emulsions has been very limited, but singularly, whilst writing these notes, a prescription for a cod-liver oil and egg emulsion was presented me to dispense. The ingredients for each dose were cod-liver oil, 1 drachm; yolk of egg, ½ a drachm; water to 1 ounce; no flavoring of any kind. It made up very well; the order of mixing was to gradually pour the oil on to the yolk of egg, with constant stirring, then dilute with water; on transference to a bottle a vigorous shake improved it. The dose 1 ounce, containing 1 drachm of oil, being for a child, seemed to me unduly diluted, and wanting in finish, so after a few experiments the following improved formula was arranged:

Take of:

Cod-liver Oil	4 ounces.
Yolk of Egg	2 "
Common Salt	35 grains.
Saccharin	2 "
Oil of Cloves	8 minims.
Water to make	8 ounces.

Rub the oils gradually with the yolk of egg, salt and saccharin, till an emulsion is formed, make up to 8 ounces with water and shake well.

The product is a thin, but most perfect emulsion, which can be flavored with any desired aromatic in place of cloves. Such a combination seems admirable in many ways; its taste is very mild, the nutritious value of the oil is enhanced by the yolk of egg, and the emulsion can be made by the merest tyro without risk of failure.

Having saccharin at our disposal, it provides us with a useful substitute for sugar in emulsions. Its advantages are that it adds nothing to the thickness of the product, and cannot give rise to fermentation. The method found most convenient for using saccharin, is a 10-per-cent solution, made by rubbing the saccharin smooth with a little water, then adding bicarbonate of sodium till effervescence ceases; 20 grains of the saccharin takes 8 grains of the soda salt. The product is a neutral saccharin salt of soda, freely soluble in water and easily miscible with neutral or alkaline fluids, but giving a precipitate of saccharin with acid solutions.

Salt is occasionally taken for masking the taste of cod-liver oil; it combines well with oil in emulsions. The taste of the oil is well covered, especially if a little oil of clove be added in addition to salt. No argument is needed to justify such a combination, as it forms a salted animal food; moreover, the salt is admirably adapted to keep the oil sweet and free from rancidity.

To keep emulsions for long periods is not desirable. They are best freshly made. Should it be desired to preserve them, recourse must be had to such antiseptics as boric or salicylic acid, or better perhaps a simple tincture of benzoin, or even pure chloroform. The latter is a most powerful antiseptic, imparting an agreeable sweetness; one minim may be added to each ounce of emulsion.

The last four or five years, it has been noticed as a growing practice among medical men and others, to call all preparations holding finely divided suspended matter emulsions. It is a common occurrence in my pharmacy to be asked to prepare an emulsion of boric acid, salicylic acid, or iodoform, in olive oil or glycerin. If it is correct to apply the word emulsion to such preparations, then we may extend its meaning to all examples of uniform suspension, so that a bismuth or rhubarb mixture becomes an emulsion. This widening of the meaning of the word is, in my opinion, perfectly legitimate, and even consistent with our own practice. When we emulsify a solid resin, as copaiba or benzoin, our whole aim is to get the solid finely divided and evenly distributed ; this accomplished, the product is called an emulsion. Therefore it is reasonable enough to argue that the suspension and equal distribution of any finely divided solid in a soft or liquid medium equally constitutes an emulsion. It does not matter whether benzoin or bismuth be suspended, the mechanical conditions are precisely the same. . . .

In conclusion, I wish to acknowledge the assistance of Mr. C. Collingwood Fenwick in conducting the experiments which this paper involved.

Mr. Joseph Ince, in discussing the foregoing paper, said : The chief merit of the paper was the direct practical experiments which controlled the more theoretical portion. Referring to some of the transatlantic methods which had been mentioned, he thought that the style of American pharmaceutical journalism was more to be deprecated than American pharmacists, as too much stress and importance was placed upon the single experiments of one man. Thus, a recent American writer said a good and perfect emulsion would stand heat, and gave this as a distinguishing test. He could not point out too strongly that this was not a true test, as only age and durability could distinguish a perfect from an imperfect emulsion ; moreover, his experience invariably showed that emulsions, however well made, would inevitably separate on the least application of heat. For that reason the least heat, even mechanical, in performing the operation should be avoided. There were three principal methods by which emulsions could be made. First, mucilage of acacia ; this unquestionably was the easiest and most fitted for the tyro. Second, powdered gum ; this, the continental method, required more experience and dexterity. Third, the instantaneous mixing of oil, gum, and water together, by no means so easy as the other methods, but undoubtedly superior when it could be done. He confirmed Mr. Gerrard's experience that the gum acacia at the present day was distinctly inferior to that in use several years ago, for he now found it almost impossible to keep it in the form of mucilage for a week and sometimes not more than three days. The value of senega as an emulsifying agent, he considered, had been much overrated, although convenient for rapid emulsifying ; but, in his experience, the emulsion thus made would not keep even an hour. Quillaia, as far as he was aware, was not used to any extent in English pharmacy, although it had found much favor in America.

Mr. H. Collier (Guy's Hospital) thought that the name emulsion should be strictly confined to the minute division and suspension of fixed and volatile oils, balsams, and oleoresins. For this purpose he knew of nothing so good as quillaia or senega. He exhibited an emulsion of mercury made eight years ago with tincture of senega, which he considered perfectly emulsified, for the globules were divided as in gray powder. Chloroform might also be quickly emulsified in the same manner, and, if left for a considerable time, would not separate. If it were thought necessary that an emulsifying agent should add viscosity, so as to keep permanently for a very great length of time, senega and quillaia fail. This feature, however, he did not consider essential, and he knew of many instances where taking a viscous emulsion was thought to be as bad as taking the oil itself, whereas emulsions made with senega were very fluid and totally unlike the oil. Besides, the great advantage was that instant agitation would produce the emulsion, and this in hospital dispensing when necessary was of great importance. He firmly maintained the exceptional value of senega, although willing to admit its deficiency in adding viscosity and permanency.—*Pharm. Journ.*

Camille-Jean-Marie Mehu died on November 29th, in Paris, aged 52. Deceased was born at Dijon (Côte d'Or), in Burgundy, and graduated as pharmacist of the first class in 1862, at the Paris College, and in 1865 as doctor of medicine at the Paris Faculty. In 1862, he was appointed the pharmacist-in-chief to the Necker Hospital, a post he filled for some nineteen years, when he was transferred, in the same capacity, to the Charité Hospital. He was, in 1880, elected a member of the Academy of Medicine for the section of pharmacy, and, in 1881, represented it, as well as the Paris Pharmaceutical Society, as their delegate to the London International Pharmaceutical Congress. He was an honorary member of many pharmaceutical societies, including those of Chicago, Philadelphia, etc., and, finally, last May he was elected an honorary member of the Pharmaceutical Society of Great Britain.

NEW FORM OF PERCOLATOR.

E. G. PERRY, of Birmingham, England, suggests a modification of the form of percolator, which differs from that directed by the U. S. Pharmacopœia in two particulars—the one, and the most important, consisting in its being longer in proportion to its diameter. The U. S. P. percolator is more conical than Mr. Toogood's, and has a depth, three and a half times the diameter at the top, while Mr. Toogood's has a depth five times its larger diameter. This is a decided advantage [!], inasmuch as the higher the column of material and menstruum in proportion to their bulk, the more complete is the exhaustion with the same quantity of menstruum. The other difference between the new percolator and the U. S. P. one is in the construction of the stem. In the U. S. P. percolator, this is narrowest at its extremity, and the cork which is fitted in the neck has to be inserted from the inside; Mr. Toogood's percolator has a regular bottle neck, in which the cork can be inserted in the ordinary way. This, though apparently a small matter, is a source of much comfort practically. The percolator is made in the following sizes: 12 oz., 25 oz., 66 oz., 100 oz., and 160 oz.—*Chem. and Drugg.*

(Our British contemporary is not the first to suggest this form of percolator, Prof. Oscar Oldberg having preceded him by three or four years and percolators of this form being made already by Whitall, Tatum & Co.—ED. AM. DRUGGIST.)

A NEW EXTRACTION APPARATUS.

O. FOERSTER recommends the form of apparatus devised by him and here illustrated. It consists of four parts:

1. A receiver of the form A, in which the solution of the dissolved matter is finally freed from the volatile solvent by heat.
2. A tube B, about 3 Cm. wide, and 19 Cm. long to the contracted portion. The latter is carefully ground so as to fit air-tight into the neck of the receiver A.
3. The extraction tube proper. This is about 22 Mm. wide, and 150 Mm. long to the contracted portion. The latter is long enough to reach down into the receiver A, and is obliquely cut off at the end. It fits quite loosely into the tube B, and its exterior is provided with some knob-like projections to permit the free passage upwards of the vapors of the volatile solvent. This tube is charged with the material to be extracted, which is confined in it by means of two loose tampons of perfectly purified cotton, at the bottom and at the top of the contents.
4. The condenser D, of the form shown in the cut. It is made entirely of glass, and ground at its lower part so as to fit air-tight into the mouth of the tube B.

The use of the apparatus is easily intelligible without further details.—After *Zeitsch. f. Anal. Chem.*, 1888, 30.

Practical Hints about Aluminium.

ALUMINIUM is at the present time made in such quantities, and so cheap that its technical use will become greatly extended. It has, however, some peculiarities which must be known or understood to render experiment with it, or its practical use, successful.

When aluminium is to be melted, to make a casting, for instance, this must not be done in clay crucibles, since it reduces the silicia contained therein to silicium, whereby it becomes gray and brittle. It must be melted in lime crucibles ; or if clay crucibles are used, they must be lined with carbon, or, well-ignited cryolite. Graphite crucibles, however, are the best.

A good solder for aluminium is made by melting together 3 parts of zinc, 2 parts of tin, and 1 part of lead, and rolling this out into thin sheets. The aluminium surface to be soldered must be scraped clear of all oxide, and coated with paraffin. A piece of the solder is then placed upon each portion and heated. This causes the paraffin to melt ; on further heating, the solder melts and unites with the aluminium. The two surfaces thus coated are then soldered together in the usual manner.

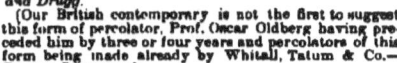

Utilization of Waste Products.[*]

Mr. Alfred H. Allen, the President of the Society of Public Analysts, of England, lately delivered the following interesting address upon a very practical subject:

Dirt has been cleverly defined as "matter in the wrong place." Similarly, we may define waste as "a valuable product, the use of which remains unknown."

In almost all manufactures we find the production of the primary article attended with the formation of one or more secondary products which it is the natural aim of the technologist to utilize. Thus, in the manufacture of iron from the ore, we get slag and combustible gases as secondary products.

Sometimes the secondary product becomes, through a change in commercial conditions, the primary aim of the manufacturer, the article for which the product was first conducted occupying the second place. A remarkable instance of this occurs in the manufacture of soda by the Leblanc process. The first stage in its manufacture consists in treating common salt with sulphuric acid. There is thus obtained sulphate of soda, which is the primary product, and is ultimately converted into the more serviceable forms of caustic soda and carbonate of soda, while, at the same time, there is produced a large quantity of hydrochloric acid in the form of gas. This, formerly, had but a limited application, and was allowed to escape in the neighborhood of the alkali works, many of which were situated at St. Helen's and Widnes in Lancashire, with the result that the vegetation for miles round suffered most severely. Under the first Alkali Act, manufacturers were compelled to condense 95 per cent of this hydrochloric acid. This, at first, was regarded as practically an impossible feat, but it was found by passing the gas up a tower filled with coke, down which a stream of water was allowed to trickle, that condensation could be readily effected. Alkali inspectors were appointed to see that the Act was properly carried out, and the arrangements soon became so perfect that, instead of merely complying with the Act, and condensing 95 per cent of the acid gas, the condensation of 99 per cent became common. It became necessary, however, to find some outlet for the liquid hydrochloric acid which was produced by the condensation, and this soon became utilised for the production of chlorine, which itself was absorbed by slaked lime to form the ordinary chloride of lime or bleaching powder. The manufacture of chlorine from hydrochloric acid was conducted by heating the latter with a mineral known as black oxide of manganese, an article which is familiar to Sheffield steel-melters. The secondary product of the reaction was a very acid liquid containing chloride of manganese, which, from its corrosive character, proved very objectionable when run into drains or rivers. By the genius and industry of the late Mr. Walter Weldon, the manganese in this secondary product was recovered, and a perfectly neutral and harmless effluent produced. The result was an enormous saving in the cost of producing chlorine, and a consequent impetus to the manufacture of chloride of lime, which is employed in very large quantities, not merely as a disinfectant, but for bleaching cotton and linen; its manufacture is, in fact, at the present time, one of the great industries of the country. Meanwhile, the sulphate of soda, which I have already referred to as the primary object of the treatment of common salt with sulphuric acid, has become of less value than formerly, owing to the competition of the so-called "ammonia process" of manufacturing soda carried out at the works of Messrs. Brunner, Mond & Co., at Northwich. This process runs the Leblanc method of soda manufacture so hard that the latter may now be said to be struggling for its existence, and the profit on the manufacture of soda by it has practically disappeared. But the ammonia process does not result in the production of hydrochloric acid, nor consequently of chlorine or chloride of lime, and as chloride of lime is required in such enormous quantities, it has become the primary object of the alkali manufacturer, who may now with greater propriety be called an "acid manufacturer," his principal raw product being the hydrochloric acid which he used to send up his chimney-stacks because he thought it too much trouble and too expensive to condense it.

The utilization of the waste products from the manufacture of coal-gas is one of the most curious chapters in the history of chemistry. Thus, when coal is distilled there are obtained, as primary products, illuminating gas, coke, tar, and ammoniacal liquor. The quality of these products largely depends on the temperature and other conditions under which the distillation is conducted. Thus, when coal is distilled primarily for the purpose of producing illuminating gas, as in our ordinary gas-works, the coke is of inferior quality, while the tar is superior. For many years it was a matter of regret with technologists that no successful attempts had been made to utilize the waste gas and tar produced when coke was the primary object of the manufacture, as in coke-ovens. Now, however, this is successfully done, but the tar produced varies greatly in character, according to the special kind of coke-oven, that from the Simon-Carvé ovens being very similar to ordinary gas-works tar, while that from the Jameson and other coke ovens is of very little value.

Every one is familiar with the general fact that gas-works tar is now the raw material from which countless products are obtained, remarkable for their color, their medicinal value, and other useful applications. These products have been actually created by the chemist. Many of them have no existence in the animal or vegetable world, while others which have a natural existence, as, for instance, benzoic acid in gum-benzoin, can now be produced from coal-tar by synthetical means at a mere fraction of the cost of the natural product. The same thing is true of alizarin, which is the basis of the so-called Turkey-red dye, so familiar to all of us. The production of alizarin from coal-tar has resulted in the entire abandonment of the cultivation of madder, the natural source of alizarin, and the same may any month happen to the culture of indigo, a coloring matter which can now be produced in a state of purity from coal-tar, but not, so far, at a price which will enable it to compete successfully with the natural product. For some purposes, however, the artificial indigo is found more convenient, and hence already receives a somewhat limited application.

Similarly, there have been recently made from coal-tar a number of bodies remarkable for their antipyretic and antifebrile characters, and more than one of the active principles of plants known as alkaloids have been synthetically prepared; in fact, the artificial production of quinine itself from coal-tar may now be regarded as fairly within the range of practical possibilities. The cochineal industry is another which is threatened with extinction by the production of the azo-scarlets from coal-tar, though these bodies are very different chemically from the coloring matter of the cochineal insect.

The production from coal-tar of the intensely sweet substance called saccharin is another instance of the creation of a new product likely to have an extensive practical application, and that in cases in which sugar is unsuitable.

There is a curious mistake which has occurred so frequently when non-scientific persons have been in conversation with me that I feel it will not be out of place to refer to it on this occasion. Continually we have the iridescence observed on a pool of water where tar has been spilt regarded as a practical illustration of the existence of brilliant coloring matters, and people seem to think that these exist ready-formed in the tar. Of course the iridescence in question is purely an optical effect, due to the same cause as the brilliant hues of the soap-bubble, and can be produced by any film which is sufficiently thin. A drop of colorless oil of turpentine on the surface of a dinner plate of inky water will show the colors as brilliantly as the soap-bubble or the pool of tarry water.

As a matter of fact, all the known constituents of coal-tar, with very few exceptions, are colorless bodies. The black color itself is probably due to free carbon, and when the tar is distilled the fresh distillates have but little color. It is true that certain fractions are known as "red oils" and "green oils," but a little coloring matter goes a long way in such cases.

It is as much a mistake to suppose that the aniline dyes and other colored substances derivable from coal-tar exist ready-formed in the crude material, as it would be to look for ready-made cakes of scented toilet soap in a cocoanut or a live sheep.

People often are inclined to ridicule the long names given by chemists to the products of the laboratory, but in defence it must be remembered that these products of organic synthesis are so numerous that casual names would be perfectly useless, and hence names which to any competent chemist are descriptive of their nature, origin, and general properties, are absolute necessities. The scientific name of a synthetic organic substance may be compared to a placard bearing the full name of a man, together with his occupation and address, his titles of honor, and very often whether he is strong in his attachments, is right or left handed, and looks with both eyes in the same direction, to say nothing of giving the names and occupations of his parents and ancestors, and the number, ages, and dispositions of his children. It is no exaggeration to say that the full systematic names of many chemical substances are capable of affording to the chemist, conversant with that particular branch of the subject, an amount of information comparable with the case just supposed.

To take a simple example of a not very complex kind, there is a certain artificial coloring matter commercially called "Helianthin." It dyes silk a fiery orange hue, and is used by chemists in place of litmus to indicate the point of neutrality. The trade name of helianthin or "Orange III.," indicates nothing of the nature of the substance, though otherwise convenient. Now the systematic chemical name of this body is ammonium dimethylanilidoazobenzenesulphonate.

This name, which at first strikes one as ludicrously long, is really descriptive of the nature and origin of the

---

[*] A paper read before the Sheffield Literary and Philosophical Society.

substance. Thus, expressing the elements carbon, hydrogen, nitrogen, oxygen, and sulphur by their initial letters, we find that the name of the substance indicates it to have the following descent.

The name benzene is applied by chemists to a hydrocarbon composed of six atoms of carbon and six of hydrogen, expressed by the formula, C_6H_6 or $C_6H_5.H$.

Azobenzene signifies benzene in which one atom of hydrogen has been replaced by nitrogen (azote) thus:— $C_6H_5.N$, or preferably doubled, $C_6H_5.N:N.C_6H_5$.

Amidoazobenzene will be azobenzene in which one atom of hydrogen is replaced by the group NH_2, called amidogen. Methylamidoazobenzene will be a body in which one of the hydrogen atoms of the amidogen is replaced by the group methyl, CH_3, and the dimethyl derivative one in which both such hydrogen atoms are replaced. A sulphonic acid is a body in which the group SO_3H replaces a hydrogen atom, and a sulphonate is a salt of such acid. Ammonium salts contain the compound group, NH_4, which plays the part of a metal and hence can replace hydrogen in an acid. Now, with this general explanation it becomes easy to trace from its name the genealogical descent of ammonium dimethylamidoazobenzenesulphonate, thus:—

1. Benzene $C_6H_5.H$
2. Azobenzene $C_6H_5.N:N.C_6H_5$
3. Amidoazobenzene $C_6H_5.N:N.C_6H_4.N\begin{Bmatrix}H\\H\end{Bmatrix}$
4. Dimethylamidoazobenzene $C_6H_5.N:N.C_6H_4.N\begin{Bmatrix}CH_3\\CH_3\end{Bmatrix}$
5. Dimethylamidoazobenzenesulphonic acid. $C_6H_4\atop SO_3H\Big\}N:N.C_6H_4.N\begin{Bmatrix}CH_3\\CH_3\end{Bmatrix}$
6. Ammonium dimethylamidoazobenzenesulphonate. $C_6H_4\atop SO_3(NH_4)\Big\}N:N.C_6H_4.N\begin{Bmatrix}CH_3\\CH_3\end{Bmatrix}$

By adding up the various atoms of carbon, hydrogen, etc., in the substance it will be found that the empirical formula of helianthin is $C_{14}H_{14}N_3O_3S$. But such a formula gives comparatively little information as to the nature of the substance. In fact, the empirical and constitutional formulæ are related to each other in much the same manner as are the commercial and systematic names of the substance.

Having the systematic name of the substance, and being thus able to plan out its constitutional formula, a chemist will find it a comparatively easy matter to devise methods for its formation; but without a knowledge of the constitution of a substance, he will be working in the dark, and will have but little chance of success. That is just the present position of the chemist with respect to albumin and some several allied bodies, which, in addition, are very difficult to purify, and have empirical formulæ of extreme complexity. It is evidently by studying the products of decomposition of a body that we can best attain such a knowledge of its constitution as will enable us successfully to essay its synthesis, as has been done with alizarin, indigo, salicylic and benzoic acids, oil of bitter almonds, and many other substances.

(To be continued.)

AN APPARATUS FOR PREPARING SULPHUROUS, CARBONIC, AND PHOSPHORIC ANHYDRIDES.

H. N. WARREN describes the apparatus here illustrated as being very suitable for the preparation of anhydrous sulphurous, carbonic, and phosphoric acids.

It consists of a glass vessel A, provided with 3 tubulures, otherwise resembling a large Woulff's bottle, the large tube B being provided with a stopper for the purpose of introducing fresh material from time to time into the small dish C. D is a tube conveying a current of air to support the consumption of the combustible material, and the generated gas is carried off by the tube E to the vessel intended to receive it.

Supposing the apparatus is to be used for making anhydrous sulphurous acid. A piece of sulphur having been dropped down the central tube, it is ignited by touching it with a red hot wire, and the stopper of the central tube is then inserted. A slight blast of air is maintained by means of bellows, connected with D, until the whole of the sulphur is thoroughly kindled, when a somewhat more powerful blast may be applied. When the apparatus is in full working order, from two to three pounds of carbonate of sodium may be converted into sulphite of sodium in less than half an hour, or several gallons of water may be saturated.

The author states that, by connecting the apparatus with a powerful refrigerator, a large quantity of liquid SO_2 has been obtained by him in a short time.

He also states that it will be found advantageous during the preparation of sulphurous anhydride to introduce a layer of water, about one inch in depth, into the generating vessel. [The cut shows the capsule C sufficiently elevated over the bottom to prevent its coming in actual contact with the water. If the capsule is of iron, such contact would, probably, be immaterial.]

Carbonic and phosphoric anhydrides may also be generated in this apparatus, by introducing slight modifications. But in the case of phosphorus, the air must be allowed to enter only gently, since a rapid current would invariably cause the fracture of the vessel.—*After Chem. News*, December 9th, 1887.

APPARATUS FOR DISTILLATION UNDER DIMINISHED PRESSURE.

DISTILLATION under reduced pressure is an operation frequently employed in the chemical laboratory and in manufacturing establishments in operations on the large scale. But it will, no doubt, also become more generally used in the laboratory of the pharmacist, as it involves but little additional trouble or expense, and, moreover, permits a much larger amount of work to be done in a less time, and at a considerably lower temperature than when the usual plan of distillation is followed.

"Diminished pressure," of course, implies the use of some method by which air or vapor is exhausted. This may be accomplished either by an aspirator, or by means of one of the well-known filter pumps. The latter need only be connected, by means of suitable tubing, with the receiver, while the latter is connected air-tight with the condenser. If the receiver has a faucet or other arrange-

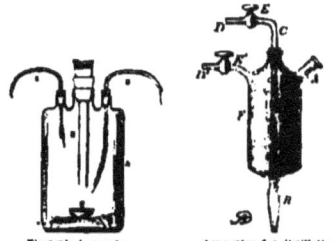

Warren's Apparatus.   Apparatus for distillation.

ment which permits its being occasionally emptied, it is unnecessary to disconnect any of the fittings. Otherwise, this is indispensable.

A very useful attachment to the end of the condenser, which permits the use of a separate and easily detachable receiver, has been devised by Prof. L. Meyer, primarily for another purpose.

It consists of the glass vessel F, which is fitted to the end of the condenser by means of the neck A. Into its neck is fitted a glass tube C, passing through a soft cork, and just tight enough to permit the tube being raised or lowered without causing leakage. The lower end of the tube is ground so as to fit into the inner construction of the neck. The outer surface of the neck B is also ground so as to fit air-tight into a series of interchangeable receivers. Both tubulures E and E are connected with the air-pump.

When the distillation is started, and the condenser, the vessel F, and the receiver are connected, the air or filter-pump is started, the tube C being drawn up far enough to permit the condensed liquid flowing at once into the receiver. When this is full, the tube C is pushed down, and whatever condensed liquid passes over now, collects in the vessel F. Meanwhile a new receiver is attached, and after a few minutes, when the air has been exhausted from it through the tube C, the latter is again raised, when the liquid already collected in F, and any that will subsequently pass over, will flow into the new receiver. The same manipulation may be repeated as often as necessary.—*After Zeitsch. f. Instrumentenkunde*, 1887, 440.

Co-operation among Swiss Pharmacists.—A number of pharmacists in Geneva have formed an association for the purchase of drugs in a wholesale way, and the common manufacture of pharmaceutical preparations, with a view of being better able to meet the increasingly severe competition to which they are subjected. The association further proposes to compete for the supply of medicines to friendly societies, charitable institutions, hospitals, the military and police departments, and other public bodies, at specially reduced prices. Ten Geneva pharmacists have so far joined the association.

Flexible Mucilage.—To 20 parts of alcohol add 1 part of salicylic acid, 3 parts of soft soap, and 3 parts of glycerin. Shake well, and then add a mucilage made of 93 parts of gum arabic and 180 parts of water. This is said to keep well, and to be thoroughly elastic.

Flucsilicate of Sodium as a Disinfectant.

Mr. E. Davies lately read before the Liverpool Chemists' Association a paper containing the following statements: The element, silicon, is in the mineral kingdom what carbon is in the organic. Being a tetrad and being able to join itself to other atoms of silicon, it can form compounds of great complexity; its oxide, silica, one of the most abundant minerals, is the anhydride of two acids, ortho- and metasilicic acids. Neither of these acids can be obtained pure, owing to the readiness with which each loses water, but the metasilicic is the more definite of the two. Its formula is H_2SiO_3, and if for the dyad, oxygen, we substitute the monad, fluorine, we get fluosilicic acid, H_2SiF_6.

This acid may be obtained by heating together silica, fluorspar, and sulphuric acid, and passing the tetrafluoride of silicon into water, when we get both fluosilicic and metasilicic acids. $3SiF_4 + 3H_2O = H_2SiO_3 + 2H_2SiF_6$. If the fluosilicic acid is then neutralised with sodium carbonate, if the acid is strong, most of the fluosilicate of sodium separates in minute crystals, which may be filtered off and dried.

Sodium fluosilicate is only slightly soluble in water, 1 part dissolving in 150 parts of water. The solution has a saline, not unpleasant taste; it is powerfully antiseptic and disinfectant. Meat immersed in a saturated solution of it remained perfectly sweet after four days at a temperature of 25° C., whilst similar meat in distilled water was disgustingly putrescent and swarmed with bacteria; no living organism was visible in the fluosilicate. Urine was also preserved for a similar time by the addition of one-fourth of its bulk of the solution.

As a disinfectant, its effects was shown by the addition of one-fourth of the bulk of the water from the putrescent meat above mentioned, from which it removed all unpleasant odor and destroyed the living organisms. It is stated to be innocuous to health, and is therefore a valuable addition to the list of antiseptics and disinfectants.

Mr. W. Thomson, of the Royal Institution Laboratory, Manchester, is the discoverer of the properties of this substance, and has patented it under the name of salufer.
—*Pharm. Journal and Trans.*

Varieties of Albumen in Urine.

The forms of albumen met with in urine are:
(1). *Serum Albumin*, a substance which, according to Hammersten, constitutes 4.518 per cent of the blood serum. It is almost constantly present in urine which contains any variety of albumen. Although a less diffusible body than serum globulin it is capable of passing through membrane.—(2). *Serum Globulin* or Paraglobulin, the globulin of the blood serum, of which it constitutes 3.103 per cent. It is met with in almost all albuminous urines, its proportion to the serum albumen varying in different instances.—(3). *Peptone*, a product of gastric and pancreatic digestion of albuminous substances, also occurring in the process of transformation of tissues and of inflammatory effusions. It is a readily diffusible substance, occasionally met with in the urine in association with or apart from serum albumen.—(4). *Propeptone*, or Parapeptone, or Hemialbumose, a substance or group of substances intermediate between albumen and peptone, constituting a stage or stages of transformation from the one to the other. It is highly diffusible, and is occasionally met with in the urine under conditions corresponding to those under which peptone occurs.—(5). *Acid Albumen*, or Syntonin, one of the derived proteids obtained by the action of acids upon albumen. It is easily produced artificially by the addition of acid to albuminous urine, but may occur naturally in certain cases.—(6). *Alkali Albumen*, another derived proteid, produced by the action of alkalies upon albumen. It is readily produced artificially, but is also found naturally in the urine.—(7). *Hæmoglobin*, the combination of hæmatin and globulin naturally existing in the red corpuscles of the blood. It sometimes appears in the urine, particularly in cases of hæmaturia and hæmoglobinuria, also in certain septic conditions, and after inhalation of arseniuretted hydrogen, transfusion of blood, and otherwise.—(8). *Fibrin*, a proteid substance which does not normally exist as such in the blood. It is met with in the urine in hæmaturia, in some cases of chyluria, and in certain varieties of renal casts.—(9). *Mucin*, the chief constituent of mucus, is a derived proteid substance. It frequently becomes superadded to the urine after secretion, and may be derived from any part of the urinary tract. (10). *Lardacein, Waxy* or *Amyloid Material*, familiarly known as a pathological substance within the body, is said to be occasionally demonstrable in renal casts.

Of these ten varieties the last four are of little practical importance—mucin alone being indeed worthy of special comment, and that mainly because of the difficulties which its presence raises in regard to the reliability of certain tests for serum albumen.

The following are the tests for the albumens, put in tabular form.

Synthesis of a Sugar.

The announcement from Würzburg that Professor Fischer and Herr Tafel have succeeded in preparing artificially a compound possessing the properties and having the composition of a true sugar—in fact, differing from glucose chiefly, if not entirely, in its behavior towards polarised light—marks another important advance in the progress of organic chemistry. This synthesis is the outcome of a long series of researches which have been laid before the Berlin Chemical Society, and recorded in the *Berichte*, but its attainment probably first came within the range of perceptible possibilities during an investigation of the conditions attending the oxidation of polyatomic alcohols. Previously to this subject being taken up by Messrs. Fischer and Tafel, the products obtained as the result of such oxidation had with one exception, been acids, the probability being that the aldehydes or ketones first formed escaped observation through lack of suitable methods for their separation. The exception, mannite, yielded to Gorup-Besanez a sugar that was named mannitose, but which has since been proved, by its behavior towards phenylhydrazin, to be identical with levulose. In consequence of this result, Messrs. Fischer and Tafel experimented upon other polyatomic alcohols; glycerin, erythrite, and dulcite being oxidized with nitric acid, and phenylhydrazin being used for the detection of the aldehyde or ketone. This was an application of an observation made previously by Professor Fischer, that the varieties of sugar which reduce alkaline copper solution form, with phenylhydrazin, crystalline compounds difficultly soluble in water and therefore easily isolated. The manner of formation of these compounds is represented by the following equation:

$$C_6H_{12}O_6 + 2C_6H_5N_2H_3 = C_{18}H_{22}N_4O_4 + 2H_2O + 2H_2$$

Each of the three products of oxidation mentioned yielded a hydrazin derivative which corresponded in composition, manner of formation, and properties, to compounds of phenylhydrazin with sugars. Glycerin, especially, yielded a beautiful crystalline product, having the composition $C_{15}H_{18}N_4O$, which seemed to have been formed, in all probability, from glycerin aldehyde ($CH_2OH.CHOH.COH$) or the isomeric ketone ($CH_2OH.CO.CH_2OH$), though it was not possible to isolate the aldehyde. It may be convenient to mention here that the term "phenylglycerosazon" has been applied to the glycerin derivative, the term being modified when applied specially to other derivatives, so as to indicate the origin of the compound.

In order to study more closely the origin of this glycerin compound, it was determined to attempt to prepare glycerin aldehyde another way. To effect this, acrolein was treated with bromine to form bibromacrolein, which was found to be easily attacked by baryta water, with the result that the bromine was replaced by hydroxyl radicals, the product being a very soluble substance that energetically reduced Fehling's solution, and possessed all the properties of an aldehyd-alcohol. It having been suspected that a sugar might be formed in this way, a preliminary attempt was made to isolate such a product, if it existed, by means of phenylhydrazin, and this was so far successful that a substance of the osazon class was obtained, having the composition $C_9H_{12}N_4O_2$, and scarcely distinguishable from phenylglucosazon, the compound formed by glucose with the same reagent, except in being optically inactive. This result, at least, left little doubt that a sugar had been formed from the bibromacrolein under the influence of the baryta, and probably according to the following equation:

$$2C_3H_4Br_2O + 2Ba(OH)_2 = C_6H_{12}O_6 + 2BaBr_2.$$

The next difficulty, therefore, to be overcome was to regenerate the sugar from the hydrazin compound, to which the name "phenylacrosazon" has been given to indicate its origin from acrolein. It was then found, in the course of purifying the substance resulting from the combination of phenylhydrazin with the products of the decomposition of bibromacrolein, that two isomeric compounds were present, one of them insoluble in ether, the other soluble in the presence of resinous impurities, but nearly insoluble when pure, and these were designated respectively α-phenylacrosazon and β-phenylacrosazon. Some of the β-phenylacrosazon, which was the preponderant constituent, was submitted to the action of reducing agents, resulting in the formation of a base which, when analyzed as an oxalate, gave figures corresponding to the formula $(C_3H_{11}NO_2)_2C_2H_2O_4$. This base gave all the reactions of glucosamine; it reduced Fehling's solution vigorously when warmed, but it was optically inactive. The neutral oxalate dissolved in ice-cold water was then treated with a calculated quantity of sodium nitrite and a little oxalic acid, which caused the evolution of all the nitrogen from the base. After this reaction had finished, the liquid was exactly neutralized with soda solution, evaporated in a vacuum, and the residue extracted with alcohol, which left upon evaporation a sugar in the form of a light brown syrup, free from nitrogen or ash, having a sweet taste, reducing Fehling's solution very strongly, and combining with phenylhydrazin to reproduce phenylacrosazon. It has not yet been ascertained with certainty whether it is fermentable. In fact, the only point of difference yet observed between it and a natural sugar is that it is perfectly inactive towards polarized light.—*Pharm. Jour. and Trans.*

Commercial Cocaine.

The editor of the *Chemist and Druggist* makes the following statement in one of the recent issues:

"There recently came under our notice a case in which a chemist had reported to a manufacturer that the cocaine hydrochlorate made by the latter was impure. The manufacturer averred, however, that the hydrochlorate conformed to Maclagan's test, giving a 'perfectly clear solution with ammonia,' and this he took as a proof that the salt was free from amorphous alkaloid. Our attention was called to the matter, and we find that another manufacturer in Germany has reproduced the test in the following form :

"'To 0.1 gramme hydrochlorate of cocaine, dissolved in 100 grammes of distilled water, 5 drops of liquor ammonia Ph. B. are added. The solution should remain perfectly bright. (McLagan's [sic] test.)'

"There is no mention here, it will be seen, of the separation of cocaine hydrate, on the addition of ammonia, and it is rather a strange fact that, on testing the product of this manufacturer, we find it not to conform with his own test, but to the original one. We have tested other samples, and find that one of German origin quite responded to the modified test above quoted, affording no precipitate, one of them only giving a faint milkiness. Three other specimens gave immediate precipitates with ammonia, which in a few seconds became crystalline, and, on subsiding, left the supernatant solution clear. These were therefore pure : the first two were not ; but we may add that when, in the latter case, the volume of water was considerably decreased, a precipitate of an amorphous character was afforded. It is perfectly obvious that some manufacturers are working up to what they consider a standard of purity, which is really one of impurity. The result is that they produced a cocaine hydrochlorate which is very bulky, is in the form of micaceous scaly crystals, and dissolves readily in water. The pure hydrochlorate is much heavier and dissolves more slowly."

Urinal Cakes.—These are much used for the disinfection of urinals. One form of these is made by fusing together sulphates of copper, iron, zinc, alum, and soda, and moulding into cakes.

A SIMPLE FILTER PUMP.

A VERY simple and efficient filter pump may be made as follows: Select a piece of stout glass tube, 3 inches long, and ¼ inch bore; fit this with corks, one with two holes, and the other with one hole. Then take three pieces of ordinary glass tubing, ⅛ inch bore, and draw two of them out as shown in the left-hand figure, cut the one at *a*, and the other at *b*; bend the third piece at an angle of 90°. Insert the tube *x a*, and the bent piece through one cork, and *x b* through the other, so that *x a* will project inside of *x b*. Attach *x a* to a water-supply. On allowing water to run through the apparatus, a vacuum will be produced in the tube N, and, if connected as shown in the cut, filtering will proceed rapidly. The apparatus gives a vacuum of 28.5 inches of mercury.—ROBERT LAW, in *Chem. News*, December 9th, 1887.

APPARATUS FOR SEPARATING LIQUID AND SOLIDIFIED CONSTITUENTS, BY MEANS OF COLD.

IN the course of an investigation on certain organic compounds of antimony, A. Michaelis and U. Genzken encountered the problem how to separate a liquid mixture, consisting of two substances, one of which is solid, the other liquid at ordinary temperatures, into its two component portions. Mere cooling and pouring off the liquid portion, even when several times repeated, was insufficient, in the special case under consideration, to accomplish the object.

Success was finally attained by using the apparatus here described, which has some resemblance to that proposed some sixteen years ago by Koerner and Lougiinine,[*] but

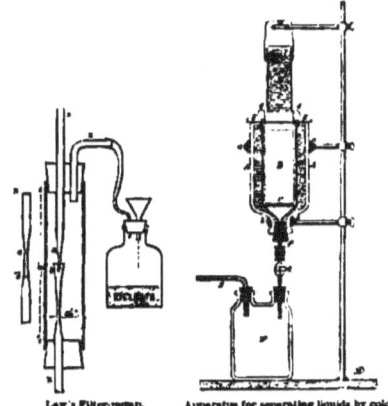

Law's Filter-pump.   Apparatus for separating liquids by cold.

which the authors have considerably improved. This apparatus is likely to be serviceable for the preparation of many other substances, requiring separation from accompanying liquids. [*Note by Ed. Am. Dr.*—It seems to be especially useful for the separation of solid stearoptens from volatile oils, or of the more solid fatty acids from the more liquid ones, etc., etc. The authors had no occasion to use a large apparatus. We shall give the measurements just as they are in the original paper. For practical or manufacturing purposes, of course, the dimensions may be correspondingly increased.]

A is a glass-bottle without bottom, about 10 inches high and 3 inches in diameter. The neck of this bottle carries a perforated rubber-stopper, through which a small leaden tube *f* passes, which is connected, by a funnel-shaped piece, with the cylinder *B* constructed of tinned iron. This cylinder has a diameter of about 3 inches. It is open at the top, and is adjusted at such a height that its rim is at the same level with the rim of the bottle. *E* is a tinned iron ring, projecting beyond the rim of the bottle, and intended to keep the open space between cylinder and bottle snugly covered. The cylinder has a perforated bottom or diaphragm at the bottom, immediately over the conical attachment.

C is an additional perforated, but loose bottom which may be lifted out or let down by means of two wires with handles (*d d*) attached.

D is a water-tight cylinder of tinned iron, 2½ inches in diameter, about 6 inches high, and provided with a handle and a well-fitting lid.

---

[*] According to Lougiinine (*Ber. Deutsch. Chem. Ges.*, 4, 514), first described by Koerner in a memoir entitled : "Sul luogo chimico nelle contenze aromatiche."

The leaden tube f is connected, with interposition of a glass stop-cock, with one neck of a Woulff's bottle, while the other neck is connected with an aspirator, or pump.

The manner of using the apparatus is as follows:

A freezing mixture is prepared by mixing comminuted ice and salt (which easily accomplishes a fall of temperature as low as − 15° C. (5° F.), and the space between the bottle A and the cylinder B completely filled with it. The ring E is now put on, and the diaphragm C let down to the bottom of the cylinder. The stop cock below f having been closed, enough of the liquid which is to be operated upon is poured into the inner cylinder to fill it about three-quarters full. Next the cylinder D, previously also filled with the above-mentioned freezing mixture, is cautiously let down into the apparatus, so as to just dip into the liquid, and the whole arrangement then left to itself for a time, in a room which should be as cold as possible.

In the special case for which the authors employed the apparatus, half an hour sufficed to accomplish the purpose. It had then become a pasty mass. The time required, and the condition of the mass, under other circumstances, will of course vary considerably, but no difficulty will be encountered in adjusting the process for any special purpose.

When the crystallization or solidification of the solid constituent appears to have proceeded as far as possible, the stop-cock is opened, and the mass compressed, first gently, then more strongly, by the cylinder D being slowly pushed down. At the same time, the aspirator or pump, connected with g, is started, so as to withdraw the liquid portion as rapidly as possible. When this is accomplished, the cylinder D is withdrawn, and the solidified contents removed by lifting out the extra diaphragm C.

[This process may, of course, be repeated once or more times, when the object is to obtain as much as possible of the liquid and of the solid constituent separately. In the experiment conducted by the authors, the main object was to obtain a certain quantity of the solid constituent. No attempt was, therefore, made to deprive the liquid portion of the small quantity of solid still retained in solution.]

The last adhering traces of the liquid portion may, in most cases, probably be removed in the manner described by the authors, namely, packing the solidified mass between layers of blotting paper and subjecting it to strong pressure. The attempt to separate the solid from the liquid portion by pressure, while all or nearly all the liquid is still present, usually results in failure, since most or all of the solid matter will re-dissolve. But when only traces of the liquid accompany the solid, the loss of the latter, upon pressure, is insignificant, even when operating at the ordinary indoor temperature.—After, *Liebig's Annal.*, 242, 164.

Mixture of Glycerin and Mucilage of Acacia.

Wm. Duncan, in a paper published by the *Pharm. Jour. and Trans.*, says that his attention having been drawn by a friend to the fact that, when glycerin is added to mucilage, a jelly is formed, and asked if he could explain it. He is in the habit of using this mixture as an excipient for Blaud's pills, and had noticed that, if it be allowed to stand for any time before using, the mixture thickens, a sort of jelly-likebody being formed at the junction of the two liquids. Mr. Duncan then writes:

"Thinking that glycerin might be a precipitant of arabin, I at once jumped to the conclusion that this was the explanation of the formation of the jelly, but on stirring together equal bulks of the two liquids in a glass measure, no separation of arabin took place. On the contrary, the mixture remained quite bright and fluid. This agrees with the statement in "Pharmacographia," "that mucilage mixes with glycerin and that the mixture may be evaporated to a jelly without any separation." I found, however, that if the glycerin be first measured out, and the mucilage be then run on to the surface of it, care being taken not to mix the two liquids, in about five minutes a jelly is formed at the junction of the two, which slowly falls to the bottom if the measure be allowed to remain undisturbed for a couple of hours. The jelly, after being slightly washed to rid it of adhering glycerin, was found to be readily soluble in water, and the solution gave precipitates with basic acetate of lead, alcohol, and ammonium oxalate, so that probably it is simply gum arabic. If the mixture be stirred, the jelly becomes redissolved and a clear solution results. This leads me to the following explanation of the reaction: The glycerin absorbs part of the water from the mucilage, and the gum, not having sufficient to keep it in solution, is precipitated in the form of a jelly. After a time, however, if the mixture be shaken, the glycerin and water begin to dissolve the precipitated gum, and we have then a clear solution. I believe this explanation to be the correct one, as I find that, if glycerin be first diluted with 25 per cent water, no separation takes place on the addition of the mucilage."

French Chemists' Assistants.

The Paris correspondent of a London daily paper states that the Parisian *potards*, or chemists' assistants, are threatening to strike, or at least to take steps to protect themselves from what they call the "rapacity of their masters." The disaffection among the knights of the pestle and mortar is attracting public attention because it is well-nigh unprecedented. It opens up, in fact, a vista of contingencies as terrible as that shadowed forth by the chemist who was subpœnaed in the famous case of "Bardell *versus* Pickwick," and had left a small boy with hazy notions of the contents of the cabalistically marked drawers and bottles in his shop. At a recent meeting of the disaffected Parisian *potards*, it was stated that there were twelve hundred slaves who were condemned to pass their wretched existence behind a counter making up pills and potions, or in the laboratory preparing syrups and purgatives. They worked seventeen or eighteen hours in summer and sixteen in winter, and another ground of complaint was that, even when there were no customers, they had to make believe that they were doing something by dusting or arranging bottles and phials. For these reasons the ill-fated *potards* are trying to form themselves into a syndicate; but it is extremely doubtful if they will succeed, even should they form such an association, in ameliorating their lot, which is not a happy one. These men are the unlucky ones of the pharmaceutical profession, as they have no money to start in business for themselves, and they are thus forever condemned to what they call in common with the Socialists, the "exploitation of the capitalists." One of the men gave a melancholy description of the ordinary day's work of a Parisian chemist's assistant. He rises at 7 o'clock, and serves the ordinary morning customers who come for castor oil, sulphate of magnesia, tisanes, and other decoctions. At 10 he goes to the laboratory and makes up syrups, after which he returns to the shop and tries to take his lunch, in a hole between the laboratory and the office. While eating he is disturbed fifty times, and when he has finished, the hardest and most responsible work of the day begins. This consists in the making up of medicines from the doctors' prescriptions, which pour in endlessly. This work is done at a feverish rate, and continues up to 11 o'clock at night, when the wearied assistant ascends five flights of stairs to his garret. Even when in bed he is doomed to hear the frequent ring of a bell which summons him to the shop or laboratory in the small hours of the morning. To the chemists' assistants who have no money and no hope, this life is worse than slavery. By joining a syndicate they may obtain more salary, if they succeed in intimidating the employers, which is doubtful; but they can hardly expect to get more liberty or recreation, for even the masters themselves have to remain tied to their desks for long hours; the chemist who is in the habit of absenting himself from his place of business, or of spending too much time in *cafés* or similar places, being regarded by the customers as dangerous and untrustworthy.—*Chem. and Druggist.*

Loofahs.

The loofah or towel gourd (*Luffa ægyptiaca*) is indigenous to Egypt and Arabia, but is grown extensively in Western Africa and the West Indies. The plant, a cucurbitaceous one, is a climbing vine which frequently attains a length of thirty feet. It is chiefly remarkable for its ovate fleshy fruit, of which it seldom bears more than a dozen, varying in length from six inches to two feet. This fruit in the fresh state is elliptical ovate, and has a green epidermis marked longitudinally with black lines. It is the close vascular network of this fruit, freed from the epidermis, pulp, and seeds, which forms the loofah, so familiar to chemists for a dozen years or more. The natives of the countries in which the towels gourds grow have long used them as scrubbing brushes and as strainers. To prepare them for these purposes the epidermis is removed, and the peeled fruit then thoroughly washed in water and beaten so as to remove the mucilaginous pulp and the seeds. Although loofahs have long been used by natives for washing purposes, we have heard it said that their introduction into this country for similar purposes was a mere accident. A consignment of them was received here, but no one knew what they were for. They ultimately got into the hands of a merchant as payment of debt, and he more than repaid himself by selling them as a sponge substitute for the bath. When the stock was exhausted several years elapsed before another supply was received; indeed, on this occasion they were placed on the market as a perfect novelty. The loofah is imported in the entire state, our own wholesalers generally giving it the longitudinal incision which makes it a flat and serviceable flesh-brush. The gourd is also used for making fancy toilet articles, which are so highly thought of in the West Indies that a sample (a small basket) was sent to the Queen as a Jubilee present, and was shown in St. James's Palace. Recently the uses of the loofah have been greatly extended by a German manufacturer established at Halle on the Saale. He makes from them loofah soles, which have to be a large extent replaced those made of straw and felt. The loofah soles warm the feet in winter and cool them in summer, keeping them constantly dry. They are extremely elastic and easily washed with soap and water. Saddle undercloths are also made from loofahs, which have the virtue of preventing the animal from remaining wet under the saddle after sweating. But what may be considered the most important application of the loofah is in the manufacture of surgical bandage stuffs. Bandages made of this material are competing closely with the wood-wool kind, which were introduced some time ago. There are unquestionably other uses to which the loofah might be applied, and as enormous quantities are obtainable at a low rate (some bales were a year ago sold in London at the rate of five a penny), further applications are only a question of time. The seeds of the loofah contain fixed oil, but this in too small quantity (2.5 per cent) to pay for its extraction. The mucilaginous matter is so rich in bassorin that an infusion of the fruit becomes almost solid on cooling. A congener, *Luffa Bindaal*, is used in India medicinally as a remedy for carbuncle. For this purpose, an infusion of the fruit is used as a fomentation, which causes the slough to come out entire. There are other species which are possessed of medicinal properties. The two species, *L. purgans* and *L. drastica*—the fruits of which are known as American colocynth—possess powerful purgative properties, as might be expected of cucurbitaceous plants. Several are of a bitter character, *e.g.*, *L. echinata*, an Indian plant, the fruit-fibre of which, according to Dymock, is intensely bitter, and is used medicinally by the Hindoos. This loofah is quite a tiny fruit, being no larger than a nutmeg. As to the use of the ordinary loofah, we find that the uncut kind is much more lasting than the other, although as a flesh rubber it is not so effective as the interior surface.—*Chem. and Druggist.*

Tincture of Quillaia Bark.*

Mr. Peter Boa says that, having had some experience in the use of quillaia bark for other than strictly medicinal purposes, I had long ago come to the conclusion that an aqueous menstruum was the most suitable for extracting its active constituents. I was therefore somewhat surprised to find that the formula given by the British Pharmaceutical Conference Committee directed the tincture to be made with rectified spirit. It is true that no dose is specified, and as the tincture for which the formula is given is used in the preparation of liquor picis carbonis, we may reasonably assume that this was the sole object for which the tincture was designed, and, if this be so, we can scarcely find fault with it, because for the purpose in question a rectified spirit tincture would be preferable to one less strong in alcohol. However, there is an increasing demand for tincture of quillaia for internal use; in Edinburgh this has been markedly so since the beginning of this year, when Dr. Claud Muirhead, in the *Edinburgh Medical Journal*, referred in commendatory terms to the administration of the drug in bronchitis, and there is just a possibility that the B. P. C. formula may be taken as a guide to the preparation of a tincture for this purpose. It would, I think, be a pity if it were so taken, because this tincture does not at all represent the virtues of the bark. I have looked up a number of references to quillaia, and I find that all the writers on the subject agree in the conclusion that water is the best solvent of saponin, which is regarded as the active principle of the bark. Gmelin says that saponin as easily soluble in water (1 in 4), more soluble in dilute than strong alcohol, insoluble in absolute alcohol.

Hager gives a formula for an infusion, and a tincture prepared with dilute alcohol.

Grazer, an American pharmacist, recommends for emulsifying purposes a tincture with 3 parts of water and 8 of rectified spirit.

Dr. Claud Muirhead has used with success a decoction.

Collier gives a formula (*Pharm. Journ.*, Sept. 20th, 1879) for emulsifying purposes with 4 oz. of bark to a pint of rectified spirit; this apparently is the formula copied into the B. P. C. formulary, but made with only half the quantity of bark.

For the purposes of this note I have prepared tinctures of various alcoholic strengths. I take three of these for comparison:

No. 1 is made according to the B. P. C. formula.
No. 2 is made with proof spirit.
No. 3 is made with 3 of rectified spirit and 4 of water.

The time at my disposal since agreeing to bring the subject before this meeting has not been sufficient to enable me to estimate the comparative values of these tinctures except in a somewhat rough and ready way, although I believe the results may be taken to be fairly trustworthy. The quantity of saponin in a tincture may be estimated comparatively by the amount of froth which it produces when shaken up with a quantity of water. Taking the three tinctures above-mentioned, adding ½ a

---

* We have retained the spelling of this word, as the author writes it. In accordance with our views expressed on page 216 of our last volume, the spelling Quillaja is preferable.

---

drachm of each to 2 oz. of water in a 6-oz. bottle, and shaking, the following results were observed:

No. 1 gave of froth 1.
No. 2 gave of froth 1½.
No. 3 gave of froth 2.

A percolate obtained by running a quantity of water, equal to half the quantity of the original tincture, through the marc from the B. P. C. formula, gave nearly as good results as No. 3, showing that the bark had not been exhausted by any means; a percolate obtained in the same way from the proof spirit tincture residue gave very little indication of value. I may say that preliminary mixtures with the water were made with spirit added to Nos. 2 and 3 to make them equal in alcoholic strength to No. 1, in case the spirit might affect the froth test. It was not found to affect the results, and has not been added to the specimens shown to illustrate the comparative frothing power. An emulsion made with No. 1 and a fixed oil separated more quickly than one prepared with No. 3. I hope, if time will permit, to determine more accurately the comparative values of these tinctures. However, I have no hesitation in concluding from the result of my experiments that a weak alcohol is preferable to a strong for making tincture of quillaia. In fact, I see no use for any alcohol except for preservative purposes.

The question arises: What should be the strength of the tincture? Dr. Muirhead says he gave 3 ss. to 3 i. of tincture, but, unfortunately, he says nothing about the strength. He mentions, however, that the decoction, of which he gave a tablespoonful, was made with 5 of bark and 200 of water. A tincture of equivalent strength might therefore be made with 2 oz. to a pint. To make the tincture approximate in strength to senega tincture, 1 oz. to the pint would be more than enough.

There is just one point more to which I would allude. The B. P. C. formulary does not specify the part of quillaia bark to be used. Undoubtedly the white portion of the bark is the more valuable; the brown outer portion contains chiefly coloring matter. Both, however, are used together, for I have seen commercial specimens of tincture resembling in color tincture of orange peel. The specimens shown, made from the white portion, are, at most, pale straw color. In making liquor picis carbonis, color is of no consequence, and the quantity of bark ordered is greatly in excess of what the menstruum can exhaust, hence, presumably, the want of any specification on this point.—*Pharm. Journ.*

Note on Hydrobromic Acid.

Mr. John Wilson says: Some time ago my attention was drawn to some hydrobromic acid which had recently been received in stock, and which showed evident signs of decomposition.

A faint straw color was first observed, which gradually deepened, until it was an intense yellow.

A few preliminary tests showed abundance of free bromine, and the question became, "What is the cause of this unwelcome change?"

To answer this satisfactorily, it was necessary to know by which of the many different processes the solution had been made. It was labelled B. P., 1885, indicating that it had been prepared by decomposing sulphuretted hydrogen by means of bromine, distilling the hydrobromic acid formed, and making the distillate up to a specific gravity of 1.077 and a strength of 10%. The reaction which takes place is as follows:

$$10Br_2 + 4H_2S + 8H_2O = 20HBr + 2H_2SO_4 + S_2.$$

The solution is apt to be contaminated with free sulphuric acid if the distillation is carried too far, and it proved to be the case in this instance, for on the addition of a little barium chloride solution the white insoluble barium sulphate was formed.

At first it was thought that there must be other acids present to account for the decomposition, but no trace of either bromic, hydrochloric, or phosphoric acid was found after careful testing.

Light exercises a strong influence on hydrobromic acid, but in this instance it could not have been the disturbing agent, as the bottle was entirely excluded from direct sunlight, or even bright diffused sunlight. The action of sulphuric acid is something as follows:

$$2HBr + H_2SO_4 = Br_2 + 2H_2O + SO_2.$$

Sulphurous acid was specially looked for, but without success, so probably it was oxidized into sulphuric acid again, in presence of water and oxygen.

$$2SO_2 + 2H_2O + O_2 = 2H_2SO_4.$$

Oxygen is a potent agent in liberating bromine from its compounds, and in this case it no doubt supplemented the action of the sulphuric acid, as the bottles, when first noticed, were little more than three-fourths full, thus allowing space for a fair proportion of air.

In the *Pharmaceutical Journal* of October 29th, some interesting experiments of Dr. Richardson are noticed regarding the action of light and oxygen on some haloid compounds. When hydrobromic acid was exposed to direct sunlight with a small proportion of oxygen, and in the presence of aqueous vapor, only .065 of free bromine was liberated after forty-six days, but with excess of oxygen under similar conditions, 7.6% of bromine was liberated after forty-five days. No decomposition was observed when the dry gases were exposed.

With this sample there was, as I have said, no exposure to light, nor undue excess of oxygen, so I am inclined to believe that the sulphuric acid was the principal decomposing agent.

I may also mention that the specific gravity of the solution is 1.085 — rather higher than the B. P. standard. This of itself would indicate either excess of hydrobromic acid, or the presence of some impurity.

I regret that I have had no opportunity of estimating the percentage of free or combined bromine in the liquid. The results would, no doubt, be of interest, and might throw some further light on the subject. — *Pharm. Journ.*

Sodium Sulphibenzoate.

STILL another compound has been added to the group of antiseptics, under the name of "*sodium sulphibenzoate*," it is described by M. Heckel (*Comp. Rend.*, CV., 896) as being prepared by dissolving sodium benzoate in a strong solution of sodium sulphite, and was, in fact, the outcome of an attempt to combine the antiseptic properties of those two salts. The chemical and physical properties of the compound are not mentioned, beyond the statement that it is very soluble in water at the ordinary temperature; it is also affirmed to be absolutely innocuous to the human organism in large doses. But its antiseptic properties are declared to be very considerable, it being reported, as the result of clinical experiments in the hospital of Saint Mandrier, that a solution of sodium sulphibenzoate, in the proportion of 4 or 5 grains to a liter of water, used as an application to wounds, is superior to carbolic acid, and comparable in its good effects to the salts of mercury without their toxicity, or to iodoform, without its disagreeable odor. — *Pharm. Journ.*

Antipyrin in Sea-Sickness.

IN a note presented to the Academy of Sciences (*Compt. Rend.*, CV., 947), M. Dupuy calls attention to the value of antipyrin as a remedy against sea sickness. He states that he prescribed to some persons who had previously suffered terribly from sea-sickness, 3 grammes daily of antipyrin on the three days previous to embarking and the three days following, whilst some patients continued to take the medicine throughout the voyage, and he has been informed that all these persons crossed the Atlantic without suffering from sea sickness. This experience was subsequently confirmed in a communication from M. Omino-Bonnet (*Compt. Rend.*, CV., 1,028), who states that, in about sixty cases occurring during a voyage to Buenos Ayres and back, he found antipyrin invariably effective in arresting sea-sickness, though the dose required was variable. In most cases 1.50 grammes was sufficient, the complete effect being produced in about ten minutes. In other cases the dose had to be repeated, but it was never necessary to exceed 3 grammes to produce cessation of the sickness within an hour. In a few cases, where the sickness was so incessant as to prevent absorption by the stomach, the same effect was produced by the hypodermic injection of 1 gramme of antipyrin. — *Pharm. Journ.*

Crystallised Colchicin.

NOT long since, in a case of suspected colchicin-poisoning, chemists were obliged to confess their inability to prove or disprove the presence of the toxic principle. Such an opprobrium on chemical science no longer exists, as M. A. Houdé, a Paris pharmacist, has discovered processes for preparing true crystallized colchicin, and identifying as well as estimating it in combinations and mixtures. The active principle — it is not an alkaloid — is obtained as follows: Powdered colchicum seeds are exhausted by percolation with about three times their weight of alcohol of 96 degrees. The percolate is evaporated *in vacuo*, at a low heat, until all traces of alcohol have been driven off. The residue, consisting of two layers — one watery and the other oily — is shaken in a separator with a 5-per-cent solution of tartaric acid. The operation is repeated several times to thoroughly exhaust the oily stratum, which is almost twenty times as bulky as the watery, and contains most of the colchicin. The acid liquor is now shaken first with ether, free from alcohol, to remove the last traces of fatty matters — colchicin being insoluble in ether — and then with chloroform, which takes up all the colchicin, together with some impurities. To purify it, the solution is concentrated by spontaneous evaporation, and petroleum ether of spec. grav. 0.620 cautiously added. The addition at first throws down coloring matters and impurities, but it must be stopped when the clear solution has turned from a dark-brown to a very light straw-yellow, else the colchicin would also be precipitated. Finally, the liquor, on being left to spontaneous evaporation, yields crystallized colchicin in the shape of long, colorless needles. The proportion obtained from the seeds is 3 per 1,000. An important point of the process is that no alkali and no mineral acid is employed, M. Houdé having proved they have both the effect of transforming colchicin into colchicein. Colchicin splits so easily under the influence of acids that even acetic acid will decompose it and form colchicein — a crystalline substance hitherto mistaken for true colchicin. The chemical until now regarded as colchicin is a mixture of the two substances. Hence the chemical reactions of true colchicin are substantially those already described, with one notable exception, however, namely, that the intense apple-green coloration afforded with ferric chloride, and insisted upon by most investigators, is characteristic of colchicein, but totally absent with pure colchicin not contaminated with colchicein. In toxicological researches, the poison is best extracted by macerating the organs, properly divided, in alcohol of 90 degrees acidulated with a little tartaric acid, distilling off the menstruum *in vacuo*, and shaking the watery residue with chloroform. By spontaneous evaporation of the solvent, colchicin is obtained in the amorphous state, and may be readily identified. The stomach, bowels, and liver are the organs in which colchicin is chiefly localized. Scarcely any is to be found in the kidneys or the saliva, and none at all in the blood. — *them. and Drugg.*

On the Use of Asbestos for Hastening Filtration, particularly of Viscid Liquids.

W. FRESENIUS reports in *Zeitsch f. anal. Chem.*, 1888, 32, that he has found finely picked asbestos to be the best medium for facilitating the filtration of viscid liquids. He found it especially valuable in filtering solutions of peptonized liquids, such as are produced by the action of any of the digestive ferments, and which it is next to impossible otherwise to filter through paper.

He states that he had previously made use of this useful property of finely divided asbestos, when he was occupied with the determination of the water-soluble portion of a very fine flour used as infants' food. It had been impossible to obtain a clear filtrate, until asbestos was tried, when there was no difficulty whatever.

All liquids which are obtained as products of artificial digestion, for instance, during experiments on the digestibility of albuminoids by gastric juice, or pepsin, or pancreatin, etc., exhibit an extreme reluctance to pass through filters, whether these are made from paper or from asbestos, and even if a portion passes through, this is always turbid. An acceleration of the filtration by means of the filter-pump is entirely useless, as this causes a still greater turbidity of the liquid. Under such circumstances, a filtration may last as much as 8 days, or may be practically impossible. A complete washing of the undissolved matter is, therefore, likewise either difficult or impracticable.

W. Fresenius states that he has recently succeeded in accomplishing the filtration by diluting with a considerable proportion of water, and then incorporating with the mixture a small quantity of previously ignited, finely picked asbestos, and thoroughly shaking. After about 18 hours, all suspended matters will have deposited, and the liquid may be easily removed by means of a siphon. The operation of washing and shaking is repeated once or twice with fresh water, and the whole mixture finally passed through a glass funnel, the neck of which contains a pellet of asbestos. If the first portion of the filtrate runs off cloudy, it is poured back until it is clear. Fresenius states that he allowed the residue in the funnel to become tolerably dry, after which he removed it for the purpose of determining the amount of nitrogen by Kjeldahl's method. Any matter adhering to the funnel can easily be wiped off by means of a small pellet of asbestos, and added to the rest.

Note by Ed. Am. Dr. — If the principle of this method of clarifying a liquid and aiding filtration is applied to the usual processes for estimating the digestive power of pepsin, or similar ferments, we would recommend to proceed as follows:

Dilute the liquid, at the moment when the digestion is to be interrupted, with a considerable quantity of water, saturate the whole liquid with chloroform to prevent its decomposition during the time of standing and filtering, then add to it a quantity of previously ignited, finely picked and weighed asbestos, about equal in weight to the quantity of albumen (if this has been used) originally employed, and shake vigorously and frequently until the supernatant liquid, on standing, is seen to become clear. Then allow the suspended matters to subside, pour off or siphon off the liquid, treat the precipitate twice more with pure water in a similar manner, and, finally, transfer the whole precipitate, by rinsing with water, to a previously washed, dried, and tared filter of loose texture (Stewart's are the best). Wash it with distilled water until a drop of the washings evaporated on platinum foil ceases to leave a residue. Then dry and weigh the filter and contents, and from the total weight deduct that of the filter and asbestos. The remainder represents the quantity of dry albumen left undissolved.

It is believed that a closer approximation to the correct amount can be obtained by the above method, or one embodying its salient features, than by any other, provided the undissolved albumen is to be determined by weighing it.

On Pure Mercurous Iodide and Bromide.
(Protiodide and Protobromide of Mercury.)

The exact color of pure mercurous iodide has long been known not to be exactly like that under which the officinal salt presents itself in the market. Some years ago, Mr. Maclagan, chemist of the firm of McKesson & Robbins, drew attention to the fact that he had devised a process by which this salt could be obtained in a much purer and more uniform condition, and in this state the salt had a pure yellow color. Bouchardat had already obtained the salt in form of yellow, rhombic crystals (according to Descloizeaux, they belong to the tetragonal system), which, when rubbed to powder, furnish a yellowish-green product. It has long been suspected that the darkening of the salt is due to the influence of light.

A recent number of the *Berichte d. Deutsch. Chem. Ges.* (1887, No. 15, page 2,818) contains a paper by A. Stoman, relating to crystallised mercurous iodide and bromide, from which we take the following:

At the suggestion of Prof. Naumann (Giessen), the author undertook to study the products of the reaction of iodine and bromine upon mercury.

1. Mercurous Iodide.

On heating a *saturated* solution of mercurous nitrate, containing only a little free nitric acid, and being as free from mercuric salt as possible, to a boiling temperature, with an *excess of iodine*, the solution becomes covered with a yellow powder, which becomes partly dissolved. The clear, supernatant liquid, after being carefully decanted into a warmed capsule, and allowed to become cold, separates transparent laminæ, which are yellow as long as kept in the dark, and have a diamond-like lustre. If a different concentration of the mercurous solution is used, or too much nitric acid, or mercuric salt are present, the crystalline compound is not formed at all. These crystals are transferred to a filter, with as much exclusion of light as possible, and washed, first with water acidulated with nitric acid and then with pure water. Finally they are dried *in the dark*, at ordinary indoor temperature upon blotting paper which has to be frequently renewed. While damp, the crystals become darker even when exposed only to diffuse light. On exposure to direct sunlight, however, even the perfectly dry salt turns black.

These crystals, on being slightly magnified, appear as tetragonal lamellæ, and as analysis showed, constitute pure *mercurous iodide.*

On mixing a saturated solution of mercurous iodide, having the properties above described, slowly and carefully, and in the cold, with a moderately concentrated solution of *iodine* in *alcohol*, and shaking, the same crystals as above described separate almost immediately in minute scales. If, however, the iodine solution is added rapidly, a *yellow, flocculent precipitate* is produced, which analysis shows to consist likewise of pure *mercurous iodide.*

The reaction takes place, both in the presence of solid iodine, and of iodine in solution, according to the following equation:

$$2Hg_2(NO_3)_2 + I_2 = Hg_2I_2 + 2Hg(NO_3)_2$$
mercurous   iodine   mercurous   mercuric
nitrate   iodide   nitrate

When heated, the crystallised mercurous iodide suffers a change of colors opposite to that of the mercuric salt: the *yellow* color passes over into *red*. Yvon observed this change of colors in crystals of mercurous iodide which he obtained by subliming weighed quantities of mercury and iodine. He states, however, that the red tint begins to show itself at 70° C., while Stoman observed a very gradual transition from bright yellow to dark yellow, orange and garnet, without being able to find—even in repeated experiments—any agreement between the temperatures at which these tints made their appearance. On cooling, the several colors reappear in a reversed order. At 100° C., the salt was always yet pure yellow. Stoman found that the salt sublimed always between 110° and 120° C. (Yvon gives 190° C.). An attempt to prepare the salt by Yvon's process furnished an impure product.

It will be of interest to describe the method of analysis employed by the author.

For the estimation of *iodine*, the salt was mixed with zinc-dust and hot water, which resulted in the formation of iodide of zinc. The latter was then decomposed, in solution, by nitrate of silver, and the iodine calculated from the obtained iodide of silver. The zinc-dust, which contained chlorine, was previously purified by washing with hot water. Results very accurate.

To estimate the mercury, the salt was decomposed with hot nitric acid of spec. grav. 1.420, which causes the escape of vapors of iodine. The solution was then diluted with much water and treated with hydrosulphuric acid gas, causing the precipitation of mercuric sulphide. But, owing to the presence of the large excess of nitric acid (required to dissolve the mercurous iodide), there is also separated a copious amount of sulphur. This is best removed in the following manner: After the hydrosulphuric acid gas has been passed long enough, a little soda solution is added, and the mixture gently warmed on the water-bath. The ascending bubbles of gas cause the particles of mercuric sulphide suspended at the upper margin of the solution to become loosened, and to fall to the bottom. The supernatant liquid, which has become completely clear after standing 12 hours, is then poured on the filter as completely as possible, and the latter washed with cold water. After cautiously neutralizing the remainder [of the liquid] with soda solution, the precipitate is warmed with a solution of sulphite of sodium, transferred to the filter, and washed with warm water.

Ammonia and caustic alkalies color mercurous iodide greenish; on heating, a black color appears and the iodides of the corresponding alkalies are at the same time formed. The black residue, containing the whole of the mercury, is partially soluble in hot hydrochloric acid, but some metallic mercury is left behind. Iodide of potassium likewise imparts a green color in the cold, a black color on warming.

Stoman declares the statement, that mercurous iodide precipitated by iodide of potassium has a *green* color, to be an *error*. This is not the case with pure mercurous iodide. On adding solution of iodide of potassium to one of mercurous nitrate, the nascent mercurous iodide is decomposed by fresh potassium iodide, and colored green. But on dissolving iodide of potassium in a small quantity of water, and rapidly adding an *excess* of dilute solution of mercurous nitrate, so that both become mixed at once, there is obtained a *yellow precipitate* consisting of pure *mercurous iodide*. The usually followed process for preparing mercurous iodide, viz., to rub together molecular quantities of iodine and of mercury, furnishes an *impure* product, precisely like that which is obtained by pouring solution of iodide of potassium into one of mercurous nitrate. The product being in these cases impure, it is more easily affected by light, and hence the green color. This curious coincidence [of similar colors being obtained by different processes] has been especially instrumental in confirming the idea that *pure* mercurous iodide was *green*, while it is, in fact, *yellow*.

The amorphous, yellow salt obtained by means of iodide of potassium may be dissolved in hot solution of mercurous nitrate, when it will be obtained in crystalline lamellæ, like that first described above.

2. Mercurous Bromide.

On shaking a solution of mercurous nitrate (such as above described) with bromine, a precipitate is obtained like that resulting from the action of bromide of potassium upon mercurous compounds. Under the microscope, it appears as a mass of minute, tetragonal lamellæ with blunted ends. The precipitate and liquid are poured off from the excess of bromine, and heated with 2 or 3 times its volume of solution of mercurous nitrate, when it will be dissolved either wholly or partially. The liquid is filtered into a previously warmed capsule and then allowed to cool, when *pure white scales*, of a *mother-of-pearl lustre*, of the same forms as those just described, will separate. These are pure *mercurous bromide*. The formation of this salt is less dependent upon strength and condition of the solution of mercurous nitrate, and the yield is also larger than in the case of the iodide. The crystals of the bromide are transferred to a filter and washed like the iodide. They are less sensitive to light, but are likewise decomposed—at least partially—on exposure to direct sunlight.

From the author's results, it follows that the most rational method to prepare *pure mercurous iodide* is to add to a concentrated solution of iodide of potassium a solution of mercurous nitrate, containing as little free nitric acid and as little mercuric salt as possible, care being taken that the solutions become mixed as quickly as possible.

There seems to be, however, no way to entirely prevent the gradual self-decomposition of the yellow mercurous iodide, since the least exposure to light appears to affect it. [Upon the degree with which light has acted on the salt, no doubt, depend the varying effects which are obtained with the salt by physicians. The purer the salt is the less harshly does it affect the organism. And to retain the salt in as pure a condition as possible, renders it necessary that it be carefully kept from the light. In the case of this salt, perhaps more than in any other, there is really an advantage to have it put up, as soon after manufacture as possible, in a form in which it can be carried and administered without risk of further alteration. The best method is undoubtedly in the form of granules or pills, coated so that the light will not penetrate further than the surface.—Ed. Am. Drug.]

Runaway Pharmacists.—When the cholera epidemic broke out in Sicily about two months ago, several local pharmacists fled from the afflicted districts. They returned when the scourge disappeared, and have now been sentenced by the Messina Court of Justice for dereliction of duty to a fine of 2 l. each and the prohibition of exercising their business for the space of three months.

Imitation Maple Sugar.

A curious patent has been granted to Josiah Daily, of Madison, Ind., for a process to make imitation maple sugar. How Mr. Daily managed to obtain such a patent, or to convince the examiners that his invention was original, is a mystery to us. To a certain extent, perhaps, there may be a little originality about it, in so far as he derives the flavoring from hickory bark and wood, instead of the maple itself. But we have heard of this trick many years ago, though, perhaps, it may not have been given out in print.

He directs the extract of hickory to be made either by preparing a decoction of hickory bark or wood, or by percolation, or by drawing the sap from the tree.

For making artificial maple syrup, he appears to prefer the commercial syrup obtained from the sugar houses, and directs adding to each gallon about three tablespoonfuls of the decoction. On boiling down such a syrup, artificial maple sugar will be obtained.

Maple sugar is a sort of luxury, which many persons have no great longing for. A very large number, also, who profess to know all about it, are regularly "taken in" with their annual purchases. The new patent will perhaps enable the latter to save a little more, by showing them how to make it themselves.

Cod-Liver Oil Emulsion.

At a recent meeting of the Edinburgh Chemists' Assistants' Association, Mr. James Mackenzie, among other subjects, brought forward a formula for a Cod-Liver Oil Emulsion. It is as follows:

Tragacanth .... 1 drachm.
Acacia .... 1½ drachms.
Arrowroot, Bermuda ...... 1 drachm.
Cod-Liver Oil .... 8 oz.
Water .... 6 "
Spirit of Chloroform .... 1 drachm.
Saccharin .... 3 grains.
Oil of Cinnamon (Cassia) .. 3 minims.

Put the powders in a dry mortar, add a little of the oil, and rub well together until it has a creamy appearance; then add the remainder of the oil, and mix. When the powders are well diffused throughout the oil, add the water all at once, and use the pestle diligently until the emulsion is formed. Dissolve the Saccharin in the Spirit of Chloroform, and to the solution formed add the Oil of Cassia, and incorporate this in the emulsion. The Saccharin should be dissolved in 3 fluidrachms of Alcohol by the aid of heat, and 3 drops of Chloroform added to the solution.

Note.—The weights are intended to be avoirdupois, the drachm being meant for ⅛ av. oz.

Naregamia Alata—The Ipecacuanha of Goa.

Mr. David Hooper directs attention to a plant described by Dr. Dymock in his "Vegetable Materia Medica of Western India," and which seems to have been little known or used away from its habitat. The natives of Goa use it as an emetic and as a remedy for bile, rheumatism, and indigestion, and usually in the form of decoction. The *Pharm. Journal* of October 15th gives a botanical description of the plant and the drug. The latter consists of the root, with the slender stems attached. The root-stock is contorted and warty, and with the roots is pale-brown; the mealy suberous layer may easily be removed by rubbing. The stems are a dirty green, with the bark more firmly adherent. A transverse section of the root exhibits a brown outer layer of bark, with a light-colored interior and a yellowish wood. Application of iodine solution shows the presence of starch in the fibrous portion. The drug is with difficulty powdered in a hand-mortar. Its activity resides in its cortical portion, which forms one-third of the whole. The powder is light-brown, with a peculiar aromatic and pungent odor, and a slightly bitter and nauseous flavor. It contains an alkaloid, an oxidizable fixed oil, and a wax, the former receiving from Mr. Hooper the name *naregamine*. These three are extracted by ether; an alcoholic extract consists mainly of sugar; an aqueous extract yields a gum and a crystalline alkaloid resembling asparagine. The experiments which have been made in India and England show that its effects re quite the same as those caused by the Ipecacuanha of commerce.

Phenacetin.

In the beginning of the preceding year (1887), a new antipyretic was announced, to which the name "p-acetphenetidin," an l "acetylamidophenol" had been applied. Subsequently more definite information was given as to the chemical constitution of this compound, from which it appeared to be analogous to antifebrin or acetanilide. The compound for which the shorter and more convenient name of "*phenacetin*" has now been chosen, appears to have been tested therapeutically, and its properties are referred to more in detail (*Pharm. Centralhalle*, Nov. 24th, p. 583). It is described as a faintly reddish, odorless and tasteless powder, which dissolves with difficulty in water, somewhat better in glycerin, but most freely in alcohol, especially if hot. It is insoluble in acid and alkaline liquids, and experiments as to its solubility in the acid juices of the stomach and in pancreas have given only negative results. Professor Von Bamberger states that phenacetin administered in doses of 0.5 to 0.7 gramme to healthy persons seemed to produce hardly any effect, the influence upon body temperature being barely perceptible; but when administered to fever patients, even in the relatively small doses of 0.3 to 0.4 gramme, it never failed to produce a marked antipyretic effect. In the first tentative experiments, doses of only 0.2 to 0.4 gramme were administered, which produced a regular fall of temperature, but this was of slight intensity and of short duration. As, however, the safety of the remedy became manifest, these doses were increased to 0.6 and 0.7 gramme, which quantity has not been observed to produce any disagreeable or injurious symptoms.—*After Pharm. Journ.*, (Dec. 3d).

New Method of Preserving Butter.

Mr. Pierre Grosfils, of Vervier, has communicated to the Société d'Encouragement de Vervier a new process for preserving butter, which may, perhaps, be applied to also to other fats. M. Grosfils describes the various phases of his research as follows: He first mingled 1 gramme of salicylic acid with 1 kilo of butter, but after some weeks the product had altered. He thought that the cessation of the antiseptic action of acid was due to its crystallization in the non-liquid substances which were mingled with it. After numerous experiments, he found that lactic acid prevents this crystallization. This acid is, in fact, a good solvent for salicylic acid. It has the advantage of being hygroscopic, of possessing antiseptic power, and, finally, of being uninjurious in food.

The first result of the discovery of M. Grosfils was to be able to diminish the amount of salicylic acid used to preserve the butter. Instead of mixing 1 gramme of acid per kilo, he put the butter in a liquid containing 0.05 per cent of salicylic acid and 3 per cent of lactic acid. He successively divided the salicylic acid into still smaller doses, until at last he had the proportion of 1 gramme of acid to 5,000 parts of water. The final composition consisted then of 98 parts water, 2 parts lactic acid, and 0.0002 of salicylic acid. This composition allows of the indefinite preservation of butter of good quality even at a high temperature and in hot countries. If the butter has already undergone some alteration, a stronger dose must be used.

But the author points to the following fact: The lactic acid contained in the antiseptic liquid in doses stronger than 2 per cent gives the product a taste which, without being offensive, is a little too sour to leave the article salable. In such case, the butter should be washed with water, or, better still, with scalded milk, to which a little carbonate of soda has been added, to prevent any coagulation of the casein. This washing will not only remove the lactic acid and its taste but also the salicylic acid solution, to such a degree that what remains will be imperceptible.

The process is stated to be most economical, as the antiseptic liquid will serve indefinitely, being unalterable. Care must be taken each time to use the same quantity of butter.

The preparation of a kilo of butter by this process, it is stated, will not cost more than one or two centimes.—*Monit. Indust.* and *Sci. Am. Suppl.*

A Convenient Method for Preparing Pure Hydrosulphuric Acid Gas.

Clemens Winkler recommends sulphide of barium as a convenient source of hydrosulphuric acid gas, particularly when it is wanted absolutely free from arsenic. He states that he has used the above compound for this purpose for the last twenty years.

The kind of sulphide of barium suitable for this purpose is prepared by mixing sulphate of barium, powdered charcoal, and a fusible salt soluble in water, for instance, chloride of sodium, and heating them together. The best proportions are:

Sulphate of Barium .... 100 parts.
Charcoal, powdered .... 25 "
Chloride of Sodium .... 30 "

The two first-named substances are finely ground together, the chloride of sodium then added, and the mixture formed, with the aid of a little water, to a slightly damp mass, which is tightly packed into clay crucibles of suitable size (for instance, 10 inches high and 4 inches in diameter). The crucibles and contents are then dried with a moderate heat, some coarsely powdered charcoal put on top of the mass, and the lids luted on with clay, a small hole being left for the escape of gases. The crucibles are then heated for several hours to an incipient white heat, after which the heat is gradually moderated, the crucibles taken from the furnace and allowed to cool.

On turning the crucibles over, the sulphide of barium will drop out in form of partly fused, very hard cones, which possess the shape of the crucible in a contracted form. By strong blows with a hammer, these cones may be broken into suitable pieces which, when brought in contact with dilute hydrochloric acid (in a Kipp'sor other form of generator), evolve a steady and abundant stream of hydrosulphuric acid gas, and are gradually dissolved, leaving only a slight carbonaceous residue.

Sulphide of barium should be kept in a moderately warm and dry place in well-closed vessels; tin boxes are very convenient, both for preserving and for transporting it.—After *Zeitsch. f. Anal. Chem.*, 1888, 26.

Determination of Sodium Phosphate in Glacial Phosphoric Acid.

Anton Bettendorff reports that he had been requested to examine a specimen of commercial glacial phosphoric acid for arsenic, and on using for this purpose the test with stannous chloride, which requires a previous solution of the substance in hydrochloric acid of spec. grav. 1.190, he obtained a copious quantity of brilliantly white, small crystals, which turned out to be chloride of sodium, while the phosphoric acid itself was nearly all dissolved in the liquid.

The glacial acid itself being free from chloride, it was evident that the sodium existed in it as sodium phosphate. The presence of this salt in commercial glacial phosphoric acid is well known, but its determination by means of converting the salt into chloride of sodium had not been suggested before. The author finds that 1 part of chloride of sodium requires, at a temperature of 12° C., 1,348 parts of fuming hydrochloric acid of spec. grav. 1.190 for solution.

The difficult solubility of chloride of sodium in fuming hydrochloric acid, therefore, explains its formation and separation from the glacial phosphoric acid containing sodium phosphate.

In order to study the reaction, the author dehydrated some sodium phosphate, and subsequently ignited it in order to remove the carbon compounds which are always present in it. 3.701 Gm. of the resulting sodium pyrophosphate were introduced into 50 C.c. of fuming hydrochloric acid of spec. grav. 1.190, and the mixture set aside for twelve hours. The resulting chloride of sodium was separated from the liquid by passing it through a filter of spongy platinum, and washed several times with fuming hydrochloric acid. The weight of the melted chloride of sodium amounted to 3.2065 Gm. (by calculation, 3.2531 Gm.). The filtrate evaporated, and the residue ignited, furnished perfectly transparent metaphosphoric acid which was soft at ordinary temperature, and weighed 2.298 Gm. (instead of the calculated 2.7247 Gm.). Hence, the decomposition between pyrophosphate of sodium and fuming hydrochloric acid is complete at ordinary temperature. With a weaker acid, the decomposition is incomplete, considerable amounts of pyrophosphate of sodium remaining in solution.

The addition of sodium phosphate is made only for the purpose of hardening the product, so as to enable its being cast in sticks. If a pure glacial or metaphosphoric acid is required, this may be easily prepared in the following manner:

Reduce sodium pyrophosphate, previously ignited, to powder, treat it with hydrochloric acid of spec. grav. 1.190, separate the chloride of sodium formed, then remove any arsenic present in the residuary liquid, evaporate the liquid finally obtained in a platinum vessel, and ignite the residue.—After *Zeitsch. f. Anal. Chem.*, 1888, 24.

The Assay of Sulphurous Acid.

Bunsen's method of assaying sulphurous acid by means of standard solution of iodine suffers from one defect, namely, that the sulphurous acid must be in very high dilution, containing not more than 0.03 to 0.04 per cent of SO_2.

Bunsen supposed that the reason why, in more concentrated solutions, sulphurous acid failed to completely fulfil its functions as a reducing agent was this, that the generated sulphuric acid acted upon the hydriodic acid produced during the action, by oxidizing the latter and itself returning to the state of sulphurous acid.

This reason did not appear satisfactory to Prof. J. Volhard, who determined to ascertain the true cause of the peculiar phenomenon alluded to, and also, if possible, to find a way to free the volumetric method of assay from the defect inherent in it.

Experiments showed that ordinary diluted sulphuric acid dissolves iodide of potassium to a colorless liquid. Only after standing some time does this become brown, no doubt caused by the oxidation of hydriodic acid through the oxygen of the air. Even a stronger sulphuric acid does not set iodine free; only concentrated sulphuric acid is able to accomplish this. Consequently, Bunsen's explanation of the retrograde reaction, when sulphurous acid, iodine, and water are brought together, cannot be correct.

In order to ascertain the true cause, Prof. Volhard instituted a series of experiments to follow the reaction quantitatively step by step, and under varying circumstances. Bunsen himself had already pointed out that the concentration of the solutions exerted a great influence; and Finkener had found that the reaction between iodine and sulphurous acid yielded uniform results only when the sulphurous acid is allowed to flow into the iodine solution under stirring. If the latter is poured into the former, there is always a smaller quantity of iodine consumed. According to Finkener, the difference in iodine amounts to only 0.5 per cent, but this is a mistake.

Volhard confirms Finkener's statement, that sulphurous acid is *completely* converted into sulphuric, when the former is allowed to flow under stirring into the iodine solution; and this is the case, not only when the acid is very dilute, but even when it contains nearly up to 2 per cent of SO_2. On the other hand, if the process of mixing is reversed, even the most dilute sulphurous acid will, in different trials, consume varying amounts of iodine, but always less than the theoretical amount. The deficiency increases with the concentration of the sulphurous acid solution. In a solution containing 0.0153 per cent, it amounted, on an average, to 5 per cent of the contained SO_2; in a solution holding 0.1 per cent, the loss represented 13 per cent of this amount; in one of 0.2 per cent, the loss reached 15 per cent; and in one of 1.8 per cent, it rose to fully 24 per cent of the SO_2.

The lesson to be derived from these results is this, that in assaying sulphurous acid, the latter should be brought to a moderate state of dilution—about 0.2 per cent (but this may vary up to 1 per cent)—and to allow this solution to flow from a burette into a measured quantity of volumetric solution of iodine mixed with a little gelatinized starch, until the iodine solution has just acquired a blue color.

Volhard remarks that in iodometric assays he prefers to carry the reaction to a blue color rather than to colorlessness. Absence of color does not admit of gradation, or reveal an excess of a reagent; but when the reaction is continued until the blue tint appears, the slightest further excess will cause a deepening of the color.

Having thus determined the best method by which uniform results in the assay of sulphurous acid could be obtained, it still remained to ascertain, if possible, the cause of failure when the process of mixing the solutions was reversed.

Volhard found that when powdered iodine was added to a saturated aqueous solution of sulphurous acid (containing about 14% of SO_2), the iodine disappeared rapidly, but the solution, instead of being colorless, acquired a light yellow color. This, on further addition of iodine, becomes brown. And when about ⅓ of the theoretical amount of iodine has been added, the solution has become opaque, and of a dark brown color from free iodine. It colors starch-paper blue, and has an intense odor of sulphurous acid. Consequently the latter, as well as free iodine, may be present together in very concentrated solution, at least for some time. After a few hours, however, the sulphurous acid disappears, but *with separation of sulphur*.

This phenomenon made it probable that hydriodic acid exerted a reducing action upon sulphurous. Indeed, when the two bodies are brought together in a gaseous form, the result is iodine, water, and sulphur, which reaction would be expressed as follows:

SO_2	+	$4HI$	=	S	+	$2H_2O$	+	$4I$
sulphurous anhydride		hydriodic acid		sulphur		water		iodine

However, the real reaction is not as simple as this scheme would show.

On adding to 1 volume of a concentrated hydriodic acid solution 1 or 1½ volumes of a saturated solution of sulphurous acid, iodine is set free. But on shaking, and, if necessary, further addition of sulphurous acid, the brown zone formed at the line of contact of the two liquids immediately disappears, and the mixture acquires a clear bright yellow color. The latter is not due to iodine, as the liquid does not color starch-paper blue; but it has an even stronger reducing action than has sulphurous acid itself, as shown by its effect on indigo solution. The liquid retains its bright yellow color for some time, but after awhile it become turbid from separated sulphur, which gradually increases in quantity, and appears partly in form of a lump (when the liquid is shaken), and partly as a firm coating on the inner walls of the vessel. After some time, all the sulphurous acid is decomposed, the time required depending on the relative proportions of the two acids. If hydriodic acid is in excess, the reaction is completed in 24 hours, but the liquid still possesses a brown color.

Now the question arises: There being no gas given off during this reaction, what has become of the oxygen which had been combined with the sulphur that has been precipitated?

Volhard found that this existed in the shape of *sulphuric acid*. At the close of the reaction, the liquid contained almost exactly 2 molecules of sulphuric acid to 1 mol. of sulphur.

From these and some further experiments detailed by the author (but omitted here) it results that when *iodine* is *gradually added* to sulphurous acid solution, a portion of the SO₂ is reduced to sulphur by the generated hydriodic acid, the amount thus reduced diminishing in direct proportion to the strength of the sulphuric acid solution. Bunsen's explanation, therefore, requires only that the word "sulphurous" be put in place of "sulphuric," when it will give the correct explanation of the phenomenon.—*After Liebig's Annal.*, 242, 93.

A BOTTLE-MAKING MACHINE.

A NEW invention, at present the property of Messrs. Sykes, Macvay & Co. (Lim.) of London, and about to be put in operation at their works in Castleford, Yorkshire, bids fair to revolutionize the manufacture of bottles. As heretofore practised, the process was the following:

The glass "metal" is heated to a semi-liquid state in large fire-clay pots of peculiar construction, into which one of the set of five hands required for turning out the bottles dips an iron tube about seven feet in length, collecting at the end of it such a quantity of the fused substance as will make a bottle of the size required. The first hand, technically known as the "gatherer," hands the tube to the blower, who, blowing in it meanwhile, shapes it roughly into a conical form on a smooth sloping stone slab. The "metal" is next quickly placed by this workman into a small hole in the floor of the workshop, in which there is an iron mould divided longitudinally and hinged at the base, connected with a chain running upwards like a bell-pull. This the blower pulls, and thereby closes the mould round the heated glass. He then again vigorously blows through the tube until the embryo bottle has attained the shape of the mould, when

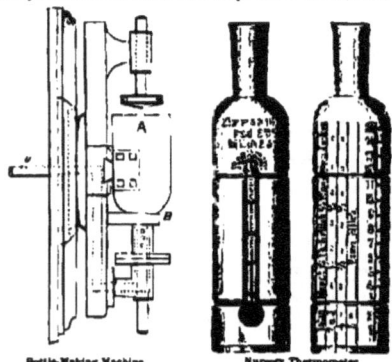

Bottle-Making Machine.   Nursery Thermometer.

by another tug at the chain it is released from the mould and handed to a boy. The latter, known as the "wetter-off," by means of a moistened steel file or chisel separates the bottle from the tube and hands it to the fourth workman, whose share in the manufacture requires the greatest dexterity of all. It is his business to trim the ragged neck and add to it a ring or lip. This he accomplishes by means of an instrument known as a "punty," a kind of four-fingered iron claw at the end of a rod, into which the bottle fits exactly, the four claws reaching just to the neck of the bottle. With the punty the bottle is pushed into a furnace and held there until the glass of the neck becomes soft. Then the "maker" applies some more molten metal round the neck, with which he forms the ring, and shapes it by means of a moulding tool called shears, consisting of a tongue fitting into the neck of the bottle, and two blades which are tightened round the neck. With this, while the bottle is being rapidly rotated with the tongue for its axis, he quickly shapes the ring. The fifth hand of the set then takes the bottle and places it with others into an annealing oven, which is heated to a very high temperature, and is allowed to cool gradually, two or three days being required for this purpose, when those that have withstood all tests and literally passed unscathed through the fiery furnace are ready for the market. The process above described, though followed with little deviation at all glassworks, has many evident drawbacks. One great disadvantage is the waste of glass metal, computed at something like thirty per cent. The bulk of this is, of course, collected again, but in remelting its quality deteriorates considerably. The blowing of the bottles is said to be an occupation almost as unhealthy as any in the manufacturing industries.

The new bottle-making machine will, it is thought, put an end to all or most of these obstacles. The apparatus is so simple, and yet, so far as can be judged from a casual visit and necessarily superficial inspection, does its work so efficiently that one marvels how such a simple idea can have so long remained unappreciated. The accompanying sketch shows the principle which underlies Mr. Ashley's invention, and represents the machine as it is working at present, though several improvements have already been patented by the inventor, and the completed machine will probably be in working order early in the spring. The principal parts of Mr. Ashley's machine are a parison mould (A), which can be drawn into a bell by means of a lever, and hermetically closed, the halves being supported by two arms. To the mould is attached a movable end, connected with an air pump, by which a vacuum can be created within the mould. The molten glass is poured into the parison mould, which holds the exact quantity required to manufacture a bottle. Another mould, called the "collar mould" (B), which is placed at the bottom of the parison mould, serves to mould the lips of the bottle. Air, forced by a pump, which is connected (w) with the stand upon which the machine is supported, is introduced into the hollow, central part of the mould, the molten glass being prevented by a button from entering the latter. The lip of the bottle is shaped first, and the mould is then quickly reversed, causing the moulten glass to fall down by its own weight. When the mass has descended to the length required, the halves of the mould are closed on it, a current of air from the pump is turned on, and the bottle quickly blown into the shape of the mould. A different mould is, of course, required for each kind of bottle. The principal improvement which is proposed to introduce into the machine now at work is to fix a number of machines—say four, six, or more—on a revolving stand, turning round as quickly as possible, one man being continually employed filling the moulds with a glass metal, another working the air-pump and closing the moulds, and a third taking out finished bottles.

The first result of the introduction of the perfected machines will be to diminish the number of the hands employed, but as a large increase of orders is anticipated, owing to the impossibility of foreign competition, which now supplies this country with about 16,000 gross of bottles per day, or two and a half times as much as we ourselves manufacture, it is thought that the growth of business will quickly necessitate the employment of even a larger number of hands than are now engaged. The inventor of the machine claims that the producing capacity of Messrs. Sykes, Macvay & Co.'s works, if sixty machines were set at work (one for each "hole" now existing), would be increased tenfold, or from 5,400 to 54,000 dozen bottles per day, while, instead of 300, only 180 hands would be required, and the cost of labor would be reduced from 3s. 10d. to 3d. per gross. The exploiters of the patent propose to allow other firms to use the machine upon payment of a royalty, but all the machines will be made at the Sykes-Macvay Works, and duly numbered and registered.—*Chem. and Drugg.*

A NEW NURSERY THERMOMETER.

THE adjoining illustration from a German source shows a felicitous combination of a thermometer with a bottle, which is also provided with a scale of proportions for mixing the ingredients of infants' food. The thermometer is likewise useful for regulating the temperature of a room or of a bath. The combination is the suggestion of Ernst Witter, of Unterneubrunn, near Eisfeld.

New Name Proposed for Antipyrin.—Considering that the compound is not an antipyretic, but a pain reliever, and that its true chemical name, oxydimethyl-quinizine, is rather inconvenient. M. Nicot, a well-known Paris pharmacist, has proposed for the appellation *parodyne*, from two Greek words (*para* and *odune*), meaning "against pain." Thus rechristened, antipyrin could be freely prescribed and dispensed without regard to trade-mark rights. French pharmacists feel sore about antipyrin, not so much, perhaps, because it is of German origin, as because a shrewd device has enabled its makers to evade the patent-medicine law, and enjoy privileges denied to French pharmacists and chemists.

Glycerin and Cocoa Cream for Chapped Hands, etc., is made from the following formula: White wax, ℥ xiv.; spermaceti, ℥ij.; cocoa butter, ℥ix.; castor oil, ℥ix.; oil of benne. ℥vi. Melt and mix; then add glycerin, ℥ij. Perfume to suit taste. This makes quite a nice preparation. Petrolatum is used instead of the oil of benne (sesame oil) by some, and is considered an improvement. Either, however, will do.

Reaction of Strophanthin.—When a trace of strophanthin is dissolved in a drop of water, together with a trace of ferric chloride, the addition of a little strong sulphuric acid gives rise to a reddish-brown precipitate, which, in an hour or two, changes color to a permanent emerald green.—H. HELBIG in *Pharm. Journ.*

Bottles.—It is estimated that 5,686,208 bottles are made daily in Europe—chiefly in Germany and Belgium—Great Britain turning out only 893,664 of the total number.

American Druggist

AN ILLUSTRATED MONTHLY JOURNAL
OF
Pharmacy, Chemistry, and Materia Medica.

Vol. XVII., No. 2.   Whole No. 164.

FREDERICK A. CASTLE, M.D., ...Editor.
CHARLES RICE, Ph.D., ...Associate Editor.

PUBLISHED BY
WM. WOOD & CO., 56 & 58 Lafayette Place, N. Y.

SUBSCRIPTION PRICE per year, ... $1.50
SINGLE COPIES, ...15

Address all communications relating to the business of the AMERICAN DRUGGIST, such as subscriptions, advertisements, change of Post-Office address, etc., to WILLIAM WOOD & CO., 56 and 58 Lafayette Place, New York City, to whose order all postal money orders and checks should be made payable. Communications intended for the Editor should be addressed in care of the Publishers.
The AMERICAN DRUGGIST is issued in the latter part of each month, dated for the month ahead. Changes of advertisements should reach us before the 10th. New advertisements can occasionally be inserted after the 15th.
REGULAR ADVERTISEMENTS according to size, location, and time. Special rates on application.

EDITORIALS.

ALCOHOLIC solutions of nitroglycerin have long been an article of commerce. That which is used for medicinal purposes is usually of the strength of one (1) per cent (see answer to query 2,097). Wholesale dealers are in the habit of ordering and obtaining their supply in form of a 10-per-cent solution in alcohol, directly from the nitroglycerin works, and many customers of the wholesale houses order the 10-per-cent solution likewise, so as to save bulk in shipping. Regarding these solutions, and particularly the 10-per-cent solution, several important facts have recently become known, regarding at least one of which it is very much desirable that those who have to handle the article shall be thoroughly posted.

The writer of this note had applied to Prof. Charles E. Munroe, U. S. Navy, at the Torpedo Station, Newport, R. I.—who is recognized as the foremost expert on high explosives in this country—for information regarding certain facts concerning nitroglycerin, for medicinal use, to be used in constructing the text of one of the articles of the forthcoming National Formulary.

Since it appears desirable that the more important portion of the information received should be made known as soon as possible, the following abstract is published here:

1. It has been repeatedly stated that a 10-per-cent alcoholic solution of nitroglycerin is non-explosive, but, so far as the pharmaceutical public is concerned, this information was not known (or known to but few) to be absolutely reliable. Prof. Munroe expressly states that this statement is correct, such a solution being *absolutely non-explosive.*

2. Prof. Munroe being asked the question, whether the admixture of an alcoholic solution of nitroglycerin with packing material, or other absorbent substances, caused by a fracture or breakage of the container, would render the packing material, etc., explosive, after the evaporation of the alcohol, answered, that the *absorbent would certainly become dangerous,* but that the rate of danger would depend upon the relative proportions of absorbent and nitroglycerin. According to his statement, a mixture of not more than 70 per cent of nitroglycerin with not less than 30 per cent of infusorial earth, or charcoal, or sawdust, etc., is non-explosive. That is, it cannot be exploded by anything else than a so-called detonator. And a mixture containing not more than 52 per cent nitroglycerin, and not less than 48 per cent of infusorial earth, etc., ceases to be explosive even with a detonator, or as the term is, cannot be detonated. But if the absorbent material should be any oxidizing substance, such as a nitrate, a chlorate, etc., etc., *even as small a proportion as five (5) per cent* of nitroglycerin may render the combination *explosive.* A strong blow or concussion, therefore, may cause an explosion. Let us suppose that a glass-bottle containing an alcoholic solution of nitroglycerin has been packed with other goods, that it has broken and the contents leaked into a package of powdered nitrate of potassium, or other oxidizing substance; on evaporation of the alcohol, this would be a decided source of danger.

For this reason, alcoholic solutions of nitroglycerin should always be kept and transported in vessels which are not liable to fracture. *The most suitable are tin-cans, such as ether is put up in.*

It has been repeatedly proposed to diminish the suspected danger arising from an accidental evaporation of the alcohol of such a solution, by adding to it a certain proportion of some non-volatile liquid, which might either hold the nitroglycerin in solution, or at least partly dilute it, after the alcohol is dissipated. Glycerin has, among other things, been proposed for this purpose, by the writer and also by others. According to Prof. Munroe, however, this is *not* advisable. He says, he would be apprehensive of danger in handling any nitroglycerin which is mixed with glycerin or with any fatty or oleaginous material. He adds: "The fact is, we have to be careful about getting such substances into nitroglycerin. Many of the accidents have been caused by the fact that the glycerin used in the manufacture has contained some small amount of fatty acids. It is possible that, on a warm day, nitroglycerin might explode from the presence of fatty acids. From my experience, I should be apprehensive of it, and would *not* recommend the use of any other solvent than alcohol."

3. In case any solution of nitroglycerin, or the latter itself in a pure state, has been spilled, Prof. Munroe advises to render it innocuous by applying a solution of sulphocarbonate of sodium. This is directed to be prepared by dissolving sublimed sulphur in a solution of sodium carbonate, by the aid of heat. A bottle full of this solution should always be kept near the vessel in which the stock-solution is kept. When any of the latter is spilled, it should be wiped up as carefully as possible, and the place or absorbent material which has soaked it up, should be thoroughly drenched with the above mentioned solution, which is technically termed "sulphur solution." Of course, the cloth which has been used to wipe it up should likewise be saturated with this liquid.

IN the course of a critical examination of a series of dates of references given in the foot-notes of a recent work on organic analysis (see page 40), our attention has been directed to the fact that much difficulty is often encountered by the absence of any definite information regarding *the date, up to which the information* furnished by the respective text *may be regarded as being reasonably complete*, or as being based upon all that has been made public up to the time of publication. In chemical works, perhaps more than in any others, the knowledge of such a date would save much waste of time, and would enable the reader or user quickly to complete the available record by referring to files of journals, annual resumés, etc., published *after* the indicated date.

Under present circumstances, an idea as to the time when a given author's text on any subject was completed (which may have been many months previous to the actual issue of the book itself), can only be obtained by examining the dates of the references which the author quotes. Some authors, in doing this, frequently quote, besides the name of a writer, the name of the journal, with volume and page, and *omit the year* of publication, which renders it mostly impossible—without the aid of special lists, or a chance of consulting the original—to fix the date of the quotation. Such a date is of great importance, as it may either show the information to be likely antiquated, or it may form the starting point for researches in literature of later date.

We would therefore propose as an improvement that, in all works of reference, for instance, such as treat on subjects of chemistry, descriptive or analytical, or on materia medica, or in fact on any subject regarding which there is a constant accession of new facts and discoveries, *the author specify the date up to which the text of any article may be considered as completed.* This may be done by appending, at the end of each paragraph (if the work is lexicographically arranged) the date, in which the number of the month is best given in Roman numerals, for instance: "(III., 17, '88)," meaning that up to the 17th of March, 1888, the literature which *had appeared up to that time* had been consulted by the author. This date should *not* mean that on which the *printing* of the article has been commenced or concluded, as this is of less importance for the reader to know than the former.

Another method for giving this same information is that which we have mentioned several years ago, by correspondence, to some of our literary friends, and which we observe carried out (though probably without any knowledge of such a plan having previously been thought of) in the new edition of the most important work of reference on the field of organic chemistry, viz., Beilstein's "Handbuch d. Organischen Chemie," vol. II., beginning with page 63. On this page, and every following, the inner margin of the page-heading bears a printed date (f. i., 13. 8. 86), which denotes the date up to which the literature referring to the subjects on that page has been completely made use of, or laid under contribution. The reader will then know at once that for any further information he will have to consult journals, books, etc., which have appeared subsequent to the 13th of August, 1886, and he will not need to consult those previously published, except to verify statements or obtain fuller details, or for other special reasons.

Of the two methods thus outlined, the second one is preferable in the case of works which are wholly written or revised by one author, or several authors conjointly. In the case of dictionaries of chemistry or other works in which the several articles are contributed by different authors, the first-mentioned plan is the better one, as each author will have to specify the particular date himself, and there may be but few bearing the same date.

We hope that the propositions here made will receive the favorable consideration of authors and publishers of works of reference.

WE gave, in answer to Query 2,080 in the foregoing number, a new process for preparing cod-liver oil emulsions, by means of mucilage of dextrin, and we now wish to draw attention to the fact that this vehicle is one of the best to emulsify and keep in suspension balsam of copaiba or other oleo-resins. The well-known Lafayette Mixture, when prepared with this mucilage, is much more permanent, and less liable to separate, than when prepared with mucilage of acacia. We have had this mixture prepared for some time by the following formula:

    ℞ Copaibæ..fl. ℥ j
      Liq. Potassæ ....fl. ℥ j
      Spir. Æther. Nit.,
      Tinct. Lavand. Co.,
      Syrupi... āā fl. ℥ j
      Mucilag. Dextrini..........................q. s. ad fl. ℥ iv

It is suggested that the establishment of a section on Pharmacy in the American Medical Association is desirable. There is some doubt as to the probability of this body accepting such advice, but there is no doubt that the majority of physicians are in need of more information respecting the articles they use, or ought to use.

HENRY CAREY BAIRD & Co., of Philadelphia, announce the publication of a new treatise on animal and vegetable fats and oils by William T. Brannt, in 1 vol. of 739 pp. 8vo, with 244 engravings. Price, $7.50.

THE *Druggists' Circular*, in its January number, announces a new feature with considerable rhetorical flourish, in the course of which it expresses a hope of pardon for asking attention

"to the fact that, so far as we can discover from extended observation, this journal is the first to be published with a regular alphabetical index for each number."

The observation of the editor could not have extended very far, for it is now about ten years since NEW REMEDIES began to publish in every number a complete and alphabetically-arranged index of its contents, and it continued to do so until it adopted its present form and title. Within that period, one of our Chicago cotemporaries (if our memory serves us) did the same thing for some time. We never claimed originality for the scheme.

Distinction of Raw and Boiled Linseed Oil.

EXCEPTION has recently been taken to the statement in the United States Pharmacopœia, under Oleum Lini, that this oil is soluble in 5 parts of absolute alcohol. Various writers have reported that a much larger quantity of the solvent was required. At the October Pharmaceutical Meeting of the Philadelphia College of Pharmacy, this matter was incidentally touched upon, and the discussion afforded at least a partial explanation of the different statements. We take the following from the *American Journal of Pharmacy* (p. 587):

"Mr. England stated that he made linseed oil with bisulphide of carbon, but that it required 10 parts of absolute alcohol to dissolve it. Prof. Maisch asked if the oil had been made from the seed ground by Mr. England, or from flaxseed as purchased. The commercial *meal* had been used. It is well known that the oil changes rapidly in ground seeds, especially flaxseed, this oil being of the class called drying oils. Mr. Moerck said that linseed oil made from *freshly-ground seed*, with petroleum spirit of light gravity, required but *five* (5) *parts of absolute alcohol*, and that made with bisulphide of carbon required about 10 parts. . . . Mr. Thompson wished to know how cold-pressed oil might be discriminated from that made by heat and pressure. It was stated that the former could be recognised by the alcohol test before alluded to, and by the mild odor and bland taste which are quite different from that made by heat and pressure."

It appears, therefore, that the solubility of linseed oil in absolute alcohol differs not only according to the nature of the solvent used, but also, in absence of a solvent, whether the oil has been pressed out in the cold, or with the application of heat. Oil extracted with petroleum naphtha, and presumably also cold pressed oil (though this needs renewed experimentation) is soluble in 5 parts of absolute alcohol. The resinification which occurs in old oil, or in hot-pressed oil, on the other hand diminishes its solubility. What share the bisulphide of carbon, as a solvent, possesses in producing the same effect is not quite clear.

A new method of distinguishing between raw and boiled linseed oil has recently been published by Finkener (*Chem. Zeit.*, 1887, 905). It is as follows:

Shake 12 C.c. of the oil briskly with 6 C.c. of glycerole of acetate of lead (see below) in a test-tube, then set the latter for about three minutes into boiling water. Boiled linseed oil will then appear as a salve-like mass, while raw oil will form two liquid layers, the lower one of which is clear like water. If the raw oil contains 25% of boiled oil, it may by this test be distinguished from pure raw oil. The lead reagent is prepared by dissolving 100 Gm. of crystallized acetate of lead in 150 C.c. of distilled water and 32 Gm. of anhydrous glycerin. The somewhat turbid solution is kept in a well-stoppered bottle. Just previous to use, 5 C.c. of the solution are mixed, in a test-tube, with 1 C.c. of 20% water of ammonia (sp. gr. 0.925), and then mixed with the 12 C.c. of oil. So-called bleached boiled oil has a much lighter yellow color than the raw oil, but behaves under the test like the latter, not the boiled oil. According to the author, this test is preferable to all others so far recommended which are based upon solubility, saponification, or oxidation of raw and boiled linseed oil, respectively.

The Pharmaceutical Society of New South Wales has adopted a novel device for obviating the inconvenience sometimes imposed upon pharmaceutical students in the colony by the necessity of travelling long distances to attend the preliminary examination. In future, whenever the candidate resides more than seventy miles from Sydney, the police magistrate of the district is to be asked whether he will undertake to superintend the examination, and return the examination papers, with the answers, to the Society in Sydney.

CORRESPONDENCE.

Tinctures by Superior Maceration.

To the Editor of The American Druggist.

The following is a practical method for making "resinous tinctures:

Break up and pass any resins, such as tolu, benzoin, aloes, myrrh, guaiacum, and other resins, through a No. 6 sieve, and suspend it in a coarse, small salt bag (previously washed and dried) by means of a string, in a wide-mouth bottle, so that the menstruum can reach the resins. The heavy solution will go down, and in one or two hours the drugs will be in solution, and does away with the six or seven days' maceration.

Yours respectfully,

HUGO OPPERMANN, Ph.G.

PHILADELPHIA, PA.

We presume that our correspondent was aware that this method is quite old and well known, but that he merely wished to point out the details which will make it useful in preparing small quantities of stock.—*Ed. Am. Dr.*

QUERIES & ANSWERS.

Queries for which answers are desired, must be received by the 5th of the month, and must in every case be accompanied by the name and address of the writer, for the information of the editor, but not for publication.

No. 2,094.—**Gallein and Lacmoid** ("Laboratory").

Gallein has been recommended several years ago already as an exceedingly delicate indicator for acids or alkalies. A small quantity of gallein added to alkaline solutions renders them reddish, while the tint of neutral solutions is pale brown.

Gallein is a name applied to a compound prepared by heating together 2 parts of pyrogallic acid and 1 part of anhydrous phthalic acid for several hours at a temperature of 190° to 200° C. It is prepared without difficulty in open vessels. At first, the hot mixture is a colorless liquid, which gradually assumes a red color, and afterwards becomes viscid and opaque. It is allowed to cool, the fused mass dissolved in hot alcohol, the solution filtered and mixed with water, which causes the separation of the gallein in form of brown flakes, which are purified by repeated solution in alcohol, and precipitation with water. The crude gallein is then heated with glacial acetic acid, whereby it is converted into an acetyl compound, which is purified by repeated crystallization. This is then decomposed with alcoholic potassa, and from the alkaline solution pure gallein is thrown down by hydrochloric acid.

Gallein is so delicate that it will indicate existing traces of alkali in such salts as chloride or acetate of ammonium, acetate, citrate, or tartrate of potassium, carbonate of magnesium, even when phenolphthalein will fail to reveal them.

The hydrates of alkalies (potassa, soda, ammonia, etc.) and of alkaline earths (lime, baryta, etc.) produce a bluish-red color with gallein; and their soluble carbonates a rose-red color. Even bicarbonates—which behave towards phenolphthalein like acids—still produce a faint rose-red tint. Alkaloids, like morphine, brucine, strychnine, cocaine, etc., likewise produce a reddish color.

We have had no extended experience with gallein so far, having only tried it experimentally. Like most new indicators, it will probably turn out to have a certain sphere within which it will be better than any other, while the others will still be useful in other directions.

Lacmoid is an artificial blue coloring matter prepared by heating resorcin with nitrite of sodium and water to a temperature not exceeding 130° C. (see this Journal, 1885, 68). This blue coloring matter undergoes the same changes as litmus in contact with alkalies and acids. It is much more delicate than litmus, and has the additional advantage that, when the coloring matter is fixed upon paper, the latter may be dipped or floated in liquids without the color being washed out from the paper. With lacmoid we have had more experience than with gallein, and can confirm the good reports of other observers. The most thorough study of this indicator has been made by Robert T. Thomson, who published his results in the *Chemical News*, vol. 52, 18.

Lacmoid paper is prepared by saturating unsized paper in a solution of 1 part of lacmoid in 1,000 parts of 45-percent alcohol. If a blue paper is wanted, about 5 to 10 drops of solution of potassa are added to the solution. According to E. Bosetti, the commercial lacmoid, before being used as an indicator, should be redissolved in water, the solution precipitated by hydrochloric acid, the precipitated matter washed, dried in the water-bath, then dissolved in alcohol, and the alcoholic solution evaporated. After repeating this process three or four times, the product will be much more sensitive.

No. 2,095.—**Copying Pad** (C. R. S.).

The hectograph mass is a combination of glue or gelatin, water, and glycerin. This combination, as used by the Hectograph Company, is protected by a patent. The proportion of the materials used is about the following:

1 part, by weight, of best glue (Cooper's extra answers well) is covered with cold water, and soaked until it is perfectly soft. The excess of water is then poured off, and the glue allowed to drain a short time. It is then transferred to a kettle, and heated (by a water or steambath) until the largest part of the water has been driven off, which may be recognized by the scant vapor given off during the stirring. The mass must be continuously stirred during the heating. Next, 4 parts, by weight, of glycerin are added, and well mixed. The pans in which the mass is to be cast, having been placed upon a perfectly level surface, the liquid mass is dipped out of the kettle, and poured into the pans, best through a conical strainer funnel, to hold back any lumps or foreign substance that may have been in the glue. After the pans are filled, the surface of the still liquid mass, which is usually covered with a sort of foam, caused by escaped air-bubbles, is carefully gone over with the smooth edge of a stiff piece of paper or stiff brush, so as to take off the scum. The pans are then covered up, and allowed to stand from twelve to twenty-four hours, so that the mass may fully set. The quantity of glycerin, viz., 4 parts, is about right for a moderately warm climate, or for summer, or where the pans are kept in warm rooms. If the pad is to be used in a cold place, or in a cold locality, the glycerin must be increased to 4½ or even 5 parts. But an essential condition of success is to boil or evaporate off all the water possible from the glue before the glycerin is added.

If a pad is spoiled, the mass, unless badly colored by the aniline ink, may be remelted and recast. Frequent repetition of this process, however, renders the mass softer, and finally it will scarcely set at all.

No. 2,096.—**Quillaja** (Supplement to Query No. 2,044, on page 218 of last volume).

We have just come in possession of a rare work, by Molina, entitled: "Saggio sulla Storia Naturale del Chili di Gio. Ignazio Molina." (2nda edit.) 4to, Bologna, 1810. This work, written in Italian, and dedicated to Eugene Napoleon, was intended by the author to serve as a revised edition of his Natural History of Chili, published in 1782. On page 192 the author writes about Quillaja as follows (we translate from the Italian):

Il Quillay, *Quillaja saponaria gen. nov. Monœc. Poliandria* [Molina was the first to determine and to name the plant or tree.] An evergreen tree, growing to a height of thirty to forty feet, with straight trunk, branched and covered with a thick, grayish bark; leaves alternate, petiolate, oblongly-ovate and dentate, of a deep-green color, etc., etc. There are, in Chili, two varieties of soap-bark, differing but little in name, and in foliage, namely, the above-described *Quillay*, and another, called *Cullay*, both receiving their names from the Chilian verbs *quillcan* and *cullean*, which have the meaning "to wash," with a certain shade of difference. The ancient Chilians, though not initiated into scientific principles, were in the habit of making careful distinctions in the names of natural objects, whenever they observed any peculiarity about them. The above two expressions and well distinguished terms have been converted on Spanish soil into one, on account of the difficulty caused by the pronunciation of the *u* in the second; hence both trees have been named Quillay, in spite of their characteristic differences. The true Quillay prefers the coast-region along the Andes; the Cullay the more elevated localities. The infusion of the bark of the Cullay renders linen fabrics somewhat yellow (as already observed by Freier), while this is not the case when Quillay is used. I believe that the Madrid botanists have formed their genus *Smegmadermos* in the section Polygamia Diœcia, upon the Cullay, as being more common than the Quillay, etc.

We quote the above, not only to explain the meaning of the original term, but also to show that the originator of the botanical term *Quillaja*, viz., Molina, spelled the word with a *j* and not with an *i*.

No. 2,097.—**Solution of Nitroglycerin. Its Assay and Mode of Keeping** (Dr. A. F. J.—and S. J. & Co.).

The only kind of solution of nitroglycerin which is used medicinally is a *one* (1) *per cent* solution in alcohol. This is, of course, meant by weight. Taking into consideration the specific gravity of nitroglycerin, which is 1.600 at 15° C. (59° F.), and that of alcohol, which is about 0.830, it will be found, on calculation, that the above proportions (by weight) are equivalent to about the following proportions by measure, provided there is no change of volume on mixing the two liquids:

Nitroglycerin.................................... 1 volume.
Alcohol.. 193 volumes.

Consequently, about 194 minims will be equivalent to 1 minim (or to 0.0076 Gm., or to 1.5 grains) of nitroglycerin. And 1 minim of the solution will contain 0.00515 Gm., or 9.079 grains, or $\frac{1}{14}$ minim of nitroglycerin.

Regarding the best method of assaying an alcoholic solution of nitroglycerin it may be stated here, that the National Formulary Committee has determined to include "Spiritus Glonoini" in the list of articles to be inserted, and has had the benefit of the advice of Professor Charles E. Munroe, U. S. Navy, at the Torpedo Station at Newport, R. I. While there are several well-known methods for testing or estimating nitroglycerin, it was deemed inexpedient to adopt any which require the previous isolation of nitroglycerin in a pure state. The experiments, however, in this direction are not yet concluded, and the results cannot be published by us at the present time.

Regarding the *mode of keeping* solutions of nitroglycerin, it should be made an invariable rule, *never* to keep the solution in vessels in which are liable to be fractured or broken. *Glass* or *stone-ware* vessels should never be used; least of all, glass. Concerning this matter, attention is called to an editorial, embodying some important information which will be of interest to many of our readers.

No. 2,098.—**Bird Lime, Brumata Lime, etc.** (St. Louis). These terms are used in English, but are sometimes misunderstood. The second word "Lime" is *not* the English word, equivalent to oxide of calcium, but is a German word, meaning *glue* in English. Bird-lime, therefore, stands for "bird-glue," that is, some preparation which is sufficiently adhesive to cause small birds, after having alighted upon it, to become so entangled in it that they may be easily caught. A preparation of this kind used to be made at one time from a decoction of *Viscum aucuparium*. But at present, artificial mixtures are usually made, chiefly composed of turpentine (that is, the natural exudation of pines), rosin and other substances. "Brumata Lime," standing for "brumata-glue," is a term as yet but little used here, but deserves to be better known. Many of our readers will have seen the peculiar yellow hairy caterpillar, with a black or brown line along the back, which infests many of our ornamental and fruit trees and causes their destruction by consuming the foliage. The "brumata-lime" is intended to prevent their propagation. It was first proposed by Mr. Becker, a school teacher at Jüterbogk (Germany), and received its name from the *Cheimatobia* (or *Aridalia*) *brumata*, the butterfly, of which the caterpillar has been mentioned above. The female of this insect cannot fly, while the males are able to do so and settle upon the tree. The females are compelled to crawl up along the trunk, and to prevent this, a ring of "brumata-lime" is applied. This is prepared by mixing 5 parts of rape oil with 1 part of lard, boiling the mixture until it thickens, then adding 1 part each of turpentine and rosin. Hager recommends to melt together 250 parts of black pitch, 100 of turpentine, 100 of paraffin, oil and 100 of crude rape oil, then to allow the mass to become partly cool, and to add 5 parts powdered benzoin, 50 of vaseline (petroleum), 2 each of carbolic and salicylic acids, and 10 of gurjun balsam.

The best time to apply the mass is about the beginning of October, or even earlier. It should be well looked after, and renewed from time to time.

No. 2,099.—**Recovery of Platinum from Laboratory Residues.**
The most systematic and carefully planned method is the following, proposed by P. Wagner and recommended by Boeckmann (*Chem.-tech. Untersuchungsmethoden*, 2d ed., I., 121).

The platinum residues are best preserved in two separate vessels, one of which is for the filters containing the potassio-platinic chloride, the other being intended for the alcoholic wash-liquids, containing platinic chloride in combination with chlorides of sodium, magnesium, barium, etc.

This liquid is operated on first. It is mixed with enough of a saturated aqueous solution of pure chloride of potassium to precipitate all the platinum. After 24 hours' standing, the supernatant liquid is siphoned off, and the residue is then washed into a porcelain capsule with the aid of some of the siphoned-off alcohol. The precipitate, which can be detached from the filters contained in the other vessel, is added to the contents of the capsule, the empty filters boiled several times with water in a second capsule, the liquids being added to the first. Next enough carbonate of sodium is added to produce a strongly alkaline reaction, the whole stirred up repeatedly, and allowed to stand on the steam-bath for about ten hours. Platinum black will then be deposited in a compact state, and the supernatant liquid will have only a faint yellow tint, due to the presence of organic substances (a lemon-yellow color would show that undecomposed platinic chloride is still present). The liquid is now poured off and allowed to run through a filter. The platinum black is boiled with water, allowed to deposit, and the liquid poured off. This boiling and washing is repeated once with pure hydrochloric acid and twice with distilled water. Finally, the platinum black is transferred to a filter, again washed and dried at the ordinary in-door temperature. A higher heat must be avoided, as the filter would be burnt up by the metal.

The platinum black thus purified is dissolved in aqua regia prepared from 5 parts of hydrochloric and 1 part of nitric acid. The best way to proceed is as follows: Put the hydrochloric acid in a wash-bottle (having a jet), and wash the platinum black from the filter into a capacious porcelain capsule, which is then gently warmed on the water-bath. Now add the nitric acid *in drops*. In one hour, solution will have been effected. Allow the solution to cool somewhat, pass it through Swedish filtering paper, and evaporate the filtrate in a porcelain capsule, upon the water-bath, until a small portion removed at the end of a glass rod begins to solidify. A very small quantity of hydrochloric acid is now carefully added, and the excess evaporated, several times in succession, until all nitric acid has been dissipated.

No. 2,100.—**Ownership of Prescriptions** (R. N. G.).
In order to obtain a list of decisions of Courts regarding the ownership of prescriptions, the most promising method would be to consult the librarian of a good law-library such as is, no doubt, existing in your city. A library attached to the U. S. Courts, or to the more important State Courts, usually possesses the published law reports of all the States of the Union, and it is then only a question of time to go through the indexes and look up the references. We cannot relieve you of this part of the work.

So far as we know, the ownership of a physician's prescription has been brought before the courts, heretofore, only in a one-sided way, and has not been argued from the standpoint of special agreement or contract. It is usually supposed that when a patient calls upon a physician for advice, the advice constitutes the commodity which the physician has to sell for the time being, and that, if he writes a prescription and delivers it to the patient, receiving his fee, the commercial transaction is completed. In other words, it is supposed that the advice, including the prescription, are tantamount to a bona-fide sale on the part of the physician, and to a bona-fide purchase on the part of the patient, so that the latter may be regarded as the owner in fee simple of the prescription. But a sale or purchase may be regarded, or rather, should be regarded, as a form of contract, entailing certain obligations upon both parties. When there are no conditions surrounding the exchange of the commodities, except the act of handing over the consideration, the transaction is absolutely completed and the contract fulfilled, as soon as the consideration is paid. But if the sale is made under certain conditions, accepted by the purchaser, the case assumes an entirely different aspect. We hold that if a physician expressly writes upon a prescription: "This prescription is intended for a special case and occasion and is not to be repeated"—or words to this effect—and if the client accepts the prescription with this condition, then the latter is bound to abide by the condition. We believe, if a case of this kind were properly argued before the Courts, it would be decided as we have outlined. But such a decision would hardly be of much practical value, because all that would be needed to evade the condition would be for the client to copy the prescription with omission of the prescriber's name and all details which might show that it was intended for a special case and occasion. Since any one may combine medicines in any way, manner, or shape, and several prescribers often happen to combine the same ingredients in the same proportions, it would be impossible for the original prescriber to identify—in a legal sense—his own prescription which he had given or sold to his patient conditionally.

Practically, therefore, even the acknowledged or assumed right of the physician to limit the use of any of his prescriptions to a particular case or time, could be easily circumvented, unless laws should be enacted which would clearly define the rights of prescriber and client.

No. 2,101.—**Detection of Mineral Wax in Beeswax** (San Francisco).
Both the bleached and the unbleached, or yellow wax, are frequently adulterated with certain kinds of paraffin, or the latter are substituted for it altogether. The usual adulterant for yellow wax is the yellow cerewin obtained from fossil wax or ozokerite. White wax is often adulterated with white cerewin, or with some variety of white paraffin obtained from the petroleum residues. The recognition of these adulterants is comparatively easy when they are present in considerable proportion. But when they are small in quantity, and perhaps other adulterants are added which partly neutralize the anomalies introduced by the former, the detection of the adulteration is not so easy.

The test for paraffin given in the U. S. Pharm., under *Cera Flava*, by heating the wax with sulphuric acid, which had been relied upon by many analysts before it was introduced into the pharmacopœia, is now regarded as untrustworthy by the most competent judges.

Among the less circumstantial methods of testing, those of Buchner and of Hager deserve mention here:

1. Buchner's Method.—Boil a sample of the suspected wax with a concentrated alcoholic solution of potassa (1 part of potassa and 2½ parts of 90-per-cent alcohol) for a few minutes in a wide test-tube. Transfer the liquid to a narrow test-tube, and place this for some time in a water-bath. If the wax is pure, the solution remains clear. If it contains ceresin or paraffin, the hydrocarbons float, as an oily layer, on the surface of the potassa solution, which is usually colored. If the separation into layers should be imperfect or sluggish, it may be brought about at once, by adding a little alcohol and again warming on the water-bath.

2. Hager's Method.—Heat 2 Gm. of the wax with 5 C.c. of a solution of carbonate of sodium, until the wax melts, then shake thoroughly, and gradually add 6 C.c. of benzol, frequently shaken. This will produce an emulsion, which should be warmed during one hour upon the water-bath to 50° C. (122° F.), and is then set aside to cool at the ordinary temperature. If the wax is pure, the upper layer is liquid and scarcely turbid. If, however, paraffin or ceresin were present, the upper layer is more or less solid, turbid, or opaque and white.

A method which requires more time, but which generally yields more definite information, even quantitatively, is:

3. Hübl's Method.—Wax consists mainly of *cerotic acid* and of *myricin*. The latter is a so-called compound ether, namely, the palmitate of myricyl. Hübl's method is based on two considerations, namely, *first*, the number of milligrammes of potassa (determined volumetrically) required to saturate the free cerotic acid, and *second*—after the cerotic acid has been neutralized—the number of milligrammes of potassa required to saponify the myricin, that is, to convert it into palmitate of potassium and myricyl alcohol.

$$C_{15}H_{31}.C_{30}H_{61}O_2 + KOH = C_{15}H_{31}.OH + KC_{30}H_{61}O_2$$
(myricyl palmitate) (potassa) (myricyl alcohol) (potassium palmitate)
(for myricin)

(Myricyl is also sometimes called mellisyl.) The proportion of free cerotic acid and myricin in wax is as 1 of the former to 6 of the latter.

The execution of the method is as follows:

Three to 4 Gm. of the wax are warmed with about 20 C.c. of 91% alcohol until the wax is melted, the mixture is well shaken, if necessary warmed again to keep it liquid, and then titrated with ½ normal potassa (containing 28 Gm. of KHO in the liter), phenolphthalein being used as indicator. As soon as the cerotic acid is neutralized, as shown by the appearance of a rose-red tint, about 20 C.c. more of the same volumetric solution are added, the quantity being exactly noted, and the mixture warmed on a water-bath for about 45 minutes. Finally, the excess of alkali, not required to combine with the palmitic acid, is determined by titrating with ½ normal acid.

The number of C.c. of the volumetric alkaline solution first consumed, when transcalculated into milligrammes of potassa, is called by Hübl "acid-number." And the number of milligrammes required to combine exactly with the palmitic acid, is called the "ether-number."

Now it has been found, that *for wax*, the "acid-number" is usually between 19 and 21, mostly 20. The "ether number" is usually between 73 and 76, mostly 75. The respectively lower and higher numbers usually occur together, hence the proportion between the "acid-number" and "ether-number" is generally very uniform, varying only by a small fraction. If the "acid number" is assumed to be 1, then the "ether-number" will be between 3.6 and 3.8, and is generally 3.7.

Now here it should be noticed that the theoretical quantity of potassa required for saponifying pure wax consisting of pure cerotic acid and myricin is less than that actually found necessary. Wax therefore must contain small quantities of other saponifiable constituents which are not known. The "saponification-number"—that is, the number of milligrammes of potassa (KHO) required to combine with *all* the acid bodies in wax—varies between 93 and 96.

Comparing with these figures, those obtained under the same circumstances with other fatty or wax-like substances, liable to be used as adulterants of or substitutes for beeswax, we find that the figures for *wax* are very characteristic, as the following table will show:

	Acid Number.	Ether Number.	Total Saponification Number.	Proportional Number.*
Japan Wax	20	200	220	10
Carnauba wax	4	75	79	19
Tallow	4	176	180	44
Stearic acid	195	0	195	0
Resin	110	1.6	112	0.015
Ceresin, or Paraffin	0	0	0	
Beeswax, yellow	20	75	95	3.75

* Supposing the figures in columns I. were reduced to "1." The figures in column IV. may be termed "proportional numbers."

If the "saponification-number" is found to be below 92, and the "proportional number" is that of pure wax, then ceresin or paraffin are present. If the "proportional number" is greater than 3.8, the possible adulterants are Japan wax, Carnauba wax, or tallow. If Japan wax is excluded if the "acid-number" is less than 20. When the "proportional number" is smaller than 3.6, the adulterant is stearic acid or resin.

Supposing a sample of wax tested in this manner has been shown to contain some ceresin or paraffin, the quantity of the adulterant may be estimated, approximately, in the following manner. Considering 95 to be the mean saponification number of pure wax, and denoting by k the saponification number of the sample under consideration (which number must have been considerably smaller than that for pure wax), we may calculate the percentage (x) of paraffin or ceresin by the formula:

$$x = 100 - \frac{100\,k}{95}$$

This equation is derived from the proportion

$$95 : 100 = (95 - k) : x$$

which may be read: As 95, or the total saponification number of pure wax, is to 100, that is to 100 parts of pure wax to which the number 95 belongs, so is the loss which the total saponification number has suffered, to the number of parts of ceresin or paraffin present. Of course, with a pure wax, k becomes 95. Hence the second portion of the equation becomes:

$$95 : 100 = 95 - 95 : x$$
$$95 : 100 = 0 : x$$
$$x = 0$$

that is, there would be none of the adulterant present.

No. 2,102.—Sulphanilic Acid (W. L. R.—M. H.).

Regarding this compound, which has been mentioned repeatedly in our pages—for instance, as a reagent, on page 231 of our last volume; as an almost instantaneous cure for iodism, page 149 of our volume for 1886, etc.—we have had several inquiries. The following note will give the essential details.

Sulphanilic acid is, properly speaking, "para-amidobenzol-sulphonic acid." Representing benzol by the usual diagram (which must only be regarded as an ideal reduction to the most simple form of a solid molecule of the substance), and distinguishing the several positions by the figures 1, 2, 3, 4, 5, 6, we have:

```
            H (1)
            |
            C
           / \
   (6) HC     CH (2)
       ||     ||
   (5) HC     CH (3)
           \ /
            C
            |
            H
           (4)
```

Any one of the hydrogens in this compound may be replaced by a monad element or group. If only one at a time is thus replaced, it is immaterial which of them is supposed to have been affected. If, however, more than *one* is replaced *at the same time*, then the properties of the products depend upon the relative position of the replacing bodies. Supposing *two* hydrogens are thus replaced. If they are contiguous, (1) and (2), or (2) and (3), or (3) and (4), etc., then the product receives the prefix *ortho-* in case it is necessary to distinguish it from others. If, however, the substitution takes place at (1) and (3), or (2) and (4), or (3) and (5), etc., with an intermediate intact member, the product receives the prefix *meta*. And if two members are passed over, that is, if the substitution takes place at (1) and (4), or (2) and (5), etc., the product receives the prefix *para*.

From benzol, C_6H_6, is derived nitrobenzol, $C_6H_5.NO_2$. This NO_2 may be supposed to be substituted for any one of the hydrogens in the benzol ring.

By treatment with sulphuric acid, under certain conditions, many organic compounds, particularly of the aromatic series, are converted into so-called sulphonic acids, that is, acids produced by the substitution of HSO_3 for one hydrogen. Thus $C_6H_5.HSO_3$ is benzolsulphonic acid. Now, as nitrobenzol already has the group NO_2 in the place of one hydrogen, it follows that, if a sulphonic acid is formed from this, the group HSO_3 will have to replace a *second* hydrogen. And now it depends which hydrogen is thus replaced. According to what has been said above, it will be readily understood that there are three nitrobenzol-sulphonic acids possible, the formula being as follows (the numbers in parenthesis indicate the position of the hydrogens replaced according to the scheme above given):

1. *Ortho*-nitrobenzol-sulphonic acid:

$$C_6H_4 \begin{cases} (1)NO_2 \\ (2)HSO_3 \end{cases}$$

In place of (1) and (2), the position may be imagined to be (2) and (3), or (3) and (4), etc., as explained above.

2. *Meta*-nitrobenzol-sulphonic acid:

$$C_6H_4 \begin{cases} (1)NO_2 \\ (3)HSO_3 \end{cases}$$

3. *Para*-nitrobenzol-sulphonic acid:

$$C_6H_4\begin{cases}(1)NO_2\\(4)HSO_3\end{cases}$$

When nitrobenzol is treated with fuming sulphuric acid, all three of the above derivatives are formed at the same time, but not in equal quantities. Usually, the *meta*-acid is produced in largest proportion, somewhere near ninety per cent.

If now, by some process, the group NO_2 is replaced by the group NH_2 (amidogen), the resulting product receives the prefix *amido*, in place of *nitro*. The process by which this is best accomplished in the present case is to convert any of the above acids, previously separated, into ammonium salts, adding a large excess of strong ammonia, and conducting a current of hydrosulphuric acid through the solution. The product will then be the ammonium salt of the amido-benzol-sulphonic acid. By decomposing this with a mineral acid, the organic acid is precipitated.

When this process is applied to the third of the above-named sulphonic acids (the "*para*"), the result will finally be:

$$C_6H_4\begin{cases}(1)NH_2\\(4)HSO_3\end{cases}$$

and this is the compound which is better known as *sulphanilic acid*. It was discovered and known long before its exact chemical constitution was understood. Practically, it is prepared in a very simple manner, the constituents used having given it its original name.

1 part of aniline and 3 parts of concentrated sulphuric acid are heated to a temperature of 180-190° C. (356-374° F.), under an upright condenser, until no more aniline is present as such. On pouring the mass into water, sulphanilic acid separates.

Sulphanilic acid is soluble in 112 parts of water at 15° C. (59° F.), more easily in boiling water. It is insoluble in ether or alcohol. The commercial acid usually has a gray or brownish color. For analytical or medical purposes, it should be white or nearly so, and should yield a clear and at least nearly colorless solution in water containing alkali.

BIBLIOGRAPHY.

ORGANIC ANALYSIS: A Manual of the Descriptive and Analytical Chemistry of certain Carbon Compounds in Common Use. For the Qualitative and Quantitative Analysis of Organic Materials, Commercial and Pharmaceutical Assays; the Estimation of Impurities under Authorized Standards; Forensic Examination of Poisons; and Elementary Organic Analysis. By ALBERT B. PRESCOTT, PH.D., M.D., Director of the Chem. Labor. in the University of Mich., etc. 8vo. New York: (D. Van Nostrand), 1887, pp. vi.; 533.

This work had been announced as being in preparation several years ago; but the last few years have been so fruitful in new discoveries or improvements in methods of testing that we fully realize the difficulty which the author must have encountered in choosing the proper time when the text of any one chapter could be considered as reasonably complete up to that moment.

On examining the work, it will at once be seen that the contents are a series of more or less detailed monographs, in alphabetical order. Some of these are treated with most particular care and fulness, having evidently formed the subjects of special or favorite investigations of the author. Neutral principles, organic acids, and alkaloids are generally treated in their respective alphabetical order, though certain groups are also treated collectively, such as Cinchona, Opium, Strychnos, etc., alkaloids. Under the chapter entitled "Alkaloids," general processes for isolating these bodies and recognizing their alkaloidal nature are given. A systematic scheme for separating alkaloids and neutral principles, based upon that of Dragendorff, is given by the author on p. 452, but we could have wished that this were more in detail, though we fully realize the fact that this would have taken considerable space, and, perhaps, been only of limited practical use, outside of a systematic work treating specially of plant analysis. The absence of a more detailed scheme of separation in the case of alkaloids, however, as well as in the case of organic acids (though minor schemes, for the separation of a small number of acids likely to occur together, are here and there inserted, *f. i.*, p. 536) is made up by very detailed methods of separation, given under the head of each separate article.

Too much praise cannot be bestowed upon the treatment of the difficult chapters of Cinchona and Opium Alkaloids, which include everything of value that had been published up to the time of the respective texts being printed, so far as we can judge from the references. A suggestion for an improvement to be introduced into works of reference like the present, which we desire to make, will be found among the editorials in this number, as we deem it of sufficient importance to draw special attention to it. The chapter on Fats and Oils is also very complete, though we think it might have been more practically useful by describing in detail, and in one connected paragraph, the best methods of separating and estimating certain bodies often fraudulently combined, such as ceresin, paraffin, etc., in beeswax. The schemes of plant analysis given are those arranged by Parsons and by Dragendorff, which cover the ground quite effectively, so far as our present knowledge of plant constituents goes. Another very instructive chapter is that on Elementary Analysis, though the execution and application of Kjeldahl's method of determining nitrogen has undergone various modifications and improvements since the author's text was completed.

Throughout the work we find a large amount of information, which is now first presented by the author, mostly based upon his own experience and experiments.

Great care has evidently been bestowed upon the editing of the work, as we have, so far, not encountered any wrong figures, and but few misprints. On page 181, foot-note, however, we miss a reference to the Important work of Schultz, "DieChemie des Steinkohlentheers," 2 vols., Braunschweig, 1882 (new edition, I., 1886). On page 177, what is given as Maclagan's (this is the proper spelling) test, is not that now recognized as such. This was published in the AM. DRUGG., 1887, page 22, but perhaps too late to be included by the author. We notice that the latter uses several unusual spellings, thus "midriatic," page 339 sqq.; "mioporoides," page 340; instead of mydriatic, etc.

Prof. Prescott's work, embodying the fruits and results of many years' study and practice on the wide field of organic analysis, constitutes an important addition to our standard and authoritative works of reference, and should be in the library of every member of the chemical and pharmaceutical professions.

ELEMENTS OF MODERN CHEMISTRY. By ADOLPHE WURTZ (Senator), etc. Third Amer. Edit. Translated and edited, with the Approbation of the Author, etc. By W. H. Greene, M.D., Prof. of Chemistry in the Central High School, Philadelphia, etc. 8vo. J. B. Lippincott Co. 1887.

We need not add anything to our former favorable notice of this work, except to say that the text appears to have been carefully revised (with one exception), and that the work is highly to be recommended as a textbook for schools. It has one weak point, however, in our judgment, though this will not make itself felt in the circles where it will be most used. We refer to the chapter on alkaloids, which is antiquated and not in accordance with our present state of knowledge. Of cinchona alkaloids, only quinine and cinchonine are treated in detail. At the present day, cinchonidine as well as quinidine are of considerable importance. The process given for the preparation of quinine has long been abandoned by all makers for a more economical one. We would suggest that this chapter be entirely remodelled, at least in a succeeding American edition, even though Prof. Wurtz may not deem this necessary for another French issue.

MANUAL OF PHARMACY AND PHARMACEUTICAL CHEMISTRY. Designed especially for the Use of the Pharmaceutical Student and for Pharmacists in General. By CHAS. F. HEEBNER, Ph.G. (New York, class '81); Instructor in Pharmacy at the College of Pharmacy of the City of New York. 8vo. New York (Publ. by the Author), 1887.

This is a book which has grown upon the author during his personal intercourse, as one of the quiz-masters or instructors with many successive classes of the College of Pharmacy. While a lecturer, *ex cathedra*, has but little chance of knowing what his hearers have learned from his lectures until an examination is held, the quiz-instructor, on the other hand, has the advantage of being constantly able to feel the pulse of the classes, as it were, so far as their comprehension of the subjects taught in the lectures is concerned. He is thereby enabled to know which matters are more slowly and with more difficulty mastered by the students, and he can arrange his drill to suit the circumstances. Experience thus gained renders quiz-instruction particularly valuable. Even a casual glance through Mr. Heebner's book will reveal its exceedingly useful character.

Of course, it can give in many cases only the leading features or the skeleton of the information which it is desirable that the student should possess. Yet, with such a ground work, well-digested, the acquisition of further knowledge is an easy matter. The book contains not only all that is essential to a knowledge of the branches it relates to, but it also embraces a large amount of information, useful and practical, which is even not found in the larger treatises, as, for instance, the method of averaging percentage on pages 32-33. (On page 33, last line, read 23.2 for 2.32).

We have so far, at our first cursory examination, observed but few misprints, and no errors of importance.

American Druggist

Vol. XVII. No. 3.   NEW YORK, MARCH, 1888.   Whole No. 165.

[ORIGINAL COMMUNICATION.]
THE UNITED STATES GALLON.
BY A. B. LYONS, F.C.S.

THE subject of Prof. Mason's paper in the January number of the AMERICAN DRUGGIST is one in which I am deeply interested, and to which I gave a few years ago a somewhat careful study, the results of which were published in the *Pharmaceutical Record* of date December 15th, 1883. The most important result reached in that study was the discovery that Prof. Barnard's corrected value for the weight of a cubic inch of water *is erroneous*. The details of the calculation by which he reaches his value are given in his work on the Metric System. The original experiments were made in 1798, by Sir George Shuckburgh Evelyn. Capt. Kater deduced from them the conclusion that a cubic inch of water at 62° F., barometer 30 inches, weighs 252.456 grains. Prof. Barnard verifies his computation, making the exact value 252.4551 grains, but points out the circumstance that Capt. Kater had assumed the specific gravity of air at 62° F. to be $\frac{1}{816}$th that of water, whereas the fraction should be $\frac{1}{817\frac{1}{2}}$, and proceeds to deduce anew the required datum. The original experiments were made with three solids of symmetrical figure—a cube, a cylinder, and a sphere. Prof. Barnard's new results from the experiments with the two former coincided very closely with those of Capt. Kater. Obviously, since the experiments were made nearly at standard temperature and pressure, it could not be otherwise, if no mistakes were made in figures. The third result, however, was larger than Capt. Kater's by nearly 0.1 grain, so that the average obtained exceeded Capt. Kater's by 0.038. We find that in the calculation he states the quotient of 28,711.714 ÷ 113.5264 as 252.9959. Capt. Kater made it 252.907. It is plain that it is the former result that is incorrect. In fact, Capt. Kater's figure, as deduced from the data referred to, is substantially correct. By an independent calculation, employing the data given by Kohlrausch in his work on physical measurements, I deduced the value 252.45533. From this we should find the true vacuum weight of a cubic inch of water at 62° F. as 252.78748, but we ought not with Prof. Mason to make this the starting point of our calculation, since the experiments were made in the air, at very near standard temperature and pressure.

At 60° F. we should find the weight of a cubic inch, as deduced from the same data, to be in the air 252.4997 + grains, or weighed in vacuo with the same brass weights 252.77198 grains, whence we should find the weight of a gallon of water, weighed in air at 30 in. barometer, and at 60° F., to be 58,327.433 grains. The value deduced from the same data in a former calculation was 58,327.406

Professor Asa Gray, of Cambridge, Mass.
[See page 62.]

grains; the difference arising from slight differences in the allowance made for the moisture presumably present in the air.

It is a waste of time, however, to carry these calculations beyond one or two decimal places, until we are more certain of the infallibility of our premises. The experiments on which these conclusions hang were made nearly a century ago. It is hardly possible that they could have had the exactness that is now possible, with the improved mechanical appliances now in universal use. There is the more reason to question their correctness, in that we must conclude that, if they are right, there is an error in the standard kilogramme amounting to half a gramme, which is simply incredible. I agree fully with the editorial comments on Prof. Mason's paper, and hope that measures will be shortly taken to clear up effectually the obscurities resting over this subject, by new and conclusive experiments, which ought to be made by our government.

PROF. ASA GRAY.

Prof. Asa Gray, the well-known botanist of Cambridge, Mass., died at his home on the 30th of January, having suffered from cerebral hemorrhage (apoplexy) something more than a month previous. In New Remedies for 1879, we published a short account of his life (with a lithographic portrait) from which and the *Scientific American* of February 11th, 1888, we take the following: He was born in Paris, Oneida Co., N. Y., on the 18th of November, 1810; graduated in medicine at the Fairfield Medical School, and at once devoted himself to the study of botany. About 1834, he was appointed botanist to the Wilkes Exploring Expedition, but resigned on account of the delay of the enterprise. While awaiting the movement of the expedition, he began work with Prof. Torrey, of New York, on the "Flora of North America," publication of which commenced in 1840. He was about the same time appointed professor of botany in the University of Michigan, then just founded, and visited Europe to study herbaria and with a commission to purchase a library for the college. His connection with the University of Michigan was brief, and in 1842 he accepted the Fisher professorship of Natural History in Harvard University, which position he held for the remainder of his life, although he was relieved of the duty of teaching after 1872. The following account of his published work includes only those of chief importance, for in addition to the labor and study connected with his herbarium, which has become the leading one of this country, he was a prolific writer.

In 1834-35, Dr. Gray published two volumes of the "North American Gramineæ and Cyperaceæ"—one of his earliest contributions to botanical literature. Each volume contained a hundred species, illustrated with dried specimens. The work was sold by subscription, and the number of copies published was necessarily limited. In it were described several new species, and the characters and synonyms of many of those already known were revised. The work, although now very rare, is still an authority upon the subjects to which it relates.

In December, 1834, Dr. Gray read before the New York Lyceum of Natural History a paper entitled "A Notice of some New, Rare, or Otherwise interesting Plants from Northern and Western Portions of the State of New York," which at once gained for him much credit among scientific men. In 1838 appeared the first part of the "Flora of North America," which he edited conjointly with Dr. John Torrey of New York. The work was, however, not completed, for by the time it had reached the end of "Compositæ" its authors were so overwhelmed with materials which rapidly accumulated that their time was occupied in studying and classifying the specimens, and it was then evident that so many additions would be needed to the portion already gone over that an appendix would embrace more space than the original text itself. Instead, therefore, of continuing the "Flora of North America," its authors published from time to time, conjointly and separately, a series of memoirs, among which the following, by Professor Gray, are noticeable: "Plantæ Lindheimeranæ"—giving a description of the plants collected by F. Lindheimer in Western Texas; in which work Dr. Gray was aided by Dr. Geo. Engelmann; "Plantæ Fendlerianæ"—a description of plants collected by Aug. Fendler, in New Mexico; "Plantæ Wrightianæ Texano-Neo-Mexicanæ"—describing the extensive collection of Charles Wright, A.M.; "Plantæ Thurberianæ," etc. During the past few years, however, the materials which had been collected and elaborated for so many years had approached such a state of completeness that the author felt warranted to proceed with the work. Accordingly he published the first volume of a "Synoptical Flora of the U.S.," which begins where the former work left off, and which, when completed, will be followed by a revised edition of the preceding portion.

In 1848 appeared the first volume of "Genera Floræ Americæ Boreali-Orientalis Illustrata," more commonly known as "Gray's Genera." The object of this work was to give one or more species of each genus of North American plants, with accurate analyses. Only two volumes, however, were issued, owing to reasons similar to those which arrested the publication of the "Flora."

Dr. Gray is the author of two volumes containing descriptions of all the plants collected during the years 1838 to 1842 by the Expedition of Commodore Charles Wilkes, except the specimens gathered on our Pacific coast. This is the most voluminous and, in many respects, his most important contribution to botanical literature.

As early as 1836 appeared the "Elements of Botany," which grew into the "Structural and Systematic Botany," and later became the "Botanical Text-Book" of the present day. This is acknowledged to be one of the best and most practical exponents of vegetable physiology in existence, and has rendered other works on this subject in this country almost superfluous. Another of his important works is the "Manual of the Botany of the Northern United States," which first appeared in 1848, and has already gone through several editions.

In 1859 he published a work on the "Relations of the Japanese Flora to those of North America," which, he thought, did more to give him a reputation abroad than any other single production.

Not less valuable, in a broad sense, are writings adapted to popular use and even to the comprehension of children. In works of this class Professor Gray may almost be said to have been the pioneer, and his "First Lessons," "How Plants Grow," and "How Plants Behave," are widely known and well appreciated.

Numerous contributions have been made by him to the columns of the *American Journal of Science and Arts*, of which he has long been one of the editors; while others, on subjects not alway connected with botany, have appeared in the *North American Review* and other magazines.

His own summary of his religious and scientific beliefs was thus expressed: "I am scientifically, and in my own fashion, a Darwinian, philosophically a convinced theist, and religiously an accepter of the creed commonly known as the Nicene, as the exponent of the Christian faith."

For many years Professor Gray held the office of President of the American Academy of Science and Arts, and in 1872 he was President of the American Association for the Advancement of Science, and at the semi-centennial celebration of the University of Michigan, in the summer of 1887, the degree of LL.D. was conferred upon him. For many years he was accustomed to contribute to the *American Journal of Science and Arts* a necrology of the botanists who had died during the preceding year; and at the time of his own death he left on his writing table the unfinished necrology for 1887.

Utilization of Waste Products.

(Concluded from page 20.)

In treating coal-tar, the first process is one of distillation, the liquid products of the operation being collected in separate fractions. Evidently the constituents of low boiling point will be the first to distil, and, by repeating the distillation, and increasing the number of fractions in which the product is collected, a very fair separation of many of the constituents of coal-tar can be effected. As will be seen on reference to Nickel's coal-tar tree, the first fraction obtained by the distillation of coal-tar is known as "first runnings," and this is followed by the "light oils." From these fractions are obtained a number of interesting products, the chief among which is the liquid hydrocarbon known as benzol or benzene. This must not be confounded with the product commercially known as "benzoline," which is a naphtha obtained by somewhat similar means from petroleum, and is quite different in chemical character. From benzene and its immediate homologues is obtained nitrobenzene—a body which, from its odor, has been inaccurately termed "artificial oil of bitter almonds," and which finds a large application in the scenting of soap, etc. By appropriate treatment, this nitrobenzene is converted into aniline, the starting point of the numerous coloring-matters familiarly known as the "aniline dyes"—a term which is sometimes incorrectly extended to include all the other colored products obtainable from coal-tar. Benzene—through aniline—is also the starting point of many of the so-called azo-dyes, which yield the magnificent yellows, oranges, and browns which have of late been so popular, while azo-reds are derived from the constituents of coal-tar known as xylene and naphthalene.

The next product of the primary distillation of coal-tar is the "carbolic oils," so called from their most important ingredient being the well-known carbolic acid or phenol, to the antiseptic characters of which we owe the stamping-out of the cattle plague, and the rendering practical the antiseptic treatment of disease. But carbolic acid is itself the starting point of an important series of artificial products. Thus it yields salicylic acid, which in its medicinal uses is scarcely less important than carbolic acid itself. By treatment with nitric acid it yields picric acid, extensively used as a yellow dye, but far more largely employed as the basis of the French explosive "mélinite." The coloring matter, known as aurin, and the products, known as the cosin dyes, are also remotely allied to carbolic acid. One of these bodies, called fluorescein, has but little dyeing power, but in solution exhibits a fluorescence or "bloom" to an almost incredible extent. Those who have observed the wonderful fluorescent fountain (exhibited by Mr. I. Levinstein in the Chemical Department of the Manchester Exhibition), the water of which is colorless, but exhibits a brilliant yellowish-green fluorescence, will be interested to know that the effect is produced by ordinary water containing 1 part per 1,000,000 of fluorescein.

Another of the leading constituents occurring ready formed in coal-tar is a hydrocarbon called naphthalene, now familiar in the form of white candle-like cylinders, and used in the production of the albo-carbon light. In

Sheffield, the choking of the gas mains by deposits of naphthalene has recently brought home to us in a striking manner the property possessed by this hydrocarbon of volatilizing at the ordinary temperature.

The higher fractions obtained by the distillation of coal-tar yield anthracene, which is the starting-point of alizarin and its analogues already mentioned, but a large proportion of this part of coal-tar must still be regarded as practically unutilized.

The pitch, which is obtained as a residue from the distillation of the tar, receives extensive applications, with which you are all familiar.

It is a lamentable fact that, notwithstanding the enormous amount of talent and ingenuity devoted to the manufacture of coal-tar products, and the immense capital invested in their production, the whole industry is now languishing in the gravest manner, and there are not wanting leading men who advocate the simple burning of much of the tar as a means of getting rid of it, seeing that its treatment cannot now be profitably conducted. Of late years several very large works have been established, not for the purpose of producing coal gas and, therefore, obtaining the tar products as one of the residuals, but for the express purpose of obtaining tar, and these works have thrown so much benzol and other primary tar products on the market as very gravely to affect the industry. To make matters worse for those interested, the ammonia, which is another of the residuals produced in the manufacture of illuminating gas, has now fallen enormously in value, the market price of sulphate of ammonia being now about £11 10s. per ton, while a few years ago it realized £22 per ton. This fall is largely due to the production of ammonia from the waste gases of blast furnaces consuming bituminous coal. This is done in Scotland to a very large extent, and Messrs. Baird & Company, at the Gartsherrie Iron Works, and the Eglinton Iron Company, at the Lugar Iron Works, two firms which are really identical, now produce an enormous quantity of sulphate of ammonia from their blast furnace gases. Another product of the cooling of this gas is a kind of tar. This differs from ordinary gas-works tar in very important respects. It yields practically no benzol, naphthalene, or anthracene, and the carbolic acid of ordinary coal-tar is represented by the analogous substance creasylic acid, together with products having an analogy to those characteristic of wood-tar. The substance known as creasote, a word which signifies "flesh preserver," was originally obtained by Reichenbach from wood-tar, and when carbolic acid was discovered by Runge in coal-tar, it was for a long time confounded with this product, and received the name "coal-tar creasote." It is probable that the antiseptic properties of carbolic acid itself would not have received such widespread and prompt recognition, but for its confusion with the original wood-tar creasote.

Under a patent I have recently obtained in conjunction with Mr. Angus, one of the partners of the Eglinton Iron Co., the constituents of blast-furnace tar, analogous to carbolic acid and wood creasote, are now about to be produced on a large scale, and will be known in commerce as "neosote," a name which signifies "new preserver" or "new preservative," and may serve to indicate the similarity of the article to creasote. It is one of the advantages of the production of this neosote that its extraction from the tar renders the residual tar or oil more suited for its application to the production of the "lucigen" and "luminator" lights. These new lights consume any cheap kind of oil, and are fed with a blast of air. One of them is now on exhibition at the Crystal Palace, and in other instances where it is used, I am informed, it is found highly successful.

It is not so long ago that blast-furnace gases were allowed to burn freely at the mouths of the furnaces, and the utilization of them for heating the boilers and blast was a distinct advance. With furnaces consuming coke, this is all that can be done, but the successful utilization of the tar and ammonia condensable from furnaces consuming bituminous coal is a further step of great practical importance.

But while interesting ourselves in the utilization of gases, we must not forget the enormous quantities of slag which form another secondary product of the reaction in the blast furnace. It is calculated by Mr. Charles Wood, of Middlesbrough, that twenty-five cwt. of blast-furnace slag is produced for every ton of pig iron obtained, which in the year of 1881 would mean a production of 8,000,000 tons of slag. The space occupied by this mass would, when loosely tipped, be nearly twice that of the great pyramid, while the bulk of the pig iron would only be about one-sixth of the size of the pyramid. The enormous quantity of this material produced has doubtless stood in the way of its utilization, and where, as in Northamptonshire, there is a constant demand for it for road making purposes at a fairly remunerative rate, there is not much encouragement to go further with it; but at Middlesbrough, it has been found of great service in the construction of the breakwater at the mouth of the Tees, for which purpose about half a million tons of slag are used annually, and a similar class of work is being conducted near Barrow with the slag from the hematite furnaces,

which, however, is less suited for the purpose. The slag used at the Tees breakwater is run from the furnaces into square iron wagons, in which it solidifies, to form blocks weighing about 3¼ tons each. By running the molten slag on to a revolving iron table, Mr. Wood converts it into "slag-shingle," which is found to be most valuable for the manufacture of concrete, and is extensively used for this purpose in connection with the Tees breakwater. By suitable means the slag is also reduced to a condition of sand, and, when mixed with lime, this forms a hydraulic cement which hardens in a perfect manner. Bricks made in this way require no burning, and are found to stand very well. In consequence of the dock extension, however, the works where the slag bricks were made has been purchased by the railway company, and so the process is temporarily suspended, but somewhat about 200,000,000 bricks have been manufactured. By projecting a blast of steam across molten slag in the act of falling, the slag becomes converted into globules, and these are drawn out into long threads of an extremely delicate character. The slag in this form is almost pure white in color, and has much the general appearance of cotton-wool, but it has not the same elasticity, and once crushed will not recover itself. Mr. Wood informs me that the slag wool is now being manufactured at the rate of 15 to 20 tons per week. It is used as a non-conducting material for covering boilers and so forth; and to put under flooring to deaden the sound. At the works of the Brittain Glass Company, in Northamptonshire, blast-furnace slag is run in a molten state into a glass furnace heated by Siemen's gas, and is there mixed with about its own weight of sand and alkali, and made into glass. The slag ornaments, which are familiar to all, are another product of a similar kind.

But blast-furnace slag is not the only slag which has lately been utilized. In Sheffield, we all know that, till recently, the only pig-iron fit for use in the Bessemer process was that which contained but a very small proportion of phosphorus. The Cleveland iron, in which phosphorus is present to an extent between one and two per cent, was utterly unfit for the purpose; but with the basic process, devised by Thomas and Gilchrist, the presence of phosphorus, so far from being an objection, is, within limits, rather an advantage. This has shifted the center of gravity of the heavy steel trade to Middlesbrough, where, under the management of my friend, Mr. Arthur Cooper, the North Eastern Steel Company have established extensive works for producing steel by the basic process. The slag which results from this operation contains a considerable quantity of phosphate of lime, and a number of ingenious processes have been devised for recovering this in a comparatively pure state. It is now found, however, that, if sufficiently finely ground, and freed from the minute particles of metallic iron disseminated through it, the slag is at once suitable for use as a manure. At the North Eastern Steel Company's works, they are making from eight hundred to one thousand tons per week of the slag, and have just erected a large mill for grinding this into powder. They have already shipped upwards of sixty thousand tons of the raw slag to Germany. There is no doubt of the valuable character of basic slag as a manure, but farmers may be excused for being somewhat sceptical of the value of many of the materials offered them, as it seems to be held by many of their professed friends that anything which is good for nothing else is sure to be suitable for manure. Of course, there was a basis of truth in the manurial value attached to sewage, but it is now well known that the practical value was greatly overestimated, and that those responsible for the disposal of the sewage must be content to get rid of it with as little expense as possible, and not dream of making a profit.

Another waste product which is deservedly appreciated as a manure consists in the sweepings and combings from woollen manufacturies, known as "shoddy." Formerly this was applied to the land in the raw state. The grease with which it was saturated acted as a preservative, and therefore detracted from its value as a manure, but no one would now think of neglecting to extract the grease from the wool before employing it on the land. The recovered grease is now recognized as a valuable secondary product, and, when purified, the stearin or solid portion makes its appearance in the form of night-lights, and the olein or liquid part goes back to the woollen manufacturers to be used again.

In the manufacture of soap, glycerin is produced in enormous quantities as a secondary product. Of the two chief processes of treating fats, one produces good glycerin, but inferior soap, and the other produces good soap, but inferior glycerin. The quantity of glycerin hitherto thrown away in the soap-leys has been something enormous, but now much of it is recovered. Thus, at the works of Messrs. Gossage, at Widnes—the largest soap works in the world—the soap-leys are boiled down, the salt separated, and the concentrated liquid distilled, whereby glycerin is obtained, which receives an enormous application in the manufacture of nitroglycerin. This, when soaked up in about one-third of its weight of a porous earth, called kieselguhr, forms the well-known explosive, dynamite, which is produced in one single works to the extent of several tons per day. The glycerin produced from the waste soap-leys at Messrs. Gossage's works was often found unsuitable for its intended purpose, in consequence of containing sulphocyanides and other cyanogen compounds. By a process patented by myself and Mr. Benjamin Nickels these products are wholly removed from the soap-leys, and thus a glycerin can be obtained from the impure source employed at Widnes as good in quality as that of any other origin. Curiously enough, this process, which has been now successfully at work at Widnes for some time, will shortly become unnecessary, owing to the introduction of an improved process of preparing the alkali used for saponifying the fat. By this process, due to Mathieson and Hawliczek, it will be freed from the objectionable sulphur and cyanogen compounds which hitherto had passed into the glycerin. At the same time the cyanogen compounds are destroyed, they will be converted into the useful form of ammonia. Truly, "the whirligig of time brings round its revenges."

MECHANICAL MORTARS.

The firm of Beyer Frères, of Paris (Rue de Lorraine 16–18), manufactures an apparatus consisting of one or more mortars provided with a mechanical pestle for contusing and grinding tough substances. The lower ends of the pestles are of steel, and have a sort of star anise shape, at least at the lower surface. They are raised by arms which release them when they are drawn up to their full height. During each lifting, they make a partial revolution around their axis so that the surface of the pestle never strikes the contents of the mortar exactly in the same place. To prevent the escape of dust, cloth or leather is tied over the mortar during the operation. If desired, the mortars themselves may be so arranged that they will gradually revolve during the operation, but under ordinary circumstances this is not advisable, as it increases the cost of the apparatus without material increase of its efficacy.—Dr. St. Mierzinski in "*Die Riechstoffe*" (Weimar, 1888).

Iodine Trichloride as an Antiseptic.

STILL another iodine compound has been brought forward as a disinfectant and antiseptic, but this time it is the application rather than the substance that presents the character of novelty, the trichloride of iodine (ICl_3) being one of the best known of the reputed compounds of the two halogens. It can be prepared by direct combination of the elements, in passing an excess of dry chlorine gas over moderately warm iodine; if the chlorine be not in excess, the monochloride is formed. It is also formed upon mixing iodic acid with strong hydrochloric acid, or by the action of phosphoric chloride (PCl_5) on iodic anhydride (I_2O_5). But the most convenient method of preparing it is said to be (*Pharm. Zeit.*, Dec. 3d, p. 692), to pass a full current of chlorine through wide tubes into a three-necked flask into which also iodine is sublimed from a small retort fitted to the centre neck. The iodine trichloride is formed in delicate orange-yellow crystals, which, if contaminated with the liquid monochloride, are somewhat darker colored. The compound which consists of 54.39 per cent by weight of iodine and 45.61 per cent of chlorine, has a penetrating, pungent smell, somewhat like that of bromine, and melts at 25° C. with loss of chlorine. In water it is tolerably freely soluble, the solution being pale yellow, strongly acid, and less strongly smelling than the dry preparation. It is also soluble in ether and in alcohol, but the alcoholic solution appears to undergo alteration even in the cold. This is more apparent upon warming a small quantity of the alcoholic solution and leaving it to evaporate spontaneously, chloral being left as a residue, recognisable by its characteristic odor. The behavior of the compound towards strong bases shows that the chlorine first enters into reaction. Aqueous solutions keep better the more concentrated they are; weak solutions undergo gradual decomposition, with the formation of hydrochloric and iodic acids and monochloride of iodine, the change being promoted by the action of direct light. According to Professor von Langenbuch the germicide action of iodine trichloride exceeds that of carbolic acid by far, and approaches that of mercuric chloride, over which the compound has the advantage of being relatively non-poisonous. He recommends the use of an aqueous solution of the strength of 1 in 1,000 to 1 in 1,500, as a substitute for a 4-per-cent carbolic acid solution, or a 1 in 1,000 to 2,000 sublimate solution, for the disinfection of the hands, instruments, or wounds. The slight yellow discoloration caused to the skin can be easily removed by means of ammonia or sodium thiosulphate (hyposulphite) solution. Further, he recommends a solution of 1 in 1,200 as an injection for gonorrhœa, or as an internal remedy for dyspepsia dependent upon the presence of bacteria, the dose in the latter case being a teaspoonful every two hours.—*Pharm. Journ.*

Zanzibar Cloves.

AN Australian traveller, Baron von Nagy Rako, in an article on the commercial importance of Zanzibar and the Somali coast, published recently in the Handels-Museum, gives some particulars on the cultivation of cloves in Zanzibar. He observes that the culture of this spice is the only one to which any particular attention has been paid by the Arab landed proprietors, and which they conduct upon rational principles. A large clove plantation contains from 10,000 to 15,000 trees, laid out in regular avenues. From 120 to 130 hands are required to attend to a plantation of this size. The Arabs employ only slave labor, thereby rendering European competition, which would entail the employment of free laborers, almost impossible. On the island of Pemba, there is a single plantation of 10,000 trees, owned by a European, a Frenchman, named Coltoni; but it is said that he is about to withdraw from the cultivation, finding it no

Sifting machine.

longer profitable. The buds are gathered with the branches, which are broken off from the tree by hand; the cloves are then taken from the twigs, sorted, separated into two qualities, spread out and dried. Only a few spots on the island of Zanzibar and Pemba (an island north of Zanzibar) are suitable for the cultivation of cloves, and all attempts to grow them in neighboring parts have failed. In quality the Zanzibar cloves are superior to those grown in Pemba, but the production in the latter island is still about three times larger. The largest and best crop is gathered shortly after the rainy season; a second, but smaller and of inferior quality, is harvested a few months after the first.—*Chem. and Drugg.*

A SIFTING MACHINE.

THE operation of sifting can be greatly accelerated in many cases by employing the apparatus here illustrated or constructed on the same principle. This has open sieves, sitting in frames which are intended to receive the sifted powder. Of course, the substance to be sifted in these cases must not have the tendency to throw out fine dust. But, if the sieves are suitably covered, they may be used even for such purposes. As will be seen by examining the illustration, the sieves rest upon a frame-work to which a shaking motion is imparted by the lateral rod hung upon an eccentric.*

---

* After *Mierzinski; Die Riechstoffe.* Weimar, 1888.

BALL-MILL.

Many substances, particularly those which are hard and brittle, may be reduced to powder by inclosing them in rapidly revolving drums containing one or more iron balls. Such a mill is illustrated in the accompanying cut. The drum is mounted upon an oblique axis, running upon a journal made of phosphorus bronze, and is inclosed by a flattened globular steel mantle. The mounting and whole action of the machine is very simple and effective. When the drum is set in motion, the iron ball or balls, rolling and thrown about, cause the substance inclosed in the drum and mantle to be gradually reduced to a uniform powder.*

A RAPID INFUSION APPARATUS.

The infusion apparatus shown in the cut is an improved form of one previously proposed by Mr. Muerrle, of Pforzheim, Germany.

The illustration shows the apparatus in section. At a, there is a funnel-shaped opening, for filling water into the reservoir b, which is situated altogether on the outside of the apparatus. By the tube c, the reservoir communicates with the boiler d, which is placed at such a height that only a small quantity of water can be contained in it at any time. The steam surrounds the infusion vessel e, and after being condensed by passing through to the tube f, returns again to the reservoir.—After *Pharm. Zeit.*, 1887, 651.

Marking Inks.

The following practical information is taken from one of the most recently published numbers of Karmarsch & Heeren's "Technisches Wörterbuch" (Vol. IX., 496).

1. *Silver Marking Ink.*—2 parts of nitrate of silver are dissolved in 20 parts of distilled water, and mixed with a sufficient quantity of mucilage of gum arabic containing

Ball mill.

lampblack (about 1 part of lampblack for every 2 parts of gum arabic contained in the mucilage). The fabric upon which this ink is to be applied must first be prepared so that it may present a smooth surface, and to prevent the capillary dispersion of the liquid. For this purpose, the place which is to be written upon is first saturated with a strong mucilage of starch or of gum arabic, then dried and smoothened with a hot iron. This is done not only in the case of silver marking ink, but also when others are to be used. If the ink, which is to be applied, has an acid reaction, which is the case when nitrate of silver is used, a little carbonate of sodium (about 1 part for every 10 of mucilage) is added to the mordant. For writing, horn- or quill-pens are to be used, and the writing should be allowed first to dry slowly, after which it is to be exposed to direct sun-light, which causes a gradual production of a black color by decomposing the nitrate to metallic silver and suboxide of silver. These latter adhere to the fibre so tenaciously that they will resist washing a long time.

In place of a simple solution of nitrate of silver, one of the ammonio-nitrate may be used, and, in that case, the addition of soda to the fabric is unnecessary. Good proportions are the following: Dissolve 6 parts of nitrate of silver in 15 parts of distilled water; add 8 parts of carbonate of sodium, and afterwards some water of ammonia, in drops, until the precipitate caused by the carbonate of sodium is redissolved. Finally, 6 parts of mucilage are added. Writing made with this ink becomes quickly black on drying and exposure to light.

* From *Miersinski: Die Riechstoffe*. Weimar, 1888.

Another method is, to dissolve chloride of silver in water of ammonia, and to add some mucilage. This ink is applied the same as those before described, upon the previously-mordanted fabric. The addition of lampblack has no other object but to color the fluid so that the writing can be seen while fresh. Any other color, such as indigo or carmine, may be substituted for it.

2. *Gold Marking Ink.*—On using a solution of chloride of gold, in place of one of nitrate of silver, red marks may be produced, instead of black. The so-called "Italian Marking Ink" is prepared in the following manner: 1 part of chloride of gold, or better, chloride of gold and sodium, is dissolved in 10 parts of water, and when the solution is to be used, a small portion of it is mixed, just previously to being employed, with an equal quantity of mucilage. Quill-pens are used for writing, and the fabric is to be previously mordanted with a solution of 1 part of stannous chloride and 10 parts of gum arabic in 100 parts of water, then dried and ironed. After the ink has been

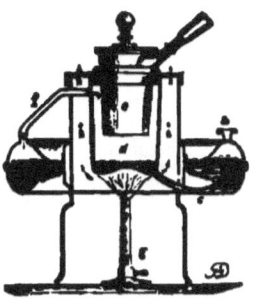

Muerrle's infusion apparatus.

applied, the fabric is exposed to a gentle heat, and after the writing has assumed a handsome red color, the place is repeatedly washed with water.

Another way is to write with a solution of chloride of gold upon the fabric, previously impregnated with some starch and then ironed. On exposing the writing to the sun-light, it will gradually assume a purple color.

3. *Platinum Marking Ink.*—If a solution of platinum chloride be substituted for silver or gold salts, the marks or writing will show a black or blackish-gray color. The marking ink is made by dissolving (1 part of) platinic chloride in (10 parts of) water and adding a little mucilage. The place to be marked must previously be treated with a little solution of stannous chloride and gum arabic. After the writing is made, the fabric is gently heated, when the marks will assume a black or blackish color.

4. *Osmium Marking Ink.*—On writing, upon a fabric, with a dilute solution of osmic acid in water, 1 part in 50, the marks will soon assume an intense dark-blue color, and will be found to be very permanent. The osmic acid solution must be quite dilute, because stronger solutions are apt to destroy the fabric itself, and the latter must be previously mordanted and ironed. Quill-pens or gold-pens should be used for writing.

5. *Aniline Black Marking Ink.*—One of the most indelible marking inks, resisting both acids and alkalies, is the so-called aniline-black.

Make a solution of 4 parts of hydrochlorate of aniline, and 10 parts of gum arabic, in 10 parts of glycerin and 40 parts of water. And another solution of 15 parts of chloride of copper, 10 parts of chloride of ammonium, 20 parts of chlorate of sodium (*not* the chloride), in 100 parts of water. Just before use, mix a sufficient quantity of the two solutions, using 1 part of the second for every 5 parts of the first-named. The writing is applied to the unsized fabric, and the latter then exposed to steam for some time. [It is preferable to hang up the fabrics in a room which is heated to a temperature of 25° to 30° C. (77° to 86° F.), and to leave them there for several days until the marks turn black. Afterwards they should be washed with a solution of soda (1 in 280), then dried.]

A new Deodorant for Iodoform.—Several months ago, Mr. H. Helbing (*Arch. d. Pharm.*) reported that the ethereal oil of *Evodia fraxinifolia*, a rutaceous plant of middle Asia, possessed the remarkable property of completely masking the odor of iodoform, not only causing that of the latter to disappear, but even its own.

We are informed that steps have been taken by a large manufacturing firm of essential oils to procure supplies of the above oil.

Notes on Ethereal Oils.*

1. *Nature and Occurrence.* —The aroma of plants is, in most cases, due to the presence of strongly odorous constituents, which are termed ethereal (or essential, or volatile) oils if they are liquid, and stearoptens or camphors if they are solid. The latter are always crystallizable, though many of them are odorless and tasteless.

The leaves, barks, and seeds of many plants from the families of Pomeæ and Pruneæ (Amygdaleæ), which, of themselves, are colorless, furnish, when they are comminuted and macerated in cold water, a peculiar, strongly smelling mixture of benzaldehyde and hydrocyanic acid, which is commonly designated as oil of cherry laurel or of bitter almond. Mustard seed, which is likewise colorless, furnishes oil of mustard only after a splitting up of the sinigrin. It would, therefore, be quite proper to exclude these liquids from the class of ethereal oils.

This convenient term cannot be sharply defined. With the exception of oil of mustard, probably all other so-called ethereal oils are likewise mixtures of several compounds. In some plants, as, for instance, in cinnamon, various species of citrus, members of the pine and labiate family, the oils derived from different organs of one and the same plant are not identical.

Most ethereal oils are known to possess an agreeable odor. In some cases, however, this may be declared without doubt as repulsive. Among the plants which diffuse a disagreeable odor when their leaves are crushed, may be quoted as examples: several species of Ferula, Melianthus, Eucalyptus pendula, Allium and Umbellularia (Oreodaphne) californica. Many flowers, f. i., those of Ailanthus glandulosa, Ceratonia Siliqua, Cratægus, and also some kinds of wood, likewise exhale bad odors.

From the class of cryptogama, only few of which have an aroma, no ethereal oil has so far been made known. There are also some phanerogamic families, as the Palms, the Polygonaceæ, Malvaceæ, Gentianaceæ, and Liguliforæ (among the Compositæ), which do not yield ethereal oils. On the other hand, certain other families are remarkable through their great richness, f. i., the Abietineæ, Zingiberaceæ, Piperaceæ, Myrtaceæ, Laurineæ, Dipterocarpaceæ, Rutaceæ, Umbelliferæ, Labiatæ, and some sections of Compositæ. Very large quantities of ethereal oils are likewise produced by the numerous eucalyptus trees of Australia, and the species of citrus of Southern Europe and India.

It is generally possible to distinguish special receptacles in or upon the different organs of plants which contain the ethereal oils. In the first eight among the above-mentioned families, for instance, these receptacles lie in the inner cellular tissue. In the Labiatæ, however, and also in many Compositæ, they are situated as scales or pediculated glands upon the epidermis.

In the tissue of sandal wood (from Santalum album and other species), which contains considerable of oil, no special oil receptacles are found. And in many plants yielding only minute quantities of oil, such as the flowers of Rosa, Sambucus, Tilia, etc., the domicile of the ethereal oil has not been made out.

The largest proportion of ethereal oils is afforded by the so-called balsams and turpentines (which are mixtures of resin and ethereal oil), also by gum-resins. Very rich in oil are also cloves, caraway, and other umbelliferous seeds, and the rinds of lemons.

The animal kingdom does not afford any ethereal oil.

2. *Preparation.* —Though the boiling points of the compounds belonging to this class (excepting abietene) is considerably higher than 100° C., they are nevertheless abundantly volatilized with steam, and are mostly obtained by distillation with water. But in the case of species of citrus, it is sometimes preferred to extract the oil, from the cells which contain it, by pressure, because the delicacy of the aroma is injured through distillation.

The preparation of essential oils is often carried out with the most simple contrivances, when small quantities are to be prepared, or when the crude material is to be worked up at once at the place of growth. . . . In large factories, the manufacture of the ethereal oils is carried on, with the aid of steam, on the largest scale with utilisation of every available technical invention. Recently, vacuum apparatus is also employed, so as to extract the oils with the least possible alteration.

During the distillation of ethereal oils it happens sometimes that fatty acids pass over. So, for instance, in the case of that of laurel, nutmeg, orris, capsicum, and tea. The small quantities of these fatty acids may possibly be derived from compound ethers (esters), either through the decomposition, by the boiling water, of fats existing in the plant, or due to the presence of esters belonging to the series of monatomic alcohols, which pass over along with the ethereal oils. When such esters are decomposed in the course of the distillation or rectification, the oil, which was previously neutral, acquires an acid reaction, as, for instance, oil of valerian, etc.

---
* Translated, and partly abstracted, from the second, enlarged edition of Prof. F. A. Flueckiger's *Pharmaceutische Chemie*, 2 vols., 8vo, Berlin (Gaertner), 1888. The work is kept in stock by O. E. Biechert or B. Westermann & Co., of New York.

Otherwise, the development of acids in ethereal oils is due to gradual oxidation by exposure to air. This occurs most prominently in oil of cinnamon.

The oils which are obtained by pressing, at least oil of bergamot, contain minute proportions of chlorophyll.

3. *Properties.* —Odor and taste of the ethereal oils correspond to the aroma of the plants from which they are obtained, though often with some difference.

The stearoptens are colorless, likewise a large majority of ethereal oils. But many of them, when freshly prepared or after being exposed for some time to the air, present a yellowish, brownish, or deep-brown color, and can be rendered colorless by rectification. Some oils have a peculiar more or less pure bluish-green tint, often covered by a brown one ; for instance, the oils of Artemisia Absinthium, Achillea Millefolium, Achillea moschata, Calamus root, Chamomile flowers, Arnica flowers and root, the root of Asarum Canadense and Asarum Europæum, Caraway seeds, Cascarilla bark, etc.

Blue oils are obtained by distilling the following drugs or their oils : Sumbul root, German chamomile, pichury seed, patchouli herb, valerian root, etc., etc. The North American sage brush (*Artemisia Ludoriciana* Nutt. †) likewise yields a fine specimen of oil belonging to this class.

When such oils are rectified, the first fractions coming over are colorless, the next are brownish, then greenish, and finally, in most cases, deep-blue, which are often again followed by less deeply colored drops. . . . This magnificent blue color is afforded particularly, and from the very beginning, by the oil of German chamomile (Matricaria), . . . and still more so by empyreumatic oils obtained by the dry distillation of asafœtida, galbanum, and sumbul root. These blue oils are probably identical with each other.

Certain green oils derive their color from chlorophyll, particularly oil of bergamot.

A fine yellow color is characteristic of oil of turmeric.

A few ethereal oils are fluorescent, for instance, that of sage, neroli, etc. The most magnificent fluorescence is produced in oil of peppermint, if it is shaken with glacial acetic and nitric acid. . . .

Ethereal oils possess different degrees of fluidity. While most of them are very mobile, others are viscid, particularly those which correspond to the composition $C_{10}H_{16}$ or $C_{10}H_{10}$, but not those of the formula $C_{10}H_{18}$. Among the more viscid oils are oil of copaiba, cubebs, poplar buds, pepper, olibanum, sandal wood, and the specifically lighter portion of oil of cloves. The residues remaining after the rectification of many ethereal oils are likewise quite viscid and appear to be formed by polymerization, that is, by the coalition of several molecules.

Most ethereal oils attack cork-stoppers, and bleach the latter through the formation of ozone.

The specific gravity of the large number of ethereal oils of the composition $C_{10}H_{16}$ and its multiples is less than that of water, and varies between 0.850 and 0.940. Some of the naturally occurring oxygenated oils possess a higher spec. gravity than water, as the oil of Asarum Europæum (1.018), oil of cloves, cinnamon, and sassafras. The oil of parsley fruit splits at 15° C. into a lighter portion floating upon water, and into a heavier portion (sp. gr. 1.140) sinking to the bottom. Oil of arnica root sinks in water between 0° and 15° C., and floats upon warmer water. Heavier than water are likewise the oils of Hyssopus officinalis and of Mentha Pulegium ; so also oil of mustard, bitter almond, and gaultheria.

Very many oils are mixtures of hydrocarbons with oxygenated portions. The latter always have a higher specific gravity, the determination of which is of practical importance, because the oxygenated portion is, in all cases, the real bearer of the valuable properties (particularly of the odor) of the oil. Carvol is the desirable portion of oil of caraway, having the spec. gr. 0.960. The finest oil of peppermint, richest in menthol, has the spec. gr. 0.920. Where the manufacturer removes the hydrocarbons of the ethereal oils, the latter become very materially improved in aroma and rendered more concentrated in valuable constituents. In such oils, the specific gravity itself serves as a criterion ; the nearer to 0.960 an oil of caraway is, or the nearer to 0.920 an oil of peppermint, the more valuable will it prove to be. . . . [The portion now following, relating to melting and boiling point, polarization is for the present omitted.]

Ethereal oils are miscible with a large number of liquids in any desired proportion. For instance, with anhydrous alcohols, esters, many organic acids, ether, chloroform, acetone, carbon disulphide, etc. But there is a considerable difference in the behavior of the non-oxygenated and the oxygenated portion of an ethereal oil towards alcohol. The latter, even when considerably diluted with water, can dissolve very notable quantities of the oxygenated portions of oils. The hydrocarbons, however, particularly those of high boiling point, often require several times their volume of alcohol (sp. gr. 0.850) to produce a clear solution. It must be remembered that freshly distilled oils behave different from older, resinified oils, which latter are more easily soluble in alcohol.*

4. *Composition of Ethereal Oils.* —Many ethereal oils

have the ultimate composition represented by the formula C_nH_n, but their vapor densities, and some other observations render it probable that some of them are constructed after the formula C_nH_n, and others again after the formula C_nH_n, or C_nH_n; some of them are mixtures of these hydrocarbons. Most ethereal oils belonging here are attacked by metallic sodium, and are therefore apparently accompanied by oxygenated oils, which are no doubt often present only in minute quantities. Curiously enough, the formula C_nH_n belongs also to gutta-percha, caoutchouc, and that portion of damar resin which is soluble in absolute alcohol; yet, the molecule of these bodies must be expressed by a multiple of the formula C_nH_n. At a higher temperature, however, they yield the simple compounds, C_nH_n and C_nH_n, of a fluid consistence.

On the other hand, hydrocarbons corresponding to the two last-mentioned formulæ, when exposed to a moderate and protracted heat, are transformed into denser and less volatile, so-called *polymerized* compounds. Polymerization appears to occur, for instance, during the rectification of many ethereal oils, as they leave behind viscid residues. This occurs particularly if they are distilled without steam.

Among the very large number of ethereal oils, which are certainly constituted according to the formula C_nH_n, several groups may be distinguished, especially if the classification is made to include also the *terpenes* which are prepared artificially from naturally occurring oils and resins. The term *terpene* is commonly applied to ethereal oil having the composition C_nH_n. Some of these compounds are solid, melt at 50° C., and boil below 150° C. The liquid terpenes, boiling near 160° C., form only liquid compounds with bromine. On the other hand, a large number of terpenes boiling at about 176° C., when combined with bromine, yield crystals ($C_nH_nBr_2$) melting at 105° C., as, for instance, the hydrocarbons occurring in the oils of species of *Citrus*, of caraway, dill, etc. A number of other terpenes, for instance, those of oil of Levant wormseed (cinene), oil of cajuput, and also those produced by heating caoutchouc, boil between 180° and 182° C., and form crystalline bromine compounds ($C_nH_nBr_2$) having a higher melting point, viz., at 125 C.

The terpenes combine with dry hydrochloric acid gas to crystals having the composition $C_nH_n.HCl$, or $C_nH_n.(HCl)_2$, at the same time assuming a dark color, even if they are kept cold. The acid gas is best prepared by allowing sulphuric acid of spec. grav. 1.840 to flow gradually into hydrochloric acid of spec. gr. 1.170.

Ethereal oils of the composition C_nH_n, or C_nH_n, yield no solid compounds with hydrochloric acid.

Under certain circumstances, probably all ethereal oils of the composition C_nH_n (but not the others having the same percentage composition), combine with 3 molecules of water to a body, which is probably identical in all cases, viz., *terpin*. This occurs also naturally, for instance, in the trunks of *Dryobalanops aromatica* Gaert., also in some Californian pines, and is occasionally deposited by the oil of *Ocimum Basilicum*, L.

Another hydrate, namely, $C_nH_n.OH_2$, is represented by the stearopten of cubebs. From elemi are obtained *amyrin* ($C_nH_n.OH$, and *bryoidin* ($C_nH_n.3OH$). Some oils, as those of rosemary and lemon, and the hydrocarbons of oil of dill and of cajuput, easily yield the above-mentioned crystals (of terpin hydrate); other oils, such as that of elemi and carvene, with greater difficulty. But even in such cases it may be obtained by placing only a thin layer of the oil upon the diluted acid.

[From a subsequent chapter, we insert here the method of preparing *terpin hydrate*: On mixing together, in a capacious flask, at the ordinary indoor temperature, 1 part of nitric acid (sp. gr. 1.200), 2 parts of alcohol (sp. gr. 0.830), 4 of water, and 8 of oil of turpentine, it requires a period of one to two years to convert about 18% of the oil of turpentine into terpin hydrate in form of large, well-developed, and but slightly colored crystals belonging to the monoclinic system. The greater the surface of contact between the oil and the lower aqueous layer, the more rapid is the production of terpin. On pouring a mixture of 1 part of alcohol, 1 of nitric acid, and 4 of oil of turpentine into flat dishes, it requires only a few days to obtain 20% of terpin hydrate from the oil. It is of advantage afterwards to partially neutralize the acid. Strong light, and also heat, retard the formation of the substance.]

Some oils, of the same percentage composition as the terpenes, correspond to the formula C_nH_n, as is shown by their vapor density. The oils of this class also possess a higher specific gravity, a higher boiling point, a lesser degree of miscibility with alcohol, and yield other oxidation products.

Some oils, as those of *Cicuta virosa* L., *Thymus vulgaris* L., *Cuminum Cyminum* L., *Monarda punctata* L., contain also cymene (cymol) which is identical with the same body (cymene) artificially prepared from the oils having the composition C_nH_n. This cymene does not form crystals either with hydrochloric acid or with water; but with fuming sulphuric acid it yields the crystallizable, deliquescent cymene-sulphonic acid $C_nH_n.SO_2OH$.

Besides hydrocarbons of the composition C_nH_n and C_nH_n, oil of rose contains a crystallizable hydrocarbon belonging to the class of paraffins (or saturated hydrocarbons).

Small quantities of such bodies have also been found in the ethereal oils of the orange family and in the fruits of *Heracleum* and *Pastinaca*. The turpentines of the Californian *Abies Sabiniana* Douglas and *Abies Jeffreyi* yield a considerable quantity of a heptane C_7H_{16} of the spec. grav. 0.694. This body, named *abietene*, boils at 98.4° C., has a strong odor of orange, and turns the ray of polarized light to the right.

Many oils are mixtures of hydrocarbons (C_nH_n) with oxygenated oils. The name of the former are usually made to terminate in—*ene* (in German in—*en*), and those of the latter in—*ol*. For instance, oil of caraway consists mainly of

carvene, $C_{10}H_{16}$, and
carvol, $C_{10}H_{14}O$.

oil of thyme, of thymene, and thymol. Hence the body which has been called cymol should be rather named cymene.

The oxygenated oils and stearoptens possess a very varied composition; most of them contain only 1 atom of oxygen; for instance:
$C_4H_{10}O$—menthol.
$C_{10}H_{14}O$—carvol, carvacrol, thymol, myristicol, eucalyptol, cumin alcohol.
$C_{10}H_{16}O$—common camphor, oils of *Mentha Pulegium* and *Artemisia Absinthium*, citronellol (from *Andropogon Nardus* L.); stearopten of the oil of *Chrysanthemum Parthenium* Pers., caryophyllin, inula- (or alant-) camphor, and alantol (or inulol), and urson from *Arctostaphylos* and *Epacris*.
$C_{15}H_{24}O$—Blumea camphor, amber camphor, Borneo camphor. The formula also belongs to the liquid existing in many ethereal oils, sometimes constituting their major portion, for instance in that of oil of wormseed, cajuput, and eucalyptus globulus. This body, named *cineol*, is also probably found in the East Indian lemongrass oil (from species of *Andropogon*), and in the oil of *Ormithopus astericoides* Cassini.
$C_{10}H_{20}O$—menthol, the crystallizable portion of oil of peppermint.
$C_{15}H_{24}O$—the stearopten of oil of matico.
$C_{15}H_{26}O$—the stearopten of oil of patchouly.

The following are richer in oxygen:

$C_{10}H_{16}O_2$—the stearopten of the oil of *Ledum palustre* L.
$C_{10}H_{10}O_3$—saffrol from sassafras.
$C_{12}H_{14}O_2$—cubebin.
$C_{12}H_{14}O_2$—parsley-camphor.
$C_{10}H_{10}O_3$—stearopten from oil of *Primula*.

Only a few oils are aldehydes, in a chemical sense; for instance, oil of bitter almond, $C_6H_5.CHO$. The chief constituents of oil of cinnamon, cumin, and Spiræa likewise belong to this class, which unites with the bisulphites of alkalies to crystalline compounds. Some other ethereal oils, as that of peppermint, ylang-ylang, and citronella, also contain small quantities of aldehydes.

Oil of rue also contains a body yielding a crystalline compound with bisulphites, but this belongs in the class of the ketones....

Alcohols (in a chemical sense, viz., methyl- and ethyl-alcohol) have been met with in the ethereal oils of many umbelliferous fruits, . . . and in some others, compound ethers (esters) are found; for instance, salicylate of methyl in the oil of *Gaultheria procumbens* (etc.). The oils of the fruits of *Heracleum giganteum* and *H. Sphondylium* L. contain a whole series of compound ethers of fatty acids with the hexyl and octyl radicals. . . .

Among the constituents of the oils of *Lepidium sativum* L., and *Tropæolum majus* L., the combination C_6H_5N has been recognized as the nitrile of phenyllactic acid ($C_6H_5.CH_2.COOH$). When boiled with alcoholic potassa, this eliminates ammonia, and hydrochloric acid precipitates phenyllactic acid from the solution. . . .

Isosulphocyanates are represented among the ethereal oils by fractions contained in oil of mustard and Cochlearia, which contain a large percentage of sulphur (like garlic). . . .

Compounds belonging to the class of phenols occur as chief constituents in the oils of anise, staranise, fennel, estragon, cloves, and thyme, and small quantities also in those of calamus and sassafras. At least, fractional distillation is able to separate from these certain portions which are colored violet or green by alcoholic ferric chloride. Very curious is the case with which carvol may be converted into a phenol.

Under the influence of air and light, and also that of heat during distillation, ethereal oils suffer certain changes which are comprised under the name *resinification*. They acquire, thereby, a viscid consistence and finally become quite stiff and almost solid. But the changes occurring during this process have not yet been fully made out. None of the resins thus produced appears to occur in nature. . . .

A NEW APPARATUS FOR ESTIMATING UREA.

Messrs. Cazeneuve and Hugouneng describe, in the *Journ. de Pharm. et de Chim.* (1887, 248), a new apparatus for estimating urea, the principle of which consists in this, that the urine, properly filtered and diluted, is subjected to heat in closed vessels, whereby the urea is converted into carbonate of ammonium which may be estimated volumetrically.

The authors use the apparatus shown in the cut. *A* is a cylindrical copper vessel, the upper part of which contains an oil-bath, likewise made of copper, and heated by a gas-burner or other controllable source of heat. The heat is regulated by the arrangement *R*, which is constructed on the general plan of thermo-regulators, any increase of heat beyond a determined point causing the automatic closure of the main supply of heat, and its automatic re-opening as soon as the temperature begins to fall below the normal point. *T* is a thermometer for controlling the latter. *C* and *T* are two short brass tubes, electro-plated with platinum internally, made strong enough to stand a pressure of 60 atmospheres (900 lbs. per square inch). Their upper portion is provided with a thread, and a shoulder of lead serves as a washer to make the connection absolutely gas-tight, when the cap is screwed on by means of a wrench.

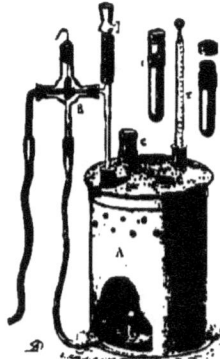

Cazeneuve & Hugouneng's urea apparatus.

The apparatus is used in the following manner: A portion of urine is shaken in a test-tube, holding about 30 C.c., with animal charcoal (not previously washed with acids), and filtered. The urine will pass through of a neutral reaction, and sensibly bleached. In the case of urine loaded with pigment, such as is voided in certain diseases, the treatment by animal charcoal is less effective, but the subsequent alkalimetric estimation is nevertheless exact.

Next, by means of a pipette, exactly 10 C.c. of urine are introduced into the tube *C*, about 20 C.c. of distilled water are added, the cap is carefully screwed on, and the cylinder heated to a temperature of 180° C. (356° F.) for half an hour. The tube is then removed, allowed to cool, the contents then transferred to a beaker, together with the washings, and the liquid titrated with sulphuric acid.

The best indicators to use are either methyl-orange or phenolphthaleine.

The authors recommend to use, for the volumetric test, a sulphuric acid containing 40 Gm. of absolute acid per liter. In this case, it is only necessary to multiply the number of cubic centimeters of acid consumed with 3, in order to obtain the quantity, in grammes, of urea contained in the amount of urine examined.

The authors append a table, comparing the results obtained by this method with those obtained by others. From their figures it appears that the new process yields more accurate results than any other so far proposed.

It might be supposed that the other constituents of the urine would interfere with the results. But this is shown not to be the case. The authors say:

If the urine is colored and acid, the bone black renders it almost colorless and neutralizes the acid. If it contains salts, such as chlorides, sulphates, phosphates, etc., it might be supposed that these would produce a double decomposition with the carbonate of ammonium; but it was found that nothing of the kind occurred so long as the solution was neutral. Regarding other nitrogenous constituents of the urine, it has been shown by Hugouneng that these are not decomposed under these circumstances at all.

If the urine contains glucose, however, the above method is not usually applicable. In such cases, a heat of 180° C. will render the urine dark colored so that a volumetric assay, in the presence of a colored indicator, becomes impossible. If albumin is present in the urine, this must first be removed by nitric acid and heat, the acid then carefully neutralized by soda, and the resulting liquid then tested like normal urine.

Test Papers.

Some practical remarks by Mr. Eugene Dieterich, on the preparation of test-papers, in the *Pharm. Centralhalle*, supplemented by notes of our own, will be of service to some of our readers.*

For preparing test-papers, either blotting or fine writing paper is used. Since all these papers contain more or less free acid which is often distributed very unequally, they should be placed during 24 hours in diluted water of ammonia (1 in 10), then pressed to remove the excess of liquid (or better, washed with water to remove all soluble matters, Ed. Am. Dr.), and then dried by exposure to air. The wet sheets are preferably hung up upon strings or wooden rods.

If blotting paper is to be impregnated, this is done by passing the sheet through the litmus solution, removing the excess of liquid by drawing the paper over a glass rod, and then hanging up to dry.

[*Note by Ed. Am. Dr.*—The most convenient vessels to dip the paper in are flat-bottomed dishes with straight sides, such as photographers use for washing prints. They may be had of agate ware in various sizes, and are very handy for many other purposes. The solution is poured into the tray, which must be adjusted so as to stand level, and the paper, held at both corners of one of its edges, floated upon the liquid, a narrow margin of the edge by which it is held being kept out of the liquid, as it is apt to tear if wholly impregnated. A glass rod is laid across the floating sheet near the line where the impregnation begins, and the paper then gently drawn over the straight edge of the dish. The glass rod keeps the paper submerged, and, drawing the paper over the edge of the dish, removes the excess of liquid. In this manner, litmus paper of any size may be prepared very rapidly, the sheets being impregnated as fast as an assistant can hang them up.

Incidentally, we may remark that the tint of the liquid and of the impregnated paper must be watched during the operation, as it is apt to be affected by acid or alkaline vapors or effluvia, even from the hands of the operators.]

If writing paper is to be treated, this is best done by coating it with the litmus or other test solution on one side only, by means of a brush, and then drying it.

[Even in this case, the plan of floating the paper on the surface of the liquid contained in a flat-bottomed tray with straight sides is preferable, and much more expeditious. The paper must be laid on so that it is held up in form of a trough, the lowest convex portion of which is first brought in contact with the liquid, either side being then gently laid down. The object of this is to exclude air-bubbles. The paper should be laid on so that a narrow margin projects over the straight edge of the tray, by which the sheet is at once drawn forward, as soon as it has become fully flattened out on the surface of the liquid.—Ed. Am. Dr.]

In chemical laboratories, test-papers are usually prepared from blotting paper.

In technical works, however, writing paper is preferred for this purpose. While both are equally sensitive, the writing paper has the advantage that it permits a more exact recognition of the change of color (though this makes its appearance more slowly), because the liquid does not penetrate the fibre of the paper, and the paper therefore acts as a white back-ground to the colored layer. Hence test-papers made from writing paper are especially suitable for testing the reactions of liquids by applying drops with a glass rod.

In order to obtain highly sensitive test-papers, it is absolutely necessary to insure the complete neutralization of any acids that may be present, except when making red litmus paper. Nor should the colored solutions be applied in too concentrated a state, as their sensitiveness diminishes with the concentration, and increases with their dilution.

The highest limit of sensitiveness is best expressed by referring to aqueous dilutions of sulphuric acid or hydrochloric acid on the one hand, and caustic potassa or ammonium on the other hand.

If we say, a test-paper has the limit of sensitiveness at 1 : 30,000 of Sulphuric Acid, this means, that the paper will still detect the acidity of a watery solution containing 1 part of Sulphuric Acid in 30,000 of the liquid.

It is to be noted that the sensitiveness of test-papers is greater towards hydrochloric than towards sulphuric acids, which finds its explanation in the lower molecular weight of the former. The same is the case in its beha-

---

* These are taken from a supplement, issued in instalments to the above-mentioned journal by the *Neue pharmaceutischen Manual*, von Berlin (Springer), which should be in the hands of every pharmacist, as it contains a very large number of practical and useful formulæ.

vior towards ammonia, compared with that of potassa, the former having the lower molecular weight.

1. *Blue Litmus Paper.*

Litmus	80 parts
Phosphoric Acid	q. s.
Distilled Water	to make 1,000 parts

Macerate the Litmus (previously crushed to a coarse powder) with enough Distilled Water to make the liquid, after filtration, amount to 1,000 parts. To this add Phosphoric Acid in drops, until the blue color begins to assume a faintly reddish tint.

Then impregnate paper with the solution, as directed above.

The highest sensitiveness of this test-paper is
1 : 40,000 toward sulphuric acid
1 : 60,000 " hydrochloric acid.
In practice, a sensitiveness of at least
1 : 30,000, and 1 : 45,000
respectively, may, therefore, be demanded.

2. *Red Litmus Paper.*

Litmus	80 parts
Phosphoric Acid	q. s.
Distilled Water	to make 1,000 parts

Macerate the Litmus (previously crushed to a coarse powder) with enough Distilled Water to make the liquid, after filtration, amount to 1,000 parts. To this add the Phosphoric Acid, in drops, until the liquid is decidedly red. Allow the solution to stand twenty-four hours, decant it from the brownish, flocculent precipitate that will have formed, and filter again.

Proceed to impregnate paper with this solution, as directed above.

Limit of sensitiveness:
1 : 10,00 toward potassa
1 : 60,000 " ammonia.
In practice, a lowest limit of 1 : 15,000, and 1 : 45,000 respectively, may, therefore, be demanded.

3. *Azolitmin Paper.*

(Azolitmin is the pure coloring matter of litmus, which is now made for sale by several manufacturers. It costs in Europe about $3.80 per ounce.)

Azolitmin	1 part
Carbonate of Sodium, in crystals	⅓ "
Phosphoric Acid	q. s.
Distilled Water	to make 1,000 parts

Dissolve the Azolitmin and the Carbonate of Sodium in 1,000 parts of Distilled Water, neutralize with Phosphoric Acid, and impregnate paper with the solution as directed above.

This paper undergoes the same changes of color as litmus paper itself.

Limit of sensitiveness:
1 : 40,000 towards sulphuric acid.
1 : 60,000 towards hydrochloric acid.

4. *Turmeric Paper.*

Turmeric, in coarse powder	15 parts
Alcohol	500 "
Distilled Water	500 "

Macerate the Turmeric with 100 parts of the Alcohol during a fortnight. (Or better, reduce the Turmeric to a moderately fine powder, and percolate the 100 parts of Alcohol slowly through it. In this case, the percolate need not be filtered.—ED. AM. DR.) Filter the tincture, and add to it the remainder of the Alcohol and the Water. Impregnate paper with this liquid, as described above.

Limit of sensitiveness:
1 : 15,000 towards potassa.
1 : 40,000 towards ammonia.
In practice, a lowest limit of 1 : 10,000 and 1 : to 30,000, respectively, may be demanded.

5. *Congo Paper.*

Congo-red	1 part
Alcohol	7,500 parts
Distilled Water	2,500 "

Dissolve the Congo-red in the mixed liquids, and impregnate paper with the solution.

Limit of sensitiveness:
1 : 3,000 towards sulphuric acid.
1 : 2,500 towards hydrochloric acid.

(According to this, Congo-red appears to be an exception to other indicators, as it is less sensitive to hydrochloric than sulphuric acid.)

[*Note on Congo-red.*—Congo-red was proposed about two years ago as a good indicator for acids and alkalies (see AM. DRUGG., 1886, 13). At first it was proposed as an indicator for free acids in presence of alum. It is turned *blue* by acids and *red* by alkalies, just the reverse of litmus. Though its sensitiveness is not very great, it may yet be used to advantage in some cases, where the result obtained with litmus paper remains doubtful, owing to the specific color of the liquid to be tested.

Congo red is a name given by the "Aktiengesellschaft für Anilinfabrikation" in Berlin to a product discovered by Paul Boettger, and patented by him on Feb. 27th, 1884. It is prepared from tetrazodiphenylchloride and naphthionic acid. It has the remarkable property of dyeing cotton without requiring a mordant, and has become the starting-point of a large number of new colors of similar properties.—ED. AM. DRUG.]

The Manufacture of Bromide of Potassium.

THE enormous scale upon which the manufacture of potash salts, and of other products derived from the immense mineral deposits of Stassfurt and vicinity is carried on, can scarcely be appreciated without a visit to the locality. Among the many valuable products obtained from this source, *bromine* occupies an important rank, and we shall shortly have occasion to give a more detailed account of the manufacture of this substance, and its general industry. At present we lay before our readers a report on the manufacture of bromide of potassium, based upon practical experience.*

The first step in the process of manufacturing bromide of potassium is the preparation of *bromide of iron.* Crystallised bromide of iron (ferrous bromide) contains 6 molecules of water—$FeBr_2.6H_2O$—and crystallizes in rhombic plates, the solution of which turns brown on exposure to air, with separation of oxybromide of iron. When warmed with more bromine, it absorbs a certain quantity of the latter, forming either ferric bromide, Fe_2Br_6, or ferroso-ferric bromide, Fe_3Br_8 or $Fe_2Br_6 + FeBr_2$.

At Stassfurt, it is chiefly the last-mentioned salt which is used in the manufacture of bromide of potassium. It contains from 65 to 70 per cent of bromine, about 0.2 to 0.4 per cent of chlorine (in form of ferric chloride), about 17% of iron, and 12 to 1½% of water.

In some places, the bromide of iron (ferrous) is obtained as a by-product during the bromine manufacture, by allowing the escaping vapor of bromine to pass over iron filings kept damp with water. In other places, where the manufacture of bromide of potassium is carried on at a large scale, the iron salt is specially prepared. In this case, special precaution is taken to avoid contamination of the product by chlorine. This is done by conducting only the first fraction of the vapors of bromine (when freshly set free from its native compounds, by means of sulphuric acid and dioxide of manganese)—which are then free from chlorine—directly into the moist iron filings. The latter are generally contained in cast-iron vessels or stone-ware vessels holding four to five gallons. Subsequent portions of the escaping bromine vapors are conducted into Woulff's bottles and there condensed.

Whenever all the iron-filings appear to be dissolved, the solution of ferroso-ferric bromide is passed through a linen strainer, or through a filtering medium consisting of gravel and sand, previously washed with hydrochloric acid. This filtration removes various impurities, chiefly carbon. The filtering medium is washed with water, and the washings are used for moistening a new lot of iron-filings.

As soon as a sufficient quantity of the bromide of iron solution has accumulated, it is warmed in a cast-iron boiler, and the necessary additional quantity of bromine added. In order to attain the high percentage of bromine required, the bromine must be free from chlorine. Instead of getting rid of the latter by distilling the crude bromine, and utilizing only the first portions of the distillate, the same object may be accomplished by shaking the crude bromine in the cold with a solution of bromide of iron containing already too much chlorine. This causes all the chlorine to combine with the iron, as long as there is any undecomposed ferrous bromide present.

The brownish-red solution of ferroso-ferric bromide is now evaporated in a boiler to a viscid consistence, and then poured out into flat-bottomed boxes made of sheet-iron, in which the product congeals to a brownish-black, crystalline mass, which is broken out, and firmly packed into small-sized casks.

The total annual production of this ferroso-ferric bromide at Stassfurt and vicinity is at the present time about 120,000 kilos or 264,000 pounds, of which the largest part is used in the manufacture of bromide of potassium.

Both bromide and iodide of potassium had been made, previous to about 1863, by various processes, some of which suffered from more or less drawbacks. As soon, however, as a pure and cheap bromide of iron became available, this agent was selected as the starting point of the manufacture by those who were the most competent judges. It was probably first applied to iodide of potassium by Baup and Caillot, who directed to decompose a solution of iodide of iron containing 100 parts of iodine,

---

* But all fine powders, or dust, should be removed by filtration.

* After *Handbuch d. chemischen Technologie.*—Bd. I, 2 *Die Stassfurter Kali-Industrie.* Von Dr Emil Pfeiffer. 8vo, Braunschweig, 1887.

by means of 80 parts of carbonate of potassium, at a boiling temperature kept up for some time, so as to cause the iron precipitate to become more compact and easier to wash when on the strainers. The sixth edition of the Prussian Pharmacopœia adopted a suggestion made by Frederking, namely not to employ the simple ferrous iodide (FeI_2), but to add to this salt one-third more of iodine, so as to convert it into the ferroso-ferric iodide (Fe_3I_8). This resulted in producing eventually, after boiling out the carbonic acid gas, the ferroso-ferric oxide, which separates in a more granular and compact form and is more readily washed out. Frederking's plan was not to decompose the whole of the iodide of iron, but to evaporate the whole mixture to dryness, then to dissolve out all soluble matter by water. This part of Frederking's plan, however, was not adopted by the Prussian Pharmacopœia, in which the ferroso-ferric iodide was decomposed by an excess of hot solution of potash, and the excess of alkali in the filtrate afterwards neutralized by aqueous solution of hydriodic acid.

To transfer this method upon *bromide of potassium*, it is only necessary to substitute 65 parts of bromine for 100 parts of iodine. The present manufacture of the German bromide of potassium is based upon Frederking's plan, with one exception. It has been found that when a ferroso-ferric salt is precipitated by potash, ferric oxide is first precipitated, and afterwards pure ferrous oxide. To avoid this the ferroso-ferric bromide is gradually added to the boiling solution of the carbonate of potassium (not *vice versa*), contained in a large iron kettle heated by an open fire or by steam.

The respective quantities of the two substances are previously weighed, in accordance with the percentage strength of the bromide of iron. 100 parts of the latter salt, as used in the manufacture, and containing 65 to 70 per cent bromine, require 56.2 to 60.5 parts of carbonate of potassium.

Towards the end of the reaction the liquid is carefully tested, from time to time, with litmus paper in order to attain a neutral, or not more than faintly alkaline reaction. The boiling is continued for some time, so that the iron may be precipitated as completely and compactly as possible. The liquid is then strained through well-washed gravel and sand, or better, through a regular filter press. Any wash-water is preserved and used in place of plain water for the next operation. The strained liquid is then evaporated to dryness.

The dry mass is afterwards redissolved in 1 to 1½ parts of water, and this solution, when it has deposited suspended impurities, is already very pure. The largest portion or the sulphate of potassium contained in the carbonate employed (such as is produced at Stassfurt) will be found in the sediment formed in the solution on standing, which sediment must be carefully removed.

The mother-liquids are now evaporated to 20° B., and may even be boiled down to 50° B., but, if hard crystals are desired, it is necessary that they be allowed to form at a moderate heat, and protected from dust or concussion.

On a small scale, the best plan is to use capacious porcelain or stoneware capsules placed in a sand-bath. When working on a large scale, it is customary to use enamelled iron vessels. The author of the work from which we quote states that these enamelled vessels are made in great perfection by the firm of de Dietrich et Co., of Niederbronn (Alsace). Plain, uncoated iron can be used only when the salt is to separate quickly, in soft crystals, from a hot saturated solution. If the crystals remain in contact with the iron for any length of time, they assume a yellowish tint.

When a considerable quantity of crystals has separated, the mother-liquid is siphoned off, and the crystals transferred to a wooden vessel with perforated bottom, where they are allowed to drain. The first crop of crystal obtained is usually pure enough to be at once put on the market. Those which are yielded by the mother-waters usually require to be rinsed off with water, the rinsings being used for the next operation.

If the solution was alkaline, carbonate of potassium will gradually accumulate in the mother-liquors. This may be removed by saturation with hydrobromic acid. Any sulphate of potassium present may be removed by precipitation with an equivalent quantity of bromide of barium. Chloride of potassium, however, which is only 0.53 times less soluble than the bromide, is so difficult to remove that the manufacturers try to avoid it by purchasing crude materials as free from chlorine as possible.

As soon as a mother-liquor begins to show a larger percentage of chlorine than is allowable, it is preferable and more economical to work it up for bromine, than to try and separate the bromide and chloride of potassium.

Bromide of potassium has a great tendency to decrepitate when heated. It is, therefore, best dried at 40° to 50° C. (104°-122° F.) upon stoneware plates, or upon sheet iron coated with amber varnish, which has been made to adhere by exposure to a rather high temperature.

As the German Pharmacopœia permits a small percentage of chlorine, the usual article of commerce is not made above this standard, though a salt absolutely free from chlorine may also be had on demand, but for a higher price.

The annual production of bromide of potassium in Germany, at the present time, amounts to about 120,000 kilos (264,000 pounds), of which about 65,000 kilos (143,000 pounds) are turned out by the "Chemische Fabrik auf Actien, vormals E. Schering," of Berlin. The next largest maker is probably Heinrich Byck, of Berlin. Johann Diedrich Bieber, of Hamburg, had reduced his manufacture, at the time of the author's writing this chapter, from 15,000 to 8,000 kilos, owing to the high price of bromine. E. de Haën, of List near Hanover, and others handle (or handled at that time) American bromide, though the continuance of this depends upon the fluctuations of the market.

Complexion Beautifier.

The *Chemist and Druggist* suggests the following formula for removing freckles and roughness and pimples from the face, neck, and hands:

Diluted Nitric Acid	2 fl. dr.
Alcohol	5 fl. oz.
Extract of White Rose	½ fl. oz.
Oil of Neroli	10 minims.

Mix and add:

Peroxide of Hydrogen	2 fl. oz.
Glycerin	3 fl. oz.
Tincture of Cochineal	1 fl. dr.
Water	enough to make 40 fl. oz.

Let the mixture stand three weeks, and filter.

Wet a corner of a napkin with the lotion, and apply it to the face, neck, arms, and hands, each time after washing; then dry.

Powdered Camphor.

Mr. J. W. England suggests that the camphor should first be reduced to powder with the aid of a small quantity of alcohol or ether, triturating it in a mortar to thorough dryness and then incorporating with it 54 of petrolatum. This proportion of petrolatum is too small to affect the characteristic properties of the camphor, but it is sufficient to prevent aggregation of the particles of the powder. After a time slight caking may occur, but it breaks down readily to fine, velvety powder upon applying slight pressure.—*Am. Jour. of Pharm.*

Bottle Cement.

Mix together

Rosin, in powder	3 parts
Soda, caustic	1 part
Water	5 parts

and afterwards incorporate

Plaster of Paris	4½ parts

After about three-quarters of an hour, the mixture will become hard. It is very adhesive, not porous, and is but little affected even by boiling water.

It must be applied to stoppers while fresh.

A Supposed New Anæsthetic.

In the Berlin Medical Society, Dr. Lewin recently had a good deal to say about an active principle which he had extracted from "Haya," an African arrow poison, and which he introduced as a *local anæsthetic*. The alkaloid was found to be identical with erythrophleine, which Merck had prepared some years ago from *Erythrophleum guineense*, the "Mancono bark." It is a little surprising that the reputed anæsthetic qualities of this body should have escaped notice at this time, and there seems to be room for a little suspension of judgment as to the value of the "discovery." The search after new anæsthetics is almost too eagerly prosecuted, and the experience afforded us by the history of drumine and stenocarpin should moderate any tendency to excitement about this new body, which, like them, seems to be the product of mercantile rather than scientific researches.—*Chem. and Drugg.*

Coconut or Cocoanut.—Prof. Balfour directs the attention of botanists (*Ann. Bot.*, p. 185) to the fact that *cocoanut* should correctly be written *coco*, and that, since *coca* is becoming an important therapeutic agent, it is all the more necessary that a correct orthography should be followed, so that less confusion may arise than at present appears to exist, he having known people who were content in the belief that the coconut palm was the source of both *cocoa* and *coca*. Dr. Balfour appears, however, to have overlooked the fact that the name *coco* is commonly applied to the root of *Colocasia antiquorum*.—*Pharm. Journ.*

[In this connection, we are reminded of a label recently seen on an English article in which "cokernut" was the orthography adopted.—Ed. A. D.]

Some New or Improved Iron Preparations.

EUGENE DIETERICH communicates, through the *Pharm. Centralhalle*, some improved formulæ for certain neutral or indifferent iron preparations, of which we select those of more general interest, using the nomenclature in vogue in this country:

1. FERRI OXIDUM SACCHARATUM SOLUBILE.
Soluble Saccharated Oxide of Iron.

Solution of Oxychloride of Iron	86 parts
Syrup	150 "
Solution of Soda	7.5 "
Sugar	enough to make 100 "

Heat together the Iron Solution and the Syrup in a capsule on the water-bath, gradually add, under stirring, the Solution of Soda, and evaporate to dryness. Reduce the mass to powder and incorporate with it enough Sugar to make 100 parts.

Note.—The solution of oxychloride of iron is equivalent to "Dialyzed Iron," and is intended to designate the preparation of the German Pharmacopœia ("Liquor Ferri Oxychlorati"), having a spec. grav. of 1.050. The solution of soda is that of the German Pharm., containing nearly 15 per cent of pure soda, and of the spec. grav. 1.159–1.163.

The product of the above formula is a light-brown powder, without odor, having a sweet, scarcely ferruginous taste, and easily soluble to a clear liquid in one-half its weight of water. 100 parts contain 3 parts of iron.

It is soluble in milk and liquids containing albuminoids without altering them.

It differs from the corresponding preparation of the Germ. Pharm. by its greater solubility.

2. FERRI OXIDUM DEXTRINATUM SOLUBILE.
Soluble Dextrinated Oxide of Iron.
("Dextrinate of Iron.")

Dextrin, pure	q. s.
Solution of Oxychloride of Iron	200 parts
Solution of Soda	35 "
Distilled Water	q. s.

Dissolve 80 parts of pure (yellow, soluble) Dextrin in 80 parts of Distilled Water, dilute the liquid with the Solution of Oxychloride of Iron (Germ. Pharm., see above), filter, and wash the filter with a little water. Heat the filtrate in a capsule to between 70° and 90° C., gradually add, while stirring, the Solution of Soda (Germ. Pharm., see above), and evaporate to dryness.

The dry, dark-brown, glassy, transparent mass, having a red-brown color by transmitted light, is reduced to a fine powder, and mixed with enough pure dextrin to make 100 parts of product.

This appears as a chocolate-brown powder, or as reddish-brown transparent scales (if dissolved to a syrupy consistence and dried on glass), without odor, scarcely possessing a ferruginous, but rather a dextrin taste, and is soluble in 1.5 parts of water.

100 parts of it contain 10 parts of iron.

It is also soluble in milk and other albuminoid liquids without altering them.

3. LIQUOR FERRI ALBUMINATI.
Solution of Albuminated Iron.

Dried Egg Albumen (Merck's)	5 parts
Cinnamon Water	50 "
Solution of Oxychloride of Iron (Pharm. Germ.)	12 "
Solution of Soda (Pharm. Germ.)	0.75"
Alcohol	12 "
Distilled Water	enough to make 100 "

Dissolve the Egg Albumen in the Cinnamon Water (which, according to the Germ. Pharm., contains about 10 per cent of alcohol). Dilute the Iron Solution with 40 parts of Distilled Water and add the alcohol. Now mix both solutions, immediately add the solution of soda, and set it aside. After several hours, filter the liquid through a pellet of cotton, and then pass enough water through the latter to make the product weigh 100 parts.

A more handsome product is obtained by reducing the dried egg albumen to 2.5 parts. Fresh egg albumen may, of course, also be used. In this case, five (5) times as much must be taken as of dry. With fresh albumen, the solutions turn out more clear and transparent.

4. LIQUOR FERRI PEPTONATI.
Solution of Peptonated Iron.

Dried Egg Albumen (Merck's)	1 part
Pepsin (undiluted)	0.05 "
Solution of Oxychloride of Iron (Germ. Pharm.)	12 parts
Syrup	3 "
Brandy	10 "
Distilled Water	enough to make 100 "

Dissolve the Egg Albumen in 19 parts of Distilled Water, add the Pepsin [the author specifies Witte's pepsin. But we have at least as active, if not more active pepsins in this country], and digest during 4 hours at 40° C. (104° F.). On the other hand, mix the Iron Solution with the Syrup and 55 parts of Distilled Water, mix this liquid with the solution of the peptonized albumen, and heat the whole, in a steam-bath, to 90°–95° C. Then allow it to cool, add the Brandy, and finally, enough water to make 100 parts.

Let the mixture stand during eight days; then pour off the clear solution from the insignificant sediment.

5. GELATINUM FERRI OXIDI.
Iron Gelatin. Iron Jelly.

White Gelatin, best	8 parts
Solution of Oxychloride of Iron (Germ. Pharm.)	12 "
Syrup of Orange Flowers	20 "
Brandy	15 "
Solution of Soda (Germ. Pharm.)	0.5 part
Water of Ammonia	0.5 "
Distilled Water	enough to make 100 parts

Dissolve the Gelatin in 30 parts of Distilled Water by the aid of heat. Mix together the Iron Solution, Syrup, Brandy, and 90 parts of Distilled Water, and add this liquid to the warm Gelatin solution contained in a capsule. Then immediately add the Water of Ammonia and Solution of Soda (previously mixed together). On cooling, there will result a transparent jelly of an alkaline reaction, a reddish-brown color, and pleasant taste. 100 parts of it contain 0.45 parts of iron.

Notes on some New Remedies.

THE Pharmacopœia Committee of the German Pharm. Association characterizes several new chemicals in the following manner:

1. ANTIFEBRINUM (*Acetanilid*).

Colorless, shining, crystalline laminæ, odorless, having a faintly burning taste, melting at 122°-123° C. (ah. 253° F.), boiling at 295° C. (563° F.), and, when ignited, burning without leaving a residue. Soluble in 194 parts of cold, and in 15 parts of boiling water; in 3.5 parts of alcohol, and easily in ether and chloroform. The aqueous solution has a neutral reaction.

The hot prepared aqueous solution is colored red by ferric chloride. When heated with solution of potassa, acetanilid evolves vapors having an aromatic odor.

If 0.1 Gm. of acetanilid is boiled for one minute with 1 C.c. of hydrochloric acid, a clear solution should result, which, when mixed with 8 C.c. of water and 1 drop of melted carbolic acid, and afterwards with solution of chlorinated lime (1 in 10), assumes an onion red color; on supersaturating the liquid with ammonia, the color changes to indigo-blue.

On adding ferric chloride to a cold saturated solution of acetanilid, its color should not be changed.

2. ADEPS LANÆ (*Wool Fat. Lanolin*).

The purified fat of sheep's wool, mixed with water.

A yellowish-white mass of thick ointment-like consistence, a faint, peculiar odor, melting at about 40° C. (104° F.), insoluble in water, but absorbing several times its own weight of this liquid, without losing its consistence. Ether as well as chloroform dissolve it to a turbid liquid of neutral reaction. When heated on a water-bath, it leaves behind a mass, which is clear [and nearly colorless] when melted. When cold it has a honey-yellow color and a tough, ointment-like consistence, is easily dissolved by ether and chloroform, but is only partially soluble in alcohol, even when absolute and hot. On pouring the chloroformic solution of the anhydrous wool-fat, made in the proportion of 1 of fat to 50 of chloroform, on the surface of concentrated sulphuric acid, a deep reddish-brown zone will gradually form at the line of contact of the two layers.

When set fire to, wool-fat burns with a luminous, strongly smoky flame, and when completely ignited, leaves a scarcely perceptible ash (0.1 to 0.3 per cent) which, when moistened with a little water, does not change the color of red litmus paper.

When wool-fat is heated on the water-bath, it should not lose more than 30 per cent of its weight. When heated with solution of soda, it should not evolve any ammoniacal gas. 2 Gm. of wool-fat, dissolved in 10 C.c. of ether, should not be altered by a drop of solution of phenolphthalein, but the solution should be colored deep red upon the addition of a drop of standard solution of soda.

3. SALOLUM (*Salol*).

A white, crystalline powder of very faint, aromatic odor and taste, melting at 42° C. (108° F.), and, when ignited, burning with a sooty flame, and leaving no residue. Salol is insoluble in cold, and but little soluble in hot water; but it dissolves in 10 parts of alcohol, 0.33 parts of ether, and abundantly in chloroform and in liquefied carbolic acid.

The alcoholic solution of salol is colored violet by ferric chloride. On boiling salol with solution of caustic soda, it dissolves to a liquid which when allowed to cool and then acidulated with hydrochloric acid emits the odor of phenol, and contains a white precipitate. The latter, when filtered off and washed, is soluble in boiling water, and the solution acquires a bluish-violet color by the addition of ferric chloride.

Salol should not redden moistened litmus. When shaken with 50 parts of water, it should yield a filtrate which does not assume a violet color upon addition of 1 drop of ferric chloride, and should not be at once affected either by solution of nitrate of silver, or by nitrate of barium.

4. SACCHARINUM (*Saccharin*).

A white, partly micro-crystalline powder, odorless, and having an exceedingly sweet taste, still perceptible in solutions containing 1 in 50,000. When heated in a glass tube, it turns brown, and evolves vapors having the odor of oil of bitter almond; upon ignition, it is consumed without leaving more than a trace of residue.* With 400 parts of cold, or 75 parts of boiling water, it yields a solution of acid reaction. It is also soluble in 30 parts of alcohol, less easily in ether. Caustic alkalies dissolve it readily, becoming saturated thereby.

A solution of saccharin neutralized by alkalies, but not a purely aqueous solution of saccharin itself, furnishes a brownish-yellow precipitate with ferric chloride. On adding hydrochloric acid to the precipitate, this is decomposed, and saccharin set free. When heated with several times its weight of carbonate of sodium, saccharin becomes carbonised with evolution of vapors of benzol. On dissolving the residue from ignition in water, filtering the solution, and supersaturating this with nitric acid, separates a white precipitate upon the addition of barium nitrate.

0.18 Gm. of saccharin, mixed with 8 C.c. of water, should be dissolved by 1 C.c. of normal solution of potassa to a neutral liquid. The resulting solution, mixed with several cubic centimeters of normal solution of potassa, and heated to boiling, should not become colored.

If a portion of saccharin, placed on a filter, is washed with several times its weight of ether, and the filtrate afterwards mixed with ten times its quantity of water, ferric chloride should neither produce a precipitate in the liquid, nor should it impart to it a violet color.

Test for Acetanilid (*Antifebrin*).

PROF. F. A. FLÜCKIGER publishes the following test of identity for acetanilid or antifebrin.

Triturate 2 parts of the substance with 1 part of caustic potassa, and enough chloroform to dampen the mixture, transfer the latter at once to a test-tube, and warm it very gently. The mass will continue to become hot, even after it has been removed from the source of heat, and will turn brown. If more than 0.02 Gm. (about ⅓ grain) of acetanilid was taken, an energetic reaction ensues. The warmed mixture emits the unmistakable characteristic odor of *isocyanphenyl*, or *phenylcarbylamine*, C₆H₅NC. As this compound, when boiling (at 167° C.), is partly decomposed, it follows that the temperature should not be allowed to rise too high. There is another reason why this must be avoided, namely, because isocyanphenyl, when heated to 200°–220° C., is converted into the isomeric benzonitril. As this compound has an odor of oil of bitter almond, it might itself be taken as a proof of the identity of the acetanilid. But the presence of an excess of alkali and heat causes it to be converted into benzoate of the alkali and ammonia. Consequently, the final product of the reaction would be odorless, or would at most have the odor of ammonia. It is, however, quite easy to attain and to maintain the proper temperature required to produce the very characteristic isocyanphenyl.—*After Apotheker-Zeit.*

Reduction of Ferric Chloride by Pepsin and Allied Substances.

MR. WILLIAM DUNCAN makes the following communication to the *Chemist and Druggist*:

To the fact that the old tinct. ferri murriatis of the Edinburgh Pharmacopœia always contains ferrous chloride is ascribed its alleged superior efficacy to the tincture of the present pharmacopœia. The following experiments which I have made seem to favor this view, and bear out a theory that ferric salts are reduced in the alimentary canal before absorption, and that their therapeutic value is in direct proportion to the amount of this reduction. Two grains of pepsin, B. P., were shaken up with 100 minims of water, and 10 minims of liq. ferri perchloridi, B. P. (free from ferrous salt), added, the whole being well shaken together. After standing for five minutes, 10 minims of 2% potassium ferricyanide solution were added, when a blue color was at once developed, showing that reduction of the ferric chloride had taken place. The same experiment was repeated with eight different samples of pepsin, all of which gave a similar result. With some, however, the reduction seemed greater than in other cases. It was also noticed that it increases with the length of time the pepsin and iron are left in contact. A control experiment was made in each case with pepsin and ferridcyanide, but only in one case was any blue color developed, and this most probably was due to an impure hydrochloric acid having been used in making the pepsin preparation. The ferricyanide apparently does not undergo reduction, as the mixture does not become blue on the addition of a drop of pure ferric acetate solution. Possibly an albuminoid compound may be formed with the iron and the pepsin, the iron being reduced during combination: but I could find no evidence of such reduction with white of egg and ferric chloride. Similar results to these obtained with pepsin were given by ox-gall, pancreatin, papain, and saliva. The same experiments were made with liq. ferri acetatis and liq. ferri dialysatus. The former showed a slight reduction, the latter none at all, even after standing in contact with the pepsin for twenty-four hours. It is generally recognised that ferric acetate is less active therapeutically than ferric chloride, and dialyzed iron is least active of all, some therapeutists even denying that it has any efficacy, and this is apparently quite in accordance with the foregoing results. I do not regard these experiments as conclusive or complete, but the results are suggestive, and, as such, I record them, hoping that the investigation will be carried further.

Analysis of Mixed Paints.

THOMAS T. P. BRUCE WARREN writes the following note to the editor of the *Chemical News* on the analysis of mixed paints, in reply to the query of a correspondent:

"A weighed quantity of the pigment ground in oil is placed in a plugged filter tube, and is carefully washed with carbon disulphide until all traces of oil are removed. The disulphide is evaporated when the weight of oil is obtained.

"Mixed paints may be treated in the same way, using petroleum spirit instead of carbon disulphide. The oils, etc., thus extracted will consist of linseed oil, boiled oil, perhaps resinous matter, etc., turpentine, shale spirit, or petroleum; these two latter are largely used to replace turpentine.

"To separate and estimate the oils, chloride of sulphur is added, when the oils will be precipitated, and the weight of turpentine, etc., may be obtained by difference. Resin, if present, may be extracted by alcohol from the matter removed by carbon disulphide; alcoholic solution of soda in some cases is necessary for this purpose.

The pigments are thus obtained in a dry state, free from oil, and may be examined in the usual way.

It is a common practice to burn off the oils, etc., but this is a mistake, as we ought to know something of the body-giving materials, as well as that of the *vitreious* used in rendering the paint 'fit for use.'"

Note by Ed. Am. Drugg.—The first step of the operation mentioned by Mr. Warren is not as easy of execution as the description would make one believe. He directs to place a weighed quantity of the pigment into a plugged filter tube, and to wash with carbon disulphide until the oil, etc., is completely removed. Our experience has shown us that mere plugging of a filter-tube will not prevent suspended matters from passing out with the liquid. In fact, a solution of oil-paints in carbon disulphide has a very strong tendency to run through filters quite opaque at least for a time, until the larger pores of the filter paper are stopped up. We have succeeded best by placing a weighed portion of the ground paint into a small filter made of Schleicher and Schull's heaviest filter paper (No. 597), folded so as to form a cylinder with nearly flat bottom, rather than as a cone. This filter containing the paint is placed into the extraction tube of a continuous extraction apparatus, not directly, however, but inside another larger filter, coming up higher along the sides of the tube. Carbon disulphide is passed through the filter, at nearly a boiling temperature, before the tube is connected with the continuous extraction apparatus, so that the first portions of the solution, in case they are cloudy or opaque, may be passed through again. When the liquid passes perfectly bright, the tube is connected with the apparatus, and the process need no longer to be watched. Care must be taken that the boiling or volatilisation of the menstruum does not take place too rapidly, so that the filters in the tube may not overflow with condensed liquid, which may carry with it some of the pigment in a finely divided state.

Fluorohydric Acid has been examined by a committee of the Paris Academy of Medicine with reference to its effect upon the bacillus of tubercle, and a very favorable report has been made on the subject. It seems that the bacilli are speedily destroyed by a minimal proportion of fluorhydric vapor.—*Nature.*

---

* The German original says "bis auf einen unmerklichen Rückstand," which would be equivalent to "an imperceptible residue." But a residue which is imperceptible is tantamount to "nothing." The words "trace merklichen" should be substituted for "unmerklichen."

Preserving the Colors of Botanical Specimens.

A METHOD of preserving the natural colors of flowers recommended by R. Hegler in the *Deutsche botanische Monatshefte*, consists in dusting salicylic acid on the plants as they lie in the press, and removing it again with a brush when the flowers are dry. Red colors in particular are well preserved by this agent. Another method of applying the same preservative is to use a solution of 1 part salicylic acid in 14 of alcohol by means of blotting paper or cotton wool soaked in it and placed above and below the flowers. Powdered boric acid yields nearly as good results. Dr. Schönland, in a paragraph contributed to the *Gardener's Chronicle* (Jan. 21st, p. 82), recommends as an improvement of the method of using sulphurous acid for preserving the color that, in the case of delicate flowers, they might be placed loosely between sheets of vegetable parchments before immersion in the liquid, or as to preserve their natural form.—*Pharm. Journal.*

Assay of Sublimate Dressings.

PROF. BERNDTS some time ago proposed to estimate the amount of corrosive sublimate in dressings by extracting them with water containing chloride of sodium, and then to estimate the quantity of mercury volumetrically by permanganate. Alfred Partheil now points out that this method is inapplicable when glycerin is present in the fabric, as is the case for instance with the liquid prescribed for the army, which is composed of

Corrosive Sublimate	80 parts
Alcohol	5,000 "
Glycerin	2,500 "
Distilled Water	7,500 "
Fuchsine	¼ part

and which quantity is calculated to be sufficient for 10 kilos (about 22½ lbs.) of fabric.

He communicates two methods for estimating the mercurial salt, one for approximate, and the other for accurate determination.

1. *Approximate method.*—Treat a piece of the sublimate gauze weighing 5 Gm. with 100 C.c. of warm solution of chloride of sodium, filter the liquid and treat it with hydrosulphuric acid. If a decided brown color is produced, this may be taken as indicative of the presence of enough corrosive sublimate to warrant the antiseptic condition of the fabric.

2. *Exact method.*—Exhaust a weighed quantity of the dressing, by displacement, with a warm solution of chloride of sodium, until the percolate ceases to be affected by hydrosulphuric acid.

[This is best done by removing the percolate in fractions to the vapor-chamber and passing through each fraction, separately, a current of the gas. If the latter ceases to affect the color of a fraction after having passed 5 minutes, the fabric may be regarded as exhausted.—ED. AM. DR.] The mercury in the percolate is then precipitated by hydrosulphuric acid gas, and the vessel set aside until next day, when the precipitate is collected upon a filter and washed. The filter with precipitate is then transferred to a beaker, with about 50 C.c. of water, and a current of chlorine passed through until all the mercuric sulphide is dissolved and the filter nearly destroyed. The liquid is now filtered, the filtrate (with washings) first freed from excess of chlorine, and the mercury precipitated as mercurous chloride (calomel) by adding phosphorous acid. The resulting precipitate is allowed to deposit during twenty-four hours, then transferred to a weighed filter, washed, dried at 100° C., and weighed.—*Pharm. Centralh.*

Asbestos Sheet as an Absorbent for Milk, etc., in Analysis.

DR. W. JOHNSTONE recently read a paper before the Society of Public Analysts, in which he reported that he had been using asbestos sheet or cloth in place of blotting paper as an absorbent for milk, in place of Adam's coils. The latter, it will be remembered, are coils of blotting paper, completely freed from fatty matter by ether and dried, which are used for soaking up a portion of the milk to be analysed. They are then dried, and the increase of weight of the dry coil for the loss which the absorbed milk has suffered by drying) represents the milk-solids. On treating the coil afterwards with ether, in a continuous extraction apparatus, the amount of butter is ascertained.

The substitution of pure asbestos is a decided advantage, inasmuch as this permits the ash to be determined in the same sample. For this purpose, the asbestos coil is simply ignited, after the fat is extracted, when the increase of weight will represent the ash.—*After The Analist*, 1887, 234.

Note by Ed. Am. Drugg.—Asbestos sheet has been used by one of us for more than a year for this purpose. It is best used in strips, one inch wide, six inches long, and made of sheets not over one-sixteenth inch in thickness. The strips are soaked in water; when soft, they are rolled up in a coil, tied with thin platinum wire, and then dried. They should be carefully trimmed, so as to remove all loose fibres which might accidentally fall off, thus vitiating the correctness of a weighing. A number of coils are made at once, macerated for twenty-four hours in dilute hydrochloric acid, then thoroughly washed, until the wash-water no longer reacts for chlorine. Next they are dried and extracted with ether, which may be done either by repeated maceration or by extracting them successively in a continuous extraction apparatus. They are then thoroughly dried, finally ignited, and weighed. The weight may be written upon them with lead pencil.

Nitrosulphonic Acid.

HUGO BORNTRAEGER draws attention to the usefulness of the so-called nitrosulphonic (sometimes also called nitrosulphuric) acid, which constitutes the substance otherwise known as "the crystals of the leaden chambers." It consists of a saturated solution of nitrous or hyponitric in concentrated sulphuric acid, and is formed whenever the supply of steam is insufficient to produce hydrated sulphuric acid. When these crystals come in contact with water, strong effervescence ensues, and nitric oxide gas escapes.

This compound may be prepared, among other ways, by passing dry sulphur dioxide (sulphurous acid gas) into cold, fuming nitric acid, until the liquid becomes syrupy.

Borntraeger finds that it is a very useful substance, on account of its loosely combined nitrogen oxides. He mentions the following uses:

1. A mixture of equal volumes of nitrosulphonic and concentrated hydrochloric acids dissolves, *when freshly mixed*, the well-known and annoying brown deposits caused by adhering manganic oxide in flasks or burettes, which have contained solutions of permanganate, or in which the latter has been decomposed.

2. The like mixture, likewise freshly prepared, most rapidly dissolves gold without requiring heat.

3. Nitrosulphonic acid is the most effective agent to liberate iodine from its combinations.—*Repert. d. Anal. Chem.*, 1887, 741.

Picric Acid as an Explosive.

AT the sitting of the Academy of Sciences, held on December 12th, Professor Berthelot read a paper on the "Various Modes of Explosive Decomposition of Picric Acid." Prefacing with an exposition of the general belief in the explosive property of the chemical, and alluding to Colonel Majendie's report on an explosion of recent occurrence in England, he related the following experiments: When a certain quantity of picric acid is heated in an open flask or capsule, it first melts, then volatilises, giving out fumes which burn with a smoky flame, but no explosion takes place. But when a test-tube, about one inch in diameter, is heated over a gas jet so as to produce a visible red, but without melting the glass or deforming the tube, on dropping into it some crystals of acid, weighing only a few milligrammes, a sharp detonation occurs, with a bright white light and characteristic noise. When the experiment is performed in nitrogen gas, a few flakes only of carbon are deposited; in ordinary air the result is the same, but no carbon is left. On increasing the quantity of picric acid, without, however, exceeding a few centigrammes, the addition may cool the bottom of the tube sufficiently to prevent immediate detonation, but the chemical is at once volatilized, and soon an explosion with flame occurs, occupying a great part of the tube. This explosion is not so sharp as the more local detonation, and more carbon is apparently deposited. An explosion of the same nature may be produced with a few milligrammes of material by using a glass tube coated with carbon of a previous explosion. With a decigramme of acid and a new tube the reaction will be slower still, yet a series of deflagrations with red flame will be observed, while the vapors will catch fire at the mouth of the tube. Finally, with larger quantities, the acid is decomposed, there being abundant fumes and partial volatilisation, but without deflagration. Other nitrogenized bodies, less oxygenated than picric acid, such as nitro- and binitro-benzin, nitronaphthalines, etc., were experimented with and afforded concomitant results, leading to the conclusion that the mode of decomposition of all these nitrated bodies depends on the initial decomposition temperature. Respecting picric acid more especially, M. Berthelot's conclusions are as follows: Should a nitro compound, such as picric acid, while burning in the air in large masses, happen to heat the sides of the containing inclosure to a degree sufficient to induce incipient deflagration, the deflagration might contribute to further increase the temperature of the inclosure, and the phenomenon might occasionally be transformed into a detonation. It would even puffice that the detonation should occur in an isolated point, either during a fire, or owing to the local overheating of a boiler or apparatus, to enable it to originate the explosive wave and propagate itself by influence throughout the whole mass, causing a general explosion.—*Chemist and Druggist.*

THE
American Druggist

AN ILLUSTRATED MONTHLY JOURNAL

OF

Pharmacy, Chemistry, and Materia Medica.

VOL. XVII., No. 3.   WHOLE No. 165

FREDERICK A. CASTLE, M.D. .... EDITOR.
CHARLES RICE, PH.D. .... ASSOCIATE EDITOR.

PUBLISHED BY

WM. WOOD & CO., 56 & 58 Lafayette Place, N. Y.

SUBSCRIPTION PRICE per year, ... $1.50
SINGLE COPIES, ...15

Address all communications relating to the business of the AMERICAN DRUGGIST, such as subscriptions, advertisements, change of Post-Office address, etc., to WILLIAM WOOD & CO., 56 and 58 Lafayette Place, New York City, to whom order all postal money orders and checks should be made payable. Communications intended for the Editor should be addressed to care of the Publishers.

The AMERICAN DRUGGIST is issued in the latter part of each month, dated for the month ahead. Changes of advertisements should reach us before the 10th. New advertisements can occasionally be inserted after the 19th. REGULAR ADVERTISEMENTS according to size, location, and time. Special rates on application.

EDITORIALS.

THE New York Assembly Bill, introduced some weeks since by Mr. J. Wesley Smith of the XIII. District (New York City), which, if it became a law, would make it unlawful to sell proprietary medicines in the State without labels upon each package giving in English language a statement of the ingredients of the contents, has very naturally awakened opposition from persons interested in the manufacture of nostrums. On the 28th of February, the Committee on General Laws, to which the bill had been referred, gave the opponents of the bill a hearing, and the newspaper accounts of the proceedings are interesting to pharmacists. Assuming that such a hasty report is correct, it is certainly rather comical, in view of his own remarks, to read S. V. Pierce's comments regarding "ignorant druggists."

S. V. Pierce, S. Humphrey, M. W. Fenner, and J. D. Hodge are said to have submitted statements to the effect that in the State of New York there are 108 manufactories of patent medicines, employing capital amounting to $3,512,430, and putting out annually, medicines valued at $4,339,178. In the whole United States there are 563 manufactories of these goods, with a capital of $10,620,880, and an annual production valued at $14,682,-493.

Mr. Pierce is reported to have said:

"There has rarely been a more outrageous measure introduced in the Legislature. It is a measure to put money into the pockets of ignorant druggists, and to confiscate one-half of the stock of the druggists of the United States. I hope, gentlemen, you will be slow to give your influence to such a bill. It is argued that proprietary medicines are harmful. I have not heard such a complaint. I challenge any one to show that these medicines had ever killed or harmed any one. Few physicians would submit to such a test. It is preposterous for us to print the names of the drugs we use on the labels of our bottles. If we should, I fear the Greek names would raise Cicero from the dead. Can it be that the Legislature would put such an absolute power as this in the hands of the State Board of Health? That Board is composed of allopathists. What sort of confidence would any friend of Dr. Humphrey have that such a Board would decide fairly on his homœopathic medicines? Why, there are 5,000 proprietary medicines. Of course, any allopathic board of physicians would say that all homœopathic medicines are useless. Would you destroy all proprietary medicines at a blow? The real intent of this bill, in my opinion, is to destroy the sale of proprietary medicines. It is well known that people are on their guard against counterfeits of proprietary medicines. They notice at once any change in labels. If we should have to change all our labels we would be subjected to a loss of hundreds of thousands of dollars by people distrusting the genuineness of the preparation. The labels are all registered at Washington and are our patent right."

There is a great deal of ignorance and unwarranted assumption in the foregoing statement. The argument that a change in the form of labels already known would injure the sale of articles covered by them is no doubt to a certain extent correct. But the bill does not call for any change in labels. It only requires that a label be attached which will tell what the contents consist of, irrespective of other labels which the package may have. If the opponents of the bill admit that the publication called for would cause such financial loss, it is equivalent to admitting that people will not buy their medicines if they know what they were composed of. What the promoters of the bill probably urge upon the Legislature is the fact that it is not in the interests of the public that medicines may be vended and urged upon the community as certain cures for a great variety of diseases, without anybody besides the maker knowing what they are composed of. With few exceptions, proprietary medicines belong one of two classes: They either contain active drugs which, if used improperly, are capable of harmful effects, or they are practically inert, and the act of vending them for the prices charged, and with the claims to efficacy with which they are accompanied, is a fraud upon the purchaser; although, to tell the truth, we have little sympathy for the person who has no better reason for spending his money for such trash than the information gained from advertisements and clergymen's certificates.

So far as the interests of physicians are concerned, there is good reason for doubting whether the present state of affairs is not more conducive to their business interests than the proposed reform would be; for there are people who do not use patent medicines, because they are so intelligent to take medicines about which nobody knows anything; if, however, they were assured of the nature of the contents, they would sometimes resort to their use in preference to consulting a physician. It is doubtful whether doctors really lose very much business in consequence of the sale of "patents," for most persons who use them to any considerable extent do so for the relief of imaginary ailments, and as a result of such aids to diagnosis as are to be gained from patent medicine advertisements. When they are really sick, they go to a doctor for advice, and take what he prescribes. Indeed, the almanac sometimes overdoes the matter, and by its long and circumstantial narration of symptoms which are alleged to indicate the existence of some terrible malady, an emotional subject is so thoroughly scared that he does not stop at the drugstore, but goes at once to some eminent physician and pays him a good fee to secure a thorough examination of his physical condition. So far as concerns the apothecary, the intelligent class of patients are more likely to ask for a medicine which the latter can recommend from personal knowledge. So long as patents can be sold at a profit, it does not much concern the apothecary whether their composition is known or not; but if the customer is disposed to want information in this direction, it is a great saving of trouble and responsibility to be able to point to a pile of almanacs and counter bills and say that in them can be found all the published information of the subject.

It is rather severe on the homœopathic fraternity to have S. Humphrey put forward as a representative of homœopathy. One might with greater justice speak of R. V. Pierce as a representative of the sect of Faith Curers, for it certainly requires an exercise of sublime faith to believe a tithe of the statements made in the advertisements of his wares. On similar grounds we shall very likely hear some of our grocers spoken of as "leading druggists."

It is to be hoped that those who were instrumental in causing this bill to be presented to the Legislature are prepared to show that the interests of the general public are the only ones to be considered in this connection, and that neither the manufacturers of nostrums, the doctors, nor the druggists have any right to special consideration. If it was justifiable for the Legislature to enact (as it did a short time since) a law prohibiting the manufacture of oleomargarine in the State, notwithstanding it was proven to be a wholesome article of food; that many hundreds of thousands of dollars were invested in the business, and that its nature was perfectly well known to the entire community, there is then, certainly, sufficient reason for requiring some better guarantee of the nature of compounds sold for medical purposes than the authority of a man who, although a manufacturer of them, is so illiterate as to say that the names of drugs are derived from the Greek language.

If our municipal and suburban health boards were made up of men competent to fill the position they occupy, the initiation of such legislation as this would not be left to citizens generally, or to individual members of any profession.

WE are informed that a bill has been introduced in Congress which provides for a pharmacopœia to be constructed by representatives appointed by the Government from the army and navy, and by the American Medical and Pharmaceutical Associations. This reads very much like a similar scheme offered, a short time before the Convention of 1880, for revising the Pharmacopœia of the United States of America, and it is not unlikely that this one is from the same source.

There is no reason for doubting that such a law may be enacted, and that a pharmacopœia may be constructed accordingly; but it must at the same time be granted that it cannot take the place of the Pharmacopœia of the United States of America, the copyright for which is held by the Committee of Revision and Publication appointed by the Convention of 1880. That committee has instructions from the Convention to submit a complete plan for revising the pharmacopœia, for which a convention will be called in 1890; and it has also accumulated considerable money which may be available for the expense of revising the work. As the call for the next convention will be issued about the 1st of May, 1889, it is already time that the subject should be generally considered. And as this call, by direction of the Convention of 1880, will invite delegates from the several incorporated medical societies, the incorporated medical colleges, the incorporated colleges of pharmacy, the incorporated pharmaceutical societies, the American Medical Association, the American Pharmaceutical Association, the Army, the Navy, and the Marine Hospital Service, it is difficult to understand how a more representative body of delegates could be obtained.

It is hardly possible that the convention thus provided for can fail to be held, and in the event of another pharmacopœia being published, according to the provisions that may be adopted by the General Government, there must necessarily result a confusion of authority which must be anything but profitable. Congress can no more legislate the Convention of 1890 out of existence than it can abolish or prevent any other gathering of a scientific association. Neither can it adopt the title of the pharmacopœia as now held by the Committee of Revision and Publication.

THE joint committee of the Iowa Legislature have prepared a bill regulating the sale of liquors which greatly concerns pharmacists in that State. According to the press reports, it authorizes permits to sell only to registered pharmacists. Applications for permits must be made to the district judge in open court, and must be signed by a majority of the property owners in the ward and not less than twenty-five women, the wives of property-holders. A bond is also required in the sum of $3,000. The statements set forth in the application must be proved in open court, and any person may appear to resist the application. Permits can only be granted to each 2,500 of population. If no pharmacists apply, the court may appoint some discreet person to sell. All liquors must be purchased through the County auditor by those holding permits. Purchasers from pharmacists must make oath to their application, and if not known to the pharmacist must be identified. The penalty for false statement of a purchaser is the same as for perjury. No liquor can be sold to minors, intoxicated persons, or those in the habit of getting intoxicated. The penalty for violation by a pharmacist is a fine of $100, and all the penalties of the Clark law.

In view of the disgrace which is becoming attached to legitimate pharmacy on account of the habit of a few who make pharmacy a disguise for a rum-shop, it is to be hoped that the pharmacists of Iowa will give this bill cordial support.

IN connection with the answer to a query on page 56, relating to the stability of solutions of corrosive sublimate intended for antiseptic purposes, it seems fair to say that there may be good reason to doubt whether it is desirable to render the solution permanent. It is not improbable that the efficacy of this preparation consists very largely in the nascent chlorine liberated during the conversion of the bichloride into calomel; and while, from a pharmaceutical point of view, it may be more satisfactory to have a solution which does not deposit the calomel, therapeutically such a solution may be the least desirable.

THE following reports of proceedings at the annual meetings of pharmaceutical associations have been received: Ohio State Pharmaceutical Association (June 8th, 9th, 10th, 1887); North Carolina Pharmaceutical Association (Aug. 4th, 5th, 1887); California Pharmaceutical Society and College of Pharmacy (1886-7); Texas State Pharmaceutical Association (May 10th, 11th, 12th, 1887); Missouri State Pharmaceutical Association (June 28th, 29th, 30th, 1887); New Hampshire Pharmaceutical Association (Sept. 27th, 28th, 1887); New Jersey Pharmaceutical Association (May 18th, 25th, 26th, 1887); Wisconsin Pharmaceutical Association (Aug. 9th, 10th, 11th, 1887). Reports of the North Carolina Board of Pharmacy; of the Missouri State Pharmacy Law; of the New Jersey State Pharmacy Law, and of the Wisconsin State Board of Pharmacy are contained in the respective publications.

Pharmaceutical Degrees in the United States.

THE *Omaha Druggist* is authority for the following list of teaching colleges of Pharmacy and the number of degrees conferred by them to date:

University of Kansas	3
Purdue University	11
University of Wisconsin	21
Albany College of Pharmacy	44
Pittsburg " "	46
National " "	77
Louisville " "	98
California " "	116
Massachusetts College of Pharmacy	197
Cincinnati " "	239
Maryland " "	350
St. Louis " "	365
Chicago " "	429
University of Michigan	450
New York College of Pharmacy	960
Philadelphia " "	2,529
Total	5,933

Heinrich Anton de Bary, Prof. of Botany at the University of Strassburg, died on the 19th of January at the age of 57 years. He was born in Frankfurt-on-Main, his father having been a physician of Belgian parentage. When 18 years old, he studied medicine in Heidelberg, and afterwards at Marburg and Berlin, where he became acquainted with Alexander Braun, the botanist. After receiving his degree, he became professor of botany successively in Freiburg, Halle, and Strassburg. His most important publication related to the comparative anatomy of phanerogams, ferns, and especially of cryptogams. The cause of his death was a cancerous affection of the mouth.

Babbit Metal is an alloy of copper, tin, and antimony made by fusing 2 parts of tin with 1 part of an alloy made by fusing together 12 parts of tin and 8 of regulus of antimony, then remove from the fire and add 4 parts of copper, and when that is incorporated, other 12 parts of tin. Protect the fused mixture from oxidation with a covering of powdered charcoal. The composition of the finished product is 3.7 parts of copper, 7.4 of antimony, and 88.9 of tin.—*Chem. and Drugg.*

A CHILD in Toronto swallowed two drachms of common insect-powder, and tetanic symptoms, with coma, followed. Death, however, was averted. Such symptoms as these are rare, and show that the various species of pyrethrum are not quite free from toxic properties.

J. Farris Moore, M.D., of Baltimore, died of apoplexy on Friday, February 3d, after an illness of two days. He was born at Port Penn, Del., February 20th, 1826, and when 16 years old, he entered the drug-store of George W. Andrews, of Baltimore. In 1847, having graduated from the Maryland College of Pharmacy, he commenced business on his own account in Wilmington, Del., and meanwhile attended lectures in the Jefferson Medical College of Philadelphia, receiving his medical degree in 1849. After the third year passed in Wilmington, he returned to Baltimore and, in partnership with Mr. J. K. B. Emory, opened a drug-store on the corner of Harvard and Madison streets. Mr. Emory retired from the firm in 1858, and Dr. Moore continued the business until his death.

Dr. Moore was one of the incorporators of the Maryland College of Pharmacy on its reorganization in 1856, and at various times was its secretary, president, professor of pharmacy, and, at the time of his death, was professor of botany and materia medica. In 1863-64, he was the president of the American Pharmaceutical Association, and twice served on the Committee for Revision of the U. S. Pharmacopœia. In 1870, the Maryland College of Pharmacy conferred upon him the honorary degree of Doctor in Pharmacy.

Joseph Roberts, of Baltimore, president of the Maryland College of Pharmacy, died in Baltimore on January 31st, of pneumonia. He was born in Baltimore on the 15th of February, 1824, and after a preliminary education in the West Nottingham Academy he came in 1841 to New York and entered the store of the late John Milhau. In 1845 he graduated from the New York College of Pharmacy, and in 1846 returned to Baltimore, where he commenced a business on his own account, which continued until his death. He was also a member of the manufacturing firm of George Page & Co., and for the past ten years was president of the Maryland College of Pharmacy, having been actively connected with its affairs since his return to Baltimore in 1846. He was twice vice-president of the American Pharmaceutical Association, and its president in 1885-86.

QUERIES & ANSWERS.

Queries for which answers are desired, must be received by the 5th of the month, and must in every case be accompanied by the name and address of the writer, for the information of the editor, but not for publication.

No. 2,103.—"Ross Jug" (W. L. B.).
Another name for this compound is "Pot-pourri," a formula for which you will find on page 119 of the AMERICAN DRUGGIST for June, 1886.

No. 2,104.—Elixir of Paraldehyde (J. D. C.).
The following formula has been used with moderate success, though many physicians who have tried paraldehyde have given up its use, chiefly from the disagreeable breath acquired by those who take it:

Paraldehyde .... 2 fl. oz.
Spirit of Chloroform................. 2 fl. drch.
Tinct. of Vanilla........................ ½ fl. drch.
Syrup of Raspberries............... ½ fl. oz.
Aromatic Elixir.........enough to make 4 fl. oz.

Dose for adults: 2 fluidrachms, containing 1 fluidrachm of paraldehyde.

No. 2,105.—Blue Mass (J. D. C.).
If you will consult the article by Mr. Sommer on "The Manufacture of Mercurial Preparations on a Large Scale," published in the AMERICAN DRUGGIST for March, 1885, you will get the information you desire.

No. 2,106.—"Extract of Bay Laurel" (J. D. C.).
This correspondent inclosed, in his letter, the label of a manufacturer of "Extract of Bay Laurel," used in the preparation of bay rum, and asks what it is made of.
We presume that it is nothing else than a combination of essential oils (chiefly oil of bay), which are afterwards to be dissolved in alcohol and diluted by water. A very good combination, acknowledged to be such, is that given by the U. S. Pharm. under Spiritus Myrciæ. If we translate the *parts by weight* of the formula into weight and measure, and split the formula in two, we obtain:

1. *Mixture of Essential Oils* (equivalent to the above Extract of Bay Laurel).

Oil of Myrcia (Bay)......................1,640 minims
Oil of Orange Peel....................... 116 "
Oil of Pimenta .... 96 "

Mix them.
To make 4 pints of bay rum use ½ fluidounce of this mixture (see next).

2. *Bay Rum*.

Mixture of Essential Oils .... ½ fl. oz.
Alcohol, deodorized ....40 fl. oz.
Water.................enough to make 64 fl. oz.

No. 2,107.—To Exterminate Roaches (A. S.).
There is no reliable method for exterminating or keeping away roaches with *harmless* substances, unless care b taken that all water or moisture be excluded from usual hiding places. If this can be done, however, a mixture of equal parts of powdered borax, powdered quassia and best insect powder will usually accomplish the object. The cupboards and places may also be painted with a strong decoction of quassia, or with shellac varnish in which picric acid had been dissolved. The shellac varnish, for this purpose, is best made with solution of borax. It should also be brushed into all the cracks and joints of the woodwork.

No. 2,108.—Query referring to Proprietary Articles (A. and J.).
We are in receipt of the following from California:
"Will you kindly furnish us with the formula for— (we omit the name of the remedy, in the interest of our correspondent)—and at the same time inform us if any claim can be made against us for putting it up, and selling it under that name, or as having been put up under their formula. Our reason for doing this is, because the proprietors have put it in the hands of grocers, and they are advertising the latter as the dispensers of their remedies. Of course, this does not prevent us from handling their preparations, for we have them on our shelves, but, by doing the above, we can run it out of the market."

Our correspondent's tale is one that could be duplicated and rehearsed in about the same strain all the country over.

The grievances which retail dealers in medicines have gradually accumulated against the proprietor and manufacturers of so-called patent medicines have been so thoroughly ventilated during the last few years that we need not waste space on this subject. All that we wish to state, or to reiterate, is this, that we regard it a great pity that so many pharmacists appear to find it necessary, for increasing their income, to keep these preparations on their shelves.

As to the intentions of our correspondents, who propose to imitate the nostrum which they mention, we would say that everything depends on the legal status of the proprietary article. If the label or the title of the mixture is protected under copyright or other U. S. law —which we have no means of ascertaining—then it would be hazardous in undertaking such an imitation. As to whether such an imitation, even if unobstructed by law, would be just and fair, we cannot say exactly, as we do not know the article from personal inspection; but there is a general principle, which we have long upheld, that no nostrum, which is praised as a cure for what are generally known as incurable diseases, deserves any consideration or recognition. As to whether the throwing on the market of a cheap imitation would kill the article, depends again upon its local reputation, the spunk of the proprietors, and various other circumstances. It is hard to give good advice from a long distance in such cases. From our observations of similar incidents in this section, we should judge that the article would eventually run itself out, if it were tabooed and severely left alone by *all* pharmacists. The public would eventually realize that a grocer's place is, after all, not a guaranty for internal remedies.

No. 2,109.—Chloro-chromic Test for Hydrochloric Acid (J. A. A.).
It is not generally advisable to employ this test when other halogens than chlorine and bromine are present. To apply the test successfully, even when only chlorine is present, it is necessary that the substance to be tested shall be added to the reagent, in powder or otherwise, undiluted. The reagent is prepared by boiling, in a large test-tube, about 5 Gm. of bichromate of potassium with about 10 Gm. of sulphuric acid until the liquid is bright red. The substance to be tested is now introduced and the tube immediately closed with a stopper bearing a small bent tube which is made to dip into water rendered alkaline by potassa or soda. The test tube being held by a support, heat is applied so as to expel the brownish-red gas, consisting of chlorochromic anhydride. This is absorbed by the water and is decomposed by the alkali present, a chromate being formed which colors the solution more or less yellow. If bromine was present in the original sample, this is also driven over, but is absorbed by the alkali to a colorless bromide. If, however, iodine is likewise present, the reactions become too complicated and uncertain. Iodine is, of course, also expelled, but a portion of it is again set free in the receiver, though it may finally also be converted into iodide. It is much better to separate any iodide present in the beginning as follows: Precipitate the three halogens by nitrate of silver, wash the precipitate thoroughly by decantation, and then boil it, while still moist, with about 100 times its weight of a solution of carbonate of ammonium (made by dissolving 1 part of translucent commercial carbonate of ammonium in 9 parts of water of ordinary temperature, and add, for every 10 C.c. of the liquid, 5 C.c. of water of

ammonia of the spec. gr. 0.960) during 2 or 3 minutes. Allow it to settle, decant the liquid, and repeat the extraction with the ammonium solution. This reagent removes all the chloride and a trace of bromide of silver, and leaves behind all the iodide of silver and nearly all the bromide. Having thus all the chlorine in the ammoniacal solution as chloride of silver, the latter may easily be obtained by supersaturating with an acid. But if the chlorochromic test is to be used, a small portion of the ammoniacal solution is just barely neutralized with sulphuric acid (it may remain slightly alkaline, but should *not* be acid); the liquid evaporated to dryness, and the residue fused together with about an equal bulk (or more, if necessary) of bichromate of potassium. This mixed salt is then dropped into concentrated sulphuric acid, and heat then applied. Or the dry residue may be dropped into the mixture of bichromate and acid previously prepared.

No. 2,110.—**Syrup of Lactophosphate of Calcium** (supplement to Query 2,089 in January number).
One of our correspondents points out that in Formula No. 2, in which Lactate of Calcium is made the starting point for preparing the syrup, the quantity of this salt should be 218 grains, instead of 220.
This is quite true, if the purely theoretical quantity is to be used. But as we have previously said that, *practically*, the molecular weights of lactate of calcium—$Ca(C_3H_5O_3)_2.5H_2O$; 308—and of phosphate of calcium—$Ca(PO_4)_2$; 310—may be regarded as identical, we chose the figure 220 for the quantity of lactate of calcium, to replace 220 parts of phosphate of calcium. In the preparation of such an article as syrup of lactophosphate of calcium, such a trifling discrepancy is immaterial. It is much more likely that a prescriber would remember the strength of this syrup if he could recall the uniform value "220 grains to the pint" than if he had to remember a separate figure for each.
Rother's formula, given on page 28 of our volume for 1884, is correct, as published by the author in the *Amer. Journ. of Pharm.*, 1883, page 607, which you may consult for learning the reasons which induced him to increase the quantity of lactic acid. Of course, a neutral calcium lactate made from a 75-per-cent lactic acid would require much less of the latter, the 150 parts of calcium carbonate requiring actually only 180 parts of the acid for this purpose. Rother, however, doubles this, as he wants to produce the acid calcium lactate.

No. 2,111.—**Putty Powder** (J. D. C.).
The process of making putty-powder is as follows, according to Oliver Byrne:
"Putty powder is the pulverized oxide of tin, or generally of tin or lead mixed in various proportions; the process of manufacture is alike in all cases. The metal is oxidized in an iron muffle, or a rectangular box, closed on all sides, except a square hole in the front side. The retort is surrounded by fire, and kept at the red heat, so that its contents are partially ignited, and they are continually stirred to expose fresh portions to the heated air; the process is complete when the fluid metal entirely disappears, and the upper part of the oxide, then produced, sparkles somewhat like particles of incandescent charcoal. The oxide is then removed with ladles, and spread over the bottom of large iron cooling-pans, and allowed to cool. The lumps of oxide, which are as hard as marble, are selected from the mass, and ground dry under the runner; the putty powder is afterwards carefully sifted through lawn. As a criterion of quality, it may be said that the whitest putty powder is the purest, provided it be heavy; some of the common kinds are brown and yellow, whilst others, from the intentional admixture of a little ivory-black, are known as *gray putty*. The pure white putty, which is used by marble-workers, opticians, and some others, is the smoothest and most cutting; it should consist of oxide of tin alone; but, to lessen the difficulty of manufacture, a very little lead (the linings of tea-chests), or else an alloy called *shruff* (prepared in ingots by the pewterers), is added to assist the oxidation. The putty powder of commerce, of good, fair quality, is made of about equal parts of tin and lead, or tin and shruff; the common, dark-colored kinds are prepared of lead only, but these are much harsher to the touch, and altogether inferior. Perhaps the most extensive use of putty powder is in glass and marble works; but the best kind serves admirably as plate powder, and for the general purposes of polishing.
"Putty powder for fine optical purposes is prepared by the following method, which is the result of many experiments: Metallic tin is dissolved in nitro-muriatic acid, and precipitated from the filtered solution by liquid ammonia, both fluids being largely diluted with water. The peroxide of tin thus washed in abundance of water, collected in a cloth filter, and squeezed as dry as possible in a piece of new clean linen; the mass is now subjected to pressure in a screw press or between lever-boards to make it as dry as possible. When the lump thus produced has been broken in pieces and dried in the air, it is finely levigated, while dry, on a plate of glass with an iron spatula, and afterwards exposed in a crucible to a *low* white heat. Before the peroxide has been heated or while it is in the levigated *hydrous* state, the putty powder has but little cutting quality, as under the microscope particles then appear to have no determined form or to be amorphous, and on being wetted to resume the gelatinous condition of the hydrous precipitate, so as to be useless for polishing; whereas, when the powder is heated, to render it anhydrous, most of the particles take their natural forms—that of lamellar crystals—and act with far more energy (yet without scratching) than any of the ordinary polishing powders. The whole mass requires to be washed or elutriated in the usual manner, after having been heated, in order to separate the coarser particles. A little crocus is usually added to putty powder by way of coloring matter, as it is then easier to learn the quality of the powder that remains on the polishing tool."

No. 2,112.—**Phenol-Mercury, or Carbolate of Mercury** (Indianapolis).
The composition of the phenol-mercury made by Merck is said to correspond to the formula $(C_6H_5O)_2Hg$, which is the mercuric salt. How it is obtained is not known. But Fischer, in his "*Neuere Arzneimittel*," states that the following process yields a product very similar to that made by Merck:
Dissolve 188 parts of melted carbolic acid, and 56 parts of caustic potassa, on a water-bath, in just sufficient alcohol, using a porcelain capsule. Now add, under stirring, an alcoholic solution of 135 parts of mercuric chloride. This will gradually produces yellowish precipitate. Continue stirring until the contents of the capsule are nearly dry and almost colorless. Next pour upon it some hot water, transfer it to a filter and wash it, first with pure water, and then with water containing acetic acid. Finally allow it to drain on porous tiles and crystallise it from alcohol. It is, however, stated that the attempt to crystallize the compound occasionally fails.

No. 2,113.—**Methylic Alcohol or Wood Spirit** (S. W. R.).
Up to within a few years ago, the quality of wood spirit, also called wood naphtha, wood alcohol, has been very unsatisfactory. Even that which is yet sold by most of the large dealers in chemicals does not appear to be sufficiently pure, or, at least, not to be as pure as it can now be had directly from the refiners. We have handled wood alcohol during the last year which is as far superior to the kinds formerly available as chemically pure sulphuric acid is ahead of crude oil of vitriol. The best grade is almost free from any odor revealing its origin, and the second grade nearly so. Of course, they possess a specific odor of their own, which is by no means disagreeable, rather the opposite.
Whoever has occasion to burn alcohol as a fuel, will find it much more economical to burn wood alcohol than the ordinary alcohol of fermentation. The price of the former is very much lower, for good grades nearly one dollar less per gallon than the latter. This makes a large saving by the barrel. Wood alcohol is also a good solvent for shellac and other resins, and may be used in a variety of ways in place of the common alcohol.

No. 2,114.—**Phosphorus Paste** (Wilmington).
It is usually recommended to melt phosphorus under water in a bottle, and then to shake the corked bottle until the water cools, when the phosphorus will be found minutely divided. An improvement of this method is given by Dr. Bruno Hirsch (in *Handbuch der praktischen Pharmacie*, von Beckurts u. Hirsch. Stuttgart, 1887). Introduce the phosphorus into a strong bottle containing a concentrated solution of common salt or sugar, place the bottle in hot water, and, when the phosphorus is melted, expel the air from the upper part of the bottle by carbonic acid gas produced by adding to the water some bicarbonate of sodium and hydrochloric acid. Then close the bottle firmly, wrap a cloth about it, and shake it until the contents are cold. If solution of common salt has been used, this may gradually be replaced by decanting and washing with water. If a sugar solution, this may be added to the mass into which the powdered phosphorus is incorporated. The mass is prepared from flour, fat, and other ingredients easily devoured by rats. Good proportions are, for every 3 parts of phosphorus, 60 parts of rye flour, 60 parts of lard or other bland fat, and 40 parts of sugar (or its equivalent in form of solution).

No. 2,115.—**Estimation of Diastase in Malt or in Extract of Malt** (Cleveland).
Of all published processes, that of C. J. Lintner, published some years ago in the *Journal f. prak. Chem.* (1885, p. 282), is probably the most reliable. It is as follows:
Heat 2 Gm. of air-dry starch with 10 C.c. of very dilute hydrochloric acid (containing $\frac{1}{10}$ per cent HCl) and about 60 C.c. of water in a closed flask for thirty minutes on the water-bath, under frequent agitation. Neutralize the liquid with 10 C.c. of very dilute soda solution ($\frac{1}{10}$ per

cent NaOH), and make up the volume to 100 C.c. at the ordinary temperature. If malt is to be tested, prepare an extract by treating 1 gramme of finely ground or crushed malt with 500 C.c. of water during six hours at the ordinary temperature, and then filtering. Ten test-tubes are then charged, each with 10 C.c. of the starch solution, and afterwards the malt extract is added to each in successively increasing quantities: 0.1 C.c. in the first, 0.2 C.c. in the second, and so forth. The test-tubes are allowed to stand for one hour at the ordinary temperature. Next, 5 C.c. of Fehling's solution are poured into each test-tube, and the whole series immersed for ten minutes in boiling water. According to the quantity of the sugar present, the reagent will be more or less reduced. That tube will most nearly represent the full diastatic value of the malt which contains a colorless liquid over the precipitated red cuprous oxide, while the liquid in the immediately preceding tube still has a faint bluish tinge.

If the malt extract, prepared as above directed, is found to be too weak to produce any reaction, a fresh lot of a stronger extract may be prepared.

Extract of malt is tested in the same manner. But several preliminary experiments will be required to find, approximately, to what degree the extract should be diluted.

No. 2,116.—**The Uses of Hops ("Nevada").**

This correspondent asks, among other questions relating to similar subjects, the following:

"What is the reason that hops are generally preferred, and even actually prescribed by law in some countries, as an ingredient in making beer or ale?"

Were we to attempt a full answer to this question, we would have to go back a long space in history to show that the selection of hops was probably one which may be regarded as the natural outcome of long-continued experiments, carried on in a crude way, by the inhabitants of central Europe during the middle age, and perhaps even previously. It was to be expected that the remarkable properties of hops—a plant which is a native of this portion of Europe—would eventually be recognized and utilized. We shall not attempt to give a historical resumé of the introduction and uses of hops, but merely a condensed statement of the present views regarding the function and use of hops, entertained by the leading authorities on the domain of brewing.

In the first place, hops impart to beer and ale a peculiar agreeably bitter taste, and, at the same time, the essential oil contained in it adds a peculiar fine aroma. But the most important property is this, that the extract of hops is one of the most energetic poisons of bacteria, and thereby prevents secondary fermentation. According to Hayduck, these effects are solely due to the bitter resins which are only very slightly soluble in water, and of which a mere trace is sufficient to render inert the ferments of lactic and butyric acids and those of putrefaction, while, on the other hand, the alcoholic ferments are not in the least affected by them. Further, the tannin contained in hops is stated to contribute to its preservative virtues, since this is capable of throwing down any soluble (or dissolved) albuminoid, and any dissolved, but unsaccharified starch, though these statements regarding the function of the tannin are not sufficiently proven.

No. 2,117.—**Stability of Solutions of Corrosive Sublimate (M.).**

The author of the query has been in the habit of keeping on hand various solutions of corrosive sublimate for surgical use, as antiseptic, and has observed that some of them gradually deposited a sediment which turned out to be calomel. He asks us for information which might enable him to prevent this.

This very subject has been reported on, during last year, by Prof. Victor Meyer, in a paper in the Berliner Berichte (p. 1,725). Prof. O. Angerer, of Munich, had pointed out that solutions of corrosive sublimate made with *ordinary* (not distilled) water could be rendered permanently stable, if a quantity of chloride of sodium equal to that of the mercurial salt was added to them. The problem of preserving solutions of bichloride is very important, as the successful employment of the antiseptic treatment of wounds, in case of war, involves the lives of thousands of soldiers. In order to avoid the necessity of carrying about bulky volumes of liquid, Dr. Angerer had suggested to prepare pastils of bichloride of mercury and of chloride of sodium in definite proportions.

Prof. Meyer's results may be summarized as follows: When *distilled* water is used for preparing bichloride solutions—the experiments were made upon such as contained 1 part of salt in 1,000 of liquid—only a faint white precipitate was produced within thirty-six hours. Practically, the whole of the bichloride remained unaltered, no matter whether the bottle was kept open or stoppered. On the other hand, when ordinary water is used (as is likely to be the case in war times), there is apt to be more or less decomposition of the mercury salt. The decomposition, however, is greatly retarded or diminished by the presence of chloride of sodium, though this is never able to prevent it completely. On using notoriously bad wellwater and filtered lake-water, the decomposition was still greater, even when the proportion of chloride of sodium was raised to 4 parts for every 1 part of mercurial salt.

Our experience confirms the above. We have for a long time been in the habit of preparing, for use in the public hospitals of New York, a glycerite of bichloride of mercury, containing 1 grain of the salt in every 2 minims. In addition, there is about ½ grain of chloride of sodium in this quantity. When this solution is made, there is always a more or less decided formation of calomel (which is, however, greatly diminished by the use of the chloride of sodium). In order to make the final product as accurate in proportions as possible, we make the original solution somewhat stronger, then allow it to become perfectly clear by standing, pour off the clear liquid, and, having added alcohol to the residuary portion, pass this through a filter. The calomel is retained by this, washed and dried. Making allowance for the amount of bichloride hereby lost from the original amount, we adjust the product so that it will represent 1 grain of the mercurial salt in 2 minims. It is advisable to take about 1/10 part more of bichloride, at the start, than is theoretically required, so as to leave a sufficient margin for dilution. We think that such a solution, *slightly tinted with fuchsine*, would be very handy for carrying about with the field hospitals and medicine chests.

No. 2,118.—**Amylene and Amylene Hydrate** (Several inquirers).

In the recent literature, the term *amylene* has two different applications or meanings. For those of our readers who have studied at least the elementary and essential parts of organic chemistry, the following explanation will be sufficient.

A saturated hydrocarbon compound is understood to be one in which the number of hydrogen atoms is double that of the carbon atoms, increased by two. CH_4 methane, C_2H_6 ethane, C_3H_8 propane, C_4H_{10} butane, C_5H_{12} pentane, etc., etc. This class of bodies is also called *paraffins*. They are saturated and do not enter into any combinations under ordinary circumstances.

Another series of bodies is comprised under the term *alkylenes*. These are unsaturated hydrocarbons, containing a number of hydrogen atoms, just double of that of the carbon atoms. They are, therefore, capable of combining with two more monads, or their equivalent. These bodies are also known as *olefines*, and they are uniformly named by terms ending either in *-ene* or *-ylene*: CH_2 methene or methylene (this appears only in compounds); C_2H_4 ethene or ethylene; C_3H_6 propene or propylene; C_4H_8 butene or butylene; C_5H_{10} pentene or *amylene*, etc. *Amylene*, therefore, in this sense signifies the olefine of the pentane or amyl series, and is really a generic term for not less than five different compounds, all of them being isomers of each other. These five different modifications or isomers bear distinctive names, more or less expressing the nature of the constitution; for instance: normal amylene or propyl-ethylene (this is called "normal" in a chemical sense, but because it is the most common; in fact, it is a body which has so far only been obtained in every small quantities; the most common is the next one); trimethyl-ethylene or ordinary amylene from fusel oil; and three other varieties.

Incidentally we will state that the last-mentioned kind of amylene is best prepared in the following manner: To 3 parts of coarsely powdered, previously fused chloride of zinc, 2 parts of fusel oil are added, and the mixture frequently shaken during 24 hours. It is then distilled from a sand-bath, and the portion coming over between $36°$ and $38°$ C. collected separately.

Amylene, in recent medical literature, is also often understood to be equivalent to *Amylene Hydrate*. It is preferable to the latter term, but medical writers are very often obstinate in their choice of nomenclature.

This last-mentioned substance is the tertiary amylic alcohol, having the composition $C_5H_{12}O$, or $(CH_3)_2CC_2H_5$. OH, also known as dimethyl-ethyl-carbinol.

Amylene hydrate has been introduced in therapeutics as an efficient hypnotic, capable of replacing chloral hydrate. It has this advantage over the latter, that it does not seriously interfere with the respiration or the action of the heart. In potency, it stands between chloral hydrate and paraldehyde, the latter being the weakest.

B. Fischer some time ago gave the following data for characterizing amylene hydrate of good quality in the *Pharm. Zeit.*:

"Amylene hydrate is a clear, colorless, oily liquid of penetrating odor, reminding one of camphor, oil of peppermint, and paraldehyde. It is soluble in about 12 parts of water, and miscible with alcohol in all proportions. When pure, it boils at $102.5°$ C. (the commercial product between $98°$ and $103°$), and when cooled to $-18.5°$ C. it congeals to needle-shaped crystals which melt at $-12°$ C. Its specific gravity is 0.826 at $0°$ C. and 0.812 at $12°$ C.

"When treated with concentrated sulphuric acid, amylene hydrate assumes a yellow to brown color. To insure the absence of the poisonous amylic alcohol (of fusel oil, produced by fermentation), the following tests are recommended: 1. Dissolve 1 Gm. of amylene hydrate in 18 C.c.

of water, and tint it slightly with permanganate. The color should not fade within 15 minutes (absence of ethylic and ordinary amylic alcohol). 2. Treat a similar solution with bichromate of potassium and diluted sulphuric acid, and warm gently; no green color should appear within half an hour (absence of the alcohols before mentioned). 3. Treat a similar solution with a few drops of solution of nitrate of silver and a trace of ammonia, then warm gently. The liquid should remain clear and should not yield a silver mirror, or precipitate any silver (absence of aldehydes, which are present in most primary alcohols)."

No. 2,119.—Assay of Aconite Preparations ("Laboratory").

It is one thing to assay a preparation made by one's self from undoubtedly genuine aconite root, and one which has been purchased ready-made, the only voucher for its being prepared from aconite being the label of the seller or manufacturer. In the last-named case, tests of identity must precede or go hand-in-hand with the assay process. The most reliable practical test is the peculiar tingling sensation which is imparted to the tongue and fauces by even minute proportions of aconitine. The utmost caution is to be exercised in tasting precipitates suspected to contain aconitine. The substance itself should never be brought in contact with the tongue. Only very dilute solutions may be thus tasted. The limit of recognition is stated to be about 1 in 10,000. However, as it appears that our correspondent rather desires information how to test aconite preparations, the genuineness of which he is convinced of, we will briefly mention three methods by which this may be accomplished.

1. *By Mayer's Solution* (after Dragendorff).—By one or more previous approximations, a solution of the alkaloids is first prepared, of such a strength that it contains 1 part of alkaloid in 150 to 200 of water. This is best done by mixing the extract of aconite (if tincture, it should be reduced to an extract at a very low temperature) with pure caustic lime, drying the mixture at a low temperature, and then extracting it with ether in an extraction apparatus. Acidulated water is then added to the ethereal solution, the aqueous layer separated and exposed a short time until the dissolved ether has volatilized, or nearly so. The solution having then been adjusted to about the strength mentioned above, Mayer's solution is very gradually added to it. The end of the reaction is ascertained by filtering a drop or two through a very small filter upon a watch-glass, and adding a drop from the burette. If a further precipitate occurs, the watch-glass and filter are drained and washed with a few drops of water back into the original vessel.

It is well known that the precipitate caused by Mayer's solution often settles only very slowly, and it sometimes becomes a very tedious process to obtain enough clear solution by filtration to make a test for the end-reaction. The operation may be much abbreviated by proceeding in the following manner:

Place into a series of rather long and numbered test-tubes equal quantities of the solution to be tested. Add to each, successively, a measured quantity of the reagent, increasing in a regular ratio (which will vary for different alkaloids), agitate gently without soiling the upper parts of the test-tubes, cork them and let them stand, until a clear layer of liquid begins to appear at the surface. When this has become sufficiently high, add to each test-tube, by means of a pipette held close to the clear layer, one drop of Mayer's solution. If there be two successive tubes, in one of which the solution produced a cloudiness, while it failed to do so in the other, then the true alkaloidal value lies between these two tubes, and a new series of trials is to be made, between these limits, with smaller intermediate fractions.' If precipitates appear in all the tubes, the original solution was too concentrated, and the preliminary trial must be repeated until in one and the same series a positive and negative result is obtained. Now each cubic centimeter of Mayer's solution has been ascertained (under the rate of dilution above-mentioned) to correspond to 0.0274 Gm. of aconitine alkaloid. But as the precipitate is not quite insoluble, it is necessary to add 0.00005 Gm. of alkaloid for every cubic centimeter of the total liquid containing the precipitate. The result is a sufficiently close approximation for practical purposes.

2 *By Volumetric Acid* (after Dieterich).—Triturate 0.2 Gm. of pure caustic lime (from marble) with 3 Gm. of distilled water, dissolve in it 2 Gm. of extract of aconite, and then thoroughly incorporate 10 Gm. more of powdered pure caustic lime. Introduce the mixture, wrapped in filtering paper, into an extraction apparatus and extract with ether during 45 minutes. Evaporate the ether from the solution, dissolve the residue in ½ C.c. of alcohol, add 10 C.c. of water, and 1 or 2 drops solution of rosolic acid (as indicator). Now titrate with $\frac{1}{10}$ normal sulphuric acid (containing 0.49 Gm. of absolute sulphuric acid per liter) until the alkaloid is neutralized. Every cubic centimeter of the acid corresponds to 0.00333 Gm. of aconitine.

No. 2,120.—Domestic "Disinfectant" (Several inquirers).

We receive every now and then an inquiry, from different parts of the country, regarding the most suitable domestic "disinfectant." In further explaining the purposes for which this is to be used, our correspondents usually mention such as refer to toilet-rooms, nurseries, sick-rooms, cellars, wash-rooms, etc., and the chief object appears generally to be to have a good *deodorant*, rather than a disinfectant. In fact, in nine cases out of ten, when a lay person asks for a disinfectant, it may be presumed that he means a deodorant. The selection of a simple and efficient agent, or combination of agents, for this purpose had for some time engaged our attention, not because there was any lack of such, but because so many things have to be taken into account in recommending a substance of this kind for domestic use.

The following may be regarded as the principal requirements or demands to be made of it:

1. It should be *efficient* for the purposes for which it is designed. It is not necessary that it be strongly antiseptic, nor need it be a very active disinfectant, though if both of these properties could be combined with the property of deodorizing, it would be a very great advantage. It is, however, impossible to do this, without having recourse to agents which are not safe to use in the hands of the common people.

2. It should be *colored*, preferably with a tint which makes it impossible to mistake the liquid for a beverage. A good color would be red, or green. The former is, however, producible only by such agents as are prone to decomposition, especially in the presence of metallic salts, and solutions colored therewith are liable to become entirely colorless in the course of time. For this reason, we prefer a green or greenish color, unless there is some objection to this. Frequently it happens that domestic "disinfectants" are wanted for treating woven fabrics, such as children's underclothing, diapers, night-dresses, bed-clothing, etc. In such cases it would not do to employ any coloring matter, or, in fact, any ingredient which would be likely to stain the fabrics. However, common sense will tell any one that a *colored* liquid is unsuitable for this purpose.

3. The liquid should have a distinctive *odor*. After trying a great many substances, both in the public hospitals of New York and in some private houses, we have come to the conclusion that a combination of oil of thyme with oil of pine leaves, or even oil of thyme alone, is the most suitable. It is pleasant, and at the same time reminds one so much of liniments that the odor alone will repel children from meddling with it.

4. It should be comparatively *concentrated*, so that it could be suitably diluted at home. And finally,

5. It should be *cheap*.

Now it would be easy to suggest a variety of combinations complying with the general rules here laid down. Upon the basis of an experience extending over a number of years, we believe that the best combination, taking everything into consideration, is one of Sulphate of Iron, and Sulphate of Zinc. To these may be added enough beta-naphthol and oil of thyme to saturate the solution.

In order to counteract the tendency of the sulphate of iron to oxidize by contact with the air, a minute quantity of hypophosphorous acid may be added to the liquid.

The following formula, based upon the considerations above advanced, is that which has been in use for some time, and has given good satisfaction:

Compound Solution of Zinc and Iron.

Sulphate of Zinc, commercial.......... 16 tr. oz.
Sulphate of Iron, crystallized.......... 16 tr. oz.
Hypophosphorous Acid (10%)............ 120 minims
Oil of Thyme............................ 60 "
Naphthol............................... 15 grains
Water.................................enough to make 5 pints

Dissolve the two Salts in 4 pints of boiling Water, add the Naphthol and the Oil of Thyme, and shake or stir the mixture frequently while it cools. Then add the Hypophosphorous Acid and make up the volume, with Water, to 5 pints. Shake or stir the mixture frequently during a few days, then filter it through a wetted filter.

This solution will have a very handsome green color, and resist oxidation for a long time.

For use, it may directed to be diluted with from 5 to 10 parts of water, the strength depending upon the work it is expected to do.

Application for Sore Nipples.—
Balsam of Peru,
Tr. Arnica .... āā 3 ʒ.
Expressed oil of Almond,
Lime Water............................ āā 3 ʒ.

Mix. Shake well, and apply to inflamed nipples with a camel's-hair brush after cleansing them with borax and water.—Dr. J. H. Scarff, in *Maryland Med. Jour.*

The Syndicate of the Rouen Pharmacists have entered into an agreement with the Municipal Council, whereby for every wounded person brought into a pharmacy, and attended to there, the city is to pay an indemnity of 3f. for day and 5f. for night attendance. When the patient is able to pay, the city may afterwards collect the amount from him—if it can.

BIBLIOGRAPHY.

TEXT-BOOK OF THERAPEUTICS AND MATERIA MEDICA.—Intended for the use of Students and Practitioners. By ROBERT T. EDES, A.B., M.D., etc. Philadelphia: Lea Brothers & Co., 1887, pp. 552, 8vo. Cloth, $3.50; Leather, $4.50.

As a text-book for students in medicine this is a remarkably good one. It gives the essential features of the subject in a crisp, attractive form which, for a subject so essentially dry, is quite novel and attractive. The author has evidently profited by his long experience in teaching, and avoided on the one hand too great elaboration of details, and on the other the condensation characteristic of a mere cram-book. Little, if any, description is given of crude drugs, for the reason that "its value would be far surpassed by a few hours in a cabinet of materia medica or in a well-furnished drug store;" but some attention is paid to the pharmaceutical relations of the articles referred to. An excellent feature of the arrangement is the use of prominent type for the titles of articles of greatest value—a matter of no small importance to the student who has, as yet, acquired but little definite knowledge from individual experience. Throughout the entire work the author's personality is apparent in the criticisms, suggestions, and comments, which indicate at once that the construction of the book was not a mere matter of compilation, but was the result of thought and observation.

Remedies which have but recently been introduced receive a very fair show of consideration, and in stating the dose of each article the equivalent in the metric system is given.

If anything is needed to increase the value of the work, it would be some advice respecting the need for greater attention on the part of physicians in writing *legible* prescriptions.

LITHOGRAPHERS' AND PHOTOGRAPHERS DIRECTORY. A Directory for Photographers, Lithographers, and for all Allied Arts and Trades in the United States and Canada, Mexico, Central and South America. New York: The Lithographer Publishing Co., 1887-88, p. 208, 8vo. $3.00.

THIS is the first edition of a very useful work of reference for all who are in any way interested in the arts to which it relates. In the addition to the directory proper, the work contains chapters of general interest on the history of lithography, photography, and kindred graphic arts.

PROCEEDINGS OF THE AMERICAN PHARMACEUTICAL ASSOCIATION, at the 35th Annual Meeting, held at Cincinnati, Ohio, September, 1887. Also the Constitution, By-laws, and Roll of Members. Philadelphia, 1887, pp. 729, 8vo.

THE general character of this volume is in keeping with those which have preceded it. The work contains not only a large number of papers, but also a brief summary of the scientific progress of the year and the text of laws recently enacted in several States, of especial interest to pharmacists.

YEAR BOOK OF PHARMACY: Comprising Abstracts of Papers relating to Pharmacy, Materia Medica, and Chemistry Contributed to British and Foreign Journals from July 1st, 1886, to June 30th, 1887. With the Transactions of the BRITISH PHARMACEUTICAL CONFERENCE at the 24th Annual Meeting, held at Manchester, August, 1887. London: J. & A. Churchill, 1887, pp. 631, 8vo, muslin, 10s.

THE present number of this valuable series differs but little in its general character from those which have preceded it. These year books deserve greater popularity among pharmacists as works of reference, and as a means for affording students in pharmacy an opportunity for valuable information. The volumes are convenient in size, and the contents are well arranged and cover a wide field of pharmaceutical literature.

DIE RIECHSTOFFE, und ihre Verwendung zur Herstellung von Duftessenzen, Haarölen, Pomaden, Riechkissen, etc., sowie anderer Kosmetischer Mittel (6th ed.), von DR. ST. MIERZINSKI (70 illust.), 8vo. Weimar (Voigt), 1888. [Price, in New York, $2.50.]

THE author's name has long been favorably known through his work on ethereal oils, perfumery, and cosmetics, which lies before us in a new and greatly enlarged edition. Every page of this bears testimony to the fact that the author has carefully collated the literature which has appeared up to the time of publication, and that he speaks from experience, gained by practical acquaintance with the substances and compounds which he describes, which is not always the case in works of this kind.

The preliminary chapters treat of the apparatus and machinery employed in the manufacture of the various natural or artificial products employed in perfumery. From this chapter, we have selected a few specimens, with illustrations, which will be found elsewhere in this number. The next chapter treats of the natural products themselves, their origin, mode of collection or production, etc. Among these are the essential oils, to which the author devotes special attention, and the treatment of which betrays his thorough practical familiarity with the subject. Next follows a chapter on the so-called pomades, both those which are prepared from delicate flowers for the subsequent extraction by alcohol, and those which are compounded for cosmetic purposes. Among the chapters which follow are such as treat of hair-oils, hair restoratives, sachets, cold creams, handkerchief extracts, colognes, and every other conceivable form of perfumery, with the exclusion of soaps. A very large number of formulæ are given, regarding which we have the author's assurance that they are all reliable and bona-fide, which, according to him (and also according to our own experience) is by no means the case with many of the formulæ found in other similar works.

SUGGESTIVE MEDICATION.

The recent discovery by Dr. Luys is in course of revolutionizing the medical world. This realized physician has recognized that it is not necessary to introduce medicinal substances into the organism of invalids to produce their effects; a simple exterior contact being sufficient. Among the curious references which serve as illustrations of this theory we choose the following, which appears to us decisive.

1.—*Before the Experiment:* The physiognomy of the subject expresses all the symptoms by which we recognize the victim of constitutional obstinacy [sic].

2.—*Operation:* Dr. Luys applies delicately between the eyes of the subject a medico-chirurgical appliance the brilliant surface of which rapidly causes hypnotism.

3.—*Result:* There follows a stage of agitation, somewhat fatiguing, happily attended with great relief, which brings about a cure.

4.—The features of the patient express the satisfaction of a function accomplished.—*L'Illustration.*

The book lacks an index, but this is, in a measure, made up by a very detailed and well-arranged table of contents.

We recommend this work, as the latest and probably most reliable guide on the subject, to our readers.

Frosted Glass.

Verre Givré, or hoar-frost glass, is an article now made in Paris, so called from the pattern upon it, which resembles the feathery forms traced by frost on the inside of the windows in cold weather. The process of making the glass is simple. The surface is first ground either by the sand-blast or the ordinary method, and is then covered with a sort of varnish. On being dried either in the sun or by artificial heat, the varnish contracts strongly, taking with it the particles of glass to which it adheres; and, as the contraction takes place along definite lines, the pattern produced by the removal of the particles of glass resembles very closely the branching crystals of frostwork. A single coat gives a small, delicate effect, while a thick film formed by putting on two, three or more coats, contracts so strongly as to produce a large and bold design. By using colored glass, a pattern in half-tint may be made on the colored ground, and after decorating white glass, the back may be silvered or gilded.—*Invention.*

THE BOTANIST.

American Druggist

The Norwegian Cod-Liver Oil Industry.

FROM a lengthy report of U. S. Consul-General R. B. Anderson, of Copenhagen, published in the *Reports from the Consuls of the U. S.*, we take the following:

1. *Preparing the Fish.*

On the way home from the fishing grounds each night when the sails can be used and the men are free, the day's catch is immediately prepared. The head is removed and saved. Then an incision is made near the tail of the fish in order to let the blood out. The liver and spawn are saved in holders brought especially for the purpose, and the entrails are cast into the sea. The fish designed for drying without salt are now tied together by the tails, two by two, without washing, and hung over racks on shore, where they remain drying in the sun until June 12th, it being forbidden by law to take them down sooner, as many men live at great distances from the drying grounds and in the absence of the law mentioned the temptation to appropriate other men's property was found to be too strong for the first comers to resist. The fish to be salted are usually sold to small smacks, which are sent by the merchants of the cities lying further south to cruise and buy them up. In these vessels the cod are salted in layers in the hold. After being opened to the backbone along the whole length of belly, the bone is removed to the third joint, opposite the navel. The fish receives no washing under this process, even though it is a well-known fact that a little care in this direction would give the finished cod a much better appearance. After completing a load the smacks depart for the small islands lying outside the cities of Throndhjem, Aalesbund, Christiansund, and Molde, where the fish are alternately piled in stacks to press the moisture out of them, and then spread on cobblestone pavements or the natural rocks to dry in the sun until ready for export.

2. *Fish Oil.*

Oil occupies by no means an insignificant position among the products of Lofoden, though in amount it varies through the several years far more than the other cod products. From 1876 to 1880 the production averages 45,000 hectoliters* per year, while in 1883 not more than 8,000 hectoliters were secured, and in 1886, 35,000. The value of the product also varies, according to quality and the amount produced, from 25 kroner ($6.66) to 350 kroner ($93.33) per barrel. The preparation of this oil is carried on partly at factories and partly as a sort of domestic industry. The liver saved, as before stated, is sometimes sold to the local factories and sometimes collected in barrels which, at the end of the season, the fisherman takes to his home in order to prepare their contents. In this way the livers often stand many weeks, and upon their arrival a certain quantity of their oil has already been freed by the rotting of some of the liver cells. This is poured off, and then, by repeated boilings over open fires, the rest of the oil is boiled out. In this way four sorts of oil are obtained — raw medicinal, clear (yellow), partly clear (light brown), and refuse or train (brown).

The livers sold to the factories are treated in other ways, and from them is obtained the well-known product which is sold as steam refined cod-liver oil. As much of this is exported to America, where it is admitted to be superior to the Newfoundland oil, I took pains to ascertain the process by which it is prepared and for this purpose I visited the celebrated factory at Stamsund, established by the late Peter Möller. Here I was well received by the present owner, the son of Peter Möller, who gave me every facility for seeing his works and assisted me in getting a clear description of his method of preparation, laying special stress upon the fact that there was no secret connected with the process. His own success, he claimed, was due chiefly to a careful selection of the livers and a scrupulous cleanliness at every stage and point of treatment. The very first requirement for the production of a good article of oil is that the liver should of the best sort and perfectly fresh. The fish from which it is taken should have been caught the same day as the boiling is done.

When care is observed, and if the thermometer be under the freezing point, the liver may also be used the day following the catch.

After being most carefully sorted, the sick livers being known by their greenish tinge, and lean, scanty ones by a red, or often really black color (both of these to be unhesitatingly thrown out), the livers, with the gall-bladders removed, are well washed and tried out by one of three processes. The first of these is used in many of the refineries, as the capital required for a plant is not great

* One hectoliter = 26.4 gallons.

and the oil obtained may be excellent, if sufficient care be observed in its preparation. In this process the principle is simply even heating of the raw material in water-baths.

The second method, used in the factory I visited, and which I myself witnessed, consists in gradually heating the livers in iron kettles about and under which steam is circulated freely, the temperature being automatically regulated by ventilators.

The third method is the most rapid, simple, and cheap of all, and is mostly used on board vessels which are sent to Lofoden for the sole purpose of trying out oil. It consists of passing steam under some pressure directly into the mass of livers, which, heated, rapidly give up their oil. After being obtained by any of these processes and poured off, the oil is cooled more or less, and during a longer or shorter time, during which treatment the stearin separates itself in a ratio proportionate to the degree of cold and the time cooled.

The better sort are kept for a long time at a temperature not above zero C., and are then pressed in cold rooms, filtered, and bottled. If all the oils prepared by either of the first two of these methods are not equally good and clear, the reason lies in the fact that the process has not been conscientiously followed and not in any secret of preparation. The fault generally lies in the choice of the livers. Strong competition often makes it unprofitable to discard large masses of raw material, simply because it is somewhat old or tainted, especially when it is known that the resulting oil cannot be recognized until after the lapse of some time.

By the third process of trying out the oil—that is, by rapid and high heating of the livers through direct contact with the superheated steam—more oil is obtained, but of a far inferior quality, as it quickly acquires a disagreeable taste, and can be detected by its appearance a short time after preparation. Long experience and extensive experiments at the better factories have demonstrated that the oil should never be heated above 70° C. Oil which has been subjected to a higher temperature oxidizes on contact with the air the more rapidly the higher the temperature it has reached. How far the separation of the stearin is of any gain or loss from a therapeutic standpoint is still an open question, but the demand of the public that the oil shall remain clear, even in cold weather, makes the present process necessary. In respect to the amount of stearin contained, there is a great difference between the Lofoden and Newfoundland oils. While the former yields from 10 to 15 per cent of its bulk in stearin at a temperature zero C., the latter, under the same conditions, never gives more than 5 or 6 per cent.

The last filtering of the oil cannot be done too carefully, as there are always minute particles of liver cells held so finely in suspension that only the most painstaking filtering can remove them. At first they are invisible, but they collect, and later show themselves as a sediment at the bottom of the bottle or vessel in which the oil is preserved.

As to the difference in quality between the American and Norwegian cod-liver oil, I think I am safe in saying, as may in fact be seen from the statements already made, that it arises chiefly from the different circumstances under which the fishing is carried on.

At Lofoden the boats used are small and open, and the circumstances require that they shall be ashore every night, and thus the factories can obtain the livers of each day's catch when not more than a few hours old. On the other hand, the fishing on our coast is carried on in decked vessels, fitted for long cruises, touching shore only at long intervals, so that by the time the livers can get to the factories they are old or partly putrefied. To remedy this, and thus bring the large industry in cod-liver oil mainly or wholly into American hands, I would suggest that our oil refiners send out clean, nicely-fitted steam refining vessels, which should cruise the fishing-grounds, buy the livers fresh from the fishing smacks, and try out the oil on the spot and in the manner above described. This plan is thought perfectly practicable by several persons largely interested in the Lofoden industry with whom I have talked. I consulted Dr. F. P. Möller, whose father, Peter Möller, was the first to produce steam-refined cod-liver oil about thirty years ago, about this proposition, and he admitted that if adopted it would be of no small advantage to our American fishermen.

To Dr. F. P. Möller I am largely indebted for the detailed description of the methods and processes of producing medicinal cod-liver oil. As the American coasts produce such an abundance of cod, it would seem to me that by the plan suggested we might ourselves produce all the cod-liver oil for our own consumption and even compete in the European and other foreign markets.

The Manufacture of Lithium Salts for Medicinal or Technical Purposes.

THE element lithium is one of those which are widely distributed and occur in many localities, but only in a few places in such quantity that its extraction becomes profitable. Its most abundant source is the mineral *lepidolite*, consisting of silicate of aluminium and fluorides of alkalies, among them also lithium, which amounts to about 3 per cent of the total constituents. The most abundant deposit of this mineral which is easily accessible, is a layer, occurring between granite and gneiss in the mountain of Hradisko near Rozena, in Moravia (Austria). Lithium occurs also in some other minerals, up to about 7$, but these are of too rare occurrence to serve as sources of manufacture. Many mineral waters contain lithium, but mostly in very small quantity. Some of them, however, contain a sufficient amount of it to warrant their employment as forms of administration of lithium for medicinal purposes. There are several valuable springs of this kind in the U. S., for instance, one at Ballston, another near Buffalo, and one in Virginia. The Mur-spring at Baden-Baden contains 0.2952 Gm. (about 4 9 grains) of chloride of lithium in the liter, and a hot spring in Cornwall (England) is said to contain 0.372 Gm. (about 6 grains) per liter, the total quantity of water produced in one day containing about 300 kilos of the chloride of lithium. Lithium has also been discovered in the ash of many plants, in the blood and milk, and in other substances.

The general method of preparing lithium salts from the crudo minerals consists in decomposing the latter by acids or, if this is impracticable, to fuse the mineral with lime and extracting the mass with water. The resulting solution is then freed from all bases except alkalies. And the usual method formerly practised for separating the lithium from the other alkalies was based upon the slight solubility of carbonate of lithium in water, compared with that of the carbonates of the other alkalies. If a concentrated solution of an easily soluble lithium salt (for instance, the chloride) is mixed with a solution of carbonate of sodium, or potassium, or ammonium, carbonate of lithium is precipitated. There is, however, some lithium left in solution, and, besides, the precipitated carbonate of lithium contains a considerable proportion of the carbonate of the alkali used for precipitation. Sometimes the precipitate appears to have been put on the market without further purification, and hence the complaints which have recently been made by some French writers (see elsewhere in this journal) that the commercial salicylate of lithium, received from Germany, is contaminated with salicylate of sodium. The precipitate above spoken of can only be deprived of the accompanying alkalies by repeatedly dissolving it in hydrochloric acid, precipitating with carbonate of ammonium and pressing. When chloride of lithium occurs in the solution alone with chloride of sodium, the two may be separated by alcohol or a mixture of alcohol and ether, which dissolve the former, but not the latter salt.

As *lepidolite* is the most common mineral of lithium, though occurring only in a few localities, it is usually employed as the source of the commercial lithium salts. According to Cooper, this mineral contains only 0.7% of lithia and 0.99% fluoride of lithium; according to other authorities, the lithium amounts to about 3 per cent. There are probably some localities in the U. S. where this mineral occurs, but so far we have not heard of any place which affords it in sufficient quantity, and readily accessible.

Among the processes employed on the large scale for extracting the lithium from the mineral, the following method, used by E. Schering of Berlin, is the best. It is based upon that of Joss, which is briefly as follows: The eluriated mineral is digested for some time with concentrated sulphuric acid in stone-ware vessels. The excess of sulphuric acid is afterwards driven off by heat, the mass extracted with water, the solution precipitated by ammonia (which separates alumina, silica, iron, etc.), the filtrate from this evaporated to dryness, and the residue ignited. The latter consists of alkali sulphates which are separated by alkali carbonates.

In Schering's factory, this method is modified in the following manner:

The mineral, lepidolite, is finely powdered and sifted, transferred to a basin of stone-ware situated so as to be surrounded by warm air, then mixed to a thin magma with concentrated sulphuric acid, and digested until the mass becomes lumpy. It is then calcined on a hearth, and, while still warm, completely lixiviated with water. Before the resulting solution is evaporated, it is mixed with enough sulphate of potassium to combine with the aluminium present to alum. During the evaporation, the latter separates as a fine precipitate, which is removed, and any alum that may finally remain in solution is decomposed by milk of lime. After filtering and washing, the united liquids are mixed with chloride of barium, whereby all the bases present are converted into chlorides, while sulphate of barium falls down. The whole mixture is then evaporated to dryness, and the residue extracted with absolute alcohol, which dissolves out the chloride of lithium and chloride of calcium. After removal of the alcohol (which is, of course, recovered), the calcium salt is decomposed by oxalate of ammonium, and if any contaminating metals should still be present, these are gotten rid of by sulphide of ammonium. The filtrate is again evaporated to dryness, once more extracted with absolute alcohol, and, upon the removal of the latter, almost absolutely pure chloride of lithium is left behind.

To convert this into the carbonate, which is the starting point for all other salts of lithium, it is dissolved in a small quantity of water, and precipitated by carbonate of ammonium and water of ammonia. The resulting carbonate of lithium is finally washed with alcohol of 60$, whereby the remaining traces of chlorides may be removed.

Anthrarobin, a new Dermatic Remedy in Place of Chrysarobin.

PROFESSORS LIEBERMANN and SEIDLER showed, in 1878, that the active principle of goa-powder was not chrysophanic acid, as had been announced by Attfield, but a body in which the quinone group of chrysophanic acid was in a partial state of reduction, and which, therefore, was able to absorb a considerable quantity of oxygen under certain conditions. This body was called chrysarobin by the discoverers, and it is under this name that it has been introduced into several pharmacopœias.

Liebermann's theory that the therapeutic activity of the commercial so-called chrysophanic acid resided exclusively in the readily oxidisable chrysarobin received confirmation by the fact that pyrogallol (pyrogallic acid) was subsequently found by Dr. Jarisch to be an equally effective agent, though be selected it for other reasons. Prof. Liebermann, however, reports that Dr. Jarisch agrees with him now as to the true interpretation of the therapeutic activity of pyrogallol.

Prof. Liebermann has recently had occasion to devote renewed attention to this subject, being engaged in studies of the reduction of chrysophanic acid to chrysarobin, and of the leuco-bodies (colorless derivatives) obtained from the coloring matters of anthraquinone. The leuco-derivatives of alizarin, flavopurpurin, anthrapurpurin, anthragallol, etc., etc., all possess the property, when in alkaline solution, of absorbing oxygen with the greatest energy, whereby they are converted into the corresponding coloring matters. If Prof. Liebermann's theory regarding the action of chrysarobin were correct, then all these bodies should turn out to possess similar therapeutic effects.

In testing this question, useful results could be expected only from such compounds which could be prepared on a large scale. Among these, the most promising were alizarin, flavopurpurin, and anthrapurpurin.

Prof. Liebermann first describes his attempt to prepare the leuco-derivatives of these bodies by heating them with glacial acetic acid and granulated zinc, but does not recommend this method, as it is not economical. However, the first specimens employed in making the therapeutic tests were prepared in this manner.

The best agents for accomplishing the reduction are zinc dust and ammonia, which had already before been employed by Liebermann himself and others as efficient reducing agents. It is only necessary to boil the respective coloring matters, during fifteen minutes, with zinc dust and dilute water of ammonia (details will be found in *Berichte d. D. Chem. Ges.*, xiv., 1,260, and xv., 1,040), and to filter the ammoniacal solution into hydrochloric acid, whereby the leuco-substances are precipitated. They are then washed and dried, and in this state are sufficiently pure for medical use.

The first body thus prepared by Liebermann was derived from flavopurpurin. For this and several succeeding trials, only the chemically pure substances were used. As soon as it was ascertained that all of these derivatives possessed about the same therapeutic energy, it was no longer necessary to employ chemically pure bodies, but the cruder, technical substances were subsequently employed.

The leuco-derivative of alizarin had already, some time ago, been prepared by Rœmer (not for therapeutic purposes, however), and had been named *desoxyalizarin*. In accordance with this term, the corresponding derivatives of the other coloring matters should be called *desoxyflavopurpurin*, *desoxyanthrapurpurin*, etc., but Liebermann, recognising the unsuitableness of these terms in medicine and pharmacy, proposes to apply the generic name "*anthrarobin*" to the leuco-derivatives of the crude technical alizarin. This name is to recall not only the fact that the new substance is derived from the anthraquinone group, but also its chemical and therapeutic relationship to chrysarobin. If it is necessary to make a special distinction between the anthrarobins derived from the several members of his group, then the following designations may be used, as proposed by Liebermann:

1. *Anthrarobin* (without further specification) is to denote the product obtained from commercial alizarin ("blue tint").
2. *Anthrarobin* "P," or "F" is to denote that prepared from the commercial purpurins.

And it is under these names that the new substance will be put on the market by the manufacturers, Messrs. Jaffé and Darmstædter, of Charlottenburg.

Anthrarobin, as it will appear in commerce, is a yellowish-white powder which is scarcely affected by the air if kept dry. It is insoluble in water and aqueous acids, but most easily soluble, even in the cold, in dilute solutions of the alkalies, ammonia, and alkaline earths, yielding brownish-yellow solutions. The latter, however, are not permanent, but absorb oxygen from the air with the greatest avidity. Most energetic in this respect are the solutions made with fixed alkalies. The color of these solutions is at first green, then becomes blue, and finally changes to alizarin-violet. This change of color, which can be used as a reaction of identity, is best observed when dilute solutions are shaken in a test-tube, the tints being most prominently noticeable along the inner walls of the test-tube (held against white paper), where the air has exerted the greatest effect. The absorption of the oxygen of the air may be easily demonstrated by shaking about ½ Gm. of the substance mixed with a solution of an alkali in a test-tube firmly closed with the thumb. It will be found that the tube will remain attached to the thumb by suction, owing to the rarefaction of the air in the tube.

Anthrarobin is soluble only with difficulty in benzol or chloroform, but in glacial acetic acid or in alcohol it is much more soluble than chrysarobin. Of alcohol (90-95s), 5 parts are sufficient to hold it in solution in the cold. The technical product yields a brownish-yellow solution with alcohol. If this menstruum is to be used, it is best to use it at a boiling temperature, which effects solution at once. But long boiling must be carefully avoided, as the body is liable to be decomposed. Cold alcoholic solutions are slightly oxidised when exposed to the air, but in a well-corked bottle they may nevertheless be kept, with but little change, for weeks. The alcoholic solution may be diluted with glycerin without precipitation. In fact, glycerin dissolves the substance likewise.

The technical product contains about ½ per cent of ash, among which is a trace of oxide of zinc, but this is of no importance.

Dr. Behrend, of Berlin, has made experiments with the new body in his dermatological clinic. He reports having successfully treated with it 9 cases of herpes tonsurans, 1 of pityriasis versicolor, 1 of eczema marginatum, and 3 of psoriasis. He also states that anthrarobin is applicable to precisely the same skin affections as chrysarobin. Its effect is somewhat less energetic than that of the latter, but is still more intense than that of pyrogallic acid.

Anthrarobin, however, possesses this advantage over chrysarobin, that it does not inflame the skin. Hence it may be used also upon the head and on the face. It imparts to the skin a light brown tint. Stains which are caused by it upon linen and white fabrics may be easily washed off with soda and soap, which cannot be done in the case of chrysarobin.

Prof. Liebermann thinks that the introduction of this new body possibly marks only the beginning of a whole series of other active remedies, the effects of which depend upon their avidity for oxygen.—*After Berichte d. D. Ch. Ges.*, 1888, 447.

Dhaura—a Useful Gum from India.

In a communication on Indian dyes and methods of dyeing followed in India, read recently before the Liverpool Section of the Society of Chemical Industry (*Journ. S. C. I.*, Dec. 31st, p. 79), Mr. Elworthy calls attention to the gum known in India as "dhaura" derived from *Anogeissus latifolia*, which he thinks would be found a useful gum in English dye works, as yielding a thick viscid liquid much superior to dextrin or "British gum," and at the same time cheaper than gum-arabic. When mixed with a small proportion of hydrochloric acid, Mr. Elworthy says, the liquid gum keeps good for several months, and although its adhesive qualities are lessened by this addition, it still answer very well for labels. This gum, it may be mentioned, is referred to with approbation by Dr. Watt, in his "Economic Products of India." Professor Dymock also speaks of it (*Mat. Med. W. Ind.*, p. 324) as a valuable gum, occurring in vermicular pieces, very slightly colored, translucent, tasting like gum arabic, and readily soluble in cold water, with which it forms a strong, almost colorless mucilage, having a faint peculiar odor. The tree is common in the Concan and Khandeich and the gum is collected by the Bheels.—*Pharm. Journ.*

It is estimated that one-half of all the drugs imported into the United States is consumed in the manufacture of patent medicines.

A New Antiseptic.

Messrs. ELLENBERGER and v. HOFMEISTER have recently published a paper in the *Archiv für exper. Pathol. u. Pharmacol.* upon some new derivatives of naphthol, namely, certain acids derived both from alpha and beta-naphthol which they found to be more powerful antiseptics than either salicylic or carbolic acids.

One of these compounds is alpha-oxynaphthoic acid, (or alpha-naphthol-carbonic acid). This is prepared in a similar manner to salicylic acid, naphthol being substituted for phenol. In fact, it is prepared by bringing together, under strong pressure, and at an elevated temperature, alpha-naphthol sodium and carbonic acid gas. Its constitution is expressed by the formula:

$$C_{10}H_6.OH.COOH.$$

The *Chem. and Drugg.* thus abstracts a portion of the paper: The compound is nearly insoluble in water; 100 C.c. in the cold only take up 0.0535 gramme. The acid sublimes unchanged between 90° C. and 100° C., and melts at 186° C. with evolution of carbon dioxide. It is soluble in the alkalies and alkaline carbonates, forming salts which are colorless and of neutral reaction, and more soluble in both hot and cold water than the acid itself. Thus 100 C.c. at 18° C. dissolve 6.37 grammes of the salts. The acid is precipitated from its salts by hydrochloric, sulphuric, nitric, aracetic acids, but not by carbonic acid gas. Solutions of the salts ultimately decompose when kept even at normal temperatures. The sodium salt, on the addition of fuming red nitric acid, changes to a beautiful violet or blue color, slowly passing into red by which reaction the acid may be always identified and distinguished from beta-oxynaphthoic acid, with which it is isomeric, but which, with fuming nitric acid, affords only a greenish-yellow coloration.

Alpha-oxynaphthoic acid and its combinations with alkalies have been studied by the authors with regard to their antiseptic properties, and also in regard to their effects upon the body in health and disease, and upon the various organs of the animal structure. Fresh meat juice began to putrefy in from about twelve hours when kept at from 37° C. to 40° C. The addition of 1: 20,000 of a-oxynaphthoic acid was found to retard the decomposition to forty-eight hours, and with a proportion of 1: 2,500 no bacteria could be detected in unboiled liquids after seven days. When the liquid had been boiled, an admixture of 1: 1,200 was found to be amply sufficient for the prevention of putrefactive change. In the proportion of 1: 600 decomposition was stopped in liquids undergoing rapid change. The sodium salt, however, had to be added in the proportion of 1: 300 to prevent decomposition, and when this was actively progressing the salt named was powerless to check it. The effect of the β-acid was very similar.

It is surmised that these compounds will also turn out to be antipyretics, like salicylic acid, and if they are to be used as such, probably they will be used in form of sodium salts.

Experiments thus far conducted to ascertain the destructive effect of these agents upon bacteria are reported to have given very favorable results.

If these substances are to be used in medicine, it will be necessary to rechristen them.

Alpha-Naphthol.

A FEW weeks since (*Pharm. Journ.*, Dec. 3d, p. 437), a reclamation was put forward in respect to the superiority of beta-naphthol as an insoluble antiseptic and its relatively non-toxic properties.

Alpha-naphthol has now in its turn become the subject of a panegyric by M. Maximowitch (*Compt. Rend.*, CVI, 346). This compound, like beta-naphthol, from which constitutionally it differs only in the position of the hydroxyl group—is insoluble in cold water; but in water at a temperature of 70° C. it dissolves to the extent of 4 parts in 10,000, the solution being of a violet color. It is readily soluble in alcohol and ether, and in a liter of dilute spirit containing 400 c.c. of absolute alcohol it will dissolve to the extent of 10 grammes. M. Maximowitch has studied the antiseptic value of alpha-naphthol by noting its effects upon fourteen different kinds of microbes cultivated in different media. He found that when added to cultivations in liquids of the bouillon class, in the proportion of 0.1 part per 1,000, it completely arrested the development, amongst others, of the microbes of glanders, chicken cholera and pneumonia, the bacillus of typhoid fever, and the organisms of suppuration, *Staphylococcus albus* and *S. aureus*. For cultivations in gelatin, the same proportions were effective, but for agar-agar the dose had to be stronger in some cases. Urine, after being shaken with alpha-naphthol in alcoholic solution or in powder, did not ferment. When introduced into the organism of rabbits, alpha-naphthol was found to be three times less toxic than beta-naphthol and 700 times less toxic than mercuric iodide, the toxic dose for a man weighing 65 kilos, being calculated as 585 grammes.—*Pharm. Journ.*

Salicylates.

THE salicylates of various bases are now coming more into use in Germany, according to a correspondent of the *Chem. and Drugg.* Bismuth, though not so much prescribed as in England, is in some favor as salicylate, and is found beneficial in chronic dyspepsia and diseases of the digestive tract generally. Magnesium salicylate is also in use, being given in doses of from 1 to 1½ drachms daily. As an antiseptic dressing, and particularly in combination with sodium chloride, salicylate of mercury is much recommended, being applied as a 4-per-cent solution with the adjunct named.

Terpin Hydrate.

TERPIN HYDRATE has but slight taste, has no odor, and is solid. It appears as small needles when crystallized from a mixture of turpentine and water, or it may be obtained in large, rhombic crystals by allowing alcohol (3 parts), turpentine (4 parts), and nitric acid (1 part), to stand in shallow dishes for 3 to 4 days. It is slightly soluble in water or turpentine, but never readily by alcohol, ether, or hot water. It is best given in pills or in wafer. An emulsion may be used, but is not an agreeable form. It may, however, be dissolved in glycerin, and after solution an equal amount of some syrup may be added. From 16 to 24 grains to the ounce of the latter can be given in teaspoonfuls every 3 to 4 hours. It has been given in doses as large as 10 and 15 grains, but there is risk of disturbing the kidneys. It has the advantage over other terebinthinates of being tasteless, while its usefulness seems to be quite as great.—PROSSER JAMES in *The Lancet.*

Morphine Hydrate.

AT a recent meeting of the Pharmaceutical Society of Great Britain, Mr. D. B. Dott read a paper on morphine hydrate, of which the following abstract is given by the *Chemist and Druggist*:

It is generally stated that morphine hydrate crystallises with one molecule of water of crystallization, which it does not lose below 100° C. Who is responsible for this statement the author has been unable to ascertain—it is probably due to some early chemist—but, however that may be, the statement is universally accepted and has been corroborated by Matthiessen and Wright, who, with other authorities consulted, say that the molecule of water is only driven off above 100° C. The author was surprised to find, on submitting the matter to test, that these statements are wrong, and he has conclusively proved that at 90° C. morphine hydrate loses its combined water. In the course of the observations, there were indications that the hydrate is hygroscopic, and subsequent experiments warrant this conclusion; also that the formula of the hydrate should be $C_nH_{21}NO_3.1\frac{1}{2}(H_2O)$; or, more correctly, $2C_{17}H_{19}NO_3.9H_2O$.

Caramel.

CARAMEL or sugar-coloring is prepared in the following manner:

10 parts of crushed sugar are heated in a copper kettle with 3 parts of water. At first the sugar will dissolve, but after a while it will again solidify to a firm mass which must be broken up. When the pieces have again become liquefied, the mass becomes dark-colored and begins to foam, necessitating a continued stirring. The heating is now continued, over a gentle fire, until the mass has become black and pitch-like. Then the kettle is removed from the fire and 10 parts of boiling water poured in, which must be done cautiously and gradually, or the contents might run over. Finally, the kettle is replaced, the contents allowed to boil up a few times, and then again removed and allowed to become cold. During the boiling, the tendency of the contents to rise too high may be overcome by adding, from time to time, a little cold water.

The caramel thus produced is soluble in liquids containing up to about 50 per cent of alcohol. In strong alcoholic liquids, however, it is only partially soluble.

Carbolate of Camphor.

DR. M. B. COCHRANE communicates a note to the *Therapeutic Gazette* on a new compound, to which he gives the name of carbolate of camphor, and which appears to possess the antiseptic properties of carbolic acid, and the carminative properties of camphor, without the cauterising properties of the former. It is prepared by dissolving camphor in a 95-per-cent solution of carbolic acid to saturation. The carbolic acid will dissolve about three times its weight of camphor, and the product is a thin, clear, oleaginous mixture, having a strong odor of camphor and a very faint odor of carbolic acid. To the taste it has a strong and, at first, slightly pungent flavor of camphor, but no flavor of the acid. It dissolves readily in vegetable oils and in vaseline, mixes with sulphuric ether, dissolves salicylic acid, cocaine, iodoform, and, in the proportion of forty grains to one ounce, disguises the odor of the latter. Taken internally, in ten-drop doses, administered in capsules, it produces a sensation of warmth in the stomach which is not unpleasant, and which continues for an hour or two. When applied to the skin it produces a slightly warm sensation for a few moments, and when applied to an abraded surface it smarts for a moment and then all pain ceases. When mixed with an equal quantity of cotton-seed oil, and applied to a fresh wound on gauze or cotton, and kept well covered, no suppuration follows, nor does vesication or pain.—*Chem. and Drugg.*

Strophanthus Seeds.

No less than six varieties of strophanthus seeds met with in French commerce are described by M. Blondel (*L'Union Pharm.*, p. 52). 1st. *Strophanthus hispidus* seeds, from Guinea and Senegambia, which are brown, velvety, acuminate below, bearing a long awn, of which the velvety part is almost as long as the naked part of the awn. 2d. Seeds of the *Strophanthus* of the Niger, which are also brown and pubescent, but with a rounded or truncate base, are much larger and have a more developed awn. 3d. *Strophanthus Kombé* seeds from the centre and east of Africa, which are hairy and glistening, of a greenish or bluish-green tint, truncated or rounded below, the lateral sides bulged or often incurved in front, and having a long awn with very spreading hairs. Under this variety M. Blondel thinks two or three forms may exist, distinguishable by the greater prominence of the raphe and the anatomical structure of the integuments and albumen. 4th. The woolly *Strophanthus* seeds of Zambesi are remarkable for their thick coat of white and shining hairs, sometimes five millimeters long, hiding their real shape and size, which is relatively small. 5th. The *Strophanthus* seeds of Sourabaya. 6th. The smooth *Strophanthus* seeds of the Gaboon, which are thin, yellow, and without pubescence. The two last kinds are not at present in commerce. M. Blondel has also met with strophanthus seeds in commerce which had been exhausted with alcohol. These are recognisable by the almost entire absence of bitterness and by the hairs being somewhat agglutinated by extracted resin.—*Pharm. Journ.*

The Oil of Mountain Pine.

THE Mugho, or Mountain Pine, is the *Pinus Pumilio* of Lambert, and from which exudes the once-prized Hungarian balsam. By distillation of the young branches with water a volatile oil is obtained, long known as "*Oleum Templinum*," or "*Krummholzöl.*" This is the most potent agent in the so-called "pine-cure" practised at Reichenthall and other German spas. At these resorts the vapor of the water, as it escapes into the inhalation rooms, is medicated with the volatile oil. The pine baths at these spas are not medicated with the *Krummholzöl*, but with a much cruder product, *viz.*, an extract obtained by evaporating a decoction of the wood and branches, and perhaps, also, the residue after the distillation of the oil. Moreover, the baths are mostly employed in rheumatism, gout, and other affections for which thermal baths are suited; while the inhalations are chiefly used in diseases of the respiratory tract. By improved apparatus and greater care in the selection of material, a much finer product is now obtained—in fact, a very pure essential oil—*Oleum Pini Pumilionis*; and this is what has lately been imported under the fanciful name *Pumiline*. This essential oil possesses in a high degree the odor of the most fragrant variety of the pine, and, moreover, is less irritating than other fir oils. Sprinkled or sprayed about a sick-room, it imparts a lasting and grateful fragrance to the air, which is not oppressive, and appears to be disinfectant; or it may be thrown into a little warm water and allowed to evaporate; or it may be diffused by a steam or hand-ball atomiser. The oil may be taken internally, and is admirably adapted for inhalation. It is better to diffuse the oil through water by the aid of magnesia, powdered silex or prepared talc, in the proportion of 40 to 60 grains of the oil to a scruple of magnesia and an ounce of water. A teaspoonful of this mixture added to a half-pint of cold water is to be stirred in inhaler, when the addition of a half-pint of boiling water gives a convenient temperature. The addition of this oil to creasote and other essential oils is advantageous, as it disguises the disagreeable odor of some and adds its fragrance to others. It mixes well with eucalyptol, and is much milder in its action than the *Oleum Pini Sylvestris* (Ph. R.). Internally it may be taken in doses of 5 minims or more, in capsules, on sugar, or in lozenges, like terebine; or a mixture may be made with the aid of gum tragacanth. Externally it may be applied on spongiopiline or flannel as a stimulant and counter-irritant.—PROSSER JAMES, M.D., in *The Lancet.*

Benzoate of Sodium is recommended by Parszevsky as a remedy in uræmic poisoning. From ℈j. to ℈ij. may be given daily in solution or in capsules. It causes diminution and, finally, arrest of convulsive paroxysms and causes sleep of a healthy character. Excretion of albumin is also diminished or caused to cease entirely.

ECCENTRIC STIRRER.

A VERY efficient stirring apparatus, particularly serviceable in the preparation of cold cream, emulsions, pomades, soft ointments, and similar preparations, is the apparatus designed and manufactured by Beyer Frères, of Paris (Rue de Lorraine 16-18).

As will be seen from the cut, it may be set in motion by hand; but it is an easy matter to apply a pulley attachment, and this would probably be preferred by most users who have steam at their command. The construction of the apparatus itself is so easily understood from the illustration that it needs no further description.—Dr. St. Mierzinski in "*Die Riechstoffe*," Weimar, 1888.

Bottling Magnesium Citrate.

BOTTLES containing solution of citrate of magnesium may be securely corked by the following method used by N. Vanderbelt, Detroit. A tube of tinned copper 4 inches long is made of such size that the small end will be of the same diameter as the inside of the neck of the bottle, the opposite end should be large enough to receive the cork to be inserted. The cork is then easily forced into the bottle with a wooden piston having a shoulder to prevent its forcing the cork beyond the small end of the tube. The corks should be thoroughly boiled before inserting. The best corks to use are straight corks; such as are used by bottling houses.—*Pharm. Era.*

Electrified Balsam.

MR. C. V. BOYS has described an interesting experiment he has made with electrified gums and balsams. If sealing wax or any similar resinous material is melted in a cup and put on the conductor of an electrical machine, it throws out threads and fibres which break into beads. The cup containing the resin should be inclined from the operator and the electrical machine before the latter is worked, else both will be covered by an invisible sticky web. Burnt india rubber also sent out the filaments; but Canada balsam appears to show the phenomenon best. When a candle flame is held near a cup throwing out such filaments, they shoot to the flame, and sometimes cover the candle, and sometimes discharge into the flame and turn back into the cup. In a few minutes a large quantity of these sticky threads can be made, and, as they break into beads, Mr. Boys points out that this plan can be used to powder the substances.—*Chem. and Drugg.*

Fermentation of Milk-Sugar.

FOR some time chemists have disagreed in respect to this question, some saying lactose cannot ferment, others maintaining that it can. M. Bourquelot, in a memoir presented through M. Berthelot to the Academy of Sciences, has explained this apparent anomaly in a satisfactory manner. His experiments demonstrate that pure lactose, freed from the glucose which naturally accompanies it in milk-sugar, cannot be made to ferment with any sort of yeast, provided this be also purified from all fermentable sugar. But when glucose—the variety, for instance, extracted from milk-sugar—is added to the solution, fermentation immediately begins, and both sugars (lactose and glucose) split into alcohol and carbonic acid in the usual manner. The larger the proportion of glucose, the more rapid the transformation. With 50% of glucose eight days were sufficient for complete fermentation; with 16 per cent, twelve were necessary; and with 3 per cent, twenty-one days. Other experiments made with some crystallized lactose given by Professor Jungfleisch, and purified maltose, demonstrated that under their influence lactose will also ferment in substantially the same manner.—*Chem. and Drugg.*

Narceine related to Naphthalin.—From recent investigations of Messrs. Ad. Claus and Al. Meixner, of Freiburg i. B., published in the *Journ. f. prakt. Chem.*, it appears that narceine, one of the alkaloids existing in opium, is closely related to naphthalin. It is, however, not yet demonstrated that narceine contains the naphthalin nucleus *as such*, but only so much, that it contains a nucleus which, under certain conditions, may change to that of naphthalin, and yield derivatives belonging to the latter body.

RAPID FILTERING APPARATUS.

A RAPID filtering apparatus which may be used for viscid liquids, and is reported to work very effectively, is that constructed and sold by August Zemsch, of Wiesbaden.*

This apparatus consists of an upper and a lower portion or frame, and may be used either in a vertical or a horizontal position. At its lower portion (or upper, if reversed) is the inlet for the liquid to be filtered, and at the other end is the outlet. Between the upper and lower portion, a filtering plate is interposed which may be of different material, according to the nature of the substance to be filtered. If filtering paper is used, the joint formed by the frames is rendered sufficiently tight by the edge of the paper being inclosed by the flanges. If other filtering material is used, rubber washers may be placed between the flanges. Besides paper, flannel, cloth, felt, wire-gauze, etc., may be used as filtering surface, and charcoal or other solid filtering mediums may be placed between the filters. Before the turbid liquid enters the apparatus it may be passed through a strainer or sieve to keep back such solid particles as would soon choke the filtering surface. If this is not convenient, the filter inside of the apparatus may be covered with a sieve-like plate or some wire-gauze. The metallic parts of the apparatus may be tinned, nickel-plated or enamelled, according as it may be desired.

The turbid liquid enters at the bottom of the apparatus, passes through the filter and issues at the top. At least, this is the intention, the object no doubt being this, that the filtering surface may not be too soon clogged by adhering solid particles.

[In the illustration, the liquid apparently enters at the top, and passes out below. Of course, if the liquid is not too turbid, the filtration will take place in this manner just as well.]

Eccentric Stirrer.

This filtering apparatus is made either with a single or with a double frame, such as is shown in *b*. In this case, the apparatus is placed horizontally, and the turbid liquid enters between the filtering surfaces, passing through the latter into the outer receptacles.

Hydrobromic Acid.

HUGO ANDRES (in *Rundschau*) states that, in his judgment, the most economical method of preparing hydrobromic acid is to decompose barium bromide with sulphuric acid. Barium bromide is easily prepared by triturating together 100 parts of barium carbonate and 95 parts of ammonium bromide with a few drops of water, until a fine, uniform powder is produced. This is gently heated for some time, until no more carbonate of ammonium can be detected by a glass rod dipped in hydrochloric acid. The residue is dissolved in water, the solution filtered, and the filtrate evaporated. The resulting salt, barium bromide ($BaBr_2$), is dissolved in 3 parts of water, and the barium precipitated by the calculated quantity of diluted sulphuric acid (1 of acid, 3 of water). The filtrate is then suitably diluted to obtain the desired strength of hydrobromic acid, which may be obtained by taking the specific gravity. A 10% acid (at 15° C.) has the spec. grav. 1.077; a 25% acid one of 1.209.

Cocaine as an Antiseptic.

DR. KENTON, of Nancy, calls attention to the antiseptic properties possessed by cocaine, as being worthy of attention (*Lancet*, Feb. 11th, p. 299). He states that while administering cocaine internally, in doses of twenty-five centigrammes, or even more, he has remarked that the different secretions—sweat, urine, products of suppuration, and even fæces—all lose their fetid odor. He, therefore, suggests that cocaine should be tried experimentally as an internal antiseptic, as for instance, in the place of carbolic acid or corrosive sublimate in the adynamic stage of typhoid fever. He believes that if administered by the mouth or more especially in the form of enemata, cocaine would act both as a neurosthenic and as a disinfectant.—*Pharm. Journ.*

---

* Figured and described in: *Die Riechstoffe.* Von Dr. St. Mierzinsky, Weimar, 1888.

Gelatin Coating for Pills.

JOHN FINDLAY recommends as the best solution in his experience for use in coating pills extemporaneously with gelatin the following:

Gelatin (sheet)	1 oz.
Glycerin	2 oz.
Distilled water	8 oz.

These ingredients are to be placed in a saucer or deep plate, which is set over a pan half full of water standing on a small gas stove. When the gelatin is dissolved the gas is turned low so as to keep the mixture merely warm. The pills are stuck on needles, and when they have been dipped are stuck in a quantity of putty contained in a flat tin pan or plate, where they are left from four to six hours to dry. The pills may be varnished subsequently with a solution of tolu one part, ether four parts, which gives them a fine gloss, but diminishes their solubility.—*Pharm. Journ.*

A Quick Filter.

A. B. CLEMENCE recommends to use a combination of an ordinary filter, with the point cut off and replaced by absorbent cotton, as a superior quick filter, especially in connection with the filter-pump:

The filter is made as follows: A three-inch filter paper is folded as usual, and the apex cut off, leaving a hole about ⅓ inch in diameter; a wad of cotton (the absorbent cotton of the druggists) is pressed into the apex, and, when wet, may be either with a pump or by the mouth, pressed tight enough to hold the residue. Even without a pump, this filter will run so fast that close watching will be needed to keep the funnel full. Wash, as usual, with hot dilute hydrochloric acid and with hot water, when the residue cotton and paper is ready for the weighed crucible. Burning with a blast lamp completes an estimation in forty minutes from the time of weighing the material. [The author is describing the application of the filter to the estimation of silicon in pig iron.] The weight of the ash of the cotton will, of course, vary with the amount used, while that of the paper will be the same in each case, but it never need be more than 0.0005 gramme, and this small amount may be disregarded in most cases.—*Journ. Anal. Chem.*

Verifying Graduated Glass Tubes.

M. BERTHELOT describes (*Compt. Rend.*, 105, No. 15) a method employed by him in verifying the graduation of glass tubes employed in gas analysis, which is, however, equally applicable to any graduated tube or burette.

The author fills the tube with mercury when in an upright position, the closed end being downwards, until it overflows, taking care that no air-bubble is introduced. A small flat piece of glass, rather thick, is pressed down upon the open end of the tube, which is then inverted; the whole—tube, mercury, and glass plate—is then weighed on a balance sensitive to 0.01 Gm. or beyond. When this is done, the arrangement is taken out and placed above a small capsule, and one corner of the glass plate is raised slightly so as to permit a certain quantity of air to enter, and a corresponding quantity of mercury to escape. The contact of the plate and tube is re-established, the arrangement is placed upright on a nearly horizontal plane, and the graduation corresponding to a horizontal plane tangential to the surface of the meniscus is read off with a lens. He then weighs, as may be most convenient, either the mercury which has escaped into the capsule or the entire system formed by the tube, the mercury and the plate, which gives the mercury escaped by difference. This weight, divided by the exact density of mercury at the temperature of the experiment, furnishes with great precision the volume of the entire space now occupied by air and limited to the graduation. In this manner the graduation of any tube may be verified and a table of correction drawn up.

Suppository and Ointment Slab.

A CONVENIENT suppository and ointment slab, having several advantages over the loose pill tile, may be prepared as follows.

Obtain a piece of plate glass about 12x14 inches, and paste on one side a piece of perfectly white paper, having previously drawn on the side next to the glass, near one end, a scale divided into halves and quarters. The paper should then be sized with mucilage and given two coats of shellac varnish, to render it impervious to oils and fatty substances, should any work under the slab. Next obtain a half inch board 14x24 inches and place the slab at one end, and in such a manner that there shall be an inch space on each side.

A strip of wood the same thickness as the glass should be tacked on each side of the slab, leaving an eighth inch space between the strips and the edges of the slab. The space should be filled with cement made of glycerin and litharge. After the cement has hardened it should be rendered impervious to fats by treating with a few coats of shellac. The remainder of the board unoccupied by the slab should be covered with a piece of board of the same thickness placed crosswise. The whole should be arranged to slide under the top of the prescription desk in such a manner that it may be drawn out just far enough to use.

The scale serves for the accurate division of the suppositories and the white background enables the operator to see when the ointment is uniformly mixed.

Should some prefer part of the slab ground, the object may be accomplished by placing emery or pumice stone and water on the slab and rubbing with another piece of glass.—*Pharm. Era.*

A Simple Pastil Mould.

MR. J. W. BOWEN, one of the members of the Board of examiners for England and Wales, has recently devised a very simple mould for pastils, which deserves to be generally known. It is intended more particularly for use at the dispensing counter, there being a growing tendency amongst medical men to prescribe pastils containing medicaments in doses to suit special cases. The want

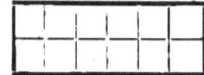

of some apparatus which would insure accuracy of division was Mr. Bowen's guiding spirit in the matter. He takes a square piece of plate and cements on three of its sides narrow slips of plate-glass, as shown in the figure. The square is then divided into smaller squares by means of grooved lines, and a piece of glass to slip up to any row required, there to be secured by means of cork, serves to give the requisite surface. The diagram shows part of the plate arranged for a dozen pastils. The plate being ready, the pastil mass is poured into it, and when it sets the glyco-gelatin sheet is removed, when it is found that on the under surface are ridges corresponding to the grooves in the plate. All that remains to be done is to cut through these ridges with a pair of scissors, and the pastils are finished.—*Chem. and Drug.*

The Size of Drops.

ATTENTION has been called from time to time to the various conditions which modify the size of drops. For example, it was shown, in a paper published in this journal in July last, that drops increase in size as the quantity of fluid in the bottle from which they are dropped decreases. Mr. A. F. Reid calls attention in the *Chemical News* to two conditions which modify the size—viz., time and temperature. In his experiments he used a 100-grain pipette and found that water at 2° C. dropped from this at the rate of one drop per two seconds gave 141 drops to 100 grains, but only 136 drops when 2 or 3 drops are formed per second. At 170° F., water dropped at the rate of 2 or 3 drops per second gives 156 drops to 100 grains and the number falls 1 drop for every 10° F. decrease of temperature until 110° F.; then the number falls 2 drops for every 10° F. fall, from 90° F. to 40° F. at the normal temperature (60° F.) 141 drops weighed 100 grains. It is well known that the size of drops varies with the nature of the liquid. The following are the drop measurements of 100 fluid grains of some liquids at 12° C. at the rate of about two drops per second.

	Drops
Absolute alcohol	287
Ether	452
Carbon disulphide	436
Sulphuric acid	840
Hydrochloric acid	182

Mr. Reid suggests that this method may be used in determining the relative quantities of alcohol and water in mixtures of these liquids. Mr. Reid does not appear to have tested the influence of the size of the pipette aperture upon the size of the drops.—*Chem. and Drugg.*

Impure Salicylate of Lithium.

SOME sensation has been caused among French pharmacists owing to the appearance in the market of salicylate of lithium containing from 12 to 15 per cent of silicylate of sodium. Investigation has shown that this is not added, but is due to the use of impure carbonate of lithium in making the salicylate. The carbonate is made from lepidolite, which contains a considerable proportion of carbonate of sodium, a salt which it is difficult to get rid of. Consequently when the carbonate of lithium made from this source is used to saturate salicylic acid, salicylate of sodium is contained in the product. M. Guyot, who writes on this subject in *Répert. de Pharm.*, states that the impure salt comes from Germany, and mentions further that German carbonate of lithium frequently contains alumina and calcium carbonate.—*Chem. and Drugg.*

Note by Ed. Am. Dr.—Regarding the source of lithium carbonate and its manufacture, compare an article elsewhere in this number.

Oil of Green Cloves.

We are dependent upon Zanzibar as the chief source of the supplies of cloves and their oil which come to our markets, and the existence there of an ad valorem duty of 30 per cent—the principal source of the sultan's revenue—makes it highly important that other sources of supply should be fostered. The Moluccas are, perhaps, the next most important producers of cloves, and next to them are the Straits Settlements, Mauritius, and the Reunion. Cloves are remarkable for the large amount of essential oil which they contain, no official drug exceeding them in this respect. From 16 to 22 per cent has generally been considered to be the range of the yield, but of late years Zanzibar cloves have stubbornly refused to give more than 17 per cent. The Mauritius cultivators have recently endeavored to improve upon this by using the cloves in the green or undried condition, and the experiment has been attended with excellent results. A small consignment of the oil thus prepared has recently been received in London. In color, odor, and taste this oil resembles ordinary oil of cloves; if anything, the odor is more fragrant, owing to the flower-buds being put into the still before they are dried. The oil has a specific gravity of 1.048 at 16° C., is soluble in less than its own weight of rectified spirit, and conforms to the reliable chemical tests for oil of cloves. It therefore corresponds with the official requirements, and is entitled to become a commercial article.—*Chem. and Drugg.*

The Nilgiri Cinchona Plantations.

Although about 300,000 cinchona trees were destroyed by a landslip in the Nilgiris in June of last year, and 20,000 more by a hail storm earlier in the season, the sales of febrifuge during the year 1886–87 were 385 lbs. in excess of those of the previous twelve months. Yellow and hybrid trees were largely substituted during the year for red cinchonas. The bark of the two former being rich in alkaloids, it is the object of Government, by working out the red-bark growths, to procure cinchona estates which will give quinine and some combination of quinine and cinchonidine at almost as cheap a rate as the febrifuge obtained at present from the red-bark trees. The cost price of the raw material used in the local febrifuge factory during the year amounted to Rs. 73,548, while the outturn yielded Rs. 113,153. Deducting from the money received for febrifuge and bark during the year and value of the stock in hand at the close, the working expenses, there was a profit of Rs. 18,464, a much less favorable result than was obtained in several former years. Commercially, therefore, the year was a bad one; but this is counterbalanced by the cheapening of the drug, which, after all, was the principal object of the Government in introducing cinchona cultivation into India. Meanwhile the Government has asked the superintendent to keep down expenditure on the plantations and to push on the experiments in the manufacture of quinine.

Annatto Cultivation in Guadeloupe.

Annatto thrives best in Guadeloupe at an altitude not exceeding 400 meters. Holes, having a diameter of fifty or sixty centimeters and thirty or forty centimeters in depth, are dug at a distance of three to four meters, and in each of these a few seeds are laid. When the young shoots appear, one of the strongest is left to grow and all the others are pulled up. The young plants require a careful hoeing around them for nearly a year on the whole extent of the plantation. In nurseries the seeds are sown in well-prepared beds, and at a distance of about thirty centimeters between each row, and when the plants have attained a height of about forty to sixty centimeters they are placed singly in each hole. The plant grows very fast, requiring little care after the plantation has attained a certain size. It blossoms one year after being transplanted, and bears a few pods, but is far from having reached its full size, which may be four to five metres. In a rich soil the trees will shade the whole ground in four or five years. The ground is hoed at least two or three times a year, until the trees have attained their full size. Annatto flowers twice a year, the spring blossoms always yielding the largest crop. As soon as the pods in the bunches commence drying and opening, the bunches are cut, packed in baskets, and transported to the shed prepared for the purpose. Every pod must be then picked with the hands, the seeds attached to the white film inside being as much as possible left untouched. The empty pods are used as manure. The picking in Guadeloupe is usually performed by women and children, who are paid at the rate of about five centimes per kilogramme.

The crop is gathered from July 15th to the end of August, and it is estimated that one hectare (2.47 acres) of annatto yields on an average 1,500 kilogrammes of green seeds for the two crops, or about seven casks of pulp, weighing from 350 to 400 lbs. each.—*Chem. and Drugg.*

TESTING FOR SMALL QUANTITIES OF CARBONIC ACID AND OTHER GASES.

Oscar Roessler recommends to use the simple apparatus here described.

A small test-tube is drawn out at its lower end, the latter bent slightly upwards, and the extreme end (*b*) cut off. From another thin-walled glass tube a capillary funnel (*e*) is formed, so as to fit into the test-tube in such a manner that the orifice is about ¾ inch from the bottom. The sample to be tested is placed into the outer tube (at *a*), and if carbonic acid is to be tested for, a small quantity of clear solution of baryta is placed into the capillary funnel—just enough to be retained therein by capillary attraction. The small column of liquid will occupy the space indicated by *d*, and a single drop of the solution will hang at the orifice (*e*). The whole apparatus, put together as shown in the cut, is now dipped into dilute hydrochloric acid, which will enter at *b*, attack the sample at *a*, and, if this contains carbonic acid, will liberate this and cause the drop of baryta solution to become opaque. Even if the apparatus is taken out of the acid, the orifice at *b* will remain closed, as this will retain a small portion of the acid by capillary attraction. The reaction may be repeated a number of times. It is only necessary to cause the drop (*e*) to fall off by a gentle shake, when it will immediately be replaced by another from the space *d*, until no more can be shaken out. The old drop, falling into the acid liquid, will of course again give up its carbonic acid.

In the same manner other gaseous bodies may be detected.

For instance, supposing nitric acid is to be searched for, the funnel (*e*) is charged with a concentrated solution of green, crystallized sulphate of iron, and the sample, mixed with an excess of chloride of sodium, is placed at *a*. The apparatus is then immersed in concentrated sulphuric acid. The latter causes the escape of vapors of chloronitrous and chloronitric acids, and causes the drop of iron solution to assume an intense brownish-black color.

According to the author, so small a quantity as 0.02 milligrammes (about 1/3200 grain) of carbonic acid gas may be detected with this apparatus.—*Berl. Ber.*, 1887, 2,639.

APPARATUS FOR SEPARATING IMPALPABLE POWDER.

When powders are to prepared of greater fineness than would be possible to obtain by means of a sieve or bolting cloth—for instance, when a powder is to be incorporated into toilet soaps—this may be accomplished by a sort of dust-collector.

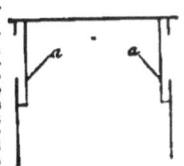

This consists simply of a pasteboard tube, about 1 foot in diameter and 9 feet high, standing on a square box provided with a well-fitting door. Immediately over the latter, a blast-tube enters the apparatus. The tube enters first horizontally, but its point is bent upwards at a right angle. The upper end of the large pasteboard tube is covered with a pasteboard cap (shown in section in the accompanying illustration). This cap has an interior flange *a a*, forming a gutter in which lodge the finest particles of the powder which are thrown upwards. A removable lid covers the top.

When a substance has been reduced to powder in the mortar, it is transferred into a suitable tube, the latter connected, at one end, with bellows, and the other end of the tube connected with the blast-tube entering the apparatus before described. Upon operating the bellows, the powder will be forced into the chimney from below upwards. The coarser particles of the powder will, of course, fall immediately back into the box at the bottom, and the finer particles somewhat later; but the finest dust will ascend and collect in the gutter at the top, whence it may be removed from time to time. When the charge has all been blown into the apparatus, and the suspended particles have all settled, the sediment in the bottom of the box is removed to the mortar and subjected to renewed trituration.

The long pasteboard chimney is constructed of several sections fitting one over the other, so that it may be lengthened or shortened, like a telescope, according to the nature of the substance of which the fine powder is to be collected.*

---

* After Blasziewski, *Die Riechstoffe*, Weimar, 1888.

Drying Agent for Gases.

Morley has examined the drying power of phosphorus pentoxide (anhydrous phosphoric acid) towards currents of air or gases. He finds it to be the most powerful absorbent of moisture so far available. On passing a current of air through suitable tubes containing phosphorus pentoxide, the author ascertained that only ¼ milligramme of moisture was left unabsorbed in a volume of 10,000 liters, or 2,615 gallons.

Sozoiodol.

"Sozoiodol," the name given to a new iodine compound which has been recommended by Dr. Lassar for use in the treatment of certain skin diseases, is a fresh instance of the bewildering confusion that is continually augmenting through the arbitrary and unsystematic manner in which multitudinous new chemical competitors for favor are named. A first impression might naturally be that sozoiodol has some relationship with iodol; but this would be wrong, since iodol is an iodized pyrrol, whilst it is stated that sozoiodol is a benzene derivative. Looking in another direction, it has been described by more than one writer as a compound resembling ortho-oxyphenyl-sulphurous acid—which bears also the shorter name of sozolic acid—but with a third hydrogen of the benzene nucleus replaced by iodine. This, however, has proved also to be incorrect, as the compound is now authoritatively stated to be an acid sodium salt of "iodparaphenol-sulphonic acid" (*Pharm. Zeit.*, Dec. 24th, p. 374). It is represented by the following curious formula:

$$2C_6H_3 \begin{cases} I \\ -O.H \\ S.O_2Na \end{cases} + C_6H_3 \begin{cases} I \\ -O.H \\ S.O_2H \end{cases}$$

Sozoiodol occurs as a white, shining crystalline powder, which does not melt upon being heated to 200° C.; but when heated sufficiently in a test tube, it is decomposed, and gives off violet iodine vapor. It is quite odorless, has a faintly acid taste, is soluble to the extent of seven per cent in cold water, and more soluble in hot water; it is also difficultly soluble in cold alcohol, but more freely in hot.—*Pharm. Journ.*

Filtration of Mercury.

Mercury often becomes contaminated with alloys or other impurities which may be removed by simple filtration. This may be done in glass funnels, the stems of which are drawn out to a fine capillary tube. But this becomes often clogged after a short time, and then ceases to act; besides, it acts very slowly.

Prof. C. Bahn, of Aschaffenburg, recommends a method which has long been practised in Bunsen's laboratory. A filter is made of writing paper and numerous fine holes pricked into it. Instead of making these round with a needle, it is better to use the point of a pen-knife, which causes the little holes to be oblongly triangular. The holes should be pricked both vertically, in the direction of the radius of the filter, and horizontally, at right angles with the former; part of the holes should be pricked from the outside inwards, and the others in the opposite direction. Even with this arrangement, the filtration sometimes proceeds only very slowly, but it may be accelerated by using a filter-pump.

A still better way to purify mercury by filtration, according to the same author, is the following: Select a glass tube, of about the thickness of a lead-pencil, and about a yard long. Expand one end to the shape of a funnel, and the other to a tulip-shaped bulb, or expand this end in a wave-like form, such as is customary when rubber tubing is to be stretched and tied over the end of a tube. A piece of linen or chamois is firmly tied over the latter end, and the tube then suspended. On pouring the mercury into the funnel, it will be pressed through the pores of the filtering medium with a pressure considerably exceeding that of the atmosphere.—*Zeitsch. f. Instrumentenkunde.*

Syrup of Hypophosphite of Iron (ferrous).

Mr. H. C. Everson, in a paper published in the *Pharm. Journ.* (Dec. 24th), states that the usual methods for preparing syrup of hypophosphite of iron (ferrous) result in the production of *ferric* hypophosphite. The formula given by the formulary of the British pharmaceutical conference, however, does produce the ferrous salt, but suffers from other drawbacks. He proposes a new method by which this syrup may be produced without difficulty. We reproduce the process here, transcalculating the British weights and measures into those of the United States as closely as practicable. The author started from the fact that metallic iron dissolved in hypophosphorous acid gives a solution of ferrous salt. He, therefore, dissolved a calculated quantity of iron wire in a sufficient quantity of hypophosphorous acid of spec. grav. 1.136, boiling them in a flask, the neck of which was closed by the nozzle of a small funnel to prevent evaporation and exposure. After the iron was dissolved, the solution was filtered, while hot, upon the sugar, and the latter stirred until it was dissolved. The result was a bright syrup containing 1 grain of ferrous hypophosphite in each fluidrachm (British), and was free from ferric salt, for potassic ferrocyanide gave only a very pale blue precipitate. The whole operation was effected in a very short space of time, and the author states that the syrup has kept perfectly bright in full bottles.

The formula is as follows, reduced to make 16 fluidounces (U. S.).

Iron Wire, pure and fine.................... 41 grains.
Hypophosphorous Acid, spec. grav. 1.136...885 grains.
Sugar... 11½ troy oz.
Water...........................enough to make 16 fl. oz.

Boil the iron wire with the acid and 7½ fluidounces of water until it is dissolved; filter the solution, while hot, on the sugar, and stir until solution is effected. When cold, complete the volume to 16 fluidounces.

Analysis of Papaw Juice.

The juice of the papaw, *Carica Papaya* L., from which the vegetable ferment papain (or papayotin) is derived, has been analyzed by Domingo Alberto Niobey of Rio de Janeiro. He found it to contain:

Caoutchouc-like substance............................. 4.535
Wax-like substance................................... 2.484
Soft Resin... 0.110
Hard Resin... 2.776
Albuminoid substance................................. 0.006
Papain... 5.303
Bitter extractive.................................... 1.282
Saccharine extractive................................ 1.059
Organic Acid (malic)................................. 0.443
Pectin and Salts..................................... 7.100
Water.. 74.971

—*Deutsche Chem. Zeit.*

[Of all these constituents, the one which interests us most is the papain. The author's estimate of its quantity comes probably very close to the truth, though the apparent exactness of the analysis, going into the third decimal, and accounting for every constituent in 100 parts without having to record any loss, does not strike us as being altogether convincing, not to mention the peculiar classification or denomination of some of the constituents.—Ed. Am. Dr.]

Metallic Oxides.

A paper on the dehydration of metallic oxides by heat has recently been contributed to the Chemical Society by Drs. Carnelly and Walker, and is published in full in a recent issue of the journal of the society. It is of considerable interest to pharmacists, for the observations which the authors have made regarding argentic, bismuthic, ferric, and mercuric oxides may be found to alter our ideas regarding the chemical composition of the pharmacopœial compounds equivalent to those named. Drs. Carnelly and Walker prepared these oxides (properly speaking, hydroxides) by processes very similar to those prescribed by the Brit. Pharm., the chief difference being that, instead of drying the compounds by the heat of a water-bath, as the Pharmacopœia directs, they were dried in the air. So obtained, the silver compound had the formula $AgOH$; on heating up to 100° C. it remained stable, and was only fully converted into Ag_2O between 180 - 270° C. The air-dried mercuric "oxide" (corresponding to hydrarg. oxid. flav.) had the formula $Hg(OH)_2$, and remained almost stable up to 100° C., began to dehydrate at 110° C., and was not completely dehydrated until the temperature of 175° C. was reached. Bismuth "oxide" required even a higher temperature for complete dehydration. As precipitated it has the formula $Bi_2O_3.3H_2O$, but on heating it immediately begins to lose water, and at a temperature of 415° C. its formula still showed combined water ($Bi_2O_3.H_2O$), complete dehydration only taking place at 600° C. In the case of these three "oxides" the Pharmacopœia directs the freshly precipitated substance to be dried by means of a water-bath, and assumes that the products are respectively Ag_2O, HgO, and Bi_2O_3; but it is evident from Carnelly and Walker's results that the Pharmacopœia formulæ are open to doubt, and require corroboration. There should be no doubt about the matter were the Pharmacopœia compounds air-dried, but as they are dried at a temperature something under 100° C. immediately after their precipitation, it is just possible that they are hydroxides or hydrates, to use a more common expression. For this reason, it is desirable that the subject should be investigated in anticipation of the next edition of the Pharmacopœia, and the composition of ferri peroxidum hydratum may be included. The Pharmacopœia gives the formula of this as $Fe_2O_3.H_2O$. Much found that the hydrate precipitated in the cold and dried at 100° C. has the formula $Fe_2O_3(H_2O)_3$. The air-dried hydrate made by the above-named chemists contained five molecules of water, became $Fe_2O_3(H_2O)_3$, at 55° C., and at 130° C. the composition corresponded with the Pharmacopœia formula. It may be mentioned that the precipitate obtained by decomposing antimony tetrate with an alkali was true Sb_2O_5, and this compound remained stable on heating up to 360° C., when it began to absorb oxygen.—*Chem. and Drugg.*

Coca Cultivation in Ceylon.

A CORRESPONDENT in the *Tropical Agriculturist*, who has been growing coca for some years chiefly for the seed, and is now extending the cultivation in view of leaf harvest, which promises to be most remunerative, writes as follows concerning the cultivation of the plant: Germination commences on the tree, as may be ascertained by dissection of the fruit. Seeds should, therefore, be sown while quite fresh on the surface of good loam, and shaded from the sun. After this no special cultivation is required. The plants can be put out like tea, three to four feet apart, in good land and sheltered, which they prefer to poor soil and exposed ridges. Markham states that the average yield of leaf in Peru was 800 pounds per acre, and that the profit from a coca farm was 43 per cent. This seems too good to be true: but even at 9d. per pound (present price of leaf in London averaging 1s. 3d.) the profit should be considerable. Machinery is not required, and the trees may be allowed to run at their own sweet will, leaves being taken off as fast as they arrive at maturity. Fruit bearing commences at eighteen months, and, when seed is no longer required, can, of course, be checked, and the energies of the plant directed to producing leaf.

The Turkey Sponge Fisheries.

SPONGE fishing extends all along the coast of Batroon, Tripoli, Latakia, and the island of Ruad, north of Tripoli. It is not confined only to native fishermen, for many Greeks come over from Kalimno, Stanchio, Rhodes, and Samos, in their little crafts, to share this traffic with the Syrians. The catch commences in June and extends to October, this season being the most suitable owing to the calmness of the sea. The diver generally remains at the bottom of the sea from sixty to eighty seconds, unlike the Australian pearl-shell fishers, who often remain under water for hours at a time. This is due to the fact, that the native Syrian diver has simply an open net around his unprotected body and uses no instrument of any kind in collecting his sponges; he cannot be induced, like the Turks, to adopt the diving dress or "Skafander." The depth to which Syrian divers descend is from 25 to 175 feet; below these depths no good sponges are said to be found. Three kinds of sponges are known here—prime, seconds, and the red ones, taken near Batroon. The latter are by far the best. They have to be cleaned and freed from sand and then pressed. The best qualities are exported from Beirut to Paris direct, the others go almost exclusively to Trieste, while the Greeks send their share of the catch to different markets in Europe. The average annual catch is estimated at about $150,000 in value. The local authorities exact a tax of 10 per cent from those engaged in the business.—U. S. CONSUL BISSINGER in *Consular Reports*.

Vanilla Culture in Mexico.

THE *Republican*, of St. Louis, some time ago, contained the following note on vanilla cultivation in Mexico, communicated by C. B. Pedretto, of Mexico:

"Vanilla flourishes in two places in Mexico, Papanton, in the State of Vera Cruz, and Misantin, but the first place is the most important. This town, of about 10,000 inhabitants, is in the land of the Toconaco Indians, who are as indolent and improvident as any people on earth. Vanilla is found wild in the forests around Papantes clinging to the trees and bushes for support. When the beans ripen in November or December the natives go out into the forests to gather them. All kinds are put into old sacks together and brought into Papantes to market. Here there are a number of buyers, Spaniards or Americans, and the competition reminds one of what is to be seen in a street where second-hand stores prevail. The old women are generally in the lead, half-naked, and with haggard faces begrimed with dirt. Then come the children, equally pitiable in appearance, and finally the old men bring up the rear, their long, stiff hair, matted and dirty sometimes, standing out twelve inches, while their beards, filthy and long, lend a finish to the picture that is most revolting. The beans are purchased by middlemen at the rate of 43s. or 50s. per 1000, taken as they are put up by the natives. One thousand good-sized green vanilla beans will weigh 60 lbs.; the same when cured about 10 lbs. The first fine morning, planks are arranged and covered with quilts on which the beans are laid after being divested of their stems. The sweating process, as it is called, then takes place, and has to be repeated seven times before all the water has evaporated. Then the beans are heated slightly and placed on shelves to dry and air. After this they are assorted in lots of fifty beans, graded according to length. In fine weather the curing process takes three weeks, but such weather rarely prevails, and the curing sometimes takes from four to five months. Last year the beans sold for 50s. per 100, which was about a pound, but owing to a heavy crop this year and the growing competition in the business, the best beans only bring 30s. a pound or 100, and the inferior from 30s. to 42s. The principal markets for vanilla beans are New York, St. Louis, and Chicago. They are bought chiefly by wholesale druggists and fine confectioners, and are becoming an important article of Mexican commerce. Last year, from the vicinity of Papantes alone, 50,000,000 beans were exported.

Dextrin as an Adulterant of Extracts.

A. PANNETIER directs attention (*L'Union Pharm.*, Feb., p. 50) to the frequent adulteration, in France, of pharmaceutical extracts with dextrin. This seems to be added with a double motive. While increasing the bulk, it also allows the evaporation to be stopped at an earlier stage of the evaporation. It is detected by adding subacetate of lead to the aqueous solution of the extract to precipitate tannin, gum and coloring matters; filtering and removing the lead by hydrogen sulphide; after again filtering, the liquid is evaporated to about one-fifth of its bulk and its own volume of 90% alcohol is added, when the presence of dextrin is detected by a precipitate being formed. The extracts containing dextrin present a fine appearance rather than otherwise.—*Pharm. Journ.*

Adulteration of Anise with Conium Seed.

SOME time ago, attention was called in the pharmaceutical press (by Mr. C. L. Lachman, of Bethlehem, Pa., in this Journal, 1887, p. 81) to a prevailing dangerous adulteration of the anise of commerce with conium or hemlock seed. A Turkish journal, in mentioning this adulteration, places on record a case which occurred some time ago at Tchataldja, a village in the neighborhood of Constantinople. A policeman there noticed a party of gypsies actively engaged in gathering hemlock seeds in the fields. Knowing this seed to be a poison, he stopped the collectors, and asked the purpose for which they gathered it, and it transpired that the gypsies collected the hemlock for druggists who paid them at the rate of 1d. per pound, and used the seeds as an adulterant for anise. The local authorities thereupon visited the drug dealers in the neighborhood, and seized large quantities of adulterated anise.—*Chem. and Drugg.*

Sophistication of Strophanthus Seeds.

AT a recent meeting of the Paris Society of Pharmacy (reported in the *Chem. and Drugg.*), M. Planchon spoke of strophanthus seeds, showing fine enlarged drawings of the various sorts, communicated by M. Dauvel. The variety of seeds in commerce is very great and frauds appear to follow apace. M. Blondel has called attention to a deceit often practised, it was said by English houses. The seeds were *exhausted* with strong alcohol. The fraud is detected through the dull appearance of the drug, and the absence of bitterness. Lately, however, the same gentleman received strophanthus kombé seeds, from England also. They looked very bright and fine, but the absence of bitterness led to a closer examination, which proved the seeds to have been exhausted with *weak* alcohol and mixed with some good seeds. The defrauders—very smart people, evidently—had profited by the caution published by M. Blondel, and changed their menstruum, so as to exhaust the drug without injuring its appearance. In the same discussion M. Petit said he had received specimens of Senegambia seeds priced at 250f. a kilo, while another called Nyanza strophanthus was offered at 43f.

Detection of Strychnine for Toxicological Purposes.

IN toxicological research, strychnine is generally detected by the process devised by Girdwood and Rogers, which has various objectionable features about it. Mr. R. A. Cripps, by a modification of Sins' process, has succeeded in separating the alkaloid much more quickly. He digests the solid substance in six times its weight of methylated spirit, containing a little tartaric acid. This is done for several hours at a temperature a little below the boiling point of the spirit. The liquid is then filtered, evaporated, and the residue dissolved in 1 oz. of water, and 20 minims of spirit added. The solution containing suspended matter is then repeatedly shaken with a mixture of equal parts of chloroform and ether, until all coloring matter is washed out. The chloroform washings are rejected, the aqueous fluid is rendered alkaline with ammonia, and again shaken with chloroform-ether to dissolve out the alkaloid, which again is re-extracted with acidulated water, the solution rendered alkaline with ammonia, and the strychnine finally dissolved out with chloroform-ether. The method can also be used quantitatively with very satisfactory results, if the ethereal and other liquids be washed by a second or even a third treatment with the solvent employed. To test its accuracy, 0.9 grain of strychnine was introduced into a dead cat, and the stomach, etc., treated as described; 0.85 grain of pale yellowish, well-defined crystals was obtained.—*Chem. and Drugg.*

Cotton-Seed Oil in Olive Oil.

To detect the adulteration, M. Ernest Millau recommends to dissolve in three times their volume of 90% alcohol the fatty acids separated from the oil in the usual manner. The liquor being placed on a water-bath, one-tenth of its volume is added of 3-per-cent solution of nitrate of silver. After a few minutes' ebullition, should any cotton-seed oil be present, the nitrate will be reduced, and the fatty acids, blackened and paste-like, come up like a scum to the surface. No such reaction is observed with the fatty acids of pure olive oil. With this method 1 per cent of cotton-seed oil can be detected, and dangers of error be avoided, as the preparation of the fatty acids and their solution in alcohol insures a removal of natural organic and mineral impurities. Such is the substance of a memoir presented on February 20th to the Academy of Sciences by M. Dobray, in the name of M. Ernest Milliau. — *Chem. and Drugg.*

Detection of Spermaceti in Oil of Rose.

Spermaceti is known to have been used to some extent as a secondary adulterant of oil of rose, after this had previously been adulterated by the admixture of oil of rose-geranium or other oils containing only a small proportion of stearoptens. Genuine oil of rose congeals at about 30° C. to a semi-transparent mass, apparently consisting of spicules or scales. To produce this appearance in spurious oil, spermaceti has been used.

G. Heppe recommends the following test to discover this adulteration. Agitate a portion of the suspected oil with 1½ to 2 volumes of liquid glacial acetic acid. After a few minutes, the mixture will solidify to a crystalline mass. Transfer the mass to a small filter and wash it with water, until it has lost nearly all odor of oil of rose. Then wash it with a little solution of soda, and lastly again with soda. The undissolved residue consists (usually) almost entirely of spermaceti. It may be identified by transferring it to a dry test-tube and heating it until it turns brown, when a characteristic odor of fatty acids will be evolved. — *Zeitsch. f. anal. Chem.*

Rapid Assay of Peroxide of Hydrogen.

Contamine recommends the following method for rapidly assaying peroxide of hydrogen.

Measure off several cubic centimeters of the peroxide, render it neutral by the addition of ammonia, introduce it into a measuring cylinder, divided into $\frac{1}{10}$ cubic centimeters and closed at one end, read off the volume, and then introduce a few crystals of permanganate of potassium wrapped in tissue paper. Close the orifice of the tube and shake briskly. The reaction will take place at once; every molecule of the peroxide corresponds to 1 molecule of oxygen. When the liquid has assumed the red tint of the permanganate, the reaction is terminated. The measuring tube is then opened under water, and the level again read off. The difference between the first and second reading gives the quantity of the oxygen, contained in the peroxide, in cubic centimeters.

Every C.c. of the usual commercial peroxide of hydrogen, when decomposed by permanganate, yields on an average 10 to 12 C.c. of oxygen. — *Dingl. Pol. Journ.*

Assay of Commercial Carbolic Compounds.

The following is an abstract of a paper by J. Muter and L. du Koningh in *The Analyst* (12, 191; after *Journ. Chem. Soc.*):

1. *Carbolic Powders.* — Where the phenols exist in the uncombined state, they are extracted by methylated spirit from 75 grammes of the powder. Where the powder contains a lime base, a preliminary thorough trituration with a small excess of dilute sulphuric acid is necessary. The alcoholic extract is mixed with 200 C.c. of a 5-per-cent solution of sodium hydroxide, and the mixture is then evaporated to half its bulk. At this point any tar oils and naphthalene will separate, and are to be filtered off. The filtrate is further concentrated to 50 C.c. and transferred to a graduated tube. This, which is known as Muter's carbolimeter, is wide in the lower portion. At 65 C.c. it is narrowed to a neck, which is graduated up to 110 C.c. in 0.25 C.c. divisions. It is stoppered, and is furnished with a long, thin, stirring rod, the volume of which must be allowed for. 65 C.c., 25 C.c. of strong hydrochloric acid are slowly added with stirring, and then enough dry common salt to render the phenols insoluble. The tube is plunged into water of 15.5° and the volume of the phenols read off.

2. *Liquid Carbolic Acid.* — If this contains excess of water, it will not give a clear solution with three volumes of benzene (benzol). The amount of water is ascertained by shaking 20 C.c. of the sample with 80 C.c. of a saturated solution of sodium chloride, and observing the diminution in volume. Tar oils are estimated by shaking 20 C.c. with 80 C.c. of soda solution (5 per cent), and a small quantity of benzene (10 C.c. for dark specimens, less for pale ones). The increase in the volume of the benzene gives the amount of tar oils. The remainder is taken as phenol and cresols.

New and Delicate Test for Morphine.

When a solution of ferric chloride is added to a solution of a salt of morphine, a bluish-green coloration is produced. At the same time, in consequence of the reducing power of morphine, a part of the ferric chloride is reduced to the ferrous condition, as shown in the following equation:

$$2Fe_2Cl_6 + 2H_2O = 4FeCl_2 + 4HCl + O_2.$$

There is, however, a point of dilution (apparently about 1 in 2,000) at which the coloration is imperceptible, though the reaction represented in the above equation appears to take place even in the most dilute solutions.

On this reaction is based a delicate test for morphine and its salts in solution; for if such a solution be treated with ferric chloride and then with ferricyanide of potassium, the latter will interact with the reduced ferrous chloride with the formation of Turnbull's blue, which appears either as a deep blue precipitate or a greenish-blue coloration, according to the strength of the solution of the alkaloid.

In a solution of one part of a salt of morphine in 20,000 parts of water, the coloration is intensely green, and in a solution of one part in 50,000, the shade is still deep, though lighter. A solution of 1 in 100,000 gives the same result on standing a few moments, the coloration, even in this dilute solution, being unmistakable.

Other reducing substances would, of course, give the same results, but in the absence of such substances, the above is a delicate confirmatory test for the presence of morphine. Several other alkaloids submitted to the above test did not give the coloration.

This reaction might be made the basis of a colorimetric process for the approximate estimation of morphine in very dilute solutions. — J. Lister Armitage in *Pharm. Journ.* (March 10th).

Separation of Paraffin from Liquid Hydrocarbon.

R. Zalozieцкi has found that solid hydrocarbons (that is paraffins) may be separated from liquid ones by taking advantage of the great difference of their respective solubilities in amylic and ordinary alcohol. According to his investigations, 1 part of *paraffin* requires for solution

at	parts of
16°–18° C.	450,000 ethylic alcohol (75%)
16°–18° C.	370 amylic alcohol
2°– 4° C.	1,050 do.

One part of paraffin is also soluble at 16°–18° C in 12,000 parts of a mixture of equal volumes of ethylic alcohol (of 75%) and amylic alcohol, and 42,500 parts of the same mixture at 2°–4° C.

It follows from these data that ethylic or common alcohol of 75% dissolves practically no paraffin at all; also, that the solvent power of amylic alcohol for paraffin is very much diminished by adding ethylic alcohol; and lastly, that a lowering of temperature reduces the solvent power very materially.

As the proposed method promises to be of considerable practical usefulness in the examinations of various kinds of petrolatum or other petroleum products used in pharmacy or the arts, the method of executing the process will be briefly described here. It may be stated that the author has succeeded, by means of his process, in separating and estimating the amount of natural paraffin existing in crude petroleum — a matter of considerable practical as well as scientific interest.

For the purpose of assay, a sample of the substance weighing between 10 and 20 grammes, or measuring the same number of centimeters, is placed into a beaker, mixed with five times its weight of amylic alcohol, and afterwards the same amount of ordinary alcohol (of 75%) is added. The mixture is allowed to stand, well-covered, during several hours (the longer, the better) in a cold place, if possible below 4° C. (40° F.), then passed through a dry and cold filter, and the residue on the filter washed with a cold mixture of 2 parts of amylic and 1 part of ordinary alcohol of 70%. The exact determination of the weight of the precipitated paraffin is best accomplished by extracting the residue with ether or benzin in a continuous extraction apparatus. For this purpose, the filter, with contents, is lifted out of the funnel, rolled somewhat together lengthwise so as to fill out the whole bore of the tube connected with the flask holding the volatile menstruum, and a condenser having been fitted to the tube, heat is applied to the flask which causes the vapors of the volatile menstruum to pass up, and afterwards to return condensed. At the same time, the filter and contents are kept hot by the ascending vapors. The contents of the flask are then deprived of the volatile menstruum by heating in a drying closet, and the residue weighed. To dry the residue completely, a temperature of 125° C. (257° F.) maintained for two hours is sufficient.

When examining crude oils, or other crude petroleum products by this method, the author recommends to use a larger quantity of the alcohol mixture — about ten times that of the sample to be analyzed—and to let the mixture stand at least twelve hours in a cold place. This will do away with difficulties encountered in filtering. The final residue on the filter should be washed with the mixture before indicated, until the latter ceases to run off colored.

This method may also be used to determine the quantity of paraffin mixed with fatty acids, neutral fats, resins, resin oils, etc. All these bodies are completely soluble under the above-mentioned conditions, in the alcohol mixture. But the admixture of paraffin to *wax* cannot be detected by it, as beeswax is likewise precipitated by the mixed alcohol.—*After Dingl. Polyt. Journ.*, 297, 276.

Preparation of Hydriodic (and, incidentally, Phosphoric) Acid.

PROF. LOTHAR MEYER has recently published a paper (in *Berichte d. D. Chem. Ges.*, 1880, 3,581) on the preparation of gaseous hydriodic acid, which contains valuable hints for those who desire to prepare this acid for medicinal or technical purposes.

Prof. Meyer points out that the drawbacks inherent in all hitherto used methods of preparing pure hydriodic acid may be avoided by a very slight improvement, consisting only in the precaution to have *at all times* an excess of iodine present. The usual methods direct to add iodine to an excess of phosphorus. This is the cause of the generation of phosphoretted hydrogen and phosphonium iodide. (Phosphonium is the hypothetical group PH_4, corresponding to ammonium NH_4. Phosphoretted hydrogen, or phosphine, PH_3, is capable of combining with haloid acids: $PH_3 + HCl = PH_4Cl$ which is phosphonium chloride, PH_4I phosphonium iodide, etc.) The excess of iodine is so decidedly necessary that it is even faulty to remove any free iodine which may have been carried over by the gas with moistened phosphorus, as this may be the cause of accidents.

The reaction which takes place between phosphorus and iodine:

$$P + 5I + 4H_2O = H_3PO_4 + 5HI$$
phosphorus — iodine — water — phosphoric acid — hydriodic acid

requires for every 100 parts of iodine nearly 5 parts of phosphorus and 12 parts of water, provided a very concentrated *hydriodic acid* is required. These proportions should be maintained, except that about 20 parts of water are preferably taken. The process is conducted in the following manner:

The 100 parts of iodine are placed into a tubulated retort the neck of which is turned upward, and about 10 parts of water are poured in. The other 10 parts of water are mixed to a thin magma with 5 parts of red phosphorus, and this is transferred to a funnel the neck of which is stoppered, not by a faucet, but by a long glass rod ground into the lower end of the funnel. This glass rod, and particularly its lower ground end, should not be too thick, as the magma of phosphorus would otherwise not easily pass by it. The funnel having been fitted in the tubulure of the retort, and the receiver, containing a suitable quantity of water, having been connected with the retort, the glass rod is *very carefully* drawn up so that *one* drop (no more) of the phosphorus magma may fall upon the iodine. This stage is the only one where *caution* is necessary. Should the operator, induced by the apparent failure of any reaction or its feeble progress, allow more phosphorus to reach the iodine in the beginning, the action would become uncontrollable and an explosion will generally result.

[*Note by Ed. Am. Drugg.*—We find, on trying this method on a small scale, that it is not always easy to restrict the quantity of phosphorus paste, in the beginning, *to just one drop*, if the funnel is charged with the whole of the magma, as above directed. The safest plan is to put into the funnel at first only so much of the magma that a raising of the glass rod cannot allow more than *one* drop to fall in. Afterwards the funnel may gradually be filled with the remainder.]

If the phosphorus is added at first quite slowly, and the reaction is allowed to moderate before adding more, the time will soon arrive when larger quantities of the phosphorus may be added at once, so that the whole operation may be completed within about fifteen minutes (when 100 Gm. of iodine are taken in operation). The whole reaction then takes place quietly and requires no heat until near the end. Any free iodine mechanically carried over by the hydriodic acid is almost wholly condensed in the neck of the retort. In order to prevent its passing over as far as possible, it is advisable to connect the retort with the condenser by means of a long, moderately wide glass tube, directed upwards, and to pass the current of gas first through a U-tube containing a little water. The best form of receiver is a pair of Woulff's bottles, connected by a siphon. In the first of these, the delivery tube ends immediately below the cork, the gas being absorbed by the water contained in the bottle with avidity. If desired or thought advisable, several of such bottles may be connected by tubes ending below the corks. When the reaction has almost ceased, a gentle heat is applied to the retort, whereby also some aqueous vapor is driven over which causes the iodine adhering to the walls to return to the retort. Should the iodine tint (of the contents of the retort) not disappear even after heating for some time, a *very small* quantity of iodine together with a few drops of water may be introduced. But care must be taken not to apply heat in presence of an *excess* of phosphorus, as this would cause the evolution of phosphonium iodide.

If the operation is to be repeated a short time afterwards, the residue may be left in the retort, and new quantities of iodine and phosphorus added. But if it is desired to utilize the ingredients of one operation to the utmost, the neck of the retort is directed downwards (after all the hydriodic acid has come over), a receiver, with well-cooled condenser, attached and heat applied, which causes the aqueous hydriodic acid remaining in the retort to distil over. If any free phosphorus should still have been present, a little iodine is added, or better, the liquid is diluted and filtered off from the phosphorus before being distilled. Finally there remains in the retort colorless, syrupy phosphoric acid.

Prof. Meyer obtained, from 100 Gm. iodine, 5 Gm. phosphorus, and 35 Gm. water, altogether 95 Gm. of hydriodic acid instead of the theoretical quantity 100.8 Gm.). Of this amount, 57.3 Gm. came over directly as gas, and the balance (37.5) was distilled over in aqueous solution. When only 20 Gm. of water were used, he obtained 74.4 Gm. as gas, and 23.7 Gm. by distillation, together 98.1 Gm. The amount of water to be introduced in the receiver should be such that the resulting product will have the desired strength.

New Method for rapidly Evaporating Non-inflammable Solutions.

J. W. GUNNING describes a new method, employed in the Government laboratories of the Netherlands, for rapidly evaporating sugar solutions by means of heat applied over the *surface* of the liquid, instead of from the bottom, so as to avoid the spattering which is liable to take place when heat is applied in the usual manner. This method of heating is, of course, applicable to all other non-inflammable solutions, when the object is to evaporate them as rapidly as possible, with a view to ignite the residue.

The apparatus is very simple, and is readily understood without a drawing. It consists simply of an iron plate standing on four legs, having four openings, one near each corner, through which the tubes of four Bunsen burners are adjusted at such a height that the tops of the burners will be a little higher than the edge of the capsules (which should be platinum or other non-oxidizable metal) which will be placed on the iron plate. A second iron plate is then adjusted over the burners. When the four flames are lit, the upper iron plate causes the flames to spread out along the plate, and both the direct flame as well as the radiation from the upper heated plate will cause a rapid evaporation of the liquid in the capsules.—*After Zeitsch. f. anal. Chem.*, 1887, 726.

Standardising volumetric Solution of Iodine.

WILHELM KALMANN has proposed a new method for standardizing or determining the exact titre of iodine solutions intended for volumetric use.

His method is based on the fact that, when iodine is brought in contact with a sulphite, the following reaction takes place:

$$Na_2SO_3 + 2I + H_2O = Na_2SO_4 + 2HI$$
sodium — iodine — water — sodium — hydriodic
sulphite — — — sulphate — acid

that is, the whole of the iodine is converted into hydriodic acid. If the latter be now titrated with a soda solution of known strength (best very dilute), in presence of methyl-orange as indicator, the quantity of soda consumed until the liquid assumes a yellow tint corresponds to the amount of iodine. The sulphite of sodium used may contain sulphate as an impurity, but must not contain either hyposulphite or carbonate, because the free hydriodic acid would act upon either of these salts and falsify the results.

In practice, the operation is carried out as follows: A measured quantity of the iodine solution is put in a beaker, and then gradually mixed with just enough of a solution of sulphite of sodium (of any desirable strength) to cause the liquid to lose its color. All the iodine is now present as hydriodic acid. A few drops of solution of methyl-orange are now added (which imparts a rose-red tint to an *acid* liquid), and afterwards a $\frac{1}{10}$ normal solution of soda (or one even more dilute than this) is gradually allowed to flow in from a burette, until the rose-red tint of the liquid passes into yellow.

This method may also be used, vice versa, to determine the quantity of a sulphite, or of a mixture of sulphite and hyposulphite, provided no uncombined bases or carbonates are present. Supposing we had a mixture of sulphite and hyposulphite of sodium. On adding to an aqueous solution of the mixture standard iodine solution as long as this is decolorized, the iodine consumed would represent both that which has reacted with the sulphite and produced hydriodic acid, and that which has reacted with the hyposulphite to form iodide of sodium. On now determining the quantity of hydriodic acid produced, as outlined above, we obtain the amount of sulphite present in the mixture. And the quantity of iodine consumed in excess of that represented by the hydriodic acid, is concerned in the reaction with the hyposulphite.—*After Zeitsch. f. anal. Chem.*, 1887, 727.

Resorcin in Sea-sickness.

RESORCIN is another addition to the long list of remedies for sea-sickness. Dr. Andeer states (*Lancet*, Jan. 7th, p. 39) that a single dose of from ten to twenty grams given early before vomiting removes the giddiness and nausea, and enables the patient to sleep comfortably. In persistent cases, large doses two or three times a day are said to produce excellent results. A ten-per-cent solution of resorcin has also been found useful in cases of laryngeal tuberculosis by Dr. Fronstein, who says that, although resorcin is not so powerful an anæsthetic as cocaine, it acts more satisfactorily in allaying the pain and distress caused by laryngeal ulceration of tubercular origin.—*Ph. Journ.*

A Suggestion for Bougie Moulds.

MOULDS for making urethral bougies are not yet considered as necessary implements in all "well-regulated pharmacies," yet sometimes a prescription is presented requiring some of those articles to be made, and we have to resort to tinfoil. Generally an elastic gum bougie is taken as a model on which to wrap the tinfoil; but the bougie being of the same thickness nearly all its length, there is considerable difficulty in drawing off the mould from the model. Often when we have succeeded in doing this we find that the bougie has acted as piston and drawn the sides of the mould together, rendering it useless. This trouble may be obviated by using a piece of glass tubing same size as a No. 8 bougie. First draw out the end to a point and cut it off about an eighth of an inch from where the narrowing begins, then fuse again until the end is rounded off as the bougie is to be, taking care not to allow the aperture to close. This tube now forms the model upon which to shape the tinfoil moulds. The tinfoil slips more easily from the glass than from the elastic gum, and the little hole at the apex allows air to enter as the tube is withdrawn.—S. J. ELLIOT, in *Chem. and Drug.*

Antipyrin as an Anodyne.

THE list of affections or morbid conditions in which antipyrin has been found beneficial is constantly increasing. Not long ago, Prof. Ryerson reported that it produced very marked and prompt relief, taken internally as an anodyne, in acute and painful affections of the eye. This is confirmed by Dr. Wetherby (*Med. Record*), who had a patient afflicted with intense conjunctivitis of the right eye, extreme photophobia and lachrymation, and most intense periœleal pain extending from the eye to the head and neck. He happened to have read Prof. Ryerson's article, and ordered for the patient six powders of antipyrin, of 15 grains each, with the instruction to take one immediately on reaching home, and to lie down. It turned out that only one powder was required to produce relief, the patient sleeping quietly during the whole night. Of course, a local treatment was employed for the inflammation in the eye, but whenever this was subsequently followed by a dose of antipyrin the patient remained free from discomfort and pain. Dr. Wetherby thinks that the antipyrin not only acted as an anodyne, but that it also had a controlling action on the inflammation, since the eye improved more rapidly than any other he had ever treated, which was similarly affected.

The Use of Salol in Rheumatism.

DR. DERCUM, in the *Journal of Nervous and Mental Disease*, speaking of the use of salol when wintergreen oil is not well borne, says: In my own experience, salol has special virtues of special application. It is an almost tasteless, fatty, insoluble powder, which is as bland and uniritating to the mucous membrane of the stomach as so much powdered paraffin would be. It is apparently not acted upon by the gastric juice, but depends for its digestion upon the pancreas. At least it is decomposed in the small intestine into salicylic and carbolic acids. This change likewise takes place when salol is mixed with pancreatic secretion or with pancreatic tissue outside of the body.

As far, then, as the stomach is concerned, it is innocuous and inert, and it frequently proves a grateful relief to that viscus, especially when the oil of gaultheria or the salicylate of sodium has been given for some time. Judging from my own experience, it is slower in producing its physiological action than the other salicylates.

The effect is not as pronounced and much less prompt. That it is, however, efficient in the same class of cases as the oil of gaultheria there can be no doubt. I generally prescribe fifteen or twenty grains to be taken every three or four hours. The effect is gradually produced, and is manifested in large doses by more or less "cinchonism." Curiously enough, I have noticed that the ringing in the ears is less, but the deafness more marked, than from the gaultheria. Occasionally patients will mention the darkening of the urine due to the presence of carbolic acid.

Now and then patients object to the drug on account of its greasy feel and greasy taste, and sometimes of their own accord ask to be placed back on the gaultheria. Occasionally, of course, it is well to alternate the gaultheria, instead of with salol, with the sodium salicylate.

The Therapeutic Use of Quillaja Bark.

PROF. R. KOBERT, of the University of Dorpat, has published the first number of a collection of investigations made at the pharmacological institute of the University, one of which has as subject the active constituents of Quillaja, or soap-bark, and the author of which is Dmitrij Pachorukow, of Irkutsk, Siberia. We shall quote only a few of the more prominent results.

Prof. Kobert had already ascertained, some years ago, that the commercial saponin did not represent the full therapeutic power of soap-bark, or of whatever either source was used for its preparation. It had been customary to designate as saponin the precipitate which was produced by adding alcohol to a cold aqueous infusion of the drug. Kobert, however, found that the filtrate, which had previously been rejected, contained a very active substance, and finally he succeeded in finding a method by which the two most energetic substances contained in soap bark, namely, quillajic acid and sapotoxin could be separated from each other.

Kobert's sapotoxin forms the principal subject of the author's paper. This substance is exceedingly powerful, but is contained in the bark only in a very small percentage.

Sapotoxin is remarkable through its solvent action upon the red corpuscles of the blood. But the same property also belongs to quillajic acid, and to the commercial saponin, though in a much lesser degree. Even in a dilution of 1 in 10,000 did the first-mentioned substance (sapotoxin) completely dissolve the red corpuscles.

Fortunately, however, this takes place only when the sapotoxin, etc., is directly introduced into the circulation (by injection). None of these substances are absorbed either by the *stomach* or *intestines*, the only effect which is produced, even by relatively large doses, being a local irritation with occasional vomiting. Even a mere hypodermic solution is followed by only slight effects, as it is but very slowly absorbed, which is shown, among other things, by the great local irritation thereby produced.

Sapotoxin, when actually absorbed, or when injected (in concentrated solution) into any involuntary muscle, diminishes or entirely destroys its vitality. It is also a poison, both for the motory and the sensory nerves, not only in their terminations, but also in their main branches.

In spite of the apparently energetic and toxic action of sapotoxin—which, however, does not exert itself except when this principle is directly injected into the venous system—the employment of quillaja bark is not only theoretically indicated, but also advisable on practical grounds, especially in place of senega. Kobert had shown, already in 1883, that the valuable constituents of senega varied very much in different specimens of the drug, while those of quillaja were constant and were, moreover, present in nearly 8 times the quantity compared with those of senega. Besides, quillaja bark contains sugar, and is free from the exceedingly irritating and disagreeable substance which renders the administration of senega so objectionable. He also showed that the preparations of quillaja are better borne than those of senega; that the former is as valuable an expectorant as the latter; and that quillaja but rarely causes vomiting or diarrhœa.

Upon the basis of Prof. Kobert's experiments, Dr. Goldschmidt investigated the therapeutic effects of quillaja. He found that the latter promoted expectoration by inciting cough, and that it, at the same time, diluted the secretion, thereby facilitating its ejection. Other experimenters have confirmed these results.

From the experiences thus gained, the author—and, in fact, Prof. Kobert and his whole school—advocate the employment of quillaja and its preparations in place of senega as an expectorant. The preparation which has usually been employed, and with uniform success, is the following (converted into U. S. terms):

B Quillaja...	gr. 75
Tr. Opii...	ṃ 40
Syrupi..	fl. ʒ 1
Aquæ...	q. s. ad fl. ʒ 6

With 7 fluidounces of water make an infusion from the Quillaja, in the usual manner. Strain, add the Tincture of Opium and Syrup, and lastly, enough water, previously passed through the strainer, to make 8 fluidounces.

Dose: A tablespoonful every 2 hours.

THE
American Druggist

AN ILLUSTRATED MONTHLY JOURNAL

OF

Pharmacy, Chemistry, and Materia Medica.

Vol. XVII., No. 4.   Whole No. 166.

FREDERICK A. CASTLE, M.D. .... Editor.
CHARLES RICE, Ph.D. .... Associate Editor.

PUBLISHED BY

WM. WOOD & CO., 56 & 58 Lafayette Place, N. Y.

SUBSCRIPTION PRICE per year, ... $1.50
SINGLE COPIES, ...15

Address all communications relating to the business of the AMERICAN DRUGGIST, such as subscriptions, advertisements, change of Post Office address, etc., to WILLIAM WOOD & CO., 56 and 58 Lafayette Place, New York City, to whose order all postal money orders and checks should be made payable. Communications intended for the Editor should be addressed in care of the Publishers.

* The AMERICAN DRUGGIST is issued in the latter part of each month, dated for the month ahead. Changes of advertisements should reach us before the 10th. New advertisements can occasionally be inserted after the 18th. REGULAR ADVERTISEMENTS according to size, location, and time. Special rates on application.

EDITORIALS.

THE *Pharmaceutical Record*, having in mind certain proceedings in the New York City courts against pharmacists who used Croton water in place of distilled water, called for in prescriptions, says:

"We should like to know how much the effect of medicine is hindered when Croton water is used in prescriptions, and how much more efficacious the same remedy would be if dispensed with distilled water. We can readily understand that there are some kinds of water that are unfit for use, and that in some instances distilled water should invariably be used; but how much more effective would a dose of rhubarb and magnesia be if mixed with distilled water in place of filtered Croton water."

We hope that our contemporary may have its desire for information satisfied, although we cannot see that the information is likely to be of any practical value.

In connection with the question of substituting Croton for distilled water when the latter is prescribed, it is of no earthly importance to the pharmacist who desires to cultivate a prescription business, whether one is preferable to the other or not. The fact for him to keep in view is that he makes a business of preparing prescriptions according to formulas furnished him, and is receiving remuneration for doing so. Let him, therefore, use all the skill he is possessed of in the first particular and then get as good pay for doing it as he can. There are sufficient occasions for the exercise of professional opinion in other directions more profitable than this and he need not concern himself with the question raised by the *Pharmaceutical Record* for a moment, when he gets a prescription calling for *distilled* water. Indeed about as unprofitable a thing as he can do is to give his patrons an impression that he exercises his own judgment in regard to the propriety of following the text of prescriptions or using something which *he* thinks more desirable than the article prescribed.

It is not many years since a very accomplished pharmacist in this city practically ran himself out of a good business by volunteering advice to his customers with regard to the propriety of using what their doctor prescribed, or taking, instead, something which *he* could give them for less money than the prescription would cost them. It required only a few attempts of this kind to cause the doctors in his neighborhood to "boycott" his store and advise their patients to beware of him.

There is little doubt that the majority of physicians might learn something of the pharmacists who prepare their prescriptions; and in the case of choosing between distilled or filtered water, they might find, by a little attention to the matter, that the latter would answer quite as well for most purposes, but it is doubtful whether it would be politic for the pharmacist to volunteer the information; for it may be accepted as a rule that the greater the ignorance of a doctor is respecting such matters, the more intolerant he is of criticism in regard to them.

Our advice is to use distilled water when the prescription specifically calls for it, and be sure to use that which will bear the Pharmacopoeial test, and then get pay for the extra labor which is involved. That is *business*.

DR. CHARLES HARRINGTON, of the Harvard Medical School, furnishes to the *Boston Medical and Surgical Journal* of March 1st a communication in which he narrates the circumstances attending the purchase of English wall-papers with the manufacturers' guarantee that they were non-arsenical. Tests made after their receipt by the Boston purchaser showed that arsenic was present and accordingly the Boston house objected to receiving and paying for them. The English manufacturer, thereupon, reiterated his claim that the papers were non-arsenical, and in proof thereof sent a testimonial from Prof. John Attfield, Ph.D., F.R.S., F.I.C., F.C.S., who said:

"Not one of these samples is an arsenical wall-paper; that is to say, not one of the pigments or color-giving substances on the papers is arsenical, and the paper itself of these paper-hangings is not arsenical."

"Pseudo-sanitarians sometimes report non-arsenical wall-papers as containing some ridiculously minute trace of arsenic. These alarmists might just as truly report some samples of common table salt as containing arsenic, for the delicacy of certain of the tests for arsenic is so great that traces can be detected in many things. But such traces are absolutely without significance from any sanitary point of view, either in salt, wall-paper, or anything else. Arsenical wall-papers have well-defined arsenical characters, were formerly common, and may now occasionally be met with. Neither of these samples is an arsenical wall-paper."

Following the receipt of this, analyses of these papers were made by Henry B. Hill, Professor of Chemistry in Harvard College; Dr. Charles S. Sanger, Professor of Chemistry in the United States Naval Academy; and by Dr. Harrington, who is the Assistant in Chemistry and Instructor in Hygiene in the Harvard Medical School, and the following table shows the results of their examinations as compared with those made by Prof. Attfield.

	AMOUNT OF ARSENIC IN GRAINS PER SQUARE YARD.			
No.	Hill.	Sanger.	Harrington.	Attfield.
1	4.66	4.08	4.40	....
2	0.85	0.72	0.90	....
3	0.98	0.73	0.82	....
4	0.63	0.71	0.76	....
5	0.21	0.23	0.26	....
6	0.13	0.04	0.14	....
7	0.10	0.08	0.12	....
8	0.21	0.23	0.22	....

According to the American analyses, *all* of the papers contained more than the permissible limit recommended to the National Health Society of England by its committee. In view of the reputation which Prof. Attfield has in this country, this result is certainly very surprising, but it shows how desirable it is to take such guarantees with great reluctance and caution. It is well understood by pharmacists and chemists that there are always to be found a certain number of chemists holding prominent professional positions who can be depended upon to furnish certificates which favor the interests of those who employ them, but we are loth to believe that Prof. Attfield is to be classed among them. He certainly owes it to himself to offer some explanation of such a decided variation between the results of his own analyses and those of the American analysts in the present instance.

Correction.

In the article on "Gleditschia triacanthos" by Mr. Abraham L. Metz, on page 1 of our January number, the words "Nessler's reagent" are used in place of "Mayer's reagent," which latter was used by the author, and which he meant to write (see second column, middle). Mayer's reagent, as will be known to most of our readers, is a solution containing 13.546 Gm. of mercuric chloride, and 49.8 Gm. of iodide of potassium in one liter of water, and is a very sensitive test for alkaloids.

Pharmaceutical Substitution.—A short time ago, a German association set itself the task of proving that the German pharmacists habitually substituted one ingredient for another when not in stock. Bogus prescriptions were, therefore, prepared containing unknown and absurd articles. One prescription read:

Aconit. Nap.
Tuber Cinereum.

Notwithstanding the fact that "Tuber Cinereum" is the "tubercle of gray substance at the base of the human brain," this article with aconite was actually dispensed and paid for in fifty-eight Berlin pharmacies. Other fancy ingredients, such as *Urticaria rubra*, *l'emphygus foliaceus*, etc., etc., were dispensed in seventy-seven pharmacies; only twelve refused them. When the hoax was complete, the whole bundle of prescriptions, together with the compounds dispensed, were submitted to the editors of the journals. The organs of German pharmacy admit the truth of the charge. The Berlin Pharmaceutical Society, at their last meeting, discreetly resolved to take no notice of the matter.

The *Practitioner* announces the publication of a general index to its series of volumes, 39 of which have issued since its foundation. This will be a welcome piece of information to the readers of this valuable periodical.

The Nebraska Pharmaceutical Association is to meet in Lincoln on the 8th, 9th, and 10th of May.

The Louisiana Pharmaceutical Association holds its next meeting in New Orleans on the 10th of April. Exhibitors should address Charles K. Hall, care of E. J. Hart & Co., New Orleans, La., accompanied with a fee of $10.

College of Pharmacy of the City of New York.—At the Annual Meeting, held on March 13th, the following officers were elected:
President: Ewen McIntyre. Vice-Presidents: H. J. Menninger, George C. Close, W. L. Vennard. Treasurer: David Hays. Secretary: J. N. Higeman. Trustees for three years: Charles Rice, H. W. Atwood, B. F. Hays, J. T. Macmahan, F. F. Knapp.

The examinations of the two classes occupied not less than nine days, owing to the intervention of the severe storm of March 12th. As we are about to go to press, we can only state that the commencement exercises were held on March 28th at Steinway Hall, General W. T. Sherman delivering the address to the Graduating Class, and Mr. A. T. Brown, of the graduating class, delivering the valedictory.

Roll of Graduates of 1888:
1. Roll of Honor: George C. Diekman (Gold Medal).
2. Harvey S. Miles (Silver Medal). 3. Albert Niederer (Bronze Medal). 4 to 13: Oswald Richter, Otto Raubenheimer, F. G. Cough, F. P. Tuthil, Emil Weiss, W. R. Betts, Mrs. Rose Smith Brunner, John Harding, L. Freiberger, Gust. Richel.

The remainder of the graduates are the following:

Charles F. Antz, New York City; Martin Arnemann, Jr., New York City; George S. Baldwin, Gilboa, N. Y.; Charles W. Bartlett, Watertown, N. Y.; Anthony Bobata, New York, N. Y.; George B. Bosch, New York, N. Y.; Arthur Tappan Brown, Sag Harbor, N. Y.; Eric Buelter, New York, N. Y.; Frank K. Burr, Iowa City, Iowa; Charles V. Chase, Davenport, Iowa; J. Taylor Clark, Clifton Park, N. Y.; J. Miller Campton, New York, N. Y.; Evan Moss Davis, Brooklyn, N. Y.; John George Deckert, Brooklyn, N. Y.; August Diehl, Phillipsburgh, N. J.; Frederick E. Dodd, Newark, N. J.; Cheon L. Doty, Glens Falls, N. Y.; Charles B. Ely, Milton, Pa.; Denis A. Falvey, Flushing, N. Y.; Henry Fink, New York, N. Y.; August Frank, New York, N. Y.; John P. Frawley, Bangor, Maine; Ferdinand Freund, New York, N. Y.; Howard P. Guiney, Sioux City, Iowa; Leopold Hahn, New York, N. Y.; John Otto Herbig, College Point, N. Y.; Edward Hoelz, New York, N. Y.; John M. Horton, Whiteville, N. Y.; Louis W. Jansen, Brooklyn, N. Y.; Robert Johnson, New York, N. Y.; W. W. Johnston, Newtown, N. Y.; W. A. Joye, Flatbush, N. Y.; John J. Kalisher, New York, N. Y.; Edward Katz, New York, N. Y.; William W. Kepler, Bloomfield, N. J.; John J. Kerwin, New Rochelle, N. Y.; George G. King, Rochester, N. Y.; J. Howard Leggett, Princeton, N. J.; Carl Ernst Levin, New York, N. Y.; Victor G. Lockwood, Mianus, Conn.; Rudolph William Martini, New York, N. Y.; Philip Mathy, New York, N. Y.; Charles Miebling, New York, N. Y.; Edward F. Miller, New York, N. Y.; William P. Miller, Siegfried's Bridge, Pa.; A. Eustace Muss, New York, N. Y.; William H. Nicholson, New London, Conn.; Emil Nowaik, New York, N. Y.; William C. Oettinger, Brooklyn, N. Y.; Neville J. Patterson, New Rochelle, N. Y.; Herman Popper, New York, N. Y.; Walter S. Reed, Long Branch, N. J.; John Graham Reeves, Yonkers, N. Y.; William P. Rich, Newark, N. J.; Armin Richter, Buffalo, N. Y.; Drahomir Ruzicka, New York, N. Y.; Albert Schurr, New York, N. Y.; Charles B. Sears, Auburn, N. Y.; Alfred B. Seebass, New York, N. Y.; James G. Shaffer, New York, N. Y.; Maxwell P. Simons, New York, N. Y.; Andrew G. Slonaker, New York, N. Y.; Miss Angela de Socarras, Puerto Principe, Cuba; G. F. Sorrow, New York, N. Y.; Albert Staudenmeyer, New York, N. Y.; David Strauss, Elizabeth, N. J.; Richard Sunderman, Bergen Point, N. J.; Fred. Clarence Viele, Glens Falls, N. Y.; August Volland, New York, N. Y.; Louis Wedel, Brooklyn, N. Y.; Leon Wernert, New York, N. Y.; Joseph Wuelfrath, New York, N. Y.; Herbert Ziebarth, Brooklyn, N. Y.; Arthur Ziegler, Hoboken, N. J.

The following students were examined in all branches except pharmacy:

Henry S. Blackmore, Mount Vernon, N. Y.; Major C. Brown, Gallipolis, Ohio; A. A. Jackson, Norwalk, Conn.; Ernest Stichl, Brooklyn, N. Y.

Special in Chemistry:
Theodore P. Van Ness, Newark, N. J.

Cincinnati College of Pharmacy.—The 16th Annual Commencement was held February 16th, and degrees were awarded to:
J. B. Adams, C. A. Apmeyer, G. D. Cabeen, A. Diebold, F. P. Dieringer, Miss Cora Dow, W. Ellis, C. L. Goeltz, H. L. Grimes, W. E. Jones, E. C. Jungkind, J. Kiehl, G. F. Maxwell, H. W. Weid, H. Voeckel, T. D. Wetterstroem, H. Folger, P. Miller.

Prizes were awarded to Cora Dow, for proficiency in Materia Medica; H. L. Grimes, for practical pharmacy; C. A. Apmeyer in chemistry, and to G. Ridenour, for the best general examination average. In the Junior Class, Victor Muehlberg won both medals in botany and examination.

Pittsburgh College of Pharmacy.—The tenth annual commencement of this college took place March 20th. The salutatory was delivered by Hugo Blanck, A.M., Ph.D., the professor in chemistry. W. T. English, of the Western Pennsylvania Medical College, delivered the annual address to the class. The degree of Graduate in Pharmacy was conferred by President Geo. A. Kelly on:

Elmer E. Knight, Turkey City, Pa.; Wilson Curtis Brewster, Butler, Pa.; Theodore Cappell, Pittsburgh, Pa.; Anthony John Houck, Allegheny, Pa.; Chas. Wallace Davis, Allegheny, Pa.; George B. Little, Washington, Pa.; James P. Beckley, Glassburo, N. J.; Chas. B. Shroom, Greenville, Pa.; Christ Ernest Strung, Pittsburgh, Pa.; S. Howard Jackson, Wilkinsburgh, Pa.; Ernest Christian Stiefel, Pittsburgh, Pa.; William G. Minnick, Allegheny, Pa.; Alexander Walter Boggs, Pittsburgh, Pa.; Charles William Kahl, McKeesport, Pa.; William H. Lewis, Belle Vernon, Pa.; John F. Murphy, Pittsburgh, Pa.; Henry Finkelpearl, Pittsburgh, Pa.

Geo. B. Little, of Washington, Pa., delivered the valedictory address. Prof. Proudfit awarded the Shady Side senior prize, gold medal, to Wilson Curtis Brewster and the Shady Side junior prize, silver medal, to Elmer E. Tribby, respectively for best examinations in pharmacy. Prof. S. Henry Stevens, on behalf of friends and members of the Board of Trustees, presented to Elmer E. Knight, of Turkey City, Roscoe's Chemistry complete in six vols. for highest general average and best senior examination in chemistry, and to Theodore Cappel, Square's Compendium to the British Pharmacopœia, for best senior examination in materia medica and botany.

The following juniors passed a successful examination and are entitled to enter the senior class.

Elmer E. Tribly, W. M. Cooke, P. T. Kearns, Oscar Mangold, D. B. Watson, Jas. W. Kinney, Benj. E. Camp, Walter F. Schwartz, W. C. Murphy, Howard Marshal, Isaac K. Dantzler, John A. Copenhaver, Samuel L. Weotling, Franklin L. Fry, A. C. Hyde, Byron Curtis Henderson, Wm. M. Frantz, Melvin A. Paterson, Henson C. Newlon, Harry L. Greer, Chas. F. Birchard, Jas. Armstrong, and Frank F. Garber.

The examining committee consisted of Messrs. Fred. H. Eggers, A. C. Robertson, Louis Emanuel, Parry M. Glein, Prof. Francis C. Phillips, besides the faculty, Prof. S. H. Stevens, Prof. Hugo Blanck, and Prof. Adolph Koenig.

The Maryland College of Pharmacy held its commencement on the 22d of March, the following-named gentlemen constituting the graduating class:

Albertson, J. E.; Atkinson, J. M.; Baxley, H. M.; Blair, S. O.; Brack, Jr., Chas. E.; Brown, Jos. D.; Buschman, Wm. G.; Charsee, B. W.; Dauger, Andrew (2); Dalton, Jr., H.; Dawson, Wm.; Dietz, O. J.; Douglass, Eugene (3); Dressel, Henry G. (1); Fermaner, Louis G.; Forien, Wm. F.; George, Alfred; Hauser, F. C.; Hill, W. J.; Lankford, G. A.; Link, Joseph; Lippey, Geo. H.; Luck, Charles A.; Maschal, Chas. S.; Modena, W. J. (5); Reh, Henry G.; Roeder, Jr., S. T.; Scherer, Wm. (4); Sherman, Louis F.; Simmonds, Sidney J.; Stewart, J. W.; Sunwalt, Jas. B.; Thillman, H. D.; Tierney, James A.; Trainor, F. S.; Tumbleson, A. L.; Waiz, J. L.; Witherspoon, W. J.; Wolf, Henry G.

The prizemen are indicated in the above list by numerals, (4) taking the "Senior Analytical;" (5) the "Practical Pharmacy," and J. A. Hardison the "Junior College."

FORMULAS.

Corn Remedy.

Salicylic Acid	10 parts.
Lactic Acid	10 "
Collodion	80 "

Mix them. The addition of lactic acid is said to increase the efficacy of this combination very materially. [Heretofore, extract of cannabis indica has usually been added as one of the ingredients.]—*Rundschau* (Prag).

Application to Diphtheritic Membranes.

Papayotin	75 grains.
Distilled Water	90 minims.
Glycerin	½ fluidounce.

For local application to diphtheritic membranes, by means of a camel's-hair pencil.

Incense.

Benzoin	6 oz.
Storax	5 "
Cascarilla, grd.	3 "
Myrrh	1 "
Olibanum	3 "
Cinnamon, grd.	½ "
Cloves	½ "
Nitrate of Potassium	½ "

Mix them.—(After *Chem. and Drugg.*).

Aromatic Vinegar.

Tincture of Benzoin	1 fl. oz.
Alcohol	1½ "
Acetic Ether	1½ "
Extract of Jasmin	1½ "
Acetic Acid	3½ "
Oil of Rose	10 drops
Oil of Neroli	5 "
Oil of Wintergreen	5 "

—(After *Dieterich.*)

Aqua Magnesiæ.

Sulphate of Magnesium	50 parts
Carbonate of Sodium, cryst.	60 "
Distilled Water,	
Carbonic Acid Gas, each	q. s.

Dissolve the Sulphate of Magnesium in 100 parts of Water and filter. Also dissolve the Carbonate of Sodium in 100 parts of Water. Then pour both solutions, at the same time, in a thin stream, into 4,000 parts of water which is being constantly stirred, and contained in a capacious vessel. The resulting precipitate (of hydrocarbonate of magnesium) is washed by decantation with distilled water (which should be quite cold), until nitrate of barium ceases to render it turbid. About eight repetitions of the washing process are required. Then mix the residue with enough water to make the whole weigh 1,000 parts. Next pass a stream of Carbonic Acid Gas through the liquid, contained (in a suitable vessel), until the precipitated salt is dissolved, and transfer the solution into bottles holding about 6 or 7 ounces, which should be stored in a cool place, lying on their sides.—After *Dieterich.*

Liquor Aluminii Chloridi.

Solution of Chloride of Aluminium.

Sulphate of Aluminium	25 parts
Chloride of Barium	25 "
Water	q. s.

Dissolve the two salts, each in 50 parts of warm Water, mix the solutions, and heat the mixture on a water-bath to about 160° F. Then allow to cool, filter, and pass enough Water through the filter to make 100 parts of product.—After *Dieterich.*

Instead of using chloride of barium, chloride of calcium may be used. In this case, however, the mixture of the two salts should be set aside, in a cold place, for at least one week, in order that the excess of sulphate of calcium, not retained in solution, may separate. And when filtering the solution, it will hardly pay to wash out the small amount retained by the precipitate. Of course, when a solution of a definite strength is required, the first-mentioned formula should be used. But when the liquid is wanted as a disinfectant, the second method may be employed.

Pastilles for Fetid Breath.

Coffee, roasted and powdered	3 oz.
Charcoal, powdered	1 "
Boric Acid	1 "
Saccharin	10 grains
Tincture of Vanilla	q. s.
Mucilage of Acacia	q. s.

Reduce the solids to a moderately fine, uniform powder, flavor it with the Tincture and then mix it with enough Mucilage to make a mass which is to be divided into troches or pastilles weighing 10 grains.

Hamburg Bitters.

Galanga Root	30 tr. oz.
Ginger	24 "
Laurel Berries	24 "
Nutmeg	18 "
Cassia Buds	14 "
Pepper, Black	8 "
Orris Root, pow'd	7 "
Cloves	5 "
Lovage Root	7 "
Capsicum	½ "
Alcohol	20½ pints.
Water	10½ "

Macerate the solids, properly comminuted, with the previously mixed liquid during one week, then express and filter. Percolation is not so suitable, as the aromatics would have to be reduced to a fine powder, which could only be done at the sacrifice of some of their aromatic constituents.

Chartreuse.

1. Yellow. *By weight.*

Oil of Angelica	24 parts
" Cajuput	3 "
" Calamus	1 part.
" Cloves	3 parts.
" Coriander	3 "
" Hyssop	3 "
" Mace	4 "
" Melisse	3 "
Alcohol, deod.	3,000 "
Sugar	1,200 "
Water	1,800 "
Tincture of Saffron......enough to impart a yellow tint.	

2. Green.

Made in the same manner, but the sugar is reduced to 900 parts, and the green tint is produced by the addition of a little solution of indigo.

3. Colorless.

In this case the proportion of sugar is reduced to 10 per cent of the final product.—*Industrieblätter.*

"Soluble" Essence of Lemon.

The following formula is given by the *Chem. and Drugg.* (the measures being converted into those of the U. S.):

Oil of Lemon	10 fl. oz.
Alcohol	125 fl. oz.
Chloride of Calcium	300 grains.
Phosphate of Sodium	1½ av. oz.
Carbonate of Sodium	½ av. oz.
Water	19 fl. oz.

Dissolve the Oil in the Alcohol and add to it the Chloride of Calcium dissolved in 5 fl. oz. of the water. Then dissolve the two Sodium salts in the remainder of the Water, add this to the alcoholic solution, shake well and repeatedly during four days, and filter.

Mistura Antifebrini.

(Antifebrin Mixture. Acetanilide Mixture.)

Antifebrin	60 grains
Brandy	4 fl. drachms
Water	6 " "
Syrup	6 " "

Dissolve the Antifebrin in the Brandy, then add the other ingredients:

Dose: A tablespoonful.

Menthol Snuff.

Menthol	30 grains
Chloride of Ammonium	90 "
Boric Acid, powd.	60 "

Triturate the substances together so that they will form a fine powder. (Dr. Beehag.)

Chloride of sodium might be substituted for the chloride of ammonium.

Blue-Black Ink.

Aleppo Galls, "blue"	4½ av. oz.
Cloves, bruised	½ av. oz.
Water, cold	40 fl. oz.
Sulphate of Iron, purified crystals	1½ oz.
Sulphuric Acid, pure	35 min.
Sulphate of Indigo	½ oz.

Macerate the galls and cloves in the water during a fortnight, then press and strain through linen, add the sulphate of iron previously powdered, dissolve and add the acid and indigo solution. Shake or stir the mixture well, then set it aside for a week, and filter it.

The galls should be free from insect perforations. The sulphate of indigo should be used in the form of a thinnish paste, neutral or nearly so.—After *Chem. and Drugg.*

Anti-Gout Collodion.

Flexible Collodion........................	½ fl. oz.
Ether....................................	½ fl. oz.
Salicylic Acid............................	60 grains.
Hydrochlorate of Morphine.................	15 "

Triturate the Hydrochlorate of Morphine to a fine powder, then mix it with the Collodion and Ether in which the Salicylic Acid had previously been dissolved.

When using the preparation, mix it thoroughly by shaking.

Apply it, by means of a brush, to the gouty joint.—*Morain; L'Un. Pharm.*

Loocock's Lotion for the Hair.

MR. JOSEPH INCE communicates to the *Chem. and Drugg.* the following formula, as having been devised by Mr. Alexander, and afterwards brought into prominent use by Sir Charles Lubbock. The only change that was made is the reduction of the quantity of oil of mace.

Expressed Oil of Nutmeg..................	5 fl. oz.
Olive Oil................................	20 fl. oz.
Stronger Water of Ammonia................	20 fl. oz.
Spirit of Rosemary.......................	40 fl. oz.
Rose Water ....to make	20 pints

(The figures are approximated to U. S. measure.) The above should be mixed with skill, best by gradually pouring the combined oils, under stirring, into the Stronger Water of Ammonia previously diluted with the Spirit, and afterwards slowly incorporating the Rose-water.

Bryan's Pulmonic Wafers is said by *The New Idea* to consist solely of sugar and corn-starch.

Hall's Catarrh Cure.—*The New Idea* says that this is a solution of iodide of potassium in the compound tincture of gentian of the British Pharmacopœia.

Pasta Mack, an English preparation advertised for the toilet and bath, is said by Eckenroth (*Pharm. Zeitung*) to be a mixture of 27% rich starch, 73% effervescing powder, perfumed and compressed into tablets.—*West. Dr.*

Hagan's Magnolia Balm.—*The New Idea* gives the following formula for a preparation which is substantially the same as the proprietary article: Oxide of Zinc, 4 dr.; Glycerin, 1½ fl. oz.; Water, 2 fl. oz.; Carmine, ½ gr.; Oil of Bergamot and Oil of Lemon, of each 1 minim.

Fleury's Tasteless Cascarine.—Advertised as harmless and as a new remedy for biliousness, costiveness, headache, dizziness, and torpid liver, is said by *The New Idea* to be subnitrate of bismuth and calomel triturated with cane sugar.

Mother Siegel's Curative Syrup is said to be composed of compound decoction of aloes, borax, capsicum, gentian, oil of sassafras, oil of wintergreen, dandelion, molasses, and alcohol.

Dalby's Carminative is said to consist of carbonate of magnesium, oil of peppermint, anise, nutmeg, laudanum, tincture of assafœtida, spirit of pennyroyal, compound tincture of musk, and peppermint water.

Seven Sunderland Sisters' Hair Grower.—The following formula gives a product substantially identical with the "secret" article. Bay rum, 7 fl. oz.; Distilled Extract of Witch Hazel, 9 fl. oz.; Common salt, 1 dr.; Hydrochloric Acid (3s) 1 drop; Magnesia, q. s. Mix the bay rum and extract and shake with a little magnesia; filter, and in the filtrate dissolve the salt and then add the acid. The acid removes the yellow color acquired by the mixture with magnesia.—*The New Idea.*

Snuff for Coryza.—Dr. Pierre Viger recommends the following:

Powdered Starch,	
Boric Acid,	
Tincture of Benzoin............	equal parts.

Triturate the ingredients together, then dry with gentle heat, and put into a suitable box.

Soaps.—Some transparent soaps are very good, some very bad. Good transparent soap is prepared from ordinary soap of good quality, which is cut into shavings, dried, and then treated with alcohol. The alcohol is evaporated, and a transparent soap is left. There are two advantages in this treatment. First, when soap is cut into shavings, any free soda tends to get less by contact with air. Second, the treatment with alcohol removes all excess of soda. The absence of free alkali renders the soap better suited for use on the skin. Many of the bad transparent soaps are prepared from impure materials, and the translucency is secured by the addition of sugar, some specimens containing as much as 25%.—*The Hospital.*

Permanganate of Potassium, dissolved in water in the proportion of 3 to 5 grains to the ounce, is the latest remedy for frost bites of moderate degree or for slight burns.

Salicylic Collodion.—Bivert, an apothecary of St. Petersburg, finds the following to be a good formula:

Collodion.................................	100 parts
Salicylic Acid (crystals)...................	10 "
Venice Turpentine........................	1 "
Chlorophyll.............................	q. s.

This collodion is especially useful as a corn-remover.

The Treatment of Furuncles by Intestinal Antisepsis.—Bouchard, in *L'Union Médicale* of January 21st, 1888, reports good results in general furunculosis from

Naphthol (β),
Bismuth, salicylate,
Magnesia................................ āā gr. 5.

repeated four times daily.

Formula for Benzol.—Macalister gives the following formula for administering benzol as a remedy for hooping-cough:

Pure Benzol..............................	♏ lj.
Alcohol,	
Compound Tinct. Chloroform............	āā ♏ ijss.
Simple Syrup.............................	♏ xx.
Mucilage............................ad	ʒ j.

From 4 to 3 drachms may be given, according to age.

NOTE.—Compound Tincture of Chloroform of the British Pharm. is prepared by mixing: Chloroform, 1 fl. oz.; Alcohol, 4 fl. oz.; Comp. Tinct. of Cardamom, 3 fl. oz.

Creosote Mixture for Bronchitis.—Ferrand's formula is:

Creosote................................	gtt. lj.
Essence of Lemon.......................	gtt. lj.
Syrup of Orange Flowers................	gtt. xxx.
Water..................................	gtt. cxx.

A teaspoonful may be taken at intervals of 2 to 3 hours.

Amylene Hydrate, reported to be useful in doses of 60 to 90 grains in cases of alcoholism, morphiomania, epilepsy, and tuberculosis, may be given in either of the following forms. The dose to be taken on retiring:

Amylene Hydrate........................	gr. lx.
Distilled Water..........................	ʒ z.
Syrup of Raspberry.....................	ʒ j.
Oil of Peppermint.......................	q. s.

Peppermint water may be substituted for plain water, if preferred.

Emulsion of Terebene.—According to England (*Amer. Jour. Pharm.*), the following gives a milk-white and perfect emulsion having the odor and flavor of terebene, and miscible with water without separation:

Terebene,	
Cotton seed Oil..........................	āā q. cls.
Powdered Acacia........................	ʒ vl.
Powdered Sugar.........................	ʒ j.
Water..................................	q. s. ad f ℥ iv.

Mix.

Extract of Coffee.—Paul Noirot, of Paris, is the patentee of a new method of preparing extract of coffee which is said to yield a very satisfactory product.

Roasted and ground coffee of the best quality is treated with boiling water in the usual manner, and the infusion caused to freeze by appropriate refrigerating apparatus. The ice crystals are rapidly crushed, and separated, in a centrifugal machine, from the dense accompanying extract which does not itself freeze. This extract, which is thus freed from about 90 per cent of its aqueous constituent, is then completely deprived of water, in a vacuum apparatus, and the residue made into tablets or cakes.

Milk Jelly.—As a variation in milk diet, the following is recommended by Prof. Liebreich:

Heat 1 quart of milk with 1 pound of sugar, and when the sugar is dissolved continue the heat, at a boiling temperature, for about ten minutes. Now cool it well, and then add, *slowly* stirring, a solution of 1 ounce of gelatin in a cupful of water. Next add the juice of 3 or 4 lemons and 3 wine-glasses full of wine, brandy or other liquor. Set the glasses containing the mixture in a cool place, so that the contents may gelatinize. It is necessary to have the milk quite cold before the other ingredients are added, as it would otherwise curdle.

Milk-Powder.—Dried milk, in form of powder, may be prepared by evaporating skimmed milk in a suitable apparatus, preferably in vacuo and under continued stirring, at a temperature of 60° to 70° C. (140°-158° F.) to a syrupy consistence, then mixing it with 30 to 50 per cent of its weight of finely powdered sugar, and continuing the heat, with constant stirring, between 30° and 55° C. (86°-131° F.) until the product has assumed a dry, granular condition.

QUERIES & ANSWERS.

Queries for which answers are desired, must be received by the 5th of the month, and must in every case be accompanied by the name and address of the writer, for the information of the editor, but not for publication.

No. 2,121.—Tablet Triturate Moulds (O. E.).
These moulds, made of hard rubber, are manufactured and sold by A. G. Newman, 1180 Broadway, New York.

No. 2,122.—Invisible Ink (F. W. S.).
A very good preparation of this kind may be made with certain cobalt salts.
For instance:

Chloride of Cobalt	50 grains.
Distilled Water	1 fluid oz.
Glycerin	10 minims.

Dissolve the Chloride of Cobalt in the Distilled Water, and add the Glycerin.
Writing executed with this ink is invisible on paper, but on warming the writing turns blue. On exposure to damp air, it becomes again invisible.

No. 2,123.—Preston Salt (S. & L.).
This is an ammoniacal smelling salt made by mixing together equal parts of chloride of ammonium and of freshly slaked but dry caustic lime. In place of the chloride, the carbonate of ammonium may be used. The mixture is introduced into the bottles and firmly pressed. Then a few drops of some agreeable perfume—according to the fancy of the maker or consumer—are added. If ordinary corks are used to stopper the bottles, they should be previously soaked in hot paraffin. If glass-stoppers are used, they should occasionally be coated with a minute quantity of petroleum ointment.

No. 2,124.—Hall's Solution of Strychnine (D. E. S.).
The formula most generally in use appears to be the following:

Acetate of Strychnine	16 grains
Diluted Acetic Acid	½ fl. oz.
Alcohol	4 fl. oz.
Compound Tinct. of Cardamom	1½ fl. oz.
Water	enough to make 16 fl. oz.

Some formularies or authorities give the quantity of acetic acid much larger. Some of them even direct strong acetic acid to be used, which is evidently a blunder. The object of the Compound Tincture of Cardamom is to impart a specific color and taste. But for this purpose a comparatively small amount of the tincture is amply sufficient.
Dr. M. Hall originally used the following formula:

Acetate of Strychnine	1 grain
Acetic Acid	20 min.
Alcohol	2 fl. drch.
Water	6 fl. drch.

and directed 10 drops to be taken three times daily as a tonic in nervous exhaustion. But, naturally, he often had to alter the proportions. However, through the employment of the preparation as a "house-mixture" in hospitals, a variety of supposed standard formulæ gradually originated.

No. 2,125.—Kremel's Method of Assaying Pepsin and Pancreatin (Chicago).
Several years ago, Mr. A. Kremel, of Vienna, published a method of assaying pepsin which is based upon its action upon powdered *non-coagulated* egg-albumen, the author holding that the employment of coagulated albumen is faulty. Without arguing this question here, it may be said that it really matters but little whether the one or the other kind of albumen is taken, as the *relative* digestive strength of the different kinds of pepsin can be measured by either method. Kremel's method is as follows:

Egg-albumen is dried at about 40° C. (104° F.) and reduced to powder. One gramme of this, together with 0.1 Gm. of pepsin, are put into a flask of the capacity of 100 C.c., together with 50 C.c of a very dilute hydrochloric acid, containing 0.2% of HCl, and heated during three hours at a temperature of 38° to 40° C. The liquid is next exactly neutralized by a previously determined quantity of carbonate of sodium, then heated on a water-bath to about 90° C., and, after the undigested albumen has been coagulated, allowed to cool. Enough water is now added to make the liquid measure 100 C.c., the solution filtered, 50 C.c. of the filtrate evaporated to dryness in a porcelain capsule, the dry residue again dissolved in distilled water, and the solution very carefully filtered through a small wetted filter into a platinum capsule. The filter having been washed, the united liquids are evaporated, and the residue dried at 100° C. and weighed. (If a very exact determination is required, the percentage of nitrogen may be determined in this residue, and the quantity of peptone deduced from this.) The residue is now mixed with carbonate of ammonium and ignited. The amount of ash thus obtained is deducted from the weight of the dry residue. The remainder corresponds to the weight of peptone yielded by 0.5 Gm. of albumen. According to Kremel, uniform results are obtained when the above process is scrupulously adhered to. If modifications are introduced, the results will differ.

The same author directed pancreatin to be examined in the following manner: digest 1 Gm. of dried egg-albumen (prepared as directed in the preceding paragraph) with 0.1 Gm. of pancreatin and 50 C.c of water at 38° C., during three hours. Then add 0.2 to 0.3 Gm. of chloride of sodium, and 1 drop of diluted acetic acid, coagulate the unaltered albumen on a water-bath, at 90° C. and then continue as directed above, under pepsin. Kremel examined six specimens of pancreatin, of which he found that 0.1 Gm. of each formed from 0.110 to 0.380 Gm. of peptone.

There is one feature of Kremel's process which might with advantage be transferred to other methods of assay. This is the neutralization of the acid liquid when the reaction of the pepsin upon the albuminoids wants to be arrested. The adoption of this plan will probably be a useful feature when making comparative assays of different kinds of pepsin.

No. 2,126.—Epsom Salt Springs (A. E. S.).
So far as known to us, the richest Epsom salt springs, the water of which is utilized and sold for medicinal purposes, are situated in Hungary. The well-known Hunyadi János spring contains in 10,000 parts: 184.9 parts of magnesium sulphate and 196.6 parts of sodium sulphate.

The Hunyádi Laszlo spring, situated at a short distance from the before-mentioned (all of which are in the neighborhood of Buda-Pesth), contains still more, viz. : 261.6 parts of magnesium sulphate and 211.0 parts of sodium sulphate.

And recently, a still richer vein has been struck, namely the Hunyádi Lajos spring, which contains: 318 parts of magnesium sulphate and 187 parts of sodium sulphate in 10,000 parts. This is equal to about ⅓ troy ounce of Epsom salt in one pint.

There are a number of "Epsom" springs in other countries, notably at Epsom, England, from which locality the salt has taken its name. The United States also contains a number of such springs, but none of them contains an amount of the salt which is at all comparable to that of the Hungarian waters.

No. 2,127.—"Tasteless" Cascara Sagrada (F. M. J.).
The preparations of Cascara Sagrada (*Rhamnus Purshiana*) generally suffer from the drawback that they are extremely bitter, and that it is very difficult to disguise this bitterness. Even the so-called "elegant" preparations, for instance, Elixir of Rhamnus Purshiana, as usually made, is by no means palatable. Mr. Graser, of San Francisco, has, recently announced (*Pharm. Rundsch.*, January 9th) a method by which this bitterness may be removed. He mixes 1 pound of the powdered bark thoroughly with a milk of 1 oz. of magnesia and 10 fl. oz. of water, then packs the mixture into a percolator and lets it macerate for twelve hours. He then pours on 10 fl. oz. of alcohol, and afterwards, when this has been absorbed, diluted alcohol to cover the drug.

After macerating twenty-four hours, percolation is started, and a fluid extract prepared in the usual manner. The product is said to be of a mild, agreeable, somewhat astringent taste, free from bitterness, and fully representing the medicinal properties of the drug.

Another method consists in extracting the bark with strong alcohol, and precipitating the bitter resin. Regarding this, experiments are being at present made by one of our correspondents.

No. 2,128.—Devices for holding Labels (E.).
This correspondent asks a question which will be of interest to many of our readers and, we believe, that a variety of excellent suggestions could be offered on the subject. We invite the attention of our readers to the matter.

Query: "What, in your opinion, is the best device for holding a large number of labels?"

We presume our correspondent has reference both to wholesale and to retail business. Of course, there is a variety of ways to keep labels. The most general, probably, is to keep them in drawers having partitions. But these often take up much valuable space that might have been utilized for other purposes.

Of other methods we may mention here *two*, which are very useful and are probably less known than they deserve. One is, to have all the shelves of the stock-room made of double boards, with an intervening space which need not exceed 1 or 1½ inches in height, into which tin or wooden drawers are inserted which hold the labels corresponding to the articles on the shelf above. These drawers may be made neatly fitting, with intervening partitions, and nicely finished, if the surrounding fittings are handsome and part of a dispensing establishment. For the ordinary stock-room, however, they may be inserted without intervening partitions, merely placed loosely side by side, though an upright piece or partition may be required in intervals of about 24 inches or less to prevent the upper shelf, by the weight it carries, from being pressed down on the little drawers.

Another plan which we have used with satisfaction is to have a square case constructed, through the centre of which passes a rod which is fastened to the floor and to the ceiling. The case is adjustable at any desired height, and is revolvable about the rod. Every one of the four vertical faces contains as many pigeon-holes, with or without drawers, as the size of the case may permit, or the number of labels may require. One or more of these label cases may be arranged at the side of, or even over the work tables, provided they are adjusted high enough to be out of the way of ordinary packages. A simple touch of the hand will revolve them, and persons at either side of the table or counter may use them. They can be made quite ornamental, if so desired.

One of us has used a case of this kind, constructed after his design, and having 64 pigeon-holes on each of the four faces, for more than 12 years.

Our correspondent also asks us who makes "Peterson's patent label case." We would refer him to our advertisement pages, where he will find that this case is sold by R. W. Tansill & Co., 55 State Street, Chicago.

No. 2,129.—"Fruit-Sugar" (Ex.).

"Fruit-Sugar" is another name for "invert-sugar," and designates a mixture, in equivalent proportions, of dextro-rotary glucose (also known as dextrose or ordinary glucose) and of laevo-rotary glucose (or levulose). Fruit-sugar occurs in many fruits, in honey and in certain saccharine exudations, though it may there be accompanied by an excess of one or the other variety of glucose. But true "invert-sugar," consisting of equal molecules, can readily be prepared by warming cane-sugar with dilute acids, when the following reaction takes place:

$C_{12}H_{22}O_{11}$ + H_2O = $C_6H_{12}O_6$ + $C_6H_{12}O_6$
cane-sugar water   dextrose   levulose

Invert-sugar is an article of commerce, though only in a few countries. It is specially recommended for the preparation of preserves, and artificial wines. It ferments much more easily than ordinary sugar, and is more readily decomposed on being heated (to about 60° C.), for which reason it is preferable to common sugar in cakes. It has also a more agreeable taste than the other sugars, and for this reason it deserves more attention. According to the *Industrie Blätter*, it may be obtained from the "Zuckerfabrik Maingau" at Hattersheim, Germany.

No. 2,130.—Preparation of Normal Starch for Assays and Tests (R. J. S. & Co.).

This subject belongs to the same query which our correspondents have directed to us regarding diastase, but we have preferred to treat of it as a separate query, so as to enable us to index it properly, in view of its practical utility.

When starch solutions are required for the purpose of estimating the amylolytic power of certain ferments, as, for instance, of "pancreatin," diastase, etc., it has been customary to gelatinize starch in the usual manner, that is, by first mixing it with a little cold water, then diluting with more water, and afterwards boiling the mixture until a translucent jelly or liquid is produced, which, if too concentrated, is then further diluted to the desired point. Starch solutions thus prepared are still more or less viscid, even when dilute, and most ferments act upon them rather slowly.

This drawback may be entirely avoided by adopting the plan proposed by Lintner (*Journ. f. prakt. Chem.*, 1886, 380). Instead of using heat and water alone to burst the cell-walls of the starch, he employs hydrochloric acid of a certain strength which accomplishes the same purpose. He directs to proceed in the following manner:

Any desired quantity of best potato-starch is mixed with hydrochloric acid containing 7.5 of the pure acid, in such quantity that the acid stands over the starch. After standing during seven days at the ordinary temperature, or during three days at 40° C. (104° F.), the starch has lost its property of forming a jelly or paste. At the same time, the structure of the starch (aside from small fissures) has remained the same. The starch is now washed by decantation with cold water until every trace of acid has been removed, as shown by delicate litmus-paper. The water is drained off as far as possible, and the starch then dried by exposure to air.

The resulting product is easily soluble in hot water to a clear liquid. Solutions containing 2 per cent remain clear for several days, or have only a faint opalescence, but after that time they become turbid. Concentrated solutions, such as contain 10 per cent and over, congeal, on cooling, to a salve-like mass.

Starch, or starch solution, thus prepared, reduces Fehling's solution only in a most minute degree, too feebly to require its being taken into account. (It will, however, be necessary to examine every lot of starch thus prepared to insure its indifference against Fehling's solution.) Hydrochloric acid of 10 per cent at once gelatinizes starch, and in this respect hydrochloric acid is much more energetic than sulphuric, which must be at least of a strength of 15 per cent, and used at a temperature of 40° C. (104° F.) to bring the starch to the same condition.

No. 2,131.—Antipyrin incompatible with Spirit of Nitrous Ether (Texas).

The following prescription was presented to a friend of one of our correspondents:

R Antipyrini..gr. 15
Spir. Æther. Nit.....................................fl. ʒ 2
Tr. Aconit. Rad......................................gtt. 8
Syr. Lactucarii......................................q. s. ad fl. ʒ 2

M. et signa: *Dose:* One teaspoonful.

This prescription was prepared and produced a green solution, and one teaspoonful was given to a patient, a little boy of 5 years of age, and who was not by any means sick or confined to his bed, but seemed to be ailing with a little fever. After taking the first teaspoonful, the child was thrown into convulsions, and died in about two hours.

In explanation of the reaction taking place between antipyrin and spirit of nitrous ether, we would state that the incompatibility of the former with nitrous acid or nitrites, in presence of acids, has long been known. In fact, the reaction has been used both as a test for nitrous acid as well as for antipyrin.

In dilute solutions containing nitrous acid, antipyrin causes a bluish-green coloration. In concentrated solutions it produces a precipitate of bluish-green crystals, consisting of *iso-nitroso-antipyrin*. The reaction is as follows:

$C_{11}H_{12}N_2O$ + HNO_2 = $C_{11}H_{11}N_3O_2$ + H_2O
antipyrin   nitrous   iso-nitroso-   water
             acid   antipyrin

Now it is well known that nitrites, in general, are active poisons. Even small doses of an alkali nitrite, for instance nitrite of potassium or sodium, say 5 to 8 grains, produce a throbbing and a sensation of bursting in the head, with vertigo, eructations, nausea and vomiting, evanosis, and often convulsions. Free nitrous acid is still more energetic, even in very small quantities. The new substance produced by the reaction between antipyrin and spirit of nitrous ether appears to belong to that class of bodies in which the effect of the presence of an active radical is greatly intensified. Yet neutral nitrites do not produce the above-mentioned reaction with antipyrin. It is necessary that the nitrous acid be in the free state. If this is the case, the bluish-green or pale green color will appear on the addition of a solution of antipyrin. When this color is once developed, it is not destroyed or removed by the addition of an alkali. But if the free nitrous acid is first neutralized with an alkali, the addition of antipyrin will fail to produce any color reaction.

No. 2,132.—Syrup of Iodide of Calcium (North Carolina).

This syrup is usually directed to be made by dissolving iodide of calcium in syrup. Attention has, however, been repeatedly drawn to the unsatisfactory quality or condition of the commercial iodide of calcium. It is a very unstable salt, apt to become colored by the liberation of iodine and the formation of secondary products. Recognizing these facts, Mr. O. Eberbach, some years ago, recommended a new formula for preparing this syrup, in which a definite quantity of iodine was employed as the starting point. This was converted first into ferrous, and afterwards, by the addition of more iodine, into a ferroso-ferric iodide, and the latter subsequently decomposed by adding a milk of lime to the boiling solution until all the iron salt is decomposed. In this reaction, ferroso-ferric oxide is thrown down, and iodide of calcium remains in solution. By simple filtration and washing of the residue on the filter, the whole of the iodide of calcium is extracted as a colorless solution, from which the syrup is then made. The resulting product is very satisfactory.

There is, however, one serious drawback connected with this process, namely, there is no visible criterion to tell when the exact quantity of milk of lime required to decompose the iron salt has been added, and the usual consequence will be that lime will be added in excess and render the resulting solution strongly alkaline. This may be avoided by a slight modification. Instead of using milk of lime to decompose the iron salt, carbonate of calcium may be used. This produces a copious effervescence, the cessation of which promptly indicates the end of the reaction. Besides, even if there is a large excess of the carbonate used, it cannot enter into solution, but remains mixed with the precipitated oxide of iron.

When small quantities of the syrup are to be prepared, we recommend the following process:

Iodine..552 grains.
Iron Wire, fine and cut..................200 "
Precipitated Carbonate of Calcium..200 "
Distilled Water............................q. s.
Sugar..11 troy oz.
Syrup.........................enough to make 16 fl. oz.

Mix the Iron Wire with 414 grains of the Iodine and 3 fluidounces of Distilled Water, and apply a gentle heat, until the Iodine is combined and the liquid has acquired a greenish color. Filter the liquid through a small filter, and wash the flask and filter with 1 fl. oz. of Distilled Water. To the filtrate, contained in a flask, add the remainder of the Iodine, and heat the solution gently, taking care that no iodine is lost by evaporation. Heat 4 fl. oz. of Distilled Water in a capacious capsule to boiling, and add to it alternate small portions, first of the Precipitated Carbonate of Calcium, and then of the solution of Iodide of Iron, stirring briskly, and waiting each time until the violence of the reaction moderates. From time to time add a little Distilled Water, to replace that lost by evaporation. When all the Calcium salt and Iron solution has been added, continue the heat until the solution is quietly boiling. Then filter it through a wetted filter, and wash the latter with enough Distilled Water to make the product, when cold, measure 8 fl. oz. In this dissolve the Sugar by agitation, then make up the volume with Syrup to 16 fl. oz., and strain, if necessary.

We find it preferable to add small alternate portions of the carbonate of calcium and the iron solution, rather than to add the whole of one constituent first, and afterwards the other. Further, it is far better to add the iron solution to the water containing the carbonate of calcium than *vice versa*, as the oxide of iron produced separates in a much more compact form and is more easily separated by filtration.

When making the process on a large scale, however, we recommend the use *both* of hydrate of calcium (as milk of lime) and of carbonate of calcium. Working on the small way makes it somewhat difficult to adjust the quantity of hydrate of calcium (lime) so as to still leave the end of the reaction to be accomplished by means of the carbonate of calcium. But when operating on the large scale, the time required for the duration and subsidence of the effervescence is so considerable, and the vessels must be chosen so large, that a modification becomes necessary. We suggest to use milk of lime during the first part of the reaction, and to use the carbonate of calcium only towards the end. The quantities of ingredients, calculated for a pint of syrup, then are as follows:

Iodine.................... 552 grains.
Iron Wire................. 200 "
Lime...................... 100 "
Precipitated Carbonate of Calcium........ 70 "
Distilled Water........... q. s.
Sugar..................... 11 troy oz.
Syrup..................... enough to make 16 fl. oz.

Slake the Lime with a sufficient quantity of Water, and add it, as apparently dry powder, in the same manner as is directed in the formula for the carbonate. Lastly, add the Carbonate in the same manner, and continue as directed.

No. 3,133.—**Preparation of Active Diastase** (R. J. S. & Co.).

Lintner, who has published the most detailed report on the properties, preparation, and assay methods of diastase, recommends for its preparation the process below given in Journ. f. prakt. Chem., 34).

It may be obtained from any kind of malt. But it is preferable to employ undried barley-malt, though air-dried malt may also be used. But roasted malt is less advantageous.

Previous to Lintner's investigations, it was customary to extract the diastase from malt by water or glycerin, and to precipitate the diastase from these liquids, either directly by precipitation with alcohol, or after heating the liquid to 70° C. (158° F.). Or, it was precipitated from its glycerin solution by alcohol, or by a mixture of alcohol and ether. Another method was that proposed by Bruecke, who caused the production, in the solution, of a voluminous precipitate of phosphate of calcium which carried the diastase along with it. But this method, as well as several others, in which heat is employed, have been found entirely unsatisfactory. After an extended series of experiments, Lintner found that the most active diastase is obtained by treating crushed undried barley malt with 2 parts of water. Considering the full effect of *pure* diastase upon pure starch to be represented by the number 100, then the product furnished by the method just mentioned had an activity represented by 96. Air-dried malt, treated under the same circumstances, yielded a product corresponding to 55.5 per cent of the absolute effect.

The following is the process recommended by Lintner for obtaining diastase of satisfactory power.

Macerate 1 part of undried barley malt or air-dried malt (deprived of the sprouts by sifting) with 2 to 4 parts of alcohol of 20 per cent during twenty-four hours or longer. The object of the alcohol is to permit a protracted digestion without running the risk of inducing fermentation or acetification. The liquid is then separated as far as possible, and precipitated by not less than 2 nor more than 2½ times its own volume of absolute alcohol. It is not advisable to use more, since the excess would precipitate pectous substances and but little more diastase. A little of the latter always remains dissolved by the alcohol, but the amount is too small to pay the labor of recovery. On stirring, the precipitate caused by the absolute alcohol separates in yellowish-white flakes which rapidly settle to the bottom. The supernatant liquid is poured off, the precipitate transferred to a filter, the alcohol drawn or aspirated off from it as rapidly as possible, and the residue on the filter then transferred to a mortar, where it is triturated with absolute alcohol. The mass is then again transferred to a filter, washed with absolute alcohol, the precipitate then triturated with ether, and after this has been drawn or washed off, the residue dried in vacuo over sulphuric acid.

The systematic dehydration thus directed to be effected by means of absolute alcohol and ether is necessary in order to obtain the diastase as a flocculent, yellowish-white powder of great activity. If the powder was not thoroughly dehydrated, it becomes dark colored when dried in vacuo, and acquires a horny consistence, suffering at the same time in strength.

No matter how long the diastase may be dried over sulphuric acid, it always retains a small quantity of alcohol, which can only be removed by drying at 105° C. (221° F.). But as this temperature would be injurious to the ferment, this drying is inadmissible except in a portion which is to be employed for other purposes than to test the fermentative power of the sample. Even the best known method of assay is not entirely free from defects, hence no further source of error should be introduced.

Diastase precipitated as above directed promises to be of considerable use in laboratories for the assay of certain articles of food. It remains active for a long time.

Lintner regards 1 Gm. of crude diastase to equal about 50 Gm. of good undried barley malt.

The precipitated diastase is wetted by water only with difficulty. It is therefore necessary to triturate it before using it with a little water in a mortar, whereby a turbid liquid is produced.

Crude diastase persistently carries down with it a considerable quantity of mineral constituents. When freshly precipitated it contains 16 per cent of ash, and after being reprecipitated six times, it still retains 10%. This may be reduced by dialysis to 5 per cent. The mineral impurity accompanying it is phosphate of calcium.

Lintner found that, by repeated purification, the nitrogen constituent of the diastase gradually rose to a little over 10 per cent. There appears to be no doubt whatever that diastase contains nitrogen, though this had been denied by Payen and Persoz.

During the first precipitation of the crude diastase, the latter carries along with it some non-nitrogenized matters which partly reduce Fehling's solution. The principal portion of these matters resembles dextrin in its nature. But by repeated precipitations these substances are removed.

CORRESPONDENCE.

To Soften Hard Skin on the Hands.

SIR:—Many people now suffer from a formation of hard skin on their hands called eczema, and it happens with people who can least afford the annoyance, because they are overworked both in body and mind, and more often than not, confined in close offices during the day.

I think many will find relief if, after they have washed their hands, they would put on some agnine or other wool fat, and rub it well in with pumice stone. It will be found that all the hard skin will come off, leaving a smooth, comfortable surface. Wipe the hands, but do not rub off the whole of the wool fat, and in a few minutes the hands will become soft and phiable, and remain so for hours. Yours truly, THOS. CHRISTY.
LONDON, ENGLAND, February 28th, 1888.

Benzoate of Sodium as a Remedy for Follicular Tonsillitis.—Boislinière highly recommends the following formula as a remedy for follicular tonsillitis:

Benzoate of Sodium................ 3 i.–3 iv.
Glycerin,
Elix. Calisaya bark.............. āā 3 i.

M. A teaspoonful every hour or two. No gargle or local applications are required and instead of the disease lasting two to five days, as is the case where it is uninfluenced by medication, it is cured (in an average based on 75 cases) in 20 hours; the extremes being 12 and 36 hours. It seems to him apparent that the febrile element of the disease is controlled, and that its use, even with children, is unattended with risk.

Fluid Extract of Quebracho colorado is recommended by Dr. Bordeaux, of Brussels, as an application for wounds. Being applied with a soft brush, like collodion, it causes transient pain, and in about an hour dries so as to form an artificial scab which can only be loosened with the aid of hot water. It requires the aid of no other dressing and greatly favors healing by first intention.

HOW DR. SCHNAPSKUEBEL'S WORLD-RENOWNED STOMACH BITTER WAS DISCOVERED.

Carbolate of Camphor which is recommended as a wound-dressing, is made by dissolving camphor in 95% solution of carbolic acid to saturation. The acid will dissolve about 3 times its weight of the camphor and the product is thin, clear, oleaginous, and has an odor of camphor rather than of carbolic. To the sense of taste it is slightly pungent and characteristic of camphor without the flavor of carbolic. Ten-drop doses may be taken internally with the aid of a capsule. Its external use causes for a few minutes a sense of warmth, and on abraded surfaces smarting for a few moments follows its use. Injected hypodermically it causes stinging, quickly followed by anæsthesia. When mixed with an equal amount of cotton-seed oil and applied to a fresh wound with gauze or cotton, it prevents suppuration.

A Menthol Snuff for the treatment of laryngeal diseases, recommended by Dr. A. G. Buhay in the *Edinburgh Med. and Surg. Jour.*, consists of menthol, 3 ss.; Ammon. chlor., ʒiss.; Pulv. Acidi borici, ʒi.

When finely pulverized, this will be found a useful insufflation in chronic laryngeal catarrh, laryngeal phthisis, nasal catarrh and ozæna, and syphilitic rhinitis.

The same authority recommends a 25% per cent solution of menthol in olive oil as an application on acute pharyngitis and tonsillitis. When applied to the nasal mucous membrane it should be from 5 to 20% per cent only.

Another formula, for local application, consists of, Iodine, gr. vi.; Iodide of potassium, gr. xx.; Menthol, 3 iss.; Glycerin, 3 vi.; Water, 3 iij.

American Druggist

Vol. XVII. No. 5. NEW YORK, MAY, 1888. Whole No. 167.

[ORIGINAL COMMUNICATION.]

CONCENTRATION BY LOW TEMPERATURES.

BY J. U. LLOYD.

I HAVE noticed with interest the paper in the AMERICAN DRUGGIST April, p. 76, regarding the method of concentrating a liquid preparation of coffee by the application of a low temperature, the paper being as follows:

"EXTRACT OF COFFEE.—Paul Noirot, of Paris, is the patentee of a new method of preparing extract of coffee which is said to yield a very satisfactory product.

"Roasted and ground coffee of the best quality is treated with boiling water in the usual manner, and the infusion caused to freeze by appropriate refrigerating apparatus. The ice crystals are rapidly crushed, and separated, in a centrifugal machine, from the dense accompanying extract which does not itself freeze. This extract, which is thus freed from about 90 per cent of its aqueous constituent, is then completely deprived of water, in a vacuum apparatus, and the residue made into tablets or cakes."

I believe that it will be found that advantage has been taken by other persons of similar methods to free organic solutions from aqueous liquids, in most cases, perhaps, where nothing has been published in that direction. Where prolonged heat is destructive, the method is often, I believe, in the future destined to be of exceptional value.

It is well known that the "mother liquor" contains most of the impurities of solutions from which crystalline bodies have been separated, and, in the case of most organic extractive matters, the natural combination is often neither crystalline nor easily frozen. Indeed, it is not always necessary to reduce the solution to the congealing point in order to cause precipitations either of valuable or of inert constituents in abundance, and the operator, by studying each particular substance in its relationships concerning other associated substances, can dissociate the natural constituents of many organic liquids, and either cast aside the precipitate or retain it as the investigations demonstrate is desirable.

I have no doubt that the reason so many persons have insisted on using evaporation, or heat application exclusively, is because of a general view which is to the effect that this is about the only feasible method of concentration. It is the easy one, the authoritative one as recorded in books, and to question the possibility of an *opposite* course in face of printed authorities seems irrational.

The fact is, however, when we purify *crystals* we actually reduce the bulk of the original liquid, which might properly be the desired product, and often is, and the crystallization of water from organic liquids, leaving the extractive matters, is, it seems to me, simply an application of the well-known laws that govern the purification of salts.

Of course, the previous application of heat is usually necessary, but, if the crystals (as water) are objectionable, a reduction of temperature will often accomplish that for which evaporation is now employed. I presume that all operators will recognize instances in which the evaporation of an extractive liquid can be accomplished to a certain extent without the development of a "burnt" odor or without apparent dissociation, but that further reduction is destructive even at lower temperatures than before. In these instances, the application of a low temperature applied at this stage of the concentration, after the plan suggested in concentrating the preparation of coffee, may more often be found effectual than is generally supposed.

I have found that in some cases if such a liquid be reduced to a very low temperature (short of freezing) and then cautiously mixed with the proper amount of alcohol, it will separate into two layers, one of which will often contain the larger amount of the inert matter, and by this method most of the water can be excluded. By studiously applying this rule, and by using various neutral solvents such as ether, or mixtures of ether, alcohol, chloroform, etc., in an appropriate manner, some very desirable and unusual dissociations of natural plant constituents may be accomplished with but little applied chemistry or evaporation. Such a study has been part of my individual duty for many years, and from the result of my labors I assume that, at some time in the future, less heroic chemistry and less heat evaporation will be employed in purifying many plant constituents, or separating them into natural sections, than is freely accepted now as a necessity. Some years ago, I was perplexed over a substance that I desired to obtain and that was associated with a glucose in a plant product. This I vainly tried to remove, but it seemed impossible to precipitate it, and any single solvent that I employed would dissolve both of them or neither.

At last I wrote to the late Prof. Henry B. Parsons, then in the Agricultural Office at Washington, for assistance. He was at this time working in this very direction (sugar cane, I think), and replied that he could give me no aid, and that with unfermentable and uncrystallizable sugars the elucidation of a simple scheme to apply to such problems was a desideratum of the day. Afterward, I effected that separation by means of a very cold solution of the glucose-like liquid in cold alcohol, to which I slowly added sulphuric ether until two layers formed. The upper layer contained the substance desired, with some glucose, and by evaporation and re-application of the process, I obtained it pure.* Since, I have evolved many detail methods with laboratory products of unofficinal and irregular character, where this manner of procedure is desirable, and, in my opinion, the present method of plant analysis, or preparation of plant products, will be considerably modified by the application of such schemes at a very near day in the future, and it may be that the present destructive methods, whereby organic compounds are evolved (or rather produced) from plants by stiff chemical reagents, will be supplemented at least by others which we seem now to have generally overlooked. In a work applied to the constituents of gelsemium, about a year ago, I had reason to prepare for Prof. Flückiger, of Strasburg, some pure gelsemic acid. This I obtained easily in a state of absolute purity and in a considerable amount, without the use of any chemical whatever, simply by the application of the foregoing principles. As thus obtained, it was in the form of great needle-like crystals, pure white, and it excited the admiration of Prof. Flückiger and also Prof. Prescott, to whom a part of it was afterward sent as a specimen.†

I do not write this paper to advance as new the suggestions therein made, for, I presume, that such applications of well-known factors are probably far from being new, and only in detail laboratory manipulation under special conditions do I suppose that I have even in my own field accomplished anything of value, but it is true that such work has been a necessity with me for years. Indeed, I was led to the consideration of the part of the subject connected with concentration by low temperature, by information derived, when a boy, from reading a narrative of the life of Colonel James Smith, in which he gives the method the Indians of North America employed to make maple syrup, and which I afterward applied to my studies. Since the appearance of your paper on the preparation of a coffee concentration, I have looked this narrative up and reproduce it as follows:

"Shortly after we came to this place [the northern part of Ohio as I would make it.—L.], the squaws began to make sugar. We had no large kettles with us this year, and they made the frost, in some measure, supply the place of fire in making sugar. Their large bark vessels, for holding the stock water, they made broad and shallow; and as the weather is very cold here, it frequently freezes at night in sugar time; and the ice they broke and cast out of the vessels. I asked them if they were not throwing away the sugar. They said no; it was water they were casting away; sugar did not freeze, and there was scarcely any in that ice. They said I might try the experiment, and boil some of it, and see what I would get. I never did try it; but I observed that, after several times freezing, the water that remained in the vessel changed its color, and became brown and very sweet."‡

It will be seen that the aborigines of North America were acquainted with methods of concentration by means of both evaporation and low temperatures, and it is evident to me that in working galenical preparations, one of our oversights has been to confine ourselves to that which is most commonly known and easily applied. This paper of Colonel Smith, 1799, appears to me to contain the essential features of that of Mr. Noirot.

---

* Such a liquid often holds a constituent quite tenaciously, that a mixture of the two liquids will scarcely separate from its natural combination. In studying the application of this method to plant dissociations, care must be taken to avoid the addition of too much ether, otherwise the entire material will be precipitated. By the use of different neutral solvents, chloroform, benzol, etc., some unusual separations may be accomplished.

† My work in this way demonstrated to my satisfaction that the alkaloid gelsemine is not combined in gelsemium with the so-called prussic acid, although it is in complex combination. Gelsemic acid (æ-colin) exists free in the drug.

‡ This is an exceedingly interesting narrative, taken from Drake's "Indian Captivities," the title being as follows: "An Account of the Remarkable Occurrences in the Life and Travels of Colonel James Smith (late a citizen of Bourbon County, Kentucky), during his Captivity with the Indians, in the Years 1755, '56, '57, '58, '59, in which the Customs, Manners, Traditions, Theological Sentiments, Mode of Warfare, Military Tactics, Discipline and Encampments, Treatment of Prisoners, etc., are better explained, and more satisfactorily related, than has been heretofore done by any author on the subject. Together with a Description of the Soil, Timbers, and Waters, where he travelled with the Indians during his captivity. To which is added, a brief account of some very uncommon occurrences which transpired after his return from captivity; as well as of the different campaigns carried on against the Indians to the westward of Fort Pitt, since the year 1755 to the present date 1799. Written by himself."

[ORIGINAL ABSTRACT.*]

The Use and Administration of the Pancreas and its Preparations.

ONE of the most efficient methods of utilizing the special ferments of the pancreas is to employ this organ in a crude condition or to prepare from it an aqueous extract which should be used as soon as possible.

According to Engesser, the best method of preparing the pancreas is the following. The organ—preferably derived from the hog—which should be as fresh as possible, is deprived of membranes, thoroughly cleansed with a cloth, and carefully freed from fat. It is then scraped with a rather blunt knife or chopped to a paste in a chopping machine, and then rubbed through a hair sieve. The resulting magma may be added to food as such. It may be preserved for a short time by mixing it with common salt or one-third its quantity of extract of beef, in a wide-mouthed bottle which must be well corked and kept in a cold and dry place; during summer preferably in an ice box. If this preserved pancreas is used, it is advisable to treat it, on the evening before it is wanted, with about 1 pint of water and 8 to 10 drops of diluted hydrochloric acid in order to liberate the larger portion of the ferment.

An aqueous solution of the ferments of the pancreas may be prepared by treating the organ, previously chopped and freed from fat, as in the preceding case, with water (1 pint for every pancreas) warmed to 30° C. (86° F.), then adding a little common salt, and setting the mixture aside for 5 or 6 hours. It is next transferred to a strainer or a fine hair sieve and the liquid portion drained off without pressure. This liquid is comparatively less active than the pancreas paste, and must be used while fresh, but in some cases it is preferable.

The best method of administering the pancreatic ferments, according to Engesser, is to add the pancreas paste (above described) to the food itself.

Since pancreatic ferments become inert when exposed to a temperature exceeding 45° C. (113° F.), the particular kind of food to which the pancreas is to be added must have a temperature below that just named. In practice, it may be said that the proper temperature is reached when a portion of the food taken into the mouth ceases to produce a sensation of heat or burning. In order to cover the taste of raw meat caused by the addition of the pancreas paste, the food to which it is added should be well spiced. Or some lemon-juice, a few drops of wine-vinegar, etc., may be added to correct the taste. [These additions are not regarded as interfering with the activity of the pancreatic ferments, at least not with all of the ferments.] In order to hide the presence of the pancreas paste to the eye, it is advisable to select a form of food (soup, etc.) which has an opaque appearance.

It is well known that soup, when introduced into an empty stomach, passes rapidly through this, and descends to the inferior portions of the intestinal canal more rapidly than other kinds of food.

Hence, in order to subject the latter likewise to the action of the pancreas, it is necessary to have several courses of soup alternate with the other dishes, or to direct the soup to be taken in portions during the whole meal. Another method which is recommended is to serve with every course some kind of sauce mixed with pancreas paste.

Since it is not always possible to procure fresh pancreas for the preparation of the paste, Engesser proposes to prepare a *powdered pancreas* of good keeping qualities. For this purpose, the properly cleansed organ is very finely comminuted, and reduced in a vacuum apparatus at a temperature of 40° C. (104° F.) to an extract. This is treated during about forty-eight hours with absolute alcohol, after which the latter is allowed to drain off, and the remainder adhering to the mass driven off by a heat not exceeding 40° C. The dried residue appears in form of a light-brown, coarse powder, which is easily taken or administered either in wafer-capsules or with water. As it is very hygroscopic, it must be kept from dampness with great care.

This preparation does not represent an isolated ferment of the pancreas, but the parenchyma of this organ hardened by means of alcohol. It is important to state this, since it is well known that trypsin—the peptone-forming ferment of the pancreas—is destroyed by the acid gastric juice, for which reason those commercial pancreatic products, which contain or profess to contain the trypsin (for instance, those of Savory & Moore, of London; Defresne, of Paris; Witte, of Rostock) become inactive in the stomach, as has been shown by Ewald.

Eye Water.—A western exchange recommends a formula for an eye-wash consisting of 2 drops of liquor plumbi diacetatis in one ounce of elder-flower water, upon which we have the criticism to make that a salt of lead should *never* be used as an ingredient in a collyrium; the reason being that an acetate is especially liable to conversion into carbonate, and in case there is any erosion of the cornea, the lead is deposited in the form of white film which *tattooes* the eye, so to speak, and leaves a permanent blemish. [ED, A. D.]

---

* From "Die neueren Arzneimittel." Von Dr. W. F. Loebisch. 8vo, Wien und Leipzig, 1889 (2d ed.).

Notes on Cocaine.

FROM a rather lengthy paper on Cocaine and its Salts by Dr. B. H. Paul, published in the *Pharm. Journ.* of March 17th, we take the following, which relates to the best practical method of testing the hydrochloride (or hydrochlorate) of cocaine: a remarkable alteration of cocaine takes place when the base is precipitated from a water solution of the hydrochloride by ammonia or some other alkali. My attention was first directed to the change in applying to samples of the hydrochloride the test suggested by Maclagan. This test consists in adding two drops of ammonia to a solution of one grain of the salt in two fluidounces of water. With a good sample a dense precipitate is produced, either at once or on stirring the liquid with a glass rod, and this precipitate soon acquired a very distinct crystalline condition. When the tested solution was left standing for some hours, it was observed that the precipitate had become less bulky, and at first it seemed probable that this change might be due to more complete crystallization; but, after the lapse of twenty-four hours, or more in some instances, the precipitate entirely disappeared, and, on examination of the solution, it was found that the cocaine had been entirely converted into benzoylecgonine, which readily crystallized on evaporating the solution over sulphuric acid. This is an alteration that always takes place to some extent when the base is precipitated, and, therefore, it may give rise to appreciable loss in the preparation of cocaine if such a precipitate is left for any length of time in contact with the liquid from which it has been thrown down....

As regards the method of testing this salt, I do not think that the chloroform test is of much service. In my opinion, a much better place of ascertaining the relative quality of different samples of cocaine hydrochloride is to determine the amount of alkaloid obtainable by precipitation of a water solution with ammonia. The chemically pure anhydrous salt, $C_{17}H_{21}NO_4HCl$, contains 88.25 of cocaine, and when the solution precipitated is not too dilute, a precipitate closely approximating to that amount should be obtained if the salt tested does not contain impurities that are more soluble in water than cocaine is.

It is sometimes stated in books that the precipitate produced by ammonia in solutions of cocaine salts is redissolved on adding excess of ammonia. This is a mistake, the solubility of cocaine in water is but little, if at all, increased by the presence of a large excess of free ammonia. The disappearance of the precipitate after the lapse of some time is not due to its being redissolved, but is the result of the decomposition already mentioned. Ammonia is, in fact, the best precipitant of cocaine, and to illustrate this fact I may state that, when a solution containing only $\frac{1}{15}$th of cocaine hydrochloride is mixed with ammonia and shaken, the alkaloid is immediately separated in the form of distinct needles. This degree of solution is nearly the same as in Maclagan's test, and it appears to be near the limit of solubility of cocaine, for with a solution containing $\frac{1}{300}$ of hydrochloride the separation of crystals is doubtful. At any rate, with such a dilute solution there is danger of the imagination being used in a manner that is not scientific. In applying this test, it is important to collect the precipitate as soon as possible after it has entirely deposited in order to avoid loss from the decomposition already mentioned. By leaving the precipitate for eighteen hours in contact with the ammoniacal liquid, there may be a loss of about 3 per cent of the cocaine....

For the purpose of ascertaining the presence of an amorphous base in cocaine salts, there is, I think, no method of testing at present known better than precipitation with ammonia. This should be carried out in the way directed by Maclagan, and also with a stronger solution, so as to observe the character of the precipitate and ascertain the amount obtainable.

Messrs. F. F. Boehringer & Sons, of Mannheim, the well-known manufacturers of quinine and other alkaloids, have recently published a circular in which they assert that the most reliable test for the purity of cocaine and its salts, in their opinion, is the following modified permanganate reaction:

Dissolve 0.1 Gm. of hydrochlorate (etc.) of cocaine in 1 Gm. of water, add 3 drops of diluted sulphuric acid (sp. gr. about 1.112) and afterwards one drop of a 1-per-cent solution of permanganate of potassium. The violet tint of the liquid must remain unchanged during at least one hour. The vessel in which the test is performed should be carefully covered to prevent the access of dust.

While this test is quite exacting and moderately reliable, it should, in our judgment, be always combined with Maclagan's test (see pp. 22 and 62, 1887).

Sutherlandia frutescens has lately reached England from Cape of Good Hope with a reputation as a cancer remedy. It appears in commerce as the foliage and stems of a leguminous shrub, bearing bladder-like, thin-shelled pods, something like those of bladder senna. It is sometimes cultivated in English gardens for the sake of its large, scarlet flowers, where it is known as Cape bladder senna. The powdered leaves and roots have been used at the Cape as an ophthalmic remedy.—*Proc. Med. Journ.*

Note on Strophanthus and Strophanthin.

From a paper by Catillon, recently published in the *Archives de Pharm.*, we take the following:

The seeds of *Strophanthus Kombé* contain in 100 parts:

Fatty Matter, soluble in ether and alcohol	32
Dry Extract, soluble in alcohol of 70%	16
Gummy and albuminous substance	11
Insoluble Residue	34
Water and Loss	8
	100

The fatty matter is of an intense green color, and imparts this tint to the tincture if the seeds themselves are treated with strong alcohol. This is a drawback, as the fat has a repulsive odor and is apt to produce nausea. Hence it must be eliminated both from the extract and the tincture, which is best done by first exhausting the seed with ether. When the fat is removed, they are extracted with alcohol of 70%, which yields a yellow tincture free from gummy or albuminous substances. On evaporating such a tincture, an alcoholic extract of great activity is obtained, which yields, with water, a milky solution, and which is difficult to handle when dry, as it excites sneezing like veratrine. When dissolved in a mixture of water and glycerin, however, this extract yields a clear solution which may be used hypodermically.

Mr. Catillon thinks it is a mistake to employ the tincture of strophanthus. This has several disadvantages. It is, in the first place, bitter; besides, it is liable to vary in its effects, because the market sometimes affords seeds which have been partly or wholly exhausted. For this, and other reasons, Mr. Catillon believes a dry extract, prepared by evaporating the tincture, to be preferable. This may be given in doses of 0.001 Gm. or $\frac{1}{60}$ grain, best in form of granules, twice daily. Dr. Bucquoy has even given as much as four such granules a day, without accidents.

The dose of strophanthin is one or two granules containing $\frac{1}{5}$ of a milligramme, or about $\frac{1}{12}$ grain each.

From one kilogramme of strophanthus seeds (from *Strophanthus Kombé*), Mr. Catillon has extracted 9.5 Gm. of strophanthin, crystallized in microscopic needles, which are transparent when damp, but become opaque on drying. They have a neutral reaction towards litmus paper, and their solution is not affected by the usual characteristic alkaloidal precipitants. With tannic acid, strophanthin yields a bulky, white precipitate, soluble in an excess of strophanthin. In such a solution of strophanthin, sulphuric acid produces a greenish precipitate becoming black after a while. In the cold, this reaction does not occur until after the lapse of several hours; it is brought about more speedily by raising the temperature. If a crystal of strophanthin is treated, directly, with a drop of sulphuric acid, a fine emerald green color is produced, passing into reddish-brown, and afterwards into black. This reaction has been announced by Gerrard as characteristic of the amorphous principle. In moist air, the black color changes again to greenish.

If strophanthin is treated with hydrochloric acid, the solution, which is colorless while cold, turns green by being slightly heated. This reaction, which is analogous to that produced with digitalin, is, therefore, no longer to be regarded as characteristic of the last-named substance. On the other hand, digitalin is not colored by cold sulphuric acid, while, with sulphuric acid and ferric chloride, and by the application of a gentle heat, it gives a blue color, in contradistinction to strophanthin which yields a green one.

Nitric acid colors strophanthin pale rose-red, which becomes orange-yellow by a gentle heat.

A solution of strophanthin, on being shaken, produces foam. If it is brought together directly with Fehling's solution, it does not affect the latter. But if it is first digested with dilute sulphuric and hydrochloric acids (1:10), it reduces the test solution, 10 C.c. of the latter being reduced and rendered just colorless by 0.15 Gm. of strophanthin. The latter, therefore, is a glucoside. It contains no nitrogen, and is not related to the group of the alkaloids.

Strophanthin is soluble in 13 parts of cold absolute alcohol, and in 3 to 4 parts of boiling alcohol. On pouring a hot alcoholic solution of strophanthin into cold water, the substance at once separates in form of crystals. The hydrated crystals dissolve easily in water; but after they are dried, it requires about 30 parts of water to dissolve them. The substance is insoluble in ether and in chloroform free from alcohol.

On evaporating its alcoholic solution, strophanthin forms, upon the walls of the capsule, a vitreous, transparent layer, separating in micaceous, brilliant scales. From this amorphous condition, the substance passes into the crystalline on moistening it with a little water.

Half a milligramme ($\frac{1}{131}$ grain) injected into a rabbit weighing 27 ounces caused death in less than an hour.

A **Two-per-cent Solution** of carbolic acid, sprayed lightly about the bed-covering, is said to be a certain preventive of trouble from gnats and mosquitoes.

NOTE ON EVODIA AND XANTHOXYLUM HAMILTONIANUM.

Some time ago the announcement was made that the volatile oil of *Evodia fraxinifolia*, an East Indian plant, had an extraordinary power to cover the odor of iodoform. We also had information, obtained through a prominent wholesale house, that steps had been taken to secure either the oil, if obtainable, or the fruits of the drug itself. Mr. H. Helbig, of London, now writes to the *Chemist and Druggist* that there was some error committed in the identification of the fruits which had been at first brought to London. It turns out now that the odoriferous fruit is derived from *Xanthoxylum Hamiltonianum*. The fruits of the true Evodia consist of four carpels united into a star-like shape, each of which contains two longitudinal and three rounded angular seeds pointed at the two ends. The seeds are of a dark-brown, faintly lustrous appearance. The epicarp is parchment-like, more or less speckled, and dirty earthy-brown in color. The fruits of *Xanthoxylum Hamiltonianum* consist of 3 to 4 carpels similarly arranged, and the pericarp is brown and dotted with minute warty points. The seeds are heart-shaped, and have a resplendent black color. The fruits of this plant are only about half as large as those of *E. fraxinifolia*, though they are much more elegant in form and appearance, but the seeds of the last-named are the smaller.

a. Fruit of *Evodia fraxinifolia* (viewed from the apex), two of the carpels of which have dehisced. *b.* Seeds of the same. *c.* Fruit of *Xanthoxylum Hamiltonianum*, with 4 carpels, all of which have dehisced (viewed from the apex). *d.* A dehisced fruit of the same (viewed from the base). *e.* A seed of the same. Cuts are same size as original fruits and seeds.

The fruit of *Evodia fraxinifolia* is quite valueless, and does not seem to contain an essential oil.

Some New Remedies.

Cedrine is a bitter principle extracted from the seeds of *Simaba Cedron* Planch., which have been highly valued in New Granada, Colombia, etc., as a remedy against the bites of venomous snakes; also in yellow fever, intermittent fever, and various intestinal troubles. Cedrine is in form of yellowish transparent crystals, easily soluble in water, less so in alcohol. The substance is extremely energetic and toxical.

Ephedrine Hydrochlorate is a crystalline alkaloid from *Ephedra vulgaris* var. *Helvetica*, forming colorless needles, soluble in 4 parts of water, and easily soluble in alcohol. It has mydriatic properties.

Iodine Trichloride has been found to be a very efficient antiseptic and disinfectant, chiefly on account of its liberating the chlorine readily. It is an orange-red powder, the odor of which strongly irritates the mucous membranes. It is best used in solution of 1 in 1,200.

Condurangin, a glucoside from condurango bark (*Gonolobus Condurango*—the Mattaperro Condurango bark). This has been used in gastric diseases with alleged success. It is an amorphous powder, soluble in water, alcohol, or chloroform.

Vieirine, an alkaloid derived from *Remijia Vellozii* D. C. (one of the cuprea barks), which stand in very close relationship to the cinchonas. Has been used as a febrifuge.—From E. *Merck's Circular* (Feb. 21, 1888).

Substitute for Gum-Arabic.

The high price of gum-arabic has stimulated inventive genius to discover substitutes suitable for the various purposes, technical as well as pharmaceutical, in which that substance has found employment. The latest is a preparation patented by Schumann. It is merely dextrin free from sugar, and is prepared in the following manner:

Two hundred (200) parts of starch are boiled with 1,000 parts of water, and 1 part of sulphuric and nitric acid in a closed boiler, at a pressure of 2 to 3 atmospheres, until the pasty mass begins to become thin fluid. At this moment the boiling is at once stopped, and the acid neutralised. The boiling is then recommenced at a pressure of 3 to 5 atmospheres, until all the starch is converted into what is technically known as "gommeline." This consists of dextrin, glucose, cellulose, the salts derived from neutralising the acid and other substances. The cellulose and salts are separated, the remainder filtered through bone-black, and the filtrate concentrated, first in a vacuum apparatus, and then in open vessels, to a density of 40° Beaumé. It is put on the market either in this condition as a viscid liquid or is further concentrated until it is obtained as a solid, forming glassy lumps when broken up. The product is perfectly transparent, not hygroscopic, and is as adhesive as gum-arabic.

Creolin.

UNDER the name *creolin*, a substance has recently appeared on the European market which has been lauded as an energetic and non-poisonous disinfectant. It appears in form of a thickish, dark-brown liquid of a tarry odor, is miscible with water in all proportions, forming a sort of emulsion, and also soluble in alcohol and fixed oils. With ferric chloride, it gives no reaction for carbolic acid. It has been introduced by a Hamburg firm, but no clew was given regarding its nature, except the statement that it is prepared in England by distilling a certain kind of coal, and that it is obtained from the distillate by treating the latter, in a certain way, with caustic alkalies.

Several analysts subsequently reported that it was essentially a resin soap containing carbolic acid.

More recently, B. Fischer and E. Biel have examined it and have come to the conclusion that it is prepared from certain fractions of the distillate obtained from gas coal, which have been carefully freed from the lower boiling phenols (carbolic acid). In fact, Biel thinks that creolin is a by-product of the manufacture of carbolic acid. Probably the higher homologues of this substance are selected and rendered soluble in water by being combined with soda. It contains from 20 to 40 per cent of aromatic hydrocarbons boiling between 210° and 300° C., and valueless as disinfectants, besides leucoline and other pyridine bases, naphthalin and anthracene.—*Chem. Zeit.*

Chloral Hydrocyanate.

CRYSTALLIZED chloral hydrocyanate is announced by Merck as an excellent substitute for bitter almond and cherry-laurel water. The substance in question is the nitrile of trichlorolactic acid ($C_2H_2Cl_3NO$ or $CCl_3.CH\text{-}(OH).CN$). It is prepared by digesting 1 part of chloral hydrate, during twenty-four hours, with 1 part of hydrocyanic acid of 10–12 per cent, then digesting several hours under an upright condenser, and finally evaporating on the water-bath.

The substance crystallizes from carbon disulphide or from water in thin, rhombic plates. It is soluble in water, alcohol, and ether. Alkaloids decompose it into chloroform, hydrocyanic and formic acids. The crystals have an odor recalling that of hydrocyanic acid and chloral. Chloral hydrocyanate is a very stable compound, even the aqueous solution keeping for a long time unchanged.

Its therapeutic effect is the same as that of hydrocyanic acid. 6.452 parts, by weight, of chloral hydrocyanate correspond to 1 part of anhydrous hydrocyanic acid. A solution of 0.065 Gm. of the salt in 10 Gm. of distilled water corresponds to the bitter-almond water of the German Pharmacopœia, which is 1 in 1,000. And a solution of 12.9 parts in enough distilled water to make 100 parts will produce a solution containing 2 per cent of hydrocyanic acid, such as is officinal in the U. S. Pharmacopœia.

Phthalate of Cocaine and of other Alkaloids.

SOME time ago, Mr. Bombelon announced that he had found a compound of phthalic acid and morphine to possess advantages superior to those of any other salt of this alkaloid, as it was not only very soluble, but also much more stable.

Upon the experience thus gained, E. Merck, of Darmstadt, has commenced to prepare the corresponding salts of some other alkaloids, for the present of cocaine and caffeine. A phthalate of strychnine was also attempted to be made, but without success. As Merck himself states, "combinations of organic bases with mineral acids (as in the case of morphine hydrochlorate and sulphate, for instance) are liable to suffer from a tendency toward decomposition in various ways. They are prone to show slightly acid reactions after being kept in solution for some time, though originally produced as neutral salts; they are, furthermore, apt to undergo decomposition through fungi, etc. From these drawbacks the phthalates are reported to be free. But the property of the phthalates most valuable to the medical practitioner, as compared with the salts of other, and especially of mineral acids, is their far higher degree of *solubility in cold water*. Morphine hydrochloride, for instance, is soluble in 25 parts of water; morphine sulphate, in 14.5 parts [it requires over 20 parts—ED. AM. DR.]; and morphine phthalate about 5 parts. Moreover, any surplus of this salt, in proportion to the menstruum, *does not* crystallize from the solution, but is deposited at the bottom of the vessels in the form of an oily liquid, thus separating at once and wholly from the concentrated solution; while, in the case of crystallizing salts, small crystals are liable to remain suspended in the liquid."

Morphine phthalate appears in beautiful, transparent, glassy *scales*, thus affording a ready means of distinguishing it at a glance from the more innocent salts (of quinine, etc.)—fatal confusions with which have sometimes occurred in the case of the muriates, sulphates, and others.

Cocaine phthalate ($C_{17}H_{21}NO_4.C_8H_6O_4$) is a colorless, viscid fluid, very readily soluble in water and in alcohol. The solutions show an acid reaction.

Caffeine phthalate ($C_8H_{10}N_4O_2.C_8H_6O_4.H_2O$) is a white, amorphous solid, of a soft, friable consistence; easily soluble in 5 parts of water, and in hot alcohol. The solutions have an acid reaction.

Acid Corrosive Sublimate Dressings.

ACCORDING to Laplace, the addition of tartaric acid to sublimate and albumen solutions insures the full activity of the antiseptic; indeed, it appears that the combination of an acid with the sublimate increases its antiseptic power, so that weaker solutions may be used. The solution employed is the following:

Corrosive Sublimate	1 part
Tartaric Acid	5 parts
Distilled Water	1,000 "

Gauze, cotton, etc., are soaked for two hours in a solution containing 0.5 per cent of the sublimate and 2 per cent of acid. Laplace obtained very satisfactory results with this dressing in the treatment of suppurating wounds.

[On theoretical grounds we should have supposed that the addition of tartaric acid rather introduced a fresh source of putrefaction or fermentation. However, theory may here be at fault, and the facts be as stated.—ED. AM. DR.]

Chapman's Copaiba Mixture.

OUR attention has recently been drawn, by Mr. E. V. Zoeller, of Tarboro, N. C., to the fact that the formula which is usually known as *Chapman's Copaiba Mixture* differs materially from that originally published by Dr. Chapman. Prof. Remington, at Mr. Zoeller's request, ascertained that the original formula of the preparation was published in Prof. Nathaniel Chapman's "Elements of Therapeutics and Materia Medica" (5th ed., Philadelphia, 1827). It is as follows:

Copaiba	fl. oz. ½
Spirit of Nitrous Ether	fl. oz. ½
Compound Spirit of Lavender	
Tincture of Opium ("Tr. Theb."),	
Acacia, in powder	āā drch. 1
Water	fl. oz. 2

Dose: A tablespoonful.

There is neither sugar nor syrup in this.

Now the formulæ quoted in works of reference differ very materially from the above. Those which are probably most generally consulted are Griffith's "Formulary" (ed. by Prof. Maisch, Philadelphia, 1874), and Remington's "Practice of Pharmacy." We shall place these side by side, distinguishing the former by "G," and the latter by "R":

	G.	R.
Copaiba	fl. oz. 4	4
Spirit of Nitrous Ether	fl. oz. 4	4
Comp. Tinct. of Lavender	fl. oz. 1	2
Tinct. of Opium	fl. dr. 4	1
Acacia, powd.	grains 60	120
Sugar	grains 60	60
Distilled Water	fl. oz. 4	4

The dose of either is given as a tablespoonful.

It is probable that the formula given in Griffith's Formulary has found the most extensive employment, as this work has been almost the only one consulted in such cases for a number of years after its publication.

The original formula, when increased so as to make *one pint*, may be written as follows:

Copaiba	3½ fl. oz.
Spirit of Nitrous Ether	3½ fl. oz.
Comp. Tinct. of Lavender	} ½ fl. oz.
Tinct. of Opium	}
Mucilage	1 fl. oz.
Water	enough to make 16 fl. oz.

The Domestic Use of Saccharin.

A CORRESPONDENT writing in the *Scientific American* of February 18th, 1888, relates his experience in using saccharin as follows:

Sugar being a prohibited article to me, I naturally became interested in Fahlberg's "saccharin," and obtaining a supply as soon as possible, began experimenting with it. Using it alone to sweeten lemon juice or stewed cranberries, I found it very difficult to mix, and tried various dodges to remedy it, all of which had some drawback or other until I thought of dissolving it in glycerin.

I found that for general purposes the formula of glycerin one pound, saccharin one drachm, heated to solution, was the best. Two teaspoonfuls of above to the juice of one lemon made up to eight fluidounces make a lemonade sweet enough for almost any one, and three teaspoonfuls to four ounces of stewed cranberries make a dish "fit for a king."

I gave a sample of the above to a gentleman to whom sugar was tabooed, and who was then using saccharin alone, and asked him to try it with cranberries and report. When next seen he said very enthusiastically, "That's splendid. I've bought a barrel of cranberries, and would not go back to sugar if I could."

The advantages of the mixture over pure saccharin are: That the glycerin gives it a body, and the mixture very closely resembles in taste and appearance the best white honey; that it dissolves readily in water, milk, tea, and coffee, wines and liquors; and that it can be very readily measured.

AGITATING MACHINE.

A MACHINE for continuous agitation, very useful for the preparation of alcoholic extracts from pomades, for extinguishing mercury by succussion, for ageing perfumes, and various other purposes, is that shown in the cut, which is manufactured by Beyer frères, of Paris (rue Lorraine, 16, 18). The mechanism producing the shaking motion is not clearly shown in the cut, but it is brought about by an eccentric position of the eye of the guiding rod.*

Distilled and Aromatic Waters.

MR. ADOLF VOMACKA makes some practical remarks of distilled and various aromatic waters in his journal *Rundschau* (Prag).

Distilled Water. Not every kind of water is suitable for the preparation of a *pure* distilled water.

The most effective method to obtain absolutely pure water is deemed by the author that which is officially prescribed by the Pharmacopœia of the Netherlands. According to this authority, the water, previous to distillation, is to be treated with permanganate of potassium until the violet color of the liquid remains permanent. Next, a solution of alum is to be added so as to render the water faintly acid, the water then allowed to stand so as to become clear by settling, the clear liquid transferred to the still, and the middle portion of what passes over to be preserved as pure distilled water.

Aromatic Waters. In the author's judgment, the most advantageous method of preparing aromatic waters, if the essential oils are to be used as starting points, is the following:

Cause the essential oil to be soaked up by filtering paper, introduce the latter (torn into shreds) into distilled water warmed to between 35° and 45° C. (95°–113° F.), shake thoroughly and frequently while the liquid cools to the ordinary temperature, and then filter.

As an aromatic water thus prepared is saturated with the essential oil at the temperature at which it was filtered, the product should not be exposed to a lower temperature, as this would cause a separation of a portion of the oil.

Torments of Trade.

ONE of our friends has placed into our hands a batch of order slips, collected during the past year or so, and written upon all kinds of paper, which call for the following articles:

1. Alcohol and bergamont.
2. 15 cents' Worth Verkmann, and 5 cents' Worth of catel oil.
3. United States Pharmacian Cathoric Pills for Billious ness.
4. 10 c. balsam pivey, 10c. Oil cubab, 10c. Spirits nitre, little alum.
5. Rochll salts.
6. Nisi fuda Oil.
7. 5 c. Flek send; 1 c. stemp.
8. cross of Supimate For Bed Buggs.
9. 5 cents worth of Frase Whitenig quirls (meaning French chalk drops).
10. 1 ounce of Laudlom, 8 grongs of calmon, 8 grongs of White Vilr, 8 Vinl water.
11. Send 1 bottle of Citron of Magnesia.
12. 5 ct of Jalv Water.
13. 25 cts Pencil Costic; 10 cts. Camel Powder; 10 cts Waden.
14. Castor Oil and Bagamant mix for hiar.
15. Darling Slave (meant for Dalley's salve).
16. 10 ct. of Jockey Club, 5 cts roschell salts.
17. jauhel water.
18. Powderd Allem.
19. Bornux Powder.
20. Capsine pors plaster.
21. five cents worth of Cattera Pills.
22. five cents worth of Opperating Pills.
23. 5 cent worth of Drop Chock.
24. Horse Foots Acid; Citrid micagnu.
25. Will you please give me a subscription for some medine for a destreem in the bowels I am trouble with contopaction very much and I am trouble with indacation and I have a destreem of bearing down always and I can't taste anything for it hearts so. Please give me something to removed my bowels right away as I am in great destreem.
26. 5 c antibilious pills and some sweet spirit to send a man into perspiration please say how much to take.
27. Hancode Water.
28. Nuts vomit.
29. centure Liment.
30. Ewance Vinella.
31. 5 cents Worth of oppecack and Scullis. 5 c. Capupified oil.
32. 5 cents worth of Red Percipretate ointment to rub on my little girls head.
33. tinctor of lade.
34. 5 cts. sulpher of zinz.
35. 5 c Syrup of Apack.
36. cott Li Oil.
37. Paregoric Elixor 1 ounce, Tincture Telun, Syr. Squills Sulfur Ether ½ oz. of each.
38. 10 cts Balsam Copaive, 5 cts Red lavender, 5 cts Tincture of steele, 5 cts of sweet nitre.
39. Balladona Blaster.
40. 1 oz. Nitre, 1 oz. Either, 1 oz. Laudnan, 5 cts cape aleoa.
41. 5 cents worth Ines (anine).
42. 5 c. Bnatiles, negro head (black fumigating pastiles).
43. Physilican Salve.
44. Baldrian Tee 5 cts.
45. Draggins Bloat, incens, Black candle.
46. 5 cents worth spermesatte.
47. 1 Bottle of Adanson Cough Balsam. And please give a Remendy Something for to break up a person who is chocked up. Something whoes tubes are chocked up.
48. 5 cents sneeg leaves.
49. Please give boy a little of Just the thing.

Shaking machine.

Pocket weighing scale

POCKET WEIGHING SCALE.

A RECENTLY patented weighing scale for the pocket is well adapted for use by physicians whose practice obliges them to dispense their medicines, or as a part of the outfit of medicine chests. To the bottom of the case is secured a post, with which is connected the scale standard by means of a pin, the lower end of the standard being slotted. The upper end of the standard is also slotted to receive the scale beam, mounted on a pivot pin, one end of the scale beam carrying a block to which the pan is secured. The pan is held in horizontal position when in use by a spring on the under side of the beam bearing against the block; but when the scale is to be folded within its case, a quarter turn given to the pan withdraws a catch, and allows the pan to be folded down. A spatula is held against the rear side of the case by a post or pin.—*Sci. Amer.*

Reaction of Cotton-Seed Oil.

ACCORDING to M. Labiche, when cotton-seed oil is treated with subacetate of lead and caustic alkali, it gives almost immediately an orange-red reaction. This is peculiar to this oil, for almond, castor, olive, poppy, rape, and cod-liver oils give a milky mixture, which is also the case with butter when thus treated. The author mixes equal parts of the oil and a saturated solution of neutral acetate of lead, and adds ammonia, stirring briskly. The acetate decomposes, and the nascent oxide reacts upon the oil. Then the red color appears. After standing, the surface turns orange-red, and the lower portion becomes grumous. If 20 per cent of cotton seed oil be present, the coloration appears at once; lesser quantities show on the surface after the mixture has remained standing for a time.—*L'Un. Pharm.* and *The Analyst.*

Tongate of Soda.

The *National Druggist* publishes a query from S. M. Meadows, of Milwaukee, Wis., as to the nature of tongate of soda. Tungstate of sodium is probably meant—sometimes used for rendering fabrics fireproof.

---

* From Miersinski; "Die Riechstoffe." Aug. Wetmar, 1888.

Opium Assay.

Messrs. E. F. Teschemacher and J. Denham Smith have contributed a lengthy paper to the *Chemical News*, in which they review most of the various recent methods of opium assay, including those of the newer pharmacopœias, that of Dr. Squibb, Prof. Flückiger, and assert that none of these processes extract as much morphine from opium as that which they have themselves devised. The paper is too lengthy to be reproduced here in full, and it is impossible to argue in the face of figures prevented. Only a critical examination of the author's process can establish the justice of their claim. They say themselves that they invite and shall welcome experimental criticisms on their method, but "must be pardoned for neglecting to notice *obiter dicta* guesses, or opinions unsupported by experimental proof."

The authors describe their own process, concisely, in the following manner:

1. Thoroughly exhaust 200 grains of opium (if the sample permits this amount) with warm distilled water.
2. Concentrate this watery extract to a thin syrup, in a shallow dish, over a water-bath, which the authors prefer should not boil.
3. Transfer this thin syrup to a suitable flask which permits the use of a soft cork, using a few drops of water successively to wash out the dish. Add to the contents of the flask 50 fluidgrains (about 53 minims U. S. measure at about 72° F.] of alcohol, spec. grav. about 0.820, and about 600 fluidgrains [633 minims U. S.] of ether. Mix gently, but thoroughly, and then add some 50 fluidgrains (53 minims U. S.] of ammonia, spec. grav. 0.935.
4. Shake the contents of the flask well to precipitate the alkaloids in arenaceous crystals, with occasional agitation during the ensuing eighteen hours.
5. Transfer the contents of the flask to a vacuum filter, and permit all the adherent liquid to be drawn away, washing out the flask with "morphiated water" (see below), and continue its use till the liquid passes colorless. Now wash with morphiated water, till this also passes colorless.
6. Now dry, slowly at first, finishing at 212° F. Transfer the dried substance to a mortar, reduce it to a very fine powder, and digest it thoroughly in benzene [benzol], to dissolve the narcotin and such of the opium alkaloids, other than morphia, which may be present.
7. Transfer this mixture to a vacuum filter, wash out the mortar carefully with benzene, which use to wash the powder thoroughly. This, then, will be morphine, free from other opium alkaloids and narcotin, but still containing coloring and possibly other organic matters, to the extent of 3 to 10 per cent. Dry and weigh this powder.
8. Now ascertain the percentage of crystallised morphine by titration of this powder with standard hydrochloric acid and litmus as the indicator, by weight. This acid is so made that 1,000 grains by weight shall exactly neutralise 100 grains of pure morphine crystallised from water, washed with ether, and gently dried finally at 212° F.

Preparation of Morphiated Spirit.—Digest a large excess of morphine in alcohol of 80 per cent, for several days, with frequent agitation. Filter for use.

Morphiated Water.—Proceed as for the preceding, substituting water for alcohol.

As an illustration of how far the processes of assay used by other analysers differ from that of the authors, the latter mention the fact that there is a universal complaint among those who have opiums tested that "Teschemacher and Smith are always too high." Further the authors say: "In illustration of the above, some friends of ours recently shipped ten cases of opium to New York, averaging 10.20 per cent morphia [of course, as determined by the authors' method]. Of these ten cases, six were rejected as containing less than 9 per cent morphia. We bear further that these rejected ones yield 7.40 to 7.98 per cent; this second place of decimals, instead of 8 per cent, points to an accuracy which will, we fear, be for a long while the distinctive characteristic of the New York Customs' analysts. If they be correct, the happy consignee will secure four chests at 13.5 per cent morphine, instead of 10.20 per cent—a gain of 3.30 per cent, solely due to the lawful action of the Customs of the United States."

The authors do not seem to like the expression "assay of morphia," which Prof. Allen uses. They say: "Do not let us Englishmen corrupt our own language. Surely, 'assay' to a chemist involves the idea of furnacing of some sort. Regarding this criticism, we would say that each branch of literature or science is constantly trying to simplify and render more concise and pregnant the terms it has to use to denote certain matters or facts. 'Assay of opium' will certainly never be associated, in the mind of any chemist, with furnacing; and it surely is more expressive than 'Valuation of opium,' and briefer than 'Determination of morphine in opium' or similar terms.

Diabetic Foods.—According to Dr. Harrington, of the Harvard Medical School, the diabetic foods commonly sold contain but a trifle less starch than ordinary bread, and he points out the danger which attends their use by persons suffering from diabetes who accept as true the assertion that these foods are non-starchy.

On the Determination of the Amount of Morphine in Opium.

Rowland Williams, F.C.S., etc., publishes the following paper in the *Chem. News* as a contribution to the question recently raised by Messrs. Teschemacher and Smith, regarding the best process of assaying opium. An abstract of the paper of the two last-named authors is given elsewhere in this number. The importance of the subject makes it advisable to give the present paper, in abstract, in the same number:

Having had considerable experience in the examination of opium for the percentage of morphia, I have read with much interest the paper by E. F. Teschemacher and J. Denham Smith, which recently appeared in the *Chemical News* [see this Journal, opposite column].

About two years ago, two Persians came to work in my laboratory, with the object of ascertaining the most reliable method for estimating morphia in opium. When in their own country, these gentlemen are engaged in the opium trade, and wished to be able to guarantee the amount of morphia in each consignment before shipment, so as to avoid disputes and allowances, as far as possible. My Persian pupils stayed with me about six months, during which period we examined a large number of samples of opium, and investigated some of the most promising processes I could find in various works which I consulted on the subject. A short account of a few of our results may, perhaps, be of interest to some of your readers.

At first we worked almost entirely by the *British Pharmacopœia* process, and our experience was very similar to that of Teschemacher and Smith, viz.: fairly concordant amounts of morphia could be obtained from duplicate estimations, but the morphia was by no means pure. We always employed a carefully graduated cylinder, marked at 1,040 fluidgrains, for measuring the aliquot portion of 1,400 fluidgrains, as a "wide-mouthed 6-ounce bottle" is obviously quite unfit for such a purpose. In other respects, we followed the directions as closely as possible. We were in the same predicament as Teschemacher and Smith with regard to taking 1,040 grains of the filtrate, as there seems no clear reason why this quantity should be regarded as equivalent to 100 grains of the opium; nevertheless, 1,040 grains were always used in our estimations. We made two or three dozen determinations of morphia by the B. P. process, but finally abandoned it altogether, as we had already gained sufficient experience to warrant our coming to the conclusion that any method in which lime is employed is, for many reasons, unsuitable for the estimation of morphia in opium.

We next turned our attention to Flückiger's method. Several samples were examined by this method, and it must be admitted that it generally yields very clean, white crystals, being in this respect a decided improvement on the B. P. process. This is, no doubt, partly due to the preliminary digestion of the dried opium with ether, which is said to remove narcotin, wax, and coloring matter, and partly owing to the non-employment of lime, which, I believe, generally produces a dark-colored morphia. Afterwards we tried the United States official method, which is, in many respects, very similar to the B. P. process, and in our hands yielded almost the same results.

In the following table are given results obtained from four samples examined by the different methods:

	Morphia per cent.		
	British.	German.	American.
Sample No. 1	10.8	10.3	11.1
" " 2	10.5	...	10.8
" " 3	7.4	7.1	8.1
" " 4	12.3	10.6	11.9

A glance at these figures will show that in every case the German method gave the lowest result, and the American the highest, except in Sample No. 4.

Our work in connection with these three processes had by this time convinced me that it was undesirable to take aliquot portions of filtrates, as this method of operating is undoubtedly liable to cause serious errors. I therefore began a series of experiments, in which weighed quantities of the opium were thoroughly exhausted with water, and the extracts concentrated to a syrup, at a gentle heat on the water-bath, before precipitating the morphia. My general plan of procedure was to place 100 grains of the opium in a porcelain basin, add 1,000 grains distilled water, and macerate frequently with a rubber-tipped glass rod. The digestion was allowed to go on all night, and the next day the strong aqueous solution of the opium, containing nearly all the morphia, was passed through a Swedish filter, taking care to leave the bulk of the insoluble matter in the basin. This residue was stirred up with several successive small quantities of water (each acting for ten minutes), and the total extract evaporated on the water-bath until it became of a syrupy consistence. This was washed into a suitable bottle, using the smallest possible quantity of water for the purpose; 100 grains of alcohol (sp. gr. 0.825) and 300 grains of ether (sp. gr. 0.730) were then added, and the bottle gently rotated for a few minutes. Finally, 30 grains ammonia (sp. gr. 0.880) were added, the bottle frequently shaken, and allowed to stand twenty-four hours. The morphia was then thrown on to a weighed filter, and washed as completely as possible, first with morphiated spirit, and then with morphiated water, as suggested by the late Mr. E. F. Teschemacher. The filter was then dried at 212° F., and the increase of weight represented the amount of crude morphia in 100 grains of the opium. . . .

During the last few months, I have slightly altered my method of estimating the amount of morphia in samples of opium which have occasionally been sent to my laboratory for examination. I now prefer to work on at least 200 grains of the opium (if that quantity be available), digest all night with ten times the amount of cold distilled water, and, eventually, completely exhaust with cold water in the manner above described. It will be noticed that I say with cold water, because I think this preferably to using warm distilled water as recommended by Messrs. Teschemacher and Smith. There can be no reasonable doubt about cold water extracting all the morphia from opium, and I fail to see the advantage of employing warm water, as there is then a risk of dissolving certain other ingredients of opium which are more soluble in warm water than in cold. Even if these impurities are removed by the subsequent washings with the various purifying agents, it seems a pity to introduce them at all if their presence can be avoided.

To return to the description of my present method. The total aqueous extract is evaporated on the water-bath to a small volume, transferred to the precipitating vessel, 100 fluidgrains alcohol (sp. gr. 0.825) and 600 fluidgrains ether (sp. gr. 0.725) are added, and the remainder of the process conducted as usual.

With regard to the late Mr. E. F. Teschemacher's process, published in the *Chemical News* (Vol. xxxv., p. 47), I must confess that it has always seemed to me to be so complicated that I thought loss must inevitably ensue at some stage or other; consequently, I have very rarely employed it, but have latterly placed implicit reliance on the method which I have just described, and which, I believe, gives very accurate results. I propose, however, in the case of future samples of opium, to try the effect of purifying the precipitate of morphia by digestion with benzin, previous to the final weighing and titrating with acid, as Messrs. Teschemacher and Smith attach so much importance to that point.

Messrs. Teschemacher and Smith mention a case in which duplicate samples of opium were submitted to several chemists after being examined by themselves. All these chemists agreed closely with one another, but they found lower percentages of morphia than Messrs. Teschemacher and Smith. As I have good reason for believing that I was one of the analysts in question, perhaps I may be allowed to say that my results were obtained by the process upon which, as already mentioned, I have latterly stated my faith.

CHEMICAL LABORATORY, 9 Albert Square,
MANCHESTER, March 24th, 1888.

APPARATUS FOR UPWARD FILTRATION.

F. C. J. BIRD, having occasion to filter a large quantity of syrup containing both a ferrous salt and a finely divided precipitate, constructed an apparatus which had the advantages of excluding air and keeping the filtering medium in the most advantageous position, viz., at the surface of the liquid. The apparatus, as described by him in the *Pharmaceutical Journal*, consists of A, a stoneware jar of about 2 gal. capacity, placed on a shelf, 5 or 6 feet above the vessel M. It is secured to a board, C, which has a perforation, q. B is of wood, 3 in. wide, and with holes, X and I. C, A and B are fastened together by string, or otherwise. J is the filter, consisting of a circular box, closed at the top and open at the bottom, and about ½ in. less in diameter than A. J is divided by a partition into two chambers, the upper one being air-tight. The tube I passes through this chamber and communicates with the lower half of J, and is connected with a glass tube, H, by means of rubber tubing. Three layers of filtering medium—calico, paper, and flannel (the latter being outside)—are fixed over the mouth of J. E is a bar of wood, to which the glass tubes, H and I, are attached, the system of tubes being counterbalanced by the weight F, which should be so arranged that J may fall to the bottom of A when it contains no fluid. K is a piece of rubber tubing. L is a glass tube reaching nearly to the bottom of M, and having a valve formed of a single turn in the tube.

A being filled with the liquid to be filtered, a cork is inserted in the lower end of T and the rubber tube V detached from I, the system of tubes is then filled with some bright liquid, the connection by means of V is again made, and a layer of ⅓ inch of colorless petroleum oil is poured on the surface of the liquids in the two vessels (O and O) when the liquid to be filtered requires to be protected from air. By removing the cork from the lower end of T, filtration commences. All joints must be bound with waxed thread or wire, and thick rubber tubing be used to prevent its collapse. J should be well varnished with shellac.

FILTERING PERFUMES.*

WHEN larger quantities of perfumed liquids are to be filtered, which would be injured by being exposed in open filters to the air, an apparatus like that here shown will be found very serviceable.

A is a cylindrical vessel with a neck passing through the stopper in a receptacle C, which is connected, by means of the tube d, with a filter pump. Into A a few disks of felt are carefully packed near the lower end, and a reservoir containing the liquid to be filtered is adjusted so as to keep the cylinder A suitably supplied. On starting the filter pump, the liquid will be aspirated through the felt and thereby filtered. The first portions of the filtrate, if not quite clear, should be returned.

FILTERING FLASK.

F. ALLIHN has devised a new filtering flask for use with the filter-pump. Its neck is ground to receive a glass funnel, which serves as a stopper, and the connection with the pump is established by means of a lateral tube.

These flasks, with corresponding funnels, are now manufactured in several sizes, and may be had through dealers in chemical apparatus.—*Zeitsch. f. Anal. Chem.*

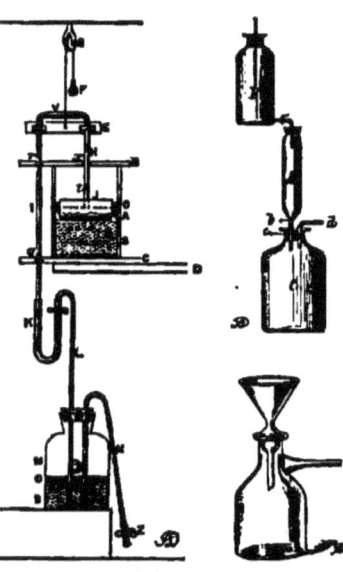

New filtering appliances.

Antifebrin in Headache.

DR. W. FAUST praises the prompt effects of antifebrin as a remedy in almost any form or kind of headache, provided it is taken in sufficient amount. He states that he finds it difficult, or rather useless, to discriminate between the various causes of headache, so far as this remedy is concerned, as it gave relief in nearly every case. Its most prompt action is observed in those cases where the pain is due to an irregular distribution of blood within the vessels of the head, and particularly that which is due to engorgement. He declares it the most effective agent to relieve alcoholic headache. It should be given in full doses from 8 to 16 grains.

The editor of the *Industrie-Blätter*, in commenting upon the preceding report, recommends caution in the use of the remedy, and believes that it should not be used promiscuously or without the advice of a physician. He quotes the case of a woman residing in Berlin, who was attracted by an advertisement recommending antifebrin against "Katzenjammer," and took 4 Gm. (60 grains) of it in two doses, at short intervals. After three hours, she lapsed into a deep coma, from which she was, however, brought back by strong stimulants.

Remedy for Lumbago.—Dr. C. G. Hollister, of Meadville, Pa., recommends the following as a specific for lumbago:

Iodide of Potassium,	
Bromide of Potassium	of each, ⅜ ss.
Tincture of Colchicum Seeds	f. ʒ iss.
Syrup of Orange peel	f. ℥ ij.
Water	enough to make f. ℥ vi.

M. One teaspoonful to be taken 3 to 4 times daily, or increased up to causing loose movements of the bowel.—*Med. and Surg. Rep.*

---

* After Mierzinski: "Die Riechstoffe," 8vo. Weimar, 1888.

The Composition of Carbonate of Ammonium.

At a recent meeting of the School of Pharmacy Students' Association (London), Mr. A. E. Chaston read a paper on "Commercial Carbonate of Ammonium."

The author first proceeded to describe the various compounds which ammonia forms with carbonic anhydride and water, viz., the normal carbonate $(NH_4)_2CO_3,H_2O$, the half acid carbonate,

$$(NH_4)_2CO_3,2NH_4HCO_3,2H_2O$$

the acid carbonate NH_4HCO_3, the super acid carbonate of Rose $(NH_4HCO_3)_2CO_3$, and the carbamate

$$NH_2NH_4CO_2.$$

Passing to the consideration of the commercial salt, he mentioned the formulæ that had been assigned to it by various chemists, and pointed out that whereas in the British Pharmacopœia of 1867 it was required to contain 28.8 per cent of NH_3, corresponding to the formula $(NH_4HCO_3)_2 NH_2 NH_4CO_2$, it is now required to contain 32.48 per cent, which corresponds with the formula assigned to it by Divers, viz., $NH_4HCO_3,NH_2NH_4CO_2$. In order to ascertain whether the salt as usually supplied to pharmacists meets the requirements of the Pharmacopœia, he had obtained specimens from various sources, and estimated them with the following results, which show that they all fall short of the standard fixed upon by that authority:

Salt.	Percentage of NH_3.	Impurities.	Odor when neutralized.
Ordinary.	28.83	Trace of chlorides.	None.
"	30.69	Trace of chlorides and sulphates.	Empyreumatic.
"	29.95	Slight trace of chlorides.	Slightly aromatic.
"	30.5	Slight trace of chlorides.	Slightly aromatic.
"	30.3	None.	Slightly aromatic.
Resublimed.	30.1	Trace of chlorides.	Slight.
"	31.15	None.	None.
"	30.1	Slight trace of chlorides.	"
"	29.6	Slight trace of chlorides.	"
"	30.15	Slight trace of chlorides.	"

The portions operated on were carefully selected from the interior of the lumps, quickly weighed, and put into an excess of volumetric solution of oxalic acid; after boiling to expel CO_2, the excess of acid was titrated by volumetric solution of soda. The specimens were also examined qualitatively for impurities, and for odor after neutralization, with very satisfactory results.—*Pharm. Journ.*

Note on a Test for "Hydronaphthol."

Mr. Alfred L. Beebe, Assistant Chemist of the New York City Health Department, has communicated the following note to *The Analyst* (London, March, 1888).

"Hydronaphthol," so called, has lately come into considerable prominence as an effective antiseptic for use in the preservation of various food products. A reliable method for its detection is therefore desirable. So far as the writer is aware, no distinctive test has as yet been given for the detection of this substance when present in minute quantities, and the results of some experiments in this direction may therefore prove of interest.

"Hydronaphthol," as is well known, is really a trade name for β naphthol. It is sparingly soluble in cold, much more readily in hot water, and is easily extracted from its water solution by shaking with ether. The ethereal extract, evaporated to dryness and taken up with hot water, or the water solution direct in absence of interfering substances, made slightly alkaline with ammonia, cooled, and slightly acidified with dilute nitric acid, gives, on addition of a drop of fuming nitric acid, or a nitrite, a beautiful rose color, analogous to that developed in the test for nitrites in water.

In making the test, care should be taken that the ammonia and nitric acid are respectively added in slight excess only, and that the nitric acid used is so dilute as to cause no heating of the solution by its combination with the excess of ammonia present. If these precautions are not observed, a dirty salmon color is apt to be developed by the addition of the fuming nitric acid, and the distinctive character of the test thereby destroyed.

The reaction is one of extreme delicacy, one part in ten thousand of hydronaphthol being readily detected.

Experiments are now being made by the writer to determine the limit of the delicacy of the test, and also to arrive at a practical method for separating "hydronaphthol" from food-products to which it may have been added, in a condition suitable for the application of the test outlined above. The results of these experiments, if successful, will be published in due course.

Fluid Extract of Bursa Pastoris, in doses of ½ drachm, is said by Dr. Ehrenwall to be equally serviceable as ergot in controlling uterine hemorrhage.

The Production of Peroxide of Hydrogen during the Oxidation of Terpenes.

Regarding the production of peroxide of hydrogen, which has long been known to occur during the oxidation of terpenes and essential oils, Prof. C. T. Kingzett publishes the following data, which give an account of the rate of oxidation, and the quantity of peroxide of hydrogen produced.

Some years ago, I subjected samples of camphor oil to oxidation by air in the presence of water, with a view of ascertaining if the products are identical with those which are furnished by terpenes generally, and found that peroxide of hydrogen was freely produced. This result was in itself a proof that the oil contained one or more terpenes, because I had previously proved that all terpenes yield peroxide of hydrogen when they are oxidized in this manner. Since then, I have on several occasions employed camphor oil on a large scale in manufacturing operations as a substitute for ordinary turpentine or eucalyptus oil in my process of preparing disinfectants, with fairly satisfactory results. In one experiment there was obtained from 120 gallons of the oil during 52 hours' oxidation, a quantity above 1,000 Gms. of peroxide of hydrogen, its capability of producing that substance remaining, of course, anything but exhausted. In another trial, a quantity of 320 gallons, during a similar period, yielded 3,379 Gms. of peroxide of hydrogen (calculated as pure H_2O_2), the density of the oil having increased to .925. This partially oxidized oil yielded a further quantity of H_2O_2, nearly equal in amount to that originally produced during a further period of oxidation, but after that time, although it still continued to yield the peroxide in diminished amount, the oxidation proceeded much more slowly than happens with turpentine oil at that stage.

In another and more recent trial in which 110 gallons of camphor oil was submitted to oxidation during 100 hours, 74 gallons of partially oxidized oil of sp. gr. .925 resulted, and this, upon further oxidation during 246 hours, yielded 62 gallons of oxidized oil of sp. gr. .950. A sample of this oxidized oil is now produced.

Fallacy of Color Reactions for Aconitine.—Various authorities have described certain color reactions which were said to be obtained by treating aconitine by different reagents, such as phosphoric acid, sulphuric acid with sugar, phospho-molybdic acid and ammonia, etc. A. Jürgens has, however, recently shown that *pure* aconitine does not yield any color reactions at all. The only reliable test of the identity of aconitine is its physiological effect.

The author found the composition of pure aconitine to correspond to the formula $C_{33}H_{43}NO_{12}$. On evaporating the alkaloid from an ethereal solution, it crystallizes in anhydrous, columnar crystals.—*Inaug. Diss.* (St. Petersburg), *Zeitsch. f. anal. Chem.*

Detection of Gentian-Violet and Fuchsin in Wine.—According to Bernède, both gentian-violet and fuchsin may be detected in red wines by shaking 10 C.c. of the suspected wine with 5 C.c. of a reagent prepared by dissolving 10 Gm. of carbolic acid in 1 Gm. of alcohol and 60 Gm. of ether. If the wine is pure the ethereal phenol solution will form a colorless layer over the wine, but if the above-named coloring matters are present, the layer will have a red or violet tint. This test is said to detect so small a quantity as 0.1 milligramme of fuchsin, or 1 milligramme of gentian-violet in 1 liter of wine.—*Dingl. Polyt. Journ.*

Quantitative Estimation of Chloroform.—L. de Saint-Martin recommends the following method of estimating the quantity of chloroform in chloroform water or other liquids. It depends upon the decomposition of the chloroform by means of alcoholic potassa, and the subsequent estimation of the chlorine as chloride of silver.

Introduce 10 C.c. of the chloroform water into a strong glass tube closed at one end, and drawn out at the other, then add 2 C.c. of very concentrated solution of potassa, and 20 C.c. of alcohol. Seal the open end of the tube in the flame, and heat the glass tube in a water-bath during three hours. Then allow it to become cold, break off the pointed end, and transfer the contents to a beaker. Wash the tube with distilled water, and add this likewise to the beaker. Now titrate the solution, in the usual way, with a decinormal solution of nitrate of silver.

The author has found that a saturated chloroform water (presumably at 15° C., though the author omits to state the temperature) contains 0.64 Gm. of chloroform in 100 Gm. or 1 in 156. Prof. Regnault had given the rate of solubility as 1 in 111. [Most authorities give it as 1 in about 200 parts.]

New Mass for the Polygraph.—The following has recently been recommended as a good combination for preparing a mass for the polygraph:

Treat 100 parts of isinglass with cold water until it is softened; then boil it with 400 parts of water until it is practically dissolved, and add 600 parts of glycerin. Strain the mixture, and pour it into the forms. One-half of the isinglass may be replaced by gelatin.—*After Polyt. Journ.*

Bleaching Wood with Hydrogen Peroxide.—The advantage of this method of bleaching, recently recommended by Dr. P. Ebell, is that the wood retains its original structure. A previous treatment is not advisable, except in the case of fresh wood, when steaming causes a saving in the peroxide. Small pieces of wood are bleached in a few days. The bleach-bath is best kept alkaline with ammonia. If it is heated to 34°, the wood bleaches more rapidly, but this entails a loss of peroxide through evolutions of oxygen. Moreover, the final effect of using a cold bath is more satisfactory. After slowly drying, the wood appears perfectly white, a plane surface remains unchanged, and the curls and streaks, though now colorless, are nevertheless more distinct than previous to bleaching.—*Jour. Soc. Chem. Ind.*

Menthol in Phthisis.—Mr. A. J. Buhay reports, in the *Edinburgh Medical Journal* for January, the account of a favorable experience with a 20% solution of menthol in laryngeal and pulmonary phthisis. The solution is injected with a special syringe into the larynx or trachea with the aid of a laryngeal mirror. In the case of laryngeal phthisis, two or three injections, of 15 minims each, are made at each sitting. Deep inspiration should follow the injection, whereby the anæsthetic effect is increased. No untoward effects follow and the treatment should be repeated once or twice daily for about two months. If possible, the patient should hourly, during the day, inhale 5 or more minims of the same solution added to a pint of boiling water or to a pledget of cotton-wool placed in a respirator. The treatment causes pain and discomfort in the larynx to disappear and relieves dysphagia. Ulceration ceases and smooth cicatrices result.

Calycanthus glaucus (Carolina Allspice).—Dr. Eccles writes, in the *Brooklyn Medical Journal* for March, 1888, that the shrub within whose seeds he discovered the alkaloid was, during the late civil war, used in decoction of roots, leaves, and bark by the Confederate soldiers for the cure of intermittent fever, and, as claimed, with success. It is still used in domestic practice by the natives of the region where it grows. A fluid extract of an allied species is already upon the market, so that somewhere in the country it is being prescribed for some purpose. If in its crude form it has proven of advantage, this new concentrated form should be still more efficient. The seeds contain nearly two per cent of this alkaloid, and a smaller amount of probably two others. The odor of the volatile one of these last is distinctly that of pyridine and as it is unlikely that two should exist having the same smell, we may at present assume it as probably such.

Toxic Effects of Antipyrin.—Dr. A. Sturge, of Nice, reports the following unusual effect of 5 grains of antipyrin upon a lady liable to migraine. Five minutes after the dose was taken the "deadly sickness" characteristic of the migraine seemed to give way and an "expanding sensation" was felt, passing upward from the stomach, violent sneezing followed, the face and eyes became suffused, and tears and nasal mucus flowed freely. Breathing became difficult, and attended with a sense of suffocation, and there was complete inability to remain in a recumbent posture. A violent cough with free expectoration followed. After these symptoms had lasted a half-hour, itching of the inner surface of the thighs and an eruption of urticaria supervened and extended to the abdomen. These was a coppery taste in the mouth and a smell of the same character. The pulse was quick and very full and there was tinnitus aurium. These symptoms lasted about ½ hour.—*Br. Med. Jour.*, February 3d, 1888.

Tannin Wool.—Benjamin Ward Richardson writes in the *Asclepiad*, No. 17, 1888, that in treating ozæna and other diseases attended with fetid odors, tannin wool turns out to be of great practical service. I had thought that the manufacture of this preparation had become a general fact; but as many medical friends have at various times written for the method, it may be of service to give the details here.

To make tannin wool, add to distilled water heated to 148° F. pure tannin up to saturation, stirring carefully all the time. When the water is saturated, add to it pure cotton wool, bit by bit, until all the solution is taken up by the wool. Lastly, put the saturated wool in an evaporating dish, and dry it slowly until it is quite dry. It is then ready for use, but must always be kept in a closed bottle. It must be neatly teased out before being used; but it is well to keep it in the rough state.

A good stock of tannin wool is at all times a useful thing to keep at hand. It is a ready styptic and possesses good antiseptic properties. It can easily be iodized by making an ethereal solution of iodine, saturating a portion of the cotton with the solution, and allowing the ether to evaporate. One grain of iodine to an ounce of the cotton is sufficient to make a very good specimen; and an iodized cotton made in this proportion is one of the best applications for bed-sores that can be adopted. It rarely irritates, it removes odor, and often favors the healing of the sore.

AN ELECTRIC THERMO-REGULATOR.

LOVITON'S apparatus, which was introduced about the middle of last year, and regarding which we have had several inquiries, is constructed in the following manner:
The essential portions are:
A, The battery. B, The manometer. C, The burner.

Any kind of battery or cell will answer the purpose, provided it has enough power. A Delaurier element is recommended by the inventor. Probably a medium-sized Bunsen element will answer the same purpose.

The manometer (B) consists of an elongated, thin-walled glass bulb R, through the upper portion of which is fused a tube open at both ends, but contracted at its lower end. A few drops of ether (or other easily expanding liquid) are first poured down the tube, and afterwards enough mercury to fill the bulb as far as possible. The few drops of ether will float on the surface of the mercury and be completely protected from access with the external air. Of course, any material elevation of temperature to which the bulb containing the mercury is exposed causes the ether to become vaporised, and the vapor, expanding with increase of temperature, depresses the mercury in the bulb, while that in the tube correspondingly ascends. A platinum wire, F, passes through the wall of the bulb and dips into the mercury. In the upper orifice of the tube, a platinum wire, F', is adjusted at such a height that the mercury, on expanding, will reach it at the temperature which is to be maintained constantly.

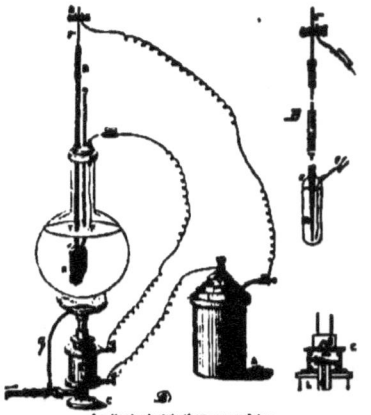

Lovitton's electric thermo-regulator.

The burner L consists of the interior gas-tube l (see separate small cut), and an exterior armature, L. Over the orifice of the interior tube, a very light disk of iron, n, is attached by means of a hinge. When the electric circuit is closed by the mercury in the tube B, reaching the platinum wire F', the gas tube becomes magnetic and attracts the disk of iron, which then closes the exit of the gas. As soon as the current is interrupted, the disk is raised again by the mere pressure of gas, and the burner is automatically relighted by a small, independent flame furnished by the tube q.

The application of the apparatus is shown, in a general way, in the illustration at the left, where a flask is supposed to be the receptacle in which a liquid is to be maintained at an even temperature.

The manometer and an accurate thermometer having been placed in the liquid, and the flame of the burner lighted, the rise of temperature is watched until it reaches the desired point, when the wire F' is pushed down so as to just reach the mercury in the manometer tube, and it is then firmly adjusted at this height. The electric current will then extinguish the flame of the burner, and as soon as the temperature falls slightly, the flame will become relit. This will take place alternately for any length of time, so long as the bulbs of the manometer and thermometer remain immersed in the liquid.

In practice, of course, it will be found impossible to keep the temperature exactly at an invariable point. There will always be slight fluctuations above and below it, but this is immaterial.—*After Journ. de Pharm. et Chim.*

Freshly Powdered Ergot.—Prof. Pajot carries in his obstetric bag an ergot-mill, resembling a small coffee-mill, compact in form, and designed to grind ergot freshly for use. He thinks that only the freshly powdered drug is reliable. [It is evidently a mill with two cranks.—ED. A. D.]

Notes on Essential Oils and Allied Products.
(From the Bericht von Schimmel & Co., of Leipzig, April, 1888.)

"*Algalia*" is the fanciful name of a mixture, sold on the American market, which consists, according to Sch. & Co., of about 80 per cent of oil of cedar or oil of copaiba, with about 20 per cent of oil of musk seed.

Oil of Almonds, expressed.—It is, of course, well known to some, but by no means to all of our readers, that the expressed oil of almonds, or "sweet oil of almonds" of the market is not exclusively derived from almonds, but that manufacturers also use the kernels of peaches and apricots as a source of the oil. [Conscientious manufacturers quote the oils obtained from the different sources separately. Others again carry on their lists only the "almond oil," without specifying what it was made from.]

Up to within a short time ago, Messrs. Schimmel & Co. (according to their own statement) had never been called upon to put themselves on the defensive regarding the quality of their product. The special importance, however, which has recently been attached to Hübl's test—the so-called iodine-number indication, the relative capacity of an oil to combine with iodine—has rendered it necessary to show its possible fallacy. In the preparations for Hübl's test, it is necessary to make a solution of iodine and of mercuric chloride in alcohol, the iodine value of which is afterwards determined by hyposulphite. Schimmel & Co. point out that the iodine-mercurial solution is liable to great alteration during the first few hours. If this alteration is taken in consideration, or allowed for, the results obtained by them upon oils of different origin, and pressed by themselves, was as follows:

"Almond Oil"	Iodine Number	Spec. Grav.
from Bitter Almonds	96.3	0.918
from Syrian Peach or Apricot Kernels (1886)	96.9	0.918
from Syrian Peach or Apricot Kernels (1887)	99.3	0.918
from Hungarian Peach Kernels	105.4	0.919
from Pea-nuts	92.4	0.918

The determinations were carried out according to Benedikt ("Analyse der Fette und Wachsarten").

Without denying in general the scientific value of Hübl's method, Sch. & Co. yet show that it does not yield reliable results in the above case. The iodine-number of pea-nut oil, which is one of the principal adulterants of almond oil, is too near to the iodine number of the different commercial almond oils, and the latter do not sufficiently agree among themselves to render any conclusion based on these numbers trustworthy. Besides, a mixture consisting, for instance, of equal quantities of pea-nut and Hungarian peach-kernel oil would yield an iodine-number which is unobjectionable; and by mixing equal quantities of Syrian peach-kernel oil and pea-nut oil, the iodine number of true oil of almonds would be attained.

Oil of Ambrette Seeds.—This product, which has appeared in the American market, is declared by Sch. & Co. to consist of oil of copaiba flavored with musk seed.

Oil of Balsam of Tolu.—This oil, only introduced recently, promises to be of great utility in perfumery, but is very expensive, costing about $3.50 per ounce. It has the spec. grav. 0.945, contains a terpene $C_{10}H_{16}$ (so-called tolene), also ethers of cinnamic and benzoic acids. Cinnamic alcohol appears to be likewise present.

Oil of Betel Leaves.—The oil distilled at Leipzig from betel leaves imported from Siam yielded a distillate having a spec. grav. of 1.030, while the oil distilled from the leaves in Java is much lighter, having the spec. grav. 0.945. The reason of this difference is probably this, that the apparatus and process employed in Java is incapable of driving out the higher-boiling portions. For this reason it is illogical, in this and similar cases, to regard an oil distilled in the East, at the place of growth, as superior to one distilled from the same substance in Europe or elsewhere, where the technical appliances and facilities are much better. It is stated that the next edition of the Pharmacopœia Neerlandica will recognise this oil as an officinal article.

Oil of Boldo.—Good boldo leaves contain more than 2% of oil. The latter has a pepper-like, narcotic odor, and a mild, indifferent herbaceous taste. Its spec. grav. is 0.918. It boils between 175°-250° C., it contains a terpene $(C_{10}H_{16})$, and several oxygenated compounds.

Oil of boldo has been used successfully in affections of the liver, in gall-stone, and also in gonorrhœa and other troubles.

Oil of Camphor.—The crude by-product obtained during the production of camphor in the East, and from which safrol is now extracted on a large scale, is shipped to Europe in constantly increasing quantities. Schimmel & Co. received during 1887 not less than about 600 tons. This firm states that they have tried to obtain the body announced by Yoshida as existing in that fraction of the crude oil which boils between 208° and 222° C., and which this author called *camphorogenol*, but even after eight repeated fractionations, they were unable to obtain a homogeneous product. They have come to the conclusion that the higher boiling fractions of the crude camphor oil contain, besides camphor, safrol, eugenol, and a sesqui-terpene $(C_{15}H_{24})$, the substance designated by Wallach *terpineol*. Though this has not yet been isolated, yet its presence is rendered almost certain by the fact that fractions boiling between 214° and 220°, when boiled with diluted sulphuric acid, yield large quantities of a terpene $(C_{10}H_{16})$ in which *terpinen* could be proven to be present. Besides, these fractions yielded terpin-hydrate, when treated with diluted nitric acid and alcohol.

Oil of Cananga.—After the rectification of a large quantity of this oil, the residue left in the still was found to contain benzoic acid. This exists not only in the oil of cananga (obtained from Java and Siam), but also in oil of ylang, probably in form of an ether. It is, therefore, probable that both of these oils will eventually be made synthetically.

Oil of Cedar (-Wood).—The employment of this useful oil in the manufacture of soap, where it is used as a basis of other perfumes, and may almost be regarded as a sort of "oil of sandal wood for the middle classes," has increased to large proportions, so that Sch. & Co. often find difficulty in procuring a sufficient amount of cedar wood chips. It has become necessary to pay better prices for the latter, to prevent the lead-pencil manufacturers from burning them. The American oil of cedar is not distilled on purpose, *per se*, but is obtained as a secondary product, in the drying rooms of the cedar wood in the factories.

Oil of Cedar Leaves.—This oil, obtained by distillation from the leaves of the same tree (*Juniperus virginiana*) which yields the preceding oil, is now again obtainable. It is entirely useless for perfumery. In odor it resembles oil of savine, with which it is said to share the same medicinal properties.

Oil of Cinnamon, Ceylon.—Schimmel & Co. draw special attention to two simple and practical tests which may be used to distinguish genuine oil of Ceylon cinnamon. 1. When dropped into water, the oil must sink, as it is specifically heavier. [This would, however, not distinguish it from several other essential oils, not even from oil of Chinese cinnamon.] 2. It must at once produce the impression of exceeding sweetness, far superior to that of sugar, and this sweet taste must persist to the very end. In low-grade sorts, a clove-like taste is first developed, which is followed only after some time by a sweet impression. An oil of this kind is not worth more than oil of cassia, but large quantities of it are exported from Ceylon.

Oil of Citronella.—During the year 1886-1887 (October 1st to September 30th), the quantity of this oil shipped from Ceylon amounted to not less than 523,214 pounds. More than one-half of this, namely 280,311 pounds, were shipped to New York, about 230,000 pounds to London, and small quantities to other places.

Oils of the Citrus Family.—According to a report of the Italian Statistical Bureau, the number of *agrumi* trees (orange, lemon, and bergamot) in existence is as follows:

In Sicily	10,115,796
In Reggio	4,811,377

and the yield of fruit was as follows:

1882	1,658,542,800
1884	3,011,908,400
1885	2,829,622,800

A large number of experiments have been made to replace the old-fashioned method of hand-pressing by machinery, but without great success. The chief difficulty lies in the irregularity, both in shape and in size, of the fruits. During 1886, the total export of oils of the citrus family from Italy amounted to 277,106 kilos. Adding the home consumption, the total yield may safely be put at 300,000 kilos. Assuming that about 1,500 fruits on an average are required for the production of 1 kilo of oil, the oil industry of 1886 would have absorbed a total quantity of 450,000,000 fruits. During 1887 the export of oils and value of same was as follows:

	KILOS.	VALUE.
Messina	265,812	£5,116,240
Palermo	24,404	339,780
Catania	10,000	157,895
Reggio	45,913	901,834
Total	336,128	£5,515,749

Oil of Cloves.—As stated in previous reports, a large proportion of what is commonly sold as "oil of cloves" is simply "oil of clove-stems." This is quite a common custom—according to Schimmel & Co., who speak presumably on the experience chiefly gained among conscientious houses—among the drug trade, and much less so among perfumers who know how to distinguish between the two kinds.

Oil of Green Cloves.—The prospective introduction of oil of cloves, distilled from the green cloves themselves at the place of growth, has been announced some time ago, but only small lots have been shipped over. And, according to Schimmel & Co., the specific gravity does not appear to be satisfactory. This is only 1.048 at 18° C., while absolutely genuine oil of cloves has one of 1.060.

Oil of Cognac, Artificial.—This is the ether of a fatty acid, and has recently found a new application in the soap industry, for producing a fruity odor. About 100 to 200 Gm. (3½ to 7 oz.) for every 220 pounds of soap produce the same effect as the "polysolve olein" introduced some years ago. The latter, consisting of sulpholeates, causes in cocoa-nut oil soap the formation of similar ethers.

Oil of Crisp Mint.—The American oil is now preferred even to the German, owing to its fine aroma.

Oil of Damiana.—From Damiana leaves, such as they are sold on the New York market, Schimmel & Co. obtained 0.9 per cent of an essential oil of a viscid, greenish oil of a chamomile-like odor, spec. grav. 0.970. In its high boiling portions it contains a blue oil.

Oil of Eucalyptus.—The oil derived from *Eucalyptus amygdalina* is losing its standing, as it has been shown that it contains no eucalyptol at all. Nevertheless, the production of this and other inferior kinds is constantly increasing. On the other hand, the oil of *Eucalyptus globulus* is coming more and more into use, and it is in Algiers which seems to be the principal source of production. Of equal value as the Algerian oil is that produced in California (Alameda county) by certain firms engaged in the manufacture of preventives against boiler incrustation. Messrs. Schimmel & Co. have, however, found that it is feasible to carry the eucalyptus leaves to Leipzig and distil the oil there. And it is upon self-distilled oil that the new facts below recorded are based.

The absolutely genuine oil of *Eucalyptus globulus* has yielded, on examination, very interesting and surprising results. In general, it agrees with that which is sold in the market as distilled in Africa or California. It has the spec. grav. 0.925, and turns the plane of polarisation five degrees to the right. The spec. grav. of the before-mentioned commercial oils varies between 0.915 and 0.925. They are all dextrogyre, though in different degrees. In six different samples, the percentage of eucalyptol was found to vary between 50 and 70 per cent. Eucalyptol is optically inactive, and this property may be regarded as one of the criterions of the purity of the oil.

While distilling the leaves of *Eucalyptus globulus*, Sch. & Co. noticed the occurrence of aldehydes of the fatty acids. Valeraldehyde was positively identified; butylaldehyde and capronaldehyde appear likewise to have been present. The larger proportion of these substances was dissolved in the aqueous portion of the distillate, but the valeraldehyde was found to exist also in the oil itself.

In connection with the above, Sch. & Co. give some very interesting facts regarding the essential oils of other species of eucalyptus. We quote their own words:

"We owe the information to a countryman of ours, Mr. C. Th. Staiger, chemist in Brisbane, who distilled these oils himself, partly by request of the committee charged with the [Intercolonial] exhibition. This is so much the more gratifying as it has been heretofore impossible for us to procure samples of these oils from our agent, although the latter was surely in a position to comply with our request. It was even impossible for us to procure samples of the oils exhibited at the Colonial Exhibition."

[Incidentally we would state, though this information is not even implied by Messrs. Schimmel & Co., that private communications we have received from trusted correspondents in Australia assure us that very considerable quantities of the remarkable oil presently to be described have annually been produced in Australia by a few manufacturers. But none of these products seems ever to have reached the market, and it remains a mystery what has become of them. When the extensive reports on eucalyptus were published at about the time of the Philadelphia Exhibition in 1876, and after Prof. F. v. Mueller's large work on eucalyptus had been completed, orders for some of these oils, notably for that of *Eucalyptus citriodora*, were sent to Australia, but none could be procured. If it *was* made in quantities, and did *not* appear on the market, the question arises where did it go to; who used it; and as what did it make its appearance?]

"These oils far surpass all our expectations, and we are confident that we shall soon be able to introduce them upon the market.

"For the present, we possess only small samples which are already several years old and partly resinified. The following data are therefore only preliminary:

1. Oil of *Eucalyptus Bayleyana* (strongly resinified), spec. grav. 0.940, boils between 150°-185° C.

2. Oil of *Eucalyptus microcorys* (strongly resinified), spec. grav. 0.933, boils between 160°-200° C.

Both of these resemble the oil of *E. globulus*. Like the latter, they contain a terpene ($C_{10}H_{16}$) and eucalyptol ($C_{10}H_{18}O$), but of the latter much less than the "globulus" oil, viz., only about 30%.

3. Oil of *Eucalyptus Dealbata*, spec. grav. 0.885, boils at 206°-216° C.

4. Oil of *Eucalyptus maculata*, spec. grav. 0.900, boils at 210°-230° C.

5. Oil of *Eucalyptus maculata*, var. *citriodora*, spec. grav. 0.903, boils at 209°-220° C."

The latter three sorts resemble each other very much. They possess a highly agreeable odor, resembling melissa, which is particularly prominent in the oil of *E. dealbata*. These oils will, no doubt, prove very valuable and of practical utility. Chemically, they are quite characteristic. None of them contains any terpene, but they consist of a ketone, $C_{10}H_{14}O$, which is the bearer of the melissa-like odor, and besides a substance $C_{10}H_{18}O$ (?) which is probably an alcohol, and has a fine odor recalling that of geranium.

6. Oil of *Eucalyptus Staigeriana*, spec. grav. 0.880, boils at 170°-230° C.

7. Oil of *Backhausia citriodora*, spec. grav. 0.900, boils at 223°-233° C.

Both of these oils are distinguished by their intense lemon- and verbena-like odor, particularly the last named, which is derived from a tree belonging to the same family as Eucalyptus.

8. Oil of *Eucalyptus Hæmastoma*, spec. grav. 0.890, boils at 170°-250° C. This differs in odor from all the rest, and recalls that of oil of cumin. It contains terpene and cymol. Among its oxygenated constituents is one having the odor of *oil of pepermint*, possibly menthol.

"Regarding the oil of *E. amygdalina*, we would state that this differs from all other eucalyptus oils, and probably contains no oxygenated constituents at all. At least 90 per cent of it consists of a well characterised terpene ($C_{10}H_{16}$), and there may possibly be present a minute quantity of cymol. The spec. grav. of the oil is 0.890; it boils at 170°-180°, and it is dextrogyre, the deviation observed in three samples (in a hundred mm. tube) being, respectively, —27°, —26.4°, —26.6°. The latter property alone, therefore, distinguishes it from the oil of *E. globulus*."

"*Formosa-wood oil*" is offered by houses in Southern France as a substitute for the expensive oil of orris. Now, there is, in the first place, no such thing known anywhere as "Formosa-wood," and besides, the oil, as sold, consists of oil of copaiba distilled from orris root. It also contains a very little oil of bitter almonds, and some 2 per cent of fixed oil.

Oil of Geranium, Turkish, or Oil of Palmarosa.—This oil, which is entirely different from the oil of geranium distilled in Africa and Spain, is produced in the northern provinces of India, and (while formerly carried to Europe by way of Turkey) is now imported direct. Sometimes it is found adulterated with oil of gurjun balsam or oil of cedar.

The ordinary East Indian oil of geranium, known as *Oil of Gingergrass*, is rarely found even in tolerably fair quality, being *always* adulterated with oil of turpentine, so that no dealer or importer is able to guarantee its quality. Whether the adulteration is practised at the place of distribution or after its arrival at Bombay has so far not been ascertained, but this will eventually be done.

Helenin, or alant-camphor, elecampane camphor, has been reported by Dr. Dono to be an efficient remedy in chorea. He used it successfully in three cases, in doses of ¼ grain three to four times daily. It has also been used with advantage in bronchitis and convulsive cough. The substance is in fine, brilliantly white, needle-shaped crystals, and must be carefully protected against heat, as it readily melts.

Heliotropin.—The users of this very useful perfume are warned that it will not stand heat without injury. It should be kept in a cool place. The best plan, however, is to dissolve the substance immediately upon receipt in (deodorized) alcohol and to keep the solution in a cold place.

The crystallized heliotropin, when exposed to heat and light, is apt to cake together and to gradually darken in color. When it assumes a brownish tint, decomposition has so far advanced that the substance is practically useless.

Oil of Jaborandi.—The leaves of the officinal jaborandi yielded 0.4 per cent of an essential oil of very strong odor, and a mild, fruity taste. Spec. grav. 0.875.

Oil of Japanese "Birch Tar."—This is the provisional name applied to a tarry oil obtained from Japan, also known as *matsu oil*, which may possibly be found applicable to medicinal purposes. It has the spec. grav. 0.973 and contains 4 per cent of phenols of an agreeable, guaiacol odor. That portion of the oil which is insoluble in alkalies burns nearly all below 180°. Only about 10 per cent pass over at a temperature beyond 200° C.

The German oil of birch tar has the spec. grav. 0.965, and contains nearly 40 per cent of phenols.

Oil of Kesso Root.—The Japanese "Valerian" root, derived from *Patrinia scabiosæfolia* Link, yielded, on distillation, as much as 7 per cent of oil. It much resembles that distilled from European valerian root.

Oil of Kiku.—This oil, obtained from a Japanese plant, was mentioned in the report of Sch. & Co. of last year, but the source was not given. We stated at the time [AMER. DRUGG., 1887, 129] that we had searched the large Japanese botanical encyclopædia "Sô-moku-sumetts," and thought it referred to *Pyrethrum chinense* Sabin. Mr. J. Murai, of Tokio, has now informed Sch. & Co. that the oil is prepared, in the western part of Japan, from *Pyrethrum indicum* Cass.

Oil of Lemon.—One of the most prominent producers of the oil [in Sicily] has long been engaged in the perfection of machinery for extracting the oil, so as to do away with manual labor. Sch. & Co. state that they have had opportunity to examine the plans, and they believe that success is near at hand. This would render the chance of an adulteration of the oil—which is now carried on by the growers in the most barefaced manner—impossible.

[As it is manifestly impracticable, under present circumstances, to transport the whole crop of fruits grown over the large territory where citrus trees are grown to manufacturing centers, because there are not enough hands concentrated there to work up the immense crop by hand, it is customary to extract the oil—if the treacle process is used—at or near the place of growth, wherever there is a large enough crop and a sufficient number of people to handle it. Many of these localities are, of course, without proper control or supervision, and, for this reason, a good deal of sophistication is practised to increase the yield improperly. Should the experiment of introducing machinery for extracting the oil succeed, a few manufacturing centres could easily work up the fruit gathered over large areas and shipped to the factory. But we foresee the troubles which this is likely to raise among the population, especially in the country districts. The common people are poor, and their chances or means of earning a livelihood are limited. As soon as the opportunity of employment at their old occupation, and the chance of the small producer to manipulate his own product is taken away, there is likely to be raised an outcry against the "grasping monopolists." It is well to think of this now, so that means may be discovered, if possible, to make up to the people the apparent loss which they will experience in their accustomed employment.]

Oil of Lemon-grass.—The shipments of this oil from Cochin-China by direct steamer are of rare occurrence, as the steamers usually refuse to carry liquid and strongly odorous substances. [In this connection, we can only express our surprise that the method of shipping such products in tin cans or other suitable metallic receptacles has not long ago been more generally introduced. Sch. & Co. have lately begun to import oil of citronella in 40-lb. tin cans. It will not be difficult to do this also in the case of patchouli, oil of lemon-grass, and similar other products which are strongly odorous. The chief difficulty to be overcome will be the apparent expense in carrying to the place of export the empty tins. But in some cases this may be offset by exporting *alcohol* in such tins; in other cases, the tin cans may be shipped unmade, packed in boxes as plates ready for soldering.]

Oil of Matico.—Owing to the scarcity of matico leaves rich in oil, this product has become expensive. [Those who use matico leaves for pharmaceutical purposes will do well to carefully examine the leaves offered to them for purchase.]

Menthol.—A combination of iodol with menthol is being recommended under the name *menthiodol*, against neuralgia. It is prepared as follows: 4 parts of menthol are cautiously melted in a porcelain capsule, and 1 part of finely powdered iodol added, under constant stirring, until a homogeneous mass is produced, which is cast into cones. Should they turn out too hard, a little camphor may be incorporated with them.

Oil of Mirbane.—This substitute for oil of bitter almonds is sometimes used for perfuming the denaturalized alcohol which has been legalised in Germany (where the denaturalisation is effected by means of certain pyridine bases) or in England (where the same object is accomplished by wood spirit). It seems again necessary to point out that this substance is *poisonous*. Even a prolonged inhalation of the vapors of oil of mirbane is apt to be followed by vomiting and diarrhœa, and 5 to 6 Gm. may produce a fatal result.

Oil of Musk-Seed.—This oil (from *Abelmoschus moschatus* L.), only recently introduced, promises to become an article of great importance. It is not improbable that the bearer of the odor contained in the oil may turn out identical with that existing in musk itself. The genuine oil of musk-seed has the spec. grav. 0.900 at 25° C. It congeals when cooled to + 10° C. (50° F.), and then remains solid at the average indoor temperature.

Oil of Orris.—The reason why some manufacturers of oil of orris offer this product at lower prices than others is this, that they first treat the orris root with sulphuric acid, whereby the starch is converted into glucose, etc. On distilling the altered root, a larger quantity of product is obtained, but this is of inferior quality.

Oil of Patchouli.—The quality of patchouli leaves shipped from the East is not always satisfactory, as they are frequently mixed with stems and already exhausted leaves. The leaves of *Urena lobata* var. *sinuata* have also been used as an adulterant. On the other hand, those of *Pogostemon suavis* Tenore, and *Plectranthus Patchouly* Clarke, are said to have the same odor. During last year, a single house at Penang shipped not less than 30,000 oz. of oil of patchouli to Europe, and a portion of this lies still unsold at London and Paris.

Oil of Peppermint.—The Japanese product continues to keep the whole peppermint market in a most depressed condition. Sch. & Co. feel certain that a catastrophe will take place sooner or later, as the market is unable to absorb the produced quantity. According to the reports of the German Consul at Yokohama, the annual production of the oil (two harvests per year) amounts to 400,000 pounds. Even supposing that only half of this amount is produced, and that one-half of the product is consumed in the country itself, there would still remain 100,000 pounds for export, an amount about equal to the total annual production in the United States.

Oil of Pine-Needles.—The kind most in request is the oil distilled from the needles of *Pinus Pumilio.* Some continental manufacturers of "forest odors" combine this or similar oils with too much of other substances, such as musk, which diminish its refreshing qualities. The ozonizing effect of these pine-oils is best produced either by spraying them through the sick-room, or by burning them in appropriately constructed lamps (such as Jaeger's ozone lamp). It is not necessary to burn, for such purpose, the most expensive of the pine-oils; a cheap and very serviceable combination consists of equal parts of the best quality of oil of *Pinus sylvestris* and oil of *Larix sibirica.* The latter is known in the trade as "Siberian pine-needle oil."

Oil of Sandal Wood.—The Brit. Pharmacopœia gives the specific gravity of oil of sandal wood as 0.960, and that of the United States as 0.945. Both figures are wrong. Schimmel & Co. find that it should be 0.970 to 0.975 at 15° C. The oil distilled in India shows a specific gravity up to 0.990, but this should not be regarded as normal, as the oil is distilled in a crude manner over a naked fire. Application of steam and improved rational apparatus has never produced an oil with a specific gravity higher than 0.980.

Oil of Wintergreen.—A report has been circulated some time ago that oil of wintergreen is largely adulterated with oil of camphor. Special inquiries made by the manager of the New York branch of Schimmel & Co. have shown that this statement lacks foundation.

Oil of Wistaria.—A product sold in the American market is stated by Schimmel & Co. to consist of balsam of copaiba, Turkish oil of geranium, balsam of Peru, and a little oil of ylang. It is probably supposed that the oil is believed to be obtained from the bark of *Wistaria Sinensis* Curt. Genuine wistaria oil, when warmed with potassa, is stated to be converted into a white substance having the odor of cumarin. The American "oil of wistaria" failed to respond to this test.

Testing Sulphate of Quinine.

In the judgment of Messrs. C. F. Boehringer & Sons, the recent discussions on the respective merits of the different tests proposed to ascertain the purity of commercial sulphate of quinine, have shown that none of them can equal, in accuracy or sharpness, the oxalate test, if conducted in the following manner:

Put 1 Gm. of commercial sulphate of quinine (or 0.85 Gm. of the completely dried sulphate) into a small tared flask, and dissolve it by means of 35 C.c. of distilled water at a boiling temperature. Next add a solution of 0.3 Gm. of neutral crystallized oxalate of potassium in 5 C.c. of distilled water, and then add enough water to make the contents of the flask weigh 41.3 Gm. Transfer the flask to a water-bath kept at a temperature of 20° C. (68° F.), shake it occasionally, filter after half an hour through glasswool, and to 10 C.c. of the filtrate add 1 drop of solution of soda (sp. gr. 1.160). No turbidity should occur in the course of a few minutes, if the sulphate was pure.

Chinese Ginger.—Up to the present time, China has exported ginger only in a candied form. Recently, however, a company has been formed there which dries fresh ginger by special apparatus, and thereby renders it capable of being exported. It is said that the fresh roots are deprived of about 90 per cent of their weight by the removal of water and of starch, and that the remaining 10 parts constitute the valuable aromatic portion. The process reduces the root to powder. A sample of this powder was submitted to Schimmel & Co., of Leipzig, who acknowledged that it had a finer aroma than any other kind of ginger they had ever met with. As to regular future supplies of the article and its price, nothing certain is known as yet.

Preservation of Organic Liquids.—For the purpose of preserving milk for some time, so as to keep it in good condition for analysis, E. Schroder recommends to add to it a drop (or more, according to the quantity) of essential oil of mustard. This will not interfere with the course of the analysis. It will no doubt answer equally well in the case of other organic liquids.

The New Austrian Pharmacopœia will appear in December next. The pharmacognosy section is said to be compiled by Professor Vogl; the chemical section, from A to K, by Professor Ludwig, and from K. to Z, by Professor Barth; while Mr. M. R. Schneider will edit the whole. The authors are very reluctant to give any details about the progress of the work.

THE
American Druggist

AN ILLUSTRATED MONTHLY JOURNAL

OF

Pharmacy, Chemistry, and Materia Medica.

Vol. XVII., No. 5.   Whole No. 107.

FREDERICK A. CASTLE, M.D.............................EDITOR.
CHARLES RICE, Ph.D.................................ASSOCIATE EDITOR.

PUBLISHED BY

WM. WOOD & CO., 56 & 58 Lafayette Place, N. Y.

SUBSCRIPTION PRICE per year, ... $1.50
SINGLE COPIES, ...15

Address all communications relating to the business of the AMERICAN DRUGGIST, such as subscriptions, advertisements, change of Post-Office address, etc., to WILLIAM WOOD & Co., 56 and 58 Lafayette Place, New York City, to whom order all postal money orders and checks should be made payable. Communications intended for the Editor should be addressed in care of the Publishers.

The AMERICAN DRUGGIST is issued in the latter part of each month, dated for the month ahead. Changes of advertisements should reach us before the 10th. New advertisements can occasionally be inserted after the 18th.

REGULAR ADVERTISEMENTS according to size, location, and time. Special rates on application.

EDITORIALS.

A CASE of suicidal poisoning recently occurred in this city which brings up the question of the utility of the present law regulating the sale of poisons. A man having a reputation for inebriety engaged a room at a hotel, wrote to his wife a parting message, and sent a hall-boy to the nearest drug store with a dollar and with instruction to bring him some laudanum and lint to be applied to an injured arm. He got the laudanum, and was, some time after, found dead.

Another poisoning case, also of recent occurrence, bears upon the same question. A servant in a boarding-house was sent to a druggist with an empty Hunyadi-water bottle and instructions to get a bottle of water like it. What he asked for, however, was "bug poison," and it seems that the druggist filled his bottle with a mixture of corrosive sublimate, carbolic acid, and similarly noxious agents, and labelled the bottle very thoroughly as a container of poison. The lady, who had sent for the water, did not look at the labels, but swallowed a quantity of the contents of the bottle and suffered pretty serious results, as might be expected.

These two instances illustrate very well the majority of the cases of poisoning which occur. In one case the poisoning is done with deliberate intent; in the other, it is the result of pure stupidity. In neither case does the existence of a law regulating the sale of poisons by druggists seem to have had any utility, and so far as can be judged from the experience of the few years that have passed since its enactment, the public would be just as well if such a law did not exist, for pharmacists generally do not comply with it, and there is no one who takes sufficient interest in the subject to secure its enforcement. There is ground for a belief that there would really be less risk of accidental poisoning if there were fewer legislative restrictions and fewer distinctive poison bottles; if each person appreciated that he must exercise precaution in taking the contents of any bottle, and if the responsibility of misadventure rests upon himself and not upon the druggist. The utter inability of the druggist to prevent misuse of poisons is well shown in the second case mentioned above, and also in a recent case in Canada, in which two rogues attempted to blackmail a druggist by putting a poisonous mixture into a bottle in place of a harmless one, which he had dispensed on prescription, and claiming that carelessness on his part had caused harm. The poison in this instance was got from another druggist with a fraudulent prescription, and the contents of the bottles were changed.

There is a growing tendency to model the restrictive laws of this country after those which exist in Europe without sufficient regard for the fact that the system of government, and the machinery by means of which the laws are administered, are quite different, and laws which may accomplish their purpose there, because it is somebody's business to see that they are enforced, are of no practical value here, because it becomes everybody's business to attend to their enforcement. So far as suppression of accidental or intentional poisoning is concerned, however, there appears to be quite as much, if not more, trouble abroad than there is here, and we repeat that we are inclined to think that there would be less of it here, if the present poison laws were abolished.

IN a recent report on the composition of "Coleman's Liebig's Extract of Meat and Malt Wine," published in the *Zeitschrift f. angewandte Chemie* (1888, 136), Mr. Heinrich Trillich justly condemns the unprincipled use which is being made of the name of the illustrious Liebig, in order to prop up all sorts of trashy preparations in the estimation of the public. There are " Liebig's Beef Wine," " Liebig's Canadian Extract of Beef," " Liebig's Perfect Health Sweets," " Liebig's Perfect Health Lozenges," " Liebig's Extract of Malt," etc., etc.—the series might be greatly extended—all of which appear under false pretenses. Liebig authorized the use of his name only in connection with a very few products, the most important of which is the Extract of Beef manufactured at Fray Bentos, Uruguay.

It is a pity that such an abuse should be made of the name of a man who will always stand in the front rank of the pioneers of modern chemistry, though no has long departed from our midst. But—*vulgus vult decipi: ergo decipiatur*.

THE following advice, published in *Science* for Nov. 14th, 1884, ought to be regularly printed in every volume of transactions of a scientific body:

"We venture to make a few suggestions which seem to us worth considering by those who are called upon to manage scientific meetings, especially the annual gatherings which bring from a great distance, at a great expense, those who are desirous of securing the utmost advantage from the meeting. *First*, Let the committee in charge make arrangements of a positive character for the conduct of the meeting, and require conformity to their regulations. Among these rules should be, (1) a strict adherence to the allotted time; (2) the presentation, in advance, of an abstract of what is to be read, and this should be printed, particularly if it contains any tabular statement, mathematical formulas, chemical formulas, or other rigidly technical statements; (3) the allowance of a definite time for discussion, questions, answers, and comments. *Second*, Let every speaker or reader form the habit of stating, in general terms, the purpose of his investigation, its relations to other work, and its results, refraining from going into minute details unless he is sure that a considerable part of the audience can follow him. Let him always remember that there are some statements which the mind cannot readily receive through the portal of the ear; and there are but few which cannot be simultaneously presented, both to the eye and the ear. The diagram, the printed formula, the abstract may cost the speaker a little expenditure; but it will save the hearer a vexatious outlay of time and attention. *Third*, Let there be a liberal margin allowed for social intercourse outside of the meetings, not merely for public receptions and excursions, but for those informal introductions and interviews which to many persons are the best part of scientific gatherings. We should not then hear it said so often: 'This would have been a very pleasant meeting, were it not for the papers which were read.'"

Memorial of the Late Henry B. Parsons.

THE Alumni Association of the School of Pharmacy of the University of Michigan have issued the following circular:

The committee desire to state that they have met with nothing but encouragement. All the alumni express a decided interest in the object and a wish to further it.

The record of H. B. Parsons has reflected honor upon his alma mater. In this record we all feel a just pride, and it is fitting that his fellow-alumni and friends should perpetuate his memory by a memorial suitable and lasting.

As the committee must be guided in the selection of a memorial by the amount raised, and as the time is now limited for the selection and completion of the work, the committee would respectfully solicit your subscription to the above and would ask that, if possible within two weeks from the receipt of this, you send your subscription to A. B. Stevens, 15 Church st., Ann Arbor.

Respectfully your Committee,

A. S. PARKER.
OTTO SCHERER.
A. B. STEVENS.

Gustavus Johannes Luhn, of Charleston, S. C., died on the 4th of April, after an illness of but a few days' duration. He was a native of Genthin, province of Saxony, where he was born on the 7th of June, 1839. After having been educated in Berlin, he came, at the age of 18 years, to this country. He already had some knowledge of the drug business, and continued the study of pharmacy after his immigration; residing successively in New York, Baltimore, and Richmond. In 1868, he commenced business on his own account in Charleston, and rapidly acquired a position as the leading pharmacist of the city, and a business which had few equals in the Southern States. He was the organizer and first president of the South Carolina Pharmaceutical Association, and for some time was a member of the Board for Examining Applicants for Apothecary's License. In 1876, he was elected first vice-president, and in 1878, president of the American Pharmaceutical Association. Mr. Luhn was well known in all his relations as a man of great business ability and strict integrity, and his death will be a severe loss to the community in which he lived. A bibliographical sketch and portrait of Mr. Luhn, were published in this journal (NEW REMEDIES), in 1879, p. 15.

Daniel C. Robbins, of the well-known New York firm of McKesson & Robbins, died suddenly in Brooklyn on the 18th of April. He left his house in the afternoon for a walk and seemed in as good health as usual. As he turned a street corner, he was noticed by some firemen to stagger and grasp an awning post for support. They carried him at once to their engine-house, which was close at hand, and summoned an ambulance surgeon, but he became unconscious and soon died.

Mr. Robbins was in his seventy-third year. He was born in Roslyn, L. I., and at the age of thirteen left home to engage in business. He served his apprenticeship with a druggist in Poughkeepsie and then came to this city, where he became chief clerk for the firm of Olcott & McKesson, of Maiden lane, more than fifty years ago. He soon rose to be partner in the firm, which later became McKesson & Robbins. For many years they have carried on business in Fulton street, and have been one of the leaders of the drug trade of the country. Mr. Robbins was also president of the New York Quinine and Chemical Works at No. 114 William street. He was for many years a member of the Chamber of Commerce, and served on important committees. He was a member of the New York Historical Society and the Mercantile Library, and of the principal Brooklyn charities.

Joseph T. Brown, the oldest druggist of Boston, Mass., died at his residence in Jamaica Plains, on the 23d of April, at the age of 78 years. He was born in Little Compton, R. I., and learned business in Boston with one of his three brothers, all of whom were druggists. He was greatly esteemed in his community and was connected with many societies and public organizations. He was eminently successful both as a business man and as a member of society.

Jules Emile Planchon, the French botanist, died in Paris, on the third of April, at the age of sixty-five years.

Alumni Association of the College of Pharmacy of the City of New York.—The officers elect are: President, Charles F. Heebner; First Vice-President, William Wright, Jr.; Second Vice-President, John Pfeiffer; Third Vice-President, George C. Dickman; Treasurer, Domingo Peraza; Secretary, G. A. Palmer; Registrar, L. M. Royce; Executive Board for three years, C. O. Douden and C. W. Brunner; Delegates to the Annual Meeting of the American Pharmaceutical Association to be held at Davenport, Iowa, H. U. Brunlich, John Pfeiffer, P. W. Bedford, Thomas T. Main, and Arthur F. May.

St. Louis College of Pharmacy.—The twenty-third annual meeting of this college resulted in the election of the following officers: President, F. W. Sennewald; Vice-President, Louis Schurk; Recording Secretary, G. H. Chas. Klie; Corresponding Secretary, Chas. Gietner; Treasurer, Solomon Boehm. The Board of Trustees stands as follows: H. E. Hoelke, J. E. Koch, H. Frielingsdorf, C. F. G. Meyer, Geo. Ude, and Dr. H. E. Ahlbrandt. Mr. Ude was elected Chairman.

The Alumni Association of the Louisville (Ky.) College of Pharmacy had its annual meeting and banquet on the evening of March 11th. The officers of the Association are: Oscar Dilly, President; Peter Schlosser, First Vice-President; Robt. J. Frick, Second Vice-President; Edw. Constantine, Recording Secretary, Frank Keifer, Corresponding Secretary; Phil. Heuser, Treasurer; Executive Board, Dr. B. Buckel, Otto E. Mueller, Otto Haugen, Adolph Schackner.

Philadelphia College of Pharmacy.—At the sixty-seventh commencement of this college, held March 20th, 1888, the Honorary Degree of "Master in Pharmacy" was conferred upon the following gentlemen: Professor Joseph P. Remington, William J. Jenks, and Thomas S. Wiegand.

As showing the increasing national reputation of the Philadelphia College of Pharmacy, it may be interesting to note, that of the one hundred and thirty-seven graduates who took their degrees on March 20th, 1888, one-half were from States widely separated from each other: California and Texas, Iowa and Massachusetts, South Carolina and New York, Wisconsin and Georgia; in all twenty-four States were represented.

The Estimation of Corrosive Sublimate in Dressings.

DR. KASSNER reports that the methods recently recommended for estimating the quantity of corrosive sublimate in dressings and other substances is liable to error, particularly when glycerin forms one of the other constituents. If the method of estimation is based upon a reduction of the mercuric chloride to mercurous by the use of a ferrous salt, and the rate of reduction afterwards determined by an oxidizing agent (permanganate or bichromate), the presence of glycerin will naturally render the result altogether erroneous.

The author conceived the idea that, by adding a known quantity of potassa to the mercuric chloride, he could precipitate the whole of the mercury as mercuric oxide (HgO), and subsequently determine the amount of undecomposed potassa by titration. On trying this method in practice, however, he always obtained short results, no doubt owing to the fact that some of the mercuric chloride escaped the action of the potassa, by the formation of an oxychloride of mercury. It then occurred to him to employ an *alcoholic* solution of potassa, and this was found to work satisfactorily.

A solution of 0.5 Gm. of corrosive sublimate in water was added to exactly 20 C.c. of ½ normal potassa solution, together with about 40 C.c. of water and 30 C.c. of 96-per-cent alcohol. The whole was then filled up to 100 C.c. with alcohol. The solution was filtered, and the filtrate titrated with a ½ normal acid. It was thus found that 0.5 Gm. of mercuric chloride had consumed 14.8 C.c. of ½ normal potassa solution, which corresponds to 100.18 per cent.

On repeating this process of assay in the presence of glycerin, practically the same results were obtained.

The best indicator to use in the above reaction is methyl-orange. This is neither affected by the presence of carbonic acid, nor by mercuric chloride. Besides, it would at once indicate the presence of an acid reaction in the mercuric chloride solution before the addition of the potassa, in which case, the acid would have to be previously neutralized.—*After Pharm. Post*, No. 11.

Anhydrous Chloride of Magnesium.

THE preparation of anhydrous chloride of magnesium has heretofore been connected with great technical difficulties. It is well known that this salt is one of the most hygroscopic substances known, and parts with its absorbed water only with the utmost difficulty. The usual method by which it was obtained anhydrous was to add chloride of ammonium to its aqueous solution, whereby a double chloride of magnesium and ammonium is formed, which, on heating, first loses water and, at a temperature of about 400°C., gives off chloride of ammonium, leaving anhydrous chloride of magnesium behind. Walther Hempel has found that, by passing a current of hydrochloric acid gas through a dense aqueous solution of chloride of magnesium, the whole of the water may be removed. On a small scale, this may be done by placing the salt in a crucible, with perforated cover, through which the current of acid gas is passed, while the crucible is heated.—*After Ber. D. Ch. G.*, 1888, 897.

Incompatibility of Antipyrin and Carbolic Acid.

WHEN aqueous solution of antipyrin and of carbolic acid are brought together in certain proportions, a cloudiness is produced, which, in more concentrated solutions, increases to the formation of a precipitate in form of an oily layer, consisting probably of 2 molecules of phenol and 1 molecule of antipyrin. Dr. G. Vulpius, who examined this reaction, found that a 2-per-cent solution of phenol is not rendered turbid even by twice its volume of a 1-per-cent solution of antipyrin, but by more concentrated solutions of the latter.

In practice, it is not advisable to employ carbolic acid for the purpose of sterilizing antipyrin solutions, as the addition of an amount of the former sufficient to produce sterilization would certainly cause turbidity or a precipitate.—*Pharm. Post*, No. 8.

Boric Acid as an Internal Remedy.

BORIC acid has heretofore been regarded by many authorities as a noxious agent when administered internally, some of them having reported that it gradually produces sterility, others that it injuriously affects the red corpuscles of the blood, etc.

Dr. Gaucher has recently reported to the Paris Medical Society of Hospitals the results of his experiments on rabbits, to whom he gave daily doses of 0.5 Gm. (about 8 grains) of boric acid. This did not prove toxic until after the lapse of 11 or 12 days. Accordingly, a toxic dose for man would be represented by about 75 Gm. (or about 2½ oz.) in twenty-four hours.

Encouraged by these experiences, Dr. Gaucher tried the effects of boric acid upon consumptives, in doses of 0.5 to 1 Gm. (8 to 16 grains) per day given per os. After a few days' treatment, the fetid odor of the discharges disappeared, and in two cases, the general condition of the patient improved. Not the least gastric disturbance was observed.—*Rep. de Pharm.*, No. 3.

FORMULAS AND ITEMS.

Ayer's Hair Vigor.—According to the *Pharmac. Zeitung* (No. 53), Ayer's Hair Vigor consists of a 3-per-cent solution of acetate of lead in water, containing a little glycerin and some sulphur.

Hair-Dye Pomades.—Haskovec recommends as basis for hair-dye pomades the following:

Lanolin	100 parts.
Lard	30 "
Oil of Rose Geranium, etc.	q. s.

And as dyeing agents for gray hairs which had originally been chestnut-brown:

Nitrate of Bismuth	5 parts.
Citric Acid	3 "
Glycerin	30 "

For gray hairs which had originally been black the following is recommended:

Extract of Walnut Shells	2 parts.
Pyrogallic Acid	3 "
Water	enough to dissolve.

—*After Casop. cesk. lék.*

Catarrh Cures.—*New Idea* says that the following formulas substantially represent the articles named:

Sage's Catarrh Cure.—Powdered Hydrastis, 1 oz.; Common Salt and Borax, of each 10 gr.

Ely's Cream Balm.—Carbonate of Bismuth, 15 grains; Thymol, 3 grains; Oil of Wintergreen, 3 minims; Vaseline, 1 oz.

Remedy for Coryza.—Dr. Fritsche recommends, as a remedy for coryza, to take 4 grains of salicylic acid five or six times daily, in intervals of two or three hours, and to use the following mixture for smelling:

Glacial Acetic Acid	2 parts.
Carbolic Acid	1 "
Oleobalsamic Mixture	5 "
Tincture of Musk	1 part.

A sufficient quantity of this mixture is poured upon cotton contained in a small, wide-mouthed bottle, and each nostril alternately applied to it at first every half-hour, afterwards in longer intervals, for about ten minutes each time, the vapor being inhaled. An improvement is said to occur already after a few hours, but the treatment may have to be continued for several days.—*After Berl. Klin. Wochenschr.*

Strychnine is said by T. Lauder Brunton to be a very efficient remedy for relief of sleeplessness in those who suffer from over-work or fatigue. It may be used in the form of tincture of nux vomica or granules [or tablet triturates] containing strychnine, moderate doses only being needed.

Formulas for Chapped Hands.—One which is said by the *Western Druggist* to be superior to many of the advertised articles consists of: Quince Seed, 2 oz.; Rose Water, 16 fl. oz.; Glycerin, 32 fl. oz.; Tincture of Benzoin, 2 fl. oz. Macerate the Seeds in the Rose Water twenty-four hours, strain, and add the Glycerin and Benzoin.

The following is also said to be satisfactory: Balsam of Peru, 1 dr.; Purified Wool-Fat, 1 oz.; Perfume to suit.

Lyon's Kathairon for the Hair.—Castor Oil, 1 fl. oz.; Tincture of Cantharides, 1 fl. dr.; Oil of Bergamot, 20 minims; Stronger Water of Ammonia, 1 drop; Alcohol, sufficient to make 3 fl. oz.—*New Idea.*

Van Buskirk's Fragrant Sozodont.—Alcohol, 1 fl. oz.; Water, 1½ fl. oz.; Soap, 129 grains; Oil of Wintergreen, 2 minims; Red Saunders, q. s. Dissolve the Soap in the mixture of Alcohol and Water, add the color and perfume, and then add enough Water to make 3 fl. oz.—*New Idea.*

Van Stan's Stratena.—Acetic Acid, 4 oz.; White Glue, 3 oz.; French Gelatin, 4 dr.; Shellac Varnish, 4 fl. dr.; Distilled Water, 4 fl. oz. Dissolve the Glue in the Acid with heat, and the Gelatin in water with heat. Mix the two solutions gradually until homogeneous, then add the Varnish, and put into bottles.

A Fraudulent Formula.—According to the *Chemist and Druggist*, several British chemists have been confronted by the following "Genuine Hop Compound for Bitters," advertised in the *Christian World* and elsewhere by S. Gould, a M.R.C.S., Eng., of Bradford: Hops, Assur Bark, Colru Bark, Kradna Root, Rolique Root, Noil Root, Rork Root, Tacher, 4 pieces of Lump Sugar. Upon examination, Gould's packets were found to be Hops, Burdock, Mandrake, Licorice, Dandelion, Dock, and Wild Cherry. The ingenious suggestion that the words were transposed, *e. g.*, rolique root = liquore root, noil root = (dandő) lion root, and so on, seems plausible.

Condurango is esteemed by Prof. Franz Riegel, of Giessen, as superior to other stomachics, the best form for administration being a wine.

Chewing Gum.—A western contemporary says that pure balsam Tolu and white sugar are the basis of the best chewing gums in the market. With which opinion we differ. Spruce gum is, above all things, the best chewing gum, but the majority of the chewing gums now sold have Balata gum (otherwise known as gum chicle) as their basis.

Arsenic for Warts.—Dr. B. S. Pullin reports, in the *Bristol* (Eng.) *Medico-chirurgical Journal*, several cases in which doses of 1 to 3 minims, twice daily, of liquor arsenicalis, Ph. Br., rapidly cured an outbreak of warty growths upon the hands.

Antiseptic Gargle.—The following solution is recommended for sterilizing the mouth after the teeth have been cleaned with a tooth-brush and soap.

Thymol	3½ grains
Benzoic Acid	45 "
Tincture of Eucalyptus	180 "
Water	11,250 "

M.

Asclepias syrica (milkweed) is highly recommended by Dr. B. F. Reynolds, of Smithville, Mo., as an efficient remedy for lumbago. A decoction of roots, gathered between August and April, should be used in doses of half a teacupful four or five times daily.—*Med. and Surg. Rep.*, March 31st, 1888.

Improving Cider by Freezing.—When cider is cooled to −18° to −20° C. (−4° F.) a portion of the liquid soon solidifies and the temperature rises to −3° to −4° C. (26–24° F.). The portion still liquid has a higher specific gravity than the original cider. The solidified portion melts to an almost colorless liquid, having a sp. gr. 1.0 and containing only 0.5 per cent of alcohol. Cider containing 4–5 per cent of alcohol yields on freezing a concentrated cider containing 7–8 per cent of alcohol and 60–80 Gm. dry extract per liter; this composition corresponds to that of the richest Normandy cider. Both the taste and aroma of the cider are obtained in a concentrated form by freezing it. The fermentation is slowed, but not stopped even after 212 hours.—*Compt. R. and Journ. Soc. Ch. Ind.*

A Domestic Remedy for Ivy-Poisoning.—Duffield writes to the *Scientific American* of March 24th, 1888, as follows:

For many years I suffered terribly from this cause, but, remembering that all poisons are acids, and that alkalies neutralize acids, I bathed the poisoned member in a strong lye made from wood-ashes, and obtained instant relief. Subsequently, I found that the dry ashes alone, rubbed over the poisoned member, were equally effective. Since this discovery, I have had no further trouble, and, having tried this simple remedy repeatedly on myself and on many others with like good results, I am now thoroughly convinced that wood-ashes will, in every case, prove a sure and sovereign specific for all cases of ivy-poison. [*Note by Ed. Am. Dr.*—The same object may be attained equally well, and in a much cleaner manner, by applying bicarbonate of sodium in powder.]

Gelatin Plaster Casts for Anatomical Specimens.—Some time ago, Mr. C. W. Cathcart, M.B. (Edinburgh Infirmary) proposed a new basis for making casts of anatomical specimens. The basis is made as follows: Take of "No. 1" gelatin, say six ounces, soak it till quite soft and swollen, afterward dry it slowly until just pliable. As it has now the minimum of water necessary, melt it in a water-bath and add six ounces (measure) of clear glycerin. When the two are thoroughly mixed, the material is ready. To render it opaque, add, while it is still hot, and therefore fluid, small quantities of a thick paint made by rubbing up oxide of zinc in glycerin. When a skin color is wanted, a little vermilion is required to give a warm, life-like hue. Should other things be cast, the prevailing color can be given with water color, as required (tubes of moist water color sold at two pence each will be found convenient). Several pounds of this mixture may be made at once, and portions used as required.—*Scientific American*, March 3d, 1888.

Opium in Tonquin.—*L'Economiste Français* says that some attempts made in Tonquin to cultivate opium last year under the direction of M. Frederick have produced unexpectedly good results, considering that sowing took place three months too late, and that the ground set apart for the experiment was far from favorable. It is now certain that opium of a good quality, or rather the white poppy which produces opium, will succeed capitally at Tonquin. An effort will now be made to organise its culture on an extensive scale.

Dr. Giral's Febrifuge Powder.—Sulphate of Quinine, 15 centigrammes; Arseniate of Sodium, 5 milligrammes; Pulverized Gum Acacia, 2 grammes; Carmine Lake, 5 decigrammes. Divide into 8 powders and take one, every morning, in a cup of tea.

QUERIES & ANSWERS.

Queries for which answers are desired, must be received by the 5th of the month, and must in every case be accompanied by the name and address of the writer, for the information of the editor, but not for publication.

No. 2,134.—Phosphomolybdic Acid (Ithaca).
Phosphomolybdic acid, which is used as a reagent for alkaloids, and also certain alkali metals, is prepared from the well-known yellow compound which is formed when phosphoric acid is brought into contact with molybdate of ammonium in a solution containing nitric acid. For this purpose, 1 part of molybdic acid may be dissolved in 4 parts of water of ammonia (or a sufficient quantity to neutralize the acid), and the solution is poured into 15 parts of nitric acid of spec. gr. 1.200. After standing several hours, the solution is passed through purified glass wool. The filtrate is then mixed with a quantity of phosphoric acid insufficient to decompose the whole reagent. The resulting crystalline precipitate is freed from the mother-water by the filter-pump, then washed with water, and next boiled with nitro-muriatic acid, which decomposes the ammonia group, and produces a solution of the phosphomolybdic acid. This may be obtained in yellow prisms by evaporating the solution. The prisms contain 20 molecules of water. On allowing the solution to evaporate spontaneously, the crystals will contain as much as 50 molecules of water.

No. 2,135.—Terebene (M. D.).
Our attention has recently been directed by the correspondent to some terrebene occurring in the market, which is entirely unfit for medicinal purposes, as it is simply refined oil of turpentine, with its optical properties but little, if at all, altered. This kind of terebene, when administered to patients, produces the same symptoms as common oil of turpentine. It acts as an irritant to the whole intestinal canal, produces bloody urine, etc. Unfortunately, the large majority of pharmacists do not possess the means to test medicinal terebene. The only reliable criterion here is the polariscope. Ordinary oil of turpentine (American) turns the plane of polarised light with sodium flame about 14 degrees to the right. Terebene produced from this, or any other kind of oil of turpentine, is entirely indifferent to polarised light, and should therefore fail to turn its flame either to the right or to the left.

There are, however, notable physical differences between optically active and inactive terebene. The former has a decided turpentine odor, and a most pronounced and sharp turpentine taste. Inactive terebene is much less harsh; in fact both the odor and the taste are blunted off and rendered mild. However, this is not equally realised by everybody, hence a mere examination by smell and taste is not sufficient to ascertain the quality of the substance.

No. 2,136.—Paraldehyde (Buffalo).
The compound known as paraldehyde is a peculiar modification of the aldehyde of the ethyl series, produced by the combination of several molecules, that is, by polymerization.

Ordinary ethylic aldehyde is C_2H_4O. When three molecules of this are combined together, the resulting compound —$(C_2H_4O)_3$ or $C_6H_{12}O_3$—is known as paraldehyde.

Paraldehyde is manufactured for medicinal purposes by oxidizing ethylic alcohol. Four parts of alcohol of 80° are mixed with 5 parts of manganese dioxide, 3 parts of sulphuric acid, and 4 parts of water; or 100 parts of alcohol are mixed with 150 parts of potassium bichromate and with 200 parts of sulphuric acid previously diluted with 3 times its volume of water. The mixture is distilled, the distillate warmed to 50° C. (122° F.), the vapors conducted into ether, and the solution saturated with gaseous ammonia. This causes the separation of crystalline aldehyde-ammonia, which is distilled with diluted sulphuric acid. The escaping vapor of aldehyde is conducted through a chloride of calcium tube warmed to about 22° C. (72° F.), and then through a cold condenser. The pure aldehyde thus produced is now polymerised, that is, converted into paraldehyde by adding to it small quantities of chloride of zinc and hydrochloric acid. The mixture becomes heated, and almost the whole of the aldehyde is converted into paraldehyde. The resulting product is now cooled to 0° C. (32° F.), the separated crystals collected, pressed at the same temperature, and distilled. These operations are repeated until the whole of the product distils over at the uniform temperature of 124° C. (255.2° F.).

No. 2,137.—Detection of Soda in Milk.
It is not an uncommon occurrence that dealers in milk try to hide an incipient acidulous condition of the fluid by the addition of soda. This is particularly the case in summer time, and is sometimes done to entirely fresh and normal milk, with a view of preventing its turning sour.

Though the quantity of the addition—usually consisting of carbonate or bicarbonate of sodium—is comparatively small, yet it is entirely improper. The presence of soda, when it amounts to not less than 0.1 per cent, or about 1 Gm. per liter (15 grains per quart) may be readily detected by the following process:

Mix 10 C.c. of the milk with 10 C.c. of alcohol, and a few drops of solution of rosolic acid (1 : 100). If the milk is pure it assumes only a brownish yellow color, but if either carbonate or bicarbonate of sodium are present, it will acquire a more or less distinct rose-red tint. When only a small amount of these salts is present (say 0.1 per cent), the color test will be best recognised by comparing the suspected sample with pure milk treated in the same manner. Phenolphthalein is unsuited for this test.

No. 2,138.—Detection of Antipyrin in Urine ("Emulsion").
Antipyrin has the property of being volatilised with the vapor of boiling water. This is the case, however, only when it is present in an uncombined state. When antipyrin is taken internally, a portion of it enters into some combination, which is not yet clearly made out, but seems to have a great similarity to certain copulated compounds, having sulphuric acid as one of its members. Phenol and many other substances related to this have the peculiarity of appearing in the urine as compound sulphuric acids ("phenol-sulphuric acid, etc., etc.). Ordinary tests fail to show the presence of phenol in such cases, until after the compound has been split up by hydrochloric acid or some other agent.

When urine, containing a small amount of antipyrin, is distilled, no trace of this body passes over. But it will do so promptly on boiling the urine with hydrochloric acid. If the urine contains a large proportion of antipyrin, however, most of it is present in the *free* state, and may be distilled over with water.

Urine containing free antipyrin, or the distillate obtained after the urine has been treated with hydrochloric acid, is rendered red by ferric chloride, and bluish-green by nitrite of sodium, or by moderately dilute nitrous acid, which latter is best prepared by allowing nitric acid to act upon a little starch, and diluting with water.

No. 2,139.—Detection of Saccharin in Wines or other Liquids ("Syrup").
A method recently recommended by C. S. Schmitt is the following:
Render a measured quantity, say 100 C.c. of the liquid, strongly acid by means of a dilute sulphuric acid, and then shake the liquid with three successive portions, of 50 C.c. each, of a mixture composed of equal parts of ether and petroleum ether. As soon as each of these portions has separated, it is at once removed and filtered. A little solution of soda is added to the united filtrates, and the whole then evaporated nearly to dryness. The residue is heated, in a silver or porcelain capsule during half an hour, to 250° C. (482° F.); the fused mass dissolved in water, the solution placed in a separating funnel, supersaturated with sulphuric acid, and the salicylic acid (which had been produced by the previous reaction) extracted with ether. The filtered ethereal solution is evaporated to dryness, the residue dissolved in a little water, and tested with a few drops of solution of ferric chloride. If the liquid contained saccharin, the well-known reddish-violet color, caused by salicylic acid, will make its appearance.

So small a quantity as 0.005 per cent of saccharin could still be detected by this test.

Of course, the liquid should first be tested directly for salicylic acid, and if any of this is present, it should be removed by shaking the acidulated liquid with ether, until it no longer gives any reaction for salicylic acid.

No. 2,140.—Composition of Cheese (Avenue).
According to the report of the New York State Dairy Commissioner for 1886, the composition of 79 cheeses prepared in the large factories during 1885 and 1886 was as follows (57 of these bore the State brand, that is, the official certificate of the Commissioner):

	57 Cheeses With State brand.			22 Cheeses Not branded.
	Lowest.	Highest.	Mean.	Mean.
Water, %	4.42	40.04	29.93	23.14
Fat, %	22.50	52.63	31.55	31.95
Casein, %	27.67	55.27	38.12	37.74
Ash, %	2.41	7.16	4.39	4.52
			99.98	109.35
Fat in dry mass....	26.10	55.00	43.50	44.98
Fat contained in insoluble Fat Acids..	85.90	89.80	87.64	
Fat contained in Soluble Fat Acids.....	4.20	8.87	5.32	

No. 2,141.—Ink Eraser (Sherley, Mass.).
A very efficient ink eraser may be prepared by powdering together equal quantities of citric and oxalic acids. When any ink-marks or writing are to be erased on paper, a little of the powder is carefully sprinkled over the writing, and then touched with the moistened end of a small piece of wood (a match), or the blunt end of a pen holder will answer. As soon as the ink-marks have disappeared, the moist spot is dried with blotting paper. If the ink-spots are on linen, etc., a little of the powder is placed upon it, and then enough water applied to almost dissolve it. In this case, less care is required, and the treatment may be repeated once or twice, if necessary. Of course, the method will only remove iron ink, not nigrosin ink. The latter can only be removed mechanically.

No. 2,142.—Fragrant and Antiseptic Mouth-Wash (O. S. W.).

We have published various formulas for preparing mouth-washes, the most pleasant and refreshing one being that which will be found on page 199 of our last volume. Since this was published, we have received a suggestion from a competent authority to omit the sugar, as this is liable to interfere with the antiseptic character of the liquid. We think this suggestion a good one, and now propose the following amended formula, which has been practically tested. The essential oils used in its preparation should be of the very best and freshest quality:

Safrol	360 min.
Oil of Pinus Pumilio	120 "
" Curaçao	120 "
" Vetivert	6 drops.
" Wintergreen	24 "
" Anise, Bazony	6 "
" Rose Geranium, Afr	6 "
Naphthol	60 grains.
Deodorized Alcohol	24 fld. oz.
Solution of Saccharin	1 "
Glycerin	6 "
Purified Talcum	2 tr. "
Water enough to make	6 pints.

Dissolve the essential Oils and the Naphthol in the Absolute Alcohol, add the Glycerin, the purified Talcum, and afterwards 3½ pints of Water, previously heated to a temperature of 122° F. Stopper the vessel securely, and shake the contents frequently until they are quite cold. Then filter through a netted filter, returning the first portions of the filtrate until it runs through clear, and pass enough Water through the filter to make the product measure 16 fluidounces.

The "solution of saccharin" directed in the above formula is one containing 4 grains of saccharin in the fluidrachm, which is the strength recommended by the National Formulary Committee. It is prepared as follows:

Dissolve 512 grains of Saccharin and 240 grains of Bicarbonate of Sodium in 10 fluidounces of Water (taking care that the reaction is made to take place in a sufficiently large vessel to prevent loss from the resulting effervescence), then filter the solution, add to it 4 fluidounces of Alcohol, and pass enough Water through the filter to make 16 fluidounces.

The cost of this preparation, calculated upon the basis of fair market prices for the several ingredients, is about 18 cents per pint.

No. 2,143.—Phenacetin (Subscriber).

This name has been recently applied to the substance known as para-acetphenetidin which was introduced about a year ago as an antipyretic by O. Hinsberg and Prof. Kast. We have had no experience with this agent so far, at least we have not witnessed its effects, though we have had it under our hands. Its constitution is represented by $C_6H_5.OC_2H_5.NH(CO-CH_3)$; that is, it may be regarded as the acetal-compound of the ethylic ether of para-amido-phenol. Or, it may be regarded as being derived from aniline $C_6H_5.NH_2$, where one atom of hydrogen of the NH_2 group is replaced by acetyl $(CO-CH_3)$, and 1 atom of hydrogen of the group C_6H_5, by the ether-radical OC_2H_5. The relationship of phenol, aniline, acetaniline (or antifebrin) and phenacetin will be understood by examining the following formulas:

C_6H_5	$C_6H_5.OH$	$C_6H_5\begin{cases}H\\NH_2\end{cases}$	$C_6H_5\begin{cases}H\\N(CO-CH_3)\end{cases}$
benzol	phenol	aniline	acetanilide

$C_6H_5\begin{cases}OH\\NH_2\end{cases}$	$C_6H_5\begin{cases}OC_2H_5\\NH_2\end{cases}$	$C_6H_5\begin{cases}OC_2H_5\\NH(CO-CH_3)\end{cases}$
para-amido-phenol	ethylic ether of para-amido-phenol or phenetidin	acetyl-phenetidin (para) or acetphenetidin, or phenacetin

Phenacetin is a microcrystalline powder of a faint reddish tint, odorless and tasteless, very difficultly soluble in water, more so in glycerin, and very easily in boiling alcohol. It is insoluble in acid or alkaline liquids, but is slowly absorbed when introduced into the stomach. It has been found to be a very efficient antipyretic, without any disagreeable effects, to judge from the reports so far received. It is best administered at first in a medium dose, viz., 5 grains, in order to be sure that it may not, after all, produce undesirable symptoms. And when it is to be repeated, it may then be given in full dose, viz., 10 to 12 grains.

The following reactions are given by E. Utscher (in the *Apotheker Zeit.*) for identifying this substance. On adding 1 drop of solution of ferric chloride to 30 C.c. of water containing 0.05 Gm. (ab. ¾ grains) of phenacetin, no change is produced until a gentle heat is applied, which causes a reddish tint, the same as would be produced by an equivalent quantity of acetate of sodium or of acetanilide. But if 0.05 Gm. (say ¾ gr.) of phenacetin are boiled with 1 C.c. of normal hydrochloric acid, then about 20 C.c. of water and 1 C.c. of normal potassa solution added, the further addition of 1 drop of ferric chloride solution will produce, on gentle warming, a magnificent violet tint. Sulphuric acid containing nitrous acid produces in a liquid containing phenacetin a deep brown color, while acetanilide under similar conditions scarcely shows any color at all. When treated with a few drops of fuming nitric acid, acetanilide yields a brownish-red solution, soon turning to a handsome blue, which gradually disappears; phenacetin yields a liquid having a persistent yellow color, which turns orange upon the addition of potassa.

No. 2,144.—Lipanin (Philadelphia).

This is the name applied to a new product prepared by C. A. F. Kahlbaum, of Berlin, intended to fulfil the functions of cod-liver oil in such cases where the latter is not well borne. Lipanin is, of course, a proprietary article, it having apparently become a point of honor, or rather an object of rivalry, for the different large manufacturing firms to search around for new resources of unlimited profit, by acquiring the exclusive ownership of a product largely used in medicine (for instance, antipyrin, thallin, lanolin, mollin, ichthyol, etc.) or in the arts.

Lipanin is stated to be a very fine quality of olive oil containing 6 per cent of oleic acid.

No. 2,145.—Gums used for Varnishes (K.).

This correspondent asks what "gums" are used in the manufacture of varnishes for wood work.

The so-called "gums" are of course, not *gums* in a chemical sense, but chiefly *resin*. In commercial parlance, however, they are usually classed as "gums." The number of those used for making wood varnishes is very large, and it would take too much space even to enumerate them here. We would recommend to our correspondent to procure a copy of "Die Harze und ihre Producte." Von Dr. G. Thenius. Wien (Hartleben). This will give the information desired. He may also consult the chapter on "varnish" in any of the technical encyclopædias.

No. 2,146.—Hoffman's Balsam of Life (Q).

Hoffman's Balsam of Life, or Balsamum Vitæ Hoffmanni, is the *Mistura Oleo-balsamica* of the German Pharmacopœia. It is merely a solution of certain essential oils and of balsam of Peru in alcohol. Calculating the original formula, which is in parts by weight, into the approximate equivalents by measure, the following quantities will yield a product practically equivalent with that of the Germ. Pharm. Oil of Lavender, Oil of Mace, Oil of Thyme, Oil of Lemon, Oil of Orange-flowers, of each 3 ℈.; Oil of Cloves, and Oil of Cinnamon, of each ♏ xxv.; Balsam of Peru, ♏ lxxx.; Alcohol, enough to make 16 fl. oz.

No. 2,147.—Pomade Vaseline and Vaseline Cold Cream (W. B. S.).

It is a very simple matter to prepare this. All that is necessary is to select some combination of aromatics suitable for hair preparations, and to incorporate them with vaseline. For common purposes the best grades of commercial petrolatum will answer. But when a nice preparation is wanted, vaseline should be used. The very best substance, however, is the beautiful, whitish-translucent base, known as *albolene* (for which McKesson & Robbins, of New York, are the agents).

Among the host of combinations which might be given for perfuming this or similar preparations, the following (suggested by Dieterich) may be quoted:

1. | | By weight. |
|---|---|
| Oil of Bergamot | 80 parts. |
| " Lemon | 40 " |
| " Lavender | 40 " |
| " Cassia | 4 " |
| " Cloves | 4 " |
| " Wintergreen | 2 " |
| Cumarin | 1 part. |

Mix them. When the cumarin is dissolved, set the mixture aside for several days in a cold place, and filter.

2. | | |
|---|---|
| Oil of Bergamot | 80 parts. |
| " Lemon | 40 " |
| " Lavender | 40 " |
| " Neroli | 10 " |
| " Cinnamon (Ceylon) | 4 " |
| " Cloves | 4 " |
| " Wintergreen | 2 " |
| " Ylang | 1 part. |
| Cumarin | 1 " |

3. | | |
|---|---|
| Oil of Bergamot | 60 parts. |
| " Lemon | 30 " |
| " Lavender | 20 " |
| " Neroli | 14 " |
| " Rose | 10 " |
| " Cinnamon (Ceylon) | 4 " |
| " Wintergreen | 2 " |
| " Ylang | 1 part. |
| Cumarin | 2 parts. |
| Tonquin Musk | q. s. |
| Oil of Orris | q. s. |

Mix the oils. To every 1,000 grains of the mixture add 21 drops of oil of orris, and 1½ grains of musk. Macerate eight days, then filter.

Vaseline Cold Cream may be prepared as follows:

White Wax	75 parts.
Spermaceti	75 "
Oil of Almonds, expressed	450 "
Vaseline	300 "
Distilled Water	300 "
Borax	10 "
Flavoring	q. s.

The flavoring recommended by Dieterich is composed as follows: Oil of Rose, 20 drops; Oil of Bergamot, 20 drops; Oil of Rose Geranium (French), 5 drops; Oil of Rhodium, 2 drops; Oil of Orris, 2 drops; Tincture of Civet (1 : 10), 5 drops; Cumarin, ½ grain. 24 drops of this mixture are to be added for every 16 avoirdupois ounces of cold cream to be obtained. The manipulation is the same as that for the officinal Unguentum Aquæ Rosæ.

By substituting *albolene* here likewise, the product will be perfectly white.

No. 2,148.—**Sherbet Powders** (K. G. K.).

These are simply flavored lemonade powders, and may be produced in various ways, with a variety of flavors. Cooley gives the following formula, on what authority we do not know:

Orange peel powdered, 12 grains; bicarbonate of sodium, 3½ av. oz.; oil of cedrat [oil of Citrus medica], 12 drops; oil of orange peel, 60 drops; tartaric acid, 4 oz. Dry each powder carefully by itself, then mix the whole quickly and put in a bottle, which must be securely stoppered.

We should imagine that, by grating the peel of fresh oranges and lemons against loaf-sugar, and then reducing this to powder, a finer aroma could be imparted.

No. 2,149.—**Mountain Balm.**

One of our correspondents writes to us from Philadelphia that he has recently on several occasions ordered "mountain balm," meaning the Eriodictyon Californicum or Yerba Santa, from wholesale houses, and that he has in each case received the *Red Mountain Balm*, viz., Monarda didyma. He desires to know whether this has occurred to any of our other readers.

We can state that we have ascertained, upon inquiry made among dealers in crude drugs, that it is customary to designate the Monarda didyma as "Mountain Balm" in the trade and price-lists. There is a certain custom prevailing in the nomenclature of crude drugs which has undergone but little alteration. If the Eriodictyon Californicum is required, we advise our correspondent to order it either by that name, or, perhaps better, by the name "Yerba Santa." He will then obtain what he wants.

No. 2,150.—**Chandler's Chlorodyne** (D. F. S.).

As is well known, there is not one among the many formulæ heretofore proposed to make a preparation equivalent to chlorodyne which does not produce a materially different result. That known as Chandler's forms no exception to this rule, but is perhaps more frequently used than others at the present time. The formula is as follows:

Hydrochlorate of Morphine	gr. 16
Alcohol	fl. dr. 10
Glycerin	fl. dr. 18
Fluid Extr. of Cannabis Indica	fl. dr. 4
Chloroform	fl. dr. 4
Tincture of Capsicum	min. 32
Oil of Peppermint	min. 16

The formula which has been worked out by the National Formulary Committee, and which will soon be at the disposal of the profession by the appearance of the work, is believed to be the most rational and satisfactory so far produced. As it is expected that the Formulary will be out before the appearance of our *next* issue, we refer our readers to the work itself.

No. 2,151.—**Hall's Solution of Strychnine** (S.).

The following formula is that most generally used. The quantity of Acetic Acid is often given differently, mostly larger; but Dr. Hall himself used only a dilute acid, and besides, changed the proportions repeatedly.

Acetate of Strychnine	4 grains
Diluted Acetic Acid	60 minims
Alcohol	1 fl. oz
Compound Tincture of Cardamom	15 minims
Water, enough to make	4 fl. oz.

The mixture should be allowed to stand, exposed to the light, during a few days, so that all the coloring matter which cannot be retained in solution may precipitate. It may then be filtered, and will remain clear for a long time.

The dose of this preparation is from 5 to 20 minims, or more, if necessary, to be used with caution.

No. 2,152.—**"Four-per-cent Solution"** (Junior).

We are asked the question: "What is a 4-per-cent solution? Is it 4 grains of cocaine (or any other soluble substance) to 100 grains of water? Or about 40 grains to 2 fluidounces of water?"

This question has been raised repeatedly of late, and we are glad to have an opportunity of stating our views regarding it.

When speaking of *percentage*, it is necessarily implied that the proportion, existing *in* 100 parts or corresponding *to* 100 parts, should be given in the same designation of *either* weight or measure.

If both the fractional part and the whole product are *liquid*, there may be a doubt engendered, as to whether *weight* or *measure* is intended. For instance, when we speak of "80 per cent alcohol." This, of course, means an alcoholic liquid, containing 80 per cent of absolute alcohol, and 20 per cent of water. But it still remains uncertain whether weight or measure is meant. To remove any doubt, it is necessary to specify either "by weight" or "by measure" in such cases.

When, however, one of the two substances, either the fractional part or the whole product is a *solid*, it is necessary to discard the *measure* and to confine one's self exclusively to *weight*. Both the liquid and the solid can be weighed. But only *one* of them could be measured. Hence, to quote the example mentioned by our correspondent, a 4-per-cent solution of a solid in water must necessarily be one which contains 4 parts of the solid in 100 parts, or in other words, every 100 grains of which contain 4 grains of the solid. There is no possible way of getting a *measure* in here.

Our correspondent commits a very common error—possibly only a slip of the pen—by using the expression: "Is it 4 grains of cocaine (etc.) *to* 100 grains of water." A solution thus prepared would, of course, weigh 104 grains, and consequently it would *not* contain 4 per cent of cocaine. A true 4-per-cent solution is made by dissolving 4 grains of the solid in 96 grains of water, the product weighing 100 grains.

Whenever the solution of a solid substance is prescribed in terms of percentage, this *is always* to be understood as being by *weight*.

Two fluidounces of water weigh about 911 grains. If 40 grains of cocaine were dissolved *in* 2 fluidounces of water, the product would weigh 951.4 grains, and would really contain only 3.8 per cent of the solid in solution.

To mention other examples, belonging here, we read of 1% solutions of corrosive sublimate, 1% solutions of nitroglycerin, 5% solutions of carbolic acid, etc., etc. *All* of these are presumed to be made by *weight*. In practice, it is certainly more easy to make them by weight than by measure. Tare a bottle, place into the proper weight of the solid and then add enough of the liquid to make up the final weight.

No. 2,153.—**Saccharin** (C. A. W.).

This substance, the chemical name of which is anhydro-ortho-sulphamine-benzoic acid, and which is now manufactured on a large scale under the patents of Fahlberg and List, may be procured from any wholesale dealers of drugs in the country.

No. 2,154.—**Analytical Balance** (Mass.).

It is very difficult to advise any one regarding the purchase of an analytical balance, if the advice is hampered by conditions, or when it is not known what kind of work is expected to be done with the balance. It is certainly much more preferable to write to makers or dealers in balances, and to ask them to send a catalogue or price list. This will give more practical information than any advice we could give here. Our correspondent may consult the index of advertisements under "Scales."

No. 2,155.—**Tasteless Syrup of Iodide of Iron** (Brockton, Mass.).

What is called tasteless syrup of iodide of iron contains the iron in a condition differing from that of the officinal syrup. The latter contains 10 per cent, by weight, of the green ferrous iodide (proto-iodide), while the so-called tasteless preparation contains the red ferric iodide (sesqui-iodide). It is also customary to make the latter weaker than the former, the most usual formula making the tasteless syrup contain about 3.5 grains of ferric iodide in each fluidrachm, while the officinal syrup contains about 8 grains of ferrous iodide. If the proportion of *metallic* iron in the two preparations is compared, the syrup of ferrous iodide (U. S. P.) represents about 1.44 grains in each fluidrachm, and the syrup of ferric iodide ("tasteless") about 0.46 grains. It would be pharmaceutically possible to raise the strength of the latter so as to equal the former in *iron*, but this would render the preparation too irritating; at least, it would require the administration of a smaller dose at a time. And, besides, it could then scarcely be designated any longer as tasteless. The best formula for preparing the tasteless syrup is the following:

Iodine	400 grains.
Iron Wire, fine and cut	200 "
Citrate of Potassium	630 "
Sugar	10 troy oz.
Distilled Water, enough to make	16 fl. oz.

Mix the Iron with 4 fluidounces of Distilled Water in a flask, add 267 grains of the Iodine, and apply a gentle heat until the Iodine is combined and the solution has acquired a greenish color. Then heat the contents of the flask to boiling, filter the liquid, and wash the filter with ½ fl. oz. of hot Distilled Water. To the hot filtrate add the Citrate of Potassium, and afterwards the Iodine, and agitate until the liquid has assumed a greenish color. Pour this upon the Sugar contained in a bottle, agitate until solution has been effected, and, when the liquid is cold, add enough Distilled Water to make 16 fluidounces.

No. 2,156.—**Chicle** (R.).

Chicle, also known by the name *balata*, *zapoto*, is the dry milky juice of *Sapota Muelleri*, a member of the Sapotaceous family so largely represented in the tropics. In Mexico, where this particular tree is at home, it is called *zapoto chica* or *zapotillo*, and the native Indian name is *riconzopotl.* The "gum" is sometimes called "bully tree gum," "tuno," or "leche de popa." The designation "gum" is scientifically incorrect, as it really belongs under the class of resins, variety caoutchouc. It is not a spontaneous oxidation, but is obtained by running a belt around the tree in a cork-screw fashion, beginning at the ground, and making only about 1 or 1½ turns all around. The sap or milk is received in vessels placed below. This is boiled to drive out the water, and it is then cast in blocks varying in weight from 1 to 25 pounds, in which shape it comes into the market.

Chicle, or "gum chicle," has been found specially serviceable as an ingredient in the rubber composition for porous and other rubber plasters, as an ingredient of certain kinds of chewing gum, and as an excellent insulating medium for electric wires. It also resists the action of ozone better than any other known substance, and for this reason, tubing made of chicle, or mainly of this substance, are very serviceable when ozonised air is to be conducted through it.

No. 2,157.—Chromatizing Catgut (J. F. L. Co.).

Regarding chromatizing catgut, we would say that the best surgeons in this country and in Europe have long given up its practice, as it is dangerous, owing to the weakening effect of the chromic acid upon the catgut, thereby rendering it liable to break at critical moments, and to cause death of the patient by secondary hemorrhage from a tied artery.

At Bellevue Hospital and in all the other large hospitals in New York City, the use of chromatized catgut has long been abandoned. The only kind now used is that which is prepared by soaking the *very best* raw catgut (violin or banjo strings of suitable size) in oil of juniper for twenty-four hours, and afterwards preserving it in alcohol.

There is no excuse for practising economy in the quality of the catgut. Only the *very best* should be used, as the life of a patient will often depend upon the soundness of an artery-ligature.

If chromatized catgut *must* be prepared, then Lister's original method is probably the best.

Dissolve 1 part of chromic acid in 4,000 parts of water, and add 200 parts of pure carbolic acid. Into this solution at once introduce 200 parts by weight of the catgut to be prepared, and macerate it for forty-eight hours. Then take it out, dry it quickly, and keep it in a solution of 1 part of carbolic acid in 5 parts of some bland oil (olive or cotton-seed oil).

No. 2,158.—Removing Mildew Spots (R. & Co.).

To remove mildew spots from fabrics, the most reliable way that we know of is to treat the spots with a clear filtered solution of chloride of lime, or with a solution of Labarraque, which is to be applied for a short time, depending on the depth of the stain or the quality of the fabric. Very delicate fabrics, including silk, will not stand a strong solution; in such cases, it should be diluted with water. It is also advisable to use a preliminary treatment with commercial solution of peroxide of hydrogen, after which the spots may often be removed by washing with soda and water, or one of the above-mentioned bleaching liquids may be applied before finally washing. Some mildew spots are very obstinate. If the fabric was pure white, the bleaching process will usually succeed. The farther from pure white the tint of the fabric is, the less successful will be the operation.

Formulas asked for.

1. Harriet Hubbard Ayer's Face Powder.
2. Recamier Cream.
3. Shiloh's Consumption Cure and Vitalizer.
4. Cosmetic Lotion (Palmer's).

CORRESPONDENCE.

Pharmacopœial Titles.

DEAR SIR:—Since the revision of the U. S. Pharmacopœia of 1880, I have not observed one package of chemicals or alkaloids properly labelled according to the revised edition. I have especially noticed packages from manufacturing chemists. Can we not correct this fault?

Yours truly,
Bempona, Mass. J. E. McKEON.

Prescription Charge.

Editor AMERICAN DRUGGIST.

DEAR SIR:—I send herewith the copy of a prescription which I have been asked to put up, provided I could do so for $1.40. I told the person who offered it that $2.50 was the least I would do it for. Here is the ℞:

Camphor.....................................	ij.
Oil of Origanum.............................	iv.
Oil of Wormwood.............................	ij.
Olive Oil....................................	iv.
Water of Ammonia............................	ij.
Alcohol.....................................	Oij.

The actual cost of this I figure at about $2.00, and how any druggist can prepare it for $1.40 and make anything out of it I cannot comprehend. Possibly some of your readers can enlighten me.

I contend that no druggist could compound it and put in all the articles at that price, and that this goes to show the disadvantage an honest and conscientious druggist has as against an unscrupulous one who, no doubt, leaves out the whole or a part of the oil of wormwood, which is the most expensive ingredient, costing 50 cents per ounce for American, and $1.25 for French.

Yours respectfully,
Chester, Pa., April 11th, 1888. F. E. E. H.

[Our correspondent may have been deceived in the statement that some other man had supplied it for $1.40. It is not unlikely that this was purely a product of the would-be purchaser's imagination, and that he meant $2.40. In a similar case, it would be well to find out the name of the man who is alleged to have made such a charge and ascertain if it was reported correctly. In the event of your having another case of the same kind, might it not be well to get out your prices-current and show the customer that you can't sell drugs for less money than you pay for them, and that any one who professes to do so must either be a fraud or a very charitable person?—ED. AM. DRUG.]

Effect of Cocaine on Leeches.

DEAR SIR:—It may interest some of your readers to learn of an incident lately experienced by the writer.

A physician, while treating a patient, prescribed a five-per-cent sol. cocaine, to be applied with a camel-hair brush; also two leeches.

The doctor applied the sol. cocaine to his patient on the part affected and wiped the part dry, then forced the leeches alternately to their required duty, which they failed to perform, and were returned to me lifeless. Well, two more were supplied, very nice ones, and returned in the same condition as those formerly.

Then came the much-annoyed and vexed physician, saying: "When I send for leeches, I don't want embryos. My time is too valuable to be fooled away these busy times," etc.

At first, not knowing that the leeches were applied to the parts directly absorbing the sol. cocaine, I said nothing. Finally, questioning the circumstances, the doctor could see the point without glasses. M. E. J.

Cincinnati College of Pharmacy.

Editor of the AMERICAN DRUGGIST.

DEAR SIR:—The annual meeting of the Alumni Association of the Cincinnati College of Pharmacy was held February 16th, at which the following officers were elected: President, Edw. Muehlburg; First Vice-President, A. W. Bain; Second Vice-President, Chas. J. Kaefer; Recording Secretary, E. H. W. Stahlhuth; Corresponding Secretary, A. Wetterstroem; Treasurer, Emil Henn; Executive Board, L. W. Sauer, C. J. Kaefer, H. Serodino, and C. A. Fieber; Entertainment Committee, C. J. Kaefer, Edw. Muehlburg, E. H. W. Stahlhuth, W. F. Schell, and C. J. Lammert; Committee on Queries, L. W. Sauer, C. J. Kaefer, and O. E. Plath.

A banquet was tendered the graduating class at the Highland House, which was participated in by the Alumni and invited guests.

At a special meeting March 14th, the Alumni met to discuss two bills which were introduced into the House and Senate respectively, relating to the practice of pharmacy in this State. The latter was a bill which had been reported favorably by the Senate committee; it was an amendment to section 4,407 repealing the original section and virtually re-enacting it, thereby opening a way for persons three years in the drug business to become registered without examination.

The Alumni immediately appointed a committee, consisting of Messrs. Bain, Muehlburg, and Kaefer, to go to Columbus and defeat the bill by all fair means.

At a subsequent meeting the committee reported that they had had an audience before the Hamilton County delegation, and pointed out the dangers to the pharmacy law in the bill, and so impressed the delegation with their opinions that it was defeated the day it came to a vote.

The House bill allowing physicians of five years' practice to become pharmacists is laid over for the time being.

Respectfully yours,
ALBERT WETTERSTROEM,
Cor. Sec'y Alumni C. C. P.
Cincinnati, Ohio, March 28th, 1888.

Denver School of Pharmacy.—The Denver (Colorado) University has added a department of Pharmacy, which will open in September next.

Nobel, the famous inventor of dynamite, recently died at Cannes, on the Mediterranean.

BIBLIOGRAPHY.

PRACTICAL MICROSCOPY. A Course of Normal Histology for Students and Practitioners of Medicine by MAURICE N. MILLER, M.D., Director of the Department of Normal Histology in the Loomis' Laboratory, University of the City of New York. Illustrated with 136 Photographical Reproductions of the Author's Own Drawings. New York: William Wood & Co., 1887; pp. 217, 8vo.

ASIDE from the general excellence of this work, there is nothing in it which calls for special comment in this connection, unless it be to express the regret that the author did not embrace the opportunity for giving a more complete list of the various reagents and fluids employed in microscope work, which now have to be sought for in numerous publications.

We observe some carelessness in the selection of language, which should be corrected in another edition.

ESSENTIALS OF CHEMISTRY AND TOXICOLOGY, for the use of Students in Medicine, by R. A. WITTHAUS, A.M., M.D., etc. New York: William Wood & Co., 1888, pp. 294. (3d ed.) $1.00.

AN INDEX OF MATERIA MEDICA WITH PRESCRIPTION WRITING. Including Practical Exercises. By CHARLES H. MAY, M.D., and CHARLES F. MASON, M.D. New York: William Wood & Co., 1887, pp. 267, $1.00.

THESE two works belong to the series of Wood's Pocket Manuals and embrace facts which are of leading importance and which, in larger works, are difficult of access on account of the amount of relevant matter with which they are accompanied. They are quite as well suited to the wants of pharmaceutical as of medical students, and their convenient size enables them to be kept at hand during laboratory work and lectures, when the information they give is most opportune and most easily remembered.

600 MEDICAL DON'TS or the Physician's Utility Enchanced. By FRED. C. VALENTINE, M.D., etc. New York: G. W. Dillingham. London: S. Low, Son & Co., 1887, pp. 144.

OF all the books that we have seen composed of medical axioms, this is by far the best. Too many of this class of hand-books have been the work of persons dominated by an -ism or a -pathy, and are correspondingly unreliable as authorities; this one, however, shows no evidence of such a bias, but is full, from cover to cover, of practical suggestions and uncommon good sense. The usefulness of many physicians would, without doubt, be greatly enchanced, by observing the truths which this little manual contains in the advice given to their patrons, and non-professional readers would likewise increase their chances of a long and comfortable life by following its precepts.

TOILET MEDICINE. A Popular Scientific Manual on the Correction of Bodily Defects and the Improvement and Preservation of Personal Appearance; together with Formulæ for all the Special Preparations Recommended. Second Edition. By EDWARD WOOTON, B.Sc., etc. New York: J. H. Vail & Co., 1888, pp. 114, 8vo.

IN many respects, this is a useful book, but it contains too little matter relating to the subject implied by its title, and too much of wholly irrelevant matter, or of matters which are not suitable for use by non-professional persons. Moreover, much of the information and advice given is not consistent with the views of medical men at the present time, and, in a few instances, might result, if followed, in injury.

Bulletin of Medical Societies.—The following bulletin of medical meetings of National and State Associations, compiled by the *Medical Standard*, will be serviceable to intending exhibitors of pharmaceutical products.

ASSOCIATION.	PRESIDENT.	SECRETARY.	PLACE AND TIME OF MEETING.	LOCAL SECRETARY.
Am. Climatological	A. L. Loomis, New York	J. B. Walker, Philadelphia		
Am. Dermatological	I. E. Atkinson, Baltimore	G. H. Tilden, Boston		
Am. Genito-Urinary	E. L. Keyes, New York	R. W. Taylor, New York		
Am. Gynæcological	R. Battey, Rome, Ga	J. T. Johnson, Washington, D.C.	Boston, September 21	
Am. Insane Hospital	E. Grissom, Raleigh, N. C.	J. Curwen, Warren, Pa.	Old Point Comfort, Va.	
Am. Laryngological	R. P. Lincoln, New York	D. B. Delevan, New York		
Am. Medical Associa'n	A. Y. P. Garnett, Washington	W. B. Atkinson, Philadelphia	Cincinnati, May 8	
Am. Neurological	J. J. Putnam, Boston	Græme Hammond, New York		
Am. Ophthalmological	W. F. Norris, Philadelphia	W. F. Wadsworth, Boston	New London, July 19	
Am. Orthopædic	N. M. Shaffer, New York	L. H Sayre, New York		
Am. Otological	J. S. Prout, Brooklyn, N. Y.	B. J. J. Vermyne, New Bedford, Mass.	New London, July 19	
Am. Public Health	G. M. Sternberg, Baltimore	I. N. Watson, Concord, N. H		
Am. Rhinological				
Am. Surgical	D. H. Agnew, Philadelphia	J. R. Weist, Richmond		
Cong. Physicians and Surgeons	J. S. Billings, Washington	W. H. Carmalt, New York	Washington, September 18	
STATE SOCIETIES.				
Alabama	E. B. Sholl, Birmingham	T. A. Means, Montgomery	Montgomery, April 11	B. S. Baldwin.
Arkansas	W. P. Hart, Washington	L. P. Gibson, Little Rock	Fort Smith, April 25	L. L. Saunders.
California	R. H. Plummer, San Francisco	W. A. Briggs, Sacramento	San Francisco, April 15	C. G. Kenyon.
Colorado	S. E. Solly, Colorado Springs	S. A. Fish, Denver	Colorado Springs, June 19	R. F. Adams.
Connecticut	F. Bacon, New Haven	S. B. St. John, Hartford	New Haven, May 23	W. Y. Carmalt.
Dakota				
Delaware	J. H. Hopkins, Milton	C. R. Layton, Georgetown	Georgetown, June 8	C. R. Layton.
Florida				
Georgia	A. G. Whitehead, Waynesboro	A. B. Ashworth, Atlanta	Rome, April 18	
Illinois	W. O. Ensign, Rutland	D. W. Graham, Chicago	Rock Island, May 15	C. Truesdale.
Indiana	S. H. Charlton, Seymour	E. S. Elder, Indianapolis	Indianapolis, June 5	M. Rowe.
Iowa	J. C. Hinsey, Ottumwa	S S Lytle, Iowa City	Des Moines, May 16	J. M. Emmert.
Kansas	L. A. Buck, Peabody	J. E. Minney, Topeka	Topeka, May 1	W. S. Lindsay.
Kentucky	J. G. Brooks, Paducah	J. S. Bailey, Stanford	Crab Orchard Springs, July 4	J. G. Brooks.
Louisiana	J. Jones, New Orleans	P. B. McCutcheon, N. O.	Monroe, April 21	
Maryland		T. Barton Brune, Baltimore		
Massachusetts	T. H. Gage, Worcester	F W. Goss, Boston	Boston, June 12	J. B. Swift.
Michigan	T. A. McGraw, Detroit	G. Duffield, Detroit	Detroit, June 14	H. O. Walker.
Minnesota	C. F. McComb, Duluth	C. H. Witherle, St. Paul	St. Paul, June 21	A. E. Senker.
Mississippi	S. L. Quice, Natchez	W. K. Todd, Clinton	Jackson, April 18	J. F. Hunter.
Missouri	F. J. Lutz, St. Louis	J. H. Duncan, Kansas City	Kansas City	
Nebraska	G. H. Peebles, David City	A. S. V. Mansfelde, Ashland	Lincoln	
Nevada				
New Hampshire	S. W. Roberts, Wakefield	G. P. Conn, Concord	Concord, June 19	J. A. Watson.
New Jersey	J. W. Ward, Trenton	W. Pierson, Orange	Lake Hopatcong, June 7	J. G. Ryerson.
New York	S. B. Ward, Albany	W. M. Smith, Syracuse	Albany, February 5, 1889	F. C. Curtis.
N. Y. Association				
North Carolina	T. S Haigh, Fayetteville	J. M. Baker, Tarboro	Fayetteville, May 8	
Ohio	S. F. Forbes, Toledo	G. Callahan, Toledo	Columbus, June 6	
Oregon	K. A. J. McKenzie, Portland	C. Strong, Portland	Portland, June 12	
Pennsylvania	R. J Levis, Philadelphia	W. B. Atkinson, Philadelphia	Philadelphia	J. H. Packard.
Rhode Island				
South Carolina	T. Simons	J. L. Dawson	Columbia, April 14	
Tennessee	P. D. Sims, Chattanooga	A. Morrison, Nashville	Knoxville	S. Cheatham.
Texas	S. R. Burroughs	F. E. Daniels, Austin	Austin, April 18	
Utah				
Vermont	E. R. Campbell, Bellows Falls	D. C. Hawley, Burlington	St. Albans, June 26	D. C. Hawley.
Virginia	B. Blackford, Lynchburg	L. B. Edwards, Richmond	Norfolk, November	
Washington Territory	E. L. Smith, Seattle	C. H. Merrick, Seattle		
West Virginia	L. S. Bruck, Morgantown	J. L. Fulterton, Charleston	Huntington, May 16	J. D. Myers.
Wisconsin	L. G. Armstrong, Boscobel	J. T. Reeve, Appleton	Milwaukee, May 1	

American Druggist

Vol. XVII. No. 6.   NEW YORK, JUNE, 1888.   Whole No. 168.

[ORIGINAL COMMUNICATION.]

MENTHA AND UVA URSI.

BY JOSEPH SCHRENK.

MENTHA.—In his work on the anatomy of officinal leaves and herbs,* A. Meyer remarks on *Mentha piperita* and *M. viridis:* "The anatomical characteristics are little distinctive." I think that the occurrence of menthol crystals in the glandular hairs of *Mentha piperita*, and their absence in those of *M. viridis*, will enable us to distinguish the smallest fragments of the two drugs with almost absolute certainty. I have examined the leaves of spearmint collected in various localities, and was unable to detect any of the prismatic, needle-like crystals of menthol, which are found, sometimes singly, but most frequently in large conglomerations, in almost every glandular hair of *M. piperita*. As the crystals are doubly refractive, they can be seen very easily by means of the polariscope. In ordinary light it is often impossible to distinguish them. A fragment of the leaf is soaked in water, and may then be examined without any further preparation with a ¼ or ½ in. objective.

It is remarkable how long these crystals will remain in the dried leaves. Fragments from an herbarium speci-

authors, however,* consider it as a form of *M. aquatica*, L., of which species Wittstein† remarks, that "of all the German mints it is probably the most efficient and hardly inferior to *M. piperita*. Further investigations will show whether the leaves of this variety *crispa* (*i. e.*, of *M. aquatica*) always contain menthol crystals or not, and whether, in case they do, the varieties of other species ought to be rejected. Thus far a few samples of the commercial imported "Folia menthæ crispæ" obtained from different sources have given entirely negative results.

It seems to be doubtful if the crystals in the glands of *M. piperita* are pure menthol. Chemically pure menthol appears of a clear white in polarized light, while the crystals in the glands of *mentha* are distinctly yellow. This color might be caused by the oil in which the crystals are imbedded and through which the light has to pass; but even when the oil is removed the yellow color remains. More remarkable, however, is the fact that alcohol, in which menthol is easily soluble, does not dissolve the crystals, for leaves that have been kept in alcohol for

Fig. 2.

Explanation of the Figures.—Fig. 1.—Upper part of inflorescence, in August, of *Mentha piperita* L. Fig. 2.—The same, of *Mentha viridis* L. Fig. 3.—Hair on leaf margin of *A. Uva ursi.* Fig. 4.—Lower cell of a hair, with adjoining epidermis cells. Fig. 5.—Junction of the two cells of hair.

men gathered in Europe in 1827 contain them in as perfect a condition as leaves of plants collected quite recently.

The pharmacognostical descriptions of Mentha refer to the histology of the *leaves* only. But as, according to our pharmacopœia, the *tops* also belong to the drug, it is perhaps worth while mentioning that the bracts of the inflorescence, as well as the calyx of *M. piperita*, are beset with numerous glands containing oil and menthol crystals. Even the lobes of the corolla are sparingly glandular on their outer surface.

Of other species examined (*rotundifolia, aquatica, arvensis, sativa, canadensis*) the only one which exhibited menthol crystals was *Mentha aquatica* L., both the type and the variety *crispa*. A specimen of the former, gathered in Germany about 1840, gave the same results as the leaves of its variety collected on Long Island in 1878, and those of an interesting hybrid of *M. piperita × aquatica*, obtained from C. Müller and W. Retsdorff (of the Berlin Agricult. Inst.).

In the German pharmacopœia "Folia menthæ crispæ" takes the place of our "mentha viridis" (which is considered as an adulteration of *M. piperita*). There seems to be considerable diversity of opinion in regard to this variety "*crispa*," for, on consulting the authorities, we find that no less than *five* species are mentioned, each furnishing a variety of that name.‡ The majority of the

several weeks have still retained them. Even heating in water up to the boiling point does not affect them, while menthol melts at about 40° C. Continued boiling, however, will remove them, although even then some glands will exhibit groups of unchanged crystals.

A peculiar difference in the inflorescence of the two species seems to have escaped notice thus far. With both,

Fig. 3.   Fig. 4.   Fig. 5.

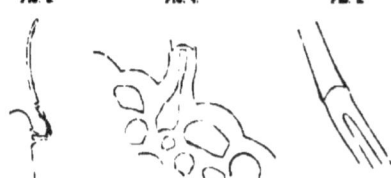

the spike of flowers terminating the main stem is much higher than all the lateral ones, at the *earlier* stage of flowering, in July. But when the terminal spike of *Mentha piperita* has done flowering (in August), it is soon overtaken and even overtopped by the lateral, lower branches, so that the upper part of the cymose inflorescence assumes the appearance of a corymb (Fig. 1). *Mentha viridis* does not behave in that manner, the terminal spike always remaining much higher than all the others (Fig. 2). Along the side of a brook in Washington County, N. Y., where the two species grow intermingled in greatest abundance,

---

* "Anatomische Charakteristik offic. Blätter und Kräuter," p. 39.
† A. Meyer, l. c.
‡ Lanessan (the Ph. d. Pharm. germ... p. 100) considers it merely as a form of *M. piperita*, var. *glabrata*. Wittstein (Pharmacogn. d. Pfl.; p. 540), says that the "crispa" is bolstered to be a variety of *M. viridis*, and the Linnean *M. crispa*, a variety of *M. aquatica*. In Husemann and Hilger's Pflanzenstoffe we find it mentioned as *M. sylvestris* var. *crispa*. Hager (Comm. z. Pharm. germ.; p. 732) gives the following synonyms: *M. crispa* L., syn *M. aquatica* L., var. *crispa* Benth. *M. crispa* Unger, syn. *M. sylvestris*, var. *crispa* Benth. *M. crispata* Schrader, syn. *M. viridis* L., var. *crispa* Benth. There is also a *M. arvensis*, var. *d crispa*, Benth., etc., etc.

* Amongst them Flückiger, Pharmacogn., p. 646, and Mohme, Lehrb. d. Pharmacogn., p. 187.
† L. c.

I could tell the individuals belonging to either, by the difference described, from a considerable distance. Some herbarium specimens of *M. piperita* and also of *M. aquatica* that I have seen since show the same habit. It would be of interest to learn if the same observation was or will be made by others in different localities.

Uva Ursi.—In his treatise on leaves cited above, A. Meyer states[*] that he found it impossible to detect the "one-celled, thin-walled hairs" on the leaves of Arctostaphylos Uva ursi Sprengel mentioned by Wiegand,† and that leaves from very different sources, and at various stages, were examined without any affirmative result. Even scars left by the falling off of hairs are said to be wanting. Vogl, in his beautiful "Anat. Atlas zur Pharmacognosie" (1887), does not mention or figure any hairs either.‡

I am unable to account for the difference in the results arrived at by such accurate observers as the authorities mentioned and those which I obtained. Leaves of Uva ursi collected by the writer in different localities, as well as those of the commercial drug, were found to possess abundant hairs on and near the margin, and along the midrib and its principal branches. The younger leaves, of course, and those from herbarium specimens, exhibited the hairs in greater profusion than the old ones or those of commerce; but even in the latter cases, their former abundant occurrence could be safely inferred from the scars they had left.

These hairs are not one-celled, however, but consist invariably of two cells (Fig. 3). The lower is of varying length, sometimes quite short, but sometimes one-third of the length of the entire hair (which is frequently one millimeter). It has very thick, cuticularized walls (Fig. 4), and is jointed to the long, thin-walled, and tapering upper cell (Fig. 5); this easily breaks off, so that, after much handling, only the lower cells remain which are wedged in between the strongly cuticularized walls of the epidermis cells. The hairs are either straight or curved or undulating in various ways.

[ORIGINAL COMMUNICATION.]

CARBOLATE OF MERCURY.

BY CHARLES ALBUS, PH.G., LOUISVILLE, KY.

Syn.: Phenol-Mercury, Phenate of Mercury, Hydrargyrum Carbolatum.

HAVING made numerous experiments to ascertain the best method of preparing this new compound of mercury, I give the following process which I found to be the best one:

Bichloride of Mercury.................271 grains
Carbolate of Potassium (Phenol-Potassium)..264 "
Alcohol,
Distilled Water, } each a sufficient quantity.
Carbolic Acid,

Dissolve the Bichloride of Mercury in 8 fl. oz. of Alcohol. Into this pour the Carbolate of Potassium, previously dissolved in 8 fl. oz. of Alcohol; then add about ½ fluidrachm of Carbolic Acid and set the mixture aside for 36 hours, with frequent agitation. The precipitate first formed has an orange-red color, changing in the course of 36 hours, to white. It is then put on a filter and washed with distilled water until the washings cease to give a violet-blue color with ferric chloride (showing absence of free carbolic acid) and a white precipitate with nitrate of silver (showing absence of any chloride). Finally, wash the precipitate with Alcohol, allow it to drain, and dry it by a gentle heat (between 90° and 100° F.).

Properties.—As thus obtained, it is a white amorphous powder, odorless and tasteless; insoluble in water, very sparingly soluble in alcohol, scarcely soluble in cold, but readily soluble in boiling hydrochloric acid. When strongly heated, it first gives off water, and is then decomposed, yielding, as decomposition products, metallic mercury, carbon, then some non-inflammable gases, and, lastly, some inflammable gases which burn with a bright, luminous flame.

Tests.—When treated with nitric acid and heated, it produces a permanent blood-red solution. If the powder be dissolved in boiling hydrochloric acid, and then 1 part of this solution be treated with solution of soda, a yellow precipitate falls.

If to another portion some solution of iodide of potassium be added, a bright red precipitate falls, soluble in an excess of the iodide.

If a copper coin be immersed in another portion, a coating of metallic mercury on the coin takes place.

On agitating a portion of the compound with water, the latter should remain unaffected by test-solution of nitrate of silver (absence of chlorides).

[Regarding phenol-potassium, see our vol. for 1887, p. 94.]

General Antidote.—Where the nature of a poison is unknown, the following is recommended: Equal parts of calcined magnesia, wood charcoal, and hydrated oxide of iron, with a sufficient quantity of water.—*Rundschau.*

---
* P. 6.
† "Pharmacognosie," p. 269.
‡ The anatomical structure of "Folia Uva Ursi" is illustrated on Plates 6 and 7.

[ORIGINAL COMMUNICATION.]

A DELICATE TEST PAPER FOR HYDROCHLORIC ACID.

BY S. J. HINSDALE, OF FAYETTEVILLE, N. C.

THE test paper of which the mode of preparation is given below, is much more delicate than litmus, as it will, for instance, readily reveal the presence of 1 part of hydrochloric acid in 150,000 parts of water. To prepare it, proceed as follows:

Take unsized white paper of a neutral reaction, preferably the best, white filtering paper, cut it in pieces of about 6 by 7 inches, and impregnate it with Tincture of Turmeric made from 1 part of turmeric and 8 parts of alcohol. Hang the sheets up on threads, and when they are dry, pass them, one by one, through a bath composed of
1 part of freshly prepared Lime Water, and
1½ parts of Distilled Water.

This should be accomplished in 15 to 20 seconds. Then immediately pass each sheet, rather quickly, through a bath of *Water*, and hang it up to dry. When dry, the paper will have a deep orange color. Shallow dishes are best for the several baths through which the paper is to be passed.

The paper should be kept in a dry place, and should not be exposed to light. I prefer to keep it in a wide-mouthed bottle covered with paper. When dipped into a liquid containing even minute quantities of an acid, the moistened portion assumes a pure yellow color.

In very dilute solution, the change of color is not as rapidly brought about as in more concentrated ones, but, nevertheless, the reaction is more delicate than with litmus. With unboiled water it will produce the reaction either at once or in a short time, owing to the dissolved carbonic acid. After boiling, pure water will not affect the paper. If a free acid, therefore, is to be detected by means of this paper, the solution should be boiled to expel the carbonic acid. Then, if a yellow color is produced, some free acid (besides CO_2) must be present.

As the paper is liable to fade, it is best prepared as wanted. Ordinary turmeric paper, prepared as above directed, may be kept in stock. For use, a few sheets of this are first drawn through the diluted lime-water, afterwards through water, according to above directions, and the paper quickly dried.

Solvents of Urinary Calculi.

DR. HERMAN GOLDENBERG of N. Y., has studied the effect of various solvents upon urinary calculi, with a view to ascertain the most favorable method of treatment of lithiasis, under different circumstances. Instead of performing his chief experiments in a test tube, by trying the solubility of uric acid, or uric acid concretions in solutions of various supposed litholytics, he treated the uric acid, etc., with urine passed by persons who had purposely taken regular doses of the litholytic remedies, and made a parallel set of experiments with normal urine not containing the latter.

It was found that the greatest solvent action was exerted by the waters of the Desirée spring of Vals, 100 C.c. of urine passed under the daily administration of one bottle of this water being capable of dissolving about 0.01 Gm. of uric acid. The "Grand Grille" of Vichy possesses nearly the same power. Next come Fachingen, the Helenen-quelle of Wildungen, and finally, the Oberzalzbrunn Kronenquelle. The latter has only one-fifth the solvent power of the Desirée.

It is now pretty certain that the main factor in the litholytic power of the waters is the percentage of carbonate of sodium.

Experiments to substitute aqueous solutions of this salt, in such strength as to resemble the natural waters, had similar effects upon the calculous deposits, but caused disagreeable effects upon intestinal peristalsis, and by rendering the urine alkaline, produced an abundant precipitation of phosphates. Similar effects were produced by *Contant's powder*, which is composed of:

Lithium Carbonate.........................1 part
Sodium Bicarbonate............................2 parts
Potassium Citrate ....4 "

Also, to a less extent, by magnesium boro-citrate, which, however, is well borne in long-continued doses.

The author advises, in acute cases, to employ the most active remedies, particularly such mineral waters as contain the largest amount of sodium carbonate. But these should not be long-continued. In chronic cases, the milder remedies are to be preferred, and aside of mineral waters, the most beneficial or least harmful appears to be the boro-citrate of magnesium.—*After Med. Record.*

Sodium Sesquicarbonate is a new salt, which has been put on the market by English manufacturers as a substitute for ordinary sal soda, over which it has the advantage of a much smaller amount of water of crystallization. The composition is $Na_2CO_3.NaHCO_3.2H_2O$, and is therefore a combination of 1 molecule of sodium carbonate, 1 mol. of sodium bicarbonate, and 2 mol. of water. It is very soluble, and is readily prepared of great purity. It is obtained by bringing together a solution of sal soda and carbonic acid gas in proper proportions, and crystallizing the solution at a temperature above 35° C.

CAPSULES AND CAPSULE-MAKING.

We owe this particular form for the administration of medicines to Mothes, who invented gelatin capsules in 1836. They afford one of the best means of administering nauseous medicines, especially liquids, and for this purpose their use has gradually extended. If it were known that a dozen capsules could be made in as short a time as is required to make a dozen suppositories, we feel sure that every pharmacist would add this branch of the pharmaceutic art to his every-day employment.

The details of the operation of capsule-making are, as will be seen from the description which follows, comparatively simple. The requisites are moulds, or olives, as the French call them. These are egg or olive shaped, solid heads of iron or britannia metal, each of which is fixed upon a metal rod; a dozen or more of the moulds are fixed into a slab of wood or cork, with perforations for the purpose, and at the back of the slab, in the centre, a handle is fixed. A good slab or holder may be made from a large cork bung. The appearance of the moulds fixed on the holder is seen in the following figure:

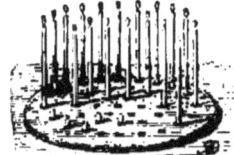

Moulds for soft capsules.

The moulds are the only part of the requisite apparatus which are not home-made. A slab of wood with quarter-inch perforations bored with a centre-bit (the holder as shown, for example), or even a suppository mould, serves to support the capsules in the process of filling, and most liquids are poured into the capsules by means of an ordinary glass syringe. The fifteen minims capsule is the common size, but the size may vary from five minims to one or even two drachms. If the moulds are made locally, the chemist should supply the moulder with the shape from which to work. For this purpose use clean yellow wax, fifteen grains for each fifteen minim mould; warm the wax and form it into the proper shape, with as smooth a surface as possible. The moulder will of course make the metal mould perfectly smooth; the slightly greater bulk, proportionately, of the wax allows a fair margin for this purpose.

Capsule-making machine.

A form of capsule which is very popular in France is the perle, or globule. They are either spherical or flattened forms of the capsule, and are made in a different way. Viel's apparatus for making these, as perfected by Thevenot, is shown in the accompanying figure.

A is the cast-iron bed or support of the machine resting upon a strong deal table; B, a hollow movable cylinder, has a moulding plate at its extremity corresponding to c. To these, bands of a gelatinous film are conveyed from the spools d. The liquid to be capsuled is placed in the receptacle E, from which it passes to the capsule. The whole apparatus is worked by means of the wheels J, K; J forms the gelatinous moulds, and K works the apparatus which closes the moulds. The gelatinous film referred to is made of Irish moss mucilage dried. The moulds turn out the two parts with edges which are subsequently made to adhere by strong pressure of a part of the apparatus worked by the wheel K, and which consists essentially of a counterpart of the capsule made of steel.

Capsules are either hard or soft. The former were the first introduced, but the latter are now deservedly the more popular, for they are more easily swallowed. The solution for hard capsules is made according to the following formula, although the quantity of liquid used in this and other cases must vary with the quality of the gelatin:—

	Oz.
Gelatin	6
Gum acacia	1
Powdered sugar	1
Water	5

Steep the gelatin in the water, when soft add the gum and sugar, and heat until dissolved, removing any scum which rises to the surface.

Various formulas have been proposed for the soft capsules. The following have been found to give good flexible masses:

		Parts.
(1)	Gelatin, gum acacia, sugar, each	80
	Honey	10
	Water	100

Make a solution as above.

		Parts.
(2)	Gelatin	25
	Glycerin	10
	Sugar	8
	Water	45

Steep the gelatin in the water, add the sugar and glycerin, and dissolve by the heat of a water-bath.

A stock of No. 2 may be kept and dissolved as required by means of a water-bath. To make the capsules, have the gelatin mixture melted and heated to 104° F.; prepare the moulds by oiling them very slightly with olive oil. This is best done by oiling a soft cloth, such as a piece of lint, and applying this over the whole of the mould surface and a little way up the supporting-rod. Lift the mould-holder by the handle and immerse the moulds completely in the gelatin mixture; in a few seconds remove steadily and begin to rotate the moulds in a circular fashion, so that the gelatin may set perfectly even. A little practice suffices to make the operator perfect in this operation. In a couple of minutes the gelatin has set sufficiently to allow the whole to be set aside. In about a quarter of an hour the capsules may be removed by grasping each lightly with the finger and thumb and gently pulling off. Place each one upon its closed end in one or other of the supporters already described, and when the whole have been removed cut off their tails with a pair of scissors. They are now ready for filling, and in the case of liquids this is simply done with a syringe; for powders use a small flannel funnel made of paper. The open end is closed by dipping a glass rod in the liquefied gelatin solution and placing the drop which it removes upon the open end. Sometimes a superior finish is given to the capsules by afterwards dipping this end of the capsule half-way up the gelatin solution and drying rapidly, but one must be an adept before this refinement is attempted. After they are finished it is necessary to expose the capsules to the air for a few hours, in order to dry them thoroughly.—*Chem. and Drugg.*, April 14th.

A New Antiseptic Soap.

At a recent meeting of the Society of Chemical Industry held at Edinburgh, Mr. John Thomson reported on the results of his experiments on the preparation of an antiseptic soap.

The mercuric salts being so powerfully antiseptic, the author experimented with a number of them, but found only one of them to resist decomposition when introduced into soap. This salt was the red iodide (biniodide), which has long been known to be more powerfully antiseptic than even the bichloride. Biniodide of mercury combines with soap of almost any kind without in any degree losing its antiseptic properties. A variety of soaps prepared by the author and containing mercuric iodide were tested by several bacteriologists and were found to be most efficient. The tests were made by introducing silk-threads impregnated with various septic material (of known origin) into a solution of the soap of known strength (usually 1 in 120) and leaving them there 10 minutes, which time was sufficient to render them perfectly aseptic.

The biniodide soap has been tried in the treatment of cases of eczema with most marked success, especially where the irritation has been produced by the fermentation of accumulated secretions.

It has also been used in parasitic skin diseases, such as favus and ringworm, with marked success.

The biniodide soap contained from 1 to 3 per cent of biniodide, dissolved in iodide of potassium.—*Journ. Soc. Chem. Ind.*, 1888, 192.

Notes on Opium Assaying.

At the request of Dr. William K. Newton, the New Jersey State Dairy Commissioner, a series of investigations was undertaken for the purpose of determining the relative value of several of the more recent and best reputed methods of assaying opium and its preparations. The principal object was to ascertain that method which, being at the same time the most convenient and least liable to error on the part of the analyst, would give accurately the proportion of morphine, when the same fell within a reasonable limit above or below the legal standard, rather than to seek for a method which would give most accurately the percentage of morphine, *whatever its amount*.

The processes which were thus studied by the author, assisted by L. W. McCay, D.Sc., were the following, in which the description of the manipulations is given in a condensed form:

1. *Squibb's Method.*—The opium is thoroughly extracted with cold water, the solution is concentrated to a small volume, alcohol is added, then ether, and finally ammonia. The precipitated morphine (after the aqueous solution has first been washed with more ether) is collected on a filter placed within another of equal weight, crystals and filter are washed successively with a little ether and then water, the filters and morphine dried at 100° C., using one filter to counterbalance the other. A portion of the weighed morphine is treated with lime-water and any undissolved residue is deducted from the weight of the morphine. The method is a modification of a process devised by Flückiger, and resembles that of the German Pharmacopœia, II.

2. *Stillwell's Method.*—This is based upon Squibb's, from which it differs mainly by the use of saturated solutions of morphine in alcohol with a little ammonia, and in water, to more thoroughly wash the precipitated morphine, and in the use of hot alcohol to separate the weighed morphine from the impurities insoluble in the alcohol.

3. *Method of the United States Pharmacopœia.*—This is one of the various lime methods; the opium is extracted by digestion with slaked lime and water; an aliquot portion of the filtered solution is shaken with alcohol and ether, then chloride of ammonium is added, and after washing the aqueous solution with more ether, the precipitated morphine is collected on a filter placed within a counterbalanced filter, the filter is washed with a little ether, and then the crystals of morphine are transferred to the filter and washed with a little water. When dry, the filters and morphine are weighed, using one filter to counterbalance the other.

4. *Dieterich's Method* (known as the "Helfenberg" Method).—The opium is extracted with cold water, an aliquot portion of the filtered solution is treated with a slight excess of ammonia and at once filtered off from the precipitated narcotine and other organic matter; an aliquot part of this second filtrate is mixed with ether and then with more ammonia, and after washing the aqueous solution with more ether, the precipitated morphine is collected chiefly in the precipitating flask and partly on a small filter; washed with a little water saturated with ether, and then dried and weighed, the morphine being brushed from the dry filter into the flask for weighing.

5. *A Modification of Dieterich's Method, devised by the Author,* in which, instead of using an aliquot portion of the aqueous extract of opium, the whole of the solution is used, after the opium has been thoroughly extracted with water as directed in Stillwell's method.

6. *Kremel's Method.*—The opium is extracted with lime-water, an aliquot part of the filtered solution is treated with ether and ammonia, and the rest of the process conducted nearly as in Dieterich's original process.

We shall not reprint here the author's detailed report on processes Nos. 1 and 2. Regarding process No. 3 (that of the U. S. Ph.), Prof. Cornwall states that, when very carefully executed, it gave better results than was anticipated on theoretical grounds. He desires, however, to draw attention to the very considerable difference in results which the operator has it in his power to obtain with the precipitated morphine, according to the way in which he follows the U. S. Ph. directions as to "pressing it between sheets of bibulous paper," before drying it at an elevated temperature.

The results come out about 0.4 per cent lower in the cases when the morphine crystals and filters were pressed between paper *until they would give up no trace of moisture* to the bibulous paper, than when they were simply pressed so as to merely render them dry to the eye. To obtain proper results, the pressing must be most thorough. The U. S. Ph. method is liable to variations, depending largely on the care and fidelity of the analyst, and it is moreover not as convenient a method as that presently to be described.

The author then described Dieterich's two methods (summarised under 4), and then gives his own modification of Dieterich's process.

He had ascertained by careful experiments that it possessed very important advantages. With laudanum (*i. e.*, a liquid which holds the morphine in solution) it succeeded extremely well. But with opium it gave low results, even allowing for the morphine which the mother liquor could have held in solution. The probable cause appeared to be imperfect extraction of the opium. On changing the method of extraction to that recommended by Stillwell, very satisfactory results were obtained.

Cornwall's Modification of Dieterich's Process.—Place 6 grammes of opium in a beaker, add 60 C.c. of water, stir occasionally (breaking up all the lumps), and finally let stand, covered, over night for twelve hours. Filter into a graduated cylinder, wash the residue on the filter until the filtrate and washings amount to 75 C.c., and set this aside. Carefully return the residue to the beaker, stir well with 20 C.c. of water, let stand ten minutes, and filter through the same filter; repeat the operation twice more, each time with 12 C.c. of water, finally pressing the residue with a glass rod. Evaporate the last three washings, about 44 C.c. in all, in a dish 4 to 6 inch. diameter, on a water-bath below boiling heat. When down to about 15 C.c., add the first strong extract, rinsing the cylinder with a little water, and evaporate the whole to exactly 50 C.c., including the water necessary to rinse the solution into the measuring cylinder. (We would have said: add the first strong extract, wash the cylinder with a little water, and evaporate the whole to a volume somewhat below 50 C.c. Then allow it to become cold, and add enough water to make exactly 50 C.c.—Ed. Am. Drug.)

Add of normal ammonia, 2 C.c. (plus the amount necessary to exactly neutralize the dilute sulphuric acid, if any such had been added—in the writer's case this was 0.5 C.c.), mix thoroughly and at once filter, as directed in Dieterich's original process. Of this filtrate take a volume corresponding to 4 grammes of opium. In the writer's case, this was of course obtained by the proportion—6 : 4 :: 52.5 : x =35 C.c. In general it would be—6 : 4 :: 50 + a : x; a denoting the number of C.c. of normal ammonia already added.

To this portion of the filtrate add 13 to 14 C.c. of ether, mix by rotating the flask, and then add 4 C.c. of normal ammonia as directed in Dieterich's original process exactly according to which the assay is now to be completed. The writer's results in three trials with the opium were: 13.23, 13.40, and 13.20 per cent.

In the last trial the extraction was made with one-half more water, including first extract and washings, than in the others, indicating complete extraction with the smaller quantity of water. In the last trial the opium was also rubbed very fine with some of the water at first. These results confirm the objections made by Squibb and Stillwell to the use of aliquot parts of aqueous extracts of opium to represent the whole of the morphine present in the opium. In applying Dieterich's methods to tinctures and officinal extract of opium, of course no such objection exists.

By this simple modification, Dieterich's process for opium is brought into agreement with other methods of acknowledged accuracy, while its convenience in comparison with them may well be likened to the superiority of volumetric over gravimetric methods of analysis. The tedious and risky weighing, washing, and drying of bulky precipitates and filter papers is reduced to the simple handling of a small flask and an easily dried, highly-crystalline precipitate.

We have not had time to test the applicability of Dieterich's method, thus modified, to poor opiums, but in view of its results with laudanum, as compared with those of the U. S. Pharm. method (which is there at its best), there is no doubt that it embraces a range wide enough to cover all the variations of the average grades of opium, or that it is admirably adapted to determine whether an opium preparation is below the legal standard.

Prof. Cornwall concludes his paper with the following summary:

Squibb's method, owing to the limited washing, is liable to give too high results.

Stillwell's method provides the means of arriving with certainty at correct results, with opium of any grade.

The U. S. Pharm. method, while open to theoretical objections, appears to be well adapted to opium of average quality, if very carefully executed; it is less liable to error in the case of officinal extracts and tinctures of opium than with opium itself.

Dieterich's methods, as improved by himself, are accurate for officinal extracts and tinctures, but still too low in the case of opium.

Dieterich's method, with the complete extraction finally adopted by the writer, gives accurate results for opium, and is the method least liable to error in comparatively unskilled hands.

Kremel's method gives too low results for opium, and is in any case inferior to Dieterich's, both as to accuracy and convenience.

---

* No dilute sulphuric acid was added in this first trial during the extraction. The argument of the results shows that the larger percentages obtained by the writer with Squibb's method were not due to the use of acid.

AUTOMATIC STILL.

REFERENCE has recently been made in the columns of the *Pharmaceutical Journal* to automatic stills, or stills that might be made automatic.* The arrangement here described is one that may readily be adapted to, and is specially suited for, the old-fashioned stills which are in frequent use among pharmacists for the purpose of distilling water. The idea is extremely simple, but I can testify to its thorough efficiency in actual practice. The still is of tinned copper, two-gallon capacity, and the condenser is the usual worm surrounded with cold water.

The overflow of warm water from the condenser is not run into the waste pipe as in the ordinary course, but carried by means of a bent tube A, B, C to the supply pipe of the still. The bend at B acts as a trap, which prevents the escape of steam.

The advantages of this arrangement are obvious. It is perfectly simple, and can be adapted at no expense. It permits of a continuous supply of hot water to the still, so that the contents of the latter may always be kept boiling rapidly, and as a consequence, it condenses the maximum amount of water with the minimum of loss of heat. If the supply of water at D be carefully regulated it will be found that a continuous current will be passing into the still at a temperature of about 180° F.; or if practice suggest the desirability of running in the water at intervals, this can be easily arranged. It is necessary that the level

SAFETY-VENT.

WHEN solutions are to be prepared without access of air, the stopper of the flask may be provided with a tube having the shape of that shown in the cut. The upper end of this is closed by fusion, and a lateral hole blown into it near the end, a piece of rubber tubing being slipped over it. Any excessive pressure in the interior will find relief by lifting the rubber valve, while pressure from the outside will render it only more impermeable.—After *Zeitsch. f. Anal. Chem.*, 1888, 176.

NEW FUNNEL.

O. N. WITT some time ago described an improvement for funnels, consisting of a perforated plate of glass, metal, or porcelain which was to be laid in the funnel, and over which a filter-paper was to be laid, which was to be held in place by a second filter.

This arrangement, which is used very largely in factories and laboratories, has the disadvantage that the filter is generally not tight, so that the filtrate runs through cloudy, at least in the beginning.

To obviate this difficulty, Dr. R. Hirsch has caused porcelain funnels to be made, in which the perforated plate is permanent fixture. In these funnels, only *one* filter is required, and the funnel may be emptied or refilled

Automatic filter.   Mabes's automatic still.   Witt's funnel.   Safety-vent.

at A should be two inches or thereabout higher than the level of the bend at C, otherwise there may not be sufficient head to force a free current of water against the pressure of steam. It will also be found that the still should only contain water to the extent of about one-fourth of its capacity when distillation is commenced, as the water in the condenser becomes heated much more rapidly than the same volume is vaporized. By this expedient a still of two-gallon capacity will yield about half a dozen gallons per day, a much greater quantity than could ever be obtained under the old system, which required the still to be re-charged with cold water every time 1½ gallons had been taken off.

The objection to all such continuous or automatic arrangements is, of course, that the condensed water contains all the free ammonia that may have existed in the water originally, but it is only in cases where the water is exceptionally impure that this disadvantage will become really serious. The method here outlined has no doubt occurred to many, and may probably be in regular use, but not having seen any previous mention of the idea I have thought that it might be useful to some pharmacists who prepare their own distilled water.—T. MABEN in *Pharm. Journ.*

AUTOMATIC FILTER.

THE apparatus figured here has recently been introduced in France, its purpose being to overcome some of the difficulties which accompany the use of ordinary funnels. The advantages claimed for it are (1) that filtration goes on regularly without the introduction of a foreign body between the stem of the funnel and the neck of the bottle (!); (2) the flow of liquid stops automatically when the liquid reaches a certain height in the bottle, so that overflowing is impossible; and (3) the funnel may be taken from one vessel to another without the loss of any of its contents. The parts of the apparatus are: v, a tin tube lined with vulcanized india-rubber, into which the extremity of an ordinary funnel is fitted; R, a stop-cock; c, an india-rubber stopper for fitting into the neck of the bottle; T, a tube connecting through the stop-cock with v, t, a small tube to allow the escape of air from the receiving vessel as filtration proceeds; to this is attached a piece of india-rubber tubing with a hook whereby it may be attached to the funnel. When the liquid in the vessel reaches t, it flows up the tube, thus stopping the exit of air, and filtration ceases.—*Chem. and Drugg.*

---

* *Pharm. Journ.* [3], vol. xviii., p. 777.

without risking the displacement of the plate, as is the case with Witt's funnels.

The appearance of the funnel, as heretofore constructed of glass, is shown in the cut. The porcelain funnel has the same construction.—*Zeitsch. f. Angew. Chem.*, 1888, 160.

Indian Sarsaparilla (Hemidesmus).

AT a recent drug sale in London there came up for disposal a number of packages of hemidesmus, or Indian sarsaparilla root, which comprised the first consignment of the drug received here after a rather unusual interval of thirteen years. It was perfectly natural, therefore, that before these packages came up for sale the drug should have been reported to be scarce—indeed, it was unobtainable, but as retail druggists are so rarely called upon to supply either the root or its preparations, the fact that the drug is scarce or otherwise is not likely to create much excitement. Yet it happens that in St. Bartholomew's Hospital, the largest medical institution in the metropolis, Indian sarsaparilla takes the place of the smilax root, so that all preparations of sarsaparilla used therein are characterised by the absence of what is generally known as sarsaparilla, and the hospital has the distinction of using more hemidesmus than all other consumers put together. Before the last arrival the hospital stock became exhausted, and one of the customs of the institution appeared to be threatened with extinction. The physicians of the hospital report that they find the preparations of hemidesmus to be as satisfactory as those of sarsaparilla. That is, perhaps, not saying much; nevertheless, when Dr. Ashburner introduced it in this country in 1831 it was said to increase the appetite, to act as a diuretic and improve the general health, plumpness, clearness and strength succeeding to emaciation, muddiness and debility. It was also said to be useful in affections of the kidneys, scrofula, cutaneous diseases, and thrush. It had long been used in India, where it is held in high reputation, and is known under the name of *Nannāri root* and *Ananto-mūl*. It is the root of *Hemidesmus Indicus*, which is the same plant as the *Periploca Indica* of Willdenow and the *Asclepias pseudosarsa* of Roxburgh. The root has a strong odor resembling tonka bean, this characteristic being particularly marked in the recent consignment.

"Listerin," according to *Fortschritt*, consists of: Benzoic acid and borax, each 8 grammes; boric acid, 16 grammes; thymol, 2.4 grammes; eucalyptol and oil of wintergreen, each 10 drops; oil of peppermint, 5 drops; oil of thyme, 2 drops; alcohol, 180 grammes, and sufficient water to make 1,000 grammes.

Notes on Commercial Drugs and Chemicals.

(From Gehe & Co.'s Handelsbericht, f. April, 1888.)

Acetanilid (Antifebrin).—The consumption of this antipyretic is quite large. It has been called, not without reason, the "antipyrin for the poor," as it is capable, in very many cases, to replace antipyrin perfectly, either by its power to reduce temperature, or by its specific effects in articular rheumatism, migraine, or neuralgia. It is certain to retain its place in the materia medica, though the time may arrive when it will be no longer deemed so important to reduce the temperature of the body.

The melting point of pure, dry antifebrin lies between 112°–113° C., its boiling point at 295° C. In determining the latter, it will be noticed that every commercial brand of acetanilid (or antifebrin) will assume in the retort, when kept during about fifteen minutes at the boiling point, a series of colors beginning with yellow and passing through rose into brownish-red. This coloration is accompanied by a decomposition of the contents of the retort, which may easily be ascertained, after cooling, by their odor and reactions. How far this decomposition depends on the presence of traces of pseudo-toluidine, or rather its acetyl compound (corresponding to acetanilid), has not yet been determined.

Alpha-Oxynaphthoic Acid.—This new acid is now obtainable in the market, and has been pronounced to be a very powerful antiseptic and antizymotic. It cannot be used as a substitute for salicylic acid, for the purpose of preserving food, as it is rather poisonous. But it is supposed that it may be used internally in diseases of the intestines and febrile diseases when prescribed by physicians. Its chief field of usefulness will, however, be that of disinfection. [The long name would eventually have to be curtailed, to popularize the substance. Probably "Naphthoic Acid" would be sufficient.—Ed. Am. Dr.]

Alum Pencils.—Gehe & Co. now manufacture also vaginal balls of alum.

Aluminium.—The electrolytic method of preparing aluminium has not yet been brought to such a point that the metal can be sold at materially reduced prices. At present, aluminium is chiefly used in the manufacture of bronzes and for physical and optical instruments, being here usually alloyed with a little silver. If it should, however, be possible to bring the cost of preparing it down to about 1 dollar per kilo, its employment would become so universal that it would revolutionize the metal industry.

Anthrarobin.—This new chemical, prepared by Prof. Liebermann as a substitute for chrysarobin, and regarding which our readers will find a detailed account on page 62 of our last April number, is now on trial. It is said to act more slowly than chrysarobin. It is almost insoluble in water, but soluble in about 10 parts of absolute alcohol; also in 10 parts of glycerin at 100° C. It is usually applied either in form of ointment (containing 10 to 20%), or as 10% tincture or in solution in glycerin.

Antipyrin.—The statements made by Prof. Germain Sée, regarding the anodyne and analgesic action of antipyrin, have been declared by several competent authorities to be exaggerated. It is not denied that the effect, as claimed, is produced, but its duration is asserted to be only temporary; and besides, if frequently used, the remedy often fails to give relief altogether.

The manufacturers of antipyrin supply it both in the crystalline form and in powder.

Balsam Peru.—Gehe & Co. report that Denner's test, first announced at the late meeting of Naturalists at Wiesbaden, for the detection of benzoin and storax in balsam of Peru, has been found by them to be very valuable. On first appearance the test is very circumstantial, but when only the presence (not the quantity) of the before-mentioned adulterants is to be demonstrated, the test may be shortened in the following manner:

Mix 5 Gm. of balsam Peru, 5 Gm. of solution of soda (containing 15% NaHO), and 10 Gm. of water in a test tube. Shake the mixture with 2 successive portions of 15 Gm. of ether, and decant the ether each time as far as possible. Heat the residue to boiling and acidulate it with hydrochloric acid. Then add cold water, and remove the resin which separates from the liquid. Dissolve this resin in 3 Gm. of solution of soda (15%), dilute with 20 Gm. of water, heat to boiling, and precipitate with solution of chloride of barium. Transfer the precipitate to a filter, drain, dry it in a water-bath, and extract it with alcohol. Evaporate the alcoholic solution, dissolve the residue with concentrated sulphuric acid, add chloroform and shake. If benzoin or storax had been added to the balsam, the chloroform will assume a violet to blue color. Even small quantities of the adulterants are still recognized by this test.

Cardamoms.—In 1880–81, the export from Ceylon amounted to only about 16,000 lbs. In 1885–86, it has risen to 216,050 lbs., and in 1886–87 to 321,560 lbs. "Long" cardamoms are scarce; the variety usually cultivated is that known as Malabar and Aleppi.

Chinotarine—a name applied for convenience's sake to a synthetic compound, viz., dichinolindimethylsulphate—has been found to possess properties similar to that of curare and "curarine." Gehe & Co. do not seem to have much faith in its vitality.

Cola-Nuts reach the market in larger quantity than formerly. As they contain both theobromine and caffeine, they are beginning to attract more attention. It is difficult to transport them without spoiling, as they cannot be thoroughly dried at the place of production.

Creosote is coming into increased use as a remedy in phthisis. It is now being administered also hypodermically in form of a 3-per-cent solution in oil of almonds.

Cubebs.—It is not improbable that the present value of cubebs will not be maintained much longer, since more attention is now paid to the cultivation and collection of the drug in Java. The demands made upon the quality of cubebs are not alike in all countries. It is, therefore, often difficult for the dealer to comply with all requirements. While in Germany the requirements of the pharmacopœia are considered as sufficient, in other countries the additional requirement is made that, when cubebs are triturated with sulphuric acid, they should assume a purple color. The failure of this reaction is regarded as a proof of their spurious character. But, in fact, the test only shows the presence of cubebin, while both the essential oil and cubebic acid may have been extracted from the drug. (Gehe & Co. report having seen cubebs which but little resembled the officinal drug. They were small, shrivelled, scarcely 1.5 millimeters in diameter, with a stem 2 or 3 times as long, and evidently gathered in the first stage of fruiting. Yet, as they yielded a larger percentage of extract, they commanded a higher price.

Ethyl Bromide, which had of late been again recommended as a substitute for chloroform, does not seem to have found universal favor, even in its purest state.

Guajacol.—In place of creosote, which has found employment as a remedy in phthisis, Sahli has commenced to use one of its constituents, viz., pure guajacol (or guaiacol), which is administered in the following form:

		Gm.
℞ Guajacol		1.5–2.0 gr. 20–30
Aquæ Destill		180. fl. 3 6
Alcohol		20. fl. 3 ⅔

Dose: A teaspoonful 2 or 3 times a day, in water, after meals.

Absolutely pure guajacol may now be had in the market. The usual commercial article often contains only about 35 per cent of it. Its purity may be determined by its spec. grav., which is 1.117 at 15° C., and by it being insoluble in 2 vol. of glycerin (sp. gr. 1.19), and in 2 vols. of benzin. It boils at 200°–202° C.

Guarana has reached the market again in sufficient quantities. It is not in active demand at present, probably owing to the cheapness of caffeine.

Hydrochloric Acid.—Wherever the new ammonia process for the manufacture of soda has been introduced, the commercial value of hydrochloric acid (which is not obtained as a by-product in this process) has materially advanced. [This is not yet the case in this country, but is likely to occur within the next five years.—Ed. Am. Dr.] Efforts have been made during a number of years to utilize the immense quantities of solution of chloride of magnesium which are obtained at the Stassfurt mines as a waste product. A special aim has been to substitute magnesia for lime in the regeneration of ammonia from the chloride of ammonium produced during the conversion of the chloride into the carbonate of sodium. If this succeeds, as there is reason to expect, and the chloride of magnesium can also be utilized to generate both chlorine and hydrochloric acid, a complete revolution in this branch of chemical industry will be brought about.

Hydroxylamine Hydrochloride.—The strongly reducing action of this compound, which places it side by side with pyrogallic acid, renders it not improbable that it will be found to possess valuable properties for the treatment of such skin diseases as are amenable to pyrogallic acid and other reducing agents in general.

Iodol has been only in moderate demand, no doubt owing to its high price. If the alleged successful employment of *sozol* in place of iodoform should turn out to be authentic, neither iodol nor iodoform would have a very hopeful future. The two compounds *sozoiodol* and *iodosozol* (respectively, iodo-paraphenol-sulphonic, and indo-orthophenol-sulphonic acids) have so far been but little used.

Iron Reduced.—Gehe & Co. state that there is no reduced iron in the market which is entirely free from sulphur.

Morphine.—The production of this alkaloid is at present larger than the market can absorb. In former years, both the Persian and East Indian opium were absorbed either by consumption at home or by export to China, but since the latter country produces nearly all the opium it requires itself, the above-mentioned varieties of commercial opium begin to make themselves felt as factors in the morphine industry.

Olive Oil.—Regarding the adulteration of this oil with seed oils and particularly with refined cotton-seed oil, many reports have recently been received from Italy. It is said that Lucca oil, in flasks, which is a favorite brand in England (and also in the U. S.), consists often only of cotton-seed oil. From Nizza it is reported that cotton seed oil, bleached and rendered odorless, is simply mixed with 20 to 25s of fine olive oil, and put on the market as "huile à manger." It is said that this kind of oil, when used for dressing salad, runs off the lettuce leaves, while genuine oil of olive adheres to them and "combines" with the vinegar. [We doubt this.—Ed. Am. Dr.]

Phenacetin.—This new antipyretic has found much favor. According to present reports, 1 Gm. of it has about the same effect upon the temperature of the body as 2 Gm. of antipyrin, or 0.5 Gm. of antifebrin. It is just as free from disagreeable secondary symptoms as antipyrin; and particularly does not produce the cyanosis so often occurring with antifebrin. Used as an antineuralgic, it calms and deadens pain much more energetically than antipyrin, and is of great benefit in migraine, insomnia, and neurasthenic affections. It may therefore be regarded as an intermediary link between antipyrin and antifebrin.

Picric Acid appears to be still used for the manufacture of explosives for war purposes, though it is not known exactly in what manner. This seems to be, at least in part, the reason why the price of carbolic acid has not experienced a very material decline.

Quinine and Salts.—The question of what is the best test to determine the purity of sulphate of quinine has been well discussed during the past year, but has not been thoroughly settled. It is pretty certain that the final choice will much depend upon the decision of pharmacologists, as to what percentage of cinchonidine (or other cinchona alkaloids) may be left in commercial sulphate of quinine without interfering with its therapeutic value. Supposing that they were to decide that an amount not exceeding 2.5 per cent may be tolerated, then Schaefer's oxalate test will probably be preferred as the most simple one. Should a larger percentage be tolerated, and the test afford at the same time an approximate quantitative estimation, the modified Kerner's test (see our last January number, page 8) will probably be preferred. Gehe & Co. believe that the difficulty of selecting the most suitable test for sulphate of quinine can be overcome by dropping the sulphate and selecting the hydrochloride as the chief officinal salt. This contains a larger percentage of quinine, and would, of course, cost somewhat more from this fact alone. But this salt may easily be prepared without being contaminated with cinchonidine, while the preparation of a sulphate entirely free from cinchonidine or containing only a definite low percentage of this alkaloid, is a difficult and somewhat expensive operation.

Rhubarb of fine quality remains as scarce as ever. Of the best quality, Shensi, only about 400 piculs are reported as representing the harvest of 1887, against 2,000 piculs in good years. Shanghai received, in 1887, only 4,248 piculs altogether, against 6,324 piculs in 1886 and 7,887 in 1885. In London there are now only 900 chests, against 1,800 at the same time last year. Even the inferior sorts have recently brought higher prices.

Sodium Silico-fluoride.—This compound, which was patented in England under the name *Salufer* ("healthbringer"), is occasionally asked for in Germany. It is said to be an efficient antiseptic, and, as it is not irritating, to be a good substitute for corrosive sublimate.

Sodium Sulphbenzoate.—This compound is obtained by saturating a concentrated solution of sulphite of sodium with benzoic acid, and may be regarded as a double salt, consisting of bisulphite and benzoate of sodium.

It is used in ½ per cent aqueous solution as a substitute for corrosive sublimate and iodoform.

Sulphurous Acid.—Besides the commercial 10-per cent aqueous solution of sulphurous acid, of spec. grav. 1.024, the pure acid, compressed to a liquid, has recently been introduced into chemical industry for the preparation of sulphites in the manufacture of cellulose, and for preparing glue (being employed in place of hydrochloric acid). The liquefied acid is prepared in Westphalian and Silesian factories on a large scale.

Thioresorcin.—Under this name, a sulphur substitution product of resorcin will probably soon be introduced into the materia medica. It is at present being tested regarding its availability as a substitute for iodoform. It is in form of a yellowish, inodorous powder insoluble in water, difficultly soluble in alcohol, but easily in dilute alkalies.

Quinidine Sulphate.—Sulphate of quinidine, at one time almost a drug in the market, at other times in considerable demand, and justly esteemed as being practically equivalent to quinine in therapeutic value, is becoming more and more scarce, because manufacturers of quinine at the present time use Javanese or East Indian barks almost exclusively, and these contain either no quinidine at all, or so little of it, that its separation does not pay.

Bismuth with Mucilage.

Jos. F. Burnett takes exception to advice recently given by a recent writer in the *Pharmaceutical Journal* that when bismuth is prescribed, a mixture of mucilage must be added to suspend it. He says: A mixture containing bismuth and tragacanth was made, in some quantity, by myself last summer, and however carefully made, or however elegant its appearance when made, in the course of a few days the bismuth had set at the bottom of the bottle, and no amount of shaking would again diffuse it. In fact, one might as well turn a few feet of cord into a bottle full of water and attempt to diffuse that. When tried with mucilage of acacia, the result was not one bit more satisfactory. I would, therefore, maintain that a bismuth mixture is much the better, in the long run, without gum at all, and no medical man who foresaw such a result as I have laid before you would be likely to order it. Is, then, the dispenser justified in spoiling a mixture which has to be kept a week simply for the sake of the appearance it may bear the first day? If a suspender be desired, I can give glycerin my unqualified approval, for I have used and am using any amount for this purpose, and I always find it all that can be desired. Of course, I do not suggest the addition of glycerin where the practitioner has not prescribed it, for I would dispense his mixture as written.

Crystallized Mercury Salts.

W. Sievers has studied methods for preparing both mercuric and mercurous preparations in a *crystalline* state, not by sublimation, but in solution. A few notes, of practical use, are here given from the author's paper (in *Ber. d. Deutsch. Chem. Ges.*, 1888, 648).

1. *Mercuric Bromide.*—This is produced by adding an excess of bromine to a solution of mercuric nitrate of the spec. grav. 1.197, rendered slightly acid by nitric acid. After a short time crystalline laminæ separate. It is necessary that the solution have the exact spec. grav. above mentioned. The crystals may be redissolved in a solution of mercuric nitrate (sp. gr. 1.197), when the salt will separate in form of white laminæ of a tetragonal appearance. From alcohol and water, the salt crystallizes in needles.

2. *Mercuric Chloride (Corrosive Sublimate)* was prepared by passing a current of chlorine gas through a solution of mercurous nitrate of the spec. gr. 1.197, when the salt separated in fine needles. These may be purified by recrystallization from hot water, or from alcohol.

3. *Mercurous Chloride (Calomel).*—A concentrated solution of mercurous nitrate was prepared by mixing 1 vol. of strong nitric acid and 4 vol. of water, and keeping this in contact with mercury for some time. Chlorine was then passed through it to saturation. This caused the separation of a crystalline and an amorphous precipitate. The former was removed by washing with hot water, and the amorphous precipitate dissolved in another portion of the mercurous nitrate solution by protracted boiling. On cooling, it crystallised in small laminæ, which were washed, first with very dilute nitric acid, then with pure water. They were pure mercurous chloride or calomel. They had a yellowish-white color. Light gradually turns them gray, owing to the formation of mercuric chloride and metallic mercury.—*After Berich. d. D. Ch. Ges.*, 1888, 647.

The Percentage of Morphine in Poppy Heads and Seeds.

E. Dietrich, of Helfenberg, has examined the flower of the red poppy (*Papaver Rhœas*) and the capsules and seed of the common poppy, to ascertain the quantity of morphine which they contain. For this purpose, he prepared extracts from these several organs, either with water or diluted alcohol, the menstruum having considerable influence upon the amount of extracted alkaloid, as will be seen further on.

Of each of the extracts thus prepared, 5 Gm. were dissolved in 30 Gm. of water, the solution filtered and mixed with 3 C.c. of normal ammonia. In all cases, not even a trace of narcotin was separated, and the solutions were simply set aside after the addition of 10 Gm. of acetic ether. After forty-eight hours, the separated morphine was collected on a filter, and the remainder of the morphine, remaining in the filtrate, was recovered by shaking the liquids with chloroform.

The total quantity of morphine thus collected was as follows:

	Morphine %.
1. Red poppy (fine) extracted with water.	0.7.
2. Red poppy (inferior) extracted with diluted alcohol,	0.11.
3. Poppy heads (fine) extracted with water,	0.032.
4. Poppy heads (inferior) extracted with diluted alcohol.	0.16.
5. Poppy heads, unripe, dried, extracted with diluted alcohol,	0.086.
6. Poppy seed, white, extracted with diluted alcohol,	0.035.
7. Poppy seed, bluish, extracted with diluted alcohol,	—

—*After Rundschau* (Prag), 1888, No. 16.

The Applicability of various Indicators for Acids and Alkalies.

The following scheme, taken from an article on "Indicators" in the *Rundschau* (Prag), presents the chief distinctions of the different substances used as indicators in a very perspicuous manner:

The nature and use of these indicators is so well known that merely a few notes will be sufficient here.

1. *Solution of Litmus.* As is well known, commercial litmus contains, besides the pure blue coloring matter known as azolitmin, another of a dingy-violet color which may be left in the aqueous extract when litmus *paper* is to be prepared, but which is best removed when a *solution* of litmus is wanted. For this purpose, the crude litmus is treated with successive portions of boiling alcohol until this ceases to take up any more color. The remaining mass is then extracted with water, gently heated, neutralized with dilute sulphuric acid, to expel all carbonic acid, and then brought back to a violet (not blue) tint by a drop or so of solution of baryta.

Solution of litmus must not be kept in tightly stoppered bottles, as this would soon render it colorless by decomposition of the coloring matter. It requires contact with the air, but this should be done so as to prevent the access of dust, bacteria, etc., as much as possible.

[We have found that a litmus solution prepared with the addition of about 4 ounces of pure chloride of sodium in the pint will keep for a long time. The chloride of sodium does not interfere with its use, and should a pure litmus solution be at any time required for a special case, it can be easily prepared. The best way to keep the solution is to put it into a bottle having a tubulure at the bottom, into which a cork, with tube and pinchcock, is inserted, through which any desired quantity may be withdrawn when needed. The neck of the bottle is to be stopped with a wad of purified cotton. In place of the tubulure at the bottom, a siphon tube may be introduced through the neck and fastened in a fixed position.—Ed. Am. Dr.]

2. *Methylorange.*—This is also known as Poirrier's Orange III., and is, chemically speaking, dimethyl-anilinediazobenzolsulphonic acid. This is especially valuable, as it is indifferent against carbonic acid, even in the cold. With the least trace of acid (except citric, acetic, and tartaric, in which its action is uncertain) it assumes a reddish tint, which is rendered yellow by alkalies. It must be used in high dilution (about 4 drops of a 1 in 1,000 solution) to render the change of tint quite decisive. Sometimes it is well to use litmus paper in connection with it, so as to obtain a preliminary clue as to the probable moment when the change of color is to be expected.

[In this case particularly, but also when using other indicators, much uncertainty may be avoided by placing in front of the vessels containing the liquid to be tested *two* similar vessels (beakers, etc.) containing either another portion of the same liquid (if this can be spared), or else pure water, to each of which the same quantity of the indicator has been added as the test-portion itself. One of the two auxiliary portions is then treated with an alkali until the color has just passed into yellow. In the case of other indicators, the corresponding operation will, of course, produce another tint. Having before one's eyes two liquids, one of which represents the exact tint of the test-liquid before the addition of the reagent, while the other shows the tint at which it is desired to arrive, a much more delicate titration becomes possible, and it is not generally necessary to repeat the experiment more than once.—Ed. Am. Dr.]

3. *Rosolic Acid.*—This substance is soluble in ether, acetic acid, cold alcohol (much more in boiling), benzol, and disulphide of carbon. It is almost insoluble in water. Its solutions have a yellowish-red color, which changes to red with fixed alkalies. It is useful as an indicator under the conditions given in the scheme.

4. *Tincture of Cochineal*, as an indicator, is prepared by macerating 45 grains of powdered cochineal with a mixture of 1 fluidounce of alcohol and 3 fluidounces of water.

Black Leather Varnish.

Shellac	150	parts
Venice Turpentine	15	"
Yellow Wax	15	"
Nigrosin, alcohol-soluble	40	"
Alcohol	enough to make 1,000	"

Melt the Venice turpentine and yellow wax at a gentle heat, and gradually add the shellac previously dissolved in 800 parts of alcohol. Next add the nigrosin, in very fine powder, and lastly enough alcohol to make 1,000 parts.

In place of the nigrosin, 50 parts of lampblack may be used. This should first be triturated with a small portion of the alcoholic solution so as to get a perfectly smooth mixture.

The leather which is to be varnished or blackened should first be cleaned with a warm solution of green soap in water, or with a mixture of 3 parts of alcohol and 1 part of water of ammonia, then allowed to dry completely, and the black varnish then applied with a soft brush. After it is dry, it is rubbed over with a dry brush.

Applicable in all cases.	In presence of carbonates, and heat.			Solution of Litmus.
	In presence of caustic alkalies, hot or cold.			
Applicable only under given conditions.	Only in cold liquids.	In absence of citric, acetic, and tartaric acids, and of nitrites.		Methylorange.
	In cold or in hot liquids.	Only when ammonia is absent.	....	Phenolphtalein.
		Only when organic acids are absent.		Rosolic Acid.
		Only in absence of acetic acid and metallic salts.		Tincture of Cochineal.

The Injurious Effect of Certain Gases and Vapors.

Experiments made on this subject by Prof. Pettenkofer and K. B. Lehmann, with the following substances go to show that the general information contained in the text-books needs considerable correction.

Hydrochloric Acid Gas.—Animals exposed to air containing 3.4 per cent of the gas for 1½ hours were seriously affected; rats withstand the gas best; cats and rabbits died on the following day from the above dose. A strong man can only stand 0.05 per cent of the gas for a short time, and the limit for workmen who have become used to it is put at 0.1 per cent.

Ammonia resembles hydrochloric acid gas in its action, but it is not so injurious. 0.3 per cent in air is dangerous, and 0.5 per cent to those accustomed to it.

Chlorine.—0.001 per cent to 0.005 per cent affects the respiratory organs; 0.04 per cent to 0.06 per cent produce dangerous symptoms, and 0.6 per cent soon proves fatal.

Bromine acts like chlorine. Men cannot stand more than 0.002 per cent to 0.004 per cent if not habituated; if habituated, not more than 0.01 per cent. This shows that fumigation with chlorine or bromine in the case of cholera epidemics is of no value, since to produce fatal effects on bacteria they must be exposed to air containing 3 per cent of chlorine for three hours, or it it contains 0.4 per cent for 24 hours.

Sulphuretted Hydrogen is less poisonous than chlorine or bromine, doses of 0.7 per cent in air being needed to kill animals exposed to it for 5 hours.

Carbon bisulphide was found to vary greatly in its action in different samples, although quite free from sulphuretted hydrogen, the chief poisonous action appearing to be due to unknown impurities it contained. A cat placed in air containing 2.3 Mgr. of carbon bisulphide to the liter for 7 hours expired 10 hours afterwards.

Aniline.—0.1 per cent in air proves dangerous, cats being especially sensitive, while rabbits and guinea-pigs are comparatively less affected.

Nitrobenzene vapor, even in large quantities, produces no serious effect.

The authors consider that these gases and vapors do not only produce local effects and changes on the body or on the blood, but that the central organs of the nervous system are acted upon, also that the more highly developed the organism is, the greater is its sensibility.—*Journ. Soc. Chem. Ind.*

APPARATUS FOR FRACTIONAL DISTILLATION.

The following form of apparatus, made from refined copper, is proposed by G. E. Clandon and E. C. Morin for the distillation of large quantities of liquid in a short time. It consists of (Fig. 1) an oven A, a boiler B, a column C, an apparatus D for separating foam, a cooler E, besides subsidiary apparatus, such as a manometer K, and test-vessel F. The oven A has two series of ring burners, each of which can be regulated at will; the boiler is provided with a cock M, a gauge L, a charging pipe n, and a cork for the manometer K; the boiler is slightly inclined towards the cock. The column C consists of an external sheath consisting of ten plates as shown at H; in the axis is a tube, the water flowing through which may be regulated; at upper end of the column is a thermometer.

Clandon and Morin's fractional still.

The signal manometer K (Fig. 2) consists of a pin ending in a piece of platinum wire passing through the copper piece b; this is fastened by means of d; c is in contact with b, while f is insulated from b, and is in contact, by means of g, with the platinum wire dipping into the mercury. When the gas flame and flow of water are properly regulated, c is so placed that the end of the point of the platinum wire is a few millimeters above the level of the mercury, so that an increase of temperature and of vapor pressure can at once be signalled. The test-vessel F (Fig. 3) serves to determine the specific gravity of the distillate and to change the receivers, the apparatus (Fig. 4) serving to signal when the receiver is full, consists of a glass tube a opened at the lower end and at the side. In a is a small float e. A plate of wood or ebonite, fastened by two bolts, bears a copper rod f, on to which a second piece g is fastened by means of the screw h. If the receiving flask is full, the float comes in contact with the small platinum plates l and m whereby the circuit is closed and the electric bell rung.

It is necessary, for the apparatus to work well, that the distillation should be commenced slowly, and the gas flame gradually raised. A mixture of alcohol and water can be distilled at the rate of 4-5 liters per hour, while a mixture of butyl and amyl alcohols can be distilled at double the rate. The apparatus also serves for the distillation of crude petroleum, benzin, and aniline. Its efficacy is equal to that of the Le Bel Henninger column with fifteen bulbs; it is constructed by Wiesnegg, of Paris.

Hydrofluoric Acid as a Destructive Agent for the Tubercle Bacillus.

Dr. F. L. Trudeau, of Saranac Lake, N. Y., has made a series of culture experiments with the aid of rabbits to test the value of hydrofluoric acid in tuberculosis suggested by Bastien, Charcot, Bouchard, Seiler, Chevy and more recently by Garcin. The result of his experiments "warrants the assumption" that hydrofluoric acid, even when quite freely diluted with both water and air, is capable of destroying the tubercle bacillus." He has not reached any definite conclusion as to the availability of the remedy or its efficacy as a therapeutic agent.—*Med. News*, May 5th.

Ghatti—a Substitute for Gum Arabic.

At a meeting of the School of Pharmacy Students' Association, April 5th, A. Mander read a paper on a variety of East Indian gums which had been mentioned as possible substitutes for gum arabic, in the course of which a description was given of *Ghatti* gum and its behavior under several pharmaceutical conditions. The gum is pale and consists of rounded or vermiform pieces of varying sizes, clear internally, but dull and roughened on the surface, apparently caused by shrinkage in drying; from brownish-yellow to perfectly colorless and transparent. More carelessly picked specimens have woody and other foreign matter adhering.

With the same proportion of water as the other gums it formed a pale yellowish-brown semi-solid mass, very powerfully adhesive.

When diluted, the solution gave a translucent, slightly gelatinous precipitate with basic lead acetate, was precipitated by alcohol, gelatinised by borax, but only a slight opalescence was produced with ammonium oxalate. By incineration, the gum yielded 2.55 per cent of an ash, consisting chiefly of potassium and calcium carbonates and traces of sulphate.

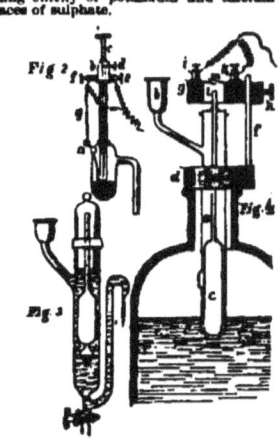

A mucilage was made with 1 oz. of the gum to 3 fl. oz. of distilled water.

On straining, a few grains were separated which had swollen to a translucent jelly, and these remained undissolved when treated with more water. The mucilage thus obtained is scarcely as bright as that from picked gum arabic, but quite equal to that given by ordinary good samples as to color, and at the same time more viscid. It is tasteless, inodorous, and of superior adhesive properties to mucil. acaciæ.

The emulsifying power was tried with olive oil, this being selected in preference to almond or castor oils as a more crucial test. The experiments showed that the emulsions afforded by ghatti mucilage are, as regards consistence, etc., quite equal to those by acacia, but preferable as to color, being of almost pure snowy whiteness. On microscopical examination, the oil particles in the emulsion made with ghatti and 2 parts of oil appear as nearly as possible identical in size with those given by acacia and 1 part, or half the quantity, of oil.

After standing fifteen days, the "ghatti" emulsions showed no separation of oil, and since the mucilage was made with double the proportion of water used for acacia, it must be acknowledged that the emulsive power of the gum is very remarkable.

The prevention, or long delaying, of the chemical reaction between mercuric chloride and calcium hydrate in the presence of acacia mucilage is well known, and experiments were made to ascertain if ghatti also possessed this power. That it does so in a very striking degree is evident. It is evident that ghatti gum is an article commercially obtainable at a low price and which, though differing considerably in appearance from the Acaciæ Gummi of the Pharmacopœia, possesses in a marked degree many characteristics which have been supposed to be peculiar to the latter. If more care were taken in the gathering and selection, there seems to be little doubt that picked qualities would speedily rise to considerable commercial value and pharmaceutical interest.

So far as I am aware, nothing has been published about ghatti gum, but it is scarcely probable that its peculiar properties have escaped notice by those who use large quantities of gum for confectionery or other purposes where a good article is essential. Of course, such delightful compounds as "chewing-gum," etc., of presumably Yankee origin, and containing in some instances 7 per cent solid paraffin, are beneath notice; but the transparency of an aqueous solution which could be improved by suitable treatment, together with the light color, freedom from taste and low price of ghatti, suggests its use in better articles where gum arabic is stated to be a chief ingredient. We may venture to note in passing that it is rather strange that one special kind of pastilles should not have advanced in price proportionately to the scarcity of the African gum, and the statement that they are sold at a loss appears at least contrary to usual commercial principles. For the ordinary opaque medicated lozenges ghatti seems well suited, and as large quantities have evidently been used somewhere, it would be interesting to trace their destination: perhaps lozenge makers could supply a clue.

Most of us are familiar with the vexing fact of labels apparently well gummed refusing to stick when damped, or certain envelopes have supplied similar instances. One well known firm sustains a reputation for avoiding this inconvenience, by using a secret composition, into which ghatti may or may not enter, but the advantages which this gum offers, either alone or in combination, for preparing adhesive substances are not small.

The prices brought by ghatti gum in the English market are as follows, showing a slight increase:—Qualities described as "good" brought, Aug. 30th, 1887, 63s.; Nov. 15th, 1887, 70s.; Feb. 28th, 1888, 75s.; Mar. 3d, 79s.; Mar. 17th, 80s. Qualities marked "fine" and "very fine" have brought 93s. and £5 15s.

The botanical sources cannot be definitely stated, and they are not easily ascertained. Their names afford little, if any, clue if correct, but are unreliable, as often transposed in re-packing, so comparison must be made with authentic specimens before we can decide, though the following notes may be of interest:—

By some authors it is stated that all Indian gum in the London market is the produce of East Africa, being brought in Arab vessels to Bombay, and thence exported to England. This, though probably true some years ago, cannot be so now, since very little, if any, is sent from that part of the African coast, so we must look to the gum-yielding trees of India itself.—*Pharmaceutical Journal*, April 14th.

Detection of Adulteration in Lard.

Mr. Shippen Wallace has studied this subject on behalf of the New Jersey State Dairy Commissioner, and we take the following from his paper published in the official report:*

Hübl has published a method which enables us now to determine, with comparative certainty, the kind of fat under examination, and, in certain instances, whether it is pure or adulterated (*Dingler's Pol. Journ.*, 253-261). This method is based on the fact that nearly all fats are composed of the glycerin ethers of the members of three groups of fatty acids; the acetic, acrylic, and tetrolic series. The relative proportion of these acids, in any variety of fat or oil, is constant, within certain limits, and differs only in different kinds of oil, but the members of the three groups of acids exhibit a very different behavior towards chlorine, bromine, or iodine. While, under ordinary circumstances, the acids of the acetic series are indifferent, those of the acrylic and tetrolic series readily unite with different quantities of the halogens. If, therefore, it is possible to make a fat unite with a halogen, so that the amount of the latter which enters into the compound may be accurately determined, the number thus obtained would be a constant, and would be dependent upon the amount of unsaturated acids in the fat. While the application of this principle to the determination of fats was not original with Hübl, yet he was the first to make use of iodine, and to elaborate a practical method. His method is as follows: 25 grammes of iodine are dissolved in 500 C.c. of 95-per-cent alcohol and 30 grammes of mercuric chloride in the same amount of alcohol. These two solutions are then mixed together and allowed to stand for twelve hours before using. The strength of the solution is then determined by means of a standard solution of sodium hyposulphite, whose strength has previously been determined in the usual manner. From 0.2 to 1.0 gramme of the oil or fat is then weighed off and dissolved in 10 C.c. chloroform, and 25-30 C.c. of the iodine solution added, and, after standing in a closed flask for not less than three hours, the amount of unabsorbed iodine is determined by means of the hyposulphite solution. By a simple calculation, the number of grammes of iodine taken up by 100 grammes of the oil or fat is then found, and this number is the "constant" for the fat examined. Hübl examined a large number of fats and others have verified the reliability of his process. He gives

for lard.................................... 59 per cent.
" tallow................................... 40 "   "
" cotton-seed oil......................... 106 "   "

* Report of the Dairy Commissioner of the State of New Jersey, 1887, 8vo., Trenton, 1888.

Mr. Wallace examined some thirty samples of lard of known purity, and obtained 59.2 as the average iodine number, the maximum being 62.8, and the minimum 57.4 per cent. Cotton-seed oil having such a high iodine degree, its presence would be indicated, when mixed with lard, by a higher figure than that for pure lard; and if with tallow, by a lower figure. The amount of admixture can be approximately estimated by means of the following formula:

$$x = \frac{100\,(I-y)}{m-y}$$

where x is the percentage of one fat (which being known, at once gives the percentage of the other fat y). I is the iodine degree or iodine number of the mixture; m is the iodine degree of the fat x, and y that of the fat y.

As it is, however, quite easy to blend together tallow and cotton-seed oil in such proportions as to produce a mixture having the same iodine number as pure lard, some additional methods must be resorted to when a sample of lard appears to comply with Hübl's test and yet is suspected of being adulterated.

One of the most reliable tests now available is that of Becchi, which has been several times slightly improved and is now performed in the following manner: A solution is prepared composed of 85 parts of amylic alcohol and 15 parts of rape-seed oil. Another solution containing 1 Gm. of nitrate of silver in 200 C.c. of 95-per-cent alcohol is also prepared. Now take 50 C.c. of the melted lard to be examined, and 1 C.c. of the alcoholic solution of silver nitrate, and then from 8 to 10 C.c. of the mixture of rape-seed oil and amylic alcohol. Shake the mixture thoroughly, and then heat it in a water-bath for five minutes. If the lard contains no cotton-seed oil, the color of the mixture remains the same as before heating, the mixture of lard and rape-seed oil producing a pale straw color. If cotton-seed oil is present, there will be produced a brownish color of a varying shade, from a light to a deep dark, according to the quantity of cotton-seed oil present. In performing the test, the following precautions must be observed: In heating the mixture, the tube containing the same is placed in the water-bath and subjected to, at the most, five minutes' heating in the boiling water; longer than this will often produce a slight discoloration, which may be misleading, although after practice one will not mistake the color. It is also well, at the time the suspected lard is thus examined, to conduct at the same time and to submit to the same length of heating an examination of a sample of pure lard; by this means, if the time is exceeded, and a discoloration is produced, it can readily be seen whether it has been caused by the cotton-seed oil or overheating. In all the tests I have thus made, I have found the mixture to begin to color in about three minutes, and, at the end of five minutes, the darkening has been perfectly evident, while during the same time the pure lard has not been changed, or at the most, has become what one might term one shade darker. The cause of the mixture becoming darkened is owing to the decomposition of the silver nitrate. Owing to the difficulty in obtaining rape-seed oil, what I have used I extracted and purified myself. In all samples of suspected lard, if one will follow the methods here given, he cannot fail to meet with correct and proper results:

I. Hübl's method, which will indicate either adulteration with tallow alone or cotton-seed oil alone, or indicate pure lard.

II. Use Becchi's test, as described, which will prove the presence or absence of cotton-seed oil.

III. Use the sulphuric acid test as a further confirmation (see Oleum Gossypii, U. S. Pharm.). By these last two, if Hübl's method should yield a figure which should classify the suspected lard as pure, one can readily confirm or disprove it, while if Hübl's should indicate cotton-seed oil, they would make the proof complete. Lard stearine yields figures, by Hübl's method, within the range of pure lard, and while some manufacturers make use of this article in the manufacture of summer lard, yet it is not an adulteration in the same sense that cotton-seed oil and tallow are. I have not mentioned other claimed adulterants of lard, as they are easy of detection; water we sometimes find, one sample I examined containing 11.80 per cent. When this is found, it is either caused by carelessness in the manufacture, or is intentional, as it can readily be guarded against.

Rapid Preparation of Tincture of Iodine.—C. Dandt recommends to dissolve 1 part of iodine in 9.2 parts of *absolute* alcohol, and then to add 0.8 parts of water. Iodine dissolves very quickly in absolute alcohol, but comparatively slowly in common alcohol.—*Pharm. Zeit.*

The U. S. Ph. directs the tincture to contain only 8 parts of iodine, instead of 10. If it is to be made quickly Dandt's plan may be followed. In this case, the following proportions are to be used:

Iodine.................................. 8 parts.
Absolute Alcohol....................... 86   "
Water.................................. 6   "

SAFETY STOP-COCK FOR GAS BURNERS.

Accidents happen not unfrequently through the flame of a gas-burner or gas-stove striking back to the orifice where the undiluted gas issues, and by overheating the rubber-tubing sets fire to the latter and to surrounding fixtures. [Two serious conflagrations, caused by an accident of this kind, are known to the editors of this journal.] Various plans have been heretofore proposed to prevent damage from this cause. But, while all these plans provide for the extinction of the burning gas or flame, none of them insures the interruption or stoppage of the current of gas. Klobukow has recently described a device which appears to accomplish the object by causing the gas delivery tube to be compressed by springs set into action after the fusion of a composite ring holding them apart.

The apparatus is a peculiarly constructed stop-cock with strong springs *f* and *f*, which is applied to the gas-burner in the manner shown in the cut.

The rubber-tubing attached to the burner passes through a ring *r*, and between two parallel bars *ab, cd*, which are kept apart by the levers *mn, op*, the ends of which are held in place by a ring *l*, made of low-fusing metal. As long as this ring holds the ends of the levers, gas will pass through the tube. As soon as the ring *l* is taken off or broken the springs at *f* will come into action and cause the two parallel bars *ab, cd*, to be pressed together, thereby shutting off the supply of gas.

The ring *l*, upon which the action depends, and which is situated where the effect of heat (caused by the striking back of the flame is first noticed), is made of a composition suitable to the temperature which is not to be exceeded. The best material to make the rings of is the fusible metal of Wood or Lipowitz, which melts at a temperature of 74° C. (165.2° F.) and 71.5° C. (161° F.)—*After Zeitsch. f. Anal. Chem., 1888, 168.*

Safety stop-cock for gas burners.

Hydrofluosilicate of Quinine.

The preparation of the acid and neutral hydrofluosilicates of quinine is reported by Dr. Cavazzi (*Archiv*, March, p. 228), who believes that these salts will prove useful as possessing at the same time antipyretic and antiseptic properties. The salts are described as being formed upon treating with silicon fluoride a solution of anhydrous quinine (*sic*, but query quinine hydrate?) in carbon bisulphide or absolute alcohol. From an alcoholic solution the neutral salt separates first in white flocks, consisting of microscopic crystals which are completely insoluble in carbon bisulphide and ether, and only very slightly soluble in alcohol, but very freely soluble in water. Upon passing in more silicon fluoride, the acid salt is formed, the crystals dissolving to give a fluorescent liquid. The two salts may also be formed by bringing together quinine hydrate and hydrofluosilicic acid in aqueous solution in molecular proportions and evaporating.—*Pharm. Journ.*

Caffeine from Tea.

At a recent meeting of the London Chamber of Commerce (reported in *Chem. and Drugg.*), the question of the manufacture of caffeine came up for discussion, with a view to have some changes made in the British custom laws to permit the importation, duty free, of damaged tea or tea sweepings. Of course it is well known that manufacturers of caffeine generally have recourse to tea, as the source of the alkaloid, and for their purposes it is immaterial whether the tea is damaged or not, as long as it contains a sufficient amount of caffeine. According to Mr. Thomas Christy's statement, made at the meeting before mentioned, there are between 3,000 and 4,000 pounds of caffeine annually made in Germany from tea sweepings which were refused admittance into England. He advocated an alteration in the regulations, so that the home industry might be benefited thereby. He suggested that the sweepings or any damaged or inferior tea, which it was intended to admit for such purposes, should be treated with enough petroleum to render it unfit for consumption. This treatment would not at all interfere with the manufacturers' process for extracting the caffeine.

The British customs officials, who are known to be crusty, unwilling to go out of old well-trodden tracks, and afraid of doing anything for which there is no "precedent," do not seem to take very kindly to this proposal, though they thought that "the request might be brought before the authorities."

Testing for Arsenic in Metallic Iron.

J. O. Bergman, of Gothenburg, points out (in *Pharm. Centralhalle*, No. 8) that the presence of arsenic in powdered iron (Ferrum pulveratum) cannot be detected either by the process prescribed by the German Pharmacopœia, or that of the German Pharmacopœia Committee, because *arsenide of iron* is insoluble in diluted hydrochloric acid.

Woehler demonstrated, as far back as in 1840, that when arsenical iron was dissolved in dilute sulphuric acid no arsenetted hydrogen (AsH₃) was evolved. Eggeris showed, in 1870, that on dissolving iron in arsenical sulphuric acid, no arsenetted hydrogen is given off after the escape of pure hydrogen. Ahlberg, in 1883, demonstrated that the facts thus ascertained when sulphuric acid was present, were valid also in presence of hydrochloric acid.

Hence, in examining powdered iron (or any kind of metallic or reduced iron, suspected to contain arsenic—Ed. Am. Dr.], the arsenic will be found in the residue left behind undissolved by the acid. In this it may be detected either by Bonnendorff's method—dissolving the residue with concentrated hydrochloric acid and the smallest possible quantity of potassium chlorate, or by distilling with ferric chloride, ferrous sulphate, and hydrochloric acid of spec. gr. 1.190 (Schneider's process), in the usual manner.

Strophanthus.—

Fraenkel reports in the *Deutsche med. Wochenschrift* the results of a series of trials of strophanthus, and says that as a heart tonic it is efficient, but can in no sense approach the digitalis excepting in individual cases where, owing to some peculiar condition, it acts more favorably. It acts best in functional disorders such as are caused by alcohol or tobacco, and also in the relief of ascites caused by engorgement of the portal circulation.

The Reaction between Zinc and Sulphuric Acid.

It is usually supposed that the reaction between zinc and sulphuric acid in the presence of water always takes place after the following scheme:

Zn	+	H₂SO₄	=	ZnSO₄	+	H₂
zinc		sulphuric acid		sulphate of zinc		hydrogen

Pattison Muir and R. H. Adie, however, have made this reaction the subject of a detailed investigation, and have come to very important results. It has, indeed, been known before that sometimes other gases, such as hydrosulphuric and sulphurous acid were formed during the reaction, but the conditions for their production were not known.

Muir and Adie find that the purer the employed metallic zinc is, the smaller are the quantities of secondary products (hydrosulphuric and sulphurous acid) produced, no matter whether a concentrated or a dilute sulphuric acid is used. When 1 molecule of this acid is diluted with 10 to 12 molecules of water, *hydrogen* is almost the sole product of the reaction, even on boiling. If the zinc used is almost chemically pure, and the reaction takes place at a temperature of 160° C., dilution of the acid diminishes both the quantity of generated hydrosulphuric acid, as that of sulphurous acid. If commercial zinc is used, the proportion of the last-named acid is diminished. With *commercial* zinc, even so dilute an acid as one composed of 1 mol. of H₂SO₄, and 100 mol. of water, still produces some hydrosulphuric acid at temperatures between 0° C. and the boiling point.

Platinised zinc behaves like the commercial substance. An acid of the concentration 1 mol. H₂SO₄ and 2 mol. water generates with commercial zinc, at 100° C., scarcely traces of either hydrosulphuric or sulphurous acids. At 165° C., however, it produces copious quantities of the former with traces of the latter. At 180° C., hydrosulphuric acid gas is given off in streams, almost free from sulphurous. Under the same circumstances, an almost pure zinc generates both gases in large quantities. Free sulphur is separated in notable quantities only when platinized zinc is used. At low temperatures, however, or with acids containing less than 2 mol. of water, free sulphur was never met with, even when hydrosulphuric or sulphurous acid was given off.—*After Journ. Chem. Soc., 1888, 47.*

Adhatoda Vasica.

DAVID HOOPER describes in the *Pharmaceutical Journal* of April 7th a shrub growing in India (where it is very common) which has some remarkable properties. As a medicine, the leaves of the vasaka, as it is called in the vernacular, have been long in use as an expectorant and antispasmodic in conjunction with an aromatic. It is also used as an ingredient in popular anthelmintics. In Bengal, the leaves have been smoked for the relief of asthma. In the arts, the yellow coloring-matter extracted by water is used in connection with indigo to produce a green dye. It is in agriculture that the leaves are of unique value. Dr. G. Watt says that in the Sutley valley the fresh leaves are scattered over recently flooded fields prepared for the rice crop, and the native cultivators say that the leaves not only act as a manure, but also as a poison to the aquatic weeds that otherwise would greatly injure the rice. Fields not treated in this way are covered with a green scum, but after the leaves are added they are supposed to kill the floating duck-weed and the submerged charrer, and prevent their propagation.

The author of the paper reports the following experiments: A sample of pond water containing *Spirogyra* and numerous animalculæ was mixed with a few drops of a strong infusion of adhatoda leaves. The chlorophyll gradually disappeared from the weeds and the cells became broken up. Oxygen was given off with less frequency, and at length ceased. Some insect pupæ rose to the surface and then died. Numerous *Paramecia* remained active for some time, but eventually succumbed to the action of the poison. In twenty-four hours the water showed only a brown mass lying on the bottom of the glass, while a corresponding specimen, which had not been treated, contained the green aquatic weeds evolving oxygen and living animalculæ.

A solution of sulphate of vasicine was added to water in a basin containing a live frog. The frog immediately sank, without the slightest movement and was unmistakably dead in a short time. Some small leeches adhering to the frog before the vasicine was dropped into the water, at once left it and came to the surface, those that did not succeed in escaping from the vessel were in an hour's time quite lifeless.

An aqueous solution of an alcoholic extract of the leaves was tried upon flies, fleas, musquitoes, centipedes and other insects, and in every case the results were poisonous. The solution appeared to kill them without previous intoxication.

On higher animals the leaves do not seem to have such an effect. A quantity of the alcoholic extract representing 225 grains of the leaves was given to a small dog and was not followed by inconvenient symptoms.

Some Practical Notes on Filtration.

FROM an article on this subject, by Mr. Eug. Dieterich, printed in the *Pharm. Centralhalle*, we take the following:
In order to obtain clear filtrates, the filter should be moistened with the same liquid which is to be passed through. In the case of tinctures, alcohol or dilute alcohol is used, as the case may be; for aqueous solutions, water, etc., etc.

In filling up the filter (which must be pushed down in the funnel to the furthest point where it will lie flat), the liquid should be poured down its side.

For liquids which pass only slowly through filters, it is not unusual to use vacuum-pumps or aspirators. The author (Mr. Dieterich) does not regard these with favor, as he finds that they soon become clogged with sediment. Besides, suction under a high vacuum usually produces a turbid filtrate. [This is probably to be understood as referring to Mr. Dieterich's experience in filtering pharmaceutical liquids on a large scale.]

When a piece of filtering paper is to be laid upon a muslin strainer, the paper should, before being wetted, be crumbled or crushed by hand, so as to make it more readily adapt itself to the folds or curves of the muslin.

Felt or flannel filtering bags do not usually filter clear at once, but require the repeated passage of the liquid before they will do so. If no clear filtrate can be obtained in this manner, the following plan may be adopted:

Soak a sufficient quantity of filter-paper or its clippings in just enough cold water, and rub it to a pulp. Then dilute it with hot water and pour some of the mass upon the walls of the filtering-bag, which must previously have been wetted and pressed. The fabric eagerly seizes upon the water and the paper pulp remains adhering to the surface. The superfluous water is allowed to drip off, a funnel with wide tube is then inserted and the bag filled with the liquid. [Care should be taken that the latter be not allowed to fall into the bag from a great height, as this would disturb the paper. A good plan is to permit a rubber (or other) tube, connected with the reservoir containing the turbid liquid, to reach to the bottom of the filtering-bag, its orifice ending in a small capsule or cup. The flow of liquid is controlled by a stop-cock. An arrangement of this kind will effectually prevent any disturbance of the filtering-surface.—ED. AM. DRUG.]

The author states that he works by the plan described by him, and that he uses a half-woollen ordinary flannel, which is regarded merely as an exterior shell, the greatest care being bestowed upon the coating of paper-pulp.

No matter whether a funnel has a large or a small funnel-tube attached to it, it is always necessary to contract the orifice where the point of the filter rests, to prevent its bursting. In funnels with wide necks, this is best done by a wad [of cotton or tow].

Funnels with ribbed walls are preferable. The walls must not be curved, but perfectly straight.

A Root Resembling Ipecacuanha.

FRANCIS RANSOM lately reported to the Pharmaceutical Society of Great Britain that a root called false Ipecacuanha had lately appeared for sale in the London market. It was dark-colored externally, not annulated, but marked longitudinally. The powdered root was of a red color; it contained much starch, but no glucose. When broken, the root was found to possess a corky portion which was distinctly porous and otherwise unlike true ipecacuanha. There was no difficulty in recognising the root as that of *Psychotria emetica*. A similar root is sometimes referred to a *Richardsonia scabra*. Long ago Pelletier reported, as the result of an analysis, that the root contained 9 per cent of emetine; but he subsequently admitted that his alkaloid was far from being pure, so that this analysis cannot be relied upon. To test the matter further, the author extracted 20 grammes of the powdered root with ammoniated chloroform by continuous percolation. Part of the percolate was shaken with water acidulated with sulphuric acid, and this solution, separated and tested with Meyer's and other alkaloidal reagents, gave an exceedingly slight indication of the presence of alkaloid. Another portion of the ammoniated chloroform percolate was shaken with water acidulated with acetic acid, and this aqueous solution on evaporation responded feebly to the test for emetine. This indication was followed up by a quantitative test, which resulted in 0.027 per cent being found as the quantity of alkaloid in the root. It therefore appears that striated ipecacuanha is of little value, so far as chemical tests can show, and these are corroborated by physiological effects. Thus, 60 grains of the powder had no effect upon the author; a dog swallowed 1 oz. of it and showed no signs of discomfort; and Professor Cash, of Aberdeen, has experimented with it and finds it to be inert. A museum specimen of the same drug gave similar results.—*Chemist and Druggist*.

Preparation of Pills or Granules of Aconitine or Digitalin

IN view of the extremely powerful action of crystallised aconitine or digitalin, and the risks attending any inaccuracy in dispensing them, Benoit and Champigny recommended (in the *Journ. de Pharm.*, 1888 [April], 408) to dissolve the alkaloids by a suitable solvent and to triturate the solution with milk-sugar, and a small quantity of harmless coloring matter, which will enable the eye to distinguish when the triturated powder has become perfectly uniform. For nitrate of aconitine, the authors recommend, as a solvent, boiling water [which we consider unadvisable, as it may cause decomposition—ED. AM. DR.]. For the alkaloid aconitine and the neutral principle "digitalin" (that is, the crystallizable principle known by that name), they recommend chloroform. This solvent has special advantages. It will serve as a sort of test of identity, inasmuch as the crystallizable aconitine or digitalin are very easily soluble in it, and any impurities which they might contain would be left behind.

To guard against inaccuracies in weighing, the authors recommend to weigh out never less than 1 centigramme (say ½ grain), and to make a large enough batch of pills or granules of the desired strength to consume the whole amount weighed out, though several hundred may have to be made at one time. They give the following formulas:

1. *For Nitrate of Aconitine.*

	Gm.	
Nitrate of Aconitine	0.01	½ grain.
Sugar of Milk, powd.	4.00	60 grains.
Acacia, powd	1.00	15 "
Excipient	q. s.	

As excipient, the officinal "mellite" (or syrupus mellis) is recommended, with addition of 10 per cent of glycerin. Syrup of honey is prepared by adding to 4 parts of honey 1 part of water.

Dissolve the alkaloidal salt in 1 Gm. of boiling water, and pour the solution, drop by drop, upon 2 Gm. (30 grains) of sugar of milk, constantly triturating. Rinse the tube in which the solution had been made with a few drops of hot water, which is to be added to the mass in the mortar. Then gradually incorporate the remainder of the sugar of milk, afterwards the acacia, and lastly make a suitable mass with the aid of the excipient. Divide the mass into 100 granules (each containing 1/130 grain of nitrate of aconitine) and keep them in a dry and well-stoppered bottle.

Chloroform for Preserving Dispensing Solutions.

Jos. F. Burnett writes, in the *Pharmaceutical Journal*: Any one who has to get through a large amount of dispensing in a short time has his ingenuity put to work to devise every means he can to expedite his work. One of the first and most natural ideas is to keep every drug or chemical (which is likely to be required) in solution. I now keep large numbers of dispensing solutions, in fact many more than ever I previously did. Then crops up the difficulty that many soon spoil, ferment, develop fungoid growths, etc., etc. Where such is the case I use chloroform water, B. P., for the solvent, and in not a single instance have I found it fail to keep the solution perfectly. I may note in passing that I have the permission of the medical staff to use any such device as this, for the dose of chloroform introduced into a mixture by adding, e. g., 80 minims of a 1-in-10 solution of quinine is neither here nor there. I have by me quantities of pulv. rhei rubbed down with aq. chlorof., likewise pulv. cret. aromat.,solutions of quinine, fer. am. cit., pot. acet., pot. citr., and a host of others, some of which are some months old, and are as good as the day they were made. A couple of drachms of chloroform will keep for a fortnight as much as three gallons of fresh infusion of gentian. Infusion of calumba or buchu made four times the strength of the B. P. (i.e., conc. 1 to 3) keep perfectly when one drachm of chloroform to the quart is dissolved in them. With infusion of buchu I consider this a distinct advance on using spirit (which the 1 to 7 preparation of the wholesale houses contains), for the chloroform does not throw down any mucilaginous constituent. These are but a few examples of the use of chloroform as a preservative.

Reaction between Chloral and Cyanide of Potassium.

ATTENTION has been called by Messrs. Blarez and Deniges (*Bull. Soc. Pharm. Bord.*, Feb., p. 48) to an interesting reaction observed in dispensing a prescription ordering chloral hydrate and potassium cyanide together in an ointment. It was found that, when equal weights of these two compounds were powdered in a mortar and mixed, after an interval varying from half a minute to three minutes, effervescence occurred in the mass, which became yellow and then brown, hydrocyanic acid being given off freely. It was also found that when the ingredients were present in other than equal proportions, the reaction took place less quickly, but that the retardation was greater when the potassium cyanide was in excess than when the chloral hydrate preponderated. The intervention of water or alcohol also retarded the reaction in proportion to the quantity added, until a certain amount of stability was attained when the relation of the liquid to the solid was 8 to 1, but even dilute solutions were decomposed when boiled. In contact with lard the decomposition commences at once, so that such an ointment would be an improper preparation. If such a combination be really desirable, it is suggested that a solution should be prepared not stronger than 1 in 10, by adding the chloral hydrate and the potassium cyanide to the water separately. In the reaction which takes place, dichloracetic acid, hydrocyanic acid, and potassium chloride are formed. —*Pharm. Journ.*

Testing Olive Oil.

AT the Station Agronomique at Nice, according to M. Brulle (*Compt. Rend.*, cvi., 1,017), a mixture of nitric acid and egg albumen is used to detect the presence in olive oil of other vegetable oils. About 0.1 gramme of albumen in powder being placed in a test tube, 2 C.c. of nitric acid is added, and then 10 C.c. of the oil to be tested, after which the mixture is heated gently over a flame in such a way that the acid and the oil shall be kept at practically the same temperature. When the nitric acid commences to boil, the test tube is inclined so that the ebullition affects the mixture of the oil and the albumen. If the sample be pure olive oil, the color of the mixture is now yellow with a greenish tint, but if it contains 5 per cent of seed oil, it takes a free amber-yellow color which is darker with a larger proportion of foreign oil, until with 50 per cent of the color is deep orange. This test has been found to hold good for mixtures of olive oil with oils of cotton-seed, earthnut, sesame, poppy-seed, colza, camelina, and linseed. One exception has been met with, under the name "*acetine exotique*," which gives a rose tint with whitish spots. Nitric acid alone gives colorations that approximate to those mentioned, but only with colored oils; it is without perceptible effect upon mixtures containing poppy-seed or earthnut oil, which are relatively colorless.

A New Form of Suppository.

A new form of suppository has been suggested by Dr. S. G. Dixon (*Therap. Gaz.*, p. 241), which differs in the broader end being terminated in a cone, so that the whole represents a double cone, of which the upper is only half as long as the lower. The upper or shorter and broader end is inserted first, and the suppository, by reason of its shape, is easily retained and forced upwards by the sphincter muscle.

Sulfonal.

THE Berlin correspondent of the *Chemist and Druggist* writes that a new soporific, called, for short, sulfonal, has been announced. It is produced by the oxidation of a mixture of ethylmercaptan and acetone, and is otherwise known as diethyl-sulphonic-dimethyl-methane, or

$$\begin{matrix}CH_3\\CH_3\end{matrix}>C<\begin{matrix}SO_2C_2H_5\\SO_2C_2H_5\end{matrix}$$

It is in the form of tabular crystals, without odor, taste, or color; is soluble in from 18 to 20 parts of boiling water, or 100 parts of water at ordinary temperatures. In alcohol, or alcohol and ether, it is more soluble. It is not decomposed by oxidising agents, acids, nor alkalies. Prof. Kast administered it to 20 healthy men and showed that as much as 1 drachm can be taken without unpleasant effects; Prof. Cramer, of Marburg, gave 300 doses to 60 persons; Prof. Bäumler gave 120 doses to 30 persons in private practice, and the proper dose appears to be 15 to 30 grains, or as much, perhaps, as 45 grains for robust males. Almost always deep and tranquil sleep commences within half an hour and lasts from five to eight hours, and is not followed by the slightest after-symptoms. It was particularly useful when insomnia was caused by illness or attendant upon insanity. In administering it, a powder of 15 grains may be given in a wafer, or mixed with water.

Guarana.

DR. H. H. RUSBY, in a lecture before the Philadelphia College of Pharmacy describing his recent experiences in South America, described the cultivation and preparation of guarana, in the course of which he said: As cultivated in the region about the lower Madeira river, it is planted like a vineyard, excepting that it is planted wide apart and is poled like hops. It is kept within bounds by pruning. The opening of the seeds is shown by the opening of the pods. The fruit resembles a hickory-nut and is contained in a husk consisting of three instead of four parts. They are shelled out by hand, washed, and then roasted for six hours. The roasting loosens a papery shell which is detached by placing the nuts in a bag and beating them with sticks. The best variety of guarana is that in which the seeds have not been broken finely. Enough water is added to form a mass and the seeds are thus kneaded by hand to the consistency of dough. Foreign substances are not generally added, as is commonly believed. The dough is then spread on the upper floors of a large building and subjected to a uniform heat by means of fires which give off little smoke. Great experience is needed in this stage of the process. By the natives guarana is used by filing off a portion of the mass and mixing it with a glass of cold water. It contains two or three times as much caffein as coffee and its effects are very refreshing, but when used in excess causes trembling and muscular weakness.—*Amer. Journ. Pharm.*

Oil of Hyoscyamus.

A FATTY oil, containing in solution some of the chlorophyl and active principles of certain narcotic plants, is a favorite remedy in continental practice, and such as that mentioned in the title is not unfrequently prescribed here. For this reason, the National Formulary has adopted a formula for its preparation. This formula is based upon an improvement of the one previously in use (Pharm. Germ.), suggested by E. Dieterich, of Helfenberg, who recommended to digest the comminuted plant with alcohol and ammonia, so as to set free the alkaloids, and then to digest it with the oil which dissolved the active principle. Recently, Dieterich has gone a step further and recommends to extract the desirable constituents from the plant by percolating with a suitable menstruum. For this purpose, 100 parts of the finely powdered herb are moistened with a mixture of 100 parts of alcohol, 40 parts of water of ammonia, and 36 parts of ether, then packed in a percolator, allowed to macerate one hour, and then exhausted with ether. The ethereal extract is mixed with 500 parts of olive oil, and the ether then distilled off.

An oil of hyoscyamus thus obtained possesses a very fine green color, a strong, narcotic odor, and contains practically the whole amount of alkaloid contained in the herb.

Hectograph Sheets.

Soak 4 parts of best white glue in a mixture of 5 parts of water and 3 parts of solution of ammonia, until the glue is soft. Warm the mixture until the glue is dissolved, and add 3 parts of granulated sugar and 8 parts of glycerin, stirring well, and letting come to the boiling-point. While hot, paint it upon white blotting-paper with a broad copying-brush, until the paper is thoroughly soaked, and a thin coating remains on the surface. Allow it to dry for two or three days, and it is then ready for use. An aniline ink should be used for writing, and before transferring to the blotting-paper, wet the latter with a damped sponge, and allow it to stand one or two minutes. Then proceed to make copies in the ordinary way. If the sheets are laid aside for two days, the old writing sinks in and does not require to be washed off.—*Chem. and Drug.*

Photoxylin.

Geo. M. Beshores, having attempted the manufacture of photoxylin, a substance used in Russia in place of gun-cotton, has described the method employed by him. Wood-pulp was obtained of the manufacturer both in the loose, fibrous form, and as condensed by rolling into thick and porous sheets. After careful drying, the pulp was nitrated in the following solution:

Nitrous acid, 48° Baumé	8½ lb. av.
Sulphuric acid	4½ lb. av.
Potassium nitrate, granular	5 oz. av.

The acids having been mixed in an earthenware crock and allowed to cool to 90° F., the potassium nitrate was added and thoroughly incorporated. Four oz. av. of the well-dried pulp was immediately placed in the mixture and allowed to remain for 12 hours. It was then removed and thoroughly washed. The addition of a few drops of ammonia to the wash water facilitated the removal of the acid. Nitrocellulose thus prepared leaves little or no residue on burning and is entirely soluble in a mixture of 50% of concentrated ether and 50% of alcohol. Three per cent of this photoxylin is sufficient to make a very thick collodion which leaves a very tough film when applied. An addition of 5 drops of castor oil to the fluidounce renders it flexible. This solution (also called "photoxylin") has the advantage over ordinary collodion of giving a stronger film.—*Amer. Journ Pharm.*

Delicate Test for Nitrous Acid.

In the course of a paper on the estimation of nitrous acid (in *Journ. Chem. Soc.*, 1888, 364), Prof. Frankland states that when he has to test qualitatively for minute quantities of nitrous acid, he always relies upon Zambelli's modification of the sulphanilic acid test. This is as follows:

Add to the solution suspected to contain a nitrite, first 1 drop of a saturated aqueous solution of sulphanilic acid, then a drop of an aqueous solution of phenol, and render the mixture alkaline with ammonia. If any nitrous acid is present, the liquid will assume a color varying from faint yellow to intense reddish yellow (like the color of a strong solution of potassium bichromate), according to the quantity of the nitrous acid present. This test is capable of indicating the presence of 1 part of nitrous nitrogen in 40,000,000 parts of water. And whilst its delicacy is extreme, it has the further advantage that the reagents employed are permanent in solution.

The estimation of the amount of nitrous acid present by this method, as will be known to those of our readers who are familiar with water-analysis, is made by ascertaining, experimentally, the depth of tint corresponding to varying proportions of nitrous acid, and then using a standard scale of colors (such as a glass prism the color of which deepens towards the thick end, or a hollow prism filled with a colored liquid), each shade of which is known to correspond to a definite amount of nitrous acid.

Anthrarobin Preparations.

The new substitute for chrysarobin, proposed by Prof. Liebermann, will probably be obtainable in the market here by the time that this number is in the hands of our readers. Regarding its nature and properties, compare our April number, page 62.

Behrend has given the following combinations in the *Therap. Monatshefte*:

Anthrarobin Ointment.

1. Ten (10) per cent.

Anthrarobin	10 parts
Olive Oil	30 "
Lanolin	60 "

or:

Anthrarobin	10 parts
Olive Oil	15 "
Lard	75 "

2. Twenty (20) per cent.

Anthrarobin	20 parts
Olive Oil	40 "
Lanolin	40 "

or:

Anthrarobin	20 parts
Olive Oil	30 "
Lard	50 "

Anthrarobin Tincture.

1. Ten (10) per cent.

Anthrarobin	10 parts
Alcohol	90 "

2. Twenty (20) per cent.

Anthrarobin	20 parts
Alcohol	80 "

Anthrarobin Solution.

1. Anthrarobin	10 parts
Borax	5 "
Water	80 "

or:

Anthrarobin	10 parts
Glycerin	90 "

Fly and Mosquito Bane.

A good preparation to prevent the bite of flies and gnats, and also mosquitoes, is the following, recommended by Dieterich (and Vomacka).

Expressed Oil of Bay	10 parts
Oil of Eucalyptus	20 "
Ether	20 "
Alcohol	70 "

Dissolve the Expressed Oil of Bay (Oleum Lauri expressum) in the ether, and the Oil of Eucalyptus in the Alcohol. Mix the two solutions, and filter rapidly in a covered funnel.

This compound may be used on domestic animals as well as by man, or it may be applied to places about the house which it is desired to protect against the visitation of flies, etc.

Phosphate of Copper as a Remedy in Phthisis.

Dr. Luton believes phthisis amenable to cure or amelioration by the administration of phosphate of copper "in a nascent state," and dissolved in an alkaline menstruum. He recommends pills containing each

	Gm.	
Acetate Copper, neutral	0.01	⅙ grain
Phosphate Sodium, cryst.	0.05	"
Liquorice Root	q. s.	q. s.
Glycerin	q. s.	q. s.

Also a mixture :

Acetate Copper, neutral	0.65	1 grain
Phosphate Sodium, cryst.	0.39	10 grains
Mist. Acaciæ	1.25	4 fl. oz.

Dose: A tablespoonful.

—*L'Union Pharm.*

Antineuralgic Salve.

(Galezowski.)

Menthol	15 parts
Cocaine (alkaloid)	5 "
Chloral	2 "
Vaseline	100 "

Mix intimately. To be applied to the painful part.—*Rép. de Pharm.*

Alizarin Ink Powder.

Tannic Acid	450 parts
Sulphate of Iron (cryst.)	540 "
Chloride of Sodium	200 "
Bisulphate of Potassium	75 "
Indigocarmine, dry	50 "
Picric Acid	4 "

Mix the sulphate of iron (reduced to a coarse powder) and chloride of sodium, and dry them in an iron pan over a naked fire, constantly stirring. Lastly reduce the mass to a fine powder. Rub the bisulphate of potassium to a fine powder in a mortar, and mix this intimately with the picric acid. Then mix this mass with that first prepared and lastly incorporate the other ingredients. [Picric acid is poisonous, and under certain conditions, explosive. It should be manipulated as directed above.]

The resulting product is a green powder which, when dissolved in 15 parts of water, yields a superior ink, which turns jet-black.—*Vomacka*.

Crayons for Writing on Glass.—The following process answers well for the production of pencils that will write readily on clean dry glass.

Take of

Spermaceti	4 parts
Tallow	3 "
Wax	3 "

Melt together in a small dish, and stir in finely powdered, and thoroughly mixed

Red lead	6 parts
Carbonate of potassium	1 part

Keep the mass melted and stirred for about half an hour, and then pour into suitable moulds, and cool as rapidly as possible.

If the mixture be introduced into glass tubes of convenient size, the solid cylinder can be pushed out when cooled and sharpened, the tube being used as a handle. Of course, French chalk will also answer.—*Br. and Col. Drug.*

Testing the Tightness of Tin-Cans.—Tin-cans are best tested as to their tightness by filling them with compressed air and immersing it in water. Any air-bubbles ascending through the water would show the existence of a leak, which it is then easy to close by soldering. There is no risk of any water getting into the cans, during the trial.—*Droguist. Zeit.*

Dextrin as an Adulterant of Extracts.—Pannetier says that the addition of dextrin to extracts, before complete evaporation, gives them a good appearance and consistence, and that this practice has reached an alarming point in the extracts sold in France.—*Nat. Drug.*

The following is mentioned by the *Brit. and Col. Drug.* as an efficient test for such alterations: Dissolve 5 grammes of the suspected substance in 50 grammes of cold distilled water. Throw down tannins, gums, alkaloids, etc., with solution plumbi subacet.; collect, and wash the precipitate. Mix the filtrate and washings, and remove the lead salts by a current of sulphuretted hydrogen. After filtering and washing the lead precipitate, it is evaporated, if necessary—though generally this operation is superfluous where the adulteration is of any magnitude—and mixed with an equal volume of strong alcohol. If the extract contained dextrin, it is thereby precipitated, and may be collected and weighed. A small proportion of salts insoluble in alcohol will be associated with the dextrin, but these may be ignored in approximate determinations.

Syrup of Tolu.—The Swedish pharmacopœia proscribes the following method of preparation: 80 parts of balsam tolu are by degrees dissolved in 100 of rectified alcohol, filtered, and poured into 2,000 parts of boiling water, and well stirred. Permit to stand for two to three days, filter off the fluid, and without the application of heat prepare with 1,900 sugar a syrup tolu, which is perfectly clear, has a strong odor, and an agreeable taste. The syrup is rather thin, however; it would be better to use 2,500 of sugar.—*Chem. and Drug.*

Cosmetic uses of Glycerin.—J. S. Charles writes to the *Scientific American* on the usefulness of glycerin and enumerates the following:

As a dressing for ladies' shoes it renders the leather soft and pliable without soiling garments which come in contact.

For excessive perspiration of the feet one part of burnt alum with two parts of glycerin should be rubbed on the feet at night and a light, open sock worn. In the morning the feet should be washed with tepid water.

For bunions and corns equal parts of Cannabis Indica and glycerin should be painted on the surface and covered with canton flannel.

For the face, oatmeal made into a paste with 2 parts of glycerin and 1 of water may be applied at night under a mask as a complexion improver.

As a supplement to a bath 3 oz. of glycerin in 2 quarts of water will render the skin fresh and delicate.

For coughs, 1 to 2 tablespoonfuls of glycerin in pure rye whiskey or hot rich cream will afford almost immediate relief.

For consumption, 1 part of powdered willow charcoal in 2 parts of glycerin is a panacea.

For diseased and inflamed gums, 2 parts of golden seal, 1 part of powdered burnt alum, and 2 parts of glycerin, rubbed on at night, after first removing any tartar.

Aluminium is coming into use as a material for dental plates. It is nearly as light as rubber; but little more than ⅓ the weight of gold; has neither odor nor taste; is not affected by the elements of food or the secretions of the mouth and costs, bulk for bulk, about ¼ the present price of silver.

Lipanine—A Substitute for Cod-Liver Oil.—Mr. Mering, starting with a theory that cod-liver oil owes its superiority to other fatty oils to its richness in oleic acid—white oil contains from 0.18 per cent to 0.71 per cent, and brown oil 2.54 per cent to 5.07 per cent—the author has tried experiments with a mixture of olive oil (100 parts) and oleic acid (6 parts), to which he has given the name of lipanine, and to which he attributes the following advantages:

Lipanine would have no disagreeable taste and would be perfectly digestible, because of its high emulsive power, oleic acid saponifying with the alkalies of the bile and pancreatic juice. For this reason it could be administered for long periods in large doses without injury to the digestive faculties. In fact, M. Mering reports that for a period of six months he administered this remedy to forty patients, of whom thirty were children, and that all took it without repugnance and without subsequent ill effects. The dose varied from one to four teaspoonfuls, according to the patient's age, and this was continued from six weeks to three months. Most of the patients were scrofulous or rickety, some consumptives or diabetics. All of them under this treatment increased in weight, their general condition improved, their strength returned, and these good results were obtained also among a great number of children in charge of Professor Kohts. In a word, these effects would appear absolutely comparable with those obtained with cod-liver oil, but the advantages of lipanine in its freedom from taste, easy toleration by the stomach, and capability of administration in the hottest summer weather are equally obvious.—*Med. News*, from *Rev. Scient.*

Fertilizer for House Plants.—Potassium carbonate, potassium phosphate, magnesium carbonate, sodium silicate, of each 1 part; potassium nitrate, 2 parts; sulphate of iron, 3 parts, in 3,000 parts of water. A little of this solution poured occasionally about the roots of plants is said by the *Droguisten Zeitung* to greatly favor the growth of house plants.

Pure Quinine Salts.—C. F. Boehringer & Sons, of Waldhof, near Mannheim, now turn out, besides the commercial quinine salts, a series specially made from "pure" sulphate of quinine. The latter, as is well known, is prepared by starting from the crystallized bisulphate of quinine, which, when crystallizing, leaves all but traces of other accompanying alkaloids behind. The new pure quinine salts possess the same crystalline form as the usually commercial varieties.

[As the price of these pure quinine salts is but little in advance of that of the ordinary salts, in which the amount of secondary alkaloids sometimes rises to 18 per cent and more, the time will surely come when the pharmacopœial requirements will exclude any but the pure salts.—Ed. Am. Dr.]

Tight Corks.—Mr. Bousquet, of Bordeaux, recommends as a good method of cleaning and preserving corks, the following process (which will also make them practically air and water-tight.—Ed. Am. Dr.).

Put the corks in a steam or water-bath until the "mildew" is removed. Then, while they are hot, immerse them in a dilute solution of albumen (1 pound of dry albumen to 180 pints, U. S. measure, of water). Fish-glue may be substituted for albumen, especially when cork-slabs are treated. For this purpose, dissolve 2 lbs. each of fish-glue and of salicylic acid in 25 gallons of hot water and plunge the corks or cork-slabs into it. When the water has become cold, put the corks in a solution of tannic acid (containing 7 oz. in 25 gallons) and dry them at a gentle heat.—*Chem. and Drugg.*

Modified Tincture of Ipecac and Opium, U. S. P.—Wm. H. Clark, of Madrid, N. Y., finding that this tincture, as made by the officinal process, is liable to ferment, owing to deficiency in alcohol (17.78% of absolute alcohol, by weight), uses strong instead of dilute alcohol, which gives a percentage of 20, by weight, of absolute alcohol and avoids any trouble from this source.—*Amer. Journ. Pharm.*

Innocuousness of Boric Acid.—Dr. Gaucher concludes from experiments on animals that men would have to take 75 grammes of boric acid in 24 hours to get toxic effects. To several tuberculous patients he gave 1 gramme daily. After a few days of treatment the fœtor of the sputum disappeared, and in two cases the general condition was improved. He also found it beneficial in cystitis. It did not disturb the stomach.—*Amer. Journ. Pharm.* from *Rép. de Pharm.*

Clarifying Wine of Gentian.—Mr. Vigier, of Paris, says that wine of gentian, which is very apt to have a muddy appearance, can be quickly clarified by adding about 1 part per 1,000 of carbonate of magnesium, shaking it, and then filtering. In a discussion on this subject, Mr. Crinon quoted Portec, a good authority on wines, as saying that this cloudiness is due to a combination of the vegetable albumin of the gentian with the red coloring-matter of the wine and that the addition of tannin, which separates the albumin at once, is preferable to the use of carbonate of magnesium.—*Chem. and Drugg.*

Dehydrating Lard.—In order to deprive lard or other fatty substances of accompanying water—and it is well known that lard, for instance, may be made to contain a very considerable proportion of water—it is recommended to add to the melted lard a sufficient quantity of effloresced and dried sulphate of sodium (Glauber's salt), which will combine with the water and form an aqueous layer at the bottom.

In place of dry sulphate of sodium, dry chloride of magnesium may be used if this can be readily obtained.—*Polyt. Centralbl.*

Note on Peanut Oil.—It has heretofore been held that the lowest melting fatty acid existing in peanut oil was a peculiar one, differing from the fatty acids found in other vegetable oils, and was designated as hypogeic acid. Ludwig Schoen has recently had occasion to examine peanut oil pressed from seeds by himself, and he finds, as the result of very detailed analyses reported in the *Ber. d. D. Chem. Ges.*, 1888, 873, that the supposed hypogeic acid is a myth, only the common, well-known oleic acid being present in the oil, aside from the usual fatty acids of higher melting points.

The American Druggist

AN ILLUSTRATED MONTHLY JOURNAL

OF

Pharmacy, Chemistry, and Materia Medica.

Vol. XVII., No. 6. Whole No. 168.

FREDERICK A. CASTLE, M.D. .... EDITOR.
CHARLES RICE, Ph.D. .... ASSOCIATE EDITOR.

PUBLISHED BY

WM. WOOD & CO., 56 & 58 Lafayette Place, N. Y.

SUBSCRIPTION PRICE per year, ... $1.50
SINGLE COPIES, ...15

Address all communications relating to the business of the AMERICAN DRUGGIST, such as subscriptions, advertisements, change of Post-Office address, etc., to WILLIAM WOOD & CO., 56 and 58 Lafayette Place, New York City, to whose order all postal money orders and checks should be made payable. Communications intended for the Editor should be addressed in care of the Publishers.

The AMERICAN DRUGGIST is issued in the latter part of each month, dated for the month ahead. Changes of advertisements should reach us before the 10th. New advertisements can occasionally be inserted after the 10th.

REGULAR ADVERTISEMENTS according to size, location, and time. Special rates on application.

EDITORIALS.

From time to time we have propositions to adopt some surer mode of writing prescriptions or of expressing the quantities of ingredients to be used, and it is often remarked as an argument in favor of the novel scheme that it is calculated to lessen mistakes by the prescriber and dispenser. There can be no doubt that any method, so long as it is generally understood, would lessen the liability to mistakes, provided prescriptions in which it is adopted are properly written, and in this, we believe, lies the gist of the whole matter. What is needed at the present time is not an improvement in method so much as an improvement in chirography, and the ingenious person who will invent a method for obliging doctors to write prescriptions in a way that will enable them to be read is the one whose coming is longed for.

We would like to see a general movement, on the part of pharmacists, having for its object an attempt to induce physicians to abandon the use of abbreviations, the use of the genitive, and the employment of Latin directions to the dispenser. Uncertainty as to the proper termination to be given to the Latinized name of a remedy is the reason why the custom of abbreviating the name has grown to be the rule, and the writing of the whole name the exception. There are excellent reasons why the use of Latin for the names of articles used in prescriptions should continue, but there is no reason why these names should not be written out in full. Theoretically it is very nice to understand that the ℞ is to be taken to mean "Take," and that the titles following it are to be put in the genitive, but practically it is of no value. Indeed, it is really of harm, since, as above remarked, it leads to abbreviating the names to avoid an exposure of ignorance of what the proper Latin for the genitive should be. If, on the contrary, every physician expressed the title of each ingredient in the nominative, writing it out in full, just as it stands in the pharmacopœia or dispensatory, who would have reason to complain? Certainly not the pharmacist, neither the patient, neither would the foreign reader of our medical literature. The only one who would be likely to object would be a lazy doctor, and objectors of that class will always find fault with anything which in any way threatens to disturb their shiftless lives, without regard to its importance as affecting the lives and welfare of others.

There is quite as little sense in attempting to give directions to the dispenser in Latin as there is in the pretense that is made of using the genitive. These should be written out plainly in English, and so much as is desired to be put on to the label should be so indicated.

The time has passed for hocus-pocus and mummery, for wearing professional garments and wigs, carrying gold-headed canes, and concealing the nature of medical directions in mongrel Latin, and it is quite time that the sentiments of the general public should be enlisted to prevent the writing of prescriptions which are enigmas for pharmacists, to say nothing of the non-professional person of average intelligence. It is time that the person for whom a prescription is written should refuse to accept from a physician an illegible scrawl upon whatever scrap of paper comes first to hand, in the belief that a medical prescription is something which requires a special education on the part of any one who may desire to read it. Every physician cannot be expected to be a genius, but no man is fit to be a physician who cannot read and write, or who cannot write an order for the compounding of a poisonous mixture in a manner which will admit of its being read by others without the possibility of mistake.

With all the progress that has been made in medical science, this feature of the art of medicine is no better to-day than it was a century ago; indeed, we doubt very much whether the generality of prescriptions of the present day would compare favorably with those of a century since, as regards their chirography, and we do not see how it will be otherwise unless it is brought about by a popular movement.

Illy-considered attempts have been made several times, in this and other States, to compel the use of English titles in writing prescriptions. This is, of course, impracticable, but, aside from the use of Latin for scientific names, the enactment of such a law is a thing to be desired. Rather let us have a law *obliging* physicians to use the recognised scientific titles of remedies, and obliging them to write them out in full, without abbreviation, in their prescriptions; and prohibiting the use of anything but the commonly used language of the locality for any directions, remarks, or other matter contained in the prescription.

College of Pharmacy of the City of New York.—The programme for the coming summer and winter course shows a number of important changes, both in the personnel of the instructors and in the method of instruction. Professor Chandler, now connected with the College, as professor of chemistry, for nearly twenty years, has been made General Director of the Chemical Instruction, both didactic and in the laboratories, and the instruction and lectures will be given by Prof. Arthur H. Elliott, Ph.D., who has been for many years Prof. Chandler's principal assistant. Prof. Chandler will deliver lectures on such topics as he will himself select. Prof. Elliott will devote his whole time and energies to the College, and will, no doubt, make the new departure a marked success. In order to carry out the modified plan of laboratory instruction, suitable alterations are being made. The lecture room of the College, well known to be one of the best in the city as to acoustics, will be provided with comfortable desk chairs, thus enabling the students to be more undisturbed and better able to take notes. The lecture course and the laboratory attendance have been materially increased in length, commensurate with the enlargement of the scope of instruction. Every thing points to a most prosperous and successful lecture season.

At the last meeting of the College, Mr. Frank F. Knapp tendered his resignation as trustee, being unable, by business engagements, to attend to the duties of the office.

Massachusetts College of Pharmacy.—The Association of Alumni gave a dinner to the graduating class, on the 25th, at the Hôtel Vendome in Boston. The officers of the Association for 1888 are: President, M. L. H. Leavitt; vice-presidents, H. A. Baker, M. J. Wilber; secretary, L. W. Griffin; treasurer, J. G. Godding; auditor, B. L. Spiller.

Ohio Pharmaceutical Association.—The next meeting will be held on the 12th inst., at Columbus. The committee having charge of arrangements advise that a through ticket be bought at the nearest available point to Columbus, and that a certificate be obtained of the ticket agent. The indorsement of this certificate by the secretary will entitle the holder to the advantages to be derived from reduced rates on return tickets. Mr. H. C. Cook, of Columbus, is the local secretary.

Albany College of Pharmacy.—The officers of the Alumni Association for the ensuing year are: President, Chas. N. Gilbert; vice-presidents, F. D. Ostrander, C.

Stewart; secretary, W. A. Livingston; treasurer, E. F. Hanling; historian, W. H. Conky; executive committee, F. J. Smith, L. Sautler, Jr., F. M. Clement.

The prizes awarded at the last commencement were: Seneca S. Smith, $25, for best general examination in senior class; James Gardner, $20, for best thesis; Comstock, $20, for best general examination in junior class.

The *Australian Chemists' Review* is the title of a new 16 page 4to. monthly, edited by Dr. Hodgson, and published in Croydon, Sydney, N. S. Wales.

Jules Emile Planchon, whose death in Paris on the 3d of April was mentioned in our last issue, was the brother of the Director of the Paris School of Pharmacy. He was born at Ganges (Hérault) in March, 1823, and studied first at Montpellier, devoting himself specially to botany and natural sciences. Having obtained in 1844 the degree of Doctor of Sciences, he went to England to perfect himself, and had from 1844 to 1849 charge of the Kew Botanical Gardens herbarium. Thence he was successively a professor at the Ghent Institut Horticole (1849-51), the Nancy School of Medicine and Pharmacy (1851-53), and finally the Montpellier College of Pharmacy, of which he was the director till within a few years. At one time (1873) he was sent on a government mission to America to study phylloxera. A corresponding member of the Academy of Sciences, Academy of Medicine, and of many British and American societies, he was at his death the Director of the Montpellier Jardin des Plantes. As a botanist, M. Emile Planchon's name is well known everywhere, and his works and papers were many and important.

CORRESPONDENCE.

The Detection of Morphine.

Editor of the American Druggist.

There have been lately published several "analyses" to the effect that a certain profusely advertised proprietary preparation contains a considerable amount of morphine, while other "analyses" flatly contradict that statement, and it seems as if the celebrated "hopeine" case, which two years ago created so much excitement in Europe, would thus find a pendant on this side of the Atlantic.

There can be no doubt that the exposure of any such fraud is highly commendable, but it should be done in a thoroughly scientific manner not open to any criticism. This has, however, been sadly neglected on both sides of the new controversy.

There has, on the one side, as far as the record goes, no *pure* morphine been separated and identified, with the exception of a precipitate having the appearance of "crude" morphine and responding to a few morphine tests. All authorities agree that the different morphine reactions are only then of value when produced by that alkaloid in its *pure* state, which it is extremely difficult to obtain from a preparation that probably contains some other alkaloids or organic substances which in their reactions may correspond with morphine. It is not necessary to go here into the details of the most approved methods of purifying morphine obtained in a crude state, for every chemist who attempts to detect morphine in a liquid of complex organic nature ought to know all of it; but it is necessary to call attention to the indefinite wording of analyses purporting to establish serious frauds. They should at least show that the "analyst" is fully conversant with the subject treated upon, so that the conclusion arrived at may be shared by others; but it would be sheer foolishness to draw any conclusion from the vague statement that a substance resembling "crude" morphine has been subjected to some morphine tests.

On the other side, the assertion that no morphine at all has been found should be accompanied with a brief statement of the "modus operandi" by which that fact has been established beyond any doubt.

Dr. C. H. Frinos, Chemist.

[*Note by Ed. Am. Drugg.*—We agree with our correspondent as to the difficulty of separating morphine from accompanying organic principles, so as to obtain the color reactions in a condition which will admit of no doubt of the identity of the alkaloid. But we believe that the weight of evidence, presented in the case of the proprietary article alluded to by our correspondent, is at present altogether on the side of the experts who reported the existence of morphine.]

Strophanthus.

To the Editor of the American Druggist.

SIR:—No doubt you will have seen a very interesting book lately published by Mons. Blondel, of Paris, on Strophanthus. A great deal of his information and facts have been based on what I have furnished him with. His experiments are leading to such important results that I have arranged with him not to publish anything further until he has visited England. To-day he has come to stop with me at Sydenham, where he will examine the different live specimens of strophanthus plants, and also the numerous specimens which could not be conveniently transported to Paris. With his first day's work he expresses himself "more than amazed" with the information he has got here. Suffice it to say, my advice to your readers is much as it was to Mons. Blondel, not to form any conclusion at present as to which strophanthus is the best, and further what the names of the different varieties are.

When Mons. Blondel has finished his work we shall then have the true chemical values of the different seeds and also roots and barks to guide us, as to their properties. I give you one instance to support these remarks. From a pinch of seed sent by the African Lake Company, I put before Mons. Blondel several plants grown from this "pinch of seed," and he could not believe they were all strophanthus, owing to their remarkable differences in foliage, until I turned the roots out and showed him that they had very near the same formation. The leaves and stems were entirely dissimilar, although the plants came from one pinch of seed. This has been equally the experience at the Botanical Gardens in Scotland. The Director had sown the seed received last year.

There is so much work waiting to be done that I should esteem it a great favor if any of your readers could forward me reliable information and samples of the different varieties of the coca. I want the large leaf variety, yielding a large quantity of cocaine. The leaf is as large as that of the Bay Tree *Laurus Nobilis*. I have now five varieties.

Yours truly,
THOMAS CHRISTY, F.L.S.

London, April 28th, 1888.

Revision of the Pharmacopœia.

THE Committee of Revision of the Pharmacopœia has determined to employ the time intervening between now and the next convention (1890), in compiling, from the literature which has appeared since 1882, a report on all subjects likely to be of practical use for their successors, in preparing a new edition of the U. S. Pharmacopœia. In addition, it has been resolved to ask the active assistance of every *State Pharmaceutical Association*, for the purpose of collecting reliable *statistics* regarding the frequency with which the various drugs, chemicals, and preparations, recognized by the present pharmacopœia, are prescribed or legitimately used. The object of these statistics is to furnish to the next Committee of Revision trustworthy data from which to decide what shall be admitted or discarded. Another important matter which it has seemed to the committee should be decided before the next convention meets, is the system of *weights and measures* to be employed in the working formulas of the pharmacopœia. It will be remembered that the Revision Committee of 1870 had been directed to employ *parts by weight*, and that much fault was subsequently found with them for not obeying this instruction. The Revision Committee of 1880 received the same directions, and actually complied with them, thereby affording the members of the profession an opportunity to test the system practically. Much has been written since then, both in favor of and against it, and a good deal of uncertainty still exists as to which side has the best of the argument. It is expected that a discussion of this question—particularly so far as it affects preparations which are *prescribed or administered by measure*—and a definite expression by each State Pharmaceutical Association, as representing the collective views of the pharmacists residing in each State, will enable the next Committee of Revision to make a satisfactory choice of methods.

For the purpose of facilitating the collection of statistics, the Committee of Revision has caused a complete list of pharmacopœial titles to be set up and electrotyped (see note 1), from which every State Association may have such a number of copies printed as it may require at cost price (see note 2).

In compliance with the directions of the Committee of Revision, the undersigned chairman respectfully requests State Associations to appoint a Committee on Pharmacopœia, to take charge of the collection of statistics and of any other kindred subject that may be referred to them by the association, and that such committee be instructed to forward a synoptical table of the results to the Chairman of the Committee of Revision, etc., before January 1st, 1889.

Regarding the system of *weights and measures*, it is requested that the result of the deliberations, or the vote of each State Association, be transmitted to the Chairman of the Committee of Revision, etc., as soon after its annual meeting, to be held in 1889, as possible—at all events, before January 1st, 1890.

CHARLES RICE,
Chairman of the Committee of Revision and Publication of the Pharmacopœia of the United States of America.

Post-office address: Bellevue Hospital, New York.

April 9th, 1888.

NOTE 1.—Specimen copies of the List of Pharmacopœial Titles will be sent to the Secretary of each Association, and to the Chairman of the Committee on Pharmacopœia, at as early a date as possible.

NOTE 2.—Orders for copies, drawn by the proper officers authorized therefor, should be sent to the Chairman of the Committee of Revision, etc., at the above-given address. The price per 100 copies will be about $6.75.

QUERIES & ANSWERS.

Queries for which answers are desired, must be received by the 5th of the month, and must in every case be accompanied by the name and address of the writer, for the information of the editor, but not for publication.

No. 2,159.—Creasote or Creosote? (C.)
The article our correspondent refers to is a paragraph in a recent issue of the *Chemist and Druggist*, in which the spelling of creasote is discussed. The Edinburgh Pharmacopœia used to spell "creazotum;" this was altered by the London Pharm. to "creasotum." The U. S. Ph. adopted this likewise, but the Germ. Pharm. selected "kreosotum." The *Chem. and Drugg.* points out that Roscoe and Schorlemmer quote a passage from Reichenbach's original memoir, in which he states that he formed the word from *kreos* (the contracted genitive of *kreas*, flesh) and *suzein*, "to save," in allusion to its extraordinary power of preserving animal matters from decay. And the editor of the *Chem. and Drugg.* believes that the form *creosote* is the more correct one.
Being asked our opinion on the subject, we have to say that while *crea-sote* is defensible on the analogy of such Greek compounds as *krea-donia* "meat-bestowal," *kreanomia*, "meat-distribution," etc., which occur in the literature, yet the form with o—as representing the genitive —is much more common. In earlier authors the o is short (o); in later ones the long o (ω) is more usual. Thus we find: *kreo-boros* "meat-eating," *kreo-poles* "meat-dealer," etc., etc. We, therefore, are likewise in favor of returning to the former spelling: *creosote*.

No. 2,160.—Guensburg's Reagent (E. S. F.).
This is also known as *phloroglucin-vanillin*. It is prepared by dissolving 2 Gm. of phloroglucin and 1 Gm. of vanillin in 30 Gm. of alcohol.
If a drop or two of any liquid containing hydrochloric acid be mixed with a drop of the above reagent, on a small porcelain capsule or other white surface, and a gentle heat then applied, a crimson red tint will develop itself along the margin of the liquid, which will become spread over a larger surface when the liquid dries up. This reaction takes place even when the acid is very dilute (up to 1 in 20,000). Lactic acid does not produce the reaction; hence it may be used to demonstrate the presence or absence of hydrochloric acid in the gastric juice, and it has been first recommended for this purpose by Dr. Germain Sée.

No. 2,161.—Banishing Ants, Moths, and Bed-bugs, etc. (Nevada).
The following practical hints, partly derived from others, partly tested by our own experience, may prove useful to our correspondent.
Ants.—These are usually very obstinate and persistent in maintaining a footing when they have once gained it. The best method to get rid of them is the following. Upon a small board, of convenient size to be quickly carried about, spread a thin layer of syrup, and put the board where the ants are apt to congregate. When as large a number as can be expected have gathered, the board is quickly carried away, and the ants destroyed. This is repeated as long as any considerable number make their appearance. When they are becoming less numerous, the syrup may be poisoned, so that the ants may carry the poison to their nests. If the nests can be found, this may be rendered uninhabitable for them by insect powder.
Bedbugs.—A tincture prepared from best insect powder may be applied with advantage to all places where bed-bugs have been found to locate themselves. Tincture of colocynth has also been used for this purpose. The most efficient remedy which we have found is a solution of bichloride of mercury in glycerine, about 1 in 50. This must be applied with care and judgment, being brushed as a thin layer into the cracks and recesses of the bedsteads, etc. It should not be used where there are children or other persons about who do not understand the nature of the substance. In barracks—such as our correspondent appears to allude to—it would be quite efficient and comparatively harmless.
Moths.—When moths have once permanently invaded a piece of furniture, furs or heavy woven fabrics, it is next to impossible to destroy their larvæ. But it is quite easy to protect untainted material from their inroads. This is best accomplished by packing the fabrics, if this is possible, into tight boxes, a layer of camphor or of *naphthalin* being put between each two layers of the fabric. The camphor may be used in pieces of about the size of a walnut, and wrapped in paper. The naphthalin is best reduced to a coarse powder, and placed between a couple of sheets of paper, as a thin layer.

No. 2,162.—Manufacture of Acetanilid (or Antifebrin) and Antipyrine (J. R. H.).
It will not pay you or any one else to manufacture acetanilid (or antifebrin) on a small scale, as it is one of those substances which can only be made profitably in aniline works and on a large scale. Aniline forms one of the necessary ingredients of the process, and you would have to purchase your aniline from your own competitors, who have, moreover, better facilities to work it up and to dispose of the waste products economically than you have. However, we will briefly describe the process: 100 parts of pure aniline (free from toluidine) are boiled with 80 parts of glacial acetic acid, in a vessel provided with a reflux condenser, for several days, until a small sample of the mixture, when dropped into dilute solution of soda, ceases to separate free aniline, which would be recognized by its odor. When the whole of the aniline has been found to have entered combination, the mixture, now containing acetanilid and acetic acid, is subjected to fractional distillation. At 120° C., the acetic acid is distilled off, and at 295° C., the acetanilid distils over. On cooling, the distillate congeals to a crystalline mass, which is purified by recrystallization from boiling water, with the intervention of animal charcoal. As "acetanilid," the product can be sold and used just the same as "antifebrin," which name has been given to it by A. Cahn and P. Hepp, who discovered the fact that the long-known acetanilid had antipyretic properties. We consider the principle upon which proprietary rights can be granted to a previously well-known and non-patented article, so as to protect it when disguised under another name, as unjustifiable and against public policy. There is such a thing as patenting the *new application* of an existing non-patented article. Had this principle been applied in the case of acetanilid, then the patenters would have to word their claim thus:
"Patent claimed for the application of the [long-known substance] acetanilid, to the treatment of the sick."
Probably it was deemed too selfish and necessary to appear to exact a toll from the sick and infirm, by making the claim as stated. Consequently, another plan was adopted, namely, to rechristen the article, to have the rechristened article manufactured by a special firm, and to discountenance and discourage the use of the unchristened article, though this may be just as pure as the other.
Antipyrine stands on a different ground. This substance was not known before its existence as well as its antipyretic action was announced by the discoverer, and under the circumstances, he had a perfect right to patent it. But the manufacture of this compound is a very complicated and difficult operation, which requires ingredients and apparatus only available in works specially constructed for the purpose. Of course, on the small scale it could be made also with simple apparatus, but the loss by secondary products that could not again be utilized would be so great that it would not pay. The stages of the operation have been described on page 164 of our volume for 1887.

No. 2,163.—Raspberry Vinegar (W. S. F.).
We take the following from our files:
1. Mix 1 pint of raspberry juice (from fruit) with 2 pints of best white wine vinegar; allow to stand a few days, and strain, if necessary.
2. To 3 pints of white wine vinegar add 3 pints of ripe raspberries, bruised, and macerate for 24 hours. Then press, strain, and for each pint of strained liquid add 1 pound of sugar. Boil, skim, and cool the mixture, and to each pint of product add 2 oz. of brandy (Dick).

No. 2,164.—Salicylic Acid as a Preservative (S. S. U.).
We are asked the following question:
"Does salicylic acid prevent 'grape wine' or other fermenting liquids from undergoing fermentation in a warm temperature, and cause it to retain its bouquet in partially empty vessels?"
The average quantity of salicylic acid necessary to be added to pure grape wine to prevent further fermentation is about 1 oz. to 75 gallons. This amount will usually be sufficient, even in a warm temperature, provided care be taken that the wine is not exposed with too large a surface to the open air. In partially empty vessels, the protection afforded by salicylic acid is rather uncertain. It all depends what kind of microscopic germs (bacteria, fungi, etc.) the air which has access to the liquid will bring to it. Most or all of these may be of that kind which lose their vitality in contact with the salicylated liquid, or some may retain their vitality and at the proper time begin their insidious growth at the expense of the wine. Supposing the wine to have been properly fermented, mixed with salicylic acid, and to be contained in a cask quite full. If now the bung-hole is secured with pure cotton (previously sterilized by heat) and securely fastened, and if the access of micro-organisms to the contents of the cask be otherwise prevented, then the wine, etc., will keep perfectly.

No. 2,165.—Ink Eraser (J. M. H.).
We have answered a query regarding ink erasers in last number. See answer to query 2,141 (page 96).

No. 2,166.—"Elixir of Guarana and Celery" (Concord).

There is no standard formula for such a compound. The National Formulary, which is on the point of being issued, contains a formula for elixir of guarana which is as follows:

Fluid Extract of Guarana	2 fl. oz.
Aromatic Elixir	8 fl. oz.
Compound Elixir of Taraxacum	10 fl. oz.

Mix them, allow the mixture to stand a few days, if convenient, and filter.

Now if there is any fluid extract of celery root or of celery seed to be combined with the above, this may easily be done. In this case, probably the following proportions might be suggested:

Fluid Ext. Guarana	2 fl. oz.
Fluid Ext. Celery Root (or Seed)	2 fl. oz.
Aromatic Elixir	2 fl. oz.
Comp. Elixir of Taraxacum	10 fl. oz.

No. 2,167.—Collecting Medicinal Plants (E. S. C.).

Since the collection, garbling and sorting of medicinal plants or parts of plants has become to a large extent monopolized by certain houses, the necessity for knowing the proper season when to gather each one has become so much less urgent that the pharmaceutical literature of this country has no recent work to offer on the subject. The most useful and practical directions for collecting such plants or their parts are given in several issues of the "Apothekerkalender," for inst., on page 89 of that for 1888. (Oskar Schlickum, Apothekerkalender, 16°, Leipzig). These pharmaceutical almanacs are very useful, and contain a variety of practical information.

No. 2,168.—Cracking of Necks of Shop-Bottles (Several subscribers).

We have had our attention recently called by several of our friends to a peculiar fatality affecting shop-bottles which must have occurred quite as frequently in former times, but which does not seem to have been discussed in public. That is the frequent cracking of necks of shop-bottles. We have been shown a number of such, and have been asked for an explanation of the "phenomenon."

If we may judge from the bottles we have examined, and from the reports we have received, this cracking of necks seems to occur more frequently in the case of those bottles which contain an aqueous liquid. The nearer to purity the water is, that is, the less material it holds in suspension, the more common does the accident seem to occur. We have seen it happen with bottles containing aromatic waters, saline solutions, solutions containing lime, soda, potassa, etc., but comparatively rarely with bottles containing tinctures and highly volatile liquids. On reflection, and taking into consideration the conditions under which the accident occurs, we have formed the following theory:

Stoppers of shop-bottles have different shapes. Some are quite tapering in the body; in others, the sides are nearly parallel. They are usually ground rather coarsely, and the inner surface of the neck of the bottle always has the same "grain" as the stopper fitted for it. When a bottle in which the stopper is inserted, expands by heat, its neck, of course, expands likewise, and, as the thick stopper cannot expand at an equal rate in the same time, it may sink, if it is tapering, by its own weight, a minute distance further down the neck than it was originally situated. When the bottle cools again, and the glass contracts, the neck cannot contract in proportion; if the stopper has sunk deeper, and if the pressure becomes too great, or unequal (from inequality of contact), the weaker body, that is, the neck of the bottle, will give way. If the stopper was not very tapering, but had nearly parallel sides, this accident will not be so likely to occur. Nor will it readily occur if the ground surfaces of neck and stopper are very smooth, and afford a chance of sliding, particularly if the surfaces of neck and stopper are in uniform contact. But it seems to depend also upon the contents of the bottles, whether the accident is liable to occur or not. If the contents are quite volatile, as f. i., alcoholic liquids, ether, etc., any increase of temperature will cause the evolution of volatile vapors of a corresponding tension, which tension may not only be sufficient to prevent the stoppers from sinking, but may even drive the stopper upward in jerks, or project it completely from the neck, as will often have been noticed by many of our readers. If the contents, however, are aqueous or nearly so, the tension of the aqueous vapor eliminated may not be sufficient, at a moderate elevation of temperature, to project the stopper or even to keep it from sinking. For this reason, aromatic waters, which are nearly pure water, may, even theoretically, be expected to cause the accident oftener than other liquids.

Now as to the remedy. We believe that if the ground surfaces were finer, or if they could be made to slide upon each other, the trouble could be almost or entirely avoided. We would advise, in the case of all liquids which exert no solvent action on paraffin or vaseline, to coat the body of the stopper with a very small amount of either of these substances. It is not necessary to smear on a thick layer. Just enough to remain scarcely perceptible to the fingers will be sufficient. And as the accident appears to be so rare with volatile liquids, particularly such as may exert a solvent action upon the two substances named, it will not be necessary to coat the stoppers of these bottles at all.

We would be pleased to learn whether our explanation is assented to, and whether the remedy suggested by us is efficacious.

No. 2,169.—Material to Resist Fusing Phosphoric Acid (Pittsburg).

This correspondent is desirous of finding some material which shall resist the action of fusing phosphoric acid. He has tried everything in the shape of available laboratory utensils, but finds that even platinum vessels are soon attacked.

We can give but little encouragement to our correspondent, as he has encountered a problem which has been a "sticker" to many before him. At the present time, the discovery of some material which would resist fusing phosphoric acid would be a most profitable matter, as it would permit the practical application of Jurisch's method of producing ammonia from chloride of ammonium by means of fusing phosphoric acid, without waste of the latter.

In analytical operations, phosphoric acid *may* be fused by itself (though this will be but rarely required). But afterwards it will be necessary to ascertain whether the acid has taken up any of the elements of the vessel in which it was fused.

No. 2,170.—Plumbate of Potassium and Plumbum Causticum (P.).

When a soluble salt of lead is precipitated in aqueous solution, by potassa or soda, the precipitate consists of hydrated oxide of lead and is soluble in an excess of the precipitant. The resulting solution contains the compound K_2PbO_2 (or Na_2PbO_2) which may be termed plumbate (or plumbite) of potassium (or sodium).

In order to obtain a definite compound free from impurities, proceed as follows:

Dissolve any desired quantity of nitrate of lead in water and precipitate the solution with caustic potassa, until a drop of the liquid, transferred to a piece of red litmus paper, produces a blue stain, showing that all the lead has been precipitated and alkali begins to be in excess. Wash the precipitate about six times by decantation with hot water, then transfer it to a filter and continue the washing until the soluble matters are extracted. Transfer the moist magma to a beaker, apply the heat of a water-bath and add to the mass successive portions of a moderately concentrated solution of potassa, under constant stirring, until nearly the whole (but not all) the precipitate is dissolved. Now filter, and evaporate the liquid to whatever degree of concentration may be desired. If this is carried too far, both the oxygen of the air and the carbonic acid will affect the product. Some red oxide of lead will form as well as carbonate, and the oxide of lead will be insoluble when water is used to redissolve the compound.

It has, however, been ascertained that the presence of the secondary products just mentioned does not interfere with the therapeutic action of the true plumbate of lead remaining. Hence the solution may be evaporated to dryness, and afterwards fused, either in a porcelain or a platinum crucible, until a gray, or reddish-gray mass remains.

A lower-fusing preparation, called "*Plumbum causticum*" has been proposed by Gerhard. It is prepared as follows:

Litharge, in very fine powder	20 parts.
Caustic Potassa, fused	80 "

Mix and reduce them to powder, place the mixture in a porcelain crucible, cover it and heat gradually until the mixture fuses and the reddish color changes to gray. Then pour it into moulds.

No. 2,171.—Marking Ink (M. M.).

Among the large number of formulæ for marking inks, the following is perhaps the most economical:

Sulphate of Copper	1 troy oz.
Nitrate of Silver	½ "
Water of Ammonia	1½ fl. oz.
Bitartrate of Potassium	150 grains.
Dextrin	150 "
Sugar	75 "
Soda	150 "
Lampblack	15 "
Distilled Water	3½ fl. oz.

Dissolve the Sulphate of Copper in the Water of Ammonia, and the Nitrate of Silver in enough of the Distilled Water. Then mix the two solutions. Dissolve the Soda, Dextrin, and Bitartrate of Potassium in the remainder of the Water, and finally incorporate the Lampblack.

The sulphate of copper may be replaced by nitrate of silver, which renders the compound more expensive, and more intense in color. But even when the copper salt is employed the product is satisfactory.

The ink may be used like ordinary ink, and applied to any fabric without previous preparation. The place to be marked should, however, first be ironed over, and when the ink is dry, a hot iron should be passed over it.

No. 2,172.—Liquid Franconia (C. H. R.).
We are not personally acquainted with this preparation. It is a proprietary article made in Fulton, N. Y., and (as you say) recommended for chapped hands. As we do not know its composition we cannot give a formula to produce a product like it. Perhaps some of our readers can.

No. 2,173.—Elixir of Hydriodate of Quinine (G. B. N.).
An Elixir of Hydriodate of Quinine has occasionally been prescribed by some physicians of Brooklyn. The following formula was devised by Mr. L. F. Stevens:

Sulphate of Quinine........................ 72 grains.
Iodide of Potassium........................ 120 "
Alcohol..................................... 2 fl. oz.
Compound Elixir of Quinine................. 4 "
Aromatic Elixir.............enough to make 16 "

Triturate the Sulphate of Quinine with the Compound Elixir of Quinine, add the Iodide of Potassium and Alcohol, and lastly enough Aromatic Elixir.
To make a plain Syrup of Hydriodate of Quinine will only be possible if a sufficient quantity of an acid, preferably hydriodic acid, is used to aid solution. But the above elixir seems a better preparation.

No. 2,174.—Borocitrate of Magnesium (F. M.).
This compound has recently been in somewhat increased demand, probably owing to the favorable reports made regarding its solvent power over calculous deposits, and its comparative innocuousness. The salt, as well as the solution of the salt, may easily be made in the following manner:

1. Borocitrate of Magnesium.

Carbonate of Magnesium..................... 1 part.
Citric Acid................................ 2 parts.
Borate of Sodium........................... 2 "
Water...................................... 2 "

Dissolve the Citric Acid in the Water at a boiling temperature, then add the Carbonate of Magnesium and afterwards the Borax. Filter and concentrate the solution by evaporation, and spread it upon plates of glass or porcelain, so that the salt, when dry, may be obtained in scales. Or, evaporate the solution to dryness, and reduce the mass to powder. Keep it in well-stoppered bottles.
Both citric and boric acids being tribasic, it would require, theoretically, 3 molecules of magnesia to saturate both acids. The actual quantity above directed, however, saturates only two-thirds of the acids, thus rendering the product agreeably acidulous.

2. Solution of Borocitrate of Magnesium.

Carbonate of Magnesium..................... 1000 grains.
Citric Acid................................ 2000 "
Borate of Sodium........................... 2000 "
Water...............enough to make 52 fl. oz.

Dissolve the Citric Acid in 8 fluidounces of Water at a boiling temperature, then add the Carbonate of Magnesium, and afterwards the Borax. Filter, and then add enough water to make the solution measure 52 fluidounces.
The solution contains about 10 grains of the dry borocitrate in each fluidounce.

No. 2,175.—Clarifying Liquids (Several subscribers).
Fermented liquids are generally clarified by means of isinglass. The imported Russian isinglass is best, but the domestic article, known as American isinglass, which is simply the dried swimming-bladder or sound of the hake, may also be used. 1 ounce of this, cut fine, is soaked in about a pint of the liquid, and when it is dissolved as far as possible, mix with more to make about 1 gallon. About 2 pints of this is enough for clarifying a barrel. The two pints are poured into a pail, and enough of the liquid from the barrel is poured to fill the pail about two-thirds, the contents being energetically stirred with a sort of whisk to raise a frothy heat. The whole is then mixed with the contents of the barrel, and in a few days clarification will have been effected.

No. 2,176.—Hard Soap (H.).
Unless you have some experience in soap-making, we fear that your first attempt to make hard soap, even when following exact instructions, will not be very successful. The best hard soap is made by saponifying tallow with caustic soda. To do this properly, the proportions between the two must be adjusted so as to saponify the whole of the fat, without leaving any great excess of uncombined alkali. It is impossible to give specific directions, as the quality of the commercial caustic soda is liable to change. But, on an average, it may be estimated that about 1 part of soda are required for 6 parts of fat. We cannot spare the space for a minute description of the soap-making process, and must refer you for this to special works on this subject, the titles of which will be supplied to you by any importing bookdealer, such as J. H. Vail & Co., 21 Astor Place, New York.

No. 2,177.—Removal of Foreign Taste from Fermented Liquids (S. C.).
One of our southern subscribers asks us how he may remove the burnt taste from a lot of vinegar which he has made from some "burned" molasses.
In reply we would say that there is no practical way to accomplish this. A portion, or perhaps the most of the foreign taste may possibly be removed by percolating the vinegar through coarse animal charcoal. But the operation would entail more expense than the vinegar is worth.
Another query by the same correspondent refers to the development of an acid in a fermented liquid he is preparing. We surmise this is one of the products of fermentation, but can give no reliable advice as to a remedy on the meagre information supplied to us. On general principles we should try the use of chalk, added as a milk, after fermentation has been established. But it must be used very sparingly, or the flavor of the product will be injured.

BIBLIOGRAPHY.

THE PRESCRIPTION. Therapeutically, Pharmaceutically, and Grammatically Considered. By OTTO A. WALL, M.D., Ph.G., Professor of Materia Medica and Botany in the St. Louis College of Pharmacy,... (etc.).... St. Louis, Mo., 1888.

We have long been aware that the author, who is well known as an accomplished physician, pharmacist and botanist, has been engaged upon the preparation of this work, and our expectation that the ground would be most thoroughly covered, is fully realized. The author has not only incorporated everything that should be known by those who wish to construct, write, read, understand and dispense prescriptions correctly, but he has interlarded a large mass of historical information which renders the work exceedingly interesting. In many places he introduces critical remarks, which either point out incongruities in existing methods, nomenclature, etc., or suggest improvements. While it could not be expected that an intimate acquaintance with the Latin language could be brought about by an abstract of the grammar, such as is given in this work, yet everything that is essential for writing and reading Latin prescriptions is given in a very concise and intelligible manner, in few rules, and without quoting endless exceptions, which only frighten the beginner.
We can recommend the work as a trustworthy guide both to physicians and pharmacists, who will derive much benefit from its careful perusal or study.

THE BEGINNINGS OF PHARMACY. An Introductory Treatise on the Practical Manipulation of Drugs and the various Processes Employed in the Preparation of Medicines.... By R. ROTHER, Grad. of the University of Mich., Dept. of Chemistry, etc. 8vo, Detroit, 1888.

This book is constructed upon an entirely novel plan. The "beginner in pharmacy" is supposed to receive his lessons from his employer, who takes him gradually through the stock-room, the laboratory and dispensing establishment, and imparts to him, in connection with every drawer, package or container, the history, properties and uses of the medicinal articles contained therein. These object lessons are rendered very instructive by the author, who contrives to convey a large amount of practical information, either on the special drugs under consideration, or incidentally, on general topics. The chapters on pharmaceutical operations are also very instructive, but could have been made much more so by appropriate illustrations. A large amount of space is devoted to the discussion of "Incompatibles." This chapter is hardly adapted to the understanding of beginners, as the manner of treatment and the language used in the explanation of facts or reactions often presupposes a considerable familiarity with chemistry or physics. This is not a serious drawback, however, as it is easily overcome by an intelligent beginner, either through self-study, or with the aid of an instructor.
In the chapters devoted to "Etymology" and "Orthography," we have encountered some statements which we must take exception to. From the former we will select only one example. The author derives *hydrastis* from the "Greek *hyein*—to rain, and *dran*—to draw." This is, of course, wrong. The *d* of *hyd-r-astis*, belongs to the first part of the word, the root being *hyd* (Sansk. *ud*; English *water*), or, in an expanded or secondary form *hydr*. Hydrastis may be regarded as a normally formed derivative of *hydrainein*, to wet, to irrigate. On page 326, the author makes the remarkable statement that "A grain weight is termed in Latin *grana*, being a noun of the third declension. Its genitive singular is *granatis*, the nom. plur. *granata*, and the gen. plur. *granatum*." By no means. There never was a noun *grana*, *granatis*, of the third declension. "A grain," as designation of a small weight, is *granum* (i, second decl.), and occurs also as *granus* (i, second decl.), but the former is the most common. The earliest document from which *granum*, as weight, is quoted (by Ducange, Glossar. Med. et Infim. Latinitatis. Niort., Vol. IV, 101) is dated 1240, though it occurred no doubt long before. (*Grana* (æ, first decl.) and *granata* (æ, 1) also occur, but not as names for weights. "A grain," therefore, is *granum* in Latin, gen. sing. *grani*, nom. plur. *grana*, gen. plur. *granorum*.

American Druggist

[ORIGINAL COMMUNICATION.]

A COLORIMETRIC TEST FOR INDICATING THE MORPHINE STRENGTH OF LAUDANUM.

BY S. J. HINSDALE, OF FAYETTEVILLE, N. C.

Dissolve *one grain* of potassic ferri-cyanide in sixteen ounces of water, and add to it *twenty drops* of liquor ferri chloridi.

Place in a 5 or 6 ounce tumbler *one drop* of tincture of opium, U.S.P., and add to it *two drachms* of the above iron mixture; allow it to stand *one minute*, add *three ounces* of water, and observe the shade of blue color developed. You can now try other samples of tincture of opium and compare the shades of color with that produced by the officinal tincture, which will indicate in *some degree* its morphine strength as compared with the officinal tincture.

A drop of a solution composed of *seven grains* of sulphate of morphine (which equals about *three* grains of the *alkaloid*) in *one ounce* of diluted alcohol, treated as above, will develop about the same shade of color as that produced by the officinal tincture, being about the same strength.

It is well to have ready prepared solutions of sulphate of morphine, containing, say, 2, 3, 4, and 5 grains of the *alkaloid* to the fluidounce of diluted alcohol.

They are convenient to compare with the shades of color produced by samples of laudanum.

It is of the utmost importance that the *drops* should be *uniform in size*. I think it best to use a pipette, which must be rinsed with the tincture to be examined. *The iron solutions should be freshly prepared.*

In testing samples of laudanum, it is best to test the *officinal* tincture at the *same time*, using *two* separate tumblers or measures. The observation of color should be made within five minutes after adding the water, holding the glasses over a white surface, and looking down through the liquid.

This iron solution is convenient to use for the detection and estimation, in some degree, of morphia in many mixtures, provided they are free from *tannin*.

Two ounces of a mixture composed of *one drop* of Magendie's solution of morphine in *one gallon* of water, if mixed with *one drachm* of the iron solution, will develop a decidedly bluish-green color. But as the same quantity of a solution of *one grain* of tannin in *fifty gallons* of water, treated in the same way, will produce a *deeper* color, it shows that this solution is of no value as a test for morphia *when tannin is present*.

It was Mr. Armitage's communication about Morphia in *Pharmaceutical Journal and Transactions*, abst. in the April number of the AMERICAN DRUGGIST, p. 70, which induced me to prepare and experiment with this iron solution.

It is possible that a colorimetric test may be made with it to estimate the tannin strength of nutgalls and other vegetable substances.

THE TREATMENT AND DISTILLATION OF PEPPERMINT PLANTS.

BY ALBERT M. TODD.†

(Paper read before the New York State Pharm. Assoc. in response to query No. 31.)

"It has been claimed that the herb peppermint when freshly cut yields more oil than when dried. Is this so, and does the increased yield of oil compensate for the increased expense of shipping the fresh herb to the distiller?"

This question has long been a disputed one, and the discussions have attracted the interest of both scientists and manufacturers. That the importance of making a determination which would be satisfactory and final will be better understood, I will, before stating the results of my experiments, give a brief description of our novel industry, which is rapidly increasing in importance and proportions, prefacing the description with the single remark that distillation is effected with threefold the rapidity from the dry, than it is from the green plants.

There are now (in 1888)* cultivated annually in the United States (almost wholly in the States of Michigan and New York), over twenty thousand tons of peppermint plants, yielding over one hundred and twenty thousand pounds of essential oil, thus requiring on the average the production and handling of about three hundred and fifty pounds of plants in the undried state, for a single pound of the essential oil. There are now in America about two hundred and fifty small distilleries where the crude or natural oil is produced, each distiller distilling, beside his own crop, the plants of about ten neighboring growers on the average, making the number of persons engaged in the industry, as principals, over two thousand five hundred, besides a large number of workmen employed in the cultivation and distillation.

The distillers' charge for working up the plants of other growers has by custom been based upon the number of pounds of oil obtained rather than upon the quantity of plants, the present rate in Michigan being twenty-five cents for each pound of essential oil. This custom is most satisfactory to the grower, as he pays only according to his receipts, but it will be seen that it is not equitable for the distiller *unless the plants are well dried prior to distillation.*

The manufacturing system may be briefly noticed as follows: The plants having been cut when in full bloom, are drawn to the distilleries either with or without curing, according to the notion of the grower. The essential features of the distillery are, first, a large boiler for the generation of steam; second, a pair of large wooden vats about six feet in height and of equal maximum diameter, which are connected with the boiler by steam-pipes, which enter them at the bottom (two vats being used so that one may be emptied and refilled while the other is running; third, a condensing apparatus, which consists of a series of pipes coated with pure tin, either with or without the ordinary "worm," over which cold water is made to flow continuously; this condensing apparatus being connected by a duplex or "changing valve" with the top of the distilling vats at pleasure; lastly, the "receiver," in which the essential oil is collected, the ordinary form of which is a metallic vessel about twelve inches in diameter and three feet in height from the bottom of which an exterior pipe leads to a height nearly equal with the body of the vessel. Recently I have constructed a much more efficient and elaborate receiver for rapidly separating essential oils both heavier and lighter than water; but as this paper is not intended as a technical treatise on apparatus, it will not be described here.

About three inches above the bottom of the distilling vats are placed "false bottoms" containing many perforations, underneath which the steam enters from the boiler. Upon this perforated false bottom is placed a strong iron hoop having a diameter nearly equal with the vat, and supplied with heavy cross-bars. Two pairs of strong chains are secured to this hoop, meeting at the top of the vat in a pair of rings, one of which is fastened on either side of the vat, at the top, while it is being fill-d. This apparatus, as will be seen, is for the purpose of drawing the charge from the vats after distillation.

The apparatus being in position, the plants are thrown in by a workman with an ordinary hay-fork, while two or three others are engaged in "tramping them down." After the vat is about one-third full, a small supply of steam is let in, which softens the plants and greatly assists in packing. When filled, the vat is closed with a steam-tight cover, and the other charge being now distilled, the entire amount of steam is turned on in the new one. The

A. steam boiler; B. steam pump for supplying the boiler with water, and, if need be, for furnishing water to the worm tank; D, worm and worm-tank; E, end of worm from which condensed steam and oil are discharged. The top of the vat passes through the floor above from which the peppermint is introduced into the distilling vat and on to which it is removed when exhausted of oil.

---

* From an article by the editor, published in NEW REMEDIES for April, 1888, p. 99.

† During the past few years, the consumption of peppermint has rapidly increased, so that statistics of production and distilleries now given show a marked increase over those given in my former papers on analogous subjects, which may be found as follows: In the "Proceedings of the American Pharmaceutical Association" for 1885, page 187; AMERICAN DRUGGIST for September, 1886, page 161.—A. M. T.

steam comes up through the perforations of the false bottom, and is diffused evenly through the plants. The oil is contained in minute cells entirely in the leaves and blossoms. The action of the steam is twofold: it softens the tissues of the oil-cells, and at the same time, by its heat, causes an expansion of the particles of oil, so that they burst forth from their miniature prisons, and are carried off with the current of steam. The steam, now charged with the essential oil, upon reaching the top, escapes into the condensing apparatus, where it assumes the form of oil and water. Separation takes place in the receiver; the water, being heavier, sinks to the bottom, and is forced by the pressure from within upward and out through the exterior pipe referred to. The oil collects on the top, and is dipped off at pleasure.

As stated, distillation can be effected with threefold the rapidity from the dry plants, for the effect of drying is to soften the plants, allowing a greater quantity to be used for a charge, while such large charge can also be distilled in one-half the time required for a smaller quantity of green plants. But many growers, fearing that a loss of oil results from drying, by diffusion in the atmosphere, cannot be prevailed upon to bring their plants to the distilleries other than in a green state. *The extremes* of difference which I have noticed are as follows: From a charge of two thousand pounds of fine plants, well covered with leaves and blossoms, thoroughly dried, I have obtained *twenty pounds* of essential oil in *thirty minutes*, an hourly rate of two tons of plants and forty lbs. of oil; from a similar charge of very coarse plants, with few leaves and blossoms, distilled in the green state, *less than two pounds* were obtained, *requiring one hour for their distillation*.

Upon a clear day in September, in the middle of the day when no dew or moisture was present, two loads of peppermint plants were cut down side by side at the same time. Both loads were immediately raked up in the fresh state, containing all the natural juices of the plant, then drawn to the scales and weighed. One load was immediately distilled, the other load being spread upon the ground and dried for two days in the sun. At this time the plants had become freed from nearly every particle of moisture, the leaves being so dry and brittle as to break off quite readily in handling. This second load, which had thus been dried in the sun and open air, was now spread out in a loft and exposed to a farther drying and the action of the atmosphere for a little over six months.

The first charge of peppermint, *which was distilled in the green state*, weighed 3,532 lbs. and produced 6 lbs. 9 oz. of essential oil, being one pound of oil for each 355.35 lbs. of plants, or 0.2814 per cent. After the second load had been dried and exposed to the atmospheric action, as stated, for a little over six months, it was then taken from the loft and distilled. I would say here that all the oil in the peppermint plant, as indeed in most, if not all, essential oil plants, is obtained from the leaves and blossoms and this load of plants being extremely dry, and having been handled over a number of times, lost in the handling some of the leaves and blossoms. However, in distilling, the yield was more than one pound of essential oil for each 362.5 lbs. of original green plants, which slight loss (about 2 per cent in the amount of essential oil) is certainly to be accounted for fully by the portion of blossoms and leaves which rattled off in the re-handlings. The charge of peppermint, which was thus fully dried, had shrunk 49.4 per cent of its original weight.

It will thus be seen that, although the plants are very aromatic both before and after cutting, *there is no perceptible loss of the essential oil by the most thorough drying prior to their distillation*, the oil being so tightly sealed in its little prisons cells that a force greater than that existing in the atmosphere or the rays of the sun is necessary to free it. Indeed, I have noticed that the leaves which fall off from the plants in dry seasons, and remain upon the ground over winter, even though subjected to the action of rains and snows as well, are often found months afterward to be so strong that one would hardly suppose that any of the strength had passed off. It is known, though, in practical experience, that when the plants are once thoroughly dried and subjected to rains, the water carries off a portion of the oil, acting in that respect as a slight distilling force.

It is not within the scope of the present article to treat of the chemical effect produced upon the oil by the action of the atmosphere, the tests of the oil, etc. Such determinations may be found by consulting the papers referred to in the note below. The principal results of the experiments recorded herein may be summarized as follows: First, in the treatment of peppermint, and such other American essential oils as have been examined, no perceptible loss of essential oil by diffusion in the atmosphere is occasioned by a thorough drying of the plants in the open air at any ordinary temperatures prior to distillation; second, when the drying of the plants is continued through many months, a slight oxidation of the oil in the leaf occurs through contact with the oxygen in the atmosphere, decreasing its solubility, and increasing its specific gravity; also slightly raising its boiling point through the formation of a non-volatile and insoluble resinoid produced by oxidation; third, a long exposure of the plants to atmospheric action prior to distillation does not perceptibly affect the crystallizing tendency of the essential oil, nor other of its physical tests except those noted, so far as investigated; fourth, to obtain the best results, both as to the quality of the essential oil and economy in transportation and manufacture, the plants should be dried as thoroughly as possible without endangering the loss of the leaves and blossoms in handling. Distillation should then take place as soon as convenient, to prevent the oxidation of the oil in the leaf by atmospheric action.

ON POWDERED EXTRACT OF NUX VOMICA.

BY W. SIMONSON, OF CINCINNATI.

(Abstract of a paper read at the last meeting of the Ohio Pharmaceutical Association, held at Columbus.)

This paper is written in reply to the query: "What is the best method of removing the oil from the seeds of *Strychnos Nux Vomica*, so that the alcoholic extract may be powdered?"

The advantages of extracts in powder over those in the soft semi-solid condition are apparent to all dispensers, in convenience, saving of time, and in greater uniformity of strength. The extractive matter of nux vomica as obtained by alcohol, and free from oil, readily yields a powder, which is quite permanent; hence the question, what is the best method of removing the oil?

Any oil solvent, while removing the fat easily and completely, takes from this drug a portion of the alkaloids to which its value as a medicine is chiefly due. Assuming that these alkaloids are the most desirable proximate principles present, that solvent is best suited to its use which removes with the oil the smallest proportion of the contained alkaloids.

Of the many solvents that could be put to this use, five are available in sufficient supply and cheapness, viz.: benzin, benzol, carbon disulphide, chloroform, and ether. In the following estimations, the usual commercial articles were used, ether being stronger ether of about 96 per cent, and nearly free from water.

25.00 Gm. of nux vomica, in fine powder, and dried at 100° C., packed in column, 75 Mm. high and 25 Mm. in diameter, was extracted by percolation with one of the above solvents until 1,000 C.c. of percolate had passed. The residue left on evaporating the percolate was brought to a constant weight at 100° C. and weighed; then dissolved in the original solvent and the alkaloids extracted by shaking the solution with four successive portions, 20 C.c. each, of sulphuric acid of 2 per cent, the fourth portion removing no alkaloids or only traces. The first three washings having been united, were washed repeatedly with chloroform, the chloroform washings shaken successively with the fourth portion of diluted acid, which was then added to the stronger solution. From this mixture the alkaloids were thrown out by soda and taken up by chloroform. The chloroform solution, drawn off into a second separator and well shaken with an equal volume of water, rendered faintly alkaline with ammonia, was, when perfectly clear, run into a tared flask. The alkaline liquids were extracted with two portions of chloroform, washed and separated as before. The united solutions, perfectly clear and colorless, were distilled to a small volume, the residue gotten in a thin film on the flask, dried to a constant weight and weighed. Weighings to 0.0001.

As these extractions were made by percolation, and as the temperature, speed of percolation, and time of alternate maceration and percolation could not be uniform in each, a second series of extractions was made, using 25 Gm. of nux vomica and 125 C.c. of each solvent, these being the same as in the first series, except that the ether now used was *absolute ether* and chloroform *purified chloroform*. After maceration during ten days, with frequent shaking, the fluid portion of each mixture was filtered in a small and well-covered funnel. In 15 C.c. of the clear filtrate the total solids were estimated, and in 70 C.c. the total alkaloids. Weighings to 0.0001.

From these figures are calculated the quantities for 125 C.c. (= 25 Gm. of drug) without allowance for increase in volume produced by dissolved substances.

1. *Table showing percentage of Alkaloid and Total Solids extracted from Nux Vomica by different solids.*

		Benzin.	Benzol.	Carb'n Disulph.	Chloroform.	Ether.
25 Gm. powdered nux vomica extracted by percolation with each solvent to 1,000 C.c. percolate.	Alkaloid.	0.080	0.090	0.085	0.125	0.095
	Solids...	1.125	1.255	1.214	1.366	1.244
	Alkaloid in Solids	5.83%	7.17%	7.00%	9.44%	7.40%
25 Gm. powdered nux vomica extracted by maceration with 125 C.c. of each solvent.	Alkaloid.	0.052	0.0685	0.092	0.1028	0.0715
	Solids...	1.065	1.110	1.196	1.387	1.130
	Alkaloid in Solids	5.55%	6.0%	7.0%	10.74%	6.23%

From these results it is concluded that benzin is the best solvent for removing the oil from nux vomica.

Operating on this fact, one part of the drug, in fine powder, was extracted by benzin, by alternating maceration and percolation until ten parts of fluid had been obtained. After drying, the prepared powder was exhausted with a mixture of 8 parts of alcohol and 1 part water. After recovering the alcohol from the percolate, the residue separated, on cooling, in form of a solid cake of fat, which was readily removed, only a small visible quantity escaping. The residual extract easily yielded a fine powder, which, however, was not permanent, cohering in time, owing to the presence of a part of the fat.

It is, therefore, impracticable to exhaust the seed with any solvent in moderate quantities, as, for the present purpose, the extraction must be very nearly complete. A preferable plan is to remove the fat from the extract while still in the thick syrupy condition. By a process modified on this principle, an extract was prepared from 50 oz. of powdered nux vomica. The yield was 4.35 oz., and, as the extraction was very thorough, one part represents about twelve parts of the drug. It contains 22.8 per cent total alkaloids, of which 40.4 per cent is strychnine, as estimated by the alkalimetric method of Schweissinger. As it is still in fine powder, though unreduced, after four months, and during extremes of weather, the following plan in detail, by which it was prepared, would appear worthy of confidence.

Prepare the extract from 100 parts of nux vomica, according to officinal instructions. To the residue of the distillation, contained in an evaporating dish or other suitable vessel, and of a thick, syrupy consistence, add, before the fat solidifies, 25 parts of commercial benzin, stir well a few minutes, and allow to stand, closely covered, for 12 hours. Pour off the upper benzin layer as completely as possible, together with a part of the fat that has resisted solution. To the contents of the dish add 10 parts of benzin, mix thoroughly and pour off the solution as before; and repeat the washing until the fat is entirely removed, about five repetitions being necessary. Evaporate the residue, on a water bath, to a stiff extract, cool, reduce to a coarse powder, and dry to a constant weight at 50° C. To the residue add 40 per cent of its weight of sugar of milk and reduce the mixture to a uniform and very fine powder.

If made from selected, light-colored nux vomica, this powdered extract will seldom assay less than 16 per cent of total alkaloids, and will be very nearly the same strength as the officinal oil-containing extract, when of firm consistence.

As the powdered extract has largely displaced the mass extract in practical dispensing, it is proper, at this place, to turn to the commercial powdered extract of nux vomica and examine what is actually used in medicine, as very few dispensers are independent of this source of supply.

Thirty-four packages, from eighteen makers, collected in the principal inland cities, and in New York City and San Francisco, were examined for total alkaloids, and percentage of fat, and alcohol-soluble extract, according to the following general method:

2.5 Gm. of the powder were extracted with 50 C.c. alcohol, at 50° to 60° C. for two hours, frequently shaking, cooled, and after twelve hours the solution poured off through a tared filter; the insoluble portion was treated as before, using 40 C.c. and 25 C.c. alcohol in succession; the residue was then washed into the filter, and the filter and contents well washed with alcohol until the filtrate passed quite colorless. Filter and contents, dried and weighed, gave alcoholic extract by difference.

To the filtrate, after distilling off the alcohol, were added 10 C.c. dilute sulphuric acid, and the remaining alcohol was removed, at 50° to 60° C., on a water-bath. The acid solution, measuring about 30 C.c., was washed, in a separator, with three successive volumes of chloroform, each washing being in turn washed with 25 C.c. of a 2-per-cent sulphuric acid. The chloroform solutions, entirely clear, yielded the fat on evaporation. Of this residue, about 1 per cent is a hard, red, brittle resin, the remainder fat, and containing but traces of the alkaloids.

From the united acid solutions, the alkaloids were precipitated by soda and taken out by 50 C.c. of chloroform, followed by another portion of 30 C.c. chloroform, further washing not extracting a weighable quantity. The chloroform solutions, washed, in succession, with 25 C.c. of 5-percent soda solution, when united, were extracted by sulphuric acid of 2 per cent, using 30, 20, and 20 C.c., the last collecting not more than traces of alkaloids. These acid solutions, after repeated washing with chloroform, were united, made alkaline, and extracted with chloroform, using 30, 25, and 15 C.c. The chloroform solutions, washed in turn with 30 C.c. of water, rendered slightly alkaline with ammonia, and *entirely* clear, were evaporated, the residue dried to a constant weight at 100° C., and weighed. Weighings were carried to 0.0001.

These residues were almost colorless, or of a pale amber color, soluble in dilute acids, giving colorless or usually light straw-yellow solutions, and were in some few instances partially crystallized.

As nothing is known concerning the preparation of these extracts, little comment can be made upon them. Those appearing to be best made, as shown by light color and the proportion soluble in alcohol contained, in the soluble part, 20 to 24 per cent of total alkaloids, the larger number being between 22 and 23 per cent. Six samples of the drug, five commercial powders of good appearance, and one rasped, gave oil-free extracts containing between 22.5 and 23 per cent. It would seem, from this, that a selected drug will yield this extract of very constant strength, so that a standard, once set up, could easily be maintained. From preceding data, that standard should be near 16.5 per cent total alkaloids. Accepting this as an average value, it is evident that much of the supply is far below what it should be according to label, although a number of makers do not prepare the powdered to equal the pilular extract.

[The author here supplies a table showing the results of assays of commercial powdered Extract of Nux Vomica, obtained from seventeen different makers from all parts of the United Sates. The total alkaloids vary from 2.30 to 18.96 per cent.—ED. AM. DR.]

Since wood alcohol has been produced of great purity, its use as a solvent for preparing solid extracts, and for similar purposes, has been proposed, on account of its much lower first cost. While this advantage may be apparent only, since the loss is much greater in working with a solvent so much more volatile than alcohol, its superior value, compared with ordinary alcohol, for preparing this particular extract has been determined, leaving the question of its greater cheapness to those who may wish to use it.

From a commercial methyl alcohol of fair quality, and free from ethyl alcohol, was obtained a distillate containing 94 per cent methyl alcohol. From this neutral liquid, and from a neutral ethyl alcohol of 88 per cent, were prepared dilutions containing of each alcohol, by weight, 90, 80, 70, 60, and 50 per cent.

To 150 C.c. of each liquid was added 30 Gm. of powdered nux vomica, dried at 100° C., and the mixtures shaken frequently daily during thirty days; then filtered in closely covered funnels. In 5.00 C.c. of each were estimated the solids; and in 30.0 to 50.0 C.c., the total alkaloids. As it is necessary, in view of the equivocal activity of brucine, to know the percentage of strychnine in the alkaloid residues, these also, in part, have been determined, using the alkalimetric method of Schweissinger.

Preparatory to this part of the work, estimations of brucine and strychnine, separately and together, were made.

It appears necessary, at this place, to make some corrections relating to this process, as its details have been widely published and may mislead others as this experimenter has been misled (Lyons, "Pharm. Assaying," pp. 116 and 117, and others).

"One C.c. of a decinormal solution of hydrochloric acid neutralizes 0.00394 brucine, and 0.00334 strychnine. Dissolve the mixed alkaloids in a slight excess of decinormal acid, and titrate back to neutrality with decinormal alkali. Divide the weight of the alkaloids in milligrammes by the number of C.c. of acid required, and subtract the quotient from 3.94; divide the remainder by 6, and move the decimal point three places to the right to obtain percentage of strychnine."

Strength of Volumetric Acid and Alkali.

As a normal solution contains in one liter the molecular weight of the hydrogen equivalent of the active reagent in grammes (Sutton), and as the strychnine molecule (mol. wt. 334) is univalent, a normal solution of strychnine contains, in 1,000 C.c., 334.0 Gm., and 1 C.c. contains 0.334; and 1 C.c. of a decinormal solution contains 0.0334, not 0.00334, as often stated, the latter figure applying to a centinormal solution. Centinormal solutions, acid and alkali, are much more convenient to use, and such were employed by the inventor of the method (AM. DRUGGIST, 1888, p. 230).

Calculation of Percentage of Strychnine.

Taken 0.334 strychnine,
and 0.394 brucine, or total alkaloid, 0.728.

Then, as 1 C.c. of *centinormal* acid saturates 0.00334 strychnine, or 0.00394 brucine, the mixture requires 200 C.c.

728 ÷ 200 = 3.64; 3.94 − 3.64 = 0.30; 0.30 ÷ 6 = 0.05, = 50 per cent of strychnine, according to the quoted rule. But $\frac{334}{728}$² = 45.88 per cent actually present.

Conversely, if 50 per cent strychnine were present, we would have 0.728 × 0.50 = 0.364 strychnine,

and if 50 per cent brucine, we would have 0.364 brucine; then, as 0.00334 strychnine require 1 C.c. of centinormal acid, and 0.00394 brucine 1 C.c. of centinormal acid, 0.364 ÷ 0.00334 = 108.98 C.c. is the amount required by strychnine,

and 0.364 ÷ 0.00394 = 92.38 C.c. is the amount required by brucine, or for the mixture 201.36 C.c. But 200 C.c. were required. The rule is not true to itself, and is therefore wholly untrustworthy.

From an algebraic solution, the following arithmetical rule may be deduced:

Multiply the number of C.c. of centinormal acid required by 3.34, and subtract the result from the weight of total alkaloids in milligrammes, multiply the remainder by 394, and divide by 60 to obtain weight of brucine. Find weight of strychnine by difference.

Example, Second of Following Tables.

In the final calculation, the experimental error is multiplied by 6.566 (¹⁹⁄₃), and the method of estimation is objectionable in this respect. Thus,

Taken 219.33 milligrammes of mixed alkaloids.¶
If all of it were brucine, it would require 55.65 C.c. N/100 acid. If all of it were strychnine, it would require 63.85 C.C. N/100 acid, a difference of 10.00 C.c. In finding the saturating power of the mixture, each 0.1 C.c. required beyond 55.65 C.c. indicates 1.0 per cent of strychnine. As the error, from all causes, can seldom be less than 0.1 C.c., the method will show, when at least 200 milligrammes is operated on, the percentage of strychnine within 1 per cent of the total quantity present. But residues are often much less than that amount, as little as 50 to 75 milligrammes, and then the error may reach as much as three or four per cent of the entire quantity of strychnine.

Both acid and alkali used in these estimations were carefully prepared, the acid standardised by sodium carbonate, the adjustment being true, as found by three trials, to one part in not less than 1,187, and alkali made exactly equal to the acid, volume for volume.

In the following table, the sixth column shows the percentage of strychnine as obtained from the volume of acid used (column 4), by calculation, according to the quoted rule, and the seventh the percentage according to the method of calculation here proposed. It is apparent how very slight errors in finding the volume needed for saturation will cause the percentage of strychnine to diverge widely from what is really present.

	Taken.				Found.		
	Weight.	N/100 C.c Acid required.	Per cent. Strychnine.	N/100 C.c. Acid used.	Weight.	Per cent.	Strychnine.
Brucine....	0.1834				0.1878		
Strychnine.	0.1358	52.55	40.96	52.35	0.1199	42.78	52.77
Brucine....	0.1284				0.1187		
Strychnine.	0.0998	62.64	40.70	62.67	0.0942	43.00	40.95
Brucine....	0.0970				0.0934		
Strychnine.	0.1500	100.44	45.6	100.53	0.1576	47.00	42.91
Brucine....	0.0987				0.0994		
Strychnine.	0.1140	59.18	53.5	59.15	0.1133	37.32	52.27

[The author also appends a table showing the amount of centinormal acid required to saturate the two alkaloids, and another, showing the relative extracting powers of ethylic and methylic alcohols, which we omit, as the general deductions are given elsewhere in the paper.—Ed. Am. Drug.]

As the strength of ethyl alcohol decreases, that of the extractive increases regularly, except in that from 80 per cent alcohol. This lower value may be due to an unnoticed accident, as that from 80 per cent was proven correct by duplicate assay. With the methyl alcohol extracts, the strength is highest at 70 per cent, and decreases with following percentages. Hence its solvent powers differ greatly from those of ethyl alcohol.

If, now, the fat removed by chloroform be subtracted from total solids, and the values of the oil-free extracts be calculated, the differences are greatly increased, as methyl alcohol dissolves very much less of the fat than does ethyl alcohol. In round numbers they compare as follows.

Ethyl, 90 p.c., 26.6%; 80, 24.6%; 70, 23.3%; 60, 20.7%; 50, 19%.
Methyl, 90 p.c., 20.6%; 80, 21.6%; 70, 21.8%; 60, 19.8%; 50 17.7%.

Next, consider the proportion of strychnine in the alkaloid residues. Only three have been determined, but as they include extremes in alcoholic strength, they are quite sufficient. The mixed alkaloids from 90 and 50 per cent menstrua were colorless, those from 70 per cent, very pale amber colored, although entirely soluble in the volumetric acid. The data are given in full in the following table, to show the accuracy of the method as applied under ordinary conditions, and the values of each mixture as found by the rule for calculation here proposed.

Table showing percentage of Strychnine in extracted alkaloids.

Source.		Weight.	C.c. N Acid.	Weight Strych alka.	Per cent Strychnine
90%	E	0.0893	24.20	0.036416	40.8
				0.052764	58.3
	M	0.0868	23.65	0.035421	40.9
				0.051279	59.1
70%	E	0.1772	48.15	0.069098	39.0
				0.102212	51.0
	M	0.1763	47.93	0.070137	39.8
				0.106163	60.2
50%	E	0.1353	36.85	0.055042	40.7
				0.080236	59.3
	M	0.1311	35.70	0.052806	40.6
				0.077894	59.4

E = Ethyl Alcohol. M = Methyl Alcohol.

The proportion between the two alkaloids is the same as extracted by the two solvents.

From the results the conclusion is reached that methyl alcohol is greatly inferior to ethyl alcohol of corresponding strength for extracting nux vomica. Did the value of the extractive matter depend solely on the contained alkaloids, it would be a useful alternative menstruum, provided the product obtained by it be adjusted to an uniform strength. But, as the fixed oil and other proximate principles have no small influence over the action of the more active alkaloids, as these substances are taken from the drug in such varying proportions by the two solvents, and as the recognised medicinal action of the extract has been based on that obtained by ethyl alcohol, the use of methyl alcohol for preparing the extract must be condemned.

Cincinnati, June 10th, 1888.

The Estimation of Oxalic Acid in Plants.

Berthelot and André have recently shown that the precipitates which are obtained in vegetable extracts acidulated with acetic acid, by means of calcium salts, are not necessarily oxalate of calcium, but may contain tartrate, uvate, citrate, and sulphate of calcium, or may not contain any oxalate at all. Besides, they may contain coagulated nitrogenous substances. Hence these precipitates should never be used directly for the estimation of oxalic acid.

In order to separate the oxalic acid, the authors recommend to proceed as follows: The vegetable extract or solution, either purely aqueous or prepared with addition of hydrochloric acid, and free from any particles of the plant, is raised to boiling, and the liquid then filtered. The filtrate is mixed with excess of ammonia, which causes a precipitate of impure oxalate of calcium, more or less colored, and mixed with flocculent substances. Next an excess of boric acid is added, which causes, if chloride of ammonium is present at the same time [and this should be added, if none is present] the resolution of other calcium salts except the oxalate, or prevents their precipitation. The mixture is now strongly acidulated with acetic acid, whereby carbonates and certain other salts are dissolved, and acetate of calcium is now added. The whole is heated during one hour, but not boiled, the object being to cause the precipitate to settle more compactly. It is then collected on a filter, and washed. But as it is not yet sufficiently pure, it is redissolved in hydrochloric acid, precipitated with ammonia, and the liquid acidulated with acetic acid. If necessary, this process is repeated two or three times.

The oxalate of calcium thus obtained is pure, and may be weighed as such, or as carbonate or sulphate.

The authors, however, prefer to estimate it indirectly, viz., by decomposing it with strong sulphuric acid into carbonic acid and carbonic oxide gases, the former of which is absorbed, while the latter is measured.—After Zeitsch. f. Anal. Chem., 1888, 403.

Improvement in Saccharin.

A great objection to saccharin is its very sparing solubility when pure. The defect is corrected by the addition of an alkaline bicarbonate, but it is often at the expense of the sweetening properties of the chemical, which sometimes acquires almost a bitter taste. Flies, bees, and other insects will not touch saccharin in any shape, but as man, who is not so good a judge of sweets, likes it, let it be at least be cooked up and served to his taste. M. P. Mercier recommends the following process. Take of—

Pure Saccharin...........................10 parts
Distilled Water...........................5 "
Sodium Bicarbonate.....................4-5 "
Alcohol (85%)............................20 "
Sulphuric Ether..........................sufficient

The bicarbonate is to be added by small portions to the saccharin mixed with the water, about half an hour being allowed to pass between each addition, and the mixture being stirred occasionally to hasten the combination and the evolution of carbonic acid gas. It is important to cease adding bicarbonate before the saccharin is entirely saturated. The operation requires 10 to 15 hours. Next the alcohol is added to the mixture, with the effect of throwing down most of the soda saccharinate, and holding in solution the excess of saccharin and impurities; and, finally, the magma is thrown on a vacuum filter, where it is washed, first with more alcohol, and lastly with sulphuric ether. On drying in the open air, a white, exceedingly sweet, and soluble crystalline powder is obtained, which possesses all the properties of saccharin. Some of the chemical features of the foregoing process may be briefly alluded to. It will be noticed, for instance, that no heat is employed. The reason is that under the influence of heat soda will readily transform saccharin into salicylic acid. Then the use of bicarbonate instead of carbonate of soda is not indifferent, as the presence of caustic soda, always to be feared in carbonate, will turn the saccharin into a para-compound possessing no sweetness. Lastly, the use of alcohol as a precipitating agent renders heat unnecessary, and removes many impurities to be found in the purest commercial saccharin.—Chem. and Druggist.

Brazilian Gum Arabic.

At the instance of the Kew Gardens authorities, the Foreign Office has applied to Mr. E. Kanthack, British consul at Pará in Brazil, for information regarding the origin of the gum which, for some time, has been consigned to England, principally to Liverpool, as a substitute for gum arabic. In answer to this communication the consul states that the gum in question is not a product of his district at all, but is found in considerable quantity in the province of Piauhy, whence it is shipped at the port of Parahyba in transit to Pará, and sent on from there to England. The gum which is thus brought into commerce consists of two different kinds. One is obtained from a tree called "jatuba," and is of a whitish and pale yellowish color, and in appearance like gum arabic. It is said to ooze out from the root or lower portion of the trunk and to dissolve by heat. The other kind is from a tree called "angico," and is of reddish color, oozing out by cutting the bark. This latter gum dissolves in water, and is considered a substitute for gum arabic. The jatuba gum has been identified by the Kew botanists as the product of *Hymenæa Courbaril*, L., known as "locust tree" in the West Indies, and as "simiri" in Guiana. It is a gum resin, resembles animi in its characteristics, and is used as a varnish gum. The angico gum, as was mentioned in *The Chemist and Druggist* some time ago, is derived from the *Acacia Angico*, Mart., and is a soluble gum, which, for certain purposes constitutes an efficient substitute for gum arabic. A supply of leaves and flowers of the tree yielding the gum may shortly be expected from Brazil, and this will probably clear up all doubts as regards the botanical source.—*Chem. and Druggist*.

In a subsequent issue of the same journal the following additional information is given:

Her Majesty's Consul at Pará states that two kinds of "gum" have appeared in the market there, viz., "Jatuba," the resin of *Hymenæa Courbaril*, a varnish gum well known in this country as Brazilian animé or copal, and angico, a reddish gum said to be obtained from *Acacia Angico*, Mart., and to be soluble in water. It is probable that the latter is the source of the Brazilian gum arabic. Certainly, however, it is not the hymenæa resin, which is quite unlike it in appearance, while "angico" is what is commercially known as a "water-gum." During the past week we have had an opportunity of testing the gum in regard to its adaptability for pharmaceutical purposes, and also of comparing it with a sample of gum imported as "gum angico," for which we are indebted to Dr. Charles Symes, of Liverpool. Our sample is in large tears, some of them weighing as much as 400 to 800 grains, with smooth and wrinkled surface, translucent, and of a dark amber color. The gum powders with difficulty, being not quite dry, and dissolves entirely in water, 1 part of the gum and 2 of water forming a mucilage as thick as the Pharm icopœial mucilage of acacia. It is not, however, so adhesive as acacia, but its ready solubility and moderate viscosity should make it a welcome addition to the confectioner's stock of acacia substitutes. Dr. Symes's specimen is quite different in appearance and property from our own sample. It is of a dark red color, and is only partially soluble in water, swelling up and forming a thick magma with twice its weight of water. In his "Notes on Brazilian Drugs," communicated to the Southampton meeting of the Pharmaceutical Conference, Dr. Symes said that 'in the Formulario on Guia Medica' of Chernoviz, it is mentioned as the product of *Acacia Angico*, and is said to be good for chest complaints; the same tree yielding an astringent bark. . . . As regards its medicinal properties, the only remark which accompanied it was similar to that of Chernovis, "usase nas molestias do peito," "useful in chest complaints." Although this gum differs so markedly in appearance from the Brazilian gum arabic, the mucilage of the latter gives very similar reactions to those which Dr. Symes noted of his gum angico, viz., no reaction with ferric chloride and lead acetates, and precipitates with ammonium oxalate and alcohol, the latter being more abundant with the new gum. It is probable that both gums are the product of allied or similar trees, and it would be important to have this point determined, for the new gum is likely to be a useful one, and if it were to be known commercially as gum angico, it is probable that consignments of the insoluble gum might be made, and so lead to disappointment.

Sulphonal.

The appearance of sulphonal as a hypnotic has been quickly followed by the publication of a test for its recognition. Dr. Vulpius recommends for this purpose (*Pharm. Centralh.*, May 17th, p. 245) the regeneration of mercaptan—of which the compound is a condensation product—by fusing a decigramme of sulphonal with an equal weight of potassium cyanide, when a thick vapor is at once given off, having the unbearable odor of mercaptan to a high degree. Mr. Ritsert, however, objects to the use of potassium cyanide, and proposes pyrogallic or gallic acid as a nonpoisonous substitute (*Pharm. Zeit.*, May 21st, p. 317). Mr. Ritsert heats one or two decigrammes of sulphonal in a dry test tube until, at about 290° C., the water-clear fused mass begins to give off bubbles of gas. From 0.08 to 0.1 gramme of pyrogallic or gallic acid is then added, which causes the clear liquid to become brown and evolve the characteristic mercaptan vapor. As to the probability that sulphonal will take permanent rank as a hypnotic, Mr. T. E. Lovegrove, writing to the *British Medical Journal* (May 26th, p. 1,113), says that his experience with it has been very discouraging. For several hours after the drug had been taken no appreciable effect could be observed in the patients, but during the following day there was extreme drowsiness and considerable cyanosis. He found it to require for solution considerably more than "eighteen to twenty parts of boiling water," and immediately on cooling it crystallised out; neither was it soluble in one hundred parts of water at the ordinary temperature. Mr. Lovegrove considers the best mode of administering sulphonal to mix it with pulv. tragacanthæ and water. According to Dr. Scholvien (*Pharm. Zeit.*, May 30th, p. 320), one part of sulphonal requires for solution 15 parts of boiling water, 500 parts of water at 15° C., 133 parts of ether at 15° C., 2 parts of boiling alcohol, 65 parts of alcohol at 15° C., or 110 parts of 50 per cent alcohol at 15° C. After recrystallisation of commercial sulphonal three times from 50 per cent alcohol, absolute alcohol, ether, chloroform, and benzol, the melting point proved to be uniformly at 125.5° C., and Dr. Scholvien thinks, therefore, that this character may be taken as an indication of a pure product. Dr. East, who introduced sulphonal, reports that he has found an allied disulphone, ethyliden-diethylsulphone, to act as a narcotic in the same doses as sulphonal, and probably in less time, but it appears to produce disturbance of the heart's action. A number of other disulphones have been experimented with, but proved to be inactive or objectionable on account of the symptoms produced.—*Pharm. Journ.*

The Spanish Saffron Trade.

In the last issue of the *Handels Museum*, Mr. Theodor Mertens, of Valencia, gives some particulars about the Spanish saffron trade. The average yield of the crop in that country amounts to between 180,000 and 225,000, a quantity four-fifths of which is quite sufficient to cover the entire consumption of Spanish saffron, so that in seasons of abundant crop, when, perhaps, 290,000 to 310,000 lbs. are harvested, a heavy stock accumulates, and three successive abundant crops generally cause the farmers to reduce their plantations. The lowest price at which saffron-growing can be made to pay, closely approaches the equivalent of 28s. 6d. per lb. At Pithiviers, in the Gatinais (France), a maximum crop of from 27,000 to 54,000 lbs. was harvested in former years, but since the severe frost which occurred in that district in 1879 the largest crop has not exceeded 11,000 lbs. (in 1887 it was only about 7,800 lbs.), and at present Spanish saffron unquestionably rules the market. The average Italian crop may be placed at 11,000 to 13,500 lbs. per annum, and in Austria saffron-growing only pays if the price is at least 53s. per lb. This Austrian is the best of all, and next to it ranks the Gatinais, the only drawback of which is that it very quickly loses its vivid color. In Spain saffron is divided into five grades, each cultivated in a different district. The centre of the export trade is Valencia, where the saffron is stored by the merchants, who generally advance money on it to the cultivators. These merchants sell it to the local agents of foreign houses, who export the drug in strong wooden cases, with an outer covering of matting, about 160 lbs. weight, and in which the saffron is packed in white paper. For export to distant countries, however, the saffron is generally packed in tins, which are placed in a wooden case. The principal buyers of Spanish saffron are a few firms in southern Germany—Mannheim, Frankfort-o-M., Hanau and Wurzburg, who pick and grade it, remove the yellow threads, leaving only the purely red filaments, or grind it, and redistribute it subsequently to all parts of the world. Pithiviers and Marseilles used to buy large quantities in Spain, but do not now take quantities of any importance. Other countries purchasing direct from Spain are England, North America (California), South America, especially Buenos Ayres, Montevideo, and certain portions on the west coast. British India and Japan. Adulteration is, of course, practiced to a very large extent; at Novelda, in the province of Alicante, for instance, all the saffron brought to market is systematically adulterated.

Glass-balls for Refilling Wine-Casks.

Wines which contain less than about 15 per cent of alcohol cannot be kept in casks, unless the latter are kept full, and protected from the air. When a portion of the contents of a cask is withdrawn, the vintner fills it up again from reserved stock, until the particular brand gives out. He then used to, and still does, resort to the practice of putting pebbles into the cask to occupy the volume of the displaced wine. But even with the best of care, some ferruginous or otherwise impure pebbles are apt to get in, which may injure the flavor of the wine. For this reason, *glass-balls* are now being used by many in place of the pebbles.

THE TECHNIQUE OF HYDROFLUORIC ACID INHALATIONS.

INHALATIONS of hydrofluoric acid gas have been used for some time with reported good success in the treatment of diphtheria and phthisis. Various forms of apparatus have been proposed for the uniform administration of the gas. Mr. Hardet, of Paris, has utilized the principle underlying the method of Dr. Bergeron for administering hydrosulphuric acid gas per rectum, and has constructed an apparatus which delivers a current of carbonic acid gas charged with the proper proportion of hydrofluoric acid.

Hardet's apparatus.

The apparatus consists of three pieces (see cut), a generator of carbonic acid, a pressure regulator, and a respiratory apparatus proper. The generator consists of a liter bottle with wide mouth, the stopper of which bears a globe-funnel and a delivery tube. The regulator consists of a small rubber bag connected with the delivery tube, and forming part of the conduit. Upon the bag rests a small, movable, and hinged trap. When the pressure of gas becomes too great, the extended bag raises the free end of the trap, and this compresses the delivery tube, thus diminishing the amount of gas generated in the flask. When the pressure diminishes, the trap is gradually released again. Another portion of the apparatus consists of a rubber bottle containing the hydrofluoric acid solution. The current of carbonic acid gas is made to pass through the acid, and the mixed vapors finally pass through a wide rubber tube into a sort of tent arranged as shown in the cut, into which the patient introduces his head. [It seems to us that the current of carbonic acid gas, mentioned in the original, should be replaced by a current of air.—ED. AM. DR.]

For use, the generator is charged with a mixture of 4 parts of tartaric acid and 5 parts of bicarbonate of sodium, and a little water is gradually added through the funnel, the lower orifice of which is best drawn out fine. The reaction is sufficiently regulated by the trap over the rubber bag. The hydrofluoric acid may be used in varying strengths, 15, 20, or 30 parts of the commercial acid, diluted with water to 100. Two sittings a day are recommended, each of three-quarters of an hour.

Another form of apparatus is that of Dr. Bergeron. This consists of two gasometers of the construction shown in the cut. When either one of the inner cylinders is pushed down into the other, the volume of air contained within it is forced through the tube T to the common outlet R, and finally passes through D, and issues at the ceiling of a small room in which the patient is made to sit. The bottle D contains a titrated solution of hydrofluoric acid. The pushing down of one of the cylinders of the apparatus naturally raises the other one, and during its ascent this becomes filled with air, which enters through the tube U, the orifice of which is provided with a valve which only opens inward. Two other similar valves will be found in the connecting tubes between U and R (see small cut on top). As the capacity of the air-space of the cylinders is known, it is easy to administer an exact dose of the vapor of hydrofluoric acid.

Bergeron does not approve the use of a dilute solution of the acid, and the passage of the air through it, as it has happened that particles of the liquid have been carried forward mechanically. He prefers to employ a strong acid and to pass the current of air over, not through it.

Seiler uses three solutions of different strength, one containing 33⅓% of hydrofluoric acid, another containing 50%, and another containing 66⅔%. A separate chamber or tent is used for each of these vapors. By the way, any glass, in windows or elsewhere, in these chambers or tents must be coated with a thin varnish to prevent the vapors coming in contact with the glass, which would thereby become dulled.

Petit and Filleau do not use an inhaling apparatus, but simply place the bottle containing the acid in the chamber, in which the patient has taken a seat, the flask being about four feet from the floor. Yet this method is not approved by Bergeron.

A very simple apparatus is that of Dupont, but the dosage of gas is rather uncertain, and it is inhaled through a cap placed over the mouth. Nevertheless, as the current of air is made to pass, not through a liquid, but through a wad of cotton, contained inside of the bottle, and moistened with the strong acid, no serious results need be feared if care be taken in administering the gas. Dupont's apparatus is shown in the accompanying illustration (see next page). It will be seen that the current of air is blown, by means of bellows, across a sort of wick, which is a part of the wad of cotton contained in the bottle. The liquid retained by the wad is gradually drawn up by capillary attraction.—After *Bull. Gén. de Thérap.*

Volumetric Determination of Potassium and Sodium.

POTASSIUM may be separated from sodium by acid tartrate. A solution of pure acid ammonium tartrate, saturated at about 90° C., diluted with an equal volume of water, is the reagent. When used, the flask containing the reagent is heated till the crystalline tartrate is redissolved.

The salts are (or should be got) in the form of chloride. Two solutions of potassium and sodium chlorides were prepared to do away with the frequent weighing out of the salts; 50 C.c. of the solution, containing about 0.3 Gm., is measured into a 100 C.c. measuring flask; 5 C.c. of ammonium tartrate for every 0.1 Gm. added; the solution is allowed to cool, and methylated alcohol is added in small portions, shaking after every addition until up to the mark. Filtered, after about three hours, into a burette, 10 C.c. is evaporated, and ignited gently till the charred mass is white. Evaporate with a solution of ammonium chloride, ignite, and titrate the sodium chloride with a solution of silver nitrate, 1 C.c. = 0.001 Cl. The sodium is found directly, and the potassium indirectly. [The author gives the results of several assays, all but one of which are satisfactory.]

The precipitations were usually done in the evening, and allowed to stand over night. Three hours were, how-

Bergeron's apparatus.

ever, found sufficient from a trial of the mixed chlorides. The filtrate from the precipitate of the solution of potassium chloride gave no fixed residue. In an early experiment, the adding of spirit at once, in quantity, lowered the quantity of sodium chloride by 0.004.

I was led to these experiments by trying to find a method of separation based on the insolubility, discovered by Wurtz, of potassium alum in aluminium sulphate. The potassium of the alum might be determined by precipitating with barium chloride, and then with ammonium carbonate, and titrating the potassium chloride formed, but the present process is simpler.—J. TRAWOO WAITS in *Chem. News.*

On the Chemical Nature of Peptone.

An important contribution to our knowledge of the nature of peptone has been furnished by R. Palm of the pharmacological institute at Dorpat. From an article by this author published in the *Zeitschrift f. anal. Chemie* (1888, 350) we take the following.

It was Lehmann who first introduced the term *peptone* in scientific nomenclature. The albuminoids, when digested in the stomach, lose the faculty of being coagulated, and of being precipitated by certain reagents, and the resulting clear solution finally has a different behavior from that of ordinary pure albumen.

On treating albumin peptones with alcohol a white, light-flocculent precipitate is obtained which, when dried on a water-bath, forms a yellowish, fissured, very hygroscopic mass, easily soluble in water to a colorless liquid. From this, the peptone is not precipitated by alcohol, heat, alkalies, acids, or neutral salts. Only solution of mercuric oxide, acetate of lead or tannic acid cause precipitates. In physiological chemistry, there are distinguished milk-, casein-, albumin-, serum-, gelatin-, and fibrin-peptones.

A qualitative test for peptone is the biuret reaction, which is given by the author in a modified manner as follows: Mix the peptone solution first with soda, and then with enough hydrochloric acid, until the precipitate first formed has been again dissolved. Next add a trace of sulphate of copper, and lastly, an excess of soda, which will cause the formation of a precipitate having at first a greenish-blue color, which changes to rose-red, by agitation, the last tint remaining even when the liquid is heated to boiling. Albumin bodies, under similar conditions, furnish solutions of a violet tint. Elementary analysis has proven that peptones have the same ultimate, chemical composition as albumins.

Fritt and Filtre's apparatus.

The author next quotes the views of all chemists who have advanced theories as to the nature of peptones. But it is evident that none of the explanations so far advanced are sufficient to furnish the correct clue.

Dr. Palm (the author) finds, as the result of his examination, that peptone (milk-peptone) *is a solution of albumen in lactic acid*. When lactic acid acts upon egg-, milk-, or serum-albumen, or upon casein, *peptone is obtained* as a result, and the same is the case when lactic acid acts upon gelatin, fibrin or chondrin. Hence *peptone* should be interpreted as a *solution of protein in lactic acid*.

A peptone of definite composition (that is, proportions) may be obtained by mixing an alcoholic solution of peptone with a sufficient quantity of ether, whereby a mixture of protein and lactic acid is separated, in stoechiometric proportion, in form of an oily mass. On the other hand, the author has succeeded in separating genuine albumen from peptone, by neutralizing the solution of the latter with ammonia (that is, by neutralizing the lactic acid), and afterwards treating the mixture with alcohol of 95%, whereby all the albumin was separated. The same result was obtained by employing alcohol (95%) acidulated with sulphuric acid. In this case, the albumin forms a compound with the sulphuric acid, which is insoluble in lactic acid. In this method, however, an excess of acid must be avoided, since the precipitate would be redissolved. The author found that after he had completely neutralized a solution of peptone with ammonia it yielded all reactions for albumin in the same manner as an original solution of pure albumin. And if the neutralized peptone solution is heated, the albumin coagulates precisely like the natural substance.

The author used milk-peptone for most of his experiments, and this contains only lactic acid. Such peptones, however, which are formed in the stomach during digestion may contain both hydrochloric and lactic acids. The reason why no albumin is coagulated when a solution of peptone is heated, is this, that it contains free lactic acid. The latter namely, like acetic acid, dissolves albumin, even if it had previously been coagulated. Besides, the presence of lactic acid in the peptones prevents the albumin from being coagulated by alcohol, or by alkalies or neutral salts. All precipitates which are produced by these agents in normal solution of albumin are easily dissolved by lactic acid, excepting the precipitate produced by mercuric oxide or tannic acid.

It remains to examine into the reason why peptones show the same elementary composition as the albumin from which they are derived. The answer is simple, viz.: "because *the method used for isolating the peptone does not yield peptone* (that is, albumin or protein and lactic acid), but only true albumin." It is, however, known from many elementary analyses, that peptones showed a smaller percentage of carbon and nitrogen than the original albumin. In these cases both albumin and lactic acid had been separated and analyzed as peptones.

"Peptone," therefore, should be understood to be a solution of protein in acids, among them sulphuric and acetic, and probably other acids.

To distinguish peptone from albumin, the author places reliance upon potassium xanthogenate or xanthate (produced by saturating boiling alcohol of 0.800 sp. gr. with potassa, and then dropping in disulphide of carbon until this ceases to be dissolved, or until the liquid ceases to be alkaline. On cooling the salt crystallizes; the crystals must be quickly removed, pressed between blotting paper and dried in vacuo). Xanthate of potassium yields a precipitate with a neutral solution of normal albumin only after addition of acids; but with peptones it yields a precipitate at once, as these already contain acids.—*After Zeitsch. f. anal. Chem.*, 1888, 359.

To Prevent Bumping during Distillation.

To prevent the annoying, and sometimes dangerous occurrence of bumping which many liquids experience during distillation—which is mainly due to a superheating of the layers of liquid situated immediately over the source of heat—A. Reissmann recommends to introduce into the flasks or retorts, spirals of rather thick platinum wire, containing small fragments of pumice. The spirals must be heavy enough to prevent the pumice from floating it. The pumice, thus compelled to sink to the bottom, has the advantage of presenting a large surface to the liquid.

E. Dannenberg recommends asbestos for the same purpose, and thinks it preferable to anything else.

W. Markownikow introduces into the liquid to be distilled several small capillary tubes, 0.3 to 1 Cm. long, and closed by fusion at one end. The presence of these will cause liquids, which are otherwise very refractory, to boil regularly and quietly, even under diminished pressure.—*Zeitsch. f. anal. Chem.*, 1888, 385.

Stray Notes on New Remedies.

Trafusia. This is the name given by an Italian manufacturer, Luigi d'Emilio, of Naples, to a condensed ox-blood, which is said to differ from similar preparations by containing the albumen in a soluble form. The new substance is completely soluble in warm or cold water, is in form of a granular powder and of a reddish-brown color, not hygroscopic and dissolving in water to a blood-red liquid. If it is to be administered to children, it is recommended to be given in chocolate, and in the case of adults, to be given with malt or spirituous liquors. The dose for children is stated to be ¼ to 1 Gm., or 1 to 3 Gm. per day. For adults, 3 to 10 Gm.

Iodine Trichloride (ICl_3). This is an orange-yellow, crystalline powder, having an astringent, acid taste, a penetrating odor, and is very volatile. Its vapor is very pungent and irritating. It is easily soluble in water, forming a brown liquid which undergoes but little decomposition if kept in amber colored bottles. Prof. Langenbeck, of Berlin, has used it in surgical operations, in aqueous solution of 1 in 1,000 or 1 in 1,500, which were sufficiently strong to destroy all kinds of bacteria, rendering it nearly equal to corrosive sublimate. Its pungent odor, and property of staining the skin is not considered to be a drawback, as it is not poisonous in the sense in which corrosive sublimate may be under certain circumstances. Iodine trichloride has also been used internally in dyspepsia, when due to bacteria [?], in doses of 1 fl. drachm of a 0.1 per cent solution. Also in skin diseases as a lotion, and as an injection in gonorrhœa.

Lipanin. We have already given an account of this new substitute for cod-liver oil, and need only add here that the substance, as sold, is stated to be prepared from pure olive oil by partial saponification, the unsaponified portion of the oil, and the liberated oleic acid being mixed to form lipanin. It is an oily liquid, resembling olive oil and contains 6½ per cent of free oleic acid. It forms emulsions with great facility. 5 C.c. of lipanin mixed with 5 C.c. of water and 3 drops of solution of soda (10%) yield a permanent and perfectly white emulsion.

Phenolphtalein Solution.—A. Gawalowski has made the observation that phenolphtalein usually (or always) has a very faint acid reaction. This is shown by the fact that if it is dissolved in alcohol absolutely free from any acid trace, it will bear the addition of several drops of normal potassa solution (from 0.2 to to 0.8 C.c. per gramme of phenolphtalein) without turning red. Only when the faint acid trace has been completely neutralized, will the rod color make its appearance upon adding more of the alkali.—From *Zeitsch. f. anal. Chem.*

A New Method of Making Mercurial Ointment.

L. JACQUEMAIRE proposes (in *Journ. de Pharm.*, May 15th, 1888) a new method of extinguishing mercury and preparing mercurial ointment. It is based on the production of a minute quantity of amalgam caused by the introduction of a minute quantity of metallic potassium, about 1 part of this being sufficient for every 1,000 parts of mercury. The amount of the former is so small that it may be entirely disregarded, and, moreover, it is probably entirely saponified by the subsequent mixture with the fatty body.

The author of course applies the new method to the particular formula prescribed by the Codex for mercurial ointment. But it would be equally applicable to other similar ones. In general, his process is as follows:

Place the requisite amount of mercury into a porcelain capsule, and warm gently [which should be done under a hood.—ED. AM. DR.], in order to dissipate any adhering moisture. Then add the potassium in small fragments. The combination takes place under slight decrepitation. Stir well with a glass rod, so as to cause the amalgam to be dissolved and uniformly distributed throughout the rest of the mercury. The mass is now poured into the fatty base, which has previously been thoroughly beaten to a homogeneous mixture. If any constituent of this is solid at ordinary temperatures, it must, of course, be previously combined with the remainder so that the only operation yet to be performed is the admixture of the mercury. A rapid and energetic trituration will cause the mercury to be immediately divided and in ten minutes to be completely extinguished.

Lanolin Preparations.

1. *Lanolinum Boricum.*

Borated Lanolin.

Boric Acid, in very fine powder	10 parts
Benzoinated Suet	30 "
Lanolin	60 "

Melt the Suet, add the Lanolin, and then incorporate the Boric Acid. Pour the mass into moulds, so as to obtain it in form of thick cylinders. Dispense them in metallic boxes with movable bottom.

2. *Lanolinum Carbolatum.*

Carbolized Lanolin.

Carbolic Acid	5 parts
Benzoinated Suet	30 "
Yellow Wax	30 "
Lanolin	65 "

Melt the Suet and Wax, add the Lanolin, and lastly the Carbolic Acid.

Pour out the mass into moulds, so as to obtain it in form of thick cylinders. Dispense them in metallic boxes with movable bottom.

3. *Lanolinum Salicylatum.*

Salicylated Lanolin.

Salicylic Acid	2 parts
Benzoinated Suet	25 "
Yellow Wax	10 "
Lanolin	65 "

Melt the Suet and Wax. Dissolve in the mixture the Salicylic Acid, and lastly incorporate the Lanolin.

Proceed as in the two preceding cases.—DIETERICH in *Ph. Centralh.*

Bolivian Cultivated Cinchona.

South Americans allowed the planters of the Old World a good start in the cultivation of cinchona before they thought fit to repair the waste and the ravages in their native forests by rearing the bark yielding trees in a systematic manner. It is perhaps a tribute to Spanish indifference to progress that a commencement in the cultivation of cinchona was first made in Bolivia ten years ago by German planters, one of the most successful being Mr. Otto Richter, of Cochabamba. Plantations exist at Mapire Longa, Yungas, and Mapire, north and east of La Paz, and in those localities over six million plants were first placed in cultivation. For some time the Bolivian cultivated calisaya, sent to our market in quill form, has been a standing feature in the London bark auctions, but quite recently one of the principal cultivators has made a bold attempt to provide us with a cultivated substitute for the so called Bolivian calisaya, which is a bark much sought after on the Continent, and for which prices are paid in excess of its mere alkaloidal value. A sample of this cultivated flat bark, recently submitted to us by the importers, shows it to have been carefully harvested. It is quite dry and powders readily, leaving little fibrous material. An assay of the bark showed us that it contains 3 per cent of total alkaloids, a percentage considerably under the standard of the British Pharmacopoeia, but comparing favorably with the quality of many samples of natural yellow cinchona. Unfortunately the appearance of the bark under notice is somewhat against it. Of course the trees in Mr. Richter's plantation are still young, and do not, therefore, yield such stout bark as the wild cinchonas which provide the ordinary flat bark of commerce. The pieces, in fact, are merely, if they may be so called, flattened quills, one-eighth of an inch in thickness and which in the ordinary process of drying would have curled up into quills, but were artificially prevented from so doing. The color is partly a deep orange, partly streaked, and spotted with rusty brown, which gives the bark a queer look. Druggists, therefore, who merely appreciate appearance shun it; but we understand that on the Continent the bark is beginning to find a ready sale, and it might be worth the while of our own export druggists to devote some attention to this new variety before it gravitates, as too many other drugs are already doing, towards rival markets.—*Chem. and Drugg.*

A Simple Method of preparing Oxygen Gas.

DUPONT recommends to use peroxide of hydrogen as a source for preparing oxygen gas, primarily for medicinal purposes, but the method is applicable to any other uses of the gas.

Peroxide of hydrogen is known to be decomposed when it comes in contact with certain pulverulent bodies, one of the most energetic being peroxide of manganese (in the cold). If pure peroxide of hydrogen solution is obtainable in the market—as it is in most large cities—the commercial article may be used. If not, it is easily prepared by any of the methods laid down in the chemical text-books. For medicinal purposes, and especially for the preparation of oxygen gas, it is best to use a solution of peroxide of hydrogen containing 20 per cent by volume of the pure compound.

An aqueous solution of peroxide of hydrogen may be concentrated either by a very gentle heat, or by freezing. If it is subjected repeatedly to the freezing process, the ice which is formed retains only traces of the compound, while the mother-liquid gradually acquires a strength up to 70 per cent by volume. If necessary, this may be purified by distillation. For this purpose, the solution is first saturated with baryta, then filtered, and afterwards distilled *in vacuo*. Hanriot has prepared solutions containing as much as 400 volumes in this manner.

To generate oxygen gas, about 100 Gm. (3½ oz.) of pure peroxide of manganese is introduced into a Woulff's bottle of the capacity of 1 quart, and solution of peroxide of hydrogen gradually, and in small portions, allowed to flow upon it. The Woulff's bottle is connected with a wash-bottle, through which the gas is made to pass before it is collected for use, or inhaled. The peroxide of manganese does not suffer any decomposition in this process; hence one and the same quantity will suffice for an indefinite period.—After *Rundschau* (Prag).

(Note by Ed. AM. DR.—The process may be made continuous by providing an exit for the exhausted liquid in such a manner that this may be discharged in proportion as fresh liquid enters. If granular peroxide of manganese is used, a small percolator with stop-cock at the orifice may be employed, the fresh peroxide being admitted at the surface of the manganese compound, and losing its excess of oxygen as it descends, finally passing out as water.)

Almadina, "potato-gum," "euphorbia-gum," or, more briefly "E. G." is a resin of African origin which has of late found its way into European drug markets in increasing quantity. It chief use hitherto has been as a substitute for or addition to india-rubber. It is not only cheaper than caoutchouc, but is said to actually improve the latter when added in certain proportions, by diminishing its porosity and imparting greater durability.—*Sci. Amer.*

Anagyris foetida, the leaves of which are used in Greece and Cyprus as a substitute for senna, is a leguminous plant, having seeds which yield a non-drying oil, two resinoids, a glucoside, and an alkaloid, called by Dr. Beck anagyrine. The formula for the latter is $C_{14}H_{18}NO_2$ (?). It is bitter, amorphous, very hygroscopic, and forms hygroscopic salts with inorganic and organic acids. The platinum compound is stable. It is best obtained by precipitation with tannin and decomposing the tannate with plumbic hydrate.

German Insect Flowers.—A Berlin pharmacist, Dr. Unger, has been experimenting with powder from the insect flowers raised at the Horticultural Society's grounds near Berlin. He finds that the powdered flowers from *Pyrethrum roseum*, *Berolinense*, act very satisfactorily, killing the insects experimented upon after forty-five minutes. The powder of *P. caucasicum*, *Berolinense*, was less active; the insects were in some degree stupefied, but even after having been kept for several hours in the powder under a glass they remained alive. The *P. carneum* powder had no action whatever. Dr. Unger considers the results obtained sufficiently encouraging to warrant the extension of the cultivation of pyrethrum, especially of the *roseum* variety. He recommends, however, the addition of lime to the soil set apart for cultivation.—*Chem. and Drugg.*

NEW YORK STATE PHARMACEUTICAL ASSOCIATION.

The tenth annual meeting of the New York State Pharmaceutical Association having been called to order in the parlors of the Prospect Park Hotel at Catskill, June 19th, at 10:45 A. M. by the President, Aaron Sager, of Cortland, prayer was offered by the Rev. W. H. Harrison, of Catskill, and the Hon. J. B. Olney, of Catskill, delivered an address of welcome to the Association. He said:

Mr. President, Members of the Association, Ladies and Gentlemen: I must say that it is with a sort of modest terror I appear before you on this occasion. In the first place, because this thing is a little out of my line; but although I am afraid of you, afraid of your nostrums, afraid of your decoctions, I have yet enough courage to say, I bid you and your ladies welcome. We have not any roaring cataract, like that which has immortalized a certain section of the State, with which to greet you, we have no Thousand Islands, but we have all hospitable homes, and we bid you a cordial welcome to them. We have our beautiful scenery, which, although we have lived here many years, still delights us, and we want you to say in relation to us, "All yours is mine, and what is mine is my own."

You have a committee of arrangements, I understand, who have undertaken to do the honors of this occasion, a very able committee, and I understand there were great discussions in that committee. Dubois insisted upon painting the town red. If you will take a walk down town you will see in what way he has done that. Other members of the committee inclined to golden brown, and on another corner you can see it exemplified by Mr. Post. I think, sir, that the town will have to be painted the color which really distinguishes our county from all others in the State, green, if you are content with that, because we generally calculate that we are green in every respect, but we will do the best we can to make it hospitable for you.

You have a programme committee, I understand, which offers to take you up into an exceedingly high mountain and show you all the kingdoms of the world and the glory of them. Do not bow down to this committee and worship them.

I think it is very appropriate that this gathering should be held on this spot. It is a historic spot. There is no right to land, either by possession or title, equal to the right by prescription. I think thus the best reason that you should select this spot for this gathering. Just below here was the Indians' burying ground, and this spot itself, I am told (I was not here at the time), is where they had the last big fight between two tribes, and right here they held the medicine dance once a year about this time. So that it is very proper that you should select this locality for the meeting of this Association.

And there is another thing of which that truthful historian, Irving, informs us. Hendrick Hudson once dwelt upon these mountains. We do not know who his family physician was, but, as I am credibly informed, he sent a messenger to Catskill village for the purpose of getting medicine. We do not exactly know who the druggist was who furnished him this medicine, but at any rate we find him half-way up the mountain when he overtakes a certain party. You know the result. Rip Van Winkle was induced to carry it to the top of the mountain, and the result was not only to put Rip Van Winkle to sleep for twenty years, but the whole locality also. I do not know exactly what it was, possibly spiritus frumenti, I am sure it was not aqua pura, but that spell which was cast over the slumbers of Rip Van Winkle, has extended to the whole population, and it is fitting that you druggists should come here and take off this spell which has prevented Catskill from having its electric lights, its street railroads and its real estate boom. This should be the result of your gathering here at this time, and if you leave enough of the prescription by which these things can be accomplished, we shall say "Amen" to your efforts.

The President called upon Dr. R. G. Eccles, of Brooklyn, to respond in behalf of the Association. He said:

Honorable sir, and friends of Catskill village and vicinity. We thank you for the reception that you have given us this morning, and as members of the Association feel that we have reached a place where we are really and in soul made welcome. You told us of the colors with which the town had been painted, and that people say the true color of the region is green. To my liking, there is no color so grand as green. It is the one color of all others that rejoices the soul. If red were as profuse as green, our eyesight would fail us, and we would not have half the appreciation of the universe that we have. There is no place where man resides, where beauty cannot be found, but this one above all others is one that is really favored by the Supreme Power that has formed the universe. The region has a reputation that is broad. Even that story that he told us about poor Rip Van Winkle being asleep has itself tended to make the region known throughout the English-speaking world.

We are glad to have come to Catskill, glad to have received such a welcome, glad we have come with such a spell as you declare has been cast by the early apothecary over the region so that it has gone to sleep. I can predict to you that this spell shall be removed, and that you shall yet have your street railroads, your electric lights, and you shall have your city built up. So we thank you for the welcome which you have given us.

The President appointed as Committee on Credentials, W. D. Balliet of Lockport. Wm. Howarth of Utica, and O. C. Weinman of New York.

The names of thirty-six applicants for membership were read by the chairman of the Executive Committee.

The President appointed as Committee on Exhibits, R. E. Phillips of Fulton, W. W. Tooker, Sag Harbor, and W. S. Gerity of Elmira.

The President then read his annual address.

LADIES AND GENTLEMEN OF THE NEW YORK STATE PHARMACEUTICAL ASSOCIATION:—Another year has passed since we threaded the beautiful islands of the St. Lawrence on the deck of the *Wanderer*. A decade has nearly passed since our Association was first organized, and I congratulate you to-day that, although we have not filled the full measure of our anticipations, we have accomplished a grand work. Pharmacy as a profession is recognized in the statute books of our State, and this recognition is due to the persistent labors of the N. Y. S. P. A. I congratulate you that so many of the members, who were identified with the early organization of the association, are permitted by a kind Providence to gather with us to-day, and while our hearts are saddened, we cherish the memory of those whose names have a place on our death-roll. We are stronger to-day because of their efforts for the advancement of our interests. Let us emulate their zeal.

It is not my purpose at this time to occupy your attention with a history of the science of pharmacy. The present and future of this Association, as representing the best interests of the pharmacists and druggists of our own and sister States, should be the object of our earnest solicitude.

The past year has been comparatively barren of good results. The treasurer can give you a solution of the difficulty under which we have labored. It is impossible to accomplish much substantial good in these days without a good bank account. The first great problem presented in putting down the late rebellion was a financial one. Fortunately, while the government was bankrupt, the resources of a prosperous and patriotic people were placed at its disposal, and soon the enginery of war was put in motion, and the great rebellion was crushed. Money furnishes the sinews of war. With a depleted treasury it has been impossible to reach our membership with such matter through the mail as was necessary to keep them advised of our affairs. Several documents have come to hand from members of our own and other associations, with the earnest request that we give them circulation among the druggists and pharmacists of our State. It has been impossible for us to comply with even this modest request.

Our committee on county organization has been financially paralyzed, notwithstanding the appropriation of one hundred dollars voted at our last annual meeting, which they have never seen.

Our legislative committee has been poor but honest, not having any funds wherewith to work the lobby. In view of these facts you will see the importance of providing a sound financial policy for the maintenance of the Association. I would advise that a special committee be appointed to formulate a plan whereby the treasury may be replenished, and our Association put upon a sound financial footing, and that such committee report at an early session of our present meeting. While, as has been remarked, little has been accomplished during the year generally, I desire to call attention to the fact that our report of proceedings for the year 1887 was issued with unusual promptness by our faithful and energetic secretary, and as elaborate as in any former year, and it has not been excelled by the proceedings of any other State association.

I have referred incidentally to the subject of county organization. I regret that so little has been accomplished on that line. The evils of unhealthy competition seem to be increasing, and the cutting of prices in many portions of our State threatens to ruin the retail trade. We can think of no adequate remedy except in co-operation for the maintenance of prices. I would, therefore, recommend that you place in the hands of your committee of county organization a sufficient sum to enable them to prosecute their labors. The substantial benefit which accrues to the members of our Association is the measure of its value. Harmonize local interests, suppress jealousy and bitterness, promote a feeling of mutual confidence among dealers, and you will accomplish a purpose which must secure the sympathy and co-operation of the druggists and pharmacists throughout the length and breadth of our land.

Our attention has been called to the Excise Law as it affects the sale of wines and liquors by druggists. A diversity of opinion prevails in reference to the proposed changes in the law. I would suggest several propositions upon which I think we can all unite.

1. That druggists selling wines and liquors only for medicinal and mechanical use should not be required to pay a license fee.

II. That druggists selling indiscriminately should pay the same fee as other liquor dealers.
III. Druggists who sell only for medicinal and mechanical purposes should be required to keep a register of sales with the names of purchasers and the purpose for which required.
IV. A penalty should be imposed upon any person who obtains wines or liquors under false representation.
I would recommend that you instruct our legislative committee to secure the passage of a law embodying such provisions.

The time seems to have arrived when a careful consideration of the Internal Revenue License in this connection is of paramount importance to this Association. All State Associations, which have already met, have placed themselves on record in regard to this question, and as the Empire State is accustomed to lead rather than follow, I feel justified in recommending prompt and decisive action. The subject should be thoroughly discussed, and a special committee created to canvass the State and prepare memorials for presentation to Congress, giving evidence thereby that the pharmacists of the State of New York feel that they have tamely submitted to this odious tax until patience has ceased to be a virtue, and now propose to carry it to the ballot box unless a hearing be accorded on the merits of the case.

In the progress of scientific research many valuable additions are constantly being made to our materia medica from the laboratory and field. The average druggist, in his daily routine, finds little time to follow the literature of the day, and thus fails to keep advised of the new remedies. I would therefore recommend that a committee be appointed on New Remedies, whose duty it shall be to prepare a report on the additions to the materia medica during the year, with samples and specimens to be placed on exhibition at the annual meetings. It is my opinion that this will add much to the interest of our meetings.

I desire to reiterate the recommendation of my immediate predecessor, Mr. Clark Z. Otis, favoring the unification of the pharmacy boards of the State, the adoption of which will do much to overcome the difficulty which now seems to embarrass the several boards in the prosecution of their work. In view of the earnest desire of the Association that every respectable druggist and pharmacist of the State shall become a member, I would advise that a committee on membership, consisting of five, be appointed, who shall have power to appoint one or more associates in each county, to solicit applications for membership.

The recommendations I have suggested will afford ample material, not only for discussion at this meeting, but for work during the year. And now, fellow-members, I trust that our deliberations may be characterized by the same spirit of harmony which has existed in years past, and that the results may conduce to our future prosperity.

Finally, I thank you for the distinguished honor which you conferred in electing me your president. I have thus far endeavored to be faithful in the discharge of my duties, and shall continue during the remainder of my term, so near its close, to preside over your deliberations impartially and in the best interests of our Association.

The chair appointed as a committee to consider the recommendations of the President's address, C. S. Ingraham, of Elmira, W. G. Gregory, of Buffalo, and W. B. Rogers, of Middletown.

The Secretary read his report as follows:

SECRETARY'S REPORT.

To the Officers and Members of the New York State Pharmaceutical Association:

The clerical work of the Secretary has been performed during the year to the best of his ability. The publication of the proceedings having been placed entirely in his hands as a matter of economy, every effort was made to curtail the report without injury to the volume. Unfortunately, a protracted business trip through the West in September necessitated much expedition to complete the book before that date. As a result, many typographical errors occurred from hasty proof-reading, which I regretted, but could not well avoid. The proceedings were issued and mailed within forty days from the meeting, the quickest time in which the proceedings of any State Association have ever been issued, and a gain of twenty-eight days on the best previous record of this Association.

At the close of our last meeting our membership numbered 798. Two names were by accident omitted from the roll, making the exact number 800. During the year five deaths have been reported as follows: Jacob Hermes, Watertown; C. W. Hinsdale, Hudson; A. B. Hollett, M.D., Havana; Stephen Keller, Buffalo; Albert Remey, Port Jervis. Eight resignations have been received. This leaves our net membership at the opening of this meeting, 787.

Acting under the instruction and advice of the Executive Committee and officers of the Association, a special appeal was sent out in the month of May to every druggist in the State, soliciting applications for membership. What result may accrue this meeting will develop.

The clerical expenses of the Secretary for the year have been as follows:

Telegrams	$2 84
Postage, General	24 70
Sundries	8 10
Express charges	4 75
Printing and stationery	15 25
Secretary's expenses attending meeting	24 42
Stenographer's salary and expenses	126 12
One thousand copies Annual Proceedings	355 00
Postage on Proceedings	46 39
Express on Proceedings	13 01
Engrossing certificates	17 50
Five hundred blank certificates	40 00
Twenty-five hundred special appeals	9 75
Postage on same	28 25
Twenty-five hundred announcements	10 80
Secretary's salary to date	300 00
Total	$1,032 67

The Secretary hereby officially acknowledges with the thanks of the Association the receipt of the following exchanges. Proceedings of the American Pharmaceutical Association, National Wholesale Drug Association, and the following State Associations: Connecticut, Florida, Georgia, Illinois, Iowa, Kansas, Massachusetts, Michigan, Minnesota, Missouri, North Dakota, South Dakota, Nebraska, New Hampshire, New Jersey, North Carolina, Ohio, Pennsylvania, Texas, Virginia, Wisconsin.

The following periodicals have been received: *Pharmaceutical Record, Pharmaceutical Era, Oil Paint and Drug Reporter, Druggists' Circular, Western Druggist, National Druggist, American Pharmacist, American Drug Clerks' Journal,* and *Medical Bulletin.*

In accordance with instructions from the Association, I procured five hundred blank certificates of membership as soon as possible after the meeting. I was obliged to wait until these were received before issuing certificates to new members, many of whom became quite impatient at the delay which on my part was unavoidable. I feel conscious of the imperfect manner in which I have executed much of the clerical work of the year. I have done the best I could under the pressure of my own business affairs, and crave your indulgence.

Respectfully submitted,
CLAY W. HOLMES,
Secretary.

The Treasurer read the report of the finances of the year, showing balance on hand of $584.

The Secretary read report of the Secretaries' Conference at Cincinnati.

REPORT OF SECRETARIES' CONFERENCE.

While your Secretary was not requested to represent the Association at the meeting of State Secretaries at Cincinnati, he felt it incumbent on him to attend, as it was through his efforts and suggestion that a call was made for such a conference. This report is presented in the hope that it may be received by this Association, and its recommendations considered.

Pursuant to the call issued by your Secretary as chairman of the committee appointed at Providence in 1886, the conference met in the parlors of the Grand Hotel, at Cincinnati, September 5th, 1887, at 9 P.M.; Alabama, Connecticut, Illinois, Iowa, Massachusetts, Minnesota, Missouri, Michigan, New York, and Ohio were represented by their respective secretaries. Your secretary was elected chairman, and Dr. Rosa Upson, of Iowa, secretary.

An interesting discussion developed the fact that such a conference would harmonize the work of all State Associations, if each association would give attention to the points considered, and adopt uniform measures. Among the recommendations of the conference, I present:

I. Would it not be desirable for State Associations to issue transfer papers signed by the president and secretary, to all persons in good standing who remove to other States, which shall admit him as a member of the association of his adopted State without payment of admission fee?

II. Shall papers read at State Associations be contributed to the public press before the proceedings are issued?

III. A plan of reorganization as set forth in the following:

Knowing that in some States a few are made to support the association and carry on legislation, etc., for the benefit of the many, who look on and receive the benefits without sharing in the expense or giving their influence to the association, the question was discussed as to how to make each member bear his proportion of the burden. The plan was proposed to be submitted to each association for their consideration. To reorganize the association so that every registered pharmacist must become a member of the association. This could only be done by concerted action between pharmacy board and association. The association should have a council composed of one druggist from each county, which should meet once a year, expense of each meeting to be paid from registration fees; expense of association should be paid from registration fees, as dues of members should be included in this fee and no other dues be collected, in this way making each man pay his part of the expense of the association, and they shall by virtue of this registration fee be members of the association. In Connecticut, two members of the pharmacy board must be members of the association. In New York, Illinois, and some other States the board and association are connected. Association might at least ask board to request each applicant for registration to become member of association. Is such a plan feasible? Would this association enter into such a plan if universally adopted? Many other points were discussed which were instructive to your secretary, and all received benefit therefrom.

All those present were authorized by their associations to attend except your own secretary, and I note that some other associations, which have since met, have placed their secretary on the delegation to the A. P. A., and directed him to attend the conference. It is my firm belief that great benefit will result from these annual conferences.
Respectfully submitted,
CLAY W. HOLMES.

Dr. Eccles read the report of the Committee on Adulterations.

The Secretary was instructed to send greeting to the Missouri and West Virginia State Associations.

Wednesday at 11 A.M. was fixed as the special order for Dr. Eccles' paper for the ladies.

The Secretary read the names of additional applicants for membership, after which the meeting adjourned.

SECOND SESSION, 3:15 P.M.

Minutes of the first session read and approved.
Fifty-four members were elected upon one ballot cast by the Secretary.

The Committee on Credentials reported the receipt of credentials from the National Druggists' Association, Connecticut Pharmaceutical Association, Cayuga and Chemung County Associations.

The Secretary read resignations from the following, which were accepted:

RESIGNATIONS.

F. L. Bates, Albion ; T. M. Glatt, Utica ; W. C. Hoag, Hess Road Sta. ; Andrew Sawyer, Troy ; W. A. A. Sloat, Newburg ; William B. Smith, Troy ; Robert Wendler, Brooklyn ; Geo. S. Whitlock, Elmira.

Accepted.

A communication was received from Prof. Jos. P. Remington, of Philadelphia, acknowledging his election as honorary member.

Prof. P. W. Bedford read a preliminary report of the Committee on Papers and Queries.

The Secretary read a communication from the Cayuga County Pharmaceutical Association inviting the Association to meet with them in Auburn next year. Same was received and referred.

The Treasurer presented a list of delinquent members. After considerable discussion this list was referred to a special committee, consisting of the Treasurer, Secretary, and Executive Committee, with power to act.

The election of officers resulted as follows :
President, Dr. R. G. Eccles, of Brooklyn.
First Vice-Pres., J. Hungerford Smith, of Ausable Forks.
Second Vice-Pres., Dr. W. W. Gregory, of Buffalo.
Third Vice-Pres., C. S. Ingraham, of Elmira.
Secretary, Clay W. Holmes, of Elmira.
Treasurer, C. H. Butler, of Oswego.
Executive committee, F. L. Norton, Delhi ; W. L. Dubois, Catskill; A. W. Rice, Hudson.
Delegates to American Pharmaceutical Association, Dr. J. H. Eaton, Syracuse ; W. R. Rogers, Middletown ; Geo. J. Seabury, New York ; Clay W. Holmes, Elmira ; Aaron Sager, Cortland.

The secretary read a communication from Dr. Charles Rice, Chairman of the Committee on the Revision of the Pharmacopoeia, requesting that a committee be appointed to co-operate with them in their labors. The Association moved to accept this recommendation.

[The names of the committee did not reach us in time for publication.]

Mr. Charles H. Ward, and Mr. Charles S. Finch, of Stamford, Conn., and Mr. N. Noble, of New Milford, delegates from the Connecticut Association, were received and accorded the privileges of the floor.

The report of the delegates to the American Pharmaceutical Association was read by Mr. George J. Seabury.

THIRD SESSION, Wednesday morning, June 20th.

Called to order at 10.30 by the president.
Minutes of the last session read and approved.
The vice-president took the chair and the committee on president's address made their report, which was accepted, and the recommendations taken up seriatim.

During the consideration of these recommendations, the special hour having arrived for Dr. Eccles' paper, the report of the committee was laid on the table, and Dr. Eccles read a very interesting paper on "Flowers and their Winged Friends," after which the meeting adjourned.

FOURTH SESSION.

Called to order at 3 P.M.
Minutes of the last session read and approved.
Consideration of the report of the committee on president's address was resumed. After each recommendation had been considered seriatim, the report was adopted as a whole.

Dr. Huested reported verbally for the committee on legislation, that no legislative work had been done during the year.

Mr. Ingraham presented a communication referring to proprietary medicines, and the publication of the formula upon the label, together with a draft of a proposed law, which was referred to the committee on legislation.

The report of the committee on county organization and trade interests was made by Mr. A. S. Van Winkle, of Hornellsville. The committee having no funds with which to prosecute their work had been unable to do anything.

Two amendments were offered to the by-laws, one directing that the proceedings should not be furnished to members in arrears for dues, the other to correct a clerical omission. They were laid over until the next session. Upon motion that a committee of three be appointed to present the names of five members to be presented to the Governor, the chair appointed C. S. Ingram, of Elmira ; R. E. Phillips, of Fulton : and A. S. Van Winkle, of Hornellsville.

The consideration of papers and queries was taken up, and answers to queries Nos. 17 and 19 were read by Prof. Bedford, and No. 2 by Dr. Eccles.

The installation of officers was then proceeded with in the usual form. The chair appointed C. Z. Otis, of Binghamton, and Dr. Huested, of Albany, as a committee to present the newly-elected officers for installation.

The committee appointed by the president to present five names to the Governor reported the following names:
A. B. Huested, of Albany ; C. H. Goss, of Albany ; Chas. F. Fish, of Saratoga ; A. W. Rice, of Hudson ; W. H. Rogers, of Middletown.

A motion was made and unanimously carried that Dr. Huested be recommended for re-appointment upon the board.

Several informal ballots were taken upon the next place of meeting. Binghamton receiving the greatest number of ballots, it was moved that our next meeting be held in Binghamton, at a date to be named by the executive committee.

The meeting then adjourned.

FIFTH SESSION, Thursday, June 21st.

Called to order at 10.30.
Minutes of the last meeting read and approved. Names of several applicants for membership were read and laid over.

The amendments to the by-laws reported at preceding session were adopted.

Telegram of congratulation was received from the Missouri State Association.

The following committees were appointed by the president:

Committee on Legislation—Dr. R. C. Eccles, Brooklyn; Aaron Sager, Cortland; Dr. B. Huested, Albany; C. W. Holmes, Elmira; Clark Z. Otis, Binghamton.

Committee on Pharmacy and Queries—Prof. P. W. Bedford, New York; C. R. Paddock, Brooklyn; Dr. A. B. Huested, Albany.

Committee on Adulterations—J. Hungerford Smith, Ausable Forks; Dr. W. G. Gregory, Buffalo; Willis G. Tucker, Albany.

Committee on County Organization—A. S. Van Winkle, Hornellsville; C. S. Ingraham, Elmira; J. B. Todd, Ithaca.

Committee on Unofficial Formulary—C. S. Ingraham, Elmira; W. C. Gregory, Buffalo; E. S. Dawson, Jr., Syracuse; T. D. McElhenie, Brooklyn; C. H. Sager, Auburn.

Committee on New Remedies—Dr. Charles Rice, New York; B. J. Beudiner, New York; Gustavus Balser, New York.

Committee on Entertainment—C. Z. Otis, Binghamton; H. A. Smith, Binghamton; J. H. Eaton, Syracuse; C. W. Holmes, Elmira.

Delegates to the National Wholesale Drug Association—Geo. R. Perry, Syracuse; Frank S. Hubbard, Buffalo; W. S. Gerity, Elmira; A. B. Huested, M.D., Albany; A. McClure, Albany; P. W. Bedford, New York; W. W. Tucker, Sag Harbor.

Delegates to Connecticut—L. E. Nicot, of Brooklyn; I. C. Chapman, of Newburg; W. B. Eddy, Whitehall.

Delegates to Massachusetts—P. W. Bedford, New York; C. F. Lloyd, Albany; J. C. Smith, Plattsburg.

Delegates to New Jersey—D. L. Cameron, Brooklyn; Geo. J. Seabury, New York; W. R. Rogers, Middletown.

Delegates to Pennsylvania—C. W. Holmes, Elmira; J. W. Bachman, Hornellsville; C. K. Brown, Deposit.

The report of the Board of Pharmacy was received and ordered published. It was moved that its recommendation be referred to the legislative committee with power to act.

Prof. Bedford read a paper on Pharmacy Boards, which was referred to the same committee.

Dr. H. H. Rusby, of Columbia College, New York, then read a very interesting paper on "Homes of South American Drugs," which was very instructive and entertaining. The thanks of the association were returned to Dr. Rusby for his paper, and he was elected an honorary member of the association by acclamation.

SIXTH SESSION.

The president, Dr. Eccles, being obliged to return home on account of sickness in his family, Vice-Pres. J. H. Smith took the chair.

Several persons were elected members of the association.

The report of the committee on exhibits not being completed, it was moved that the same be referred to the committee for publication, when received by the secretary.

The president appointed as special committee on excise laws, R. K. Smither, of Buffalo; L. E. Nicot, of Brooklyn; Geo. J. Seabury, of New York; C. W. Holmes, of Elmira, and A. B. Huested, of Albany.

Prof. Bedford, chairman of the committee on papers and queries, read a voluntary paper by Albert M. Todd, in response to query No. 31, upon treatment and distillation of peppermint plants. Also a voluntary paper by Frank P. Dalzell, of Cold Springs, upon elixir of phosphates of iron, quinine and strychnine. Several other papers were read by title and referred to the committee for publication.

Joseph Schnell, of Binghamton, was elected local secretary, after which it was moved that the association adjourn to meet in Binghamton upon the call of the Executive Committee.

Considerable discussion upon the best time for holding the meeting resulted in a recommendation to the Executive Committee that an earlier date be selected for the next meeting.

Adjourned to meet at call of Executive Committee.

LIST OF MEMBERS ELECTED.

Mason S. Brown, Strykersville; Wm. J. Smythe, Jr., Seabright, N. J.; Fredrick Herdling, Yonkers; Edward Holt, New York; James H. Bushnell, Churchville; Chas. L. Easton, Sherburne; A. J. Ditman, New York; Thomas J. Barnabee, New York; Milo E. Fletcher, Norwood; David H. Jennings, Far Rockaway; Arthur E. Todd, M. D., Gloversville; Walter A. Tuck, Gloversville; Henry D. Spingard, New York; Louis Spingard, New York; Chas. Henry Ruck, New York; Max Abramson, New York; William A. Van Duzer, Brooklyn; J. O. Barnaby, Brooklyn; H. W. Holden, Elmira, N. Y.; Henry K. Harris, M.D., New York; S. L. Hall, M.D., Mechanicsville; F. F. Henry Syvarth, Brooklyn; Wm. McAllister, Albany; J. H. Campbell, Suffern; Wm M Davis, Brooklyn; Chas. A. Swanson, Jamestown; Willis O. Tucker, Albany; Wm. B. Eddy, Whitehall; Albert J Rust, Chateaugay; Wm. A. Desl. Ausable Forks; Orville A. Manville, Whitehall; Patrick N. Barry, Whitehall; Henry E. Gillespe, Ausable Forks; Lawrence Corbett, Whitehall; John E. Corbett, Whitehall; Daniel S. Parson, Jr., Dannemora; Noah A. Overmiller, New York; W. Mason Brown, Lockport; Thos. R. Anderson, Port Jervis; Geo. E. More, Oneonta; Geo. C. Waldir, New York; L. A. Skinner, Schenectady; Wm. R. W. Pound, Lockport; Jos. N. Walker, Ellenville; Herbert E. Reed, Syracuse; Geo. B. Benedict, New York; Jas. Henry Hutchens, New York; Chas. J. Delz, New York; Evander Farrington, North Tarrytown; Chas. Ruth, Rondout; Nelson H. Kettle, Schenectady; Elmer E. Rowe, Warsaw; Albert L. Embres, Tarrytown; Chas. L. Wiggins, Newburg; Albert Smith, Newburg; Frederick R. Dennis, Marlborough; Elmer E. McNamara, Marlborough; Frederick J Walling, Brooklyn; Augustus McKinstry, Hudson; Jas. A. Eisenmann, Hudson; Harry P. Carr, Kingston; Julius F. Wingenbach, Utica; Wm. D. Olney, Middletown; T. H. S. Pennington, Saratoga Springs; John O. Gladstone, Delhi; Fred. W. Schaefer, Albany; Dayton E. Slater, Hunter.

Correction.

In our review of Mr. Rother's work, entitled "The Beginnings of Pharmacy," contained in our last issue (page 120), it should read: The author derives hydrantis from the "Greek *hyrin*—to rain, and *dran*—to be active," instead of "*dran*—to draw."

Reducing Obesity.—The Detroit *Lancet* describes the four plans for reducing obesity:—The eating of nothing containing starch, sugar, or fat, called the Banting system; the eating of fat, but not sugar, or starch, called the German Banting; the wearing of wool, and sleeping in flannel blankets instead of sheets, or the Munich system; not eating and drinking at the same time, or rather the allowing of a couple of hours to intervene between eating and drinking, the Schweninger system.

Methyltrihydroxchinolinecarbonic Acid is the elaborate title of a new substance proposed by Professor Demme in the *Therapeutische Monatshefte* as an additional antipyretic, the chemical formula being $C_9H_4NO_2 + CH_3 + C_3H_2(CH_3)NO_3H$.

By the addition of 1.0 gramme of dry sodium carbonate to every 3.66 grammes of the acid in warm solution, the sodium salt is produced, having a dark brown color. The dry compound is pale yellow. The free acid is but slightly soluble in water. In its constitution this acid closely resembles thallin. Its effect in lowering body temperature is slower and longer in appearing than is the case with antipyrin. Its dose is 0.1 gramme (ab. 1½ grains) for children between 4 and 6 years, and 0.25 gramme (ab. 4 grains) for such as are 11 to 15 years old.

A NEW DROP-COUNTER.

L. TRAUBE, of Hanover, has patented the device here illustrated (Germ. Pat. 40,277). The neck of the bottle is provided with two slits situated opposite to each other, at a and c. The hollow stopper has a small tube fused upon it, and at its opposite side contains a small interior groove, for the admission of air when the stopper is turned so as to permit the escape of drops.

A New Process for Estimating Alcohol.

IF potassic permanganate is added to alcohol, mixed with dilute sulphuric acid, an imperfect oxidation takes place, even if the mixture is heated. If, however, very dilute alcohol is first mixed with large excess of permanganate, and then suddenly with about one-third of its volume of sulphuric acid, the alcohol instantly and completely changes into carbonic anhydride and water. Water may now be added, and the excess of permanganate titrated back with potassic tetraoxalate. From the amount of permanganate decomposed, the alcohol can be readily calculated; 8.244 grammes of permanganate equal 1 gramme of alcohol. The test analyses, four in number, are very satisfactory. Further experiments are promised.—B. Rumg in *Zeitsch. f. angew. Chem.*

GLASS JET FOR WASHING PRECIPITATES.

MR. S. J. HINSDALE, of Fayetteville, N. C., has sent us several specimens of a very simple and handy glass jet or nozzle for washing precipitates. The accompanying cut illustrates the construction.

C is a cork, through which passes the glass tube a, one end of which is open, while the other is closed by a perforated rubber cork f, through which passes the inner, smaller glass tube b. The latter is bent and slightly contracted at the projecting end g. At d, a small hole is blown in the larger tube, and a ring-shaped piece of rubber tubing is slipped over the glass tube, by means of which air may be admitted or its access shut off.

The cork having been tightly inserted into a suitable flask or bottle—say, holding a pint and about two-thirds filled with distilled water—and the rubber ring being pushed over the hole d, the flask is inverted and adjusted at the proper height, in a retort-stand or other contrivance, over the filter the contents of which are to be washed. The glass jet g should be adjusted so that the little hole d will be below the highest level at which the liquid is intended to stand in the small filter. As soon as the rubber ring is slipped up, water will commence to run from the jet, until the little hole is covered, and the filter will periodically be refilled, as soon as air is admitted again. The little rubber ring is applied merely to prevent spirting while the flask is being inverted and adjusted.

SEPARATING FUNNEL.*

CURRIER has devised the separating funnel shown in the accompanying cut. Through a cork inserted into the neck of a funnel, a glass tube is passed, the inner end of which is closed by fusion, and which has an opening (made by a file) a little below the closed end. If this tube is pushed down so low that the opening is covered by the cork, nothing will flow from the tube. On pushing it upwards, the hole becomes uncovered and will permit the passage of liquid through the tube.

Orange Wine.—In the German colony Blumenau, in Brazil, orange wine is prepared in the following manner:

To make a cask of orange wine, between 800 and 1,000 oranges are required. These are subjected to a strong pressure. About 60 pounds of sugar are dissolved in 5 gallons of water, the solution brought to a boil, skimmed and set aside to cool. It is then mixed with the orange juice, and the whole allowed to ferment. When fermentation is completed, and the wine has become clear, it is bottled. [Considerable quantities of orange wine are now made in Florida by a somewhat similar process.]

---

* After Mierzinski, "Die Maschstoffe." etc. Weimar, 1888.

Preparation of Diachylon Ointment.

E. Dieterich has made experiments to ascertain the keeping qualities of Unguentum Diachylon according as it is prepared with different vegetable oils mixed with lead plaster. It is well known that all oils are liable to exhibit very remarkable and unexpected peculiarities in their different practical applications. This consideration led the author to examine mixtures of lead plaster with different oils both immediately after their preparation and after four and eight weeks, with a view to determine the amount of free oleic acid by titration. For this purpose, he dissolved 3 Gm. of the salve in 30 C.c. of ether, added three drops of solution of phenolphtalein and then added 1/10 normal alkali until the acid was neutralized.

The results are given in the following table:

Diachylon Ointment prepared with	Required milligrams of potassa after being prepared		
	2 hours.	4 weeks.	8 weeks.
Oil Almonds exp.	30.8	30.8	30.8
" Peanut	30.8	30.8	30.8
" Cotton seed	30.8	42.0	47.0
" Sunflower	31.6	33.6	36.
" Cod Liver	33.6	38.6	38.
" Walnut	30.8	42.0	47.
" Linseed	30.8	38.4	42.
" Olive, comn.	30.8	30.8	30.8
" Poppy	30.8	38.	38.4
" Rape	30.8	38.4	43.
" Sesame	30.8	30.8	30.8
" Castor	30.4	30.4	33.

Increase of acidity generally caused also an increase of rancid odor. The best mixtures, regarding flavor, were obtained with olive and castor oil, particularly the latter. —*Ph. Post.*

It will be seen from the above, that cotton-seed oil is not as good an ingredient, though it makes a very smooth and homogeneous mixture, for which reason mainly it was adopted, in this preparation, by the U. S. Pharm.—Ed. Am. Dr.

Salol Tooth Powder.

Calcium Carbonate, precip.	750 parts.
Sugar of Milk, pow'd	100 "
Orris Root, pow'd	100 "
Pumice, powd.	90 "
Salol	30 "
Oil of Peppermint.	3 "
" Geranium	1 part.
" Staranise.	"
" Cloves	"

Mix intimately.—*After Pharm. Centralh.*

Salol Tooth Wash.

Cloves	10 parts.
Cinnamon, Ceylon	10 "
Staranise.	10 "
Cochineal.	5 "
Alcohol.	1,000 "

Macerate during eight days, then add:

Oil of Peppermint.	5 parts.
Salol.	25 "

Agitate frequently, and filter after 24 hours. (Dieterich, *ibid.*)

We should have given the directions as follows: Reduce the cloves, cinnamon, staranise, and cochineal to a moderately fine powder, moisten it with alcohol, pack it in a percolator, and percolate until 970 parts of tincture are obtained. In this dissolve the oil of peppermint and salol.

Using this process, the operator can make the preparation in 24 hours, or even in less time, if small amounts are operated on.

Pepper-growing a Profitable Occupation.

The *Straits Times* recently advised planters to turn their attention to the cultivation of pepper, which, it is claimed, is a crop likely to prove a very paying one to the producers, the prices being high, and the cultivation a comparatively easy one. The latter is now almost exclusively in the hands of the Chinese, only one European, Mr. Stevenson of Klang, in the Straits Settlements, having thus far ventured upon pepper-growing. One indispensable condition for the success of pepper-growing is good choice of ground, especially as regards the situation of the land. Flats or gently sloping land of sedimentary and plutonic formation have invariably been found most suitable for the purpose, and such lands are obtainable in sufficient quantity to meet any demand likely to arise. In the neighboring native states, far-reaching and fertile plains are available in any quantity. The consumption of pepper, not only in Europe and America, but also in China, has of late proved so steady and rapidly increasing that the supply has utterly failed to overtake the demand, especially because Acheen, in former times the chief source of supply, does not now produce any quantities worth mentioning.—*Chem. and Druggist.*

Magnolia Balm.

A repetition of the analysis of Hager and F. M. Clarke has been made by the analyst of *New Idea*, and he reports that the balm consists of zinc oxide (colored with carmine) in suspension in a little dilute glycerin, and perfumed with oil of bergamot, oil of lemon, and perhaps one other odor. The following formula makes a preparation substantially the same as the proprietary article:

Zinc oxide	4 drachms
Glycerin	1½ fl. oz.
Water	"
Carmine	⅛ grain
Oil bergamot	1 minim
Oil lemon	1 "

Johore Ipecacuanha.

Mr. Trimen, the Director of the Ceylon Botanic Gardens, in his last reports refers to the introduction of ipecacuanha in India, and states that as early as 1848, or sixteen years before the first plants reached India, ipecacuanha was introduced in Ceylon, but that its cultivation in that island did not meet with any considerable amount of success, and it does not look as if we could ever expect to receive the drug in commercial quantities from Ceylon, especially if, as now seems probable, the Straits Settlements should furnish considerable quantities in the near future, for the use of the root is limited, and any successful cultivation on a large scale in various countries would soon bring the price down to a level which would cease to pay the cultivators. The sample of Johore ipecacuanha, which was recently exposed for sale in Mincing lane, does not differ materially from that which first imported. If anything it is more varied, thin and stout roots, possessing the gray and reddish surfaces, making up the parcel. The roots which we selected for analysis were a fair sample; the woody column was somewhat thick. The percentage of emetine we found in the specimen is 1.4, somewhat lower than the specimen examined by Mr. Ransom afforded; but this may be accounted for by the thickness of the woody column, and the difference is no more than may be expected of two different samples of root.

Cola Nuts.

Messrs. Jobst and Hesse, of Stuttgart, have made some experiments with cola nuts, with a view of ascertaining whether they would make a beverage which could be used in place of coffee or chocolate.

As is well known, cola nuts are very rich in caffeine, of which they contain about 1.83 per cent, and have even been found to contain 2.35 per cent.

The fresh nut is very sweet, and afterwards astringent and bitter. As they reach the European (or this) market they are half dried, and somewhat resemble chestnuts externally. The taste of the yellowish-brown flesh or kernel is insipid, somewhat recalling that of cacao shells. On the one hand, the chemical constituents of the substance proclaim it to be a stimulant of the first rank; and on the other hand, its taste does not promise much for it as a source for a pleasant beverage.

Messrs. Jobst and Hesse deprived the nuts of their shells, roasted them like coffee, and reduced them to powder. The aqueous infusion of this had a handsome color, but its taste was not particularly agreeable, reminding one strongly of acorn coffee.

Next they tried to make "chocolate" of it, but here the difficulty arises that it does not contain enough fatty matter, which makes it necessary to incorporate a good deal of butter of cacao with it, besides the sugar. And this resulted in the production of a chocolate of very handsome appearance and odor, though of a rather peculiar, and not quite agreeable taste.—*After Industrie-Blätter.*

Impurity in Hydrochlorate of Quinine.

At a recent meeting of the Paris Society of Pharmacy (*Chem. and Drugg.*), M. de Vrij made a communication on the occasional presence of hydrochlorate of cinchonidine in commercial hydrochlorate of quinine. The impurity he would attribute to the natural composition of the new cinchona barks now in the market. As a test he recommended the following:

Quinine Hydrochlorate	1 gramme.
Water of 50° to 60° C	40 grammes.
Pure neutral Chromate of Potassium	0.30 gramme.

The chromate is to be added after the mixture has been effected.

At the temperature given, the quinine is rapidly precipitated, while the cinchonidine remains in solution. On adding caustic soda to the clear liquor, the cinchonidine is thrown down, even in the cold, but more speedily by the help of a gentle heat. The solution, however, should not be too alkaline or overheated, as soda will then transform the alkaloid into a resinoid substance.

A Volatile Poison in the Exhalations of Man and some Animals.

BROWN-SÉQUARD and D'Arsonval announce the existence, in the air expelled during expiration, in man and some animals, of a highly poisonous agent. Up to the present it was known that the exhaled air contained, nearly always, some ammonia, in very minute traces, also carbonic acid gas, and besides, some organic matters, which, though they may not be putrid at the time when they are thrown out into the air, yet undergo change very rapidly, even at a low temperature.

The authors above quoted, however, have found that the lungs of man, also those of the dog and hare in a state of health, produce, and discharge with each expiration, a minute quantity of a very violent poison, which from the experiments thus far made appears to have the properties of an alkaloid. When its solution was injected into the circulation of dogs, etc., the latter rapidly died. Heat does not seem to be very much injurious to the body, as a temperature of 100° C. appeared to render it even more active than it had been previous to heating. Further accounts will be published in a short time.—*Rep. d. Pharm.*

The Gum Benzoin Trade.

BATTAS consular reports from Java state that, during the year 1887, 6,296 piculs gum benzoin were exported from Padang (west coast of Sumatra). Nearly the whole of this went to Java, small shipments to Holland, the Straits Settlements, and to America. This quantity is one of the largest on record, but it should be observed that the shipments of gum benzoin from this port are steadily on the increase. In the thirty years from 1858 to 1887 inclusive, 140,901 piculs have been exported from Padang.

The Aniline Treatment of Phthisis.

THE aniline treatment of phthisis consists of frequent administration of acetanilide (10-grain doses four or five times a day) and the inhalation of pure aniline mixed with an essential oil, such as anise, eucalyptus, or peppermint oil. A suitable mixture is aniline, 3 j.; eucalyptus oil, 3 vij.; mix. At the same time ointment of iodine or iodoform, with eucalyptus oil, is rubbed into the chest. The acetanilide breaks up in the system, aniline being one of the products. Although cyanosis and other disagreeable symptoms supervene, the decomposition of the acetanilide is apparently part of the cure, so also is careful attention to dietary. In the *Lancet* of March 24th, there are some notes on an indisputable case of four years' standing which recovered under this treatment.

Preservative Sugar.

Salicylic Acid .... 50 parts.
Sugar, in fine powder....... .... 950 "

Triturate the salicylic acid with some of the powdered sugar, in a mortar, and gradually incorporate it with the remainder.

This compound is used for preserving fruits and other articles of fruit. The salicylic acid prevents the development of the fungi and fermentation. One ounce of it is sufficient for about 6 pounds of preserves. The latter are prepared with sugar in the usual manner, transferred to suitable vessels, and a proportionate layer of the preservative sugar sprinkled on top.—*Vomacka*.

Solution of Iron in Caustic Soda.

WHEN a strong current of air is blown into a hot, concentrated solution of caustic soda, containing about 34 per cent NaOH, standing in an iron vessel, or to which finely divided hydrated ferric oxide has been added, perceptible quantities of iron are dissolved without discoloring the liquid. In fact such a solution will remain clear and colorless for several days, at the ordinary temperature; ultimately it becomes turbid, yellow, and finally red, owing to the presence of the hydrated ferric oxide, but this color disappears again on heating. When the colorless solution is diluted, the oxide is precipitated in about half an hour, but again passes into solution when the liquid is concentrated. Hydrogen sulphide at first produces a deep cherry-red coloration in the colorless liquid, and by its continued action a greenish-black precipitate forms, which settles down, leaving a clear solution, free from iron, but slightly yellow from sodium sulphide. It is suggested that the iron exists in solution as a perferrate, analogous to sodium permangate, and with the formula $NaFeO_4$, therefore.—L. G. ZIMFFI in *Chem. Zeit.* (Abst. from *J. S. Chem. Ind.*)

Reaction of Cotton-seed Oil.

A small quantity of the oil is mixed with an equal quantity of a saturated solution of normal lead acetate; ammonia is then added, and the whole shaken. Under these circumstances cotton-seed oil assumes a reddish orange color, whilst butter, olive, castor almond, and other oils give a red color.—M. LAMICHE in *Arch. de Pharm.* and *J. S. Chem. Ind.*

Lac Ferri, *Iron Milk*.

Pyrophosphate of Sodium .... 20 parts
Solution of Chloride of Iron............. 22 parts
Glycerin................................. 50 parts
Distilled Water........enough to make 1,000 parts

Dissolve the Pyrophosphate of Sodium in 400 parts of Distilled Water, add the Glycerin, and filter. Dilute the Solution of Chloride of Iron (U. S.) with 400 parts of Distilled Water, pour this slowly into the cold solution of the sodium salt, under gentle and slow stirring, and add enough water to make 1,000 parts.

If it is desired to remove the small amount of chloride of sodium produced by the reaction—though it may be left, being harmless—an excess of iron must be used, the sodium pyrophosphate solution poured into the iron solution, and the whole raised to boiling. The precipitate is then collected, washed and suspended in water. But the product will not possess a "milk-like" character, as the precipitate, in the latter case, is soon deposited at the bottom. The first mentioned process yields a permanent "milky" liquid.

[The original formula, by E. Dieterich, in *Ph. Centralh.* directs 50 parts of Solution of Chloride of Iron, which refers to that of the Germ. Pharm., containing 10 per cent of metallic iron. It has been transcalculated into that of the U. S. Ph., containing 13.06 per cent of iron.

The Camphor Trade in Formosa.

The Chinese Governor of the island of Formosa some time ago declared the camphor trade in the interior of the island a Government monopoly, thereby greatly injuring a number of private traders, who for many years had dealt extensively in the article on their own account. Troubles ensued with some of the foreign houses, and the United States Government addressed a remonstrance on the subject to the Tsung-li-Yamen in Pekin—a body somewhat resembling our Foreign Office. We now hear that this appeal has remained fruitless, the Pekin authorities, in a communication dated February 16th, fully justifying the action of the Governor of Formosa, and declaring their intention of maintaining the monopoly. It appears that in those parts of the island now thoroughly brought under Chinese control the camphor trade is free, or at any rate subjected to but few restrictions; but, unfortunately, in those districts scarcely any trees are left, while only in the mountainous interior of the island, nominally under Chinese dominion, but in reality occupied by tribes of warlike savages, the camphor laurel still flourishes. In the camphor districts of the interior the Chinese, at a considerable cost, maintain military stations, and they partly defray the expense of these by keeping to themselves the exclusive right in the camphor trade. The Tsung-li-Yamen also point out that in prohibiting foreigners from penetrating into the unsafe centre of the island they are actuated by a desire to avoid such complications with foreign governments as might result from the murder of their subjects by the aborigines. The Chinese arguments appear to be unanswerable, and we may therefore take it that the camphor monopoly will be kept up—at any rate for the present.—*Chem. and Drugg.*

Detecting Gas Leakage.

Dr. Bunte's method for detecting gas leakage by means of palladium paper has been rendered still more delicate by Herr Schauffers, who uses, to every three parts of palladium, one part of chloride of gold. The increase of sensitiveness may be partly due to catalytic action, that is, to the mere presence of the gold, perhaps to the action of traces of acetylene upon the gold solution. The solution used for making the paper contains ½ per cent of chloride of palladium, and ⅙ per cent of chloride of gold. One pint costs about nine shillings, and will steep filter paper enough for 8,000 to 11,000 tests. The main sources of error are tobacco smoke, stoves, and smoky chimneys, which let carbonic oxide into the room, the vapor of fusel oil, onion smell, mercury vapor, and sulphuretted hydrogen.

Nitroglycerin in Heart Failure.

Dr. M. H. Firnell, of Philadelphia, after reporting three cases of syncope in which hypodermic injections of two drops of a 1-per-cent solution were used, remarks (*Med. and Surg. Reporter*): "One who has seen cases of heart failure treated in the usual way can have no conception of the brilliant results which may be obtained by the hypodermic use of nitroglycerin."

Creosote Mixture for the Treatment of Phthisis.

Creosoti, ⋙xv.: Tr. Gentian., ⋙xlv.; Spir. Vini Rect, f. ʒ viss.; Vini Xerici, ad f. ʒ iij. Take of this one-third, thrice daily. The amount of creosote may be gradually increased to double this amount. The treatment should be continued for three to twelve months, and its beneficial effects are most marked in recent cases.

Borofuchsin,

recently proposed by Prof. Lubinoff, as a staining medium for tubercle bacilli, consists of: Fuchsin, 7½ grains; Boric Acid, 7½ grains; Absolute Alcohol, 4 drachms; Distilled Water, 5 drachms. This mixture is clear, slightly acid, and is not liable to spoil from age.—*Med. and Surg. Reporter.*

THE
American Druggist

AN ILLUSTRATED MONTHLY JOURNAL

OF

Pharmacy, Chemistry, and Materia Medica.

VOL. XVII., No. 7. WHOLE No. 109.

FREDERICK A. CASTLE, M.D. .... EDITOR.
CHARLES RICE, PH.D. .... ASSOCIATE EDITOR.

PUBLISHED BY

WM. WOOD & CO., 56 & 58 Lafayette Place, N. Y.

SUBSCRIPTION PRICE per year, ... $1.50
SINGLE COPIES, ...15

Address all communications relating to the business of the AMERICAN DRUGGIST, such as subscriptions, advertisements, change of Post-Office address, etc., to WILLIAM WOOD & CO., 56 and 58 Lafayette Place, New York City, to whose order all postal money orders and checks should be made payable. Communications intended for the Editor should be addressed in care of the Publishers.

The AMERICAN DRUGGIST is issued in the latter part of each month, dated for the month ahead. Changes of advertisements should reach us before the 15th. New advertisements can occasionally be inserted after the 15th.

REGULAR ADVERTISEMENTS according to size, location, and time. Special rates on application.

EDITORIALS.

SOME time ago a warfare was inaugurated by French physicians and pharmacists against antipyrine, chiefly on account of its being protected by a patent or copyright, and possibly—though not openly so stated—because the profits of the patent found their way across the border, into the pockets of the German patentee.

Here is what the *Répertoire de Pharmacie* says about the matter in its issue of May, 1888:

"At present, when the failures of this trans-Rhenish drug can no longer be counted, it is well to announce the measure which has just been adopted by the Governing Board of Public Assistance. At the meeting of May 1st, held at the Academy of Medicine, our master, M. Bourgoin, announced that the Governing Board of Public Assistance followed the principle of making its own medicines, or obtaining them by contract. It has not been able to do this so far in the case of 'dimethyloxyquinizine,' the antipyrine of the Germans, as this remedy is the subject of an unjustifiable monopoly."

"Anxious to protect its interests, and in order to avoid all suits, the Governing Body of Public Assistance has decided, upon the proposition of M. Bourgoin, that this remedy shall hereafter be dispensed in the Paris hospitals under the name *analgésine*. The thing is worth the trouble, for, during the first quarter of 1888, the hospitals have purchased 116 kilogrammes of it (about 4,092 avoirdupois ounces), at an expense of 60,000 francs calculated for the whole year, assuming that the consumption would be kept up at this rate."

"But, even from a scientific point, it had been originally pretended, that 'dimethyloxyquinizine' is a substitute for sulphate of quinine. This pretension has not been justified by the facts, and the best proof is, that the consumption of sulphate of quinine in the hospitals is now precisely the same as formerly. Hence the name *antipyrine* does not properly belong to the 'dimethyloxyquinizine.' On the contrary, it is now generally regarded as a remedy for allaying pain. If this is so, the name *analgésine* is quite appropriate for it."

"It is hoped that this new name will be accepted without objection by the medical profession. Frenchmen will then be able to manufacture the analgesine, and the Governing Board of Public Assistance will be able to obtain it by contract, like other chemical or pharmaceutical products. Besides, if a product is a specialty or monopoly, the buyer is compelled to accept it with eyes shut, all examination being impossible or illusory; or it may happen that the buyer will obtain antipyrine which turns yellow on exposure to air, and gives out a disagreeable odor of benzin."

"We report this decision, with the remark that it was not necessary to assure us of the sentiments of right and patriotism of our master. All of us who know him, can appreciate the persistence with which this eminent professor has striven to protect the French interests of pharmacy."

As a pendant to this editorial of our French contemporary, we give the following brief note from the Paris correspondent of the *Chemist and Druggist* (May 26th):

"It will probably be remembered that 'analgesine' is the new name proposed to designate antipyrine, and thus avoid conflict with those claiming property in the familiar designation. But it was alleged at a meeting of the Academy of Medicine that two country physicians have been in the habit for a long time of prescribing under the name of 'analgesine' a certain mixture of their own, entirely different from antipyrine. The parties interested in the patent rights make all they can out of this complication, while others maintain as stoutly as ever that the copyright being *de jure* null and void, any one is free to make and sell antipyrine under its best known appellation. The truth in all this appears to be that the threatened confusion of 'analgesines' is grossly exaggerated, if it existed; and that, on the other hand, while every one loudly proclaimed the antipyrine patent's invalidity, no one cares to join issue with the doughty Dr. Knorr. In the mean time the infringement suit against M. Petit is still on, but no progress has been reported lately."

It is much to be regretted that so much precipitation, and, we fear, also, national prejudices, have been allowed to become prominent factors in this movement. We do not wish to appear as the champions of Dr. Knorr or of any one else who is interested in the antipyrine patent. But every chemist knows that Dr. Knorr discovered the compound and a method for its preparation. He announced it originally as dimethyl-oxy-chinizin, but has given this theory up long ago, as a more intimate study has led him to view its constitution differently. (See this JOURNAL, 1887, 164.) Our French confrères seem to have overlooked this fact altogether. No one can patent a product of nature, but he can patent the process by which it can be obtained, if original. In France a patent is only valid if worked there, and to comply with this law the owners of the antipyrine patent erected a factory on French soil. It is true, the French laws prohibit the patenting of medicines or medicinal compounds, but so far as we know, this only applies to such as are specially designed to serve as such. Should a substance incidentally be found serviceable as a medicine, while forming the link in a chain of technical products, the case is probably different. Ethically, and theoretically, we are opposed to patents on medicines ourselves, but, as long as the law permits their issue, our own or anybody else's objection cannot interfere with established rights. Every patent is of course a monopoly, but why should one special patent be decried as an oppressive monopoly, and not all patents? A confiscation or annulment of a patent, provided it is rightfully granted, is a serious breach of contract on the part of a state. Had antipyrine remained a comparatively insignificant article, such as kairine, thalline, etc., it would probably not have been attacked at all.

The writer of the editorial above quoted is evidently not well posted on the therapeutic history of antipyrine. This body was ascertained, at a very early date after its discovery, *not* to be a substitute for quinine as a miasmatic or anti-febrile remedy, but only as an antipyretic, and even to exceed quinine and all other then known antipyretics in the power of reducing febrile temperatures. It has not been claimed to be, nor ever been regarded by competent authorities as, a substitute for quinine. But it is a true *antipyretic*, or "remedy against heat." Its anodyne and analgesic properties are a comparatively recent discovery, the remedy having been used for several years before this property became known. That the "failures of antipyrine can at present no longer be counted" is a rather wild statement, as it depends altogether on what it was tried to be used for.

We are in receipt of a letter from Dr. S. Mierzinski, the editor of the *Drogisten-Zeitung*, and author of the new work on Perfume ("Riechstoffe," etc.) from which we have given a number of extracts in our recent issues, regarding the article entitled "The Manufacture of Lithium Salts for Medicinal and Techni al Purposes" (see April number, page 62). We there gave, on the authority of Graham-Otto's "Lehrbuch d. Chemie" (new edition), the process which is now followed in Schering's factory to decompose lepidolite and to prepare from it the carbonate of lithium.

Dr. Mierzinski draws our attention to the fact that he is the author of this process, having published it, in 1868, in the *Zeitschrift d. Oesterr. Apotheker-Vereins*, p. 53.

Our respected contemporary, the *Deutsch-Amerikanische Apotheker-Zeitung*, in its issue of June 1st, has an editorial in which the writer gives his views respecting the steps at present being taken to prepare for a new edition of the United States Pharmacopœia. We shall have occasion in the future to discuss a few points alluded to by our confrère, on which we hold somewhat different opinions. At present we wish merely to direct attention to a statement which we cannot account for and is certainly based on a misconception. The writer says: [we translate]—"What reasons induced the Committee (of Revision, etc.) of the U. S. Pharmacopœia *to omit, in the later edition, the assay process of Extractum Cinchonæ Fluidum, which had been given in the edition of 1880*, is not known to us. At all events the insertion of all such tests is to be recommended, provided they afford, even only approximately, a criterion of the quality and genuineness of the preparation."—The italics of the preceding quotation are our own.

We know of no edition of the U. S. Pharm. of any date which contained an assay process of Fluid Extract of Cinchona. The U. S. Pharm. of 1880 was not issued until the latter part of 1882, and the text of this has not been altered since its appearance. Hence there has only been *one* edition of the U. S. Pharm of 1880, the title page of which bears the year 1882. Of the pharmacopœia of 1870, which appeared at beginning of 1873, the various reprints that were made of it, bore on their title pages the year of issue, which occasioned much confusion abroad, as some of these reprints were mistaken sometimes by prominent writers for new editions or revisions of the work.

Considering the fact that there are few retail establishments which offer so many facilities for decorative treatment of their contents as the drug-store, it is rather surprising how little attention is paid by pharmacists to this element of business management, and also how seldom the effect of a reflected light, strong shadows, and effective back-ground are properly considered. Taking, for example, the effect of gaslight, it is more often than otherwise the case that the lights are so placed as to dazzle, by their glare, the eyes of the passer-by, and prevent him from distinguishing the details of the objects in the interior of the store. As commonly arranged, they have, in some degree, the effect of a "jack" used by hunters in shooting deer at night, and render it difficult to distinguish objects beyond them. As an illustration of an opposite effect, observe the method of lighting employed by dealers in pictures. In this case the greatest pain is taken to screen the light so that it can only reach the observer as a reflection from the surface of the objects exhibited. To apply this principle to a drug store, the light should come from the same source in the night that it does in the day-time, namely, from the windows, where, along the upper part of the window-spaces, lamps or gas-jets should be arranged in number sufficient to light the main body of the store, and having reflectors between them and the windows which will intercept and throw towards the back of the store all rays which would otherwise pass outward, toward the street. At the back of the store should be placed objects, which, in turn, reflect the light towards the front, such as shelf-bottles with gilt labels, show-bottles with colored contents; while midway should be arranged such things as toilet-bottles in cut-glass, with sparkling facets and numerous angles. Any chandeliers in the centre of the store should be but dimly lighted to permit a brilliant light.

One of the most ingenious effects of lighting which we remember to have seen used to be in Houston Street, just east of Broadway, in this city, where, on a corner of the street, was a building surmounted at the angle by a large gilt eagle with outspread wings. On the cornice just below it were arranged a number of lights with reflectors, which threw the light upward against the eagle, and with screens which prevented the lights themselves from being seen from the street. At night the effect was very bold, and the great eagle shone out strongly against the background of dark sky in a manner which attracted the attention of every one who looked in that direction. Druggists who wish to place an illuminated sign in front of their stores may take a valuable hint from the above, and produce something much more effective than the transparencies commonly used.

In selecting a back-ground of color for the shelving which ordinarily covers the side-walls of every store, it is too often the case that pale tints are used, and the effect is to render the outlines of the bottles on the shelves indistinct. If instead, a dark color such as the maroon or Indian red used for the walls of many picture galleries were employed, the brilliancy of the glass shelf-ware with gilt labels would be greatly heightened. A wall paper with decided pattern, such as is sometimes employed, is not the thing to use. What is needed is a solid body of dark contrasting color, which will also harmonize with the predominant colors of the articles placed on the shelves. For this purpose nothing serves better than the dark red above spoken of. The complementary color of red, viz., green, is oftentimes quite effective, but for this purpose a pale green will not not answer; it, too, must be dark and decidedly green. Green will be especially effective with mahogany-colored shelf-fittings and cornice.

Some time since we inserted among the items in the advertising pages one referring to the death, in San Francisco, of one M. D. Babcock, alleged to be the inventor of the fire-extinguisher of that name.

It seems that the truth is that this allegation was purely the product of a deranged brain, and that Professor James F. Babcock, a well-known chemist of Boston, was actually the inventor. Unfortunately for Professor B., the invention has not resulted in a fortune for himself, whatever may have been the proceeds for the manufacturers.

The Connecticut Valley Dental Society and Massachusetts Dental Society are to hold a union meeting in the Institute of Technology, at Boston, on the 10th to 13th of July, inclusive; and solicit from the drug trade an exhibition of such things as druggists' sundries which are of interest to dentists.

The article on page 102 of our last number, contributed by Mr. S. J. Hinsdale, in which a new test-paper is described, should have had the heading: "A New Test-Paper for Acids," since it is as delicate towards sulphuric and other acids as against hydrochloric, which was there mentioned in the title.

American Pharmaceutical Association.

The thirty-sixth annual meeting of the American Pharmaceutical Association will be held in Detroit, Mich. First session, Monday, September 3d, at 3 p.m. Aside from the usual attractions presented by our meetings, preparations have been made by the pharmacists of Detroit for our reception, matters both scientific and recreative being elaborated to an unusual degree.

The Michigan Pharmaceutical Association holds its annual meeting simultaneously with our own, and it may be safely predicted that the members attending both associations will outnumber any collection of pharmacists in the previous history of our country.

Full information regarding hotel and railway rates will be furnished our members in the usual annual circular of the permanent secretary.

The exhibition promises to equal, if not surpass, that of any preceding period of our history. Commercial interests are now recognised as a part of the object of our meetings, and it is to be presumed that extraordinary endeavors will be made to render conspicuous, displays of commercial products. The local secretary, Mr. James Vernor, 233 Woodward avenue, Detroit, will give information regarding matters connected therewith.

Dr. A. B. Lyons, 423 Second street, Detroit, Secretary of Committee of Scientific Papers, should receive the scientific papers at as early a date as possible.

J. U. Lloyd, *President*.

Early-closing in Hamilton, Ontario.—The *Canadian Pharmaceutical Journal* published the following municipal ordinance, passed May 14th.

By the Corporation of the City of Hamilton.

"1. All shops within the municipality of the City of Hamilton, belonging to the class known as Chemists' and Druggists' shops, shall be closed at or before 8 o'clock in the afternoon of every day in the week, excepting Saturdays, Sundays, and days immediately before public or municipal holidays, and shall be closed throughout every Sunday except between the hours of 10 and 11 o'clock in the forenoon, between the hours of 3 and 4 o'clock in the afternoon, and between the hours of 8 and 9 o'clock in the evening."

The Sixth International Pharmaceutical Congress will assemble at Milan in September next. The preliminary arrangements are in the charge of the Associazione Farmaceutica Lombarda, and a very general participation of other countries has been promised. It would be a good thing for our Italian confrères if they could meanwhile manage to publish their first national pharmacopœia, which has been hanging fire now for about seven years.

Christy & Co., 25 Lime Street, London, England, wish us to inquire whether any of our readers will sell to them two complete sets of the "Working Bulletins" by Messrs. Parke, Davis & Co., the first volume of which was published in 1883.

British Pharmacopœia.—A report of the British Pharmacopœia Committee was recently presented to the Medical Council, in which it was stated that there has been a profit on the production and sale of the Pharmacopœia amounting to £1209 8s. 2d. It was also announced that a report for 1887 on the work had been received from Prof. Attfield.

The Massachusetts College of Pharmacy has elected the following officers: President, Henry Canning; vice-presidents, S. A. D. Sheppard, W. C. Durkee; secretary, C. C. Williams; treasurer, H. K. Appleton, Jr.; auditor, L. D. Drury, Trustees (until 1889): W. B. Potter, C. A. Niegmund, E. C. Marshall; (until 1890) J. O. Godding, G. M. Hoyt, E. H. La Pierre; (until 1891) L. D. Drury, W. F. Sawyer, J. C. Benedict; (until 1892) W. C. Durkee, H. K. Appleton, W. W. Bartlet; (until 1893) S. A. D. Sheppard, H. Canning, C. C. Williams.

Gluten Bread.—A recent improvement in the mode of preparing gluten bread for the use of diabetic persons is said to render it much more palatable. It resembles ordinary bread in its general aspects, and is not unlike in taste certain kinds of cakes which are readily eaten by most people. Moreover, it is easily masticated. The formula from which this new gluten bread is made is set down thus: Best quality of yeast, 20 grammes; cold water, 120 grammes; butter, 125 grammes; gluten flour, 500 grammes; and eggs, 4. For one loaf. The yeast is stirred carefully and quietly into the water, then the eggs and butter are added, and the whole melted. The gluten flour is mixed in and worked up with these ingredients, and a round loaf is thus made which is about 18 inches wide and 20 inches deep; it is placed before the fire for about an hour to cause the dough to rise, and is baked in an oven heated from below. Gluten flour is manufactured expressly for this and other kinds of cakes.—*Monthly Magazine.*

What Medical Men Said of Anæsthetics Forty Years Ago.—Commenting on the reports of the first use of ether as an anæsthetic in surgery, the Philadelphia *Medical Examiner* expressed the views of the conservatives in the following terms: "We are persuaded that the surgeons of Philadelphia will not be seduced from the high professional path of duty into the quagmire of quackery by this will-o'-the-wisp. . . . We cannot close these remarks without again expressing our deep mortification and regret that the eminent men who have so long adorned the profession in Boston should have consented for a moment to set so bad an example to their younger brothers, as we conceive them to have done in this instance. If such things are to be sanctioned by the profession, there is little need of reform conventions, or any other efforts to elevate the professional character; physicians and quacks will soon constitute one fraternity."

Vigier's Coryza Powder.—This remedy, which is greatly prised and often prescribed by French physicians, has the following formula, as given by M. Vigier himself (in the *Gazette Hebdom. de Méd. et Chirurg.*): Finely powdered starch, boracic acid, tincture of Siam benzoin, of each equal parts. To be used as a snuff, frequently and plentifully. We would remark here that powdered gum benzoin should not be used in lieu of the tincture, as is frequently done by American pharmacists in preparing snuff powders. When the gum is used, the resulting powder is tenacious, packs easily, and is difficult to draw into the nostrils. The same may be said of camphor. It is far better to use the tincture and allow the alcohol to evaporate, as in this manner a granular powder is obtained which has not the vice above referred to.—*National Druggist.*

QUERIES & ANSWERS.

Queries for which answers are desired, must be received by the 5th of the month, and must in every case be accompanied by the name and address of the writer, for the information of the editor, but not for publication.

No. 2,178.—Vapo-Cresolene (S., Buffalo).

This is a trade-mark for what is commonly known as cresol, which you will find a description of in either of the leading dispensatories or works upon coal-tar and its products.

No. 2,179.—"India-rubber" Cement for Glass, etc.

Try the following: Caoutchouc, 20 grains; chloroform, 2 fl. oz.; mastic, ½ troy oz. Dissolve the caoutchouc in the chloroform, then add the mastic, and set it aside for a week, or until solution has taken place. This cement can be used cold, and may be applied with a camel's-hair brush.

No. 2,180.—Mettauer's Aperient.

This is a mixture composed of:

Aloes		3 6
Sodii Bicarbonatis		3 10
Tinct. Lavandulæ Comp.	fl.	3 2
Aquæ	fl.	3 83

M.

No. 2,181.—Machine-folded Filters (Chicago).

The "folded filters" you refer to are those made by the well-known house of Schleicher & Schuell, of Dueren, Germany, and may be had through dealers in chemical apparatus (see our advertisements).

We are glad that we have an opportunity of drawing the attention of our readers to these exceedingly useful, labor- and time-saving filters. They are made in three qualities. No. 588, in diameters from 12.5 to 50 centimeters, for all ordinary filtrations. No. 586 made of special paper, for the filtration of viscid, syrupy or other liquids, which often cause much trouble and annoyance. And No. 580, all of large size, with hardened points preventing them from breaking.

Since we have begun to use these folded filters, we have become convinced that they are indispensable. Of course, they cannot be used for fine analytical work, when the precipitate in the part wanted, as it would be difficult to detach this.

No. 2,182.—Cure for Wrinkles (Modesto, Cal.).

This correspondent refers to an item in one of our recent issues in which "Lanolin" is spoken of as a cure for wrinkles, and wants to know whether it is to be used pure or mixed with anything.

Our private opinion on the subject is, that it would be necessary to incorporate with it a very large percentage of credulity to have much effect upon a well-developed wrinkle; or, in other words, it will work best with such persons as are most susceptible to the remedial virtues of the "Faith Cure."

No. 2,183.—Hair Oil (J. M. H.).

One of the most commonly used compounds, and one of the best we are acquainted with, is a mixture of castor oil and alcohol, about as follows:

Castor oil	7 fl. oz.
Alcohol	9 fl. oz.

This may be scented according to individual preference. It is customary to add to it certain substances supposed to act either as tonics or as detergents, such as quinine, tincture of cantharides, etc., only a small quantity of each being usually added. Tincture of quillaja may also be added to advantage.

No. 2,184.—Indelible Stencil Ink (M.).

The following formula has been furnished by one of our correspondents:

Dissolve 1 troy ounce of nitrate of silver in 4 fl. oz. of stronger water of ammonia; then add 1 troy oz. of bitartrate of potassium and 1 troy oz. of sugar, and dissolve by agitation.

Mix thoroughly 1 troy oz. of powdered acacia with 3½ fl. oz. of boiled linseed oil, and incorporate 40 grains of lampblack.

For use, mix about equal quantities of the preceding solution and mixture on a slab, and apply it by means of a stencil. The fabrics must be afterwards heated or passed over with a hot iron to make the marks lasting.

No. 2,185.—Liquid Franconia (Supplement to query 2,173).

Dr. Laurence Johnson, of this city, informs us that he made some experiments about a year and a half ago to devise a preparation having the properties of this nostrum. He finally arrived at the following formula:

Prepare a thick, almost jelly-like infusion of flaxseed, and add to it 20 per cent of its volume of glycerin, with which has been mixed sufficient salicylic acid to make the finished product contain 2 grains in each fluidounce. Perfume according to taste.

Dr. Johnson says that, while this may not be the exact formula of the article in question, it yields a close imitation, and one which is an excellent remedy not only for chapped hands, but also for many cases of eczema.

No. 2,186.—Insect Powder (M.).
This correspondent refers to the article entitled "Insect Remedies," contained on page 13 of our last January number, and desires to know whether the "Pyrethrum" there mentioned is the *Pyrethrum carneum* or "Persian Insect Powder."

In reply, we would say that there are several species of Pyrethrum (or Chrysanthemum) which have insecticidal properties. The best known are *P. carneum*, *P. roseum*, and *P. cinerariaefolium*. The two former are usually grouped together as "Persian Insect Flowers," while the last-mentioned is known as the "Dalmatian" or *buhach*. It is now generally conceded that the Dalmatian flowers are more active and energetic than the Persian. If our correspondent will consult our volume for 1887, p. 3, he will find an interesting article on the subject.

No. 2,187.—Bismuth Hair Dye (J. H. S.).
In a formula for hair-dye published on page 95 of our May number, taken from a European exchange, "nitrate of bismuth" is quoted as one of the ingredients. We have now ascertained that the subnitrate was meant, and that the formula should read as follows:

Subnitrate of Bismuth	10 parts.
Solution of Potassa (10ς)	q. s.
Citric Acid	q. s.
Glycerin	150 parts.
Water	to make 300 "

Intimately mix the subnitrate of bismuth and the glycerin by trituration, then heat the mixture in a water-bath, and gradually add to it solution of potassa, under constant stirring, until the bismuth salt is dissolved. Next add a concentrated solution of citric acid until only a slight alkalinity remains. Finally add enough water to make 300 parts, and scent according to preference.

No. 2,188.—Ink Tablets (G. B.).
The demand for these, or for ink-powder, is rather limited, though the form is extremely handy for carrying ink along on a journey, especially on routes where accommodations have to be mainly provided by the traveller himself. A few formulae for preparing such tablets are here given:

1. Extract of logwood 500 parts, alum 10 parts, gum arabic 10 parts, neutral chromate of potassium 1 part. Dissolve the salts in 500 parts of water, add the extract of logwood and gum arabic, and concentrate the mixture to the consistence of an extract. Then pour the mass out, either into moulds, or into a flat-bottomed dish, and cut it in pieces of suitable size, which may be inclosed in boxes or other receptacles.

2. Extract of logwood 100 parts, gum arabic 10 parts, indigo-carmine 5 parts, neutral chromate of potassium 1 part, glycerin 10 parts, water q. s.; proceed as in the preceding formula.

No. 2,189.—Hypophosphite of Iron (Medicus).
In preparing hypophosphite of iron by double decomposition between hypophosphite of calcium and solution of chloride of iron, "in proper proportions," it happened to our correspondent that, on washing the precipitated hypophosphite of iron, only a small quantity of it remained on the filter, the balance redissolving in the washwater. He asks us for the reason of this, and how to avoid it.

All hypophosphites are soluble in water, and so is the true, unchanged ferric hypophosphite. At least it is so stated by all authorities. The insoluble hypophosphite of iron is probably a modification, differing by the presence of some basic salt. At all events, if the solutions of the two salts are mixed while warm, and the whole then set aside for twenty-four hours, the resulting precipitate will be scarcely soluble. Should the wash-water have dissolved any, it may be recovered by concentrating the washings on a water-bath, when the salt will gradually separate. It may then be washed without material loss. This change of condition, caused by standing, in contact with water, seems to point to some molecular alteration, though this has not yet been proven.

Hypophosphite of iron is also soluble in an excess of either of the two salts from which it is prepared by mutual decomposition. For this reason, the salts should be taken as nearly in molecular proportions as possible.

No. 2,190.—Indelible Document Ink (Tyro).
The best ink for documents of importance when the writing is to remain deep black in India ink. This, of course, only adheres to the surface of the paper or parchment, and cannot penetrate the fibre. The next best ink is well-made iron ink. This should not be jet-black at the time when it is written with, but should be rather pale, the iron being in a ferrous condition. After it has penetrated the fibres of the paper, etc., and been exposed to the air for a short time, it becomes black. India ink cannot be removed by any chemicals, being highly divided carbon. Iron ink may be removed, though when old it is very resistant.

A very good, permanent ink is Reade's blue ink. This is prepared by mixing a solution of Prussian blue in oxalic acid with a good chromated logwood ink. The solution of Prussian blue is prepared by mixing pure Prussian blue first with about an equal quantity of sulphuric acid, setting the mixture aside for about eight days, then diluting with water, and washing the precipitate with water, until the washings cease to have an acid reaction. The precipitate is mixed, while still damp, with a solution of 1 part of oxalic acid in 5 of water for every 5 parts of precipitate, and solution promoted by gentle warming. The product is then mixed with the chromated logwood ink. This ink looks violet in fresh writing. It gradually turns black. Acids turn it blue, chloride of lime does not destroy it.

Another good safety ink is the following: Heat 1 part of glucose in 25 parts of water with ⅓ part of caustic potassa to boiling and add to the dark brown liquid a sufficient quantity of extract of logwood mixed with about 0.1 per cent of its weight of neutral chromate of potassium. This ink looks dark-brownish violet in fresh writing, and is not destroyed by alkalies, acids, or chloride of lime.

No. 2,191.—Cologne (J. M. H.).
Have you ever tried the formula for *Spiritus odoratus* of the U. S. Pharmacopoeia of 1880? If not, we would advise you to prepare it once and examine its merits. It does not yield a product equal to Farina's cologne, but neither does any other published formula. The best formulae for cologne are never made public by those who have discovered them after long research and the expenditure of much capital. There are some good formulae available in the current literature (see this Journal, 1886, page 116).

A most superior kind of cologne, or, more properly, handkerchief extract, may be prepared by the following formula, provided only the finest and freshest ingredients are taken:

Oil of Bergamot	80 Gm.
" " Lemon	30 "
" " Ylang	30 "
" " Neroli, big.	20 "
" " Rose Geranium	2 "
" " Rose	4 drops.
Tinct. of Musk	50 Gm.
" " Tolu	15 "
Acetic Ether	15 "
Orris Root	120 "
Deodorized Alcohol	600 "

Macerate for at least forty-eight hours, at a temperature between 100 and 110° F., replacing any alcohol lost by evaporation at the conclusion of the maceration; then add:

Milk (fresh cow's)	300 Gm.
Deodorized Alcohol	500 "
Tinct. of Benzoin	50 "
Tinct. of Musk	20 "

Cool to 60° F., and filter. To the filtrate add

Oil of Patchouli	1 Gm.
Deodorized Alcohol	19 "

The product may be diluted with deodorized alcohol, if it is found to be too concentrated.

We will append the remark that all such combinations are greatly improved by the judicious application of heat. This must be applied so that none of the volatile constituents are lost. Heating seems to blend the flavors of the different aromatics more effectually. The same thing is accomplished by age; but if the result can be obtained without loss of time, it will be an advantage.

No. 2,192.—Tincture of Nux Vomica ("Bromide").
We are asked the question how a tincture of nux vomica made after Mr. Rother's formula (Am. Jour. Pharm., 1883, p. 1; U. S. Disp., 14th ed., p. 1,466) would compare in assay with one made after the process of the U. S. Ph.

It should first be stated that Mr. Rother's formula contains the proportions of drug and menstruum prescribed by the U. S. Ph. of 1870, namely, 8 troy ounces of nux vomica represented by 32 fl. oz. of percolate. The process of the U. S. Ph. of 1880 requires the finished tincture to contain 3 per cent of an extract (weighed as dry) prepared by exhausting the drug with a mixture of 8 parts of alcohol and one part of water. On an average, this menstruum yields from 100 parts of the drug 10 parts of dry extract. The latter contains all the alkaloids contained in the 100 parts of the drug, which may be reckoned to amount to 2 parts, about half of which is strychnine. As 100 parts of the finished tincture contain 3 parts of this dry extract, it follows that the latter contain about 0.6 part of mixed alkaloids. The spec. grav. of the U. S. P. tincture is about 0.775. Consequently 100 grains measure 134 minims. 32 fluidounces of it, therefore, weigh, approximately, 23.5 troy ounces, and these, calculated as containing 2 per cent of dry extract, should contain 0.47 troy ounces of this, or 0.094 tr. oz., or about 44 grains of mixed alkaloids. On the other hand, the 8 troy ounces of nux vomica which were made into 32 fl. oz. of tincture according to the U. S. P. of 1870, or according to Rother's process, contain about 77 grains of mixed alkaloids. It will be seen from this that the tincture of U. S. Ph. of 1880 is almost only of half the strength of that of the U. S. Ph. of 1870. That is theoretically. Practically a complete exhaustion of the nux vomica by the process of 1870—obtaining 32 fluidounces of percolate from 8 troy ounces of drug—was rarely obtained, and the actual tincture made by the process, as dispensed in the shops, was probably but little stronger than that prepared by the new process.

Since the issue of the last U. S. Ph., the methods of assay of nux vomica have been more thoroughly studied, and at the next revision a more exact method of standardizing the strength of this preparation will no doubt be introduced.

No. 2,193.—Sulfonal (Several inquirers).

We have succeeded, at the time of writing this article (June 12th), in obtaining only a few ounces of this new hypnotic, which has been used by observant physicians, without producing untoward symptoms, but also without creating any special enthusiasm regarding its virtue, at least so far. It certainly will not take the place of chloral if its price is kept at the high figure at which it is sold for at present.

Sulfonal has first been reported by Dr. Kast of Freiburg to have soporific powers. It belongs, chemically, to that class of bodies which are grouped together in disulphones, that is, those which contain two molecules of the univalent group SO_2R (in which R represents any monad element or group) united to carbon. The particular body under consideration is an oxidation product of ethyl-mercaptane ($C_2H_5.SH$) with acetone ($CH_3.CO.CH_3$).

Sulfonal (or sulphonal) is prepared in the following manner: dithioethyl-dimethyl-methane is shaken with a 5% solution of permanganate, a few drops of acetic or sulphuric acid being added from time to time. The permanganate solution is added as long as it loses its color. When the color remains unaltered, numerous crystals of the oxidation product float about on the surface. The mass is now warmed on the water-bath, filtered hot, and then evaporated to one-half of its previous volume. On cooling, the new substance, sulfonal (or sulphonal) crystallizes out, and is obtained pure by recrystallization from hot water or alcohol. The composition of the substance is represented by the scheme:

$$\begin{matrix} CH_3 \\ CH_3 \end{matrix} C \begin{matrix} SO_2C_2H_5 \\ SO_2C_2H_5 \end{matrix}$$

It crystallizes in large, colorless plates (or in small laminæ), which are perfectly odorless and tasteless, soluble in about 100 parts of cold, in 18 to 20 parts of boiling water, difficultly soluble in cold alcohol, and rather easily in ether, benzol, or chloroform. Sulfonal melts at 130°–131° C., and boils at 300° C. with slight concomitant carbonization and production of a pungent odor. The distillate has a yellowish color, solidifies to a crystalline mass, and on being once recrystallized again furnishes pure sulfonal. The substance is quite resistant towards acids, alkalies, and oxidizing agents, both hot and cold. It is very easily soluble in concentrated sulphuric acid. On warming this solution, the body is gradually decomposed, and sulphurous acid is eliminated. From its solution in sulphuric acid, sulfonal is precipitated by water.

Concentrated nitric acid dissolves it easily even in the cold, and the resulting solution may be boiled some time without undergoing change. Addition of water precipitates it in this case likewise. Bromine dissolves the body without altering it. On evaporating the solution, the residue, recrystallized from alcohol or water, is found to be pure sulfonal. Caustic alkalies do not attack it even on protracted boiling.

No. 2,194.—Metaphosphoric Acid Changing to Orthophosphoric (C. G. K.).

Metaphosphoric acid, as is well known, appears in commerce under the name of glacial phosphoric acid. There are various qualities of this, some of which are quite impure, owing to the fashion of requiring the acid to be cast into sticks, which can only be accomplished by mixing with the acid some fusible salt, usually phosphate of sodium. In reality, this is not added as a salt, but is produced by the addition of a certain proportion of soda.

Glacial phosphoric acid was at one time officinal, but has been subsequently replaced by the tribasic, or orthophosphoric acid. In one respect, this was an error, as there are certain mixtures or combinations in which the presence of orthophosphoric acid is a disadvantage, as it is liable to cause a precipitate or gelatinizing of the mixture. The National Formulary, recognizing the necessity of reintroducing it, at least temporarily, has provided a formula for an "Acidum Metaphosphoricum Dilutum," of approximately 10 per cent, and, among the directions for preparing it, will be found the remark:

"This preparation should be kept in a cool and dark place, and should not be prepared in larger quantity than may be consumed within a few months."

The reason why the keeping of a large supply of this solution is unadvisable is simply this, that an aqueous solution of this acid gradually changes to one of orthophosphoric. This change is comparatively slow in the dark and when the solution is cold, but it is rapidly brought about by heat.

Paul Sabatier some time ago made experiments to determine the rate at which this change from meta- to orthophosphoric acid occurred. He found that the change produced two new acid functions, recognisable alongside of the function of the still unchanged strong acid. The former two functions may be designated as "medium" and "weak." If "Orange 3" is used as indicator, the function of the strong acid alone is visible. Phenolphthalein reveals only the strong and the medium acid. The weakest acid is only qualitatively shown by the so-called "C_4B blue."

The author's experiments on the time required for changing from one state to another were made with a solution of pure anhydrous phosphoric acid in ice-water. The anhydrous acid was obtained by calcining pure crystallised orthophosphoric acid for some time in a platinum crucible. The mass was allowed to become cold in an exsiccator, and then plunged into water at 0° C., which causes the mass to decrepitate and to throw out fragments of a gelatinous appearance which dissolve slowly.

The results below recorded were obtained with solutions containing 40 grammes of metaphosphoric acid in the liter. It was found that the change into orthophosphoric began (though slowly) from the moment that the solution was made. In order to convert the whole of the metaphosphoric into orthophosphoric acid, the following number of days was required at the given temperatures:

At ° C.	° F.	
0	32	About 150 days.
14	56	About 80 days.
31	88	About 5 days.
61	142	About 4½ hours.
95	203	About 1 hour.

A 10-per-cent solution will, of course, require a longer time to change. Nevertheless, the change will be very decided even at the end of one month. For this reason it is, perhaps, advisable to recommend that the diluted metaphosphoric acid be prepared fresh when wanted, or only in quantities sufficient to last a few days.

No. 2,195.—Detection of Lead in the Urine (Dr. A. L. M.).

When urine is to be tested for lead, in cases of suspected lead-poisoning, after the administration of suitable remedies to cause its elimination, it is necessary to collect carefully *all* the urine voided subsequently, and to examine this in portions, depending upon its volume, perhaps the amount voided in 12 or in 24 hours.

Regarding the process, we can do no better than to quote Prof. E. S. Wood's directions, published some time ago in the *Therap. Gazette*:

"The urine is strongly acidulated with nitric acid, and evaporated to dryness upon a water or steam bath. If a sufficient amount of nitric acid has been added, the residue left will be of a light-yellow color; if it is not, more nitric acid must be added to the residue, and the evaporation continued. When the residue is dry, or nearly so, it may be transferred to a sand bath and heated, when ignition takes place very quickly with more or less deflagration. If proper care be taken in managing the heat, there will be no loss of material on account of the deflagration, and a perfectly white residue will be left. After cooling, this residue is extracted with hot, dilute HCl, filtered while hot, and the filtrate precipitated with ammonia and ammonium sulphide; this precipitate is washed by decantation three or four times with boiling water, then acidulated with HCl, to dissolve the phosphate and sulphide of iron, and allowed to stand until the next day to settle. The precipitate, which will contain sulphide of lead, if any lead was present in the urine, is collected upon a small Swedish filter paper (or other filter free from any trace of iron), washed thoroughly with boiling distilled water, and treated while on the filter with hot *dilute*, pure nitric acid, which liquid is collected in a watch-glass, and evaporated to dryness on a water bath. This residue, which contains any lead present in the form of a basic nitrate, is treated with a drop of water and a crystal of potassium iodide as a *preliminary* test for lead; if lead is present, there will be a yellow streak of iodide of lead. A colored streak may also be produced if the residue contains compounds of other metals, especially copper, bismuth, or iron (compounds of the last metal sometimes becoming introduced in traces in the form of dust, or as a contamination in the filter). If a colored streak has been produced, the residue containing it is moistened with a drop of acetic acid, and washed with boiling distilled water into a small filter, the filtrate being collected in a test tube (perfectly clean). A few drops of dilute sulphuric acid are then added, the test tube stoppered, and placed aside until thoroughly settled. If any lead be present, it will be converted into the form of *sulphate of lead*, which will form a sediment at the bottom of the test tube, often so slight an amount that it cannot be seen until the test tube is gently moved, so as to cause the fluid within to rotate, when the sulphate of lead precipitate will be drawn up in the centre of the fluid in the form of a cone, when it can be easily seen even when present in very minute amount.

"Every precaution, so far as apparatus and chemicals

are concerned, is taken. The crucibles used are Berlin crucibles, and both evaporating dishes and crucibles have been found, by repeated analyses, not to yield any lead. The final test being the formation of sulphate of lead avoids any possibility of error due to the presence of traces of copper or bismuth, which would certainly exist if reliance were placed upon the color reaction with potassium iodide.... In well-marked cases of chronic lead-poisoning, even while the patient is being treated with potassium iodide, the amount of lead eliminated with the urine is very small, never exceeding a few milligrammes in 24 hours, and in the majority of cases being only a small fraction of a milligramme. The successful detection of lead in one or two liters of urine in such cases requires, therefore, that the process used should be a very delicate one, and also that it should be conducted with the greatest care."

No. 2,196.—**Pix Canadensis. Hemlock Gum** (L. F. and G. W. R. & Co.).
We have recently had several inquiries as to what commercial substance should be supplied when the officinal Pix Canadensis is demanded. In reply, we have advised our correspondents to employ the so-called "gum hemlock," as this appears to be most nearly corresponding to the description given by the U. S. Ph. The latter was based, many years ago, upon a product rather differing in appearance and properties from what is now usually obtainable. Canada "pitch" indicates, by its name, not a natural exudation of the tree, but a prepared product, having passed through some operations which bring it under the class of pitches (or residues of distillation). Now the substance known as "hemlock gum" is such a product, and is, in fact, the only one which at all approaches the requirements of the pharmacopœia.
It has been shown some time ago (see NEW REM., 1881, 23) that Abies canadensis does not yield "spruce gum." This is to be understood as meaning any kind of gum as an exudation. The spruce gum of the market is derived from Abies nigra.
Regarding hemlock pitch and tamarac, we have recently been favored by some friends of ours with data which may be of more general interest. They are in the shape of letters, derived from persons practically acquainted with this industry. From these letters we abstract the following:
Hemlock Gum. "Derived from Abies canadensis."
"Of this tree there are two species, the red hemlock and the white hemlock. The red attains the height of about 75 to 80 feet, and 3 to 5 feet in diameter at the cut, and its wood is red except about 1 or 2 inches next the bark, which is very thick and rough. The white reaches to 80 to 100 feet in height, and is not as large nor so rough in the bark as the red. Its wood is white except about 2 inches at the heart. There is but a slight difference in the leaves of the two trees, but the red is not as white beneath. Both are a silvery white beneath, and dark green above. Both are evergreens and flower in May. Northern New York, Canada, Vermont, New Hampshire, and Maine abound in large forests of this tree. The wood is very coarse and brittle, and is used largely as coarse lumber for building purposes, and lasts a great while in or near the ground. The bark is very largely used for tanning leather in this and other countries. Every year companies of five or ten men go into a large forest of hemlock and build a log shanty and cover with the bark, and cut and peel these trees from June 1st to August 1st; the trees are cut down and girdled once in a fortnight, and then with a spud or sharpened stick or iron the bark is easily peeled off, and spread out so as to expose the inside to the sun until it is dry enough to be piled up in cord piles (if it rains it is turned over), with the rough side up, and left to be drawn to depot in winter to be shipped to tanners. After the bark is all piled up, the trees are then cut by two men with a cross-cut saw into logs of the length wanted, usually from 12 to 40 or even 80 feet, and then drawn and skidded, i. e., rolled up on two logs lying on the ground 10 feet apart, so they can be easily loaded on a sled in the winter, to be drawn to the saw-mill. Then the tops are chopped into cord wood and piled for next year's wood. The boughs are in many places distilled, and yield the oil of hemlock. There is never any appearance of gum or oleoresin on a white hemlock tree, but on the red there is some found around the end of dead limbs on the bark, but none on any tree less than about 75 years old. This gum is crumbly and very easily powdered; but no gum oozes from any wound in the wood of these trees as does from the spruce, pine, arbor vitæ, balsam fir, or tammerack trees, and I have lived and worked in and chopped and cut acres of it in all stages and at all times of the year, and have not seen 5 pounds of this gum in all my life; others may. I have seen rolls of a waxy-like gum at drug stores, kept in water, and called gum hemlock, but I have never seen or found any such thing on any tree. But from the earliest history of this country (the Indians taught the white settlers to make a hemlock gum for plasters) every one, to my knowledge, has obtained the so-called "hemlock gum" by steaming the boughs and bark around the knots of the red hemlock as for gum tammerack, or by boiling and removing the scum or gum in the morning, when cold, and reducing it in a water-bath to a homogeneous mass."

No. 2,197.—**Ginger Beer** (H.).
The following is said to make a good preparation:
Place 1 oz. of best unbleached Jamaica (or African) Ginger, well bruised, 16 oz. of crushed sugar, 1½ oz. of parsley root, 360 grains of bitartrate of potassium and 2 sliced lemons into 1 gallon of boiling water. Cover the vessel and stir the contents frequently until at the temperature of about 100° F. Then add 2 oz. of yeast, and keep the vessel in a moderately warm place, so that fermentation may occur. After twenty-four hours pass the liquid through flannel, ferment for a day or two longer, then strain it again and bottle it, securely fastening the corks.

No. 2,198.—**Sticky Fly-paper** (J. D. C.).
This may be prepared by making a mass from

Turpentine	65 parts
Linseed Oil	34 "
Yellow Wax	1 part

by melting, and applying a thin layer of it to sheets of strong brown paper, previously well sized with solution of glue or gelatin and dried.
The "turpentine" is the natural oleoresin of the pine, (the officinal *Terebinthina*) and *not* to be interpreted as equivalent to rosin.
Regarding machinery to apply this to paper, we can only say that, if we had to undertake the manufacture of such an article, we would try to devise an apparatus ourselves. The principal points to be kept in view are: 1. To have the mass kept just liquid enough to flow; 2. To cause its even distribution over the surface of the paper, through a slit which may be regulated at will; 3. To feed the paper to the machine in a regular and even manner. We believe that some of the old-fashioned plaster-spreading machines may be easily adapted to this kind of work.

No. 2,199.—**To Prevent Tarnishing of Nickel or Silver-Plating** (S. C., Fort Scott, Kans.).
"Can you inform me if there is any way that brass can be nickel or silver-plated so as to stay brightly?"
No. No matter what method is employed for plating brass with nickel or silver, the latter will tarnish if exposed to the air. By coating a polished surface with colorless varnish, the tarnishing may be delayed somewhat, but the metallic surface will be injured more or less.

No. 2,200.—**National Formulary** (Several Inquirers).
The following notice received from the permanent secretary of the Amer. Pharm. Association, Prof. J. M. Maisch, will serve as answer to many inquiries received.
The "National Formulary of Unofficinal Preparations," which has been in course of preparation for some time past by a committee of the A. P. A., will be ready for issue July 2d, and will be for sale by the permanent secretary and by the acting authorized agents of the association in the different cities—also by wholesale druggists, booksellers, and others interested in the work. It contains about 190 octavo pages and gives 435 formulas for preparations in daily use by pharmacists and druggists.
Price, including postage, for formulary bound in cloth, 75 cts.; interleaved, $1.10; cloth, raised nails, 90 cts.; bound in sheep, $1.10.
To dealers a cash discount of 33⅓ per cent on these prices.

Preservation of Sulphuretted Hydrogen Water.—A. Schneider of Dresden reports in the Pharm. Centralhalle, that sulphuretted hydrogen water may be kept unchanged for a long time, if it is kept in black bottles, the stoppers of which are rendered air-tight by a *liberal* coating of vaseline. The latter cannot affect the reagent injuriously.

A New Reagent for Copper.—Aliamet recommends a cold saturated solution of neutral sodium sulphite in which a certain amount of pyrogallic acid is dissolved. On adding this reagent to an aqueous solution of copper of medium concentration, the liquid acquires an intensely blood-red color, similar to that produced by sulphocyanides with ferric salts.
The reaction is said to be capable of detecting 1-4,000,000th gramme of sulphate of copper.—*Bull. de la Soc. de Chim.*

Roses in the Caucasus.—Plantations of roses on a large scale are to be established in the province of Kutais of the Caucasus, so that there may be an extensive native manufacture of the otto of roses. At the present moment this is largely exported from foreign States, principally Bulgaria and Turkey, into Russia, and it is the object of the Minister of Domains in promoting this enterprise—which it may be mentioned, is only an expansion of an earlier experiment at Baku—to oust the foreigner and substitute a native industry.

Compound Laxative.—The *Chemist and Druggist* gives the following:—Fluid ext. senna, 12½ fl. drachms; fl. ext. of rhubarb, 4; fl. ext. of cloves, 4; fl. ext. of wormseed, 2; oil of anise, 10 minims; oil of wintergreen, 20; Rochelle salt, 256 grains; bicarb. of soda, 34; fl. ext. of liquorice, 10 fl. drachms; sugar, 4 ounces av.; water, q. s. = 8 fl. ounces. Dose, 10 drops, or a teaspoonful, according to age. This is given as a "substitute for castor oil."

American Druggist

MAIZE OIL, OR OIL OF CORN.

BY J. U. LLOYD.

(Paper read at the Annual Meeting of the Ohio Pharm. Association at Columbus.)

It is well known that Indian corn contains considerable quantities of fixed oil and, some years ago, endeavors were made to separate this oil on a large scale from the ground corn before it was mashed in the making of whiskey. The writer remembers that the late John Crawford, well known as a Cincinnati pharmacist, embarked in a venture with this object in view, and established a factory in Kentucky opposite the city of Cincinnati for the purpose of making bisulphide of carbon, which was used as a solvent to dissolve the oil. The corn meal was percolated with this bisulphide of carbon, whereby the fixed oil was removed, and the bisulphide of carbon was afterward recovered by distillation.

It was thought by Mr. Crawford that the corn meal so treated yielded a larger amount of whiskey and of finer quality than when the crude meal was worked. However, after devoting some years to this industry and establishing the process in several sections of the country in connection with distilleries, it was found, I think, that objections rendered it impracticable, and that the advantages derived from the process were more than overcome by the disadvantages that followed. In consequence, if I remember correctly, even before Mr. Crawford's death, the scheme was dropped and the industry abandoned.

It has been found in the making of starch and perhaps in other directions as well, that it is desirable to get rid of the germ of the corn, as for reasons that it is unnecessary for me to mention this germ is objectionable in these manipulations.

In order to accomplish this result, a machine has been devised which degerminizes the corn, throwing the hard starchy part of the corn in one direction and separating the germs in another, and this method can be, and is applied to the making of starch in large quantities and is found to be of great assistance and advantage.

Naturally, there was an accumulation of these excluded germs which, as is well known, constitute a considerable proportion of the corn, and they became a by-product. They were found to be valuable as a feed for stock, but really were too "rich" for such purposes, containing as they did such an enormous quantity of oil, the oil of the corn being altogether found in the germ. In order to render the material more acceptable as a feed for stock, a company was recently established for the purpose of squeezing the fixed oil from the germs and thus improving the feed meal. A plant was established a few months ago (the only one in existence, now, I learn) in the city of Cincinnati for this purpose and is now in operation. The method is very simple. The germs are conveyed from the factories, wherein they are a by-product (such as starch factories), and are first purified by separating from them a considerable amount of bran or husk of corn that adheres to them or is mixed with them. They are then steamed under pressure so as to soften them, after which, in the usual manner by means of hydraulic presses, the oil is squeezed from them.

The process is a very simple one and it yields an oil cake which, when ground into meal, is found to be exceedingly valuable as a food for stock, the manufacturers of this meal claiming that it is superior to cornmeal that is made from the whole corn.

Thus it is that in addition to the oil cake, which is the prime object of the industries, there is an accumulation of the fixed oil of corn or maize oil, which induces this paper. I accidentally came across the oil, was led to its examination, and as a result found that it is in many respects preferable, as I believe, to cotton-seed oil that has recently become officinal in the Pharmacopœia as a substitute for olive oil. I have used it in the making of ammonia liniment to which purpose it is particularly adapted, and in which, to my experience, cotton-seed oil is practically a failure.

Oil of corn saponifies *immediately*, forming with ammonia a smooth, creamy emulsion that retains its nature apparently indefinitely, as specimens that I have in my possession, and which I herewith exhibit, are quite old and are now in their original condition. It does not clot or form masses or curd-like aggregations, as we sometimes find to result with olive oil, in accordance with the manner in which the ammonia is added to it, and even if for no other use than the making of ammonia liniment, I think it should become officinal instead of cotton-seed oil. However, I doubt if there is any preparation in the Pharmacopœia that demands olive or cotton-seed oil in which it cannot be used, and probably it will be found superior in all other directions. The industry that yields this oil, in course of time, promises to increase, and the oil will likely be obtained in unlimited amounts. Indeed it can now be obtained in any quantity, car load or otherwise. It is not probable that the output will ever be less than the demand. It is peculiarly, and of necessity, an American production, and will always probably be at our command.

The price is reasonable, in car loads being now 40 cents per gallon. Of course, in smaller quantities as it will be obtained by the retail druggists, there will be an increase probably reaching to 50 cents; but even if the price should be equal to that of cotton-seed oil, or a little above it, so far as I am concerned, I say that it has proved in my hands enough superior to cotton-seed oil, for the making of volatile liniment (wherein I suggest its employment) to merit a better price.

Properties.—Maize oil has been analysed by an English chemist, and the well-known authority, Prof. Chas. O. Curtman, M.D., of St. Louis, has determined its character as follows:

"Oil from embryo of Indian corn, in unrefined state, has a specific gravity of 0.916 at 15° C., which is nearly that of pure olive oil (0.915 to 0.918).

The elaidine test shows the presence of a large quantity of oleine, intermediate in quantity between olive and cotton-seed oils.

Its color is a pale yellowish-brown; its odor and taste that of freshly ground cornmeal.

It belongs to the non-drying group of the vegetable oils, experiments showing that a very thin layer on paper does not in three weeks' time form a pellicle on the surface exposed to air. In this respect it closely resembles the oils of olive, almond, colza, rapeseed, etc.

It does not very rapidly become rancid by exposure to air, and in this regard compares favorably with the best oils.

Its use produces no specific purgative effect, any more than olive oil.

With ammonia or solutions of caustic alkalies it rapidly saponifies, forming a white soap."

Analysis by F. Williams, Liverpool, England.

Fatty Acids (free).. 0.88
Total Fatty Acids... 96.70
Unsaponifiable, Mucilagineous and Albuminous Bodies. 1.54

[ORIGINAL ABSTRACT.]

CONVERSION OF HYOSCYAMINE INTO ATROPINE.

A FURTHER and most important step in the chemistry of the solanaceous alkaloids has been made by the discovery that hyoscyamine can be converted into atropine in a very simple manner.

[This fact had been announced already, during last year, by Prof. Ernst Schmidt, in a paper read before the Naturforscherversammlung (Section Pharmacy) at Wiesbaden, but no official report was made of this paper.]

W. Will investigated the relationship of atropine, hyoscyamine, and hyoscine at the request of the Chemische Fabrik auf Aktien (late E. Schering), of Berlin. In this factory very large quantities of belladonna root have latterly been worked up under various precautions. In the course of these operations it was observed that the relative quantity of atropine and hyoscyamine differed very much, according to the process used in extracting the alkaloids—a fact which is already recorded in the older literature. But while it was heretofore supposed that the varying yield was due to an original variation in the total amount of alkaloids contained in the root, or else to the fact that one or the other process extracted proportionately more (or less) of one alkaloid, the experiments conducted at Schering's factory showed that

one and the same root yielded the more hyoscyamine, and the less atropine, the more carefully the process was conducted.

In fact, it has been ascertained that if the process is carried out to perfection, *belladonna yields only hyoscyamine and no atropine at all*. If the process, however, is less carefully conducted, more or less atropine is obtained, the total yield of alkaloids in both cases being about the same.

These results showed that during the process of manufacture, hyoscyamine is liable to be converted into atropine. To test this practically, the author was put in possession of the requisite material and factory records. He has found that hyoscyamine can indeed be quite easily converted into atropine, and that the conditions under which this change takes place can easily occur during the extraction of the alkaloids, if the methods laid down in the text-books are used.

Before the author began his experiments on the conversion of hyoscyamine into atropine, he assured himself of the identity and purity of the material placed at his disposal.

While his results of the examination of this material show that it was pure hyoscyamine, yet he found the latter to differ in a few respects from the substance as described by others. Ladenburg had announced that he could not obtain simple crystallized salts of hyoscyamine; also doubted the statements of previous authorities regarding these salts, and inclined to believe that the alkaloid they had had in hand was hyoscine. Will, however, has prepared from his lot of hyoscyamine a whole series of crystallized salts, which are undoubtedly true hyoscyamine (not hyoscine) salts.

Sulphate of hyoscyamine crystallizes from alcohol in fine, colorless needles, resembling sulphate of atropine. The crystals melt at 206° C. When dried at 100° C., the salt has the composition $(C_{17}H_{23}O_3)_2H_2SO_4$. With hydrochloric acid and chloride of gold it yields the characteristic crystalline double chloride of gold and hyoscyamine. The hydrobromate crystallizes in large crystals, upon evaporation of its aqueous solution.

Former investigations have shown that hyoscyamine in aqueous solution turned the plane of polarized light to the left, the specific rate being determined by Poehl and Ladenburg to be about $-14.3°$. Will has found that various samples of hyoscyamine placed in his hands yielded uniform but much higher figures, the mean of a series of experiments being $-20.97°$. This circumstance appears to the author a further proof that he had a purer material under his hands than any observer before him.

The author now describes *two* methods by which hyoscyamine is converted into atropine.

One is by *melting*. The author's experiment was made upon 5 Gm. of hyoscyamine, which were exposed for 5 hours to a heat of 109°-110° C. in a bath of chloride of sodium solution. The result was the almost complete conversion of the alkaloid into atropine. The conditions, however, under which this change occurs do not exist during the process of manufacture of the alkaloids, and since nevertheless a conversion of one alkaloid into the other was observed to take place in the course of manufacture, some other cause of the change had to be searched for by the author.

Conversion of Hyoscyamine into Atropine at ordinary Temperature by dilute Solution of Soda.

A solution of pure hyoscyamine in alcohol may long be preserved without undergoing any change. On evaporating the alcohol at the ordinary temperature, only hyoscyamine results again. If such a solution is introduced into a polarising tube it will be found that it does not change its rate of polarisation during several days. But if *one* drop of an alcoholic solution of soda be added to such a solution, and its polarising power be examined, it will be found that it gradually diminishes, and finally descends to 0 (atropine, in alcoholic solution, is optically inert).

One grammo of a ten-per-cent solution is thus completely rendered optically inactive within two hours by one drop of a solution of soda.

[That the resulting alkaloid was atropine was proven in various ways.]

It is, therefore, demonstrated that hyoscyamine is converted, at the ordinary temperature, completely into atropine, under the influence of a trace of alkali. And the author adds, in a foot-note, that the same effect seems to be produced by warming the alkaloid for some time with dilute hydrochloric acid.

Regarding the influence of the kind and quantity of the alkali upon the duration of the reaction, experiments are under progress. The rate of the reaction may be easily controlled by means of the polarising apparatus. It is probably proportionate to the co-efficient of affinity of the bases. Ammonia produces the change likewise, but only very slowly.

This transformation explains, in a very simple manner, the various statements made by different experimenters regarding the variation in yield of either alkaloid from the same or from different roots. During the manufacture, the alkaloid is always set free by means of an alkali, and the relative proportions of the two must be greatly influenced also by the rate of concentration of the solution, and by the length of time during which they are in contact with the alkali.

It is now also easy to understand the fact reported by Prof. E. Schmidt, viz., that the crystallized residues obtained from the mother liquors of crude atropine and crude daturine yield fresh quantities of the higher-melting alkaloid, if they are once more dissolved in hydrochloric acid, then precipitated with carbonate of potassium, and the separated oily base allowed to stand for some time until it solidified.

It is known that the study of the bases isolated from plants has repeatedly shown the former to consist of several bodies having the same empirical composition (such as quinine, quinidide, etc.), and also that the alkaloidal product obtained by various processes contains these isomeric bodies in very varying proportions. On closer study, it is quite possible that similar transformations will be found to take place under the influence of the reagents used for isolating the alkaloids.

The author announces that he will investigate these isomeric alkaloids for this purpose.

A Few Artificial Mineral Waters.

EUGENE DIETERICH gives a series of mixtures for artificial mineral water (in the *Pharm. Centralhalle*, Nos. 21 and 22), from which we select a few of those in demand in this country.

1. *Pullna Bitter Water.*

Sodium Sulphate, dry	115 parts
Potassium Sulphate	5 "
Sodium Chloride	25 "
Sodium Bicarbonate	17 "
Magnesium Sulphate, dry	190 "
Calcium Sulphate, precip	5 "

Taken in grammes, the mixture will serve for 10 liters (10½ quarts) of artificial bitter water.

To prepare an average dose, put a tablespoonful of the salt into a half-pint bottle, fill it half full of water, dissolve by agitation, and then fill the bottle with carbonic acid water.

2. *Hunyadi János Water.*

Potassium Sulphate	0.5 parts
Sodium Chloride	14.0 "
Sodium Bicarbonate	53.0 "
Sodium Sulphate, dry	190.0 "
Calcium Sulphate, precip	15.0 "
Magnesium Sulphate, dry	34.5 "
Iron Sulphate, dry	0.2 "

Taken in grammes, the mixture will serve for 10 liters (10½ quarts) of the artificial water.

Dose, as in preceding.

3. *Pyrmont Water.*

Lithium Carbonate	0.1 parts
Sodium Bicarbonate	24.0 "
Sodium Sulphate, dry	21.0 "
Sodium Chloride	34.0 "
Magnesium Sulphate, dry	27.0 "
Calcium Sulphate, precip	34.0 "
Iron Sulphate, dry	0.12 "

The same remarks, as given under 1 and 2, apply here.

4. *Ems, " Kraenchen."*

Sodium Chloride	9.0 parts
Sodium Bicarbonate	2.2 "
Potassium Sulphate	0.4 "
Calcium Sulphate, precip	1.6 "
Magnesium Sulphate, dry	2.1 "

Taken in grammes, the mixture will serve for 10 liters (10½ quarts) of the artificial water.

Dose: Put as much as will go on the point of a knife (about 20 grains) in a half-pint bottle, fill this two-thirds full with "soda water" (see below), and then fill the bottle completely with boiling water. The product is either drank by itself, or in combination with hot milk. In the latter case, the bottle is filled with boiling hot milk instead of water.

["Soda-water" is meant by the author to be carbonic water containing a small amount, about 0.1 per cent of carbonate of sodium.]

5. *Karlsbad, Kissingen, and Vichy Water.*

Formulæ for this are contained in the new National Formulary of the Amer. Pharm. Assoc., and need not be repeated here.

6. *Friedrichshall Bitter Water.*

Two formulæ for this will be found in our answers to Queries in this number.

Alpha-Naphthol as an Antiseptic.

ALPHA-NAPHTHOL is insoluble in cold water. One liter of dilute alcohol, containing 40 per cent of absolute alcohol, dissolves 10 grammes of the substance. J. Maximovitch (*Comptes Rend.*) has studied the antiseptic action of this substance towards 14 different microbes, and finds that alpha-naphthol acts more strongly antiseptic than does beta-naphthol, according to the recent researches of Bouchard. At the same time, alpha-naphthol is less injurious to the animal organism than beta-naphthol. In order to kill a rabbit, 9 grammes of alpha-naphthol must be used for every kilo of the weight of the animal, showing that it is three times less poisonous than beta-naphthol, and 700 times less than mercuric iodide.

Improved Process for making Hydrochlorate of Quinine.

L. R. WELD has patented the followed process for making hydrochlorate of quinine.

Sulphate of quinine dissolved in alcohol is boiled with a solution of sodium chloride in excess in an open or closed vessel for about 10 minutes; the proportions are about one part of quinine sulphate to four parts of sodium chloride and 50 parts of alcohol. On concentration, the sodium sulphate and chloride separate first, and then the hydrochlorate of quinine, which can readily be obtained in the crystalline state.

A KNEADING MACHINE FOR PILL MASSES, OINTMENTS, ETC.

Messrs. Werner and Pfleiderer, of London, are the manufacturers of a strong and compact kneading machine, which is very useful for making pill-masses, or mixing ointments, plasters, or other similar compounds, in quantities from about ¼ pound upwards. It is made in various sizes, to be worked either by hand or by steam-power. We give an illustration of one of the smaller sizes.

This machine is capable of working from 2 to 4 pounds of any kind of mass, in from 5 to 15 minutes, under proper manipulation. The speed of working can be altered at will, to suit the consistence of the mass, by simply shifting the handle to another shaft, there being three of the latter. A soft, pliable mass will be best worked at a higher speed, while very hard or tough masses will require a slow speed. Fig. 1 shows the machine as it appears when screwed fast to a table. Fig. 2 shows it tilted back for discharging the kneaded material. This is accomplished by simply releasing the catch which holds down the machine by the rim of the trough, and pulling the trough over by hand, at the same time slowly turning the shaft in the reverse or outward direction, so as to allow the mass to disengage itself from the blades. The interior construction will be understood by examining Fig. 3, which represents a machine of the smallest size made, intended for about 1 pound of mass.

The cubic contents, that is, the volume of liquid or solid required to fill the trough to the top of the blades is 1.2 pints for the smallest, and 3.5 pints for the next size. But the largest size, working as much as 135 pounds of mass at a time, has a cubic capacity of 13.2 gallons. The prices of the two sizes described are £4.5.0 and £7.10.0.

Assay of Argols, etc., for Tartaric Acid.

The following improved process for determining tartaric acid in argols, etc., is proposed by Goldenberg, Geromont & Co. (in *Chem. Zeit.*)

Six grains of the finely powdered substance are stirred in a beaker with 9 C.c. of HCl (sp. gr. = 1.10), a like volume of water is now gradually added, and the mixture is digested with frequent stirring for 1–2 hours throughout, at the ordinary temperature. The liquid is now made up to 100 C.c. with water, and then passed through a dry filter. 50 C.c. are then placed in a well-covered beaker, to which 10 C.c. of K_2CO_3 solution (containing 3 Gm. K_2CO_3) are added; after boiling for some time the CO_2 will be completely expelled, and the $CaCO_3$ precipitate will have completely separated in the crystalline condition; after filtering and washing the latter, the solution is evaporated to about 10 C.c., acidified with 2–2.5 C.c. of glacial acetic acid, gradually introduced with constant stirring, mixed with 100 C.c. of pure alcohol of 90°–to 96° Fr., and stirred until the precipitate is distinctly crystalline. After frequent washings by decantation the precipitate is filtered through a 8-Cm. filter, which, with precipitate and dish, must be thoroughly washed free from acetic acid by means of alcohol. The filter, with the precipitate, is now transferred from the funnel into a beaker; the dish is washed with boiling water, which is then added to the substance in the beaker, and the whole is titrated with normal alkali. The number of C.c. of alkali used, multiplied by five, gives the percentage of tartaric acid in the lees. In making allowance for the volume of the residue insoluble in HCl, it is found that 0.7 per cent should be deducted from a yield of 20 per cent tartaric acid, or 0.7+0.2n from one of 20+n per cent. In analyzing tartar and calcium tartrate, 3 grammes of the substance are digested with 9 C.c.

Fig. 1.

Fig. 2.

Werner and Pfleiderer's kneading machine.

Fig. 3.

of the HCl; the solution is then filtered (the residue being well washed) and made up to 100 C.c., of which 50 C.c. are used for the subsequent stages as above. The percentage of tartaric acid is in this case found by multiplying by ten the number of C.c. of normal alkali used.—*J. S. Chem. Ind.*

Estimation of Emetine.

Lignon gives the following process in the *Chem. Zeit.* Rub together 25 grammes of the powdered ipecacuanha root in 25 C.c. of water and 20 grammes of slaked lime, and after this has been well rubbed up add 30 grammes more of slaked lime, and treat the mixture with 300 C.c. of ether in a suitable extraction apparatus, filter the ethereal solution (about 200 C.c.) if it contains any solid matter, and make it up to 200 or 250 C.c. Place 50 C.c. of the solution in a 100-C.c. flask; to this add 10 C.c. of semi-normal sulphuric acid, and 4 to 5 drops of freshly-prepared concentrated extract of logwood. After thorough shaking, the mixture divides into a colorless ethereal layer and a yellow aqueous layer. The acids contained in the solution are neutralized by adding semi-normal ammonia, drop by drop, until the aqueous layer is colored red, and the difference between the amount found and that originally used shows the amount of alkaloid which has combined with the acid.

Croton Oil.

Kobert has recently (*Chem. Zeit.*) attacked Senier's theory that there are two principles in croton oil—one a cathartic, and the other a vesicating body. His belief is that both effects are due to Buchheim's crotonolic acid, which exists in the oil partly as a glycoside, and may be prepared by treating the oil with a hot saturated aqueous solution of barium hydrate, whereby the fatty acids are precipitated. They are collected, well washed and dried, and the oleic and crotonolic salts dissolved out with ether. After evaporation the residue is treated with absolute alcohol, which dissolves out the barium crotonolate, which is decomposed with sulphuric acid. Kobert denies that the oil is separable by means of alcohol into the two portions mentioned by Senier, and states that the solubility of the oil depends mainly upon its age. Some varieties are soluble in all proportions; while crotonolic acid itself is readily soluble in alcohol, the solubility of the oil bears no relation to the quantity of free crotonolic acid present.

Estimation of Glucose in Urine.

The urine is mixed with an equal volume of one-fifth normal baryta solution, filtered, and to 5 C.c. of the filtrate another 5 C.c. of baryta solution is added, together with 100 C.c. of 90% alcohol; after agitation, the solution is set aside for two or three hours. The precipitate is collected, washed with 20 C.c. of 90% alcohol, and thrown along with the filter into the precipitating flask, in which 10 C.c. of decinormal sulphuric acid has previously been placed. After warming and shaking, the excess of sulphuric acid is neutralized with standard baryta solution, using as an indicator not more than one drop of phenolphthalein solution (1 : 100). The barium sulphate is now filtered off, and the filtrate is evaporated to dryness, and weighed. The grape-sugar remains as a yellowish mass containing a little baryta, which is obtained as carbonate on ignition. This weighing of the sugar serves as a check on the volumetric estimation by means of the baryta precipitate, as described. The author concludes that:

I. Grape-sugar in aqueous solution can be very accurately estimated by the baryta method, either by titrating the baryta or by weighing the separated sugar. II. When baryta in sufficient excess is present, the aqueous solution of the barium sugar compound is precipitated as BaO ($C_6H_{12}O_6$) + BaO On the addition of so much alcohol that the mixture contains 81 to 86% of alcohol by volume. III. In the presence of only 68 to 70% of alcohol, the precipitate has the composition BaO($C_6H_{12}O_6$). IV. In diabetic urine, the results obtained with Fehling-Soxhlet's titration method agree closely with those yielded by the baryta method.—H. Will in *Arch. d. Pharm.*, abst. in *J. Chem. Soc.*

Note on a Modified Process of Repercolation.

FROM a "Monograph on Fluid Extracts" presented by Mr. Josiah H. Lilly to the Missouri Pharmaceutical Association, we take the following remarks on processes of percolation, or methods of exhausting the drug:

The Officinal Method is, of course, the most practicable, most largely used by pharmaceutists, the process being sustained upon the grounds of convenience and practicability. We must confess, however, that the finished preparations are prone to precipitation and open to the objection of the necessary application of heat to the excess percolate. Hence it is not perfect.

Single Percolation with Reserve Percolate.—Is a process little known and still less practised. It is applied in the following manner: Say 16 troy ounces of drug is packed, macerated in the usual manner, percolation started, and but 7½—12 fluid ounces—allowed to escape. This is put in stock as fluid extract. Percolation is then continued until one pint has been obtained. This is put aside until it is desired to prepare another quantity, when 16 troy ounces of drug is again taken, packed and macerated with the weak percolate, then *one pint* is obtained therefrom and constitutes the fluid extract. Another pint of weak percolate is obtained from this lot and set aside for future use. This method at first seems rather plausible, but upon second consideration will be condemned for its real inaccuracy.

Pressure.—It would necessarily consume much space and time to review verbatim here a published account of conducting this method. It occurs in Remington's Pharmacy, and I would suggest to those interested in this subject to give it a careful reading. Being familiar with the process in an experimental way, I must take serious exceptions to the assertion that this process can produce an acceptable extract. The sentence made use of under Fluid Extract Burdock, that "exhaustion by this process is not so complete as by one previously described, but is generally sufficiently so for practical purposes" is a loop hole that allows many a pharmaceutical problem to be easily solved.

To be more exact, issue is taken with the first method mentioned under the head of Fluid Extract Podophyllum where 100 pounds (we presume of 16 troy ounces each), of drug in No. 30 powder is taken, treated in the usual way until 120 pints of menstruum have been added, when percolation ceases; the drug is then taken, one-fifth at a time, placed under tremendous pressure, all contained liquid possible is obtained, put upon remaining drug, percolated, etc., as described.

Now mark—" The fluid expressed from the last portion, when added to the reserved portion" (not before mentioned), "which should be 95 pints, constitutes the fluid extract." Presumably the amount obtained in the last portion is but 5 pints; hence, allowing nothing for evaporation during exposure, 4 pints of menstruum was left after expression in each fifth portion—or say 16¼ of menstruum used—hence, in order for the 100 pints to contain all the active constituents, the last 20 pints of menstruum added must contain *nothing*, and the first 100 must contain *all*.

Again, according to the deduction we quote, the last portion is pressed and 4 pints remain therein. Does not this 4 pints contain as much matter in solution as that obtained by pressing others which is necessary to complete the 100 pints? It certainly does. Hence the student would be forced to the conclusion that after all the process has no real advantage over single percolation carefully conducted, because, first, pressure to secure fresher menstruum for forcing ahead the preceding portion is parallel to adding new menstruum to the whole. Second, there is no great saving of menstruum, for here we note a loss of 20 pints, which, to be sure, may be mostly recovered by apparatus used in like operations.

The second method consists of placing in a macerator 100 lbs. of drug with 120 pints of menstruum, inverting macerator occasionally for ten days, then the drug is pressed out with the result of obtaining 80 pints of fluid (this leaving 40 pints of liquid of equal strength in the macerator). The drug is then broken up and more menstruum added (thus diluting the strength of the liquid contained therein), macerated a few days, pressed again, and sufficient fluid obtained to complete the 100 pints.

Now, what have we here! First, 100 lbs. of drug and 120 pints of menstruum, the whole menstruum equally saturated; we obtain finally, after adding more menstruum to pressed drug, but 100 pints of liquid. By what miracle do the substances dissolved in the original excess of 20 pints, and the menstruum subsequently added, get into the remaining 100 pints! "Sufficiently exhausted," appears to be rather stretched in this connection, and I ask your opinion upon it. Practical experience in this field has satisfied me that these deductions are correct.

Maceration and Percolation in Vacuo.—This interesting method is now used to a limited extent by some of its enthusiastic supporters, and at one time it threatened to revolutionise the art of making fluid extracts, but while it is possible to prepare a fluid extract from the denser drugs without the use of more than 16 fluid ounces of menstruum to 16 troy ounces of drug, it is necessary to use more when treating the more bulky drugs, thus reducing it nearly to the plane of more simple processes which necessitate subsequent concentration or preservation of weak percolates for future operations.

Method of Dr. Squibb.—This method has been recognised as approaching more nearly to perfection than any previously conceived, and has certainly proven worthy of the wise mind that begot it. This being so familiar to all pharmaceutists, being an optional process of our pharmacopœia, extended comment in this connection is hardly necessary. However, it may be asserted that even in this process we have not perfection, as it necessitates the preserving of weak percolates, which, by most pharmaceutists, is considered a serious objection—a foothold for inaccuracy.

Before dismissing this subject of processes, allow me to present for your consideration and inspection a modification of the Squibb method of repercolation.

Modified Process of Repercolation.—The apparatus consists of four percolators of the later pattern, mounted with tubes and fittings substantially as prescribed by the pharmacopœia. The operation here shown (by drawings which did not, however, accompany the author's paper) is the manufacture of two pints of fluid extract of Cascara Sagrada, and has been conducted as follows:

Eight troy ounces of the granulated drug (No. 30) was moistened with the menstruum, packed in percolator No. 1, sufficient menstruum being added to cover. After macerating two days, percolation was allowed to take place (more menstruum being added), until 12 fluid ounces of percolate had been obtained; now making no reserve (as in the Squibb method), this 12 fluid ounces is used in moistening, packing, and macerating No. 2. After two days, percolation is again allowed to proceed, procuring 20 fluid ounces from No. 2 to pack and macerate No. 3, then proceeding, after two days, as before, 26 fluid ounces of percolate is secured from No. 3 to pack and macerate No. 4, then after one day we are ready to continue the process to completion.

The percolators being then arranged so that each may discharge into the succeeding number, the new menstruum is added to No. 1, and the process continues. When 32 fluid ounces of liquid shall have emerged from No. 4, the drug will be found completely exhausted and a perfect fluid extract results.

At first thought one is likely to criticise using a liquid so rich in dissolved matter for macerating new drug, and this is strengthened somewhat by the knowledge that solutions of many substances have different solvent powers from the original menstruum. But please notice that the amount of percolate obtained from each number is so regulated as to avoid a point near saturation and in practice its solvent power has not been found to interfere with the ultimate success of the operation. The great point gained in this process is perfect exhaustion, avoiding the necessity of preserving a weak percolate or subsequent evaporation.

A practical objection is the amount of extra menstruum necessarily used, but is this not more than over-balanced by the absence of weak percolate?

This is the first publication of this process and is commended for trial and comment by interested pharmaceutists.

Liquor Antihydrorrhoicus.

BRANDAU and SPENER have obtained a patent upon a new compound which they call Liquor Antihydrorrhoicus, and which is said to be a very efficient remedy against footsweat. According to the patent specifications, it is prepared in the following manner:

100 parts of butyrate and 100 parts of acetate of sodium are mixed with 160 parts of alcohol of 90 per cent, and 250 parts of concentrated sulphuric acid, and the mixture distilled. The vapors of ethyl butyrate and acetate are conducted into a glass globe having three tubulures, which is at first exposed to diffused daylight, but is afterwards protected against light. Through one of the other tubulures a measured current of chlorine gas is introduced. The third tubulure serves to connect the globular receiver with a flask containing a mixture of 3,760 parts of concentrated hydrochloric acid, 120 parts of alcohol of 90 per cent, and 120 parts of glycerin. The compound ethers, which are chlorinated in the receiver, descend into the acid mixture contained in the flask, in which they are dissolved. The whole product is finally colored red with litmus.

This solution—which seems to us rather problematical—is to be used undiluted as a bath to the soles of the feet. In case of very sensitive persons, it may be diluted. It is said to arrest the excessive sweating promptly and effectively.—*After Pharm. Centralh.*

Guaiacol is recommended by Sahli as preferable to creosote for internal use, owing to the uncertainty with regard to the purity of the latter. He proposes the following formula for its use: Guaiacol, 1 grammes; alcohol, 20 grammes; water, 180 grammes. Dose, a teaspoonful to a tablespoonful twice or thrice daily, after eating. The mixture should be kept in a bottle of black glass.—*Journ. de Pharm. d'Alsace-Lorraine; Amer. Journ. Pharm.*

COMBINED SUCTION AND PRESSURE PUMP.

A VERY compact and neat pump, suitable both for exhaustion and for pressure, and, besides, permitting an inspection of the working parts by their inclosure within a strong glass cylinder, has been constructed by Robert Muencke, of Berlin. It bears two gauges, one being for vacuum and the other for pressure. If any vessel is to be exhausted of air, this is connected by means of stout rubber tubing, with lower end of the tube coming from the vacuum gauge (c). At v there is a check-valve, to prevent the access of water. When the apparatus is to be used for pressure, as, for instance, when it is to furnish compressed air for a blow-pipe or blast-lamp, the stop-cock d is connected with the lamp. The faucet at the bottom of the cylinder serves to regulate the escape of the water.—*Chem. Zeit.* and *Chem. Centralbl.*

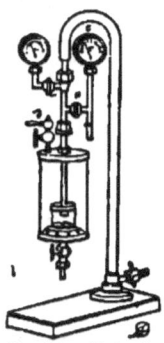

Muencke's combined suction and pressure pump.

Calamine Varieties.

There are few things more bewildering, and often inconvenient, than the many varieties of calamine in commerce, and the position is somewhat complicated by the urgent recommendation by each manufacturer of his own particular kind. Ranging through all colors from pink and red to gray and white, its composition seems correspondingly various. It is a question whether the employment (in English pharmacy) of pure carbonate of zinc in its place would not be attended with equally beneficial results; but some respect is due, perhaps, to time-honored prejudice. Moreover, it has been said, "in a multitude of councillors is wisdom," and perhaps the remark applies to the composition of this remedy. From a paper by A. R. Bennett on the subject, it appears that some samples are devoid of zinc. The qualities of a good calamine are its amorphous condition, freedom from silica, and presence of zinc. These conditions seem best fulfilled by the gray varieties.

Chloroform as a Preservative of Urine.

OF peculiar interest to the pharmacist is a communication of Prof. Salkowski to a Vienna medical journal on the use of chloroform for the preservation of samples of urine by the analyst. A 5-per-mille solution was found by him to effectively prevent the growth of micro-organisms, and he recommends it to be employed for keeping pathological liquids, and for the storage of anatomical preparations. Moreover, he suggests the employment of such a solution internally as a disinfectant and as a mouth-wash, and observes that it could be advantageously added to hypodermic injections. Salkowski's investigations confirm the principle upon which, by some manipulators, a little chloroform has been added to aqueous extracts of drugs, etc., to protect them from the growth of fungi and the effect of putrefactive change.—*Chem. and Drug.*

Refining Olive Oil without Chemicals.

ACCORDING to G. Seidel, olive oil is put into a conical tub provided with a steam-coil. About ½ inch over the bottom, a faucet is inserted, to let off the water and impurities, and about 4 inches above this, a second faucet is placed for drawing off the oil. The tube or tank may be made of any desired size, but that described by Seidel holds about 2,000 pounds. It is placed upon a stone floor, and alongside of it are placed at different levels, 5 to 6 clarifying tanks resting upon strong wooden frames. These tanks, which may also be of tinned iron, have a cylindrical form, a false perforated bottom about 1 or 1½ inch above the bottom, and above this, at the side, a stop-cock. A layer of cotton, or preferably, glass-wool, is placed on the diaphragm. Glass-wool is preferred as it may be easily washed and can be used for years, while cotton will last only for 2 or 3 operations. For every 100 lbs. of olive oil to be clarified, 10 to 15 lbs. of water are added. The oil is then brought to a boil, by means of steam, and kept so for 2 or 3 hours. It is then allowed to be at rest for 24 hours, during which time the water will separate. On opening the stop-cock the partially clarified oil is allowed to flow into the first clarifying tank. When this is full, its contents are allowed to flow into the second, and so forth. When the first tank is empty, it may be refilled from the steam tank as soon as a new lot of oil has been treated as described above.—*Industriebl.*

Carbonaphthilic Acid is said by the *Lyon Medical* to be about five times as powerful an antiseptic as salicylic acid, but very poisonous and insoluble.

WATER BLAST PUMP.

IT is well known that the principle which is applied to the construction of vacuum or filter-pumps, and which aims at the production of rarefied air in a certain inclosed space, may also be applied to the production of air-pressure.

A simple apparatus by which this may be accomplished has recently been constructed by A. Beutell.

A tall cylindrical flask, K (see cut), is provided with an outlet tube near the bottom, and its stopper carries two tubes, one (M) for the entrance of a jet of water, and the other (L) for the exit of the compressed air, which may be conducted to a blast lamp or wherever air under pressure may be needed. The column of water entering through M causes air to be sucked in through the little hole at c, and this air, after arriving in the flask, is gradually compressed by the continuously entering water.

In order that the apparatus may work properly, it is necessary to construct the tube M in a particular manner, and of certain definite proportions. Figure 3 exhibits its bore and shape in an enlarged view. A short distance above the orifice of the tube it is slightly expanded, and then gradually contracts to the place b. It then again expands to an oblong cavity, and contracts again to a neck, e, which is a trifle wider than that at b, and which must be so situated that the column of water passing through b is exactly perpendicular to the centre of the aperture at e. The tube then expands again to its original diameter, and is slightly curved, which is done to prevent any of the compressed air in the cylinder K from regurgitating upwards.

The outlet tube at A is preferably constructed as shown in Fig. 2. Instead of being made of one piece, it is there represented as consisting of two pieces joined together by rubber tubing, a sort of check-valve, G, being introduced into the rubber joint. By regulating the check-valve, that is, by approaching it more or less to the exit of the tube A, the outflow of water may be regulated. It

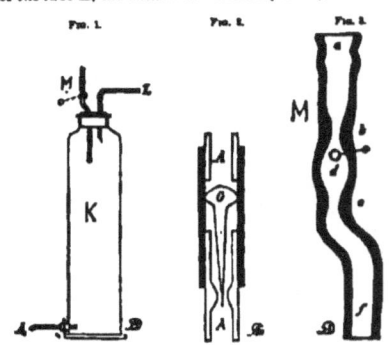

Beutell's water blast-pump.

is important to adjust this so that the cylindrical flask will always be at least half-full, and never over three-fourths filled. While the column of water falls through the aperture at b into the expanded portion of M, it aspirates air through the little orifice c, communicating with the outer air, and this air is carried along with it into the flask, where it accumulates until it is under a pressure equal to that of the column of water entering the apparatus, when the latter will cease to flow. By allowing the air to escape through L, more will be successively compressed, so that a steady blast may be obtained.

The proportions between the diameters of the expanded and contracted portions of the glass-tube M are important. If the bore at b amounts to 2.8 millimeters, that at e should be 3 millimeters. Under these circumstances, and with a pressure of water equal to a column of 61.7 cubic centimeters, the apparatus will furnish 890 liters of air for every 1,000 liters of water consumed. If the two diameters were: b, 1 millimeter, and e, 3.4 mm., one liter of water aspirates 2.35 liters of air. These proportions are, no doubt, capable of improvement.—*Chem. Zeit.* and *Ch. Centralbl.*

Poisoning by Himrod's Powder.—Geo. Throp, in *The Lancet* of May 19th, mentions a case of poisoning by Himrod's Asthma Cure, where a stupid fellow mixed a teaspoonful with water and drank it without regarding the directions. Emetics were given, cold was applied to the head, and brandy given internally, and after a time his delirium and other toxic symptoms abated. The doctor attributed to copious draughts of lime-water much of the improvement that was secured.

Improvements in Revivifying Charcoal.

From a lengthy paper on "The Mode of using Charcoal in Sugar Refining," by Messrs. Newlands in the *Journ. of Soc. of Chem. Ind.*,* we take the following passage, which gives some practical hints that may be applied to revivifying animal charcoal, even on the small scale.

Under certain circumstances, the calcic carbonate, carbon, iron, and other constituents increase to such an extent during long use (owing to the gradual waste of carbon during the process of reburning), as to render their reduction a matter of importance, and various means have been devised to attain this end. The treatment with dilute hydrochloric acid to convert the calcic carbonate into calcic chloride is the ordinary method adopted on the Continent in the beet-sugar factories, but this plan is open to the objection that a certain quantity of calcic phosphate is sure also to be decomposed, and that the framework of the charcoal will consequently be injured. To obviate this to some extent, it has been proposed to exhaust the air previous to the introduction of the acid, so as to bring the latter instantaneously in contact with every particle of the charcoal, and in this way equalize its action. To further overcome this difficulty, Beans used dry hydrochloric acid gas, which is said to have no action on calcic phosphate. Stenhouse and Duncan proposed to use dilute nitric acid in place of hydrochloric acid, and there is little doubt that it possesses advantages over the latter. Cook has suggested treating the charcoal with a solution of ammonic chloride, and then reburning so as to produce ammonium carbonate which goes off, and calcic carbonate which is afterwards dissolved out. Cook also patented the use of phosphoric acid to decompose the calcic carbonate. Patrick, Beans, and others have proposed to dissolve out the calcic carbonate by means of a saturated solution of carbonic acid. In English refineries, the calcic carbonate, in all cases, so far as we can ascertain, decreases during use, and this appears to be due to the employment of cane sugar, which is generally slightly acid. It has been proposed to reduce the carbon by reburning the charcoal after it has been saturated with a solution of ammonic nitrate, but we have not been able to ascertain if this has been done on a large scale....

Instead of revivifying by carbonization, it has been proposed (and to some extent carried into effect) by Eisfeld, and also by Phillips, to digest the charcoal after use in a solution of ammonia, potash, or soda in water or alcohol, the ammonia and alcohol been recovered by distillation. In this way the coloring matters and a large portion of other organic and mineral matters taken up from the sugar can be removed. This process has been worked on the Continent, but only experimentally in England.

A New Vegetable Rennet.

In his interesting narrative of a journey through the Kalahari Desert,* Mr. G. A. Farini relates the following occurrence which may afford to some of our enterprising hunters after novelties an opportunity to exercise their faculties.

The author and his companions had been attended by a native "black beauty," who had been sent to him as cook and "general housekeeper," etc., by one of the native chiefs. The first meal appears to have been quite a feast, according to the author's description. What happened after this we shall give in the author's own words (page 216):

"When we had finished it was her ladyship's turn to eat. Her despondent state had not affected her appetite, for she consumed enough for three men, washing down the hearty repast by drinking a small calabash of milk, which only a few minutes before had been brought in fresh from the cow, but which was now quite thick. This astonished me, for I knew that the thick milk which all Kaffirs prize so highly takes some time to get ready—at least among the Zulus, who prepare it by filling skins, which already contain a certain amount of 'leaven,' with fresh milk, and subjecting them to considerable agitation. What necromancy had been employed to 'turn' the milk so soon in this case! Had the Black Beauty's sour temper effected the change! I tried to ask by means of pantomime, but could not make them understand; they thought I asked for more milk, and sent for a fresh supply, which came in a quarter of an hour, the froth still on it, quite fresh from the cow. Seeing a little thick milk still left in the calabash, I pointed to it and then to the new. Now they understood, and one of the Ahigals went out and brought in two little berries, about the size of a red currant, and nearly the same color, but not quite so bright. Taking them between her thumb and finger, she pricked them and squeezed a drop or two of greenish fluid out of each, letting it fall into the new milk, in less than half a minute it was quite thick, but still remained perfectly sweet. The berry itself had a peculiar bitter flavor. It grows on a low bush, not unlike a rose bush, some of the seeds of which I secured, thinking this Kaffir substitute for rennet might be useful in Europe."

* "Through the Kalahari Desert. A Narrative of a Journey with Gun, Camera and Note-Book, to Lake N'gami and Back." By G. A. Farini. 8vo, London, 1886.

Reagents for Detecting Free Acids in the Stomach.

Much attention has recently been bestowed upon the nature and quantity of free acids in the stomach, as their kind, presence or absence has been recognised to be a characteristic of certain diseases. The pharmacist is frequently called upon by the physician for information or assistance in the execution of the tests, and for this reason the following synopsis, originally outlined by Dr. Boas, of Berlin, and taken from the *Pharm. Zeitung* (18-8, pp. 343), will be of practical interest:

A. *Reagents for Detecting Free Hydrochloric Acid* (HCl.).

1. *Methyl-violet.*—Mix the gastric juice [which here and in other cases may be obtained either by the stomach pump or in any other way.—Ed. Am. Dr.] with a very dilute aqueous solution of methyl-violet. If HCl is present, the tint will change to azure or sky-blue. Lactic acid produces this tint only when concentrated far beyond the limit which it can reach in the stomach.

2. *Tropæolin 00* (oxynaphthyl-azophenyl-sulphonic acid) in saturated alcoholic solution. Distribute four or five drops of this by brisk agitation about the edge of porcelain capsule, and allow the liquid to be examined to flow over it in drops and to become mixed with it. Again distribute the whole mixture about the edge, allow the excess to flow off, and warm gently over a flame. If HCl was present, there will be produced more or less extensive violet to lilac spots.

3. *Rhusch's* or *Mohr's Reagent.* 2 Cc. of a 10 per cent solution of sulphocyanide of potassium, and 0.5 Cc. of a neutral solution of ferric acetate are diluted with water to 10 Cc. A few drops of this ruby-red solution are put into a porcelain capsule, and one or two drops of the liquid to be tested is then allowed to flow down upon it. If HCl is present, a faint violet or lilac tint will form at the point of contact, becoming mahogany-brown on mixing the liquid.

4. *Günzburg's Reagent.*—2 Gm. of phloroglucin and 1 Gm. of vanillin are dissolved in 30 Gm. of alcohol. A drop of this solution and a trace of mineral acid produce a bright-red liquid and precipitate. When testing gastric juice, a few drops of the latter (previously filtered) and a few drops of the reagent are mixed in a small flat capsule, and the latter cautiously warmed over a flame. If HCl (even only about 0.05 per cent) is present, a bright-red circle will appear at the outer rim.

5. *Coloring Matter from Huckleberries (Bilberries).* (Uffelmann).—If freshly-expressed huckleberry juice is extracted with amylic alcohol, the latter assumes a reddish-blue color, which becomes lilac on addition of HCl, while the aqueous layer has a bright currant-red color. On repeatedly saturating blotting paper with the acrylic solution, a grayish-blue reagent paper is finally obtained, which assumes a fine red color with HCl, the color remaining upon the addition of ether. Lactic and butyric acids produce this reaction only when present in larger quantity than 4 to 4.5 per 1,000; acetic acid only at 8 per 1,000.

6. *Malachite-Green* (Koester).—A solution of malachite green containing 0.025 per cent forms a bluish-green liquid, which is colored bright emerald green by HCl. Below 0.05 per cent HCl, the reaction is feeble. Organic acids do not alter the tint.

7. *"Emerald-Green"* (extra crystallised) (Jaksch).—Aqueous solutions of this coloring matter (water soluble; blue variety) are turned green by HCl, even when dilute. (Butyric, acetic, and lactic acids do not change the original color even in concentrated solution.)

8. *Tropæolin-Paper.*—This is same reagent as No. 2, only in form of test-paper.

9. *Congo-Paper.*—Paper tinted with Congo red is turned blue (according to Riegel) in presence of free HCl.

B. *Reagents for Detecting Free Lactic Acid.*

10. *Uffelmann's Reagent.*—Mix 10 Cc. of a 4 per-cent solution of carbolic acid with 20 Cc. of water, and add a few drops of solution of ferric chloride. The amethyst-blue color is changed even by very small quantities of lactic acid into bright yellow (canary yellow). The reagent must always be prepared fresh.

11. *Ferric Chloride.*—Add a few drops of dilute solution of chloride of iron to 50 Cc. of water. The resulting liquid should have not more than a faintly yellowish tint. Addition of diluted HCl, or butyric or acetic acids does not change this; but free lactic acid or lactates turn it more or less yellow.

[The original adds a method of detecting and isolating butyric and lactic acids. But this method is practically useless, and therefore omitted here.—Ed. Am. Dr.]

The New Austrian Pharmacopœia will appear in December next. The pharmacognosy section is being compiled by Professor Vogl; the chemical section, from A to K, by Professor Ludwig, and from K to Z by Professor Barth; while Mr. M. B. Schneider will edit the whole. The authors are very reluctant to give any details about the progress of the work.

IODOFORM AND OTHER PENCILS.

On page 39 of our volume for 1887, we described a class of remedies introduced by Dr. Unna under the name of pencils or *stylus dilubilis*, and gave a variety of formulas therefor. Mr. H. Hebling, of the German Hospital, London, in a paper published in the *British and Colonial Druggist*, offers some modifications based upon his experience in making them in considerable quantities. Dr. Unna's formulas provides for the use of starch, dextrin, sugar and tragacanth as a base. Mr. Hebling says:

I have used two different kinds of base. The first, made up of gelatin, glycerin and water, is prepared as follows:

Take of

Best Gelatin	10 oz.
Best Glycerin	18 oz.
Water	q. s.

The gelatin is dissolved in water and glycerin by the aid of a water-bath in a porcelain dish, the water lost by evaporation being compensated for, by addition of more. The ingredients, if not soluble in water, are mixed in a finely-powdered condition with the warm and tenacious glue, which is poured into moulds similar to those used for making caustic, previously moistened with oil or soap liniment. When cold the pencils are quite elastic, but not sticky, and they do not adhere to the skin.

In a previous article the base was recommended for such ingredients as zinc oxide, salicylic acid, and as a dressing in cases of eczema. Since then Dr. F. A. Phillipi, M.D., of the German Hospital, and Dr. Unna, have both called attention to "zinc-glue" at the Conference of the British

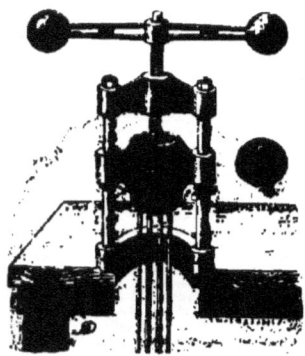

Apparatus for making Pill or Pencil Pipes.

Medical Association held in Dublin. Dr. Phillipi reported on its use in the treatment of 40 cases of ulcer of different kinds, of which 25 were cured by this preparation, and I can recommend zinc-glue to the readers of this diary as a dressing, which, if offered to doctors, will certainly give them every satisfaction.

The second way of preparing these sticks, which is quite familiar, consists of making use of cacao butter as the base. The fat is melted and allowed to half cool. At this point the various medicinal agents are introduced and reduced to fine powders if insoluble, or if soluble, like salol, betol, etc., simply added, and the whole poured into appropriate moulds. These kinds of pencils are, of course, not flexible.

When one has a large number to prepare, the operation outlined above, occupies a very long time—more, indeed, than it is often possible to spare. Recognizing this disadvantage, I began to cast about for some more rapid method of working, and finally hit upon the following. I may say that it admits of both kinds of sticks being prepared, on the large scale, with surprising rapidity, and essentially consists in abandoning the process of melting the basis, resorting instead to dry pressure. A simple machine is required which I illustrate above.

It is an apparatus which I also use for the piping of pill masses by pressure. The illustration is so clear as to render explanation superfluous.

The mode of procedure is very simple. The piston B is removed, and the prepared mass filled into the cylinder A. The cylinder being replaced is screwed down on to the contents of A, which are forced through the orifices in the plate C. This I have had in my machine so constructed that it is perforated with two holes having a diameter of ⅛ of an inch, and an equal number with a diameter of 1/16. I have also an iron plug for each of the orifices, by means of which any one of them can be filled up, according to the size of the pencils it is desired to make. The plate C being movable, can be replaced by any other of the same size

and shape, which may be bored of a suitable size for the preparation of suppositories, etc.

For elastic pencils I use a mass consisting of dextrin, sugar, starch, and tragacanth, with which the ingredients are well mixed and beaten, with the addition of a little water and glycerin, to a very hard but plastic mass. The formulas are as follows:

Iodoform Pencils, 33 per cent.

℞ Iodoform	3 i.
Amyli	3 iij.
Tragacanthæ	3 i.
Dextrini	3 i.
Sacch. alb.	ℨ ss.
Aq. et Glycer.	ââ q.s.

Salicylic Acid Pencils, 5 per cent.

℞ Acidi Salicyl.	3 i.
Tragacanthæ	3 i.
Amyli	3 i.
Dextrini	3 vij.
Sacch. Alb.	3 iij.
Aq. et Glycer.	ââ q.s.

When the masses are pressed, the pipes should be cut into pieces of about 3 inches in length, and may be polished, if necessary, by rolling on a porcelain slab with a thin board.

The method of preparing the cacao butter pencils is still more simple. The fat is first powdered, or, what is easier, comminuted by the use of an ordinary grater. It is then mixed with the ingredients. With this base elegant preparations may be obtained, which will give satisfaction to any one. The formulæ I use are:

Iodoform Pencils, 33 per cent.

℞ Iodoform pulv.	1 part.
Ol. Theobromatis	2 parts.

Cocaine Pencils, 2 per cent.

℞ Cocainæ Muriat.	1 part.
Ol. Theobromatis	49 parts.

To be cut into pieces so that each one contains ¼ gr. of cocaine salt.

Salol Pencils, 20 per cent.

℞ Salol	1 part.
Ol. Theobromatis	4 parts.

Dissolve the salol in the liquid oil, and after cooling with constant stirring, powder the mass, and treat as above described.

Opium Pencils, 5 per cent.

℞ Pulv. Opii.	1 part.
Ol. Theobromatis	19 parts.

To be divided into 1 gr. sticks.

Thalline Pencils, 5 per cent., for Gonorrhœa.

℞ Thallin. Sulph.	1 part.
Ol. Theobromatis	19 parts.

Mercurial Pencils for Syphilitic Fistula, 25 per cent.

℞ Ung. Hydrarg.	
Cera Alb.	ââ. partes.

Melt the wax. When half cool add the ointment, and allow to solidify, with constant stirring. Then press as above described.

Syrup of Lactophosphate of Calcium.

In answer to Query No. 19, *What is the best process for making Syrup of Calcium Lactophosphate*, Mr. John J. Buehler read a paper before the Ohio State Pharm. Association, in which he reported, that the following formula and process for making the above syrup, while not differing much from the U. S. P. formula, has been found to be the most satisfactory of many that have been tried.

Lactic Acid	19 fluid drachms.
Ppt. Phosphate of Calcium	2 oz. avoird.
Gran. Sugar	3½ lbs.
Hydrochloric Acid,	
Aqua Ammonia,	
Water,	
Distilled Water	ââ q. s.
Glycerin	ℨss.

Mix the Calcium Phosphate with 1½ pints of water, in ½ gallon bottle, to which add sufficient Hydrochloric Acid (about 3½ oz.) to dissolve. Transfer to an open crock (2 gallon) and add water q. s. to bring up the volume to about six pints. Add to this an excess of Water of Ammonia (about 8 oz.) to precipitate, stirring with a wood spatula or glass rod. Throw the mixture in a muslin strainer, tied over an open crock; when well drained mix the magma once more with 6 pints water and strain again, then add to the moist magma the Lactic Acid, dissolve and add enough distilled water to bring the volume to 31 fluidounces, add the sugar, dissolve by agitation. When dissolved, add the glycerin.

IMPROVED EXTRACTION APPARATUSES.

The apparatus consists of a flask, F, of about 290 C.c. capacity, into which fits tightly a sound cork C, pierced with two holes. Underneath, and in the centre of the cork C is fixed a small hook H (pin bent round will do very well); to this hook H is suspended, by means of a platinum wire, a small cotton bag, B, which contains the substance to be operated upon. On the top of this flask is a tube, T, about 7 inches long and 1½ inches in diameter; at each end of this tube is fitted a good sound cork, S and P; the cork S is pierced with two holes, similar in size and position to the holes in the cork C. The holes in these two corks are best made by placing the corks together, end to end, and boring through both corks simultaneously. Into the larger of the holes in S is pushed the tube D, about 6½ inches in length and 1½ inches in diameter (internal), and through the small hole in S is pushed the siphon tube V, which is about ⅜ inch internal diameter, and which has been previously bent round in the manner shown; the cork S is now pushed tightly into the end of T; at the top of this tube is fitted another cork P, which is pierced with a hole in the centre; through this hole the tube W passes into the condenser, R.

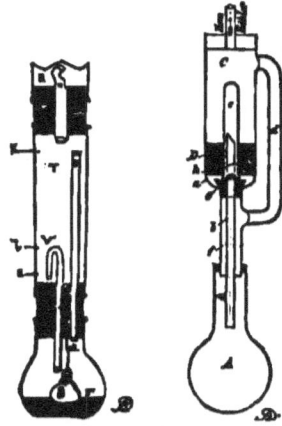

Barlow's apparatus.   Schmidt and Haensch's apparatus.

When operating I take from 3 to 6 Gm. of the substance, place on a piece of good calico, about 5 inches square (which has been previously well cleaned by boiling in a dilute solution of sodium carbonate, afterwards in water, dried and weighed); the substance is tied up in this by means of a platinum wire, and then suspended to the hook H; then about 120 C.c. of ether are placed in F, the cork C pushed in tight, with bag underneath; the bottom of the bag must be at least ½ inch from the bottom of the flask. The tube T is now fixed to the condenser R, by pushing the tube W through the hole in the cork P; then the flask is fitted to T by pushing it on to the tubes V and D, the cork C fitting closely up to the cork S; the tube D must only just pass through C, and the tube V much lower. The whole apparatus is now lowered, so that F is immersed in a large beaker or other suitable vessel of water, kept at the temperature of boiling ether. When the ether boils its vapor rises up through the tube D into the condensing tube W, flows back down W, when condensed, into the tube T, where it accumulates until it gets to the bend of the tube V at b, when it will siphon back into the flask, and so on ad libitum. After about two hours, the beaker of hot water may be removed, and the flask, with corks C and S, and the tubes D and V, taken from the tube T; tube V is removed, and then replaced by a larger one, which reaches up to the point K. The apparatus is again connected, and the distillation carried on till the ether fills the tube T to the point K. The flask is now slipped off C, the bag taken from the hook H, and both flask and bag placed in the air-bath, and dried at a temperature of 230° F., until weight is constant. The weight of the flask and its contents, minus the weight of the flask, gives the weight of the oil extracted. The contents of the bag are ready for operating on to obtain indigestible fibre, mineral matter, etc.

The advantages claimed for this arrangement are: 1st, that the tube T, with its fittings, acts precisely as in a delicately made Soxhlet tube, but is not so liable to fracture, is less costly, and can be easily fitted up out of loose material found in most laboratories; 2d, the substance operated upon is always subject to the action of boiling ether or ether vapor—a point of great importance with some substances—instead of only cold ether, as in other arrangements; 3d, that, by means of using a larger siphon tube, after the old extraction, nearly all the ether can be distilled off and recovered at one operation, and the whole extraction done in much less time than with cold ether, and with very little loss.—JOHN J. BARLOW, Chem. News, Feb. 10th, 1888.

F. SCHMIDT AND HAENSCH, of Berlin, have patented the extraction apparatus here described, which has several advantages.

The extractor proper is a rather wide tube C, ending in a somewhat narrower one, and having a lateral tube for conveying the vapors. At g, a cork is inserted, and through this passes the tube b, the upper end of which is obliquely cut off. Over this end is inverted another tube closed at one end (a test-tube will answer), the rim of which is provided with dents, made by softening it in the flame and indenting it at several places of the circumference. At a finely perforated metallic disk is inserted. Thus is covered by a piece of felt h, and upon this is placed the powder, etc., to be extracted. The tube b must be adjusted at such a height that the lowest point of the obliquely cut-off end is on a level with the surface of the powder.

When the extractor has been fitted into the flask (which is charged with ether, or another volatile liquid), and the condenser attached above, heat is applied, which causes the vapors to rise through d. Being condensed in the cooler, they fall back upon the powder which they penetrate. The saturated liquid gradually rises through the dents of the tube c until it finds an outlet through the tube b.

The advantage of this construction consists in this, that the powder is constantly covered with liquid, which causes a much more speedy exhaustion.

Naphtalin as Insect Destroyer.

H. HAGER has recently put in a plea for the abandonment of arsenic and its compounds as an insect destroyer, and for its replacement by naphtalin, benzin, petroleum, disulphide of carbon and chloroform. The latter liquid (which is not itself inflammable at ordinary temperatures) is capable of materially reducing or altogether neutralizing the inflammability of the 3 liquids previously mentioned.

It is necessary to get the naphtalin into solution. For this purpose, Hager recommends to mix 1 kilo (2 lbs.) of soft soap with 1 liter (1 quart) of boiling water, and to gradually add, under energetic agitation, 30 Gm. (300 grains) of oleic acid. If a sample of this is diluted and shaken with an equal volume of alcohol, and if it then still possesses an alkaline reaction, a little more oleic acid should be added, 10 Gm. (150 grains) being probably amply sufficient. The resulting product might be called "Mitigated Green Soap."

The parasiticide liquids may be prepared, according to Hager, as follows:

1. Liquor Naphtalini Benzinatus.

Naphtalin....................................	40 parts.
Chloroform...................................	60 "
Benzin.......................................	100 "

Mix at a temperature between 18° and 20° C. about 64-68° F.), and shake until solution has been effected.

2. Liquor Naphtalini Sulpho-carbonatus.

Naphtalin....................................	30 parts.
Chloroform...................................	50 "
Disulphide of Carbon..........................	30 "

Prepare like No. 1.

For use in a liquid form, either of these liquids is to be properly diluted, the following being a good formula:

Common Family Soap, dry.......................	35 parts.
Castile Soap, dry.............................	30 "
Water...	900 "
Alcohol (90%).................................	450 "
"Liquor Naphtalini Benzinatus"................	150 "

Dissolve the soaps in the water and alcohol previously mixed, allow the liquid to become cold, and then add the naphtalin solution. Before using the liquid, shake it thoroughly.

If an ointment is required, 85 parts of vaselin and 15 parts of cerosin are melted together and before the mass sets, 200 parts of the liquor naphtalini benzinatus mixed with it.

If either of these is to be used as a parasiticide upon animals, it should be applied with a stiff brush, in quantity only large enough to moisten the skin or to render the hair or fur slightly glossy. Under all circumstances is it preferable to use these compounds at night time, as accidents may occur by approach to or contact with flames.—Abstract fr. Ph. Zeit., 1888, p. 160.

BOTTLE-CAPSULING APPARATUS.

An ingenious contrivance for affixing metal capsules to small bottles is shown in the adjoining illustration. It is the invention of Zugler & Gross, and is said to be managed with ease by boys or girls. The tube T is fastened in a block of wood W, which can be screwed on the wall or door, etc. (about one yard above the floor). Into the opening O of this tube an india-rubber ring R is inserted, being fixed by the flange F. To use this apparatus place the capsule C slightly over the cork of the bottle B, then push the top of the bottle into the centre of the india-rubber ring, turn the bottle once or twice, and the capsule will be nicely fixed on the bottle.—*Br. and Col. Drug.*

Another capsuling apparatus of more elaborate character and costing about $11.00 in England is called the "Simplex." The proprietor, C. Molin, 37 Crutched Friars, London, E. C., specially recommends it for dispensing bottles. "A single pull on the lever brings a cord around the neck of the bottle and affixes the capsule without pleating or creasing it." Its weight is about 40 lbs. and it occupies 18x20 inches of space.

Notes on New Remedies.

Mono-brom-phenyl-acetamide.—This compound ($C_6H_4Br.NH.C_2H_2O$), which was first prepared by Cheyne in England, is supposed to combine the *sedative* effects of sodium bromide and the *antifebrile* effects of phenacetin (phenylacetamine), which two remedies have heretofore been often given in combination with good effect.

Caffeine and Sodium Citrate.—Announced as a true double salt, containing 52.5 per cent of caffeine.

[As in the case of the benzoate and salicylate of sodium and caffeine, it will probably be much preferable to prepare a compound containing just 50 per cent of caffeine, as it will be almost impossible for the physician to remember the varying percentages of caffeine of the so-called true double salts. Ed. Am. Drug.]

Simulo.—A tincture of *simulo,* which is the name of the fruit of a species of *Capparis* (Cornesse) was first prepared by Thomas Christy, of London. Simulo has been reported by White (in *The Lancet*) to be an excellent anti-epileptic, anti hysteric, and nervine tonic, in doses of 4-8 Gm. (ab. 1 to 2 fluidrachms) per day.

Citrobenzoate of Sodium.—A double salt, very soluble in water, used like the benzoates in general, in bronchitis, asthma, etc.

Sodium Sulphite, Benzoated.—This compound, not a true double salt, has been found by Prof. E. Heckel to be a most powerful and non-poisonous surgical antiseptic. It is readily soluble in water, but unstable. Heckel asserts that it is ten times as powerful as iodoform, and fully equal to mercurial salts, over which it possesses the advantage of being non-poisonous.—From *Merck's Bulletin*.

Meconarceine.

This is the name of a preparation, devised by Dr. Laborde, who declares that it contains narceine and a few other alkaloids of opium, but is free from morphine. It has long been known that narceine is a narcotic alkaloid free from the objectionable properties of opium. But its difficult solubility rendered its practical employment almost impossible. Dr. Laborde now claims to have solved the problem, but the announcement smacks much of proprietary rights, or nostrum. The new substance is said to be a definite alkaloidal product from opium, given internally, in pills, in doses of $\frac{1}{12}$ grain, and subcutaneously in solution so that one injection contains about $\frac{1}{12}$ grain.

Caffeine from Damaged Tea.—

At a recent meeting of the London Chamber of Commerce it was alleged that 3,000 to 4,000 lbs. of caffeine were made annually in Germany, mainly from damaged tea which is rejected in British custom houses. Messrs. Thomas Christy & T. P. Moran were appointed a committee to endeavor to receive admission of damaged tea under conditions which would prevent its use as a beverage, but would not interfere with the extraction of the alkaloid.

Keratinised Pills.

Some practical hints regarding the preparation of pills coated with keratin, which are intended to pass the stomach undigested and to be dissolved in the upper part of the intestinal canal, are given by Mr. Kippenberger in the *Pharm. Zeitung* (June 6th) as follows:

It is not sufficient to coat the pills with keratin, since each pill, on passing through the stomach, would absorb a certain amount of moisture through the coating of keratin, and thereby swell up. For this reason, the pills are made with the aid of a fatty excipient, and are afterwards coated with fat of such a nature that not only the coating but also the pill-mass will soften, but not melt at the temperature of the body, the softening process or solution not taking place until after they have passed beyond the stomach. A very good combination for this purpose is either of the following:

	parts.
Suet	10 8
Wax	— —
Cacao Butter	— 2

Zugler & Gross' Capsuling Apparatus.

Care should be taken to avoid the presence in the pills of any substance which easily swells up or is damp. If its constituents are such that they require much stiffening, the best substances to accomplish this are bole, powered charcoal, kaolin, gum arabic or tragacanth. The coating with fat must be done with special care, since each defect in the coating will cause the pill to burst in the stomach during digestion. The fat-coated pills are rolled in powdered graphite, which is, however, not necessary, and is only done to give a better appearance to the pills. Next they receive two successive coatings of keratin solution—either plain aqueous or prepared with acetic acid or with ammonia (see below)—and rolled in a flat capsule until they are dry. They may be given a finer finish by sprinkling them with a little graphite and rolling them for some time cautiously in a metallic box, without, however, shaking them strongly, as this might cause the coating of keratin to become broken.

The keratin solution is best prepared in the following manner. Shavings of horn are deprived of fat (by extraction with benzin, etc.), and are then subjected to artificial digestion with pepsin, hydrochloric acid, and water, in order to remove those bodies which would reduce the keratin coating during digestion in the stomach. The remaining shavings are washed, and then digested in dilute water of ammonia, at a gentle heat, until solution has taken place as far as possible. The liquid is then filtered, and the filtrate evaporated to dryness. The residue is eventually dissolved in glacial acetic acid, in the proportion of 1 in 10, or in a mixture of equal parts of water of ammonia and diluted alcohol.

The ammonia solution of keratin dries more rapidly than the others. Equal parts of the acetic and ammoniacal solution may also be mixed and applied to the pills.

Note on Phosphoric Acid Estimation.

When phosphoric acid is determined or separated, analytically, by means of ammoniacal solution of chloride of ammonium and sulphate (or chloride) of magnesium, the resulting crystalline precipitate of ammonio-magnesium phosphate usually adheres with considerable tenacity to the sides of the beaker and to the glass rod (if one is present). According to Stutzer, this may be avoided by adding to the liquid, before it is stirred, a few shreds of chemically pure, ash-free filtering-paper (Schleicher & Schuell's). Upon these shreds almost all of the crystals are formed. These shreds are prepared by agitating pieces of the filtering-paper in a bottle with water of ammonia, so as to produce a thick magma.—*Chem. Zeit.*

Molin's Capsuling Apparatus.

Drug Adulteration and Alcoholic Nostrums.

Dr. Bennett F. Davenport, one of the analysts of the State of Massachusetts, reports the following results of his examinations of articles collected in the drug trade during the preceding year.

Potassium Bitartrate, 27 samples. Were all of standard quality except two. One of these had about 60 per cent of lime sulphate, and the other nearly as much of acid phosphate of lime and starch.

Potassium Iodide, 15 samples. All but one had an excess of chlorides and of carbonates.

Oils, of the fixed and volatile mentioned in the United States Pharmacopœia, 93 samples. Of these all but 13 were of their proper quality.

Jalap, 18 samples. All but 2 fairly contained the required amount of total resin and of that not soluble in ether.

Powdered samples of the United States Pharmacopœia, spices and other vegetable drugs, 56 in number, were submitted to microscopic examination. Of these 7 were found to contain foreign ingredients; nearly all of them were mustard, and the adulterant flour.

Chloral Hydrate, 16 samples. Were all of good quality.

Pepsin, 6 samples; of which 3 did not have the required amount of digestive activity.

Iron, Saccharated Carbonate, 9 samples. Were all of good quality.

Bismuth Subnitrate, 5 samples. Were all of correct quality.

Glycerin, 7 samples. Were all of fair quality.

Menthol, 4 samples. Were of standard quality.

Alcohol, 6 samples. Were all of proper strength, and agreed as well with the United States Pharmacopœia tests for foreign organic impurities as could be expected from the customary storage of it in barrels.

Whiskey, 4 samples. But one of these agreed with the requirements of the United States Pharmacopœia—that is, was the straight, natural distilled spirit, mellowed only by time. All the others had been submitted to the processes of the mixers, blenders and other so-called improvers, who are miscalled rectifiers, at least in the ordinary meaning of the term.

Brandy, 16 samples. Not one of them was the natural article demanded by the Pharmacopœia, but every one of them had met the misadventure which had befallen the most of the whiskey samples. It does seem that at least enough to supply the legitimate pharmaceutical needs of the country should be obtainable from our own domestic production in California and some of the other States, even if there is no reasonable expectation of obtaining it from abroad.

Wine, 12 samples. The same was true of all but one of these samples as was of the brandy samples. None were the natural article called for by the requirements of the United States Pharmacopœia. They had undergone an even more varied experience than the samples of whiskey and brandy; for, wine being naturally a fluid of a more complex composition than distilled spirits, it allows of a greater range of variation in other respects besides the coloring. It is very unfortunate that the two imported wines in most general medical and pharmaceutical use, port and sherry, are more generally sophisticated than any other sold in our market. The analyses of natural native wines, however, which were made by Prof. Henry B. Parsons, and published in the Report of the United States Department of Agriculture for 1880, show that they at least conform to the requirements of the United States Pharmacopœia, which were in fact based upon them. That the ordinary manufactured wines are likely to prove any more injurious to the health of consumers than would natural wines, has not yet, I think, been fairly demonstrated. Yet to sell them for natural wines is none the less a fraud.

Spirits of Nitrous Ether. Fourteen samples have been examined, and only two of them were found to fairly contain the required percentage of ethyl nitrite. From some of them it was well-nigh totally absent. Probably this was largely due to the improper manner in which the preparation is commonly stored, as was mentioned in my last report.

Compound Spirits of Ether. Thirteen samples have been examined and 8 of them found to fairly contain the required amount of heavy ethereal oil. This is a much larger proportion than was found in any previous year.

Tincture of Nux Vomica. Thirty samples were examined, and only 8 of them were found to have just the proper amount of 2 per cent of extract. They ranged from 0.92 per cent to 5.31 per cent of extract, one thus being over six times as strong as another. There were 15 of them above and 9 below the proper strength. Their average was 2.34 per cent. This is a preparation for which there is no valid excuse for any essential variation from the exact amount, when one considers its method of preparation; for if the very simple directions of the Pharmacopœia are followed, the desired definite result will be secured.

Quinine and its Sulphates. Forty samples were examined, and all were found to be fairly within the Pharmacopoeial requirements of purity.

Citrate of Iron and Quinine. Thirty-eight samples were examined, and all but 3 were found to be fairly up to the standard required for percentage of alkaloid. This is a very great improvement over what has been found in previous years, when about three-fourths of the samples have been found to be deficient in the alkaloid. The general substitution of the unofficinal ammonia form of the preparation, however, continues, as it should not.

Opium in the forms of Gum, Powder and Pill. Twenty-seven samples were examined, and all but 2 were found to fairly contain the Pharmacopœial amount of morphine. In no previous year have many more than half of the samples been found to be up to the standard. Thus there has been a very great improvement in regard to this very important drug. The poorest yield of morphine in any sample of powder has been 11.40 per cent, and the best 14.76 per cent. The poorest gum had 9.80 per cent and the best had 13.80 per cent. The commercial drug as found sold in this State thus seems now to be of very good quality.

Opium as Tincture, simple and deodorized. Forty-two samples were examined, and but 9 were found not to be fairly of the standard quality. In no previous year have quite half of the samples been found to be up to the required standard. The highest percentage of morphine yielded by any sample was 1.59 per cent, and the lowest 0.58 per cent, which was thus only about one-third as much as in the highest, and less than half of the required amount. Their average was 1.24 per cent, the requirement being 1.20 per cent. In my report made in 1883 upon the first general collection of samples made throughout the State, the average was but 0.96 per cent, and 82 per cent of the samples fell below the standard, while some were six times as strong as others, which were only about one-fourth the required strength. Thus in this preparation, which is one of the most important of all those used in medicine, the very great improvement which has been brought about through the influence of our State adulteration law is made very manifest.

Besides the above-mentioned Pharmacopœial drugs and their preparations, I have examined the following list of 50 samples of proprietary preparations, tonics and bitters, with special reference to the relation which the percentage of alcohol which they were found upon assay to contain might bear to the admission of the presence of any claims for the absence of all alcohol, as given upon their labels and wrappers. I have also noted the doses and frequency with which they were recommended to be used, as well as the place of their origin. The alcohol found upon assay is given in per cent by volume. How far the claim of some of them for special usefulness in the reformation of intemperate habits is justified is self-evident.

Tonics.

Dr. Buckland's Scotch Oats Essence, New York City. "Enough alcohol is added to dissolve resins, and prevent fermentation." "Not a temporary and fleeting stimulant, but a permanent tonic. Its use must be regular and continued over a considerable period. An extract of double and triple strength also made. Dose, 10 to 15 drops to a teaspoonful three or four times daily, increased as needed." In the simple essence 35 per cent of alcohol was found on assay. Further examination of this article reveals a still more dangerous ingredient in its composition. The sample analyzed was found to contain one-fourth grain of morphia to the ounce of the so-called "Essence of Oats." A more insidious and dangerous fraud can scarcely be imagined, especially when administered, as this is recommended, for the cure of inebriety or the opium habit.

The "Best" Tonic, Milwaukee, Wisconsin. "A concentrated liquid extract of malt and hops. Neither alcohol nor spirits used in its preparation. Dose, from a wineglassful to a pint bottle full per day." Percentage of alcohol found, 7.85.

Carter's Physical Extract, Georgetown, Mass. Dose, 1 tablespoonful 3 times daily. 22 per cent of alcohol found on assay.

Hooker's Wigwam Tonic, Haverhill, Mass. One tablespoonful 3 times daily. 20.7 per cent of alcohol found on assay.

Hoofland's German Tonic, Philadelphia. Admits Santa Cruz rum. Wineglassful, 4 times daily. 79.3 per cent.

Hop Tonic, Grand Rapids, Mich. One tablespoonful to wineglassful, 3 times a day. 7 per cent.

Howe's Arabian Tonic, New York. "Not a rum drink." Tablespoonful to wineglass, 4 times daily. 13.2 per cent.

Jackson's Golden Seal Tonic, Boston. Admits Marsala wine. Half wineglass, 3 times daily. 19.6 per cent.

Liebig Co.'s Coca Beef Tonic, New York. "With sherry." Two to four teaspoonfuls, 3 times daily. 23.2 per cent.

Menaman's Peptonized Beef Tonic, New York. "Contains spirit." One tablespoonful to 2, 3 times daily. 16.5 per cent.

Barker's Tonic, New York. "A purely vegetable extract." "Stimulus to the body without intoxicating." "Inebriates struggling to reform will find its tonic and sustaining influence on the nervous system a great help to their efforts." Dose as tonic, 1 to 2 teaspoonfuls, 1 to 3 times daily. 41.6 per cent.

Schenck's Sea-weed Tonic, Philadelphia. "Distilled from sea-weed after the same manner as Jamaica spirits is from sugar cane. It is therefore entirely harmless, and free from the injurious properties of corn and rye whiskey." Dose, half wineglass, 3 times daily. 19.3 per cent.

Bitters.

Atwood's Quinine Tonic Bitters, Boston. Dose, half tablespoonful to half wineglass, mixed with water, wine or spirit, 3 times daily. 29.2 per cent.

L. F. Atwood's Jaundice Bitters, Portland, Me. Half tablespoon to wineglass, 1 to 6 times daily 22.3 per cent.

Moses Atwood's Jaundice Bitters, New York. Half tablespoon to wineglass, 1 to 6 times daily. 17.1 per cent.

H. Baxter's Mandrake Bitters, Burlington, Vt. One to 2 tablespoonfuls. 16.5 per cent.

Boker's Stomach Bitters, New York. Dose not given. 42.6 per cent.

Brown's Iron Bitters, Baltimore, Md. "Perfectly harmless." "Not a substitute for whiskey." Tablespoonful. 19.7 per cent.

Burdock Blood Bitters, Buffalo, N. Y. Teaspoonful to tablespoonful, 3 times daily. 25.2 per cent.

Carter's Scotch Bitters, Georgetown, Mass. Tablespoonful to wineglassful, as occasion requires. 17.6 per cent.

Colton's Bitters, Westfield, Mass. Teaspoon to 2 tablespoonfuls, 3 times daily. 27.1 per cent.

Copp's White Mountain Bitters, Manchester, N. H. "Not an alcoholic beverage." Wineglassful. 6 per cent.

Drake's Plantation Bitters, New York. "Contains St. Croix rum." Wineglassful, 3 times daily. 33.2 per cent.

Flint's Quaker's Bitters, Boston. Teaspoonful, 6 times daily. 21.4 per cent.

Goodhue's Bitters, Salem, Mass. Half wineglassful. 16.1 per cent.

Hartshorn's Bitters, Boston. Tablespoon to half wineglassful. 22.2 per cent.

Hoofland's German Bitters, Philadelphia. "Entirely vegetable and free from alcoholic stimulant. Tablespoonful, 4 times daily. 25.6 per cent.

Hop Bitters, Rochester, N. Y. One to 3 tablespoonfuls, 3 times daily. 12 per cent.

Hostetter's Stomach Bitters, Pittsburg, Pa. Wineglassful, 3 times daily. 44.3 per cent.

Kaufman's Sulphur Bitters, Boston. "Contains no alcohol." Tea to tablespoonful. It contains no sulphur, but has 20.5 per cent of alcohol.

Kingsley's Iron Tonic, Northampton, Mass. One to 2 teaspoonfuls, 3 times daily. 14.9 per cent.

Langley's Bitters, Boston. Half wineglass or more, 3 times daily. 16.1 per cent.

Liverpool's Mexican Tonic Bitters, Boston. Half to full wineglassful, 3 times daily. 22.4 per cent.

Oxygenated Bitters, New York. Tea to tablespoonful. Acid but no alcohol.

Pierce's Indian Restoration Bitters, Boston. Up to wineglassful, 4 to 6 times daily. 6.1 per cent.

Z. Porter's Stomach Bitters, New York. Tablespoonful or more several times daily. 27.9 per cent.

Rush's Bitters, New York. Wineglassful, 4 times daily. 35 per cent.

Dr. Richardson's Concentrated Sherry Wine Bitters, Wakefield, Mass. Tablespoonful to half wineglass or more, 3 times daily, "or when there is sensation of weakness or uneasiness at the stomach." 47.5 per cent.

Secor's Cinchona Bitters, Providence, R. I. Half wineglassful, 3 times daily. 13.1 per cent.

Shonyo's German Bitters, Concord, N. H. Tablespoonful. 21.5 per cent.

Job Sweet's Strengthening Bitters, New Bedford. Tablespoonful to wineglassful, 3 times daily. 29 per cent.

Thurston's Old Continental Bitters, Lynn, Mass. Tea to 2 tablespoonfuls. 11.4 per cent.

Walker's Vinegar Bitters, New York. "Free from all alcoholic stimulants. Contains no spirit." Half to full wineglass. 6.1 per cent.

Warner's Safe Tonic Bitters, Rochester, N. Y. Tablespoon to wineglassful. 35.7 per cent.

Warren's Bilious Bitters, Boston. Teaspoon to 2 tablespoonfuls, 1 to 3 times daily. 21.5 per cent.

Wheeler's Tonic Sherry Wine Bitters, Boston. Two-thirds wineglass, 2 times daily. 18.8 per cent.

Wheat Bitters, New York. Dessert to wineglass, 3 times daily. 13.6 per cent.

Faith Whitcomb's Nerve Bitters, Boston. Tablespoonful, 3 times daily. 20.3 per cent.

Dr. William's Vegetable Jaundice Bitters, Lowell, Mass. Half to full wineglass, 1 time daily. 18.8 per cent.

DETERMINATION OF THE MELTING POINT OF FATS.

IN the official methods of analysis of the Association of Official Agricultural Chemists for 1887-88 (U. S. Dept. of Agriculture), the following method of determining the melting point of butter-fat is recommended. This is, of course, equally applicable to other fats:

Apparatus.—The apparatus. Fig. 1, consists of (1) an accurate thermometer for reading easily tenths of a degree; (2) a less accurate thermometer for measuring the temperature of water in the large beaker glass; (3) a tall beaker glass, 35 Cm. high and 10 Cm. in diameter; (4) a test-tube 30 Cm. high and 3.5 Cm. in diameter; (5) a stand for supporting the apparatus; (6) some method of stirring the water in the beaker; for example, a blowing bulb of rubber and a bent glass tube extending to near the bottom of the beaker; (7) a mixture of alcohol and water of the same specific gravity as the fat to be examined.

Apparatus for determining the Melting Point of Fats.

Manipulation.—The disks of the fat are prepared as follows: The melted and filtered fat is allowed to fall from a dropping tube from a height of 15 to 20 Cm. on to a smooth piece of ice floating in water. The disks thus formed are from 1 to 1½ Cm. in diameter, and weigh about 200 milligrams. By pressing the ice under the water, the disks are made to float on the surface, whence they are easily removed with a steel spatula.

The mixture of alcohol and water is prepared by boiling distilled water and 95% alcohol for ten minutes, to remove the gases which they may hold in solution. While still hot, the water is poured into the test-tube already described until it is nearly half full. The test-tube is then filled with hot alcohol. It should be poured in gently down the side of the inclined tube to avoid too much mixing. If the tube is not filled until the water has cooled, the mixture will contain so many air bubbles as to be unfit for use. These bubbles will gather on the disk of fat as the temperature rises, and finally force it to the top of the mixture.

The test-tube containing the alcohol and water is placed in a vessel containing cold water, and the whole cooled to below 10° C. The disk of fat is dropped into the tube from the spatula, and at once sinks until it reaches a part of the tube where the density of the alcohol water is exactly equivalent to its own. Here it remains at rest, and free from the action of any force save that inherent in its own molecules.

The delicate thermometer is placed in the test-tube, and lowered until the bulb is just above the disk. In order to secure an even temperature in all parts of the alcohol mixture in the vicinity of the disk, the thermometer is moved from time to time in a circularly pendulous manner. A tube prepared in this way will be suitable for use for several days, in fact until the air bubbles begin to attach themselves to the disk of fat. In no case did the two liquids become so thoroughly mixed as to lose the property of holding the disk at a fixed point, even when they were kept for several weeks.

In practice, owing to the absorption of air, it has been found necessary to prepare new solutions every third or fourth day.

The disk having been placed in position, the water in the beaker glass is slowly heated, and kept constantly stirred by means of the blowing apparatus already described.

When the temperature of the alcohol water mixture rises to about 5° below the melting point, the disk of fat begins to shrivel, and gradually rolls up into an irregular mass.

The thermometer is now lowered until the fat particle is even with the centre of the bulb. The bulb of the thermometer should be small, so as to indicate only the temperature of the mixture near the fat. A gentle rotary movement should be given to the thermometer bulb, which might be done with a kind of clockwork. The rise of temperature should be so regulated that the last 2° of increment require about ten minutes. The mass of fat gradually approaches the form of a sphere, and when it is sensibly so, the reading of the thermometer is to be made. As soon as the temperature is taken, the test-tube is removed from the bath, and placed again in the cooler. A second tube, containing alcohol and water, is at once placed in the bath. The test-tube (ice-water being used as a cooler) is of low enough temperature to cool the bath sufficiently. After the first determination, which should be only a trial, the temperature of the bath should be so regulated as to reach a maximum about 1.5° above the melting point of the fat under examination.

Working thus with two tubes, about three determinations can be made in an hour.

After the test-tube has been cooled, the globule of fat is removed with a small spoon attached to a wire, before another disk of fat is put in.

Phenacetin.

INDEPENDENT experimental evidence has recently been published with respect to the value of the new antipyretic phenacetin, which on the whole has been in its favor. Mr. Greenfell describes in detail several cases of pyrexia treated with it in the Wandsworth and Clapham Infirmary (*Practitioner*, May, p. 344), and sums up by saying that the results show that phenacetin is an undoubted anti-pyretic. The effect is perceptible half an hour after administration; the patient generally perspires freely and feels drowsy, and after sleep is freer from pain and more comfortable. The most satisfactory dose for an adult was found to be about 8 grains. Mr. Roe (*Brit. Med. Jour.*, May 26th, p. 1,113) states that he has found phenacetin to act admirably in from four to twelve grain doses, and that it has a greater and more prolonged effect upon the temperature than antipyrin, whilst it produces no rigors, vomiting, or nausea. He has heard that it has been used with effect in the treatment of neuralgia. Dr. Koller, of Vienna, also has published his experience with the drug (*Brit. Med. Jour.*, May 26th, p. 1,126) which is fairly in accord with the foregoing. He states, however, that although the fall in temperature is not usually accompanied with perspiration, when this does occur great care is required in exhibiting the drug. In one case of this kind some alarm was caused by the fall of the temperature to 95° F.—*Pharm. Journ.*

Note on Antifebrin and Phenacetin.

THE close resemblance of antifebrin (acetanilide) and phenacetin in some of their physical properties and the difference in their cost suggest the possibility that the higher-priced phenacetin may sometimes undergo admixture with antifebrin, and for such a contingency Mr. Schwas suggests the following means of detection (*Pharm. Zeit.*, June 20th, p. 364): If 1 gramme of phenacetin be heated with 2 C.c. of soda solution, upon the addition of a few drops of chloroform and again heating, the odor given off is aromatic and not disagreeable, but in the presence of a trace of acetanilide the isonitril reaction occurs, and the extremely repulsive but characteristic smell of phenylcarbylamine becomes perceptible. Again, when acetanilide is boiled with caustic soda solution, a separation of oily drops of aniline floating on the surface of the liquid takes place, but no such separation takes place when phenacetin is similarly treated. Lastly, if the liquid resulting from heating acetanilide with caustic soda be shaken with ether, the ether evaporated, a little water added to the residue and then a drop of liquefied carbolic acid and some filtered 10-per-cent solution of chloride of lime, it is colored blue-green; a drop of hydrochloric acid changes this color to an onion-red, but saturation with ammonia restores the original blue-green color (indophenol reaction). Phenacetin similarly treated gives with the chloride of lime solution a cherry red, which is not affected by hydrochloric acid or by ammonia. In commenting subsequently upon this communication (*Pharm. Zeit.*, June 27th, p. 383), Mr. Ritsert recommends the substitution in the first test of a fragment or two of chloral hydrate for the chloroform, as the reaction is more delicate in the presence of nascent chloroform. He also points out the necessity for caution in the employment of this test, on account of the noxious properties of the vapor of phenylcarbylamine.

The occurrence of antifebrin containing unaltered aniline has been reported, so that the following test recommended by Mr. Salzer may prove useful for identifying antifebrin as well as the contamination (*Pharm. Zeit.*, June 20th, p. 364). If pure acetanilide be dissolved in cold hydrochloric acid and covered with solution of chloride of lime, a white precipitate is formed which is redissolved upon shaking the acid, but after a time there is again a separation of beautiful silky, colorless needles. In the presence of aniline, the known color reaction takes place, indicating the formation of magenta.—*Pharm. Journal*, June 30th.

Effects of Bitter Tonics.

DR. REICHMANN, of Warsaw, gives the following results of several experiments on the effects of bitter tonics upon the stomach:

1. There was a great difference in the effect of the different bitter medicines on the stomach.
2. In every stomach which was empty or not digesting, where the gastric juice was normally secreted, or where its secretion was either affected or increased, there was a much less activity of secretion immediately after taking the bitters than after taking distilled water.
3. If the bitter infusion was taken on an empty stomach, the secretory apparatus was excited to an increased activity after the disappearance of this substance from the stomach.
4. When the stomach was digesting (e. g., white of egg) and the bitters were taken, the mechanical activity of the stomach seemed to be injured by the use of the bitters.
5. After taking the bitter infusion for several weeks there was no change in the function of the healthy or diseased stomach, and after the use of the bitters was given up, the function of the stomach did not seem to be changed.

Therefore: The bitter medicines should be prescribed only in those cases in which the secretory activity of the stomach is affected; in those cases the bitter medicines should be taken about *a half an hour before eating.*—*Md. Med. Jour.*

New Use for Codeine.

A NEW use for codeine is proposed by Dr. Lauder Brunton (*Brit. Med. Journ.*), viz., for the relief of pain in abdominal disease. This is probably, as he points out, a new application of an observation by Barbier in 1834, when he came to the conclusion that codeine acts chiefly upon the sympathetic nervous system, and especially upon that part of it which is in the region of the stomach. Dr. Brunton's experience with codeine satisfies him that it has a powerful action in allaying abdominal pain, and it can be pushed to a much greater extent than morphine without causing drowsiness, or interfering with the respiration or with the action of the bowels. It is specially indicated in cases where the heart or lungs are affected, also where it is desired to relieve the pain without interfering with the action of the bowels. On the other hand, in cases where there has been much diarrhœa, as in some cases of malignant disease of the colon or rectum, the absence of any tendency to lessen peristaltic movement is rather a disadvantage to codeine as compared with morphine or opium. In cases of long continued enteralgia without organic disease, it has continued to relieve pain for months together, without the dose being increased beyond 1 grain three times a day, and Dr. Brunton found the same to be the case where the presence of a tumor, in addition to other symptoms, had led to the diagnosis of malignant disease. It is evident, therefore, that codeine is well worthy of further trial in these particular directions.—*Chem. and Drugg.*

Chlorine Water.

(Paper read at the meeting of the Ohio State Pharm. Assoc., by J. Geo. Spenzor, of Cleveland, O.)

QUERY No. 53.—*At what rate does decomposition proceed—Data are wanted as to its keeping qualities under varying conditions.*

The keeping qualities of chlorine water depend principally on the manner of its making and the method of keeping it.

I have seen chlorine water kept in amber cork-stoppered bottles be useless in two or three months, when kept in cool dark places; while if kept in amber glass-stoppered bottles and opened from to time it will be quite strong in six months. If prepared according the U. S. Pharmacopeia it will keep for a year.

I have a few suggestions to offer which may have some merit, *i. e.*: If the distilled water be first boiled to expel air and then cooled out of contact with the same, thoroughly saturating the cold water with chlorine, filling small amber glass-stoppered bottles with the chlorine water, driving out any air with a stream of chlorine and stopping the bottles with stoppers greased with tallow, the water will keep for from one and a half to two years.

Chlorine gas itself can be kept in this manner for two years.

Chlorine water gradually decomposes as air is introduced in dispensing; but if kept in small, well-stoppered bottles as directed in the Pharmacopœia, it can always be had fresh.

Another suggestion which is very serviceable is Winkler's method of furnishing chlorine from chlorinated lime. The chlorinated lime is mixed with plaster of Paris made into a paste with water and formed into balls and dried. These are then used with dilute acid in any of the forms of common generating apparatus. Used in this manner it should displace to a certain extent the old method of heating black oxide of manganese and hydrochloric acid together.

SIEMENS' INVERTED BURNER FOR RAPID EVAPORATION.

WALTER HEMPEL proposes to utilize Siemens' "regenerative burner," on a smaller scale, for the purpose of rapidly evaporating liquids.

In the accompanying cut, A is the "regenerative burner," with flame directed downwards [as supplied by the "Fabrik patentirter Beleuchtungs-apparate," Dresden (Altstadt), Fabrikgasse 5]. C is a glass cylinder resting upon a plate a, which can be adjusted higher or lower, and the outer rim formed by the cylinder and edge of the plate is filled with fine sand. The capsule containing the liquid to be evaporated is placed upon a support b, which may be raised or lowered independent of the plate. The burner being a stationary fixture, screwed fast to some gas delivery pipe, it is necessary to have the other parts of the apparatus movable. When a capsule is to be introduced or removed, the plate with cylinder is lowered by a mechanism not shown in the cut, and when the flame is required to do its work, it is again raised.

The rate of evaporation is regulated either by the size of the flame or by raising or lowering b. Evaporation takes place very rapidly, much more so in proportion than when applying heat from below in the usual manner. As the capsule does not come in contact with the flame, it does not matter what material it consists of. The author reports that he has concentrated solution of fluoride of ammonium in capsules made of wood and paper pulp. The absorption of sulphuric acid from the flame is the smaller the closer the flame is to the liquid to be evaporated, and

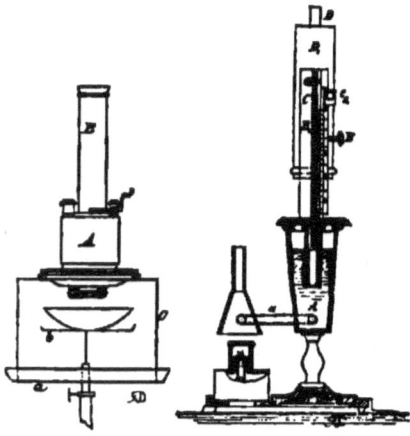

Siemens' Inverted Burner.   Kapeller's Ebullioscope.

none at all is absorbed if the flame is in contact with the liquid.—*Ber. d. D. Chem. Ges.*, 1887, 900.

Since this article has been in type, we have received from the manufacturers a circular in which the apparatus is described with greater detail. Some changes have been made in the form of support, and the admission of gas, but the main parts and the principle remain the same.

These burners are made, for the present, in two sizes, No. 1, consuming about 9 cubic feet per hour, and evaporating about ½ pint of water from a capsule 5 inch. in diameter, costs 80 marks; No. 2, consuming about 14 cubic feet of gas per hour, and evaporating about 14 fluidounces of water from a capsule of 10 inch. in diameter, costs 100 marks, at the factory.

ALCOHOLOMETRY BY MEANS OF THE EBULLIOSCOPE.

II. KAPELLER, of Vienna, has constructed an ebullioscope for determining the percentage of absolute alcohol by volume in any liquid. As the assay of alcohol in complex liquids is usually only possible by distilling off the alcohol, which often requires considerable time, and Kapeller's new method requires only some 15 or 20 minutes, this apparatus will often be found very useful.

The instrument (see cut) consists of a boiler with exterior chamber, and a tightly fitting lid bearing a condenser and a thermometer with an adjustable scale of graduation calculated for directly indicating the percentage of alcohol. Before performing any assay, the zero-point of this scale must each time be exactly adjusted in the following manner. The boiler A being filled, to the upper ring, with water, heat is applied which will cause the water to boil in about 5 minutes, whereupon the mercury in the thermometer will rise to the boiling point of water, which is, of course, liable to vary according to atmospheric pressure. But turning the screw B, the graduated scale is now so adjusted that its zero-point exactly coincides with the level of the mercury, and the scale is fixed in this position by a set-screw. The boiler is now emptied, cooled, rinsed with the alcoholic liquid to be tested, and then filled with this to the upper ring. Heat is now applied, as before. The condenser is supplied with very cold water, so as to prevent the escape of vapors of absolute alcohol, and to maintain a uniform boiling point. As soon as the column of mercury remains at a constant level, the degrees on the scale are read off, and these are so adjusted that they will at once express the percentage by volume, of absolute alcohol, in the liquid.

In the case of highly alcoholic liquids, where the graduation would not reach far enough to indicate the percentage, the boiler is filled with the liquid only to the first ring, and distilled water then added up to the second ring. The result found is then simply doubled to give the real percentage.

APPARATUS FOR DETERMINING SUGAR IN URINE.

FOR the determination of sugar in urine, Fleischer recommends to use flasks (see cut) having a lateral, open, graduated tube arising from near the bottom, and divided into two unequal compartments by a glass diaphragm through the centre of which arises a hollow glass tube. Into the lower compartment (Hg) mercury is poured, which will, of course, rise to the same level, both in the flask itself and in the lateral tube. Into the upper compartment, 10 C.c. of the urine ("Harn"), together with a sufficient quantity of yeast ("Hefe"), are introduced, and the rubber stopper then inserted. Into a second flask a like quantity of mercury is poured, and into its upper compartment 10 C.c. of water, some yeast, and 0.1 Gm. of pure grape-sugar, which may be kept on hand for this purpose, put up in gelatin capsules. Both flasks are then set aside at a moderately warm temperature until the fermentation in both is completed. Having previously noted the exact height of the mercurial columns in the lateral tubes, and knowing by observation how far the mercury has been pushed upward by the compressed air and gas in the flask charged with 0.1 Gm. of grape-sugar, a simple comparison with the other flask and tube will show how much more or less pressure of gas is in the other, and, consequently, how much more or less grape-sugar the urine contained. *Med. Chir. Rundschau; Chem. Centralbl.*

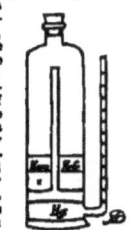

Antiseptics in Phthisis.

THE antiseptic treatment of phthisis appears to be generally recognized now as the rational method of treatment. The medicaments used are numerous, and the ways and means taken by prescribers to get the antiseptic or bactericidus, as most of them are, to act upon the consumption bacillus, are perplexing. The great fault of the therapeutic writers who are devoted to the subject are that they sound the praises of their peculiar methods of treatment before they have sufficiently demonstrated the value thereof on a large number of cases. One, two, or a dozen cures are not enough to prove the infallibility of any method. Phthisis is one of the scourges of this country, and there ought to be no difficulty in getting a hundred, or even a thousand, patients to submit to any course of treatment which fairly promises to be successful. Until that is the case, we must be content with such results as are made public. In the *Provincial Medical Journal*, Mr. F. Taylor Simpson describes a case in which he tried a method of treatment which had occurred to him. The patient was a young man of 22, who presented all the symptoms of early phthisis, "crowds of tubercle bacilli" being found in his sputum. He was ordered to sleep in a large, well-warmed room, the air of which was to be rendered aseptic by steam impregnated with oleum eucalypti and oleum pini sylvestris; to take ol. morrhuæ, ʒij., and syr. hypophosph. co., ʒi., three times a day; to eat as much as possible; and to use the following inhalation every night:

Hydrargyri Chloridi Corros.	gr. ¼
Ammonii Chloridi	gr. ½
Aquæ dest.	℥iv.

One tablespoonful to be added to a tablespoonful of hot distilled water, and thoroughly inhaled, in the form of spray, every night.

The patient began to show improvement in about three weeks, and the spray was gradually increased in strength to ½ grain of the sublimate per ounce. Improvement continued, the crepitations disappearing in two months, and the tubercle bacilli about the same time. At the end of three months, the inhalations were stopped, and the patient put on carefully regulated and nourishing diet, but by this time he had increased in weight by a stone and was quite well.—*Chem. and Drugg.*

To clean Vessels of Sulphide of Lead.

FISCHER gives the process described below, in the *Pharm. Zeit.* It is often extremely difficult to remove a dried residue of lead sulphide from glass or porcelain apparatus, the endeavor frequently ending in fracture of the vessel. Fischer recommends the addition of a small quantity of liquor soda and some hydrogen peroxide solution. The process will clean the oldest concretions off in a short time by the oxidation of sulphide to sulphate by the H_2O_2, and the solution of the sulphate of lead by the caustic soda.

Improvement in the Manufacture of Phosphorus.

A PATENT was recently granted to A. Nicolle, of Paris, for an improved process of making phosphorus.

The mineral phosphate, either natural or artificial, is treated with nitric acid, and then, on the addition of potassium sulphate, the calcium is precipitated as sulphate. This is removed by filtration, and mercurous nitrate in proper quantity is introduced. The phosphate of mercury thus obtained is distilled with carbon, when first mercury and then phosphorus are distilled over. To the calcium nitrate solution more potassium sulphate is added, and the resulting potassium nitrate crystallized.

Emulsion of Cod-Liver Oil with Hypophosphite of Calcium.

MR. W. B. ALLISON, of Hartshill, Stoke-upon-Trent, writes to the *British and Colonial Druggist*: I inclose a formula for a cod-liver oil emulsion which may be useful to some of your readers, as it is one of the best I have ever used for making a good keeping emulsion, and for the idea for which I have to thank your valuable Diary. The formula should prove especially valuable in hospital practice. I would recommend the aid of a Taylor's No. 4 Patent Churn, driven by steam power at about 70 revolutions per minute.

The following is the formula referred to by our correspondent:

Take of

Fine Norwegian non-freezing cod-liver oil ....4 galls.
Powd. Tragacanth................6 oz. 5 drms. 20 gr.
Tinct. of Benzoin or Tolu (2 oz. to Oil)........8 fl. oz.
Spirit of Chloroform............................6 fl. oz.
Glycerin......................................32 fl. oz.
Saccharin....................................240 grs.
Oil of Lemon or Cassia.........................2 fl. oz.
Hypophosphite of Calcium... 26 oz. 5 drms. 20 gr.

Place the Oil in the churn and pour in the Tragacanth powder, Tr. Benzoin, and Sp. Chloroform previously mixed together; agitate briskly until a smooth mixture is formed, then add all at once 2 gallons of Water in which the Hypophosphite of Calcium has been dissolved, and again agitate. Lastly, add the Essential Oil, Glycerin (in which the Saccharin has been dissolved by a very gentle heat), and sufficient Water to make the product measure 8 gallons. This should be churned until a thick, creamy, and perfect emulsion is formed.

Utilisation of Liquid Carbonic Acid as a Preservative.

PROF. REITLECHNER, of the celebrated vinicultural institution Klosterneuburg, reports that the employment of liquid carbonic acid in wine cellars promises to be of the greatest importance. It has been found that red wines saturated with, or otherwise protected by carbonic acid gas, retain their coloring matter much better, and that white wines preserve their peculiar bouquet. The bleaching of red wines is due to the action of the oxygen of the air. In some peculiar wines, the coloring matter does not bleach, but becomes darker. Oxygen also alters or destroys the bouquet. If, however, the wine is saturated with carbonic acid gas, these deteriorations will not occur, nor will there be any ropy deposit or active fermentation produced.

In connection with the above we would say that the manufacture of liquid carbonic acid promises to be a very profitable undertaking in this country. But it must be remembered, that for its transportation very strong metallic vessels (small steel-fountains will be best) are required, which necessitate a considerable outlay at first and which the manufacturer must make arrangements to receive back empty for refilling. Moreover, the contents of a fountain are of so comparatively moderate cost that it would not pay to transport the fountains filled and to reship them beyond a certain distance from the factory. In fact, a number of independent factories would have ample room if scattered over different sections of the country, where the gas can be utilized to advantage in large quantities. Of course, liquid carbonic acid is much more economical for those who use much of it, than gas under pressure such as is used in soda-fountains. And it can even be used in the latter to advantage. For lager-beer, ale and similar liquids which are drawn from casks, it will furnish not only the requisite pressure, to force them out of the faucet, but it will prevent them from spoiling. Fruit-juices, and many other substances, which are liable to change, can be preserved by saturating them with the gas, tightly corking and securely sealing the stopper.

The Production of Indigo in Manchuria.

THE following account of the production of indigo, given by a correspondent of the *Chinese Times*, may be of interest: On leaving Hsi-lung-ch'eng we turned due North along the eastern border of the imperial forest, through a wide valley stretching from the city to Tung-ho, a distance of over 100 miles. This valley is fully cultivated, and well cultivated up to the border of and even encroaching on the forbidden forest. One of the most important products of this as of the other valleys is indigo. Our attention was the more directed to it here on account of the unusually large number of indigo tanks we met with in this valley. Every farmer large or small has got an indigo vat or vats attached to his farm as surely as he has got a threshing-floor. The plant, probably, *Polygonum Chinese*, grows to a height of from two to three feet, and flowers in the month of August. As soon as the flowers appear the plant is cut down, and the work of manufacturing it at once proceeded with. Sometimes the method of manufacture is simple in the extreme, the only thing visible being a round pit dug in the ground. Generally, however, there are four such pits; one is simply a water pond, and is called the *shui y' ao*; two of equal size, parallel to each other, are called *tien ch'ih*; another curved tank is called the *Fung chih*. In addition there is usually a large wooden trough, called the *shui kuei*, placed between the parallel vats. The latter are filled with the stems and flowers of the plant, and covered with water, which is conveyed from the pond by an aqueduct. The indigo remains infusing in the tanks for twelve hours, by which time all the dye is supposed to be extracted, the liquid is then transferred from the vats into the wooden trough, when lime is added and the contents are violently agitated for some time by being beaten with a shovel shaped instrument called the indigo rake. This completed, the decoction is poured into the curved tank, which is faced with mortar. Here it is allowed to settle; the clear water is then drawn off, and the sediment, of a pulpy consistency, carefully removed. In this condition it is put into boxes, sold to the dealers for 130 cash a catty, shipped to Shanghai and other Southern ports, where the manufacture is completed, "and then," they say, "it comes back to us again in small round pieces, which are sold for about four times the original price under the name of Western indigo." Hundreds of thousands of catties are turned out of these primitive manufactories every year.—*Br. and Colon. Druggist*.

Coca grown in India.

C. J. H. WARDEN has published a paper on the cultivation of coca in India, from which the following salient points are taken (after *J. Soc. Chem. Ind.*):

The author has examined some coca leaves grown in India. The dry pulverized leaves moistened with alcohol, acidified with sulphuric acid were then extracted with alcohol, the alcoholic extract mixed with acidified water, exhausted with ether, and finally made alkaline with sodium carbonate and again exhausted with ether. This final extract containing the cocaine, was washed twice with water, dried and weighed, the result being the amount of crude alkaloid. The dry leaves yielded from 0.848 to 1.671 per cent of alkaloid, and from 6.36 to 12.54 per cent of ash.

The "crude alkaloid" was very faintly yellow in color, and was in no instance obtained crystalline, although many experiments were made to get a crystalline alkaloid, both by changing the mode of preparing the leaves and by modifying the mode of extraction by the use of different acids and solvents, and varying temperatures. Even Williams' method of purification (*Pharm. J. Trans.*, 1887) failed to yield crystals. The only instance of crystallisation was the deposition of star-shaped crystals on one occasion from the ethereal solution of the alkaloid obtained from the decomposition of the soluble platino-salt. This extract of Indian coca leaves yields a soluble and insoluble platinosalt, both yielding bases producing a marked anaesthetic effect on the tongue. Howard shows that in the leaves he examined, only the soluble platino-salt yielded a base producing anaesthesia, the insoluble salt giving some other base. The author found from 18.71 to 19.3 per cent of platinum in his soluble platino salt, and 18.69 per cent in his insoluble platino salt; he attributes discrepancies from the theoretical to varying amounts of cocamine in the Indian leaves.

The author observed the largest amount of coca-tannin acid was associated with the largest amount of alkaloid, and suggests that possibly the alkaloid exists in the leaves as coca-tannate. With regard to hygrine, no volatile base has been found in the Indian leaves.

Judging from the available data, which however, are obtained from leaves and plants of various ages, the percentage of alkaloid in Indian leaves is not much affected by either altitude or rainfall. The plants may require both nitrogenous and potash manures. The best mode of preparing the leaves is to dry them as rapidly and thoroughly as possible at the lowest possible temperature, and directly they are cold to pack them in air-tight boxes to avoid absorption of moisture, as the dry leaves are very hygroscopic. The leaves grown in India contain more alkaloid than the South American leaves, and the non-crystalline character of the alkaloid does not appear to detract from its physiological activity.

AN IMPROVED FORM OF LUNGE'S NITROMETER.

LUNGE'S, as well as Allen's, nitrometer has become so well known as the most convenient apparatus for measuring the volume of gas generated by certain reactions (as, for instance, in estimating spirit of nitrous ether, urea, etc.) that we need not give a minute description. Lunge has recently introduced a further improvement, which consists in the employment of the obliquely bored stop-cocks, likewise previously described by us. This form of stop-cock not only permits the alternate connection of different parts of the same apparatus, but it also prevents the gradual formation of leaky passages in the stop-cock itself.

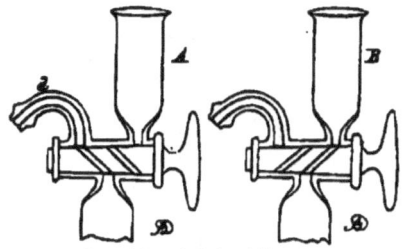

Improved Stop-cocks for Lunge's Nitrometer.

As formerly constructed, the nitrometer had the shape as shown in Fig. 1. In this case, we may suppose that the apparatus is to be used for the estimation of urea, the urine being contained in the little tube f, while the bottle e contains a certain quantity of solution of hypobromite of sodium. On mixing the two solutions, nitrogen is set free, which displaces a corresponding volume of water from the graduated tube, and by reading off of the volume subsequently, after having put the two tubes at such a level that the liquid in both is at the same height, the amount of urea may be known from the volume displaced, each cubic centimeter being equal (theoretically) to 0.0027 Gm. of urea.

As will be seen, the stop-cock is itself perforated. But since it is necessary to shake the little flask a while connected with the apparatus, it happens sometimes that the stop-cock becomes loosened, whereby air is admitted and the whole analysis vitiated. In the new form of apparatus, the stop-cock has two oblique perforations, and the little generating flask is connected with the independent neck d. By giving the stop-cock a half revolution, the two positions shown at A and B are produced, and there is no further risk of a leak.—*After Ber. d. D. Chem. Ges.*, 1888, 376.

The alleged Incompatibility of Potassium Chlorate with the Iodide.

THE generally accepted opinion is, that chlorate of potassium should not be administered at the same time as iodide of potassium, for the reason that on boiling the salts together a poisonous compound—potassium iodate—will be formed. MM. Chuche and Dragros have now come forward to disprove this opinion, and relate the following experiments to support their views: First a mixture of iodide and chlorate dissolved in water was kept in a test tube for two hours at a temperature of from 35° to 37°C. (95° to 99° F.) by means of a water-bath. The test for iodate, namely, acetic acid and chloroform, proved that none had been formed. The second series of experiments consisted in the addition of very weak lactic acid to the same chlorate and iodide solution, to be heated in the water-bath. The idea was to more exactly represent the normal condition of the digestive process. On testing, as before, a light pink color developing in the chloroform showed the presence of minute traces of free iodine. Finally, to ascertain whether the liberated iodine was owing to the formation of an iodate or to the usual effects of acids, the experiment was repeated with iodide of potassium and lactic acid, without chlorate, all the conditions remaining otherwise exactly the same. The result was, on testing, a pink coloration of the chloroform of precisely the same tint and depth as in the preceding experiments. Hence MM. Chuche and Dragros have come to the conclusion that, since no iodate was formed under conditions resembling those of digestion, the chlorate and iodide of potassium are not incompatible. Such a deduction, it is scarcely necessary to say, is rather premature. The experiments quoted only show that in a glass tube, at a temperature below 100° F., will not, as it does at 212° F., turn iodids into iodate of potassium, but they prove nothing as regards the chemical changes in the system, still less do they counterbalance the poisoning cases on record caused by the simultaneous administration of the two salts.—*Chem. and Drugg.*

NEW GAS-GENERATORS.

GREINER and FRIEDRICHS have constructed a new gas-generator. The vessel A serves to receive the acid, and the cylinder B the substance which is to yield the gas (sulphide of iron, marble, zinc, etc., etc.). E is a perforated diaphragm of porcelain, O a hollow glass stopper provided with a lateral tube which is to be connected with the gas delivery tube. D serves for withdrawing the exhausted acid, and V is a safety-valve. Further description of the apparatus is unnecessary.—*Chem. Zeit.*

G. NEUMANN describes an improved gas generator, which is shown in the accompanying illustration. It consists of a double-necked Woulff's bottle A, bearing two globe funnels with long tubes, in its tubulures. One of these (D) is adjusted at a higher level than the other. The tube of E reaches nearly to the bottom of the bottle, while the other reaches only about half-way down. The lower situated globe funnel is provided with a glass stop-cock fitted into its neck, and the other remains open. For use, the globe E is filled with the solid substance, which is to give up gas upon the access of an acid. Next, open the stop-cock E, and pour enough of the exciting liquid (acid, etc.) into the globe D until the flask is filled to the end of the tube B. Now close the stop-cock F, and pour enough liquid in until D is about two-thirds full. When the apparatus is required for use, open the stop-cock, and the column of liquid in D will soon attain its level with that in E. To prevent solid particles from clogging the tube of the globe funnel E, a rubber plate (or other contrivance) is put underneath the solid substance from which the gas is generated.

The application of this apparatus to the preparation of hydrochloric acid gas, ammonia, and nitrogen may be accomplished in the following manner:

1. *Hydrochloric acid gas.*—This is best prepared from carnallite ($K_2MgCl_2.12H_2O$) and concentrated sulphuric acid. The latter acts upon the mineral slowly, hence the current of gas will be feeble; but it is very regular, and, with one pound of carnallite, may last during two or three days.

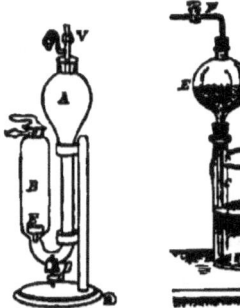
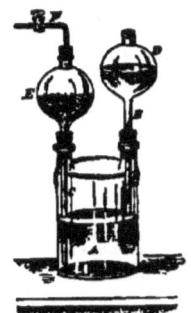

Greiner and Friedrichs' Gas Generator.   Neumann's Gas Generator.

2. *Ammonia.*—On allowing water of ammonia to come in contact with solid caustic potassa, a copious current of ammoniacal gas is given off. Two hundred Gm. of caustic potassa will generate ammonia gas during about ten hours. The residuary liquid may easily be freed, by warming, from any remaining ammonia, and may then be used simply as solution of caustic potassa. If a large quantity of solution of ammonia acts at once upon caustic potassa, the reaction is too energetic. Hence, only a small quantity of ammonia should be admitted at any one time.

3. *Nitrogen.*—This is developed by oxidizing ammonia by means of hypochlorites, such as "chloride of lime." In practice it is advisable to employ the cubically compressed chloride of lime recommended by Winkler, and a mixture of equal parts of water of ammonia and water. As the generated gas is not pure nitrogen, it must be conducted through caustic potassa, and afterwards through concentrated sulphuric acid. Sometimes the gas passes through both of these wash-liquids in an impure condition, being mixed with white vapors of chloride of ammonium, but these disappear completely if the gas is passed through a third wash bottle containing hot water.—*After Journ. f. prakt. Chem.*, 1888, vol. 37, 342.

THE graduating class of '88 in the Massachusetts College of Pharmacy was the largest in the history of the institution, numbering 30.

THE
American Druggist

AN ILLUSTRATED MONTHLY JOURNAL

OF

Pharmacy, Chemistry, and Materia Medica.

VOL. XVII., No. 8.   WHOLE No. 170.

FREDERICK A. CASTLE, M.D. .... EDITOR.
CHARLES RICE, PH.D. .... ASSOCIATE EDITOR.

PUBLISHED BY

WM. WOOD & CO., 56 & 58 Lafayette Place, N. Y.

SUBSCRIPTION PRICE per year, ... $1.50
SINGLE COPIES, ...15

Address all communications relating to the business of the AMERICAN DRUGGIST, such as subscriptions, advertisements, change of Post-Office address, etc., to WILLIAM WOOD & CO., 56 and 58 Lafayette Place, New York City; to whom order all postal money orders and checks should be made payable. Communications intended for the Editor should be addressed in care of the Publishers.

The AMERICAN DRUGGIST is issued in the latter part of each month, dated for the month ahead. Changes of advertisements should reach us before the 10th. New advertisements can occasionally be inserted after the 15th.

REGULAR ADVERTISEMENTS according to size, location, and time. Special rates on application.

EDITORIALS.

IT has long been known that certain organic proximate principles, chiefly alkaloids, are very easily affected by reagents, or by certain operations, such as heat, light, etc., to which they are exposed during the process of extraction. The presence of free alkali, particularly, has been known to be quite injurious to a number of these bodies. Yet the importance of this fact has never been so thoroughly realised as it is now, since we have been put in possession of the result of the investigations of W. Will on the correlation between hyoscyamine and atropine, a full account of which will be found on page 141 of this number. It seems to be demonstrated beyond a doubt that belladonna does not contain any atropine at all, but only hyoscyamine, and that the former alkaloid is a secondary product, resulting from the latter under the influence of alkalies or of heat. Before we had read the author's paper half through, the idea occurred to us—and would naturally have occurred to any other attentive reader—that this modifying influence must play an important part also in the case of other alkaloids, and we found at the end of the author's paper that he proposes to investigate other groups of these principles with a view of clearing up their correlation to each other. Of course, those derived from cinchona bark would first come into one's mind. The list of bases so far obtained from cinchona is very large, and the end seems not yet. It appears quite probable that, by a modification of treatment, the alkaloids extracted from any given lot of bark will be found to consist of entirely different proportions of the several bases than when the usual processes now in vogue are employed. If it were possible to isolate these bases by the agency of a substance which would leave them entirely unchanged, a great advance would be made towards a true understanding of the chemical nature of the mother bases, and of the manner in which the secondary ones are derived from it. We await further developments with great interest.

THE inspection of drugs in Massachusetts during the past year, as reported by the State Board of Health, embraced 550 samples, of which 400 were found to be of good quality, 27.27% being adulterated. The same report states that in the case of foods 35.05%, and of milk alone, 38.33% failed to meet the statutory requirements—a comparison quite favorable to the drug-trade. The effect which the enforcement of such a law has is so clearly shown, that we venture to quote a few passages from the report for the information of our readers generally:

"The examinations of drugs made through the past year shows a greater improvement than that of either of the other classes which come within the provisions of the acts relative to inspection, and this is still more manifest when it is known that the collection of samples has been even more closely limited than before to articles liable to adulteration. So great has been the improvement brought about by the administration of the law with reference to drugs, that, whereas it was difficult to find the stronger preparations of opium conforming to the pharmacopœial standard previous to the enforcement of the act of 1882, at the present time such departures from the standard are the exceptions rather than the rule."

In 1883, in a collection of 100 samples of tincture of opium collected in different parts of the State, there were 82% of the number which fell below the standard requirement of at least 1.70% of morphine. In a similar collection made during the past year, the number of samples falling below the standard was but 21.4%.

"It was predicted that great danger would follow the requirement that such preparations should uniformly conform to the standard laid down in the statutes, and that an alarming fatality would be sure to ensue, especially in view of the fact that the opium preparations are among the most valuable and widely used of the officinal articles. No such result, however, has followed, and the registration reports and the returns of medical examiners give ample proofs of this statement.

"There are certain articles, however, which still show a lamentable deficiency in meeting the requirements of the Pharmacopœia. Of these, the most marked instance is found in the compound spirit of ether, and it may be reasonably inquired whether the limited use of this preparation, once so highly valued, may not be due to the habitual omission of its most essential ingredient, the ethereal oil.

"The same remark is also applicable to the pharmacopœial spirits and wines, four in number, brandy, whiskey, rod and white wines. The two latter are rarely prescribed or called for under these names, and when they are called for it is also quite as rare to obtain a genuine, unadulterated product."

We give elsewhere extracts from Mr. B. F. Davenport's report on the various articles examined, which should direct the attention of druggists in other parts of the country to the wares most likely to be impure or of deficient strength.

WE have lately had our attention directed to the subject of labels, and particularly to some in which, with the pretext of attaching a label serving to identify the nature of the contents, and the precautions to be exercised in its use, the dispenser covers the greater portion of the vial or box with an advertisement of his business, while the essential feature of the label, so far as the purchaser is directly concerned, is of a very subordinate character. Another fault which is not unfrequently characteristic of this variety of label, is the covering of the only available space for directions with *As Directed* written in a bold hand, thus preventing the small amount of space not occupied by printed matter from being used by the doctor or the nurse for adding directions for use, or a title by means of which the contents may be known. Why a dispenser should write "as directed" on a label when the prescription contains no specific directions, we fail to comprehend. Even when the doctor uses the phrase as a sort of flourish at the end of a prescription we cannot see how it helps the nurse or the patient to have these words on the label; for it may be presumed that in any case the medicine will be used "as directed"; if not according to explicit instructions given with the prescription and intended to be copied on the label, then it must be according to either verbal or written instructions, of which the dispenser has no personal knowledge; and it would be much more reasonable to leave the space for directions blank, to enable those who wish to do so to write whatever may be desirable on it.

Our suggestion would be to leave as much blank space on every label as possible, and limit the printed matter to the title and location of the establishment dispensing it, and a sufficient space for the name of the prescriber, date of the dispensing (not the date of prescription), and the number of the prescription. The adjoining scheme will illustrate our idea of a rational label for a two-ounce, oval vial. The arrangement of matter gives the directions the greatest prominence, and the other features will show plainly as the vial is turned edgewise. If the dispenser desires to call attention to any particular features of his business let him use another style of label for the completed package which is devoted to advertising matter, excepting enough space to contain the address of the person who is to receive it, and other directions for the messenger-boy who is to deliver it. This latter label need not be attached with paste, but simply held by the twine which secures the wrapping paper.

```
┌─────────────────────────────────────────┐
│ RICHARD H. ROE,                         │
│  Graduate of the                        │
│  College of Pharmacy of the City of     │
│     New York,            DIRECTIONS:    │
│  2047 Fourth Avenue,   For              │
│     NEW YORK.          Dose ____        │
│                                         │
│                     Prescription No. 188│
│                     Dr.                 │
│                     Date.               │
└─────────────────────────────────────────┘
```

We have sometimes wondered that graduates of colleges of pharmacy, who desire to cultivate a prescription business and encourage respect on the part of the public for the professional side of the business of pharmacy, do not state the fact of their graduation upon their labels in some such way as we have indicated in the above model. It is true that the diploma is often framed and hung over the prescription counter, or in some equally prominent position, but so are the licenses to sell tobacco and alcohol and the advertisements of certain beverages, which especially are made to resemble a diploma in general appearance.

Finally, those who dispense prescriptions in New York State should be provided with an extra label in small type to be attached to containers of prescriptions coming within the provisions of Chapter XXX. of the Laws of 1887—something like the following:

> According to Chapter 635, of the laws of 1887, this prescription cannot be refilled more than once, except on the verbal or written order of a physician.

This will avoid much misunderstanding and trouble for those who have any regard for the law.¹

Another feature deserving of attention is the management of the cork of a vial. It happens frequently that corks are forced into the neck of a vial with such force that they are twisted off in the effort to extract them, and then, in most households, there is a provoking amount of trouble involved in getting out the retained fragment, and finding another cork to take its place. Quite as often as otherwise this grows out of the habit of using a cork so large that it has, practically, to be disintegrated with a cork-squeezer before it can be got into the neck of the vial, and has not enough tenuity, when once in, to hold together when an attempt is made to extract it. It would, therefore, be a good rule for the dispenser to follow, to always take the cork out and reinsert it to assure himself that it can readily be done by the person who is to use the contents of the vial.

THE labors of the Committee on National Formulary of the American Pharmaceutical Association have been brought to a close by the appearance of the printed text. To carry it through the press has been more of a task than those unfamiliar with such work are aware of. Not by way of an excuse for its late appearance, but as a testimony that reasonable care was exercised during the editing, it may be stated here that of each galley, page proof, and revise separate sets were sent directly from the printer's office to twenty members or volunteer assistants of the Committee, who forwarded any corrections to the chairman, the latter combining them and sending a corrected proof to the printer. It might be supposed that when twenty or even ten different persons read one and the same sets of proofs, and the editor is watchful, the result will be a work free from errors.

But, among works of the nature of the Formulary, this has probably never happened, at least at the first issue, except by accident. Indeed, we can recall no instance where it did happen. Hence we are not surprised to see a list of errata, but believe it might have been better to have chosen another heading, as we find only about *four or five* actual corrections of mistakes (chiefly of figures), while the balance is made up of improvements of language or of processes. We advise our readers, before using the book, to note in the text any correction or alteration quoted under "Errata," on page x. of the work.

¹ See text of law on advertising page 44.

We know from experience that the majority of purchasers of new books hardly ever peruse a preface. Of course, there are many books that might just as well be without one, but in the case of the "National Formulary," a careful perusal of the Preface is absolutely necessary to obtain a correct idea of its scope, the general principles followed in its construction, and the best method of its use. Much that we would like to say here is laid down there and explained, and as every reader of this journal will no doubt become the possessor of a copy, if he has not one already, we need not repeat it here.

One matter, however, we would desire to touch upon. It is well known that many previously published collections of formulas have given the latter in such a shape that a very considerable number of preparations had to be carried in stock, of which two, three, and sometimes more were successively required to turn out another which finally formed the constituent of still another preparation. This was a serious drawback, and particular care has been taken by the committee to remove this as far as possible by reducing the stock-preparations to the smallest possible number, and constructing their formulas so that they could be kept for some time in stock without deteriorating.

We have heard remarks made in some quarters that the existence of a "National Formulary," alongside of the Pharmacopœia, is liable to detract from the authority of the latter. There might be some force in this argument, if the former work were merely a "National Formulary," pure and simple. Which it is not. It is the "National Formulary of *Unofficinal Preparations.*" It is self-evident that from the moment when a new edition of the Pharmacopœia adopts a formula for one of the preparations in the "National Formulary," the officinal formula cancels and supersedes the other. The American Pharmaceutical Association puts forward the work merely as a convenient collection of formulæ, most of them already in existence and use, though often made of varying strength, with the recommendation that they be followed, wherever possible, so as to bring about a greater uniformity even in the more ephemeral, unofficial preparations.

As had been already announced in one of the preliminary reports, the Committee did not want to confine itself to what may be called "elegant pharmacy," but it aimed to embody in the work whatever might otherwise be of practical usefulness. Thus it happens that the work will be found to contain a number of chemicals (as Acidum Hypophosphorosum Dilutum, Acidum Metaphosphoricum Dilutum, Bismuthi Oxidum Hydratum, etc., etc.), several dressings (Carbasus carbolata, etc.), 51 fluid extracts, about 32 tinctures, 7 glycerites, 19 mixtures, 41 solutions (liquores), and a variety of other preparations. Under Pepsinum will be found a method of assay which is believed to embody the best features of all methods heretofore proposed, and which has been tested practically. The U. S. Pharm. requires that "1 part of saccharated pepsin, dissolved in 500 parts of water, acidulated with 7.5 parts of hydrochloric acid, should digest at least 50 parts of hard-boiled egg-albumen in five or six hours at a temperature of 38° to 40° C. (100°-104° F.)." When this test was published, our knowledge of pepsin and its assay did not enable us to give anything better. At the present time, however, we are better situated, and while strict adherence to the officinal digestive strength (1 : 50) is demanded of the officinal saccharated pepsin (see "Nat. Form.," No. 281), a better method of assay, specially designated for undiluted pepsin, has been introduced, which method is also applicable to diluted pepsins.

It is too soon to review the work as a whole, as the merits of most of the formulæ can only be ascertained by the experience gained upon trial.

The Publication Committee of the Council of the A. P. A., who awarded the contracts for composition and electrotyping the text, and for printing and binding the book, decided, in order to emphasize the national character of the work, to omit from the title-page any reference to a city as place of publication. We approve of the sentiment, but think it would have been better to follow the title-page of the Proceedings, or, at least, to mention—perhaps in a note on the back of the title-page—the address of the Permanent Secretary of the A. P. A., to whom intending purchasers could apply.

The well-known firm of Dodge & Olcott, manufacturers of, and dealers in essential oils, has recently announced that their laboratory records show a material discrepancy between the specific gravities assigned to certain essential oils by the U. S. Pharmacopœia [and other authorities], and those observed by themselves. In the case of those oils which had previously not been manufactured by themselves, they had to rely upon published standards, but since they have enlarged the number of their own products by distilling many essential oils themselves, which they had formerly procured from other sources, they have found that the existing standards, particularly as regards specific gravities, require more or less modification. This announcement, coming from so reliable a source, is made in the year 1888, more than five years after the appearance of the last U. S. Pharmacopœia. Even if the firm had not distinctly stated that these discrepancies have only lately attracted their attention, it might certainly have been inferred that, if these facts had been known to them or to others four or five years ago, the criticism referring to the figures of specific gravity of essential oils in the Pharmacopœia would have been made immediately or soon after the appearance of this work, as it must have been to the interest of any manufacturer to counteract or prevent any condemnation of his product, on the plea of their not corresponding to the authoritative standard. But this was by no means the case. The firm in question, with a candor, which is both honorable and rare, acknowledges that it had (like all or most others, no doubt) for a long time been relying upon the accuracy of the figures obtained by acknowledged scientific authorities, and accepted also by the U. S. Pharmacopœia, for the specific gravities of certain essential oils, particularly of such as were not manufactured by themselves. It was only after having themselves undertaken the distillation of certain oils, previously purchased from others, that they found the traditional figures unreliable and requiring modification. This is, of course, an important announcement, and will necessitate an exhaustive study of the whole subject at the hands of the next Committee of Revision of the U. S. Pharmacopœia. The necessity of a revision of the specific gravities of essential oils has also occurred to other large houses engaged in the business. The well-known firm of Schimmel & Co., of Leipzig, some time ago, rendered valuable service by publishing, as an appendix to their annual report, a table of specific gravities of essential oils, based upon the experience made in their own laboratories (see our volume for 1887, page 129). To show by a glance the discrepancies between the figures given by Schimmel & Co. and those of the U. S. Ph., we have placed them here side by side, together with those given by the German Pharmacopœia. Only those officinal (U. S. P.) oils are quoted which are contained in Schimmel & Co.'s table. The Germ. Pharm. gives specific gravities only in some cases. (Figures are printed as whole numbers, referring to water as 1000, at 15° C.)

The exact determination of the specific gravities of essential oils is a much more difficult task than is generally supposed. Some recent editorial remarks of the *Paint, Oil, and Drug Reporter*, referring to this very subject, contain an implied charge that the last Committee of Revision of the U. S. Ph. has been negligent in their work, and state that "the eyes of the pharmaceutical public are only just opening to this fact." But if it has taken the largest manufacturers and dealers, handling tons upon tons of these oils, nearly *five* years, after the appearance of the U. S. and German pharmacopœias, to pronounce definitely upon what should be the correct specific gravities, was it to be expected that a Committee of Revision, with a multitude of other work on their hands, and who could have made experiments only on the smallest scale, would have arrived, between the years 1880 and 1882, at essentially other results than authorities who had made special studies on this very subject before them, and whose results were generally accepted as trustworthy? Only during the last few years has it been recognized that the results of large manufacturers show, in quite a number of cases, material differences from those obtained in the chemist's laboratory. These differences may arise from various causes. Either there may be a loss from incomplete condensation of the lightest boiling portion, or from incomplete exhaustion of the odorous material, or from unequal degrees of heat, or—and this is one of the principal causes—from the difference in treatment which the crude oil has subsequently undergone. Most crude essential oils, which are obtained by distillation, are subsequently rectified one or more times, and here the large manufacturer has a decided advantage, as, with his superior apparatus, he encounters a much smaller loss by resinification, etc., than the experimenter on a small scale. It is therefore not to be wondered at that differences should be found between the results obtained in one or the other manner. In establishing the proper figures for specific gravities in essential oils in the next U. S. Ph., it will no longer suffice to rely upon the results of even the best experts, if those are arrived at by working on a small scale, but it will be necessary to take into account the products of the manufacturer, for the pharmacist cannot afford to distil his own essential oils, but has to purchase them in the market. The manufacturer should be relieved from the onus of having to defend his bona fide products against supposed standard figures, which may be correct and true for the conditions under which they were obtained, but which it is impracticable for him to imitate.

To accomplish this purpose it will be necessary that the next Committee of Revisions shall be put, by the manufacturers of essential oils, in possession of all data bearing upon this subject, and that the duly appointed experts of the Committee shall be given every facility to study the products of the manufacture under such conditions that full reliance can be placed upon their results.

Essential Oil of	Spec. Gravities.		
	U. S. Ph.	Schimmel & Co.	Germ. Pharm.
Almond, bitter............	1060–1070	ab. 1060	......
Anise....................	ab. 978–990	983	980–990
Bergamot................	880–890	883	......
Cajuput.................	ab. 920	925	......
Caraway................	ab. 920	......	910+*
Caraway, twice rect......	......	......	......
Cloves..................	ab. 1060	1060–65	1041–60
Cinnamon...............	ab. 1040	1030	1035–55
Coriander...............	ab. 870	887	......
Cubeb..................	ab. 920	915	......
Eucalyptus..............	ab. 900	922	......
Fennel.................	960+	965–975	960+
Juniper.................	ab. 8	......	......
Juniper, twice rect.......	......	858	......
Lemon..................	ab. 850	854	......
Mustard................	1017–1021	1024	1016–22
Orange Peel.............	ab. 860	850	......
Peppermint..............	ab. 900	903	900–910
Santal..................	ab. 945	975	......
Sassafras...............	ab. 1090	1063	......
Valerian................	ab. 980	945	......

* Meaning: not below 910; and so in other cases.

Ylang-ylang in the Philippine Islands.—The distillation of ylang-ylang is extending very rapidly throughout the Island of Luzon, especially in the neighborhood of Manila and in the province of Albay, and the European markets have unfortunately been flooded with oil, much of it of very inferior quality, although a few of the old established distillers maintain their reputation for excellence of product. The exports of ylang-ylang were 764 kilos in 1884, 1,613 kilos in 1885, and 1,487 kilos in 1886.—*Brit. Cons. Rep.*

Correction.

In our last number, page 121, the following correction should be made in Mr. Hinsdale's paper, "A Colorimetric Test for Indicating the Morphine Strength of Laudanum." Line 14 of text read: "Which equals about 5½ grains of the alkaloid."

And on page 132, in Mr. Hinsdale's article: "Glass jet for Washing Precipitates," line 23, read: "The glass jet *g* should be adjusted so that the little hole *d* will be about one-quarter of an inch above the surface of the liquid in the filter." Of course, the adjustment must be made so that the liquid will not rise too high or overflow the funnel, and this idea was in the writer's or editor's mind when the original description of the apparatus was written.

QUERIES & ANSWERS.

Queries for which answers are desired, must be received by the 5th of the month, and must in every case be accompanied by the name and address of the writer, for the information of the editor, but not for publication.

No. 2,201.—**Acetanilide** (J. R. C.).
Regarding the therapeutic effects of acetanilide or antifebrin, a large amount of literature is available. For a condensed account we refer you to this journal for 1887, pages 175, 204, 55, 210. For an exhaustive account you should consult Fischer, "Die neueren Arzneimittel," (3d ed., Berlin, 1888); and particularly Loebisch, "Die neueren Arzneimittel," Wien and Leipzig, 1888. In English literature there is no single work, as yet, which gives as much information on this and other of the newer remedies as the above-mentioned two works.

No. 2,202.—**Acetanilid or Acetanilide?** (E. S.).
The term *acetanilid* was introduced by Gerhardt in 1849, in German chemical nomenclature. It was constructed after the analogy of *chlorid*, *bromid*, etc., which have been rendered in English as *chloride*, *bromide*, etc. So also the German *Oxyd* is in English *oxide*. For the sake of preserving uniformity, and in accordance with the precedents established by leading English text-books of chemistry, we regard the spelling *acetanilide* (in English) as preferable, the syllable -*ide* to be pronounced like the corresponding part of the word *pride*.

No. 2,203.—**Test for Acetanilide** (J. W.).
The tenor of the note received from this correspondent leads us to surmise that the object is, not to prove the purity of any given sample of acetanilide or antifebrin, but to recognise its presence, and to identify it.
As reactions of identity the following will be amply sufficient. This is the method proposed by the Pharmacopœia Committee of the German Pharmaceutical Association:
On boiling 0.1 Gm. of acetanilide, for one minute, with 1 C.c. of hydrochloric acid, a clear solution results which, when mixed with 3 C.c. of water and 1 drop of liquefied carbolic acid, is rendered onion-red by the addition of solution of chloride of lime (1 : 10). On supersaturating the liquid with ammonia, the red tint changes to indigo-blue. Ritsert (in *Pharm. Zeit.*) has pointed out another and more simple color reaction. If acetanilide is boiled with hydrochloric acid, and to the cooled liquid a little solution of chloride of lime is added in such a manner that the latter shall form a layer on the former, a rose-red zone, immediately changing to indigo-blue, will form at the line of contact of the two layers.

No. 2,204.—**Acetone-Chloroform** (Senior).
It seems to us that you have confounded two different things. The acetone-chloroform you speak about in the beginning of your letter is evidently the chloroform made from acetone, now controlled by the patent granted to Roessler and Hasslacher. In this case, the word *acetone* indicates only the source from which the chloroform is made. There is no acetone in the chloroform produced by this process. If there were, the product would be unfit for use.
There is, however, an "acetone-chloroform," discovered in 1881 by Willgerodt. This exists in two modifications, liquid (oily) and solid, which are, however, not chemically identical, but merely isomeric. This body is an addition-product of acetone and chloroform, containing both bodies, boiling at 160° C., of an oily character, and colorless when fresh. Exposure to light darkens it. This body is poisonous. Whether chloroform made from acetone is ever liable to contain traces of this substance is doubtful. The acetone-chloroform (last mentioned) is prepared by heating 500 parts of acetone with 1,000 parts (an excess) of chloroform, and 300 to 350 parts of potassa in a flask during two and one-half days, under a well cooled condenser. The mass is filtered, and the filtrate fractionated.

No. 2,205.—**Koumys** (B. J. W.).
The new National Formulary gives a working formula for this preparation under No. 193. "Lac Fermentatum," as follows:

Cow's Milk, fresh	33 fl. oz.
Yeast, semi-liquid	60 min.
Sugar	1 tr. oz.

Dissolve the Sugar in the Milk, contained in a strong bottle, add the Yeast, cork the bottle securely, and keep it at a temperature between 23° and 32° C. (75° to 90° F.) for six hours; then transfer it to a cold place.
We have published other formulæ before, and will append yet another, recommended by Dr. E. C. Anderson, of Walsingham, in a paper read before the last meeting of the British Medical Association:
Steam any desired quantity of sweet "old or skimmed," milk until a fairly tough pellicle forms upon the surface; then set it aside for twelve hours, and take off the pellicle and every particle floating upon the surface. Next add of water one-fourth of the volume of the milk, and for each quart of mixture add 20 grains of sodium bicarbonate and 1½ oz. of fine white sugar or "pure clover honey" († ED. AM. DR.). Then add the ferment, namely, about a quarter of fairly new koumys. Bottle at once in champagne bottles, and securely cork and wire them. Submit them to a uniform temperature of about 80° F. for twelve to twenty-four hours. A drop or two of koumys exuding through the cork shows that the process is complete. The bottles may be shaken and put away in a cool place. It has now a slightly acid taste, and is fit for immediate use, but it will keep good for an indefinite period, except that it daily becomes more acid.

No 2,206.—**Syrup of Oxide of Iron** (Aus).
Oxide of iron, as such, is insoluble in water or other solvents. In the presence of sugar, however, and of an alkali, it is abundantly soluble, the resulting compound being a chemical combination of undetermined composition. A preparation of this kind is officinal in several pharmacopœias of Europe. The new National Formulary published by the American Pharmaceutical Association gives a formula for *Syrupus Ferri Saccharati Solubilis* under No. 368 (p. 130). This furnishes an excellent product. Care should be taken to make the correction indicated on page x, of the Formulary. This preparation is called in the Germ. Pharm. *Syrupus Ferri Oxydati Solubilis*, and it is often called, for short, syrup of oxide of iron.

No. 2,207.—**Pyroxylin** (J. K. L. Co.).
This substance, a peculiar kind of gun-cotton made from wood cellulose, was recommended last year by Prof. Wahl, of St. Petersburg, as a superior base for collodion for surgical purposes, as it formed a much tougher and stronger coating than any other. It has been used in photography under the name of Manu's gun cotton, according to information furnished to us by Dr. F. Ch. Elmer, of the Scovill Manufacturing Co., of New York. Fuller information on this subject will be found in our volume for 1887, pages 174, 198, 217.

No. 2,208.—**Standard Strength of Tincture of Strophanthus** (Several Inquirers).
Our attention has been called to the fact that several manufacturers of pharmaceutical preparations specify in their catalogues "Tincture of Strophanthus, 1 in 20," without stating whether this is meant by measure or by weight. And further, one manufacturer announces that he uses the proportions of 1 in 20 *by weight*, while others use the same proportions by weight and measure. We are asked to state which is correct.
In the case of so powerful a drug as strophanthus, uniformity in strength is very important. The authority who introduced the drug into medicine, Prof. T. H. Fraser, of Edinburgh, originated a formula for the tincture which was universally followed, and when it was subsequently modified, upon the basis of extended experience, both therapeutically and pharmaceutically, the new, modified formula was likewise generally followed. This latter formula was published by us in our volume for 1887, on page 6.
It will be found there that 1 oz., or 1 part of the seeds, freed of their comose appendage, reduced to powder and dried, is to be made into 1 pint (Brit. meas.), or 20 fluid parts of tincture.
Now, 1 Imperial pint is equivalent to 19.2 U. S. fluidounces. On calculating the volume which a tincture, made in the same proportions, but starting with 1 troy ounce of the seeds, should occupy, this will be found to be 20.2 U. S. fluidounces, or practically 20 fluidounces.
The "Unofficinal Formulary" of the British Pharmaceutical Conference contains a formula for the preparation, fixing the strength as 1 avoirdupois ounce of the seeds represented by 1 Imperial pint of tincture. The new National Formulary of the American Pharmaceutical Association has a similar formula, the strength of the preparation being 1 troy ounce of the seeds represented by 20 fluidounces (U. S.) of tincture.
It will, therefore, be seen that these two tinctures are practically identical. The British formulary has been published and in use for some time, and is probably accepted as a guide in England by all who have occasion to make or use any of its preparations. We are not aware that any one has criticised the formula as establishing a standard differing from that recommended by Prof. Fraser.
But if any one were to make the tincture *weight* for *weight*, that is, if he were to make from. say 1 troy ounce of seeds, 20 troy ounces of tincture, the resulting preparation would be very much different. Assuming that officinal alcohol has been used for extracting the seeds, and that the specific gravity of the tincture is 0.830, then 20 troy ounces of this would measure about 25.4 fluidounces. Such a tincture would, therefore, be about 25 per cent weaker.
If such a strength has been adopted by any manufacturer, it is probably due to a misconception of the term "fluid part," which is an unfortunate innovation of the last British Pharmacopœia, and has often led to error. Under " fluid part " is meant " the volume of an equal num-

ber of parts (by weight) of water." Hence, "20 fluid parts," in the above formula, is exactly equivalent to "20 Imperial fluidounces," because each Imperial fluidounce is equivalent to 437.5 grains, or 1 avoirdupois ounce of water.

No. 2,209.—Colored Sealing Wax (Milwaukee).
The following may answer your purpose, for capping bottles:

1. White:

Bleached Shellac	840 parts.
Venice Turpentine	160 "
Plaster of Paris	100 "
Magnesia	15 "
Subnitrate of Bismuth	150 "
Carbonate of Lead	335 "

Melt the Turpentine in a capacious copper kettle over a charcoal fire, and gradually add the Shellac. When a uniform melted mass has resulted, gradually add the solid ingredients, which must be in form of finest (bolted) powder, under constant stirring. Then remove the kettle, keep stirring until the mass cools short of solidifying, and pour it out into forms.

2. Yellow.

Shellac	790 parts.
Venice Turpentine	220 "
Rosin	160 "
Plaster of Paris	50 "
Magnesia	10 "
Chrome yellow	80 "

Proceed as directed under 1.

3. Green.

Shellac	500 parts.
Venice Turpentine	250 "
Rosin	150 "
Magnesia	70 "
King's Yellow (Yellow Litharge)	60 "
Mountain (Sander's) Blue	50 "
Oil of Turpentine	20 "

Proceed as before, except that the coloring matters are best triturated to a fine paste with the Oil of Turpentine, and this paste added to the melted mass in small quantities at a time. Mountain Blue is a copper color.

No. 2,210.—Friedrichshall Bitterwater (Akron).
According to Raspe, artificial Friedrichshall Bitterwater may be prepared by dissolving in 10,000 parts of water the following quantities of salts calculated as dry, expressed in parts and fractions of parts:

Sodium Bromide	1.278
Potassium Chloride	1.696
Sodium Chloride	114.999
Calcium Chloride	11.145
Sodium Sulphate	7.543
Magnesium Sulphate	109.470
Sodium Bicarbonate	9.502

The total quantity of solids contained in 10 liters will then be about the same as that contained in the natural water itself.
Dieterich gives a simplified formula in the *Pharm. Centralh.*:

Potassium Sulphate	1.0
Sodium Chloride, dry	40.0
Sodium Chloride	115.0
Sodium Bicarbonate	10.0
Sodium Bromide	1.4
Calcium Sulphate, precip.	16.5
Magnesium Sulphate, dry	133.0

Mix the salts intimately, and preserve the mixture in a well-closed bottle. The above quantity is sufficient to make 10 liters (say 10½ quarts) of artificial mineral water. But it is best to keep the salt in form of mixture. When a dose of the water is wanted, take a *tablespoonful* of the salt, introduce it into an 8 ounce bottle, fill up half full of water, shake until the salt is dissolved, then fill up the bottle with carbonic acid water, and cork immediately, or take it at once, if required.

No. 2,211.—Sachet Powders (D. & Co.).
We append a few formulæ from our files (after Hall):

1. Orris Sachet Powder.

Orris Root, coarsely powd.	2 lbs.
Musk	24 grains.
Eau de Brotfeld (see below)	1 fl. oz.
Benzoin, powd.	90 grains.
Deodorized Alcohol	2½ fl. oz.
Oil of Bergamot.	
" Lemon	680 minims.
" Cloves	1 fl. oz.
" Lavender	
" Cinnamon, Ceylon	26 drops.
" Rose	40 minims.

Macerate the Benzoin with the Deodorized Alcohol for about one week and filter. Free the powder from fine dust, then mix the liquids and incorporate them with the powders.
Eau de Brotfeld is prepared by macerating 30 drops of oil of neroli, 15 of oil of rose, 50 minims of oil of lavender, 110 of oil of cloves, 330 minims, each, of oil of bergamot and lemon, 4 grains of musk, 75 grains of vanilla (or two grains of vanillin) with 1 quart of deodorized alcohol during a few weeks.

2. Heliotrope Sachet Powder.

Orris Root, coarsely powdered	1 lb. 7 oz.
Lavender Flowers, crushed	34 oz.
Rose Leaves, crushed	3½ "
Tonka Beans, crushed	2 "
Vanilla, crushed	2 "
Musk	45 grains.
Oil of Bitter Almond	20 drops.
Oil of Rose	90 "

3. Sachet aux Millefleurs.

Orris Root, coarsely powdered	1 lb.
Benzoin, coarsely powdered	3½ oz.
Lavender Flowers, coarsely powdered	3½ "
Rose Leaves, coarsely powdered	5 "
Tonka Beans, coarsely powdered	2 "
Melissa Leaves, coarsely powdered	1 "
Vanilla, coarsely powdered	2 "
Cinnamon, coarsely powdered	1 "
Storax	1 "
Musk	20 grains.
Civet	15 "
Patchouli Essence	100 min.

Patchouli Essence may be made by dissolving 16 grains of oil of rose and 144 grains of oil of patchouli in 1 quart of deodorized alcohol.

No. 2,212.—Linne's Botanical Works (Camden).
The best and most compact work, embodying the whole Linnean system of botany, with detailed references to the original works of Linné, is the following: Caroli Linnæi Systema, Genera, Species Plantarum, Uno Volumine, etc. Ed. Herm. Eberh. Richter. 4to, Leipzig, 1840,pp. xxxii., 1,102. With an index volume of 202 pp.

No. 2,213.—Physician's License in Washington Territory (A. W. S., Pomeroy, O.).
Can any of our readers inform this correspondent whether a diploma is necessary for practising medicine in Washington Territory?

No. 2,214.—Formulæ asked for.
We do not know the composition of the following preparations. Perhaps some of our readers can supply the information.

1. Lithiated Hydrangea.
2. Ruane's Magic Oil.
3. Sandford's Liver Invigorator.
4. St. Antonius Liniment.
5. Epidermaline and Dermaline.
6. Denton's Balsam.

BIBLIOGRAPHY.

THE PHYSICIAN'S BEDSIDE RECORD, for the Systematic Recording of Clinical Notes and their Permanent Filing for Future Reference. Copyright, 1888, by GIDEON C. SEDUE, M.D. Hartford, Conn.: Plympton Manuf'g Co.

This is by all odds the best thing of the kind we have yet seen. It is 3½x6½ in. in size, has a manilla paper cover and an abundance of space for all the necessary notes of a case lasting through four weeks, and costs 50 cents per doz.

NINETEENTH ANNUAL REPORT OF THE STATE BOARD OF HEALTH OF MASSACHUSETTS. Boston: 1888, pp. 375, 8vo.

WE give elsewhere numerous extracts from this model report and commend them to the careful attention of our readers.

THE THREE ETHICAL CODES, ETC., ETC.
This is issued by the Illustrated Medical Journal Co. of Detroit, and costs 50 cents. It contains the Constitution and By-Laws of the American Medical Association, and the Ethical Codes of this Association, the American Institute of Homœopathy and the National Eclectic Medical Society. It does not contain the ethical code of the Medical Society of the State of New York and is, therefore, of much less general value.

THE NATIONAL FORMULARY OF UNOFFICINAL PREPARATIONS. First Issue. By authority of the American Pharmaceutical Association—Published by the Amer. Pharm. Association. 1888.

An editorial notice of this work will be found elsewhere in this number. Further notice will appear hereafter, as opportunity offers. Intending purchasers may obtain the work either through the book-trade, or through the authorized agents of the A. P. A., or from Prof. J. M. Maisch, Permanent Secretary of the A. P. A., at Philadelphia, Pa.

American Druggist

Vol. XVII. No. 9.   NEW YORK, SEPTEMBER, 1888.   Whole No. 171.

ESTIMATION OF TANNIN IN TEAS, NUTGALLS, AND OTHER VEGETABLE SUBSTANCES.*

BY S. J. HINSDALE, OF FAYETTEVILLE, N. C.

Dissolve one grain of Potassic Ferricyanide in *sixteen fluidounces* of water, and add to it *twenty drops* of Liquor Ferri Chloridi.

Dissolve one grain of Tannin (gallo-tannic acid), dried at 212° F., in *thirty-two fluidounces* of water.

Exhaust with boiling water *ten grains* of powdered Tea, and make the infusion up to *sixteen fluidounces* with water.

Place eight wine-glasses on a white surface, in each of which place about 100 minims of the above iron solution.

With a pipette place in one of the glasses *five drops* of the filtered infusion of tea, and in the other glasses, with the same pipette, after washing, place 10, 11, 12, 13, 14, 15 and 16 drops of the solution of tannin and observe the shades of color. After about one minute fill the glasses with water.

The number of drops of the solution of tannin used in the glass which corresponds in *shade of color* with the glass containing the tea, indicates the percentage of tannin in the tea; thus, if 16 drops are used, the tea contains 16 per cent of tannin.

The tannin strength of galls can be estimated in the same way, making the infusion *ten grains* to the *pint* and taking *one* drop instead of *five* (as in the tea).

Each drop of the tannin solution used in *this* experiment will indicate *five per cent.* Thus, if 14 drops are used, the galls contain 70 per cent of tannin. As galls seldom contain less than 40 per cent of tannin, place 8, 9, 10, 11, 12, 13 and 14 drops of the solution of tannin in the glasses.

In estimating the strength of barks and substances containing less than 10 per cent of tannin, proceed in the same way as for tea, adding to the glass containing the infusion, drops enough of the tannin solution to make the shade of color correspond with that produced by ten drops of the tannin solution, and estimate accordingly.

The iron and tannin solution and the infusions must be freshly prepared.

NOTES ON THE NATIONAL FORMULARY.

We shall, from time to time, publish such criticisms and suggestions for improvement of this work as come to our knowledge and are deemed of sufficient practical value to be put on record.

114. *Emulsio Olei Morrhuæ.* Emulsion of Cod-Liver Oil. Some of the reviewers very naturally ask the question why the "Stronger Emulsion of Cod-Liver Oil," which had been provided for by the New York and Brooklyn Formulary, was not introduced in the present work.

This matter was thoroughly discussed, and the arguments pro and con carefully considered. While on the one hand it is conceded that the keeping in stock of a strong emulsion, made in bulk, would be a great convenience for dispensing, yet the difficulty in keeping this for any length of time, and the consideration that a very large number of pharmacists would probably find it the reverse of economical to make any considerable quantity ahead, induced the committee to abandon the stock emulsion. Perhaps it might have been well to give a formula, in a foot note, so that those who desire to use it, and who have a chance of disposing of it before it can spoil, might refer to it. Yet the absence of this can do no harm, since any intelligent pharmacist will be able to devise a modification of the formula for this special purpose himself.

The *Druggists' Circular* makes the point that it would have been preferable to specify a definite and uniform flavoring in each formula of emulsions, rather than to leave the choice entirely free between seven different combinations. Of course, the meaning is that, while one special flavoring should be ordered in the formulæ, a list of other flavorings be given in a note. We believe this to be a good point and worthy of adoption in a future edition.

166. *Extractum Rhei Fluidum Aromaticum.* Aromatic Fluid Extract of Rhubarb.

In the note it should read: "If ½ fluidounce [instead of 1 fluidounce] of this preparation is mixed with 15½ fluidounces of syrup, the product will be practically identical with the official *Syrupus Rhei Aromaticus.*"

228. *Liquor Phosphori.* Solution of Phosphorus. Thompson's Solution of Phosphorus.

The *Chemist and Druggist* criticises the formula given for this preparation, as it is certain that the product cannot by any possibility retain 1/50 grain of free phosphorus in a fluidrachm. The committee, having at least four different formulæ supplied to them by members and contributors, had recourse to Thompson's original work "On Free Phosphorus," and adopted his own formula, believing that, although it is not likely to contain the full amount of free phosphorus claimed for it, it yet had been long in use, and the therapeutic effects recorded have been obtained by its use in medical literature were probably all, or at least largely, based upon a preparation made after Thompson's original directions. The *Chem. and Drugg.* points out that Mr. Williams had found glycerin to be an admirable substitute for alcohol as a solvent for phosphorus. In the proceedings of the Brit. Pharm. Conf. for 1874 (p. 588) will be found a paper by Mr. J. Williams in which he shows that a mixture of equal parts of absolute alcohol and glycerin dissolves phosphorus readily. The strength of the solution to be made, according to Mr. Williams, is between 1/50 and 1/70 grain per fluidounce. Warm glycerin alone, without alcohol, is also a good solvent of phosphorus, and the solution remains clear when it is diluted with alcohol.

225. *Liquor Morphinæ Hypodermicus.* Hypodermic Solution of Morphine. Magendie's Solution of Morphine.

The *Chemist and Druggist,* in its first notice of the "National Formulary," criticised this preparation on account of its title, claiming that the term "Magendie's Solution of Morphine" should rather be used as a synonym of No. 224, viz., "Liquor Morphinæ Citratis." In a subsequent number of the journal, however, the editor modifies his statement, in consequence of having received an interpellation from Mr. Martindale. From the editorial alluded to we quote the following:

The original formula of Magendie's solution of morphine appeared in 'Magendie's Formulary for the Preparation and Employment of Several New Remedies,'* of which at least eight editions were published, besides several English translations. The solution of citrate of morphine devised by Magendie was intended to replace a preparation with the same name introduced by Dr. Porter, of Bristol, U. S. A., which was made by treating 4 oz. of opium and 2 oz. of citric acid with a pint of boiling water, macerating twenty-four hours, and filtering. Magendie explains that Dr. Porter had formed the term *citrate of morphine* because he supposed that the preparation was composed entirely of citric acid combined with 'the alkali of opium,' and he points out that the preparation would contain 'morphine, narcotine, and all other crystallizable products recently discovered.' He then goes on to demonstrate the advantages of using pure morphine, and adds: 'The American physicians have used Porter's preparation with advantage . . . they regard his solution of citrate of morphine as more active than opium.' He then gives a formula for the solution of 'citrate of morphine.' But he also gives one for a solution of acetate of morphine, namely:

Acetate of Morphine	16 grains
Distilled Water	1 ounce
Acetic Acid	3 or 4 drops
Alcohol	1 gros [1 fl. drachm]

In France, Magendie's solution is at present prepared by dissolving 0.8 Gm. (12) grains of acetate of morphine in 30 Gm. (nb. 1 fl. oz.) of water. This is, therefore, much weaker than what is known in the United States as Magendie's solution. Martindale, in his Extra-Pharmacopœia, says that 'Magendie's solution in France is slightly stronger than that of the United States; it contains 1 part of acetate of morphine in 37½.' This is a mistake; the author should have said "somewhat weaker."

It is, however, to be noticed that the name of Magendie's solution has gradually come to be applied rather to a solution of a morphine salt of a particular *strength* than to the solution of any particular *salt* of morphine. In fact, solutions of acetate and of sulphate of morphine are indifferently known as Magendie's, provided they are of the established strength.

The editor of the *Chem. and Drugg.* acknowledges that there can be no doubt that in the United States Magendie's solution of morphine is understood to be made with the sulphate. He also states that in Europe it depends entirely upon the custom prevailing in different countries as to which morphine salt is to be used.

There can be no doubt that the selection of the sulphate would under all circumstances be preferable to the acetate or citrate, as the sulphate is an absolutely well-defined and stable salt, not requiring the addition of any acid to make a clear solution, nor liable to change by keeping. Perhaps a still better salt, considering therapeutics as well as pharmacy, would be the hydrobromide. But there is no use deviating from a long established custom.

---

* Formulaire pour la préparation et l'emploie de plusieurs nouveaux médicaments, etc. 10me. Paris, 1836 (last edition). English translation of 1st edition by Ch. T. Haden (London, 1825). Of 8th ed. by Hockly Dunglison, London, 1824. Of 9th ed. by Jos. Houlton (London, 1880), etc., etc.—ED. AM. DRUGG.

* Read at the meeting of N. C. Pharmaceutical Association, at Goldsboro, Aug. 9th, 1888.

236. Liquor Sodii Boratis Compositus. Compound Solution of Borate of Sodium. Dobell's Solution.

The *Pharm. Journ. and Trans.* remarks in reference to this formula that the solution, by the evolution of carbonic acid, will often burst the bottles containing it. This is quite true, and a cautionary remark ought to have been added, to allow the reaction to proceed before stoppering the bottle.

278. Pancreatinum. Pancreatin.

Our attention has been called to an apparent contradiction in the notes to No. 278 and No. 318. In the former, a test is given for controlling the strength of pancreatin, and subsequently the following remark is made: "Peptonized milk, as prepared by the above process, or when the process is allowed to go on to the development of a very distinct bitter flavor, should not have an odor at all suggestive of rancidity. Milk has simply a marked bitter taste when thoroughly peptonised." And in No. 318, where a process is given for making peptonized milk fit for use, the remark is made: "Milk thus peptonized should not be used when it has been kept over twenty-four hours, or when it has developed a bitter taste."

In the note to No. 278, a test is given to ascertain the digestive or peptonising value of pancreatin. There are many kinds of pancreatin, of varying strength, on the market. Some of them, though perhaps not the weakest, cause the development of a very decided and disagreeable rancid flavor in milk when the process of peptonization has been carried to a point when the milk has acquired a bitter taste. That is, when the milk is, for this very reason, unfit to be given as a food. The object here is only to ascertain whether the pancreatin is free from the objectionable, no doubt fatty, impurities which cause the production of the rancid flavor. In fact, the latter is only fully developed when the peptonising process has gone beyond the limit at which the milk could be given as food.

In No. 318, it is already supposed that a pancreatin answering the requirements of No. 278 is at hand. Then a process is given to use it for peptonising milk, which directions, if carefully followed, will result only in a *partial* peptonisation, thereby avoiding the production of a bitter taste, which would render it unfit for use. And special directions are added that milk, peptonized according to the directions, should not be used when it has been kept over twenty-four hours, nor when it has been over-peptonised, that is, developed a bitter taste.

Incidentally, it may be remarked that the improvement of the process for preparing pancreatin, given in the list of errata, is quite important and should not be overlooked. It was brought to the notice of the committee after the text of page 318 had already been printed. The product obtained by the process must be freed from the last traces of *fat*, the presence of which not only interferes with its peptonizing power, but is also probably the cause of the rancidity developed in completely peptonized milk. The *Pharm. Journal*, in copying the process for No. 318, overlooked the correction.

308. Pulvis Aloes et Canellæ. Powder of Aloes and Canella. Hiera Picra.

Dr. Frederick Hoffmann, in the *Pharm. Rundschau*, states, although this compound powder bears the traditional name of Hiera Picra in this country, yet that this term has been in use for more than a century to designate a popular compound used for preparing an Elixir Vitæ ["Bitters"]. He gives a formula under the title *Species Hiera Picra*, Syn. *Species pro Elixirio ad longum vitam*, as follows:

Aloes, 8 oz.; Myrrh, 1 oz.; Benzoin 1 oz.; Rhubarb, Agaric, Ginger, Zedoary, each, 1 oz., Saffron, ½ oz.; Theriac, 1 oz.

We would here point out that the term Hiera Picra has been used by the old Greek physicians and mediæval writers to denote various bitter compounds, generally containing colocynth or aloes as a base, with addition of aromatics. Thus Galen (*De Comp. Medic. sec. locos*, lb. VIII.) mentions a hiera containing aloes 100 parts, and cinnamon, nardus, xylobalsamum, mastic, asarum, and saffron, each 5 parts. He advises the reduction of the aloes to 90 or 80 parts. Mesue describes 6, Haly Abbas 5, Myrepsus not less than 30 different kinds. Three preparations then found their way into regular pharmacopœias, for instance, the Pharm. Augustana and many others subsequently. Gradually the formula was simplified, and that which is now known in England and the United States under this name is based upon the London Pharmacopœia of 1746.

353. Syrupus Coffeæ. Syrup of Coffee.

When the proofs and last revises were read, the title of this preparation was "Syrupus Caffeæ," it being overlooked by every one of the proof-readers that the botanical plant name of coffee is spelled *Coffea*, and not *Caffea*. Consequently the formula was left as No. 353, until it was too late to transfer it. But the error in vowels was corrected and the title changed to "Syrupus Coffeæ." It should, of course, properly have appeared after "Syrupus Cinnamomi," on page 126, the intervening preparations being advanced one number. But it seems that no one, so far, has been put to any inconvenience by the alphabetical misplacement.

401. Tinctura Iodi Decolorata. Decolorized Tincture of Iodine.

Perhaps it might have been useful to append a note to this preparation, to the effect that the extinction of color in a tincture or other preparation of free iodine implies that the iodine is no longer free, but in combination. But as all intelligent pharmacists at the present time will know this already, it was deemed unnecessary by the Committee to attach an explanatory note. Moreover, this preparation has long been known and used under the above name. It was officinal in the first German Pharmacopœia (1872), and is still so in the Russian and Swiss Pharmacopœias, under the same title.

Inks.

Mr. Eugene Dieterich reports that he has obtained very remarkable results during his continued experiments on inks, particularly those made with nutgalls. He found that both the ferrous and the ferric tannate are soluble in an excess of tannic acid, and that ferric salts yield more stable inks than the ferrous salts heretofore usually employed. Moreover, when ferric salts are used, the employment of a mineral acid is not necessary to keep the tannate in solution, a little excess of gallic acid being amply sufficient. Inks thus prepared affect steel pens but little.

We append a few of the new formulæ published in the *Pharm. Centralhalle* (No. 27).

1. *Alizarin Ink.*

Indigotin	6 parts.
Pure Water	889 "
Sugar	50 "
Solution of Tersulphate of Iron (U. S.)	62 "
Ink Body (see below)	500 "

Dissolve the Indigotin by one day's maceration in the water. Then add the Sugar and Solution of Tersulphate of Iron, and lastly the Ink Body.

[The original has 400 parts of water and 50 of solution of tersulphate of iron, intending that of the Germ. Pharm. We have substituted an equivalent quantity of the preparation of the U. S. Ph., and diminished the water in proportion.—Ed. Am. Dr.]

In place of the ink body a solution of 50 parts of tannic acid in 540 of water may be used.

The prescribed method of mixing must be scrupulously followed.

The finished ink is set aside for eight days, and the clear liquid then decanted from the trifling precipitate.

This ink flows bluish-green from the pen, and writing executed with it on paper soon turns black. The writing may be copied inside of the first 48 hours.

The ink body above directed to be used is prepared in the following manner:

Macerate 200 parts of coarsely powdered Chinese galls for twenty-four hours with 750 parts of distilled water, strain and express. Upon the residue pour 350 parts of boiling distilled water and express after one hour. Triturate 50 parts of white bole with the mixed strained liquids, raise once to boiling, remove the scum, and filter through flannel bags. Wash the latter with water until the weight of the filtrate is 1,000 parts.

2. *Blue Document Ink.*
(Blue Nutgall Ink.)

Solution of Tersulphate of Iron (U. S. P.)	44 parts.
Sulphate of Sodium, cryst.	20 "
Sugar	50 "
Ink Body	500 "
Aniline-blue (water-soluble) " I B"	4 "
Pure Water	q. s.

Dissolve the Sulphate of Sodium in 242 parts of Water, add the Solution of Tersulphate of Iron and the Sugar, and when the latter is dissolved, add the Ink Body. Lastly add the Aniline-Blue dissolved in 200 parts of Water.

In place of the ink body, a solution of 50 parts of tannic acid in 450 parts of water may be used.

Let the ink stand eight days, then pour off the clear liquid.

This ink writes with a fine blue color, dries rapidly upon paper, and after a few days becomes bluish-black.

Fresh writing made with this ink copies moderately well, but loses this property after a few hours.

For ordinary use, as for school purposes, this ink may be diluted with an equal volume of water which has been boiled and then allowed to become cold. For every 100 parts of the product, 3 more parts of sugar are added.

3. *Red Copying Ink.*
(Imperial Ink. Crown Ink. Coral Ink.)

Extract of Logwood, French, extra fine	100 parts.
Oxalate of Ammonium	30 "
Sulphate of Aluminium	20 "
Oxalic Acid	5 "
Bichromate of Potassium	5 "
Salicylic Acid	1 "
Pure Water	q. s.

Reduce the first four ingredients to a coarse powder and heat the mixture with 800 parts of Water to boiling in a copper vessel. Then add a solution of the Bichromate of Potassium in 150 parts of hot water, next add the

Salicylic Acid, and set the whole aside for fourteen days. Pour off the clear liquid, and fill it in ½-lb. or 1-lb. bottles.

In thin layers this ink has a fine red tint, and writes with violet-red color, which copies dark-violet, and also assumes the last-mentioned shade when drying. It is one of the best copying inks in existence. Writing done with it can be copied many weeks afterwards.

4. Violet-Blue Copying Ink.
(Japanese Ink. Cameroon Ink.)

Extract of Logwood, French, extra fine	60 parts
Oxalate of Ammonium	30 "
Sulphate of Aluminium	10 "
Sugar	10 "
Oxalic Acid	3 "
Bichromate of Potassium	6 "
Salicylic Acid	1 "
Pure Water	q. s.

Prepare this like No. 3, using the Water in the same proportions.

This ink is violet-blue in thin layers, flows dark-blue from the pen, dries bluish-black on paper, and yields bluish-black copies. As it is somewhat thicker than No. 3, it is preferable to use for it pens with broad nib.

5. Ink for Writing upon Zinc and Tin (also Tinned Iron).

Chlorate of Potassium	60 parts
Sulphate of Copper	120 "
Aniline-Blue, water-soluble, I B	1 part
Acetic Acid	100 parts
Pure Water	q. s.

Dissolve the Sulphate of Copper and Chlorate of Potassium in 1,400 parts of Water. Also dissolve the Aniline-Blue in 400 parts of Water and add the Acetic Acid. Then mix both solutions.

Upon zinc this ink is applied directly by writing with a steel pen. If writing, however, is to be done upon tin or tinned iron, this is to be first freed from fat or grease by ether and then to be rubbed over with a solution made from equal parts of chloride of zinc and hydrochloric acid. Of course, to write with this ink upon any surface, the latter must be thoroughly clean.

6. Document-Ink Extract.

Tannic Acid	50 parts
Tersulphate of Iron, dry	20 "
Sulphate of Sodium, dry	10 "
Sugar	20 "
Aniline-Blue, water-soluble, I B	4 "

Reduce them to a coarse powder and keep it in a tin box. When using it, pour the contents of the box into an earthen jar, add 1 quart of pure hot water, and stir until everything is dissolved. When cold, the ink is transferred to bottles.

This ink writes with a bluish color and turns rapidly black.

[The dry tersulphate of iron, for the present purpose, is best prepared by evaporating 250 parts of Liquor Ferri Tersulphatis U. S. P. on a water-bath to a syrupy condition, then adding the dry sulphate of sodium, and transferring the mass, in thin layers, upon plates of glass, which are to be placed in a drying closet until the mass is dry, when it may be reduced to powder.—ED. AM. DRUGG.]

Artificial Mineral Waters.

We have given several formulas for preparing the more commonly used mineral waters in our last issue. We now append a few more, partly for comparison, taken from the *Formulaire Pharmaceutique* of the Paris Hospitals (Paris, 1887):

1. Contrexéville Water.

Bicarbonate of Sodium	1 lb.
Sulphate of Sodium	3 "
Sulphate of Magnesium	8 "
Chloride of Sodium	1 "
Carbonic Acid Water	q. s.
to make 500 bottles or about 600 pints.	

2. Pullna Water.

Sulphate of Magnesium	3 lb.
Sulphate of Sodium	3 "
Chloride of Sodium	1 "
Carbonic Acid Water	q. s.
to make 100 bottles.	

3. Seidlitz Water.

Sulphate of Magnesium	2 lb.
Carbonic Acid Water	q. s.
to make 100 bottles.	

4. Sulphurous Water.

Monosulphide of Sodium, cryst.	200 gr.
Distilled Water	q. s.
to make 100 bottles.	

5. Vichy Water.

Bicarbonate of Sodium	6 lb.
Sulphate of Sodium	¼ "
Sulphate of Magnesium	¼ "
Chloride of Sodium	780 gr.
Carbonic Acid Water	q. s.
to make 500 bottles.	

A NEW PINCH-COCK.

B. PROSKAUER has devised a new pinch-cock of universal applicability, which will shortly be patented. It combines the advantages of the screw and the clamp. Only one hand is required to regulate or adjust it, and this makes it especially valuable for use upon volumetric apparatus. It may be applied or removed at any time without disconnecting the ends of tubing, or without altering the adjustment of the jaws of the pinch-cock.

The construction of the pinch-cock is as follows (see cut). On turning the terminal screw c, the two jaws are either approached to, or separated from each other, the jaws always remaining parallel to each other. This screw motion is used only for regulating the distance permanently, if so desired, but the jaws may at any time be pushed further apart, by placing the thumb upon b, and the index and middle finger upon the two wings a, a. On pressing against the latter, the jaws will open, and on releasing the pressure, they will again return to the position at which they had been regulated by the screw c. When the pinch-cock is used for small rubber tubing, such as is usually attached to burettes, the two jaws are made to touch each other, by turning the screw c until this takes place. The pinch-cock is then regulated only by the three fingers of one hand, as described above.

These pinch-cocks are made in all sizes by Gust. Ludwig, Berlin, Fehrbellinerstrasse No. 14), and may be obtained through dealers in chemical apparatus.

BRANDING PRESS FOR BOXES.

IN a manufacturing and wholesale business it sometimes becomes desirable to stamp a trade-mark, address, or some particular device upon the cover or end-boards of packing boxes. A machine for accomplishing this, invented by H. Keruart, of Epernay, France, is shown in the adjoining figure. The design to be used is cast in metal, reversed as in the case of ordinary printing types and blocks, and is heated by being placed on a small portable stove which also forms the base of the press. By means

Branding press.

of a suitable compression plate, adjusted for the thickness of the boards to be branded, and actuated by suitable mechanism, the boards are firmly clamped against the face of the heated design, and the impression is both indented and charred into the face of the lumber. The entire apparatus is said to weigh about 800 lbs., and is capable of branding about 350 boxes or 400 boards per diem, and of giving an impression as handsome as if done by lithography, with the labor of a single person.

Kola.

AN article published in a German daily paper on the uses of kola has drawn a commentary from the well-known African traveller, Adolf Krause. Krause is of opinion that there is only a small demand for the drug in Europe, which is not likely to increase, as it would be difficult for a new nutrient beverage to command the field in the presence of such well-established rivals as cocoa, tea, and coffee. Only if it were very cheap would such a result be possible, and this condition he regards as unlikely, as the article is very highly esteemed by the natives—a statement which he supports by quoting various prices at which it is sold there. Krause also reminds readers that a German factory had made an attempt to introduce kola chocolate without satisfactory results. The opinion prevalent on the Continent that Europeans eat kola when in Africa is contradicted, it being asserted that they only do so when nothing else is to be had. The traveller says that he himself has tried it in all kinds of preparations, including the fresh drug, and the same when roasted like coffee, but he never derived any great pleasure or benefit from its use. [An interesting account on the Kola or Gûro nut, and its high value in the interior of Africa, will be found in our last volume, page 168.—ED. AM. DRUGG.]—*Chem. and Drug.*

On the Relative Value of Different Pepsin Tests.

From a lengthy paper on this subject, by Mr. James H. Stebbins, Jr., printed in the *Journ. of the Chem. Soc.* (March, 1888), we select those portions which appear to be of most practical value to our readers.

The author first mentions Bidder and Schmidt's method of testing which was directed to be carried out as follows: Place a known weight of small cubes of coagulated white of egg in contact with a liquid containing a known weight of pepsin dissolved in hydrochloric acid of 0.2 per cent strength, and heat the mixture for about five hours at 45 C. At the end of this time the undissolved albumen is washed and weighed. The loss in weight of this albumen indicates the digestive power of the pepsin.

This method of assay, says the author, has the inconvenience of taking into account only the amount of albumen dissolved, without paying attention to the amount of albumen really converted into peptone. The same objection also applies to the next two methods discussed by the author, one of which is the test of the U. S. Pharmacopœia, while the other is Manwaring's test.

Regarding the U. S. P. test, the author says that it is unreliable and misleading, as no two persons using the same pepsin can obtain the same, or even approximate results. (This is quite true, and is not even disputed by those who devised and introduced that test in the text of the U. S. P. But it must be remembered that in 1882, when the text of the U. S. P. was printed, our knowledge of the properties of pepsin and of methods of testing it were not as far advanced as they are now. Indeed, at that time, a better test could not be devised. At the present time, however, the case stands differently. While the digestive power of the official saccharated pepsin is not attempted to be interfered with, the National Formulary, recently published, contains an improved process of testing pepsin which is believed to be fully satisfactory. It also contains the feature, found fault with by Mr. Stebbins, that the digestive power is determined from the amount of undissolved albumen remaining behind. But, in our judgment, the most weighty objections (though not all) against this method are removed by the details of manipulation.—Ed. Am. Dr.] Several of the objections made by the author of the paper need not be mentioned here, as they are superseded by the new pepsin test just mentioned in the note in brackets. But there is one point which even now deserves attention. The writer says: "It is difficult to see how accurate results are to be obtained by weighing the amount of undissolved pepsin remaining after a digestion, because it is impossible to find two samples of coagulated albumen which contain exactly the same quantity of moisture; and besides this, the quantity of moisture is very liable to vary during the weighing, owing to the loss of moisture by evaporation." [The new test directs that egg-albumen prepared by boiling fresh eggs for 15 minutes shall be rubbed trough a clean hair sieve, having 30 meshes to the linear inch. This is a great improvement over the other method, but even here, there is no absolute certainty that the rate of hydration of the prepared mass is perfectly uniform. However, it is probably conceded that the error caused by this method is too small to be of practical importance.—Ed. Am. Dr.]

The author then turns to the "Manwaring test," which is given as follows:

"The design of the following mode of testing the dissolving power of pepsin is to conform as nearly as possible to the U. S. P. test, which, contemplating the testing of the saccharated form, makes no provision for the proportion of acidulated water to be used with a pure pepsin. On the basis that 1 part of a pure pepsin is capable of dissolving 1,000 times its weight of coagulated egg albumen in 6 hours, a saccharated pepsin made with a pure pepsin of U. S. P. strength would contain 8 per cent of pure pepsin. Therefore, if 1 grain of a U. S. P. saccharated pepsin is to be tested in the presence of 500 grains of acidulated water, then 1 grain of a pure pepsin should be tested in the presence of 10,000 grains of acidulated water to equal the same proportions of water and acid used for the *actual* quantity of pepsin contained in a U. S. P. saccharated pepsin when tested according to the U. S. P."

Manwaring recommends, when pure pepsin is to be tested, to mix it previously with milk-sugar. He also directs to rub the albumen (obtained by boiling eggs for 15 minutes) through a No. 30 sieve. [These and certain other features of the test in the National Formulary are based upon Manwaring's directions.] After digesting the pepsin and albumen for 6 hours at a temperature of 100-105° F., Manwaring directs to run up the temperature quickly to above 145° F., in order to destroy the pepsin. Then the bottle and contents are to be allowed to rest over night so that the undissolved albumen may settle. The strength of the pepsin is calculated by evaporating a small portion of the supernatant liquid to dryness, and by using certain factors for multiplying (which may here be omitted), the amount of normal albumen corresponding to the dry residue is ascertained. Mr. Stebbins raises several objections to this method, among which the following are the more important.

Regarding the direction that the peptic principle should be destroyed by raising the temperature up to and above 145° F., it is to be remarked that the object is not attained in this manner. It has been shown that digestion may and does continue up to 80° C. (172° F.), though of course much more slowly than at a lower temperature. Hence, if the bottle and contents are subjected only to a temperature of 62.2 C. (145° F.), and it is then set aside during a whole night, digestion will progress to some extent all night.

Another objection is raised against the method of determining the "peptone" contained in an aliquot part of the liquid, chiefly for the reason that the portion of liquid taken for the assay contains other substances besides true peptone. Mr. Stebbins confirms an observation long ago made by others, but which it is nevertheless worth while to mention again, viz., that the accumulation of peptone during peptic digestion hinders and finally stops the action of the pepsin upon the albuminoid matter entirely. If then the liquid is diluted, digestion will commence again, and proceed until the pepsin has become inert. Mr. Stebbins does not believe in the theory that one grain of pepsin can go on digesting to infinity.

The good points in Manwaring's test, according to Mr. Stebbins, are, first, that he directs strong pepsins to be suitably diluted before assaying them. Second, that he does not weigh the undissolved albumen, which is a great source of error. Instead of this, he calculates the amount of "albumen" digested from the amount of dry residue of a measured portion of the supernatant liquid. Mr. Stebbins thinks that, while the whole method contains errors, they are not as great as those affecting the U. S. P. method.

The author now turns to the test which he considers the only approach to accuracy so far proposed. He does not, however, regard even this as absolutely accurate, as slight errors are apt to occur, but he thinks that these do not materially injure the final result. The test here referred to is that proposed by Kremel, of Vienna.

In devising this test, Kremel has made a radical departure from the usual methods, and bases his test upon the fact that, under the conditions in which artificial peptic digestion takes place, pepsin alone has the property of converting albuminoid matter into peptone, and that, therefore, from an analytical as well as from a physiological standpoint, the only correct method is to take the quantity of peptone produced as a gauge of the action of the pepsin; or, in other words, the test is made to resemble as nearly as possible the conditions existing in the natural process.

Without going into any further detail, we shall give the test, as proposed by Kremel:

One Gm. of egg albumen (soluble) dried at 40° C. and pulverized, and 0.1 Gm. of the pepsin to be tested are placed into a 100 C.c. flask, and dissolved in 50 C.c. of 0.2 per cent hydrochloric acid. The solution is heated to 38-40° C. (100.4°-104° F.) for three hours, and then exactly neutralized with sodium carbonate; it is then heated on a water-bath to 90° C. (194° F.) and cooled, after coagulation has taken place. The flask is then filled to the mark with distilled water, 50 C.c. are filtered off and evaporated to dryness in a platinum dish on a water-bath.

The residue is dissolved in hot distilled water, filtered through a moist filter into a platinum dish, and the filter carefully washed. The solution is again evaporated to dryness and weighed. The peptone is then incinerated with ammonium carbonate, and the weight of the ash deducted leaves the weight of the pure peptone, or the representative of the digestive power of the pepsin.

The good features of the above test are the following:

1. Simplicity.
2. No guess work, troublesome calculations, or the use of questionable factors.
3. No weighing of albumen dissolved in hydrochloric acid, undigested albumen, and intermediary products along with the peptone. This is all obviated by the use of soluble egg albumen, coagulation and filtration, or removal of the undigested portion as detailed above.
4. The ease with which it is possible to duplicate and still obtain concordant results.

On the other hand, the objections to this process are the following:

1. The great difficulty of procuring absolutely pure soluble dried egg albumen. This source of error, however, in my opinion, is very slight, because in each test a large excess of albumen is always used, and consequently the pepsin always has enough albumen to act upon. Besides this, it must be remembered that only the peptone formed is weighed, and not the amount of undigested albumen, as is the case with the U. S. P. test.
2. It may be objected to this test that the results obtained are expressed by the weight of peptones formed and not by the weight of albumen dissolved, and consequently the figures, being based upon dry peptone, will be much lower than when the result is expressed as so much moist or coagulated albumen. If this, however, be objected to, it is comparatively easy to obtain higher figures by a simple calculation. Assuming that the amount of dry peptone obtained is equivalent to so much dry albumen, then by multiplying the weight of the latter by 8 (Manwaring's multiplier) we would obtain the equivalent in coagulated or moist albumen. Mr. Stebbins does not think it necessary or advisable to follow this course, as it involves the use of a multiplier which is questionable.
3. It takes a little longer to make a test by this process,

but if accuracy is thereby gained, the process is to be preferred.

The author now appends a series of analytical figures showing the result he obtained with this test. Fourteen samples of pepsin were tested, both "pure," and saccharated. The amount of peptone formed by 0.1 Gm. of the several samples within three hours varied from 0.5644 Gm. to 0.1734 Gm., and the author thinks that the figures obtained fairly indicate the relative strength of the several pepsins. As it might, however, be objected that the promiscuous application of this method to both "pure" and saccharated pepsins might do the former an injustice, by not bringing out their full digestive power, the author made a second series of experiments, in which he saccharated every one of the samples of "pure" pepsin he had previously assayed. The results obtained showed that the *relative* amount of pepsin formed was actually larger than when the undiluted pepsins were used in the experiment.

As all the results obtained by strictly following Kremel's directions are comparable among themselves, Mr. Stebbins does not see how the process can well be improved upon. The mere fact that increased dilution increases the yield of peptone is not, in his opinion, sufficient reason for condemning the process. As the conditions prevailing in the stomach of a full-grown man do not differ materially as to dilution from day to day, it is safe to say that pepsins of varying strength administered to such a person will only perform a certain amount of work and no more, and that, consequently, the results obtained by this test more closely resemble the conditions prevailing inside the stomach than any other.

Adulterated Pepper.

AT a recent meeting of the Paris Society of Pharmacy — according to the Paris correspondent of the *Chem. and Drugg.*— the fascinating subject of "Pepper Adulteration" was brought forward, and gave rise to quite an interesting exchange of views.

M. Ferrand said that at the previous meeting Prof. Planchon had somewhat criticised Gilet's iodine process, and markedly expressed his preference for the microscopical investigation. Yet, as a commercial test, Gilet's method is as reliable as it is convenient. One gramme of the pepper should be wetted with 80 centigrammes of tincture of iodine, made with 90 per cent alcohol, and allowed to dry without the addition of any water. Any ground olive-seed present (which is at present a very common adulterant) will at once turn to a uniform rhubarb-yellow, while pepper turns dark-brown. When a mixture of pepper and olive-seed is thus tested, as commercial pepper is never sold in the shape of an impalpable powder, the two substances present such a contrast in color as to be immediately apparent. The variegated aspect of yellow spots among brown cannot fail to attract attention. Indeed, from the samples shown by M. Ferrand, the test will do for all practical purposes.

A member having suggested that falsifiers will now add starch to olive-seed powder, M. Ferrand replied it would not do, as commercial pepper is sold in coarse powder, and the olive-seed will show its yellow color with iodine. At the same time, microscopic examination must not be neglected, and cannot be replaced for general purposes. For olive-seed, however, Gilet's test is the thing, as no particular skill is needed, such as is required for handling a microscope. To some one's query: "How about the malaguetta seeds?" the reply was made that they are not used as adulterants proper, as they cost about as much as pepper. They are added, owing to their greater pungency, to permit the introduction of the real adulterating substances, and these must be looked for.

In the subject of pepper adulterations, Prof. Moissan related his experience when a young man employed in a wholesale drug-house. There the laurel leaves in which Italian licorice is packed being received in large quantities, were powdered, and the assistants ordered to mix some of the stuff with every parcel of powdered pepper sold. How were you to find this out?

M. Ferrand: "For the present, olive-seed, ground, is the common adulterant. It is a regular article of trade, sent out from Marseilles, sold in large quantities, properly ground, and offered of two colors, black and white, so as to better imitate the pepper color. The white is the olive-seed skilfully decorticated. The sophistication is not easily detected with a microscope, unless one is very expert indeed, while the iodine test is simple and convenient. It may be but a temporary expedient, as falsifiers will invent other frauds; yet for the present this settles ground olive-seeds."

Colin spoke — while pepper sophistications were on the *tapis* — of roasted bread-crumbs as a general adulterant which had long puzzled him. It is likely to be added, it seems, to nearly everything, and is most difficult to identify. The only distinctive feature is the presence of the hair of the wheat, recognizable by experts. To give an idea of the ingenuity of falsifiers, he said, at the museum and other libraries their chemists are on the watch for new books on adulterations, and the first to read them.

AUTOMATIC DISTILLING APPARATUS.

THE *British Trade Journal* recently described an automatic still especially intended for producing fresh water at sea, or in countries where good water for drinking or culinary purposes is not available. It is made by Brucher & Co., Wincanton, Somerset, England, and may be had in either tinned plate or tinned copper, and is said to be comparatively inexpensive (prices not given) and very simple and efficient in its action.

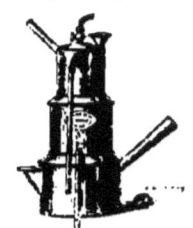

The water to be distilled is placed in the lowest receptacle or boiler, beneath which any convenient form of heating can be applied. Above this is the distilling or condensing chamber, fitted with a broad annular rim to catch the condensed vapor, and surmounted by a cone into which the steam from the boiler ascends, and where it is condensed by the lower temperature maintained in the cone by a supply of cold water flowing through the topmost compartment and circulating round this cone. These receptacles fit one into the other, and can be readily taken apart for packing and conveyance in a small space, and the cold water used for cooling can, with advantage, be made to flow into the boiler. Thus the whole becomes really automatic when once the supply is regulated. The distilled water is drawn from the bottom of the second chamber by means of a tube and nipple, and can thus be led to any receptacle prepared for it. It is made in two sizes, and would appear to be well adapted for pharmaceutical purposes.

A CONSTANT GAS GENERATOR.

A GLASS vessel, resembling a chloride of calcium drying cylinder (A) contains a perforated diaphragm and up right glass tube, which are attached, as shown in the cut, at the constricted portion of the cylinder.

The neck is closed with a doubly perforated cork, carrying a drop-funnel B, provided with a stop-cock, to the exit of which is attached a spider-like glass jet, with capillary tubes, the object of which is to distribute the liquid (for instance, acid) uniformly over the material in the cylinder (for instance, calcium carbonate). Through the other perforation of the cork passes a gas-delivery tube, which is externally (at c) connected with the drop-funnel by means of a flexible tube d. By a proper adjustment of the stop-cock a very regular and steady current of gas may be produced. The spider-like liquid-distributor is illustrated in Figure 2. — After *Chem. Zeit.*

Adulterated Liquorice Juice.

As the result of the examination of a number of samples of liquorice or "Spanish juice," based upon a comparison of the ash yielded with that obtained from samples believed to be genuine, Mr. B. Dyer is of opinion that liquorice is adulterated to an enormous extent (*The Analyst*, July, 1241). The sophisticated samples, so far as could be ascertained, appeared to be chiefly of French origin, the best samples coming from Italy. The genuine juices all contained a tolerably large quantity of starch, but this was readily distinguishable from the added starch, which was recognized in different samples as derived from wheat, barley, rice, potatoes, and perhaps rye. The samples in which adulteration are detected by the microscope showed a very low yield of ash free from silica and clay; in four cases the quantity fell below 2 per cent, and in another case below 3 per cent, whilst that from presumably genuine specimens ranged between 3 and 5 per cent. Another difference observed was in the relative proportion of potash in the ash, which in that from genuine samples amounted to from 34 to 43 per cent, whilst in that from adulterated samples it was only 18 to 30 per cent. A sample made by Mr. Dyer, by evaporating a decoction of liquorice root, gave results that agreed well, as regards the quantity of ash and its composition, with those obtained from the commercial samples of reputed genuineness, except that the proportion of phosphoric acid in the former was much higher. — After *Pharm. Journ.*

Official Tests for Arsenic and Tin, in Germany.

A GOVERNMENT order, made for carrying out the details of a law regarding the use of noxious ingredients in articles of food or use, has recently been issued in Berlin, which prescribes very minutely the methods to be followed in testing for *arsenic* and *tin*. As this method has evidently been most carefully drawn up, and embodies all improvements that have been found acceptable up to the present time, it will be of interest to place on record here at least that portion of it which refers to arsenic. It should be stated that the law particularly aims at the suppression of poisonous colors for articles of food or general use.

I. SOLID SUBSTANCES.

1. Of solid articles which are dyed throughout, 20 grammes are taken in operation. If the color is only superficial, it is scraped off, and such a quantity of it used that it corresponds to 20 grammes of the original substance. Only when the prescribed amount of 20 grammes cannot be obtained, may a smaller quantity be used for the test.

2. Reduce the sample by trituration, or in any other manner, to a fine powder or mass, and then mix it, in a capsule of genuine porcelain [Berlin porcelain], with a measured quantity of pure hydrochloric acid, spec. gr. 1.100 to 1.120, mixed with so much water that the proportion of the hydrochloric acid to the water is about like 1 to 3. Usually, 25 C.c. of the above-mentioned hydrochloric acid and 75 C.c. of water will answer the purpose.

Next add 0.5 Gm. of chlorate of potassium, transfer the capsule to a water bath, and, as soon as the contents have acquired the temperature of the latter, add, in intervals of five minutes, further small portions of the chlorate, until the liquid has acquired a light-yellow color, and has become homogeneous and thin fluid. About 3 Gm. of the salt, altogether, will usually be found sufficient. The water which is lost by evaporation must be replaced from time to time. When the desired point has been attained, 0.5 Gm. more of the chlorate are added, and the capsule removed from the water-bath. When it has become completely cold, the contents are passed through a filter placed over a flask of the capacity of about 400 C.c. When all the liquid has passed, the flask is placed on the water-bath and heated until the odor of chlorine has nearly disappeared. The filter and residue, which it usually contains, are well washed with hot water, the wash-water evaporated on the water-bath to about 50 C.c. and this portion, together with any precipitate that might possibly have separated, added to the filtered liquid in the flask. Care is to be taken that the total volume of liquid be at least six times that of the volume of the hydrochloric acid employed. For instance, if 25 C.c. of hydrochloric acid were originally used, the final liquid (filtrate and concentrated washings) must measure at least 150 C.c., but are preferably 200 to 250 C.c.

The liquid is now heated to between 60° and 80° C. (140° to 176° F.), and while being kept at this temperature, a slow current of pure, washed hydrosulphuric acid gas is conducted through it during three hours. It is then allowed to cool, the current of gas being continuously maintained, the flask then lightly covered with a piece of filtering paper, and set aside in a moderately warm place, for at least twelve hours.

4. If a precipitate has been produced, this is to be collected upon a filter, washed with water containing hydrosulphuric acid, and, while still moist, to be treated with moderately yellow sulphide of ammonium which had previously been diluted with dilute water of ammonia. Usually, 4 C.c. of sulphide of ammonium, 2 C.c. of water of ammonia (sp. gr. 0.960), and 15 C.c. of water, will suffice. Any residue remaining after the treatment with sulphide of ammonium is washed with water containing sulphide of ammonium, and the filtrate and washings evaporated to dryness, in a deep porcelain capsule of about 5 Cm. diameter, at a moderate heat. The residue left upon evaporation is covered with about 3 C.c. of crude, fuming nitric acid—the capsule being covered with a watch-glass—and the acid then cautiously evaporated at a moderate heat. If the residue which now remains has a yellow color, while yet moist, it is treated as directed in the next paragraph. But if the residue is dark-colored, it must be again treated with crude, fuming nitric acid, until it looks yellow while moist.

5. The yellow and still moist residue in the capsule is mixed with finely-powdered sodium carbonate until the mass has a strongly alkaline reaction, then further mixed with 2 Gm. of a mixture of 3 parts of carbonate and 1 part of nitrate of sodium, a little water being added so as to produce a homogeneous, pulpy mass. This is dried in the capsule, and cautiously heated until it is anhydrous or begins to melt. A higher temperature should be avoided. The resulting mass will be white or colorless. Should this not be the case, a little more nitrate of sodium is to be added, until the desired result is attained.*

6. The melted mass is treated with water, at a gentle heat, and the liquid passed through a filter. If any tin was present, this is now (almost all) contained in the residue upon the filter, in the form of white *oxide of tin,* while the *arsenic* is contained in the filtrate as *arsenate of sodium.* If a residue has remained on the filter at all, it is to be remembered that a small portion of the tin may also be contained in the filtrate. The residue is once again washed with cold water, then three times in succession with a mixture of equal parts of water and alcohol, and the washings evaporated, so that the united filtrate and washings amount to about 10 C.c. Next, diluted nitric acid is added, until the liquid just has an acid reaction. Should this produce a separation of traces of oxide of tin, this is filtered out and washed again as directed above. The filters now containing any *tin* that may have been present are then specially treated so as to isolate and determine the quantity of this metal. (The prescribed process contains nothing new and is here omitted.)

7. To demonstrate the presence of arsenic (in the filtrate), it is first converted into arsenic-molybdate of ammonium. For this purpose, the liquid is acidulated with nitric acid, freed from carbonic and nitrous acids by warming, then cooled, and, if necessary, again filtered. It may now amount to about 15 C.c. It is now mixed, in a small flask, with about an equal volume of a solution of molybdate of ammonium in nitric acid,* and allowed to stand three hours without warming. Should the liquid, owing to an insufficient washing of the first hydrosulphuric acid precipitate, contain traces of phosphoric acid, this would be now precipitated as phospho-molybdate of ammonium. If the operation, however, has been carefully conducted, no precipitate [certainly none containing any arsenic] will form.

8. The clear or filtered liquid (of §7) is now warmed on a water-bath, until it has been kept at the temperature of the latter for about 5 minutes (or better, until molybdic acid begins to separate). If any arsenic was present, this will be separated as a yellow precipitate of arsenico-molybdate of ammonium, and there will usually be also a separation of white molybdic acid. After standing one hour, the liquid is passed through a small filter, which will retain a trace of the precipitate, while the largest part of the latter will remain in the flask. The precipitate in the flask is now twice washed with a mixture of 100 parts of the above-mentioned (see note) molybdic reagent, 20 parts of nitric acid (sp. gr. 1.200) and 80 parts of water, and then dissolved, by warming, in 2 to 4 C.c. of water of ammonia (sp. gr. 0.960), with subsequent addition of 4 C.c. of water. If necessary, the liquid is again passed through the small filter [if any of the precipitate had first been collected upon the filter, it should be treated in the same manner so that contained in the flask, so as to get it all into one solution. —ED. AM. DRUGG.], and the filtrate mixed, first with one-fourth of its volume of alcohol and then with 2 drops of solution of chloride of magnesium and chloride of ammonium. [The analytical, so-called magnesia mixture made with sulphate of magnesium will also answer.—ED. AM. DR.] The arsenic will separate, either at once, or on standing in a cold place, as white and more or less crystalline ammonio-magnesium arsenate. This is filtered off and washed with the least possible quantity of a mixture of 1 part of water of ammonia (0.960), 2 parts of water, and 1 part of alcohol.

9. The washed precipitate on the filter is next dissolved in the least possible quantity of dilute nitric acid, the solution evaporated to a small bulk, then one drop transferred upon a porcelain disk, and another upon an object glass. To the drop on the disk is added a drop of solution of nitrate of silver, and afterwards, from the edge, a drop of water of ammonia (0.960). If arsenic was present, a reddish-brown stripe will be formed at the line of contact, due to the formation of arsenate of silver. The drop placed upon the object glass is rendered alkaline with the least possible quantity of water of ammonia. If arsenic is present, there will be produced, either at once or after a short time, a precipitate of ammonio-magnesium arsenate which, when viewed under the microscope, will be seen to consist of pointed crystals.

II. LIQUIDS, JELLIES, ETC.

Of liquids, etc., the quantity to be taken is such that it corresponds to about 20 Gm. of dry substance. For instance, of strawberry syrup about 30 Gm., of red wine or vinegar about 800 to 1,000 Gm. In exceptional cases, when these quantities are not available, smaller amounts may be used.

Fruit-juices, jellies, etc., are treated with hydrochloric acid and chlorate of potassium precisely as directed under I. Thin liquids, not of an acid reaction, are evaporated to a small bulk, and this treated like jellies, etc. Thin, acid liquids are distilled until only a small residue remains, and this is then treated as directed before. The distillate, in this case, is acidulated with hydrochloric acid, and likewise treated with hydrosulphuric acid in the same manner as the solution of the residue.

III. IN WOVEN FABRICS, ETC.

If the arsenical dye or color is soluble in water, it may be extracted by this liquid. Usually it will probably be

---

* If the melted mass remains black, in spite of this treatment, this is usually due to a small amount of copper, since sulphide of copper is not entirely insoluble in sulphide of ammonium.

* Dissolve 1 part of molybdic acid in 4 parts of water of ammonia (sp. gr. about 0.96), and pour the solution into 15 parts of nitric acid (sp. gr. 1.200). Let the mixture stand a few days in a moderately warm place, and, if necessary, draw it off clear from any sediment formed.

but little or not at all soluble. In all cases it is convenient to test a small portion in Marsh's apparatus in order to ascertain whether arsenic is present or not. If none is discovered, no further tests are required.

Take 10 Gm. of the fabric, cut it into small pieces, introduce these into a tubulated retort of potash-glass, of the capacity of about 400 C.c. and add 100 C.c. of pure hydrochloric acid of spec. gr. 1.190. The neck of the retort should be drawn out and bent at an obtuse angle. The retort is adjusted so that the branch extending from the retort itself is directed obliquely upwards, and the second bent downwards. The latter is introduced into a Liebig's condenser, the connection being closed by a piece of rubber tubing. The condenser tube is made to dip air-tight into a tubulated receiver of about 500 C.c. capacity, containing 200 C.c. of water. To keep it cool, it is placed into a basin containing cold water. The tubulure of the retort is connected with a Peligot tube filled with water (to form a water-joint). After about one hour, 5 C.c. of a cold saturated aqueous solution of crystallized ferrous chloride (free from arsenic) is put in the retort and the contents heated. When the excess of hydrochloric acid has been driven off, the temperature is raised so as to bring the contents to boiling, and the distillation is continued until the contents begin to swell. The retort is allowed to cool, 50 C.c. more of hydrochloric acid (sp. gr. 1.190) then added, and the distillation repeated.

The distillate in the receiver (which may have a brown color from organic matter), united with the contents of the Peligot tube, is put into a flask, diluted to 600 or 700 C.c. with distilled water, and a current of pure hydrosulphuric acid gas then conducted through it, first while heating, and afterwards during cooling.

After 12 hours, the brown precipitate (partly or entirely consisting of organic substances) is filtered out upon an asbestos filter, prepared by a suitable layer of asbestos in a funnel, the exit tube of which contains a glass stop-cock. After washing the filter a short time, the stop-cock is closed, and the residue upon the filter—while the funnel is covered with a plate of glass or watch glass—treated with a few cubic centimeters of bromated hydrochloric acid (prepared by saturating hydrochloric acid of sp. gr. 1.190 with bromine). After about half an hour's treatment, the solution is allowed to flow off through the stop-cock into the same flask in which the precipitation was carried out, upon the walls of which there are frequently slight films of the original sulphuretted precipitate. The residue upon the asbestos filter is washed with hydrochloric acid of spec. grav. 1.190.

The liquid in the flask is again mixed with an excess of ferrous chloride and transferred (with washings made with hydrochloric acid of sp. gr. 1.190) into a smaller retort, where the distillation is conducted precisely as described before.

The distillate will now usually be limpid like water. It is then diluted with distilled water to about 700 C.c. and treated with hydrosulphuric acid as directed above. After 12 hours, any precipitated sulphide of arsenic is separated by filtration upon a filter which had previously been washed successively with dilute hydrochloric acid, water, and alcohol, then had been dried at 110° C. and weighed. The residue upon the filter is washed, first with water, then with absolute alcohol, afterwards with warmed disulphide of carbon, and lastly again with absolute alcohol. It is then dried at 110° C. and weighed.

From the amount of As₂S₃, the quantity of arsenic originally present is calculated. In the case of fabrics (or wall papers) the calculation should extend to the amount present in a given square surface, best in 100 square centimeters.—After *Zeitsch. f. Anal. Chem.*, 1888, 471-478.

Color-Test for Saccharin.

Mr. David Lindo writes in the *Chem. News* (August 3d): I have failed as yet to obtain a characteristic reaction (color-reaction) for the substance in solution. The following test, which must be applied to the solid body, is believed to be original. It consists in evaporating to dryness on the water-bath the saccharin mixed with excess of nitric acid. A fragment of caustic potash (not too small) is then added, and a drop or two of water, without removing the dish from the bath. Color is at once developed, and if the dish is inclined, streaks of color, blue, violet, purple and red, flow from the caustic. The test, however, is not extremely delicate; half a milligramme of saccharin in the solid state is about the smallest quantity that will give definite results. Heat is necessary to develop the colors, and apparently a large excess of alkali. Soda does not appear to act as well as potash. Mr. Lindo adds that color reactions obtained with coal-tar products must always be suspected of not being characteristic. Whether the one here described for saccharin is peculiar to it, remains to be ascertained.

The Indiana Legislature has enacted a law prohibiting the refilling, more than once, of prescriptions containing doses of more than ¼ grain of opium or ⅟₁₆ grain of morphine without verbal or written order from the prescriber.

AN IMPROVED FILTERING APPARATUS.

P. Raikow has utilized Nickel's idea of perforated filters in a new manner.

A conical tube of porcelain (D), which is perforated with a series of holes, is placed inside of a funnel, in the manner shown in the cut, the portions coming in contact being suitably ground. The cone D is wound around with filtering paper, cut into strips of 2 to 4 Cm. width, which may be suitably tied. The liquid to be filtered is poured into the space between the funnel and conical tube. If there is much sediment, the lower holes of the filtering tube will gradually become clogged, but the upper ones will still continue to functionate.

In case it is desired to hasten filtration by a filter pump, the orifice of the cone D is closed with a cork carrying a tube which is connected with the pump. In this case, of course, care must be taken that the level of the liquid to be filtered is maintained above the top row of holes in the cone; otherwise air would be aspirated, and the action of the pump be neutralized. When the liquid becomes scant in quantity, the author recommends to push a cork (which is supposed to fit suitably, see Fig. 2) down the conical tube, so as to cover the several rows of holes which would otherwise be exposed.—After *Chem. Zeit.*

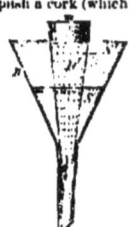

Note by Ed. Am. Drug.—In place of this arrangement, we would construct the apparatus differently. We would use not a conical, but a parallel-sided tube with rows of holes, and fasten it by passing it through a cork put into the neck of the funnel in such a manner that the connection would be water-tight, but at the same time permit the tube being pushed down through the cork when so desired. After the last of the liquid has been poured into the space between the funnel and central tube, the level of the liquid must be watched, and whenever it approaches the top row of holes, the tube must be pushed down so as not to permit any access of air.

ON FILTRATION.

Otto Hehner and Henry D. Richmond have examined the methods for inserting filters in funnels, in order to find out which is the best. If a filter is so placed in a funnel that it is at all points in contact with the latter, the liquid cannot escape, and filtration is slow. For this reason, corrugated or channelited funnels have been made, which do not, however, any longer fulfil their purpose, owing to the thin filtering paper now generally used, which stretches sufficiently to accommodate itself to the uneven surface of the funnel. The authors caused funnels to be made which contained four ridges upon their inner surface, the ridges running from the rim to the neck. Then they examined the rate of filtration through different kinds of funnels and with differently folded filters. As filtering liquid, 250 C.c. of pure water were used, and the filters kept constantly full. For each experiment a new filter was used, since even pure water gradually stops up the pores of a filter, thereby retarding filtration. The results, which express the rate of filtration of 250 C.c. of pure water in seconds of time are given below. A variety of filtering papers were used by the author, but we shall note here only the reference made to Schleicher and Schüll's papers.

250 C.c of water filtered in			seconds.			
	2	3	4	5	6	7
Schleicher and Schüll's filtering paper.	553	840	160	—	98	120
	430	160	148	—	100	200
	645	160	199	—	90	155
	750	250	162	—	188	150
Mean	577	357	165	—	119	156

Column 2 gives the rapidity of filtration (in seconds) with smooth funnel; No. 3 the same, with smooth funnel and closely cut-off stem, the paper being folded at an angle somewhat larger than 90°, so that it may not fit tight; No. 4 the same arrangement, only with substitution of the new funnel above-mentioned; No. 6, with folded filter; and No. 7 with the filter folded, as shown in the cut. This is done in the following manner: Fold the filter in the direction of two diameters crossing each other at right angles. This will produce four quadrants. Open the filter out again, reverse it, and in two opposite quadrants fold back the edges until they meet. When the filter is placed in a funnel of 60°, it will exactly fit it.—After *The Analyst*.

The Synthesis of Coniine.

In 1886, Prof. Ladenburg announced the important fact that he had succeeded in producing synthetically the alkaloid coniine possessed of every property which characterized the natural alkaloid. Previous to that time, a synthetical coniine had already been prepared, but while this corresponded with the natural alkaloid in nearly every respect, yet there were some differences which showed that the identity was not absolute. One of the chief differences was this, that the artificial coniine was optically inert, while the natural coniine turned polarized light to the right.

It has long been known that artificially prepared organic bases are optically inert, while all natural alkaloids turn the ray of polarized light either to the right or to the left. The solution of this puzzle will no doubt mark an important era in chemical knowledge, and an important step towards its solution has been made, first, by Pasteur in his researches upon dextro- and lævo-tartaric acids, and now by Ladenburg. The latter has occasion, in a recent extensive paper on pyridine and piperidine bases, published in *Liebig's Annalen* (vol. 247, p. 80), to give a more detailed account of how the synthesis of "natural" coniine was brought about, and we give the more interesting portions of this paper in the following:

Although coniine was observed already in 1827 by Gieseke and shortly afterwards more closely studied by Geiger, its correct chemical composition ($C_8H_{17}N$) was first determined by Hofmann in 1881. The latter recognized its similarity to piperidine, and subsequently showed that it could be changed, by a reduction process, to a new base, $C_8H_{19}N$.

The latter, known as conyrine, has been recognized by its decomposition products to be identical with propyl-pyridine, which may in fact be obtained by the action of reducing agents (nascent hydrogen, etc.) upon natural coniine.

Without entering here too minutely into the chemical constitution and relationship of the several synthetic compounds involved in the final building up of true coniine, we will merely state here that the next problem to be solved was the conversion of alpha-propyl-pyridine, (or conyrine ($C_8H_{11}N$) into alpha-propyl-piperidine which latter contains six atoms more of hydrogen, and is, therefore, according to its elementary composition, apparently identical with natural coniine: $C_8H_{17}N$. It was not necessary to convert the first-named base itself into the second, as there were better means available to pass from the pyridine series to that of piperidine. Alpha-allyl-pyridine was treated with metallic sodium and boiling alcohol, and produced the desired base in nearly the theoretical quantity. The crude base was converted into the hydrochlorate, the latter several times recrystallized, and the base isolated by distilling the salt in the usual manner with aqueous solution of soda. The oily alkaloid was separated from the distillate, the remainder dissolved in the condensed water, separated by potassa, and the united portions of the alkaloid thus dried over potash.

The base thus obtained coincided in boiling point, elementary composition, odor, specific gravity, behavior towards reagents, physiological effects, etc., etc., completely with natural coniine, *but there was still a difference, as the artificial base was optically inert, while natural coniine is dextrogyre.*

The important step now to be undertaken was to split the optically inactive artificial coniine into its two component isomeric bodies, which—after the analogy of certain substances investigated by Pasteur—could be anticipated to be, the one dextrogyre and the other lævogyre, in such proportions that their optical properties mutually neutralized each other. Pasteur had shown that *uvic acid* is such a compound, made up of dextro- and lævo-tartaric acid.

Ladenburg tried several methods to bring about a splitting up of the artificial coniine. One of these consisted in treating a solution of the base with fungi, which could be expected to destroy one of the active isomers, leaving the other behind. [Pasteur had shown, in 1860, that it to a solution of acid uvate of ammonium, containing traces of phosphates, some spores of Penicillium glaucum are added, the dextro-tartaric acid, of which the uvic acid is partly composed, is gradually consumed, so that lævo-tartaric acid finally alone remains.] But it was found that coniine behaved, even towards the most resisting fungus (Penicillium glaucum) so poisonously that no solutions containing over 0.1 per cent could be employed. And even after many weeks' trial, the coniine was found to have undergone no change.

The next method was one for which Ladenburg made use of a hint afforded by Pasteur's investigations. Remembering that this chemist succeeded in splitting up *uric acid*, while the latter was combined in *salts*, Ladenburg looked about for an optically active acid which would form a well-crystallizable salt with coniine. A good promise appeared to be afforded by the dextrogyre tartrate of coniine, which had been prepared some years previously by Schorm. This was a salt of coniine prepared with dextro-tartaric acid. On preparing a syrupy solution of equal molecules of tartaric acid and true *coniine*, and adding to it a crystalline fragment of the before-mentioned salt, Ladenburg found, after a short time, that the whole liquid solidified to a *hard crystalline mass*. On repeating this experiment with substitution of alpha-propyl-piperidine, that is, artificial coniine, crystals appear in this liquid likewise, but even after eight days it was only *partially* solidified. As it could not be filtered, the mass was transferred upon blotting paper, which absorbed the syrupy portion. The crystals were freed from adhering syrup by strong pressure between bibulous paper, the dry crystals decomposed by potassa, the base distilled over, and after being separated and dried examined in the polariscope. It was now found to turn the plane of polarized light to the right to the same (or practically the same) degree as natural coniine, and in all other respects, even where there had previously yet been some slight differences, the identity was absolute.

Hence this operation resulted for the first time in the complete synthesis of a natural alkaloid—if we understand under alkaloids those natural bases of vegetable origin which are related to pyridine, or at least contain a nitrogenized nucleus.

In this connection, it is proper to remark that not only Ladenburg, but many other chemists had heretofore believed that the *pyridine* which they had recognized as being closely related to the alkaloids, and which they usually obtained for their experiments from certain manufacturers, was obtained from bone-tar (product of the dry distillation of bones), as this was supposed to be a much more abundant source of the substance than coal-tar or other compounds which were also known to contain it. Prof. Ladenburg was led to the above supposition because the manufacturers used to supply the crude pyridine under the name of "Thier-Öl-basen" ("bases from animal oil"). It now turns out that in spite of this name, the commercial crude pyridine is all obtained from coal tar.

The dextrogyre portion of alpha-propyl piperidine having thus been extracted and identified with natural coniine, it remained only to separate the lævogyre portion contained in the syrup soaked up by the blotting paper. It was first tried to remove from it any of the dextrogyre salt still contained therein, but this was unsuccessful. However, by the aid of iodide of cadmium, which forms double salts with coniine and many other alkaloids, a partial separation of the lævogyre salt was accomplished, the resulting base being, however, only approximately pure.

Disinfection.

The following directions for disinfection are contained in the official *Formulaire Pharmaceutique* of the Paris hospitals:

1. Before employing any disinfectant, search for the cause of infection, with a view to suppress it. Particularly look to the tightness of sewers, construction of closets, etc.

2. *Personal Disinfection.*—Surgeons and their assistants should wash their hands first with soap and water, and afterwards with either one of the following solutions:

a. Carbolic Acid............................ 50 parts.
   Glycerin................................. 75 "
   Water................................... 1,000 "

b. Corrosive Sublimate...................... 2 parts.
   Chloride of Sodium....................... 2 "
   Water................................... 1,000 "

3. *Disinfection of Bedding, Clothing, Curtains, Carpets, etc.*—Expose the objects, during twenty minutes, to steam under pressure, in a suitable apparatus, such as that of Geneste and Herscher, at a temperature of at least 105° C. (221° F.). Dry air, even at 120° C. (248° F.), does *not* disinfect bulky articles, even after several hours; and woollen goods are rendered reddish-brown by it.

Blood, fecal matters, and colored albuminous dejections leave indelible stains upon tabries, if these are heated to about 100° C. (212° F.) The stains found on coverlets, mattress covers, etc., are first washed with a dilute solution of hypochlorite of sodium (about 1 volume of Labarraque's solution in 300-400 volumes of water).*

Shoes should be washed with the following solution:

Corrosive Sublimate..................... 2 parts.
Chloride of Sodium..................... 2 "
Water................................. 1,000 "

4. *Disinfection of Linen, etc.*—Bedclothing, linen, etc., which is soiled by dejections or blood, should first be soaked or rinsed in the above-mentioned dilute solution of hypochlorite of sodium (called *chlorozone* in the original), then wrung out, and afterwards put in the steam-heating apparatus. Or the articles may be boiled in the liquid just mentioned. Or they may be kept from six to twelve hours in a weak solution of chloride of lime, obtained by inclosing chloride of lime in a sack of stout material and hanging it into the water. About one pound of chloride of lime is required for every twenty-five gallons of water.

---
* This will be found too dilute. The strength to be used will depend upon the intensity of the stain and the nature of the fabric.

In order to avoid the scattering of germs, the fabrics should be immersed in the liquid previous to being sorted out and counted.

Leather is disinfected by applying to it, with a brush, a solution of

Corrosive Sublimate	16 grains.
Chloride of Sodium	16 "
Water	1 quart.

5. *Infectious Fecal Discharges.*—Place into the porcelain vessel (intended to receive them) beforehand some 4 or 8 ounces of a 5-per-cent solution of hydrochloric acid or of chloride of lime, or the following:

Sulphate of Copper	1½ oz.
Sulphuric Acid	1½ oz.
Water	1 quart.

6. *Sick-Rooms, Unoccupied.*—These are treated either by sulphur or nitrous fumigations.

a. Sulphur Fumigations. Close up all exits and fissures [except one or more, to be closed after the disinfecting process has been started]. Boil some water in the room for at least one hour in a vessel placed on a suitable heating-apparatus. Place pieces of sulphur into sheet-iron pans having low sides (about 12 inches in diameter, and 2 inches high), standing upon beds of sand. Add a little alcohol to each, and then ignite them. For every 35 cubic feet, 300 grains of sulphur should be used. Close the last exits. After twenty-four hours open the room and ventilate thoroughly.

b. Nitrous fumigations. Into a cup, placed inside of a stoneware jar, put crystals of nitrosyl-sulphate (sulpho-nitrous acid; the lead-chamber crystals of sulphuric-acid works), of which about 16 grains will be required for every 35 cubic feet. Then place the vessel under a faucet, and adjust the latter so that water will fall upon the crystals drop by drop, which will cause the immediate disengagement of reddish fumes. Close the room until the following day. Be particularly careful not to inhale the escaping vapor of the gas, or the air of the room, charged with the vapors, on opening it. It is best to have two vessels containing the disinfectant, one at each end of the room.

After either one of the above fumigations are completed, wash the walls and floor of the room, by means of a painter's brush, with a 2-per-cent solution of carbolic acid.

7. *Disinfection of Wagons [Ambulances, etc.].*—Sick-wagons should be disinfected in the following manner:

Wagons which can be closed are disinfected like sick-rooms, by means of the before-mentioned nitrous fumigations. Wagons lined with cloth may be likewise disinfected in this manner; but open wagons must be disinfected in a special shed which can be closed.

Wagons lined with moleskin or plush are disinfected like shoes, viz., by washing them with a solution containing 2 parts, each, of corrosive sublimate and of chloride of sodium in 1,000 parts of water.

Alaninate of Mercury.

Alanin ($C_3H_7NO_2$) is a body derived from lactic acid and propyl-glycol. It is also known as lactamine or amido-propionic acid.

In order to obtain the alaninate or amido-propionate of mercury, alanin is dissolved in 20 parts of water, the solution raised to boiling, and then gradually saturated with mercuric oxide, added in very fine powder and in small quantities at a time. The filtered solution is evaporated, and there will be obtained a white, crystalline powder, soluble in 3 parts of cold water. This solution is colorless, and keeps indefinitely, even though exposed to air and light.

De Luca recommends alaninate of mercury, in form of hypodermic injection, in doses of 5 to 15 milligrammes (1/13 to ¼ grain) per day for adults, in the treatment of syphilis. A course of forty-five days is stated to often be sufficient to bring about a permanent cure.

In children, the remedy is to be administered per os, in doses of 2 to 5 milligrammes (1/32 to 1/13 grain).—After *Arch. de Pharm.*, June.

The Camphor Monopoly at Formosa.

In reply to a communication of the American Minister to China, in which he asked that the camphor industry of Formosa should be conducted under the rules formerly in use, and not as a Government monopoly, the Yamên (Chinese Foreign Office) state that the whole aspect of the camphor industry upon Formosa has changed since the rules were made (in 1869). There is no more camphor produced in the territories adjacent to the sea-coast, though, if any camphor is procurable there, it may still be purchased by foreign merchants, whether it is "official" or not. The custom passes which foreign merchants require for travelling on business specially stipulate that they must not proceed "to places in close proximity to the country occupied by the aborigines and their trade." The provincial monopoly in camphor is in that produced in the inner mountainous region inhabited by the aborigines, which has been brought under subjection by the governor. The government has established military stations there, both as a means of keeping the aborigines in subjugation, and to protect the business.

AN IMPROVED EXTRACTION APPARATUS.

A. A. Lumsden describes an extraction apparatus (in *Chem. News* of March 29th) which has several useful features, one of which is the small quantity of solvent required, which is used over and over again until the substance is exhausted. The author says:

The apparatus I constructed for myself some years ago, and have since used exclusively without accident or trouble, is a modification of Church's apparatus, the essential improvement being in the removal of the danger of bursting the flasks, or driving out the corks, by pressure during the distillation. The extraction of a sample occupies no more than an hour as a rule, while the recovery of the ether is accomplished, and loss by evaporation is avoided, just as effectively as with any other apparatus.

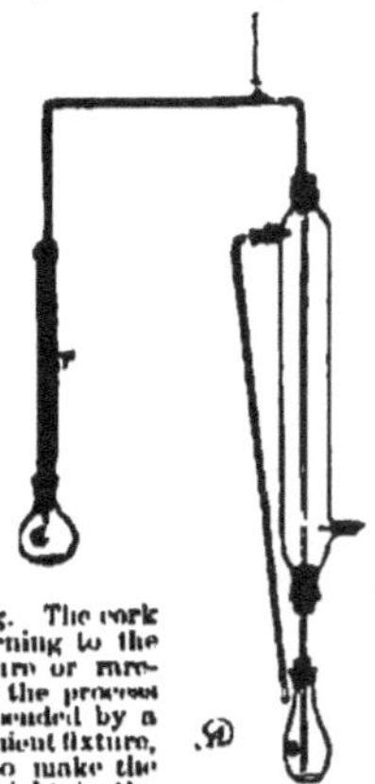

The tube *T*—a piece of ordinary combustion tube, drawn out to go through the cork of flask *a*—contains the substance, which is kept in its place by a plug of cotton pushed pretty tightly into the lower end of tube, and by a more loosely fitted plug, held down by a spiral string of common wire. The tared flask *a* is short and wide, with a capacity of 80 to 90 C.c., and is heated in the usual way by a beaker of hot water. Flask *b* has a similar capacity to *a*, but is preferably of a taller form, and is inserted in a beaker of cold water kept overflowing by a continuous stream from the tap, passing first through the condenser. The tube leading from *T* to the bottom of the flask *b* is ¼ inch in diameter and has no joining. The cork of *b* has a small V-notch opening to the air, to prevent either pressure or rarefaction in the apparatus as the process proceeds. The whole is suspended by a string attached to any convenient fixture, and can thus be adjusted to make the flasks hang at a suitable height in the beakers. When an extraction is being commenced, 2 or 3 C.c. of ether are put into flask *a*, *b* is half filled with the same liquid, and the corks are all firmly inserted. The apparatus is now lowered to its normal position, when the ether in *a* is vaporized, expelling the air. The apparatus is now lifted bodily (by taking hold of the condenser) and flask *a* is plunged into a beaker of cold water standing beside the hot one. In a few seconds, the liquid ether in *b* is completely drawn into *a*, carrying along a portion of the oil in the sample. Flask *a* is again inserted in the hot beaker, when distillation commences, and is allowed to continue until the greater portion of the ether be condensed in *b*; *a* is again dipped in the cold water, and the operation is repeated until the sample be completely extracted.

I find it convenient to use two hot-water beakers, one standing over an argand and ready to replace the other at each new distillation.

PREPARATION OF ABSOLUTE ALCOHOL.

On a small scale absolute alcohol may be obtained, according to J. Habermann, by introducing caustic lime, in small fragments, into a glass tube *b*, about 28 inches long, and 1½ to 2 inches wide, which is connected, in an upright position, with the distilling flask. The lime is, however, not poured into the tube directly, but is made to fill the space between the walls of the tube and a narrow roll of iron wire gauze *c*, which is made to occupy the centre of the tube, and the object of which is to permit the passage of alcohol vapors upward, when the lower layers of lime begin to become semi-liquid. To completely dehydrate 4 C.c. of 95% alcohol, 1 Gm. of lime is required. At first, the contents of the flask must be heated very slowly and gently on a water-bath, so that but little distils over during the first two hours. Then the receiver is changed, and the distillation made to proceed more rapidly. As soon as the lime has become semi-liquid, the tube is exchanged for another.—After *Chem. Centralbl.*, No. 24.

A Substitute for Cod-Liver Oil.

PROF. LÉPINE (in *Rép. de Pharm.*, July, 1886), after having discussed the nature of an oil emulsion in general (see page 171 in this number), turns to the subject of cod-liver oil in particular, and first quotes the observation of Berthe that bleached cod-liver oil is much less easily absorbed than the brown. The cause is this, that the latter contains between 6 and 11 per cent of free fatty acids, while the bleached contains only about 0.4 per cent. Buchheim, who recognized the importance of having free fatty acids present, some years ago proposed to add these to cod-liver oil, or to administer them separately. And quite recently Mering recommended the employment of partially saponified oil of olive. The substance Lipanin which is made by Kahlbaum, of Berlin, and has recently been introduced in medicine, is nothing else than olive oil, in which a small quantity of free fatty acids has been set free (about 6 per cent), and converted into soap.

Salkowski criticises this preparation. Instead of a partial saponification he prefers the direct addition of pure oleic acid, or of erucic and palmitic acids. The latter is objected to by Mering, as it is apt to crystallize out, while the former is liable to become easily rancid.

In place of using olive oil, Mr. Fournie, chief pharmacist of the Lyons hospitals, has selected, at Prof. Lépine's suggestion, a new vehicle to carry the free acids, viz., *butter*.

To make the preparation, the butter is first melted, washed with alkaline water, and afterwards with pure water, being thereby deprived of casein, serum, and volatile fatty acids. It is then mixed with 5 per cent of its weight of a mixture of fatty acids obtained in the following manner. A specified quantity of butter is saponified; the resulting soap is decomposed with an acid with the exclusion of air (under a current of carbonic acid gas) and at a low temperature, to avoid the formation of oxy-oleic acid. The supernatant fatty acids are removed after cooling, then washed with several portions of water at a temperature of 75° C. (167° F.), and afterwards added to the purified butter. The product is absolutely free from odor and disagreeable taste, provided the process has been carefully conducted. It may easily be mixed with medicaments, so far as they are not incompatible. This method of operation is deemed by the originators preferable to that involving the use of pure oleic acid, as this is worth some ten dollars a pound.

Regarding the effects of treatment of consumptives with this new agent, experiments have not far enough advanced to give a decisive statement. Meanwhile, as there is great activity at present among observant therapeutists, in experimenting with new agents to combat the old enemy, phthisis, the publication of the above process will afford to those who desire to do so, a chance to try it.

The Pharmacopœial Assay of Cinchona.

THE Pharmacopœia Committee of the German Pharmaceutical Association propose the following text for the article "Cortex Chinæ" (Cinchona) in the next edition of the German Pharmacopœia:

Cortex Chinæ. Bark of the branches and trunk of cultivated species of cinchona, chiefly of *Cinchona succirubra*, occurring frequently in rolls of about 60 Cm. (23 inches) in length, 1 to 4 Cm. (½ to 1½ inches) in diameter, and 2 to 4 Mm. (ab. ⅛ to ⅙ inch) in thickness. These brittle barks have a thin, grayish-brown cork, with coarse longitudinal ridges and short diagonal fissures, and have a brownish-red, fibrous interior. Under the microscope, the bark exhibits the bast-cells peculiar to the cinchonas.

On heating 0.1 Gm. of the bark in a test-tube to redness, a fine carmine-red tar is produced.

Cinchona bark yields a reddish-brown powder, which should contain not less than 3.5% of alkaloids.

Shake 20 Gm. of the powder repeatedly and energetically with 10 Gm. of water of ammonia, 20 Gm. of alcohol, and 170 Gm. of ether, and after twenty-four hours pour off 100 Gm. Add 3 C.c. of normal hydrochloric acid, and 27 C.c. of water, then remove the ether and alcohol by distillation and, if necessary, add more normal hydrochloric acid, so as to render the liquid acid. Then filter and while the liquid is cold add to it, while stirring, 3.5 C.c. of normal potassa solution, or such a quantity thereof as will be required to cause phenolphthalein paper dipped into the liquid to acquire a red tint. The precipitate is collected upon a filter, and gradually washed with a little water, until the escaping drops cease to redden phenolphthalein paper. Allow the precipitated alkaloids to drain, press them gently between blotting paper, dry them in the air sufficiently to transfer them upon a watch-glass, and then dry them completely, first over sulphuric acid and then on a water-bath. The weight of alkaloids thus obtained and dried at 100° C. should not be less than 0.35 Gm.

On treating the alkaloids thus obtained and reduced to a fine powder, with 15 C.c. of ether, added in several portions, not more than one-half of their weight should remain undissolved. On shaking the ethereal solution with diluted sulphuric acid, a few drops of the latter, mixed with several cubic centimeters of water, should give a bluish-fluorescent liquid, which assumes a handsome green color upon addition of chlorine water and excess of ammonia.

The Committee adds the following comments: The changes which are here proposed in the method of assaying cinchona bark rather concern the manipulation than the principle. In the first place, 100 Gm. of the extract are taken for assay, as these correspond to 10 Gm. of bark. [No account, however, is taken here of the weight of alkaloids contained in those 100 Gm. Supposing the bark, of which 20 Gm. had been taken for assay, to contain 4 per cent of alkaloids, then the 200 Gm. of mixed solvent would extract these and become 204 Gm. Hence it would be necessary to withdraw 102 Gm. of the liquid to represent 10 Gm. of bark. As, however, the actual percentage of alkaloid in the bark is unknown previous to the analysis, and the possible error is usually very small, we agree with our German confrères that it may be disregarded.—ED. AM. DRUGG.] On adding the 3 C.c. of normal acid, some water must be added also so as to enable the alkaloidal salt to enter solution. The ether cannot all be removed by spontaneous evaporation, as in this case the concomitant alcohol would also remain behind. It is absolutely necessary to heat the liquid so as to drive off the alcohol, in order to cause the alkaloid to be precipitated in a liquid entirely free from alcohol. The distillation must be conducted in the water-bath, and continued until nothing more passes over. The quantity of caustic alkali required for precipitation is easily ascertained by employing strips of paper impregnated with alcoholic solution of phenolphthalein. If such a strip is colored red, when dipped in the liquid, an excess of alkali is present, and the precipitation completed. In the same manner the completion of the washing is ascertained. Phenolphthalein reveals the presence of caustic alkalies with great distinctness by becoming red; but free alkaloids (though they turn litmus blue) have no influence upon phenolphthalein [that is, alkaloids from cinchona; Flückiger, however, has found that both atropine and hyoscyamine are capable of reddening phenolphthalein paper.—ED. AM. DR.].

The assay of the bark is proposed to be extended to a determination of the amount of ether-soluble alkaloids. [In the present German Pharm. this had not been provided for, but it has been in the U. S. Pharm.] This is done by treating the finely triturated total alkaloids with small quantities of ether until 15 C.c. of this have been consumed. The identification of quinine or quinidine in the ethereal solution is performed as prescribed in the text, the fluorescence being particularly prominent when the liquid is as highly diluted as the text prescribes.

The Cardamom Plant.

THE cardamom of commerce, *Elettaria Cardamomum*, a member of the natural order of Zingiberaceæ, is indigenous to the forests of Malabar, where it is found growing wild at altitudes ranging from 1,800 to 3,500 feet above sea level. A moderate degree of shade and any amount of moisture are the climatal conditions most favorable for the plant's luxuriant growth.

If the shade be too profound, the stalks which spring from the rhizome will be but few in number, but if sunlight be moderately admitted, they will increase amazingly, often exceeding seventy in number; but if exposed to sunshine for more than an hour or two daily, the plant languishes and eventually dies out. Each stalk throws out a scape, or peduncle, varying in length from 1½ to 2½ feet, on which the fruit is produced in the form of capsules, arranged in an alternate manner on each side of the shaft, at a distance of about 2½ inches from each other. From the description of the plant above given, a large crop might be expected, but the result does not fulfil the expectation to the anticipated extent, as, owing to the large amount of moisture contained in the vegetable tissues of the cases which cover the grains, one pound of the green fruit reduces down to one quarter or sometimes one-fifth of a pound, when fully dried.

In its natural climate and soil, a sandy loam devoid of clay, the plant begins to bear in the second, and yields a full crop in the fourth year. My experience does not enable me to state precisely the yield of each plant. I think that the planter may consider himself fortunate if he succeeds in harvesting, on the average, one-quarter pound of dry cardamoms per plant in the total number of sixty plants which occupy an acre, in the fourth year, less a certain percentage of loss occasioned by rats, squirrels, and snakes, all which species of vermin evince a partiality for the fruit, and are ever on the watch to pounce upon it the moment it becomes ripe; and this entails the necessity of great watchfulness on the part of the planter to forestall these marauders, and be in the happy position of that early bird which proverbially "gets the worm." Each stalk, as it completes its functions in bringing its scape to maturity, and becomes effete, is succeeded by another stalk, sprouting from the parent rhizome, which begins to bear in the course of a year; and in this order the growth proceeds with successive renovations, until the plant attains its ultimate span of existence, in the lapse of time; the extent of duration of which is not accurately known to the writer.

Until Ceylon glutted the home markets, cardamoms sold well, but they hardly fetch remunerative prices now, as the quotations have fallen from 5s. a lb. to 1s. 4d., and even less for the small kinds, of which there is a considerable proportion in all lots, and which sell for about 8d. a pound. The spontaneous way in which the plant was for a long time supposed to be exclusively produced, viz., from the concussion of the ground occasioned by the fall of a large tree felled over it, was, if not a purely fanciful idea, probably a cunning one suggested by the interested motives of those who were the fortunate holders of the cardamom hills and habitats. Whether such an origin has any better foundation to rest upon than mere imagination, it would be idle here to discuss, as there is no question of the fact that cardamoms can be reared from seed sown in shaded nurseries in the ordinary way, or from the division of the rhizome into parts containing young shoots or eyes fit for development into them. The former is undoubtedly the quickest way of forming a plantation, although it must be admitted the seed is singularly slow in germinating, taking never less than three and often as many as five months before the little spikes show themselves above ground. Within a year from this time, the plants will, with careful culture, have attained a sufficient size to be planted out into pits dug for their reception, in the shade of the forest, suitably prepared by trenching, and the thorough extirpation of root and branch of the brush-wood occupying the surface. The process cardamoms are put through, called "bleaching," is a tedious one, and if left to agents, particularly costly. It is done by exposing them to the fumes of sulphur in closed receptacles—a process which has the effect of transforming their dingy gray into a delicate pale straw color. This may be called one of the tricks of the trade, which, while perhaps it may not appreciably deteriorate or detract from the quality or flavor of the grains, captivates the public eye and secures a better price.—*Tropical Agriculturist.*

On the Nature of Oil Emulsions.

In the course of a paper on Cod-Liver Oil (in the *Répert. de Pharm.* July, 1888), Prof. Lépine discusses the mode of formation of emulsion of fixed oils, and draws certain conclusions therefrom. Though no specially new facts are there advanced, yet it is worth while to give an abstract of this portion of the paper.

When an emulsion is to be prepared artificially, we are obliged to have recourse to violent agitation. On the other hand, when an oil is emulsified in the intestinal canal, the feature of violent agitation is absent, there being merely the peristaltic action of the intestines. The author quotes the explanation which was given by Gadin Dubois' *Archiv*, 1878, 1881), to account for this. Supposing we add to the solution of an alkali contained in a watch-glass, very carefully a single drop of a fixed oil *containing about 6 per cent of free fatty acids*, there will soon be observed a whitish zone forming around the drop of oil. Upon very gentle agitation, some small particles will be observed in this zone, having an active motion, and these particles will, upon a slightly increased agitation, be recognized as minute droplets of fat which separate from the main drop. It has been assumed that the latter contains some free fatty acid. Any molecules of this which happen to be about the surface of the drop will be converted into soap by the alkali, and the resulting soap-molecules, dissolving in the water, produce centrifugal currents and movements. Under their influence, the drop of oil throws out more or less extended projections, which, upon separating, constitute minute droplets.

Each of these is coated by a thin pellicle of soap which prevents the droplets from running together. Under these conditions, the emulsion is *stable*.

In order that the experiment shall succeed, there must be a certain proportion of fatty acid in the fixed oil. The soap which is produced must be rather soluble, and not in too large a quantity, the density of the surrounding liquid must be suitable, etc. If all these conditions are fulfilled, the emulsion is perfect. All conditions being equal, cod-liver oil forms a better emulsion than any other fatty substance.

As has been shown by Hoffmann, fatty substances are frequently acid. Thus, even the purest olive oil always contains a trace of free oleic acid. But it is in the intestinal canal, as has been proven by Claude Bernard, and under the influence of the pancreatic juice, that neutral fats undergo a partial decomposition, resulting in the formation of free fatty acids. The latter then decomposes the alkali carbonates, and saponify with the alkaline bases, the resulting soaps, when dissolving, producing the above-mentioned currents. In this manner emulsions are formed in the duodenum, there being this additional feature (compared with artificial emulsions) that the presence of albuminous matter, and still more that of bile, assists the furmation of the emulsion, there being, besides, other factors which are not yet clearly made out.

Instantaneous Remedy for Hiccup.—
The following method of suddenly cutting short hiccup is, perhaps, not altogether new, but combines several features sometimes recommended singly as a cure for the trouble.

Close the external auditory canal of both ears with the end of the index-fingers with a moderate pressure. At the same time drink a small quantity of some liquid, no matter what, in repeated portions, the liquid being held to your mouth by a second person, in a cup or glass. The hiccup will then instantly stop.—*Bull. de Thérap.*

A BURETTE-FLASK.

H. MORGAN's burette flask can not only be used like an ordinary burette, but also permits the gravimetric determination of the amount of liquid contained therein or taken therefrom. The total weight of flask and burette, when empty, amounts to only 30 to 35 Gm. The burette tube is fused into the neck of the flask, and reaches to within about 1 millimeter of its bottom, having a small opening at its closed end. The lateral tube B serves for the admission of air during titrating and when filling the burette; likewise also, of course, for filling the flask. When the burette is to be filled, the flask is set on its bottom, P is opened, and by compressing the bulb B, the liquid is forced into the burette. Then the orifice P is closed.—*Jour. Anal. Chem.*, 1888, 1.

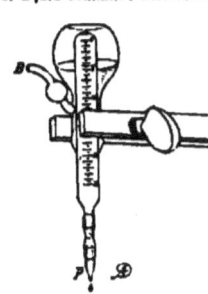

Morgan's burette flask.

A SELF-ADJUSTING BURETTE.

A BURETTE which fills itself to the zero mark or to any other mark previously determined, has been devised (and patented) by H. Oppermann, of Beraburg, Germany. (Germ. Patent No. 43,568.)

The burette B has a lateral branch near the stop cock, which is connected with the tube C in the manner shown in the cut, a separate branch connecting C with the reservoir of the reagent A.

At first, stop-cock i is opened, which causes liquid to flow from the reservoir into the upper branch of C. On opening now the stop-cock d, the contents of C will flow down and enter the burette. When enough liquid has entered the latter to fill it either to the zero point or to any other previously determined mark, the level of the liquid in both branches will be alike, the two branches communicating with each other by means of flexible tubing. The air confined in this communicating tube remains unchanged, only varying in density.

If the pinch-cock d is shut, and liquid allowed to flow from the burette, by opening the pinch-cock at i, the column of liquid in the two portions of the tube C will remain unchanged. When i is closed again, it is then only necessary to open d, which will cause exactly as much liquid to flow from the reservoir as had previously been withdrawn from the burette. In other words, the liquid will flow until the air confined in the curved flexible tube is back again at its original density.

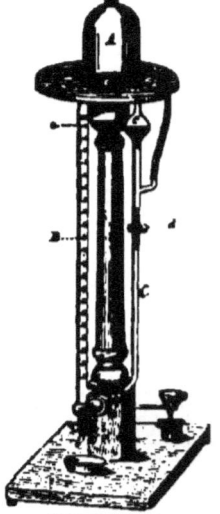

Oppermann's burette.

Micromillimeter.—A recent communication to *Nature* by Prof. Rücker calls attention to the fact that the term *micromillimeter*, which has long been in use among scientists as equivalent to the "one-thousandth of a millimeter," should no longer be used in this sense. The Committee of the British Association for the Selection and Nomenclature of Dynamical and Electrical Units laid down the rule that the prefixes *mega* and *micro* should be employed for multiplication and division by one million. The term micro-millimeter is now used by physicists who adhere to the new rule, in the sense of "*one-millionth of a millimeter.*" The Royal Microscopical Society have directed the editors of its journal to abandon the use of the term micromillimeter in the old sense, and to use instead of it, the term *mikron* which had also been employed for it formerly. This is to be represented by the Greek letter μ while the millionth of a millimeter or micromillimeter, will be designated by $\mu\mu$.

Hypodermic Injections.

The *Formulaire Pharmaceutique* of the Paris hospitals gives the following list of typical hypodermic injections, containing such a quantity of the several medicaments that the usual hypodermic dose (say about 15 minims) will correspond to the average dose for adults of the respective remedies.

We have converted the metric terms of the original into the nearest equivalents of our weights.

	In 150 min. of water dissolve	15 min. will contain about
Apomorphine Hydrochlorate,	1½ grains	$\frac{1}{6}$ grains
Aconitine Hydrochlorate,*	$\frac{1}{12}$ "	$\frac{1}{120}$ "
Atropine Sulphate,	0.15 "	$\frac{1}{100}$ "
Caffeine Hydrobromate,	7 "	$\frac{7}{10}$ "
Codeine,	1½ "	$\frac{1}{8}$ "
Curare,	0.15 "	$\frac{1}{100}$ "
Duboisine Sulphate,	0.15 "	$\frac{1}{100}$ "
Ergot, Aqueous Extract,	10 "	1 "
Eserine (Physostigmine),	0.15 "	$\frac{1}{100}$ "
Hyoscyamine,	0.15 "	$\frac{1}{100}$ "
Morphine Acetate,	1½ "	$\frac{1}{8}$ "
" Hydrochlorate,	1½ "	$\frac{1}{8}$ "
" Sulphate,	1½ "	$\frac{1}{8}$ "
Pilocarpine Hydrochlorate,	3 "	$\frac{3}{10}$ "
Quinine Hydrobromate,	25 "	2½ "
" Hydrochlorate,	7 "	$\frac{7}{10}$ "
" Sulphate (+ Cit. Acid),	7 "	$\frac{7}{10}$ "
" Sulphovinate,	40 "	4 "
Strychnine Sulphate,	$\frac{1}{8}$ "	$\frac{1}{120}$ "

The following are directed to be dissolved in *Liquid Vaseline* as a vehicle:

Eucalyptol, Thymol, Bisulphide of Carbon, Carbolic Acid, Chloroform, Iodoform, Iodine, Bromine, Phosphorus, Calomel (! suspended !), Yellow Oxide of Mercury (suspended !).

We only give the names of the substances without the strength of solution, as it is not likely that the above-mentioned vehicle will long continue to be employed.

Delicate Test for Nitrous Acid.

The most delicate test for nitrous acid so far discovered is the reaction it gives with metaphenylene-diamine, first reported by Griss. Several other allied bodies have since then been observed to give a similar reaction, and various improvements have been pointed out to make the test even more delicate and certain. Zambelli proposed the modification to employ sulphanilic acid. The liquid suspected to contain nitrous acid or a nitrate is treated with a drop of a saturated solution of sulphanilic acid, then a drop of an aqueous solution of phenol is added, and the liquid thus rendered alkaline with ammonia. According to the amount of nitrous acid present, the liquid will assume a tint varying from faint-yellow to intense reddish-yellow (like a strong solution of bichromate of potassium).

David Lindo tried the effects of various other phenols besides carbolic acid (which was the phenol employed by Zambelli), in order to find out which is the most sensitive. He found that *thymol* is sometimes preferable, and he also succeeded in making the test more decisive in other ways.

The test is performed in the manner below described.
The reagents required are:

1. Standard solution of Nitrous Acid. This is not specially described by the author, who only speaks of a solution of nitrous anhydride (N_2O_3), containing one part of this in one million. But for practical purposes an equivalent quantity of pure nitrite of potassium, or better, nitrite of silver, may be used.
2. Solution of Thymol, 10 per cent, in alcohol, or solution of Carbolic Acid, 10 per cent, in diluted alcohol.
3. Sulphanilic Reagent. A cold mixture of 1 part of pure sulphuric acid and five parts of water saturated with sulphanilic acid.
4. Solution of Ammonia, containing 6 to 7 per cent of ammoniacal gas. Fixed alkalies (pure) may be used in place of ammonia, but the latter is preferable.

Assuming, with the author, that we have a 1 in 1 million dilution of nitrous acid, then the test is made and results as follows:

Put 5 C.c. of the nitrite solution into a small test tube. Add 1 drop of the Sulphanilic Reagent, and 1 drop of the Thymol solution. Allow the mixture to be at rest during ten minutes, then add 1 C.c. of the Ammonia solution and mix well.

With a dilution of nitrous acid, such as has been assumed, the color is a yellowish-orange, increasing in depth when stronger nitrite solutions are used.

The author states that carbolic acid will possibly be preferred for *quantitative* work for the reason that it gives a pure yellow, without a tinge of orange, in high dilutions (at and beyond 1 in 1 million) of nitrites; while thymol always causes more or less of an orange tinge. For *qualitative* work, the author appears to prefer thymol, as it gives a deeper tint than carbolic acid in the same dilution of a nitrite.

The color is fully developed immediately, or almost immediately, after adding the alkali—which is a great advantage, particularly when the test is to be employed quantitatively.

The limit of the test, either with carbolic acid or with thymol, is about 1 of nitrous acid in 10 millions of water, the tints being very weak at this dilution.

The above reaction may also be used inversely as a very delicate test for the phenols which have been shown to produce the test. But as quite a number of them give this reaction, it would be impossible to identify the particular phenol. Yet, when it is known beforehand *which* of these phenols is present (as, for instance, in a solution prepared by the operator on purpose, for experimental or other purposes, or, to quote a practical example, when carbolized gauze is to be assayed for its percentage of carbolic acid, or when naphthol or thymol preparations are to be similarly assayed—Ed. Am. Drugg.), then the above test will afford a ready method of ascertaining the quantity present.—After *Chem. News*, July 27th.

The Chinese Cassia Trade.

The British Consul at Canton reports that the opposition of the cultivators of cassia in the province of Kwangsi, against the newly-formed cassia syndicate caused the viceroy, in the spring of 1887, to again grant to the old cassia merchants permission to trade with the producing districts. These old traders compete very strongly with the syndicate, and consequently the price of cassia fell to the lowest point ever known, viz., $5.60 per picul (133¼ W.), at which large contracts were made. The shipments of cassia lignea and broken cassia from Canton, during the year 1887, reached the enormous amount of 140,733 piculs, against 79,434½ piculs in 1886, while in former years an export of 100,000 piculs was considered exceptionably high.

How to Make Jujubes.

Take 2 lb. of picked gum arabic, 1½ lb. of the finest sugar sifted, 5 oz. of orange-flower water, and 1 pint of pure water. Powder the gum and then put it into a bright clean basin with 1 pint of water, and dissolve it over a slow fire, stirring constantly with a wooden spatula. When it is entirely dissolved, strain it through a towel or fine hair sieve to free it from all sediment. Put the strained gum and the sugar into another clean bright basin, and stir it over a very moderate fire while it boils and reduces to the "small pearl" (or 30° by the saccharometer); then add the orange-flower water. Stir all together on the fire, take off the scum, and pour the mixture into very smooth clean tin pans that have previously been well rubbed with oil of almonds, or with olive oil; fill them with the mixture to the depth of a quarter of an inch, and set them to dry in the drying-room at a moderate heat. When sufficiently dried, so that in pressing the surface it proves to be somewhat elastic to the touch, remove them from the heat and allow them to become cold; the jujube may then be easily detached and removed from the pans, and is then to be cut up with scissors into strips, and then the strips into diamond-shaped pieces. The jujubes can be colored with cochineal or ammoniated carmine solution, may be flavored with vanilla, rose, etc., and may be medicated.—*Brit. and Col. Confect.*

Ricin.

The well-known poisonous properties of castor-oil seeds, when eaten, have at length been explained by Dr. H. Stillmark, who has been working at the subject of the toxic principle of the seeds in Professor Kobert's laboratory at Dorpat. He has discovered in them an albuminoid body which he has named *ricin*, and classes among the "unformed ferments." This, however, does not appear to be the purgative principle. Its action, whether given by the mouth or hypodermically, is to produce hemorrhagic inflammation of the gastro-intestinal tract, affecting the small intestine and probably obstructing the bile duct, since there is usually extreme fulness of the gall bladder; the inflammation also extends to the vesical mucous membrane. Diarrhœa is by no means constant. The drowsiness and convulsions which occurred in some of his experiments on animals he attributes to possible thrombosis of the cerebral vessels. The lethal dose of ricin for man he calculates to be 6.0 milligrammes, $\frac{1}{10}$ grain for a man weighing 80 kilogrammes, this quantity being equal to about ten ordinary seeds; although, Christison once had a fatal case where only three seeds had been swallowed, and on the other hand a case is on record in which a person who had eaten seventeen seeds recovered. Ricin appears to have a peculiar effect upon blood, causing a rapid conglomeration of the red corpuscles, together with the formation of a substance like fibrin. One part of ricin to 60,000 of defibrinated blood is sufficient to cause a separation of the serum, so that the latter is capable of being passed through a filter. Crotonoleic acid, which exists in croton seeds, was found to be quite distinct from ricin. The results obtained by the experiments of Dr. Stillmark find further confirmation in a note in the *Medical Recorder* (July, p. 299), in which it is stated that fifteen children under six years of age, poisoned by eating castor-oil seeds, suffered from severe vomiting and prostration, but not from catharsis.—*Pharm. Journ.*

---

* The original gives the single hypodermic dose as 1 milligramme (1-64th grain). If Duquesnel's aconitine is used, this would be a highly dangerous dose.

Tincture of Pyrethrum as an Insecticide.

An old suggestion for the use of a strong alcoholic preparation in the place of the ordinary insect powders is revived by Mr. Harpmann, who recommends the use of a tincture prepared by macerating one part of "insect powder" in twenty parts of 96 per cent alcohol for eight days and then filtering. He says that if this tincture be sprayed in places infested by flies or other insects, it will act similarly to the powder, whilst it only causes very slight irritation to the mucous membrane and leaves hardly any stain. When used in a chamber, it is suggested that it should be combined with a little oil of lavender or some other perfume. This communication incidentally confirms the view that the toxic action of "insect powder" is not due to the fineness of the powder, as had been alleged, but to a definite compound that is soluble in alcohol and very volatile. In fact a distillate from the flowers is said to have the same effect as a pure insect powder.—*Pharm. Centralh.* and *Ph. Journ.*

Sulphonal.

Several additional papers have recently been published on the therapeutical effects of sulphonal, among which that of Professor Kast is noteworthy. He traces the somewhat considerable lapse of time which ensues before the remedy exerts its soporific influence to its comparative insolubility. Making experiments with water, with common salt solution, with an artificial gastric juice, and with the latter containing an excess of peptones, all at the blood heat, he found it required for solution 450, 250, 200, and 100 parts respectively. From these results the inference is clear that if the remedy is to be rapidly absorbed and therefore rapidly effective, it must be given in considerable quantities of warm liquids. Martin recommends sulphonal as reducing night sweats and increasing sleep in 8-grain doses for phthisical patients, while Leman records excellent results from the administration of 15-grain doses in asthma which morphine and chloral failed to relieve. Dr. Schney states that 30 grams given to an aged patient (61 years old) suffering from angina pectoris increased the symptoms of that affection, and, therefore, draws attention to its contra-indication in such cases. Dr. Fraenkel, from nearly one hundred trials of Riedel's sulphonal in cases of abnormal sleeplessness, in the usual doses, concluded that its effects were not always equal. In some cases the influence of the remedy was exerted in an hour, while in others it was observed only after the lapse of two or three hours.—*Chem. and Drugg.*

The Manufacture of Quinine in India.

From a report on this subject, we select the following description of the process employed in India (after *Chem. and Drugg.*)

The bark is first reduced to powder by means of a Carter's disintegrator and this powder is passed through a scalper, the sieves of which are made of silk and have 120 meshes to the linear inch. This extremely fine powder in the proportion of 100 parts is mixed with 8 parts of commercial caustic soda dissolved in 500 parts of water, and there is then added 600 parts of a mixture of fusel oil 1 part and kerosene oil 4 parts. Slaked lime may be used instead of the caustic soda, 15 parts of it being intimately mixed with the powdered bark before the water. The whole mixture—bark, alkali, water and oils—is next thoroughly agitated in barrels for four hours, then allowed to rest, and the oily layer drawn off from the top. This oil is again agitated for five or ten minutes with water acidulated with hydrochloric or sulphuric acid, whereby the alkaloids are dissolved out from the oil. Separation is again effected, the oil being transferred to the bark mixture, and agitated with it for two or three hours; again drawn off and washed as before in the same acidulated liquor. This process is repeated a third or fourth time, or until it is found by testing that only a small quantity of the bark has been thoroughly exhausted of its alkaloids. The quantity of acid required to take up the alkaloids from the oil depends, of course, on the quality of the bark operated on. If the bark contains 1 per cent of alkaloids, about 2 lbs. of sulphuric acid mixed in 20 gallons of water are sufficient. The after-treatment of the acidulated solution of alkaloids is simple. The solution is first neutralized with ammonia or soda and set aside to crystallize. The crystals are collected on a cloth and drained, then dissolved in about fifty times their weight of boiling water, and filtered hot through a little animal charcoal. On cooling after filtration, the crystals again form and are separated as before from the mother liquor by filtration. The crystalline mass obtained is then placed in small lumps on sheets of white blotting-paper stretched on slabs of plaster of Paris. By this means they are practically dried. They are afterwards thoroughly dried by being laid on blotting-paper in a room heated to about 10° above the temperature of the open air. The foregoing presents the salient points of Mr. Gammie's process for the manufacture of sulphate of quinine. The resulting product doubtless contains other alkaloids than quinine, but in what proportion there is nothing to indicate.

IMPROVED BURETTES FOR BARYTA SOLUTION, ETC.

The use of baryta and various other solutions, in volumetric analysis, is rendered somewhat difficult by the readiness with which they absorb carbonic acid gas from the air. When such solutions are to be frequently, or perhaps constantly, required in actual practice, it is best to adopt some plan by which the access of impure air to the liquid may be permanently prevented.

Such a plan is presented in the arrangement devised by A. Beutell. In this case, the baryta (or other) solution enters the burette from below. This is not shown here, but, as there is no chance of any air getting in at this end, there was no need of doing so. As the liquid rises in the burette, it will finally flow out from the orifice *i*, and pass through the tube *e* into a small reservoir *f*, the flow being stopped when the end of the tube *k* is covered by some of the solution. The cylindrical tube *a* is charged with caustic soda, soda-lime, or caustic baryta, and its lower end is fused into another small reservoir or wash-vessel containing enough mercury to cover the end of the tube. The object of the mercury is to compel the damp air contained within the burette while empty, and which is expelled while it is being filled, to pass out through *e k f*, rather than through *b a*. This effects a material saving of the charge placed in the tube *a*, the functions of which are to take all carbonic acid from that air which is required to enter the apparatus when liquid is allowed to flow from it.—After *Chem. Zeit.*

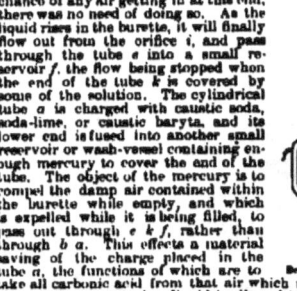

Beutell's burette.

A NEW SIPHON AND PIPETTE.

Raikow describes, in the *Chemiker Zeitung*, a new siphon which permits to draw the liquid from the top of a reservoir instead of the bottom. The principle of this siphon may be understood by examining the illustration. The siphon tube proper (A) has two stop-cocks. Over the upper one (*h*), the tube is expanded to a bulb which ends in a fine orifice. Opposite to this is the orifice of a

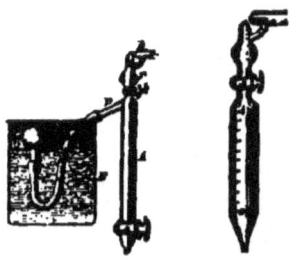

Raikow's siphon and pipette.

blowing tube *b*, arranged as in the well-known spray apparatuses. The short siphon tube *p* is connected, by means of flexible tubing with the glass float *n*, which has a hole *o*, where shown in the cut.

When the siphon is to be started, the stop-cock at *h* is opened and air blown through *b*, which will cause the liquid to be aspirated, so that the leg A becomes filled with liquid. On closing *h* and opening the lower stop-cock, the liquid will continue to flow off.

The same principle may be applied to the construction of a pipette, in the manner shown in Fig. 2.—After *Chem. Zeit.* and *Chem. Centralbl.*

Ether Drinking in Ireland.—In some places in the north of Ireland ether is largely used as a substitute for whiskey, one reason being its cheapness, inasmuch as a person can obtain for a penny sufficient ether to make him drunk. The subject of ether drinking in certain districts in Ireland has for some years attracted attention, and recently a clergyman moved a resolution bearing on the subject before the General Synod of the Irish Church. He proposed that a petition be presented to Parliament praying for the regulation of the sale of ether as an intoxicant in certain districts. The motion was adopted. There is, it is alleged, a special kind of ether prepared for drinking purposes, and it is also said that, although the excise authorities have been applied to, they have refused to control its sale.—*Br. and Col. Druggist.*

Mercury Salicylate.

This compound is being energetically pushed and recommended. As the double salt with sodium chloride is more soluble than the salicylate itself, it is better adapted for use in practical surgery. This double salt has the formula $C_6H_4.COOHgCl.ONa$ and contains 50 per cent of salicylate of mercury.—*Chem. and Drugg.*

New Method of Separating Bromine from Iodine and Chlorine.

John Tsawoo White, of Rangoon, has found that bromine may be liberated from bromides, and estimated, even in presence of iodides and chlorides, by heating the aqueous solution of the bromide or mixture with a solution of permanganate of potassium and sulphate of aluminium.

Supposing the solution to be tested or assayed contains 0.1 Gm. of bromine. Having introduced it into a distilling flask, add to it 10 C.c. of a solution of permanganate of potassium (1 : 35), and make all ready for distillation. At the last moment, add 5 C.c. of an aqueous solution of aluminium sulphate, saturated at the ordinary temperature, and then apply heat. Only bromine will be given off. This may be caught in a standard solution of iodide of potassium, and the liberated iodine—equivalent to the bromine—estimated by hyposulphite.

There seems to be, however, still some uncertainty whether the method can be used for the quantitative estimation of bromine. Meanwhile, it will, at all events, serve as a qualitative test, easily applied.—*After Chem. News,* 1888, 238; 245.

Estimation of Chloroform.

A solution of caustic potassa in alcohol of 60% decomposes chloroform slowly, but almost completely, at the ordinary temperature, and decomposition is rapid at 100° C. If the strength of the potash solution is known, the excess may be determined by titration, using phenolphthalein as indicator, and after the liquid has been carefully cooled, the amount of the potassium chloride formed may be estimated by silver nitrate solution with potassium chromate as indicator. In the cold solution the alcohol and potassium formate have no effect on the titration. In order to employ this method for the estimation of chloroform, the latter is heated with the alcoholic potash in sealed tubes [heating under a well-cooled upright condenser will also answer, Ed. Am. Drug.], and the excess of potash and amount of chloride formed are estimated.

In order to determine the quantity of chloroform vapor in air or other gases, a known volume of the gas is allowed to enter a vacuous globe into which a measured quantity of alcoholic potash is then introduced. After standing for eight or ten days, an aliquot part of the potash solution is withdrawn and titrated.—L. De St. Martin in *Compt. Rend.,* abstract in *J. Chem. Soc.*

Effervescent Carbonate of Iron.

Dr. Hermann Hager, having been requested to devise a formula for preparing an "effervescent carbonate of iron," publishes the following in the *Pharm. Centralhalle* (No. 29):

Sulphate of Iron, cryst.	40 parts
Tartaric Acid	100 "
Bicarbonate of Sodium	166.5 "
Citric Acid	8 "
Sugar	80 "
Oil of Lemon	1.5 "
Absolute Alcohol	1 part

Reduce all the solids to a fine powder, and mix them, in a porcelain [or Wedgwood] mortar, with the Oil of Lemon and Absolute Alcohol, previously mixed together. Then pass the mixture through a sieve, transfer it to a porcelain capsule placed on a water-bath, and stir the mass, while it is being heated, with a glass-rod, until it has become granular. Allow it to become cool, and transfer it to bottles which must be carefully stoppered.

Dose: Sixty to seventy-five grains in "a tumbler filled about two-thirds with water."

Although ferrous carbonate is almost insoluble in water, yet the freshly-prepared solution in water, of the above compound, is scarcely turbid, probably owing to the presence of free carbonic-acid gas.

Detection of Minute Quantities of Bismuth.

M. Léger recently made a communication to the Paris Society of Pharmacy, illustrated with experiments, on a test for bismuth which he proposes. One of the most sensitive tests for alkaloids, he said, whether they be natural or artificial, is the double iodide of bismuth and potassium. The reaction, it is true, is quite general and reliable, but not very instructive, because it has never helped us, so far, to form more definite conceptions of the constitution of alkaloids. The idea then came to M. Léger of reversing the test, and using an alkaloid to detect bismuth instead of bismuth to show up alkaloid. He found the reagent very satisfactory in all respects, especially as regards sensitiveness. For obvious reasons, cinchonine was the alkaloid selected. A solution of potassium and cinchonine hydriodate added to a liquor containing 1 per 10,000 of bismuth gave immediately a bright red precipi-

tate; with 1 in 100,000 of water a very appreciable tinge could be observed even from a distance. With 1 in 500,000 a faint hue can with some precautions be recognised. At the same time care must be taken how the bismuth solution is made; there should be no alcohol, no alkalies, or excess of sulphuric acid. To further extend the usefulness of the test, he tried to use it for quantitative estimations of bismuth, but so far without success, owing to the uncertain composition and keeping properties of the precipitate. Hence it can be only recommended as a qualitative test for bismuth, but an excellent one. In answer to a query by M. Petit, M. Léger added that mercury could not be mistaken for bismuth with the test in question. While bismuth affords a very bright red precipitate, mercury gives only a faint yellow one, and but little of it.—*Chem. and Drugg.*

Occurrence of Fluorine in the Organism.

The method adopted by G. Tammann for the quantitative estimation of fluorine is as follows: The substance under investigation is treated with powdered quartz and sulphuric acid. A current of dry air carries the silicon fluoride so formed through a narrow tube, where it is decomposed with steam and the silicic acid collected on the walls of the tube, hydrofluosilicic acid being also formed; the latter is absorbed in aqueous potash, and evaporated to dryness; the residue is taken up with hydrochloric acid, the potassium silicofluoride precipitated with alcohol, filtered, and titrated with potassa solution. Fluorine is well known to be a constant constituent of bone; it is also known to occur in ploughed earth and in wells. Horsford found weighable quantities of fluorine in the human brain, and Salm-Horstmar found that certain plants did not fully develop in the absence of fluorine.

In the present research, plants grown in culture liquids, which did not contain fluorine, were found to die quickly when fluorine was added to such liquids; thus, the addition of 0.1 gramme of potassium fluoride per litre caused death in these plants in twelve hours.

The different parts of the egg were investigated; the shell contained imponderable traces only; the white contained somewhat larger traces, but still imponderable; the yoke yielded weighable quantities; 84 grammes of fresh yolk contained 0.0009 gramme of fluorine. Attention is drawn to the fact that the brain and the egg-yolk, tissues that contain much phosphorus, are also richest in fluorine. In other experiments, brain, cow's milk, and blood, were found to contain small weighable quantities of fluorine.

From these experiments, certain conclusions are drawn, the chief purport of which is, that fluorine is of greater physiological importance in the animal economy than has hitherto been considered to be the case.—*Zeitsch. Physiol. Chem.* and *J. Chem. Soc.*

On the Cultivation of Capsicum Annuum.

It is well known that capsicum plays a considerable rôle in the culinary art of different nations. In Moravia and Hungary it is known under the name of *paprika,* and much attention is paid to its cultivation. In northern Hungary, "paprika" is called *risk* or *tesser;* and in the district of Pesth, *bdihya.* The true home, or rather centre, of cultivation of the plant is Szegedin and its environs, where some 2,500 families are engaged exclusively in its cultivation. Only two species are chiefly raised, namely: 1st, the Turkish or Serbian variety, which is sweet and fleshy—known also in France as l'iment doux d'Espagne, Piment gros carré doux; and in South America, Aji dulce—being the *Capsicum tetragonum* Miller. And 2d, *Capsicum annuum* var. *Szegedinensis.* The first mentioned variety is so mild that it is either eaten raw with salt, or is sliced and added as a condiment to potato-salad. In restaurants at Pesth it is served filled with chopped meat. The Transylvanian Roumanians and Saxonians scald and skin it, and in this form eat it under the name of *ardei.*

The pendulous, fleshy pods are distinguished by their angular form, and by the fact that their points end in four to five conical ridges.

The second variety mentioned above has laterally-curved, conical berries or pods, of a scarlet color, about 2¼ to 3¼ inches long, and generally also ridged near the point. The ripe seeds are planted at the end of March in rich garden soil. When the plants are about a finger high, they are dug out, with a lump of soil adhering to the root, and transferred to carefully prepared beds, being planted about 18 inches apart in all directions. Until the flowers appear (June to September), the beds are hoed twice or three times, and the crop is gathered as it ripens up to the time of the first frosts. The fruits are strung upon cords 9 to 12 feet long, and hung up at the southern side of the houses where the ripening process is completed. Finally, they are stored indoors in a well-ventilated place.

The preparation of "paprika," as a condiment, begins with the introduction of the pods into heated ovens, where they are rendered brittle. Then they are comminuted between ordinary millstones, and passed through a sieve. The coarser residue is once more dried and ground, and this latter, known as *cedrmüly paprika* ["paprika waste"], is much preferred, as it consists almost solely of the pericarp, and possesses both a fine color and a very mild taste.—*After Industriebl.*

Iodoform as a Hæmostatic.

IODOFORM is recommended by Chauvin and Jorisenne as a powerful, reliable, and rapid hæmostatic. They administer it in pills containing one grain of iodoform made up with extract of gentian or liquorice, three to five being taken daily.—*Med. Press und Circ.; Pharm. Journ.*

Mouth-Wash and Catarrh Cure.

Carbolic Acid	ʒ iv.
Spirit of Chloroform	ʒ iij.
Tinct. of Myrrh	ʒ ij.
Eau de Cologne, to	℥ vi.

M. To be used with water.

A gentleman who got this lotion from Mr. Stevenson, L.D.S., of Wimpole st., happened to be troubled with a nasal catarrh which a throat specialist's remedies did not cure. He sniffed a little of the mouth-wash up his nose and it stopped the sneezing and watery discharge.—*Chem. and Drugg.*

Condemning Saccharin.

THE Seine council of Hygeine, at their meeting of June 22d, received a committee report on saccharin presented by Dr. Dujardin-Beaumetz and signed by MM. Péligot, A. Gautier, Jungfleisch, Proust, and Riche. The committee declare saccharin to be not an aliment, but a medicament. They are, moreover, convinced its only use in industry will be for adulterating alimentary products. The report was unanimously adopted by the council. The probable consequence will be the prohibition of saccharin in all articles of food.—*Chem. and Drugg.*

Chloroform as a Preservative.

PROFESSOR UNNA suggests the employment of chloroform for the preparation of solutions generally and those for hypodermic injection in particular. He believes that chloroform water may, with advantage, be made the menstruum in such liquors as Fowler's solution and for liquor. morphin. hypoderm., which latter may be injected with less pain than accompanies the operation generally.—*Chem. and Drug.*

[We have long recommended this method, and have also employed it practically. It has also found mention in the new National Formulary.]

Solanine.

SOLANINE has been reported to be an efficient analgesic. But it has been found to be inferior to both antipyrin and acetanilide (antifebrin) in acute articular rheumatism. In neuralgia of old standing, however, and in neuritis it is far superior to them. It excels acetanilide in its power to control the phenomena of motor excitement.—*Arch. de Pharm.*

We wish to add that the price of Solanine is so high that its extended medicinal use is not likely to be encouraged at the present time.

Alleged Death from Sulphate of Sparteine.

MR. LAVALLE, pharmacist at Crest, reports to the *Union Pharmaceutique* that a case of death has occurred from the administration of sulphate of sparteine, in doses of about ⅓ grain. The physician had prescribed ten doses of ⅓ grain (0.05 Gm.), ten doses of 1½ grains (0.10 Gm.), and twenty-five doses of 4 grains (0.25 Gm.). The patient only took the ⅓-grain doses, one in the morning and one at night, and died on the eighth day.

The editor of the journal adds that the dose given was normal, and that the death was probably due to other causes. We agree with this view.

Boldoin as a Hypnotic.

ACCORDING to M. Juranville, boldoin, the glucoside of boldo leaves, far exceeds in its hypnotic and narcotic action opium, chloral, or any other similar agent (*Chem. Zeit.*, June 17th, p. 166). The quantity that can be administered to invalids daily without ill effects is stated to be as much as 5 to 10 grammes. The yield of boldoin from the leaves is given as 3 per cent. It may be mentioned that the hypnotic action of this glucoside was observed by Dr. Laborde at the time of its first discovery four years ago (*Pharm. Journ.* [3], xiv., 965).—*Pharm. Journ.*, June 30th.

Chutnee.—The following formula, with gooseberries as one of the ingredients, is given by the *Chem. and Drugg.*

Gooseberries	2	quarts.
Vinegar	3	"
Salt	1	lb.
Mustard Seed	1	"
Stoned Raisins	1	"
Brown Sugar	1	"
Garlic	12	oz.
Cayenne Pepper	6	"

Make a syrup of the sugar with a pint of the vinegar, boil the gooseberries with a quart of the vinegar; bruise the mustard seed and the garlic, and well incorporate the whole of the ingredients in a mortar.

A NEW METHOD OF ASH-DETERMINATION.

THE incineration of substances for the quantitative determination of the ash is in many cases a very tedious and disagreeable operation, partly owing to foaming or swelling of the mass and partly through the formation of difficultly combustible carbon.

Ludwig Reese has succeeded in devising a plan by which this process can be very materially abbreviated. The principle is merely this, that a current of hot air is conducted over the substance contained in a suitable receptacle.

The apparatus recommended for this purpose consists of a wide glass tube *AB*, of difficultly fusible glass, and a similar, smaller one *ab*, which can be pushed into the larger, and in which the incineration is made to take place. The external tube, *AB*, is 40-50 Cm. (16-20 in.) long. Its bore, as well as the length and bore of the smaller tube, depend upon the quantity of substance to be incinerated. The amount employed for this purpose by the author varied between 0.3 and 3 Gm., for which he used tubes of 16-20 Cm. (6¼-7¾ in.) in length, and 11 to 18 Mm. (7/16-¾ in.) bore. The end A of the tube *AB* is connected with a water pump (vacuum pump), but it is advisable to interpose, between it and the pump, an empty flask for the purpose of being able to observe the vapors emitted. The smaller tube *ab* is drawn out a little at one end (*a*), and this is packed with doubly folded platinum wire gauze to catch any particles which might be mechanically carried forward by suction.

The smaller tube is surrounded by a coil of platinum wire to prevent adhesion to the outer tube when the temperature is high. The incineration itself is conducted in a porcelain boat slipped into the smaller tube.

When an ash determination is to be made, the weight of the dry, inner tube including boat is first determined. The latter is then drawn out, the substance weighed into it, again replaced, surrounded with the platinum spiral, and introduced into the larger tube. Next, the end *a* is connected with the pump, and while the current of air is passing, the larger tube is heated at *C*. When the water of the substance has been thus carried off, and it begins to decompose, the flame at *C* is made a little larger, the substance at *D* also gently heated and the point *a* somewhat more strongly, to prevent the accumulation of products of distillation. Gradually the heat is raised until the vapors pass through the interposed flask in a copious current, care being taken at the same time that the substance does not swell up so as to pour or flow over the edge of the porcelain boat. Finally, when no more empyreumatic vapors are given off, the heat is again raised a little, and it is observed whether the carbon is all being consumed or not. In most cases, this will occur. Should it not take place readily, a current of perfectly dry oxygen gas is conducted over the substance, the heat being continued. Lastly a current of dry air is conducted through the tube, after the heat has been removed, the tube then withdrawn, allowed to cool in the exsiccator, and weighed.

The analytical data given by the author, who selected for this purpose notoriously obstinate substances, show that this new method saves many hours of work.—After *Zeitschr. f. Anal. Chem.*, 1886, 133.

CENTRIFUGAL EXTRACTION APPARATUS.

IN the extractor patented by Adolf Schulze, of Halle (Germ. Pat., No. 41,772), a novel feature is introduced. The extractor proper is a vessel contained in an outer shell or boiler, and can be set into rapid circular motion by a pulley attachment. The centrifugal motion thereby produced causes the mass contained in the extractor to be-

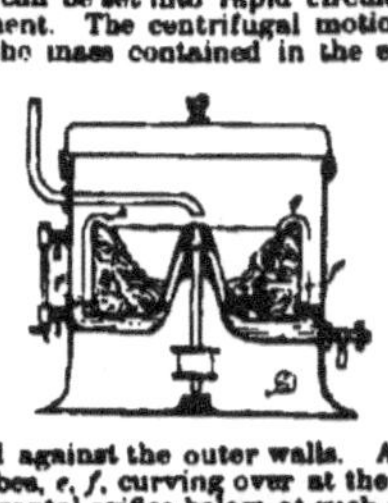

come impacted against the outer walls. Along the latter run several tubes, *e*, *f*, curving over at the top, and opening with a horizontal orifice below, at such a level that the orifice will be below the surface of the extracting liquid. When the apparatus is charged, and the pulley is set in operation, the rapid circular motion causes liquid to ascend the tubes *e* and *f*, and to be constantly ejected from the upper end over the substance to be exhausted. This operation, therefore, insures the utmost economy in menstruum.

Pharmaceutical Curiosities.

ONE of our subscribers has sent us another batch of curious orders which have occurred in his practice:
5 cent worth flack side.—5 cts. ipecca scrop.—5 cents worth Clordia Lime.—5 cents worth Senia and Mania, and a little Aniseed in it.—10 cents Seltzer powders.—Corcose of supplement for beg bugs.—The wine of ginsengo roots.—A pair of small twers [meant for tweezers] for pulling out. — Lickererspauter [meant for Liquorice powder, comp.].—Sun Coleria Drops.—Iodorform, or odorform, a yellow powder to put on a sore.—Canfreted oil [meant for camphorated oil].

Galvanized Iron Condemned.

On being consulted thereon, the Paris Council of Hygiene have disapproved of the use of galvanised iron vessels for holding or measuring liquids intended for alimentary purposes. Owing to their cheapness, large tanks and measures were sought to be introduced, but they offer the danger of rapidly contaminating with zinc most liquids happening to come into contact with them. In consequence of the decision, the administration will refuse to affix the legal stamps to any vessels of this description, and will only allow, as heretofore, tinned copper or tinned iron.—*Chem. and Drugg.*

Detecting Pus in the Urine and Other Liquids.

VITALI recommends tincture of guaiac as a delicate reagent to detect pus, even when this has been altered by fermentation, or has become dried up.
If the test is to be applied to urine, the latter is mixed with such a quantity of tincture of guaiac that it acquires a decided milky appearance. It is then warmed to between 35° and 40° C. (90°-104° F.). If pus was present, the liquid assumes a blue color. Another method is, to filter the urine, and to treat the filter, while still wet, with a little of the tincture, whereby a magnificent blue color is produced. A very gentle heat promotes the reaction, but a stronger heat prevents or destroys it. In presence of reducing agents, such as hydrosulphuric acid, sulphide of ammonium, etc., and of caustical alkalies, the reaction fails.—*Bollet. farmac.*

Anthrarobin.

AT a recent meeting of the Berlin Physiological Society, Dr. Weyl stated that he had found, as the result of experiments on rabbits and dogs and on himself, that anthrarobin (see our last April number, page 62) possesses absolutely no action on the living organism, even when taken by the mouth in relatively large doses, or hypodermically injected. It appears in an unaltered state in the urine, and he therefore concludes that, notwithstanding the great affinity for oxygen that it possesses, it passes through the body without being oxidized. Chrysarobin, on the other hand, has a powerful physiological action when taken internally. Dr. Weyl is, however, unable to confirm the statements of several authors that chrysarobin appears in the urine as chrysophanic acid. He believes it is excreted as chrysarobin, and subsequently undergoes the change to chrysophanic acid.—*Pharm. Journ.*, June 30th.

Salicylic Collodion as a Corn Cure.

GEZOW's formula containing 10% of salicylic acid in collodion, with the addition of extract of cannabis, for preventing pain and inflammation, has, of late, become almost a domestic remedy for corns in Austria, Switzerland, Germany, and parts of Russia. Cases having been reported, however, in which toxic symptoms followed its use, Ivan Binert, an apothecary of St. Petersburg, who saw such a case, declares that the symptoms were evidently caused by the cannabis. As the ingredient is rather superfluous, the salicylic acid being the sole curative agent, Mr. Binert recommends the following formula, saying that he has sold several thousands of bottles without receiving any reports of inefficiency or unpleasant effects. His formula is:

Crystallized Salicylic Acid	10 parts.
Collodion	100 "
Venice Turpentine	1 part.
Chlorophyl (for coloring)	q. s.

Volumetric Estimation of Iodine in Presence of Chlorine and Bromine.

ACCORDING to N. McCulloch (in *Chem. News*), iodine may be estimated in the presence of bromine and chlorine without previous removal of the latter elements, by the following method. The solution containing the iodine, bromide, and iodide is mixed with its own bulk of strong hydrochloric acid, and 20 to 30 fluid grains of chloroform. Standardised permanganate is dropped in, with agitation, until the iodine color at first produced in the chloroform is again discharged owing to the formation of colorless iodine monochloride. Iodine bromide in strong solution colors the chloroform faint yellowish-pink, which cannot, however, be mistaken for the iodine coloration. The process cannot be employed in the presence of free hydrochloric or hydrocyanic acids; the presence of the latter causes high results.—*Abstr. in J. Chem. Soc.*

Impure Pilocarpine.

PILOCARPINE hydrochlorate has been often noticed to fail in producing the desired effect, to the annoyance of both patient and medical attendant. This want of activity and of certainty in action, it is suggested in a communication to the *Therap. Monatsh.*, is due not so much to deterioration through keeping as to the presence of jaborine, which is formed during the isolation of the principle by the action of any acid liquid upon it.—*Chem. and Drug.*

Aluminium as a Natural Constituent of Wheat Flour.

W. C. YOUNG (in *The Analyst*) confirms the statement of Yoshida as to the occurrence of a minute quantity of aluminium in wheat, and shows that, practically, the whole of it is associated with the gluten. A sample of the best Vienna flour gave 0.0073 per cent of aluminium phosphate. The gluten from 250 grammes of this flour was dissolved in acetic acid to purify it, and the solution yielded aluminium phosphate amounting to 0.0074 per 100 of flour.—*J. Chem. Soc.*

Test for Sulphonal.

IF equal quantities of sulphonal and of potassium cyanide (or in place of the latter, of pyrogallic acid) are triturated together in a mortar, and the mixture then heated in a dry test-tube, the latter is quickly filled with dense vapors having the odor of mercaptan. If the melted mass is dissolved in hot water and a little solution of ferric chloride added, a blood-red color is produced, identical with the reaction between potassium sulphocyanide and ferric salts.—G. VULPIUS in *Apoth. Zeit.*, 3,247.

New Method of Determining the Amount of Fat in Milk, Cream, etc.

TAKE a graduated test-tube, having the capacity of about 50 C.c., and divided into $\frac{1}{10}$ C.c., introduce into it exactly 10 C.c. of the milk or similar fatty liquid (with cream, only 5 C.c. are required), then add 10 C.c. of concentrated hydrochloric acid, and boil the mixture, while moving the test-tube to and fro, until the contents assume a dark-brown color. Then cool the tube by immersing it into cool water, add 30 C.c. of ether, shake, and set it aside until the ethereal layer has separated. Measure the latter, remove 10 C.c. of it by means of a pipette, and evaporate this in a tared porcelain capsule on the water-bath, aiding the evaporation by blowing air over it. Finally, dry at 100° C. (212° F.) in a hot air-bath, weigh, and calculate the result for the total volume of the ethereal layer.
If the operation is properly conducted, the ethereal and aqueous solutions will separate sharply and clear, without the least turbidity. The ethereal solution should not show any minute aqueous particles when it flows from the pipette.
The results obtained by this method are perfectly accurate [according to the author], and do not differ, either among themselves, or from the results obtained by other analytical methods, by as much as 0.1 per cent.
The execution of the assay, if everything is properly prepared for it, does not consume more than fifteen minutes.—DR. WERNER SCHMID, in *Zeitschr. f. anal. Chem.*, 1888, 468.

Improved Method of Generating Hydrogen Gas.

HABERMANN recommends to employ for the generation of hydrogen gas, particularly when the well-known apparatus of Kipp (see this Journal, 1887, p. 167) is used—an alloy of 84 parts of zinc and 16 parts of tin, in pieces granulated in the same manner as zinc alone has heretofore been employed. When dilute sulphuric acid acts upon this alloy, hydrogen gas is produced from the first moment of contact in abundant quantity. When the zinc contained in any of the granulated pieces has been dissolved out, the remaining tin, now a metallic sponge, retains the shape of the original piece, and this prevents the access of any metal to the globular reservoir at the bottom. When pure zinc is used, and the pieces become gradually reduced in size until they are able to drop down into the reservoir, it often happens that a further generation of hydrogen takes place in the latter, which is not at all intended, and may sometimes result in the forcing out of some of the liquid contents from the apparatus.—*After Chem. Zeit.*

Oil of Bay vs. Flies.—It is stated that expressed oil of bay (*huile de laurier*) is extensively used in Switzerland by butchers to keep their shops free from flies, and that after a coat of oil has been applied to the walls none of these troublesome pests venture to put in an appearance. This remedy has also been tried and found effectual in the south of France in preserving gilt frames, chandeliers, etc., from becoming soiled. It is even remarked that flies soon avoid the rooms where this application has been employed.

American Druggist

AN ILLUSTRATED MONTHLY JOURNAL

OF

Pharmacy, Chemistry, and Materia Medica.

Vol. XVII, No. 9.   Whole No. 171.

FREDERICK A. CASTLE, M.D.................Editor.
CHARLES RICE, Ph.D..................Associate Editor.

PUBLISHED BY

WM. WOOD & CO., 56 & 58 Lafayette Place, N. Y.

SUBSCRIPTION PRICE per year, ... $1.50
SINGLE COPIES, ...15

Address all communications relating to the business of the AMERICAN DRUGGIST, such as subscriptions, advertisements, change of Post-Office address, etc., to WILLIAM WOOD & CO., 56 and 58 Lafayette Place, New York City, to whom order all postal money orders and checks should be made payable. Communications intended for the Editor should be addressed in care of the Publishers.

The AMERICAN DRUGGIST is issued in the latter part of each month, dated for the month ahead. Changes of advertisements should reach us before the 15th. New advertisements can occasionally be inserted after the 20th.

REGULAR ADVERTISEMENTS according to size, location, and time. Special rates on application.

ITEMS.

Kings County Board of Pharmacy.

A SPECIAL meeting of the Kings County Pharmaceutical Society was held on Thursday afternoon, July 26th, in their rooms, 356 Bridge street, Brooklyn, for the purpose of electing two members to fill the vacancies caused by expiration of term of office in the Kings County Board of Pharmacy, the retiring members being Mr. William P. De Forst, president of the board, and Mr. L. E. Nicot.

The meeting was called to order by President Stevens at 3:30, and the object of the meeting stated.

President De Forst read the report of the board, giving information of its doings for the past three years, showing how the law had been applied for the benefit of the dispenser, the prescriber, and the public, the last being of great importance to be considered, as they were the excuse for its enactment.

The board had met with some antagonism on the part of a few druggists who forgot to sink their personality in the duty they owed to others; the large majority of pharmacists, however, had aided with their moral influence; there had been no occasion to invoke the aid of the courts, for the few who had temporarily defied the board's authority had either, in the end, submitted to its decision or removed from the territory.

Allusion was made to the recent amendment of the law creating the grade of assistant pharmacist, which enabled the board to raise the standard of examination of those who proposed opening stores, while making it easier for those who wished only to serve as clerks.

The subject of interchange of certificates of qualification by the different boards was treated at great length; the Kings County Board favored it, provided other boards required as high conditions for qualifications as they did, and that they reciprocated by receiving the Kings County certificates.

Attention was called to the suggestion of the president of the board, three years ago, of establishing a school of pharmacy for the education of beginners in pharmacy, especially of those who would have to appear for examination; thanks were tendered to the Society for its promptness in acting on that suggestion and establishing the series of lectures. For several years they had been eminently successful, as nearly every one attending them had passed better average examinations than others; this was especially noticeable in those who had striven for the Fairlie prize; they had been the means of inducing many students to enter the College of Pharmacy, and besides had had a moral and educational effect on the members of the Society.

The point of great interest in the report was the case of the druggist who had been charged by a customer and physician with substituting on a prescription dispensed by an unregistered clerk. The druggist was tried before the board, and though he was given the benefit of all the doubts, the evidence was strong against him and he was unanimously adjudged guilty, censured, fined a sum of money, and his registration suspended.

The board had issued a circular letter to the druggists of the county warning them that the article "Rough on Rats" being proved by analysis to be mainly arsenic, would have to be sold with all the restrictions that any other poison was; replies were received from nearly every druggist in the county that they would conform to the law in that respect.

The report closed by words of congratulation to his associates on the board.

The secretary, L. T. Perkins, read the short report showing the number of men examined and registered during the last term, and turned a surplus of money over to the treasury of the Society.

The Society proceeded to nominate and elect the two members. President De Forst declined a re-election, owing to his having severed his connection with the retail business, as he believed none but those in active work in drug stores should be on a board of pharmacy. Mr. L. E. Nicot and W. M. Davis were elected, and the Society adjourned. The Kings County Medical Society re-elected the two physicians, C. E. De La Vergne and Jos. H. Hunt, who have served for the last three years. The four gentlemen will have to qualify before the County Clerk during the next thirty days, and then proceed to elect a fifth member as secretary, who must be a pharmacist.

The North Dakota Pharmaceutical Association held its annual meeting on the 7th of August. Of a total of one hundred and sixty members, thirty were present. The following officers were elected: president, C. L. Valentine, of La Moure; vice-presidents, D. F. Siegfried, of Sanborn; C. H. Trepanier, of Grand Forks; secretary, H. L. Haussamen, of Grafton; treasurer, E. C. Maxey, of Fargo; executive committee, C. R. Meredith, of Casselton; W. Flath, of St. Thomas; F. H. Divaux, of Valley City; local secretary, P. W. Hawkinson, of Fargo; delegate to A. P. A., H. L. Haussamen.

The following committees were appointed:
Queries—M. D. Fleming, Fargo; C. R. Meredith, Casselton; L. Christianson, Fargo. Revision of Pharmacy Law—The North Dakota Board of Pharmacy; Messrs. Frank Frisby, Bismarck; H. L. Haussamen, Grafton; E. C. Maxey, Fargo; L. Christianson, Fargo, and S. F. Langdon, Casselton.

The Newark Drug Clerks' Association held their regular monthly meeting on August 3d, with a full attendance.

After the reading of the minutes of preceding meeting, the secretary, Mr. Henry Ost, handed in his resignation, which was accepted. He was unanimously elected an honorary member.

Mr. Frank B. Meeker was then unanimously elected secretary in the place of Mr. Ost, resigned, and Mr. Otto C. B. Grum was unimously elected to the vice-presidency, vacated by Mr. Meeker.

One new member was elected and three others proposed who will be acted on at next meeting.

The meeting closed with an interesting address by Mr. Ost on the subject of "Beer Brewing."

The Association is now in a flourishing condition, and all drug clerks in the vicinity are cordially invited to attend any of the meetings.

The next meeting will be on Friday, September 7th.
The constitution may be obtained by addressing the secretary, Frank B. Meeker, 661 Broad street.

Chicago College of Pharmacy.—The friends of the members of the class of eighty-eight assembled in the Grand Opera House on the afternoon of July 31st to witness the bestowal of diplomas on the thirty-three graduates, who, with the faculty, occupied the stage. Honorable mention for especial excellence in studies was made of Wm. E. Greiner, of Paris, Texas. Amongst the junior students, R. F. Curti, F. Dempster, Otto Paul, and R. R. Smith received honorable mention. The Hon. Charles Ham, who may be justly regarded as the father of manual training in Chicago, delivered an address. The valedictory was delivered by Thomas W. Sanders. After the diplomas had been awarded by Wm. K. Forsythe, that gentleman delivered the address to the graduates. Martin Heinemann was the recipient of a prize microscope. Prof. H. D. Garrison made the concluding address.

The Alumni Association held a meeting in the evening, at which there was a goodly number of associates of long standing. Several new members were elected. The choice of officers resulted as follows:—President, W. A. Puchner; first vice-president, J. E. Grubb; second vice-president, A. E. Hiss; secretary, A. E. Venn; treasurer, F. F. Gazzolo; executive board, G. R. Baker, J. T. Delfosse, G. B. Farrer, A. A. Winter, E. L. Becker, and G. K. Hermer. It was voted to extend the prize gold medal to the summer term. Power was given to the Executive Board to elect new members, so that it will be unnecessary to wait until the half-yearly gathering at commencement for election to the membership of the association. A committee was appointed consisting of F. M. Schmidt, A. E. Hiss, and A. E. Venn to draw up an expression of regret for the death of the late G. W. Hunt, Actuary of the College, which occurred July 30th.

At a meeting of the College, the following Resolutions were adopted:

Whereas, The messenger of death, who sooner or later comes to all, has visited this College and taken away from us our Actuary, Mr. George W. Hunt, one who was highly esteemed among us as an officer and a man; therefore,

Resolved, That we, the students, faculty, officers, and trustees of the Chicago College of Pharmacy desire to give our testimony to the great respect in which the deceased was held by us. As an officer of the college he was ever diligent and faithful in the discharge of his duties. In all his dealings with the students he was kind, generous, and just, and he invariably won and retained their respect and love. Upon the minds of all the faculty and the other officers of the college he has left the impression of a faithful, upright man and of an affable, cultured gentleman. Those who knew him most intimately were the ones to respect and revere him most.

Resolved, That to the bereaved family we extend our sympathy in this their time of sorrow.

Resolved, That a copy of these resolutions be sent to the family of the deceased, and other copies to the pharmaceutical journals for publication.

Chicago, July 31st, 1888.

Correction.

In the formula for artificial Ems ("Kraenchen") mineral water given on page 142 of last number, the quantity of bicarbonate of sodium should be 22 parts, instead of 2.2.

QUERIES & ANSWERS.

Queries for which answers are desired, must be received by the 5th of the month, and must in every case be accompanied by the name and address of the writer, for the information of the editor, but not for publication.

No. 2,215.—Erlitzki's Fluid (Boston).
This is a liquid intended for hardening anatomical specimens. Its composition is the following:

Potassium Bichromate .... 25 parts
Copper Sulphate .... 5 "
Water .... to make 1,000 "

No. 2,216.—Perfume in Snuff (Montreal).
A good and durable perfume in snuff cannot well be imparted by making the latter on the small scale. Should you be specially interested in this, we advise you to consult "Karmarsch und Heeren, Technologisches Wörterbuch," edited by Kick & Gintl, 8vo, Prag, vol. VI, pp. 735-745, where the whole process is minutely described and many formulæ given. A copy of this important work is, no doubt, on file in some of the libraries of your city. For ordinary purposes, a good flavoring for snuff is either Tonca-Beans or the so-called American Vanilla, or Deer's Tongue, viz., *Liatris odoratissima*, the leaves of the latter being an important article of commerce.

No. 2,217.—Aluminium Bronze (A. E. W. & Co.).
Aluminium bronze is an alloy of pure metallic copper and metallic aluminium. When the proportion of the latter is between 5 and 10 per cent, the alloy has a golden color, is very resistant to atmospheric influences, is easily worked out to wire or sheet, may be readily engraved, and forms an excellent material for balances, scientific instruments, and numerous other articles. Our correspondents inquire, among other things, whether we know of any one who makes weights of aluminium bronze. So far we have not been able to ascertain. But we shall be glad if some of our readers can supply this information. It would certainly be an excellent material for this purpose.

No. 2,218.—Dilution of Strong Sulphuric Acid for Titration ("Laboratory").
When strong sulphuric acid is to be titrated, there are several methods by which the acid may be diluted. One is, to slowly introduce a known weight of the acid (dropped from a bottle the contents of which are of a known weight) into water, and when the mixture has cooled, to fill it up to the desired mark. Or, a portion of the acid may be weighed directly in a capacious flask which can be closed with a rubber stopper. The acid cannot be safely diluted with water, but by adding to it gradually some pure, crystallised sulphate of sodium, the water of crystallisation of the latter will quietly dilute the acid so that water may be afterwards safely added to the liquid. Of course, the Na₂SO₄ does not interfere with the titration at all.

No. 2,219.—Prescription Query (J. C. C., Ont.).
"In the following mixture will you kindly tell me the cause of change in color:

℞ Morph. Sulph..................... gr. 2
Tr. Cardam. Co .... ʒ 4
Aqua .... ad ʒ 3

After standing for a day or two, it changes from the original red to a dirty brown."
You will find that the change takes place whether sulphate of morphine is present or not. The cause, therefore, is to be looked for in the water. The latter causes the gradual precipitation of the coloring matter of cochineal to which the tincture owes its fine color. The liquid finally retains only that coloring matter which is derived from the other ingredients. There is no help for this, unless the ingredients or proportion are changed by the prescriber.

No. 2,220.—Renewing old Corks (O. S. G.).
In general it may be declared a poor policy to use old corks over again. Certainly this should never be done, if they have passed through unknown hands, and bear the evidence of having been used in bottles of various, or at all events unknown or doubtful contents. Of course, we refer to corks intended for bottling liquids for internal use. Only under peculiarly favorable circumstances may it be safe to use such corks a second time, and even then not without having subjected them to a thorough cleansing. When corks are returned to the original bottles with which they have been sent out (and when there is no doubt about this), there will be no harm in using them again, if they are in good condition. At the dispensing counter, however, new corks should *always* be used, the risk of contaminating a mixture for internal use by a tainted cork being something that no pharmacist should venture to run.

For bottles containing liquids or solids that are not intended for internal use, second-hand corks may be used, provided there is nothing objectionable about them. It must, however, be a rather poor enterprise or business venture that has to have recourse to the expedient of using old corks for this purpose, there being several other uses to which old cork may be put and for which it is bought up by some dealers. Nevertheless, as this is an age where nothing is supposed to be wasted, and as there may be some more of our readers who can legitimately profit by the information here given, we will append a note on cleaning used corks.

Corks which have been used should first be sorted into: 1. Such as have retained their original color entirely or nearly so, and have evidently only been wetted with odorless or nearly tasteless liquids. These corks may usually be cleaned by one or more boiling in water. They are for this purpose best tied in a bag, made of loosely woven material which is kept below the surface of the boiling water either by weights or by wedges. 2. Such corks as have become stained, but not tainted either with a bad odor or taste. Here it will depend a good deal upon the nature of the stain. Corks which have been in ink bottles, for instance, will never be entirely restorable. They, and all similar ones, are preferably laid aside, each kind by itself, and treated separately, with a view of being used for the same purpose (and no other) again. Others are treated either by boiling water to which is added from 1 to 10 per cent of solution of chlorinated soda (Labarraque's solution), or, they may be cleaned by permanganate of potassium. The new National Formulary contains a process for bleaching sponge, which directs to immerse the previously cleaned sponge in a solution of permanganate of potassium, then to wash them with water, and afterwards to treat them with a solution of hyposulphite of sodium and some hydrochloric acid. While this is an excellent method for *sponge*, it will not do for corks. The permanganate of potassium is, indeed, the chief bleaching agent, but the hyposulphite of sodium likewise contributes to it, as it is decomposed by the hydrochloric acid into chloride of sodium, sulphurous acid, and free sulphur, a small portion of which latter remains imbedded in the texture of the sponge, where it certainly can do no harm. Free sulphur, however, might do harm in a cork, as it might affect the contents of the bottle in which it is inserted. For this reason, the hyposulphite of sodium must be omitted in the case of corks, and only the acid used after the permanganate. The corks should be put into the solution of permanganate (120 grains to the pint), so that they are below the surface of the solution, and allowed to remain therein for 1 or 2 days. They are then washed in water, and when they no longer stain the latter, immersed in a mixture of 1 volume of hydrochloric acid (commercial) and 8 volumes of water. About a pint of this dilute acid will be required for each pint of permanganate solution. Lastly, they are washed with water, until all trace of soluble matter is removed from them. 3. Such corks as are tainted by odoriferous matters or have acquired a peculiar taste not removable by the treatment previously mentioned. These are best thrown away, if no other economic use can be found for them.

No. 2,221.—Blueing in Sugar (New London).
This subscriber asks whether there is any granulated sugar in the market at the present time that does not contain any blue coloring matter, such as is added to neutralise the faint yellowish tint which sugar usually has.

In reply we would say that up to the time when the Sugar Trust went into operation, there were some manufacturers whose product was free from this impurity. Since that time we have met the same difficulty which our correspondent and many others have encountered and we are still in search of a brand which can be called absolutely free from the objectionable ingredient. Meanwhile, we have recourse to rock candy for all special purposes, such as syrup of iodide of iron, etc.

No. 2,222.—Zeihl's and Frankel's Solutions (Boston).
Both of these are used for staining tissues, in bacteriological examinations. They are prepared as follows:

Zeihl's Solution.

Fuchsine	1 part
Alcohol	10 parts
Solution of carbolic acid (5 per cent.), enough to make 100 parts by weight.	

Dissolve the fuchsine in the alcohol and very gradually and slowly add the solution of carbolic acid.

Frankel's Solution.

Water	80 parts
Alcohol	50 "
Nitric Acid	20 "
Methyl Blue	q. s.

Mix the water and alcohol, gradually add the nitric acid, allow the mixture to become cold, then saturate it with methyl blue.

No. 2,223.—Modelling Wax (E. D.).
A good composition for this purpose is said to be furnished by the following formula:

Beeswax	1 part
Lead Plaster	1 "
Rosin	1 "
Olive Oil	q. s.
Prepared Chalk	q. s.

Melt the first three ingredients together, and incorporate a sufficient quantity of Prepared Chalk previously triturated with Olive Oil to a smooth paste, to impart to the mass the requisite stiffness. The Olive Oil may amount to 1 part or a little more. If desired, the mass may be tinted with a little curcuine, or carmine and annatto, or other coloring material. Those here named will probably answer for dental purposes.

No. 2,224.—Black Ink (M. F. N.).
Your query for a formula for black ink "without boiling" is partly answered by the publication of some formulæ elsewhere in this number.
Another excellent formula which we have used for years is the following:

Nigrosine, best water-soluble	120 grains.
Gelatin, Cooper's	20 "
Bichromate Potassium	10 "
Glycerin	1 fl. oz.
Water	enough to make 10 fl. oz.

Dissolve the Gelatin in about 6 fl. oz. of water, add the Nigrosine and dissolve, if necessary, by warming. Then add the Glycerin, and lastly the balance of the water in which the Bichromate of Potassium has been dissolved. Keep the ink in a dark, amber-colored bottle.

No. 2,225.—Geoffroya Inermis (E. W.).
There is no standard formula for a tincture of *Geoffroya inermis* known to us from any existing pharmacopœia. But in accordance with the recommendation of the National Formulary, all tinctures for which no authoritative formula is otherwise provided should be made of such a strength that 1 pint of the finished tincture represents 2 troy ounces of drugs.
Geoffroya inermis Willd., is a synonym of *Andira inermis* Kunth, and is known by the name of Cabbage Tree. It is a native of Jamaica, and the bark has long had a reputation as a vermifuge. An allied species, *Andira retusa* Kunth, is a native of Surinam and Cayenne. To distinguish the two kinds, it is customary to call the former "Jamaica cabbage tree (bark)," and the latter "Surinam cabbage tree (bark)." Consult Stillé & Maisch's "National Dispensatory," 3d ed., page 202, U. S. Dispensatory, 13th ed., page 1393. You will, no doubt, be able to obtain it through one of the large wholesale houses of New York. If not, we would advise you to procure it directly from Jamaica.

No. 2,226.—Saccharin and Alkaloids (Dr. A. H. S.).
The proposition to combine bitter alkaloids with saccharin, we believe, was originally made by Dr. Fahlberg, who claims the discovery of saccharin, and obtained the patents on it. The firm manufacturing saccharin, prepares several of these compounds, viz:
1. *Saccharinate of Quinine* (called by Fahlberg "Saccharin-Chinin"). This contains 36 per cent of saccharin and 64 per cent of quinine. It is a white powder of faintly-bitter taste, which may be completely covered by a further addition of saccharin. It is difficultly soluble in cold or hot water, and is best employed in form of powder.

2. *Saccharinate of Morphine* contains 39.1 per cent of saccharin and 60.4 (according to Fischer; should probably be 60.9) per cent of morphine.
3. *Saccharinate of Strychnine* contains 35.4 per cent of saccharin and 64.6 per cent of strychnine.
Incidentally we would say that we do not see the utility of the two last-named compounds. Indeed, we consider them as positively objectionable and dangerous. There will no longer be any chance of readily distinguishing the several alkaloids from each other by the taste, and a mistake may easily be made. We would at least advise that they be colored, so as to distinguish them both from the original saccharin, as well from each other.
A *saccharinate of cocaine* has been prepared by Mr. B. F. Hays of this city, and has been used to some extent.

No. 2,227.—Rapid Estimation of Lead (Croton).
The correspondent has a connection with the main water supply by means of a long lead-pipe, and wishes to know how he may make a rapid estimation, day by day, of the quantity of lead which the water may take up.
In the first place, we must remark that unless the conduit is very long, or the water has been allowed to remain undisturbed in the pipe in the intervals between making the tests (at least 12 hours), it will not be possible to detect the presence of lead, under ordinary conditions, unless the water drawn from the pipe for the purpose of analysis is concentrated to a small bulk by heat. However, assuming that the water, as drawn, contains enough lead to respond at once to tests, we would suggest the following method, based upon that recently proposed by L. Liebermann, as a modification of one previously used by Pelouse and Bischof.
Take two beakers of equal size, put into one of them 200 C.c. of the water to be tested, together with 10 C.c. of moderately dilute hydrochloric acid (1 to 5 of water), and 20 C.c. of saturated solution of hydrosulphuric acid. If the color of the mixture should become very dark, it is necessary to use a smaller proportion of the water to be examined and to complete the whole bulk of 230 C.c. by means of distilled water. Not more than a brownish coloration, insufficient to render the liquid opaque, should be produced; otherwise a smaller quantity of the water must be used for the assay.
In a second beaker are put 200 C.c. of distilled water, 10 C.c. of the previously specified hydrochloric acid, and 20 C.c. of solution of hydrosulphuric acid, and then—both beakers standing upon white paper—a solution of acetate lead, containing 1 Gm. in 1 liter, is allowed to flow, drop by drop, from a burette into the second beaker, until, after stirring, the depth of tint in both beakers is identical. The amount of lead solution consumed will give, by a simple calculation, the approximate quantity present in the suspected sample.
Of course, this method is liable to lead to error. But it has been shown that, when carefully conducted and when the tint produced is pale, the results are in satisfactory accordance with the actual quantities of lead present.

No. 2,228.—Boonekamp Bitters (J. N.).
The following formula (recalculated by us to U. S. weights and measures) is published by Hell. Others have been given by other authors.

Oil of Angelica	16 min.
" Bitter Orange	16 "
" Staranis	16 "
" Lemon	12 "
" Coriander	12 "
" Galanga	8 "
" Marjoram	8 "
" Absinth	8 "
" Peppermint	6 "
White Agaric	200 grains.
Liquorice Root, ground	2½ Troy oz.
Sugar	4 "
Water	3 quarts.
Alcohol	enough to make 10 quarts.

Macerate the White Agaric during one week with 20 fluid ounces of Alcohol, and filter. Dissolve the Oils in the filtrate. Extract the Liquorice Root by infusing it with 1 quart of boiling water. Then add to this the Sugar and 4 more pints of water; afterwards the alcoholic solution first prepared, and then 3½ pints more of alcohol. Filter, and pass enough dilute alcohol through the filter to obtain 10 quarts of filtrate.
We have given the ingredients according to Hell, and the directions according to our files. But we fail to see where the specific benefits of the product come in, so far as its medicinal properties are concerned.

No. 2,229.—Tests for Antipyrin and Antifebrin (M. O. A.).
In preceding numbers of this journal you will find a number of proposed tests for both of the above substances. In a recent issue of the *Chem. News* (Aug. 3d), Mr. David Lindo publishes some further contribution to this subject, as follows:
Knorr, who "appears to have discovered" [this should certainly read, "who discovered"] antipyrin, gives reactions by which it can be identified: 1. Even a highly di-

lute solution of the substance in water gives a red color on addition of a drop of ferric chloride solution. 2. The solution of antipyrin is mixed with a dilute solution of a nitrite, and a few drops of dilute sulphuric acid are then added. If the quantity of antipyrin is not too small, a blue color is developed; otherwise the tint will be green. Knorr also found that nitro-antipyrin is obtained by gently heating a solution of antipyrin in concentrated nitric acid. This crystallizes in white needles, is insoluble in water and alkalies, but is sparingly soluble in strong nitric or hydrochloric acids. Mr. Lindo wonders whether he overlooked a fine color reaction, which may be obtained by heating antipyrin with strong nitric acid in a small porcelain basin over the lamp until reaction commences; the lamp is then withdrawn, and when the reaction ceases, a fine purple colored liquid residue remains. On adding water and filtering, a beautiful purple-red filtrate is obtained, and a violet-colored precipitate remains on the filter. This reaction is very delicate, and has not been mentioned here before.

Regarding antifebrin, Mr. Lindo writes: I have met with no published tests (meaning evidently "color-tests") for this body, and the only one I have discovered as yet must be applied to the solid substance, of which a very minute quantity, however, will suffice. The test depends upon the fact that when antifebrin is strongly heated with concentrated sulphuric acid, sulphanilic acid is formed, or at least a body which reacts exactly like it with nitrous acid and phenols. A small quantity of antifebrin is put in a porcelain dish, a little pure sulphuric acid added, and heat applied with a naked flame until the acid fumes strongly. When cold, a little water is added, and then a highly dilute solution of a nitrite. Next the mixture is treated with a phenol, such as alphanaphthol, thymol, or carbolic acid, when the characteristic red color (see this number, page 172) will make its appearance.

No. 2,230.—Nitrite of Cobalt (Several Inquirers).
The "nitrite of cobalt" which has recently been introduced in medicine as a definite agent for administering nitrous acid, is the double nitrite of cobalt and potassium, which was originally discovered by Fischer, and is obtained as a yellow precipitate when the solution of a cobalt (cobaltous) salt, acidified with acetic acid, is mixed with a solution of nitrite of potassium. The reaction is as follows:

$8CoCl_2$ + $12KNO_2$ + $2HC_2H_3O_2$ + H_2O =
cobaltous   potassium   acetic   water
chloride   nitrite   acid

= $(KNO_2)_3 Co_2O(NO_2)_4.H_2O$ + $4KCl$ + $2KC_2H_3O_2$ +
potassium-cobaltic   potassium   potassium
nitrite   chloride   acetate

+ $2NO$
nitric
oxide

Roscoe and Schorlemmer (I., 134) give a reaction, in which 4 molecules of free nitrous acid are made to enter, besides 10 molecules of nitrite of potassium. We do not see how this agrees with the facts. The above reaction is frequently used as a test for cobalt. For this purpose the solution containing a cobalt salt is evaporated to a small bulk, then caustic soda added, and the precipitate redissolved with an excess of acetic acid. A solution of potassium nitrite is then added, the whole digested for a while at a gentle heat, and then set aside for 24 hours, when the yellow precipitate of the above-mentioned double salt will separate. As this is somewhat soluble in water, it is best washed with a solution of potassium acetate (containing a slight excess of acetic acid) and lastly with 80% alcohol. This compound is also known as "cobalt yellow," and consists, when viewed under the microscope, of minute crystals. According to Sadtler, the salt is usually anhydrous; but it may be obtained with from 1 to 4 molecules of water, according to the concentration of the solution.

No. 2,231.—Baking Powders (Subscriber).
This correspondent sends us the names of four baking powders, asking us to give their composition. Two of them are, however, entirely unknown to us, and on inquiry we cannot find that they are known or sold in the New York market. The other two are well known. As they happen to be among those reported on in a paper read at the last meeting of the Kansas Pharmaceutical Association, it may be of interest to give them for the whole series here. The analysis of these powders was made by Miss Rice at the laboratory of the University of Kansas, under the supervision of Prof. E. H. S. Bailey.*

We have arranged the results obtained by Miss Rice in form of a table to save space. The starch was in no case specially determined, but the sum of all the other solid ingredients deducted from 100, was put down as "starch." The "gas" is understood to mean the total amount, by weight, of carbonic acid gas, which 100 parts of the powder would give off, when treated with water. The solids were determined by igniting a known weight of the powder until all carbonaceous matter was destroyed. From this

* From Proceedings of the Ninth Annual Meeting of the Kansas Pharm. Association, held at Atchison, May 16th-17th, 1888. 8vo, Lawrence, 1888, pp. 67-72.

was deducted the amount of cream of tartar and of bicarbonate of sodium previously determined. The remainder was calculated to Rochelle salt, or tartrate of potassium and sodium (which need not therefore be assumed to have been originally present), or to the alum and sodium compounds, etc., formed. Regarding other details, we must refer the reader to the original paper.

Constituents of Baking Powders.	Rumford Baking Powder	Price's Baking Powder	Log Cabin Powder				
Bicarbonate of sodium...	24.70	21.17	20.81	18.82	16.38	18.97	13.42
Cream of tartar..........	55.32	55.88	31.00				
Tartaric acid............			15.27				
Bisulfate of potassium...			7.85				
Carbonate of ammonium..	1.52						
Rochelle salt.............		8.34					
Ammonia alum...........				34.15	30.07	35.71	34.06
Hydrate of aluminium, sulphate of sodium, of ammonium, etc.				1.05	16.55		1.26
Starch...................	18.46	14.63	25.57	45.93	37.00	45.32	61.24
Gas......................	13.62	11.09	10.64	9.46	8.56	9.94	7.08

No. 2,232.—Sulphide of Calcium (Montana).
The U. S. Ph. of 1880, on page 52, will give you part of the information you ask for. You speak of the work as if you were quite familiar with it, yet you do not seem to have found this preparation in it. The fact is, it is not pure sulphide of calcium, though commonly so named. It is a mixture of sulphide and sulphate of calcium containing generally accidental impurities derived from the ingredients from which it is prepared. It has long been used by the homœopaths under the name of hepar sulphuris calcareum, and was directed by Hahnemann to be prepared by mixing equal parts of finely powdered oyster shells and "pure" sublimed sulphur, then raising the mixture to a white heat, and keeping the product in well-closed bottles. It is, however, largely prepared by other processes, particularly one of the following:

1. Introduce into a clay crucible an intimate mixture of 4 parts of plaster of Paris (calcined sulphate of calcium) and 1 part of wood charcoal in powder. Heat the mixture to a red heat and further to nearly a white heat. Allow to cool, and preserve the product in well-closed bottles.

2. From 8 parts of plaster of Paris, 2 parts of powdered wood charcoal, 1 part of rye flour, and a sufficient quantity of water, prepare suitable cylinders. Dry them thoroughly and pile them alternately with a layer of charcoal in a muffle-oven, where the whole is afterwards brought to a full heat. When the charcoal is consumed, close the oven and allow to cool. Reduce the cylinders (freed from ash) to powder.

3. Make an intimate mixture of equal parts of powdered caustic lime and sulphur, press it firmly into a crucible, cover this well, and heat this during one hour so that the heating proceeds from above downwards. When cold, transfer the product at once to bottles.
The reaction is chiefly the following:

$4Ca(OH)_2$ + $4S$ = $3CaS$ + $CaSO_4$ +
lime   sulphur   calcium   calcium
(calcium hydroxide)   sulphide   sulphate

+ $4H_2O$
water

No. 2,233.—Bromidia (B. & S.).
The proprietors of the preparation "Bromidia" publish a formula, in which they claim that each fluid drachm contains "15 grains each of pure chloral hydrate, and 'purified' bromide of potassium, and ⅛ grain each of genuine imported extract of Cannabis Indica and Hyoscyamus."

Any attempt to get the extract of cannabis indica in solution in an aqueous menstruum corresponding to that which is present in bromidia, is unsuccessful. Nor does the extract yield to the menstruum any constituent that can be traced. In the case of extract of hyoscyamus, most of the active principle will probably pass into solution. There is no doubt in our mind or that of others who have examined the subject that the finished preparation contains no cannabis indica at all, though this may have been employed as an ingredient. The National Formulary has adopted a formula in which the extract of cannabis indica is retained. But it is made diffusible by means of tincture of Quillaja, and attention is drawn, in a note, to the fact that, if the mixture is filtered, the resin (extract of cannabis indica) will remain on the filter.

The formula for Tasteless Tincture of Iron you will also find in the New National Formulary, which you ought to procure as soon as possible. You may obtain it through the book trade.

Formula Asked For.

Schiffmann's Asthma Cure. What is the composition?

American Druggist

Vol. XVII. No. 10.   NEW YORK, OCTOBER, 1888.   Whole No. 172.

THIRTY-SIXTH ANNUAL MEETING OF THE AMERICAN PHARMACEUTICAL ASSOCIATION, AT DETROIT.

Monday, Sept. 3d, 1888.

President J. U. Lloyd called the meeting of the American Pharmaceutical Association to order at 3:20 P.M., on September 3d, in the Detroit Light Infantry Armory, Detroit, Mich., and introduced Rev. C. R. Henderson, who delivered a prayer, the members standing meanwhile. The meeting was then declared open and was addressed by the Hon. William C. Maybury who, in the name of the Mayor and the people of Detroit, welcomed the Association, speaking of the pharmaceutical manufacturing laboratories of Detroit as the pride of their city. Referring to the exhibit, with its wealth of beauty, he felt the traditions of his boyhood were fast being swept away. The time-honored bunch of catnip and other nauseous herbs were no longer the most prominent things that greeted the eye when visiting the apothecaries' shops, and it is now not necessary to judge of the virtue of a medicine by its bitterness of taste. Instead of screwing up the face, and dreading the nauseous dose, as was the custom years ago, now a man will walk up to the counter and take his innocent-looking capsule with as little concern as he will his soda-water. He wondered where the mystic compounder of his boyhood days had gone, who, went behind the barrier, and, while the patient was waiting, awed by the solemnity of the occasion, prepared the mystic compound.

Now the time had come when all mysteries were being opened to humanity. The druggist of to-day was allowing mystery to be replaced by greater skill and education. Thus the labors of the physician were aided by the knowledge of the druggist, and they realize that there is no labor for the individual like that which rises to the dignity of alleviating the sufferings of human life.

Mr. Alexander, of St. Louis, in a few well-chosen words, responded for the Association, returning thanks for the cordial welcome.

J. F. Judge, of Cincinnati, was called upon to read the President's address, which was a long document containing many valuable suggestions, which, upon motion of J. M. Good, of St. Louis, was referred to a committee of three, consisting of John Weber, J. L. Lemberger, and G. W. Sloan.

The Secretary of the Council read the names of one hundred and seven druggists who had been reported to the Council as desirable members for the Association, and, on motion of Mr. Seabury, of New York, they were invited to become members.

Reports of committees being called for, the following reports were read by title and laid over:

Reporter on Progress of Pharmacy, Committee on National Formulary, and Committee on Incorporation of the Association. Mr. A. E. Ebert, of Chicago, reported from the Committee on Revision of the Pharmacopœia that they had no meeting this year; the Committee would have to be reconstructed somewhat, and promised a report for the next yearly meeting. Prof. J. P. Remington, from the Committee on Management, reported that they had preferred to make no report this year, but would wait to see the effect of the working of the new system.

The roll of States was called, and, according to the new amendment of last year, each State appointed two men who were delegates, and the President appointed five men who were not delegates, to serve as Committee on Nomination for Officers of the Association for the ensuing year. They were as follows:

California—Emlen Painter, Connecticut—Frederick Wilcox. Dakota—H. M. Haussmner, J. M. Da Rold. Delaware—S. E. Stewart. Illinois—T. M. Jamieson, E. C. Day. Indiana—G. W. Sloan, Jacob Bauer. Iowa—Ross Upson, C. Wangler. Kansas—R. G. Brown, L. E. Sayre. Kentucky—G. C. Pfinget, O. E. Mueller. Louisiana—W. Boyd, Mrs. E. Rudolph. Maine—Henry Cunning. A. R. Bayley. Michigan—Geo. Gundrum, D. O. Haynes. Minnesota—Carl Simmon, J. C. Henning. Missouri—H. M. Weipley, F. G. Ublich. New Hampshire—C. B. Spofford. New Jersey—Charles Holzhauer. New York—G. J. Seabury, William P. De Forest. Ohio—J. Heckler, J. Weir. Pennsylvania—C. A. Heinitsh, J. F. Patton. Rhode Island—H. J. Aldridge, W. E. Cates. Tennessee—Al. A. Yeager, J. L. Thompson. Wisconsin—J. A. Dadd, A. H. Hollister. Province Quebec—S. Lachauer, E. Muir. Province Ontario—J. E. D'Avignon. At large—A. E. Ebert, Edmund Bocking, John Ingalls, J. Dupont, J. F. Judge.

The Committee was notified to meet at the Cadillac Hotel at 8 P.M.

The minutes of the Council were read for approval.

The Council had been organized by the selection of W. H. Rodgers as chairman, Carl Simmon as vice-chairman, and G. W. Kennedy as secretary. The usual committees had been appointed. The title of the National Formulary had been discussed and fixed and the contract for its printing and binding awarded to the lowest bidder. The Committee on Membership had sent circulars to each member calling attention to the change in the manner of electing members. A rule had been added to the by-laws of the Council in regard to trust company's bond for treasurer. The American Pharmaceutical Association had been incorporated in the District of Columbia under Act of Congress which required that seventeen or eighteen members of the thirty-five necessary should reside in that District, and be the managers of the Association and of its finances during the first year; these provisions had required no changes in the by-laws of the Association. The certificate of incorporation, which was kept by the Council, was read. An appropriation of $200 had been made for the exhibition of the preparations of the National Formulary. A change had been made in the fees for life membership, and the Council had decided hereafter not to meet on Sundays. The work of the Council was on motion approved.

A. E. Ebert offered an amendment to the by-laws that the Secretary of the Council may or may not be a member of the Council.

S. A. D. Sheppard, of Boston, Mass., offered an amendment to Art. VIII., sec. VI.

E. Painter, of New York, moved that a committee of three be appointed to select the time and place of the next meeting, and also extended an invitation from the California State Association for the American Association to hold its next meeting in San Francisco. Referring to the many times this invitation had been extended, he thought we should accept it this year as a duty we owed to them and the good it would do the Association.

Mr. Sheppard said that too much time was taken up year after year by discussing time and place of meeting in the Association, and thought that a large committee consisting of fifteen members should be appointed to consider and have authority to act in this matter, twelve of the committee to be appointed by the Association and three by the President, the said committee to give two hearings to any persons who might suggest places to them.

Mr. Painter thought the scheme good in some respects and bad in others. The committee, by giving two hearings, might take up too much time and then be unable to come to a definite conclusion.

Prof. J. P. Remington, of Pennsylvania, said that, when the Committee on Management amended the by-laws arranging the business of the meeting last year, they had thought it judicious not to take away any of the business of the Association that would be of interest to the members, and they had kept that in their mind in all their work. Now this matter of selecting time and place of meeting he considered as a matter of interest to all the members, and as such should be settled in open meeting, and then none could feel aggrieved. It might save time to refer this to a committee of three or of fifteen, but he certainly would never consent to be one of such a committee, for they would never be able to please the majority of the Association. If it was to be settled by a committee, it had better go to the Nominating Committee, they were a representative body now, as they are appointed by each State.

Mr. Painter, of New York, thought there would be too much work for the Nominating Committee to select officers and to take charge of the consideration of this matter.

Mr. Hechler thought there should be a session of the Association set aside for the general consideration of this subject.

The motion that fifteen members constitute the committee and have authority to settle the time and place was lost, and the motion that a committee of three be appointed to report to the Association was carried. The President appointed Emlen Painter, New York, J. P. Remington, Pennsylvania, and P. W. Bedford, New York.

The meeting then adjourned until nine o'clock on Tuesday morning.

Tuesday, Sept. 4th, 1888.

Second Session, called to order at 10 A.M. by the first vice-president, Mr. M. W. Alexander.

Secretary J. M. Maisch read the minutes of the previous session, which were approved.

The minutes of the Council were read and approved, also forty-seven names of proposed new members who were invited to join. A change in the rule of finance was proposed by the treasurer, that dues should be paid by the 20th of June of each year, and if not within twenty days after, a sight draft should be drawn.

The Nominating Committee reported that they had met and selected the following officers for the Association:

President—M. W. Alexander, St. Louis; *1st Vice-President*, James Vernor, Detroit; *2d Vice-President*, Frederick Wilcox, Connecticut; *3d Vice-Pres.*, Alvin A. Yeager, Tennessee; *Treasurer*, S. A. D. Sheppard, Boston; *Secretary*, J. M. Maisch, Pennsylvania; *Reporter*, C. Lewis Diehl, Kentucky. *Three members of the Council*—Henry Canning, Boston; Emlen Painter, New York; C. L. Keppler, Louisiana.

On motion, the report was received, and one ballot was cast for the president, which being done, Mr. M. W. Alexander was declared elected.

On motion, one ballot was cast for 1st vice-president, and Mr. James Vernor was declared elected.

On motion, one ballot was cast for the rest of the names reported by the Committee, and they were declared elected.

A telegram was read from the British Pharmaceutical Conference at Bath, England, which was received, and on motion of Mr. DeForest, of Brooklyn, the secretary was directed to acknowledge the receipt of the telegram, and to return cordial greeting.

The reporter on Progress of Pharmacy, C. Lewis Diehl, then read the preliminary part of his report for the past year. Extracts taken are as follows:

"Since our meeting here twenty-two years ago," he said "our national pharmacopœia has been revised twice, and the time is near at hand for another revision of that standard, for which preparations are being made both by the societies concerned in the revision and by the permanent committee of revision created in 1880. The work is likely to be more arduous than ever, for the introduction of new remedial agents has so rapidly followed the one upon the other, that it has been difficult for pharmacists to keep up with them. The widening of the scope of the pharmacopœia is not confined to the United States, as is evidenced by the action of pharmaceutical bodies abroad. The formulas and definitions will not alone be thoroughly revised, but the remedial agents that have in recent years come to notice will be very completely represented in the work.

"Scientific pharmacists have invented better, or at least more convenient, preparations than those which are in the pharmacopœia. They have invented, too, pleasanter forms of administration. Since the production of their new compounds on a large scale is cheaper than on a small scale, there are good grounds for believing that the call on the part of the medical profession for these preparations and medicines is increasing and will increase and that this call will distinctly affect pharmacy. The new compounds are welcomed partly because of their convenience and partly because their uniformity of composition is, to a certain extent, guaranteed by the producer. At dispensaries, students, with few exceptions, learn little or nothing, and even the opportunities for acquiring a knowledge of compounding drugs under practitioners who dispense their own medicine have somewhat diminished; for ready-made medicines are usurping the place of the official preparations. It is not likely that a return will be made to the old system under which medical students acquired a knowledge of pharmacy. If, then, the sole office of the pharmacist were to compound drugs, the future of pharmacy could not be regarded as satisfactory. In that end, however, the very increase of the wholesale production of compounded medicines, as simple articles of commerce, will not take from, but add to, the work of the future pharmacist, if he fulfils all the duties which seem to belong to his occupation. If pharmacy is to hold its own, each pharmacist must be, in the future, guarantor of the purity of the medicines he dispenses, not the mere distributor. The rise of pharmacy to a higher state, or its fall to a lower, depends on whether its more scientific functions are accepted or declined.

"The pharmacist is held responsible for the medicines he dispenses, whether these are prepared in his own or some one else's laboratory. While in emergencies the pharmacist may be called upon to purchase fluid extracts from the wholesale manufacturers, it is plainly his duty to prepare them in his own laboratory whenever possible. The conscientious pharmacist cannot fail to make it remunerative to himself as well as doing justice to his assistants and the public.

"During the past year, a number of papers have appeared that are directed towards an adjustment of the grievances between physician and pharmacist. Some fifty papers on the subject were elicited by the *Pharmaceutical Era*, the one by Prof. F. H. Gerrish, of Bowdoin Medical College, securing the prize offered. He regards the unsatisfactory relations between the two professions to be due to very simple causes, for which both are responsible. On the part of the pharmacists the custom of prescribing, aggravated by a lack of proper qualification and education in medicine, the custom of renewing prescriptions without the sanction of the physician; the sale and its encouragement of so-called patent medicines. On the part of the physician, the custom of verbally directing the renewal of prescriptions; the demand on the spur of the moment of whimsical preparations or for different brands of the same standard medicine; the habit of some physicians in localities where pharmacists are accessible of furnishing their patients with medicines.

"It is clearly the duty of the pharmacist to attend to the preparation, dispensing, and sale of medicine, in which event he must, or should, conform to the code of ethics of the medical profession. The renewal of prescriptions is an evil for which the physician is equally responsible. The sale of patent medicines, while it cannot be avoided, need not be encouraged by the pharmacist. The physician, on the contrary, should not whimsically designate the products of special manufacturers in his prescription, and he certainly should not supply the medicines needed in his prescription if such can be filled in the locality in which he resides. The professions of medicine and pharmacy are so intimately related that they cannot afford to quarrel!"

The report was discussed by Prof. J. P. Remington, of Pennsylvania, Dr. James, of St. Louis, Dr. Stewart and Dr. R. G. Eccles, of Brooklyn. Dr. James, referring to the allusion of substitution by German druggists, said the cases cited were all of homœopathic druggists. The homœopathic physician had found it almost impossible to obtain their medicines correctly prepared from the homœopathic stores, and had adopted the method of sending around to them prescriptions calling for the most absurd and unheard-of things, and, in a majority of cases, they were filled.

The speaker knew what he was talking about, as he was the first to translate these cases in this country, and he did not want the regular druggists blamed for it, as they have been.

Dr. Stewart thought the report dealt with an interesting subject, when speaking of the relations of the physician and druggist, and stated the American Medical Association was considering the idea of establishing a Section on Materia Medica and Pharmacy to which the American Pharmaceutical Association will probably be asked to send delegates.

He thought the American Pharmaceutical Association would do well to reciprocate by establishing a Section on Therapeutics in their Association.

Prof. Remington was glad the subject had been brought to the attention of the Association. There should be a systematic effort made to bring the two professions together, and anything that will break the policy of non-intercourse, and will promote harmony, is good and must meet with success. There is no doubt that delegates from the American Pharmaceutical Association coming with this in view would be received with open arms. One ground which they could regulate would be the prescribing of officinal preparations, instead of non-officinal ones, and thus give the druggist a chance of his life.

The speaker spoke of the success of the Committee from the Pennsylvania Pharmaceutical Association to the Pennsylvania Medical Association, and the action of the Medical Association in incorporating in their by-laws amendments to encourage such committees. He was in favor of the action of the American Medical Association establishing this Section in Pharmacy and Materia Medica in that body, but he would not recommend the American Pharmaceutical Association to take any action just yet, as the Medical Association must first invite us to meet with them, and then we can reciprocate the compliment.

Dr. R. G. Eccles, of Brooklyn, thinks the American Medical Association is making a right movement in taking this action, and thought we should at once show our appreciation of it by doing as much ourselves; for if we wait, it will look as though we were dragged into it; but if we now determine to establish a Section on Therapeutics, we would show we are as anxious as they. Only the progressive men of each society favor such a movement. There are plenty in each who are not progressive enough to see the benefit of such a movement, and they will do all they can to retard it. So the sooner we work for it the better.

Mr. Seabury, New York, said the acoustic properties of the hall in which the Association was meeting was so bad that those in the back could not hear, and moved that a Committee be appointed to interview the janitor to see if it were not possible to secure the room down-stairs. Carried, and Messrs. Merrill and Hechler were appointed such a Committee.

Mr. William P. De Forest, of Brooklyn, read the report of the Committee on National Formulary on Unofficial Preparations, which announced the completion of the labors of the committee and submitted certain propositions as to the manner of revising the work in the future. These propositions were contained in the following two resolutions (which were acted upon at a subsequent session):

1. *Resolved*, That a *Committee on National Formulary* be appointed at the meeting of the Association following the publication of the work. The said committee to hold office, unless otherwise directed by the Association, until their successors are appointed at the meeting of the Am. Ph. Assoc., succeeding the issue of a *revision* of the work, and shall report at each meeting of the Association.

2. *Resolved*, That the Council of the A. P. A. shall have authority, upon the recommendation of the Committee on National Formulary, to make all necessary arrangements for the publication of a revision, and to provide for its distribution.

The report was received, and Emlen Painter, of New York, moved a vote of thanks to those gentlemen, not members of the Committee, who had assisted the Committee in their work. This was amended by others, including the Committee, in the resolution of thanks and of a special vote of thanks to Dr. Charles Rice, the Chairman of the Committee, for his indefatigable efforts in this work. These were carried unanimously. The resolutions proposed by the Committee were read and the whole subject of the National Formulary was referred to the Section on Scientific Papers.

Report of the Council showed that the Committee on Publication had awarded the contract for publishing the National Formulary to the lowest bidder. There had been printed and distributed a first and second edition of two thousand and three thousand copies, and a third edition of three thousand was in course of distribution.

J. M. Good, of St. Louis, spoke of the impossibility of printing the Formulary in the proceedings last year, as ordered by the Association, and thought it is not necessary to have it done now, as the book had been sent to each member.

Messrs. Enten Painter, of New York, and Hallberg, of Chicago, disagreed with him, as they thought it was part of the record of the Association, and should be in the proceedings, and, on motion, it was ordered to be printed in the proceedings this year.

The Treasurer S. A. D. Sheppard, Boston, read his report. The receipts during the year were $7,937.05, and the balance from the year before was $4,719.44, making a total of $12,656.49. The disbursements during the year were $10,280.42, leaving a cash balance in the Treasurer's hands of $2,371.07.

In the items of disbursements was one of $4,000.00 which was invested in U. S. Bonds, thus making the actual expenses for the year $6,280.42. The Auditing Committee reported that the funds of the Association invested in U. S. Bonds amounted to $11,347.82.

The Committee on membership reported that a year ago the Association had 1,791 members. The new members during the last year swelled this to 1,395, but the loss due to death, resignation, and suspension was 138 members, leaving the membership at 1,257. The Committee gave a list of deceased members and a brief obituary of each.

A. E. Ebert, of Chicago, referring to the fact that a great many druggists had been invited last year to join the Association, and but a few had availed themselves of the invitation, thought the by-law should be changed and the Association go back to the old plan, for the present plan of begging men to connect themselves with the Association was lowering the dignity of such a body.

Mr. G. L. Kennedy, of Pennsylvania, said that members should be very careful as to what names they presented, for in several instances the invitation had been returned with the statement that they were already members, and had paid their dues and could not understand why they should be requested to send another five dollars or sign again the by-laws.

The Committee on Time and Place of Meeting for next year unanimously reported in favor of San Francisco, the time to be left with the council, with the understanding that it should be about August 1st.

Mr. Hallberg, of Chicago, wished to know about what the railroad fare would be, and the time necessary to be taken.

Mr. Painter said that the fare would be very much reduced if a company could be formed to go from the east, so that the expense would be but a little more than at any other place near by. That it was a duty we owed to the brethren on the Pacific coast to hold our meeting there, or else decide that we are not an Association for the whole country. We never have a very large representation from any one part of the country at any meeting, no matter where it is held, except those living in the locality the Association meets in. The regular attendants of the Association would, no doubt, attend no matter where it is held, and the effect on the druggists in California and the Pacific coast would be such as to bring them in the Association in large numbers, and thus do good to it as well as to themselves.

Mr. Senbury, of New York, thought we ought to think well before we did this, for he believed it would be an expensive trip. He put the figure at $300 as what it would cost, and that was too much for the average druggist to pay for his summer vacation.

Mr. L. E. Sayre, of Kansas, said that appealing to his pocket, it would be a question whether he could go or not, and so he might be deprived of the privilege of attending the Association for one year, but he believed in looking at it in a more unselfish way than that, and leaving himself out of the question, consider whether it was not due to the brethren on the Pacific coast for us to send the Association there. He had seen the same opposition when the question was raised in the Teachers' Convention, but when they decided to go, the matter was placed in the hands of men with great executive ability, who succeeded in getting up a grand excursion and the railroad fare there and back was only thirty-five dollars for each person. Five dollars of that went into the Treasury of the Association and they received so much that they have now a large surplus.

Mr. Ebert, of Chicago, said that a few years ago he was chairman of a committee to take a census of the members, as to how many would attend the meeting. A great many did not reply; 80 from the East said they would go

50 would not, but from the Pacific slope they received responses from 400 who said they would attend and that there would be 21 papers furnished. He approved going there and would vote for it.

Mr. Brown, of Kansas City, said the only question to be considered was, not the selfish one of each individual, but whether it would be best for the Association.

Mr. Carl Siminon, of Minnesota, made an appeal for the Association to meet in St. Paul or Minneapolis, Minnesota.

Several other members spoke upon the question, when the report of the Committee was adopted by a large rising vote. A Special Committee of five was appointed by the president to make arrangements with the railroads and report to the Council at some future time.

Association then adjourned till afternoon.

SECTION ON COMMERCIAL INTERESTS.

Tuesday afternoon, 3.30.

This being the third session of the Association, according to the by-laws it was given up to the section on Commercial Interests.

The Chairman. A. H. Hollister, of Madison, Wis. occupied the chair and called the section to order. J. W. Colcord, of Boston, the secretary, made a short report.

The Chairman stated it was the duty of this section to appoint a Committee on Exhibits and asked how it was to be done. It was decided that he should appoint them.

He named F. Wilcox, of Connecticut; J. F. Patton, of Pennsylvania; and Alexander K. Finlay, of Louisiana.

W. H. Rogers, of Middletown, N. Y., offered a resolution that the secretary of this section correspond with manufacturers, requesting them to label their products in conformity with the officinal nomenclature, and to designate strengths by ap. gr. or per ct., and abolish arbitrary signs such as "ff" marks and Baumé, and that the co-operation of the National Wholesale Dealers' Association be solicited toward securing this result.

Carried.

Mr. Rogers, the only member of a committee appointed last year, being called upon for a report, said the committee was unable to do anything, as there was a question as to where their work begins or ends and as to how much it trenches on others.

Mr. Colcord, the secretary, also spoke in reference to the same.

A motion was made to appoint a committee to report nominations for officers of the section for the ensuing year. Messrs. Alexander, Ebert, and Ingalls were made such a committee, and very soon after reported the following: A. Hollister as chairman and J. W. Colcord as secretary. The Committee explained why they decided to report the re-election of the present officers. These gentlemen had not had much chance to understand what they were to do this last year, and that in another year they could make the section more interesting.

Chairman Hollister declined a re-election, for if there was any honor in such positions they should be passed around. He had had no misapprehension of his work, and had performed it to the best of his ability, though there had been great difficulties in the way. As to his not having made a report, he had conferred with several of the members of this Association, and with the President of the Michigan Association, and it was deemed advisable by all to defer it until the evening session, when the two Associations would meet together.

Mr. Alexander said that he had had no intention of reflecting on the chairman in his remarks, but had meant the section was hardly in good working order yet, and by continuing the present officers another year, much good might be done.

Mr. Hollister said all he wanted to do was to seek the good of the Association, and if he had failed it was an error of judgment, an error of head, not of heart.

The acting chairman, Mr. Rogers, was then directed to cast one ballot for the nominees of the committee.

Mr. Canning offered a resolution that the manufacturers in the rebate system be requested to furnish no rebate goods to any wholesale firm or party who retail such goods, no matter how much they may purchase, and that the National Wholesale Dealers' Association be requested to co-operate in carrying this out.

This was debated by Messrs. H. Canning, J. W. Colcord, C. S. Hallberg, R. G. Eccles, E. Painter, and others, who thought it was a desirable move, for it was impossible for retail druggists to compete in prices with those jobbers who bought in large quantities under the rebate plan, and then sold them at a very little advance. The same resolutions had been before the Massachusetts Pharmaceutical Association and by them brought to the attention of the wholesale association. It was brought here for us to act upon.

Some thought that the question of conspiracy might be raised by any firm of wholesalers who had regular retail stores, and the wholesalers would be only too glad to have a chance to laugh at us and pay no attention to our request.

Mr. Colcord spoke of a notion store in Boston putting up nineteen thousand prescriptions in a year and a half; he said if the wholesaler continues this practice of retailing, there will be no business for the retailer, and he will soon be ground out. Anybody in Boston can go in the wholesale drug store there and buy as cheaply as the druggist can.

It was finally referred to a committee of three to report at the evening session. Committee: Messrs. Canning, Hallberg, and Eccles.

Mr. C. F. G. Meyer, of Cleveland, Ohio, was introduced as a delegate from the National Wholesale Druggists' Association, and made a speech in which he showed the wholesale dealers were in sympathy with the American Pharmaceutical Association in its scientific pursuits.

Mr. Seabury, of New York, started a discussion on the practice of wholesale dealers substituting a cheap drug for a higher priced one in filling retail orders. That firms took pains to introduce goods and to leave the orders received with wholesale dealers; and when later druggists were called upon to supply the articles, that other goods were being substituted for them, the excuse of the retailer being that he could not get them from his jobber. He believed in only one kind of substitution and that was when a physician orders an officinal article, though he designates any maker, the druggist can supply his own make, knowing it to be as good, if not better.

Dr. Eccles did not believe even in this kind of substitution, as it might be the entering wedge to vice, and, like all wedges, very thin, and makes but small opening at the first, but soon broadens into larger ones and then will admit greater things, and he reminded the Association of the story that Prof. Remington had once told of the fl. ext. cinchona which the druggist said he knew was good, because he had made it himself. It was very light-colored and proved to be only one-fifth the strength. So the mere fact of a druggist making his own preparations was not a proof they were the best, and if a druggist commences to substitute even in that small way, it will tend to make him do so when more important things come in his way. There is but one safe way: don't put up the prescription at all, or put it up as it is written. As to obtaining goods from jobbers, if the druggist insists upon getting the goods he wants, and will pay the price asked, he will always get them.

Mr. Brown, of Kansas City, doesn't believe there is as much substitution going on among druggists as there was fifteen or twenty years ago. The facility for getting goods is so great now that it is his own fault if he don't get them.

Mr. Eliel, of Indiana, coincided with Mr. Brown and thought this talk of substituting more of a bugbear than a fact.

Mr. Brown said that, if Mr. Seabury knew of any wholesaler in our Association who was guilty of substitution, he should bring charges against him and have him expelled.

Mr. Painter said he had no trouble to get the goods he wanted; the jobber, if he did not have it in stock, would make great efforts to get it for him, sending sometimes as far as Chicago for that purpose.

Mr. Ebert, of Chicago, said the charge of substitution could not be brought against the jobbers of the West, as he had never known of such a thing there for the last twenty-five years.

Mr. Colcord announced the arrangements for an excursion to Chicago and the lakes, to start Saturday night and return by Tuesday noon; cost, including state-room and meals, $16.

The meeting then adjourned until evening.

Tuesday Evening, 8:25.

The Chairman of the Section on Commercial Interests, Mr. A. H. Hollister, called the meeting to order at 8:22 P.M., and delivered an address filled with advice and encouragement to the patient druggists which pointed out the way to success and instilled ideas of duty and honesty. He said the interest connected with this section was the interest that gave them their bread and butter, which none but those fully equipped could hope to win. He advised preliminary education of apprentices as necessary, spoke of the relations of pharmacists and physicians. He believed we should form a mutual fire insurance company. The tariff, where it affects our interests, we should try to remedy, and especially have the twenty-five-dollar-tax on spirits wiped out. We should use our influence on the Government to have measures adopted looking toward the cultivation of medicinal plants, such as the poppy, the indigo plant, the plants of the citrus family, and the olive. He referred to the cutting craze as unbusinesslike and suicidal, and finished by saying the druggists of the country are looking to the A. P. A. to solve these questions and lend them to success.

A motion made by Mr. T. J. Macmahan, New York, that a committee take the report in charge and report upon the suggestions, did not meet with favor, and, on motion of Dr. Eccles, of Brooklyn, the section decided to discuss the report section by section, and if any gentlemen present had papers prepared on any subject embraced in the chairman's address, they could read them when that subject was under discussion.

Mr. Basset, president of the Michigan State Pharmaceutical Association, was introduced, and made an address.

Mr. F. D. Wells, of Lansing, Michigan, member of the Michigan State Association, read a paper on liquor legislation.

Dr. Eccles moved the Section take up the regular order of the chairman's address, commencing with the first proposition.

After some discussion, this motion was carried, and the chairman then read the first proposition, that no apprentices should be received except those having a good English education.

Mr. Whelpley, of St. Louis, moved that the proposition be referred to the Section on Pharmaceutical Education.

The second proposition, as to the relation between physician and pharmacist, led to a long discussion, which was participated in by Messrs. Painter, Remington, Hallberg, Eccles, Macmahan, Holshauer, Hollister, Alexander, and Eberbach, the main point of which was the use of the phrase by the chairman, "that the druggist should seek to make some arrangement with the physician." It was feared this would be misunderstood by outsiders to mean a monetary arrangement. It was finally settled by putting the word "professional" before arrangement.

The third proposition, that of "Mutual Insurance," brought out the fact of a Druggists' Mutual Insurance being already established in St. Louis, which was indorsed by several members. The Section adopted the suggestion of the chairman.

The fourth proposition, "Tariff on Medicines and Liquor Legislation," was then discussed by Messrs. Leo Eliel, Eccles, S. A. D. Sheppard, Hallberg, Parkill, Painter, Diehl, Remington, Canning, and Whelpley.

Dr. Eccles said there would be no harm in taking the tax off whiskey, for there are only three classes in the community. One who does not drink at all, and he would not drink any more if liquor was free. Second, the moderate drinker who has enough when he has drank his one or two glasses, and cheapness would have no effect on him; and third, the drunkard who rolls in the gutter, who has filled himself to his utmost capacity, therefore, no matter how cheap the liquor might become, he could put no more in himself. In fact, the latter would be benefited, for now when it costs him ten dollars to get drunk, with untaxed whiskey then he could do it for five dollars and have the other five dollars for his suffering family. The cheaper alcohol would benefit druggists, as it is used in the preparation of fluid extracts, alkaloids, ether, and many other necessary things. He thought the U. S. Government in taxing liquor was robbing the sick and suffering.

Mr. Sheppard informed the suggestion of the chairman, for the twenty-five-dollar tax brought us into the class of liquor sellers, and he wanted stopped.

Mr. Hallberg thought this matter should not be touched by the Association, but left to be acted upon at the polls this fall, but if anything was done, the Lawlor Bill now pending in Congress, which was simply to remove all special taxes, should be indorsed. This was opposed by several as verging too near to politics. After a very long discussion, the section passed a resolution asking Congress to repeal all special taxes.

The fifth proposition on cultivation of plants was indorsed.

Prof. J. P. Remington said, in reference to the poppy plant, that there was no doubt it could be successfully cultivated, as it has been in several parts of this country; but as to the yield of opium, it was questionable whether that could ever be made a paying project on account of the price of labor. We cannot hire help to sweep off the juice and get it in sufficient quantity cheaply enough.

The discussion on the sixth proposition, relating to the cutting craze and the retailing by wholesalers, took up a large amount of time and was participated in by many of the members.

Mr. Canning's resolution, which had been offered in the afternoon session and sent to a committee, was reported with an amendment that nothing in the resolution shall interfere with those firms who carry on a retail department in a separate and distinct pharmacy building.

Mr. Sheppard thought it a waste of breath to try to pass such resolutions. The best way for the druggist to form a co-operative partnership for the purpose of buying goods in large quantities and thus get the benefit of the rebate. If some such plan was adopted generally, it would be successful. He was not prepared to say just now how it was to be done. They had tried it in Boston and it worked very well until the jobbers refused to supply them with goods. But though it had not succeeded just then for that reason, he believed that if it were made general all over the United States, they, the jobbers, would be forced to supply the goods.

Mr. Basset, President of the Michigan State Association, thought nothing could be done about the cutting craze; that men, when they buy goods, could do as they pleased with them. It was an underlying principle in business, and we had better leave the subject alone; any movement that attempts to regulate another man's business must and will fail.

Mr. C. S. Hallberg said, the reason we were losing the trade in proprietary medicines was because we would not assume any responsibility for them.

Dr. Eccles thought we should pass the resolutions so as to establish a moral sentiment, though he didn't believe it would have any effect. One bad feature, if we did pass them and they were regarded by the wholesalers, would be, that no retailer would be able to become a wholesaler. It may stop cutters, but it would also retard the growth of the retailer, for he could never then get goods in sufficient quantity to do any little jobbing trade that comes to his hand.

Mr. Eliel spoke against the resolution. The resolution was carried by a vote of 25 to 22, but very shortly afterward, on motion of Mr. Henry Canning, its author, the vote was reconsidered.

Mr. Sheppard moved that it was the sense of this Association that some arrangement should be made by the Association that retailers should be able to buy goods under the rebate plan. Discussed by Messrs. Seabury, Basset, Remington, Painter, Dadd, Sheppard, Eccles, Hallberg, and De Forest, of Brooklyn.

Mr. Seabury said it was because the druggists of New York and Brooklyn did not stand by their unions that the trouble had become so bad, and he made a long speech complaining of their action.

Mr. Painter replied that it was the unions that had advertised the cutters, and put them on their feet and it was altogether their fault the cutters had grown so strong.

Mr. Hallberg said that, if pharmacy laws were better enforced there would be no cutters. In Chicago they had had three cutters, but that one had been shut up by the sheriff, the second had been forced to take out a five hundred dollar license fee for violation of law, and would soon go under, and the third had died.

Mr. De Forest said that as to enforcing the law and so forcing the cutter out of business, that did not apply to Brooklyn. The cutters of Brooklyn were more particular than any in obeying the law. For no matter how many times they changed their clerks, whether it was once a week or once a year, they would immediately send them down to be registered or examined. The pharmacy law had been enforced as well, if not better, in that city than in any place in the country. He knew what he was talking about, for he had had the administration of the law in that place for the last five years.

The following gentlemen were named constituting the Committee to Assist the Officers in their Work: Messrs. Leo Eliel, Chas. Holzhauer, and William Searby.

The Committee on Exhibits wanted information as to the desire of the Association of how to grant the prizes; whether grandeur or size of exhibit; and whether all exhibits no matter how slightly connected with the business, should be considered to be entitled to be in competition for the prize. After some discussion, Mr. Painter moved that the Committee take in consideration everything that was admissible and then use their own judgment.

The Section then adjourned at 11 P.M.

FIFTH SESSION.
Wednesday Morning.

At 9:55 the Association was called to order, and listened to the reading of the minutes of the last meeting, and acted upon the initiation to eighteen new members. It then gave way to the

SECTION ON SCIENTIFIC PAPERS.

The Chairman and Secretary of the Section being both absent, the third member of the Committee, Prof. J. M. Good, of St. Louis, called the Section to order and asked that officers of the Section be elected. It was decided that Prof. Good should act as Chairman during this meeting, and Prof. H. M. Whelpley as Secretary. Nominations for officers for the ensuing year resulted in Messrs. Emlen Painter, of New York, and H. M. Whelpley, of St. Louis, being elected as Chairman and Secretary, and the Chairman elect appointed Dr. R. G. Eccles, of Brooklyn, as the third member, that they to be installed at the close of the business of the Section.

Prof. Prescott, of Ann Arbor, Mich., read a paper on Artificial Salicylic Acid, prepared by Erwin E. Ewell and A. B. Prescott.

Dr. R. G. Eccles read a paper on Calycanthus Seeds and the Alkaloids found therein.

E. Painter wanted to know if the toxic effect upon animals was due to the alkaloid. Dr. Eccles questioned if the alkaloid had much if any effect, as he had eaten many of the seeds without any bad effect.

W. P. De Forest read a paper prepared by L. F Stevens, Brooklyn, entitled "Condensed Notes upon Trials for a Quinine Mask."

Prof. Remington was sorry it was not possible to get some simple elixir that would cover quinine, as in the formula adopted there was a mixture of yerba santa with the compound elixir taraxacum, which elixir was a mixture of ten or twelve different ingredients. If the yerba santa alone could be used as a cover, it would be better.

Mr. De Forest said that had been tried, but had failed to hide the unpleasant taste.

Prof. Remington said that yerba santa had an unpleasant taste itself, and that, while that had covered the taste of the quinine, evidently the taraxacum was needed to cover the taste of the yerba santa. Now something should be found to cover the taste of the taraxacum, and then we would have a perfect formula.

Mr. Hallberg wished to know whether this was not the formula in the National Formulary; and when assured it was, said that it had been used very often in his vicinity and found to be very good indeed.

A. B. Stevens, of Detroit, read a paper on Peppermint Oil.

The Chairman announced there were about fifteen more papers to be read, besides the discussion of the National Formulary.

Prof. Henry Trimble read a paper in answer to Query No. 27: "The U. S. P. denotes as Catechu the Extract of Acacia Catechu; the Br. P. uses the Extract of Uncaria Gambier. Which of these two is to be preferred?"

The author stated that his results were a surprise to him, as he did not expect, at the beginning, to come to the conclusion he did.

C. S. Hallberg, of Chicago, read a paper on the Nomenclature of Pharmaceutical Preparations.

Mr. Painter thought this should be referred to the Committee on the Revision of the United States Pharmacopœia, so that it shall be kept before the Association. This was carried.

Dr. F. E. Stewart referred to new preparations mentioned in the London *Lancet* and other English medical journals, called Valoids. They are liquid preparations in which 1 lb. represents 1 lb. of the drug, and are really fluid extracts under another name. When these preparations are put on the market, they will mix up our nomenclature.

Prof. Remington suggested that there might be a chance in these new preparations for the retailer. For if the manufacturers are going to make trouble by urging the physicians to use their different makes, these valoids, not being so well known, can be made by the pharmacist himself; but, on general principles, it is demoralizing to nomenclature to call the same articles by different names.

Prof. Oldberg said there was a slight difference between the fluid extracts and valoids, as in the latter 1 lb. of finished product represents 1 lb. of the drug, while in the former 100 C.c. represents 100 Gm. of the drug.

Mr. L. E. Sayre, of Kansas, read a paper on Loco Weed, and remarked afterward that this weed had created great excitement in the West, for one State had paid out $43,000 and another State $200,000 for its collection and extermination. Of course, there had been fraud and imposition practised by the gatherers, for, in many instances, they had not only mixed other plants resembling the loco with the loads brought to the inspector, but some had also sown the regular weed, and then gathered it, thus making a nice little income for themselves.

Prof. Remington asked if these plants were found in the mountains or the lower region.

Mr. Sayre answered they were not found in the upper regions.

Dr. Eccles said he would throw out the thought that the pods of the plants contain leguminose, an albuminous body subject to decomposition. This is closely related to casein. We know casein will change to a toxic principle tyrotoxicon which has been developed in milk used in making ice cream. Why may not the leguminose in its decomposition produce a ptomaine which would have the toxic effect upon the animal? The plant is closely related to the physostigma and this production of a poisonous principle in this way might be possible.

Mr. Sayre said the toxic effect of this weed could not be referred to the pods, for the animals are poisoned before the plant is in flower. When the plant first begins to shoot above the ground the cattle eat it very greedily, and then again in full, after the pod has shed its seeds. He had endeavored to secure a ptomaine in the decomposition products, but had not succeeded as yet. He would still continue his trials.

Prof. Oldberg said it was doubtful if the real loco weed which produces these effects was known or whether there was any plant which did produce them.

Mr. Sayre said that ranchmen agreed upon three varieties of Astragalus as being the loco weed. And as they were pretty generally observing men, they had no doubt they were correct. He would not say the loco weed was a myth, or that these symptoms were not produced by the plant, but he had his own ideas about it. There were any number of theories, all of which he would not stop to enumerate, but would mention two or three. One was, that it was caused by malnutrition.

Some thought that, as a large percentage of the plant was a fine fibre, like very light cotton stock, this being very indigestible, set up an inflammation in the alimentary tract.

Others claimed there was a little worm enveloped in the leaf which caused the trouble. He had collected all he could find upon the weed, and sent them to an entomologist for examination.

Others said it was a root that gets into the stomach. But it is well known that roots are digested and go off with the fæces.

He was inclined to the opinion that the effect supposed to be due to this plant was in reality mal-assimilation. Either the animal was overfed or ate something it could not digest.

Prof. Remington wanted to know if any experiment had been made in feeding these plants to a certain number of animals and watching the physiological effects.

Mr. Sayre said this had been done only with two animals, and a post-mortem examination held on them, but he had had no faith in the man who made the postmortem. Nothing was found out. But such an experiment would be of no account. For only about five per cent of those animals who eat this plant become attacked with locoism, or die, and if the experiment failed, it would at once be said you had not got hold of the right animal.

Prof. Maisch said the only way was to go to the bottom and try all experiments, and called attention to the fact that all or almost all of Mr. Sayre's experiments had been made with carnivorous animals, and not herbivorous, and perhaps that was why they had failed. Even man is both carnivorous and herbivorous, and the poison may not have as much effect on man as it would on animals which only eat plants.

Mr. Brown, of Kansas City, and others took part in the discussion, after which the session adjourned until afternoon.

Wednesday Afternoon.

Meeting called to order at 3:40 by Chairman Good; W. P. De Forest, of Brooklyn, acting as secretary.

Mr. J. L. Thompson, of Tennessee, presented the following resolution:

Whereas, The able and interesting paper presented to this Association by Prof. L. E. Sayre shows that he has made extensive investigations of the properties of the loco weed, and that still further investigations and experiments will prove of great value to the State of Kansas, and the other States in which the weed grows; Therefore, be it

Resolved, That the American Pharmaceutical Association earnestly recommend to the Legislature of the aforesaid State that they give to Prof. L. E. Sayre their hearty indorsement and support for further investigation of the loco poison.

Remarks, all in favor of the resolution, were made by G. L. Kennedy, E. Painter, J. L. Thompson, M. W. Alexander, and J. M. Good, and it was passed without a dissentient voice.

The subject of the National Formulary, referred to this section by the main association, was then taken up and discussed. The point of interest was how often should the work be revised.

Mr. De Forest thought it was a work of importance, and as such should not be subject to too much change or changed too often. He personally favored a change not more than once every three years, but, conversing with some gentlemen of the Association, he found they thought it should be revised oftener. In order to test the question, he moved that the National Formulary be revised once in two years.

Prof. Remington thought Mr. De Forest had the right idea. It is a work of great importance, and if changed every year, the druggists would soon lose faith in it. They don't want to change the color or taste of a preparation too often, and it would be better to put up with something slightly wrong even for three years, rather than to have an uncertainty as to how often it would be changed.

Prof. Maisch said it would be impossible at the present time to say how soon it ought to be revised. We should wait and see; it should not be revised until after the next revision of the U. S. Pharmacopœia, and then there will be some material to work upon. Maybe some of the formulæ in the present work will be taken into the Pharmacopœia, and we may want to put those that are left out of the next Pharmacopœia in this book. At any rate, it wasn't practical to say how soon the revision will come.

W. H. Rogers thought the committee had had great labor and gone to a great expense to bring the book to its present perfectness, and it would be great folly to think of making any great change too soon. It should have a chance to be in the hands of physicians, and they should have a chance to try it before any change was made. Besides, there was a business side to the question. The expense of each revision should be met by the sales. Wholesalers would discredit our work if it they knew we would have to revise it too often.

Mr. Carl Simmon thought the work should be revised at least once in two years.

Prof. C. L. Diehl favored the revision once in five years, in the mean time giving the committee a chance to send out corrections if necessary.

Mr. Hallberg said that from the beginning it had been promised that this was to be a National Formulary, and in order to do this, it was necessary to have it revised very often. New York and Brooklyn had found it was impossible to give all the necessary formulæ called for through the country, and so they had called upon the country at large to help them. Now they have done their part of the work and it should go to other parts of the country and let them have a trial at it. Some of these things that are prescribed are short-lived, and if we are going to wait for three or five years to have a formula for them, we won't get them in at all. We should not wait until their life of usefulness has passed.

Mr. Day, of Illinois, looked upon the National Formulary as an appendix to the Pharmacopœia, and thought that, as such, it should be revised much oftener.

Prof. Remington said it is a sort of supplement to the Pharmacopœia, and the proper time to revise it is after the revision of the Pharmacopœia in 1890. Better not tie the committee down to any time, but wait until we see what we shall have by the way of a revision.

Mr. De Forest then withdrew his motion and in its place moved the adoption of the first resolution of the committee (see above), amended by adding the words "and report at each meeting of this Association." Carried.

Mr. De Forest then moved the adoption of the second resolution. Carried.

Mr. De Forest, reading the latter part of the report of the committee in reference to there being but one standard or authority, moved that the suggestion of the committee be adopted, to make a distinct announcement and place the same on record, that the U. S. Pharmacopœia be the *only* standard of authority for all *officinal* preparations, and that when any preparation in the National Formulary should be taken into the U. S. Pharmacopœia, the authority of the National Formulary over that article ceases and is thereby abolished. Carried.

Prof. Oldberg hoped the time would come when the U. S. Pharmacopœia should not contain any compounds, but be merely a collection of titles and tests and working formulæ for simples. No ointments or pills, or any such compounds, should be contained in it, and then the National Formulary could contain all these things.

Messrs. Remington and Painter agreed with Prof. Olaberg, and thought that in time this may come. But as this was not the Pharmacopœia Convention, nothing could be done about that now.

Mr. Hallberg coincided with Mr. Oldberg's idea and thought it might be done at the next revision.

Prof. Remington moved that this Section ask the President of the Association to appoint five members from the central portion of the United States and one member from each State Association to act as Committee on National Formulary.

After discussion, and several amendments being offered designating certain cities, which were lost, it was carried as originally offered.

Mr. Carl Simmon offered the following resolutions, which, after a little discussion, were carried:

Resolved, That the President of the American Pharmaceutical Association appoint a committee of five to visit the American Medical Association, to submit to their consideration the National Formulary, and to use their best endeavors to get the American Medical Association to adopt this work as an authority for all unofficinal formulæ contained therein.

Resolved, That the Secretary of the American Pharmaceutical Association be requested to send notice to the different State Pharmaceutical Associations requesting them to appoint a committee from their association to visit their State Medical Associations, at their next annual meeting, for the purpose of submitting to their consideration and adoption the National Formulary as an authority for all preparations contained therein.

The Section then listened to a paper by Mr. Enno Sander, of St. Louis, on Natural and Artificial Salts.

A discussion followed, principally devoted to the formula for Carlsbad Salt in the National Formulary, and the statement made that the Association would protect any of the members, if necessary, in the use of any of the formulas.

H. W. Snow read a paper on Phosphomolybdic Acid for the Quantitative Estimation of Alkaloids.

In reply to a question, Mr. Snow said three washings was all he had to use.

Dr. Eccles said the titration should depend upon the alkaloid. In some cases, phosphomolybdic would be the best, in others, Mayer's reagent.

Prof. Remington wished to know if the reagent would keep, or if it had to be made frequently.

Mr. Snow said it was apt to change and should be made frequently.

Prof. Henry Trimble, of Pennsylvania, read a paper in answer to Query 7: "Is the Precipitated Sulphate of Iron of Constant Composition? Does it Contain the Same Proportion of Water of Crystallization as the large Crystals?"

The Chairman announced there were five papers in his hands, presented through Prof. Prescott, of Ann Arbor, from gentlemen who were not members, and he wished the sense of the Section as to the disposition of them.

Prof. Bedford, of New York, moved they be received as volunteer papers and be read. Carried.

Prof. Painter thought preference should be given to the papers of members, and then, if there was time, to have them read.

The Chairman stated there were only nine more papers to be read, five of which were the volunteer papers, and four by members.

Mr. F. A. Thompson, of Detroit, read a paper on Pepsin Testing.

Prof. Sayre said he had over twenty men at work, this last winter, on pepsin, just to see how much acid was necessary to work pepsin. It had varied, but generally required a 0.2 strength. They went over the whole ground with different pepsins, and found that one may require more acid than another.

Dr. Eccles said that he had tried a number of experiments a couple of years ago, and had found a 0.2 strength just right. The temperature was an important thing. At a high temperature, you produce a parapeptone; and at a very high temperature, there is almost nothing produced but parapeptone.

Prof. Sayre said that test-tube manipulation was not the same as Nature, and we are apt to get on the wrong track very often in our work.

Mr. Seabury, of New York, wanted to know whether the antiseptics that pepsin-makers used did not have some effect upon their product, and so cause the difference in their albumen-dissolving proportion. All pepsin-makers must use some antiseptics, such as boracic acid, benzoic acid, or salicylic acid, and some traces of this must be left in the pepsin.

Mr. Thompson said he must take exception to this statement, for there was no antiseptic used in the preparation of pepsin.

Mr. Hallberg did not see the necessity of the use of any antiseptic. Nearly all these scale pepsins are made by macerating the stomach with acid, expressing the liquid, filtering rapidly, evaporating at a temperature of 140° F. or 150° F. to a fair consistence, then neutralizing by use of soda, ammonia, or some such alkali, bringing it to a syrupy consistence, spreading upon plates of glass, and drying in a closet.

Mr. Sayre said he had manufactured pepsin for many years and had not used antiseptics. He had tried to use them, but could not, as all of them were objectionable. He had made odorless pepsin without any of these chemicals which had kept well for a very long time.

Prof. Remington thought it would be unwise, on the part of any manufacturer, to send out any pepsin with an antiseptic in, for they would certainly stop the action of the pepsin. Alcohol does not destroy the action, but only retards it, and the pepsin can be preserved by alcohol. Prof. Scheffer had started us on the track that alcohol and pepsin should not be given together, but he thinks he then made a mistake which we are gradually coming back from now.

The subject was discussed at great length, when it was moved to adjourn until next morning.

Thursday Morning.

Meeting called to order at 9:45. Minutes of the Association read and several members invited to join the Association.

The section on Scientific Papers held its last session.

Mr. Joseph F. Geissler, of New York, read a paper entitled, "Notes on the Morphiometric Assay of Opium."

Prof. Maisch asked if there was any objection to using hot water.

Mr. Geissler said the use of hot water caused the precipitation of many impurities which are not removed subsequently. Even spirit will not remove them.

Prof. Maisch said that was the trouble with the old method and agreed with his own experience.

Mr. Geissler said that when using an opium of over 15 per cent. the ammonium chloride and lime should be increased.

The loss of morphine in the mother liquor is 1 per cent.

Prof. Painter moved that all members of the Michigan Association and all those interested in pharmacy, present at the meeting, be invited to participate in debate. Carried.

Dr. Rosa Upson read a paper on "Sponges."

Mr. A. M. Todd, of Nottawa, gave a description of a new still for the distillation of peppermint oil, showing a model of the same.

Prof. Prescott thought a great deal might be gained by a small stream of water running over the condensing pipes and thus the absorption of latent heat could be used.

Prof. Painter said that to have a stream of water running on a pipe would make it necessary to use a greater length of pipe, more so than to have the pipe surrounded with water.

Mr. Todd said he had attached the Remington condenser, laboratory size, once when his regular condenser was being repaired, and he found the condensation very rapid.

On a large manufacturing scale it was found cheaper to use long pipes and apply water. His condenser was thirty feet long, seven in diameter, and took one thousand barrels of water a day. One-third that size would take two thousand barrels.

Prof. Remington said it is a well-known fact that for manufacturing on the large scale the apparatus must be specially constructed. Appliances that can be used on a small scale cannot be enlarged, and one kind of still will not do for all things.

Mr. A. E. Ebert said an important thing often overlooked is the temperature of the steam for distillation, and the temperature of the water should be calculated. It is different at different times of the year. Most distillers use water from wells of a depth of 20, 30 and 40 feet, and the usual temperature is 50 to 60° F.

If you take into consideration the temperature of your steam in distilling, and the temperature of your water in condensing, you can figure out the size and length of your condenser.

Mr. Todd said the temperature of the escaping steam is always identical, no matter if you have 4 oz. pressure or 400 lb. pressure.

Mr. Hallberg said there were over 300 or 400 charcoal furnaces in the State of Michigan, and he had heard they burned the coal in the old way, that all the vapor was allowed to escape, and nothing but charcoal was saved. He wanted to know if any method had been utilized to save the other products. This distilling apparatus had suggested the inquiry to find out whether there could not be some cheap apparatus for this purpose.

Prof. Prescott said there may be some furnaces worked in the old way, where all the products are wasted. But in the most of them the vapors are drawn by fans and the products condensed.

Prof. Prescott read a paper, by John E. Pennington, on "Assay of Powdered Ipecac."

Mr. Thompson expressed surprise at the small percentage of emetine obtained; he had obtained double the amount in his work.

Prof. Ohlberg wanted to know if Mr. Thompson in his experiments had used the bark and the ligneous cork or only the bark alone.

Mr. Thompson said he had used both.

A. B. Stevens read a paper, by E. Soebtje, on Query No. 20: "A Practical Formula is wanted for the Economical Preparations of Pure Commercial Mercurous Iodide (Yellow)."

Prof. Prescott said the success is due to the precision in making the mercurous nitrate.

Prof. Remington said there had been some controversy as to the proper color of the mercurous iodide. The British Pharmacopœia concluded to drop the green iodide, and the United States Pharmacopœia had changed its title. Some say the yellow is the proper color and the green color is due to decomposition.

A. B. Stevens said that if this formula was followed it would always be one color, and if kept from the light it will always keep yellow.

Prof. Good thought, if the bottle were kept in a drawer, that would be sufficient protection for it.

Dr. Eccles said that heat would change the color. The same is the case in the red iodide of mercury. By heating you make it quite yellow, then by rubbing it in a mortar you make it red again.

Prof. Prescott read a paper on Arsenic in Medicinal Bismuth Salts.

Dr. Eccles said his neighbor had asked him whether, if there were any medicinal doses of arsenic in bismuth salts, the medicinal effect of the drug was due to the arsenic or the bismuth.

Chairman Good.—I suppose the chairman is not obliged to answer that question (laughter).

Prof. Remington believes the effect of bismuth in bowel troubles and irritation of mucous membranes is largely due to its mechanical effects, by coating the membrane, and these solutions of bismuth salts, from which great good was hoped, had proved to be of no value in such cases.

An analogous case is that of prepared chalk and precipitated chalk; the former makes the best chalk mixture. Its molecular structure is such that it adheres to the membrane and so soothes it. He didn't believe the medicinal effect of bismuth was due to the arsenic it contained, but to its mechanical action.

A paper by Charles V. Boettcher on "Limit Tests for Calcium Tartrate in Cream of Tartar" was then read.

It was stated that many tests had been made with cream of tartar, purchased of grocers and of druggists. In almost every case the grocer's cream of tartar was very bad, containing a large quantity of terra alba, while the druggists' samples were good.

The paper was discussed by Messrs. H. M. Whelpley, G. W. Sloan, and C. S. Hallberg.

Prof. Remington then introduced Dr. S. S. Garrigues, one of the oldest members of the Association, a life member, who is a manufacturer of salt, who spoke for fifteen or twenty minutes on the way salt was manufactured in Michigan.

The Committee on Prize Essay was ordered to report to the Council.

The Section then adjourned.

Thursday Afternoon, 3:15.

This session, according to the by-laws, was devoted to the Sections on Pharmaceutical Legislation and Pharmaceutical Education, which were to be held simultaneously, or one after the other. The Section on Pharmaceutical Education not being ready for work, the Section on Pharmaceutical Legislation commenced its session in an adjoining room.

W. P. De Forest, of Brooklyn, the Secretary, in the absence of the Chairman, called the Section to order, and asked for nominations for temporary Chairman.

Mr. Alexander, the President of the Association, was by vote asked to take the Chair.

The Secretary then stated there was no report of officers, owing to the absence of the Chairman, but suggested that Mr. C. E. Day, of Illinois, who had been appointed chairman of a committee to prepare a plan whereby there could be an interchange of certificates between the different boards of pharmacy might have a report for the Section.

Mr. Day said he had sent letters to many and asked for suggestions, but received but little encouragement. He had no report to make.

The subject of interchange of certificates was discussed by Messrs. Keppler, of Louisiana; Butler, of Massachusetts; Alexander, of Missouri; Simmon, of Minnesota; Hollister, of Wisconsin; and De Forest, of Brooklyn. Mr. Simmon stated the Conference of State Secretaries had passed a resolution desiring the American Pharmaceutical Association to prepare a uniform law, so that all boards of pharmacy could recognize each other.

A telegram was read from the Chairman, R. F. Bryant, Kansas, announcing his inability to be present, and wishing a successful and interesting meeting.

It was moved that the Chairman appoint a committee of five to take in consideration the interchange of certificates by boards of pharmacy, and to draw up a plan whereby a uniform pharmacy law can be adopted. Carried.

Dr. Jamieson thought we should have a sample of the questions of each board, and the answers to them, to establish such a standard.

Mr. Day said this motion was almost precisely similar to the one of last year, and he did not think it would place us in any better position than that did.

Dr. Jamieson moved to elect officers for the ensuing year.

Mr. Day thought there was not any inducement to spend much labor on this Section, as so few members attended; the Section in the other room seemed to be drawing off our members; besides, he did not like to see this Section put at the tail end of the Association. It was as important as any of the others.

Mr. Hollister thought the two Sections of Legislation and Education should meet together, as their work was so similar.

Mr. Painter said this Section did not seem to understand what was expected of it and moved to take a recess until after the other Section had adjourned.

Mr. Hallberg gave notice that he would move to amend the by-laws, so that the two Sections should meet together.

The Section then took a recess.

At 5 o'clock it was again called to order by the Secretary, who asked the Section to again appoint a temporary Chairman.

On motion, Mr. A. E. Ebert, of Chicago, was asked to take the chair.

Nominations for officers for the ensuing year were called for and resulted in the election of C. A. Day, of Illinois, as Chairman; J. U. Hurty, of Indiana, as Secretary; P. S. Brown, of Mississippi, as third member; Mr. Ebert and Mr. De Forest both declining positions as Chairman and Secretary.

A resolution was offered by Mr. Brown, of Kansas City, that State Associations should require members of the Board of Pharmacy to pass examination before taking position.

This was discussed and the question asked who would examine the men who are to examine the members of the Board of Pharmacy.

It was finally withdrawn and the following resolution offered in its stead.

Resolved, That State Pharmaceutical Associations exercise great care in selecting competent and educated pharmacists for the State Board of Pharmacy.

A resolution was passed asking the Association to so arrange the business that the Legislative Section does not meet simultaneously with any other section.

Mr. Hallberg consented to withdraw his amendment merging the two sections in one.

The officers were installed and the section adjourned.

Very shortly after the Legislative Section commenced their business, the Educational Section was called to order by J. F. Judge, the Chairman, H. M. Whelpley acting as Secretary.

On motion, a Committee was appointed to present nominations for officers. They reported: P. W. Bedford, as Chairman; L. E. Sayre, Secretary; Prof. Patch, as the third member.

The Secretary made his report.

A paper was read by R. G. Eccles on Pharmaceutical Education.

L. E. Sayre read a paper on The Importance of a good English Training, as a part of Pharmaceutical Education.

This paper was discussed by A. B. Prescott, E. Painter, J. F. Judge, R. G. Eccles, H. M. Whelpley, J. P. Remington, and C. S. Hallberg. Prof. Prescott thought that a knowledge of English grammar was a necessary part of an apprentice's training. Prof. Painter thought a knowledge of mathematics was just as necessary as grammar. J. P. Remington thought that memorizing was the bane of all our educational systems.

The thing that confronts all our teachers is what shall be done with men of brains and no education. A preliminary educational requirement will often reject men who are the best fitted for our business and accept many others who are not. Many young men come from college perfectly familiar with certain ways of stating and answering propositions, but just change the problem a little, and they are unable to think it out.

He did not think we could establish a professorship of English in our pharmaceutical colleges.

Mr. C. S. Hallberg offered a resolution that we recommend all our colleges of pharmacy to require a preliminary education at the earliest practical time.

Mr. Sayre said he was in hearty sympathy with the motion, but he was afraid it would be laughed at, for each college had its own ideas.

Mr. Feucel, of Cincinnati, thought this looked as though the Association was trying to dictate to the colleges.

Mr. Ebert said, Colleges of Pharmacy are like all other private business enterprises. They make great promises, but after all, they are dependent upon the money they can make. The best preliminary examination was to require the students to have two years' practical experience in a prescription pharmacy, before they can pass their junior course.

Mr. Day moved an amendment that a committee of three be appointed by the Chairman to determine a standard to be recommended to the colleges.

Letters were read from E. Goodman and E. Bastin, of Cincinnati, giving their view on a pharmaceutical education. On suggestion of Mr. Bedford, these letters were to be handed to the Chairman of the Section, to be considered at the next meeting.

The Local Secretary, Mr. James Vernor, of Detroit, gave notice of the time of departure and arrival of the excursion boat to Star Island on the following morning.

A discussion took place as to the legality of holding a meeting on board the boat, and it was decided not proper.

The Section then adjourned.

Friday Morning.

The Association was called to order at 9:30. The officers of the Association were installed in their positions.

Mr. Finlay, of New Orleans, made a motion to reconsider the action of the Association as to the place of meeting, San Francisco. This was discussed and by a standing vote lost; 30 in favor of reconsideration, 34 against.

Mr. James Vernor was made a member of the Committee on Arrangements for the next meeting.

The Committee on Exhibits reported awarding prizes as follows: To Messrs. Hance Brothers & White, of Philadelphia, a gold medal for the best general exhibit, and to Feldcamp, Hallberg & Co. for the best exhibit of pharmaceutical goods prepared by retail pharmacists.

Votes and thanks were passed to the druggists and press of Detroit and to the local committee. The minutes were read and approved, and the Association adjourned to meet next year in San Francisco.

PAPERS.

Artificial Salicylic Acid.*

Notes upon methods for estimating the quantities of homologous acids present.

BY ERWIN E. EWELL AND ALBERT B. PRESCOTT, ANN ARBOR, MICHIGAN.

OF the homologous phenols associated together in the distillates of coal-tar, the first member is the chief constituent of ordinary carbolic acid, but, it is well known, the higher members are not altogether absent. Considerable percentages of higher phenols are common in carbolic acid. Since salicylic acid is in greater part manufactured from carbolic acid by Kolbe's process,† inquiry naturally arises as to what becomes of the higher phenols of carbolic acid used in this manufacture. It had been found some time ago; that when the higher phenols of carbolic acid are treated as they are in Kolbe's method, they are changed into homologues of salicylic acid; the cresols into hydroxy-toluic acids $(C_6H_3.OH.CO_2H)$, and the xylenols into hydroxy-xylenic acids $(C_6H_2.OH.CO_2H)$, just as phenol proper is changed into a hydroxy-benzoic acid.§

The presence of some other acids besides true salicylic acid (ortho-hydroxy-benzoic acid) in the article of salicylic acid of commerce was reported by Mr. Williams in 1878.|| He found the calcium salt of the foreign acid to be much more soluble in water than calcium salicylate is. By neutralizing a hot aqueous solution of salicylic acid with calcium carbonate, causing the salicylate of calcium to crystallize out as completely as practicable, and then acidulating the mother liquor, the unknown acid was obtained. In certain physical characters, this acid was found to be distinctly different from salicylic acid and from the other two hydroxy-benzoic acids. In the leading chemical reactions, however, the unknown acid was found to agree

---

* Paper read at the meeting of the Amer. Phar. Assoc. at Detroit.
† Kolbe, 1873; Jour. pract. Chem. (2), 10, 89; Jour. Chem. Soc., 9, 880; Watts' "Dict. Chem.", 7, 1. Phar. Proc. Am. Phar. Assoc., 22, 561; 27, 642; Schmitt, 1885; Jour. prakt. Chem. (2), 31, 397-411; Jour. Chem. Soc., 48, 984; Phar. Jour. Trans. (3), 6, 441.
‡ Biedermann and Pike, 1874; Ber. d. Chem. Ges., 6, 323; Watts' Dict., 7, Bd: S, 4,808.
§ For the ortho-compound, $C_6H_4.OH.CO_2H$ $(OH: CO_2H = 1:2)$. The reactions and their homologues are given in Prescott's "Organic Analysis," pp. 184, 454, 442.
|| J. Williams, 1878; Phar. Jour. Trans. (3), 8, 769; Proc. Am. Phar. Assoc., 25, 235.

with salicylic acid and the isomers of the latter. The acid liberated from the crystals of calcium salt, after purification, was found to agree in all points with true salicylic acid. Mr. Williams concluded that the acid not salicylic formed 15 to 25 per cent of the better grades of salicylic acid of the market. Very little further investigation of the presence and proportion of the homologous acids has been reported. In 1883, Dr. E. R. Squibb* gave the opinion that "the better grades of the well-crystallized acid of the market contain 4 to 5 per cent of something which is not salicylic acid," and for which, he says, he knows no test.

The physiological and therapeutic value of the homologous acids in medicinal salicylic acid are certainly deserving of careful study, in view of the large doses in which the agent is used and the somewhat variable effects reported of these doses.

1. A METHOD BY ACIDIMETRY.

The molecular weights of the homologous acids show the following differences, those of $CH_2 = 13.97$, in arithmetical increase.

Salicylic acid (hydroxy-benzoic acids), $C_6H_4.OH.CO_2H = 137.67$.
Hydroxy-toluic acids, $C_7H_6.OH.CO_2H = 151.64$
Hydroxy-xylenic acids, $C_8H_8.OH.CO_2H = 165.61$.

And of hundredth normal solution of alkali ($\frac{N}{100}$) needed to neutralize these acids and form monobasic salts:

1 gramme of salicylic acid requires 726.3 C.c.
1 gramme of a hydroxy-toluic acid requires 659.4 C.c.
1 gramme of a hydroxy-xylenic acid requires 603.8 C.c.

In the application of this method, it was assumed that hydroxy-toluic acids, $C_8H_8O_3 = 151.64$, fairly represent the total acids of molecular weight above that of salicylic acid. This can be justified both because there can be only a very small quantity of xylenics in carbolic acid of respectable quality, and because a given percentage of the xylenol-product would indicate a larger percentage of the less objectionable cresol-product. Thus, of the ($\frac{N}{100}$) alkali solution to neutralize 1 gramme of the acid,

Hydroxy-toluic acids take 66.9 C.c. less than salicylic.
Hydroxy-xylenic acids take 122.5 C.c. less than salicylic.

One per cent of a hydroxy-xylenic acid would indicate 1.8 per cent of a hydroxy-toluic acid. Then *the saturating capacity of "salicylic acid"* made from carbolic acid will stand as follows:

FOR ONE GRAMME OF THE ACID TESTED.

Salicylic acid, absolute .... 726.3 C.c. $\frac{N}{100}$ alkall.
" " with 5% hydroxy-toluic... 723.0 " "
" " " 10% " 719.6 " "
" " " 15% " 716.3 " "
" " " 20% " 712.4 " "
" " " 25% " 709.5 " "

In making trial of the calculated saturating powers of salicylic acid and its homologues, potassa and soda were found to work equally well in the standard solutions ($\frac{N}{100}$), and phenolphthalein proved thoroughly satisfactory as an indicator of the end-reaction, while litmus is wholly incapable of being used in this estimation. *The titrations are to be made as follows:*

About a fifth of a gramme of the acid to be tested, dried at or below 65° C. to constant weight, is accurately weighed, placed in a beaker of about a half-liter's capacity, some drops of the (alcoholic) solution of phenolphthalein added, and (without adding water for solution) the hundredth-normal solution of alkali is run in from the burette, while stirring, until the end-reaction is approached. The beaker is now placed upon wire cloth over the flame (or otherwise promptly heated) while gently stirred, only long enough to complete the solution of the acid, and without decided boiling, when the heat is removed, the beaker sides rinsed down with a little distilled water, and the titration completed. The weight taken : 1.000 =: C.c. required : x = C.c. for one gramme, to be compared with the table above.

In drying salicylic acid for a constant weight, it was found that this could be attained at 65° C., while at 70° to 75° C. there was a constant loss, in a short time sufficient to be registered by the balance. A portion of the purified acid from oil of wintergreen, placed between watch glasses, arranged for sublimation and heated to 115° C., promptly gave a sublimate of colorless crystals of good size. In aqueous solution, it suffers loss by boiling at common air pressure.

Acidimetry under the directions given above was tried upon a sample of purified acid from oil of wintergreen, a sample prepared for the purpose, in the way followed by Williams: one ounce of oil of wintergreen was saponified by potassium hydrate solution, the liquid cooled and acidulated with hydrochloric acid, the precipitate four times crystallized from boiling water, then hot solution filtered through strictly purified animal charcoal and re-

crystallised, and lastly twice recrystallised from alcohol. The average of several titrations of this purified salicylic acid agreed very closely with the calculated quantity, 726.3 C.c. ($\frac{N}{100}$) alkali for one gramme of the acid.

Applying the same volumetric reagents in the same way to a sample of salicylic acid of the ordinary market,* in four titrations an average of 714.3 C.c. was obtained — corresponding to a proportion of 15 to 20 per cent of homologous acids calculated as a hydroxy-toluic acid.

With titrations of good ordinary care, using verified instruments of such delicacy as every chemist requires for analytical work, acidimetry can reveal quantities of hydroxy-toluic acids as low as four or five per cent, other interfering impurities being absent.

II. A METHOD BY CONVERSION TO PHENOLS.

When salicylic acid and its homologues are distilled from lime they yield a distillate of their respective phenols, the elements of carbon dioxide being retained by the lime, so far becoming a carbonate. Subjecting commercial salicylic acid to this reaction, it was undertaken to apply to the distillate a limit test for comparison of the produced phenols, namely, the test by adding an equal volume of nine per cent solution of sodium hydrate, and then noting the number of volumes of water to be added to cause beginning precipitation. Experiments were undertaken, with mixtures of a fairly representative "creoylic acid" and good carbolic acid, to obtain limits of dilution for each 5 per cent addition of cresol in the mixture.

A "creoylic acid" of the market, of specific gravity 1.04, was found to yield results so far consistent that it was taken as an approximately representative cresol. Best carbolic acid of the market, with water just enough to liquefy it, was taken as phenol. From mixtures of these imperfectly pure articles, preliminary data were obtained, as set forth in the following table:

Volume per cent of cresol in the distillate.	Calculated per cent of hydroxy-toluic acid distilled.	After adding an equal volume of nine per cent sol. of soda, number volumes of water added before precipitation.
5	4.9	6.7
10	9.8	5.0
15	14.8	5.25
20	19.8	4.5
25	24.7	4.0
30	29.7	3.6
35	34.7	3.3
40	39.7	3.1
45	44.7	2.8
50	49.7	2.6

The conversion of the "salicylic acid" into its corresponding phenols was done as follows: 15 grammes of the acid and an equal weight of lime are thoroughly dried, well triturated together, placed in a glass retort, put over a strong heat, and quickly distilled, collecting the distillate in a well-cooled receiver. To promote the distillation, with great advantage dried iron filings may be added in equal quantity to the contents of the retort. When the distillate is complete, it is liquefied by adding just enough water.

The sample of commercial salicylic acid previously tested by the method of acidimetry was subjected to this process, and the distillate tested by an equal volume of 9-per-cent sodium hydrate, and subsequent dilution with measured water, until after stirring there remained visible precipitation. Five volumes of water were required, indicating, according to the table above, some proportion of hydroxy-toluic acid between 14.8 and 19.8 per cent, and agreeing substantially with the result by acidimetry.

It appears evident that a method by conversion of phenols can be made effectual for the estimation of homologous acids in the salicylic acid in use, and probably with closer results than those obtained by acidimetry.

III. SEPARATION BY SOLUBILITY OF THE CALCIUM SALTS. THE METHOD OF WILLIAMS.

This method, cited in the beginning of these notes, was the basis of the only estimation of the quantity of homologous acids in artificial salicylic acids which has come to the notice of the writers, and they have submitted it to a careful trial. The operation directed by Williams‡ was conducted three times successively. The products of each operation—that is, the salicylic acid of assumed purity, on the one hand, and the homologous acids assumed to be free from salicylic acid, on the other hand—were subjected to estimation by the method of acidimetry.

In each of the three operations, the salicylic acid was obtained from the crystals of calcium salicylate in excellent crystals, and in each case acidimetry gave results for pure salicylic acid. The mother liquors, treated for sep-

---

* In appearance the sample was an indistinctly crystalline powder of a slightly pinkish color.
† A. H. Allen, 1878: *The Analyst*, 3, 301; Allen's "Commercial Organic Analysis," 2, 551; Lunge's "Coal Tar Distillation," 63.
‡ 1876: *Phar. Jour. Trans.* (3), 6, 730; *Proc. Am. Phar. Assn.*, 19, 556.

† *Ephemeris*, 1, 411, Nov., 1882.
‡ *Phar. Jour. Trans.* (3), 6, 745.

aration of the homologous acids,* yielded acid agreeing with that described by Williams—acid differing greatly from salicylic in physical properties. This "homologous acid," subjected to acidimetry, gave for 1 Gm. of the acid, (1) 705 C.c., (2) 699 C.c., and (3) 697 C.c., of the 100th-normal solution of alkali, the average being 700.3 C.c. By the average of these estimations, then, the "homologous acid" still retained 61 per cent of salicylic acid against 39 per cent of hydroxy-toluic acids, and in estimation (3), where the separation was carried further than in the other two trials, there remained over 50 per cent of salicylic acid. Indeed, the process of crystallization does not promise well for estimation unless by some system of allowances and for an approach toward exact determination.

UNIVERSITY OF MICHIGAN, August, 1888.

Arsenic in the Medicinal Bismuth Salts.

BY RICHARD E. HAWKES.†

THE quantity of arsenic in the subnitrate and subcarbonate of bismuth furnished in pharmacy has been reported upon by several analysts within the past few years.‡ The desire for increasing purity in bismuth preparations has led the writer to make estimation of the arsenic contained in a collection of samples of both of the pharmacopœial simple salts, as obtained from dispensing pharmacists here and there at different times. Seven samples of subnitrate of bismuth and seven samples of subcarbonate were taken.

The quantity of arsenic was determined by weight of the mirror of the reduced element, obtained under Marsh's plan, as used by Gautier,§ and improved by Chittenden,| the details being fixed as follows: Five grammes of the bismuth salt, accurately weighed, were gradually treated with diluted sulphuric acid, in the case of the nitrate heating until all nitric acid was expelled, and the mixture diluted with water to 120 C.c. About 30 grammes of zinc were placed in a flat-bottomed generating flask of some 400 to 500 C.c. capacity. The rubber stopper of the flask admits a separatory funnel, closed with stop-cock, and a connection with a drying tube filled with calcium chloride of neutral reaction, this joined by a flexible connection to the horizontal ignition-tube, of hard glass and about ⅜ inch inner diameter for six or seven inches in length, then narrowed to about one-third its previous thickness for about two inches, and lastly bent at right angles to reach down into a short test-tube carrying 3 or 4 C.c. of silver nitrate solution. The ignition tube is supported for four or five inches by a single wrap of wire gauze, reaching within one-fourth of an inch of the narrowed part of the tube. The wire gauze is supported at its extremities, and a double or triple spread burner of the Bunsen lamp is placed beneath so as to heat the whole of the wire gauze and preserve an even, low red heat in the ignition-tube for three to five inches, or throughout its wrapped portion. If the inner diameter of the ignition-tube be over four or five millimeters (⅕ inch), it should be heated to redness for more than three inches of its length with a slow evolution of the gas. The length of the ignited portion of the tube is to be proportional to its width and to the rapidity of the stream of gas. But the reaction in the silver nitrate solution will reveal the escape from the reduction of any weighable quantity of the arsenic.

Sufficient diluted sulphuric acid is introduced into the flask to clear the air, the rate of transmission of gas being indicated by the bubbling in the silver solution, and as soon as the air is all out, the ignition-tube is heated to redness. Purity of the zinc and sulphuric acid having been previously determined, the prepared solution of bismuth sulphate is gradually introduced through the separatory funnel, with additional diluted sulphuric acid if need be, to maintain a steady bubbling in the silver solution. If a mirror be obtained at the close of the operation, the section of the tube containing the mirror is cut out, wiped clean, cooled to the temperature of the balance, and weighed. The tube is heated over a smokeless flame until the arsenic is wholly expelled, then cooled, wiped again, and the empty tube weighed again.

In each of these tests the gas was passed through the heated tube for six hours. The zinc and sulphuric acid, in a trial for the same time, gave strictly negative results.

---

* The acid not salicylic has usually been designated in the singular number and it may be that only one homologue acid occurs in the manufactured article. But as there are three isomeric hydroxy-toluic acids, to any making of the hydroxy-xylenic, and in absence of any identification of these isomers in "homologous acid," it is as well to recognize their existence in the plural. Melting points of the hydroxy-toluic acids have been reported as follows:—

Acid—CO₆H : OH : CH₃ = 1 : 2 : 3—melts at 103° C.
Acid " " = 1 : 4 : 2 — " 177° C.
Acid " " = 1 : 2 : 5 — " 131° C.

† Paper read at the Detroit meeting of the A. P. A.
‡ Chittenden and Lambert, 1882; Amer. Chem. Jour., 3, 99; Jour. Chem. Soc., 44, 578.
O. B. Ledman, 1885; "Contributions Chem. Lab. Univ. Mich.," 2 61.
The Pharmacist and Surgeon, Ann Arbor, 5, 241.
Dr. L. Hough, 1886; Proc. New York State Pharm. Assoc., p. 201; Druggists' Circular, 31, 200; Proc. Am. Phar. Assoc., 34, 234.
H. L. Rumbo, 1888; Am. Jour. Phar. Assoc., 36, 526; Proc. Am. Phar. Assoc., 36, 580.
Taylor's "Treatise on Poisons," 1875 Philadelphia, p. 578.
"Trials for Murder by Poisoning," 1863, London, p. 310.
Wharton's and Stille's "Med. Jurisprudence," II., 1884. Amery and Wood, pp. 261, 571.
§ A. Gautier, 1876; Bull. Soc. Chim. (2), 24, 200.
| Chittenden and Donaldson, 1883; Am. Chem. Jour., 4, 230.

With the selected samples of bismuth salts, results were obtained as follows:

Subcarbonate of Bismuth.

No.	Taken.	Weight of mirror.	Arsenious Acid.	Per Cent.
1	5.000	0.0025	0.00330	0.0660
2	5.000	None.	....	....
3	5.000	A trace.	....	....
4	5.000	0.0001	0.00013	0.0026
5	5.000	0.0003	0.00040	0.0080
6	5.000	0.0005	0.00067	0.0133
7	5.000	0.0004	0.00053	0.0106

Subnitrate of Bismuth.

No.	Taken.	Weight of mirror.	Arsenious Acid.	Per Cent.
1	5.000	0.0005	0.00067	0.0133
2	5.000	None.	....	....
3	5.000	A trace.	....	....
4	5.000	0.0002	0.00027	0.0053
5	5.000	0.0005	0.00067	0.0133
7	5.000	A trace.	....	....

From the experiments of others upon the limit of recovery of arsenic in its chemical separations,* it appears evident that the actual loss of arsenic, in working 5 grammes of material, should not have been at the very utmost over 0.00004 gramme, that is, the admissible error should not affect the tenths of milligram expressed in "weight of mirror." And in No. 2, subnitrate, and No. 2, subcarbonate, if arsenic were present, it was in proportion not above about 0.002 per cent; in No. 3, subcarbonate, and Nos. 3 and 7, subnitrate, not more than about 0.003 per cent.

Recounting the summarized results of the analyses cited at the beginning of this note, it appears that, of arsenious acid from bismuth subnitrate, Chittenden and L. obtained 0.013 per cent in average of 14 samples:
0.077 per cent maximum;
traces in 2 of the 14;
and none in 1 of the same.
Ledman obtained 0.0025 per cent, average of 11 samples, with 0.0108 per cent maximum,
and traces only in 6 of the 11.
Haigh obtained 0.033 per cent, average of 5,
with trace only in 1 of the same.
Rumbo obtained presence of arsenic in 2 only of 4 samples, under Fleitmann's test.

UNIVERSITY OF MICHIGAN, N. MASS. OF PHARMACY, July, 1888

Calycanthus Seed.

(Abstract of paper by R. G. G. ECCLES, M.D., read at the Detroit meeting of the A. P. A.)

At the meeting of the Torrey Botanical Club of New York City in December, 1887, Mr. E. E. Sterns exhibited specimens of the fruit of *Calycanthus glaucus* Willdenow, which he had received from Mr. J. H. Boyd, postmaster of Cagle, Sequatchie County, Tennessee. A letter from Mr. Boyd was read, which, with other interesting information, contained the following: "Hundreds of cattle and sheep have died here in the past five years from 'bubby' (the local name of Calycanthus). The seeds only are poisonous. When a brute gets a sufficient dose, from five to ten well-filled pods, it makes for the nearest water, and often falls dead while drinking, or it may live three or four weeks and then die. The symptoms are like those of a man extremely drunk, except that any noise frightens it. Stamp the ground hard, close to a brute poisoned with 'bubby,' and it will jump and jerk and tremble for several minutes. That is our method of telling when they have taken it. The eyes turn white and glassy, and while lying they throw back their head and look as if dead already. 'Bubby' does not seem to hurt the brute so much if it cannot get water. Our best remedy is apple brandy, strong coffee, and raw eggs poured down as soon as possible after finding. It is certain that 'bubby' is the most poisonous of any shrub weed in existence here, from the fact that, when brutes have once eaten it, they will take it every time they can get it. It grows on every hillside, along all branches (creeks), in every fence-corner, and almost everywhere here."

Men living miles apart have told the same story of the effects produced by eating the schenia. The Loco, or Crazy Weed of the West, has had a similar reputation; but chemical investigation failed to discover anything to which such therapeutic effects could be attributed. With calycanthus, however, we have the testimony of intelligent observers as to its toxic effects. Dr. B. W. Sparks, of McMinnville, Tennessee (*Torrey Bulletin*, August, 1888, p. 208), writing to Mr. Sterns, under date of June 11th, 1888, says: "In regard to the 'bubby,' 'sweet shrub' (*Calycanthus glaucus* Willd.), if you ask me, do I believe this plant to be poisonous to cattle and sheep ? Most as-

---

* Control Analyses, Prescott, 1883: Proc. Am. Assoc. Adv. Sci., 34, 118; Chem. News, 53, 76, et seq.

suredly it is. It will poison cattle, sheep, goats, deer, and all other ruminating animals, but does not have any effect on the horse, mule, and ass. At least this is my experience. It will poison the squirrel, rat, and dog, when ground or unground. I cannot speak for the hog family. I have known and made many experiments on rats and dogs. It is as sure death to them as strychnine or arsenic; symptoms in overdoses identical with those of strychnine, which I need not repeat. In my opinion, it contains an alkaloid allied to strychnine." (Ibid., p. 209.)

(Abstract.) During the last week in January and the first half of February, Dr. Eccles endeavored to isolate any active principle the suspected achenia might contain. The results were so far successful that an alkaloid was isolated and named *Calycanthine*, from the genus of plants in which it was procured. Another alkaloid was then suspected, which subsequent investigation failed to isolate, although there are still indications which point to its presence.

In grinding the achenia, the large quantity of fixed oil they contain is at once made manifest. In the powdered condition, a few seconds' contact with paper saturates it. To finely powder them before abstraction of this is manifestly impossible. Rhigolin, benzin, and other forms of petroleum spirit remove it completely, and they do not seem to appreciably disturb any other constituent. The barest trace of alkaloid is taken up after hours of percolation in a Soxhlet apparatus, or maceration for weeks. The oil is practically the only thing removed. One hundred grammes of achenia so treated, weigh, after washing with same kind of solvent and drying, only a little over sixty-one grammes, and the extracted oil, after evaporation, nearly thirty-nine grammes. If the alkaloid were absent, the seeds would make excellent fattening, especially as most of the remaining sixty-one parts is starch and albumin. It is really not to be wondered at that animals want to eat them after becoming accustomed to the bitter taste. No drug, according to the author, ferments as readily in the presence of water as do these seeds. Licorice root does not approach it in this respect. Possibly this accounts, in some measure, for the observed physiological effects upon ruminants.

If the alkaloid is, as Dr. Sparks suggests, analogous to strychnine, it certainly has nothing like its potency in affecting man. Twenty achenia, weighing 2.7 Gm., were freed from their pericarps, and eaten without toxic symptoms of any kind. The lot from which they were taken showed the presence of 21 per cent of alkaloid.

The alkaloid is slightly soluble in water, and very soluble in ether or chloroform. Its salts are insoluble in the latter substances, but very soluble in water. Its most characteristic color reaction is the development of a green on the addition of a strong nitric acid. The purer the alkaloid, the finer the color. Other reactions are yellow with strong sulphuric acid, a pale canary with strong muriatic acid which gradually changes towards orange, a rose red with bichromate of potassium and strong sulphuric acid, and a pink red if sugar is used instead of bichromate.

The ether extract of Calycanthus, after all the oil has been removed with petroleum spirit, contains little more than alkaloid and coloring matter, and yet it leaves some of these behind; alcohol takes up what is left. Dilute mineral acid, when agitated with the ether extract, washes out the active principle, leaving barely a trace behind. The ether becomes milky on the addition of the acid, but soon clears up on shaking. Water of ammonia or solution of soda precipitates the alkaloid from the acid solution again; and on washing this with ether, we have it in a pretty pure state. Spontaneous evaporation of the ether leaves the alkaloid in crystals. Procured in the manner here indicated, it has only the faintest suggestion of the odor of pyridine. When first taken from the powdered seeds by means of alcohol, this evaporated, dilute sulphuric acid added, made alkaline with ammonia, and washed out with ether, the pyridine odor is very decided and persistent. This seems to indicate that the pyridine is a product of chemical decomposition of the alkaloid.

[The author then refers to the existing theories regarding the relationship of alkaloids to pyridine, and points to the base obtained from Calycanthus as a possible key to unlock the mystery.]

When ten per cent hydrochloric acid is used to remove calycanthine from ether in which has been extracted, and allowed to stand a few days, it suffers some slight decomposition, forming a brown solution. The alkaloid in this solution is very readily saponified by caustic potash and heat. The new alkaloid formed has not yet been named, although isolated in handsome crystals. The change is remarkable in that it develops a strong, sweet odor, like that of oil of Ylang Ylang. The structure of this oil awaits investigation, as does that of a dense precipitate that goes down with the newly-formed alkaloid on the application of the caustic soda. The quantity of the aromatic product must be considerable, as the odor from a fraction of a grain of alkaloid lingers for days. The suggestive interruptions that crowd in here are of the most interesting character, and make one wish that he had all his time for at least a year, free from other cares and able to devote the same to the solution of the problems here involved. It certainly seems as if there must be some connection that can be synthetically bridged between benzoic acid and our most fragrant and costly essential oils, and that the way is here indicated. Cannot some of our chemists who have more time at their disposal than the writer take the matter up and give it a thorough investigation? From a commercial standpoint, it is my belief that there is money in it. The abundance of the shrub in its native habitat guarantees an almost limitless supply. The essential oil of leaves, flowers, and bark would be well worth isolating as a rich ether for soda-water flavoring. The fixed oil constitutes more than one-third of the total weight of the seed, and is, when unaffected by high temperature, of a pleasant taste and odor. This would add materially to the income of any one who would try to utilize the shrub commercially. Although the therapeutic properties of the alkaloid have not yet been developed, little doubt can be entertained of its having some specific action upon the nerve centres that can be turned to use. Certainly the decomposition product that possesses so powerful and pleasant an odor would be immediately utilized by perfumers, and should it prove to be identical with oil of Ylang Ylang, the new supply might soon outrival the old in this, our most expensive essential oil. The remaining starchy and albuminous material would make good fattening and harmless food for hogs, chickens, or cattle. The ferment might prove valuable to chemists and physicians, and certainly it is active enough, if we may judge from its prompt results. Thus, to pharmacists, physicians, chemists, perfumers, confectioners, and farmers, it opens up interesting possibilities. The whole seed can be utilized, part in one direction, and part in another. Should any one single item be inadequate to support an industrial plant, surely the combination of all would be sufficient. It certainly looks worthy of further and more careful investigation.

The Preparation of Mercurous Iodide.[*]

BY EDWARD ROETJE.

The great trouble I had in making a sample of this salt by the tedious, and I might say uncertain process of the U. S. P., led me to investigate the subject of finding an easier and better method of manufacture. That the U. S. P. method is tedious, any who has tried it can testify. That the purity of the product is uncertain, can be seen by the number of washings required.

Washing with alcohol takes out the mercuric iodide, but the iodine and mercury are present in nearly the exact proportions to form mercurous iodide, so it will be seen that for all the mercuric iodide formed, a corresponding amount of metallic mercury is left. This cannot be washed out, and so will be left as an impurity with any mercuric iodide remaining.

As far as I can find, only four other methods of preparing this salt have ever been proposed: first, by triturating mercuric iodide with the right proportion of mercury; second, by precipitation of a double salt of sodium pyrophosphate and mercurous acetate with potassium iodide; third, by treating calomel with potassium iodide; and fourth, double decomposition between mercurous nitrate and potassium iodide. The first process is open to the same objection as that of the U. S. P. The second is hardly of practical value, on account of the difficulty of making mercurous acetate, and the increase in cost by the pyrophosphate, while nearly the same objections can be offered as to number four. When made by the third method, the product is liable to contain calomel and some mercuric iodide and metallic mercury may also be formed. Number four, while having a few objections, seems to offer us a quick and certain process, giving a purer product than can be obtained by any other method unless it be number two. One of the difficulties of this method is to make a pure mercurous nitrate. This I managed to do by the following process:

Hydrargyri Nitras.

$Hg_2(NO_3)_2$, H_2O ; 541.4.

Mercury..................................10 parts
Nitric Acid.............................. 5 "
Water.................................... 4 "

Mix the acid and water, and pour upon the mercury. Set aside to react in the cold, shaking briskly from time to time to remove any coating of nitrate which may have formed around the globules of mercury. When the reaction has ceased, the crystals of mercurous nitrate are separated from the mother liquor and any metallic mercury remaining, by pouring on to a filter through the bottom of which several small holes have been punched. A second crop of crystals may be obtained by concentrating the mother liquor, or more nitric acid may be added to dissolve the remaining mercury, if any. If the crystals are to be kept for any length of time, they should be washed on the filter with a small quantity of a mixture of water 100 parts and nitric acid 1 part.

The crystals are then dried between bibulous paper without heat. I made mercurous nitrate several times by this process, testing the product each time for mercuric salt, by dissolving, precipitating, as calomel, with hydrochloric acid, filtering, and treating the filtrate with hydro-

---

[*] Paper read at the meeting of the A. P. A. at Detroit.

gen sulphide, which failed to give even the slightest trace of precipitate. One sample was kept for over a month in a bottle without any attempt to exclude light, and then tested as before, with the same result.

From this it would seem that the salt can be made pure, and, by taking ordinary precautions as to exclusion of air and light, be kept pure for use as required. After the mercurous nitrate is made, the iodide can easily be prepared by the following formula:

Mercurous Iodide.

Hg_2I_2 : 652.6.

Mercurous Nitrate............................10 parts
Potassium Iodide............................ 6   "
Nitric Acid,
Water,....................each, a sufficient quantity

Dissolve the mercurous nitrate in four hundred parts of water containing four parts of nitric acid, and the potassium iodide in four hundred parts of pure water, both in the cold. Pour the solution of the iodide slowly into that of the nitrate, stirring briskly, and allow to stand for five minutes. When the precipitate has subsided, decant off most of the liquid, and transfer the precipitate on to a filter. Wash the precipitate several times with water and dry at a temperature of not over 50° C., keeping from strong light as much as possible during the whole process.

The product obtained by this method is of a bright yellow color, instead of a green. C. H. Wood, F.C.S., in an article in the *Amer. Jour. of Pharm.*, Vol. xl., 337, gives the result of an analysis of a sample of green and a sample of yellow mercurous iodide, which proves that the yellow is purer by far, containing much less mercuric iodide and uncombined mercury than the green. My time being too limited, I did not try this experiment, but accepted the conclusions of this analyst, especially as they had been substantiated by others. From an estimation of this salt, I obtained an average of 60.83% of mercury and 38.13% of iodide, the per cent in the pure salt being 61.16 of mercury and 38.84 of iodide, a very little over 1% being unaccounted for in my estimation. One gramme of the salt being treated with 10 C.c. of alcohol as directed by the Pharmacopœia, the alcohol dropped into water gave no opalescence whatever, and 5 C.c. evaporated on a watchglass left only a very small residue, which was not red. That very little mercuric iodide is formed is shown by testing the first filtrate with hydrogen sulphide, which gives a scarcely perceptible precipitate, and the mercuric salt, if present at all, would be in the filtrate, as it contains a slight excess of potassium iodide. As no mercuric iodide is formed, no metallic mercury can be left. The first washings of a sample made according to the Pharmacopœia gave a heavy precipitate with hydrogen sulphide.

A sample of mercurous iodide made by the above process, showed no change in color after standing three months in a bottle kept in a little wooden box, thus at least partly proving its stability.

Peppermint Oil.[*]

BY A. B. STEVENS.

Much stress has been laid on the polariscope as a test for the purity of oil of peppermint.

While it is without doubt a useful, and to the larger purchasers of the oil a valuable aid, its expense is such as to place it beyond the reach of the retail dealer. Again, valuable as it is, and may be, even those whose moneyed means will admit the purchase of a polariscope cannot wholly depend upon it as a test of purity, as the variation in different samples of pure oil is great, ranging from −35 to −55°. An oil having a high polarizing power may be largely adulterated, or it may be dementholized, and still be above −35°.

It is stated by A. M. Todd (*Amer. Journ. Phar.*) that menthol has a very low polarizing power, and that an oil having a polarizing power of −74° from which 16 per cent of menthol had been removed showed a decrease of only 3°. The simple fact that the polarization was decreased at all, when the volume of the oil was reduced 16 per cent, proves that the polarization of the menthol must be greater than that of the oil from which it was taken.

The writer finds that both Japanese and American menthol have a polarizing power of from −95° to −100°. This was obtained by dissolving 10 Gm. of menthol in 20 C.c. of alcohol (giving a volume of 31.5 C.c.). The solution had a polarizing power of −33°.

As this solution was only one-third menthol, it must necessarily be increased threefold to obtain the polarization of pure menthol, viz., −99°.

The reason of Mr. Todd's failure to obtain the true polarizing power of menthol was doubtless due to the fact that he attempted to obtain it by reducing the menthol crystals to a liquid state by heat, instead of dissolving it in a non-active liquid.

The writer would recommend the following as the most reliable test for the presence of oil of camphor in peppermint oil.

Place a drachm of nitric acid (sp. gr. 1.42) in a test tube, add one drop of the suspected oil, and agitate gently, and set aside for a few minutes. The mixture will be of a yellow color, and if pure, will remain the same. If as low as 5 per cent of oil of camphor is present, the mixture will turn red within fifteen or twenty minutes.

While experimenting with various reagents, it was found that iodine was decolorized by oil of peppermint. We then endeavored to find the limit of decolorization. Therefore, a volumetric solution of iodine was prepared according to the United States Pharmacopœia, but displacing part of the water with alcohol, and we proceeded as follows:

To 2 C.c. of oil was added 5 C.c. sol. iodine and 10 C.c. of alcohol. The whole was agitated thoroughly and allowed to stand ten minutes. Then from the excess of iodine, by titration with a volumetric solution of hyposulphite of soda, by repeated experiments it was found that the reaction proceeded until nearly 10 minutes had expired, but no change occurred after that time. During these experiments it was found that alcohol prevented oxidation or decolorization of the iodine. To ascertain to what extent the alcohol prevented the action, a fresh volumetric solution of iodine was prepared without alcohol, when it was found that the quantity of iodine decolorized increased as the quantity of alcohol was decreased. To complete the reaction, it required constant agitation for 10 minutes. By this method 1 C.c. of oil decolorized 30 C.c. of iodine solution.

	Polarization.	Freezing Mixture −25° C. (13.5° F.)	Nitric Acid test for Oil Camphor.	Vol. Sol. iodine decolorized by 1 C.c. of oil.	
				With Alcohol.	Without Alcohol.
1 Pure Oil Peppermint.	−35°	Solid	Yellow.	...	...
2 Pure Oil Peppermint.	−44°	Solid	Yellow.	...	...
3 Pure Oil Peppermint.	−28°	Solid	Yellow.	1.5 C.c.	30 C.c.
4 No. 3 Dementholized Oil Peppermint.	−84°	Slightly crystalline.	Yellow.	1.6 C.c.	33 C.c.
5 No. 3 Dementholized Oil Peppermint.	−30°	Semi solid	Red	.85 C.c.	
6 No. 3 Dementholized Oil Peppermint.	−34°	Nearly solid	Light red.	1.55 C.c.	
7 No. 3 Dementholized Oil Peppermint.	−25°	Cloudy	Red	...	
8 No. 3 Dementholized Oil Peppermint.	−48°	Semi-solid	Yellow.	...	
9 No. 3 Dementholized Oil Peppermint.	−57°	Solid	Yellow.	...	
10 No. 3 Dementholized Oil Peppermint.	−48°	Solid	Yellow.	...	
11 No. 3 Dementholized Oil Peppermint.	−25°	Cloudy	Red	...	
12 No. 3 Dementholized Oil Peppermint.	−45°	Cloudy	Red	...	
Alcohol 2 parts, Menthol 1 part.	−83°		Yellow.	None	0.3 C.c.
Dementholized Oil 2 parts and Menthol 1 part.	−55°		Yellow.	1 C.c.	32.1 C.c.
Oil Pennyroyal	+53°		Yellow.	0.2 C.c.	9.7 C.c.
Oil Camphor, red	+29°		Red	0.7 C.c.	
" refined	+34°		Red	None	9.1 C.c.
Oil of Turpentine	+21°		Yellow.	...	...
No. 1 3 P. + Pennyroyal 1 P.	−29°		Yellow.	1.1 C.c.	34 C.c.
No. 1 3 P. + Oil Camphor 1 P.	−31°		Red	1.4 C.c.	23 C.c.
No. 1 3 P. + Turpentine 1 P.	−39°		Yellow.	1.6 C.c.	34.2 C.c.

Various mixtures of pure oil and some of the common adulterations were next subjected to a freezing mixture of −25° C. (12.5° F.), as follows:

Per Cent of Adulteration.

	5%	10%	25%
Alcohol	Liquid	Liquid	Liquid
Oil Pennyroyal	Solid	Nearly solid	Liquid
Oil Camphor	Solid	Nearly solid	Liquid
Turpentine	Solid	Nearly solid	Liquid

The writer is by no means content with the work done, but intends to continue it during the coming year. Mr.

---

[*] Paper read at the Meeting of the A. P. A. at Detroit.

[*] No. 1 refers to the No. 1 Oil Peppermint, above.

A. M. Todd has kindly promised a supply of oil with which to continue experiments.

The writer is indebted to Mr. H. D. Cushman for a sample of pure oil, also sample of same dementholised. We acknowledge the indebtedness and return our hearty thanks.

Phosphomolybdic Acid for the Quantitative Estimation of Alkaloids.

(Abstract of paper by H. W. Snow, Ph.C., read at the Detroit meeting of the A. P. A.)

This paper was written to show the unreliable results obtained with the phosphomolybdic acid or phosphomolybdate of sodium which the market affords when applied to the quantitative estimation of alkaloids. Even when the same maker's product was used, parallel experiments yielded different results. This circumstance, in addition to the uncertainty as to the exact constitution of the precipitate, which may possibly contain ammonia in addition to alkaloids, renders any general reliance upon the reagent for quantitative purposes unadvisable. (The author gives a detailed account of his experiments and a synoptical table of results, which is here omitted.) Yet the reagent may be used in certain cases with a tolerable degree of accuracy. In solutions containing pilocarpine, the reagent produces a faint opalescence, even when applied to 5 C.c. of a solution containing only 1 part of the alkaloid in 75,000. Gelsemine also responds to the reagent very readily. With coniine, it reacts when only 1 part in 5,000 or 6,000 are present, while Mayer's reagent will fail even with solutions of 1 in 2,000.

The reagent is prepared by dissolving 5 Gm. of phosphomolybdate of sodium in a mixture of 90 volumes of water and 10 vol. of pure nitric acid (full strength, about 69% absolute acid), so as to make 100 C.c.

The author expects useful and practical results by applying the reagent volumetrically, determining its value first upon a definite quantity of known material.

The Composition of Precipitated Sulphate of Iron.

(Abstract of a paper by Prof. Henry Trimble, read at the Detroit meeting of the A. P. A.)

As inquiry at several stores in Philadelphia revealed the fact that this official preparation is not usually kept in stock, I made the experiments on four samples prepared by myself. No. 1 was made according to the U. S. P. No. 2 according to the Br. P., with the quantity of water reduced to 20 per cent, and without boiling the solution. No. 3 according to the proportions of the Br. P., omitting the boiling; as this solution was quite dilute, the yield was small. No. 4 was made exactly according to the directions of the Br. P. This authority directs that the solution be boiled for ten minutes in an open dish, but leaves one in doubt whether to take into account the loss by evaporation or not; therefore, if the strength of the solution and consequently the proportion of alcohol affect the composition, it will be shown by samples 3 and 4. The directions for getting rid of adhering moisture and acid are not so exact as our own, consequently a slight excess of acid will be found in the Br. P. samples. In the following results, the amount of iron was determined by both gravimetric and volumetric methods, the latter being by titration with potassium permanganate. The results by the two methods were not materially different. The sulphuric acid was determined by barium chloride.

	No. 1. U S P.	No. 2 Br P from 20% Water, boiled	No. 3. Br P. Not boiled	No. 4 Br. P.	No. 5. Larger Crystals	Theoretical
Fe	20.4+5	20.86%	20.37%	20.53%		20.1%
SO₃	35.40''	35.84''	35.40''	35.44''	36.40''	34.54''
H₂O	44.12''	43.30''	44.23''	44.19''	43.07''	45.34''
Total	100.00	100.00	100.00	100.00	100.00	100.00

No. 5 settled out from the filtrate of No. 3, which was more dilute than the others and therefore contained a larger quantity of the salt. The deposit took place during three weeks, in granular crystals much larger than in the other samples.

None of the specimens when first made gave more than slight indications of ferric iron, and the determinations by potassium permanganate failed to indicate any appreciable quantity. The above results are sufficient to show that the salt is precipitated under different conditions is of constant composition. It is identical with the large crystals, keeps well in glass-stoppered bottles, but loses water, and is slowly oxidized by exposure to air.

Picrate of Iron, locally applied in aqueous solution, is reported to be one of the most effective remedies to stop bleeding from the nose. The ferric picrate is the salt in question, which has the composition $Fe_2O.2C_6H_2(NO_2)_3O$.

A NEW THERMOREGULATOR.

D'Arsonval describes a new thermoregulator, combined with drying oven, in *L'Union Pharmac.* (1888, 353).

In this apparatus the thermoregulator forms an integral part of it. It consists of a metallic box, formed of grooved or corrugated plates, such as are used for aneroid barometers, and constitutes the central part of the lower cone of the oven. The gas is admitted to the regulator by a central inlet, and passes, through two lateral branches provided with stop-cocks, to the two burners, each of which is surmounted by a small hood. The stop-cocks are so constructed that air can be admitted by turning them, whereby the flames become non-luminous, and serve as Bunsen burners. The heat of the flame is conveyed through a series of tubes passing through the liquid contained between the double walls of the apparatus, on the principle of a vertical tubular boiler. The space between the walls is filled with water from which the air has been driven out by boiling, which may be done in the apparatus itself. If a higher temperature than 100° C. is required, a sufficient amount of glycerin is mixed with the water. The upper cone of the apparatus is provided with a neck bearing a cork and glass tube. When the liquid in the apparatus expands by heat, it rises in the tube, and the additional

D'Arsonval's heat-regulator.

pressure causes the regulator at the bottom to collapse, in proportion to the pressure, thus diminishing the amount of gas conducted to the burners. Another neck is fitted with a thermometer passing into the interior of the apparatus. The inventor claims that the regulation of temperature may easily be adjusted for any desired degree. The interior is accessible through a door at the side, and is divided into several compartments. To prevent evaporation of water from the upright glass tube, the author recommends to introduce into it a drop of kerosene.

The author uses the apparatus also for obtaining temperatures below that of the surrounding air. For this purpose, he causes water from the water service (provided this has the desired temperature) to pass through the tubes between the walls.

The True Source of Star Anise.

From a paper by Mr. E. M. Holmes in the *Pharm. Journ.* of August 11th, we take the following important note on star anise:

In December, 1880, notwithstanding the publication of *Illicium anisatum* as the botanical source of star anise in Bentley and Trimen's "Medicinal Plants," Dr. Bretschneider, then medical officer to the Russian embassy at Peking, in "Notes on Some Botanical Questions Connected with the Export Trade of China," states "the plant which produces this article is still unknown to botanists," and he then goes on to remark: "The first authentic information concerning the actual habitat of the star anise tree was furnished by Mr. Piry, in his 'Report on the Trade of Pakhoi,' for the years 1878–1879, in which star anise is said to be brought for exportation in Kin-chow and Pakhoi from the province of Kuangsi, two districts in that province producing the article; Lung-chow, on the borders of Annam; and the country about Po-se, on the West River, close to Yunnan."

Dr. Bretschneider adds a translation from the well-known work on Chinese materia medica and natural history, "Pen t'sao kang mu," vol. XXVI., fol. 62, in which it is stated that star anise grows in the mountains near the Tso kiang and Yu-kiang (rivers), and that the kind most valued in China grows in Kuangsi and Kuangtung, and in Annam. Dr. Bretschneider remarked that both the above rivers are in Western Kuangsi, the first being a tributary of the West River. The city of Po-se mentioned by Mr. Piry is situated on it. The Tso-kiang is a southern tributary of the Yu-kiang. These notes appear to have attracted the attention of the late Dr. Hance, who, in October, 1881, forwarded seeds of the true plant received from Pakhoi to Kew. In the same year, fruit and fragments of the leaves were forwarded by Mr. C. Ford from the Hong-Kong Botanical Gardens to Kew. A few seedlings of the plant obtained by Mr. Kopsch, Commissioner of the Chinese Imperial Maritime Customs at Pakhoi, were grown in the Hong-Kong Gardens, and flowered in November, 1886, when the plants had attained a height of nine feet. Some seedlings sent by Mr. Ford to Kew in 1883 flowered at Kew in 1887, and from these the excellent plate given in [a recent number of] the *Botanical Magazine* was drawn.

Sir Joseph Hooker points out that the plant must be placed in quite a different section from that to which *Illicium anisatum* L. belongs, since it has broad, obtuse perianth segments, and the peduncles are not bracteate at the base. He describes it as a new and hitherto undescribed species, and names it *Illicium verum* Hooker fil. (description omitted here).

The leading feature in the plant appear to be the solitary axillary globular flowers, which do not expand fully, the segments remaining convex, the inner segments being red, and the ten stamens, in which the filament forms with the connective an ovoid body. The peduncles are curved and barely half an inch in length. It may here be remarked that a very similar plant, but with smaller and yellowish flowers, has been grown at the Botanical Gardens at Regent's Park, for the last eighteen years, under the name of *Illicium anisatum*, but the leaves of this species have a sassafras taste. They differ from those of *Illicium religiosum* in having the midrib prominent below and depressed on the upper surface of the leaf, while in *Illicium religiosum* the midrib is prominent on the upper, and not on the lower surface, and the taste is astringent and therebinthinous.

Cotton-Seed Oil.

The following is taken from a description of the cotton-seed oil industry furnished by Mr. A. E. Thornton to a reporter of the *Atlanta Constitution*:

From the platform where the seed is unloaded, it is thrown into an elevator, and carried by a conveyor—an endless screw in a trough—to the warehouse. Then it is distributed by the conveyor uniformly over the length of the building, about 200 feet. The warehouse is nearly half-filled now, and thousands and thousands of bushels are lying in store. Another elevator carries the seed up to the "sand-screen." This is a revolving cylinder made of wire cloth, the meshes being small enough to retain the seeds, which are inside the cylinder, but the sand and dirt escape. Now the seeds start down an inclined trough. There is something else to be taken out, and that is the screws and nails and rocks that were too large to be sifted out with the sand and dirt. There is a hole in the inclined trough, and up through that hole is blown a current of air by a suction fan. If it were not for the fan, the cotton seed, rocks, nails, and all would fall through. The current keeps up the cotton seed, and they go on over, but it is not strong enough to keep up the nails and pebbles, and they fall through. Now the seed, freed of all else, is carried by another elevator and endless screw conveyor to the "linter." This is really nothing more than a cotton gin with an automatic feed.

Then the seed is carried to the "huller," where it is crushed or ground into a rough meal about as coarse as the ordinary corn "grits." The next step is to separate the hulls from the kernels, all the oil being in the kernel. Hence the crushed seed is carried to the "separator." This is very much on the style of a sand screen, being a revolving cylinder of wire cloth. The kernels, being smaller than the broken hulls, fall through the broken meshes, and upon this principle the hull is separated and carried direct to the furnace, to be used as fuel. The kernels are ground as fine as meal, very much as grist is ground, between corrugated steel "rollers," and the damp, reddish-colored meal is carried to the "heater."

The "heater" is one iron kettle within another, the six-inch steam space between the kettles being connected direct with the boilers. There are four of these kettles side by side. The meal is brought into this room by an elevator, the first "heater" is filled, and for twenty minutes the meal is subjected to a "dry cook," a steam cook, the steam in the jacket being under a pressure of forty-five pounds. Inside the inner kettle is a "stirrer," a revolving arm attached, at right angles, to a vertical shaft. The stirrer makes the heating uniform, and the high temperature drives off all the water in the meal, while the fixed oil all remains.

In five minutes the next heater is filled; in five minutes the next, etc.

Now there are four "heaters;" and as the last heater is filled, at the end of twenty minutes, the first heater is emptied. Then, at the end of five minutes, the first heater is filled, and the one next it is emptied, and the rotation is kept up, each heater full of meal being "dry-cooked" for twenty minutes.

Corresponding to the four heaters are four presses. Each press consists of six iron pans, shaped like baking-pans, arranged one above the other, and about five inches apart. The pans are shallow, and around the edge of each is a semi-circular trough, and at the lowest point of the trough is a funnel shaped hole to enable the oil to run from one pan to the next lowest, and from the lowest pan to the "receiving tanks" below.

As soon as a "heater" is ready to be emptied, the meal is taken out and put into six hair sacks, corresponding to the six pans in the press. There are six hair mats, about one foot wide and six long, one side of each being coated with leather. The hair mat is about an inch thick. Now the hair sac, containing ten and a half to eleven pounds of heated steaming-meal, is placed on one end of the mat, and the meal distributed so as to make a pad or cushion of uniform thickness. The pad of meal is not quite three feet long, a foot wide, and three inches thick, and the hair mat is folded over, sandwiching the pad, and leaving the leather-coating of the mat outside. In this form, the six loads are put into the six pans, and by means of a powerful hydraulic press the pans are slowly pressed together. The oil begins trickling out at the side, slowly at first, and then suddenly it begins running freely. The pressure on the "loads" is three hundred and fifty tons. After being pressed about five minutes, the pressure is eased off and the "loads" taken out. What had been a mushy pad three inches thick is a hard, compact cake about three-quarters of an inch thick, and the sac is literally glued to the cake. The crude oil has a reddish, muddy color, as it runs into the tanks. In each mill, there may be seen lying great heaps of sacks of yellowish meal—the cakes which have been broken and ground up into meal. That, as explained above, forms the body of all fertilizers. The following is a summary of the work for the eight months' season at the Atlanta mills:

15,000 tons of seed used give:
15,000,000 pounds of hull.
10,331,250 pounds of meal.
4,688,750 pounds of oil.
300,000 pounds of lint cotton.

The meal is worth at the rate of $6 for 700 pounds, or $88,603.58.

The oil is worth 30 cents a gallon, or 7½ pounds, or $186,750.

The lint is worth $18,000, making a total of $293,393, and that does not include the 15,000,000 pounds of hull.

Note on the Digestion of Fermented Milk or Koumiss.

Mr. T. R. Powell publishes the following paper in the *Pharm. Journal* of August 25th:

As far as I am aware, no suggestion has hitherto been offered which explains the retention of fermented milk or koumiss by the stomach when all other nourishment has been rejected. The following rough experiments may perhaps throw some light on the subject, which at all events deserves more attention than it has yet received.

It is, of course, well known that, if milk to which a few grains of pepsin and a few drops of hydrochloric acid have been added, be gently warmed, coagulation takes place almost immediately, the casein or cheese separating in a more or less solid condition, a similar coagulation probably taking place whenever milk is acted upon by the gastric juice of the stomach.

To render milk more digestible, lime-water or aërated water is often added, in various proportions. Dilute, therefore, a portion of milk with a fourth part of aërated water, and add a few grains of pepsin, when it will be found that coagulation will take place almost as quickly as in a mixture of milk and water; but the condition of the two precipitates will differ somewhat, the casein separated in the presence of carbonic acid water being in a finer state of division and therefore more readily digested. If, however, lime-water be substituted for the aërated water, the effect is far more decided, coagulation being delayed for some time, and the precipitate, when it at length falls, being, as in the previous case, very finely divided.

Koumiss or fermented milk, when freshly prepared, effervesces but slightly and resembles ordinary milk; but as the fermentation proceeds, lactic acid is formed, coagulation takes place, and the thick liquid becomes charged with carbonic acid. If, at this stage, two or three ounces be drawn off by a siphon tap and gently warmed, with stirring to drive off excess of gas, there will result a thick acid fluid, thicker than milk, though an equally good emulsion; and, coagulation having already taken place in the bottle, the addition of pepsin (which dissolves more readily than in the previous experiments) causes no further precipitation, the casein being in an almost gelatinous condition.

It seems probable, therefore, that the indigestion and nausea so often produced in cases where a milk diet is desirable are the result of the coagulation of the milk—a congulation which may be delayed by the addition of alkalies; and it is further probable that koumiss is retained by the stomach, in preference to milk, for the following reasons: 1st, that congulation has already taken place; 2d, that the precipitated casein—the nourishing constituent—is in a very fine, almost gelatinous condition; 3d, that carbonic acid is present in the free state and exerts a sedative action; and 4th, that free lactic acid still further stimulates and aids digestion.

Cinchona in Colombia.

In a work just published by Dr. Alfred Hettner, giving an account of his travels in the Andes of Colombia,* the author reports that the plantations of cinchona which have been started during the last few years are making satisfactory progress. The first attempts to raise cinchonas by cultivation were made in various localities, for instance, in the hacienda "Columbin," east of Purification, but the first systematic plantation was started by Germans at the hacienda "Alexandrin," located at an hour's distance south of Los Manzanos, at the upper end of a valley, having a southern trend, and situated about 2,600 m. (ab. 8,000 ft.) over the sea-level. Dr. Hettner, who had been invited by Mr. Paul Heckel, the manager of the plantation, visited the latter several times, and found it to make a decided and continued progress. While it is confidently expected that Colombin will have ample supplies of cinchona bark, the natural source of which had almost been exhausted, it is doubtful whether the country will be able, in the future, to compete with the East Indian plantations, owing to the difficulty of getting the bark to the sea shore.

It will be remembered what excitement was caused in the bark-trade by the appearance of the so-called cuprea bark, derived from a tree closely allied to cinchona, growing in the forests to the west of Buccaramanga and Veles, the former being situated about 175 miles NNE., and the latter about 100 miles N. of Bogotá. About 60 miles ESE. of Bogotá lies Villavicencio, which was only a poor hamlet some years ago, but has blossomed out into an important trading place. It acquired some notoriety shortly after the cuprea bark had been discovered, by the fact that considerable forests situated near the place were regarded as consisting of the same kind of trees (species of Remijia) which yielded the cuprea bark at the other places. A speculative fever at once seized such a number of merchants of Villavicencio and Bogotá, who bought up quantities of the bark, and sent it to Europe. Some German firms, or their representatives, however, were more cautious, and subjected the bark to an analysis, when it turned out to contain only minimal amounts of quinine. The "cuprea" tree, which is found in various localities of the Cerro de la Paz, had always been regarded as valueless, until a peon drew the attention of a German merchant, Mr. Lengerke, to its bitter taste. The latter sent samples of it to Europe, where it was at once found to contain paying quantities of quinine. At first he carried on the collection of the bark as secretly as possible, but the secret soon leaked out, and in consequence of it, Buccaramanga was seized by a perfect whirlwind of speculation. All sorts of levers were set in motion—even dishonest ones—to secure forest land where cuprea trees were reported to occur, and open warfare was waged in the forests between the peons working for different firms. The robbing system soon brought its own punishment. All easily accessible cuprea forests having been exhausted and the market being unfavorable to the employment of this kind of bark on the part of the manufacturer, the business died out.

Strophantin and Ouabain.

NOT long since, M. Arnaud announced to the Academy of Sciences that he had discovered a poisonous glucoside in the wood of an apocynaceous tree, called in the Somali country (Eastern Africa) Ouabaio or Ouabayio. The natives use it to poison their arrows by simply extracting the wood with water, and evaporating the decoction to the proper thickness. On game the poison acts very much like strophanthus preparations, the wounded animal showing at first no apparent uneasiness, but after a short time dropping down suddenly paralyzed. A log of the wood in question was recently brought to Paris, and yielded to M. Arnaud a glucoside which he found to have the formula $C_nH_{15}O_{12}$, while $C_nH_{24}O_{12}$ proved to be that of strophantin. Owing to the great resemblance of the two glucosides, it was thought interesting to ascertain how their physiological effects would compare together. The investigation was undertaken by MM. E. Gley and F. Boudeau, and its first results have been communicated by M. Gley to the Academy. On the whole, ouabain and strophantin have been found to have very similar properties, both acting as heart-paralysers with like symptoms. But without entering into the particulars of the experiments, the main difference, if not the only one, is that ouabain will cause death more rapidly and in smaller doses than strophantin will, whether administered hypodermically or given through the stomach. For instance, the lowest deadly hypodermic dose of ouabain for guinea-pigs was found to be on an average one-tenth of a milligramme for each one kilogramme weight of the animal and twenty-five minutes' time to be necessary. With strophantin one fifth of a milligramme and fifty minutes were requisite to the same effect. With dogs the proportions, both as regards deadly dose and speedy death, were slightly less in favor of ouabain, and still less with rabbits. But at the lowest estimate ouabain may be considered to be, on an average, twice as powerful hypodermically. When given through the stomach both poisons are much less dangerous, as dogs were made very sick, but not killed, with doses twenty-five times as large of ouabain, and over one hundred times of strophantin. A remarkable feature about the new toxic substance is that, while poisonous barks, seeds, and leaves are known in great number and variety, poisonous woods are seldom spoken of.—*Chem. and Drugg.*

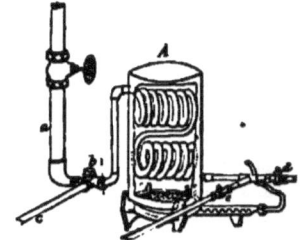

A LABORATORY APPARATUS FOR SUPER-HEATING STEAM.

THE superheater consists of half-inch copper tubing wound to a double spiral. For avoiding loss of heat by radiation, it is surrounded with a copper jacket well covered with asbestos. The whole is placed over a Fletcher burner. To start the apparatus, the three-way tap *b* is turned so that the condensed water in the steam-pipe *a* escapes through *c*. The tap *d*, which allows the superheated steam to pass on to its ultimate destination, is meanwhile closed, whereas *e* is open. As soon as the steam-pipe *a* delivers dry steam, it is allowed to enter the apparatus, and the burner is lit. The steam in the mean time escapes through *e*. The latter is closed and *d* opened when the steam has reached the temperature required. —*Chem. Zeit.* and *J. Soc. Chem. Ind.*

Solvents of Morphine.

MR. A. H. ALLEN throws doubt on Dieterich's statement that morphine is soluble in amyl alcohol in the proportion of 1 part in 1,300, in acetic ether 1 in 1,665, and in ordinary ether 1 in 1,250. These figures do not at all agree with ordinarily accepted statements, for they show that morphine is more soluble in ordinary ether than in acetic ether or amyl alcohol, which are solvents largely employed in preference to ether for extracting morphine from its solutions. Dieterich further states that morphine is soluble in 7,000 parts of cold methyl alcohol, and in 1,660 parts of ethyl alcohol. This great difference of solvent power suggested to Mr. Allen the possibility of using methyl alcohol in opium assay according to the process of the German Pharmacopœia, as this alteration might materially diminish the error due to solubility of morphine. But on putting the matter to test, Mr. Allen found that morphine was very readily soluble in methyl alcohol, so that it would be hopeless to make the substitution suggested. Dieterich also states that morphine sulphate is "very soluble" in ether, whereas Mr. Allen finds the solubility to be 1 in 82,000, and when the ether has been previously washed free from traces of alcohol, and then dehydrated by means of potassium carbonate followed by distillation, the solubility of morphine sulphate is almost infinitesimal. Thus the residue of morphine sulphate from 50 C.c. of dry ether free from alcohol was only 0.0002 gramme, corresponding to a solubility of 1 gramme of the salt in 152,000 grammes, or 225,000 C.c.

Salicylate of Sodium in Toothache.

A GERMAN physician recommends salicylate of sodium, in doses of 10 grains, every half-hour, as an internal remedy for toothache. It has been found effective both in rheumatic toothache and in caries or periosteal inflammation. Though its effect is not lasting, it is nevertheless capable of alleviating or removing the pain for one or several days.—*Zeitschr. Oest. Ap. Ver.*

---

* "Reisen in den columbianischen Anden." Von Dr. Alfred Hettner. 8vo. Leipzig, 1888.

New Formulæ from the Unofficial Formulary B. P. C., 1888.

The Committee on Unofficial Formulary of the British Pharmaceutical Conference, at the late meeting of the society at Bath, presented a series of 30 new formulæ to be incorporated with those previously reported. Among them are some which bear the same title, or practically the same, as certain preparations of our National Formulary, and are intended for the same purposes. We therefore need not quote them here. Among the remainder, the following may be found of service to some of our readers. We have recalculated all formulæ, where it appeared necessary, into the U. S. weights and measures. In the formula for Emulsion of Cod-Liver Oil, the difference would have been insignificant. Hence, the original proportions may be transferred without change to U. S. terms:

1. Emulsio Olei Morrhuæ.

Cod-Liver Oil	8 fl. oz.
The Yolk of 2 Eggs,	
Tragacanth, powdered	16 grains
Elixir of Saccharin	1 fl. drchm.
Tincture of Benzoin	1 " "
Spirit of Chloroform	4 " "
Oil of Bitter Almonds, essent	8 min.
Distilled Water	enough to make 16 fl. oz.

Measure 5 fl. oz. of Distilled Water, place the powdered Tragacanth in a dry mortar, and triturate with a little of the Cod-Liver Oil. Then add the Yolks of Eggs and stir briskly, adding water as the mixture thickens. When of a suitable consistence, add the remainder of the oil and water alternately, with constant stirring, avoiding frothing. Transfer to a pint bottle, add the Elixir of Saccharin, Tincture of Benzoin, Spirit of Chloroform, and Oil of Almonds, previously mixed, shake well, and add Distilled Water, if necessary, to make 16 fluidounces.

The "Elixir of Saccharin" is made by dissolving 384 grains of saccharin and 192 grains of bicarbonate of sodium in about 8 fl. oz. of water, adding 2½ fl. oz. of Alcohol, filtering, and then adding enough Water to make 16 fluidounces.

Each fluidrachm of this Elixir contains 3 grains of Saccharin. (The Liquor Saccharini of the Nat. Form. contains 4 grains in a fluidrachm.)

2. Syrupus Codeinæ.

Codeine	16 grains
Diluted Alcohol	5 fluidrachms
Distilled Water	5 "
Syrup	enough to make 16 fluidounces

3. Syrupus Ferri et Quininæ Hydrobromatum.

(Syn. Syrupus Ferri Bromidi cum Quinina.)

Acid Hydrobromate of Quinine	12½ grs.
Diluted Hydrobromic Acid	266 min.
Syrup of Bromide of Iron (U. S.)	6 fl. oz.
Distilled Water	enough to make 8 fluidounces.

Mix the Diluted Hydrobromic Acid with 1 fluidounce of Distilled Water, dissolve in the mixture the Quinine salt, and add enough Distilled Water to make 8 fluidounces. Then add the Syrup of Bromide of Iron.

Each fluidrachm contains 1 grain of acid hydrobromate of quinine and about 4 grains of bromide of iron.

[In transcalculating the original formula, so as to produce the strength here indicated, a proportionate amount of the Syrup of Bromide of Iron of the U. S. Ph. was directed to be used.]

4. Syrupus Ferri, Quininæ et Strychninæ Hydrobromatum.

(Syn. Syrupus Ferri Bromidi cum Quinina et Strychnina.)

This is prepared like the preceding, with the addition of 2 grains of strychnine, so that the product contains ¼ grain of strychnine, 1 grain of acid hydrobromate of quinine, and about 4 grains of bromide of iron.

5. Tinctura Phosphori Composita.

Compound Tincture of Phosphorus.

Phosphorus	5 grains
Chloroform	800 min.
Alcohol	enough to make 10 fl. oz. (U. S.)

Place the Phosphorus in a stoppered bottle, and apply the heat of a water-bath until dissolved. Then add the solution to enough Alcohol to make 10 fl. oz. Shake well. This tincture should be protected from the light, in accurately stoppered bottles.

Each fluidrachm contains 1/16 grain of Phosphorus.

6. Unguentum Oleoresinæ Capsici.

Oleoresin of Capsicum (U. S.)	1 oz.
Yellow Wax	¼ "
Benzoinated Lard	4 "

Melt the Lard and Wax at a low temperature, add the oleoresin, mix thoroughly, and, if necessary, strain through muslin. Stir until cold.

Cements and Pastes.

In his "Pharmaceutisches Manual," Eugene Dieterich gives the following formulæ:

1. Cement for Porcelain, Marble, Alabaster, Glass, etc.

a.
Caustic Lime	10 parts.
White of egg, fresh	25 "
Plaster of Paris	55 "
Water	10 "

Reduce the Caustic Lime to powder, and triturate it with the White of Egg to a uniform paste. Dilute this with the water, quickly incorporate the Plaster of Paris, and use the cement at once.

[The materials to be cemented must be ready at hand. The broken surfaces should be dampened with water so that the cement will at once adhere. The pieces must be firmly pressed together and kept in this position for about twelve hours.]

b.
Casein, fresh	100 parts.
Silicate of Sodium, syrupy	q. s.

Mix the Casein in a mortar with enough Silicate of Sodium to produce a uniform honey-like mass.

This cement is transparent and keeps for some time. It is not water-proof.

2. For Meerschaum.

Use the casein cement described under 1. b., with the addition of five parts of calcined magnesia for 100 parts of casein.

3. For Paper, Woven Fabrics, Leather, etc.

Borax	5 parts.
Water	95 "
Casein	q. s.

Dissolve the Borax in the water and incorporate enough Casein to produce a honey-like mass.

4. For Horses' Hoofs.

Ammoniac, purified	30 parts.
Turpentine (oleoresin)	10 "
Guttapercha	60 "

Melt the first two ingredients in a steam-bath and gradually add, while stirring, the Guttapercha. For use, soften the mass in hot water and then press it into the previously clean hoof-fissure. The cement may be colored black by incorporating about 2 parts of lamp-black.

5. For cementing Leather Belts, Leather upon Wood or Metal, etc.

Guttapercha	20 parts.
Bisulphide of Carbon	50 "
Oil of Turpentine	10 "
Asphalt (Syrian), powd	20 "

Dissolve the Guttapercha as far as possible in the mixed liquids, then add the Asphalt. After several days' standing the mass will be homogeneous. Should it be too thin, evaporate it somewhat so that it may be of the consistence of honey when cold.

Before applying this cement to leather, the latter must be deprived of fat by means of benzin, upon the side to be cemented.

6. For tightening Iron Vessels.

Iron Filings	85 parts.
Sublimed Sulphur	10 "
Chloride of Ammonium, powd	5 "
Water	q. s.

Mix the solids and make a thick mass with water. Apply this to the fracture, previously cleaned by scraping. After standing eight days the cement will be as hard as iron, and will resist boiling. It is very serviceable for tightening steam-apparatus with leaky bolts.

7. Cement for coating Boiler-Coverings, etc.

Litharge	85 parts.
Boiled Linseed Oil	15 "

Triturate them in a warmed mortar until a plastic mass results.

8. Cement for Retorts, etc.

Clay, powd. and sifted	60 parts.
Rye Flour	30 "
Bran	10 "

Mix them well. When wanted, take a sufficient quantity and mix it with water to a dough to be applied to the retort or flask.

9. Paste for affixing Paper to Tin.

Mucilage of Acacia	95 parts.
Glycerin	5 "

The tin must be cleaned before the label is pasted on.

A CONSTANT GAS GENERATOR.

1. *Evolution of Hydrogen.*

The apparatus used is that shown in the cut. About one and a half kilos of sheet zinc in pieces, about 1 sq. Cm. in area, are placed in the annular space A, and hydrochloric or sulphuric acid of about five times normal strength, containing 10 C.c. cobalt chloride sol. per liter, is allowed to flow on to it from the globular funnel B, by turning the cocks C and D and the stopper E, so as to permit the transference of the expelled gas from the lower vessel to the upper by means of the tube F (after the manner of a percolator).

The tube of the stopper E being prolonged nearly to the bottom of the funnel, serves to maintain a constant head, acting on the principle of Marriotte's bottle, which, indeed, may be substituted for it when the apparatus is to be used continuously for a long period.

The U-tube G, filled with mercury, is designed to allow the escape of any small quantity of gas evolved after cutting off the supply of acid, if the cork on the exit tube H should happen to be closed.

The solution of the zinc salt, as it forms, passes through the holes in the inner tube K, and rises gradually to a level with the upper end of the tube L, down which it flows into the base of the apparatus. By this means, the partly exhausted acid is kept in contact with the zinc until it is almost completely saturated, while at the same time the evolution of gas does not slacken, because of the continual dripping of fresh acid from the funnel.

The function of the adjunct marked M is merely to distribute the acid on each side of the inner tube. The object of the two stop-cocks (C and D) is to allow of one of them being left in the position that has been found to give the right flow of acid for any particular work, while the other can be closed when it is desired to stop the evolution of gas for a time.

With this apparatus a very nearly constant pressure of gas is maintained, the maximum variation of a series of 11 experiments being equal to a column of water 2.5 Cm. in height.

2. *Evolution of Oxygen.*

All that is necessary is a thin copper flask to contain the oxygen mixture (potassium chlorate with 0.1 per cent of ferric oxide), a burner with a gauze cap to prevent its catching back, and an arrangement like an ordinary thermostat (attached to the delivery tube), which is set at the desired pressure, so that on its being exceeded, the gas supply is diminished, returning to its original magnitude on the pressure falling again.—*Chem. Zeit.* and *J. Soc. Chem. Ind.*

A SAFETY RETORT FOR GAS GENERATION.

N. von Klobukow recommends the form of retort to be presently described, whenever gases are to be prepared which are liable, under certain circumstances, to become dangerous to the operator. As will be seen from the cut, the lid fits into a flange around the edge of the retort. All parts are made of malleable iron. The joint is made tight by filling the flange with a mixture of 100 parts of sand (of medium fineness) and 50 to 60 parts of plaster of Paris made into a thick paste with water, and then pressing the lid into the mass in the flange. In about 15 minutes, the retort may be heated.

The mass just described furnishes a very good cement, which does not crack, resists the passage of gases for some time (about 5 hours, certainty), and at the same time easily gives way, should there be a sudden high pressure developed within the retort. Even if the lid should be completely thrown or projected upwards, no damage from flying fragments can result.

To loosen the lid, it is only necessary to tap the lid lightly with a hammer.

If desired, the lid may be provided with an inlet, so that the retort may be periodically refilled, when the current of generated gas becomes weaker.—*Zeitsch. f. Anal. Chem.*, 1888, 467.

THE "FUMIFIER."

Dr. Robert J. Lee describes, in *The Lancet* for May 19th, an apparatus of somewhat novel construction for producing fumes for remedial and disinfecting purposes, which consists of a steam generator (Fig. 1) with

Fig. 1.

Lee's Fumifier.

an attachment shown in diagram in Fig. 2. The action of the current of steam, escaping from the small aperture in the steam generator, causes a current of air in the tube T, in the direction of the arrows, and any substance placed in the bowl B and ignited is subjected to a downward draft. By means of a damper-ring R, which opens or

Fig. 2.

closes a series of holes in the upright tube, the force of the draft through the bowl B may be regulated. In the case of vegetable substances capable of ignition—such as tobacco, stramonium, etc., no considerable previous preparation is required; but opium, arsenic, calomel, etc., may be combined with charcoal as in the case of pastilles.

Dangers of Paraldehyde.

Paraldehyde is by no means so innocent a hypnotic as it has been frequently reported. On the contrary, it should be used, according to Froehner (*Apoth. Zeit.*) with great care. In animals living chiefly upon vegetable diet, it attacks particularly the red blood-corpuscles. Under its reducing action, the blood becomes as seriously affected (by methæmoglobin-anæmia) as by chlorate of potassium, pyrogallic acid, or nitrobenzol. In addition, it has a poisonous effect upon the nervous centres.—*After Rundschau* (Prag).

Artificially Dyed Moss, etc.

According to W. Braunsdorf (in *Neueste Erfind. und Erfahr.*), moss and other vegetable structures may be dyed a fine green color in the following manner: Dissolve 3½ av. oz. of ferric chloride and 7 av. oz. of acetate of lead in 4½ gallons of hot water, and immerse the moss, etc., in this liquid for about one minute. Then remove it, drain and partly dry it, and immerse it in a hot solution of 770 grains of chromate of potassium, and 1,160 grains of ferrocyanide of potassium. Remove the excess of coloring liquid by gentle pressure between boards, spread it out on wood to dry somewhat, and finish the drying by hanging it up in an airy, but dark and warm chamber.

THE
American Druggist

AN ILLUSTRATED MONTHLY JOURNAL

OF

Pharmacy, Chemistry, and Materia Medica.

VOL. XVII., No. 10. WHOLE No. 172.

FREDERICK A. CASTLE, M.D................EDITOR.
CHARLES RICE, PH.D...................ASSOCIATE EDITOR

PUBLISHED BY
WM. WOOD & CO., 56 & 58 Lafayette Place, N. Y.

SUBSCRIPTION PRICE per year, ... $1.50
SINGLE COPIES, ...15

Address all communications relating to the business of the AMERICAN DRUGGIST, such as subscriptions, advertisements, change of Post-Office address, etc., to WILLIAM WOOD & CO., 56 and 58 Lafayette Place, New York City, to whose order all postal money orders and checks should be made payable. Communications intended for the Editor should be addressed in care of the Publishers.

The AMERICAN DRUGGIST is issued in the latter part of each month, dated for the month ahead. Changes of advertisements should reach us before the 10th. New advertisements can occasionally be inserted after the 15th.

REGULAR ADVERTISEMENTS according to size, location, and time. Special rates on application.

EDITORIAL.

NOTES OF THE MEETING.

Again we have to record the close of another of one of those delightful reunions of druggists from the different sections of the country. The meetings of the American Pharmaceutical Association have grown to be of great interest and pleasure to all who participate in them, and each year as we adjourn and bid good-by to those we have met, the feeling is that it has been one of the most delightful meetings we have ever attended. The one this year is no exception to the rule, for if ever any city tried to make the Association feel at home and provide enjoyment for it, Detroit bids fair to outrank them all. The beauty of the city with its fine broad streets, most of which are lined with magnificent trees, and the houses of an architecture so different from the routine flat-fronts of our eastern cities, where one can hardly tell his house from his neighbor's, favorably impressed the senses and made us feel we were in a place where comfort and pleasure are thought as much of as the accumulation of wealth. The attentiveness of the local druggists was remarkably displayed on many occasions. No care was spared to see that each want was attended to, and the trouble they took that this should be done was deserving of many thanks. The entertainments given were marked by an absence of formality which rendered them very enjoyable.

The meeting was well attended, and each session had more than enough present to enter into the discussions and render them interesting.

The section on commercial interest, contrary to general expectation, drew out a large crowd, and though one evening session was prolonged until eleven o'clock, the members remained and were interested to the end.

The attendance on the section on scientific papers belied the statement made in former years that but very few were interested in the papers, or that the only reason members attended the meeting was for the entertainments, for at each of its sessions, and there were three, a large proportion of members were present, either as interested spectators or participants.

Pharmaceutical legislation and pharmaceutical education were not forgotten, and the working of the new plan, of dividing the work into sections, showed the wisdom of the Association in adopting it. A few years ago, no one knew when any particular business was to be considered, and it was in the power of a person antagonistic to any measure to bring up enough business of another nature to crowd out what he disliked. As it is now, there are times for all things and reasonable opportunity for having all measures carefully considered. It would be impossible to go back to the old method, for no one wants it.

The papers furnished seemed to be a little above the average of past years, and show that the Association is not deteriorating in its scientific work.

It was pleasant to see most of the old work horses of the association on hand, but the faces of a few who have passed over the border-land were missed.

Wednesday night the reception at the Armory was well attended by young and old.

Thursday night at the Opera House was passed very pleasantly; the singing and dancing of the ballet being enlivened by the witticisms of the comedian on polka-dot neckties and other things.

The trip up the river and on Lake St. Clair, though made unpleasant for a few by the storm and consequent rolling of the boat, was thoroughly enjoyed. A mistake was made by most of the party of partaking too freely of the generous hospitality of Parke, Davis & Co., for after passing through their immense establishment and watching their process of manufacturing and gelatin-coating pills, a hearty and elaborate lunch was provided on the lawn, which seemed to meet the favor of all, but which spoiled the appetite for the banquet provided by the committee on entertainment on Star Island.

On the return to Detroit the company were entertained by music and by responses to toasts. Mr. M. W. Alexander, the President, responding to the toast, "American Pharmaceutical Association;" Mr. Geo. J. Seabury, to "Where and Why should we meet?" T. P. Cook, of Pennsylvania, to "Pharmaceutical Exhibits;" Dr. J. E. Clark, Detroit, to the "Michigan State Pharmaceutical Association," and S. A. D. Sheppard, to "Pharmaceutical Education," and volunteer toasts by other gentlemen.

The badge furnished at this meeting was a miniature pill tile, made of celluloid with the letters on the back, A. P. A. and M. P. A.; the latter meaning the Michigan State Pharmacy Association, which meeting was held at the same time. On the front was the division into twenty-four parts, usually seen on pill tiles, and below that a number, a different one for each person. There was also a little directory printed and furnished with the names of every person present and the corresponding number on his pill tile. This was very convenient; for, in travelling around the city, when one of those little pill tiles was seen, by looking at the number and referring to the directory, one could tell at once who the owner of it was.

Prof. Painter, of New York, is a very happy man, for besides being honored by an election to the council, and also as chairman of the scientific section, he has succeeded in at last persuading the Association to go to San Francisco; so next year we may expect our brethren on the Pacific slope to exert their utmost endeavors to make the meeting of 1889 a memorable one.

THE recent observations, which tend to prove that the true nature of cholera infantum and, indeed, of many other disturbances of the digestive apparatus, instead of being inflammatory, is really a condition of poisoning, are of great interest to pharmacists from a purely business point of view. Taking, for example, the summer cholera of infants, the presumption has been, until lately, that it is an inflammation—entero-colitis—and the efforts of physicians to arrest its progress have been chiefly based upon this presumption; hence the multiplicity of mixtures containing opiates, antacids, and astringents. According to the new light thrown upon this malady, it becomes apparent that it is caused by poisonous substances commonly developed in the food supplied to infants artificially fed, and caused by atmospheric germs. Insanitary surroundings and high temperature serve only as conditions favoring the development of bacteria, and when the latter gain access to the alimentary canal, they interfere with normal digestion, and by their growth give rise to leucomaines, which are a cause of acute poisoning. The watery movements from the bowel are the result of the effort on the part of the system to get rid of the poison, and little is to be gained by locking up these irritating products in the intestine. The rational treatment consists in removing the contaminated contents of the bowel, arresting the further development of bacteria, and securing a pure food supply for the future.

This change in the mode of treatment affects the pharmacist, in so far as it diminishes the demand for mixtures and abbreviates the duration of treatment. Indeed, with proper precautions regarding the purity of the food supplied for young infants, it does away with most of the need for medicines at all.

Fortunately the new condition of things offers the wide-awake pharmacist a source of profit which may, in a measure, at least, replace the loss in business which he will otherwise suffer, and that is the sale of properly sterilized milk. The method at present in favor for insuring the freedom of milk from disease germs is the subjection of it in closed vessels to a temperature of 260° F. It is found that, when thus treated, cow's milk becomes not only aseptic, but the effect of this degree of heat is to render it more easy of digestion. The casein, instead of forming a hard curd, with difficulty soluble in the intestinal secretions of the infant, forms flocculent curds, more nearly resembling those which are characteristic of human milk.

Now, the trouble involved in the proper treatment of cow's milk to secure a proper condition must often interfere with its use if it is to be carried out in every family where infants have to be fed artificially. On the other hand, no one so intimately connected with the supplying of household needs is as capable of undertaking this work as an intelligent pharmacist. Provided with a Papin's digestor, or other efficient apparatus, he can easily supply all the demands of his neighborhood; for milk thus prepared and preserved in closely stoppered bottles can be kept for many days unchanged, and he runs little risk of loss on unused stock. The convenience of being able at all times to procure properly sterilized milk without having to prepare it day by day in the house will render the majority of people willing to pay a reasonable price for it, providing pharmacists undertake the business before the public have been educated to do it for themselves, and the apparatus has become generally introduced.

In view of the prevailing tendency to encourage systematic education of pharmacists in pharmaceutical colleges in place of that formerly in vogue, and the disposition on the part of framers of laws regulating the practice of pharmacy to accept the possession of a diploma of a pharmaceutical college as evidence of fitness in lieu of an examination of the candidate, it seems proper to call attention to the condition of affairs which has grown up in the medical profession of this country. For many years it was almost invariably the custom to make the possession of a medical degree a license to practise, and any person holding a medical diploma was, so far as the legal requirements were concerned, enabled to practise medicine in nearly every State of the Union. It was not long, however, before it became apparent to some that the manufacture of degrees and their advertisement and sale for a purely pecuniary consideration might become a profitable undertaking: and some parts of the country were flooded with such diplomas, and many persons obtained them without having acquired even a smattering of medical education.

We have no reason to believe that there exist, as yet, any bogus pharmaceutical schools among us; the few colleges already in existence, like the earlier medical colleges, being reputably conducted and their diplomas being obtainable only after the candidate has presented evidence of fitness; but given the same conditions as those which existed formerly in the case of the medical profession, and we will have such bogus diploma mills organized among us, and the reputable pharmacist and the public will correspondingly suffer. If, on the other hand, pharmacy boards will only accept the results of examination by themselves or by similarly organized boards as evidence of qualification, pharmaceutical schools will then be stimulated to secure efficient instructors, to improve their methods, and increase the percentage of students who succeed in passing the licensing boards. The established schools will be protected from ruinous competition, and the standard of requirements will be kept up to a creditable limit. Students will resort to schools for education in pharmacy because the facilities offered for instruction will enable them to acquire with greater ease and rapidity the knowledge which is requisite to obtain a license to do business.

The medical profession of this country is now endeavoring to secure reform in this matter, but finds much opposition in the existence of so many medical colleges having a low grade of requirements, and it is only in a few localities that local laws have enabled the reformers to make headway against vested rights and conflicting interests.

It is to be hoped that pharmacists will take advantage of the experience of the past, and avoid the condition which will surely produce similar results.

WE are informed that the Committee of Revision and Publication of the U. S. Pharmacopœia will shortly issue to the bodies entitled to send delegates to the next convention a pamphlet containing the criticisms of importance which have been made upon the Pharmacopœia as it exists at present. We hardly need to remark upon the benefit to be derived from a careful study of these comments by those who are to participate in the Convention of 1890, or the importance of such a publication as affecting the labors of the next Committee on Revision.

A number of queries and several Society reports which have been crowded out from this number of the AMERICAN DRUGGIST will appear in our next issue.

CORRESPONDENCE.

AMERICAN DRUGGIST:
Replying to inquiry of A. W. S., Pomeroy, O., I have to say that a medical diploma is necessary in Washington Territory. The law provides that a copy of diploma be filed with the county auditor, and the party desiring to practise must register at the same time. Æ. McM.

QUERIES & ANSWERS.

Queries for which answers are desired, must be received by the 5th of the month, and must in every case be accompanied by the name and address of the writer, for the information of the editor, but not for publication.

No. 2,234.—**Liquid Carbonic Acid Apparatus.**
We do not know any firm that makes a specialty of apparatus for making *liquid* carbonic acid gas. For this purpose, a compressor or pump is necessary which must be constructed with great nicety. We have no doubt, however, that, if you will consult any of the leading manufacturers of soda-water apparatus, they will put you in communication with firms who can supply what is wanted.

No. 2,235.—**Cleaning Sponges (J. E. L.).**
We are asked to give a method of "cleansing sponges of the sand and white particles that are found in them.

On a small scale, the only efficient way to deprive sponges of sand, is to beat them well, with a stick or mallet, and to shake out the loosened particles of sand. The "white particles," or any red core, or large incrustations can only be removed by tearing or cutting out.

On a larger scale, sponges may run between crushing rollers, then through agitators, and centrifugal machines to remove sand or any other foreign particles that can be dislodged by concussion and agitation. The deeper-seated particles, however, are liable to remain under any circumstances. If the sponge is rendered antiseptic, these can do no harm.

No. 2,236.—**Removing Air-bubbles from Ointments (C. W.).**
This correspondent writes: "Can you suggest anything better than the beating process to remove air-bubbles from an ointment of vaseline which has been thoroughly agitated in compounding?"

We are sorry to say that we can suggest nothing better. If the vehicle inclosing the air were more liquid and mobile, we might suggest an aspirator or air-pump, but this would probably be insufficient to cause the escape of air-bubbles from an ointment. If it were in thin layers, however, the air may possibly be extracted in this manner.

No. 2,237.—**Swedish Matches (McC. and W.).**
The improved Safety Matches or Swedish Matches were invented and introduced by Lundstrom of Jönköping, Sweden, under a patent. The improvement consisted in

dividing the ingredients so that neither portion could ignite by friction, without coming in contact with the other. One of these portions is applied to the ends of the matches, and consists of the following substances: chlorate of potassium 6 parts, sulphide of antimony 2 to 3 parts, glue 1 part. The glue, of course, must be dissolved and the other ingredients added. The wood of the matches also requires a previous treatment, which varies in different factories. A good plan is to impregnate it with a dilute solution of paraffin, after it has been thoroughly dried. The second portion of the explosive mixture is prepared from: amorphous or red phosphorus 10 parts, sulphide of antimony or binoxide of manganese 8 parts, glue 3 to 6 parts. This mixture (the glue being dissolved) is applied to the friction surface, which had previously been roughened by a coating of glue and sand.

No. 2,238.—Coloring Matter in Pharmaceutical Preparations (Wheeling).

This subscriber asks whether we think it justifiable to add any coloring matter to pharmaceutical (that is, medicinal) preparations, referring particularly to such coloring agents as "tincture of cudbear, solution of carmine, or the tincture of compound cudbear of the National Formulary.

In reply we have to say, that a purposeless addition of coloring matter would certainly be unjustifiable. But where a special object is to be attained, provided no fraud is intended, and the coloring matter is harmless, we do not see what objection can be raised. The addition of red coloring matter to white wine, to make it pass for genuine red wine, would, of course, be a fraud. But in legitimate pharmacy, there are many cases where coloring matters are useful and advisable. In some cases preparations are colored, because it is desired to distinguish them from others, with which they might be confounded. Take the case of Fowler's solution, for instance. This is not only colored, but also flavored by the addition of Compound Tincture of Lavender, to prevent the solution, which would otherwise be colorless and tasteless, to be mistaken for an innocent solution. Elixir of Valerianate of Strychnine is directed by the N. F. to be colored with Compound Tincture of Cudbear, because the preparation, as heretofore made by manufacturers, was always colored, and it would have caused confusion to propose a new formula producing a colorless product. Compound Syrup of the Phosphates has always been colored either with cochineal or with cudbear. Why depart from this custom, when the public is accustomed to it in that condition ? Compound Elixir of Quinine (N. F.) is directed to be colored, if so desired, by the addition of Compound Tincture of Cudbear, not because it is intended that the purchaser shall be deceived as if the preparation had been made from cinchona bark, but because the elixir may have to be added, in place of Elixir of Cinchona (for which it is a perfectly legitimate substitute, as it can only be regarded as a vehicle, and not as a medicine), when the latter is not at hand, and a different color would be imparted to the product if the elixir had been left colorless. It is all very well to stand up for pure medicines. We are as much in favor of purity and standard strength, perhaps more so, than others. But we must not forget that the patient or consumer who has to take the preparations has his whims and peculiarities, and that it is often necessary to disguise disagreeable features, or to afford him protection against mistakes from dangerous preparations by some outward sign, one of which is coloring matter judiciously applied.

No. 2,239.—Solution of Gun-Cotton; its Nature (U. H.).

Our correspondent asks why it is that films of different degrees of toughness are obtained by evaporating collodions made from different kinds of gun-cotton, particularly such as are made from long and short-fibred cotton.

This is a simple question to ask, but not easy to answer. We have frequently speculated on the subject, and are surprised that it seems not to have been discussed in professional literature. In fact, at this moment we cannot recall any publication where the particular point to which our correspondent's question leads has been alluded to.

In the first place, it will be accepted as a fact, verified by all practical photographers and many others who have worked with gun-cotton and collodion, that the nature of the film (obtained by allowing a solution of gun cotton to evaporate) varies very much—as to toughness, firmness, and cohesion—not only according to the kind and quality of the cotton used, but also according to the treatment. A short-fibred cotton will always yield a weak and brittle film, even when it has been converted into gun-cotton at low temperature and with an acid of just sufficient strength. Elevation of temperature, prolonged chemical action, and very strong acids will render the resulting gun-cotton almost useless for technical purposes. In the case of a long-fibred cotton, such as that known as "Sea-Island," a cautious treatment, a low temperature, with acids of just proper strength, and carefully regulated as to time, results in the production of a film which is remarkable for its toughness, and which, when torn, very much resembles a woven fabric, or rather fine paper, with the fibres interwoven and crossed in every direction. Any overstepping of the limits above outlined will produce an inferior product, and when the treatment is carried to excess, the result will be just as bad as that obtained from short-fibred cotton under similar circumstances.

Now, it is well known that chemical compounds of definite composition and capable of crystallization may be obtained by concentration or evaporation of their solutions, and that they will, under proper management, always appear in their original forms, although we must suppose that, while they were in solution, the original crystals were disintegrated down to the crystalline or to the chemical molecules.

While it is, however, easy to account for there appearance, in a *crystalline* shape of a dissolved *chemical compound*, it is not easy to understand how a vegetable fibre or cell could be first *dissolved* and afterwards be *reformed*, so as to resemble or equal the original fibre in physical properties. We can find no explanation for this; nor have we ever heard one offered by anybody else. But there seems to us to be a way out of the difficulty. Is it *absolutely certain and proven that the whole of the gun-cotton fibre is actually in perfect solution?* Is it not possible that, having been modified in structure and chemical composition by the treatment it has undergone, a certain portion or small skeleton of it is left undissolved and is rendered perfectly transparent and invisible by the action of ether-alcohol? It will be remembered that a comparatively small quantity of gun-cotton will render a considerable amount of ether-alcohol *rigid*. And it is known that different brands of collodion, though made with precisely like quantities of gun-cotton (of different origin), are apt to differ considerably in their degree of viscosity. It is hard to account for this, if we assume that the gun-cotton is in perfect solution, unless we assume a more complex reaction during the conversion of pure cotton fibre into gun-cotton resulting in different proportions of products according as longer or shorter fibres are operated on.

We are not prepared, at this time, to do more than to throw out the suggestion that there is apparently some physical cause inherent in the fibres, as we would otherwise be hardly able to account for the differences observed in the collodion films. On the other hand, we encounter facts which appear to be positive proofs that collodion is a perfect solution, chief of which is the fact that even perfectly clear collodion may be filtered through paper, cotton, or other porous material, without appearing to lose its viscosity.

No. 2,240.—Reaction between Camphor and Salol (L. F., New York).

This correspondent writes: "I recently received a prescription for powders in which, among other ingredients, there was salol and camphor. The others were acetate of lead, Dover's powder, and sugar. On mixing them together, the powder became moist, and a little while afterwards wet. On investigating the cause, I found it was due to the camphor and salol. When these are brought together, they liquefy the same as chloral and camphor. On addition of water, a heavy, oily-looking liquid separates and remains on the bottom. Alcohol dissolves this to a clear solution. When water is added to the alcoholic solution, it becomes white, and small drops of oil appear on the side of the vessel and on top. I have not come across any article on this subject in the current literature. Will you kindly explain the reaction?"

It is known that chloral hydrate, when brought in intimate contact (by trituration, etc.) with certain bodies, such as camphor, menthol, or with phenols, such as carbolic acid, thymol, etc., brings about a liquid product, if the two substances are in suitable proportion. On the other hand, camphor, when brought in contact with some of these phenols, results in the same kind of product, though more rapidly and energetically in some cases than in others.

In the former case we have a compound of chloral-camphor, chloral-menthol, chloral-phenol, etc.; and in the second case, a compound of camphor-menthol, camphor-phenol, camphor-thymol, etc., etc.

The precise nature of these compounds has not been made out. It is assumed that the physical change, and other changes in properties, show the formation of a definite chemical compound. If this is so, then it may be further assumed that this new compound is a liquid at or, dinary temperatures, and that it possesses great solvent powers, as it is evidently able to hold in solution whatever accidental excess of either of the two constituents may originally have been present. That the combination is not a very firm one may be inferred from the readiness with which it may be broken up.

In the case of camphor and salol, our correspondent reports the fact correctly. Salol is a salicylate of phenol (representing about 38 per cent of carbolic acid). On triturating it with camphor, a more or less liquid mass results, in which the salol is evidently undecomposed; for, on treating the liquid mass with a solution of carbonate of sodium, not a trace of salicylic acid is taken up.

At present it is not possible to give a rational explanation regarding the nature and constitution of these compounds, except by way of theory, which would serve no practical purpose here.

Formulæ Asked For.

Can any of your readers furnish the formula of Hair's Asthma Cure?

American Druggist

Vol. XVII. No. 11.   NEW YORK, NOVEMBER, 1888.   Whole No. 173.

[ORIGINAL COMMUNICATIONS.]

ON TYPEWRITER RIBBONS.

BY ISIDOR FURST.

The ever recurring query as to re-inking typewriter ribbons has been kindly referred to me by the editors of this Journal.

In treating of this question the second time, I shall endeavor to put whatever knowledge I possess regarding it into such form as will enable any person of average skill to make an ink suitable for any particular style of ribbon and apply it. I mean to illustrate the principles involved and how to meet the various requirements. My reason for doing this, rather than to give a specific formula to be followed in every instance, is that often an experimenter has already produced an ink which lacks only some correction to make it entirely suitable; for "there are many ways leading to Rome." Besides, an ink which may have been suitable at one time, may fail at another because used under different conditions, and once a person knows how to correct a defect, the ink may be made to answer all purposes.

The constituents of an ink for typewriter ribbons may be broadly divided into four elements: 1, the pigment; 2, the vehicle; 3, the corrigent; 4, the solvent. The elements will differ with the kind of ink desired, whether permanent or copying.

Permanent (Record) Ink.—Any finely divided, non-fading color may be used as the pigment, vaseline is the best vehicle, and wax the corrigent. In order to make the ribbon last a long time with one inking, as much pigment as feasible should be used. Suppose we wish to make black record ink. Take some vaseline, melt it on a slow fire or water-bath, and incorporate by constant stirring as much lampblack as it will take up without becoming granular. Take from the fire and allow it to cool. The ink is now practically finished, except if not entirely suitable on trial, it may be improved by adding the corrigent, wax, in small quantity. The ribbon should be charged with a very thin, evenly divided amount of ink. Hence the necessity of a solvent, in this instance a mixture of equal parts of petroleum benzin and rectified spirit of turpentine. In this mixture dissolve a sufficient amount of the solid ink by vigorous agitation to make a thin paint. Try your ink on one extremity of the ribbon; if too soft, add a little wax to make it harder; if too pale, add more coloring matter; if too hard, add more vaseline. If carefully applied to the ribbon, and the excess brushed off, the result will be satisfactory.

On the same principle other colors may be made into ink; but for delicate colors albolene and bleached wax should be the vehicle and corrigent, respectively.

The various printing inks may be used if properly corrected. They require the addition of vaseline to make them non-drying on the ribbon, and of some wax if found too soft. Where printing inks are available, they will be found to give excellent results if thus modified, as the pigment is well milled and finely divided. Even black cosmetic may be made to answer, by the addition of some lampblack to the solution in the mixture of benzin and turpentine.

After having thus explained the principles underlying the manufacture of permanent inks, I can pass more rapidly over the subject of copying inks, which is governed by the same general rules. Personally I am not in favor of the use of copying ink; first, because the print is liable to fade, smear, and become invisible; second, because it is unsuitable for legal and other documents of value; third, because it is easier to write two or more copies at one operation with manifold (carbon) paper than to make a second press copy after the writing is done.

For copying inks, aniline colors form the pigment; a mixture of about three parts of water and one part of glycerin, the vehicle; transparent soap (about one-fourth part), the corrigent; stronger alcohol (U. S. P.) (about six parts), the solvent. The desired aniline color will easily dissolve in the hot vehicle, soap will give the ink the necessary body and counteract the hygroscopic tendency of the glycerin, and in the stronger alcohol the ink will readily dissolve so that it can be applied in a finely divided state to the ribbon, where the evaporation of the alcohol will leave it in a thin film. There is little more to add. After your ink is made and tried—if too soft, add a little more soap; if too hard, more glycerin; if too pale, a little more pigment. Probably, printer's copying ink can be utilized here likewise, because every one now has the means to modify and correct it to make it answer the purpose. I have not tried it because I am opposed to copying inks.

Users of the typewriter should so set a fresh ribbon as to start at the edge nearest the operator, allowing it to run back and forth with the same adjustment until exhausted along that strip; then shift the ribbon forward the width of one letter, running until exhausted, and so on. Finally, when the whole ribbon is exhausted, the color will have been equally used up, and on re-inking the work will appear even in color, while it will look patchy if some of the old ink has been left here and there, and fresh ink applied over it.

According to the directions here given, I have done nearly all the re-inking of my ribbons for more than seven years, and I am sure, if the reader should fail, it will be due to inattention on his part to some of the principles laid down.

New York, October 2d, 1888.

[ORIGINAL COMMUNICATION.]

LLOYD'S CONDENSER.

Prof. J. U. Lloyd, of Cincinnati, has for over a year been perfecting a novel piece of apparatus which will undoubtedly come into general use and displace many of the less efficient contrivances heretofore used for condensing purposes. In devising the new condenser, Prof. Lloyd's idea was to bring the whole of the volume of hot vapor issuing from the mouth of the still at once in contact with a sufficient space of cold surface, to cause its complete condensation, with the least expenditure of cooling liquid, or of space occupied, and without any loss by the escape of uncondensed vapors. We have had the privilege of receiving periodical information regarding the gradual evolution of the apparatus, and are now enabled to describe it to our readers, as the patent has been issued a few weeks ago (U. S. Pat. 390,243, Oct. 2d, 1888).

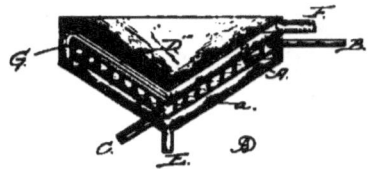

In the accompanying drawing, the figure represents a vertical section of the condenser. The condensing chamber is preferably constructed of an inverted cone-shape, but may be made of any other desired form. At its upper end it is provided with an inlet, B, for the entrance of the hot vapors to be condensed, and at its lower part, with the outlet, C, for the escape of the condensed liquid.

The interior of the condensing chamber may be perfectly smooth, but is preferably provided with a helically or other suitably arranged ribbon or flange extending from the top of the condensing chamber to the exit C.

An outer chamber or jacket, D, preferably corresponding to that of the condenser, surrounds the latter in such a manner as to leave a space, a, between the two for the circulation of a cold stream of water, which is supplied through the tube F projecting into said space, while the tube F serves as an exit for the heated water during the process of condensation.

The water chamber, at the under side of the condenser, connects with the corresponding chamber at the upper side by means of a tube, G, which establishes communication between the two. The stream of water passes from the lower chamber to the central part of the upper one, and there spreads out in a thin sheet over the upper surface of the condenser before passing out of the exit. Thus the outside surface of the vapor space is subjected to a continuous current of cold water, in a thin stratum, and a complete condensation of the vapor thus attained.

This new form of condenser is distinguished by its compactness and by its requiring so little space, while at the same time it presents to the vapors of volatile liquids a very large surface which is kept constantly cool. The condenser may be hung up out of the way, in any convenient place; all that is necessary is to connect the mouth of the still with it.

Prof. Lloyd informs us that he has substituted this form of condenser even for his largest old-style worms. It condenses vapors from a two-inch pipe as fast as they can be delivered. "The principle is: An extensive cooling surface, the condensing water being applied in a thin layer, the alcoholic or other vapors circulating on the other side of the water, and the escape of the condensed liquid at C, where the water is coldest."

The specifications of the patent are thus summarized:

"In a condensing apparatus, the cone-shaped chamber A, having double walls, the interior of which is provided with a helically arranged ribbon or flange, and with suitable inlet and outlet pipes, B and C, in combination with an inclosing receptacle or jacket, D, also provided with inlet and outlet pipes E and F, and distributing pipe G, a space, a, being formed between the said chamber and its inclosing jacket, substantially in the manner and for the purpose specified.

Effect of Hybridisation on Cinchonas.

THE following is an abstract of a paper by Mr. D. Hooper, the quinologist of the India Government, read at the late meeting of the Brit. Pharm. Conference:

In the cinchona plantations of the Madras Government there are two well-defined species of cinchona, C. succirubra and C. officinalis—the bark from the former containing less quinine with more cinchonidine and cinchonine than that from the latter. Between these two species there are also many hybrids, and as the hybrids frequently assume the quicker growing character of the succirubra parent, it was interesting to ascertain how far and in what direction the hybridization affected the production of alkaloid. Fifty samples of succirubra bark examined yielded an average of 6.5 per cent of total alkaloid, and in 100 parts of this the quinine ranged from 17.6 to 26.8 parts, the average being 22.2 parts, whilst the average of the cinchonidine was 34.1 parts. Only five out of the fifty samples failed to comply with requirements of the British Pharmacopœia for bark, that it should yield between five and six per cent of total alkaloid, not less than half of which shall consist of quinine and cinchonidine. From fifty samples of C. officinalis bark, the average yield of total alkaloid was 5.25 per cent, but in 100 parts of this the quinine ranged from 48.2 to 62.1 parts, average 55.9 parts, while the cinchonidine only averaged 26.7 parts. The results obtained in analyses of twenty-five hybrid barks showed more total alkaloid with proportions somewhat different from the theoretical quantities calculated for a typical hybrid on the assumption that it would partake equally of the character of the two parents. The quinine ranged from 30.8 to 55.3 per cent of the total alkaloid, the figures for cinchonidine increasing more or less with the decrease of the quinine, and the two together constituting four-fifths of the whole alkaloid. The highest amount of quinine in the succirubra barks was only equal to the lowest in the hybrid barks, whilst that of the highest of the hybrids merged into the lowest of the official barks.—*After Pharm. Journ.*

Preparation of Pure Hydrogen.

ACCORDING to Schwarz, a very profitable method of preparing pure hydrogen gas consists in mixing together 30 parts of zinc-dust and 22.8 parts of calcium hydrate, obtained by slaking caustic lime with a sufficient quantity of water, then sifting and drying at 100° C. On gently heating the mixture, hydrogen gas is given off in copious quantities and very regularly. 20 Gm. of zinc and 22.8 parts of calcium hydrate yield 5,200 C.c. of pure hydrogen at 0° C. and 760 mm., corresponding to 0.466 Gm. of water. The mixture cannot be kept ready-mixed, as it will gradually react even in the cold.—*Dingl. Polyt. Journ.*

The Adulteration of Sherry.

IN the last issue of the United States Consular Reports, the Consuls at Cadiz and Jerez de la Frontera return to the subject of the adulteration of sherry, on which they reported most unfavorably. Mr. Ingraham, of Cadiz, sends a translation of a circular from the Spanish Minister of the Interior to the civil governors of the provinces, directing prosecutions against the makers and vendors of adulterated wines, in accordance with a royal decree against adulteration. Adulterated wines are thus defined in the decree: Natural wines which contain: (1.) Impure industrial alcohol and alcohol from husks (cascara), if they are not rectified and purified. (2.) Salicylic acid and other antiseptic substances. (3.) Foreign coloring substances, those derived from the products of pit coal (sic), as well as of vegetable or other origin. (4.) Artificial glucose, sugar from flour, or new wine. (5.) Glycerin. In a report on the trade in sherry for last year, Mr. Ingraham says: "Old houses admit that the demand for low-priced wines compels them to yield reluctantly and compete for the market by using Berlin spirits for rectification at one-half the cost of Spanish grape alcohol, which is sold at 2s|. to 30L a butt, according to vintage, while German alcohol is selling at 13l. a butt under sharp competition and on long credit." Eleven thousand butts of this spirit were imported into Cadiz in 1886, and consumed in the province, the total average vintage of which was 75,000 butts. The Mayor of Jerez declares that all the misfortunes of the wine-growers arise from the use of the industrial spirits; that the cellars are "mysterious laboratories, whose secrets no one is allowed to penetrate," and that the spurious usurps the genuine wines. It is said that only four gallons of spirit are used in a butt of wine, but the proportion of import to the vintage is as 11 to 75, and Cadiz only imports about one-twentieth of that annually imported into Spain.—*After J. S. Chem. Ind.*

[ORIGINAL COMMUNICATION.]

HISTORICAL NOTES ON ANTIMONY AND ITS PRINCIPAL COMBINATIONS.

BY PROF. JAMES F. BABCOCK, BOSTON.

THE native trisulphide of antimony (stibnite) was known to Eastern nations from the very earliest times under the name of *kohl* or *kohol*—a word which has passed into alcohol—the modern name of spirit of wine, but which was first applied to this mineral, and afterwards to any fine powder. POPPIUS, in his *Basilica antimonii*, writes as follows: "The use of this by the Spanish women for improving the beauty of their eyelashes was very common; the powder was called alcohol (which term even to the present day is employed in chemical laboratories), whence crude and unbroken antimony is called antimony." LEMERY says: "To alcoholize or reduce into alcohol signifies to subtilize, as when a mixture is beaten into an impalpable powder (Lemery, "Course of Chemistry," translated by W. Harris, London, 1686, page 40. See also note to "Alcohol," in NEW REMEDIES, December, 1880, p. 359).

The use of the sulphide of antimony as a cosmetic was common among the Syrians, Babylonians, Arabs, Hebrews, and other Oriental nations, a custom which is several times referred to in the Old Testament. "Jezebel heard of it, and she painted her face and tired her head, and looked out at a window," 2 Kings ix. 30. St. Jerome's translation of this passage reads, *"depinxit oculos suos stibio."* "For whom thou didst wash thyself, paintedst thy eyes, and deckedst thyself with ornaments." Ezekiel xxiii. 40. In the Spanish translation, this passage is rendered *"alcoholaste tus ojos."* St. Jerome's translation reads: *circumlinisti stibio oculos tuos."*

DIOSCORIDES (1st century) writes of the crude mineral under the names of *stimmi* and *stibi*. He describes it as crystalline and frinble. In preparing it as a paint, he directs that it should be inclosed in a lump of dough, and buried in coals until reduced to a cinder; extinguished with milk and wine, it is again to be placed upon coals, and blown till ignition, but he cautions that if burned too long, it becomes lead (see below; also foot-note) (Dioscorides, v., 99). The description given by PLINY (1st century) does not correspond in all respects to the ordinary sulphide of antimony. He says: "It is white and shining without being transparent, and has the several names of *stimmi, stibi, alabastrum,* and *lardaxis*. There are two kinds of it, the male and the female. The latter kind is the more approved of, the male stimmi being more uneven, rougher to the touch, less ponderous, not so radiant, and more gritty. The female kind, on the other hand, is bright and frinble, and separates in laminæ, and not in globules. Stimmi is possessed of certain refrigerative and astringent properties, its principal use in medicine being for the eyes. Hence it is that most persons call it *platyophthalmon* (meaning eye-dilating), it being extensively employed in the callibiephuric (meaning beautifying the eyebrows) preparations of females. ... The method of preparing it is to burn it inclosed in a cost of cow dung in a furnace, which done, it is quenched with woman's milk, and pounded with rain water in a mortar." PLINY then directs the powder to be washed, and the fine portion poured off and allowed to settle. He adds: "The main thing of all is to observe such a degree of nicety in the heating it as not to let it become lead." Some writers infer from this passage and a similar one in Dioscorides that the ancients occasionally obtained antimony in a metallic state, but, as in the case of zinc, confounded it with lead, which was better known to them (Pliny, "Natural History," xxxiii., 33, 34.

The origin of the name antimony is uncertain. In the Latin translation of GEBER (8th century), the crude sulphide is called *antimonium.* Geber writes: "Antimony is calcined, dissolved, clarified, congealed, and ground to powder; so it is prepared ("Sum of Perfection," Book I., Part III., ch. 8.)."

BASIL VALENTINE (15th century) says: "The Arabians, to whom in times past this mineral was known, did in their language call it *asinat;* but the Chaldæans called it *stibium;* among the Latins at this day the name *antimony* is used,[*] by which name they first of all signified it.

---

[*] The first Latin translator of Arabic works in the Middle Ages (sometimes Africanus, of Salerno [about 1060 A.D.]). It is in his translation of a work of Isḥāḳ ibn Sulaimān (died 932 A.D.), entitled *"Liber de gradibus,"* that the term *antimonium* first occurs. At least, this passage, as occurring in a translation which is supposed to have been made previous to that of any of Geber's works, may be placed first.—ED. AM. DRUGG.

The Arabic name of antimony is *ithmid* or *ithmud* (as some authorities give). In Badī Valentine's work, the term *asinat* is probably only a misprint for *asnat*. The New English Dictionary (Murray) says: "Like many other alchemistic terms, antimony is a corruption of some Arabic word, refashioned to wear a Greek or Latin aspect—perhaps, as has been suggested, of the Arabic name *athmud, ithmid* itself, latinized *athmodium, athmodius, athmonium, antimonium*. The earlier form of the Arabic is *ithmid,* in which Latin suggests an adaptation (qasi *ithimadi*) of Greek *στίμμιδι,* variant of *στίμμι,* whence also Latin *stibium*. If this conjecture is substantiated, *antimonium* and *stibium* will be transformations of one and the same word."

The word stimmi had long been suspected to be of Egyptian origin, as it is evidently formed after the pattern of other words known to be of this origin, such as *hamu, khi, amu* (to which may probably be added *tamu,* riven heni, atapu, tipaeu, etc.) and it has indeed been found upon inscriptions dating from the 4th century before Christ (from the temple of Edfu), in which an Egyptian fleet is reported to have brought from the extreme northeast of Africa, among other commodities, also *stim* or *stmmi*, which is ms-phide of antimony. The substance itself (in lumps or in mortars discovered in the laboratories of old Egyptian temples.—ED. AM. DRUGG.

We Germans in our language have given it a name which seems to express a certain property of its nature; for since it is seen to consist of a certain streaked matter, and of it may easily be made glass, endued with various colors, which proceed therefrom, we have called it *spiraglass*, as if we should say streaked glass" ("Chariot of Antimony," London, 1678, p. 35). The French story that the name, which in that language is *antimoine*, originated from the accidental poisoning of monks, to whom Valentine had administered it, supposing it would have the same fattening effect upon them that it had upon swine, has no foundation. Valentine, indeed, mentions the fattening of swine by the use of the crude sulphide, but he says nothing of its administration to monks. He writes: "Therefore let men know that antimony not only purgeth gold, cleanseth, and frees it from every peregrine matter, and from all other metals, but also, by a power innate in itself, effects the same in men and beasts. If a farmer purpose in himself to keep up and fatten any of his cattle, as, for example, an hog, two or three days before let him give to the swine a convenient dose of crude antimony—about half a drachm mixed with his food—that by it he may be purged, through which purgation he will not only acquire an appetite to his meat, but the sooner increase and be fattened" (Basil Valentine, "Chariot of Antimony with Annotations by Theodore Kirkringius, M.D.," London, 1678, p. 86). BERGMANN remarks: "As to what is said by some, that it derives its name of antimony from its bad effects on the monks of his society, as if *antimonachal*, is entirely without foundation, as Basilius himself makes use of that appellation, which otherwise he certainly would not have done" (Bergmann's "Chemical Essays," III., 110).

VALENTINE (15th century) also gave the first detailed account of antimony and many of its preparations and combinations in his "Triumph-Wagen Antimonii," first published in Leipzig in 1604. "In this work," says Roscoe, "the characteristic properties of the antimony compounds are so completely given that up to the beginning of this century hardly any further knowledge of this subject had been gained." VALENTINE was the first to give a clear description of the method of preparing the regulus or metal, which he calls *spiraglass-res.* He does not, however, claim this as a new discovery, for he expressly states that the stellate crystalline surface shown by the metal had been observed before his time. He gives the following process: "Take of the best Hungarian speis-glass and crude tartar equal parts, and of sal nitre half a part; grind them well together, and afterwards flux them in a wind-furnace; pour out the flowing matter into a cone, and there let it cool; then you will find the regulus, which thrice or oftener purge with tartar and nitre, and it will be bright and white, shining like cupellate silver, which hath fulminated and overcome all its lead" ("Chariot of Antimony," London, 1678, p. 107). VALENTINE mentions the use of the metal for casting printer's types, and says: "Antimony is useful for many purposes, and, among others, for making the letters employed by printers." Valentine regarded antimony as an imperfect lead. He says: "Between antimony and common lead there is a certain near affinity, and they hold a strict friendship each with the other. As a tree casts out of its side its superfluous rosin, which is the sulphur of that tree, as the cherry tree and other trees which give forth such gums, . . . so the earth likewise hath abortive fruits, which in separation from the pure metals are severed and cast out." In his work entitled "Offenbarung der verborgenen Handgriffe," Erfurth, 1624, he says: "Antimony is the bastard of lead, as wismuth or marcasite is the bastard of tin." In a French manuscript, "Macrocosme ou Traité des Minéraux," quoted by Hoefer, VALENTINE gives the following method of preparing the regulus: "By the addition of tartar and salt, there may be made from antimony a regulus, which, being melted, if there be added steel-iron by a secret preparation, it will show a star, which before my time was called the philosophical star" (Hoefer, "Histoire de la Chimie," Paris, 1866, Vol. I., 483). Valentine and some of his contemporaries believed that the crystalline surface was only produced when iron was used

---

* From several passages occurring in old chemical and Oriental works, it has been surmised that *metallic antimony* was known at the time when the respective works were written. Thus, Pliny, in his "Natural History," B. M, says of sulphide of antimony: "Acte omnis autem argenti nitidus accommodatur ne plumbum flat." "But before all, care must be taken not to melt it down and become lead." A similar remark is made by Dioscorides. The meaning is simply "lead it not like lead." Whitelo and others have misunderstood the passage.

In a Sanskrit glossary of synonyms of substances used in Hindu medicine, compiled by a Ceylonese physician, Sarahari, between the years 1226 and 1250, there are, in the section on minerals (xiii., 87-8; in 120; edition of Garbe: two chapters, the first of which is rightly interpreted by Garbe as referring to the native black sulphide of antimony, as every attribute there mentioned ("black, dark colored, eye-astonishing, collyrium," etc.) exactly agrees with the crude substance. A subsequent chapter, however, speaks of another form of antimony, which Garbe refers to the pure metal, basing his opinion on a few descriptive adjectives ("rubeous," "the essence of anti-vice," "that is, of sulphide of antimony"); (cupola-azure, azure meaning; used in the list. But in the absence of any other confirmatory proof that antimony as a metal was known to the Hindus in those days, the description alluded to is most probably to be referred to a purified sulphide. Indeed, one of the adjectives used by Sarahari—"vainabyaguhya," "having the form of an anti-bill," used with the stirrer tried, unsuccessfully, to find an explanation for, refers undoubtedly to the shape the mass acquires from the vessel in which it is fused. It is even at this day that all is moulded masses of the form of the vessel in which it is melted. While in the instances quoted a knowledge of antimony as a metal is not to be assumed, it is quite probable that metallic antimony was known to Europe even before Basil Valentine, though he is the first to mention it.—ED. AM. DRUG.

in its preparation, but BOYLE discredited this explanation, and claimed that iron for this purpose was unnecessary. He says: "Upon this subject I must not omit to tell you that awhile since an industrious acquaintance of ours was working on an antimony, which, unaware to him, was, as we then supposed, of so peculiar a nature, that making a regulus of it alone without iron, the common way (for his manner of operation I inquired of him), he found, to his wonder, and showed me his regulus adorned with a more conspicuous star than I have seen in several stellate reguluses of both antimony and Mars" (Boyle, "On the Unsuccessfullness of Experiments"). It was claimed by some chemists that the crystalline surface shown by the pure metal was connected with a favourable conjunction of the stars. Of this, LEMERY says: "The star which appears upon the martial regulus of antimony when it is well purified, has given occasion to the chemists who reason upon the matter; and the greatest part of these men being strongly persuaded of the planetary influences and a supposed correspondence between each of the planets, and the metal that bears its name, they have not wanted to assert that this same star proceeded from the impression which certain little bodies flowing from the planet Mars do bestow upon antimony for sake of the remaining iron that was mixed with it, and for this reason they wonderfully recommend the making of this preparation on Tuesday rather than another day, between 7 and 8 o'clock in the morning, or else between 2 and 3 in the afternoon, provided the weather be clear and fair, thinking that that day which is denominated from Mars to be the time that it lets fall its influences most plentiful of any. . . . But all opinions of this kind have no manner of probability, for nobody's experience did ever evince that the metals have any such correspondence with the planets, as I have maintained otherwhere; much less can they prove that the influences of the planets do imprint such and such figures to metals, as these men do determine" (Lemery, "A Course of Chemistry," translated by Walter Harris, M.D., London, 1686, 212).

Notwithstanding the exact descriptions of antimony by VALENTINE, this metal was confounded with bismuth by LIBAVIUS and some other chemists of the sixteenth century. ETTMULLER described the regulus as "the most noble and most metallic part of antimony (i. e., the sulphide) or rather the concentrated mercury of antimony; this regulus is of the nature of lead or an imperfect metal" ("Chymia rationalis," Leyden, 1684). LEMERY in a work published in 1707, "Traité de l'antimoine," Paris, gave a complete description of antimony and a large number of antimonial preparations. NEUMANN in his "Chymia medica," 1756, writes as follows: "Lemery in his treatise on antimony describes no less than two hundred preparations of antimony; among which there are many good and many useless ones. That gentleman was an excellent workman, but an unhappy philosopher; we may depend on his operations, but we are not to trust his theory" (Seumann, "Chemical Works," translated by William Lewis, London, 1773, Vol. I., 200).

Native antimony was discovered by SWAB at Sahlberg near Sahl, Sweden, in 1748. (Act. Acad. reg. scient., Stockholm, 1748.)

Antimony and its combinations were especially studied by BERGMANN (1773–1783); by BERZELIUS (1812–1821); by ROSE (1825); by PHILLIPS (1830); and by FREMY (1844).

The first determination of the atomic weight of antimony was by BERZELIUS in 1818. He gave the weight as 129 (Schw. Jour., xii., 69); SCHNEIDER in 1856 claimed that 120 was more exact (Pogg. Ann., xcviii., 243); DEXTER found it to be 122 (Pogg. Ann., c., 563); this result was confirmed by DUMAS in 1859, and by KESSLER in 1861 (Ann. Chim. et Phys., 3, lv., 129; Pogg. Ann., cxii., 145). COOKE in 1878 after a very thorough examination decided in favor of 120 as the correct figure (Amer. Jour. Science, 3, xv., 41 and 107).

Explosive or electrolytic antimony was discovered by GORE in 1858 (Phil. Trans., 1858, 185; 1859, 797; 1862, 323).

ANTIMONY CHLORIDES.—The preparation of antimony trichloride is given by VALENTINE in his "Triumphwagen Antimonii," 1604. His method consisted in the distillation of equal parts of the native sulphide with corrosive sublimate. He called the product *spiraglass-öl* and says of it: "The oil which comes over is at first white, and congeals like ice or clots of butter."

An oxychloride of antimony precipitated when a concentrated solution of the chloride is added to water was known to VALENTINE. PARACELSUS (1493–1541) describes this preparation under the name of *mercurius vitæ* ("Archidoxorum," lib. 5, 20). This preparation was for a long time believed to contain mercury, but GLAUBER showed this to be an error. He writes: "Take this white powder called mercury of life, and heat it in a crucible; you will find that it is transformed into a glass of antimony, but you will not obtain a trace of mercury." GLAUBER prepared the chloride of antimony by treating its oxide with spirit of salt (hydrochloric acid) and he states that similar products may be obtained by treating arsenic, tin, and zinc in the same manner.

Towards the end of the 16th century the precipitated oxychloride of antimony was much employed by a Veronese physician, ALGAROTTI'S, under the name of *pulvis angelicus.* It was afterwards known as the powder of Algaroth. CROLLIUS in "Basilica chymica," Francof., 1609, described it under the mass of *antimonium diaphoreticum*, and BEGUINIUS in his "Tyrocinium chymicum," Paris, 1608, called it *bezoardicum minerale*. The determination of the exact nature and composition of this precipitate is due to PHILLIPS (1830), and MALAGUTI (1835) (*Phil. Mag.*, VIII., 406; *Ann. Chim. Phys.* (2), LIX., 220).

ANTIMONY HYDRIDE.—This gas was discovered in 1837 by L. THOMPSON (*Lon. and Ed. Phil. Mag.* (3), X., 353); and about the same time independently by PFAFF (*Pogg. Ann.*, XLI., 339). It was specially studied by JONES in 1876 (*Chem. Soc. Jour.*, 1876, 643).

ANTIMONY OXIDES.—The trioxide of antimony was described by DIOSCORIDES and PLINY (1st cent.), and was obtained by roasting the native sulphide.

BASIL VALENTINE prepared a crude antimoniate of potassium by the fusion of antimony with nitre; he gave to the product the name *pulvis albus antimonii*. LIBAVIUS (1560-1616) treated the residue obtained in this way with acids, and thereby produced an impure antimonic acid.

A celebrated nostrum consisting of oxide of antimony and phosphate of calcium, produced by heating the sulphide with horn shavings, and called *pulvis febrifugus Jacobi* or James's powder, was introduced by DR. JAMES, an English physician, about 1750. In the London Pharmacopœia of 1788 it is called *pulvis antimonialis*.

PEARSON made an examination and analysis of this nostrum in 1791 and disclosed its composition and mode of preparation (*Phil. Trans.*, LXXXI, 317).

The earliest mention of the native oxide (valentinite) was by MONGEZ in 1783 (*Jour. de Phys.*, XXII., 66). ROSSLER, examining a variety of this mineral from Bohemia in 1784, confirmed the composition determined by Mongez (*Crell's Ann.*, I., 334).

The number of the oxides of antimony was for some time in dispute. THENARD in 1799 mentioned six (*Ann. Chim.*, XXXII., 259), PROUST in 1804 admitted only two (*Jour. de Phys.*, LV., 328). BERZELIUS (1812-1821) determined that there were three (*Ann. Chim.*, LXXX; *Ann. Ch. Phys.*, XVII.).

The salts of antimonic acid were studied by BERZELIUS in 1818 (*Schweig. Jour.*, XXII., 69). These salts were thoroughly investigated by FREMY in 1843. This chemist suggested the antimoniate of potassium as a reagent for the detection of sodium salts (*Comptes Rendus*, XVI., 187; *Ann. Chim. Phys.* (3), XII., 499). HEFFTNER studied the same subject in 1852 (*Pogg. Ann.*, LXXXVI., 418). SCHLIPPE in 1821 described the sulphantimoniate of sodium, known as Schlippe's salt (*Schweig. Jour.*, XXXIII., 380).

ANTIMONY AND POTASSIUM TARTRATE.—BASIL VALENTINE (15th cent.) was the first to mention the medicinal virtues of antimonial preparations ("Triumphwagen Antimonii," Leips., 1604), PARACELSUS (1493-1541) contributed much towards the extension of the medical use of antimony, but he divided the medical profession into two hostile camps, which for a long time carried on a bitter contest in regard to the merits of these preparations. SEVERIN, a most ardent disciple of PARCELSUS, still further popularized the use of these medicines. In 1571 he wrote: "Just as antimony purifies gold and separates impurities from mineral substances, so it removes from the body of the sick man all impediments to the play of the natural functions of his organization ("Idea medicinæ philosophicæ," etc., Basle, 1571).

In 1556 the opponents of the medicine obtained an act of the Paris parliament forbidding the use of antimony and its compounds, and in 1603 the medical faculty of Paris took a similar step, and issued a decree which declared antimony to be a poison, and condemned its use (Sprengel, "Hist. de la Med.," III., 121). In the same year, a celebrated physician, TURQUET DE MAYERNE, was prosecuted under this decree because he had, in spite of the decree, sold antimonial preparations, and BESNIER in 1609 was expelled from the medical faculty for having prescribed them.

The decree of the faculty against Turquet, dated at Paris, December 5th, 1603, is as follows: "The College of Physicians in the Academy of Paris, legally assembled, having heard the report of the faculty to whom was entrusted the duty of examining the tract published under the name of Turquet of Mayerne, condemn it unanimously as an infamous libel, full of proved falsehoods and impudent calumnies, which could only be made by an ignorant and impudent man furious from drink. Turquet himself is judged to be unfit to practice medicine, on account of rashness, impudence, and ignorance of true medicine. All true physicians who practise among any people or in any place, are exhorted to exclude Turquet and similar monstrosities of men and opinions from themselves and their boundaries, and to remain faithful to the teachings of Hippocrates and Galen; and any one of the order of physicians of Paris is prohibited from entering into medical consultation with Turquet and those like him. Whoever does otherwise, shall be deprived of the privileges of the academy, and expelled from the number of the regents" (Hoefer, "Hist. de la Chimie," II., 239).

SYLVIUS (1614-1672) was a zealous partisan in favor of antimonial preparations as remedial agents and among others he advocated the use of regulus of antimony cast into pills like shot, which when once used were washed and kept for future employment for the same purpose—hence their name *pilula perpetua* (Sylvius, "Opera medica," Amsterdam, 1679). Goblets in which wine had been allowed to stand for some time, were also employed and it was believed that both the pills and the goblets acted only by contact and did not lose weight. VIGANI (1683) was one of the first to combat this idea. He affirms, as the result of his own experience, that the antimony gradually lost weight, and that wine was rendered emetic by the combination of the tartar contained in the wine with the particles of the metal (Vigani, "Medulla chemiæ," London, 1683). LEMERY expresses a similar opinion. He says: "When a man swallows the perpetual pill, it passes by its own weight and purges downwards; it is washed and given as before, and so on perpetually. . . . Almost all chemists have written that this pill loses nothing at all of its weight, though taken several times. It is true, indeed, the diminution is but very small, yet, nevertheless, it would not be hard to remark it in some measure. . . . When this pill had been taken and voided twenty or thirty times, it purges not so much as it did at first, as well because its more soluble parts of the sulphur are gone, as that which remains doth pass without any great effect " ("A Course of Chymistry, by Nicholas Lemery," translated by Walter Harris, M. D., London, 1686). During the period of the medical controversy on antimony (1620) CORNACCHINI, professor in the university at Pisa, published a work entitled "Methodus in pulverem," in which he gave an account of a powder, invented by the Earl of Warwick, which had acquired great celebrity in Italy. This powder was composed of scammony, crude antimony, and cream of tartar triturated together. The wonderful cures attributed to its use attracted the attention of a physician of Mecklenburg, named MYNSICHT, who in 1631 described a preparation made by boiling a solution of tartar with *crocus metallorum* (Mynsicht, "Thesaurus medico-chymicus," 1631). To this preparation he gave the name of tartar emetic. MYNSICHT was the first to clearly describe the preparation of this salt, but there are indications that it was known to some of the earlier chemists—as VALENTINE and LIBAVIUS (Hoefer, "Hist. de la Chimie," Vol. I., 480). Glass of antimony was afterwards substituted for the crocus. LEMERY writes: "This preparation is a soluble tartar, impregnated with some portion of glass of antimony which renders it emetic." SALA, whose works were published in 1647, wrote a treatise on the medical uses of antimony ("Anatomia antimonii"), in which he insisted on extreme care in the use of antimonial preparations. He says: "Whoever values his health should be on his guard against these medicines. Independently of the arsenic which is found naturally in antimony, this substance may by combination with other bodies acquire poisonous properties, just as mercury, which in itself is not a poison, may become so in the state of corrosive sublimate" (Sala, "Opera medico-chymica," Francf., 1647). In 1637 antimony wine was allowed a place in the officinal French pharmacopœia, and in 1666, upon the petition of the medical faculty, the original decree of the parliament against it was rescinded. In an essay on "Antimoniated Tartar," in 1773, BERGMANN gave a full account of its preparation and properties (Bergmann, "Opuscula," I., 101. This salt was especially studied by THENARD, 1801 (*Ann. Chim.*, XXXVIII., 39); and by PHILLIPS, in 1823 (*Ann. Philos.*, (2) IX., 372).

ANTIMONY SULPHIDES.—The early use of this mineral as a cosmetic and the references to it by DIOSCORIDES and PLINY have been already given. Among the alchemists and the early metallurgists crude sulphide of antimony was employed to separate the baser metals from gold. It was called by a variety of names, as *lupus metallorum, proteus aries, othia, saturnus philosophorum, magnesia saturni, judex ultimus*, etc. VALENTINE and GLAUBER knew that the mineral contained sulphur, but its exact composition was first definitely stated by BERGMANN in 1782 (Bergmann, "Opuscula phys. et chem.," III., 164). VALENTINE (15th Cent.) describes the preparation of the red or precipitated sulphide as follows: "Antimony (sulphide) is pulverized and boiled for two hours in a concentrated lye prepared from the ashes of the oak; strong vinegar is then added, and the liquid filtered. The antimony will thus become a beautiful red" ("Triumphwagen Antimonii," Leipzig, 1604, p. 168). GLAUBER in 1654, describes a preparation, which he calls *panacea antimonialis* or *sulphur purgans universale*, made by precipitation of a solution of the slag produced during the preparation of regulus by means of vinegar ("Pharmacopœa spagyrica"). ETTMULLER, in 1684, describes a similar preparation. He states that when crude antimony is fused with alkalies, in order to extract the regulus, the sulphur is absorbed by the flux, and that to extract it, the slag should be dissolved in water and acid added, when "there is produced a horrible stench and a diaphoretic sulphur, called golden sulphur of antimony, is precipitated" (Ettmuller, "Chymia rationalis," 1684). This preparation consisted only of sulphur, such as would be produced by adding an acid to a solution of alkaline polysulphide, but afterwards a preparation containing antimony was, by later writers, directed to be made by adding acid to a more or less oxidised solution of sulphide of antimony containing sulphantimoniate of the alkali. Precipitated sulphide of antimony was extensively used as a medicine about [the beginning of the 18th century under the name of kermes mineral. A Parisian apothecary, named DE LA LIGERIE, had bought the secret from a German apothecary, a disciple of Glauber. The administration of this preparation by a monk named Simon to a Carthusian monk, whose life had been despaired of by the Paris faculty, is said to have restored him to health. The preparation thus acquired a great reputation. Simon called this powder alkermes mineral, and it was afterwards called poudre des chartreux, being sold by the Carthusian friars in Paris at a considerable price (Lemery, "Sur une preparation appellée commencement Poudre des Chartreux ou Kermes mineral," *Mém. de l'Acad.*, Paris, 1720). Such was the celebrity for remarkable cures which this medicine acquired that the French Government purchased the secret of its preparation of De la Ligerie in 1720.

The composition of this sulphide was the subject of much controversy. It was studied by GEOFFROY in 1735 (*Mém. de l'Acad.*, Paris, 1735). ROSE in 1823 showed that kermes was amorphous sulphide of antimony (*Pogg. Ann.*, III., 441).

Hepar antimonii, or liver of antimony of the earlier chemists, was a mixture of the trioxide and the trisulphide prepared by deflagrating equal parts of crude antimony and nitre. This liver-colored mass, pulverized, and edulcorated with water, was known as *crocus metallorum* (Newman's "Chemistry," London, 1773, Vol. I., 208; Lemery's "Chemistry," London, 1686, 317).

BURETTE FOR TITRATING HOT LIQUIDS.

DR. L. L. DE KONINCK, of Liège, describes the burette here figured in the *Zeitschr. f. angew. Chemie* (1888, 187).

In certain cases, it is necessary to heat the liquids which are to be assayed or titrated, as, for instance, when carbonates are being decomposed by standard acid, or when sugar is to be determined by Fehling's solution. When a liquid is heated while situated under a burette, or when a hot liquid is placed directly under it, the burette soon becomes coated with condensed moisture, and the contents expand through the heat ascending from the liquid. The arrangement proposed by the author does away with these drawbacks. The burette is firmly clamped to a support and a special delivery tube, bent twice, as shown in the cut, and drawn out at the point, is attached to it by means of a piece of rubber tubing. [This delivery tube is best arranged, so that it may be easily turned aside and back again, so as not to have it over the heated liquid longer than is at all necessary.]

Rendering Blue Prints Brown.

IN the *Moniteur de la Photographie*, M. Gauthier-Villars gives the following formula for the conversion of the blue color of cyanotypes into brown:

I. *Solution for the Preparation of the Paper.*
Potassium ferritartrate.................. 15 Gm.
Potassium ferridcyanide .... 12 "
Distilled Water........................250 C.c.

II. *Solution for Bleaching the Prints.*
Ammonia (24°)........................100 C.c.
Distilled Water........................900 "

III. *Solution for Coloring Brown.*
Tannin................................10 Gm.
Distilled Water.......................500 C.c.

The blue prints are first well washed and then dipped into solution No. II. until the image is completely bleached. It is then washed again and immersed in the tannin-bath solution III., where it is left until it has assumed the desired tone, which may not be until after twelve hours. If at the end of this time the desired depth shall not yet be attained, a few drops of ammonia should be added. Finally, the print is washed with plain water. To blacken blue prints, Mr. Roy's method is recommended, bleaching yellow in a solution of 4 Gm. caustic soda to 100 C.c. water, then blackening in a solution of 4 Gm. of tannin to 100 C.c. water.

Note.—A detailed description of the process of making blue prints will be found on p. 117 of our volume for 1887.

AN APPARATUS FOR COMPARISON OF COLOR TINTS.

IN certain operations, it is necessary to compare tints of color produced by known quantities of one reagent upon unknown quantities of a given liquid, for the purpose of estimating the quantity of certain constituents. One of the most familiar examples is the assay of ammonia by means of Nessler's reagent. The execution of these assays is usually performed by gradually adding small measured quantities of the reagent (of known strength) to a measured quantity of a liquid containing a known amount of ammonia, until the tint has been rendered equal to that existing in a sample of the liquid under examination, likewise treated with a known quantity of the reagent.

Mr. A. W. Stokes has devised an apparatus by means of which this assay is considerably simplified, the depth of color being equalised by adjusting the column of liquid. We quote, as follows, from *The Analyst* (June, 1888):

"Whenever it is necessary to compare a number of depths of tint with one another, it is very inconvenient to have to make up a large series of standard tints. The apparatus obviates this necessity. By reference to the annexed diagram, it will be seen to consist of a base-board on which lies a sheet of white opal glass. Placed obliquely, a little way above this, is a sheet of colorless glass on which rest the Nessler tubes containing the solutions whose tints are to be compared. The mouth ends of these tubes recline towards the observer, in grooves hollowed in a horizontal bar. This bar is supported by two pillars, one of which slides a ring clasping a calibrated glass tube; this tube has a side tubulure at the base, and is thus, by means of a short india-rubber tube, connected with a

similar, but uncalibrated tube resting on the glass plate. A known quantity of the standard color, being placed in that tube carried by the ring, and diluted up to the top mark with water, if this tube be raised in its sliding collar, its standard solution will flow into the tube resting on the glass plate. The movable tube is so calibrated as to show how much liquid is present in the tube connected with it. Hence, if a Nessler tube containing liquid of an unknown depth of tint be placed beside the tube resting on the glass plate, and the tube in the sliding ring be raised or lowered till the tints agree in the two tubes that rest on the glass plate, a simple inspection of the level of the liquid left in the calibrated tube will give the quantity of standard color the unknown solution is equal to. The distance apart of the grooves in the horizontal bar is the average width between the eyes, so that, as the mouths of the tubes lie inclined towards the observer, and the light is reflected up from the opal glass through the full length of the tubes, observations are easily made. As shown, the apparatus will take three tubes for comparison with the standard color, but it may readily be made to take any number. By putting a similar pair of connected tubes on the other pillar, an unknown tint might be placed between two known depths of tint. A small slip of wood is fixed along the glass plate to keep the tubes in an inclined position. By placing blackened cards in front and behind the tubes, light can be prevented from entering the tubes except from the bottom. The apparatus is simple and readily cleaned. It can be obtained from Messrs. Townson & Mercer, of London."

Diphenylmethylpyrasol.

THE aniline works of Hoechst, on the Rhine, formerly Meister, Lucius & Bruening, have secured a patent on a new antipyretic, which has a composition similar to that of antipyrin, and which is designated as *diphenylmethylpyrazol* or, shorter, *diphenylpyrazol.*

The new substance is prepared by a process very much resembling that by which antipyrin is made.

It is reported to appear in form of white needles, difficultly soluble in water, ether, or petroleum ether, but easily in alcohol or glacial acetic acid. It differs from antipyrin by possessing a pronounced basic character. With nitric acid and ferric chloride, it reacts similarly to, but much more faintly, than antipyrin.—*After Zeitsch. f. angew. Chem.*

Notes on Commercial Drugs and Chemicals.

[From the September Report of Gehe & Co., of Dresden.]

Acetanilide (Antifebrin).—The consumption of this antipyretic is constantly increasing. Though some authorities declare it to be affected with some drawbacks—according to Lépine, for instance, it produces decided anemia—its cheapness is probably the principal cause of its more general use.

Alantol Essence.—Marpmann's Alantol Essence, prepared from elecampane, has been used with continued good success in alleviating or curing acute catarrhal affections of the air passages, due to infection.

Boric Acid.—The discovery of the borax deposits (boronatrocalcit) in Chili, upon the high plateaus of Copiapo and Antofagasta, has materially depressed the market of Italian boric acid in Europe.

Bromide of Ethyl is a favorite anæsthetic in small dental operations, where only a short anæsthesia is wanted. It is said never to cause nausea, and those under its influence recover rapidly.

Caffeine.—No article has suffered so much depreciation during the last twenty or thirty years as this. About 1860 it was worth about eighty-eight dollars a pound; ten years later only twenty-five dollars; last year only nine dollars, and at present it is only worth five dollars. But even now it does not appear to have reached bottom. English manufacturers have succeeded in persuading the Custom Department to permit them to use damaged tea duty free, for the purpose of extracting the caffeine. The new regulations require that the tea shall be denaturalized by means of a solution of lime impregnated with asafetida, which renders it unfit for domestic use.

Cascara Sagrada Bark has become so firmly established in European medical praxis that every shipment was rapidly bought up, and the supplies in Europe have lately become low.

Cinchona Bark.—There seems to be at last a turning point reached in the exports of Ceylon cinchona bark. During the period from October 1st, 1886, to July 12th, 1887, there were exported 11,703,924 pounds; and during the same period 1887–1888, only 9,183,039 pounds. On the other hand, Java's export is constantly increasing, and cultivated bark from Bolivia is also arriving in Europe in considerable quantities. The latter appears both in flat pieces (trunk-bark) and in quills (branch bark), and are very rich in quinine. It is, however, doubtful whether the cultivators reap any profit as yet from their enterprise.

As a supplement to the article entitled "Cinchona in Columbia," in our last number (page 195), the following statements of Gehe & Co. may find a place here. These are evidently based upon much more recent information.

The Cuprea bark of Colombia still appears on the market occasionally. Up to the year 1879, it had been entirely unknown, was afterwards shipped in immense quantities to Europe, and soon appeared to have become exhausted. It is, however, reported by reliable correspondence that a revival of the Cuprea industry is not at all improbable, provided fair prices could be realized. When the first samples of cuprea bark were sent to London, in order to ascertain whether these trees growing in dense forests, at a height of less than 4,000 feet beyond the sea level could be utilized by the quinine manufacturers, it was found that they were worth 2/3 to 3/3 per pound, while their collection for the market at home was probably only 0.2½ per pound. In consequence thereof, the cuprea forests on the banks of the Lebrija and Sogamoso, and in the side valleys, were overrun by wood-choppers already in 1880; in a few months everything had been laid low, and some 150,000 to 180,000 bales of bark were ready for export. Finally the taxes decreed by the Colombian government, the increasing costs of transport owing to the greater distances over which the bark had to be carried, and the lowering of the prices in Europe, caused an entire cessation of the industry. Nevertheless, the cuprea bark trees are not exhausted. The remaining roots have driven forth new stems and shoots, the bark of which, luckily, was for a long time unfit for stripping. At this time, however, some eight years after the demolition of the original forests, the trees are of a size to admit peeling. It will depend upon the prices of East Indian bark whether the new Cuprea can be brought upon the market.

Citrate of Caffeine.—The new Hungarian Pharmacopœia recognizes as citrate of caffeine a mixture of 100 parts of caffeine and 50 of citric acid. The Brit. Ph., it will be remembered, directs it to be prepared from equal parts, by weight, of caffeine and citric acid. The ordinary commercial salt is usually made by crystallizing caffeine from a solution in citric acid, in which case only about 5 per cent of the latter remains mixed with the crystallized caffeine.

Cornutin.—This active principle of ergot, discovered and introduced by Prof. Kobert, is only in slight demand, which is partly due to its readiness to suffer decomposition, and partly to its high price. Some gynecologists regard it as the best agent to produce contraction of the uterus, and to stop uterine hemorrhage. It is difficultly soluble in ether, easily in alcohol, acetic ether, or chloroform. An alcoholic solution of it, however, decomposes within a few hours, when exposed to light.

Coto Bark.—No true Coto bark has appeared on the market for some time. What was shipped to Europe as such turned out to be Paracoto Bark.

Creolin, the new antiseptic, is in very active and increasing demand. It is probable that it will become an active rival of crude and crystallized carbolic acid, when the latter is to serve as a disinfectant, antiseptic, or antiparasitic.

Gum Arabic.—The supplies of the genuine gum from the Soudan, which had been seriously interrupted during the past five years, have now ceased entirely. Consumers are compelled to use other sorts of gum, from Arabia, India, Australia, the Senegal, and even from Brazil. Gum Ghezireh, which used to be exported from ports in the Red Sea, also becomes very scarce. But a fair substitute for Ghezireh, of a whitish color, is now being delivered at Mogadore. The principal substitute on which the market has to rely is Senegal-gum, though this is also getting scarcer.

Hydrastine.—The alkaloid as well as its hydrochlorate are in regular though only moderate demand. They are reported to be especially efficacious in menorrhagia in doses of 0.05–0.1 Gm. (¾ to 1½ grains).

Kola Nuts.—Since the shippers of this valuable drug have adopted the plan to break the nut into its component parts (3 or 4), it has been possible so to dry it that it can be transported without spoiling.

Narceine and Meconarceine.—In Germany, narceine is used but rarely, but in Southern Europe it is in some demand. Recently a new substance, *meconarceine,* has been introduced, which is said to contain, besides narceine, several other (so far unknown) active principles of opium, and is said to be much more soluble than pure narceine. As long as the actual composition of the former is not made known, it will have but little chance of being regularly used.

Peroxide of Hydrogen is now obtainable also in about double the former strength, viz., 20 per cent by volume. It is, however, impracticable to warrant the stability of this solution, as it will lose gas even at ordinary temperatures.

Phenacetin.—Bayer's phenacetin is constantly extending its use. In antipyretic effect it is at least equal to antipyrin and antifebrin; and as an antineuralgic it is ahead of the latter. It is not unlikely that it will be found to possess still other valuable properties.

Powdered Glass.—Gehe & Co. announce that they have a stock of powdered glass specially prepared from the purest white glass.

Solanine.—The demand for this alkaloid has lately been so great that it could not be supplied. It is used in doses of 0.05 to 0.3 Gm. (¾ to ab. 4 grains) per day internally, or 0.01 to 0.05 Gm. (⅙ to ¾ grain) 2 to 4 times daily, hypodermically, in ischias, tic douloureux, and other nervous diseases as an analgesic and anæsthetic.

Sozo-iodol.—This substitute for iodoform, which is, chemically speaking, di-iodo-paraphenol-sulphonic acid, has recently been offered in form of a salt, combined with sodium, potassium, mercury, and zinc. It is said to equal iodoform as an antiseptic, and in some cases even to surpass it.

Succinic Acid and Amber.—A prominent firm engaged in the amber industry has offered a prize for the discovery of new channels in which succinic acid and oil of amber could be technically utilized.

Sulphonal.—This new hypnotic, chemically "di-ethyl-sulphone-dimethyl-methane," has been in considerably increased demand. But until its price becomes very materially reduced, there is no probability that it will displace the commonly used hypnotics.

Tincture of Strophantus has greatly fallen off in use. According to Prof. Eichler, digitalis is preferable to it, as it acts more rapidly.

Tasteless Liquid Extract of Cascara Sagrada.

Mr. R. Wright read a paper on the above subject, at the late meeting of the Brit. Pharm. Conference, from which we give the following, after *Chem. and Drugg.:*

Mr. Wright adopted the plan proposed by F. Graser, of using magnesia to combine with the resins, the bitter principle being left behind, and recommends the following process (in which we have substituted U. S. weights and measures):

Cascara Bark, in No. 40 powder	16 ℥
Calcined Magnesia	2 ℥
Distilled Water	32 fl. ℥
Diluted Alcohol	q. s.

Mix the powders in a large mortar, and make a paste with the water. Allow to stand for twelve hours, and dry over a water-bath. Reduce the dry mass to powder, moisten it with 18 fl. ℥ of Diluted Alcohol, and pack tightly in a series of six percolating tubes. Percolate with Diluted Alcohol, the percolate from No. 1 tube being used as a menstruum for No. 2, and so on until the last of the series is reached. Diluted Alcohol is added to No. 1 tube as required, and the first 14 fl. ℥ which pass through the last tube are reserved. Percolation is then continued until the powders are exhausted. From these percolates the alcohol is recovered by distillation, and the residue evaporated on a water-bath to the consistence of a syrup. This is added to the reserved portion, and the volume made up to 16 fl. ℥ with Diluted Alcohol.

Note.—The original formula everywhere directs proof spirit (Brit. Ph.) in place of diluted alcohol. But the latter being so near in strength to the former and better known here, will no doubt answer the same purpose.

Two New Antiseptics.

METHYLENEDOL CARBONIC Acid and Methylenedol-acetic Acid are the names of two new antiseptics. A paper has been read concerning them by Professor Penzoldt, from which it appears that the first occurs as white acicular needles, nearly insoluble in cold water, though the sodium salt is more readily taken up by that menstruum. It was found to be very efficacious in the treatment of wounds, both fresh and ulcerated. Even forty-five grains given internally were not observed to exercise any poisonous effect, or to produce any unpleasant symptoms. As the preparation of the carbonic acid compound is very difficult and expensive, the methylenedol-acetic acid has been made, and while much more cheaply prepared, it is equal to the first-named in the treatment of wounds. Further trials are to be made in order to determine if these compounds are preferable in antiseptic surgery to iodoform.— *Chem. and Drugg.*

Preparation of pure Hydrogen Peroxide from the Commercial Product.

COMMERCIAL hydrogen peroxide often contains hydrochloric, sulphuric, phosphoric, hydrofluoric acid, alumina, lime, magnesia, potash, and soda, derived from the water used in the manufacture, while baryta and traces of iron, copper, lead, and manganese are sometimes found if it has been carelessly made.

When these last are present, the product is stable only if it be sufficiently acid, though even then it is less stable than in the absence of these impurities.

The pure substance is chiefly used as an antiseptic in the treatment of sores. The commercial liquid, of about 3 per cent strength, is purified by the addition of about 1 per cent concentrated phosphoric acid (preferably pure) to precipitate iron, copper, lead, and manganese, and prevent the subsequent formation of their peroxides, which would otherwise take place. Saturated baryta water (hot or cold) is then added very gradually, until neutrality is reached; no excess must be used or hydrated BaO₂ will be precipitated, which will produce decomposition of a portion of the hydrogen peroxide.

The clear liquid is now drawn off, and is poured into an excess of cold saturated baryta water, when hydrated BaO₂ is thrown down, and is then washed until no metal except barium can be detected in the washings.

The BaO₂ is then suspended in water and added drop by drop to a solution consisting of 100 parts of distilled water to 10–12 of pure concentrated sulphuric acid until only traces of acid remain free; these are best removed by weak baryta water, for an accidental excess of BaO₂ will induce decomposition of some of the already formed hydrogen peroxide, while an excess of BaO will have no such effect. The barium sulphate is allowed to settle, and the clear liquid drawn off, if found free from both barium and sulphuric acid.

The resulting product is about 3 per cent strength, very stable, and of great purity.—MANN in *Chem. Zeit., J. S. Chem. Ind.*

Impure Iodoform.

CERTAIN commercial brands of iodoform, particularly a few which are reputed to be the purest, have been found by C. Neuss, of Wiesbaden, to yield with 10 parts of ether immediately a red solution, while other brands furnished a yellow solution retaining its tint for at least 10 minutes. In all other respects, the former responded to the requirements of the Germ. Pharmacopœia. The samples which produced the red solution were also found to impart to pure gauze (free from chlorine) at once a green color, even when light was excluded. Curiously enough, this green color returned again to iodoform yellow when the gauze was kept in the dark for some days or weeks. Iodoform which behaves as above stated, *exercises a caustic effect upon the skin.* A person who manufactured prepared gauze with this kind of iodoform, suffered from eczema for several days. It is not impossible that the secondary effects of the drug reported by numerous observers are due to the same impurity as that which causes the above-mentioned color reactions. The quality of ether used for the first experiment has only a slight influence upon the reaction, since chemically pure ether can retard it only for 1 or 2 minutes.

The chemical nature of the secondary body which yields up its iodine so readily has not yet been made out. That the iodine must be originally in combination is shown by the fact that alcohol fails to remove it from the iodoform, while the red ethereal solution undoubtedly contains free iodine. The author is convinced that neither free iodine nor hydriodic acid are present previous to the solution in ether, also that the secondary body is more easily soluble in ether than iodoform itself.—*Alter Pharm. Centralh.,* No. 39.

MEASURING FLASK WITH BURETTE.

R. SCHUETZE employs burettes bearing a globular reservoir at the top, which is connected with the burette by means of a three-way stop-cock. If the contents of the reservoir are such that only washed air may be allowed to have access to them, then the outlet of the stop-cock at *W* is connected, by means of rubber tubing, with the tube *r*, and the wash-funnel *f* is charged with a liquid suitable for keeping the contents of the reservoir free from contaminations which might be caused by air.— *Chem. Zeit.*

A LABORATORY DRYING-OVEN.

FROM a paper by Mr. A. J. Banks, published in the *Chem. News* (Aug. 3d), we take the following:

In laboratories where steam is used for the purpose of heating drying-ovens, evaporating-pans, etc., the water produced by the condensation of the steam is a frequent and troublesome annoyance. The supply pipes very often have to be carried a considerable distance before reaching the laboratory, and are not unfrequently exposed to strong draughts of air; hence considerable condensation of the steam is brought about and, in conjunction with that produced by the expansion of the steam on entering the oven, and the larger surface there exposed, the amount of water produced is a serious obstacle to the attainment of high temperatures.

With the object of overcoming this difficulty, I have

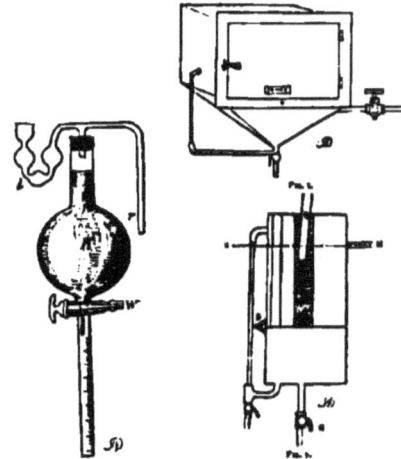

Measuring flask with burette.   Laboratory drying oven.

revised a modified form of water oven, which answers admirably. Its construction will be readily understood from the accompanying drawing, which represents an ordinary drying-oven, with the bottom of the outer covering in the form of an inverted pyramid, provided with a gauge glass to indicate the height of the water, and a stopcock or valve for running off the same. The inlet pipe is placed immediately below the inner case (see cut).

Test for Saccharin.

SOME time ago (see this Journal, September, p. 167) Mr. David Lindo published a test for Fahlberg's saccharin, which he has since found can be modified to advantage as follows: After placing the saccharin with concentrated nitric acid in a small porcelain dish, evaporate to dryness on the water bath, or by moving the flame of a spirit lamp to and fro under the dish, blowing on the surface occasionally to facilitate evaporation, and taking care that the heat does not rise too high. If the dish is allowed to cool and a few drops of strong solution of potash in 50 per cent alcohol are added to the residue, a faint yellow color only will be developed. Spread the liquid over the surface of the dish, and before it has settled to the bottom, apply heat with the lamp, as above, quickly all over the under surface of the dish. If the vapor of alcohol happens to ignite, it must at once be extinguished. A greater variety of colors will be developed in this way than by following the directions formerly given. As the dish cools and moisture is absorbed, the colors fade; by heating they can be reproduced, but not in the same perfection as at first. [See also page 214.]—*Chem. News,* Sept. 28th.

Loco Weed and the Importance of Scientific Investigation.

(From a paper read by Prof. L. E. Sayre, of Kansas, at the Detroit Meeting of the A. P. A.)

At the outset I deem it expedient to offer an apology for the heading which states the subject of this paper. It was my original purpose to present to the Association a paper upon the subject of loco weed in the usual form which characterized literature of this nature brought before a scientific organization. Accordingly, I took up the subject for investigation in the usual way, but found, after much research, a surprising condition of affairs which justifies me in using the above caption. The object of this paper, therefore, is not only to give the results of my researches, but at the same time to call especial attention to the importance of scientific investigation for the purpose of distinguishing between hearsay evidence and that obtained by the sifting method of modern science.

When I first went to Kansas, some three years ago, I found that loco weed had been exciting much public attention, on account of its alleged poisonous effects upon cattle who pastured in the locality where it abounded. Loco weed was regarded by all as a destructive poison, damaging to the cattle interests of the West. So many complaints in fact were received concerning the immense loss to the ranchmen from this pest that the legislature of Colorado finally enacted laws for its suppression by means of a wholesale eradication of the plant from the soil of that State. The following is from the act passed May 1st, 1885.

"Any person who shall dig up, not less than three inches below the surface of the ground, any loco or poison weed during the months of May, June, July, shall receive a premium of one and one-half cents per pound for each pound of such weed dug up. To be paid out of the State Treasury, as hereinafter provided. Provided that such weed shall not be weighed in a green state, but shall be thoroughly dried when weighed."

There are other sections to the act referred to which relates to the claimants producing the weed, etc. The oath required to be taken by the claimant was as follows: "I do solemnly swear or affirm that the weed here produced by me this day is loco or poison weed," giving the number of pounds dug up within two months last past. The remainder of the act relates to weighing, recording of oath, etc.

In looking over the records, I found the following as showing the distribution of funds for this purpose, during the years 1885 and 1886, which will indicate the portions of Colorado in which this pest was supposed to be most felt: Chaffee County, $1,104.07; Costilla County, $3,865.89; Custer County, $6,156.98; El Paso County, $15,638.05; Fremont County, $968.43; Huerfano County, $9,144.80; Las Animas County, $4,182.91; Ouray County, $1,384.55; Pueblo County, $4,176.32; Saguache County, $11,860.47. Making a grand total for the years 1885 and 1886 only of $63,928.56. In an interview which I had recently with the State Treasurer of Colorado, he informed me that about $200,000 has already been expended by that State for the purpose of carrying this law into effect. It will be seen, therefore, to what enormous proportions the importance of this subject had grown in the public estimation, and as can well be imagined, when I was asked to investigate the nature of the poison and its effects as a toxic agent, I felt, by so doing, I was taking up a work which might give results of the greatest consequence to all concerned.

After an immense amount of research to ascertain the nature of the poison of loco weed, I have been gradually led away from the path first mapped out by an unexpected turn of affairs. It is a grave question whether the loco weed is a poison at all. In fact, it is a question whether the animals said to have been poisoned with it in such immense numbers as to justify the State of Colorado spending $200,000 for their salvation from the dread scourge, have not died from some other cause.

I will now give you some of my experiences in conducting this investigation, during the vacation of the University with which I am connected. In the year 1886, between June and September, I took the opportunity offered of visiting numerous cattle ranches in the State of Kansas. Each year since that time I have made many similar trips over a considerable territory in the West in no man's land, across the Western portion of the State of Kansas, and a large portion of Colorado, the last summer travelling over a portion of the Indian Territory for the purpose of visiting and collecting information from ranchmen, farmers, and others who had practical experience with the loco weed. I at the same time had in view the mapping out of the extent of the growth of the plant, and ascertaining the amount of damage done by it to cattle, horses, and sheep.

In starting out on my last trip, I arranged with Prof. Burleigh (professor of veterinary science at the U. S. Experimental Station, at Manhattan, Kansas) that he should come to my assistance in any portion of the territory described, if I should find an animal suffering from the loco poison, the understanding being that he would make ante-mortem and post-mortem examination, that we might report together the phenomena resulting from the poison. One of my first experiences was as follows:

Being informed by a gentleman who had large cattle interests that at his ranch, a number of miles distant, I would find an animal showing all the signs of blood poisoning, I started out for the purpose of making investigations. I travelled all day over a rough country, went through all the experiences of a tenderfoot, lost my way on the prairie, and I finally came to the ranch referred to. There I partook of the sumptuous repast spread for me, after dinner drove out to the herd and a horse was there pointed out which was said to be "locoed." I am sorry I did not have with me a photographic apparatus, as I think the picture of this animal would be interesting. I never saw before a skeleton breathing the breath of life, as was the case in this instance, but notwithstanding the most horrid condition of the animal, there was no evidence of loco poisoning present.

It may be well before to briefly state the symptoms exhibited by an animal said to be "locoed." The first symptoms are those of hallucination. When led or ridden up to some trifling obstruction, such as a bar or rope lying in the road, he stops short, and if urged forwards, leaps over it as if it were a fence four feet high. All sense of dimension seems to be lost. A barn near at hand seems far away and one a mile off appears near at hand. He will go headlong against any obstruction or over a precipice, unconscious of the proximity of the danger. He may permit one to approach him, but is likely to run away as though frightened, and then suddenly stop short, stare, and return to his former position. Any sudden and violent motion made before the animal's eyes, such as throwing up the arms, may cause him to fall to the ground through sudden fright. Sometimes the animal is seized with a frenzy, and then is uncontrollable and dangerous. The eyes during the frenzy are turned upwards, exposing the whites which are strongly injected. These seizures may be provoked by anything which excites the animal. In addition to these symptoms, the locoed animal generally loses flesh; his gait is feeble and uncertain, eyes sunken, flat and glassy, coat rough and lustreless. He will not be led, and attempts of this kind results in obstinate resistance.

One particular symptom which the ranchman mentions as indicative of a locoed condition is the loss of sense which guides it in finding water. On the prairie, water is found by native animals sooner than by man. A cow, for instance, raised upon the prairie, no matter how far away she may be when she is thirsty, will go to the stream in the shortest and most direct way instinctively. This peculiar instinct is possessed by them to a remarkable degree, but if locoed, this sense is entirely lost.

Now during the past three years I have travelled over a large portion of the west where the loco plant is said to ravage the stock. I have visited ranch after ranch, inspecting the herds, and looking for cases of poisoning, but, either owing to the season of the year, or to some unexplained reason, I have been unable to satisfy myself in regard to the nature of the few cases found, either because the symptoms were so unlike those described as due to the poison, or because in the instances that came under my observation, the symptoms might be assignable to some other cause.

Time will not permit me to give you the results of the many observations I have made in conducting this investigation. It may be interesting, however, in this connection, to refer briefly to an ante-mortem and post-mortem examination secured in one case, where the animal was supposed to be suffering from loco poisoning. The case in question was that of a cow four years old. During this time she had been pasturing on grounds where this weed grows. The poison is a slow one, acting year by year during the time of pasturing, so that the case may be under its influence several years before the poisoning results in death. I found this animal stunted in growth, and presenting all the symptoms of malnutrition. She seemed stupid, as though suffering from the influence of a narcotic, which by the way is said to be one of the symptoms of loco poisoning. Whether walking or standing, she was in constant tremor and seemed hardly able to stand from excessive weakness. It is not necessary to detail the results of the post-mortem examination. They will be found in the Transactions of the Kansas Academy of Science, Vol. X., page 69. Suffice it to say that the pathological condition found could be accounted for without attributing it to loco poisoning.

I have given a full description of the loco plant, and a report of its chemical examination in the publication above referred to, and in papers which have been published in the Biennial Report of the Kansas State Board of Agriculture, 1885 and 1886, and in a report of the meeting of the Kansas State Pharmaceutical Association for 1888, so it is not necessary to repeat them here, especially as the plant is sufficiently described in botanical manuals. I have, however, specimens with me of three leguminous plants, each of which in different localities is said to be loco.

The specimen which I show here, and to be loco weed, is one I found growing on the Rocky Mountains, and differs from the *Astragalus mollissimus* which is commonly recognized as the loco plant. The leaves are arranged differently, the pod is hairy, but in other respects it resembles the mollissimus. This specimen is probably *Astragalus Bigelovii*. The genus Astragalus is truly a western genus. East of the Mississippi there are about sixty-four. During the past summer it has been my object to specially study the geographical distribution of the plant. I have visited numerous sections of the country and had interviews with cattle- and ranchmen in different parts of the Indian Territory, No-man's land, the western part of Kansas, Colorado, and New Mexico. The plant in the State of Kansas begins to appear on the southern border about Medicine Lodge, at about the ninety-ninth meridian, extending into the Indian Territory, in almost a direct line south, and into the State of Kansas in rather a northwesterly direction, from this eastern boundary line, it grows plentifully until the mountains of Colorado are reached. And the growth of the plant assumes a considerable importance south of the Arkansas River, extending down nearly to the southern border of New Mexico, the western boundary line being indicated by about the one hundred and ninth meridian.

In this area there are found three distinct plants of this order having physical resemblances which are known as loco. The most important one is the *Astragalus mollissimus*, the second the *Oxytropis Lamberti*, and the third which I have mentioned, which is probably the *Astragalus Bigelorii*, I have had sent to me. However, numerous other weeds claim to be genuine loco. Among them are *Malvastrum coccineum*, *Sophora sericea*, and *Amarantus altus*.*

It is most important to state that no toxic effect was observable when the plant was administered to frogs, cats, dogs, or the human species. This does not correspond with the observation made by Dr. Isaac Ott, however. His experiments were conducted with a preparation consisting of an acidulus aqueous solution, obtained by evaporating the alcoholic tincture, and exhausting the extract remaining with water acidulated with acetic acid. Dr. Ott's experiments seem to indicate toxic properties.

Feeling very certain that the specimens which I had secured possessed no poisonous properties, after testing on animals, I concluded to try some experiments on myself. Commencing cautiously with a dose of 15 minims of an alcoholic preparation of the strength of a fluid extract, which I took every three hours, I gradually increased the dose to two teaspoonfuls, and would have continued had it not been for the disagreeable effects of the alcohol. A tablespoonful of the preparation, made according to the plan pursued by Dr. Ott, produced no noticeable effect, except possibly that of slight uneasy sensation in the stomach and a slight undefinable sensation in the head.

It will be seen, then, that in spite of all the dangerous properties ascribed to loco weed, it is probably possessed of no poisonous properties whatever. In passing, I may say, I am confirmed in this opinion by Mr. Kennedy, who has recently written from San Antonio (*Pharm. Record*, July, 1888). The results, therefore, will be observed to have been negative. But they have been more or less instructive and important. If I shall be able finally to prove beyond all peradventure that loco weed has no poisonous property whatsoever, I shall have very forcibly illustrated the point of this paper, namely, the vast importance to the public of a thorough scientific investigation which the professional pharmacist should be able to make.

The majority of mankind draw this conclusion from hearsay evidence without investigation. In this case the evidence has been of such a nature that the legislature of Colorado was evidently deceived, although it must be supposed that this body contained men of great wisdom and judgment.

Then, too, observe the amount and extent of the investigation necessary to determine a point which any one not acquainted with the unreliability of hearsay evidence would naturally suppose could be settled without any difficulty whatever. Even now, after my laborious and expensive work upon it, the point cannot be accepted as a settled one, whether loco is poisonous to cattle or not. Changes in food often seriously affect stock, as is well known, and it may be possible that cattle who have been deprived of green food, and half-starved all winter, when they are turned out to luxuriant pasturage in the spring, are affected with indigestion and the evils of malassimilation on account of overfeeding; and this particular plant may be of such a character as to produce these symptoms in a very natural way, on account of its peculiar nature as a food, as I have pointed out in former papers. In this connection, the State veterinarian of Kansas has written a paper, which was published in the *Globe Democrat*, calling attention to the subject of "Equine Dyspepsia," in which he refers to nervous phenomena, which I would observe might easily be attributed among the unenlightened to poisonous food and charged to loco. . . .

Chicago College of Pharmacy.—At the meeting held September 18th, $20,000 were appropriated for current expenses, and the announcement was made that the Illinois Pharmaceutical Association had accepted the transfer to it in trust of the College. Mr. C. S. Hallberg was elected a trustee to take the place of Mr. F. M. Schmidt resigned.

* See papers on Loco Weeds in NEW REMEDIES, 1879, 880; 1880, 67.—ED. AM. DRUG.

A WIRE-GAUZE HEATING FRAME.

WHEN a considerable number of flasks, etc., are to be heated or kept warm at the same time, the apparatus devised by F. Muck, and here illustrated, may be employed. It consists of a frame made of hoop or band iron, standing upon four legs, and having a double top of wire gauze, the upper one being made in sections which may be hinged back. The wire gauze has thirty meshes to one lineal inch. The distance between the two wire-gauze surfaces is one and one-eighth inch. Flasks, beakers, etc., set upon the lower wire gauze, are heated strongly, those set on the upper one only moderately.—*Chem. Zeit.*

Muck's wire-gauze heating frame.

AN IMPROVED SIPHON.

THE siphon here shown was exhibited to a reporter of the *Pharmaceutische Zeitung* by the firm of L. Barthels of Hamburg.

The siphon is filled by dipping leg A into the liquid, closing the stop-cock at D, and then pouring enough liquid into the funnel C to fill the interior completely. On closing C and opening D, the flow will continue automatically.

An improved siphon.

Isatropyl-Cocaine, a Secondary Alkaloid in Coca.

PROF. C. LIEBERMANN some time ago received from Dr. Fritz Giesel about one kilogramme of an amorphous base obtained as a secondary product in the manufacture of cocaine from coca leaves. This represented that portion of the entire amount of secondary bases which resisted the action of permanganate. It appeared in form of a yellow, tough, sticky mass, from which the alkaloidal base could be easily extracted. The crude mass was dissolved in dilute hydrochloric acid, the solution filtered, and the latter carefully shaken with ether, which removed considerable quantities of oil of bitter almonds. From the solution of the hydrochlorate of the alkaloid, the remaining ether was expelled by a strong current of cold air, since it had been ascertained that the application of heat to expel the ether would be improper, as it caused a partial decomposition of the alkaloid. From the remaining aqueous solution, the alkaloid may now be precipitated by solution of soda or ammonia. It appears then in form of a white, cretaceous, amorphous substance, which may easily be dried upon previously ignited porcelain to a snowy white, loose powder. Since it was doubtful whether the substance was homogeneous throughout, and neither the base nor its salts could be crystallized, it was redissolved, and precipitated in fractions. The middle fraction was the main one used for the investigation, but the preceding and ulterior fractions did not appear to be materially different. The middle fraction amounted to about 70 per cent of the original quantity. In the course of the preparation of this purified fraction, it was found that the original crude alkaloid contained about 1 to 2 per cent of ecgonine.

The selected middle fraction was once more dissolved, again precipitated, and the precipitate examined for ash, when it was found that there was no difficulty whatever in depriving it of the inorganic salts generated during solution in an acid and precipitation by a base.

The base had a great resemblance to cocaine, except that it was amorphous (also its salts). It is easily soluble in the cold, in alcohol, ether, benzol, and chloroform, and on evaporating these solutions, it remains behind as a resin. In petroleum ether, however, it is difficultly soluble, wherein it differs greatly from cocaine, which is notably soluble in this liquid and crystallizes from it in handsome needles, while the above alkaloid remains behind in an amorphous condition. The author therefore used petroleum ether to free the amorphous base from traces of cocaine. Ammonia also dissolves cocaine more readily than the amorphous alkaloid.

Among tests given by the author, the following may be mentioned. Picric acid produces a yellow precipitate. Chromic acid causes an orange red one; permanganate, even in dilute solutions of the sulphate, a violet precipitate, gradually passing into red and brown, even in the cold, without the development of the odor of oil of bitter almonds. Mercuric and stannic chloride produce white, gold chloride yellow, platinic chloride very light colored, amorphous, heavy flakes which can be well washed. The alcoholic solution of the base exhibits no alkaline reaction with phenolphthalein.

Prof. Liebreich examined the alkaloid physiologically and found it to be an *active poison*. Possibly it is the cause of certain toxic symptoms sometimes observed when impure cocaine is administered. In effect it resembles neither cocaine nor atropine; it is a cardiac poison, and has no influence upon the sensory nerves.

Prof. Liebermann's attention was at this time drawn to several papers of Dr. Hesse, in the *Pharm. Zeitung* (1887, 407; 668), in which the latter announces the existence in coca of two amorphous bases, which he calls cocamine and cocmidine, and which he states have the same ultimate composition as cocaine. At first, Prof. Liebermann thought that his base was identical with one of these, but subsequent investigation showed that his base was entirely different, and, besides, had the composition $C_{18}H_{19}NO_3$, while cocaine and Hesse's amorphous alkaloids correspond to $C_{17}H_{21}NO_4$.

To determine the constitution of the body, Prof. Liebermann heated a portion of it with concentrated hydrochloric acid in a sealed tube. It was, however, soon found that the same decomposition could be brought about by heating the base for one hour in an open flask, with reflux-condenser, in contact with diluted hydrochloric or diluted (10%) sulphuric acid. Indeed, the base is so extremely sensitive towards mineral acids that if a solution of it with an excess of strong hydrochloric acid is allowed to stand at the ordinary temperature, decomposition (observable through the separation of crystalline organic acids) proceeds already during the first 24 hours, and is complete after 14 days.

It was found that one product of the decomposition was methyl. This could be collected in form of methyl-alcohol, by boiling the base for some time with diluted sulphuric acid under a reflux-condenser. Under the influence of certain acids, the decomposition is accompanied by peculiar phenomena. If the base be boiled with hydrochloric acid (sp. gr. 1.100), the solution remains clear for about half an hour. Suddenly, insoluble acids will begin to separate and in a few minutes the contents of the flask will be a thick magma. The reaction is then soon terminated.

The separated acid was found to be composed of two distinct acids, which were examined by Prof. Liebermann and found to be very closely resembling the alpha- and beta-isatropic acids, discovered by Losson and Fittig. He denominated them, respectively, gamma- and delta-isatropic acid. Both have the same composition, $C_9H_7O_2$, but different properties. Their relationship to atropic acid remains to be cleared up. It will be noticed that these acids contain no nitrogen, the whole of this remaining in the other product of the decomposition. To isolate this, the solution (in which alkalies produced no precipitate, showing that the base was soluble in water) was evaporated to dryness, and the crystalline mass freed from adhering liquid upon porous porcelain. It was now found that, if the attempt was made to use soda for setting the base free, the latter was injured. Hence Prof. Liebermann used oxide of silver to accomplish this (of course, the acid in combination with the base was hydrochloric, which forms insoluble chloride of silver with the oxide). On final separation, the base was obtained in clear colorless crystals, and turned out to be ecgonine, $C_9H_{15}NO_3$.

As a general result of the investigation, it may be stated that the crude base originally taken in operation was found to consist of equal molecules of methyl alcohol, isatropic acids, and ecgonine.

When cocaine is split up by decomposition, benzoic acid appears as the acid product. In the case of the alkaloid above described, isatropic acid takes the place of benzoic. For this reason, the author has named it *isatropyl cocaine*.

The author proposes to prepare synthetical cocaines by varying the acid.

In a postscript the author announces that he, in conjunction with Dr. Giesel, have recently found that other secondary alkaloids of coca also easily yield ecgonine as a decomposition product under the influence of acids. They have also succeeded—against the statement of Merck, who failed to succeed—in converting ecgonine into benzoyl-ecgonine, and they expect, by employing Einhorn's method of converting benzoyl-ecgonine into cocaine, to devise a technical process for converting ecgonine into cocaine. [This would enable manufacturers to turn a useless by-product into an article of value.]

English-distilled Oil of Japanese Peppermint.

Mr. JOHN MOSS, F.C.S., read the following paper at the late meeting of the British Pharm. Conference:

I have recently distilled 205 lbs. of green herb of Mentha arvensis, grown partly in my garden, close to the Mitcham peppermint fields, and partly in a garden four miles farther away. This is the plant which yields Japanese oil of peppermint. The original slips were kindly furnished by Mr. Thomas Christy about two years ago.

The yield was 4 ounces, being about ⅛ of 1 per cent, somewhat less than half the yield obtained at Mitcham. Had the plants been allowed to remain till in full bloom in September, the yield would no doubt have been much greater, but having grown so luxuriantly as to be somewhat of a nuisance, they were collected Aug. 14th, when they had attained a height of three feet, and distilled on the 16th.

The oil, after standing for a week, was brilliant, and had a decided yellow color. The specific gravity at 62° F. was 0.9107.

When determining the boiling point, a light shower of very minute bubbles began to ascend at 339° F.; at 342° F., the shower was closer and remained steady for a quarter of a minute; at 369° F., it was still denser and composed of larger bubbles, and stayed quite half a minute; at 402° F., with the barometer at 30 in., there was a steady tropical rain of large bubbles, which continued for ten minutes, and the boiling point was deemed to be determined.

The specific gravity of the oil, after determining the boiling point, was found to be 0.9117 at 62° F.

Other specimens of oil distilled in England from imported herb, which was, of course, dry, were different in appearance and physical properties from that distilled by myself. They were some months, at least, older. One labelled "Nou-roct," was distinctly green, and had a specific gravity of 0.9167 at 62° F.; a second labelled "Heck," was pale in color, with a faint green tinge, and had a specific gravity of 0.9098. They were fatter-looking oils than mine, and no doubt owed to their higher gravity and greater viscosity to resinification by age.

The specific gravity of these three oils confirms Todd's generalization that the specific gravity of pure oils falls between 0.908 and 0.917. Each of them is miscible with any proportion of rectified spirit. The odor of the oil from English-grown herb was much more powerful and penetrating, yet softer, than that distilled from imported herbs.

None of the three oils gives any coloration when subjected to the test given by Todd. It consists in adding 1 drop of oil to a mixture of 25 drops of alcohol with 1 drop of nitric acid, 1½. After a longer or shorter interval, sometimes a few hours, a permanent blue or bluish-green color is developed if oil from M. piperita be used. The test is exceedingly delicate. It is unfortunate that we possess none for the cheap Japan oil and can only, after many experiments, estimate the proportion of it in a mixture by the weakened response of the true oil present. The object of this note is to place on record certain characters of Japan oil of peppermint of undoubted genuineness.—*After Chem. and Drugg.*

On Sublimate Dressings and their Gradual Deterioration.

M. HAUPT, of Varel, Germany, writes on the above subject in the *Pharm. Centralhalle* (Sept. 20th). His paper presents several new and important facts, which are here given in abstract.

The author's attention having been drawn to the apparent gradual deterioration of sublimate dressings, he first prepared a series of strictly standard dressings in accordance with the army medical regulations, and afterwards subjected them periodically to analysis. Among all processes proposed for such an assay, he found C. Donner's method (conversion of the sublimate into sulphide, and of the latter into iodide, by means of normal solution of iodine) the most advantageous.

For the purpose of extracting the prepared fabrics, the latter are introduced into large, wide-mouthed bottles, a weighed quantity of hot distilled water is added, and the whole well stirred with a glass rod. After half an hour, the liquid is pressed out, and a definite part of it—taking in consideration the amount of glycerin contained in it—is weighed off. When the amount of liquid adhering to the fabric has thus been determined, the latter is replaced in the bottle, strong chlorine water is added, and afterwards enough distilled water to restore the previous weight. When this second maceration has been continued some time, the liquid is pressed out, and the sublimate estimated in such a quantity of the united liquids, as corresponds to one-half of the total quantity added.

The result, of course, corresponds to one-half of the weight of the fabric. But a correction must be made for the amount (one-half) of sublimate which failed to be extracted by the first maceration, and was converted into sublimate, and extracted by the second step of the process.

Next follows the determination of the mercury, for which the author prefers Denner's method. [But almost any of the usual methods of estimating mercury will answer, in our judgment.—Ed. Am. Dr.]

The author next gives a table which shows the quantities of sublimate he obtained by the first and second maceration, respectively, in a various dressings, namely: 1, sublimated cotton; 2, sublimated mull, and 3, sublimated gauze.

All samples were made at the same time, containing 0.4 per cent of sublimate. The series II. was examined when a month older than series I.; III. was examined a month after II; IV. was examined after five months, and V. after seven months. The letters *a* and *b* denote, respectively, the first (a) and second (b) extraction.

		Cotton, $\% HgCl_2$	Mull, $\% HgCl_2$	Gauze, $\% HgCl_2$
I.	a.	0.298	0.257	0.215
	b.	0.030	0.072	0.112
II.	a.	0.272	0.204	0.192
	b.	0.054	0.122	0.135
III.	a.	0.217	0.187	0.185
	b.	0.108	0.138	0.184
IV.	a.	0.189	0.169	0.073
	b.	0.136	0.155	0.246
V.	a.	0.161	0.129	0.068
	b.	0.158	0.191	0.251

On examining these figures, it will be noticed that, on adding a and b of each set together, there was never found more than 0.33 per cent, instead of 0.4 per cent, of sublimate. The author suspected that the balance was lost by evaporation during the drying. Experiments specially made for this purpose showed him that, on drying such impregnated fabrics by exposure to air, about 16 per cent of the employed sublimate is lost by volatilization. For a quantity of 0.4 per cent, this amounts to about 0.065, leaving 0.335 per cent, almost exactly the highest amount actually found.

It will also be noticed that the loss of sublimate and the rate of its reduction increases by time. The rate of reduction [to calomel probably] was most pronounced in the case of sublimate gauze, which contained after seven months only about one-fourth of the original quantity undecomposed.

The author found that sublimate dressings prepared with the aid of chloride of sodium or tartaric acid, though they lost some mercury during the drying process, yet retained all the mercury in a soluble form even after three months.

Notes on National Formulary Preparations.

(Continued from page 164.)

Form. 390, *Warburg's Tincture* and 290, *Warburg's Pills*. Mr. Theodor Louis, of New York, draws our attention to a discrepancy between the amount of aloes in equivalent quantities of the tincture (N. F., No. 390) and the pills (No. 290). He writes: "In the tincture 'with aloes,' 28 grains of aqueous extract of aloes is directed to be added to 16 fl. oz., while in the pills there is 1 grain of the extract in about 5 grains of mass. Would not ½ grain be more in harmony with the proportion of aloes in the tincture?"

Our friend and correspondent is quite correct in his criticism. If 1 pint of the tincture is to contain 28 grains of aqueous extract of aloes, then one of the pills, made with ingredients in the same proportion as the tincture, should contain ½ grain of the extract.

There is, however, something more to be said about those preparations. The original formula of Dr. Warburg directed just 4 times as much Socotrine aloes as of rhubarb or angelica. Hence, to make one gallon of the tincture "with aloes," for which formula No. 390, I., directs 448 grains of rhubarb, 1,792 grains of Socotrine Aloes would be required. Or, reckoning that Socotrine Aloes yields 25 per cent of aqueous extract, 448 grains of the aqueous extract would be required for 1 gallon of tincture; hence 56 grains for 1 pint. Now formula 390, II., directs only 28 grains. This figure has been chosen because information reached the committee that this was the quantity usually employed by prominent manufacturers, owing to recommendations of physicians who found the preparation too intensely bitter when made with the full amount of aloes. On the basis of 56 grains of extract of aloes for each pint of tincture, the quantity of extract in the pill (No. 290) would be ½ grain; but, when the strength in extract of aloes is reduced one-half, that is, on the basis of 28 grains to the pint, the quantity in *one* pill should be ¼ grain.

2. *Acidum Carbolicum Iodatum.*

It will be necessary either to reduce the amount of iodine or to omit the glycerin, as the former does not all remain in solution when the preparation becomes cold.

54. *Elixir Eriodictyi Aromaticum.*

It will be well to note the fact that 1 fluidrachm of this preparation is about the proper quantity to cover the bitter taste of 5 grains of Sulphate of Quinine.

AN IMPROVED FUNNEL FOR AUTOMATIC WASHING OF PRECIPITATES.

G. Neumann has devised the funnel shown in the accompanying illustration for the automatic washing of precipitates. The funnel *T* is closed on top by means of a ground cover, *D*. The wash-fluid flows from a reservoir through the tube passing through the cover against the upper inside wall of the funnel, or within contained filter. The funnel is set into a flask connected with the filter pump, and the latter so regulated that a uniform level of liquid is maintained in the filter.—*Chem. Centralb.*, No. 38.

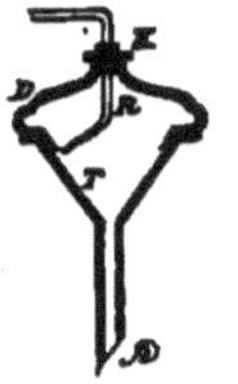

Neumann's washing funnel.

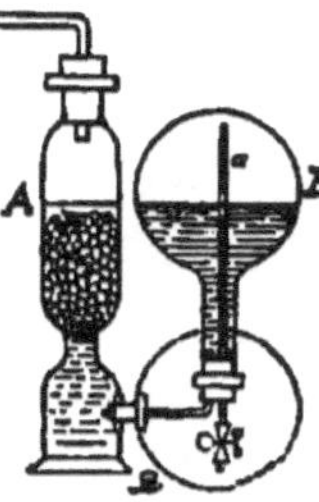

Sulphuretted hydrogen generator.

SULPHURETTED HYDROGEN GENERATOR.

P. Chautemille uses the apparatus here shown, in which the connecting tube between the two parts must necessarily be quite strong, much more so than the cut would indicate.

When the generator *A* is to be filled with sulphide of iron, the flask *B*, which contains the acid, is brought to a horizontal position. When gas is wanted, the flask is raised, as shown in the cut, whereupon the acid will rise in the generator until it reaches the sulphide. The flask may be emptied of liquid by opening the stop-cock at the neck.—*Chem. Centralb.*

Clarifying.

Clarification is a process by which any solid particles suspended in a liquid are either caused to coalesce together or to adhere to the medium used for clarifying, that they may be removed by filtration (which would previously have been impossible), so as to render the liquid clear.

One of the best agents for this purpose is albumen. When clarifying vegetable extracts, the albumen which is naturally present in most plants accomplishes the purpose easily, provided the vegetable matter is extracted in the cold, so as to get as much albumen as possible in solution.

Egg-albumen may also be used. The effect of albumen may be increased by the addition of cellulose, in form of a fine magma of filtering paper. This has the further advantage that the subsequent filtration is much facilitated.

Suspended particles of gum or pectin may be removed by cautious precipitation with tannin, of which only an exceedingly small amount is usually necessary. It combines with the gelatinous substances better with the aid of heat than in the cold. There must be no excess of tannin used.

Another method of clarifying liquids, turbid from particles of gum, albumen, pectin, etc., is to add to them a definite quantity of alcohol. This causes the former substances to separate in more or less large flakes. The quantity of alcohol required varies greatly according to the nature of the liquid. It should be determined in each case by an experiment on a small scale.

Resinous or waxy substances, such as are occasionally met with in honey, etc., may be removed by the addition of bole, pulped filtering paper, and heating to boiling.

In each case, the clarifying process may be hastened by making the separating particles specifically heavier, that is, by incorporating some heavier substance, such as talcum, etc., which may cause the flocculi to sink more rapidly, and to form a compact sediment.

Clarifying Powder for Alcoholic Liquids.

Egg-albumen, dry	40 parts
Sugar of Milk	40 "
Starch	20 "

Reduce them to very fine powder, and mix thoroughly.

For clarifying liquors, wines, essences, etc., take for every quart of liquid seventy-five grains of the above mixture, shake repeatedly in the course of a few days, the mixture being kept in a warm room. Then filter.

Powdered talcum renders the same service, and has the additional advantage of being entirely insoluble. However, the above mixture acts more energetically.—Eugene Dieterich, in *Neues Pharm. Manuale* (Ed. II.).

The Detection of Cotton-Seed Oil in Lard, etc.

FROM a paper on this subject, by Mr. Michael Conroy, read at the late meeting of the British Pharmaceutical Conference at Bath, we take the following passages, with the remark that, in our estimation, it is quite as necessary to examine the purity of the lard, for medicinal purposes, sold on our market, as that which is exported abroad.

"Fortunately, the presence of cotton-seed oil in lard is easily detected, and my object in bringing the matter under your notice is to lay before you some of the tests that I have myself tried. The first is the nitric acid test, which some years ago I had the honor of reading a paper on before the Liverpool Chemists' Association in connection with the adulteration of olive oils. It consists in heating and stirring well about ½ oz. of lard with one tenth its weight of strong nitric acid (sp. gr. 1.420) in a porcelain dish of about 8 oz. capacity, until brisk action commences, when it should be removed from the source of heat. Pure lard sets in about an hour to a pale orange-colored solid like citrine ointment; but if adulterated with cotton-seed oil, it takes a more or less deep orange-brown tint, according to the extent to which it is present. There are two drawbacks to this test, the first being that lard sometimes contains a small amount of water which reduces the strength of the acid, causing the action to be less energetic and thus leading to error. The second is that the difference in color between pure and adulterated samples is not sufficiently definite when the adulterant is under 5 per cent.

I have also tried the test proposed by M. Labiche, who says that when cotton-seed oil is treated with subacetate of lead and caustic alkali, it gives almost immediately an orange-red reaction. The author mixes equal parts of the oil and a saturated solution of neutral acetate of lead and adds ammonia, stirring briskly. The acetate of lead decomposes, and the nascent oxide reacts upon the oil, causing it to turn red. If 20 per cent of cotton-seed oil be present, the sample is said to turn red at once, lesser quantities show after some time. In my hands this test has proved an utter failure, but I think it may be due to the fact that the cotton-seed oil which I used in my experiments was highly refined; and it is quite possible that the crude oil would give this reaction.

The next test is by Ernest Milliare, and was proposed by him for the detection of cotton-seed oil in olive oil. It is an excellent test and quite applicable to lard. It is as follows: In a porcelain capsule, holding about 1 liter, 15 C.c. of the sample in question are heated to 110°. Then, whilst still continuing the heat, we pour upon the oil a mixture of 15 C.c. of a solution of soda of 30° Beaumé in distilled water, and of 15 C.c. of alcohol of 92 per cent. When the mass has become homogeneous, we add drop by drop, so as not to cool the paste and form clots, about ¼ liter of distilled water. After boiling for a few minutes, the fatty acids are separated by means of pure sulphuric acid diluted to one-tenth. As soon as the separation is complete and the sulphuric acid is in slight excess 5 C.c. of the hydrated fatty acids are collected with a silver spoon and poured at once into a test tube, about 3 Cm. in diameter and 12 in length. We add 20 C.c. of alcohol of 92 per cent, and heat slightly in the water-bath to dissolve the fatty acids. When the solution is effected, 2 C.c. of a solution of silver nitrate (30 Gms. in 100 C.c. of distilled water) are added, the tube is placed in a water-bath and heated until about one-third of the mass is evaporated. The tube is then removed from the water-bath. Whatever the origin of the sample, its fatty acids remain unaltered if the sample be pure. But if cotton oil is present, the silver is reduced and blackens the fatty acids which rise to the surface. In this manner, 1 per cent of cotton seed oil can be detected in olive oil.

In using this test for lard, instead of for olive oil, as intended by its author, a brown coloration, instead of a black one, is obtained in samples containing cotton-seed oil, while pure samples remain perfectly white, and I find it better, instead of adding the ¼ liter of cold water "drop by drop," to use boiling water. For delicacy and reliability this test leaves nothing to be desired, and its only drawback is the time it takes to perform.

Another test for the detection of cotton-seed in olive oil, dependent upon the nitrate-of-silver reaction, is given by Becchi as follows: 5 C.c. of the oil are mixed with 25 C.c. of 98 per cent alcohol and 5 C.c. of silver-nitrate solution (prepared by dissolving 1 Gm. of the nitrate in 100 C.c. of 98 per cent alcohol); the mixture is heated to 84° C. If cotton-seed oil be present, the mixture becomes colored; but not so if the oil be genuine. It is necessary to avoid heating by the direct flame, as other oils which may be present, such as linseed, colza, etc., will give colorations.

This, unlike the previous test, is not quite suitable for the detection of cotton-seed oil in lard, because lard sometimes contains traces of sodium carbonate, due to the fact that this substance is commonly used in washing lard that has become rancid. Slight traces of sodium carbonate decompose the silver nitrate, and the subsequent heating reduces it, causing samples of genuine lard to become darkened in such a manner that they might possibly be condemned as impure.

For several weeks past I have tried these and other tests with the object of finding the most reliable and expeditious, and my experience is that those dependent upon the reduction of silver nitrate are the best, and the following *modus operandi* has given me results that are entirely satisfactory and reliable, and only requires a few minutes' time:

1. Make a test solution containing 5 parts of silver nitrate and 1 part of nitric acid (sp. gr. 1.42) in 100 parts of rectified spirit (sp. gr. .838).

2. Melt a small quantity of the lard to be tested in a water-bath and pour about 100 grains of it into a dry test tube, about half an inch in diameter. To this add 20 grain measures of the above-mentioned test solution and place the tube in boiling water for five minutes, taking care that no water enters it.

Pure lard remains perfectly white, but if adulterated with cotton-seed oil, it assumes a more or less olive-brown color, according to the amount present. The color is best seen when the lard sets, and it saves time to put the test tube direct from the boiling water into a vessel of cold water.

The presence of 5 per cent of cotton-seed oil in lard gives a very decided olive-brown coloration with this test, and 1 per cent gives a color quite distinct from genuine lard. The addition of nitric acid to the test solution is intended to neutralise any traces of alkali or alkaline carbonate that may be present, and it also prevents a slight reduction of the silver nitrate which takes place in genuine lard. It must not be forgotten that some samples of lard might possibly contain sodium chloride, though I have never met with any, in which case the silver nitrate would be precipitated as chloride instead of reacting on the oil, but this would be at once seen by the white, curdy precipitate that would be formed."

Notes on Oil of Rose.

AN Austrian pharmacist who recently spent a holiday by traversing Bulgaria on a bicycle writes to the *Pharmaceutische Post* the following particulars concerning the distillation and adulteration of otto of roses. The distilling apparatus generally used in the country consists of a copper container, and the distillation product is cooked in large wooden vats. One of the largest firms in Kezanlik once tried to introduce modern distilling apparatus, such as is employed in large distilleries in Germany and elsewhere, but it was found impracticable in use. Red roses are used almost exclusively for distilling, because they yield an oil of sweeter aroma, being richer in the aromatic principle of essential oils. But in order to obtain a more easily solidifiable oil, freezing at 14° C., a certain percentage of white roses is added to the red ones, such a mixture yielding a product richer in stearopten than the other. For adulteration, geranium oil, procured from Constantinople, is most frequently used. The oils are not mixed directly, but the rose-flowers are sprinkled with the geranium oil before distillation, and the adulterant is thus more intimately mixed with the genuine oil than could be the case otherwise. To make this manipulation successful, a majority of white flowers must be used. The distillers are exclusively Bulgarians, mostly small men, although they count among their number a few large wholesale dealers, among whom Papasoglou, of Kesanlik, and Stransky and Kolmschieff, of Carlowo, are especially mentioned.—*Chem. and Drugg.*

Against the general expectation, the yield of otto of rose in Bulgaria has been a very good one this season, amounting to about 85,000 oz. The weather during the distilling period (May 22d to June 20th) and that which immediately preceded it was so favorable that an average weight of 9 okka of flowers sufficed to yield one miscal (nearly 5 grammes) of otto, while, as a rule, 12 okka of flowers are required to produce that quantity. Prices are rather lower than last season, partly because of the heavy old stock which is still held by the principal dealers, and also because the export outlook is very unfavorable, Turkey, the principal buyer, having now put a customs duty of 8 per cent *ad valorem* on otto of rose, which was formerly admitted duty free. Moreover, the Bulgarian and East-Roumelian emigrants who have settled in the Turkish vilayets of Adrianople and Broussa have founded rose plantations there, which already commence to compete severely with those in Bulgaria.

Delicate Test for Physostigmine.

IN a paper on physostigmine (in *Pharm. Zeit.*, August 15th) Mr. Eber states that chloride of gold, or the double iodide of potassium and bismuth, or the double iodide of potassium and zinc, precipitate this alkaloid even from an extremely dilute solution of the sulphate. If the precipitation is effected on a white plate or capsule, and only 0.000001 Gm. ([illegible] grain) of the salt is present, the precipitate may still be recognized. This chemical test is, therefore, much more delicate than a physiological test. On placing in contact with one drop of a solution of the salt, containing the before-mentioned minute quantity, a drop of a 5-per-cent solution of potassa or soda, a red color will be noticed at the point of contact, due to the formation of rubreserine. When the drop dries, a yellow film is left, which dissolves again with a red color in water. If baryta water is used instead of potassa or soda, a carmine color will first be produced, and this will afterwards change to blue.

A Curious Stink Plant.

WHEN Mr. G. A. Farini, on his return from an exploring tour of the Kalahari Desert in South Africa (see note on page 217 of this number), arrived at Upington, he was shown a plant without leaves, resembling a cactus, the fleshy stems growing in a bunch, with a border of flowers about ten inches across, and looking as if cut out of purple-brown velvet, marked throughout with bright golden hieroglyphics. This plant was called by Mrs. Scott, the wife of the resident commissioner, the "carrion plant," and it well deserved this name, for when disturbed it emitted an odor which was perfectly unendurable. Mr. Farini had already come across the plant on his route through the desert. At one time he was attracted towards it by the brilliant golden markings on the deep, rich-toned flower head. He dug up a specimen, but as soon as it was disturbed, it threw out such a sickly odor that he nearly gave up the job in disgust. However, he persevered, and put it into the wagon, but it soon protested against the jolting of the vehicle, and emitted such a pungent stench that the driver had to get out and walk. When they halted, it was placed behind a bush, and even then its odor made Mr. Farini's companion "sea-sick," and made the former so drowsy that he was obliged to bury it bodily beneath the sand. While doing this, the narcotic effect was so powerful that he nearly fell asleep. The second time when he encountered the plant, he was inclined to give it a wide berth, but he brought home some small specimens which were placed in the charge of the authorities at Kew Gardens. According to the appendix attached to Mr. Farini's work (page 449), the plant is a species of Stapelia. Further information on this interesting plant is much desirable, and will probably be furnished by the botanists at Kew.

Salicylic Acid as a Preservative of Volumetric Solutions.

A RECOMMENDATION made some 13 years ago by F. Mohr, but apparently overlooked, has been renewed by Hugo Bornträger, viz., to add salicylic acid to volumetric solutions with a view to their preservation. Many of these solutions owe their decomposition to micrococci existing in the distilled water.

As an example, the author mentions volumetric solution of hyposulphite of sodium, which is known to be one of the most unstable solutions, and which had been treated with a small quantity of salicylic acid ("as much as the point of a knife will hold, for every liter"). In the course of 6 weeks it was frequently tested and found to have preserved its titer decidedly better than without the preservative.—After *Zeitsch. f. anal. Chem.*, 1888, 641.

Antidote against Bite of Poisonous Serpents.

MR. G. A. FARINI, the explorer of the Kalahari Desert in South Africa (see note on page 217 of this number), relates that some of his oxen had been bitten by poisonous snakes, whereupon one of his bushmen undertook to cure them. He took a knife, made one or two incisions round the place where the bite was, which was easily seen by the swelling, and rubbed in a powder which he said was made from the dried poison-sacs of another snake. In a few hours the swelling had entirely subsided, and the cattle were as well as their half-starved state would allow them to be. Mr. Farini expressed a doubt whether this "cure" would be efficient in man, but the bushman asserted that it was. On the very next day the bushman was bitten by a full-grown capell or "spuugh slange." Coolly taking out some dried poison-sacs, he reduced them to a powder, pricked his foot near the puncture with a knife, and rubbed the virus powder in just as he had done with the cattle. Then he extracted the fangs of the freshly-killed snake, drank a drop of the poison from the virus sac, and fell into a stupor which lasted some hours. At first the swelling increased rapidly, but after a time it began to subside, and next morning he inoculated himself again. That night the swelling had disappeared, and in four days he was as well as ever.

At Mier Mr. Farini obtained information from Mr. Halliburton of another antidote, in the shape of an animal, a little saurian, called the N'auboo. Every bastard or half-breed, and every native in that region carries it in a dried and powdered state. The animal is a little lizard, with rather short legs, but capable of moving along at a great speed. It is supposed to be the most deadly of all reptiles, save the little worm called Kameroo. The natives pay a big price for them, often paying an ox for one. There is hardly a bastard in that part of the country who has not some N'auboo, in case either man or beast is bitten by a snake. It is said never to have been known to fail. The whole of the animal is dried and reduced to powder. When any one is bitten by a snake, some incisions are made near the bite, and the powder rubbed in. The swelling ("even in extreme cases") will gradually subside. When the natives have no N'auboo, they use the poison of any snake in a similar manner.

Mr. Halliburton assured Mr. Farini that he had often seen it applied, and always with success. Mr. Farini asked whether it might not amount to the same thing if a traveller were to carry along with him a live poisonous snake, so as to have the latter produce a second bite near one inflicted on the road by a stray snake. This question was probably asked to test Mr. Halliburton's veracity or intelligence. The latter replied that he did not know whether this would answer the same purpose; he at least would not want to try it, but he had positive evidence of the good effects of N'auboo.

Mr. Farini only succeeded in obtaining the head portion of one of these animals, which he brought back to England. This has been placed into the hands of competent authorities on the continent of Europe for physiological investigation.

Note on the Conversion of Hyoscyamine into Atropine.

FROM a lengthy paper by W. Will and G. Bredig on the conversion of hyoscyamine into atropine by contact with bases, in which the effect of the latter as to intensity, duration, etc., is principally studied by means of the polariscope, we take a few passages, giving some of the results obtained by the authors.

1. The conversion of hyoscyamine into atropine by bases is a purely catalytic reaction, analogous to the inversion of cane-sugar.

2. Besides this catalytic action, there is a very slow secondary reaction, consisting in the splitting up of atropine (in the cold) into tropine and tropic acid. In more concentrated solutions, this secondary reaction takes place somewhat more quickly.

3. Atropine is an optically active base, turning the plane of polarized light slightly to the left. Approximately, $[\alpha]_D = -1.69$. If it is desired to obtain atropine as free as possible from hyoscyamine, it is best treated, in the cold, with a very dilute solution of an alkali, until the optical properties are rendered constant. Conversion into the gold-salt, and recrystallization of the latter, is a less advisable process.

4. For manufacturers of hyoscyamine and atropine it may be of interest to know that, besides the fixed caustic alkalies, sodium carbonate also causes the conversion of the former into the latter base. Ammonia, on the other hand, produces the change more slowly than any other base so far examined.—After *Ber. d. D. Chem. Ges.*, 1888, 2,797.

Impurities in Reagents.

C. KRAUCH, in *Zeitsch. f. angew. Chem.*, discusses the purity of the reagents sold as "purissimum," "purum," "depuratum," etc., and shows that those terms, when applied to commercially pure chemicals, have really no definite meaning. The following is a list of "purissimum" chemicals examined and the impurities found:

Caustic potash.—Alumina, chlorine, sulphuric and nitric acids.
Caustic soda.—The same.
Ammonia.—Pyridine, pyrrol, occasionally copper and zinc.
Sodium carbonate.—Thiosulphate, arsenic, ammonia.
Sodium nitrite.—Generally pure (100 per cent).
Potassium nitrite.—Generally very impure (80 to 90 per cent).
Potassium nitrate.—Has been known to contain chlorate.
Sodium tungstate.—Chloride, sulphate, and carbonate of sodium.
Potassium chlorate.—Has been found to contain lead.
Potassium sulphocyanide.—Traces of iron and lead.
Lime.—Silica, alumina, iron oxide, and sulphuric acid.
Platinum chloride.—Often not completely soluble in alcohol.
Uranium nitrate.—Occasionally much sulphate.
Molybdic acid.—Always 10 to 20 per cent of ammonium salts.
Ammonium molybdate.—Frequently pure.
Hydrofluoric acid.—Usually not pure enough for analytical purposes.
Sulphuric acid.—Five per cent of ammonia has been found in "pure" acid.
Hydrochloric acid.—Nearly always traces of arsenic, sometimes organic chlorides.
Tartaric and citric acids.—Traces of iron, lead, lime, and sulphuric acid.
Oxalic acid.—Usually sulphuric acid and once ammonia.
Methyl alcohol.—One sample contained much acetone.
Ether.—Petroleum ether, hydroxylaldehyde.
Ferro- and ferricyanides of potash.—Usually pure.
Iodine.—Usually pure.
Nitric acid.—Usually pure.

The author, in conclusion, observes that most salts denominated in commerce "puriss.," etc., are usually impure. B. Fischer states that he had found lead and sulpuretted hydrogen in hydrochloric acid and tin in ammonia, and he, with Krauch, draws attention to the desirability of the use of standard methods, both of preparation and analysis, so that the manufacturer shall know what it is desired that he should produce, and the buyer what impurities are likely to be present.—*Journ. S. Chem. Ind.*

Delicate Test for Saccharin.

THE most delicate test for saccharin so far known is that discovered by Ira Remsen.

A minute quantity of saccharin is mixed with a little excess of resorcin and a few drops of sulphuric acid in a test tube. On heating, the mass turns yellow, red, then darkgreen, gives out a large amount of sulphurous acid, and swells up. The heat is then withdrawn for a short time, but reapplied again two or three times, so that the mass may swell up during each heat. It is then allowed to cool, diluted with water and supersaturated with an alkali. The resulting solution will have a reddish tint by transmitted light, and a strongly green fluorescence by reflected light. This reaction permits the detection of 0.001 Gm. (ab. $\frac{1}{64}$ grain) of saccharin in 5 or 6 quarts of liquid.

In order to separate the saccharin from articles of food, or drink, or medicinal mixtures, an excess of acid must be used, as the saccharin is present in form of a soluble alkali salt. Solid and difficultly soluble substances are powdered, moistened with a few cubic centimeters of dilute sulphuric or phosphoric acid, then dried and exhausted with ether. Wines and other similar liquids are acidulated and shaken at least twice with an equal volume of ether during one hour. If fats are present, these are removed, previous to acidulation, by means of petroleum ether.—*After Amer. Chem. Journ.* (The residue left by the etherial solution, if not sufficiently pure, may be got into aqueous solution by means of a dilute alkali, the solution filtered if necessary, and the saccharin separated by an acid and by ether as before. See also page 207.—ED. AM. DR.]

Antipyrin in Whooping-Cough.

DR. SONNENBERGER, of Worms, has drawn attention in the early part of this year to the remarkably beneficial effects of antipyrin as a remedy in whooping-cough. This announcement was made almost with reluctance, since antipyrin had already been blazoned forth almost as a cure-all, and it was known beforehand that any fresh announcements of new channels of its usefulness would be probably received with a shrug of the shoulder. And yet there seems to be no doubt now but that this remedy is one of the most reliable ones in the disease mentioned. This is not the place for an article on medical therapeutics, and those who wish to learn all the details of treatment and the mode of using the remedy should consult the author's original paper. But for the information of our readers, it may be stated that the author reports it to have the best effects when given as early in the disease as possible. If given in time, it causes the disease to "abort," so as to appear only as a mild bronchial catarrh. But even when administered in a subsequent stadium, it will quickly reduce the attack to a mild grade.

Quinine Mask.*

MR. L. F. STEVENS, who has spent a large amount of time and labor on the search for an efficient covering of the bitter taste of quinine, enumerates first the various propositions made by others, and afterwards turns to his own experiments, of which over 100 were made, and samples of a number of which were exhibited to the Committee on National Formulary. As it is not feasible to give an abstract of those experiments which were only intermediary, and as a satisfactory practical result was finally obtained, it will be sufficient to quote the latter. This is, indeed, the same formula as that adopted for the National Formulary, but it may be reprinted here for the benefit of those who have not yet received this work:

Elixir Eriodictyi Aromaticum.
Aromatic Elixir of Eriodictyon.
Aromatic Elixir of Yerba Santa; Elixir Corrigens.

Fluid Extract of Eriodictyon	1 fl. oz.
Syrup	8 fl. oz.
Pumice, in fine powder	½ fl. oz.
Carbonate of Magnesium	80 grains
Compound Elixir of Taraxacum,	
enough to make 16 fl. oz.	

Mix 7 fluidounces of Comp. Elixir of Taraxacum with the Syrup and Pumice, then add the Fluid Extract, and mix the whole thoroughly by agitation. Shake the mixture occasionally during a few hours, allow it to settle, and carefully decant the liquid into a funnel, the neck of which contains a pellet of absorbent cotton. Afterwards add the dregs and allow them to drain. To the filtrate add the Carbonate of Magnesium, and shake occasionally during several hours. Let the mixture stand at rest during 12 hours, if convenient, then decant the liquid, and filter it through paper. To the filtrate add enough Compound Elixir of Taraxacum, if necessary, to make 16 fluidounces.

Mr. Stevens adds the remark that the first treatment separates a bitter resin which remains upon the cotton filter, without injury to the other constituents of the yerba santa or to the aromatics. The after-treatment with magnesia neither adds to, nor detracts from the efficiency, merely causing the separation of some inert extractive matter and the solution of non-bitter resins, and aiding in producing a more elegant preparation.

Of this preparation, one fluid drachm mixed by agitation with 5 grains of sulphate of quinine, without the addition of any diluent or acid, will so cover the bitterness the quinine, that even an expert will scarcely detect it. Children take doses of 1, 2, or 3 grains of quinine, in this manner, like sweetmeats.

* Abstract of a paper entitled "Condensed Notes upon trials for a Quinine Mask," by Luther F. Stevens, of Brooklyn, read at the Detroit Meeting of the A. P. A.

Iodoform Bituminate.

"IODOFORM Bituminate" is the designation of a combination of iodoform and tar which is introduced as being devoid of the objectionable odor of the former substance. Dr. Ehrmann has used it in various cases of soft ulcers with good results. It occurs as a bronze-like powder, which seems to have a conspicuous odor of tar, and at the same time that of iodoform is not unrecognizable. It is difficult to say whether it is likely to have any extended application or not.—*Chem. and Drugg.*

Ptomaines as Constituents of Urine in Cystinuria.

In a paper published in the *Berichte der Deutschen Chem. Ges.* (1888, p. 2,744), under a title ("Das Benzoylchlorid als Reagens") which does not allude to the most important portion of the paper, L. v. Udránsky and E. Baumann announce the general applicability of benzoyl chloride as a means of separating polyatomic alcohols from their dilute aqueous solutions.

When benzoyl chloride and caustic soda are added to even highly dilute solutions of *diamines*, the latter are converted into the dibenzoyl compounds which are entirely insoluble in water, and separate as crystalline bodies.

As an example the following may be quoted:
On shaking an aqueous solution of 1 Gm. of ethene-diamine in ¼ liter of water with 10 Gm. of benzoyl chloride and 80 C.c. of a 10-per-cent caustic-soda solution, there was obtained 3.5 Gm. of dibenzoyl-ethene-diamine as a crystalline precipitate. Even from exceedingly dilute solutions this and similar compounds will separate.

Some years ago, Brieger discovered, among the products of putrefaction due to bacteria, a ptomaine to which he applied the name *cadaverine*. This was subsequently identified by Ladenburg as *penta-methene-diamine* (pentamethylene-diamine), and this was confirmed by Brieger.

Among other ptomaines discovered by Brieger, there was one having the composition of the *tetra-methene-diamine* (tetra-methylene-diamine), but which has not been proven, up to the present, to be identical with this body.

The authors of the paper here abstracted had been making systematic examinations, during some nine months, of the urine of a patient who had suffered for years from cystinuria and catarrh of the bladder. On applying to this urine the reagent just described, they found it to respond to it quite copiously. In fact, they discovered that the urine in question contained a series of diamines, among which penta-methene-diamine (or cadaverine) and tetra-methene-diamine could be sharply recognized. Fifty days' urine of the patient yielded to the authors 30 Gm. of a mixture of the crystallized benzoyl compounds, the larger portion of which (about 20 Gm.) belonged to the penta- and about 6 Gm. to the tetra-diamine. The fæces of the same patient yielded about ½ Gm. of benzoyl compounds per day, the larger proportion of these belonging to the tetra-diamine.

Repeated experiments with normal urine have shown that the latter never contains any diamines. The same has been proven in the case of normal fæces. It is possible that diamines may appear in the excretions also in other diseases, besides cystinuria, but so far nothing of the kind has been observed.

The authors have, therefore, for the first time ascertained the fact that ptomaines—or substances which have heretofore been known to be the products of bacterial putrefaction—may occur as constituents of excretions in disease. The most remarkable fact is that they occur in the urine. It is surmised that there is some connection between the appearance of these bodies and the abnormal excretion of cystin. Further experiments are promised.

Tests for Eucalyptus Oil.

THE discussion between certain English chemists and the house of Schimmel & Co., of Leipzig, regarding the presence or absence of eucalyptol in certain kinds of oil of eucalyptus, has not yet been finally terminated, but has had the effect of bringing out a number of interesting points not heretofore known.

Thus, Schimmel & Co., announce a new and delicate test to distinguish between the oil of *Eucalyptus amygdalina* and *E. globulus*:

Mix 1 C.c. of the oil with 2 C.c. of glacial acetic acid, add 1 or 2 C.c. of a saturated solution of sodium nitrite, and stir slightly. If the oil is from the amygdalina species, the separated top layer will congeal to a crystalline magma of phellandrene nitrite, but pure eucalyptol and the oil of *E. globulus* are not so affected.

The specific gravity is also a good distinguishing criterion. The *E. globulus* oil is certainly not genuine if its density is below 0.900. On the other hand, that of *E. amygdalina* rarely exceeds 0.890.—*After Chem. and Drugg.*

American Druggist

AN ILLUSTRATED MONTHLY JOURNAL
OF
Pharmacy, Chemistry, and Materia Medica.

Vol. XVII., No. 11.   Whole No. 173.

FREDERICK A. CASTLE, M.D. .... Editor.
CHARLES RICE, Ph.D. .... Associate Editor.

PUBLISHED BY
WM. WOOD & CO., 56 & 58 Lafayette Place, N. Y.

SUBSCRIPTION PRICE per year, ... $1.50
SINGLE COPIES, ...15

Address all communications relating to the business of the AMERICAN DRUGGIST, such as subscriptions, advertisements, change of Post-Office address, etc., to WILLIAM WOOD & CO., 56 and 58 Lafayette Place, New York City, to whom order all postal money orders and checks should be made payable. Communications intended for the Editor should be addressed in care of the Publishers.

The AMERICAN DRUGGIST is issued in the latter part of each month, dated for the month ahead. Changes of advertisements should reach us before the 10th. New advertisements can occasionally be inserted after the 18th.

REGULAR ADVERTISEMENTS according to size, location, and time. Special rates on application.

EDITORIAL.

WE are in receipt of a communication from our friend, Prof. C. Lewis Diehl, of Louisville, regarding the elongated form of percolator which is generally known as "Oldberg's Percolator." He draws our attention to the fact that this improved form of percolator—illustrated on page 23 of our last February number—was the outcome of a detailed study of the process of percolation undertaken for the Committee on Pharmacopœia of the American Pharm. Association. In the Proceedings, vol. 27 (1879), p. 729, will be found a sketch of the percolator recommended on the basis of the results obtained by Prof. Diehl's experiments.

While the exact dimensions for this kind of percolator are not given in the paper just quoted, he mentions that the percolator should be just twice the usual height, and his sketch of a percolator so constructed above dimensions that fully conform to the ideas of the more recent advocates of tall percolators.

In the Preliminary Notice to the U. S. Pharmacopœia of 1888 (p. xxxvi.), in the Chapter on Percolation, which was drawn up by Prof. Diehl, the exact dimensions for a tall percolator, suitable for the extraction of 500 grammes of drug, are given, and on the basis there given Prof. Oldberg constructed the percolators known by his name, but these differ somewhat from the officinal proportions.

Prof. Diehl informs us that he considers the dimensions given by him the most practicable for the quantity of drug contemplated, but that for larger quantities of drug, taller and proportionately narrower percolators would be desirable, and he thinks that this idea is plainly indicated in his before-mentioned study on Percolation, which he concludes (on page 730) by recommending "*simple percolation*," "*selecting for this purpose tall, slender, moderately tapering percolators*."

We take it that Prof. Diehl merely desires it to be understood that to him belongs the priority of recommending this form of percolator, but that he does not object to have special patterns made on this principle, designated by the designers' names.

UP to within about a dozen years or so, pharmacy in Europe, particularly on the Continent, has been so exceedingly conservative that not only were novel processes, new appliances, and new forms of preparations, which had come into use in foreign countries, not adopted or introduced, but in many cases they were entirely ignored, or looked down upon as being unworthy of notice. We can well remember the time, in our younger days, when, on general principles, almost anything claiming to be of American origin was at once suspected of being bogus, fraudulent, or calculated to deceive. This notion prevailed for a long time, even among otherwise well-informed people, and it required the severe lesson taught by the Centennial Exhibition of 1876 to open the eyes of Europeans regarding the astonishing progress and development of American industry, which in many cases had so outstripped that of the foreign exhibitors that some of the products of the latter appeared to be rather as cheap toys, or as made for uncivilized nations than calculated for real practical use. The earnest representations and uncompromising reports of Rouleaux and other foreign delegates to their governments, however, though at first wounding national pride, have had the good result to remove the prejudices existing in various industries against adopting foreign and particularly American methods and appliances. We do not wish to be understood as implying that these prejudices were at that time still universally shared. This was by no means the case. Curiously enough, one of the most powerful agents to gradually dispel, even long before 1876, the old repugnance to American goods in Europe was the sewing machine, which made its way slowly but surely into the various homes, and acted as a missionary for the future.

Those who have had, like ourselves, the opportunity of witnessing the habits, and knowing the feelings of our continental colleagues, will agree with us that one of the slowest bodies to accept new ideas from this country has been the pharmaceutical profession. We refer here particularly to Germany and other continental countries where German is spoken. However, this is not to be wondered at, if we remember how much trash, in the shape of patent and proprietary medicines, has been and is floating about on our market, making it almost an impossibility even for professional experts living abroad to distinguish the wheat from the chaff, and causing many of them to look upon the whole output of products as undeserving of notice.

The year 1876 undoubtedly marks an era in pharmaceutical international reciprocity. Not only were our own pharmacists made better acquainted with the old European ways and methods, but European pharmacists were, for the first time, made thoroughly acquainted with our best features and processes. Among these, the process of percolation, adapted to the preparation of tinctures, and particularly to that of *fluid extracts*, stands at the head. Though the principle of the process was first suggested in Europe many years previously, yet it was only applied, at least almost exclusively, in chemical laboratories or certain technical works. While the usefulness and expediency of this process were recognized by leading authorities, there were, however, serious obstacles in the way of its introduction. The principal obstacle was this, that the continental pharmacopœias prescribed the old process of macerating the drug with the whole quantity of menstruum, in the case of tinctures and similar preparations, and as this process requires no special apparatus, no expert skill, and no watching, it was not likely that pharmacists would take kindly to another process involving new appliances and demanding extra work. The fact that the old process consumed a large amount of time, compared with the new one, was hardly taken in consideration. Time—in the sense here meant—is not as valuable a commodity to the pharmacist in Germany as it is to us, because he is, to a large extent, protected against undue competition by the laws of the land.

In the course of time, certain enterprising American manufacturing firms took particular pains to draw the attention of European pharmacists to the class of fluid extracts, by making prominent exhibits at international or special expositions, by placing specimens in the hands of prominent medical experts for trial, by copious advertisements, and by other means. There can be no doubt that to these causes the more rapid recognition of the value of fluid extracts is chiefly due. It was curious, and sometimes amusing, to read papers, even coming from well-known authorities, which appeared to have knowledge only of fluid extracts of the newer drugs, introduced and specially advertised by the firms alluded to, it being altogether overlooked that these preparations had been long in use, and that our pharmacopœia recognises a large number made from the well-known, older, and universally used drugs. Gradually, however, the list of fluid extracts is extending, and it will not be long when this class of preparations will be as well made, and as generally used, in Europe as it is in this country.*

There is one point connected with this subject which we would like to draw the attention of our continental colleagues to. It is this, that we would seriously caution them not to try, *in the beginning*, to adopt new-fangled methods or apparatus, in the preparation of fluid extracts or tinctures, but to thoroughly test those which our long-continued experience has finally shown to us to be most adapted for the purpose. We do not claim that there are no further improvements possible; indeed, we shall always be on the lookout for them, and bid them welcome. But we have had a practical experience of nearly forty years in the application of the process of percolation, and have tested a multitude of variations, most of which are on record in American pharmaceutical literature. Our continental friends will probably be able to save much labor, time, and expense, if they will consult the existing literature before they strike out on a new path, which may possibly lead them to a failure which could otherwise have been avoided. We have already noticed several announcement of new percolating apparatus, from the illustration and description of which we should judge that the expected results will not be attained. Among the best we have seen is that illustrated by Eugene Dieterich, in his "Neues Pharmaceutisches Manual" (2d ed., 1888, p. 275), where the accompanying text bears evidence that the writer is thoroughly familiar with the subject. At the end of the chapter, he expressly states that no other method of extraction equals, in efficiency, that of percolation. But he adds a remark which we cannot agree to: "At the same time, no other [process] requires so much time. It will, therefore, be more suitable for working on a small scale than for operations on a large scale." Not at all; our experience has shown that the scale makes no difference. It is only necessary to use proper judgment, according to the nature of the drug, in the fineness of powder, the kind of menstruum, and the rate of exhaustion. There is no need of *always* using very fine powder, or of allowing the percolate to pass at the rate of *only* two drops per second, etc. The sole object is to exhaust the drug, and to obtain a definite volume of percolate. As long as this is accomplished, we can relax any conditions which would unnecessarily consume time.

Besides, when a preparation is in continuous demand, it would be unwise to start a new batch only when the old stock is consumed. While the last batch is being drawn upon, the new one can be made; and if it is suddenly required in unusually large quantities, it is best to subdivide it into smaller manageable portions, all of which can be worked simultaneously within the time allowed for the operation.

American pharmacists have sometimes been misrepresented by European professional writers, as being almost fanatics on the subject of percolation, wanting to apply it for everything and in every case. Any one, however, who has attentively examined our literature, will know better. We know there are certain drugs which cannot be extracted by percolation with certain menstrua, owing to swelling or other causes, and in such cases we have recourse to maceration. In fact, our aim has always been to study each drug thoroughly, and to ascertain the most favorable conditions under which all the useful and desirable constituents of a given quantity of a crude drug, of normal condition, can be gotten into permanent solution, so that the volume of the latter bears a definite ratio to the weight of the drug. In our last pharmacopœia the ratio of *weight of drug* to *volume of product* existed only to *weight of product*. We are, however, inclined to believe that the majority of the profession desires a return to the former method.

Our German colleagues have recently instituted statistical inquiries regarding the extent to which officinal or unofficinal preparations are in use in their country. The Pharmacopœia Committee of the German Pharmaceutical Association, of which Dr. G. Vulpius is Chairman, recently sent copies of a complete alphabetical list of the titles of all articles contained in the last German Pharmacopœia, which are just six hundred in number, to the directors of the pharmacies attached to the clinics of the five principal German Universities, frequented by more than one-half of all the medical students in Germany. Lists were also sent to certain veterinary institutions. The request accompanying the lists was, to cross out any article which had not been in use or demanded during the past year, and also to add the titles of such articles or preparations as had been used without being officinal. From the replies received it appears that of the 600 officinal articles, only six had not been demanded in the before-mentioned five pharmacies during that time. In addition, about 250 of the preparations officinal in the first, but not received into the last pharmacopœia, were still in use; besides about 150 older remedies which had not even been in the first edition; and finally some 200 newer remedies. Similar results were obtained by the inquiries among veterinary institutions. By actual count, there were used, during the past year, in those five pharmacies, 1,185 different articles, of which 589 were officinal in the last German Pharmacopœia, 252 had been officinal in the preceding (first) one, 157 were still older, and 187 were new drugs or preparations.

It will be seen that for about 600, or one-half of all the remedies employed, there is actually no fixed legal standard. Dr. Vulpius wishes that there were a possibility of inducing physicians to abandon old remedies which are no longer recognised, but he is not at all sanguine that this will ever be brought about. On the other hand, he would not be in favor of enlarging the scope of the pharmacopœia, by reintroducing the discarded material.

Some relief, according to Dr. Vulpius, can be rendered in two ways. In the first place, it may be legally ordered that for all articles contained in the first German Pharmacopœia which have not been received into the second edition, the text of the former shall remain in force. And secondly, for all other remedies, an agreement may be brought about among pharmacists, as to which works of reference, in the shape of supplements to the pharmacopœias or formularies, shall be commonly accepted as standards, and followed. Dr. Vulpius alludes to the fact that a similar movement has been started in this country. When writing his paper, he evidently had not yet seen the results, in the shape of the National Formulary.

The problem which our German colleagues have to face is one with which we have long been familiar, and for which the only possible solution was the preparation of some interim-standard, to be in force until a higher authority should provide a formula for any preparation contained in it. Had we not done this, we could have only attempted the next best alternative, namely, to select a number of privately published works, formularies, dispensatories, etc., which we might have agreed among ourselves to regard, for this or that preparation, as authoritative. It might have been necessary to name twenty or more different works to cover the best of all the formulas needed. And what guarantee would there have been that any new edition of any of these works would still afford us the reference wanted? We have certainly chosen the most practical solution of the difficulty, and strongly advise our German confrères to adopt the same plan we did.

We all know why old remedies do not easily disappear. Old physicians will prescribe what they have learned to use in their early days, and as many of them are exceedingly conservative, it is hard to get them to use new things. At all events, it is harder to get them to throw the old things aside. The dear public, of course, also contributes its share, and a most prominent one, in preventing many old, silly, and—as we know—valueless preparations in the case of fluid extracts. In all other liquid preparations obtained by percolation, the ratio was *weight of drug to die out*. However, it would be useless to try to enact laws which would hinder the prescriber in his choice of remedies. It is only from a higher standard of medical education, and from a closer intercourse between the pharmaceutical and medical professions, and a more frequent interchange of views and experiences among them, that a relief will come. May it not be far off.

THE recent publication of a very complete treatise on the art of prescription-writing gives rise to a query as to whether there is really any occasion for such an elaborate manual, and whether such an amount of detail connected with a very simple matter is not calculated to do harm and complicate the practice of writing prescriptions rather than simplify the work. Time was, before the present modes of diagnosis were in vogue, when a peculiar costume, a wig and cane, an oracular manner, and a mysterious formula were considered essential to successful practice. The wig, cane, costume, and much of the manner have gone, and the physician of the present day aims at appearing like other gentlemen. Of the elaborate formula expressed in a comparatively unknown language, almost the only remaining mystery consists in the abominable chirography which too often characterizes it. The medical student of the present time has less absolute need for instruction in Latin terminations than for manual dexterity in expressing his wants on paper.

Correction.

PROF. C. LEWIS DIEHL draws our attention to a passage in our abstract of the preliminary part of his Report on the Progress of Pharmacy, which is printed as if it were a part of his own text, while it should have been put in quotation marks, to show that it was from other sources. Prof. Diehl informs us that he quoted very freely, for instance, from a paper in the Year-Book of Pharmacy, on "The Future of Pharmacy," and much of this appears in our report of the Proceedings (see our October number, page 182), as though it were an original expression of Prof. Diehl. It will not be necessary to do more than to mention this matter here, so that the omission of the quotation marks may not be charged to our friend, Prof. Diehl.

South Dakota Board of Pharmacy.—The board, as lately reorganized, consists of D. S. White, of Flandreau, President; B. F. Stearns, of Aberdeen, Secretary; and J. L. Kreychie, M.D. The board has issued the following important notice:

1st. The Board will not allow any one to conduct a drug store, as has been done heretofore, without first becoming registered.

2d. According to the Pharmacy Law, Paris Green, Blue Vitriol, and other poisonous drugs should be sold only by registered pharmacists, and sales of same should be recorded in a poison register. Therefore it is illegal for any one, excepting registered pharmacists, to sell such drugs, and the Board will prosecute all such violations, upon a complaint being made. Every druggist is earnestly requested to report to the Secretary all violations of the law.

Every registered pharmacist is respectfully requested to comply with the following requirement of the pharmacy law: "*Every certificate of registration and every renewal of such certificate shall be conspicuously exposed in the pharmacy to which it applies.*"

It is also recommended that "Registered Pharmacist" labels, with name of dispenser, be put on all packages and articles put up or dispensed in drug stores.

New Hampshire Pharmaceutical Association.—The following are the officers for the coming year, elected at the annual meeting on September 25th: President, Geo. F. Underhill, Concord; 1st Vice-President, L. B. Downing, Hanover; 2d Vice-President, Gale C. Shedd, Keene; Secretary, C. B. Spofford, Claremont; Treasurer, F. A. James, Manchester; Auditor, J. Irving Hoyt, Penacook; Executive Committee, S. Howard Bell, Derry; A. D. Smith, Manchester; C. B. Spofford, Claremont.

Ernest Wende, M.D., B.Sc., of Buffalo has been appointed Instructor in Botany in the Buffalo (N. Y.) College of Pharmacy, to succeed Prof. Kellicott, who has accepted a professorship in the University of Ohio, at Columbus.

J. B. LIPPINCOTT & Co. have just published a new edition of the United States Dispensatory, with nearly 800 pages of new matter, including the incorporation of the National Formulary.

CORRESPONDENCE.

Delicate Test for Bismuth.

DEAR SIR:—I see on page 174 of the September number of the AMERICAN DRUGGIST Mr. Leger's test for bismuth. As I have frequent occasion to make tests for bismuth, in its different forms in the ores of this country, I have need of a very delicate way to test for the smallest percentages of the metal, and have employed the following, which I send with the hope that it may benefit other readers of the journal.

Powder the ore and mix 100 to 200 milligrammes with equal parts of powdered iodide of potassium and sublimated sulphur. Place it on charcoal, and use the blow-pipe. In a few minutes there will be a red incrustation on the coal. It is best to have a second piece of coal over the orifice of the one containing the mixture. I have found that assay solution containing bismuth, mixed with the above powder and heated on charcoal in the same way, will give like results. I think that as low as one-fiftieth of one per cent can be detected.

The hydrogen-sulphide test is too complicated when one has to employ the test several times a week. I have never known the test I have mentioned to fail, and its simplicity recommends it.

This method forms a preparation like the one Mr. Leger recommends. Yours very truly,

G. H. HUBERT (Druggist and Apothecary).

BEAVER CITY, UTAH, Sept. 18th, 1888.

Qualification for License.

DEAR SIR:—In the spring of 1884, A, who is a shoemaker, invested some money in the drug business with B, who had a little experience in the drug trade.

A would come to the store once in awhile after his day's work in the shoeshop, and sometimes would sell cigars or soda, until a few weeks before the registering law was enforced, when he bought out the interests of his partner B. A applied to the Board of Pharmacy, and obtained his certificate.

I would like to know whether he was entitled to it !

Yours truly, H.

This case happened in a town in Massachusetts, where the law establishing a "Board of Registration in Pharmacy" went into operation about October, 1885. Section 3 of the act provides that any person or firm engaged in the business of retailing or dispensing drugs, medicines, chemicals, and poisons on their own account, or any others (viz., then out of business) who had had three consecutive years of practical experience at the aforesaid business, could be registered as a pharmacist by the Board.

No doubt the law would have never been passed, had it affected those already in business. It was necessary to allow the bogus pharmacist to come in with the genuine, so as to get at least the door shut for the future. In our judgment, the person alluded to had a right under the law to be registered, much as we regret it. It is much to be hoped that, by this time, he has learned to distinguish sulphate of zinc from Epsom salt, or morphine from quinine. These drawbacks are incidental to the passage of any pharmacy law, and cannot well be helped.—EDITOR AM. DRUGGIST.

A Perfumed Insect.

MR. G. A. FARINI, in his work entitled, "Through the Kalahari Desert,"[*] relates the following interesting fact, which may possibly put some of our readers on the track of a new perfume:

"Three days' easy going brought us to Ghanse without any notable incident. As we drove to the water, the fore-wheel of my wagon crashed into a bush, which at once gave out a *powerful and delicious* perfume. Jumping down to examine the cause, I plucked some leaves, but found they were scentless, as was also the stem of the plant. I could not make out where where the pleasant odor came from until I touched a small *beetle*, when out came a puff stronger than ever. The little bug was an animated perfumery store, emitting the delicious scent whenever disturbed. I caught three of them, and put them in a perforated box, in which they lived for a week, the movement of the wagon affecting them sufficiently to make them give up their fragrance in such quantities as to keep the wagon perfumed like Rimmel's. When they died, the scent died with them.

It is true that the locality where these remarkable insects were met with is rather out of the way, being situated in about 21.45° S. and 21° E. (of Greenwich), between what is known as Demara Land, and Khamas Land. But as the author is known to be reliable, and has brought back so many other remarkable novelties, there is no reason to doubt the existence of the "perfumed" insect.

[*] Published by Sampson Low, Marston, Searle, & Rivington. 8vo, London, 1886, p. 231. A few other interesting extracts from this work will be found elsewhere in this number.

QUERIES & ANSWERS.

Queries for which answers are desired, must be received by the 5th of the month, and must in every case be accompanied by the name and address of the writer, for the information of the editor, but not for publication.

Liquid Carbonic Acid.—If the writer of query 2,234 in our October number will address Mr. W. B. Keller, Editor and Proprietor of the *National Bottler's Gazette*, 31 Park Row, New York, he will be put in the way of obtaining the information desired.

No. 2,241.—Dose of Extract of Hyoscyamus (H. O. D.).

"Will you please let me know whether the inclosed prescription (see below) deserves any criticism on account of the uncertainty regarding the amount of Extract of Hyoscamus which might be taken? Do you think the prescriber should have specified the amount of the same?

℞ Morph. Sulph .... gr. iss.
Ext. Belladonna .... gr. v.
P. Camphora............................. gr. xlv.
Ext. Hyoscyami.......................... q. s.

Fiant pil. 15."

In reply, we would say that authorities are pretty unanimous in considering hyoscyamus as not belonging to the very potent drugs. Stillé (in "National Dispensatory") states that the *minimum* dose of the officinal extract is 2 grains, and that this should be rapidly increased until the characteristic effects are produced. In Wharton and Stillé's "Medical Jurisprudence" (by Amory and Wood, vol. II., Philadelphia, 1884, page 429), we find the statement: "The dose of the tincture is a fluidrachm, that of the extract 5 grains, as an average." Cases of fatal poisoning by hyoscyamus are very rare; in fact, there is only one authenticated case, from the year 1715, reported by Walther, and a doubtful one about the end of the last century.

It is not likely that our correspondent would want to make very large pills from the above prescription. He will, therefore, be justified, on the strength of the authorities above quoted, to use his own discretion in the amount of extract of hyoscyamus to be used. We often see prescriptions for pills by leading therapeutists, here in New York, where the quantity of extract of hyoscyamus is left blank.

No. 2,242.—Syrup of Hydriodic Acid (Ch. H. M.).

We published a formula for a Colorless Syrup of Hydriodic Acid on page 195 of the last volume. This is the formula which was then proposed to be introduced, and has since been introduced, into the National Formulary published by the American Pharmaceutical Association. We advise you to send for that work at once—address Prof. J. M. Maisch, of Philadelphia—as it contains not only this, but 454 other formulas which you may need in your business.

No. 2,243.—Shampoo Liquid (E. S.).

The readiest agent to produce a good lather upon the hair of the head is a solution of potassa or soda, or a dilute water of ammonia. The latter, however, owing to its penetrating odor, is not usually liked. The following combination will be found serviceable:

Solution of Potassa (U. S.).................. 4 fl. oz.
Borax...................................... 1 tr. oz.
Bay Rum................................... ½ fl. oz.
Tincture of Quillaja (N. F.)................. ½ fl. oz.
Water..............................enough to make 16 fl. oz.

This may be scented according to taste. An increase of alcohol will reduce the lather-producing property.

E. Dieterich recommends the following preparation:

Fresh Eggs................................. 3
Spirit of Soap (N. F.)...................... 1½ fl. oz.
Carbonate of Potassium.................... 180 grains
Water of Ammonia......................... 180 minims
Oil-Sugar of Cumarin....................... 8 grains
Oil of Rose................................ 2 drops
" " Bergamot .... 2 "
" " Geranium, French..................... 1 drop
" " Almonds, essent..................... 1 "
Rose Water................................ 27 fl. oz.

Thoroughly beat the 3 Eggs and then dilute with the Rose Water. Then add the other ingredients.

Oil-Sugar of Cumarin is directed to be prepared by triturating 1 part of cumarin with 999 parts of sugar of milk.

No. 2,244.—Constitution of Antipyrine (Several Inquirors).

Several authorities still continue to assign to antipyrine a chemical name (dimethyl-oxy-chinizin) and constitution which has long been given up as untenable by the discoverer, Dr. L. Knorr. In order to give to our readers the exact words of Dr. Knorr's claim, we print here the essential portion of the U. S. patent granted to him on October 28th, 1884, entitled, "Preparation of Dimethyl-Phenyl-Oxypyrazol."

My invention consists of a new product, dimethyl-phenyl-oxypyrazol, from phenyl-hydrazine, the latter yielding, as products of a series of operations, new compounds, which I have found to be valuable medicaments.

The following is a description of my method of proceeding:

By mixing the body well known as acetylacetic ether with a molecular quantity of phenyl-hydrazine, water is eliminated, and a condensation product is formed, termed "phenyl-hydrazine-acetylacetic ether," of the formula:

$$C_6H_5 - N_2H = \overset{CH_3}{\underset{C - CH_2 - CO.C_2H_5}{|}}$$

When this product is heated to a temperature of 100 to 150° Centigrade, until a sample perfectly solidifies on cooling or on immersion into ether, a mass will result which, after crystallization from water or from some other medium, represents pure methyl-phenyl-oxypyrazol. Its formation from phenyl-hydrazine-acetylacetic ether takes place under production of alcohol, as expressed in the equation:

$$C_6H_5N_2HC\!\!<^{CH_3}_{CH_2CO.C_2H_5} = C_{11}H_{12}N_2O + C_2H_5OH.$$

When the methyl-phenyl-oxypyrazol thus formed is heated with methyl chloride, bromide, or iodide, it is readily converted into dimethyl-phenyl-oxypyrazol.

Dimethyl-phenyl-oxypyrazol is distinguished by the following properties: It crystallizes from ether in lamellae of a pearly lustre, melting at 113° Centigrade. It is soluble in alcohol, water, and acids, from which solutions it is precipitated by concentrated alkalies. Its aqueous solution turns red on addition of ferric chloride, and green when a nitrite is added. When a concentrated aqueous solution is mixed with the solution of a nitrite, green crystals separate on standing.

What I claim as new, and desire to secure by Letters Patent, is:

The new product dimethyl-phenyl-oxypyrazol, the result of the process herein described, the same being distinguished by the properties herein mentioned.

No. 2,245.—Thapsia and Silphium (U. O.).

The only species of Thapsia used in medicine at the present day is *Thapsia garganica* L., a common umbelliferous plant of Algiers, particularly frequent in the province of Constantine. Its root, which was used in a fresh condition by the Arabs, and is even by some modern authorities stated to be injured by drying, contains an irritant resin, which is extracted in an impure form, and used in the preparation of Thapsia plaster, officinal in the French Pharmacopœia. This plaster, when applied to the skin, produces in about twenty-four hours an immense number of small miliary vesicles upon a reddened skin, without liability to spread, and also without pain.

Internally, thapsia root produces irritation of the alimentary canal and acts as a cathartic. But it has only been used so by the Arabs, and never by modern physicians.

Ancient writers report similar effects to have been obtained from a plant named by them Silphium. A juice (probably dried gum resin) was obtained from this which was also distinguished by the appellative "Cyrenaic." In fact, both the plant and its root or juice was known as *Silphium cyrenaicum*. It is highly probable that this was the plant now known as *Thapsia garganica* L. At all events, the identity of the two is accepted by most authorities, and the two names are frequently placed side by side as synonyms.

While the name "Silphium," as used by ancient authors, thus denoted an umbelliferous plant growing in Northern Africa and the Levant, Linné made an entirely new use of the name by transferring it to an American genus of Compositæ, of which there are about half a dozen species known, mostly indigenous in the Middle or Southern States. One of these species, viz., *Silphium laciniatum* L. (formerly named *Silphium gummiferum* Ell.; see Elliott, "Sketch of the Botany of South Carolina and Georgia," Charleston, 1821-1824, Vol. II., 406), has been reported by Dr. H. D. Garrison (*Eclectic Med. Review* and elsewhere) to be an excellent remedy in asthma. It has been used for the heaves or asthma in horses (Dodd, J. H., "The Amer. Horse and Cattle Doctor"). Asthma or heaves in horses is said not to exist in the prairies where this plant grows. Dr. King (in the "American Dispensatory") says that this species (which he calls "rosin weed," and which he does not regard as identical with *S. laciniatum*, or "compass weed"), is, like the "laciniatum," reported to be emetic, to have effected cures in intermittent fever, and to be beneficial in dry obstinate cough. Porcher ("Resources of the South. Fields and Forests," Charleston, 1869, p. 460) adds that the "rosin weed," which is sometimes called the "polar" or "compass plant," because its leaves are said to point north and south, is said to be powerfully diuretic. An alcoholic fluid extract is recommended in doses of 20-40 drops. The dose for a horse is 2 fl. ounces morning and evening (Tilden's *Journ. Mat. Med.*, November, 1867).

If, therefore, any physician prescribes a fluid extract or other preparation of Silphium (without further specifications), it may be inferred that the American composite plant *Silphium laciniatum* is meant, and by no means the ancient *Silphium cyrenaicum* which is now Thapsia gar-

ganica and a liquid preparation of which will probably act, internally, somewhat like croton oil.

No. 2,246.—The Keeley Motor ("Uncap").
This subject is rather outside the scope of the AMERICAN DRUGGIST and we decline to offer any opinion as to the present status of the alleged discovery. The question: "Do you think it possible that—as Mr. Keeley claims—a single pint of water and a match is capable of giving out or producing such a tremendous force as he claims to have discovered . . . ?" is, however, worthy of consideration. In the first place, we are not aware that any such claim has ever been made by Mr. Keeley, and think that our correspondent has been misinformed. One of us has had opportunity for seeing an exhibition of the working of some of the mechanism alleged by Mr. Keeley to be influenced by the force which he claims to have discovered, and have listened to many accounts of the personal experience of others, and we do not remember to have seen or heard of the "match" or of any form of applying heat.

It seems to us very likely that Mr. Keeley has discovered *something* which furnishes a means of force hitherto unappreciated, but that he has thus far failed to reduce its use to a practical basis. Meanwhile, a fear that some one else may get hold of the principle, succeed in putting it into practice, and reap the pecuniary results has led him to exercise as much secrecy as possible and exhibit only *results*. It must be remembered that no one in this country can obtain a patent for a natural force or product, but only for the mechanism or process for applying it. It will, therefore, be understood how Mr. Keeley or anybody else would exercise a great deal of caution in allowing his secret to become the property of others, assuming, of course, that he *has* one.

Those who have any knowledge of scientific matters are aware that there are many exhibitions of force proceeding from conditions which are not well understood, and which are difficult of comprehension, and that there is nothing more remarkable in Mr. Keeley's claims for "vibratory energy" than existed in the case of steam or electricity. We are aware that the motor which refuses to *mote* and Mr. Keeley have been the butt of many jokes, and that ridicule is a very difficult thing to contend against. We are also aware that a great deal of money has been invested on the *probability* of his being able to do what he claims to be able to accomplish. We suspect that Mr. Keeley finds himself in the position of the man referred to by the *Detroit Free Press* who "bit off more than he could chaw;" and while we would caution our correspondent against any investment in Keeley stock, unless he has more money than he knows what to do with, we would also deprecate unseemly ridicule of something which is not generally understood, and mention that, before the days of steam navigation, a prominent member of the British House of Parliament said, in open debate, that he would eat the boiler of the first steamboat which succeeded in crossing the Atlantic Ocean. It is very likely that the next generation will know more than this one does about many matters, and "Keeley's motor" *may* be one of them.

No. 2,247.—Dextrin (St. Louis).
Commercial dextrin appears in various tints, and does not by any means usually represent a homogeneous substance. Being produced on a large scale from starch, it depends much on the source of the latter and on the process employed, whether the product approaches purity or not. The usual impurities which are present are unaltered starch, due to an insufficient reaction, or sugar, owing to a too long-continued reaction. The former may be removed by one of the processes given below. Sugar may be removed by dissolving the dextrin in water, filtering, if necessary, and precipitating with alcohol. The sugar will remain in solution, while the dextrin (and any accompanying starch) will be precipitated as a doughy mass.

The yellow dextrin of commerce, also known as British gum, is prepared by heating starch in iron vessels to a temperature of about 460° F. (440° to 500° F.). This kind of dextrin is usually free from unconverted starch, and wholly soluble in about 2 parts of water. The white dextrin is prepared by different processes, chiefly by the intervention of acids, and at much lower temperatures.

The National Formulary has adopted a formula for making Mucilage of Dextrin (chiefly as a vehicle of emulsions), in which it is specially pointed out that the *white* variety of commercial dextrin, which still contains unaltered starch, is to be used for this purpose.

If it is desired to remove free starch from dextrin, this may be done by intimately mixing 100 parts of the crude dextrin, previously mixed with 1 part of precipitated carbonate of calcium, with 200 parts of water, agitating repeatedly, macerating two days, then pouring off the clear solution from the sediment, and passing the liquid through flannel. The strained liquid is evaporated to a syrupy consistence and may then be spread on plates, dried, and reduced to powder. If the sugar is to be removed at the same time, the syrupy liquid is poured in a thin stream, and under constant stirring, into a large vessel holding 200 parts of alcohol. After twenty-four hours, the supernatant liquid is poured off, the gummy precipitate transferred to a capsule, and evaporated to the consistence of extract over a water-bath. The mass is then transferred in thin slices to plates or spread on a parchment paper, dried and powdered. The drying in either case should be done at a temperature not exceeding about 100° F.

Yellow dextrin usually contains also a peculiar dark-brown substance, probably saccharine, to which the specific dextrin odor is due. According to Dieterich, this may be removed by stirring up the dextrin (100 parts) with a mixture of 5 parts of water of ammonia and 150 parts of alcohol, allowing to macerate 24 hours, then transferring to a funnel stopped up with cotton; care being taken to lose as little alcohol as possible—and, when the liquid has run off, washing with 100 parts of alcohol poured on in about 10 separate portions. The dextrin thus purified appears, when dry, of a whiter color, and is nearly odorless and tasteless. The alcohol used in purifying dextrin may be recovered by distillation, the free ammonia being previously neutralized by sulphuric acid.

No. 2,248.—Moth Destroyers and Preventives (D. A O'C.).
Camphor and naphthalin are mostly relied upon as preventives against the ravages of moths. They may be either wrapped in paper and placed between layers of clothing in trunks, or paper may be impregnated with an alcoholic solution of either of these substances, and laid between the layers. In the case of articles of furniture infested with moths, a cautious application of a spray of such solutions will usually suffice. The odor will gradually disappear on exposure. Among other preparations recommended are the following:

1. *Moth Essence.*

Oil of Patchouli	75 min.
Oil of Mirbane	75 min.
Naphthalin	300 grains.
Carbolic Acid	300 grains.
Camphor	750 grains.
Oil of Turpentine	1½ fl. oz.
Alcohol	to make 1 quart.

Mix, macerate a few days, and filter. Impregnate filtering paper with the liquid, put it between the substances to be preserved, in a secure box, and keep this in a cool place.

2. *Moth Paper.*

Naphthalin	10 parts.
Carbolic Acid	5 parts.
Ceresin	5 parts.

Melt them together, and apply the hot mass, with a brush, to unsized paper laid upon a warm surface, away from lights or fire.

3. *Moth Powder.*

Capsicum, powd.	1 part.
Naphthalin, fine powd.	4 parts.
Insect Powder	5 parts.

Mix. This powder is best applied by sprinkling it over paper laid between layers of fabrics, another paper being laid on top of the powder. Dieterich recommends to sprinkle it upon the fabrics (wool, etc.) themselves.

4. *Moth Species.*

Patchouli, herb	150 grains.
Rosemary, flowers	300 grains.
Thyme, flowers	300 grains.
Sage, flowers	300 grains.
Naphthalin	300 grains.
Oil of Mirbane	90 min.
Oil of Turpentine	60 min.
	3 fl. oz.

Cut the vegetable substances and mix them. Dissolve the naphthalin and oils in the alcohol, sprinkle the solution over the herbs, and place these between the articles to be preserved. (Dieterich.)

No. 2,249.—Estimation of Mineral Wax in Beeswax (Columbus).
Horn's method of estimating paraffin, ceresin, mineral oils, etc., in fats and waxes was published in the *Zeitsch. f. angewandte Chemie*, No. 16, of 1888. As we believe that the method will interest also many others of our readers, we publish it here in abstract.

The first step is to saponify the fat or mixture under examination. For this purpose, some 5 or 6 Gm. of the substance to be examined are put into a porcelain capsule of 8 to 10 C.c. diameter, then a piece of caustic potash or soda, about 2 to 3 Gm. in weight, is added, at all events enough to have an excess of alkali. Some 50 C.c. of absolute alcohol are added, and the whole is stirred with a glass rod, warming it meanwhile over a water-bath. All fatty substances will thus be speedily saponified, and a dry soap obtained. An addition of sand or of carbonate of sodium to the mass, when it has become mushy, is not necessary if it is only constantly stirred with the rod as soon as it gets thick. The dried soap is now introduced into a cylindrical roll of filtering paper. Most of the particles adhering to the dish may be scraped off with a spatula; the remainder may be easily removed by warm chloroform. The paper roll having been introduced into a Soxhlet apparatus, the chloroformic solution is poured on top, and the apparatus having been properly adjusted and charged with chloroform, the contents of the roll (which is left open above) are exhausted.

The chloroformic solution of the paraffin or mineral oil is poured into a weighed glass capsule, the chloroform evaporated on a water bath, and the residue dried during two hours at a temperature of 105° to 110° C., since it obstinately retains chloroform for a considerable time.

In the case of beeswax, it must be remembered that this contains more than 50 per cent of unsaponifiable matter (myricyl-alcohol) as a natural constituent, which is soluble in chloroform. Hence a method of separating the paraffin, etc., from the myricyl-alcohol must here be added. Five or 6 Gm. of wax are saponified and treated precisely as above directed, and the final residue of myricyl-alcohol and paraffin (if this is present) boiled with acetic anhydride, which converts the myricyl-alcohol into a compound ether and dissolves it, while the paraffin collects at the surface in drops. The solution is poured upon a stout filter in a funnel, placed in a hot-water apparatus, and the paraffin, which remains on the filter, repeatedly washed, first with boiling acetic anhydride, then with water. A loss of paraffin is not to be feared. The washed paraffin and filter is then put into a small beaker, dried at 100° until the adhering water is dissipated, then dissolved in petroleum ether or chloroform, the solution evaporated in a tared capsule, and the dried residue weighed. In place of acetic anhydride ($C_4H_6O_3$), anhydrous or glacial acetic acid ($C_2H_4O_2$) may be used, but in this case the compound ether produced is apt to separate if the temperature is at all allowed to decrease.

No. 2,250.—Prescription Query (A. M. D.).

"Please state how the following prescription should be compounded:
Potassii Chloratis............................. 3 iiss.
Quininae Sulphatis........................... gr. xl.
Syrupi Pruni Virg............................. ʒss.
Syrupi.. ʒi.
Aquae..................................... q. s. ad ʒiv.
M. Sig. ʒss. every four hours."

As the prescriber did not order any acid to bring the sulphate of quinine into solution, we assume that he wants it mechanically incorporated. Further, we have to note that the quantity of chlorate of potassium is larger than could be dissolved in an aqueous 4-ounce mixture. If there is no chance of communicating with the prescriber, we see no way out of it but to dispense the prescription with the undissolved portion suspended, to attach a *shake* label, and to give particular instructions to the recipient that this be not forgotten. In preparing the mixture, we would mix the two syrups with 3 fluidounces of water, triturate the liquid thoroughly with the chlorate of potassium and sulphate of quinine, then transfer the mixture to a graduate or 4 oz. vial, and rinse the mortar with enough water to make 4 fluidounces.

BIBLIOGRAPHY.

THE NATIONAL FORMULARY OF UN-OFFICINAL PREPARATIONS. First Issue. By authority of the American Pharmaceutical Association. Published by the American Pharmaceutical Association, 1888, pp. 176, 8vo, sheep and muslin.

THE conservative tendency of the last Committee of Revision of Publication of the Pharmacopœia has quite naturally borne fruit in the present form. Much labor has been required to prepare the 435 formulas which the book contains in a manner calculated to be acceptable to pharmacists and physicians distributed over such an enormous territory, and suited to the needs of so many widely separated localities, and it is a matter worthy of congratulation that the work has been accomplished so creditably. After the committee have gratuitously labored so long and faithfully, it is only fair that pharmacists generally should do their share to secure the adoption of the formulas by prescribers, for the benefit to be derived from an extensive sale is not the immediate pecuniary result so much as the relief of the pharmacists themselves from the necessity for carrying a stock of nearly similar articles of various manufacture. In other words, the more effort is made individually to secure the adoption of the work as a standard, the more individual benefit will be derived from it.

PTOMAINES AND LEUCOMAINES, or the Putrefactive and Physiological Alkaloids. By VICTOR C. VAUGHAN, Ph.D., M.D., Professor of Hygiene and Physiological Chemistry in the University of Michigan, etc., and FREDERICK G. NOVY, M.S., Instructor in Hygiene and Physiological Chemistry, etc. Philadelphia: Lea Bros. & Co., 1888, pp. 316, 8vo, muslin, $1.75.

PROF. VAUGHAN has probably done more than any one else in this country to advance our knowledge of this curious and important group of bodies. The work here referred to is a very successful attempt to embrace the known facts regarding them within limits which permit of their easy acquirement. There are some details which more particularly concern the physicians, but nearly everything contained in the work is of interest to chemists, and there is nothing which is not of the greatest importance as throwing light upon many obscure forms of illness. The study of the facts here presented cannot fail to exert great influence upon medical practice in the immediate future, and the medical profession especially are under many obligations to the authors for collecting, in such convenient shape, so much recent knowledge.

THE EAR AND ITS DISEASES: Being Practical Contributions to the Study of Otology. By SAMUEL SEXTON, M.D., Aural Surgeon to the New York Eye and Ear Infirmary, etc. Edited by CHRISTOPHER J. COLLES, M.D., Assistant Aural Surgeon to the New York Eye and Ear Infirmary. With Numerous Original Illustrations. New York: William Wood & Co., 1888, pp. 441, 8vo, muslin.

DR. SEXTON'S writings on the subject of aural diseases are already frequently met with in medical journals and government reports, and the materials for this volume have already in large measure appeared in the form of such scattered papers. Their collection and publication in their present form render them especially valuable. In many features this work is unlike its predecessors in this department of medical literature, and it occupies a place by itself, so that its purchaser will not be duplicating his sources of information.

MANUAL OF CHEMISTRY. A Guide to Lectures and Laboratory Work for Beginners in Chemistry. A Textbook especially adapted for Students of Pharmacy and Medicine. By W. SIMON, Ph.D., M.D., Professor of Chemistry and Toxicology in the College of Physicians and Surgeons; Professor of Chemistry and Analytical Chemistry in the Maryland College of Pharmacy, Baltimore, Md. Second edition, thoroughly revised and greatly enlarged, with forty-four illustrations and seven colored plates, representing fifty-six chemical reactions. Philadelphia: Lea Brothers & Co., 1888, pp. 479, 8vo, muslin, $3.75.

IN noticing the first edition of this work, we have already recognized its peculiar meritorious features, and a careful inspection of this greatly enlarged second edition more than justifies our former opinion. The book being specially designed for students in pharmacy and medicine, the author was enabled to confine his treatment of the subject within definite boundaries, omitting that which would only interest the general student who has to go over the whole ground of the science. The work is, of course, primarily intended to be used under the guidance of a teacher, but it is so practically arranged that it may well be used for self-study likewise. A distinguishing feature is the addition of a series of plates, showing, by colored strips, the various color-reactions of the more important metals, particularly of those which are liable to be confounded or mistaken for one another. We are so impressed with the usefulness of this feature—which we distinctly except from the class of so-called "coaching" or "cramming" aids—that we could have wished it rather more extended. In fact, we would prefer to have the plates separate from the book, perhaps best in form of a chart, on which all final color-reactions, which are capable of being illustrated, are shown. However, this idea is thrown out merely as a hint.

The work is gotten up in very handsome style, and in spite of the expense in preparing the colored plates, is sold at a very moderate price.

A TEXT-BOOK OF PHARMACOLOGY, THERAPEUTICS, AND MATERIA MEDICA. By T. LAUDER BRUNTON, M.D., D.Sc., F.R.S., etc. Adapted to the United States Pharmacopœia by FRANCIS H. WILLIAMS, M.D., Boston, Mass. Third Edition. Philadelphia: Lea Bros. & Co., 1888, pp. 1,261, 8vo, cloth, $5.50; leather, $6.50.

SINCE its first appearance, this work has rapidly become one of the most favorite text-books on its topic. We have already, in a notice of a former edition, spoken of its various features and the comprehensive manner in which its author has embraced the recent literature of pharmacology (used in its widest sense). As a hand-book for general reference respecting the knowledge of recently discovered remedies, it has no equal in our language and should be in every well-equipped pharmacist's working library. This latest addition has been considerably increased in size by additions of new matter.

THE PRESCRIPTION: Therapeutically, Pharmaceutically, and Grammatically considered. By OTTO A. WALL, M.D., Ph.G., Professor of Materia Medica and Botany in the St. Louis College of Pharmacy, etc. St. Louis, Mo., 1888, pp. 184, small 8vo, muslin.

THIS is unquestionably the most complete hand-book on the subject of prescription-writing that has yet appeared in this country, and the student of pharmacy or medicine who desires a work of the sort need not wait for something more comprehensive, as its appearance in the future is extremely improbable.

E. SACHSSE & Co. Preisliste ätherischer Oele. Leipzig-Reudnitz.

American Druggist

Vol. XVII. No. 12.   NEW YORK, DECEMBER, 1888.   Whole No. 174.

THE CORK INDUSTRY.

During former years we have several times published descriptions of the methods of procuring cork-wood and manufacturing bottle-corks, but a recent article in the *Gartenlaube*, by Fr. Helbig, contains a number of items of interest, particularly with reference to the art of cork-making in Germany, which we reproduce, in part, here.

The use of cork-wood for stoppering bottles does not seem to date back further than the fifteenth century. Previous to that time, much harder and tougher substances were used for such purposes. Bremen appears to have been the first commercial city which imported cork-wood from its more southerly home, and applied it technically. This may be concluded from a report printed in the State Almanac of Oldenburg of the year 1789, in which it is stated that the industry of cutting corks was already established, by a Bremen merchant named Hensch, in the beginning of the the preceding century, at Stuhr, a village in Oldenburg, situated about one mile from Bremen. From Stuhr, the industry spread over the lowland of Oldenburg, and gradually became independent of Bremen. Among other places, a cork-factory was established at Hasbergen, near Delmenhorst, by Friedrich Cordes, who had learned the art under Hensch, of Bremen. In 1796, the brothers Cordes employed 26 workmen, quite a large number for that period. Gradually other factories sprang up, but during the last thirty years most of these have been transferred to Delmenhorst, which has become the chief centre of the cork industry of Germany. . . .

The cork-oak (*Quercus suber* L.) is confined almost exclusively to Spain, Portugal, and Algiers. Attempts to grow it elsewhere have, so far, not been successful, owing to the absence of the proper climatic and geological conditions. The trees must have attained an age of 25 to 30 years, before they can be stripped of bark. But even this first bark—called in Spain *corcho virgen*, "virgin cork"—is unsuitable for making corks. It is only used for ornamental purposes, such as decorations for garden-pavilions, flower-stands, etc. The cork-wood proper grows only after the first bark has been taken off. When the bark is stripped off, great care must be taken not to injure the cambium layer below it. The latter will then produce a new white bark suitable for corks. This new layer requires for its full development a long time, some 8 to 10 years in Portugal, and from 11 to 14 years in Spain and Algiers, before it can be taken off. The stripping is done during the summer, from May to September. The usual process is to cut the bark cautiously with light hatchets in a circle around the tree, at intervals of about a meter; longitudinal cuts are then made, and the bark loosened and pried off with the handles of the hatchets. After a cork-oak has once begun to yield bark, it may, under favorable circumstances, last from 100 to 150 years. The freshly stripped corkwood differs, of course, greatly, both in quality and thickness, according to the size and age of the tree it is taken from. After it has been stripped off, it is first piled up in heaps, and then conveyed to factories where it is prepared for market. First it is soaked in water, and the rough outer bark scraped off. Next it is boiled for a few minutes, in large chaldrons, and then pressed into a flat shape. Finally it is assorted into grades, of which about ten are recognized, and sent to market in bales holding 60 to 70 kilos.

The great difference between the several grades of commercial cork-wood may be seen from the price, which runs from about $2.50 to $37 per 100 kilos. The best quality, suitable for wine and champagne corks, comes from Catalonia and a few other Spanish districts, and also from Estremoz and several other places in Portugal. Some very good grades are also furnished by Algiers. But most of the other cork-wood collected in Portugal is so soft that it is chiefly useful only for beer and druggists' corks.

After the cork-wood has reached the manufacturer, it is first sorted, the best qualities being reserved for wine or mineral water bottles.

In the factory of Cordes and Ellgass, each workman receives usually 50 kilos of cork-wood assigned to him at a time, from which he is expected to produce 30 kilos of large bottle corks and 15 kilos of small druggists' corks. The remainder is allowed as waste. The thinner cork-wood used for druggists' corks has usually a much thicker bark and furnishes more waste. The workman first cuts the wood into strips corresponding to the length of the corks to be made from it. Next he detaches the bark, cuts the strips into cubes, and from these he cuts the corks. This he does by means of two sharp knives, with broad blades, one of which is used for cutting into strips and cubes, the other for round-cutting. He uses no other tools. Considerable judgment is necessary to adjust the sizes of the strips and to select the various portions so as to obtain as large and perfect corks, and as many of them as possible. Even the smallest piece which will yield a cork must be utilised.

A skilful workman can turn out, each day, about 1,500 bottle or 2,000 druggists' corks. The work is not done in a factory, but at the workman's home, and the whole family often assists in the work. The small corks are usually finished by the children.

During the last twenty years, this industry has also been introduced in the neighborhood of Eisenach, where the same home manufacture is carried on. Each workman has a piece of leather strapped around his thigh, upon which he sharpens his knife, which becomes rapidly dull by cutting the soft, porous wood. Upon the chest he carries a large square piece of cork wood, suspended by a strap around the neck. This he uses as a support when stripping off the bark. Before each cutter is placed a willow basket, into which the finished corks are thrown. The people engaged in this industry are usually poor, and the wages low, as must naturally be the case where child labor is employed.

Machines for cutting cork do not appear to have made much headway in Europe, at least for the finer qualities of cork. For common grades, however, machines are used which can turn out some twenty thousand corks in ten hours.

After being delivered in the factory, the corks are passed through graded sieves for the purpose of separating the different sizes, and afterwards they are sorted over two or three times, to separate the grades.

Champagne corks, which receive their peculiar shape only when driven by power into the bottles, are almost exclusively manufactured in Spain and France. Of late years, they are often put together from different selected small pieces, which are glued upon each other by a peculiar cement, after which the corks are cut to the proper shape. This is done because the finest and softest grade of cork-wood is rather scarce and very expensive, the manufacturers' price for the best quality of champagne corks being about $36 per 1,000.

While the localities above mentioned comprise the most numerous factories, there are, of course, many others elsewhere. In fact, there is scarcely any city of note which has not one or more of them.

Oils of Cinnamon Bark and Leaf.

The *Sandaresa*, a Cingalese paper, strongly advises the natives of Ceylon to give up the distilling of cinnamon leaf oil, which they now manufacture in large quantities, and distil bark oil instead. Several persons, the journal in question observes, manufacture and export cinnamon leaf oil in spite of the small remuneration they get through it. In the Negombo district the distillation is not done by the proprietors, but by outsiders who pay a small sum in consideration of the leaves they get. If a distiller were to produce 100 bottles per month (which is the highest average he could attain), and well these at the rate of 1 rupee per bottle, he would get barely 15 rupees profit. On large estates leaves are obtainable during eight months of the year, and if the distiller is very active he will be able to earn 120 rupees per annum. The sum paid to the estate owner for the leaves and fuel is only 5 rupees per month. But it is clear that the cinnamon estates must lose by the carrying away of the leaves in consideration of such a small sum as 5 rupees, the leaves being a valuable fertilizer. Ceylon exports annually about 10,000 bottles of cinnamon oil which, on account of its low price, is used in the manufacture of soap and perfumery. If there were no leaf oil, the manufacturers would have to use oil made of bark, and thereby cause a good demand for low quality bark. To make up for 10,000 bottles leaf oil, they would at least require 5,000 bottles of bark oil, and to manufacture this quantity, 2,500,000 lbs. of coarse bark, at the rate of 500 lbs. per bottle, would be wanted. Therefore, it is advisable to leave off the small profits obtained through the distillation of leaves, in consideration of the higher demand arising in the market for the bark.—*Chem. and Drugg.*

A New Alkaloid from Calabar Bean.

Messrs. Böhringer & Sons, of Mannheim, announce the discovery of a new alkaloid in Calabar bean, to which they have given the name *eseridine*. This alkaloid has been known to them for some years, and they have made a careful investigation of its chemical and physical properties, and Dr. W. Eber, of Berlin, has reported upon the physiological action of the base. As a result, it appears that eseridine is not nearly so active a poison as physostigmine, but it is closely related to it chemically. From the particulars which have been communicated, the properties of the old alkaloid and its new associate may be thus contrasted:

Physostigmine, $C_{15}H_{21}N_3O_2$.	Eseridine, $C_{15}H_{23}N_3O_2$.
Melting point 105° C.	Melting point 132° C.
Very soluble in ether.	Sparingly soluble in ether.
Crystallises with difficulty and becomes amorphous on exposure to the air.	In crystalline white powder and large transparent crystals, permanent in the air.
Combines readily with acids to salts.	Forms salts with difficulty.

Perhaps the most important point regarding the new alkaloid is the fact that it so closely resembles physostigmine (there is only the difference of one molecule of water in the formulae) that, when heated with acids, it changes to physostigmine. Certain properties of the new base, chiefly its physiological effect, make it probable that it is closely related to, or some form of, the tetanising alkaloid calabarine which was discovered in calabar beans by Harnack and Wiskowski some fifteen years ago, and the existence of which has recently been called into question.—*After Chem. and Drugg.*

Creosote Pills.—F. Hachfeld mentions in the *Pharm. Zeitung* (No. 82) that creosote pills are best prepared by first triturating the requisite quantity of creosote with an equal weight of powdered gum Arabic, then adding water and briskly triturating so as to make a perfect emulsion. To this may then be added any convenient indifferent substances to give firmness and plasticity to the mass, so as to permit its being rolled out into pills. These are preferably coated, as patients object to the taste which is very persistent.

THE ART OF DISPENSING.

GENERAL SUGGESTIONS.

The Dispenser.—Be careful! This is the first thing to be learned by the one who wishes to become a dispenser; it comprises a great deal, not only the avoidance of mistakes in preparing medicines, but also the cultivation of habits of order and cleanliness. Untidy or soiled clothing, a disarranged or dirty prescription counter give the public an unpleasant impression and cause loss of patronage. Such practices as pressing cork with the teeth, holding powder envelopes or papers in the mouth, shaking up mixtures with the fingers over the mouth of the bottle, breathing on pill masses, wiping spatulas on the hands and clothing, should be avoided. Decent and becoming manners are essential, scolding the boy or assistants or joking with them before the customer, are out of place and should never be practised. Dispensing is the most responsible part of the pharmacist's duties, considered so by doctors and patients alike; the closest attention and most scrupulous care must, therefore, be manifested at all times at the dispensing counter.

Quality of Drugs.—The medicines employed in the preparation of prescriptions should be of the finest quality procurable for money, and officinal or other preparations made from them should be prepared in strict accordance with recognized methods. Second qualities of some goods may be necessary for certain purposes in other sales, but the pharmacist should not for a single moment permit the entrance of a thought about second qualities in the dispensing department. Differences will occur in medicines prepared at different establishments, but always retain the satisfaction of knowing that these cannot result from the use of inferior drugs in your pharmacy.

Let the question of profit gained from the dispensing of prescriptions be a secondary one; that will take care of itself. Dispense medicines with the feeling that an artist has in his work, and so will you make your vocation a pleasant labor.

Insure, by occasional testing, that preparations are of proper strength; this, in a great many instances, is now a comparatively easy thing to do, by the use of the tests directed by the pharmacopœia; if it be not possible to test everything that is used at the dispensing counter, at least those that are liable to deteriorate, such as Spts. Etheris Nitrosi, or dilute Hydrocyanic Acid, should receive your attention.

But *make* time to devote to testing, and although you pay the best price for your drugs, do not take for granted that you will always receive the best, nor let it prevent you from submitting them to examination before placing in stock.

A little practice in testing will soon make you perfect, so do not be discouraged if your first efforts are not as successful as you could wish; you will grow in love with the work as you progress, and the results will often be astonishing; besides, it will tend to make you much more dexterous and insure a confidence in your dispensing work which can never be otherwise attained.

Style in Externals.—The pharmacist, however, may lose all the pecuniary benefit of his conscientiousness, though using the most costly drugs and being particular in their examination, if he should be wanting in neatness or style in sending them out. The dispenser who economises on his drugs is a rogue, but he who economises on his bottles, corks, pill boxes, twine, or paper is a fool. Customers judge by the externals, and generally they would be right in concluding that a man who passes out his drugs in a low class bottle with a brittle cork or wrapped in common paper may have used drugs of equally low quality. Especial care should be taken when renewing a prescription, if it be a liquid, to see the bottle is thoroughly cleansed, both inside and outside, removing all sediment that may have dried on; if powders or pills, always dispense in a new box.

Labels.—Neatness, distinctness, and simplicity should govern the selection of labels. Therefore have a neat label for the dispensing department, with as little beyond your name, qualification, and address as you can help. Let the directions to the patient, and not your name or address, be the most prominent part of the label. Particular attention should also be paid to the handwriting. These are important particulars, for patients are exceedingly apt to form an estimate of the qualifications of the compounder of a prescription from the style of his penmanship, reasoning that, if he is careful, clean, and neat in the one particular of which they are competent to judge, *i. e.*, the handwriting on the label, he will exercise similar qualifications in the more vital operations involved in compounding and dispensing, for upon the technicalities of the latter they cannot hope to pass judgment.

Bad penmanship is too easily accepted as a sort of natural defect and a good many people even pride themselves on it. Some perseverance, however, is all that is necessary to make a bad writer into a good one, and the youth who will not take the trouble to cultivate that first branch of his art had better abandon any thought of fitting himself to become a dispenser of medicine.

In round labels there is little room for variety, but in

this case it is all important, owing to the small space for directions, to have little room wasted on the name and address.

Labels should always be neatly trimmed by carefully cutting off with a pair of scissors the surplus paper at the margin. Many pharmacists neglect to do this, but when done, it adds greatly to the appearance. Tinted paper is often used for labels, and undoubtedly in some instances looks very well, but care should be exercised in the selection, for the printing and writing on many colors, when stained by the contents of the bottle, especially when this is of an oily nature, will be completely hidden. It is advisable, and almost always necessary, to relabel when renewing prescriptions.

The practice, too often seen, of placing a fresh label over an old one to save the trouble of removing it should never be permitted. It is a lazy, slovenly habit, and may produce mistakes from the accidental removal of the top label and exposure of another unlike in nature or dose. The old label can be quickly removed by dampening with water and holding it over the flame or before the fire for a few seconds; this softens the mucilage, and the label may be removed with ease. A stout knife, with a good edge, may be used, if in a hurry, to scrape off the label, then a damp towel will remove any pieces of paper left. A better plan than either of these is to lay the bottle in a pan of water

lotion labels with "Poison" at the top, and another series without, can be kept. Mixture labels the same way, one with "The Mixture," another with immediately below these words, "Shake the bottle well before using."

CAPPING BOTTLES.—Bottles are generally finished off by being capped or having the top of the cork waxed. When capped, it is with either sheepskin—split skins they are called commercially—or paper. When the skins are used, they should be well wet with water (if not pure white, lime water will bleach them), and then put on the bottle smoothly; it requires a little practice to get the skin over the cork and tied under the neck of the bottle without many laps showing, but it can be done by any one who will take time to do it, and repays one for the trouble. A paper cap should consist of a double thickness. For the top layer, it is customary to use glazed, colored paper; for the lower, a clean, white, thin paper; but for salves and electuaries, in place of the latter, waxed or paraffin paper. When tying a cap, another piece of soft paper should be laid over the external layer, to prevent soiling the latter during the pressure required to adjust it. After the smoothing, the soft paper is to be removed, and the cap fastened with two turns of fine twine. The ends of the twine may be sealed to the top of the cap, as shown in the figure.

Caps of all sizes pleated by machinery are now supplied

Gathering cork in Algiers. (See page 221.)

for a few minutes—this may be done while the new label is being written—the label will in most instances be easily removed. The latter plan serves a double purpose also of aiding in cleaning the bottle. The label being taken off entire can be used for comparing with the prescription to prove the right one has been prepared.

ADVENTITIOUS LABELS.—Poison, Shake the mixture well before using, For external use only, and other adventitious labels are best placed on the shoulder of the bottle or around the neck. If placed at the foot, the hand holding the bottle may cover them, or a hurried person may overlook them. At the shoulder they will be read first. Moreover, it frequently happens that the patient will only tear off the upper part of the wrapper, hence a label at the bottom in such an instance would be of no avail because not seen. In some establishments economy is practised by having rubber stamps for the words "Mixture," "Lotions," etc., instead of separate printed labels; this may be justifiable in a very few instances, but as printing is so reasonable now, it is much more desirable, certainly looks neater, and gives a better finish to use the printed ones.

These words may be printed on the label and they can be given a prominence so as at once to attract attention by the use of different kind of type, or printed with a different color of ink, than the rest of the label. One series of

to the trade at a very moderate price, and are planted much more evenly than any done by hand. See Fig. on p. 224.

All that is necessary is to place them over the size of cork they are made for, and to tie under the neck of the bottle with a string. When tying, whether it be a cap on the bottle, or the wrapping paper around the bottle, always tie with a loop so that the string can be removed without any difficulty. The practice of waxing the top of corks should be discouraged for prescription work, for generally the first time the bottle is opened the wax is broken, and the cork ever after presents an unsightly appearance; besides, there is a liability of some of the wax dropping inside the bottle or resting on its mouth, disgusting a fastidious patient. If wax be used, put it on very light and stamp it with your initials or name; always dampen the metal stamp before pressing it on the hot wax. Some pharmacists paint or varnish the top of the cork, which of course has to be done some time before they are wanted for use. The neatest and handiest of all methods is to have a round gummed label just the size of the cork, on which may be printed the name and address of the pharmacist; these are readily moistened and fastened to the top of the cork.

ONE THING AT A TIME.—Always finish a prescription that has been commenced. Write the label and paste it on the bottle or box before starting on another. A disregard of this rule will cause more mistakes than anything else, for if a prescription is only partly completed, laid aside, and attention concentrated on something else, it is very easy to forget what was put in, and an article will often be duplicated or left out in consequence when work on the prescription is renewed.

If the label is not attached at once when the prescription is finished, it will often happen the wrong label will go on the wrong bottle, and lead to serious consequences, as, for instance, a liniment label attached to an internal remedy mixture; even if both prescriptions are for internal administration, the difference in doses may lead to confusion, and if discovered by patient or doctor, to doubt and loss of patronage. Never take any chances when at pharmaceutical work; a dispenser's reputation is obtained only after great effort, is too easily lost, and never fully regained to allow one to take risks that can be avoided.

Of course, these remarks, except as to labelling, do not apply to prescriptions for infusions or other preparations that cannot be finished at once or do not need constant attention. In such cases set the jar on one side, mark on a piece of paper its contents and what is to be done with it, and paste this on its side. You can then attend to other prescriptions. When a prescription is finished and labelled, at once clear up all the mess, or have it done for you, and put away all bottles, measures, spatulas, and mortars that have been used; these should in no case be allowed to accumulate on the prescription counter, for they are bound to hamper a man in his work and divert his mind from an earnest study of his prescription, which is so essentially necessary to him. The practice that many dispensers have of bringing together on the counter all the bottles or packages containing the ingredients ordered in the prescription is not a commendable one. It is safer to go to the shelf for each article, as it is needed to be weighed or measured; it may cause a little more trouble, but trouble should not be considered if mistakes can be prevented. When fitting up a store or a prescription department, have bottles so arranged that the most ordinarily used articles will be handy, and that will reduce the trouble to a minimum.

Two persons should never work at the same prescription, except when checking off. The one who prepares it should copy it, if it is to be copied, write the label, and hand the medicine to the customer, unless, as in some large establishments, his duty is to stay in the prescription department entirely, then he should pass it to the clerk who waits upon the customers.

PRESERVING PRESCRIPTIONS.—In many pharmacies it is customary to copy the prescription into a book, retaining the original one on a file; in others the prescription is pasted into a book; still another custom is to merely file the prescription.

The first method is probably the best, for it insures a critical reading of and familiarity with the prescription that is so essentially necessary. The great objections that may be urged against it are, first, the time it consumes, which is an important thing to consider when you have an impatient customer waiting; and, second, the danger of copying it down wrong—all are liable to error, even the best of pharmacists. If such an error should occur, the prescription may be renewed several times before it is discovered, for generally when prescriptions are renewed the copy is referred to and not the original paper. When copying is practised, it should always be done before the prescription is prepared.

The second method is good, and takes but little time. It is better to paste the prescription in the book immediately after preparing it, but, if for good reasons it should be deemed best not to do this at once, it should be placed with others of the day on a small file, and either the last thing in the evening or the first in the morning pasted in the book. The third method of merely filing prescriptions is the most objectionable, especially when they are stuck on a long wire, which is the general way, and this hung on a nail in a corner. The papers soon become dusty, fly-marked, torn, and some lost. It is a very slovenly way, and cannot fail to unfavorably impress customers and physicians who see them and may often wish to refer to them. The best way to keep prescriptions on file without pasting in a book is to have small boxes, each capable of holding about one hundred papers, each numbered on the outside from 1 to 100, as, for instance, 15,501 to 15,600, 15,601 to 15,700, 15,701 to 15,800, etc.; it is easy to refer to any number, and the prescription, being covered, is free from dust and flies; the principal objections to it are the liability of the paper not being replaced in its exact order, or of others being withdrawn when one is taken out, and possibly lost.

READING PRESCRIPTIONS.—When handed a prescription, do not attempt to read it before customers; for, if an attempt be made to read it carefully then, they will at once jump to the conclusion that either the doctor has made an error, or the pharmacist does not understand it, and questions will be asked, annoying remarks made, or a request for a return of the prescription for preparation by another pharmacist. Carry it back to the prescription counter, and when shielded from the customer's gaze, take plenty of time to study it carefully; think which of the articles will act on each other; which of the liquids, if there are more than one, the solids are soluble in. Note the quantities and calculate what proportion of each ingredient there will be in each dose; refer to the dispensatory or other work to ascertain any dose of which you are in doubt. Don't let pride stand in the way, if there is a doubt in the mind about anything on the prescription; do not hesitate to consult with others about it; superiors, of course, if possible; inferiors rather than not at all.

PREPARING PRESCRIPTIONS.—Having become satisfied that the prescription is thoroughly understood, copy it, if it is to be copied; then get the mortar, graduates, and spatulas needed, and proceed to weigh or measure out the ingredients, commencing with the smallest quantities first, unless there are reasons for doing otherwise. It is always best to use a mortar to mix or dissolve solid matters in the liquids, for the mixture can be thereby made much more evenly. The small lumps into which most powders will aggregate will be broken up more readily in the mortar than when shaken with a liquid in a bottle, if, indeed, in the latter case they separate at all. Many substances cause great frothing when shaken up. This will be avoided if the mixture is made in the mortar. Powders, when put into a bottle, are apt to cake in the bottom, and cannot be loosened without great difficulty, and in some cases not at all; the use of the mortar obviates this. Even in cases of readily soluble ingredients, it is better to use a mortar, for every preparation that is to be clear of sediment, should be filtered, or strained through a cloth, to separate the particles of dirt that will always be found after dissolving a solid; if the ingredients had at once been put into the bottle, this would require a pouring-out and a consequent rinsing of the bottle. Reserve some of the liquid with which you rub up the solids to rinse out the mortar with. After weighing a powder carefully, wipe the scale pan; this is essential, for if a dark powder, like aloes, should have been used, and next a white one, like sugar, too much of the latter may be on the scale pan and have to be returned to the stock bottle. If the pan was not wiped after using the aloes, a portion of the latter will be gathered up and pass into the bottle with the sugar, giving it a taste, and possibly a color, that does not belong to it. The practice of wiping the scale pan each time it is used will insure its being clean when the prescription is finished. Having weighed all that is necessary, put away the weights, relieve the beam from the weight of the scales, and close the doors of the case. Do not treat the scales roughly. It is evidence of carelessness and indifference, on the part of the dispenser, to throw a weight, or a substance to be weighed, upon the scale pan. It should be put on gently, and the indicator watched meanwhile; when that begins to move, there is probably enough on.

If hand-scales are used, hold them in the left hand by the thumb and finger, the indicator being prevented from oscillating too far by the third and fourth fingers. By this means they can be held up to the level of the eyes. It is always safer to judge the weight while the indicator is moving, noticing that it goes as far one side of the centre as the other, rather than to take the weight as it stands still in the centre, for a trifle more or less of the substance being weighed may not overcome the friction when the balance is at rest, or a slight portion of dust or rust on the bearing points would destroy its delicacy of movement; these would not have the same retarding power while the balance is in motion. Never guess at a quantity, no matter if the substance is the mildest drug known; it will be sure to cultivate carelessness. Train the eye, however, so that you do not put very much more or less at once on the scale than is needed. Learn to be rapid in manipulation, but do not practise haste at the expense of accuracy.

CHECKING.—The dispenser should never pass out a prescription without without having his work checked. No matter how skilful he is, nor how much care he exercises, it will make him feel much more comfortable to know that his skill and care has been rendered doubly sure by some one besides himself going over his work. Many an error may be detected in this way which otherwise might not have been discovered until too late to rectify. In any case, the prescription should not be allowed to leave the hand without a final reading, attention being concentrated on it, the quantities as well as the substances being carefully noted. It is a good plan to mark on the label the initials of the dispenser and of the one who checked it. A form like this could be used:

Dispensed by R. G.
Checked by A. D.

Particular care should be taken to see that each customer receives his right medicine. There are probably as many, if not more errors made this way than in any other. Two

REYNOLD'S PHARMACY.
PRESCRIPTION CHECK.
680.

REYNOLD'S PHARMACY.
PRESCRIPTION CHECK.
680.

PRESCRIPTION DEPARTMENT
REYNOLD'S PHARMACY,
PLAINFIELD, N. J.
Please present to a Check when calling for your Prescription.
680.

customers come in at the same time, and each hands in a prescription probably from the same physician. Unless some precaution is at once taken to identify each customer with his own prescription, the chance is they will each receive the wrong one; even if a second or third is handed in some time after the first, there is apt to be confusion. Many times prescriptions are left to be called for, and other members of the family come for it; it is difficult to know which one to give unless provisions have been made beforehand to guard against the trouble. Many establishments adopt the system of having checks with duplicate numbers. One number is given to the party ordering the medicine and the corresponding number attached to the prescription. This need not be confined to stores doing a large prescription trade, for no matter how small the business, too much care cannot be exercised to prevent a mistake.

H. P. Reynolds, of Plainfield, N. J., suggests* a form of check, which can be printed six or eight on a sheet, and gummed by hand, or bought all ready for use for about $3 a thousand. The coupons only are gummed, and are scored in printing, to enable them to be torn off. When a prescription is received, the check is handed to the customer, and the coupons are affixed to the prescription, one of them projecting, to be attached to the completed and wrapped package, to serve for its identification on the presentation of the check.

Whether checks are used or not, when a prescription is handed in, at once ask for the name of the party it is for or who hands it to you, and at once write this name on the face or back of the paper. When the prescription is finished, or ready to be delivered, call out the name and inform him the prescription is ready.

Note on Sulphonal.

In spite of its comparatively high price, sulphonal appears to have taken a decided hold among observant therapeutists, as an efficient and harmless soporific. The only difficulty connected with it is its pharmaceutical intractability, it being so little soluble in the usual menstrua which can be used for the internal administration of remedies. The following notes, taken from the *Pharm. Centralhalle* (No. 36), may afford some hints to prescribers or dispensers.

Kast (*Therap. Monatsh.*, 1886, 316) finds sulphonal to be soluble in water, at the temperature of the blood (37°-38° C.), in the proportion of 1 in 450. The solubility is decidedly increased by the presence of salts, a 2-per-cent solution of chloride of sodium at 40° C. dissolves sulphonal in the proportion of 1 in 250.

Baumann has already pointed out that concentrated mineral acids dissolve sulphonal easily; but even when they are highly diluted, they exert a solvent action upon the substance. In a solution of hydrochloric acid containing 2‰ HCl—about the proportion existing in the gastric juice —the solubility was found, at blood-temperature, to be 1 in 272 and 1 in 280. 100 C.c. of artificial gastric juice, mixed with 0.5 Gm. (8 grains) of sulphonal at blood-temperature, effected complete solution in 1 to 2 hours. This represents a proportion of 1 in 200. On neutralizing this solution with soda, the sulphonal did not crystallize out during several hours.

In presence of salts and peptones, sulphonal is still more easily soluble. But alkalies exert scarcely any influence upon its solubility.

Kast recommends, as the best method of administering sulphonal, to give it in form of powder (15 to 45 grains) mixed with at least 7 fl. oz. of some warm liquid in the early part of the evening, say between 7 and 8 o'clock. It may be given with a part of the evening meal or in the tea. Under these circumstances it is most readily dissolved.

To detect sulphonal in the contents of the stomach or intestines, they are shaken with ether, which takes up both the dissolved and the undissolved sulphonal. The ethereal solution is evaporated, the residue treated with hot water, the solution freed from fat by filtration, the filtrate again shaken with ether, and the ethereal solution again evaporated.

According to Schwarz, minute quantities of sulphonal may be detected in the following manner: Place some powdered wood charcoal and a trace of sulphonal into a test-tube, cover this with moistened blue litmus paper, and heat the contents over a flame. A dense cloud having the odor of mercaptan will form, and at the same time the litmus paper will be strongly reddened by the simultaneously produced vapors of formic, acetic, and sulphurous acids.

Another reaction is given by Schwarz as follows: Heat sulphonal for some time with caustic soda and powdered wood charcoal over a flame. The fused mass then contains sulphide of sodium, and therefore yields the usual reactions with nitro-prusside of sodium, or solution of lead salts, or on addition of an acid. This reaction may be performed even with very minute quantities of sulphonal upon a platinum wire, but a protracted ignition is necessary for success.

Observers differ somewhat in their statements as to the proper doses. According to Rosin, it is not a prompt soporific in doses of 1 Gm. (15 grains); but 2 Gm. (30 grains) act promptly; and may be considered as equivalent to ⅓–½ grain of morphine. In children a prompt effect it produced, according to Schwalbe, by doses of 4 to 8 grains. Schmey warns against administering sulphonal to persons suffering from angina pectoris or arteriosclerosis.

Dr. Mathes records in the *Centralblatt f. klinische Medic.* (*Chem. and Drugg.*), the results of a series of clinical trials of the soporific, which were carried out under the supervision of Professor v Ziemssen in Munich. The doctor gave ninety-nine single doses to twenty-seven patients, and the therapeutical virtues of the compound may be judged from the fact that a complete effect was obtained in 72 per cent of the administrations, while in 9.25 per cent the remedy was somewhat less successful, making 81.25 per cent of cases in which it more or less

Capped and sealed bottle.

Machine pleated cap.

Gummed cork-tops.

accomplished the desired end. In 18.75 per cent of the total number of times it was given, the results were negative. The dose was found to vary with the individual, so that no hard and fast line of maximum and minimum could be drawn. For a majority of doses 15 grains was found to be sufficient, and in all instances it was observed to be desirable to administer the compound some hours before the sleep was desired, as its effects are only slowly produced. It is preferable to other hypnotics in being free from taste and odor, and without any tendency to interfere with the vital functions.

Partial Vacuum for Desiccators, Percolators, etc.

A GALLON tin is fitted with a rubber stopper, through which passes a glass tube bent at right angles and attached to a rubber tube, which can be closed by a screw pinchcock. About half a pint of water is placed in the tin and boiled until the air has been removed, that is, until the steam is wholly condensed when passed into cold water. The source of heat is then withdrawn and the rubber tube closed with the pinchcock. The tin is cooled by placing in cold water. The rubber tube is now attached to the vessel to be exhausted, and the cocks opened. If the vessel be about a liter in capacity, three-fourths of the air will be taken from it, and if the operation be repeated a second time, the quantity may be further reduced to one-sixteenth of an atmosphere, and this for most practical purposes is a vacuum.

I find that an ordinary gallon tin will bear the required pressure; that a two gallon tin of usual thickness will not do so; neither will an essence-of-lemon copper, which is generally so useful for laboratory purposes, answer in this case; but its failure in this respect may be turned to account as a lecture experiment to illustrate the great force of atmospheric pressure.—W. H. SYMONS in *Pharm. Journ.*, Sept. 15th.

[If any of our readers happens to have what Mr. Symons calls a "gallon tin" which is of any particular value, we caution him not to place implicit faith in the above statement that it will not collapse if treated as directed.—ED, A. D.]

---

*American Druggist, February, 1888.

Glycerin Suppository as a Laxative.

A PROPRIETARY preparation introduced in Europe under the name of Oidtmann's Purgative has been the means of leading the attention of physicians to the fact that glycerin administered per rectum seems to be one of the most prompt and efficient laxatives in existence. The preparation before mentioned has been examined by various chemists, who found it to contain a high percentage of impure glycerin, but it is presumed the "inventor" did not know himself that the principal activity of his compound resided in this ingredient. It has since then been reported by various authorities that glycerin, introduced as enema, is an exceedingly prompt evacuant. Several methods have been proposed to apply the agent for this purpose practically, but none of these are as advantageous as the method of Dieterich, who prepares suppositories containing 90 per cent of glycerin in the following manner:

Dissolve 10 parts of extra-hard "dialyzed" stearin soap in boiling water, add to the solution 90 parts of pure glycerin, filter the whole in a steam-funnel, and evaporate to 100 parts. Then pour the mass into suppository moulds.

The suppositories thus prepared are firm and transparent, hygroscopic, and when exposed to the air soon become coated with water blisters. The combination of soap and glycerin appears to be a very judicious one, as soap alone is well known to act as a laxative.

It is said that the laxative effect occurs between one and ten minutes after introducing the suppository, and is so easy and free from discomfort that this promises to come soon into general use.

[The efficacy of these suppositories as a laxative is denied by Dr. Boas, of Berlin, who says that the mixture of which the suppository consists is insoluble in the rectum, owing to its high melting-point (76° C.). Another correspondent of the *Pharm. Zeit.*, Mr. A. Heck, asserts that they are readily melted in the rectum within ten minutes, and that they have a prompt effect. Before use, they should be rubbed over with a little glycerin or oil.—ED. AM. DRUGG.]

Dieterich makes two sizes of suppositories, weighing respectively about 10 and 40 grains, which are wrapped in tin-foil for protection.—*After Zeitsch. d. Oester. Apoth. Ver.*, No. 26.

Note by Ed. Am. Drugg.—The "dialyzed" stearin soap mentioned in the formula is no doubt the same for which Dieterich gives a formula in his *Pharm. Manuale* (2), p. 310:

Stearic Acid	1,000 parts.
Sodium Carbonate, cryst.	585 "
Alcohol	100 "
Sodium Chloride	240 "
Water	3,750 "

Melt the Stearic Acid, and gradually add it, under stirring, to a solution of 560 parts of crystallised Carbonate of Sodium in 3,000 parts of Water, heated on a steam-bath. When all the stearic acid has been added, add the Alcohol, cover the vessel, and allow it to stand at least six hours on top of the steam apparatus [that is, in a warm place]. Then cause the soap to separate by adding a filtered solution of the Chloride of Sodium, and the remainder of the Carbonate of Sodium (25 parts) in 750 parts of the Water, transfer it to a cloth strainer, allow to become cold, and press.

If it is desired to remove the salts which are contained as impurities in all commercial stearic acid, the soap solution is not salted out, but is filled into parchment paper bags (gut or parchment "cases"), which are hung into hot water. The salts will thus gradually dialyse out. But this latter operation can be carried out with advantage only on the large scale. The yield of salted-out soap obtained from the above-named quantities amounts to at least 1,100 parts.

Camphoric Acid.

CAMPHORIC acid was first recommended by Reichert as a remedy in affections of the mucous membrane of the respiratory passages. Lately it has been thoroughly tested by Nissel in the medical clinic at Greifswald. It was found that a 1-per-cent solution of it, effected by means of an alkali, when used by way of inhalation upon consumptives, almost always produced a diminution of expectoration and of a desire to cough. The same solution was found useful in chronic cystitis, being used as injection. Its greatest usefulness, however, was found to be the reducing effect it had upon the night-sweats of consumptives. For this purpose it was given in doses of 1 Gm. (15 grains), or even 2 Gm. (30 grains); or 1 Gm. (15 grains) three times daily.—*After Deutsch. Med. Wochensch.*

Note by Ed. Am. Drugg.—Camphoric acid is prepared from camphor by the prolonged action of hot nitric acid. The following is an outline of the process. To 150 Gm. of camphor contained in a capacious flask placed on a water-bath add 4 pints of nitric acid of spec. grav. 1.270, and fit a long glass tube into the neck by means of plaster of Paris, the glass tube serving as an upright condenser. Then heat the water-bath to boiling and keep it so until the vapors in the glass tube have nearly or entirely ceased to have a reddish tint, for which a period of about 50 hours may be necessary. Now concentrate the contents of the flask, neutralize with soda, filter, and decompose the salt with hydrochloric acid. The camphoric acid will separate, and is recrystallised from boiling water.

Camphoric acid is in form of white scales or crystals, soluble in 160 parts of water at 12 C., and in 12 parts of boiling water. Its sodium as well as potassium salts are deliquescent. The lithium salt requires 1, and the magnesium salt 2.5 parts of water for solution. Camphoric acid is a bibasic acid, its formula being $H_2C_{10}H_{14}O_4$, or $C_{10}H_{16}O_4$, while camphor has the formula $C_{10}H_{16}O$.

Chlorodyne.

THE new Hungarian Pharmacopœia, among other new preparations, gives a formula for "Chlorodine," which differs very considerably from those previously known under this name, and certainly does not appear to resemble the proprietary article known under that name. The formula, transcalculated into our weights and measures, is as follows:

Extract of Cannabis Indica	1½ grains.
Acetic Ether	q. s.
Chloroform	90 min.
Tincture of Ginger	300 "
Syrup of Orange Peel	70 "

Dissolve the Extract of Cannabis Indica by rapid trituration in thirty drops of the Acetic Ether, and add the Syrup of Orange Peel. Then gradually incorporate, while stirring, the Tincture of Ginger, transfer the mixture to a bottle, and add the remainder of the Acetic Ether and the Chloroform. Keep in a well-closed bottle. It should have a greenish-yellow color, and remain free from sediment.

Improving the Taste of Cascara Preparations.

IN view of the recent discussion on the activity of cascara preparations which have been rendered palatable by treatment with alkali, the following comments by Dr. John Irving, of Leytonstone, are of interest, and apart from that the notes give some hints which pharmacists may advantageously follow up. Dr. Irving calls attention to the repulsive-looking mixture which the ordinary fluid extract forms with water, and states that this unsightliness may be entirely and satisfactorily obviated without either glycerin or syrups. A very small quantity of water of ammonia, dropped into the watery mixture, will clear it to a bright ruby color, seen by transmitted light, the transparency of which is not altered by a flavoring agent, such as tinct. aurantii, nor by a sweetener, like saccharin.

Fl. Ext. of Cascara	℥ 30
Water of Ammonia	gr. 2
Tinct. of Orange	℥ 15
Solut. of Saccharin (5%)	q. s.
Water	fl. ℥ 1½

One dose.

Again, ammonia permits cascara to be dispensed with some preparations of iron, such as citrate of iron and ammonium, the mixture, though dark in proportion to the amount of extract used, being a perfect solution:

Citrate of Iron and Ammonium	gr. 30
Water of Ammonia	℥ 10
Fl. Ext. of Cascara	℥ 30 to 60
Sol. of Saccharin (5%)	q. s.
Water (aromatic)	to make fl. ℥ 6

Dose: A fluidounce thrice daily.

This combination is especially serviceable, with (or without) small doses of digitalis, where the heart is enfeebled and constipation exists, with tendency to œdema of the extremities; in such a case, the liquid extract of cascara, given with the iron in regulated small doses, three or four times a day, serves an obvious twofold purpose: (1) it counteracts the binding effect of iron in relieving the bowels, and (2) assists the circulation by removing excess of fluid. In a similar way, cascara may be combined with liq. bismuthi et ammon. citratis in digestive derangements. Numerous other mixtures will doubtless suggest themselves; the only point to be kept in mind is that the medicine containing the cascara must be somewhat alkaline, and made so with ammonia, or, as has been suggested, with potassa.—*After Brit. Med. Journ. and Chem. and Drugg.*

The Cutch Trade of Burmah.

THE *Rangoon Gazette*, discussing the manufacture and trade in cutch in Burmah, says that the export of cutch is the next most important to that of rice, and it has been steadily increasing during the past twenty years. The Acacia Catechu, or cutch tree, is found in large forests throughout the whole country; the core of the tree is a dark red wood like mahogany; the wood is chipped and boiled, the inspissated extract thus obtained being the cutch. In October the cutch boilers form themselves into small companies, and select a spot where there are good robust trees. The boiling pans are firmly fixed in holes in the ground, the trees are felled, the branches lopped, the bark and outer wood removed, and the core reached. The children chip the dark red wood, which is placed in the pans with a little water, care being taken that it does not get overheated or burnt. When of the required consistence, the contents of the pans are spread out on mats to evaporate, the woody refuse being thrown away, and the sap alone retained. In a short time the mats can be manipulated into small blocks of a regular size. The colors are red, dark red, or black, the shades depending principally on the quality of the chips and the time taken in boiling. The light red and red cutch is considered the best, and with betel nut and other ingredients is chewed by the Burmese, and is exported to India for the same purpose. The dark red and black are prepared largely for the markets of Europe and America. The characteristics of pure, unadulterated cutch are uniformity of appearance, bitter, acrid, or pungent taste, smell like opium, and friability. Formerly the quality could, as a rule, be relied on, but of late years, owing to the steady demand, keen competition, and enhanced prices, a stimulus has been given to the trade, and great liberties have been taken with the cutch in mixing and adulterating. A spurious cutch is used; fibrous matter, sand, or earth are sometimes added to increase the weight, and the Chinese dealers have a habit of putting good, bad, and indifferent into one consignment, which is then sold for a good sample.—*Chem. and Drugg.*

Insect Powder and Hellebore.

According to Marpmann, the poisonous action of insect flowers is due to a volatile principle, soluble in alcohol and very volatile, as by distillation a product is obtained which is as active. Hellebore is sometimes used as an adulterant of insect powder. That this is not a poison to flies can be shown by putting them under bell jars with the different powders. With insect powder, the flies, after several minutes, drag the hind legs, fall on the backs, and are stupefied. On the contrary, with hellebore they are alive after twenty-four hours.—*Chem. and Drugg.*

Avoidance of Weighed Filters.

Professor DE KONINCK, of Brussels, calls attention to the advantage of a method long ago recommended by Prof. Fresenius, by which the weighing of filters containing precipitates may in many cases be avoided. It is well known that the drying of filters to a constant weight and the keeping them dry during weighing is often difficult. Besides, when the precipitate is to be ignited with the filter, it is sometimes impossible to prevent the reduction of a part of the precipitate, whereby loss is incurred.

The remedy proposed is to wash the filter with a liquid which will completely dissolve the precipitate, and which will not bring into the resulting solution any substance that cannot be driven off at the temperature to which the precipitate proper would have to be exposed.

The author, for instance, recommends, when potassium is to be determined as the double chloride of platinum and potassium, and after this precipitate has been properly collected on the filter and washed in the usual manner with moderately strong alcohol, to detach the precipitate as far as possible from the filter, then to replace the filter in the funnel, and to wash the rest of the precipitate through by means of boiling water. This solution is then evaporated, the detached precipitate added, the whole dried and ignited. There being no danger of reducing any of the salt by contact of organic matter from the filter, more accurate results are obtained.

The same may be done when determining arsenic as ammonio-magnesium arsenate, or phosphorus as ammonio-magnesium phosphate, and so in many other cases.—*Zeitsch. f. angew. Chem.*

[It could also be well applied in determining alkaloids, as it is well known that the use of counterbalanced filters is usually a source of inaccuracy.—ED. AM. DRUGG.]

RECEIVER FOR DISTILLATION IN VACUUM.

In place of the apparatus designed by Raikow, Edgar v. Boyen recommends the construction shown in the accompanying illustration, which does not need a detailed description. The vacuum is, of course, established by aspiration (by means of a pump, etc.), at the lateral tubes of the flasks A and B. Communication with either one or the other receiving flasks is established by a proper adjustment of the stopcocks $a b$ and $a' b'$. To make the apparatus less fragile and complicated, it is so arranged that it consists of several pieces to be joined together by stout rubber-tubing.—*Chem. Zeit.* and *Chem. Centralbl.*

A DIALYZER FOR EXPERIMENTAL PURPOSES.

The glass vessel g has thick walls, is expanded above, and in the inside of its neck, at x, has three projecting ledges. Upon these is placed a funnel t, the stem of which is cut off, and in the inside of the funnel is placed a parchment filter $p f$, folded in the manner proposed by Hehner & Richmond (see September, page 167). The filter projects 1½ Cm. beyond the edge of the funnel. The substance to be dialysed is put into the filter, and the vessel is filled, by means of a sprite-flask, with distilled water to the height of 1 Cm. over the edge of the filter (that is, to the mark $w h$). This causes the filter to float in the position it occupies, and all conditions for a successful dialysis are now very favorable. The dialysate may be seen to flow off or descend from the orifice of the funnel, while fresh water passes in over the edge of the funnel. When the water is to be renewed, the funnel with filter is lifted out by means of a pair of crucible tongs. The whole apparatus is covered by a plate of glass.—A. SCHNEIDER, in *Pharm. Centralh.*, 144.

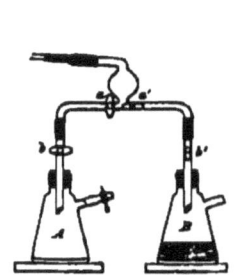

Boyen's apparatus.

Receiver for fractional distillation.

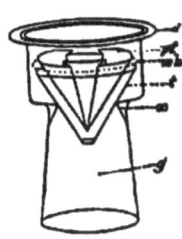

Schneider's dialyzer.

RECEIVER FOR UNINTERRUPTED FRACTIONAL DISTILLATION.

When a liquid is to be distilled under reduced pressure or under a vacuum, which is accomplished by connecting the receiver with the air pump or with a Bunsen filter pump, and when it is at the same time desired to receive the distillate in several fractions without disturbing the vacuum, the apparatus shown in the cut may be used. This is an adapter and condenser combined. It is made of glass, and supplied by Alt, Eberhard, and Jaeger, of Ilmenau, in Thuringia.

The receiver is a glass vessel, with adapter-tube i, and aspirator-tube e, provided with a glass stopper k which ends in a curved hollow tube s, having a number of round holes o, which are situated so that they exactly correspond to the opening between the arm i and the body of the vessel. Whenever any of these holes is brought in exact position with this opening, the outlet of the stopper (a) is exactly over one of the five exit nipples, for instance, that at t, all of which are carefully ground at the outside, and form an integral part of the apparatus. To each nipple belongs a bottle, fitting the ground neck tightly. When the distillation has been started, and the proper degree of exhaustion attained, the first distillate is received in any of the attached bottles. As soon as a different fraction of the distillate is required to be collected separately, it is only necessary to carefully turn the stop-cock k, so that the orifice at a will point into another vessel.—*Chem. Zeit.*

Kennedy's Medical Discovery.—This nostrum is reported to be prepared after the following formula: Helenium autumnale, 1 oz. ; Licorice root, ½ oz.; Apocynum cannabinum, ¼ oz. ; Boiling water, 8 oz. ; Proof spirit, 10 fl. oz. ; macerate for 48 hours, strain, and add sugar, 4 oz. ; Tinct. Gaultheria, 1 fl. oz.

Testing the Purity of Chloroform.

M. C. Traub states that perfectly pure chloroform should respond to the following tests.

1. When a considerable volume of it, say 100 C.c., is evaporated, it should leave no residue.

2. It should be absolutely free from acid. To determine this, 25 C.c. of alcohol are poured into a glass-stoppered cylinder of 50 C c. capacity, and 10 drops of a neutral alcoholic solution of purified litmus added. Next, enough chloroform is poured in to fill the cylinder completely, so that it will contain no air when the stopper has been inserted. It is then thoroughly shaken (that is, frequently reversed, so as to mix the contents thoroughly), and set aside in a dark place. The tint should not be altered within twenty-four hours.

3. It should be indifferent towards colorless, concentrated sulphuric acid. It will stand this test only when it has been kept in glass-stoppered bottles. If cork has been used to stopper the original bottle, the chloroform is liable to abstract from it gradually certain organic substances which will impart color to the sulphuric acid.

4. It should not produce a blue or bluish tint when added to solution of iodide of zinc and starch (absence of free chlorine or loosely combined chlorine compounds).

5. When shaken with water, the latter should, after being separated, remain unaffected by nitrate of silver.

6. If hydrogen gas be developed from pure zinc and diluted sulphuric acid, in the presence of some of the chloroform, the gas should not affect filtering paper moistened with a 50x solution of nitrate of silver.—*After Schweiz. Woch. f. Pharm.*

Wear of Platinum Vessels.

P. Vieth reports in *The Analyst* on the loss of weight which platinum capsules, used only for milk analyses, have suffered in the course of years. The figures given are of interest, as it is not uncommon among chemists, to assume the weight of platinum dishes which have been cleaned without scouring, and which have not been subjected to red heat, to remain practically constant.

The weight of the capsules employed varied between 10 and 14 Gm. each; internal diameter 4 Cm., the greatest depth 1.5 Cm. Each capsule was used 250-300 times a year. At each operation it was charged with 5 Gm. of milk, heated for three hours in a steam-bath, and afterwards 3 more hours in an air-bath at 100°C., and then weighed. The cleaning was performed by soaking the capsules for half an hour in hot water containing some carbonate of sodium, and then wiping them out with a wisp of straw. Next they were put into a fresh solution of washing soda, and finally rinsed with pure water.

Sixty eight capsules, which had been in constant use during 7 years, lost during this time 14.119 Gm., that is, each on an average 0.2076 Gm. Eight capsules, which had been used upwards of 5 years lost 0.594 Gm., or 0.0747 Gm. each. And 23 capsules, used only during 2 years, had lost 0.227 Gm., or 0.0099 Gm. each.

Comparative Efficacy of Antiseptics.

Dr. G. Riedlin has made experiments to determine the comparative efficacy of several agents reputed to be antiseptic, regarding their power to destroy, or prevent the development of, bacteria in culture-gelatin. Though the conclusions to be derived from this series of experiments may not be altogether transferable or applicable to all other methods of antisepsis, yet they are of value so far as they show the penetrating power of the various agents.

1. *Iodoform.* This behaves towards the several bacteria either as an almost indifferent powder, or as a feeble antiseptic. Towards cholera bacilli, however, it acts as a powerful antiseptic; its vapors alone are sufficient to prevent their development in a 10 per cent culture-gelatin down to a depth of about 10 millimeters.

2. *Oil of Turpentine.* In a 1 per cent solution, this acts as a powerful preventive of bacterial development. Addition of 1 part of oil of turpentine to 200 parts of culture-gelatin renders the latter sterile. But a 1x emulsion of the oil is insufficient to kill the Bacillus anthracis. When poured upon gelatin, the oil penetrates to a depth of about 10 Mm., and thus far renders it sterile.

3. *Oils of Lavender, Eucalyptus* and *Rosemary* are the best antiseptics among other essential oils, particularly when used undiluted. The two first named penetrate culture-gelatin to a depth of 10, the latter to 15 millimeters.

4. Next after these oils comes *oil of cloves*. Others, such as the oils of thyme, fennel, peppermint, anise, juniper and camphor are of little account as antiseptics.

5. *Iodol* has proved to be inert and indifferent towards bacteria.

6. *Balsam of Peru* is a rather powerful antiseptic, being especially destructive to the cholera bacillus. It penetrates culture-gelatin to a depth of about 8 Mm.

7. *Sulphichthyolate of Sodium* in 5 per cent aqueous solution is a very feeble antiseptic.

8. *Aniline*, best in saturated aqueous solution, is a most prompt antiseptic. A 10x culture-gelatin prepared with $\frac{1}{2}$ of solution of aniline is incapable of propagating bacteria.—*Centralbl. f. Ther.*

THE
American Druggist
AN ILLUSTRATED MONTHLY JOURNAL
OF
Pharmacy, Chemistry, and Materia Medica.

Vol. XVII., No. 12. Whole No. 174.

FREDERICK A. CASTLE, M.D. .... Editor.
CHARLES RICE, Ph.D. .... Associate Editor.

PUBLISHED BY
WM. WOOD & CO., 56 & 58 Lafayette Place, N. Y.

SUBSCRIPTION PRICE per year, ... $1.50
SINGLE COPIES. 15

Address all communications relating to the business of the American Druggist, such as subscriptions, advertisements, change of Post-Office address, etc., to William Wood & Co., 56 and 58 Lafayette Place, New York City, to whose order all postal money orders and checks should be made payable. Communications intended for the Editor should be addressed in care of the Publishers.

The American Druggist is issued in the latter part of each month, dated for the month ahead. Changes of advertisements should reach us before the 15th. New advertisements can occasionally be inserted after the 18th. Regular advertisements according to size, location, and time. Special rates on application.

EDITORIAL.

Half-strength Fluid Extracts.

We have received two letters of inquiry asking us to give our views regarding the new class of liquid preparations which were proposed by Prof. J. U. Lloyd in his recent address, as president, to the American Pharmaceutical Association, in the following words:

"I suggest that a class of *liquid preparations of plants* be made conspicuous in our Pharmacopœia that may be used by all physicians. Let each of these preparations represent the drug *one grain to two minims*, as far as it is practical to make them by percolation and maceration, one pint being derived from 8 ounces of drug, without the evaporation of any reserved percolate. Let the class of fluid extracts and tinctures be merged into and give way as much as possible to this class of preparations, which, from its nature, may be made without any elaborate apparatus, and need not be purchased from manufacturers, all such preparations being easily made by an apothecary. Physicians will at once understand that two minims of each of these preparations will represent practically one grain of crude material, thus approaching a definite strength, as near at least to a certainty as the science of medicine can now diagnose and prescribe in disease." Prof. Lloyd's further remarks on this subject are omitted here, excepting his statement that he, himself, would deem the introduction of this new class of preparations into the Pharmacopœia unadvisable, if the class of tinctures and fluid extracts could not at the same time be abolished.

If we were in the fortunate position of having to construct our *first* pharmacopœia, with nothing preceding it, we would be fully justified in adopting the very convenient plan afforded by Prof. Lloyd's plan between the tinctures and fluid extracts. These two last-named preparations, however, have gone so thoroughly over into the flesh and blood, as it were, of the pharmaceutical and medical professions that, even if a new class of preparations, such as suggested by Prof. Lloyd, were actually introduced, either officially or by private enterprise, the tinctures and fluid extracts would still be prescribed. And here is just the difficulty. The strength of the different preparations or the doses might be confounded. Besides, a liquid percolate obtained by passing the menstruum, however slowly, through 8 ounces of drug, so as to obtain a pint of percolate, will in many cases not fully represent the active constituents of the 8 ounces. To do this fully, it would be required to exhaust the drug and then to adjust the volume to 16 fluidounces. But we understand Prof. Lloyd's objection to this very well. He thinks that a slight deficiency of the product in soluble matters not extracted, and therefore absent in the pint of liquid, is amply made up by the better quality of the product in other directions, as it has not been subjected to heat, and will probably be less likely to precipitate. However, to return to the principal objection: Physicians will most certainly keep on prescribing tinctures and fluid extracts, for does not past experience teach us how hard it is to cause old preparations to be relegated to oblivion? We agree with Prof. Lloyd that the introduction of the new preparations would be advisable *only* if the old ones can be entirely replaced by the new. But as this is not likely to happen, we foresee no chance for the latter even in the distant future.

Use of Vanillin.

COMMERCIAL vanillin is not made from vanilla, but from the cambium sap of the pine, which contains coniferin or coniferyl-alcohol. The latter is converted into the former by a process of oxidation. The discoverers of the chemical constitution, and of the method of artificial preparation of vanillin, Messrs. Tiemann & Haarmann, have gradually improved the process; so that the commercial product is fully equal in aroma to the natural vanillin contained in vanilla beans. And the vanillin is now sold at a price which makes it decidedly more economical to use it than an equivalent amount of the beans themselves. There are several manufactories in Europe which do not seem to have as yet combined to a "trust." In consequence, the price has been depressed more and more.

At one time it was supposed that artificial vanillin would ruin the vanilla industry and trade, just as artificial alizarin has practically ruined the madder industry. But, curiously enough, this has not been the case. Vanilla holds its own extremely well. In fact, there is much more vanilla grown and sold at the present time than before vanillin was known as a commercial product. And yet, the latter is also consumed in constantly increasing quantities.

There is one reason for this. It is well known that an extract of vanilla made from the bean contains other matters besides the vanillin, among them what is usually termed "extractive" and a good deal of coloring matter. Now these substances have the power of binding or holding the odor of vanilla much more energetically than a simple neutral solvent would. Therefore, if two liquids are made of as near equal strength in odor and taste of vanillin as possible, one from vanilla bean and the other from vanillin, and if these two liquids are used, in equal proportions, to flavor equal amounts of any inert or insipid mixture, it will be found that the one flavored with the extract of the bean will retain its odor longest. But this property is not always required of the flavoring. When used for culinary purposes, it is seldom required to preserve the odor or taste of some flavored delicacy more than 48 hours. On the other hand, when chocolate or other confectionery is made on the large scale for the market, it is necessary to insure the stability of the odor and taste for as long a time as possible. Hence while artificial vanillin is perfectly satisfactory in the former case, the natural bean is preferred in the latter. It is usually considered that 1 oz. of vanillin is equivalent to 40 oz. of good vanilla beans.

Handling of Acids.

A CORRESPONDENT informs us that he has met with a serious accident, caused by the spattering of some drops of muriatic acid into his eyes, while loosening the glass stopper of a five-pint bottle containing it. He suggests that we caution our readers against similar mishaps, and he thinks that it would be a useful thing to repeat such cautions occasionally, even without waiting for the occurrence of an accident. We think this suggestion deserves attention, and, in compliance, will append here some cautionary remarks, which do not claim to embrace all that could be written upon the subject, but which may afford some practical hints at least for the younger and less experienced members of the profession:

When emptying carboys of acid, see that they are securely held. Do not tilt them over with one hand, while holding a receiving vessel in the other, unless they are so hung or placed that you have absolute control over them. A good way is to put the carboy on an elevated place, say about 18 to 24 inches high, so that when it lies on its side, its upper edge will be about three inches within the edge of the platform. If the carboy has a wooden strip or side-rail, instead of a handle, it is best to tilt it on the side where this is situated, as this assists in keeping command over the carboy while it is tilted. If you have a carboy-swing, be sure you see that the carboy is securely fastened, and that allowance be made for the change in centre of gravity as it becomes more empty.

Never stand in front of a carboy while emptying it, but sideways, and use a receiving vessel with a substantial handle. Do not hold a bottle with a funnel under the mouth of the carboy, nor hold any vessel so that if it should overflow the acid would run over your hands.

Choose such a place for emptying carboys, or any other containers of acid, as will suffer the least injury should the vessel be broken, or any of the acid be spilled.

Remember that the larger or the flimsier the container is, the more care and circumspection must be exercised. A person may have emptied a hundred or more carboys without any mishap, when unexpectedly an accident will happen, and in nine cases out of ten this is due to pure carelessness.

Never carry large containers of acid in contact with your body. Should they accidentally break, a most serious burn (sometimes turning out fatally) may be the result.

When opening acid bottles, for instance the usual five-pint sizes, first remove the cement from around the stopper, and wash and wipe the neck carefully to remove every trace of foreign matter. Then, if the stopper cannot be easily loosened by hand, place a coarse towel over the stopper and bottle, and while bearing with the thumb of one hand against the edge of one side of the stopper, tap the other side gently with the wooden (*not* metallic) handle of a spatula, when it usually will become loose. Should it be very obstinate, and the bottle at the same time appear to be of rather thin glass, place the bottle into a sufficiently deep and large acid-proof jar to receive the contents in case the bottle should break. The reason why a towel should be put over the stopper is almost self-evident. Our correspondent would have had no occasion to write to us had he used one. If a bottle of acid is exposed to a warm temperature, evidently some pressure will be developed within the bottle. By moving the bottle about, the neck and bottom of the stopper will be wetted with the acid, and if afterwards the stopper is suddenly loosened, the compressed air or gases will throw out any particles of liquid which are between the neck and stopper.

All acids are not equally dangerous. Hydrochloric or muriatic is perhaps the least risky. Sulphuric acid comes next, as it does not evolve any gases. The greatest care, however, must be exercised with nitric acid, and still more so with aqua regia.

When compelled to work for any length of time with acids, it is well to have a vessel of fresh water close at hand, to wash off any drops that may have come in contact with the hands or face. Sometimes it may be advantageous to wear india-rubber gloves, though most of those sold for this purpose are rather clumsy.

In packing acids, it should be made a rule to put them in a box by themselves, if at all possible. It would certainly be dangerous to pack sulphuric acid promiscuously with such articles as chlorate of potassium and organic substances.

In storing acids, equal care must be exercised. As a rule they should be kept in a place so arranged that, if the containers should be broken, the acid would be unable to reach other substances.

When diluting acids with water, remember always to pour the acid, gradually and under stirring, *into the water*, and not the water in the acid. In the case of sulphuric acid, for instance, the latter method may develop such an amount of steam at once that the whole liquid may be scattered about and do much damage. The last time we saw this happen was about a year ago, when several carboys of acid accidentally fell from the rear end of a truck in front of a factory of mineral waters. The acid collected in a pool in the gutter, and one of the workmen connected with the establishment, wanting to wash it into the sewer, turned a small stream of water upon it by means of a hose. The consequence was a violent evolution of steam, almost resembling an explosion, and a number of the bystanders received more or less of the spray, to the damage of their skin and clothes.

WE publish elsewhere in this number the first portion of a series of papers on the art of dispensing, which will be continued in subsequent issues. The basis for these articles will be the recent publication by the *Chemist and Druggist*, a notice of which will be found among the book reviews on page 232; but to adapt it to the needs of American pharmacists, many features will be changed and new matter and illustrations will be introduced. Much of the materials which have appeared in NEW REMEDIES and THE AMERICAN DRUGGIST since its first publication, and which is allied to this subject, will also be incorporated; so that in many respects these papers will be a *resumé* of progress in the art of dispensing during a period of nearly twenty years.

It is thought that a republication of this character will be particularly acceptable, since it will serve to instruct beginners, and suggest to others ways in which their business may be promoted.

OWING to the space required for the index of this volume, a number of answers to queries are unavoidably delayed, and other interesting matters are obliged to lie over.

LINDSAY AND BLAKISTON'S "Physician's Visiting List" for 1889 has come to hand, and has, in the thirty-eighth year of its publication, become a thoroughly established requisite in the business of many practitioners. The introductory text embraces a number of new features.

THE sixteenth edition of the Dispensatory of the United States of America has reached us, and will be noticed in our next issue. It has been re-arranged, thoroughly revised, and largely re-written. The entire incorporation of the National Formulary, covering sixty-eight pages, is one of the new features. The price of muslin-bound copies is $7.00.

WE have just received from our esteemed friend, Dr. Bruno Hirsch, of Berlin, parts 3 and 4 of the second volume of his Universal Pharmacopœia, which we have had occasion to speak of in our previous volumes. The work contains a systematic digest of all European and the U. S. Pharmacopœias, and is not only of the greatest practical utility to every working pharmacist or dispenser, but is an indispensable work of reference for every one who intends to share in the labor of revising the pharmacopœia of his country, or to make recommendations to his Committee of Revision. The nature of the book hardly admits of a review, though there are innumerable places where the export author has interwoven instructive or emendatory remarks of his own. In view of the fact that so much activity is at present shown in the pharmaceutical profession in preparing for a new revision of the U. S. Pharm., we deem it our duty to draw the attention of our readers to this work.*

Henry A. Cassebeer, Sr., a well-known retired pharmacist of this city, from 1846 to 1850 one of the trustees of the College of Pharmacy, died on Nov. 18th, aged 75 years.

---

*The title is: "Universal-Pharmakopöe. Eine vergleichende Zusammenstellung der zur Zeit in Europa und Nordamerika gültigen Pharmakopöen." Von Dr. Bruno Hirsch (vol. I., 16 Marks, and vol. II., 1-4 nos). 8vo. Göttingen. It may be obtained through importers of books, such as G. E. Stechert or B. Westermann & Co., of New York.

QUERIES & ANSWERS.

Queries for which answers are desired, must be received by the 5th of the month, and must in every case be accompanied by the name and address of the writer, for the information of the editor, but not for publication.

No. 2,251.—**Black Polish for Leather** (Jamestown). Perhaps the following combination, which is used in the German army for blackening leather, will answer your purpose:

Shellac .... 12 oz.
Borax .... 4 "
Nigrosin .... 1 "
Water .... 80 "

Dissolve the Borax in the Water (hot), and then dissolve the Shellac in the mixture; lastly add the Nigrosin, previously rubbed with a little of the solution so as to break up the small lumps.

No. 2,252.—"**Diamond Nail Enamel**" (S., Oswego). We are unable to give you the composition of the particular brand of this proprietary article which you inquire about. Its composition is not known to any but the maker, so far as we know. At least, it has never been analysed and reported upon.

No. 2,253.—**Russia Leather Odor** (W. H. R.). The nearest approach to the odor of Russia leather may be produced by using the common oil of birch (oleum betulae lentae). Of course, in preparing the leather, the various processes it passes through impart to it a special odor besides, or modify the original odor inherent in the skins. Genuine Russia leather is made from cows' skins, which are tanned with willow bark, and afterwards rubbed over with oil of birch.

No. 2,254.—**Tincture of Ichthyol** (K.). We do not know whether a formula for such a preparation has been recommended by the dermatologist you mention. The only account we have seen of such a preparation was a brief reply to a correspondent of the *Pharmaceut. Zeitung*, in which the editor stated that under Tincture of Ichthyol the writer probably meant a 10-per cent solution of the substance in a mixture of alcohol and ether. You are probably aware that the manufacturers of ichthyol preparations make and sell several such solutions of different strength, and also a series of salts containing sulphichthyolic acid. When "ichthyol," without further specification, is demanded, the sulphichthyolate of ammonium is supplied. All the other salts are sold under their respective names; for instance, sulphichthyolate of sodium (sometimes called "sodium-ichthyol"), etc.

No. 2,255.—**Gluten-Bread for Diabetic Persons** (E. V.). A recent communication of Dr. Woltering, of Münster, to the *Allg. med. Cent.-Zeit.* (No. 62) gives the following method for making diabetic bread.

Take 1 lb. gluten, and having mixed a little compressed yeast with a few tablespoonfuls of lukewarm water, mix this with the gluten and incorporate about ⅓ pint of water so as to make a dough, which is exceedingly sticky. Let it stand 1½ to 2 hours at a temperature of 86°–104° F., then place it into suitable tin moulds coated with butter, and bake it in the oven. After 1 or 2 hours the bread should be turned. It depends upon the degree of heat, how long the baking is to continue. Experience is the best teacher. In place of the yeast, baking powder may be taken, and this is even preferable. Mix 1 lb. of gluten with 1½ heaped tablespoonfuls of baking powder, and pass the whole through a sieve. Next make a dough with ⅓ pint of water (which in this case is scarcely at all sticky), fill the moulds, and at once put them in the oven. The finished bread is somewhat brittle, has a hard, brown crust, and a light gray porous crumb. Its taste is slightly bitter and acidulous, but its nutritive value is very high, as it contains about 55 per cent of protein substances.

No. 2,256.—**Yield of Wintergreen, Sassafras, etc., in Essential Oils** (Prscud, N. C.). Gaultheria or wintergreen or "mountain-tea" leaves yield, on distillation, about 0.8 per cent (8 per 1,000) of essential oil. Birch-bark, also called mahogany birch, which is the most common source of commercial oil of wintergreen, yields only 0.25 per cent, but the oil made from this costs less to the manufacturer. Sassafras root, in chips, yield on distillation from 1 to 2 per cent oil. The bark of the root is the portion used medicinally, and this contains a good deal more oil. But distillers use the whole root, finely chipped. Pennyroyal from Mentha Pulegium (Europe) yields about 0.3 per cent of oil. What the American pennyroyal (Hedeoma pulegioides) yields is not exactly known.

It is, of course, to be understood that much depends upon the condition of the fresh material to be distilled. If it is obtained at the proper season, in prime condition, and subjected to careful distillation in a proper apparatus, much larger percentages of oil may probably be obtained. Before entering upon such an industry, however, you should collect together from the existing literature all that can be learned on the subject (consult particularly the annual Proceedings of the Amer. Pharm. Assoc.), and besides, you ought to see the workings of such stills, and understand their management.

No. 2,257.—Vanillin (C. R. W.).
Artificial Vanillin is prepared in the following manner.

1. **Preparation of the glucoside *Coniferin*.** The trunks of pines or other coniferous trees, freshly felled in spring, are stripped of bark, the cambium layer is scraped off, and the juice thus obtained heated to boiling, whereby the albumen is coagulated. It is then strained, evaporated to one-fifth and set aside to crystallize. The crystals are purified by recrystallization from boiling water with the aid of animal charcoal.

2. **Preparation of Vanillin.** 10 parts of coniferin are dissolved in boiling water, and the solution added, in a fine stream, to a mixture of 10 parts bichromate of potassium, 15 parts of sulphuric acid, and 80 parts of water. The whole is warmed for about 3 hours to boiling, under an upright condenser. The vanillin which has been formed is dissolved out by ether, or distilled out by a current of steam. It is purified like coniferin. The chemical changes are the following:

$C_{16}H_{22}O_8$ + H_2O = $C_6H_{12}O_6$ + $C_{10}H_{12}O_3$
coniferin water glucose coniferyl-alcohol

$C_{10}H_{12}O_3$ + O = $C_8H_8O_3$ + CH_2O
coniferyl-alcohol oxygen vanillin aldehyde.

The *National Formulary* contains a formula for *Tinctura Vanillini Composita*, for the rapid preparation of an "extract of vanilla" made with vanillin. In this preparation, a very small quantity of (artificial) cumarin—the odorous principle of the Tonka bean—has been added, which serves the purpose of making the odor and taste of vanillin more stable and persistent.

On page 229 will be found a further note on vanillin.

No. 2,258.—Bromide and Ammonio-Bromide of Copper (Norfolk).
Our correspondent inquires where he can procure *soluble* bromide of copper, which he has seen recommended as a reducer for over-exposed photographic images or prints. He has procured some from Philadelphia, but finds it almost insoluble.

The same trouble seems to have been met with in Europe, for a few months ago we noticed a paper by de Koninck (in the *Zeitsch. f. angew. Chemie*), in which this very subject is discussed and a remedy proposed. This chemist recommends to use the ammonio-bromide of copper, which can easily be obtained in fine emerald-green crystals by the following process: To a weighed quantity of copper-turnings, in a flask provided with a glass-stopper, about twice their weight of water is added, and afterwards, gradually, enough bromine, until the metal has dissolved, and an excess of bromine is present. The flask must be kept cool to prevent loss of bromine. Next, the dark brown solution is freed from the excess of bromine by heating it in a capsule over a water-bath. To the residuary solution, containing a known quantity of cuprous bromide, an equivalent amount of bromide of ammonium is added, that is, 300 parts of the last-named salt for every 100 parts of metallic copper used. The dark red liquid is then filtered and concentrated to the crystallizing point.

A concentrated solution of this salt is dark red; a dilute one faintly bluish-green. The transition from one tint to the other takes place at ordinary temperature in a solution of 1 part of the salt in 3 of water. The higher the temperature, the more water may be added before the red color turns to green.

A solution of 1 in 1,000 is a very energetic reducer of the photographic image.

John Carle, one of the oldest wholesale druggists in the country, and probably the oldest in New York City, died on October 28th, aged 81 years. He was born at Cedarswamp, Long Island, in 1804. When twelve years of age, he entered the employment of his uncle, Silas Carle, druggist, at Fulton and Water sts., New York. During more than seventy years he was actively engaged in the wholesale drug business (firm of John Carle & Sons, Maiden lane and Water st.), and even during the last few years he loved to assist his only remaining son in the management of the affairs of the house. He filled the office of trustee of the College of Pharmacy during eight annual terms between the years 1832 and 1868, and that of vice-president in 1862. For more than twenty-five years he was a trustee of the Bowery Savings Bank. Mr. Carle was a well-known figure in down-town commercial circles, respected by all, of sterling integrity, and leaves a bright memory of himself behind him.

The Lancet says that a free-lunch counter has been introduced at the Wolverhampton Hospital as a means of attracting dispensary patients.

CORRESPONDENCE.

THE CULTIVATION OF PEPPERMINT; SMYRNA TOBACCO, ETC.

The Editor of the American Druggist.

SIR:—You may have noticed in the last week's number of the *Chemist and Druggist* newspaper that Mr. John Moss, the well-known chemist's opinion upon the oil of peppermint he distilled from the foliage which I had grown at Sydenham, was, that if the oil was properly treated and the plants grown on a similar soil to the Mitcham, he believes that the flavor would be in every way equal, and naturally the yield would be very much larger.

I hope that some of my friends in America who are readers of your paper will take this matter to heart, and try growing a few hundred of plants of menthas in rows three feet apart; because it is certain that after a little experience in distilling these separate oils you will soon be able in America to produce a mentha that will equal the Mitcham variety of peppermint, by noting the soil.

We have had a great discussion in the English press lately upon the irritating effect produced by smoking cigarettes, especially those of the Egyptian variety. It is well known to many of us who have sought to produce the peculiar flavor known as the Turkish tobacco prepared in different parts of the world (but with very indifferent result) that there is a tobacco largely grown in the neighborhood of Smyrna which has the special property of producing this irritation at the back of the throat, and it is employed for this purpose as giving piquancy to Turkish tobacco when mixed with it and also in imparting an agreeable flavor.

Very few natives can endure this tobacco when smoked in a pure state except those brought up in the neighborhood.

Hoping that these few lines will lead to research by some of your numerous readers, for suitable soil, I remain, sir, Yours truly,

THOS. CHRISTY, F.L.S.

London, Oct. 10th, 1888.

[It is our impression that a favorable climate will have quite as much influence as a suitable soil in favoring the growth of peppermint. It is quite certain that plenty of moisture is requisite, and very likely that the moist, warm air of some of our southern States may furnish the proper condition. If Mr. Christy will consult the publications of the agricultural department of the United States, he may find the information he desires.—ED. A. D.]

Cultivation of Sponges.—In November, 1881, we published an account of the results of trials, on this side of the Atlantic, of the method suggested by Prof. Oscar Schmidt, of Gratz, Styria, for the propagation of sponges by fixing pieces detached from living sponges, by means of wooden skewers, to sandy bottoms, where they are left to themselves to grow. Recent reports state that the Austro-Hungarian government have undertaken the protection of this industry on the coast of Dalmatia.

The Geochronoscope is the latest attractive feature for the pharmacy. Mr. James Anderson, of the Dundee drug stores, has developed the idea from an invention by a local clock-maker. The geochronoscope consists of a round cylinder on which is placed a map of the world. While examining this instrument, it struck Mr. Anderson that, if it could be attached to a clock and moved by the clock in such a way that the cylinder would revolve once every twenty-four hours, the relative time in any part of the world would be shown at a glance. Mr. Kelt took up the idea and has made for Mr. Anderson an instrument which is perfect in every particular. The clock is mounted on the geochronoscope. A thin, elastic cord, stretched from above to below the cylinder, acts as a meridian index, and as the cylinder revolves, every part coming under this index is noon. There are twenty-four longitude lines on the cylinder, and these being numbered the same as an ordinary clock, the telling of the time in any given part is as simple as telling the time on an ordinary clock.—*Chem. and Drugg.*

Note on Antipyrine.—In a mixture of nitric and sulphuric acids, antipyrine assumes a cherry-red color. On adding to a small quantity of alcoholic solution of antipyrine a few drops of nitric, and afterwards some sulphuric acid, a brisk reaction ensues, and a red color appears. On now immediately adding some drops of distilled water, a green precipitate is thrown down, which is insoluble in water. The addition of the same acids to an ether-alcohol solution of antipyrine does not produce these phenomena, until after the ether has evaporated.—*Journ. de Pharm. et Chim.*

Chevreul, at the Academy of Sciences meeting of September 17th, was replaced in the financial committee by Admiral Mouchez. It is rumored the old chemist has become childish, and his health causes anxiety.—*Chem. and Drugg.*

BIBLIOGRAPHY.

ANGEWANDTE PFLANZENANATOMIE. Ein Handbuch zum Studium des anatomischen Baues der in der Pharmacie, den Gewerben, der Laudwirtschaft und dem Haushalte benutzten Pflanzlichen Rohstoffe. In Zwei Bänden Erster Band. Allgemeiner Theil. Grundriss der Anatomie, von DR. A. TSCHIRCH, Docent der Botanik an der Universität Berlin. Mit 614 in dem Text gedruckten Holzschnitten. Wien und Leipzig: Urban & Schwarzenburg, 1888, pp. 548, Royal 8vo —[APPLIED VEGETABLE ANATOMY, Vol. I., by DR. A. TSCHIRCH, Lecturer on Botany and Pharmacognosy in the University of Berlin.]

THE term "applied vegetable anatomy" appears here for the first time, and is used in a similar sense as the expression "applied chemistry." The aim of the author is to give, in the present volume, a theoretical foundation for the practical exercises and investigations of all those who are interested in the examinations of such vegetable substances as are of importance to pharmacy, the various branches of industry and agriculture, and to every household. Very properly the author remarks in the preface that, although without the least doubt the microscope is of the first importance in the identification of drugs, woods, flour, fibres, etc., it will furnish absolute proof only in the hands of a person who has become intimately familiar with the anatomical structure of the objects to be examined. For, just as the chemist must acquire a thorough knowledge of the theoretical principles of his science before he can put it into practice, every practical microscopist will have to base his work on his acquaintance with general vegetable anatomy. In this volume, however, the author proposes to discuss such anatomical questions only as refer, in some way or other, to a practical application in microscopical diagnosis.

An introductory chapter gives the most approved methods of preparation, apparatus, and reagents, and some very valuable hints as to the method of study for self-instruction. Still the author remarks: "Although all of us have been using our eyes since we were born, very few of us have really learned to 'see,' i. e., to observe. . . . For these reasons, practical, microscopical exercises under the direction of an instructor are almost indispensable." The dislike, not to say prejudice, of many German investigators against all kinds of apparatus not absolutely necessary, manifests itself now and then, e. g., when the author speaks rather disapprovingly of the use of the turn-table and circular cover-glasses. When making permanent mounts in glycerin, etc., it is certainly much safer, more convenient, and cleanlier to prepare a shallow cell on the slide for the reception of the object than to place a square cover-glass directly on the drop of glycerin, without any cement ring on the slide. For this and similar manipulations a simple turn-table is a very great convenience, and its use can be learned without the least difficulty.

A very large portion of the book (about 200 pages) is devoted to the study of the individual cell, its contents, and the structure of the cell-wall. The careful and exhaustive treatment of the cell-contents best characterizes the progress of vegetable anatomy and its modern tendencies. The chapter on starch alone occupies twenty-five pages; appended to it is a list of all the plants of which starch is obtained in the different parts of the world. The interesting carbo-hydrate amylodextrin, a substance intermediate between dextrin and starch, is also discussed; it was discovered, e. g., in maris and in germinating seeds of sinapis alba. A condensed compilation of the investigations referring to the seat of the various alkaloids in the plant tissues is very valuable. The same may be said of a table containing the most important plants furnishing volatile oils; it shows the amounts in per cent, and also whether the oil occurs in schizogenetic or lysogenetic receptacles, in oil-cells, in glandular hairs, or uniformly distributed in the cell-contents.

After a full account of the morphology of the cell-membrane follows a thorough discussion of its chemical composition; the description of the origin of the mucilages, resins, gums, etc., is of particular interest.

The second part of the book treats of the various cellular tissues. The author strictly follows the principles of the modern so-called "physiological vegetable anatomy" (Haberlandt), according to which the classification of the tissues is not based upon the topographical arrangement, nor upon the order of their development, but exclusively upon the functions which they have to perform in the living plant. Accordingly we find the hairs, so important for diagnostic purposes, together with the cork and "bork" formations, under the head of "epidermal system," while bast and libriform fibres are treated, with sclerenchyma and collenchyma, as belonging to the "mechanical system." Then all the other tissues are fully described and respectively referred to the systems of absorption, assimilation, conduction, storage, and, finally, of secretion and excretion. The last-named tissues and their products are discussed in a very complete and instructive manner on 78 pages.

The book is profusely supplied throughout with most beautiful and correct illustrations. With many of them we are familiar, as they are taken from Flückiger and Tschirch's "Principles of Pharmacognosy"* (some also from Berg's Atlas and other standard works), but a large number are original. Altogether this book, without any doubt, will occupy a prominent place among our standard botanical works for a long time to come.

It is intended to publish a second volume, in which the most important drugs, articles of food, fibres, etc., will be described in detail.

J. S.

THE ART OF DISPENSING: A Treatise on the Methods and Processes Involved in Compounding Medical Prescriptions. *The Chemist and Druggist.* London: 1888, pp. 280, 8vo. Muslin, $1.00. [H. V. Dakers, 45 Liberty St., New York.]

THIS is a reprint of much of the literary portions of the *Chemical and Druggist's Diaries* for 1880 and 1885, together with such other materials by eminent British pharmacists as serve to make the work systematic and adapted to the needs of students, teachers, and practitioners in pharmacy. Having been especially prepared for British readers, it is not equally well adapted for use in this country, owing to the differences in weights and the composition of articles officinal under similar titles; but one who will bear these exceptions in mind will find it in all other respects a most valuable guide.

Credit is given to Prof. Remington's "Practice of Pharmacy" for a number of the illustrations; but Prof. Remington, we would presume, had he been able to choose, would have preferred to have waived the formality; for such slovenly reproductions are of no credit to any one, and in the present condition of the art of book illustration, positively disgraceful. In the case of fac-similies of difficult prescriptions, the defects of the engraving increase unnecessarily the difficulty of deciphering what are already sufficiently illegible examples of chirography.

THE EXTRA PHARMACOPŒIA, with the Additions introduced into the Pharmacopœia (1885) by William Martindale, F.C.S., etc. Medical References and a Therapeutic Index of Diseases and Symptoms by W. Wynn Westcott, M.B. Lond. Fifth Edition. London: H. K. Lewis, 136 Gower St., W. C., 1888, pp. 462.

THIS fifth edition embraces most of the notable advances made in therapeutics and materia medica since its predecessor appeared, and in spite of its diminutive size (1x3¾x6 inches) contains a wonderful amount of information. For ready reference, either on the pharmacist's prescription-counter or the prescriber's table, it will be found extremely valuable. The bibliographic references in the case of recently-introduced remedies is alone worth much more to any physician than the price of the book.

GIFT UND GEGENGIFT. Ein Hülfsbuch für vorkommende Vergiftungsfälle. VON CRACAU. 12mo, Leipzig; pp. 449.

THIS is one of the most complete reference books on poisons and their antidotes which has come to our notice. The contents are as follows: 1. Introduction. 2. The poisons, their chemical, physical, and toxic properties, their use in medicine and the arts, and the corresponding antidotes. 3. List of antidotes. 4. Non-poisonous substances, which may under circumstances become the carriers of poison. 5. Secret nostrums known to contain poisons. 6. Symptoms of poisoning. So far as we have examined the book, the statements therein made are correct and reliable, and we recommend it to those of our readers who have a command of the German language.

CHEMICAL LECTURE NOTES. Taken from Prof. C. O. Curtman's Lectures at the St. Louis College of Pharmacy. By H. M. WHELPLEY, Ph. G., Professor of Microscopy, etc., at the St. Louis College of Pharm., etc.; 2d ed., revised and enlarged. 8vo, St. Louis, 1888.

THE object of this book is, of course, not to replace any text-book on chemistry, nor to serve as a substitute for the didactic lectures and demonstrations, but as a skeleton or guide for reviewing the subjects taught in the lecture-room. We notice that a rather considerable portion of the book has been devoted to chemical physics, which subject is evidently one of the specialties of the author, to judge from the well-digested plan and manner in which the subject is presented. The book may be profitably used by students of other colleges of pharmacy.

GUIDE BOOK FOR DISTILLERS and Manufacturers of Arrac, Cognac, Gin. Rum, Cordials, Liqueurs, etc. By E. SACHSSE & Co., Leipzig, pp. 48, 8vo.

THIS is a guide to the manufacture of wines and liquors, with the aid of the essential oils for which this house is noted. Formulas are furnished for pretty much everything that is considered drinkable, the oils or essences required to impart the characteristic flavor or appearance being secret and the property of this firm.

WILDER, HANS M. Price and Dose Labels of Drugs and Preparations generally kept in a Retail Pharmacy, including, besides those officinal in last Revision of the U. S. Pharm., many other new and rare Drugs and Chemicals, with the Latin, French, and German Synonyma, narr. 8vo, New York, 1888.

---

* Translated by Dr. F. B. Power (Wm. Wood & Co.)

INDEX.

The asterisk (*) indicates illustrated articles.

CORRECTIONS, 74, 132, 136, 158, 178, 212.

A

Acacia Angico Mart., as a source of gum, 125
Acetanilid, 51, 106
  increased demand for, 206
  manufacture of, 118
  mixture, 75
  test for, 52, 152
  therapeutic use of, 152
Acetone-chloroform, 159
Acid, alpha-oxynaphtholic, 63, 196
  anhydrous phosphoric as drying agent for gases, 68
  boric, commerce in, 206
  boric, innocuousness of, 115
  boric, internal use, 24
  camphoric, 126
  carbonic, apparatus for estimating,* 5
  carbonic, apparatus for liquefied, 159
  carbonic, liquid, as a preservative, 154
  carbonic, liquefied, 218
  carbonaphthilic, 145
  fluorhydric, 52
  glacial phosphoric, determining sodium phosphate in, 33
  hydriodic, preparation of, 71
  hydriodic, syrup, 218
  hydrobromic, 29
  hydrobromic, preparing, 44
  hydrochloric, chlorochromic test, 16
  hydrochloric, delicate test-paper for, 102
  hydrochloric, probable increase of price, 106
  hydrofluoric, inhalations,* 120
  hydrofluoric, use in consumption, 109
  iodated carbolic, 211
  lactic, free, reagents for, 141
  metaphosphoric, change of, 132
  methyltrihydroxyquinoline carbonic, 112
  nitro-sulphonic, 53
  nitrous, delicate test for, 114, 172
  oxalic in plants, 124
  phosphomolybdic, 96
  phosphomolybdic as test for alkaloids, 193
  phosphoric, estimation, 149
  phosphoric, material to resist fusing, 119
  phosphoric, preparation of, 71
  picric, as an explosive, 53, 107
  rosolic, as an indicator, 168
  salicylic, as a preservative, 118, 213
  salicylic, estimating homologous acids, 188
  succinic, 206
  sulphanilic, 37
  sulphuric and zinc, reaction between, 111
  sulphuric, rules for dilution, 178
  sulphurous, assay, 33
  sulphurous, liquefied, 107
Acids, apparatus for preparing,* 25
Acids in the stomach, reagents for, 148
  handling, 229
  various indicators for, 168
Aconite preparations, assay of, 52
Aconitine, fallacy of color reaction, 86
  nitrate, pills or granules of, 112
  pills or granules, 112
  with menthol, 15
Adhatoda vasca, 112
Agaricin, 17
Alantol essence, use of, 206
Alizarin, production of, 24
Albolene, 87
Albumen in urine, varieties of, 26
ALTER, Chas., on carbolate of mercury, 102
Alcohol, estimating, 132
  methylic, 57
  preparation of absolute,* 152
Alcoholometry by means of ebullioscope,* 153
Alkalis, 80
Algerian pharmacy, 13
Alkalies, various indicators for, 168
Alkaloids, effects of heat upon, 156
  phosphomolybic acid as test, 193
Almadina as substitute for caoutchouc, 128
Aloes and canella, powder of, 162
Alpha-naphthol, 63
  as an antiseptic, 112
Aluminium, 106
  bronze, 178
  hints about, 23
  in wheat flour, 178
  uses of, 115
Alum pencils, 105
Amber, oil, prize for industrial use for, 206
American ideas in Europe, 215
Amidoazobenzene, definition of, 23
Ammonia, injurious effects of vapor, 108
  production of, 43
Ammonium carbonate, composition of, 88
  chloride, solution, 75
Amylene and amylene hydrate, 58
  hydrate, formula, 76
Anæsthetics fifty years ago, medical opinions on, 137
  local, 16
Anagyris fœtida, a Grecian substitute for senna, 128
Analgesine, another name for antipyrine, 135
Analyses of wall-paper, English vs. American, 73
Analytical balance, 94
Angico gum, 125
Anhydride, carbonic, apparatus for,* 25
  phosphoric, apparatus for,* 25
  sulphurous, apparatus for,* 25
Aniline, 42
  as an antiseptic, 228
  injurious effects of, 108
Animal poisons, volatile, 134
Anise, adulterated with conium seed, 62
Annatto cultivation in Guadeloupe, 67
Antharobin, 62, 106, 176
  preparations, 114
"Antiboldos," 13
Antifebrin, 3, 51, 100
  manufacture of, 118
  reactions of, 152
  tests for, 172
  use in headache, 87
Antimony, historical notes on, 202
Antineuralgic salve, 114
Antipyrin, 106
  and carbolic acid, incompatibility, 94
  as an anodyne, 72
  color reactions, 231
  extensive use of, 14
  French objections to, 135
  incompatible with spt. of nitrous ether, 78
  in sea-sickness, 30
  in urine, detection, 96
  in whooping cough, 214
  manufacture of, 118
  poisoning by, 89
  proposed name for, 34
  tests for, 172
  text of the patent, 28
Antiseptics, comparative efficacy, 228
  in phthisis, 153
  new, 2, 7
Anthracene, 43
Ants, modes for abolishing, 115
Aplantesis, 12
Argols, assay of, 142
"Armenian Pills," 16
Arsenic as a remedy for warts, 95
  bismuth free from, 20
  in bismuth salts, 190
  in metallic iron, testing for, 111
  official test for, 160
Asbestos as filtering medium, 30
  use in milk-analysis, 53
Ash determination,* 175
"Assar Bark," 95
Atropine, oleate, in suppositories, 18
"Australian Chemists Review," the, 117
"Ayer's Hair Vigor," 95
Azobenzene, composition of, 23
Azolitmin paper, 49

B

Babbitt-metal, 55
BABCOCK, J. F., historical notes on antimony, 202
Baking powders, composition of various, 180
Ball-mill,* 45
Balsam, electrified, 65
  Peru, 106
  Peru, as antiseptic, 228
BARY, Prof. H. A. de, death of, 55
Bay laurel, extract, 56
Bay-rum, 66
Bed-bugs, modes for exterminating, 115
Beeswax, estimation of mineral wax in, 213
Benzene, composition of, 23
Benzol, formula, 79
  in whooping cough, 14
BIBLIOGRAPHY:
  Angewandte Pflanzenanatomie, Tschirch, 232
  Chemical Lecture Notes, Whelpley, 323
  Die Riechstoffe, Mierzinski, 60
  Elements of Modern Chemistry, Wurtz, 40
  Essentials of Chemistry and Toxicology, Withaus, 100
  Gift und Gegengift, von Cracau, 323
  Guide Book for Distillers, etc., Sachsse & Co., 323
  Index of Materia Medica with Prescription Writing, May and Mason, 100
  Lithographers and Photographers' Directory, 60
  Manual of Chemistry, Simon, 220
  Manual of Pharmacy and Pharmaceutical Chemistry, Hæhner, 40
  Medical Don'ts, Valentine, 100
  Nineteenth Annual Report of the State Board of Health of Massachusetts, 180
  Organic Analysis, Prescott, 40
  Physician's Bedside Record, Segur, 180
  Practical Microscopy, Miller, 100
  Proceedings of the American Pharmaceutical Association, 60
  Ptomaines and Leucomaines, Vaughan and Novy, 220
  Text-Book of Pharmacology Therapeutics and Materia Medica, Brunton, 220
  Text-Book of Therapeutics and Materia Medica, Edes, 60
  The Art of Dispensing, 232
  The Beginnings of Pharmacy, Rother, 120
  The Ear and Its Diseases, Sexton, 220
  The Extra Pharmacopœia—Martindale and Westcott, 232
  The National Formulary of Unofficinal Preparations, 160, 220
  The Prescription, Wall, 120
  The Three Ethical Codes, 160
  Toilet Medicine, Wooton, 100
  Year-Book of Pharmacy, 60
Bird-lime, 38
Bismuth, delicate test for, 217
  detection of, 174
  free from arsenic, 20
  hair-dye, 128
  oxyiodide, improved preparation of, 12
  salts, arsenic in, 190
  with mucilage, 107
"Bitters," alcoholic strength of various, 151

INDEX.

Bitter tonics, effects of, 112
Board of Pharmacy, South Dakota, 217
Boldoin as a hypnotic, 178
"Boonekamp Bitters," 179
Borofuchsin, 134
Bottle-capsuling apparatus,* 148
   cement, 50
   making machine,* 84
   specific gravity,* 3
Bottles, production in Europe, 34
Bougie moulds, 72
Bougies, medicated,* 147
Blaud's pills, 17
Bleaching feathers and hair, 19
   powder, manufacture of, 24
   wood with hydrogen peroxide, 82
Bloxam, Prof., death of, 12
Blue prints, 24
   prints, to render brown, 205
Bread, gluten, 230
   gluten, improved, 137
Bronchitis cure, "Dobell's," 14
Bromidia, composition of, 180
Bromine, injurious effects of vapor, 108
   separation from iodine and chlorine, 144
Brumata lime, 38
"Bryan's Pulmonic Wafers," 76
Bully-tree gum, 99
Burette flask,* 171
   for baryta solution,* 173
   for titrating hot liquids,* 205
   self-adjusting,* 171
Burettes, filling-flask for,* 7
Burner, improved Bunsen,* 8
   Siemens' inverted, 183
Bursa pastoria, uses, 66
Butter, preserving, 32

Cabbage-tree bark, tincture of, 179
Caffeine and sodium citrate, 149
   citrate, nature of, 205
   depreciation in cost of, 205
   from tea, 111
   from damaged tea, 149
   phthalate, 84
Calabar bean, new alkaloid in, 222
Calamine varieties, 145
Calcium iodide, syrup, 78
   lactophosphate, syrup, 57, 147
   sulphide, 180
Calomel, crystallised, 107
Calycanthus glaucus, use in malarial fevers, 89
   seeds, constituents of, 180
Camphor and salol, reaction, 200
   carbolate of, 64, 80
   ice, 14
   monopoly at Formosa, 168
   powdering, 30
   trade in Formosa, 134
Camphorogenol, 20
Capsicum annuum, cultivation of, 174
   ointment of oleoresin of, 198
Capsules and capsule making,* 103
Caramel, 84
Carbolic acid and antipyrin, incompatibility, 24
   compounds, assay of, 70
Carbon bisulphide, injurious effects of, 108
Cardamom plant, cultivation, 170
Cardamoms, 106
CARLE, John, death of, 231

Carolina allspice, use in malarial fever, 89
Cascara bark, European demand for, 206
   preparation, improving taste of, 236
   sagrada, "tasteless," 77, 205
CASSEBEER, H. A., death of, 230
Cassia-trade, Chinese, 172
Castor-oil mixture, 14
   pomade
Catarrh "cures," 93, 175
Catgut, chromatising, 82
Caustic, sulphate of zinc, 15
Cedrine, 83
Cellulose for finings, 7
Cement for glass, India-rubber, 137
Cements, varieties of, 196
"Chandler's Chlorodyne," 26
"Chapman's Copaiba Mixture," 84
Chapped hands, formulas for, 95
Charcoal, revivifying, 146
Chartreuse, 75
Cheese, composition, 96
Chemists' assistants, French, 26
CHEVREUL, 231
Chewing-gums, 95
Chicle, 24
Chinese trade guilds, 12
Chinotoxine, 105
Chloral and cyanide of potassium, reaction, 113
   hydrocyanate, 84
Chlorine, injurious effects of gas, 108
   water, 152
Chlorodyne, 126
   Chandler's, 26
Chloroform as a preservative, 113, 145, 175
   estimation, 174
   quantitative estimation, 88
   test, 222
Chutnee, 175
Cider, improvement by freezing, 23
Cinchona, assay of, 170
   bark, production of, 206
   Bolivian, 125
   fluid extract, assay of, 136
   in Colombia, 195
   plantations in the Nilgiris, 67
Cinchonas, effect of hybridization, 202
"Cinchonid-Sulph. Fort.," 20
Cinnamon oil, production in Ceylon, 222
Clarifying liquids, 211
Cloves, Zanzibar, 44
Coal-tar products, 42
Cobalt, nitrate, 180
Coca cultivation in Ceylon, 69
   grown in India, 134
   secondary alkaloid in, 209
Cocaine as an antiseptic, 65
   commercial, 27
   manufacture of, 7
   notes on, 82
   on leeches, effect of, 29
   phthalate and other alkaloids, 84
   saccharinate, 172
Cochineal, tincture, as an indicator, 108
Coconut, orthography of, 50
Codeine, new use for, 152
   syrup, 126
Coffee extract, 76
   syrup of, error in orthography, 162
Cola-nuts, 108, 133
Colchicin, crystallised, 30
College of Pharmacy, Albany, 115
   Chicago, 177, 202
   Cincinnati, 15, 74, 92
   Denver, 92
   Maryland, 74

College of Pharmacy, Massachusetts, 116, 137, 155
   New York, 74, 116
   Philadelphia, 94
   Pittsburgh, 74
   Toronto, 14
Collodion, anti-gout, 76
   salicylic, as a corn cure, 176
Cologne, 138
Coloring-matter from buckleberries as a reagent for free hydrochloric acid, 144
Coloring pharmaceutical preparations, 201
Colors of botanical specimens, preserving, 53
Color tints, apparatus for comparing,* 205
Coniferin, preparation of, 231
Conline, synthesis of, 168
Compound laxative, 140
Concentration by cold, 81
Condenser, Lloyd's,* 201
Condurangin, 83
Condurango as a stomachic, 95
Congo paper, 49
   red as a reagent for free hydrochloric acid, 144
Conium seed as adulterant of anise, 69
Contrexéville water, artificial, 163
Copaiba mixture, Chapman's, 84
Copper, bromide and ammonio-bromide, 231
   phosphate as a remedy for phthisis, 114
   reagent for, 140
Copying pad, 37
"Cordu Bark," 95
Cork industry,* 221
   management of prescription, 137
   removing, 173
   tight, 115
Corn-remedy, 75
Corn-salve, 14
Cornutin, 20
   inutility of, 206
Corrosive sublimate, crystallised, 107
   sublimate dressings, 55
   sublimate dressings, acid, 84
   sublimate dressings, deterioration of, 210
   sublimate in dressings, estimation of, 84
   sublimate, stability of solutions, 58
Coryza remedy, 95
Cosmetics, 80
Cuto bark, scarcity of, 206
Crayons for writing on glass, 114
Creolin, 3, 84
   demand for, 206
Creosote mixture, 76, 134
   orthography of, 118
   use in phthisis, 106
Cubebs, increased cultivation, 105
Cutch trade of Burmah, 226

Dalby's Carminative, 75
Dandruff, remedies for, 14
Dating scientific work, 35
Dental societies, meeting of, 136
Dentifrices, salol in, 133
Dextrin as an adulterant of extracts, 69, 115
   as an emulsifier, 19
   as a substitute for gum-arabic, 83
   mucilage, 19
   nature and uses, 219
Dhaura-gum, 83
Dialyzer, experimental,* 227
"Diamond Nail Enamel," 230
Disease, estimation of, 57
   preparation of, 76
Digitalines, pills or granules, 113

Digitalis, preparation of infusion, 10
Diphenyl-methylpyrazol, 205
Diplomas in Washington Territory, 109
Diploma-mills, laws encouraging, 109
Diphtheria, remedy for, 75
Disinfection, domestic, 82
   French directions for, 188
Dispensatory, U. S., new edition of, 217
Dispensing, art of,* 222
Distillation, Chandon and Morris's apparatus,* 109
   to prevent "bumping," 187
Distilling apparatus, automatic,* 183
   in vacuum, receiver for,* 227
   receiver for fractional,* 227
   under diminished pressure,* 25
"Dobell's solution," liability to develop carbonic acid, 162
"Dr. Giral's Febrifuge Powder," 95
Drop-counter, Traube's,* 132
Drops, size of, 86
Drug adulteration, in Massachusetts, 134
   Clerks' Association, Newark, 177
Drugs used in patent medicines, 63
   inspection in Massachusetts, 156
Drug-store decoration, etc., 136
Drying-oven,* 207

Early closing in Hamilton, Ont., 137
"Eau de Castile," 13
"Eau de Cologne," trade in, 13
"Eau de Fève," 13
"Eau do Fleur de Lys," 13
"Eau des Fleurs," 13
"Eau Figaro," 13
"Eau Magique," 13
"Eau Royal de Windsor," 13
Elixir terpinhydrate, 14
"Ely's Cream Balm," 95
"Emerald Green," as a reagent for free hydrochloric acid, 144
Emetine, estimation of, 143
Ems water, 142
Emulsion, cod liver oil, 1, 32
Emulsions, 11, 21
Ephedrine hydrochlorate, 83
"Epitème," 13
Epsom salt springs, 77
Ergot mill, 80
Eriodictyon, elixir, 211
Erlitzki's fluid, 178
Eseridine, 222
Ether drinking in Ireland, 173
Ethyl bromide, lack of demand for, 108
   bromide, use as anæsthetic, 206
Euphorbia gum, as substitute for India-rubber, 128
Evaporating non-inflammable solutions, 71,* 133
Evodia, 83
Examining Board, Georgia, 15
Extraction apparatus,* 148,* 169
   apparatus, centrifugal,* 175
   apparatus, Foervier's,* 21
"Extract of Meat" titles, abuses connected with, 93
Extracts adulterated with dextrin, 69
"Eye-water," 82

Fat in milk, cream, etc., determining, 176

INDEX

Fats, determining the melting point of,* 131
Feathers, bleaching, 12
Fermented liquids, removing foreign flavor, 120
Ferric chloride as reagent for free lactic acid, 148
Fertilizer for house plants, 115
Filter, an improved,* 167
  a quick, 86
  automatic, 105
  pump, Law's,* 27
Filtering apparatus, Zunch's, 65
Filters, avoidance of weighed, 227
  machine folded, 137
Filtration, apparatus for upward, 87
  notes on, 112,* 187
Fire extinguisher, original inventor, 136
Flask and burette,* 207
  filtering, 87
"Fleury's Tasteless Cascarine," 78
Fluid extracts abroad, 213
  extracts, half strength, 228
  extracts, suggestions relative to, 218
Fluorine, occurrence in animal bodies, 174
Fly-paper, sticky, 140
Fonds, dialetic, 86
Formula, a fraudulent, 85
Four-per-cent solution, 98
Frankel's solution, 172
Friedrichshall bitter-water, 160
"Fruit sugar," 78
Fuchsin, detection, 88
"Fumifier," the,* 197
Funnel, separating, Currier's,* 132
  Will's,* 105
Funnels, drying frame for,*
FURST, IsMon, on the re-inking of typewriter ribbons, 201

G

Gallein, 37
Gallon, the United States, 2, 41
Gargle, antiseptic, 95
Gas-burner, safety stop-cock for,* 111
  generator,* 158, *165, *197
  hydrochloric acid, injurious effects of, 108
  hydrosulphuric acid, preparing, 32
  leakage, detecting, 134
  manufacture, by-products of, 24
Gases, drying agent for, 68
  injurious effects of various, 108
  testing for small quantities,* 67
Gelatin pill-coating, 66
  plaster-casts, anatomical, 95
Gentian, clarifying wine of, 115
Gentian-violet, detection, 88
Geochronoscope, 231
Geoffroya internis, tincture of, 172
Ghatti, a substitute for gum Arabic, 109
Ginger beer, 140
  Chinese, 92
Glass-balls for refilling wine casks, 125
  frosted, 60
Gleditschia Tricanthos by Abr. L. Metz, 1
Glucose in urine, estimation of, 143
Glue, convenient, 14
Glycerin and cocoa cream, 34
  and mucilage, mixture of, 28
  cosmetic uses of, 115
  production of, 43

Glycerin suppository as a laxative, 229
Graduated glass tubes, verifying, 66
Graduates in Pharmacy, recognition of, 20
Granules of aconitine or digitaline, 112
GRAY, PROF. ASA, death of,* 42
Guaiacol, use in place of creosote, 106, 144
Guarana and Celery, Elixir, 118
  cultivation and preparation, 113
Guensburg's reagent, 118, 148
Gum Arabic, Brasilian, 125
  Arabic, complete stoppage of supply, 206
  Arabic, ghatti as substitute for, 109
  Arabic, substitute for, 81
Gum benzoin, trade in, 184
Gums used for varnish, 97
Gun-cotton, solution of, 200

H

"Hagan's Magnolia Balm," 76
Hair, bleaching, 13
  dye, bismuth, 138
  dye pomades, 85
  lotion, Locock's, 76
"Hall's Catarrh Cure," 76
"Hall's Solution of Strychnine," 98
Hamburg Bitters, 78
Haya as a local anæsthetic, 20
Heating frame,* 209
Heat-regulator, 193
  regulator, electric,* 89
Hectograph sheets, 113
Helenin, 91
Helianthin, production and uses, 24
Heliotropin, 91
Hemlock gum, 140
Hiccup, instantaneous remedy for, 171
Hiera Picra, origin of, 162
"Hinrod's Asthma Cure," poisoning by, 145
HINSDALE, S. J., on colorimetric test for morphine, 121
  S. J., on a test-paper for hydrochloric acid, 102
"Hoffman's Balsam of Life," 97
Hops, uses of, 17
HUBERT, O. H., on a delicate bismuth test, 217
Hunyadi Janos water, 142
Hydrastine, moderate demand for, 208
Hydrogen gas, generating, 175
  peroxide as bleacher for wood, 59
  peroxide, increased strength of, 206
  peroxide, preparation of pure, 207
  peroxide, rapid assay of, 70
  peroxide resulting from oxidation of terpenes,*
  preparation of pure, 202
  sulphuretted generator for,* 211
  sulphuretted, injurious effects of, 108
Hydronaphthol, test for, 68
Hydroxylamine hydrochloride, use of, 106
Hyoscyamine into atropine, conversion of, 141, 213
Hyoscyamus extract, dose of, 213
Hymenæa Courbavil L., as a source of gum, 125
Hypnon, 3

I

Ichthyol, tincture, 230
Incense, 75
Indexing contents of monthly numbers, priority in, 36

Index to *The Practitioner*, 74
Indigo in Manchuria, production, 134
Infusion apparatus,* 45
Injections, convenient solutions for hypodermic, 172
Ink, alizarin, 152
  blue-black, 75
  blue nut-gall, 162
  Cameroon, 163
  coral, 162
  Crown, 162
  document, 163
  eraser, 96, 118
  for writing on zinc and tin, 163
  Imperial, 162
  indelible document, 138
  indelible stencil, 137
  invisible, 77
  "Japanese," 163
  marking, 119
  nigrosin, 172
  powder, alizarin, 114
  red copying, 162
  marking, 45
  tablets, 138
  type-writer, 201
  violet-blue copying, 163
Insect, a perfumed, 217
  flowers, German, 128
  powder, 138
  powder, hellebore as adulterant, 227
Insecticides, 13, 17, 83, 114
Intestinal antisepsis for furuncles, 78
Iodine, "Churchill's," 20
  decolorized tincture, 162
  rapid production of tincture, 110
  standardizing solutions of, 71
  trichloride, 127
  trichloride as an antiseptic, 44
  volumetric estimation of, 126
Iodoform and other pencils,* 147
  as a hæmostatic, 175
  as antiseptic, comparative value, 92
  bituminate, 214
  deodorant for, 45
  impure, 207
Iodol, as antiseptic, 228
  moderate demand for, 106
Ipecac and opium, U. S. P. tincture modified, 115
Goa, 32
Jahore, 133
  root resembling, 207
Iron, albuminate, 18
  and quinine, syrup of hydrobromate, 196
  effervescent carbonate, 174
  galvanized, harmful use of, 176
  hypophosphite, 138
  in caustic soda, solution of, 134
  jelly, 51
  metallic, testing for arsenic in, 111
  milk, 134
  picrate, as a styptic, 193
  preparations, improved, 51
  reduced, sulphur in, 106
  reduction of chloride by pepsin, etc., 52
  sulphate, composition of precipitated, 193
  soluble dextrinated oxide, 51
  soluble saccharated oxide, 51
  solution of albuminated, 51
  solution of peptonated, 51
  syrup of hypophosphite, 51
  syrup of oxide, 152
  tasteless syrup of iodide, 98
"tasteless" tincture, 17
Isatropyl, cocaine, 209

Ivy-poisoning, remedy for, 95

J

Jatuba gum, 125
  "Johst-Zimmer" company, 13
Jujubes, 172

K

"Keeley's motor," 219
  "Kennedy's Medical Discovery," 227
KIRCHHOFF, Prof. G. R.,* 2
Kola, 163
  nuts, improved mode of shipping, 206
Koumys, 158
"Kradna Root," 85

L

Label-paste, 14
  Labels, containers for, 77
  remarks concerning, 156
Lactroid, 87
"La Fayette Mixture," improved, 26
"Lait antipellique," 13
"Lait de Manille," 13
"Lait de Ninon," 13
Lanolin, 81
  preparations, 128
Lard, dehydrating, 115
  detection of adulteration in, 110
  detection of cotton-seed oil in, 212
Laudanum, colorimetric test for morphine, 121
Lead, estimation of, 179
  glycerite of subacetate, 20
  in urine, detection, 139
  sulphide, to clean vessels from, 134
Legislation in Iowa relative to sales of liquor, 55
  in N. Y. State relative to sale of nostrums, 24
Lemon, "soluble" essence, 75
Licensing pharmacists in Massachusetts, 217
Lime, syrup of lactophosphate, 92
LINNÉ, botanical works of, 160
Lipanin, 97, 127
  as substitute for cod-liver oil, 115
"Listerin," 105
Lithium salicylate, impure, 68
  salts, manufacture, 62
Litmus paper, 49
  solution as an indicator, 108
  tincture, 16
"Liquid Franconis," 170, 187
Liquids, apparatus for shaking and separating,* 7
  clarifying, 120
"Liquor antihydrorrhoicus," 144
Liquorice juice, adulterated, 185
LLOYD, J. U., on concentration by low temperature, 81
"Locock's Hair Lotion," 76
Loco weed, 185, 208
Loofahs, 29
LUHN, G. J., death of, 23
Lumbago, remedy for, 87
LYONS, A. B., on the United States Gallon, 41
"Lyons' Kathairon for the Hair," 95

M

Magnesia water, 75
Magnesium bromide, solution, 18
  borocitrate, 120
  chloride, anhydrous, 94
  citrate, bottling, 66
"Magnolia Balm," 133
"Malachite Green" as a reagent for free hydrochloric acid, 148
Matches, Swedish, 199

Meconarceine, 142
  nature and use, 206
Medical societies, meetings of, 100
Medicinal plants, collecting, 119
Mentha, notes on,* 101
Menthiodol, 22
Menthol, 22
  snuff, 75, 80
  with aconitine, 15
  use in phthisis, 89
Mercuric bromide, production of, 107
Mercurous iodide, preparation of, 121
Mercury, aluminate, 162
  biniodide, soap of, 103
  carbolate, 57, 102
  filtration, 68
  protiodide, 31
  protobromide, 31
  salicylate, 174
  salts, crystallized, 107
Methylol, 5
Methyl orange as an indicator, 108
  violet as reagent for free hydrochloric acid, 145
"Mettauer's Aperient," 137
Metz, A. L., on Gleditschia triacanthos, 1
Michu, C. J. M., death of, 23
Micromillimeter, 171
Mildew, removing, 29
Milk, digestion of fermented, 124
  powder, 78
  jelly, 78
  sterilized, 129
  weed as remedy for lumbago, 95
Mill, ball,* 45
Mineral waters, artificial, 163
  waters, various, 142
Modelling wax, 179
Mohr's reagent for free hydrochloric acid, 145
Monobromphenylacetamide, 142
Moore, Dr. J. F., death of, 56
Morphine, detection of, 117
  hydrate, 64
  in laudanum, colorimetric test, 121
  law against refilling prescriptions, 167
  origin of Magendie's solution, 161
  over-production of, 106
  percentage in poppy heads and seeds, 107
  phthalate, 84
  saccharinate, 172
  solvents of, 125
  test for, 70
Mortar, mechanical,* 44
Moss, artificially dyed, 197
"Mother Siegel's Curative Syrup," 76
Moths, means for destroying, 118, 219
"Mountain Balm," 98
Mouth wash, 178
  fragrant and antiseptic, 27
Mucilage, flexible, 25

Naphthalene, 42
  Naphthalin as an insecticide, 148
Naphthol derivatives as antiseptics, 63
National formulary, 20, 140, 157, 186
  Pure Food Convention, 15
Narceine, infrequent use of, 206
  related to naphthalin, 65
Naregamia alata, 32
Necrosote, 43
Neuralgia powder, 14
Nickel, to prevent tarnishing, 140
Nitrobenzene, 42
  injurious effects of vapor, 108
Nitroglycerin in heart failure, 134
  safety in handling, 35

Nitroglycerin solution, assay, and mode of keeping, 37
Nitrometer, Lunge's improved,* 155
Nobel, death of, 22
"Noli Root," 25
Nomenclature, chemical, rationale of,* 84
Nostrums, alcoholic strength of various, 180
Nux vomica, powdered extract, 122
  tincture, 188

Obesity, reducing, 132
Oil, almond, expressed, 90
  ambrette seed, 178
  bay to prevent flies, 178
  betel leaves, 90
  birch tar, Japanese, 91
  boldo, 90
  camphor, 90
  cananga, 90
  cedar (leaves), 90
  cedar (wood), 90
  cinnamon, 90, 222
  citronella, 90
  clove, 90
  clove, as antiseptic, 228
  cod-liver, detection of vegetable oils in, 6
  cod-liver, emulsion of, 161, 194
  cod-liver, Norwegian industry in, 61
  cod-liver, substitute for, 170
  cod-liver, with hypophosphite of calcium, emulsion of, 154
  cognac, artificial, 91
  corn, 141
  cotton-seed, detection in lard, etc., 212
  cotton-seed, manufacture, 194
  cotton-seed, reaction, 85, 134
  cotton seed, tests for, 110
  crisp mint, 91
  croton, 143
  damiana, 91
  emulsions, nature of, 171
  essential, extraction of, 16
  eucalyptus, as antiseptic, 228
  eucalyptus, tests for, 214
  formosa wood, 91
  gingergrass, 91
  green cloves, 67, 90
  hair, 177
  hyoscyamus, 113
  jaborandi, 91
  Japanese peppermint, 210
  geranium, 91
  kuso root, 91
  kiku, 91
  lavender, as antiseptic, 228
  lavender, Mitcham, 5
  lemon, 91
  lemon grass, 92
  matico, 91
  mateu, 91
  mirbane, 92
  mountain pine, 64
  musk-seed, 92
  mustard, essential, as preservative of organic liquids, 92
  olive, adulteration of, in Italy, 107
  olive, detection of cotton-seed oil in, 70
  olive, refining without chemicals, 145
  olive, testing, 113
  orris, 92
  palmarosa, 91
  patchouli, 92
  peanut, composition of, 115
  peppermint, Japanese, 92
  peppermint, Mitcham, 5
  peppermint, still for,* 187

Oil, peppermint, tests of, 122
  pine-needle, 92
  raw and boiled linseed, to distinguish, 36
  rose, detection of spermaceti in, 70
  rose, notes on, 212
  rosemary, as antiseptic, 228
  sandal-wood, 92
  Tolu balsam, 90
  turpentine, as antiseptic, 228
  valerian-root, Japanese, 91
  wintergreen, 92
  wistaria, 92
Oils, citrus, 90
  essential, notes on, 90
  essential, specific gravities of, 184
  essential, table showing yield of, 4
  essential, yield of, 230
  ethereal, notes on, 46
  eucalyptus, 91
  vegetable in cod-liver oil, detection, 6
Ointment, diachylon, preparation of, 133
  mercurial, new mode of making, 123
Ointments, kneading machines for, 143
  removing air-bubbles from, 122
Oleine for darkening hair, 14
Opium assay, 86, 104
  law against refilling prescriptions, 167
  prevention of after-effects, 12
  Tonquin, 95
Ouabain, 195
Oxides, metallic, dehydration of, 68
Oxygen gas, simple mode for making, 128
  test-paper for, 14

Paints, analysis of mixed, 52
Pakoe-Kidang, 16
Panawar Jambi, 16
Pancreas and its preparations, uses, 32
Pancreatin, use of, 162
Paraffins, separation of, 70
Paraldehyde, 26
  dangers from, 127
  elixir, 28
Paradyne, 34
Parsons, H. B., memorial of, 23
"Pasta Mack," 76
Pastilles, aromatic, 75
Pastil mould,* 86
Pawpaw juice, analysis, 89
Pepper, adulterated, 165
  cultivation, 133
Peppermint, cultivation of, 221
  treatment and distillation,* 121
Pepsin and pancreatin, assay, 77
  manufacture of, 186
  tests, relative value of, 164
Peptone, chemical nature, 127
Percolator,* 23
Percolators, Prof. Diehl's suggestions relative to, 213
Perfume in snuff, 178
Parfume, filtering, 87
Permanganate, standardizing solution of, 14
Pharmaceutical Association, American, 136, 181, 198
  Louisiana, 74
  Massachusetts, 116
  Nebraska, 74
  New Hampshire, 217
  New York State, 129
  North Dakota, 177
Pharmaceutical Congress, Sixth, 137
  curiosities, 178
  degrees in the U. S., 55
  matters in Kansas, 15

Pharmaceutical section proposed in Amer. Med. Assoc., 36
  Society, California, 15
  Society of New South Wales, 76
  substitution, 74
Pharmacists' fees for service to the injured, 52
  runaway, 91
  Swiss, co-operation among, 25
Pharmacopœia, Austrian, 92, 146
  British, sale of, 137
  National legislation relative to, 55
  preliminary words relative to next revision, 117
  publication of criticisms concerning the U. S., 149
  universal, Hirsch, 230
  U. S., date of issue, 136
Pharmacopœial matters in Germany, 216
Pharmacy Board, Kings County, N. Y., 177
Phenacetin, 32, 97, 152
  increasing demand for, 206
  use of, 107
Phenol mercury, 57
Phenolphtalein solution, 127
Philicome, fluid, 14
  pomade, 14
Phloroglucin, vanillin as a reagent, 118
Phosphorus, compound tincture, 196
  improvement in manufacture, 154
  paste, 87
  Thompson's solution, 161
Photoxylin, 114, 159
Physostigmine, test for, 212
Pill masses, kneading machine for,* 143
Pills, creosote, 222
  keratinized, 142
  of aconitine or digitaline, 112
Pilocarpine, impure, 178
Pinch-cock,* 163
Pipette,* 173
Planchon, Jules Emile, death of, 115
Platinum from laboratory residues, recovery, 38
  vessels, wear of, 228
"Plumbum causticum," 112
Poisons, efficiency of laws regulating sales of, 23
Polish for leather, black, 230
Polygraph mass, 88
Pomade, castor-oil, 14
  "Philicome," 14
  "Royal Windsor," 14
Poppy heads and seeds, percentage of morphine in, 107
Potassium bromide, manufacture of, 49
  chlorate with pot. iodide, alleged incompatibility, 155
  cyanide and chloral, reaction, 113
  permanganate, for frostbites, 76
  plumbate, 119
  volumetric determination, 126
"Pot-pourri," 36
"Poudre Pilivoire de Loforet," 13
Powders, apparatus for separating,* 67
Precipitates, funnel for washing,* 211
  Hinsdale's apparatus for washing, 112
Prescription charges, 29
  difficult, 18, 178, 220
  ownership of, 38
  writing, 118, 217
Press for branding boxes,* 163
Preston salt, 77
Putty powder, 57

Proprietary articles, queries relative to, 56
Psychotria emetica, 112
Ptomaines in urine, 214
Pyrethrum, cultivation of, 128
  poisoning by, 55
  tincture as an insecticide, 173
Pyrmont water, 142
Pullna Bitter Water, 142
  water, artificial, 163
Pumiline, 64
Pump, combined suction and pressure,* 145
  water-blast,* 145
Pus, detection of, 178

Quebracho as an application for wounds, 72
Quillaia bark as an emulsifier, etc., 29
  tincture, 29
  therapeutic uses, 72
Quillaja, source of, 37
Quinidine sulphate, demand for, 107
Quinine hydrochlorate, improved process for, 142
  hydrochlorate, impurity in, 133
  hydrofluosilicate, 111
  manufacture in India, 173
  means for masking the taste of, 188
  mixtures, 11
  saccharinate, 178
  salts, pure, 115
  sulphate, tests for, 8, 92, 117
  Yerba santa as a disguise for, 214

Reagents, impurities in, 213
Red fire, 17
Rennet, vegetable, 146
Repercolation, modified process, 144
Resorcin in sea-sickness, 72
Retort for gas generator, safety, 127
Rheach's reagent for free hydrochloric acid, 146
Rhubarb, aromatic fluid extract, 161
  scarcity of, 107
Richardsonia scabra, 112
Ricin, 172
Roach exterminator, 56
Robbins, D. C., death of, 84
Roberts, Joseph, death of, 56
"Rock Root," 85
"Rulique Root," 85
Rose-jug, 56
Roses in Caucasus, 140
"Royal Windsor Pomade," 14
Russia leather odor, 230

Saccharin, 52, 98
  a coal-tar product, 24
  color test for, 167
  detection, 98
  domestic uses, 84
  French prohibition of use, 175
  improvement in, 124
  in pill-coating, 15
  products of decomposition, 5
  solubility, etc., 16
  syrup of, 14
  test for, 207, 214
Sachet powders, 180
Safety-vent,* 105
Saffron trade, Spanish, 125

"Sage's Catarrh Cure," 85
Salicylates, uses of, 64
Salicylic collodion, 78
Salol, 51
  and camphor, reaction, 210
  tooth powder, 133
  tooth-wash, 133
  use in rheumatism, 72
Sal soda, manufacture of, 24
"Salufer," 107
Salve, Galezowski's antineuralgic, 114
Sandal-wood, 13
Sarsaparilla, Indian, 105
"Schnapsknebel's Stomach Bitters," 85
Sassafras, yield of, 230
SCHRENK, Prof. Jos., Pharmacological notes by, 101
Sealing-wax, colored, 180
Seidlitz water, artificial, 163
Separating liquids and solids by cold,* 27
Serpent-bite, African antidote, 213
"Seven Sunderland Sisters' Hair Grower," 78
Shaking Machine,* 85
Shampoo liquid, 218
Sherbet powder, 98
Sherry, adulteration of, 175
Shop bottles, cracking of, 112
Sifting-machine,* 44
Silphium, source and uses, 218
Silver, to prevent tarnishing, 140
Simulo, as a nerve tonic, 142
Siphon,* 173, 209
Slag from iron furnaces, uses of, 43
Snuff for Coryza, 75
Soap, antiseptic, 103
  dialyzed stearin, 226
  hard, 120
  manufacture by products from, 43
Soaps, 75
Soda, caustic, solution of iron in, 133
  in milk, detection, 98
Sodium benzoate as remedy for tonsillitis, 72
  benzoate, use in uræmia, 84
  citrobenzoate, 149
  fluosilicate as a disinfectant, 26
  phosphate in glacial phosphoric acid, 33
  salicylate in toothache, 133
  sesquicarbonate, 102
  silico-fluoride as an antiseptic, 107
  sulphibenzoate as an antiseptic, 107
  sulphichthyolate, as antiseptic, 228
  sulphite, benzoated, 142
  sulphibenzoate, 30
  tungstate, 85
  volumetric determination, 126
Solanine, increased demand for, 206
Sore nipples, application for, 59
Sozoiodol, 66
  as a substitute for iodoform, 206
Sparteine, alleged poisoning by, 173
Spence-metal, 20
Sponge fisheries, Turkish, 89
Sponges, cleaning, 189
  cultivation, 231

Staranise, source of, 193
Starch for assays and tests, 78
Steam, apparatus for superheating,* 195
Stenocarpine, 1
Still, automatic,* 105
Stink-plant, an African, 213
Stirrer, eccentric,* 65
Strophanhlin, 195
  reaction, 34
Strophanthus and Strophanthin, notes on, 85, 117
  compared with digitalis, 111
  diminished call for, 206
  preparation of, 12
  seeds, 64
  sophistication by English houses, 85
  standard strength of tincture, 152
Strychnine, detection of, 89
  for relief of sleeplessness, 25
  Hall's solution, 77, 98
  saccharinate, 178
Sublimate dressings, assay, 33
Sugar, bluing in, 179
  imitation maple, 32
  in urine, apparatus for determining,* 133
  of milk, fermentation of, 65
  preservative, 134
  synthesis of, 7, 26
Sulphonal, 113, 159, 195
  demand for, 206
  notes on, 225
  test for, 176
  uses of, 173
Sulphurous water, artificial, 163
Suppositories, atropine, 14
Suppository and ointment glycerin, as a laxative, 226
  new form, 113
Sutherlandia frutescens, an alleged cancer remedy, 82
Syrup, saccharin, 14
Syrups, purification by dialysis, 7

Tablet moulds, 77
"Tacher," 85
Tannin in vegetable substances, estimation of, 161
  wool, 89
Tape, air-tight,* 3
Tea, caffeine from, 111
Terebine, 26
  emulsion, 76
Terpenes, production of peroxide of hydrogen during oxidation of, 82
Terpinen, 90
Terpineol, 90
Terpin hydrate, 64
  hydrate, elixir, 14
  solubility
Test-paper for oxygen, 14
  papers, manufacture of, 42
Thapsia, source of, 218
Thermometer, nursery,* 34
Thioresin, as a substitute for iodoform, 107
Tin cans, testing tightness of, 115
Tinctures by superior maceration, 37
Tin, official test for, 166
Titles, pharmacopœial, neglect of, 89

Tobacco, Smyrna, 231
Toilet preparations, nature of, 13
Tolu, syrup, 115
Toothache remedy, 14
Tooth powder and wash, salol, 133
Torments of trade, 85
Towel-gourd, 23
Trefusa, 127
Tropæolin 00 as reagent for free hydrochloric acid, 146
Tropæolin paper, 142
Turmeric paper, 49
Typewriter ribbons, re-inking of, 201

Uffelman's reagent for free lactic acid, 146
Urea, apparatus for estimating,* 44
Urinal cakes, 27
Urinary calculi, solvents of, 102
Uva Ursi, notes on,* 101

Vacuum apparatus, simple, 225
Vaginal balls, alum 106
Valoida, nature of, 185
"Van Buskirk's Fragrant Sozodont," 85
Vanilla culture, Mexican, 69
Vanillin, preparation of artificial, 231
  use of, 229
"Van Stan's Stratena," 85
"Vapocrsoline," 137
Vapors, injurious effects of various, 102
Varnish, black leather, 108
Vaseline pomade and cold-cream, 97
Vichy water, artificial, 163
Vieirine, 83
"Vigier's Coryza Powder," 137
Vinegar, aromatic, 75
  raspberry, 117

"Warburg's tincture," notes on, 211
Waste products, utilization of, 24, 42
Water, sulphuretted by hydrogen, preservation, 140
  used in dispensing, choice of, 73
Waters, aromatic, 85
  distilled, 85
Wax, mineral, in beeswax, detection and estimation, 38, 219
Weighing scale, pocket,* 52
Weppe, E., appointment of, 217
Wine, detection of gentianviolet and fuchsin, 88
  natural iron in, 14
  orange, 132
Wintergreen, yield of, 230
Wool-fat, 51
  fat for softening hard skin, 72
  products from waste, 43
Wrinkles, cure for, 137

Xanthoxylum Hamiltonianum, 83

Ylang-ylang in the Philippine Islands, 162

Zeihl's solution, 179
Zinc and sulphuric acid, reaction between, 111
  caustic sulphate, 15

www.ingramcontent.com/pod-product-compliance
Lightning Source LLC
Chambersburg PA
CBHW031748230426
43669CB00007B/535